Chicagoland

Darlington

Daytona

Kansas

Las Vegas

Martinsville

Michiga

Richmond

Infineon

Talladega

Bristol

California

Charlotte

Chicagola

ead-Miami

Indianapolis

Kansas

Las Vegas

Kentucky

Phoenix

Pocono

Richm

s Glen

Atlanta

Bristol

California

///NASCAR™

THE COMPLETE HISTORY

GREG FIELDEN
with BRYAN HALLMAN
and THE AUTO EDITORS OF CONSUMER GUIDE®

Publications International, Ltd.

Louis Weber, CEO
Publications International, Ltd.
8140 Lehigh Avenue
Morton Grove, IL 60053

Permission is never granted for commercial purposes.

ISBN: 978-1-68022-989-9

Manufactured in China.

8 7 6 5 4 3 2 1

The editors gratefully acknowledge the cooperation of the following people and entities who supplied photography to help make this book possible:

Auto Club Speedway, Dale Barbee, Gary Beem, Jack Cansler, Phil Cavali, Chrysler Photographic, Chrysler-Plymouth Performance Publicity, Dodge Public Relations, Chris Dolack, ESPN, Greg Fielden, Ford Motor Company, LaDon George, David Griffin, Matt Griffith, Phil Hall, Bryan Hallman, Mark Hawkins, Gil Haywood, Mike Horne, International Speedway Corporation, Dave Jensen, Brett Kelley, Don Kelly, Tom Kirkland, Mike Laczynski, Las Vegas Motor Speedway, Vince Manocchi, Larry McTighe, Motorsports Images & Archives Photography, NASCARMedia.com, Victor Newman, Bill Niven, Petty Enterprises, James Price, Jeff Robinson, David Schenk, Ted Seminara, Texas Motor Speedway, Kevin Thorne, Wieck Media Services, Inc., Chuck Yadmark, Doug Yockey

Special thanks to Bonnie Hallman for her invaluable assistance and inexhaustible patience.

A note about statistics: The statistics quoted in *NASCAR: The Complete History* have been compiled by the author. Many of the numbers do not match official statistics recognized by NASCAR, but they do represent the best efforts of one of racing's most respected historians.

contents

Foreword

Late in the 20th century, NASCAR drove past USAC, Trans-Am, Can-Am, Indy, NHRA, and Formula One to become America's most-followed motorsport. Then NASCAR raced past hockey, golf, basketball, and baseball to become one of the most-watched sports on U.S. television.

As with many success stories, NASCAR began with one man and his dream.

William Henry Getty France was a skilled promoter whose word was his bond. In 1948, his National Association for Stock Car Auto Racing gave the fledgling sport honesty and respectability. A national championship series created publicity, and ensured a constant flow of membership and sanctioning fees to Daytona Beach to help grow the sport.

France never rested on his laurels. He dreamed of a high-banked superspeedway faster than Indianapolis and created a tri-oval masterpiece in Daytona Beach with borrowed money on public-owned land. A decade later, France built an even bigger and faster speedway in Alabama.

Bill kept his sport healthy in the late 1950s when Detroit automakers pulled out in the wake of congressional pressure and concerns over fatalities throughout racing. He fought off unionization in '61, and in 1969, he climbed into a race car and drove high-speed laps to prove his track was safe. France started his own radio network in 1970 to ensure weekly live coverage, and helped struggling team owners stay in business.

Junior Johnson was one of its early stars, a mountain of a man who won 50 races driving, then six titles as team owner. Junior brought RJ Reynolds to NASCAR, and "Grand National" became the "Winston Cup" series in 1971.

A two-time champion and NASCAR Hall of Famer, Ned Jarrett became the first expert analyst on NASCAR Sprint Cup Series broadcasts. Ned's blend of racing savvy and next-door-neighbor friendliness helped make the sport welcome in millions of American living rooms.

Richard Petty, NASCAR's all-time leading winner and first seven-time champion, set the standard for

driver behavior. His smile, grace, and humility made him a perennial fan favorite.

France's son, Bill, Jr., and CBS announcer Ken Squier brought NASCAR to network TV. When CBS first televised the Daytona 500 live in 1979, its thrilling, crashing, fist-fighting finish created millions of new fans and gave the sport its biggest jolt of momentum.

By the mid '80s, most races were shown on network or cable TV. Where television went, Madison Avenue quickly followed, bringing a wide range of sponsorships: beer and building supplies, crackers and camera film, detergent and deodorant, financial services and America's military.

A brash, upstart high school dropout became NASCAR's next megastar. Dale Earnhardt turned his raw driving talent into seven championships, unrivaled hero worship, and a marketing empire worth millions. Earnhardt's style redefined the limits of on-track behavior. When he stepped over the line, the line often moved with him. Earnhardt's fatal crash on the final lap of the 2001 Daytona 500 cost the sport its biggest star, yet propelled NASCAR to a new proactive stance on safety.

Bill France, Jr.'s son, Brian, extended NASCAR's marketing reach, and succeeded his dad as chairman and CEO. Brian led negotiations for 2001's landmark network television deal. Now every NASCAR Sprint Cup race is televised live by FOX, TNT, or ABC/ESPN.

NASCAR president Mike Helton integrated Sprint as the series' new title sponsor and the Chase for the NASCAR Sprint Cup playoff format to determine the series champion. With some of the best pure racing in years, twice the season's final race began with three drivers having a legitimate shot at the title.

In 2007, Toyota joined Chevrolet, Ford, and Dodge to become the first foreign nameplate to race at the sport's top level in 44 years. Impact-absorbing walls and a new "Car of Tomorrow" platform offered drivers a safer environment.

The NASCAR Hall of Fame opened in uptown Charlotte in 2010, mere miles from where the first sanctioned race was held in 1949.

Jimmie Johnson and team owner Rick Hendrick have cemented a dynasty, winning five consecutive NASCAR Sprint Cup Series championships. Johnson and Jeff Gordon stand within striking range of records held by Petty and Earnhardt. But when the fans vote at the souvenir stands, Dale Earnhardt, Jr., is the runaway leader and overwhelming fan favorite.

2013 views the sport on an upswing with TV ratings and crowds on the rise. Brash young champion Brad Keselowski, social media, Danica Patrick, and heated rivalries all contribute. New Camry, SS, and Fusion NASCAR Sprint Cup cars *look* like "*stock*" cars for the first time in many years.

I've enjoyed the challenge and thrill of broadcasting this sport for nearly 40 years because of the sport's rich history, its engaging personalities, its explosive action, and most of all…because you never know who's going to win until the checkered flag waves.

Mike Joy
FOX Sports
@mikejoy500

March 2013

Before NASCAR

The first recorded closed-circuit auto race in the United States took place in September 1896 at a horse-racing track in Narragansett Park in Rhode Island. A small fleet of Duryeas, a Morris, and a Salom Electrobat competed in an event of undisclosed distance. Frank Duryea was declared the winner in an automobile he built himself. The newfangled sport of auto racing had begun.

With the dawning of the twentieth century, a variety of auto speed shows turned up in all corners of the globe. Races were conducted on public streets, hastily built speedways, rutted dirt tracks originally designed for other uses, and along the sandy shoreline of Florida's Daytona Beach.

In February 1903, the first organized speed tournament was staged on the sands of Ormond Beach, Florida, near the famous Ormond Hotel. Alexander Winton, sitting atop an eye-jabbing creation that bore his name, blistered the hard-packed sands in his Winton Bullet at a 68.19 mph clip.

Although attended by only a handful of chilly, curious onlookers, Winton's feat would kick off an annual affair in the resort town of Daytona Beach. Every winter, innovators, wealthy sportsmen, and a few genuine screwballs made their way to Daytona to test the speed limits of a potpourri of vehicular oddities. Within a few years, the eyes of the world focused on the mechanical magic taking place on the sands of Daytona and Ormond Beach.

The winter events eventually became an international happening. Speeds increased at alarming rates as world-record speeds were challenged and surpassed. By 1935, the 300-mph barrier was well within reach. Sir Malcolm Campbell, an English gentleman, strapped himself into a five-ton machine powered by a 2227-cid engine on March 7, 1935, and pierced the sands at a speed of 276.82 mph. Campbell,

knighted for his deeds in speed, surpassed 300 mph on one trip down the shoreline, but his two-way average dipped due to rough conditions. Campbell was disgusted that an official 300-mph speed hadn't been reached. Shortly after Campbell's Daytona jaunt, the speed trials were moved to the more suitable conditions offered by the vast salt flats of Bonneville, Utah. The city officials of Daytona Beach contemplated losing the aura and lure of auto racing.

In March 1936, the town of Daytona Beach organized a race for stock cars in an effort to keep auto racing active in the coastal hamlet. A 3.2-mile beach and road course near the center of town became the new racing "closed course." Milt Marion, driving a V-8 powered Ford, motored to victory on the choppy and rutted course. An obscure, lanky youngster named Bill France finished fifth.

The 240-mile event was an artistic and financial failure. With the slim hope of other stock car racing events sponsored by city officials, it appeared racing was over in Daytona Beach.

Bill France held out hope and decided to try his hand at promoting his own stock car racing events on the beach and road course. He achieved moderate success with his low-buck, small-time promotions.

In 1938, an event of major proportions was promoted in the deep South. The one-mile Lakewood Fairgrounds Speedway in downtown Atlanta was selected to host a "National Championship Stock Car Race." A 150-mile marathon race for late-model, American-made stock cars would be the featured attraction on Armistice Day, November 12, 1938. Lloyd Seay, a pencil-thin, self-confident 18-year-old, had driven hundreds of miles at breakneck speeds on the back roads of North Georgia (often eluding

the hot pursuit of the police), but none on a racetrack. A green kid with unimaginable skill, Seay stunned many as he galloped to victory in the Lakewood race, outrunning a gathering of hard-core renegades who spent most of their lives deliberately crusading on the wrong side of justice. His maiden voyage in auto racing had made history, yet it was consigned to the mere memory of trackside patrons.

Other stock car racing events began popping up on rough dirt tracks across the South—and a few north of the Mason-Dixon line. A good many of these "facilities" had been carved beneath the raw edge of a tractor blade over the period of a few days. Few, if any, measures were taken for the safety of gladiator or spectator. The events were marked by little publicity, virtually no organization, crooked promoters, and nonexistent rule books. Plus, the behavior of the contestants was a crapshoot.

Often, a promoter disappeared with the gate receipts well before the checkered flag fell. Some actually hung around and paid the drivers a few bucks for their daring exploits. The sport was growing so fast it had burst its proverbial ragged britches. Stock car racing was in dire need of some organization.

Bill France stepped to the forefront. A driver of considerable merit, France had joined the traveling band of rowdies in 1940 and began winning races regularly. In July, France finished first in a 200-mile race at Ft. Wayne, Indiana, the biggest race of the 1940 season. He also won at Daytona and finished second in a big race at Langhorne. At the end of the year, France was acknowledged as the "1940 National Stock Car Racing Champion," although there was no formal point system in place to document his title.

In his travels, France also gained a working knowledge of promoting automobile races. A man of exceptional intelligence and a keen sense of fairness, France absorbed what the drivers, teams, race officials, and indeed the sport itself, needed to flourish.

The relentless racers crisscrossed the eastern United States in 1941, enduring an exhaustive schedule that included four championship races at Daytona promoted by France. Near the end of the year, Lloyd Seay, then 21, was achieving new standards in high-speed artistry. He won at Allentown, Pennsylvania; High Point, North Carolina; Daytona Beach, Florida; and Atlanta, Georgia. He was madcap, rambunctious, and always spectacular. But after his victory at Atlanta, he was shot to death by his own cousin in a dispute over the family moonshine business. The brightest star of this relatively new sport had been snuffed out.

Within a few more weeks World War II broke out, which brought the sport of auto racing to a screeching halt. All of America's resources had to be channeled into the war effort. Every racing event in the country was canceled. Over four long years, the engines remained silent.

The first postwar stock car racing event was staged on September 3, 1945, at the venerable Lakewood Speedway in Atlanta. Bill France finished second to madman Roy Hall, who was taking a break from his regular incarcerations in local and federal correctional facilities.

With a running start into the 1946 campaign, dozens of "racing organizations" sprung up virtually overnight. France competed in the dusty and dangerous events on occasion, but hung up his goggles in early 1946 to devote his full attention to promotions. At the end of the 1946 season, Ed Samples was declared the national champion of stock car racing.

The complex landscape of stock car racing was in a state of flux and the sport was about to change. Bill France would be the man behind that change.

Before NASCAR

February 1903 The first organized speed tournament in the Daytona Beach, Fla., area is staged at Ormond Beach. Alexander Winton blisters the hard-packed sands at 68.19 mph.

March 7, 1935 Sir Malcolm Campbell guides his five-ton Bluebird down the sands of Daytona Beach at 276.82 mph in a record speed run. The historic event marks the close of speed trials on the Daytona Beach shoreline.

March 8, 1936 Daytona Beach city officials conduct a 240-mile late-model stock car race to replace the speed trials. Milt Marion prevails on the 3.2-mile sand and macadam course. A young Bill France finishes fifth.

September 4, 1938 Smokey Purser finishes first in a 150-mile race on the Daytona Beach-Road course, but is disqualified when he fails to submit his car for postrace inspection.

November 12, 1938 Promoters at Atlanta's Lakewood Fairgrounds stage a "National Championship Stock Car Race" on the one-mile dirt track. Nineteen-year-old Lloyd Seay wins the race, which is shortened due to darkness.

September 17, 1939 Roy Hall, a known moonshine runner, drives his Ford to victory in a 150-mile race on a tiny dirt track in Salisbury, N.C. Bill France finishes second.

March 10, 1940 "Rapid" Roy Hall drives his 1939 Ford to a big victory in the 160-mile stock car race on the Daytona Beach-Road course.

July 28, 1940 Bill France drives Andy Beardon's 1939 Ford to victory in a 200-mile event at Ft. Wayne, Ind. France fills in for Roy Hall, who is in a Georgia jail on a moonshine charge.

September 1, 1941 Lloyd Seay wins the 150-mile National Championship race at Atlanta's Lakewood Speedway. The following day, Seay is shot to death by his cousin in a dispute over the family moonshine enterprise.

November 2, 1941 Jap Brogton prevails in the Lloyd Seay Memorial race at Lakewood. It is the final stock car race event before World War II.

The program cover for the Third Annual International World's Championships at Ormond Beach and Daytona Beach in January 1905 featured a White Steam Car and a trio of curious water nymphs. The original speed trials on the shores of the Atlantic took place in Ormond Beach, just north of Daytona. The '05 speed runs attracted entries from all over the world, but Bostonian H. L. Bowden, driving a Mercedes, turned the quickest time through the Measured Mile at 109.75 mph.

Frank Lockhart, a mechanical genius who could barely read or write, handcrafted the Stutz Blackhawk in 1928 and took it to Daytona. Equipped with a V-16 engine with a modest 182 cid, Lockhart pierced the Measured Mile at 198.292 mph. He was running well above 200 mph on a return run when the right rear tire blew, and the car tumbled for more than 1000 feet. The 26-year-old 1926 Indianapolis 500 winner was killed instantly.

In the early twentieth century, steeply banked board tracks sprang up all over the United States, instantly becoming the fastest closed-circuit racing facilities in the world. From 1910 to '28, two dozen of these speedways were constructed of pine board laid on edge. Some board tracks were banked as high as 49 degrees, and speeds were astonishing. One board track, Fulford by the Sea near Miami, Fla., opened in February 1926. Peter DePaolo won the only race staged on the 1¼-mile track. A hurricane later that year leveled the place, leaving lumber scattered over a large area. The track was never rebuilt.

Ray Keech wheeled Jim White's monstrous 36-cylinder Triplex down the Daytona shoreline in April 1928. The Triplex was an awful beast to handle, and it beat Keech to a pulp on several warm-up runs. Despite the poor handling, Keech tied two runs together at 207.552 mph for a new world's Land Speed Record. The future Indy 500 champion dismounted the car and vowed never to get back in. The following year, local garage operator Lee Bible drove the Triplex and lost his life in a nasty accident.

Perhaps the most glamorous car to ever blister the sands was also the last. Malcolm Campbell's Bluebird V, a 30-foot long bodyshell built around five tons of complicated machinery, was an outstanding example of the art of aerodynamics. With 2227 cid churning out 2700 horsepower, Campbell ran a 276.82 mph two-way average on March 7, 1935, with a one-way run of over 330 mph. On the return run, part of the cowling ripped away and Campbell spun sideways, causing him to fall short of the 300 mph mark.

A stock car race sanctioned by the American Automobile Association replaced the land speed vehicles in Daytona Beach in 1936. Young Bill France was one of the 27 entrants in his #10 Ford V-8 coupe. France qualified at 69.22 mph on the 3.2-mile sand and pavement course, 18th quickest.

Before NASCAR

A variety of stock automobiles competed in the inaugural auto racing event at Daytona Beach on March 8, 1936. Coupes, hardtops, sports cars, and convertibles were all eligible. Spectators could get a close-up view of the cars as they hammered through the north turn, whether in a trench on the inside of the curve or along the outer rim of the course.

Bill France wheels his lightweight Ford through the south turn on his way to a fifth-place finish in the 1936 Daytona Beach-Road race. Fords took the first six spots. Many of the speedier but heavier cars got bogged down in the thick sandy corners while the nifty Fords sailed over the ruts with relative ease.

Wealthy sportsman Jack Rutherford guides his #29 Auburn bobtail speedster through the rutted north turn in the inaugural 1936 Daytona Beach-Road stock car race. Rutherford was among the quickest qualifiers but he failed to finish the car-killing contest. Only 10 cars in the starting field of 27 were running at the finish.

Milt Marion is congratulated for his victory in the 1936 Daytona Beach-Road race. Driving a '36 Ford, Marion was flagged the winner when officials halted the race 10 miles short of its scheduled 250-mile distance. Marion's mount was a test vehicle for the Permatex Corp., which was testing gaskets in the event. Marion collected the $1700 top prize.

Ed Eng, driving the #14 Hudson, chases Smokey Purser's fleet Ford through the south turn during the Sept. 5, 1937, Daytona Beach-Road race. The 50-mile contest was the second stock car race presented on the midtown course. Purser won the race and earned $43.56; the total purse was only slightly more than $100.

Bill France poses with his team of assistants prior to the start of the July 10, 1938, race at Daytona Beach. Youthful Marshall Teague, later to become a top ranked driver, is on the left next to France. Ted Swaim, an American Indian who later would excel as a driver and flagman, is between France and Cannonball Bob Baker, a young racer from Daytona. France ran second in the race while Baker finished out of the money.

Joe Littlejohn, in the #7 1939 Buick, leads Roy Hall's '39 Ford in a battle for the lead during the March 10, 1940, Daytona Beach-Road race. Littlejohn led the first 28 laps of the 160-mile contest before Hall made the decisive pass.

The four horsemen of the early Daytona Beach-Road racing days (left to right), Smokey Purser, Bill France, Roy Hall, and Sammy Packard, pose beside Hall's winning '39 Ford following the March 10, 1940, event. Purser and Hall each won three races at the demanding course while France won twice. Packard was a top contender, but never won.

Bill France poses beside the #1 Graham that he drove to the fastest qualifying time for the March 2, 1941, 8th Daytona Beach race. France qualified at 77.838 mph in a quick trip around the 2.2-mile course. France failed to finish the event, falling victim to mechanical problems. As France sped into the sandy corners, the big car drooped low and sucked sand into the engine. On the fourth lap, the engine

The crowd-pleasing Cyrus Clark cuts a quick swath through the north turn in the July 27, 1941, Daytona Beach race. Newspaper reports referred to Clark as "the lunatic from Miami." Clark's wild antics behind the wheel netted him a 10th-place finish in this event.

Joe Littlejohn and #14 Roy Hall hook up in a dramatic side-by-side battle in the north turn at Daytona. In the early 1940s, the Beach-Road races were popular spectator attractions. Crowds would line up a dozen deep along the inside of the course to watch the goggled daredevils roar past.

Bernard Long, sand curling off his spinning tires, zips around Bill France in the north turn during the July 27, 1941, Daytona Beach-Road race. Long scored his lone Daytona win driving this #9 '40 Mercury. France was driving a '40 Graham, but wasn't a factor in the 160-mile contest.

Fearless Lloyd Seay teeters on two wheels in an acrobatic jaunt through the north turn of Daytona's Beach-Road course. Seay was always spectacular. The youthful Dawsonville, Ga., driver flipped twice in one event, yet still finished fourth. On Aug. 24, 1941, Seay led the entire distance to win the 160-mile event at Daytona. Eight days later he was shot to death by his cousin.

Lloyd Seay

NASCAR FOUNDER Bill France, Sr., regarded Lloyd Seay as the "greatest stock car driver who ever lived." That's high praise from the man who organized and nurtured stock car racing into the slick production it is today. It is even more remarkable considering Lloyd Seay never competed in a NASCAR race. He was murdered nearly eight years before NASCAR was incorporated.

"I raced against Lloyd before the war," France said in 1984. "He was the best pure driver I ever saw, and I have seen 'em all."

Seay was born in the north Georgia hills on Dec. 14, 1919. An adventurous sort, Seay grew up on the rough side of the tracks and hung around the lawless characters of his rural surroundings.

In his early teens, Seay became involved in whiskey tripping, transporting "hooch" from one point to another—usually with the police and revenue agents in hot pursuit. His exploits behind the wheel of a car on the twisting switchback roads of Georgia became legend. "He was wide open all the way," said Raymond Parks, a tycoon among race-team owners before and immediately after the war.

Stock car racers of the time dealt in thrills and spills, defying sanity and logic. Seay's ability to hang a car on the edge made him an instant threat to win races, particularly with the support of Parks and Red Vogt, the game's top mechanic. At the age of 18, Seay entered his first stock car race at Atlanta's Lakewood Speedway—and prevailed.

A hard-boiled speed merchant, Seay's rise to stardom was meteoric; success was a constant companion. He could find as many ways to win as there were opportunities.

In 1941, Seay won three races of national importance. In the Aug. 24 race on Daytona's Beach-Road course, Seay bolted from his 15th starting position to lead the opening lap. He romped to victory, finishing 3½ miles ahead of runner-up Joe Littlejohn. Seay then won with ease at High Point, N.C., on Aug. 31.

Next, Seay packed up and headed for his home in Atlanta and the annual championship event at Lakewood Speedway on Labor Day, Sept. 1. Seay started near the back of the field, having missed qualifications while in North Carolina. By the 35th lap, he had grabbed first place. Seay outran the field the rest of the way to post his third win in nine days.

Only hours after accepting accolades for winning one of stock car racing's most sought-after prizes, Lloyd Seay was shot to death by his cousin, Woodrow Anderson. According to police reports, the two got into an argument over some sugar Seay purchased on Anderson's credit.

Raymond Parks, who admired the youngster and had provided him with a speedy race car, arranged for an unusual tombstone to rest over Seay's burial place. Seay's famous #7 Ford coupe was engraved in relief and the driver's window was carved out. Inserted in its place was a photo of Seay, mounted in a crystal cube.

Largely unknown today, Lloyd Seay generated excitement and showed fans what stock car racing was all about simply by how he drove a race car. The moment when he geared up for the start of a race brought out his electric, elegant best.

This portrait of hard-charging youngster Fontello Flock was taken during his early years as a race car driver. Flock, who later shortened his name to Fonty, was severely injured at Daytona in 1941. His injuries took six years to heal, but Flock was able to return to racing following World War II. He went on to become one of racing's most endearing heroes.

Wild-eyed Bob Flock, eldest of the famous Flock racing gang, was one of stock car racing's top-ranked speedsters when racing resumed after the end of World War II. For a short time, Flock was banned from racing at Atlanta's Lakewood Speedway because he had a criminal record stemming from a number of moonshine hauling charges.

A number of speedways in the mid 1940s were dirt ovals originally designed for horse races. The turns were flat, devoid of banking, and surrounded by a wooden fence on the inside. Bill Snowden dashes through a flat corner in a four-wheel drift, demonstrating the quickest way around a flat horse track.

Louis Jerome Vogt, known to all in the racing circles as "Red," was stock car racing's greatest mechanic in the formative days. Cars groomed by his oily hands won 11 races on Daytona's Beach-Road course, including seven in a row during one stretch.

Stock car racing became a popular sporting attraction in the South following World War II. Here, a gaggle of cars kick up huge clouds of dust on a ½-mile dirt track as a standing-room-only crowd watches the action.

The one-mile circular Langhorne Speedway near Philadelphia was one of America's most famous dirt tracks. Built in 1926, the track hosted a variety of motor racing events for open-wheel Champ cars, sprints, motorcycles, and stock cars. Ted Nyquist and Bill Schindler are on the front row for this '46 stock car race.

1947-49: The Birth of NASCAR

In early 1947, visionary Bill France took a bold, decisive step by announcing the formation of the National Championship Stock Car Circuit, a new touring series for stock car jockeys. France saw the potential of a unified, organized series. After all, the action on the dirt speedways was exciting to watch, with burly goggled gladiators engaging in bumper-to-bumper combat before thousands of screaming fans. The stock jalopy buggies with their souped up engines were also getting a serious second look. Southern stock car races were enjoyable spectacles, but it was time for the sport to grow beyond its Southern roots.

France had first made a pitch at the American Automobile Association to include stock car racing in its repertoire of auto-racing sanctions. The AAA had sanctioned big-time open-wheel racing since the early part of the twentieth century, and it was clearly the leader in the industry. In exchange for AAA group insurance and sanction, France wanted to conduct a stock car racing series under the AAA banner. Effectively, the AAA told France to get lost—stock car racing would never make a viable branch of motorsports.

Undaunted by the AAA's cold reception to what he thought was a good idea, France carried on by himself. The sport was catching on quickly in the small towns of the South. Predictably, about a half dozen stock car racing

organizations seemingly came out of the woodwork to grab a piece of the action. By forming the NCSCC, complete with a series of races with points standings and a standard set of rules, Bill France put himself one step ahead of the competition. The NCSCC would be a touring series for American-made stock cars, and the top points winners would share in postseason money. A thousand bucks and a nice trophy were promised to the champion.

Although a modest degree of skepticism existed among the contestants—none had ever been offered a points fund after the racing season—most of the drivers and car owners sided with France's carnival of courage. They were willing to give this newfangled idea an honest shot.

France's National Championship Stock Car Circuit began in January 1947 at Daytona Beach and concluded at Jacksonville in December, having sanctioned nearly 40 events. Attendance at most of the races exceeded capacity and surpassed the visions of the ever-optimistic France. Posted awards were paid, points accumulated, and a champion was named. Truman Fontello Flock, known in the dusty dirt track domain as Fonty, logged seven race wins en route to a narrow victory over Ed Samples and Red Byron in the NCSCC championship chase. Fonty won seven races in 24 starts.

Just as he had promised, Bill France delivered the post-season payoff. Flock received a huge four-foot trophy and $1000. A total of $3000 was doled out to the top drivers. Promises were fulfilled—how unique for stock car racing!

During the final weeks of the 1947 season, France was spreading the word to track operators, drivers, owners, and any interested party that a big powwow would take place in December in Daytona Beach. Big Bill, a man of strong will and deep convictions, wanted to take the sport to a national level, but he knew he needed the support of the contestants. He welcomed all to the Streamline Hotel for a series of meetings that began on Dec. 14, 1947.

Thirty-five men shimmied up a creaky wooden staircase to the top floor of the Streamline Hotel. At 1:00 P.M. on that Sunday afternoon, France called to order the "First Annual Convention of the National Championship Stock Car Circuit." The meeting marked the first of four days of seminars that would outline the direction the sport was headed. During that initial meeting, France is quoted as saying: "Gentlemen, right here within our group rests the outcome of stock car racing in the country today. We have the opportunity to set it up on a big scale. We are all interested in one thing: improving present conditions."

Bill Tuthill, a racing promoter from New York, became France's right-hand lieutenant, as well as the chairman of the meetings. At the end of the four-day seminar, France had appointed technical and competition committees with all factions—drivers, mechanics, and owners—represented. Louis Jerome Vogt, ace-mechanic of the era, coined the name for the organization: National Association for Stock Car Auto Racing. Virtually all of the renegade racers seemed to think France's new circuit was a good idea.

One of the most important elements to come out of the meetings was an insurance policy and a benevolent fund for injured drivers. With assistance from Daytona Beach attorney Louis Ossinski, NASCAR was formed into a private corporation with France as President. E. G. "Cannonball" Baker, a well-respected racer from the Roaring '20s, was appointed National Commissioner.

NASCAR also expanded its boundaries to include operations in the Northeast and Midwest, forming a pair of regional series outside the deep South. Houston Lawing was appointed publicity director for NASCAR, and his typewriter became an important piece of traveling hardware.

The first official NASCAR-sanctioned stock car racing event took place on a special 2.2-mile portion of Daytona's 4.1-mile Beach-Road course on Feb. 15, 1948. Fifty cars took the green flag and more than half were out of the race by the halfway mark. Red Byron sailed into the lead with 16 laps remaining and sped to victory.

The 1948 NASCAR championship season consisted of 52 races, each packed with its own distinct flair and drama. Hopped up prewar coupes, known as "Modifieds," comprised each field. The Modified championship races were staged in seven different states from Birmingham, Ala., to Langhorne, Penn. Fourteen different drivers earned at least one trip to victory lane on a variety of speedways. A few female drivers, including Sara Christian, Louise Smith, and Ethel Flock, competed alongside the fellows.

Crusty veteran Robert "Red" Byron won the 1948 NASCAR championship on the strength of 11 wins. In a close title chase, Byron edged Flock by only 37.75 points. The early NASCAR points system included fractions of points.

Byron, a gunner in dangerous air battles during the war, emerged as the personification of the American Dream. A decorated war hero, Byron had spent more than two years in Army hospitals while doctors tried to keep him alive and piece his mangled left leg back together. He returned to stock car racing after the war, and, incredibly, resumed his winning ways. NASCAR publicist Houston Lawing referred to Bryon as "the disabled war veteran."

Byron trailed Flock during most of the 1948 title chase. With a flourish at the end of the campaign, Byron won four of the last seven races and finished no worse than second. He snatched the points lead from Flock with three races remaining. Byron and Flock swapped one-two finishes in each of the last three races as both rose to the occasion. The two title contenders, who collectively won half the 52 races,

had been brilliant and spectacular throughout the season. Byron collected $1250 in postseason money for winning the inaugural NASCAR championship while Flock pocketed $600 as his runner-up prize.

Bill France and his loyal sidekicks, operating out of a rolling trailer that also served as an office, pulled off the exhaustive 52-race season with few glitches. The Modifieds were immensely successful, and France wanted to capitalize on the rising popularity. He drew up plans to introduce a Roadster Circuit in 1949. The chopped up, topless cars were the wheels of the assertive American youth. Maybe there would be an interest in Roadster racing somewhere other than California.

While the Roadsters auditioned at a few tracks in early 1949, paying spectators showed only a passing interest. They still thrilled at watching the aging prewar family sedans in competition on the short-track battlegrounds. By late spring 1949, the Roadster Circuit fizzled out, never having left its imprint on the canvas of NASCAR motorsports.

The Modifieds kicked off their 1949 campaign on Jan. 16 with a 200-miler on Daytona's Beach-Road course. Home-grown boy Marshall Teague overtook Ed Samples' disabled machine two laps from the finish and sped to victory. Fonty Flock, who ran fifth at Daytona, won the next three races at Ft. Lauderdale, Jacksonville, and Morrow, a small town south of Atlanta. Fonty jumped to a healthy points lead.

About the same time NASCAR threw in the Roadster towel, Bill France started toying with the idea of a circuit for late-model American cars. Prior to the war, nearly every

stock car race was entirely comprised of late-model sedans. A shortage of new, postwar automobiles delayed any serious thought of racing late models—until May 1949, when France announced plans to conduct a "Strictly Stock" race in June.

News of Bill France's latest brainstorm spread quickly. With its central location, Charlotte Speedway was chosen to host the 150-mile race for stock late-model cars. The two-year-old facility was a rough ¾-mile dirt track surrounded by scraggly fences of undressed lumber. Charlotte had become a regular stop on NASCAR's annual Modified tour, and its seating capacity of 10,000-plus was a factor in France's decision. The field for the June 19, 1949, Strictly Stock race would be open to the fastest 33 cars in qualifications, *à la* the Indianapolis 500.

Race trim for the cars consisted of a number painted on the door, optional protective screens to keep mud and rocks out of the radiator, and some masking tape securing the headlights. Many of the cars were driven to the track, and less than 30 had entered. Some accomplished drivers with helmets in hand had no car to drive. By the same token, there were plenty of new—and perhaps speedy—American cars parked in the infield that belonged to racing enthusiasts. Tim Flock spotted a '49 Oldsmobile 88 resting in the infield. The owner of the car, Buddy Elliott, was sitting on the hood, watching practice. Flock actually talked Elliott into letting him drive that brand-new car in the race.

Amazingly, Tim took the car out and qualified second. Bob Flock, Tim's older brother and personal mentor, put a new

Hudson on the pole. Glenn Dunnaway found a 1947 Ford owned by Hubert Westmoreland, and he, too, got a ride just before qualifying. Dunnaway was told the car could possibly be a moonshine runner, which probably meant it was a pretty fast car. Dunnaway qualified seventh.

On race morning, the crowd of cars along Wilkinson Boulevard leading to the speedway was enormous. Five solid miles of cars broke the serenity of a lazy Southern Sunday. Although written reports indicated more than 20,000 spectators were on hand for the historic event, about 13,000 paid to get in.

The 200-lap, 150-mile race was a hoot. Thirty-three new cars slapped fenders, sent up billowing clouds of red dust, and thrilled the trackside audience for a shade over two hours. Bob Flock's new Hudson succumbed to engine problems early, but he hopped in a car that was started by Sara Christian and resumed the chase. Several cars dropped out with overheated engines. Lee Petty rolled his Buick Roadmaster four times shortly after the halfway point without injury.

As the race neared its conclusion, Dunnaway had put his bootlegger Ford out front. He passed Jim Roper's sputtering Lincoln in the final laps and cruised to victory, earning $2000 from the overall purse of $6000. Roper held on for a second-place finish.

After the race, the NASCAR technical committee, headed by Al Crisler, thoroughly inspected the top finishing cars. Crisler soon realized he had a problem on his hands. The winning 1947 Ford that Dunnaway had driven was equipped with stiffened springs, affording better traction in the corners. Custom work on an automobile's springs was essential to deliver moonshine quickly to its secret destination, and it figured prominently in Dunnaway's victory ride at Charlotte. But stiffened springs didn't jibe with the Strictly Stock guidelines that NASCAR stressed. Crisler disqualified the car with France's blessing. Westmoreland challenged the ruling in court, but the case was dismissed. Jim Roper became the winner of the first race on the circuit that would eventually become known as the NASCAR NEXTEL Cup Series.

Seven other Strictly Stock races were staged during the 1949 season, including events near Pittsburgh and in upstate New York. Attendance figures were tremendous: 20,000 at Langhorne; 17,500 at Occoneechee Speedway in Hillsboro, N.C.; and 11,733 at Hamburg, New York. The Strictly Stocks had become a booming success.

Red Byron, twice a winner during the inaugural 1949 Strictly Stock season, captured the championship and shared top honors with Fonty Flock, who was crowned champion of the Modified circuit. Byron won $1000 in points money, while Flock enjoyed a $1250 points purse since the Modifieds staged more shows and therefore had more money in the kitty.

As the decade of the 1940s drew to a close, NASCAR's festival of noise and color had achieved a new level of respectability within professional motorsports. NASCAR's growing popularity was Bill France's doing through his steadfast determination, unique attitude, polished people skills, and eye toward the future.

1947

January Bill France announces he will direct a series of stock car races under the National Championship Stock Car Circuit banner in 1947. France's slogan for the new touring series is "NCSCC: Where The Fastest That Run, Run The Fastest."

January 26 Red Byron captures the inaugural NCSCC event, billed as the "Battle of Champions," on the Beach-Road course at Daytona.

May 18 Fonty Flock wins the inaugural event at North Wilkesboro (N.C.) Speedway. The race is a smashing success, with over 10,000 spectators in attendance.

June 15 Bob Flock drives his Ford to victory in the NCSCC event at Greensboro, N.C. Ed Samples, the recognized 1946 stock car racing champion, rolls three times but continues in the race.

June 29 Jimmie Lewallen slips past Fonty Flock on the final lap to win the 80-lap NCSCC race at High Point, N.C.

August 10 Bob Flock leads most of the way and wins the 200-mile marathon race at Langhorne Speedway's circular one-mile track in Pennsylvania. Forty-five cars start the race, but only 19 finish.

August 17 Bob Flock starts last, charges to the lead in the opening lap, and sprints to an overwhelming victory in the 100-mile race at Daytona Beach.

September 7 The new track in Martinsville, Va., opens to a large crowd. Red Byron finishes first in a 50-lap event that is marred by deplorable dust conditions.

September 14 A huge crowd of 20,000 turns out for the 160-lap race at North Wilkesboro. Marshall Teague wins as more than 1000 carloads of racing fans are turned away due to lack of parking space.

October 17 Bob Flock falls out of contention for the championship when he fractures his back in a spill at Spartanburg, S.C., and is forced to miss the rest of the season.

This rare color photograph shows "Big Bill" France posing beside the utility vehicle he drove around during the 1947 season. Prior to the incorporation of NASCAR, France operated the National Championship Stock Car Circuit, as noted on the door of the black Ford.

Top contending driver Buddy Shuman stands beside the 1939 Ford he ran at North Wilkesboro Speedway. The track, which opened on May 18, 1947, actually owned Shuman's car. Tracks often fielded top running cars to ensure quality cars would run at their races. Shuman scored his first win of the '47 season one week later at Birmingham, Ala., beating Bob Flock and Glenn Dunnaway in a close finish.

Fonty Flock, who hadn't raced since being severely injured in the summer of 1941, returned to stock car racing in '47. Here, Flock hugs the inside rail and leads #15 Bill Snowden and #14, big brother, Bob Flock.

The one-mile Lakewood Speedway in downtown Atlanta was the scene of many important stock car races, even though it operated independently and wasn't a part of the National Championship Stock Car Circuit. The infield lake left little room for a pit area. The grandstand, which seated up to 18,000 spectators, was located near the entrance to the first turn.

Crashes were plentiful in the action-packed 1947 NCSCC events. The drivers often snagged bumpers and tipped over, triggering massive pileups. Safety paraphernalia was virtually nonexistent. Nearly a dozen drivers required hospitalization during the season, but none were killed.

Here, two cars run door-to-door down the front chute at a 1947 NCSCC race. Note the close proximity of the observation tower to the track surface. Unprotected officials stand dangerously on the edge of the speedway.

1947

December 12 Red Byron gallops to victory in the 1947 NCSCC finale at Jacksonville, Fla. Fonty Flock, winner of seven races during the season, is declared the champion. Flock finishes 235 points ahead of two-time winner Ed Samples. Nine-time winner Red Byron finishes third in points.

December 14 Bill France meets with 35 others who share a concern for the future of stock car racing at the Streamline Hotel in Daytona Beach. A set of rules is established and Red Vogt coins the name National Association for Stock Car Auto Racing, which becomes NASCAR. Fonty Flock, winner of the NCSCC title, will be listed as "1947 NASCAR Champion" in all early season press releases.

Glenn "Fireball" Roberts began his stock car racing career in 1947 at age 18. The teenager, who got his nickname for his prowess as a baseball pitcher, displayed raw but unrefined talent in his rookie season. One of his best finishes was seventh place at Daytona on Aug. 17.

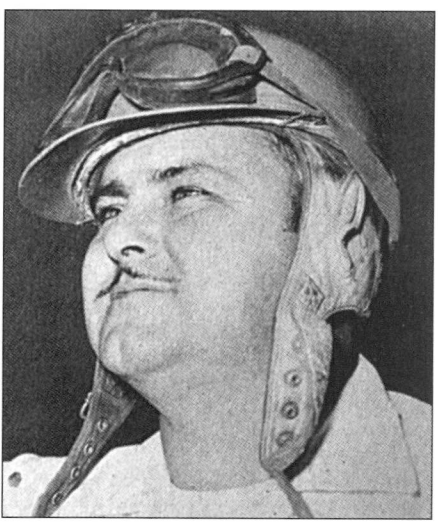

Jimmie Lewallen was one of the front runners in NCSCC competition, winning twice and finishing eighth in the final points standings. Lewallen scored victories at High Point, N.C., and Toccoa, Ga., during the 1947 campaign.

A jam-packed hillside crowd watches the start of the opening stock car event at Elkin Speedway in North Carolina on Aug. 9. Pole-sitter Glenn Dunnaway leads the charge in the #55 car. Johnny Rogers won the 75-lap event on the ½-mile dirt track.

Bill Snowden powerslides through the corner on a dirt track in 1947. The St. Augustine, Fla., veteran was one of the most capable and well-respected drivers on the NCSCC tour.

Red Byron, his uniform soiled by dust, poses beside his Red Vogt-tuned #22 Parks Novelty Machine Co. Ford after a victory at Lakewood Speedway in Atlanta. Byron participated in major independent stock car races and won nine of 18 starts on Bill France's new NCSCC tour.

Newcomer Lee Petty competed sparingly during the 1947 National Championship Stock Car Circuit season, driving the #87 '37 Plymouth owned by Ed Blizzard. Petty didn't begin his racing career until he was 33 years old. He would go on to form Petty Enterprises, the winningest outfit in NASCAR history.

Bowman Gray Stadium in Winston-Salem, N.C., opened in June 1947 with a variety of stock car races. The tiny ¼-mile track featured narrow dimensions, but the drivers still ran three-abreast. Bowman Gray hosted weekly events, but didn't stage any NCSCC championship meets in '47.

Dust swirls as a closely bunched pack of cars speeds down the front chute in a 1947 NCSCC event. Swayne Pritchett, driving the #17 Ford, takes the high line down the straightaway. Pritchett was a part-timer in the NCSCC, finishing 18th in the final points standings.

1947

Buddy Shuman guides his 1939 Ford through the south turn during the Aug. 17 race on Daytona's Beach-Road course. Shuman finished sixth. Bob Flock led every lap in driving to victory.

Fisticuffs were plentiful in the early days of stock car racing. Drivers would often engage in heated battles on the racetracks, then settle personal differences in the pit area after the event was over.

Red Byron (left) and Fonty Flock were two of the top contenders for the inaugural National Championship Stock Car Circuit title. Byron won the most races, taking nine checkered flags in only 18 starts. Flock prevailed seven times in 24 starts and won the NCSCC championship because he competed in more races.

Bob Flock was in the thick of the championship chase until he fractured his back in a nasty spill in the Oct. 17 NCSCC event at Spartanburg, S.C. Despite laying out of action for the final six weeks of the season, Flock finished fifth in the final points standings.

Bill Snowden limps around the corner with a flat left front tire as a rival closes in rapidly. Flat tires were a major problem in the formative days because virtually all the rubber used came from local garages. Race-tire technology was still a concept for the future.

Marshall Teague drives his Hill Motor Co. #4 Ford around a track without a protective helmet. Teague was injured in a spill at North Wilkesboro and missed several races. He still accumulated enough points to rank 10th in the championship chase at the end of the 1947 NCSCC season.

Fonty Flock poses with the handsome championship trophy he received for capturing the NCSCC title. The inscription on the trophy reads: "Won by Fonty Flock—Atlanta, Ga.—Driving for Parks-Vogt Racing Team—1765 Total Points Won—National Championship Stock Car Racing Circuit."

In December 1947, the spic-and-span Streamline Hotel was the scene of a series of meetings that laid the groundwork for the NASCAR circuit. The historic hotel still stands today on Highway A-1-A in Daytona Beach.

Bill France

WILLIAM HENRY Getty France, known simply as "Big Bill," brought an imaginative and resourceful mind to the sport of stock car racing. A driver of considerable merit in his early days, Big Bill's most valuable asset was his ability to organize a growing sport. For the better part of a decade, he toured scores of small, dimly lit dirt tracks, crisscrossing virtually every trail east of the Mississippi and developing a working knowledge of promoting a sport that—at the time—wasn't worth promoting.

Born on Sept. 26, 1906, in Washington, D.C., France was the son of a Virginia farmer. He was mechanically inclined as a youngster and enjoyed watching the old board-track races in Laurel, Md. In 1934, France and his budding family migrated to Florida and settled in Daytona Beach.

France donned a helmet and competed in a number of auto races, including the first race on the sands of Daytona in 1936. By '40, he was regarded as the number-one stock car racer in the country.

Big Bill hung up his goggles in 1946 and focused his efforts on promoting the sport of stock car racing. France peered into an uncertain future with crystal clarity, honing and nurturing racing into a major enterprise. "He had more foresight than anyone could have imagined," said Glen Wood, patriarch of the famous Wood Brothers Racing team. "He certainly got stock car racing going when no one else considered it."

In 1947, France developed the National Championship Stock Car Circuit, a precursor to the NASCAR touring series. It proved to be the canvas on which France would unleash his uncanny gift for auto-racing promotions.

France perceived the untapped potential of organized stock car racing and its rough-hewn personalities. He believed he could create nuggets of gold out of a series of events that no other individual had been able to make interesting to a mass audience.

France combined all his instincts into a unified theory that promoting stock car racing's personalities would help his circuit to be embraced by a growing sports-minded society. The implications reached far beyond a mere sporting event to marketable entertainment.

France organized and incorporated NASCAR in 1948. NASCAR guaranteed prize money would be paid, created a benevolent fund for injured drivers, and made heroes of the drivers by honoring champions determined by points standings. "Everything he did, he did right," says Richard Childress, one of the top team owners in NASCAR history. "He didn't just look out for himself. He cared for everybody. That's the thing I admire most about him."

France provided steady leadership that led NASCAR into the future. In 1959, he opened the Daytona International Speedway, realizing that a rapidly expanding sport needed finer facilities. He took a firm and unwavering stance against possible Teamsters Union involvement in NASCAR in '61, defeating the powerful entity. He courted the television networks as NASCAR advanced into the electronic media, getting races on TV as early as 1960 and signing the first live-broadcast racing deal with ABC in '70. And he took the bull by the horns during the energy shortage in '74, guiding the sport through an uncertain time when the mere existence of auto racing was threatened by politicians.

"He was a great innovator as far as having the foresight into racing, what he was after, and what he was trying to accomplish," said Hall of Famer Junior Johnson. "He had a dream and stood by that dream. His efforts are what we see in our sport today. There have been a lot of heroes come through this sport. But Bill France is *the* hero of our sport."

1948

February 15 Red Byron wins the first NASCAR-sanctioned auto race in a 1939 Modified Ford owned by Raymond Parks and tuned by Red Vogt. Of the 62 cars that enter, 50 start. A crowd of 14,000 pays $2.50 each to watch the historic moment at the Daytona Beach-Road course.

February 21 Louis Ossinski, an attorney and aide to Bill France, completes the paperwork for the new stock car racing organization. NASCAR becomes incorporated.

February 24 Fonty Flock wins the NASCAR Modified race at Jacksonville, Fla. The steering wheel breaks on Flock's 1939 Ford, but he drives the late stages using only the remaining steering spoke.

May 23 NASCAR stages three championship events in different locations on the same day. Gober Sosebee wins at Macon, Ga., Bill Blair captures the feature in Danville, Va., and Johnny Rogers tops the field at Dover, N.J.

May 30 Veteran driver Paul Pappy outruns 19-year-old rookie Fireball Roberts to win the 40-lap Modified championship race at Jacksonville. It is the first time Roberts emerges as a stout contender.

June 20 NASCAR makes its first trip to Alabama. Fonty Flock wins the Modified feature at Birmingham. On the same day, Tim Flock scores his first NASCAR win at Greensboro, N.C.

July 25 Slick Davis becomes the first NASCAR driver to be fatally injured. The tragedy happens in an event at Greensboro, N.C. Curtis Turner starts on the pole and wins the race. Billy Carden wins another NASCAR Modified race held on the same day in Columbus, Ga.

August 15 Al Keller spanks the 48-car field in a 200-mile NASCAR Modified race at Langhorne's circular one-mile dirt track. Runner-up Buck Barr finishes 18 laps behind Keller. Only 14 of the 48 starters manage to finish.

August 20 NASCAR is forced to cancel a number of scheduled events due to an outbreak of polio in North Carolina.

The first event of the 1948 season took place at the Pompano Beach Speedway, a huge 1¼-mile dirt track that didn't have grandstands. While the Jan. 4 event wasn't officially part of the NASCAR schedule, the field was filled with NASCAR drivers. Buddy Shuman won the 62½-mile race as the throng stood along the outer rim of the track.

Buddy Shuman, winner of the stock car racing debut at the Pompano Beach Speedway, is pictured with NASCAR president Bill France. Shuman won one of the two heat races and outran Louie Taylor and Bill Snowden to win the feature.

NASCAR President Bill France (right) and National Commissioner Cannonball Baker present Fonty Flock and Ed Samples (left) with trophies before the start of the inaugural NASCAR-sanctioned event at Daytona on Feb. 15. Flock won the National Championship Stock Car Circuit title in 1947 and Samples finished second in the points standings. Samples was acknowledged as the '46 stock car racing champion.

Fonty Flock's #1 Al Dykes 1939 Ford lies in a patch of palmetto bushes after tumbling off the course during the first NASCAR race at Daytona's Beach-Road course. Flock was shaken, but not seriously hurt after flipping end-over-end nearly a dozen times.

Femme fatale racer Sara Christian guns her Ford through the tight corner at Macon Speedway in Georgia on April 4. Christian was the most accomplished female driver in the early days of NASCAR. Note the dozens of spectators perched on the rooftop of a nearby structure for unobstructed viewing.

Red Byron is presented with a trophy for winning the Feb. 15 NASCAR race at Daytona. The post-race ceremonies were conducted as darkness descended on the Beach-Road course. Standing to the right is NASCAR Commissioner Erwin "Cannonball" Baker. The young lady is unidentified.

Fonty Flock waves to the sellout crowd as he takes the checkered flag to win the NASCAR race at New Atlanta Speedway on March 27. The crowd was so large that spectators stood atop the two-foot high concrete retaining wall. No protective catch-fence was in place at the ½-mile dirt track.

1948

September 5 Curtis Turner bags the doubleheader at North Wilkesboro Speedway. Turner wins the opener from the pole. An inverted start for the second event fails to slow Turner, who slashes through the field to beat runner-up Bob Smith, who owns the cars he and Turner are driving.

November 14 Red Byron wins the season finale at Jacksonville, Fla. Byron, winner of 11 of the 52 NASCAR-sanctioned events, edges Fonty Flock by 32.75 points to capture the inaugural championship. Flock is the top winner, taking the checkered flag 15 times, but he finishes 32.75 points behind Byron. Byron collects $1250 in points fund earnings.

Bill Snowden in #16 runs just ahead of #22 Red Byron and #17 Swayne Pritchett at Augusta Speedway on April 11. Bob Flock won the race, finishing ahead of Fonty Flock and third-place finisher Pritchett. A month later, Pritchett lost his life in an independent race at Jefferson, Ga., when his throttle hung open after he received the checkered flag.

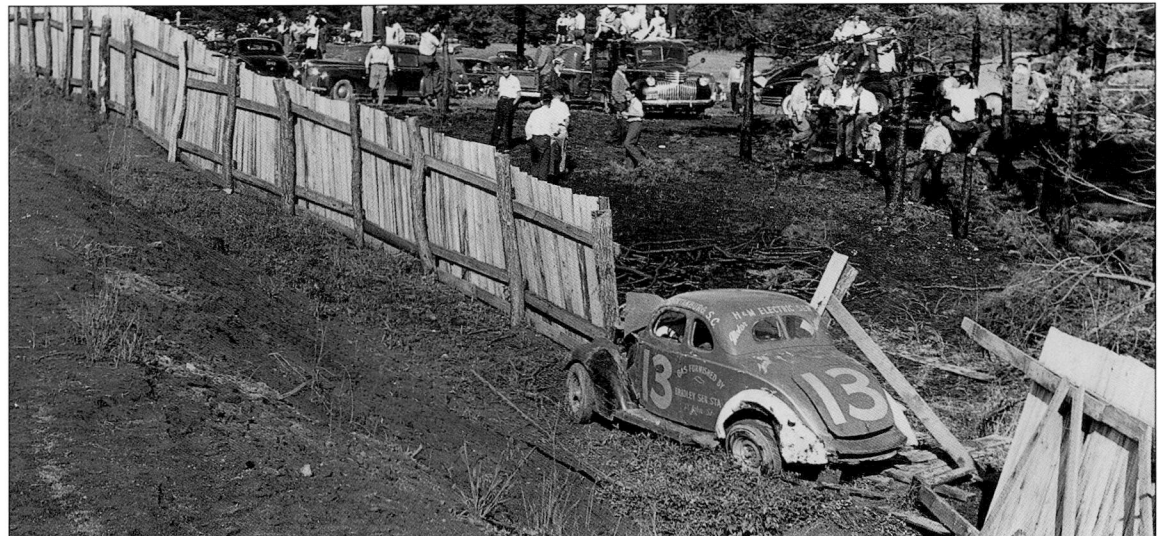

Ed Southers' battered #13 Ford rests on the outskirts of the Lakeview Speedway in Lexington, N.C., after crashing through the wooden fence during the inaugural event at the ⅝-mile dirt track. Southers was unhurt in the accident. Red Byron won the 30-lap contest.

Two cars spin in tight traffic during one of the early NASCAR races. In many cases, cars spun into a dusty infield and managed to return to action. Note the whitewall tires on the car at the far left.

Front-row starters #90 Tim Flock and #55 Glenn Dunnaway lead #9 Ed Samples and #14 Bob Flock in the opening heat race on June 6 at Lakeview Speedway in North Carolina. Note the narrow pit area where cars slated to compete in the next heat race are parked. Bob Flock won the 30-lap feature, with Tim Flock running a close second.

▼ The one-mile Occoneechee Speedway presented its inaugural race on June 27. The NASCAR Modifieds competed in a 100-mile jaunt, one of the biggest events on the '48 calendar. Jack Etheridge cocks his #6 Ford into the corner, just ahead of #7/11 Sara Christian. Others pictured are #7 Frank Mundy, #14 Bob Flock, and #44 Marshall Teague. Fonty Flock beat Teague to take the victory.

NASCAR's newfangled form of motorsports played host to many capacity crowds during the 1948 Modified campaign. Thousands of spectators would pay between $2 and $4 to watch the carnival of craziness.

Bob Flock throttles his way past an overturned vehicle during one of the 1948 NASCAR events. NASCAR sanctioned 52 championship events in its inaugural season. Flock won five times and finished seventh in the final points standings.

A group of cars hustle down the front chute at Occoneechee Speedway in Hillsboro, N.C. The one-mile track was located on the Occoneechee Farm, which was once an Indian reservation. Five men, Dobe Powell, Enoch Staley, Bill France, Charlie Combs, and Ben Lowe, pooled their resources and efforts to build the picturesque track. Fonty Flock bagged both ends of a doubleheader on Sept. 9.

Young Tim Flock began his racing career in 1947 and scored his first victory at Greensboro, N.C., on June 20, 1948, behind the wheel of Charlie Mobley's '39 Ford. Flock learned the tricks of the racing trade at Atlanta's Lakewood Speedway when big brother Bob took him on the course and promptly rode him into the trees. Bob's teaching method was odd, but he did it to prepare Tim for what would happen when he entered actual competition.

Buddy Shuman was one of NASCAR's most ardent supporters in its formative years. He competed in most of the events and was a contender in many. Shuman won two races in 1948 plus the nonpoints race in Pompano Beach. He also scored four runner-up finishes and wound up fifth in the final points standings.

Wrecks were a part of the NASCAR landscape in 1948. Most drivers were able to walk away from bone-jarring crashes such as this. One driver, W.R. "Slick" Davis, lost his life in a crash at Greensboro on July 25, becoming the first fatality in NASCAR competition.

Fonty Flock

A CORNERSTONE of the folklore of NASCAR's early years. Truman Fontello Flock was more than an accomplished throttle stomper. Known as Fonty, he was intelligent, well-spoken, and one of the few drivers of the late 1940s who felt at ease with the media. Always humorous and witty, he conducted himself admirably and helped NASCAR become a marketable commodity in its formative days.

As a teenager, Fonty sharpened his natural talents on rough dirt tracks under the tutelage of his older brother Bob. By the time he was 20 in 1941, Flock was regarded as one of stock car racing's best drivers. His rapid ascent to elite status took him to Bill France's touring series.

Fonty was crowned the champion of the 1947 National Championship Stock Car Circuit, the forerunner to NASCAR. He finished second in the '48 NASCAR standings and won the '49 Modified title. During the first three years France conducted Modified races, Flock won 34 races in a few more than 100 starts.

When the new Strictly Stock Late Model tour became part of NASCAR's traveling show in 1949, Flock was again one of the central figures. He finished fifth in the inaugural Strictly Stock standings. Flock scored his first NASCAR Grand National win in '50 at Langhorne Speedway, then enjoyed his finest season in '51. Winning eight races and 12 poles, Flock took a close second to Herb Thomas in the '51 Grand National title chase.

Flock was leading the points standings and on pace to capture the 1952 NASCAR Grand National championship until he broke his shoulder in a crash at Martinsville. He was unable to start the following week at Columbia, S.C., and had to have relief help from Jack

NASCAR Grand National Career Record 1949-1957
Starts: 154
Wins: 19
Top 5s: 72
Top 10s: 11
Poles: 33
Career Winnings: $73,758

Smith at Atlanta. Under NASCAR's points system, relief drivers earned points based on the amount of laps driven. When Flock had to relinquish the seat to Smith, he only earned a fraction of the points for the duo's seventh-place finish.

With his arm still in a sling, Fonty drove the next race one handed in Macon, Ga., and miraculously finished second. A victory at Darlington pushed him back into the top five in points. At season's end, Fonty ranked fourth in the NASCAR Grand National standings.

Fonty quit NASCAR early in the 1954 season and campaigned in a Midwestern stock car series. He returned to NASCAR in '55 and won three races. After the '55 season, Flock only competed in selected events. He won one of seven starts in '56 and remained inactive most of the '57 season.

With the eighth annual Southern 500 coming up on Labor Day 1957, Herb Thomas asked Flock to drive his Pontiac in the race. Having won the event in '52, Flock jumped at the chance, but Darlington's fickle blacktop held a trump card.

Flock wrestled with the ill-handling car for the first few laps. On the 28th lap, the car escaped his control and spun at the entrance of turn three. Split seconds later, Bobby Myers and Paul Goldsmith smashed full-bore into the idle Flock. Flock and Goldsmith were seriously hurt. Bobby Myers was killed instantly.

It was the final NASCAR start for Fonty Flock. He announced his retirement from a hospital bed.

During his career in Strictly Stock competition, Flock compiled enviable numbers. He was universally regarded as NASCAR's uncrowned champion.

1948

Brothers Fonty and Bob Flock lead the pack into the first turn in one of the 1948 NASCAR events. Fonty, driving the #1 Al Dykes Ford, was the top race winner in '48 with 15 victories. He finished a close second to 11-time winner Red Byron in the final points standings. Byron took the points lead for the final time after the 49th of 52 races in what turned out to be a memorable championship race between two larger-than-life motorsports heroes.

NASCAR Executive Secretary Bill Tuthill signed all of the checks for the NASCAR points fund. Buddy Shuman finished fifth in the 1948 NASCAR points standings, earning $300. Champion Red Byron received $1250, runner-up Fonty Flock received $600, Tim Flock got $400 for third, and fourth-place Curtis Turner cashed a $350 check from the First Atlantic Bank in Daytona Beach.

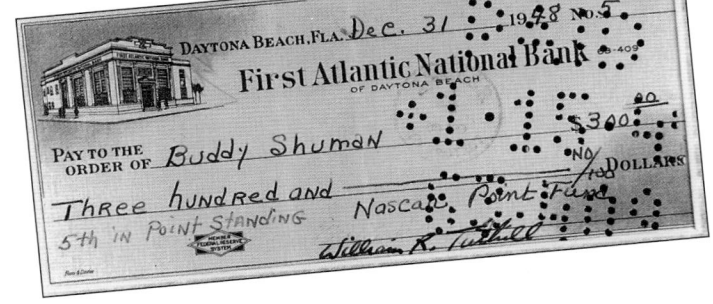

Sara Christian earned the admiration and respect of her male counterparts with an uncanny ability to handle a high-speed automobile. Bob Flock, one of the roughest characters in the early NASCAR days, even sponsored her through his Bob Flock Garage during the latter part of the 1948 NASCAR season.

Gordon Mangum in the #2 and #00 Buck Baker were two of the many early NASCAR pioneers. Mangum raced out of Virginia and Baker was a former bus driver out of Charlotte. Baker failed to win any feature events in 1948, but did manage to finish 10th in the final points standings.

Inaugural NASCAR champion Red Byron chats with Bill France before the start of a race. Byron, a decorated war hero, represented NASCAR well during his championship reign. Quiet but intelligent, Byron's demeanor was quite polished compared to some of his hell-bent comrades. In the 1948 NASCAR campaign, Byron won 11 races and finished second on six occasions.

1948 NASCAR MODIFIED POINTS RACE

Rank	Driver	Points	Starts	Wins	Top 5	Top 10	Winnings
1	Red Byron	2996.5	34	11	25	32	$13,150
2	Fonty Flock	2963.75	40	15	30	34	$14,385
3	Tim Flock	1759.5	25	1	20	24	$5660
4	Curtis Turner	1540.5	26	7	20	22	$6435
5	Buddy Shuman	1350	21	2	15	18	$4365
6	Bill Blair	1188.5	21	1	11	18	$4055
7	Bob Flock	1181.5	20	5	12	16	$4710
8	Marshall Teague	1134.5	16	1	9	12	$3835
9	Bill Snowden	1092.5	14	0	6	14	$2665
10	Buck Baker	952.5	22	0	7	18	$2605
11	Billy Carden	866.5	16	2	8	15	$3115
12	Johnny Grubb	733	19	0	8	16	$1965
13	Speedy Thompson	623	19	0	7	14	$2110
14	Roscoe Thompson	471	10	0	5	7	$1470
15	Jimmie Lewallen	437	13	0	4	10	$1175
16	Al Keller	415	4	1	1	3	$1775
17	Jimmy Thompson	386	16	0	1	10	$1130
18	Jack Smith	384.75	9	0	4	7	$1210
19	Pee Wee Martin	354	12	0	4	8	$795
20	Fred Mahon	353	4	0	3	3	$1255
21	Ed Samples	320.5	13	0	5	9	$1350
22	Swayne Pritchett	290	3	0	2	3	$555
23	Wally Campbell	286	8	0	3	5	$670
24	Carson Dyer	246.5	5	0	3	4	$660
25	Walt Hartman	245	7	0	1	5	$530
26	Skimp Hersey	238.5	14	1	1	6	$895
27	Bob Smith	225	11	0	3	7	$570
28	Olin Allen	220.5	6	0	0	4	$365
29	Fireball Roberts	218.5	6	0	2	3	$670
30	Cotton Owens	218.5	5	0	1	3	$605
31	J.L. McMichaels	217.5	4	0	3	3	$415
32	Jim Paschal	194	10	0	1	5	$360
33	Frank Mundy	183.5	2	0	1	1	$235
34	Doug Wells	183.5	8	0	0	3	$485
35	H.D. Trice	180	3	0	2	3	$445
36	Chick DiNatale	168	1	0	1	1	$100
37	June Cleveland	167.5	3	0	1	3	$505
38	Lee Morgan	166	5	0	1	2	$305
39	Pete Harris	158	2	0	1	3	$240
40	Buck Clardy	155	3	0	1	3	$440
41	Bill McKeehan	155	1	0	0	0	$80
42	Leonard Tippett	150	2	0	2	2	$380
43	Hugh Lanford	149	7	0	1	4	$400
44	Joe Eubanks	148.5	7	0	1	4	$445
45	P.E. Godfrey	136	10	0	1	5	$400
46	Bob Apperson	125.5	8	0	1	5	$295
47	Jerry Wimbish	110	2	0	1	2	$265
48	Frank Reynolds	109	9	0	0	5	$340
49	C.E. Robinson	92.5	2	0	1	2	$215
50	Bob Richey	87.5	3	0	0	3	$170

Red Byron, a decorated war hero, prevailed in an intense battle for the 1948 NASCAR championship after a season-long struggle with '47 title-winner Fonty Flock. Byron grabbed the points lead in the 49th of 52 national championship races and edged Flock by 32.75 points.

Byron won 11 races during the 1948 campaign, including four in a row in April and May. Flock finished first in 15 races, including six wins in the final two months.

Byron and Flock swapped the points lead five times during the season. Byron snared the lead for keeps after winning the Oct. 17 race at North Wilkesboro.

Young Tim Flock wound up third in the points standings, followed by seven-time winner Curtis Turner and two-race winner Buddy Shuman. Bob Flock claimed five wins, but only managed to finish seventh in the final points standings.

1949

January NASCAR heavily promotes its new Roadster division featuring chop-bodied convertibles. The first race scheduled at Daytona is cancelled due to work on the newly designed Beach-Road course. Other events are slated for the Broward Speedway north of Miami.

January 16 Marshall Teague wheels his 1939 Ford Modified to victory in the 202.1-mile NASCAR season opener. The lead changes hands nine times among six drivers. Of the 75 cars that start, only 38 finish the grind.

January 23 NASCAR President Bill France promotes a 100-mile race at the new Broward Speedway. The huge two-mile speedway consists of a paved circle used as taxiways at the Ft. Lauderdale-Davie Airport. Red Byron sets the pack in qualifying with a speed of just over 115 mph. Lloyd Christopher wins a preliminary 10-mile "Strictly Stock Late Model" race. Fonty Flock wins the 50-lap feature at an average speed of 97 mph.

February 27 A second experimental Strictly Stock Late Model race is added to the three-event racing card at Broward Speedway. Benny Georgeson drives a 1947 Buick to victory in the 10-mile contest. Roadsters and Sports Cars are the headlining attraction, but much interest is focused on the new Strictly Stock event. Bob Flock wins the Roadster race at an average speed of 104.5 mph.

March 27 Fonty Flock wins his fourth Modified championship race in a row in the 40-lap feature at North Wilkesboro Speedway. Red Byron, the 1948 NASCAR champion, is unable to compete due to illness.

May Given the interest piqued by two late-model events earlier in the season, NASCAR's Bill France scales back on his promotions of Roadster events and schedules a 200-lap, 150-mile Strictly Stock race at Charlotte Speedway in mid June.

May 15 Red Byron speeds to victory in 40-lap Modified race at Charlotte Speedway. More than 10,000 spectators are in attendance, one of the biggest crowds of the season.

Marshall Teague pushes his #8 Cox Motor Co. 1939 Ford sedan through the south turn along the way to victory in the Jan. 16 Modified race on Daytona's Beach-Road course. Teague took the lead with two laps remaining when leader Ed Samples blew his engine. Teague outran and outlasted a huge 75-car field in the '49 NASCAR Modified division season opener.

Fonty Flock, behind the wheel of Joe Wolf's #47 Ford, holds a narrow advantage over a pack of cars in the March 27 NASCAR Modified race at North Wilkesboro Speedway. Chasing Flock are #16 Bill Snowden, #90 Tim Flock, #22 Red Byron, #44 Frank Mundy, and #7 Bob Apperson. Fonty Flock won 14 races during the 42-race '49 Modified season. He took the points lead following the third event of the season and remained atop the standings for the rest of the year.

Red Byron, NASCAR's 1948 Modified champion, competed in selected Modified events in the '49 campaign. Byron's Park's Novelty & Machine Co. '39 Ford won twice, both victories coming at Charlotte Speedway's dirt track. Despite running less than half the races, Byron wound up seventh in the final Modified points standings.

Tim Flock, wheeling Charlie Mobley's #90 Ford, powers his way past #16 Bill Snowden en route to victory in the May 22 Modified race at North Wilkesboro Speedway. Cotton Owens' abandoned #71 machine rests against the wooden guardrail. Tim Flock was a championship contender in 1949, winning nine races and finishing second to brother Fonty in the final points standings.

Sara Christian was NASCAR's most famous female racer in the early days. The Atlanta housewife was among the 33 starters in the inaugural NASCAR Strictly Stock (today's NEXTEL Cup) race at Charlotte on June 19. Christian drove a Ford entered by her husband Frank. She qualified 13th and drove the first part of the race. During a pit stop, Bob Flock took over and drove to a 14th-place finish.

Female racer Louise Smith is all smiles after her spectacular tumble out of the Occoneechee Speedway during a practice run. After the car was dragged out of the woods, Smith climbed inside the crumpled machine to pose for photographers. One of the most popular competitors in NASCAR's early days, Smith always had an entourage of enthusiastic supporters in her pit area.

Thick, blinding dust billows off the churning tires of the NASCAR Modifieds during the 35-mile race at Hillsboro's Occoneechee Speedway. A total of 36 cars entered the race, which was the 12th of the 1949 Modified season, and Fonty Flock scored his seventh win. Customary procedure for the Modified card included time trials, a pair of heat races, a consolation event, a semifeature, and, finally, the main event.

1949

June 19 More than 13,000 spectators attend the inaugural Strictly Stock National Championship race at the ¾-mile Charlotte Speedway. Glenn Dunnaway crosses the finish line first in a 1946 Ford, but is disqualified when NASCAR inspectors find illegal springs on the former moonshine car. Jim Roper is declared the official winner in a Lincoln. NASCAR Publicity Director Houston Lawing reports more than 5000 fans were turned away due to lack of grandstand space.

June Hubert Westmoreland, owner of the car Dunnaway drove at Charlotte, files a $10,000 lawsuit against NASCAR for disqualifying his car in the 150-mile Strictly Stock race.

Late June With the astounding success of the Charlotte Strictly Stock race, Bill France quickly announces the second race for late-model cars will be held at Daytona in July.

July 10 Red Byron gallops past Gober Sosebee with six laps remaining to win the 166-mile Strictly Stock race on the Daytona Beach-Road course. A less-than-expected crowd of 5000 watches the event. Three female drivers, Ethel Mobley, Louise Smith, and Sara Christian, compete. Mobley finishes 11th.

August 7 A 200-mile Strictly Stock race replaces the scheduled Modified feature at Occoneechee Speedway in Hillsboro, N.C. Bob Flock wins in an Oldsmobile after a six-car crash takes out Red Byron and Sara Christian. Over 17,000 spectators turn out to watch the event.

September 11 Curtis Turner wheels his Oldsmobile to a big victory in the 200-mile NASCAR Strictly Stock race at Langhorne Speedway. More than 20,000 spectators turn out for the celebrated event. Sara Christian finishes sixth in the field of 45, and race winner Turner invites her to join him in victory lane ceremonies.

October 2 Lee Petty records his first NASCAR Strictly Stock victory in the 100-mile race at Heidelberg Speedway near Pittsburgh. Sara Christian finishes fifth, the best finish ever for a female driver in NASCAR's premier stock car racing division.

This panoramic view shows the wall-to-wall crowd that attended the first Strictly Stock race on June 19 at Charlotte Speedway. Initial press releases said 22,500 paid to attend the 150-miler, but later accounting tabbed the throng at 13,000. The race featuring late-model stocks was an instant hit, and NASCAR President Bill France quickly began to arrange other events that featured current-model automobiles.

▲ This is the only known photograph of the winning Lincoln that Jim Roper drove to victory in the first NASCAR Strictly Stock event. Roper read about the race in the *Smilin' Jack* comic strip, syndicated by cartoonist Zack Mosley. The news of the upcoming Strictly Stock race was published in daily newspapers across the country. Roper made the long haul from Great Bend, Kan., and pocketed the $2000 winner's prize.

▼ NASCAR Commissioner Erwin "Cannonball" Baker greets Red Byron after a race. Byron won the second Strictly Stock race at Daytona Beach and climbed atop the NASCAR points standings, a lead he never relinquished. With the mushrooming popularity of the late-model stocks in 1949, Byron cut back on his Modified racing. The veteran driver would become the first champion of what is now the NASCAR NEXTEL Cup Series.

A sell-out crowd is on its feet as second-row starters #22 Red Byron and #19 Otis Martin cruise down the front stretch during the pace lap of the first-ever NASCAR Strictly Stock race at Charlotte Speedway. Glenn Dunnaway's Ford, pictured on the inside of the third row, drove to victory. However, his car, which was a moonshine runner, was disqualified for illegal rear springs, leaving Jim Roper with the win.

Circular Langhorne Speedway in Pennsylvania was the site of the fourth NASCAR Strictly Stock race of the 1949 season. The one-mile dirt track contained no straightaways. Drivers who tackled the fickle monster had to run flat out for the entire distance in a four-wheel drift. Langhorne Speedway was one of the most punishing and dangerous racing facilities ever built.

Ed Tyson's #62 Ford leads the #52 Buick of Lou Volk and Erwin Blatt's #23 Ford on the front bend of Langhorne Speedway on Sept. 1 as the sell-out crowd of 20,000 looks on. Volk finished 10th after starting 34th in the 45-car field. Blatt ran 14th, and Tyson took 21st. Volk won $125 for his top-10 effort, while Blatt and Tyson each pocketed $50.

Ken Schroeder guns his #77 1949 Buick around Langhorne Speedway during the Sept. 1 Strictly Stock race. The Strictly Stocks were just that—highway-legal automobiles. Headlights were taped, protective screens were placed over the grilles, doors were strapped shut, and the numbers were often applied with masking tape. Tommy Coates is in the #91 Ford and Bob Flock is in his #7 Olds. Flock ran second to Curtis Turner in the 200-mile contest.

1949

October 16 Bob Flock captures the eighth and final 1949 Strictly Stock championship race at North Wilkesboro Speedway. Red Byron is crowned the first Strictly Stock champion, finishing 117.5-points ahead of runner-up Lee Petty. Byron won two of his six starts.

October 23 Promoter Sam Nunis schedules a 150-mile Strictly Stock race at Atlanta's Lakewood Speedway with the National Stock Car Racing Association (NSCRA) as the sanctioning body. NASCAR's Bill France copromotes the event, which attracts a crowd of 33,452. Tim Flock wins in an Oldsmobile.

November 13 With the financial success of the Lakewood Speedway Strictly Stock race, promoter Nunis schedules an encore event for Nov. 13. The race is curtailed by rain and completed the following week. June Cleveland wins in a Buick before 22,000 spectators.

November 28 NASCAR announces that the victory dinner to honor divisional champions will take place in Daytona Beach on Feb. 1, 1950. Red Byron is honored as the inaugural NASCAR Strictly Stock champion, while Fonty Flock is crowned the champion of the Modified division.

December 5 The Central States Racing Association, a rival Midwestern-based stock car racing sanctioning body, announces it will sanction the inaugural Southern 500 at the new Darlington Raceway in 1950. Track president Harold Brasington attempted to get NASCAR to sanction the first 500-mile stock car race, but Bill France turned down the offer fearful the Strictly Stock cars couldn't go a full 500 miles.

December NASCAR's public relations office releases the winner of the first Most Popular Driver poll. Curtis Turner garners the most votes by NASCAR racing fans, finishing ahead of Red Byron. Other awards, via a poll of fans, went to Byron (Best Strictly Stock Car Driver), Turner (Best Modified Driver), Sara Christian (Best Woman Driver), and Joe Wolf (Outstanding Mechanic).

December 16 Judge John J. Hayes dismisses the lawsuit filed by Hubert Westmoreland, and rules NASCAR is allowed to disqualify cars that don't comply with technical specifications.

Sara Christian competed in six of the eight Strictly Stock races in the inaugural 1949 season. She finished an impressive sixth at Langhorne in her #71 Oldsmobile, and race-winner Curtis Turner invited her to join him in the victory lane ceremonies. Less than a month later, Christian finished a strong fifth in the 100-miler at Heidelberg Speedway in Pittsburgh. It remains the best finish for a female driver in NASCAR's top division.

Lee Petty drove in six Strictly Stock races in 1949, including the inaugural event at Charlotte. Petty drove a borrowed Buick Roadmaster in the Charlotte race and rolled the car four times on lap 108. After that, Petty switched to a lightweight Plymouth, figuring a lighter car would handle better in the corners. Petty racked up his first victory in the Plymouth in the Oct. 2 race at Heidelberg Speedway.

Herb Thomas, a farmer and truck driver from Olivia, N.C., caught the racing bug in the late 1940s and entered four of the Strictly Stock races in '49. Driving a Ford, Thomas' best effort was a fifth-place finish at North Wilkesboro. He wound up 25th in points and won a grand total of $225 for the entire season. It was the beginning of what would eventually turn out to be a stellar career in the NASCAR stocks.

Fonty Flock's huge Buick Roadmaster negotiates the fourth turn at North Wilkesboro Speedway during the final Strictly Stock race of the season on Oct. 16. Flock finished third and won $400. Flock won the 1949 NASCAR Modified championship and finished fifth in the final Strictly Stock points standings, the only driver to log top-five finishes in the same season in both of NASCAR's top two divisions.

NASCAR's team of inspectors made every effort to ensure that the Strictly Stocks were within the rules. Henry Underhill checks under the hood of Lee Petty's Plymouth prior to the North Wilkesboro event. Major Al Crisler, NASCAR's Technical Director, checks out the suspension, while Bill Middlebrook makes sure the steering mechanism is safe. By the way, that's 12-year-old Richard Petty in the background, peering over his father's car.

Red Byron

ROBERT N. BYRON'S name is prominently etched in NASCAR's record books, having won the inaugural championship in 1948 and the first NASCAR Strictly Stock title (now known as the NASCAR NEXTEL Cup Series) in '49. Known as "Red" throughout his life, he refined the art of slinging dirt.

Byron, from Anniston, Ala., claimed he first drove an automobile at age five and owned a car when he was 10. "It was a Model T Ford and that was in 1926," Byron said.

Young Red stripped the Ford down, slashed off the fenders, stiffened the suspension, and doctored the engine. He accepted the challenges of older kids to participate in unorganized races around a homemade track carved out of a local cow pasture. It was there that he won his first race.

Byron's professional racing career began when he was only 16. In the 1930s, he was interested in any form of speed on four wheels, be it open wheelers, chopped-up roadsters, powerful Midgets, or stock cars. During his early adulthood, Byron rose through the ranks of educational (small-time) racing and developed into a consistent winner.

With the outbreak of World War II, Byron's racing career was put on hold. He enlisted in the U.S. Army Air Forces and served as a flight engineer on a B-24 bomber. He completed 57 missions in Europe, but was shot down on his 58th over the Aleutian Islands. Critically wounded, Byron spent more than two years in Army hospitals.

He left the hospital in 1945, able to walk on his own with the aid of a cane. Byron had authored countless feats of courage and resilience in the war, and he laid plans to return to auto racing.

In February 1946, Byron made a triumphant return to racing in a Modified event in Orlando, Fla. He nosed out Roy Hall and Bill France in a three-car finish. When he parked in the make-do confines of a roped-off victory lane, Byron had to be helped from his car. His left leg, so badly damaged in the war, had been placed in a steel stirrup that was bolted to the clutch. When he unbuckled the chin strap of his Cromwell helmet, he looked like a man twice his age of 30.

Despite his game leg and his frail appearance, Red Byron could dazzle and bewilder the best stock jockeys in the business. He developed patience and savvy to complement his undiminished aggression, and it paid off with back-to-back NASCAR championships.

Byron only competed in 15 races from 1949 to '51 in NASCAR Strictly Stock and NASCAR Grand National competition. He posted two wins and registered nine top-10 finishes.

Declining health forced him to hang up his goggles in 1951, but he remained active in racing. He worked with Briggs Cunningham, who was trying to develop an American sports car that could win Grand Prix races, then became manager of a Corvette team with the same goal. Neither project succeeded, but Byron enjoyed sports cars. When he died of a heart attack in a Chicago hotel room on Nov. 7, 1960, at the age of 44, he was managing a team in Sports Car Club of America competition.

1949

Ken Wagner's Lincoln leads #14 Roy Hall, #22 Red Byron, and Bill Blair's Cadillac in the Oct. 16 Strictly Stock season finale at North Wilkesboro Speedway. Wagner earned the pole position with a speed of 57.563 mph, but retired due to mechanical problems. Hall finished sixth in his Oldsmobile. A week later, on Oct. 23, Hall was critically injured in a spill during a Modified race at High Point, N.C.

After the close of the 1949 NASCAR Strictly Stock season, independent promoter Sam Nunis staged a late-model race at Atlanta's Lakewood Speedway. NASCAR President Bill France assisted Nunis with administrative duties, opening the door for NASCAR regulars to compete. A huge crowd of 33,452 attended the event, which was officially sanctioned by the rival National Stock Car Racing Association. Tim Flock won in an Oldsmobile.

Fonty Flock poses with his sister, race car driver Ethel Flock Mobley, before the Oct. 23 Atlanta race. Mobley drove in two Strictly Stock events in '49, including the Daytona Beach race that had three female drivers in the lineup. Ethel was the wife of Charlie Mobley, who fielded Modified cars for Tim Flock.

Red Byron, the 1949 Strictly Stock champion, pitches his #22 Oldsmobile into the first turn in the first postseason Lakewood Speedway late-model race. Byron encountered mechanical problems that removed him from contention.

Red Byron breezes through a turn at Atlanta during the second late-model race promoted by Sam Nunis on Nov. 13. Byron finished fourth in the event, which was won by June Cleveland. Note the tarpaulin strapped to the fence high above the track to keep people from watching the race free of charge.

Carl Green, manager and operator of the Hanger Restaurant located near the Atlanta Municipal Airport, poses with Harold Kite prior to one of the Lakewood Speedway races. Green might have cooked a tasty steak and provided comfortable accommodations at his hotel, but his forte certainly wasn't spelling.

1949 NASCAR STRICTLY STOCK POINTS RACE

Rank	Driver	Points	Starts	Wins	Top 5	Top 10	Winnings
1	Red Byron	842.5	6	2	4	4	$5800
2	Lee Petty	725	6	1	3	5	$3855
3	Bob Flock	704	6	2	3	3	$4870
4	Bill Blair	567	6	0	3	5	$1180
5	Fonty Flock	554	6	0	3	3	$2015
6	Curtis Turner	430	6	1	1	4	$2675
7	Ray Erickson	422	4	0	2	3	$1460
8	Tim Flock	421	5	0	2	3	$1510
9	Glenn Dunnaway	384	6	0	1	3	$810
10	Frank Mundy	370	4	0	2	2	$1160
11	Bill Snowden	315	4	0	1	3	$660
12	Bill Rexford	286	3	0	2	2	$785
13	Sara Christian	282	6	0	1	2	$760
14	Clyde Minter	280	2	0	2	2	$760
15	Gober Sosebee	265	3	0	1	2	$1305
16	Jim Roper	253	2	1	1	1	$2130
17	Sam Rice	231	2	0	2	2	$680
18	Jack White	200	1	1	1	1	$1580
19	Dick Linder	180.5	3	0	1	1	$830
20	Billy Rafter	160	1	0	1	1	$480
21	Archie Smith	145	2	0	0	1	$225
22	Joe Littlejohn	140	1	0	1	1	$300
	Jack Russell	140	3	0	0	2	$175
	Mike Eagan	140	1	0	1	1	$300
25	Herb Thomas	132	4	0	1	1	$225
26	Sterling Long	100	2	0	0	1	$150
	Frank Christian	100	1	0	0	1	$175
	Frankie Schneider	100	1	0	0	1	$150
	Lloyd Moore	100	1	0	0	1	$150
	Roy Hall	100	1	0	0	1	$150
31	Slick Smith	99	4	0	0	1	$275
32	Al Keller	80	1	0	0	1	$200
33	John Wright	80	1	0	0	1	$100
	Al Bonnell	80	2	0	0	1	$150
35	Otis Martin	69.5	4	0	0	1	$200
36	Jimmy Thompson	65	2	0	0	2	$175
37	Charles Muscatel	60	1	0	0	1	$75
	Raymond Lewis	60	1	0	0	1	$75
	Al Wagoner	60	1	0	0	1	$75
40	George "Skip" Lewis	40	1	0	0	1	$50
41	Lou Volk	30	2	0	0	1	$125
42	Buddy Helms	27.5	1	0	0	1	$75
43	Bob Apperson	25	3	0	0	0	$150
44	Bill Bennett	24	1	0	0	0	$100
	Ted Chamberlain	24	2	0	0	0	$100
46	Buck Baker	20	2	0	0	0	$50
	Jack Etheridge	20	1	0	0	1	$75
	Ellis Pearce	20	1	0	0	1	$50
49	Bobby Greene	19.5	2	0	0	0	$50
50	Ken Wagner	19	3	0	0	0	$100

Red Byron won his second straight NASCAR title and became the first champion of the new Strictly Stock late-model tour on the strength of a pair of wins during the abbreviated eight-race campaign. Byron finished 117.5 points in front of runner-up Lee Petty, who won once.

Byron took the lead in the points standings after his victory at Daytona Beach, the second Strictly Stock race of the inaugural season. His second victory at Martinsville in September locked up the championship.

Byron drove Oldsmobiles for Raymond Parks during the campaign. Chief mechanic Red Vogt kept the cars in top running order all season. Byron only finished out of the top 10 in two of his six starts.

Two-time winner Bob Flock came in third in points with Bill Blair and Fonty Flock rounding out the top five.

1950s: The Manufacturers Take Notice

Things were happening fast for Bill France as the calendar flipped to 1950. After only eight Strictly Stock races staged in '49, NASCAR's newfangled late-model racing division was already a hot commodity. It became NASCAR's number-one series, replacing the Modifieds as the headlining attraction, and a new title had replaced "Strictly Stock." The late-model division became the "NASCAR Grand National Circuit."

The development of NASCAR's Grand National Circuit and the advancement of the American passenger car were a natural mix with perfect timing. The automobile manufacturers, with accelerated research and mechanical development, were producing more powerful passenger cars to whet the appetite of a youthful car-buying public.

For the 1949 model year, Oldsmobile and Cadillac introduced all-new, high-compression, lightweight V-8 engines. The NASCAR rule book still mirrored the manufacturers spec sheets, and the nimble, smooth-handling, and powerful Olds became the car of choice of NASCAR racers. Oldsmobile won 15 of the first 24 NASCAR Grand National events, and a good many of the Oldsmobile dealerships in the South noticed a measurable increase in the amount of showroom traffic. Despite a stellar record on the racetracks, General Motors executives maintained only a passing interest in the sport.

Perhaps the first manufacturer to take a closer look at NASCAR's Grand National Circuit was the Nash Motor Co. Very few competitors had selected Nashes to race in NASCAR competition, and Nash wanted to rectify that. The company offered cash prizes as contingency money in a few races and promised to deliver a new Nash to the 1950 NASCAR Grand National champion. Bill Rexford, a newcomer from New York, won one race and accumulated more points than any other driver in the 1950 season. He won $1500 in points fund money plus the new Nash Ambassador.

Nash also became more actively involved in the sport. Nash provided an Ambassador for Bill France and Curtis Turner to drive in the inaugural 1950 *Carrera Panamericana* in Mexico, and recruited and signed Curtis Turner and Johnny Mantz at the beginning of the '51 season to drive

Ambassadors in NASCAR Grand National competition. Turner was NASCAR's most dynamic star, a flamboyant driver who won four times during the 1950 season while driving Oldsmobiles. Mantz had driven a Plymouth to victory in 1950 at the inaugural Southern Five-Hundred at Darlington in NASCAR's first superspeedway event.

Turner finished seventh in the 1951 Daytona Grand National while Mantz ran ninth. Marshall Teague won in a Hudson Hornet. In the second event of '51, Turner drove his Ambassador to victory in the 150-lap race at Charlotte Speedway. Turner led most of the way, and Nash public relations let the country know about its magnificent automobile.

The Charlotte win was destined to be the first and last for Nash. Turner ditched his Ambassador by late April and returned to his trusty Oldsmobile. "The Nash is an upside down bathtub that overheats all the time," Turner said.

Daytona winner Marshall Teague felt the Hudson Hornet was the best-designed automobile for NASCAR racing. Hudson had developed a chassis in the late 1940s with wraparound perimeter-style frame rails that enabled the body and floorpan to hang closer to the ground. The chassis also extended outside the rear wheels, giving the car a well-enclosed "low-rider" look. From ground to rooftop, it was a foot lower than many of its contemporaries. This "step-down" effect gave the Hudson a lower center of gravity and enhanced handling.

Teague flew to the Hudson Motor Co. headquarters in Michigan to tell them what a nice car they had developed—and how suited it was to NASCAR racing. Teague also convinced Hudson to support his racing efforts and showed how winning on the NASCAR tracks would sell more Hudson cars to the public. The Hudson executives listened to the articulate and well-spoken Teague and agreed to give it a try.

Hudson introduced a heavy-duty suspension option, called a Severe Usage Kit, which was ideal for speedways. Since it appeared Hudson's parts catalog, it was legal in NASCAR Grand National races. Hudson also offered dual carburetors—called Twin H Power—and the entire performance package was a powerful force in stock car racing.

Hudson won 12 of the 41 races in the 1951 NASCAR Grand National campaign. Oldsmobile won more races, but the Hornets grabbed the two biggest prizes, the Southern 500 and the Grand National championship with Herb Thomas.

One of the most significant events in the formative years of NASCAR Grand National racing was Bill France's effort to convince the Detroit Junior Chamber of Commerce to book the Grand National Circuit at the Michigan State Fairgrounds. Again, the timing was perfect as the Motor City was gearing up to celebrate its 250th anniversary in the summer of 1951.

NASCAR took its unique brand of automobile racing to the doorstep of the manufacturers' home base, and virtually every make of American car was represented in the starting grid. Most of the race cars were products of local dealerships and not directly backed by the manufacturers. Tommy Thompson won a memorable duel with Curtis Turner to give the Chrysler nameplate its first NASCAR victory. The race made a lasting impression on many of the manufacturers.

With its factory program running smoothly, Hudson dominated in 1952, capturing 27 of the 34 NASCAR Grand National races. No other make won more than three times. Tim Flock captured the championship in his Ted Chester-owned Hudson Hornet, winning eight races in 33 starts. Thomas finished a close runner-up to Flock in the title chase.

Thomas rebounded in 1953 and became the first driver to win two NASCAR Grand National titles. Thomas established a new NASCAR record by winning 12 races in a single season and finished comfortably ahead of Lee Petty in the final standings. Hudsons won 22 of the 37 NASCAR Grand National races. Hudson's prowess on NASCAR's speedways made the other manufacturers take notice.

By the mid 1950s, GM, Ford, and Chrysler were developing more powerful vehicles for highway use. Chevrolet and Ford produced V-8 engines, dual carburetors, increased horsepower, a refined chassis, and a lighter overall package. Chrysler came up with the hemi engine. Meanwhile, Hudson fell behind, making only peripheral refinements.

Virtually all of the Hudson drivers shifted their allegiance to other makes. Herb Thomas went to GM and Tim Flock found himself in a Chrysler. Marshall Teague made an even bigger switch, leaving NASCAR to join the rival AAA tour.

The 1955 season was pivotal for NASCAR. Mercury Outboard magnate Carl Kiekhaefer appeared virtually overnight with a powerful Chrysler 300. He brought the car to Daytona without a driver. Tim Flock, who quit NASCAR in '54 after he was disqualified from the Daytona victory, was the logical choice to drive Kiekhaefer's Chrysler. A deal was struck, and Flock won the '55 Daytona race in his first start

with Kiekhaefer. Ironically, Flock won after the Buick of Fireball Roberts was disqualified on a technicality.

Kiekhaefer's team wasn't directly backed by Chrysler. An independent effort, Kiekhaefer used the NASCAR playground as an advertising medium for his Mercury Outboard engines. The crusty, no-nonsense perfectionist from Fon du Lac, Wis., brought his considerable resources to NASCAR and played the game seriously. He was the first to utilize covered transporters to haul cars from track to track, he paid handsome salaries to his drivers, and he sent a fleet of uniformed mechanics to each race to service his multicar team. Kiekhaefer also had his lieutenants keep detailed records of track conditions, dirt-track textures, and even weather conditions, noting how all these factors affected the performance of his cars. Kiekhaefer's professional discipline and deep pockets lifted him head-and-shoulders above the other "shade tree engineering" NASCAR race teams.

Kiekhaefer's cars dominated NASCAR. Flock won 18 races during his 1955 championship season. The Kiekhaefer Chryslers won 22 of the 39 races in '55. His cars led every lap in 11 races and finished first and second four times.

By late 1955, GM and Ford had pulled out all the stops to derail the Kiekhaefer/Chrysler express. Chevrolet's NASCAR operation was headed by three-time Indianapolis 500 winner Mauri Rose along with Frankie Del Roy. The Ford team countered with a unit headed by 1925 Indy 500 winner Peter DePaolo and retired NASCAR driver Buddy Shuman. The big showdown came at Darlington's Southern 500, NASCAR's premier superspeedway race and, to date, the only 500-miler.

The battle of the Big Three manufacturers captured the fancy of Southern racing fans. Chevrolet jumped full bore into a national advertising campaign focusing on NASCAR stock car racing. Daily newspapers were saturated with ads about the new speedy Chevy, billboards lined the highways, and television commercials beamed across the network airwaves. A frenzied peak of anticipation grew each day leading up to the Darlington race. All of the grandstand seats were sold out more than 24 hours in advance.

Herb Thomas drove his Smokey Yunick-tuned Chevrolet to victory in the Southern 500, finishing a lap ahead of another Chevrolet manned by Jim Reed. Kiekhaefer's Chrysler with Tim Flock aboard wound up third.

Joe Weatherly was Ford's top threat, but he broke a wheel while leading with less than 50 laps to go. Fords broke the

ice in a 300-miler on the huge 1½-mile dirt track in LeHi, Ark. Speedy Thompson and Marvin Panch, in a pair of DePaolo Engineering Fords, took the first two spots.

The battle between Chevrolet and Ford escalated in 1956. The two giants collectively spent better than $6 million to win NASCAR stock car races and sell their products to the motoring public. Pontiac and Mercury also got into the mix.

Despite the spending sprees by Chevrolet and Ford, Kiekhaefer's Chryslers and Dodges cleaned house. His cars won 30 of the 56 NASCAR Grand National events, finished 1-2 in six races and 1-2-3 four other times. Kiekhaefer compiled an amazing 16-race winning streak during the early summer and finished the season with five straight victories. Lead driver Buck Baker, who replaced Tim Flock when he quit in April, won the NASCAR championship. Ford won 14 times while Chevy only won three races.

Near the end of the 1956 season, Kiekhaefer withdrew from NASCAR. He had accomplished all he had set out to do and his teams had performed splendidly. But his team was constantly booed by spectators and was always under the watchful eyes of NASCAR inspectors. Kiekhaefer's cars were protested repeatedly and torn down on dozens of occasions. They always passed the intense inspections. Kiekhaefer could never understand why his efforts weren't appreciated. He got out of NASCAR as suddenly as he had arrived.

Kiekhaefer's departure left Chrysler without a top-ranked team. The MoPar unit quickly patched together a team for the 1957 NASCAR Grand National season, but Chrysler was far behind Chevrolet and Ford, both of whom were spending millions on their racing efforts.

The horsepower race was in full gallop as the 1957 campaign got underway. Each manufacturer had swarms of press agents to beat the drums of publicity in newspapers, magazines, radio, and television. The manufacturers produced optimum equipment in souped-up vehicles. Fuel-injected engines and superchargers were available to the public, and, therefore, eligible for NASCAR competition.

The directors of the Automobile Manufacturers Association were disturbed about the excessive advertising of brute horsepower. The nation's highways had become lethal with record numbers of fatalities, and fatal crashes in several

racing series were making headlines. The AMA felt the increased loss of life on the highways was linked directly to the escalating horsepower race and unchecked advertising. The automakers were feeling the heat, and threats of federal regulation meant they had to do something.

On Thursday, June 6, 1957, heads of several car companies, sitting as directors of the Automobile Manufacturers Association, unanimously recommended that the industry take no part in, or assist in any way, automobile races or other competitive events that emphasized speed or horsepower.

The Association believed: "The automobile manufacturers should encourage owners and drivers to evaluate passenger cars in terms of useful power and ability to provide safe, reliable, and comfortable transportation, rather than in terms of capacity of speed." The resolution also spread to ad campaigns. The AMA recommended that the industry "… should not advertise or publicize actual or comparative capabilities of passenger cars for speed, or specific engine size, torque, horsepower, or ability to accelerate or perform, in any context that suggests speed," and furthermore, the AMA would "disassociate itself entirely from auto racing."

When the resolution came down, the automotive industry retreated from NASCAR stock car racing. The unlimited gravy train of racing goodies from Detroit and Dearborn to the Southern racing teams dramatically slowed down.

The racing equipment remained in the hands of the teams. Most had the resources to finish out the 1957 season. Buck Baker won 10 races and captured his second straight NASCAR Grand National championship driving his own Chevrolets.

Despite the AMA ban on active participation in auto racing, the manufacturers were itching to get back into the sport. To abide by the AMA resolution yet still get the latest equipment into the hands of the competitors, the manufacturers just had to be a little more discreet. The new batch of 1958 equipment found its way to select NASCAR team owners. John Holman said his newly arrived '58 Fords were the courtesy of 32 Carolina Ford dealerships, not the Ford factory. Jim Rathmann, who owned a Chevrolet dealership in Florida, found himself surrounded with Chevrolet's latest high-speed equipment and some of the first '58 sheetmetal. Pontiac was well-represented too, with the addition of Smokey Yunick to its team.

Forty-nine cars showed up for the 1958 Daytona Beach NASCAR Grand National race, which was won by Paul Goldsmith in a Yunick-prepared Pontiac. Curtis Turner's Holman-Moody Ford finished second. The '58 season never broke stride. Fifty-one events comprised the NASCAR Grand National season, and a pair of 500-milers at Trenton, N.J., and Riverside, Calif., were added to the slate. Lee Petty took the checkered flag in seven races in his Oldsmobile and won his second championship.

Construction had already begun on a massive new, 2.5-mile speedway in Daytona Beach, and it was generating plenty of interest across the country. With a huge new speedway opening in February 1959, it was a temptation none of the manufacturers would be able to resist. This magnificent new racing palace represented a golden opportunity for publicity and exposure for the latest American cars.

The Holman-Moody shops in Charlotte took delivery of a fleet of new Ford Thunderbirds, stuffed them with potent 430-cid Lincoln engines, and offered them to racers. Full-page ads in racing publications offered four of the seven Holman-Moody T-Birds for sale, race-ready, for $5500 each. All four were sold and all seven of the cars competed in the first Daytona 500 on Feb. 22, 1959.

GM was also well-represented at Daytona. Pontiac supplied a new Catalina to Bill France to tool around Daytona. New 1959 model cars were put on display throughout the Daytona area throughout February and the town was decorated with hundreds of banners, all prominently displaying the GM logo. At the speedway, Chevrolet had plenty of new '59 Impalas on hand with the latest GM high-performance goodies, and Smokey Yunick had his '59 Pontiac with Fireball Roberts at the helm.

Defending NASCAR Grand National champion Lee Petty took delivery of a new 1959 Oldsmobile from Newton-Chapel Motors in Reidsville, N.C., a few weeks before Daytona. Petty paid $3500 for the new showroom automobile and made the car race ready in his Randleman, N.C., garage.

The first Daytona 500 attracted the most media representatives to an auto race outside of the Indianapolis 500. The show turned out to be better than a Hollywood production. For 500 miles, devoid of a single caution period, America's finest machinery battled around the new Daytona International Speedway in dizzying fashion. Speeds were alarming—certainly faster than any stock car had gone and within a whisker of the top speeds turned at Indy.

Fireball Roberts' new wide-track Pontiac was the quickest, coming from 46th starting position to assume command by the 23rd lap. A fuel-pump failure knocked him out of the race following his first pit stop. Jack Smith's Impala picked up the lead, and he had things in hand until his tires started to blister. The Holman-Moody Thunderbirds were swift and agile, but many lost tires at the tremendous speeds.

In the late stages, the race boiled down to a two-car struggle between Petty's Oldsmobile and the Thunderbird driven by Johnny Beauchamp. The two drivers swapped first place a dozen times during the last 50 laps. In the final laps, Petty and Beauchamp were running together, joined by Joe Weatherly's Chevy, which was two laps down.

All three crossed the finish line door-to-door. The finish was so close Bill France called Beauchamp the winner, while most other observers felt Petty had reached the checkered flag first. Everyone had an opinion as to who had won the 500-miler, so Bill France stepped in to announce the results were "unofficial" until all available evidence could be studied in the form of photos and film.

After 61 hours, Lee Petty was declared the official winner. Film of the finish proved Petty had reached the finish line first by about one foot. He averaged 135.521 mph, 33 mph faster than any other NASCAR Grand National race.

The race was an electric success and it generated more publicity than any other stock car race to that point in history. A trackside audience of 41,921 watched history unfold.

The theater of NASCAR stock car racing was expanding. The sprawling facility at Daytona delivered cachet for the entire sport and momentum was building. Within weeks, several entities announced their intentions to build high-banked superspeedways, most notably in Atlanta, Charlotte, and California. NASCAR stock car racing was about to venture into a new chapter of ultrafast speedways.

1950

January Entering its second season, NASCAR's Strictly Stock late-model division is renamed the "Grand National" division because, NASCAR president Bill France explains, "Grand National indicates superior qualities."

February 5 Harold Kite drives a Lincoln to victory in the 200-mile NASCAR Grand National race at the Daytona Beach-Road course in his first start. Kite finishes 53 seconds ahead of runner-up Red Byron in the caution-free event.

April 16 Curtis Turner wins the 150-mile NASCAR Grand National event at Langhorne Speedway, his second consecutive triumph on the circular one-mile track. Tim Flock takes the points lead in the race for the championship.

May 5 NASCAR president Bill France and Curtis Turner enter a Nash Ambassador in the *Carrera Panamericana*, a 2172-mile endurance race across the rough Mexican terrain. The race starts in Juarez, Chihuahua, and ends in El Ocotal on the Guatemalan border. France and Turner crash out of the race.

May 30 Bill Rexford passes Curtis Turner with 80 laps to go and wins the 200-mile NASCAR Grand National event at Canfield, Ohio. The 200-lap, 100-mile race, run opposite the Indianapolis 500, is called the "Poor Man's 500."

June 8 Tickets go on sale for the first 500-mile stock car race at the new Darlington Raceway. Prices range from $3 general admission to $10 for lower row "box seats." The event is sanctioned by the Central States Racing Association after NASCAR turns down the initial offer from track president Harold Brasington.

June 25 Jimmy Florian scores the first NASCAR Grand National win for the Ford nameplate in the 100-mile race on the high banks of Dayton (Ohio) Speedway. Florian opts not to wear a shirt while driving in the searing-hot race.

July 18 Darlington Raceway officials officially title the 500-mile Labor Day race as the "Southern Five-Hundred." Harold Brasington also announces NASCAR will cosanction the $25,000 race. The original sanctioning body, the CSRA, has had difficulty attracting entries. Raceway officials report the field will be limited to 45 cars.

Red Byron gallops out of Daytona's south turn during his runner-up effort in the opening event of the 1950 NASCAR Grand National season on Feb. 5. Byron was among the leaders in the points standings, but had all of his points stripped when he drove in independent "outlaw" races. NASCAR had a strict policy in the early years that licensed drivers must stay within the sanctioning boundaries or accept the loss of all championship points.

Harold Kite, a former Army tank driver, hitched a ride in the Rogers Auto Service Lincoln and authored a surprise victory in the 200-mile Daytona Beach Grand National event. Kite qualified third and led all but 10 of the 48 laps around the 4.1-mile Beach-Road course. He is one of only six drivers to win a NASCAR Grand National event in his first career start.

While most of the attention was focused on the NASCAR Grand National late-model division, NASCAR still conducted Modified races throughout the South. Curtis Turner got a little out of the groove and plowed through the wooden retaining barrier in the March 26 Modified race at North Wilkesboro. Buddy Shuman slips past unscathed on the low side.

NASCAR published its first annual yearbook in 1950. Loaded with hundreds of photos and statistical accounts from the inaugural 1949 season, the *1950 NASCAR Yearbook* is one of today's most sought-after racing collectibles. It originally sold for a dollar, but today it can command as much as $250.

Red Byron's #22 Oldsmobile scoots under June Cleveland's Buick in the April 2 Grand National at Charlotte Speedway. Byron started on the pole, led for 42 laps, and finished second. Cleveland started seventh and raced among the leaders until he hooked a rut and flipped over on the 85th lap. Cleveland was unhurt in the mishap.

▲ Bob Flock's immaculate #7 Oldsmobile, complete with whitewall tires, speeds through a turn at Charlotte Speedway. Flock qualified on the front row, led five laps early in the event, and wound up second, half a lap behind his brother Tim. The Charlotte NASCAR Grand National event was one of only four races that the eldest member of the Flock gang competed in during the 1950 campaign.

▼ Bill Blair, driving the #2 Cadillac owned by Sam Rice, puts a lap on Charles Muscatel's #7 Mercury in the early going of the 150-miler at Langhorne Speedway on April 16. Blair's Caddy succumbed to a broken steering linkage, while Muscatel fell out early with overheating problems.

▲ Harold Kite drove the #21 Lincoln to victory in the 1950 season opener at Daytona, but Tim Flock was behind the wheel for the April 2 race at Charlotte. Edmunds Motor Co., a dealership in the Carolinas, had replaced Roger's Auto Service on the side of the car. Flock started fifth and passed Red Byron on the 48th lap to take the lead. The 25-year-old Flock drove to victory, his first in NASCAR Grand National competition.

1950

July 23 Curtis Turner records his fourth victory of the year in the 100-mile NASCAR Grand National race at Charlotte Speedway. Lee Petty, who ranked third in the points standings, had all 809 points removed by NASCAR. During the three-week lull, Petty competed in a nonsanctioned stock car race, and NASCAR decided to strip all of his points for failing to compete within NASCAR sanctioning boundaries.

August 13 Twenty-one-year-old Fireball Roberts guns his Oldsmobile to victory in the 100-mile NASCAR Grand National event at Occoneechee Speedway in Hillsboro, N.C., making him NASCAR's youngest winner. Darlington Raceway officials announce that the inaugural Southern Five-Hundred field will be expanded from 45 to 75 cars.

August 19 Curtis Turner qualifies his Oldsmobile at 82.034 mph to win the pole for the inaugural Southern Five-Hundred at Darlington Raceway. Fifteen days of qualifying will determine the 75-car field. The quickest five cars each day earn a starting berth.

The promoters at North Wilkesboro Speedway conducted the "Wilkes County Championship Fan's Car Race" as an accompanying event to the Modifieds. The race took place on June 11. The cars weren't painted with race graphics and all had been driven to the race. Third-place starter Gwyn Staley, brother of North Wilkesboro Speedway promoter Enoch Staley, won the 10-lap race in a pickup truck.

HAROLD BRASINGTON AND THE INAUGURAL SOUTHERN 500

HAROLD BRASINGTON, a South Carolina farmer, was 14 years old in 1925 when his father took him to watch an auto race on Charlotte's high-banked boardtrack. The wide-eyed adolescent marveled at the blazing fast speeds the racers produced on the 1¼-mile oval. Earl Cooper's 122.03 mph victory in the 250-mile race had a lasting impression on Brasington. "That race set me on fire," said Brasington. "I thought it was the greatest thing I had ever seen."

Bitten by the racing bug, Brasington occasionally made the trek to Indianapolis Motor Speedway for the Memorial Day Indy 500. Amazed by the daunting crowds that paid to watch the AAA Indy cars battle for 500 miles, Brasington began fostering dreams of building a big racing facility in his native South Carolina. "I saw Louis Meyer win at Indy in 1933," said Brasington. "Ever since that day, I wanted to build a racetrack."

Brasington didn't own a parcel of land big enough to accommodate a track the size he envisioned, but he knew a gentleman who did. J. Sherman Ramsey had a tract of land just off U.S. Highway 151 in Darlington. "I had been talking with Mr. Ramsey for a few weeks about building a track down here," Brasington said. "I told him that I'd already been to Indianapolis and I'd checked into it pretty good, and I was sure it would go. Mr. Ramsey . . . was willing to take a chance. We shook hands on the deal. No contract or no nothing. We started right there—on a handshake."

Brasington wanted to build a multipurpose 1¼-mile paved track with modest banking, a facility that would be ideal for stock cars, motorcycles, and open-wheel Indy Cars. With support from Ramsey and local businessmen Bob Colvin and Barney Wallace, construction began in late 1949 on the Darlington International Raceway. Brasington wanted the inaugural event to be a 500-mile stock car race.

Ramsey told Brasington he could proceed with the construction, but the minnow pond located near the second turn couldn't be disturbed. "We had to draw the track back in where the minnow pond was," Brasington explained. "That's the reason it is pear-shaped."

During a NASCAR Strictly Stock race at Hillsboro, N.C., Brasington spoke with Bill France about backing his 500-mile pipe dream. France said he would discuss the matter at a later date, but the NASCAR president harbored reservations about stock cars lasting a full 500 miles. If the 500-miler was held and all the cars broke down, France felt it would create chaos and possibly ruin stock car racing. "Bill France did not show for that other appointment," Brasington said years later. "I was thinking he was not interested."

Needing an established sanctioning body to support his race, Brasington went to Ohio to meet with officials of the Central States Racing Association. Norman Witte, one of the founding fathers of the CSRA in 1932, listened to Brasington's proposal. "Mr. Witte came down to Darlington with his PR man Bob Smith," recalled Brasington. "They took one look at the work being done and agreed to sanction the race. For the advertising, Smith tagged it 'The Southern Five-Hundred,' and it's been the name of the race ever since."

Jimmy Florian drove his Ford to victory in the June 25 NASCAR Grand National race at Dayton Speedway, giving the Ford nameplate its first big-league NASCAR win. Temperatures soared into the 90s on that hot Ohio day. Florian removed his shirt before the race started in a meager effort to deal with the weather. At the time, NASCAR had no rule requiring drivers to wear a shirt when driving in a race.

Curtis Turner wheels his #41 Oldsmobile 88 past the packed grandstands while driving to victory at Langhorne. Five different drivers swapped the lead in the 150-lapper on Langhorne's one-mile circular dirt track. Turner led the final 36 laps and won $1500 for his efforts. Turner's Eanes Motor Co. Oldsmobile was shod with Dunlop tires, whose name was painted prominently across the door.

Unfortunately, the CSRA was unable to attract many entrants. "About six months into it," Brasington said, "we had half the tickets sold, but we didn't have but five entries. Bob Colvin and I went to see Bill France, and I said, 'We need help.' France decided to sanction it along with the CSRA. I say Bill France has done more for racing than anybody."

With NASCAR cosanctioning the race, entries began filing in. By the time practice and qualifications began in August 1950, more than 80 cars, with their drivers and mechanics, were jammed into Darlington's cramped pit area.

Fifteen days of time trials established the 75-car field for the first inaugural Southern Five-Hundred. Curtis Turner put his Oldsmobile on the pole with a four-lap average speed of 82.034 mph as the top first-day qualifier. On the 13th day of qualifying, Wally Campbell turned in the quickest time of the month with a five-mile average speed of 82.400 mph. He would line up 60th on the starting grid.

An overflow crowd of 25,000 turned out to watch the inaugural Southern Five-Hundred on Labor Day 1950. The size of the crowd astonished Brasington. "I didn't figure there was any way that many people would come to see the race. I was pleasantly surprised."

As the huge 75-car field dashed into the first turn, outside front-row starter Gober Sosebee grabbed an early lead as second-position starter Jimmy Thompson spun. Incredibly, all of the cars were able to steer clear of Thompson's sideways Lincoln.

In the early laps, cars began pitting to have flat tires replaced. Red Byron, NASCAR's 1949 Strictly Stock champion, made countless pit stops due to tire failures. Byron's Cadillac blew 24 tires during the 400-lap, 500-mile race.

Prior to the race, Johnny Mantz, a veteran of the AAA Indy Car tour, had figured a hard tire compound might do the trick on Darlington's high-speed banks. Mantz located a number of hard truck tires that were similar in texture to those used on the AAA circuit. As the speedy cars made repeated trips to the pits, Mantz cruised around the track at a planned speed of about 75 mph. By the 50th lap, Mantz was out front, a lead he would never relinquish.

At the end of 500 miles, Mantz had lapped the field no less than nine times. It was a runaway victory authored by an experienced veteran who was driving the slowest car in the field. Mantz had qualified 43rd at barely over 73 mph. Fifty of the 75 starting cars finished the race, proving to Bill France that Strictly Stock automobiles could indeed run 500 miles at breakneck speeds.

The inaugural Southern Five-Hundred was a huge success, and it was a key ingredient to the success of NASCAR during its formative days.

September 4 Johnny Mantz of Long Beach, Calif., drives a Plymouth to an overwhelming victory in the Labor Day Southern Five-Hundred, nine laps ahead of runner-up Fireball Roberts. Mantz collects $10,510, the largest purse so far in stock car history.

September 30 NASCAR promotes a 25-mile, nonpoints race for NASCAR Grand National cars at the ¼-mile Civic Stadium in Buffalo, N.Y. Won by Bobby Courtwright, the race is the "pilot" event for the upcoming NASCAR Short Track Grand National Circuit.

October 29 Lee Petty captures the NASCAR Grand National finale at Hillsboro, N.C., as 23-year-old Bill Rexford wraps up the national driving championship. Rexford edges Fireball Roberts by 110.5 points.

October 30 1949 NASCAR champion Red Byron, who ranked sixth in the '50 NASCAR Grand National standings, has all 1315.5 points stripped for participating in a non-NASCAR-sanctioned race at Atlanta's Lakewood Speedway. Byron drove at Atlanta rather than the NASCAR Grand National finale at Hillsboro. The Lakewood race was sanctioned by the National Stock Car Racing Association (NSCRA).

December 18 NASCAR announces $23,024 in points fund money will be distributed to drivers in all stock car divisions based on final points standings. NASCAR Grand National champion Bill Rexford will receive $1375.

"We had to draw the track back in where the minnow pond was. That's the reason it is pear-shaped."
—Harold Brasington on Darlington International Raceway

There was a wide groove at Dayton Speedway in Ohio for the June 25 NASCAR Grand National race. More than 12,000 spectators jammed the covered grandstands at the steeply banked dirt track.

Dick Linder, the highly regarded racer out of Pittsburgh, keeps his #25 Oldsmobile ahead of a trio of challengers in the Aug. 24 NASCAR Grand National race at Dayton. It was Linder's first of three wins in the 1950 NASCAR season. A versatile driver, Linder quit NASCAR racing in '52 and made the move to the AAA Indy Car series. He lost his life in a crash at Trenton in '59.

Construction began on the new Darlington International Raceway in 1949. The brainchild of Harold Brasington, the 1¼-mile track was built as an all-purpose facility with the NASCAR stocks as the headlining attraction. Originally, NASCAR president Bill France wasn't interested in sanctioning a 500-mile stock car race, fearful that the stock automobiles would never go the distance. At the eleventh hour, NASCAR jumped on board and cosanctioned the inaugural Southern Five-Hundred with the Central States Racing Association, which had agreed to support the race all along.

Seventy-five cars line up three-abreast on the front chute of Darlington Raceway on Labor Day, Sept. 4. Curtis Turner, Jimmy Thompson, and Gober Sosebee qualified for the front row. Fifteen days of qualifying determined the inaugural Southern Five-Hundred field. Sosebee went down in the record books as leading the first green flag lap in Darlington history. Thompson spun out in the first turn, but, miraculously, every car avoided hitting him.

▼ Johnny Mantz wheels his 1950 Plymouth around the low groove in the Southern Five-Hundred. The black Plymouth, which was owned by Bill France, Alvin Hawkins, and Hubert Westmoreland, was used as a utility vehicle during the two weeks leading up to the Southern Five-Hundred. Finally, on the ninth day of qualifying, Mantz got the car into the race-day field with an average speed of 73.460 mph. Mantz went on to win by nine full laps, and his average speed in the race was quicker than his qualifying speed. Mantz used durable truck tires in the race and cruised to victory when his speedier rivals had to make several pit stops to replace blown tires.

▲ Joe Eubanks in the #4 Mercury leads a gaggle of cars down the back chute during the inaugural Southern Five-Hundred at Darlington. Eubanks, who finished 19th, was driving a car groomed by Bud Moore, who was participating in his first NASCAR Grand National event. Eubanks completed 359 of the 400 laps and finished ahead of 56 other competitors, but he didn't earn a single penny for his efforts. The payoff included the top 18 positions, plus some qualifying money that went to the quickest drivers in time trials.

Wally Campbell and Tim Flock, in a pair of Oldsmobiles, pace the field at the start of the 200-mile NASCAR Grand National event at Langhorne Speedway on Sept. 17. The circular Langhorne track was devoid of straightaways, and the curved front chute afforded an excellent view for the spectators. Bill France took note of the contour of Langhorne's front chute and built a similar curve into the homestretch when he built the Daytona International Speedway nine years later.

1950

Ebenezer "Slick" Smith drove this Nash Ambassador in the Sept. 24 NASCAR race at North Wilkesboro Speedway. Smith crashed midway through the race and wound up 20th in the field of 26. Bill France and Curtis Turner had driven the Nash in the *Carrera Panamericana* during the summer. The Nash Motor Co. was the first manufacturer to actively support NASCAR racing. This Ambassador, which served as a pace car when it wasn't being raced, was one of the perks provided for NASCAR president Bill France.

(Left to right) Twenty-year-old Fireball Roberts, Red Byron, and Johnny Mantz congratulate each other in victory lane following the first Southern Five-Hundred at Darlington. Byron was originally flagged in second place, ahead of Roberts. Following a lengthy study of the scoring sheets, race officials discovered Roberts had completed one more lap than Byron in the 500-miler. Mantz collected $10,510 for the win, while Roberts took home $3500, and Byron pocketed $2000.

Buck Baker's #87 Oldsmobile runs inches ahead of Lee Petty's Plymouth and Tim Flock's Oldsmobile during the Oct. 15 NASCAR Grand National event at Martinsville Speedway. Herb Thomas won the 100-miler with Baker finishing second and Petty third. Flock's Olds threw a wheel and wound up 12th. Baker's Griffin Motors Olds was the first car entered in the inaugural Southern Five-Hundred at Darlington.

Ewell Weddle, in the #78 Lincoln, cuts to the inside to protect his line against Fonty Flock's #7 Oldsmobile and Clyde Minter's #38 Buick in the Oct. 29 race at Hillsboro, N.C. Weddle, who finished 14th in the field of 29, nicknamed his car the "Warbash Cannon Ball." Note that Weddle's goggles have slipped down below his chin.

Herb Thomas (left) and Lee Petty pose with their Plymouths following the 1950 season finale at Hillsboro's Occoneechee Speedway. Petty won the race and wound up third in the final points standings. Over the course of the season, Petty scored more points than any other driver. But, in July, he competed in a non-NASCAR-sanctioned event and lost all 809 points he had earned up until that time. The 809-point penalty cost Petty the NASCAR Grand National championship.

Fireball Roberts (right) congratulates Bill Rexford for his 1950 championship as Bill France looks on. Rexford fell out of the final race at Hillsboro early, opening the door for Roberts to snatch the title. Needing to finish fifth or better to win the championship, Roberts decided against a conservative approach. He charged into the lead and was running third when his engine blew. The mechanical failure gave the championship to the 23-year-old Rexford. He remains the youngest title winner in NASCAR history.

1950 NASCAR GRAND NATIONAL POINTS

Rank	Driver	Points	Starts	Wins	Top 5	Top 10	Winnings
1	Bill Rexford	1959.0	17	1	5	11	$6175
2	Fireball Roberts	1848.5	9	1	4	5	$6955
3	Lee Petty	1398.0	17	1	9	13	$5580
4	Lloyd Moore	1398.0	16	1	7	10	$5580
5	Curtis Turner	1375.0	16	4	7	7	$6935
6	Johnny Mantz	1282.0	3	1	1	2	$10,835
7	Chuck Mahoney	1217.5	11	0	3	6	$2760
8	Dick Linder	1121.0	13	3	5	8	$5570
9	Jimmy Florian	801.0	10	1	3	6	$2695
10	Bill Blair	766.0	16	1	5	7	$4320
11	Herb Thomas	590.5	13	1	4	6	$2945
12	Buck Baker	531.5	9	0	2	5	$2195
13	Cotton Owens	500.0	3	0	0	1	$1100
14	Fonty Flock	458.5	7	1	2	3	$2170
15	Weldon Adams	440.0	4	0	2	3	$1305
16	Tim Flock	437.5	13	1	4	7	$4080
17	Clyde Minter	427.0	8	0	3	3	$1280
18	Dick Burns	341.5	8	0	2	3	$930
19	Art Lamey	320.0	4	0	2	3	$830
20	Bob Flock	314.0	4	0	1	3	$1180
21	George Hartley	298.0	8	0	0	2	$875
22	Gayle Warren	287.0	10	0	1	2	$550
23	Frank Mundy	275.5	8	0	0	3	$550
24	Jim Paschal	220.5	6	0	1	2	$850
25	Jack White	211.5	7	0	1	3	$525
26	Roscoe "Pappy" Hough	207.5	5	0	0	2	$325
27	Ray Duhigg	202.5	5	0	1	2	$450
28	Leon Sales	200.0	2	1	1	1	$1000
	Jimmy Thompson	200.0	4	0	0	3	$525
30	Harold Kite	187.0	3	1	1	1	$1550
31	Neil Cole	183.5	2	0	1	1	$300
32	Buck Barr	180.0	2	0	1	2	$575
	Red Harvey	180.0	1	0	1	1	$750
	Ted Swaim	180.0	1	0	1	1	$750
	Jack Smith	180.0	3	0	1	1	$775
	Bucky Sager	180.0	2	0	1	1	$750
37	Pepper Cunningham	177.5	2	0	0	2	$300
38	Ewell Weddle	173.5	3	0	1	1	$600
39	Donald Thomas	164.0	2	0	0	2	$300
40	Bill Snowden	163.0	4	0	1	2	$325
41	Chuck James	140.0	1	0	1	1	$400
	Jimmie Lewallen	140.0	3	0	1	1	$400
43	Dick Clotheir	133.5	5	0	0	2	$350
44	Paul Parks	124.5	6	0	0	1	$375
45	Al Gross	124.0	2	0	1	1	$550
46	Jack Reynolds	120.0	2	0	1	1	$300
47	Jim Delaney	114.0	2	0	0	1	$175
48	Carl Renner	108.0	2	0	0	1	$250
49	Jack Holloway	107.5	2	0	0	2	$225
50	Robert Dickson	105.0	6	0	0	2	$275
	J.C. Van Landingham	105.0	1	0	1	1	$450

Despite mechanical problems in the season finale at Hillsboro, N.C., 23-year-old Bill Rexford held off Fireball Roberts by an eyelash to capture the 1950 NASCAR Grand National championship.

The 1950 title chase was quite memorable. In the 19-race campaign, the points lead changed hands nine times among seven different drivers. Rexford took the points lead in the next-to-last race at Winchester, Ind., and finished 110.5 points ahead of Roberts.

Roberts, the 21-year-old youngster out of Daytona Beach, could have won the title with a fifth-place finish in the season finale. With Rexford on the sidelines, Fireball elected to charge to the front rather than employ a conservative approach. Roberts led twice for nine laps, but blew the engine in his Oldsmobile and wound up 21st.

In addition to Rexford and Roberts, other drivers to lead the standings during the season included Curtis Turner, Lloyd Moore, Tim Flock, Red Byron, and Harold Kite.

1951

January Bill France announces that the NASCAR Grand National division will venture into the far west in 1951. Johnny Mantz, winner of the 500-mile race at Darlington, will be the Regional Director of NASCAR events in California.

January 22 Bill Holland, winner of the 1949 Indianapolis 500, is suspended from AAA Indy Car racing. Holland, who has never finished worse than second in four starts in the Memorial Day classic, is kicked out of AAA for one year for competing in a three-lap Lion's Charity race at Opa Locka, Fla., on Nov. 14, 1950. The AAA has a strict rule forbidding its drivers to participate in any race other than its own.

February 11 Marshall Teague wheels his Hudson Hornet to victory in the season-opening NASCAR Grand National race on Daytona's Beach-Road course. Bill France is successful in luring suspended AAA driver Bill Holland into the NASCAR fold. Holland drives a Nash Ambassador, but encounters early mechanical trouble and finishes 47th in the 54-car field.

April 1 Curtis Turner drives a Nash Ambassador to a big win in the 150-lap NASCAR Grand National race at Charlotte Speedway. Bill Holland, in the Plymouth that Johnny Mantz drove to victory in the 1950 Southern Five-Hundred, survives a wild tumble on the 132nd lap.

April 8 Marshall Teague wins the first NASCAR Grand National event on the West Coast. Driving his Hudson Hornet, Teague leads all 200 laps at Carrell Speedway in Gardena, Calif. Frank Mundy drives a rental car to an 11th-place finish, winning $25. Mundy waited until after dark to return the car so the attendant wouldn't notice the bald tires.

April 16 Officials at Darlington International Raceway schedule a 250-mile AAA Big Car race for July 4. At the request of AAA officials, the 200-mile NASCAR Grand National race slated for July 3 at Darlington is canceled. The AAA told Raceway officials it would refuse to conduct an Indy Car-type race in conjunction with NASCAR.

As one of the perks for capturing the 1950 NASCAR Grand National championship, Bill Rexford was presented a new Nash Rambler during the '51 Daytona Speedweeks activities. Don Willis, general manager of a Daytona Nash dealership, gave the keys to Rexford. The Nash Motor Co. was the first automotive manufacturer to provide active sponsorship and contingency awards in NASCAR racing.

Marshall Teague slaps his Hudson Hornet into the south turn during the 1951 NASCAR Grand National season opener at Daytona on Feb. 11. Teague took the lead from Tim Flock with 12 laps remaining and sped to his first career NASCAR Grand National win. Teague said he had only one close call in the 160-miler. A photographer had darted onto the track to take a picture, and Teague commented that he "had to veer quick to miss him."

Curtis Turner poses with his Nash Ambassador in the makeshift victory lane following his win in the April 1 150-lap race at Charlotte Speedway. Turner was one of the drivers for the 1951 factory-backed Nash team. Turner, who referred to the car as "an upside down bathtub," flashed past Fonty Flock in the 47th lap and finished a couple car lengths ahead of runner-up Lee Petty to register the only career NASCAR win for the Nash nameplate. Less than a month later, Turner parked his Nash and returned to his more reliable Oldsmobile.

Red Harrelson's Ford and Tim Flock's Oldsmobile are on the front row for the start of the April 8 NASCAR Grand National event at Lakeview Speedway in Mobile, Ala. Fonty Flock pulled double-duty in this 150-lap event on the ⅜-mile dirt track, acting as the event promoter, and finishing second to winner Tim Flock. The rain-plagued race was postponed from March 18 and was hampered by additional rains in April. The track surface broke up badly during the race. One news reporter wrote "… the cars were in bad need of periscopes to see above the holes in the track."

Due to horrible track conditions in the April 8 event at Mobile, the NASCAR Grand National cars took a beating in the 112.5-mile race. Here, the trunk of Herb Thomas' #92 Plymouth has been jarred open by the choppy surface. Frank Luptow's #88 Olds bounces after hitting a deep rut, and Weldon Adams' #72 Plymouth, which has already broken down, rests at the top of the turn. Luptow and Adams failed to finish, while Thomas motored home third.

Fonty Flock leads the pack on the pace lap for the April 15 NASCAR Grand National event at Hillsboro's Occoneechee Speedway. Flock started on the pole and led the entire way in the scheduled 150-miler. A thunderstorm hit the one-mile dirt oval after 95 laps were completed and race director Bill France was forced to halt the event. Frank Mundy finished second in a Studebaker and Bill Blair, who started on the front row beside Flock, wound up third.

Coleman Lawrence sports one of the fashionable early driver's uniforms in 1951—denim coveralls and a short-sleeved shirt. Lawrence hailed from Martinsville, Va., and was a part-time racer during NASCAR's early years. Lawrence drove a Ford most of the time and entered 22 races from '51 to '53. He managed to finish in the top 10 in six events. His total winnings for his 22 starts amounted to $875.

1951

May 6 Curtis Turner hops into his reliable Oldsmobile and wins the 100-mile NASCAR Grand National event at Martinsville Speedway. Turner parked his Nash Ambassador due to repeated overheating problems.

Late May NASCAR joins forces with the Detroit Junior Chamber of Commerce and will celebrate the 250th anniversary of the Motor City with a 250-mile NASCAR Grand National race at the Michigan State Fairgrounds. Posted awards of $12,500 will be distributed to the drivers who qualify for the event.

June 16 Driving a Studebaker, Frank Mundy wins the 100-mile NASCAR Grand National event on a Saturday night at Columbia Speedway in South Carolina. It is the first NASCAR Grand National event to be staged under the lights, Mundy's first career NASCAR Grand National victory, and the first win for the Studebaker nameplate.

July 8 Fonty Flock prevails in a wreck-strewn 100-mile race at the Bain-bridge, Ohio, Fairgrounds. Only five cars finish the brutal event on the one-mile dirt oval.

Tim and Fonty Flock lead the charge at the start of the 100-mile NASCAR Grand National race at Martinsville Speedway on May 6. Like most tracks of the early '50s, Martinsville had no protective barrier to separate the racing surface from the pit area. It was an issue that wasn't addressed for another decade or so. Curtis Turner, who started in the fourth row, drove his Oldsmobile to victory, assuming command when leader Marshall Teague crashed. Frank Mundy's Studebaker, which started sixth, finished second.

Marshall Teague dives into the corner at Martinsville Speedway. Teague drove his Hudson to victory in three of the first six races of the season, but demolished his "Fabulous Hudson Hornet" in a hard crash at Martinsville. The Daytona Beach native led the points standings early in the season, but curtailed his efforts near midseason. He won five of his 15 NASCAR Grand National starts in 1951.

HERB THOMAS

HERB THOMAS of Olivia, N.C., was NASCAR's first superstar. Thomas, the first driver to collect more than $100,000 in career earnings, won 48 NASCAR Grand National races and was the leading race winner for three consecutive seasons. He bagged the Southern 500 at Darlington three times and captured the NASCAR championship twice. He did all of this in just seven full years on the major league stock car racing circuit.

Thomas was the hardest charger in the early days of NASCAR. When he didn't win, he usually wrecked or blew the car up trying to do so. "It's win or bust with me," Thomas said. "Second place is never good enough."

Thomas' rustic beginnings in stock car racing were like most others of the day. In 1946, he went to watch a Modified race at Greensboro, N.C., and the following week he had a car out on the track himself. While competing in a few scattered Modified races, Thomas ran strong but rarely finished. He didn't win a single race.

When Bill France orchestrated the Strictly Stock circuit in 1949, Thomas built a late-model automobile for competition. He struggled once again, coming up winless until late in the

'50 season when he won at Martinsville. "My money was running low," Thomas recalled years later. "I was really disgusted. I thought about quitting racing and going back to the sawmill business. But when I won Martinsville, I decided to stick around a little longer."

The Martinsville triumph set the stage for the 1951 season. Thomas drove three different brands of cars—Hudson, Plymouth, and Oldsmobile—and put them all into victory lane. He won seven events in 33 starts and snared the NASCAR Grand National championship.

From 1952 to '54, Thomas came home first in 32 races and finished no worse than second in the points standings.

During his title defense in 1955, Thomas had a bad spill at Charlotte's dirt track. The car tumbled over and Thomas was tossed onto the track surface. He was rushed to the hospital where he was laid up for several weeks. From his hospital bed, he made a bold prediction: "Don't worry about me, I'll be racing again by the time the Darlington 500 comes up in September. And I'll win it again, too."

He was out of the hospital by August and won his second start at Raleigh, N.C., in a 100-miler. The next week, Thomas

NASCAR president Bill France tends to the injured Bob Flock after a spill in the May 6 NASCAR Grand National event. Flock's Oldsmobile rolled over a couple of times, and, lacking roll bars, the roof collapsed on the driver's head. Flock wasn't seriously injured, but did make a trip to the hospital for treatment.

An Oldsmobile convertible pace car leads the field onto the track at the start of the NASCAR Grand National race at Ohio's Canfield Fairgrounds Speedway. Bill Rexford earned the pole, the only time in his career that he was quickest qualifier. Tim Flock flanks Rexford on the front row. The covered grandstands were packed for the May 30 event. Staged on the same day as the Indianapolis 500, promoters named the race the "Poor Man's 500" even though it consisted of just 200 laps. Marshall Teague won, earning $1000. Lee Wallard won the Indy 500, a victory worth $63,612.

The NASCAR Grand National stockers engage in close battle during the June 10 event at Columbus Speedway in Georgia. Jim Paschal's #60 Ford is tucked behind a '50 Oldsmobile as Tim Flock's #91 Olds nips Paschal's heels. Bud Erb, in the #97 Mercury, clings to the window ledge and drives with one hand as the speedy trio make the high-side pass. Flock went on to win the 100-miler as Paschal came home fourth. Erb wound up 18th, several laps off the pace.

made good on his promise, driving a Chevrolet to victory in the Southern 500. Despite missing 22 of the 45 races in 1955, Thomas still finished fifth in the final points standings.

Thomas' last full year in racing was 1956, a season in which he should have won the title a third time. Instead, a set of circumstances ended the career of America's best stock car racer.

Thomas started the 1956 campaign in his own Chevrolets, but joined Carl Kiekhaefer's powerful Chrysler and Dodge team at midseason. After winning three NASCAR Grand National races for Kiekhaefer, Thomas bowed out and returned to his self-owned team. "He was sending me to places I didn't want to go," Thomas said of the demanding Kiekhaefer. "He sent me all the way to California for a 100-miler when I wanted to stay closer to home where there were a lot more races. I finally quit him because I felt I could do just as good in my own cars."

With five races left in the season, Thomas was on top of the points standings. But Kiekhaefer leased a couple of tracks late in the season, quickly arranged for a NASCAR sanction, and gave his drivers Buck Baker and Speedy Thompson additional shots to overtake Thomas.

One of those races was a 100-miler at the Cleveland County Fairgrounds in Shelby, N.C., on Oct. 23. Thomas started 13th, but charged into contention by the halfway point. He took

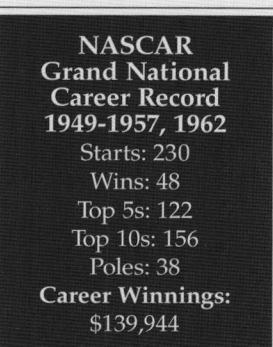

NASCAR Grand National Career Record 1949-1957, 1962
Starts: 230
Wins: 48
Top 5s: 122
Top 10s: 156
Poles: 38
Career Winnings: $139,944

second place from Thompson down the backstretch. Before they reached the third turn, Thompson tagged Thomas' rear bumper, sending the two-time champion headfirst into the outside guardrail.

Thomas' car pierced the steel plate retaining barrier and was a sitting duck for the onrushing pack of cars. At least six cars plowed into Thomas. He was lifted from the car unconscious, suffering from a cracked skull. Critically injured, he underwent brain surgery and missed the rest of the season. Buck Baker went on to win the championship for Kiekhaefer.

Miraculously, Thomas recovered from the devastating injuries. He made two token appearances in 1957, then retired. "It's too much dog-eat-dog out there now," Thomas admitted at the time. "I used to pass everyone in the turns. Now they pass me in the turns. It's time to hang it up."

Thomas did make one other appearance at North Wilkesboro in 1962, but the competitive spark was gone. "Shucks," Thomas said, "there's no use in running if you can't be first. So I quit again, and I quit for good."

Herb Thomas won 48 NASCAR Grand National races in 230 career starts, a 20.9 winning percentage, which remains the best on the all-time list.

1951

July 14 Tony Bonadies wheels a Nash Ambassador to victory in the 400-lap NASCAR Short Track Grand National race at Lanham, Md. Bonadies is the only driver in the 25-car field to run the entire distance without making a pit stop.

August 12 Newcomer Tommy Thompson outlasts Curtis Turner in an epic slugfest to win the Motor City 250 at Detroit. Driving a Chrysler, Thompson survives a motorized rubdown with roughneck Turner, takes the lead with 18 laps remaining, and collects $5000 for the victory.

September 3 A record 82 cars start the 2nd annual Southern 500 at Darlington. Herb Thomas and Jesse James Taylor finish 1-2 in Hudson Hornets.

October 14 A total of 106 cars compete in the NASCAR Modified and Sportsman race at Langhorne Speedway. Dick Eagan, driving in relief of Hully Bunn, is declared the winner after a crash halts the race after 83 laps. Don Black is critically injured in the massive pileup, which unfolds for more than one minute. Fritz Holzhauer was badly burned in an earlier incident. Photos of the big crash will appear in the Dec. 9 issue of This Week magazine, which appears in Sunday editions of newspapers across the country.

November 7 NASCAR publishes its first official newsletter from its new offices on Peninsula Avenue in Daytona Beach. The NASCAR Newsletter consists of four pages.

November 11 Tim Flock takes the lead on the 14th lap and breezes to victory in the 100-mile NASCAR Grand National event at Lakewood Speedway in Atlanta. It is the first official NASCAR race staged at the venerable one-mile oval. Young Jesse James Taylor, runner-up in the 500-miler at Darlington, is critically injured in an early spill.

November 12 NASCAR announces it intends to sanction a Speedway Division for open-wheel cars powered by stock engines. The first appearance of the Speedway cars is slated for the 1952 Daytona Speedweeks activities.

Team owner Perry Smith, a Studebaker dealer from Columbia, S.C., and veteran driver Frank Mundy became a powerful force in 1951. Mundy won three races, earned four poles, and finished a strong fifth in the points standings. After the season, Smith was flying an elderly lady for medical treatment in Chicago on a mercy mission when his single-engine plane went down in bad weather. The beloved Smith and his passenger perished in the accident.

Marshall Teague takes the high line as he passes Mike Klapak's Nash Ambassador and Ray Duhigg's Plymouth in the June 24 NASCAR Grand National event at Dayton (Ohio) Speedway. Teague finished sixth in his Hudson Hornet, a couple laps behind winner Curtis Turner. For Klapak, a gifted NASCAR Sportsman driver from Warren, Ohio, it was one of his rare NASCAR Grand National starts. Duhigg competed in NASCAR from 1950 to '55, then quit to join a rival Midwestern stock car organization. Duhigg lost his life in a crash at Salem, Ind., in October '55.

Fonty Flock drove his #14 Oldsmobile flat out during the 1951 NASCAR season. One of the most-gifted high speed artists in NASCAR history, Flock won eight races that year and finished second to Herb Thomas in the NASCAR Grand National points standings. The entire Flock gang drove for team owner Ted Chester during most of the season. Fonty drove the Red Devil Olds, while Tim wheeled the Black Phantom car. Bob's Olds was nicknamed the Gray Ghost. Fonty won the most races in '51 and led the most laps.

Herb Thomas takes the checkered flag in winning the July 15 event at Heidelberg Speedway near Pittsburgh. Thomas hooked up with Oldsmobile team owner Hubert Westmoreland for this one event. The 100-mile race was one of the most brutal in NASCAR history. The starting field consisted of 42 cars, but only five finished. Many were wiped out in a series of wrecks. Dust conditions were particularly bad that afternoon, which adversely affected the drivers' vision.

Bill Holland's #175 Cadillac was wiped out in the epic Aug. 12 slugfest on Detroit's flat one-mile dirt oval. Holland came to the NASCAR circuit after being kicked out of the AAA Open Wheel tour. The 1949 Indianapolis 500 winner competed in a three-lap charity race in Opa Locka, Fla., in '50. For that honorable act, the AAA booted Holland out for competing in a non-AAA-sanctioned event. It still stands as one of the most ridiculous executive decisions in auto-racing history.

Marshall Teague and Fonty Flock lead the charge into the first turn at the start of the Motor City 250 at Detroit's Michigan State Fairgrounds. The event was one of the most important in NASCAR history. Bill France took NASCAR's unique brand of stock car motorsports to the doorstep of the automotive industry. A wall-to-wall crowd of 16,352 watched the action-packed contest, and to NASCAR's delight, the automobile executives took a keen interest, too.

The inaugural Motor City 250 wasn't only a much-anticipated affair, it turned out to be one of the most thrilling events in NASCAR history. Newcomer Tommy Thompson, driving a Chrysler, locked horns with the rambunctious Curtis Turner in the final laps. As both dueled for the lead, the big Chrysler and Turner's Olds collided in the third turn. As they zoomed down the front chute, Turner's busted radiator spit out a geyser of steam, leaving Thompson with a clear path to victory. Fifteen different makes of cars dotted the field, a NASCAR record.

1951

November 25 Frank Mundy throttles his Studebaker to a win in the 150-lap NASCAR Grand National finale at Lakeview Speedway in Mobile, Ala. Bob Flock crashes his Oldsmobile in the early laps and suffers a broken neck. Herb Thomas wraps up the tightly contested NASCAR Grand National championship chase by nosing out Fonty Flock by 146.2 points.

December 8 Perry Smith, owner of the Studebaker Frank Mundy drives, perishes in a private air crash near Greensburg, Ind. Smith was on a mercy mission, carrying an ill 80-year-old woman to a hospital when his Navion flew into icy weather and crashed into a rural countryside.

Marshall Teague, the fastest qualifier for the second annual Southern 500, shakes hands with raceway vice president Bob Colvin as track president Harold Brasington looks on. Herb Thomas, clinging to a pair of handsome trophies, won the race, leading 301 of the 400 laps. Thomas earned 1250 points for his Darlington win, which figured prominently in his championship run. Most of the short track races in 1951 awarded 200 points to the winner. In NASCAR's early years, the higher the posted awards, the greater the number of points distributed.

With 82 cars taking the green flag, the Sept. 3, 1951, Southern 500 had the largest starting field in NASCAR Grand National history. Herb Thomas started second, and won easily. Darlington Raceway had several wide grooves during its early years. Some drivers elected to run on the relatively flat apron, figuring the inside groove was the shortest way around. Other cars ran on the banking near the guardrail, opting for a faster, but longer route around the 1¼-mile paved oval. Lee Petty ran the low groove in his #42 Plymouth and finished 15th. Fireball Roberts, in the #11 Oldsmobile, rode the entire race in the high lane, which carried him to a fifth-place finish.

With Herb Thomas in the 1951 NASCAR Grand National championship chase, fellow Hudson driver Marshall Teague offered to let the title contender drive his car in a number of late-season events. Thomas' own operation was getting a little ragged around the edges during the final weeks of the exhaustive campaign. Teague's cars were well rested, having been driven in only selected events. Thomas put Teague's #6 Hudson on the pole at Jacksonville for the Nov. 4 event, and drove to a convincing victory. Frank Mundy's #23 Studebaker qualified second and finished fifth.

A Nash pace car heads onto the track to lead the field for the start of the 100-mile NASCAR Grand National event at Atlanta's Lakewood Speedway on Nov. 11. Pole-sitter Frank Mundy led the opening lap in his Studebaker, but was quickly passed by Bob Flock. Flock kept his Oldsmobile in the lead until younger brother Tim raced past in his new Hudson. Tim led the final 87 laps to rack up his seventh win of the season.

Young Jesse James Taylor drove his #31 Hudson Hornet to a runner-up finish in the 1951 Darlington Southern 500 in only his fifth career NASCAR Grand National start. He seemed destined for success until he was badly injured in a spill at Lakewood Speedway in Atlanta on Nov. 11. Taylor's head injuries kept him sidelined for five years. He attempted a comeback in late '56, but only drove in five more races before hanging up his goggles for good.

1951 NASCAR GRAND NATIONAL POINTS RACE

Rank	Driver	Points	Starts	Wins	Top 5	Top 10	Winnings
1	Herb Thomas	4208.45	35	7	16	18	$21,050
2	Fonty Flock	4062.25	34	8	20	22	$15,535
3	Tim Flock	3722.50	30	7	19	21	$15,155
4	Lee Petty	2392.25	32	1	11	19	$7340
5	Frank Mundy	1963.50	27	3	8	11	$7095
6	Buddy Shuman	1368.75	7	0	1	6	$2755
7	Jesse James Taylor	1214.00	10	0	1	3	$3700
8	Dick Rathmann	1040.00	15	0	4	7	$3480
9	Bill Snowden	1009.25	12	0	3	9	$2365
10	Joe Eubanks	1005.50	12	0	3	3	$3350
11	Lloyd Moore	996.50	22	0	4	8	$2335
12	Fireball Roberts	930.00	9	0	2	3	$2110
13	Jimmie Lewallen	874.25	12	0	4	8	$2180
14	Bob Flock	869.00	17	1	4	9	$3680
15	Jim Paschal	858.50	16	0	4	7	$2360
16	Bill Blair	840.00	18	0	4	7	$2735
17	Gober Sosebee	784.00	10	0	4	5	$2953
18	Erick Erickson	773.50	12	0	4	6	$2285
19	Tommy Thompson	755.00	5	1	1	2	$5435
20	Donald Thomas	743.50	17	0	4	7	$1645
21	Johnny Mantz	725.00	6	0	2	4	$2025
22	Lou Figaro	684.20	13	1	3	4	$2135
23	Buck Baker	644.50	11	0	4	5	$1650
24	Dick Meyer	626.50	6	0	3	4	$1650
25	Harold Kite	625.00	2	0	0	5	$800
26	Billy Carden	509.75	11	0	2	5	$1460
27	Jimmy Florian	462.50	9	0	2	5	$1100
28	Jim Fiebelkorn	455.00	17	0	1	4	$1355
29	Ronnie Kohler	432.00	5	0	2	3	$1100
30	Danny Weinberg	423.50	6	1	2	3	$1470
31	Roscoe Hough	423.00	9	0	1	4	$760
32	Woody Brown	421.00	3	0	0	2	$1125
33	Neil Cole	382.00	5	1	3	3	$2050
34	Paul Newkirk	375.00	1	0	1	1	$500
35	John McGinley	372.50	6	0	2	2	$1300
36	Marvin Panch	371.50	3	0	1	2	$1075
37	Oda Greene	366.50	6	0	2	3	$825
38	Jack Goodwin	362.50	3	0	0	1	$725
39	Jack Smith	360.50	7	0	2	2	$1275
40	Bob Caswell	350.00	3	0	1	1	$1325
41	Lloyd Dane	323.50	7	0	2	3	$975
42	Cotton Owens	312.50	5	0	0	1	$225
43	Fred Steinbroner	306.50	6	0	2	3	$700
44	Ewell Weddle	293.50	7	0	0	2	$435
45	George Seeger	278.00	9	0	1	3	$910
46	Sam Hawks	262.50	3	0	1	1	$650
47	Don Bailey	239.50	10	0	1	2	$625
48	Bud Farrell	227.50	5	0	1	2	$700
49	Harvey "Bud" Riley	226.50	8	0	1	2	$475
50	Freddie Lee	224.00	6	0	1	1	$450

With his overwhelming victory in the Southern 500 at Darlington on Labor Day, Herb Thomas leapt atop the NASCAR Grand National points standings and led the rest of the season. Thomas, winner of seven races during the 41-race season, wound up only 146.2 points ahead of runner-up Fonty Flock, who won eight races.

Thomas remained within striking distance of the points lead throughout the first half of the season, but didn't take the lead until his big victory at Darlington, when he earned 1250 points. Distribution of points in 1951 was parallel to the posted awards, and the Southern 500 was the richest race on the NASCAR Grand National schedule. Fonty Flock finished eighth at Darlington and earned 375 points.

The points lead changed hands nine times among four drivers during the course of the season. Tim Flock finished third in points after leading the standings for 13 races. Lee Petty and Frank Mundy rounded out the top five in the final tally.

1952

January 20 Tim Flock wins the 100-mile season opener at Palm Beach Speedway in West Palm Beach, Fla. Bernard Alvarez escapes injury when his Olds flips over and the roof caves in. NASCAR rules are amended to now require the use of steel roll bars on all race cars.

February 6 NASCAR distributes over $40,000 in points money at the annual Victory Dinner at the Princess Issena Hotel in Daytona Beach. Herb Thomas collects $2264.50 for winning the 1951 NASCAR Grand National championship.

February 9 A two-way radio is first used in NASCAR competition. Al Stevens, who operates a radio dispatch service in Maryland, drives in the 100-mile Modified and Sportsman race at Daytona while talking to pit boss Cotton Bennett. Stevens finishes 27th in the 118-car field and third in the Sportsman class. Tim Flock is flagged the winner, but is disqualified when NASCAR technical inspectors find "improper" roll bars in his '39 Ford. Jack Smith is declared the official winner.

April 12 Buck Baker wins the 100-mile NASCAR Grand National race at Columbia, S.C., and Lee Petty vaults to the top of the points standings. Fonty Flock, points leader entering the race, sits out due to injuries suffered at Martinsville. E.C. Ramsey crashes into a passenger car that attempts to cross the track during the race. Ramsey's Ford and the passenger car are heavily damaged.

April 17 Marshall Teague, who ranks sixth in the NASCAR Grand National points standings, is stripped of all points when he quits NASCAR and joins the rival AAA tour. Teague will drive in the AAA Stock Car division and has his eyes peeled for a possible ride in the Indianapolis 500.

May 10 Buck Baker drives a Cadillac-powered open-wheel car to victory in the 200-mile NASCAR Speedway division race at Darlington Raceway. Dick Rathmann prevails in the accompanying 100-mile NASCAR Grand National race, which was added to the program to boost attendance.

It was a grand sight to watch the NASCAR Modifieds fan out 12-abreast up the two-mile straightaway along the shoreline of Daytona's Beach-Road course. The cars had to be in some semblance of order when approaching the hairpin curves on the north and south end of the course. Spectators parked their cars in what was regarded as the "infield," just off the inner edge of the racing surface.

While the late-model NASCAR Grand Nationals were clearly the featured attraction by 1952, the older model Modifieds never disappointed the spectators in terms of excitement. Here, a couple of Modifieds have gone over the rim of Daytona's south turn and have landed near the front row of the grandstands. The officials perched in the observation tower were clearly at risk, with nowhere to run for safety when an errant car tumbled in their direction.

Qualifications on Daytona's Beach-Road course were unique from that of any other racetrack. Rather than touring the entire 4.1-mile course in a race against the clock, NASCAR Grand National competitors made brisk runs through the measured mile. The quickest through the timing traps from a running start earned the pole. Here, Tim Flock's Hudson Hornet prepares for his southbound run before the 1952 Daytona NASCAR Grand National race. Flock experienced mechanical trouble in the Daytona event, finishing 55th in the field of 61.

Curtis Turner hustles through the south turn in the Feb. 10 Daytona Beach NASCAR Grand National race. While the wooden north-turn grandstands afforded the best view of the Beach-Road course, the south-turn bleachers attracted an equally enthusiastic throng. However, the south-turn bleachers were situated inside the track, so patrons could only see a fraction of the 4.1-mile course. The concrete blocks that held the south turn stands are still in the ground today.

Marshall Teague hoists a pair of trophies following his victory at Daytona. Teague, a savvy businessman as well as an accomplished race car driver, entered four Hudson Hornets in the race. Teague and Herb Thomas finished first and second in their "Teaguemobiles," while Pepper Cunningham finished 26th and Mike Klapak wound up 47th after rear gearing problems. The Daytona race was one of Teague's final NASCAR starts. In the spring of '52, Teague quit NASCAR and joined the rival AAA tour.

Herb Thomas kicks up dust as he exits the fourth turn at North Wilkesboro (N.C.) Speedway during the March 30 NASCAR Grand National event. Thomas started on the pole and led all 200 laps to rack up his ninth career NASCAR victory. Buck Baker, who started on the front row with Thomas, sits in the pits as his crew attempts to repair a broken radiator.

Flagman Alvin Hawkins presents Dick Rathmann with the checkered flag after the April 6 NASCAR Grand National event at Martinsville Speedway. Rathmann, a hot shot Californian, drove Walt Chapman's Hudson Hornet to his first career victory in the 100-mile contest. Rathmann started ninth and worked his way into contention late in the race. He made the decisive pass with 20 laps to go.

1952

June 29 Tom Cherry bags the 100-mile NASCAR Speedway Division race at Langhorne Speedway, the final event staged for the new open-wheel class. A paralyzing nationwide steel strike and a blisteringly hot summer are factors in the early demise of the once-promising series.

July 1 The first NASCAR Grand National event staged outside the U.S. takes place at Stamford Park in Niagara Falls, Ontario. Buddy Shuman outruns Herb Thomas by two laps in the 100-mile race as Hudson Hornets finish first and second.

July 4 Curtis Turner tames a 56-car field to win the 200-mile NASCAR Modified-Sportsman race at Darlington Raceway. Rex Stansell is fatally injured in a late-race crash. NASCAR inserted the Darlington race into its crowded Modified-Sportsman schedule to counter the AAA Indy Car race staged at the new Southland Speedway in Raleigh, N.C.

August 17 Bob Flock, making his first start since breaking his neck in a crash at Mobile, Ala., on Nov. 25, 1951, wins the 100-mile NASCAR Grand National event at Asheville-Weaverville Speedway. Flock's little brother Tim finishes second and holds on to his narrow points lead.

August 20 NASCAR issues a new rule that will reprimand drivers who are guilty of reckless highway driving. E.G. "Cannonball" Baker, NASCAR's commissioner, recommends the rule to Bill France. "There is no excuse for speeding on the highways," says Baker. "If NASCAR members are convicted of such highway violations, they will face fines, suspension, and loss of championship points."

September 1 Fonty Flock, wearing bermuda shorts and a short-sleeve shirt, takes the lead just before the halfway point and motors to victory in the third annual Southern 500 at Darlington.

September 14 Lee Petty drives his Plymouth to victory in the tragic 250-mile NASCAR Grand National event at Langhorne Speedway. Rookie driver Larry Mann, competing in only his sixth race, overturns on the 211th lap and dies of massive injuries. Mann defied a long-standing racing taboo by painting his Hudson green.

Buck Baker stands beside his B.A. Pless-owned #89 Hudson Hornet, which he drove to victory in the April 12 NASCAR Grand National race at Columbia Speedway in South Carolina. Pless entered a car in only 19 NASCAR races and won twice. Baker won one race in 10 starts in the Hornet, while Buddy Shuman won once in eight starts. Jimmy Thompson drove the Pless Hudson in one race. Shuman's triumph in the July 1, 1952, race at Niagara Falls, Ontario, was the first NASCAR Grand National race staged on foreign soil.

Fireball Roberts and Fonty Flock share the front row at the start of the 100-mile NASCAR Grand National event at Darlington Raceway on May 10. The 80-lap contest was tossed into the NASCAR schedule at the 11th hour as a companion event to a new Speedway Division race. The Speedway Division was an open-wheel tour featuring Indy-style cars powered by stock engines. Roberts led in the early laps, but Dick Rathmann drove his Hudson to the win.

Dick Rathmann poses in victory lane with Darlington Raceway President Bob Colvin (holding the checkered flag) at the conclusion of the 100-mile race on May 10. Advance ticket sales for the NASCAR Speedway Division race at Darlington were lagging below expectations, so the 100-miler for the popular NASCAR Grand Nationals was arranged to stimulate sales. A healthy crowd turned out once the late-model stocks were booked. The spectators got to see a doubleheader for the cost of one ticket.

Front row starters Fonty and Tim Flock lead the relatively small 19-car field to the green flag at the start of the 100-mile NASCAR Grand National event at Hillsboro, N.C. Tim led most of the way and scored his third win of the season. The victory pushed Flock to third place in the points standings, and he found himself in the thick of the championship hunt after falling far behind with a 55th-place finish at Daytona. The Flock brothers, Lee Petty, and Herb Thomas were engaged in a spirited battle for top honors.

The NASCAR Speedway Division ran its second race at Martinsville Speedway on May 25. Only 17 cars were ready for the 100-miler, but the new open-wheel cars generated a pretty good crowd. Bill Miller is in the pole slot in his "Olds 88 Special." Flanking him on the outside is Buddy Shuman in the "GMC Special." Tex Keene, in an open wheeler powered by a stock Mercury engine, came from his 16th starting spot to win the race. A total of seven Speedway Division events were staged in 1952, and Buck Baker was crowned champion.

Lee Petty smiles from victory lane after his July 11 victory at Morristown Speedway in New Jersey. Petty's narrow victory over Tim Flock was his first NASCAR Grand National win in nearly a year. Petty was NASCAR's steadiest driver throughout his career. He won his share of races, but more importantly, he rarely tore up his equipment. NASCAR's points system has always rewarded consistency and "Poppa" Lee was always in the running for the title. In his first 11 years, Petty never finished lower than fourth in the final NASCAR points standings.

Tim Flock rides under the checkered flag to win the second annual Motor City 250 at Detroit's one-mile Fairgrounds Speedway. The 250-miler in the automotive city's backyard was destined to be the final NASCAR race at the old Fairgrounds track. Plans were underway for a third event in 1953, but NASCAR and track promoters squabbled about sanctioning fees. Looking for a cheap way out, track operators elected to go with a Midwestern stock car organization for the '53 race.

Bob Flock (left) missed the first half of the 1952 season. Flock had crashed and broken his neck in the '51 season finale at Mobile, Ala. At the time, he wasn't aware of the extent of his injury. Flock drove to Pensacola, Fla., where he visited a doctor to seek advice to deaden the pain in his neck. Doctors determined he had broken his neck. Out 10 months, Flock made a memorable comeback by winning the Aug. 17, 1952, NASCAR Grand National race at Weaverville, N.C., in his first start since recovering from his injury.

1952

September 28 Herb Thomas creeps to within 174 points of leader Tim Flock in the NASCAR Grand National title chase with a victory in the 100-mile event at Wilson, N.C. Thomas averages only 35.398 mph, and takes almost three hours to complete the race. It is the slowest average speed in NASCAR Grand National history.

November 16 Donald Thomas, with relief help from older brother Herb, wins the 100-mile NASCAR Grand National event at Lakewood Speedway in Atlanta. The 20-year-old Thomas becomes the youngest driver to win a NASCAR Grand National event.

November 30 Herb Thomas speeds to victory in the 1952 NASCAR Grand National season finale at West Palm Beach as Tim Flock captures the championship. Flock flips his Hudson in a 164th lap mishap, but his 12th-place finish is enough to edge Thomas for the title by 106 points.

December 8 NASCAR stock car racing and newly crowned champion Tim Flock are featured in the Dec. 8 issue of *Time* magazine.

Number 16 Banjo Matthews and #58 Johnny Patterson, driving a pair of Hudson Hornets, battle side-by-side down the back chute at Darlington Raceway during the third annual Southern 500 on Sept. 1. Patterson, barely 20 years old, came from the 42nd starting spot to finish a startling second. Matthews, who was making his NASCAR Grand National racing debut, came from 57th to finish fifth. Patterson's Hudson was owned by Grady Akers, and Matthews was wheeling a car set up by prewar racing hero Bill Snowden.

Bobby Myers pushes his #6 Ford under Slick Smith in the early laps of the Southern 500. Smith was teammates with Fonty Flock on the Frank Christian-owned, Red Vogt-tuned Oldsmobile team for the race, which was the richest of the year. Smith qualified 19th in the 66-car field, but fell out early with engine problems. Myers, in his third NASCAR Grand National effort, ran 145 laps before his engine expired.

John B. Thomasson, who raced under the name of Perk Brown his entire career, was one of NASCAR's top-ranked short-track stars. In 1952, Brown and team owner R.G. Shelton decided to take a fling at the NASCAR Grand National tour. Driving a Hudson, Brown quickly served notice that he could compete with the NASCAR's best, scoring a couple of third-place finishes. Except for an occasional appearance, Brown limited his NASCAR Grand National efforts to 19 starts in '52. He went back to the weekly Modified races near his hometown of Spray, N.C., choosing to sidestep the extensive traveling schedule the NASCAR Grand Nationals demanded.

Fonty Flock waves to the crowd as he thunders under the checkered flag to win the Southern 500. Fonty became the first pole winner to win the Southern 500, leading all but 59 of the 400 trips around the egg-shaped raceway. After his victory lap, Flock stopped on the frontstretch, hopped on the hood of his car and led the crowd of 32,400 in singing *Dixie*, the South's "national" anthem.

MARSHALL TEAGUE

MARSHALL PLEASANT TEAGUE, one of racing's most brilliant minds, was also one of NASCAR's most accomplished pioneer racers. A native of Daytona Beach, Teague began his racing career on Dec. 2, 1945, at Seminole Speedway in Orlando, Fla. Still a Second Lieutenant in the United States Army, Teague was one of 22 drivers entered in the Orlando event. His name appeared on the entry list as "Lt. Marshall Teague," joining headliners Bill France, Roy Hall, Fonty Flock, Sgt. Red Byron, and Buddy Shuman. Teague finished second to France in his first effort.

The mechanically inclined Teague was a semiregular competitor in stock car racing events in the late 1940s, winning races from 1946 to '48 with regularity. By the time the newfangled late-model NASCAR Strictly Stock/Grand National division became the hot tour in '49 and '50, Teague had prepared a low-profile Hudson Hornet to drive in Bill France's organization.

Teague won his fifth career start at Daytona, driving the Hornet to a decisive victory. During the 1951 NASCAR Grand National campaign, Teague won five of his 15 starts, and provided technical assistance and a car for Herb Thomas to drive in selected '51 races during Thomas' title run. Teague didn't show up in the final points standings since he elected to go against France's orders to refrain from driving in Mexico's *Carrera Panamericana* in the winter of '51. The Mexican race was an exercise NASCAR approved of in 1950, but the '51 contest was strictly "hands off." Teague competed anyway, and finished sixth in his class. The Mexican road-race incident strained the relationship between Teague and France, a rift that would last until the day Teague died in 1959.

Teague had to pay a hefty fine of nearly $600 to be reinstated with NASCAR for the 1952 Daytona Beach race. Teague successfully defended his Daytona championship, then won at Jacksonville, and was among the contenders for the NASCAR championship.

All that changed on April 12, 1952. NASCAR's Bill Tuthill mailed a letter to Teague alerting him that his championship points had been taken away due to participation in a non-NASCAR-sanctioned race at Tampa, a charge Teague denied.

NASCAR Grand National Career Record 1949-1952
Starts: 23
Wins: 7
Top 5s: 9
Top 10s: 11
Poles: 2
Career Winnings: $10,060

In reaction to the letter, Teague quit NASCAR, joined the AAA Stock Car tour, and blazed a path of success. Teague won his first AAA start at Toledo on May 4, and went on to take the AAA Stock Car championship in 1952 despite missing several early season events.

The former NASCAR driver won several AAA laurels in 1952, including a coveted AAA Stock Car Driver of the Year Award. Teague was cited for "his willingness to cooperate with his fellow drivers in preparing their automobiles. He is always available for advice and, on several occasions, helped prepare the car which defeated him."

Teague realized a dream when he landed a ride for the 1953 Indy 500. Driving the Hart Fullerton Special, Teague qualified 22nd in his first effort in a high-powered open-wheel car. He had advanced into the top 10 when an oil leak ended his run with 31 laps remaining. He finished 18th.

Teague ran both the AAA Stock Car and Championship Big Car open-wheel tour in the 1950s. He took the '54 AAA Stock championship, his second title in three years. Top-flight rides in the Indy 500 were few and far between, but Teague did get a ride in Chapman Root's Sumar Special in the '57 Indy 500. Teague responded brilliantly, finishing seventh after starting 28th.

When the Daytona International Speedway opened in 1959, Root prepared a streamlined Sumar Indy Car so Teague could take a stab at the existing closed-course record. The car had closed wheel covers and a canopy for aerodynamic enhancement. During a warm-up lap on Feb. 11, the car lurched sideways in the west banking and flipped over. The seat, with Teague still strapped in by the safety belts, broke loose from the chassis and tumbled across the steeply pitched pavement. Teague died instantly, and the Daytona Beach native became the first victim at his hometown speedway.

Teague is recognized in a number of racing Halls of Fame, including the National Motorsports Hall of Fame (1966), the National Old Timers Auto Racing Club National Hall of Fame (1988), the TRW/NASCAR Mechanics Hall of Fame (1989), and the American Auto Racing Writers & Broadcasters Hall of Fame (1991).

With Hudson's total domination of NASCAR Grand National races in 1952, the Hudson Motor Co. unleashed an avalanche of advertising in the print and electronic media. This two-page spread in a nationally distributed magazine featured NASCAR drivers Dick Rathmann, Tim Flock, Herb Thomas, Buddy Shuman, and Marshall Teague. Hudson was one of the first manufacturers to advertise lofty records in NASCAR racing to sell more passenger cars.

Fonty Flock poses with his Southern 500-winning Oldsmobile. The snazzy attire—slip-in sandals, bermuda shorts, and a pull-over polo shirt—was Flock's "driver's uniform" during the Labor Day spectacle. NASCAR had no rules in place governing the type of garb worn during an event. Drivers often wore what was most comfortable for the time-consuming ride. It took Flock nearly seven hours to complete the 500-mile race.

Tim Flock poses with his championship trophy and the Ted Chester-owned Hudson Hornet he drove during the 1952 NASCAR Grand National campaign. Flock started 33 of the 34 races, won eight times, and finished in the top 10 in 25 events. Counting his postseason awards, Flock took home $22,890 during his stellar season.

Herb Thomas went on a winning spree in the fall, winning three out of four races in a four-week span. Following his victory in the Oct. 26 event at North Wilkesboro (N.C.), Thomas crept to within 146 points of NASCAR Grand National leader Tim Flock. The margin was closer than it seems. The NASCAR points system for most short-track events awarded 200 points to the winner with a drop of eight points for each position. That meant Thomas was within 20 finishing positions of Flock after 32 of the 34 races.

Donald Thomas, younger brother of Herb Thomas, registered his only NASCAR Grand National victory in the Nov. 16 race at Atlanta's Lakewood Speedway. Thomas started on the pole and ran among the leaders the entire race. When Herb dropped out on the 86th lap, Donald pulled off the track and allowed his older brother to finish the race. NASCAR awarded championship points to relief drivers in 1952. Herb carried the car to victory, giving the win to Donald.

1952 NASCAR GRAND NATIONAL POINTS

Rank	Driver	Points	Starts	Wins	Top 5	Top 10	Winnings
1	Tim Flock	6858.50	33	8	22	25	$22,890
2	Herb Thomas	6752.50	32	8	19	22	$18,965
3	Lee Petty	6498.50	32	3	21	27	$16,876
4	Fonty Flock	5183.50	29	2	14	17	$19,112
5	Dick Rathmann	3952.00	27	5	14	14	$11,248
6	Bill Blair	3449.00	19	1	10	13	$7899
7	Joe Eubanks	3090.50	19	0	4	9	$3630
8	Ray Duhigg	2986.50	18	0	4	10	$3811
9	Donald Thomas	2574.00	21	1	5	14	$4477
10	Buddy Shuman	2483.00	15	1	3	7	$4587
11	Ted Chamberlain	2208.00	18	0	0	6	$1277
12	Buck Baker	2159.00	14	1	3	6	$3187
13	Perk Brown	2151.50	19	0	3	6	$2187
14	Jimmie Lewallen	2033.00	20	0	2	7	$2052
15	Bub King	1993.00	10	0	2	5	$2737
16	Herschel Buchanan	1868.00	5	0	4	5	$2468
17	Johnny Patterson	1708.00	5	0	2	2	$3618
18	Jim Paschal	1694.00	15	0	1	7	$1483
19	Neil Cole	1618.00	11	0	1	7	$1793
20	Lloyd Moore	1513.50	8	0	2	4	$2193
21	Gene Comstock	1339.00	8	0	1	3	$785
22	Banjo Matthews	1240.00	3	0	1	1	$1000
23	Ralph Liguori	1230.00	12	0	1	6	$920
24	Jack Reynolds	1177.50	10	0	2	6	$1450
25	Dick Passwater	1148.00	6	0	1	3	$945
26	Bucky Sager	1119.50	10	0	1	3	$710
27	Frankie Schneider	931.00	6	0	3	4	$1350
28	Otis Martin	873.50	5	0	0	2	$275
29	Coleman Lawrence	846.00	8	0	0	3	$375
30	Ed Samples	827.00	8	0	2	4	$1535
31	Fred Dove	780.00	8	0	0	3	$390
32	Slick Smith	746.00	5	0	0	3	$725
33	Iggy Katona	742.00	5	0	0	2	$525
34	Jack Smith	729.00	8	0	0	2	$820
35	Tommy Moon	726.00	6	0	2	3	$1145
36	Rollin Smith	700.00	1	0	0	0	$350
37	Speedy Thompson	656.00	2	0	0	0	$305
38	Jimmy Thompson	650.00	1	0	0	0	$300
39	George Farrell	648.00	6	0	0	2	$325
40	Weldon Adams	634.00	6	0	0	2	$275
41	Clyde Minter	632.00	5	0	0	3	$375
42	Elton Hildreth	614.00	6	0	0	1	$375
43	Dave Terrell	612.00	5	0	1	3	$475
44	Tommy Thompson	602.50	5	0	0	1	$525
45	Bob Moore	579.50	5	0	1	3	$575
46	Jim Reed	567.00	7	0	1	3	$475
47	E.C. Ramsey	560.00	7	0	0	0	$260
48	Jimmy Florian	551.00	6	0	0	2	$175
49	Ed Benedict	526.00	5	0	1	2	$360
50	Curtis Turner	505.00	7	0	1	1	$265

The battle for the 1952 championship came down to the final event of the season at West Palm Beach. Tim Flock, who took the points lead from Herb Thomas at Langhorne in September, clinched the title by simply starting the 100-miler. Flock smacked the wall and flipped down the front chute in the West Palm Beach finale, but he had accumulated enough points to seal the championship.

"I think I'm the only guy who ever won a championship on his head," cracked Flock afterward.

Thomas, who had taken the points lead at Darlington, only held it for two races before Flock was back in front. The margin at the end of the season was 106 points.

Flock and Thomas both won eight races during the 34-race campaign. Lee Petty, Fonty Flock, and Dick Rathmann, all multiple race winners, filled out the top five in the final NASCAR Grand National points standings.

1953

January 13 NASCAR announces it will require that drivers mail entry blanks to NASCAR headquarters and speedway promoters to earn championship points. Many promoters have complained that they don't know who will compete and have been unable to properly promote their events.

February 1 Lee Petty and Jimmie Lewallen finish first and second in the 1953 NASCAR Grand National opener at West Palm Beach. Both drive Dodge Diplomats prepared in the Randleman, N.C., Petty Engineering shops.

February 11 NASCAR conducts its fourth annual Victory Dinner at the Princess Issena Hotel in Daytona Beach. Lee Petty is named Most Popular Driver, the first time the award has been given out since 1949.

February 15 Fonty Flock runs out of fuel on the final lap as Bill Blair drives to victory in the NASCAR Grand National event on the Beach-Road course in Daytona. It is the first NASCAR Grand National race to be determined by a last-lap pass.

April 5 Dick Passwater scores an upset victory in the 150-lap race at Charlotte Speedway. Five different drivers lead in the final 25 laps, and Passwater takes the lead with just three laps to go.

May 16 Tim Flock, with riding companion "Jocko Flocko," prevails in a 100-mile NASCAR Grand National event at Hickory, N.C. Jocko, a rhesus monkey, has a driver's uniform and a custom-made seat. It is the first time a NASCAR Grand National winner has a copilot.

May 30 The one-mile superspeedway in Raleigh, N.C., joins NASCAR and presents a Memorial Day 300-miler. Fonty Flock comes from his 43rd starting position to win. Tim Flock falls to third in the final laps when he pits to remove monkey copilot Jocko Flocko from his car.

June 21 Dick Rathmann leads all the way to win the International 200 at Langhorne Speedway, the first NASCAR event open to both domestic and foreign cars. Lloyd Shaw wins the pole in a Jaguar. Oldsmobile driver Frank Arford is killed in a qualifying mishap.

New beauty, style and luxury for the

NATIONAL STOCK-CAR CHAMPION*

*HUDSONS WIN TRIPLE STOCK-CAR CROWN

FABULOUS 1953
HUDSON HORNET
and its lower-priced running mate, the
1953 HUDSON WASP

◄ ▼Hudson continued to live by the credo "Win on Sunday, sell on Monday" early in 1953, as this ad from *Time* magazine shows. The key to Hudson's success was its unibody step-down design that provided better cornering than its rivals. Also early in '53, a new Hudson Hornet was presented to '52 NASCAR Grand National champion Tim Flock. The car's value was almost equal to the amount of postseason award money the champion received.

The beachside portion of the Daytona north-turn grandstands contained a small observation tower for NASCAR officials. The timing wire that stretched across the sand was the finish line of the Measured Mile for performance trials and qualification runs. During the stock car races on the 4.1-mile Beach-Road course, officials could keep an eye on the long two-mile beach straightaway in case an accident warranted a yellow flag.

The opening laps of the Feb. 14 Daytona Modified-Sportsman race was punctuated by a multicar entanglement in the north turn. The starting field consisted of 136 cars, the largest in NASCAR history. The flimsy wooden guardrail was reduced to splinters as a dozen or so cars piled into each other. Cotton Owens, driving a Modified Plymouth, won the 100-mile race.

The start of the annual NASCAR Grand National event on Daytona's Beach-Road course was always a spectacular scramble with hordes of drivers trying to make their way through the hairpin curves. Fifty-seven cars started the Daytona race on Feb. 15. Here, #54 Obie Chupp and #8 Gene Comstock dice for position in thick clumps of traffic. The splintered guardrail in the north turn is a remnant of a wild day of action in the Modified-Sportsman race. The entire barrier had been destroyed in Saturday's race and wasn't replaced for the Sunday NASCAR Grand National race.

Dick Rathmann guns his #120 Hudson Hornet off the north turn and onto the paved backstretch at Daytona. He started ninth and finished 12th. Rathmann competed in NASCAR racing from 1951 to '55, winning 13 of his 128 starts. In '56, he departed NASCAR and joined the United States Auto Club tour, running stock cars and Indy Cars. Rathmann drove in nine Indy 500s, qualified on the pole once, and posted three top-10 finishes.

Driving a 1953 Lincoln that competed in the annual *Carrera Panamericana*, Tom Cherry whips a quick lap at Daytona. Cherry finished ninth in what turned out to be his only start in NASCAR's premier stock car racing series. Two different numbers were painted on the durable Lincoln—the #120 that it had in the grueling race over the rugged Mexican terrain, and the #38 that it officially carried in the NASCAR Grand National event.

The north-turn grandstand is packed with fans as Fonty Flock's #14 Olds leads the charge onto the paved section of Highway A-1-A in the Daytona Beach NASCAR Grand National event. The old wooden structure located at the hairpin turn on the north end of the 4.1-mile Beach-Road course had a seating capacity of about 4000 and was accessible by a single stairway. Tickets for the weathered and splintered seats cost about $4, and they were always filled when the NASCAR Grand Nationals came to town.

1953

July 4 Junior Johnson wins the 200-mile NASCAR Modified-Sportsman race at Darlington Raceway. In a same-day NASCAR Grand National event at Spartanburg, S.C., title contender Tim Flock is run over by a car as he takes a nap in the infield. Flock's injuries will keep him out of action for several weeks.

July 22 NASCAR embarks on a western tour with NASCAR Grand National races in South Dakota, Iowa, and Nebraska.

July 31 NASCAR conducts another race with international flavor in the NASCAR Short Track Grand National Division. Jim Reed, driving a Ford, captures the 400-lapper at Norwood Arena in Massachusetts. Foreign entries lead the early stages, but fade at the end.

September 1 Buck Baker takes the lead with 10 laps remaining to win the Southern 500 at Darlington. It is one of the most competitive events in NASCAR Grand National history, with four drivers swapping the lead a record 35 times.

September 19 NASCAR's first nighttime superspeedway, a 220-mile Modified-Sportsman race at Raleigh Speedway, is marred by tragedy. Bill Blevins and Jesse Midkiff are killed in an opening-lap crash. Officials are unaware that Blevins' car has stalled on the backstretch during the pace lap. The 60-car field gets the green flag and the crash occurs seconds later.

November 1 Herb Thomas wraps up the NASCAR Grand National championship with a 14th-place finish in the 100-mile finale at Atlanta's Lakewood Speedway. Thomas becomes the first driver to win two titles.

November 27 NASCAR announces it will have both owner and driver points standings in 1954. Team owners have complained that some drivers have failed to split the points fund money, which has always been awarded to the drivers. Points money for the owners and drivers will be identical.

December 12 NASCAR president Bill France discloses plans for a 2.5-mile superspeedway in Daytona Beach. France estimates the facility will cost $1,674,000 to build and could open as early as 1955.

Fonty Flock is pushed by teammate Slick Smith during the final lap at Daytona. Flock started on the front row and led the entire distance until his fuel tank ran dry on the last lap. Smith, playing the role of good samaritan, pushed Fonty's #14 Oldsmobile across the finish line, but NASCAR disallowed the assist and awarded Flock second place. Bill Blair went on to win.

Bill Blair whips his Oldsmobile around the north turn during his victory ride at Daytona. Blair was declared the winner when NASCAR officials ruled that Fonty Flock's car couldn't be pushed across the finish line by another car. Blair's victory was the first NASCAR Grand National race determined by a last-lap pass.

Herb Thomas throws his Hudson Hornet into the first turn at Harnett Speedway in Spring Lake, N.C., on March 8. Thomas led all 200 laps on the ½-mile dirt track to take his 17th career NASCAR Grand National win. He became NASCAR's all-time Grand National race winner in this event, and held the distinction until Lee Petty surpassed Thomas' 48 wins in 1960.

NASCAR newcomer Dick Passwater lifted eyebrows with a victory in the April 5 race at Charlotte Speedway. The Indianapolis lad took the lead with three laps to go and scored a narrow victory over Gober Sosebee. Passwater moved to as high as second in the NASCAR Grand National points standings while driving Oldsmobiles fielded by Frank Arford. When Arford was killed qualifying for a race in Langhorne, it left Passwater without a ride. He returned home and drove in only one more NASCAR event in his career.

Tim Flock's #91 leads #82 Joe Eubanks in a stirring battle during the May 16 race at Hickory Speedway. Flock edged Eubanks to score his first win in nine months. Hickory Speedway was originally measured as a ½-mile dirt track and was billed as the fastest ½-mile track in the South. In reality, the track was a tiny .363-mile oval, and lap times made it appear that speeds were greater than they actually were.

Lee Petty powered his #42 Dodge to victory in the controversial May 17 race at Martinsville Speedway. Herb Thomas finished first, but when NASCAR officials studied the score sheets, they discovered that, on paper, Petty had traveled the 200 laps first. Fudging in the scoring stand, a standard practice at the time, was regarded as a method of gaining a competitive edge. Petty kept the $1000 first prize because no error in the scoring cards could be detected.

In 1953, NASCAR began issuing staged publicity photographs of mock racing action to local newspapers. Accompanying a prerace press release, photos like this showed up on the desks of local sports editors a couple weeks in advance of an upcoming race. Cars were parked sideways on the track, wheels cocked to the right to depict the action readers might see if they attended a NASCAR Grand National event. Here, the cars of Fonty Flock (#14), Herb Thomas (#92), Tim Flock (#91), and Curtis Turner (#41) sit idle on the track.

This aerial photo shows the paper-clip-shaped Raleigh Speedway in North Carolina. The one-mile paved super-speedway opened in 1952, but promoters elected to bring in AAA Indy Cars for their inaugural show while shunning NASCAR's stock car series. By '53, Raleigh Speedway was in NASCAR's fold. The first NASCAR race was staged on May 30, 1953, opposite the celebrated Indy 500.

Fonty Flock, in the #14 Hudson Hornet, and Hershel McGriff's #5 Oldsmobile battle during the inaugural 300-miler at Raleigh Speedway. Flock was unable to take a qualifying run due to engine problems. He was forced to start 43rd in the field of 49. Flock sliced his way through the field, grabbed the lead on the 196th lap, and led the rest of the way to post a magnificent come-from-behind victory. In so doing, Flock equaled Johnny Mantz, who started 43rd and won the 1950 Southern 500.

Number 14 Fonty Flock ducks under the #21 Lincoln of Glen Wood in the Raleigh 300. Wood, an established short-track star, was driving in his second NASCAR Grand National event and his first on a paved super-speedway. He finished 20th, 26 laps behind winner Flock. Wood, the patriarch of the famous Wood Brothers, was in the early stages of building the Virginia-based operation into what would become one of the most successful teams in NASCAR history.

The NASCAR Grand National circuit staged a western tour in the summer of 1953, taking its wild, sideways traveling show into South Dakota, Nebraska, and Iowa. Herb Thomas, wheeling his baby-blue #92 Hudson Hornet, won two of the three races and finished second in the other event. The venture was the NASCAR Grand National division's first and last visit to those three states.

▼ A crowd of nearly 40,000 turned out to watch the fourth running of the Southern 500 on Labor Day, Sept. 7. The infield of the Darlington Raceway was jammed with racing fans and the frontstretch grandstands were filled to capacity. The 59 cars that comprised the starting field were traditionally lined up in their post positions before the start of the race. The race produced 35 lead changes, a record that would stand for nearly 10 years.

Buck Baker's #87 Oldsmobile leads Mike Magill's #23 Lincoln and the #60 Chevrolet driven by Tyre Rakestraw in the early laps of the Southern 500. Magill, who cut his teeth in open wheelers, crashed through the fence on the 245th lap and suffered a fractured leg and broken ribs. Baker went on to win while Rakestraw finished 22nd.

JOCKO FLOCKO

IN THE EARLY part of the 1953 NASCAR Grand National season, Hudson team owner Ted Chester was visiting a pet shop in Atlanta to buy a birthday gift for a member of his family. While browsing through the pet shop, Chester noticed a rhesus monkey, one of the smallest and most personable of all primates.

Chester purchased the monkey with a crazy idea in mind. He thought putting the small monkey in lead driver Tim Flock's car during NASCAR Grand National events would make for an entertaining gimmick.

"Ted came to me and told me about this monkey he wanted to put in the race car with me," reflected Tim Flock years later. "I thought Ted had been hittin' the jug too much. He couldn't be serious. But the more I got to thinking about it, the more I liked it. Ted said the monkey already had the name 'Jocko,' and he gave him a last name of 'Flocko.' I decided Jocko Flocko could ride with me anytime."

The problem confronting Chester and Flock was gaining NASCAR's permission. "We did it the best way," said Flock. "We didn't ask NASCAR. We hid Jocko until it was time for the cars to line up for the start. It was a great surprise when we made our first laps in the race. Other drivers would look over at my car as I passed them, and they almost ran into the guardrail when they saw Jocko looking back at them."

Jocko Flocko's first ride in a NASCAR Grand National race car was at Charlotte on May 5, 1953. The Flock-and-Flocko duo managed to post a fourth-place finish.

NASCAR's code of conduct wasn't as stringent in 1953 as it is today. So, since he had already ridden with Flock in a race, Jocko was allowed to ride in other events. Prior to other races, Tim would carry Jocko over to the grandstand fence to the delight of spectators. Many would feed him peanuts. "Jocko loved peanuts and he loved people. He was a big hit with the kids."

NASCAR Grand National Career Record 1953

Starts: 8
Wins: 1
Top 5s: 1
Top 10s: 6
Poles: 0
Career Winnings: $3945

Jocko Flocko finished sixth at Macon, fifth at Langhorne, second at Columbia, then rode home a winner with Tim Flock in the May 16, 1953, NASCAR Grand National race at Hickory. "It was one whale of a victory lane party," cracked Tim.

Team owner Chester rigged a customized seat for Jocko, had a seamstress sew him a well-fitted driver's uniform, and even provided a small helmet for him. "Jocko would sit up there and have a blast as I tore around the track," said Flock.

Two weeks after the Flock/Flocko win at Hickory, Jocko competed in his final NASCAR event. "Back in those days, before we had special durable racing tires, there was a cable attached to a trap door over the right front wheelwell," said Flock. During the race, the driver would pull on the cable, which would open the trap door so we could check the tire wear.

"Well, Jocko had seen me tug on that cable a number of times," Flock continued. "In the 300-mile race at Raleigh, we had a little problem with Jocko. Late in the race, while I was running second, he broke loose from his seat and he jumped down on the floorboard. He yanked that cable and opened the trap door—right as I ran over a rock on the track. The rock zinged Jocko right between the eyes. He went crazy. He jumped on my neck and started scratching me to the point I almost wrecked a couple of times. Finally, I had to make a pit stop so we could put Jocko out of the car.

"I'm the only driver in NASCAR history to lose a race because we had to pit to get rid of a monkey," Flock said with a chuckle.

After the incident, Chester and Flock decided against having Jocko ride along in competition. "It disappointed the kids, so I told them I had to fire Jocko because he couldn't sign autographs."

For the record, Jocko Flocko rode in eight NASCAR Grand National events. Although his name doesn't appear in NASCAR record books, Jocko won once, logged six top-10 finishes, and won a total of $3945.

Fireball Roberts steers his crippled #11 into the pits in the Southern 500 at Darlington. The right front wheel collapsed on the 198th lap, forcing the hotshot from Daytona to retire from the event. Prior to his misfortune, Roberts led for 41 laps in the Ed Saverance-owned Oldsmobile. In the formative years at Darlington Raceway, the pit area was located on the inside of the frontstretch and was devoid of any protective retaining barrier. A fatal pit accident in 1960 prompted raceway officials to build a wall to keep cars from spinning into the crowded pits.

Number 92 Herb Thomas mixes it up with #14 Fonty Flock and #99 Matt Gowan during a 1953 NASCAR Grand National event. This is one of the rare shots showing Thomas' Hudson without the inscription "Fabulous Hudson Hornet" on the doors. Thomas took the lead in the points standings after the third race in early March and held it to the end of the 37-race campaign.

Drivers meetings in NASCAR's early days were held on the front straightaway just before the start of the race. Drivers, owners, pit crewmen, and race officials all gathered and stood around listening to the instructions. This photo was taken on Oct. 18 at Martinsville Speedway, an event that Jim Paschal drove to his first career NASCAR Grand National win. That's 16-year-old Richard Petty standing near the rear of the meeting in front of the door of Lee Petty's #42 Dodge.

Tim and Fonty Flock, in their speedy Hudson Hornets, head the field for the NASCAR Grand National finale at Atlanta's Lakewood Speedway on Nov. 1. The dazzling Flocks traded the lead in the early going before Buck Baker took command in the late stages. The flat one-mile dirt track was one of the most famous speedways in the South. Along with NASCAR's Grand National races, Lakewood hosted Sprints, Indy Cars, Motorcycles, and even had boat races in the infield lake during its tenure from 1915 to '79.

1953 NASCAR GRAND NATIONAL POINTS RACE

Rank	Driver	Points	Starts	Wins	Top 5	Top 10	Winnings
1	Herb Thomas	8460	37	12	27	31	$28,909.58
2	Lee Petty	7814	36	5	25	31	$18,446.50
3	Dick Rathmann	7362	34	5	22	25	$20,245.35
4	Buck Baker	6713	33	4	16	26	$18,166.20
5	Fonty Flock	6174	33	4	17	17	$17,755.48
6	Tim Flock	5011	26	1	11	18	$8281.86
7	Jim Paschal	4211	24	1	6	9	$5570.75
8	Joe Eubanks	3603	24	0	7	15	$5253.60
9	Jimmie Lewallen	3508	22	0	7	13	$4221.80
10	Curtis Turner	3373	19	1	3	5	$4371.45
11	Speedy Thompson	2958	7	2	5	7	$6546.45
12	Slick Smith	2670	23	0	0	10	$2301.45
13	Elton Hildreth	2625	25	0	1	5	$1996.45
14	Gober Sosebee	2525	17	0	2	9	$2721.45
15	Bill Blair	2457	23	1	6	8	$4534.30
16	Fred Dove	1997	20	0	0	4	$1239.30
17	Bub King	1624	14	0	0	5	$1035.30
18	Gene Comstock	1519	13	0	0	3	$989.30
19	Donald Thomas	1408	17	0	0	4	$1764.30
20	Ralph Liguori	1336	12	0	2	3	$1097.60
21	Pop McGinnis	1113	13	0	2	5	$975.00
22	Otis Martin	1068	8	0	0	2	$610.00
23	Andy Winfree	954	7	0	0	3	$300.00
24	Bob Welborn	761	11	0	2	6	$1160.00
25	Johnny Patterson	753	11	0	1	2	$645.00
26	Ted Chamberlain	738	9	0	0	3	$500.00
27	Neil Roberts	738	2	0	0	1	$400.00
28	Buddy Shuman	713	5	0	0	0	$395.00
29	Arden Mounts	644	10	0	0	1	$395.00
30	Bobby Myers	644	2	0	0	1	$390.00
31	Clyde Minter	636	8	0	0	3	$430.00
32	George Osborne	612	2	0	0	0	$300.00
33	Jim Reed	590	3	0	1	1	$635.00
34	Gordon Bracken	538	6	0	0	1	$215.00
35	Don Oldenberg	527	4	0	1	2	$375.00
36	C. H. Dingler	520	5	0	0	3	$250.00
37	Elbert Allen	488	4	0	0	2	$250.00
38	Mike Magill	486	3	0	0	0	$235.00
39	Lloyd Hulette	486	1	0	0	0	$250.00
40	Bill Harrison	480	3	0	0	3	$450.00
41	Tommy Thompson	463	3	0	1	1	$865.00
42	Coleman Lawrence	446	8	0	0	1	$250.00
43	Dub Livingston	435	6	0	0	1	$225.00
44	Buck Smith	400	5	0	0	1	$175.00
45	Jimmy Ayers	384	4	0	0	2	$150.00
46	Bob Walden	356	4	0	0	3	$275.00
47	Eddie Skinner	352	4	0	0	1	$200.00
48	Bill Adams	346	2	0	0	1	$250.00
49	Mel Kreuger	336	3	0	0	1	$175.00
50	Johnny Beauchamp	328	3	0	0	1	$150.00

Herb Thomas took the lead in the 1953 points standings in early March and never looked back as he sailed to his second NASCAR Grand National championship. The Olivia, N.C., Hudson driver won 12 events in the 37-race season and finished a comfortable 646 points ahead of runner-up Lee Petty, who won five races.

Thomas and crew chief Smokey Yunick (shown at left) were true to the test of an exhaustive schedule. In July and the first week in August, the tour made stops in New York, South Carolina, New Jersey, Georgia, South Dakota, Nebraska, Iowa, and North Carolina—in that order! Thomas won four races during that criss-crossing sojourn over America.

Thomas led virtually every major category during his championship run. He won the most races, led the most laps, scored the most top-five and top-10 finishes, completed the most miles and set a new record with $28,909.58 in prize money and post-season awards.

1954

September 12 Hershel McGriff drives an Oldsmobile to victory in the 100-mile NASCAR Grand National race at Macon, Ga. Tim Flock finishes second in his first start since quitting the tour following his disqualification at Daytona.

October 10 The recently completed Memphis-Arkansas Speedway opens to a crowd of 12,000. Buck Baker wins the 250-miler on the huge 1½-mile high-banked dirt track.

October 24 Lee Petty finishes last in the season finale at North Wilkesboro (N.C.) Speedway, but secures his first NASCAR Grand National championship. Petty finishes 283 points ahead of runner-up Herb Thomas. California driver Lou Figaro loses his life in a tumble three laps from the finish.

Starting fourth, Tim Flock gained control of the 160-mile Daytona Beach event by the third lap. He motored to a one minute, 28 second lead over runner-up Lee Petty when the checkered flag dropped. Upon a postrace inspection, NASCAR technical director Jim Ross noticed the carburetor on Flock's Olds looked a little different. Since the NASCAR rule book paralleled the manufacturers' parts catalog, Ross had to telephone Oldsmobile headquarters in Lansing, Mich. When NASCAR determined the venturis in the carburetor had been relieved ⅛ inch, the car was disqualified. Lee Petty was declared the official winner.

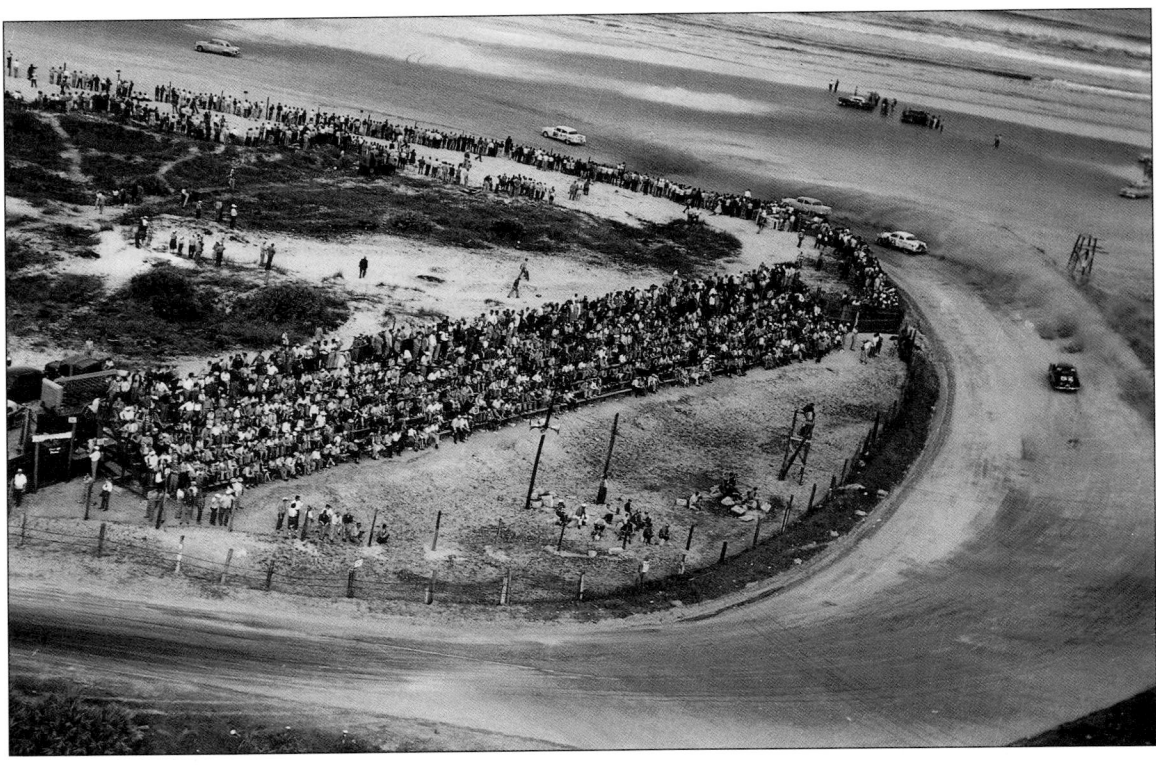

The narrow turns on the Daytona Beach-Road course gave some fans a unique opportunity. Many of the infield spectators would line up on the dunes to watch the cars scamper up the beach straightaway. They could then hop across the palmetto bushes and view the cars when they came back down the paved A-1-A roadside. The general admission ticket price for this exhaustive pleasure was $3.

Lee Petty started on the pole in the 1954 Daytona Beach NASCAR Grand National and led only the first two laps. But Petty was awarded first place when Tim Flock's winning Oldsmobile was disqualified. NASCAR freely disqualified winning cars that didn't comply with specs in the 1950s, a practice that has been discontinued.

Curtis Turner and Herb Thomas are at the front of the field during the pace lap for the March 7 NASCAR Grand National race at the unmanicured Jacksonville Speedway Park in Florida. The wooden fence had decayed due to weather (and errant cars). Thomas kept out of the fence and drove to victory, finishing two laps ahead of runner-up Fonty Flock, who started fifth.

Number 3 Dick Rathmann and #4 Tommy Moon battle side-by-side as #51 Gober Sosebee looks for an opening on the dusty surface of Jacksonville Speedway Park. Rathmann fell out of the event while Moon went on to finish 10th. Sosebee placed 16th. Rathmann's John Ditz-owned team had Pure Oil as a sponsor. Pure was NASCAR's first corporate contingency sponsor. As such, the company put up awards at every race for any car carrying its decal, and paid additional money to top finishers sporting its decal. Rathmann's sponsorship was in addition to Pure's contingency program.

A new, sporty Chevy Corvette paces the field at the March 28 event at Savannah's Oglethorpe Speedway. The Thomas brothers, Herb and Donald, make up the front row. Al Keller, who started third, scored his first NASCAR Grand National win. The Oglethorpe Speedway located just north of Savannah, has always been a dirt track and is still in operation today.

Following his Daytona Beach disqualification, Tim Flock quit NASCAR in a huff. He went back to Atlanta to operate a gas station. Team Owner Ernest Woods put Tim's brother Bob in his Helzapopin' Oldsmobile for the NASCAR Grand National race at Savannah. Woods simply whitewashed Tim's name from the roof, leaving "Flock." Bob qualified 10th and finished 12th after encountering a long pit stop.

Herb Thomas prevailed in the second annual Memorial Day weekend 250-miler at Raleigh Speedway. Thomas beat runner-up Dick Rathmann by a comfortable margin. The event was run without a caution flag. NASCAR's Bill France knew it was imperative to stage a big stock car race close to the time of the annual Indy 500. Originally, the race was staged at the ½-mile dirt track in Canfield, Ohio, but moved to Raleigh's newer one-mile super-speedway in 1953.

▶ Al Keller poses with his Jaguar sports coupe at New Jersey's Linden Airport. NASCAR's first road-course event was staged over two miles of the airport's runways on June 13. The event was open to both American stock cars and foreign sports cars. Nearly half of the entries in the 43-car starting field were foreign cars. Keller won the race in the Jag, leading the final 28 laps of the 100-mile race.

▲ Gober Sosebee, affectionately nicknamed "The Wild Injun," dabbled in NASCAR Grand National racing during his career. Best known for his exploits in the Modified circuit, Sosebee was one of stock car racing's free spirits, a veritable "outlaw" who rarely raced for just one sanctioning body. Twice, Sosebee lost all championship points when he wandered outside NASCAR's strict guidelines. In his 71 NASCAR Grand National starts, Sosebee won twice, including the 100-miler at Macon, Ga., on April 25, 1954.

Ralph Liguori, who raced out of the Bronx, was a regular in NASCAR Grand National competition in 1954. Driving a Dodge, Liguori logged 10 top-10 finishes in 23 starts and finished 10th in the final points standings. His best finish of the year was a third place at the ½-mile Wilson Speedway dirt track in North Carolina on May 9.

Elbert Allen in the Cherokee Garage Oldsmobile battles with Bill Irvin's #147 Plymouth in 1954. Allen was a part-timer from Atlanta, and was well acquainted with Gober Sosebee, who raced and operated out of his Cherokee Garage. Allen borrowed Sosebee's car and competed in four 1954 NASCAR Grand National races, with a 12th-place finish as his best effort.

NASCAR's First Road Course

UPON ITS INCEPTION, NASCAR's Grand National circuit drivers were required to make only left hand turns. A variety of oval races made up the entire annual tour in all NASCAR divisions—Grand Nationals, the Short Track Circuit for Grand National cars on tracks less than ½ mile, Modifieds, and Sportsmen. The competitors tackled their first road course on June 13, 1954, when promoters Ed Otto and Red Crise organized an "International 100 Mile Race."

Otto and Crise developed a two-mile, five-turn course on the concrete runways and taxiways on the Linden, N.J., airport. To add interest, foreign cars were made eligible for NASCAR's maiden voyage into the road-racing waters.

The foreign-car element wasn't a first in NASCAR competition. On rare occasions, NASCAR had permitted foreign sports cars to compete on the Grand National circuit. The most notable achievement was Lloyd Moore's Jaguar winning the pole for the June 21, 1953, race at Langhorne, a race eventually won by Dick Rathmann in a Hudson. That event featured 10 foreign makes mixing it up with the domestic NASCAR Grand National stock cars. The NASCAR Grand Nationals took the first five positions, and a Volkswagen managed to finish 19th in the field of 38.

For the Linden event, Otto-Crise Promotions decided to promote a race within a race, awarding a bonus for the highest finishing foreign sports car equipped with an engine smaller than 2000 cubic centimeters (about 122 cid).

The two-mile course consisted of four left-hand turns and a single right-hand bend. Total posted awards of $5020 attracted a full field of cars. Twenty-one foreign cars and 22 domestic stock cars qualified for starting spots. A total of 13 different makes started the race. Nimble Jaguars, MGs, Morgans, Austin-Healeys, and a Porsche lined up next to the full-size domestic Hudsons, Oldsmobiles, Dodges, Plymouths, Fords and a couple of tiny Henry Js.

Buck Baker was the quickest qualifier at 80.536 mph in his trusty Olds 88. Herb Thomas qualified second in a Hudson, while M.R. "Eric" Peterson was third in a Jaguar. New Yorker

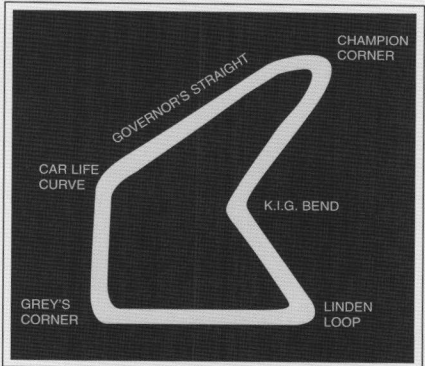

LINDEN, NEW JERSEY, AIRPORT COURSE

Al Keller, a part-time NASCAR driver since 1948, qualified seventh in a Jaguar coupe owned by bandleader Paul Whiteman. Keller had scored his first NASCAR Grand National win on a ½-mile dirt track in Savannah, Ga., that March, and he gladly accepted a ride to compete in NASCAR's inaugural road-course event.

A crowd of nearly 10,000 paid $4 each to sit in the reserved grandstands and $3 to roam around the course. The race got underway at 3:00 P.M. with pole-sitter Baker leading the charge. Hershel McGriff, driving a Jaguar, challenged Baker on the ninth lap, but found himself spinning off the course after being sideswiped by the tough NASCAR regular. Herb Thomas dashed into the lead when Baker and McGriff tangled.

Thomas and Baker traded the lead two more times before Keller breezed into the lead just before the halfway point. Keller's lightweight Jaguar scampered away from the field over the last 25 laps and finished ½ mile in front of runner-up Joe Eubanks' Hudson. Baker recovered from his duel with Keller to finish third. Jaguars took the nextthree spots.

During victory lane ceremonies, Keller announced he was quitting the NASCAR Modified tour to join the rival AAA racing series. Like Marshall Teague who preceded him, Keller's compass was squarely fixed on the coordinates of Indianapolis Motor Speedway and the famed Memorial Day 500-mile race.

Keller would start his first Indy 500 in 1955. In that event, Keller was involved in the awful crash that took the life of Indy legend Bill Vukovich, who was well on his way to scoring his third consecutive Indy win at the time of the accident. Keller made five starts in the Indy 500, with a fifth-place effort in '61 as his best finish. On Nov. 19, 1961, Keller was fatally injured in a fiery spill at Phoenix while competing in an Indy Car event.

While NASCAR's first road race at Linden was deemed successful, it would be another two-and-a-half years before the NASCAR Grand Nationals would again compete on a road course, and road racing would never become NASCAR Grand National racing's stock and trade.

1954

Curtis Turner makes a late pit stop in the Southern 500 at Darlington, which may have cost him a victory in the celebrated Labor Day event. Turner, driving an Elmer Brooks-owned Oldsmobile, led for 266 of the 364 laps, but the lengthy pit stop late in the race allowed Herb Thomas to take the win. Brooks fielded a car only 10 times in 1954, his only year active in NASCAR Grand National racing. Turner won one race and finished second at Darlington, but Brooks bowed out of racing after his brief fling.

Joe Littlejohn was one of the most versatile individuals in stock car racing, both before and after the war. A top-ranked driver in early stock car racing well before the formation of NASCAR, Littlejohn also successfully operated a number of speedways around his hometown of Spartanburg, S.C. On July 4, 1954, he added another feather to his cap. During Herb Thomas' record qualifying time at Asheville-Weaverville Speedway, Littlejohn was riding shotgun in the car. With the blessing of Thomas (and apparently NASCAR officials), Littlejohn became the only passenger to ever ride in a race car during a qualification lap.

Herb Thomas salutes from Darlington's victory lane after scoring his second win in the Labor Day Southern 500. Thomas became the first driver to win twice at Darlington, and the first man to score two superspeedway wins in a single season. The talented Hudson driver also won on the one-mile superspeedway in Raleigh that May.

Rookie driver Blackie Pitt makes a quick stop for fuel in a 1954 NASCAR Grand National event. The young driver out of Rocky Mount, N.C., had very little experience before tackling the NASCAR tour in '54. NASCAR publicity director Houston Lawing, who felt there was a need for a Rookie of the Year award, noticed the improvement Pitt displayed in his rookie season. Although NASCAR didn't officially recognize a Rookie of the Year until '57, Lawing referred to Pitt as "the 1954 Rookie of the Year" in many of his press releases.

Buck Baker finished third in the 1954 NASCAR Grand National points standings and won four races in #87 during the campaign. His biggest victory of the season was the Mid-South 250 at the new Memphis-Arkansas Speedway. The track was a high-banked 1½-mile dirt oval, a beast of a track that was both deceptive and dangerous. Baker only led the final 17 laps, taking the lead when Lee Petty snapped an axle and had to pull out of the race.

Lee Petty produced one of the most consistent seasons in NASCAR history in 1954 in claiming the championship. He won seven races and finished in the top 10 in 32 of his 34 starts. Petty was perhaps the steadiest of the NASCAR pioneers, taking care of his equipment while attaining maximum performance. Prior to a coil burning out in the Southern 500, Petty had been running at the finish in 56 consecutive NASCAR Grand National events stretching back into the '53 season.

1954 NASCAR GRAND NATIONAL POINTS

Rank	Driver	Points	Starts	Wins	Top 5	Top 10	Winnings
1	Lee Petty	8649	34	7	24	32	$21,101.35
2	Herb Thomas	8366	34	12	19	27	$29,974.05
3	Buck Baker	6893	34	4	23	28	$19,367.87
4	Dick Rathmann	6760	32	3	23	26	$15,938.84
5	Joe Eubanks	5467	33	0	11	24	$8558.45
6	Hershel McGriff	5137	24	4	13	17	$12,999.23
7	Jim Paschal	3903	27	1	5	11	$5450.70
8	Jimmie Lewallen	3233	22	0	5	10	$4668.37
9	Curtis Turner	2994	10	1	7	8	$10,119.84
10	Ralph Liguori	2905	23	0	2	12	$3494.84
11	Blackie Pitt	2661	27	0	0	6	$1924.11
12	Dave Terrell	2645	30	0	0	8	$2224.84
13	Bill Blair	2362	19	0	2	10	$2649.84
14	Laird Bruner	2243	24	0	2	6	$2079.84
15	Gober Sosebee	2114	18	1	4	7	$3149.84
16	Joan Soares	2072	9	1	2	4	$3261.56
17	Marvin Panch	1935	10	0	3	7	$4746.56
18	Eddie Skinner	1794	15	0	0	1	$1016.56
19	Joel Million	1779	9	0	0	1	$1091.56
20	Elton Hildreth	1710	14	0	0	2	$1151.56
21	Arden Mounts	1705	12	0	0	1	$875.00
22	Fireball Roberts	1648	5	0	0	2	$1080.00
23	Speedy Thompson	1480	7	0	1	3	$1165.00
24	Johnny Patterson	1417	4	0	1	1	$1240.00
25	Erick Erickson	1337	6	0	1	3	$1365.00
26	Ray Duhigg	1245	12	0	2	5	$1375.00
27	Slick Smith	1122	6	0	1	2	$950.00
28	Clyde Minter	1116	12	0	0	6	$900.00
29	Gwyn Staley	1088	2	0	0	1	$670.00
30	Lloyd Dane	984	4	0	3	4	$1600.00
31	Donald Thomas	980	9	0	3	4	$1675.00
32	Ted Chamberlain	920	10	0	0	1	$475.00
33	Danny Letner	915	4	1	2	3	$1975.00
34	Elmo Langley	864	2	0	0	0	$450.00
35	Tim Flock	860	5	0	1	3	$1050.00
36	Fred Dove	832	12	0	0	2	$525.00
37	Bill Widenhouse	805	6	0	0	0	$425.00
38	Gene Comstock	780	1	0	0	0	$400.00
39	Walt Flinchum	756	8	0	0	2	$425.00
40	Charles Cregar	716	5	0	0	0	$405.00
41	Bill Amick	700	6	0	1	1	$250.00
42	Harvey Eakin	698	7	0	0	0	$425.00
43	Lou Figaro	690	3	0	0	2	$425.00
44	Ken Fisher	668	5	0	0	1	$400.00
45	Jim Reed	631	9	0	2	3	$965.00
46	Russ Hepler	624	6	0	1	1	$525.00
47	Allen Adkins	624	2	0	2	2	$1150.00
48	Van Van Wey	602	3	0	0	0	$495.00
49	Tony Nelson	568	3	0	0	1	$325.00
50	Johnny Dodd, Jr.	552	1	0	0	1	$150.00

Parlaying consistency, Lee Petty took the points lead in mid May and cruised to a 283-point victory in the 1954 NASCAR Grand National championship chase.

Two-time champion Herb Thomas gave chase, but was unable to catch the smooth-driving Petty. Petty logged 32 top-10 finishes in the 34 races he started. Thomas won 12 times and had 27 top-10 finishes. Buck Baker, who led the standings for six weeks in early spring, wound up third in the standings on the strength of four wins.

Petty won seven races during the season, including the Daytona Beach NASCAR Grand National event. He only finished out of the top five in 10 races. The 1954 championship was sweet revenge for Petty, who lost the '50 title when NASCAR docked him 849 points for competing in a non-NASCAR-sanctioned event.

1955

Herb Thomas and Tim Flock lead the charge at the start of the NASCAR Grand National event on Charlotte Speedway's dirt track. The large letters on the side of each car were part of an experimental scoring method NASCAR used briefly in 1955. When 26 or fewer cars were in the starting grid, a typewriter was used to keep score as the cars completed each lap. An expert typist was seated in the scoring stand to assist scorers, documenting each lap while never having to take her eyes off the track.

Herb Thomas' Buick hooked a rut on the 42nd lap of the May 1 100-mile NASCAR Grand National event at Charlotte Speedway and tumbled several times. Thomas, who was running fourth at the time of the mishap, was tossed from his car and the two-time NASCAR champion suffered a badly broken leg, severe bruises, a concussion, a lacerated arm, and shoulder injuries.

Number 300 Tim Flock, #301 Fonty Flock, and #87 Buck Baker battle in close quarters in the 100-mile NASCAR Grand National at Martinsville Speedway on May 15. Tim won the race in his Kiekhaefer Chrysler, his fifth of the season. Fonty encountered brake failure early and wound up 23rd in the 27-car field. Baker ran sixth in his Oldsmobile.

Mack Hanbury's #140 Hudson plows nose-first into the chain-link fence during the May 29 race at Forsythe County Fairgrounds Speedway in Winston-Salem, N.C. Perk Brown's #5 Mercury and Jim Paschal's #78 Oldsmobile slip beneath the incident. Hanbury, a part-timer from Hyattsville, Md., competed in just 10 races during his brief tenure in the NASCAR Grand National ranks.

Bob Welborn guides his Chevrolet around Bowman-Gray Stadium in Winston-Salem after winning a NASCAR Short Track Grand National event on June 23. NASCAR conducted a separate series for Grand National cars in the 1950s on tracks shorter than ½ mile. Welborn won two Short Track Grand Nationals in '55. He also competed in 32 premier NASCAR Grand National races, finishing fourth in the final points standings.

Lee Petty drove a Chrysler in the 1955 NASCAR Grand National season. The patriarch of the Petty kingdom won six races in 42 starts and led the points standings most of the season. He ended up third in championship points behind Tim Flock and Buck Baker.

TIM FLOCK

VETERAN NASCAR drivers will often talk of the "school of hard knocks." Generally speaking, it is a driver's initiation into the fraternity. Experienced drivers aren't afraid to swap sheetmetal with rookies.

But perhaps no other driver endured the on-the-track training that Julius Timothy Flock had to encounter. Flock, the 1952 and '55 NASCAR Grand National champion, was the youngest of the Flock clan, the most famous family in the early days of stock car racing. Older brothers Bob and Fonty, plus sister Ethel Flock Mobley, all drove in NASCAR Strictly Stock and Grand National competition. "I worshiped Bob and Fonty when they were driving," recollected Tim. "But they said I'd never be a race driver. I always tried extra hard to beat Fonty on the track because he wouldn't let me race as a kid."

Despite the objections of his older siblings, Tim was determined to squeeze his way into the sport of speed. When he was 18, Flock went to a Modified race at North Wilkesboro and talked Bruce Thompson into letting him drive his car. "It seemed like everyone bumped into me, and I was glad the rear end finally froze up and I had to quit the race," said Tim.

Finally convinced Tim was going to become a race car driver, Bob and Fonty decided it would be best to tutor their younger brother in the arts of racetrack survival. "They took me out to the old Lakewood track in Atlanta and showed me all the tricks," remarked Tim. "They would knock me through the fence—just to demonstrate how it was gonna be and that I'd just have to deal with it. I learned quite a bit in a short period of time."

Flock hooked up with team owner Ted Chester and won the 1952 NASCAR Grand National championship. In '53, Flock was again a contender for the title until an unusual accident laid him up for several weeks. "We had raced in

NASCAR Grand National Career Record 1949-1961
Starts: 188
Wins: 39
Top 5s: 102
Top 10s: 129
Poles: 39
Career Winnings: $109,656

Syracuse, N.Y., on July 3 and had to race again the next day in Spartanburg, S.C." said Flock. "After we arrived in Spartanburg, I laid down in the infield to catch a few winks. We had driven all night from Syracuse and we were plumb wore out. Next thing I knew there was an automobile tire—with the automobile attached—parked on my head. A spark plug representative hadn't seen me. He accidentally backed over my head. I was out of action for most of the remainder of the year."

When he came back in 1954, Flock finished first at Daytona's Beach-Road course, but was disqualified when NASCAR officials determined his carburetor wasn't stock. Flock quit racing in disgust, headed back to his hometown of Atlanta, and operated a gas station. "I went flat broke doing that," Tim said.

For 1955, Flock returned to NASCAR to drive Chryslers for Carl Kiekhaefer. Flock enjoyed a phenomenal year, winning 18 races and 18 poles, both records at the time. He easily captured his second NASCAR Grand National championship.

In early 1956, Flock bailed out of the Kiekhaefer team, citing health reasons. "I had ulcers real bad," said Flock, "and I couldn't take Kiekhaefer's drill-sergeant attitude anymore. I had to quit to save my own life."

Flock was only a part-time participant in NASCAR for the remainder of his career. His final victory came on the road course in Elkhart Lake, Wis., beating the Kiekhaefer team in their own backyard. In 1961, Flock was booted out of NASCAR by Bill France for assisting Curtis Turner in his efforts to organize the drivers to join the Teamsters Union. When the ban was lifted in '65, Flock decided against resuming his career.

During his tenure in NASCAR racing, Flock won 39 NASCAR Grand National events, and he remains one of stock car racing's most honored legends.

This staged photograph was arranged by NASCAR and Purolator photographers. Several photos like this appeared in Purolator newspaper and magazine advertisements. All of the cars had the Purolator decal prominently displayed on their hoods. The cars were motionless, strategically positioned to simulate close competition on a dirt track.

Junior Johnson's first full season of NASCAR Grand National racing was 1955. Having entered only five races in '53 and '54, Johnson hit the tour with a vengeance in '55, winning five races and finishing sixth in the final points standings while driving an Oldsmobile. Had NASCAR issued Rookie of the Year honors, Johnson would have been the hands-down choice. Rookie of the Year honors weren't officially awarded until '57. Ken Rush would become the first recipient of the top freshman award.

After recovering from his Charlotte spill that left him with a badly broken right leg, Herb Thomas was able to attend several NASCAR Grand National events. He vowed to be healed in time to compete in Darlington's Southern 500 on Labor Day, and he promised to win the race. Despite being unable to start 22 of the 45 races on the 1955 schedule, Thomas still finished fifth in the final NASCAR Grand National points standings.

Fireball Roberts leads the chase into the first turn at the start of the Sept. 5 Southern 500 at Darlington Raceway. Roberts led the opening four laps and was running in the top five when a blown tire sent his Buick into the wall on the 30th lap. Roberts was sidelined and finished 66th in the 69-car field. Tim Flock trails in the #16 Chrysler. Flock usually ran #300 in '55, but Darlington officials prohibited the use of three-digit numbers.

Herb Thomas guns his Smokey Yunick #92 Motoramic Chevy down the frontstretch during the closing stages of the sixth annual Southern 500. Thomas, in only his third start since returning from injuries suffered at Charlotte, took the lead late in the event. He finished a lap ahead of runner-up Jim Reed, making good on the promise he made after his May wreck. It was Thomas' third win in the Labor Day race, a mark that wasn't surpassed until 1978.

Victory lane ceremonies at Darlington were held on the front chute before a special platform was built for the winner. Following the 1955 Southern 500, a mass of humanity surrounds Herb Thomas' winning Chevrolet. Race officials did their best to rope off an area for the celebration, but there was no holding back several hundred spectators who wanted a closer look at the winner and his car.

The pit area at most of the dirt tracks in the 1950s contained the bare necessities—an unkempt wooden plank that served as a protective wall, and a few termite-infested posts supporting the fence. That's 18-year-old Richard Petty to the far left, keeping an eye on his father Lee's progress.

A flock of Flocks: (left to right) Fonty, Bob, and Tim pose with a pair of the speedy Carl Kiekhaefer Chryslers. All three of the Flock brothers worked and drove for the Kiekhaefer team in '55. Bob only competed in one race that year, but served as a crew member for his brothers in many races.

1955 NASCAR GRAND NATIONAL POINTS RACE

Rank	Driver	Points	Starts	Wins	Top 5	Top 10	Winnings
1	Tim Flock	9596	39	18	32	33	$37,779.60
2	Buck Baker	8088	42	3	24	34	$19,770.90
3	Lee Petty	7194	42	6	20	30	$18,919.29
4	Bob Welborn	5460	32	0	12	24	$10,146.76
5	Herb Thomas	5186	23	3	14	15	$18,023.47
6	Junior Johnson	4810	36	5	12	18	$13,802.78
7	Eddie Skinner	4652	38	0	4	15	$4736.85
8	Jim Paschal	4572	36	5	12	18	$10,585.88
9	Jimmie Lewallen	4526	33	0	4	15	$6439.51
10	Gwyn Staley	4360	24	3	12	20	$6546.43
11	Fonty Flock	4266	31	0	8	16	$13,099.11
12	Dave Terrell	3170	25	0	7	14	$3654.11
13	Jimmy Massey	2924	11	3	12	14	$3509.11
14	Marvin Panch	2812	10	0	3	10	$4384.11
15	Speedy Thompson	2452	15	0	4	8	$7089.11
16	Jim Reed	2416	14	0	4	4	$2702.74
17	Gene Simpson	2388	22	2	3	5	$2157.74
18	Dick Rathmann	2298	20	0	4	4	$4367.74
19	Ralph Liguori	2124	12	0	1	7	$1972.74
20	Joe Eubanks	2028	14	0	7	8	$2007.74
21	Blackie Pitt	1992	20	0	0	7	$1785.00
22	Harvey Henderson	1930	17	0	1	6	$1810.00
23	Banks Simpson	1852	7	0	0	0	$870.00
24	Dink Widenhouse	1752	15	0	0	6	$1660.00
25	Johnny Dodd, Jr.	1496	13	0	1	7	$1695.00
26	Bill Widenhouse	1444	5	0	1	3	$1065.00
27	Lou Spears	1272	3	0	0	1	$810.00
28	Larry Flynn	1260	1	0	1	1	$1175.00
29	Cotton Owens	1248	2	0	1	2	$900.00
30	Gordon Smith	1212	15	0	0	2	$975.00
31	Billy Carden	1172	13	0	2	3	$1340.00
32	Arden Mounts	1170	12	0	0	4	$1025.00
33	Joe Million	1136	8	0	2	6	$1685.00
34	Curtis Turner	1120	9	0	4	4	$2605.00
35	John Lindsay	1052	6	0	0	3	$575.00
36	Nace Mattingly	992	3	0	1	1	$700.00
37	Bill Blair	974	12	0	0	0	$440.00
38	Donald Thomas	932	10	0	2	4	$1240.00
39	Ed Cole, Jr.	924	13	0	0	0	$645.00
40	Mack Hanbury	900	8	0	0	2	$575.00
41	Danny Letner	892	4	1	2	2	$1780.00
42	George Parrish	880	12	0	0	1	$750.00
43	Banjo Matthews	860	3	0	0	2	$745.00
44	Carl Krueger	748	7	0	0	1	$585.00
45	Ted Cannady	744	9	0	0	0	$450.00
46	Allen Adkins	740	4	0	2	2	$1160.00
47	Joe Weatherly	724	6	0	1	4	$2575.00
48	John McVitty	684	7	0	0	2	$550.00
49	Lloyd Dane	674	5	0	1	2	$780.00
50	Fred Dove	668	7	0	1	2	$750.00

Tim Flock thoroughly dominated the 1955 NASCAR Grand National season, winning 18 races in 38 starts along the way to his second championship in four years. Flock finished 1508 points in front of runner-up Buck Baker, but he didn't take the points lead until the 33rd race of the season in mid August.

Consistent Lee Petty led the points standings most of the season, but was no match for the determined Flock, who drove the powerful Kiekhaefer Chryslers. Petty's consistency kept him on top of the points standings, but he tapered off in the second half of the season. Petty won six races and wound up third in the final standings.

Herb Thomas rallied back from injuries suffered at Charlotte in May to finish fifth in the standings. He was on the sidelines for over three months, but rebounded strongly.

Flock's record of 18 wins wasn't surpassed until 1967 when Richard Petty won 27 races.

1956

November 13, 1955 Tim Flock wins the NASCAR Grand National season opener at Hickory Speedway as the new campaign gets underway early. Former NASCAR star Buddy Shuman, recently appointed head of Ford's NASCAR factory effort, tragically dies in a hotel fire the night before the race.

December 11, 1955 Joe Weatherly and Jim Reed, the first two finishers in the 100-mile race at West Palm Beach, are both disqualified for technical violations. Herb Thomas is declared the official winner.

February 26 Tim Flock outruns and outlasts a huge 76-car field to score his second straight win in the Daytona Beach NASCAR Grand National event. African-American driver Charlie Scott posts a 19th-place finish.

April 8 Tim Flock racks up his third win of the season at North Wilkesboro, N.C., then surprises the racing world by quitting the championship Kiekhaefer Chrysler team. Buck Baker will replace Flock in the coveted ride.

May 6 Speedy Thompson drives a Kiekhaefer Chrysler to victory in the 100-mile race at Concord, N.C. It marks the fourth consecutive NASCAR Grand National event that the Kiekhaefer team has swept the top two spots.

June 3 Herb Thomas scores an easy win in the 100-mile event at Merced, Calif., giving the Carl Kiekhaefer team its 16th consecutive NASCAR Grand National victory. It is a record that will likely live forever in the NASCAR record book.

June 10 Ralph Moody wheels a DePaolo Engineering Ford to victory at West Memphis Speedway, halting the 16-race win streak by the Kiekhaefer team. Two drivers, Clint McHugh and Cotton Priddy, are killed in accidents during the race weekend.

July 4 Fireball Roberts records his first superspeedway triumph in the 250-miler at Raleigh Speedway. Carl Kiekhaefer files a protest against the weight of Roberts' flywheel. No scales are available at the speedway, so NASCAR officials take the flywheel to a local fish market to be weighed. Roberts' win is upheld by NASCAR.

The ramshackle NASCAR press headquarters in 1956 were a far cry from the luxurious, air-conditioned structures in use today. A windblown, listing tent, anchored by a rope tied to posts hammered into the sands of Daytona Beach, served as the pulse for the gathering media representatives during Speedweeks.

More than 80 cars started the 1956 Daytona Beach NASCAR Modified-Sportsman race. Tim Flock, in the red #47-A '39 Chevrolet, led the entire distance and won in a runaway. The car, one of the most modified cars to ever appear in the NASCAR Beach races, was owned by Joe Wolf. The Chevy coupe featured a '56 Olds Rocket 88 engine with a batch of handcrafted goodies conjured up by Wolf. The engine was set back 26 inches, putting the driver's compartment where the back seat would normally be located.

Bob Pronger, wheeling the #99 Ford, runs just ahead of rim-riding Fireball Roberts in the inaugural NASCAR Convertible race on Feb. 25. Pronger, a rugged competitor from Blue Island, Ill., drove sparingly in NASCAR's Grand Nationals and Convertibles in the '50s. He was both controversial and colorful during his brief tenure in NASCAR. His death is shrouded in mystery. He disappeared early in 1971, and was officially declared "missing at the hands of Mafia agents" on June 17.

► After posting its first-ever NASCAR Grand National win in 1955 and starting the '56 Short Track season strongly, Chevrolet called attention to its racing success in national print ads. Chevrolet's efficient 265-cid V-8 was the reason behind the success, putting out 225 horsepower, up 45 hp from '55. Chryslers and Fords still dominated the win column in NASCAR Grand National racing, but Chevrolet did manage three wins in the top division.

Charlie Scott shakes the hand of Wendell Scott prior to the Daytona Beach NASCAR Grand National race. The two Scotts, who weren't related, were the first African-American drivers in NASCAR. Wendell finished 33rd in the '56 Modified-Sportsman race and became the first full-time African-American NASCAR Grand National driver five years later. Charlie finished 19th in the Daytona Beach event driving one of six cars entered by Carl Kiekhaefer.

Eccentric team owner Carl Kiekhaefer had six drivers under contract for the Feb. 26 Daytona Beach NASCAR Grand National event. Pictured from left to right are: Charlie Scott, Tim Flock, Fonty Flock, Frank Mundy, Buck Baker, and Speedy Thompson. Tim Flock won and his brother ran 10th. The others finished outside the top money positions. A total of 76 cars started the race, the second-largest field in NASCAR Grand National history.

Jim Wilson's #576 1956 Dodge lies upside down after an early spill in the south turn at Daytona. Buddy Krebs' Dodge is also turned turtle. Both Wilson and Krebs were driving new Dodges for team owner Harvey Walters, and both were eliminated in the same crash.

Tim Flock and Speedy Thompson hustle through the north turn in the early laps of the Daytona Beach NASCAR Grand National race. The Kiekhaefer cars started on the front row. Thompson fell victim to mechanical problems and wound up 71st. Flock went on to win, leading all 37 laps on the 4.1-mile Beach-Road course.

1956

August 4 Lee Petty dismounts his car in disgust on the 32nd lap, climbs the flagstand, grabs the red flag from the official starter, and waves the scheduled 100-mile NASCAR Grand National race at Tulsa, Okla., to a halt. Dusty conditions blinded the drivers and Petty acted on his own to prevent a catastrophe. The race is never completed or rescheduled.

August 12 Tim Flock, with his Mercury's windshield wipers flapping, drives to victory in the 258-mile NASCAR Grand National event at Elkhart Lake's Road America. NASCAR's first appearance in Wisconsin goes off on schedule despite a steady rain.

September 30 Curtis Turner is declared the winner of the scheduled 100-mile NASCAR Convertible race at Asheville-Weaverville Speedway when a 14-car crash wipes out all but one car running in the event. Turner's Ford is the only car still in running condition when officials terminate the event after 181 of the scheduled 200 laps.

October 14 Curtis Turner captures the 1956 NASCAR Convertible Circuit finale at Orange Speedway in Hillsboro, N.C., recording his 22nd victory of the year. Turner wins seven of the last eight races, but loses the championship by 836 points to three-time winner Bob Welborn.

October 23 Buck Baker's Kiekhaefer Chrysler tiptoes around a nasty crash involving former Kiekhaefer teammate Herb Thomas and wins the 100-mile race at Shelby, N.C. Speedy Thompson, also member of the Kiekhaefer team, triggers the crash, which leaves Thomas gravely injured. Baker pulls to within 118 points of Thomas with three races remaining.

Junior Johnson climbed out of the rear window of his overturned Pontiac after a crash in the late stages of the Daytona Beach NASCAR Grand National. Johnson had spun out twice earlier in the race, but continued to charge into the north and south turns with reckless abandon. His courage finally caught up to him with a series of tumbles as he approached the north turn.

◀ ▼ (Left) Photographers examine the spectacular sequence shown below: Russ Truelove's tumble midway through the Daytona Beach NASCAR Grand National. Truelove's Mercury was one of the quickest cars, qualifying fifth. The beach conditions were awful, though. Truelove hit a soft patch in the sand and flipped almost a dozen times near the north end of the beach. Afterward, Truelove stepped out of the smoldering machine through the passenger door.

> "I couldn't take Kiekhaefer's drill-sergeant attitude anymore. I had to quit to save my own life."
>
> —Tim Flock

Ralph Moody's Ford darts out of control as Lee Petty passes in his #42 Dodge. Moody, driving one of the Peter DePaolo Engineering Fords, ran among the leaders until the mishap. Incredibly, Moody flopped over on his wheels and motored on to a third-place finish. Petty finished 12th.

NASCAR President Bill France greets Tim Flock following his win in the April 8 race at North Wilkesboro (N.C.) Speedway. After the race, Flock notified team owner Carl Kiekhaefer that he was quitting the formidable team due to stomach ulcers. Flock won 21 of his 46 starts with Kiekhaefer in a little less than 14 months.

Upon Tim Flock's departure from the Kiekhaefer team, the crusty team owner hired Herb Thomas to join Buck Baker and Speedy Thompson on the successful Chrysler and Dodge outfit. Thomas won three races while driving for Kiekhaefer, but he, too, quit the team late in the year and returned to cars he owned himself.

All was somber in the pits at the Memphis-Arkansas Speedway in LeHi, Ark., before the June 10 NASCAR Grand National race. The track was a 1½-mile ribbon of deceitful dirt, and was regarded as one of the most dangerous tracks in the history of NASCAR. Two drivers died on this 1956 race weekend. Clint McHugh was killed in qualifying and Cotton Priddy died of injuries suffered in the race. Ralph Moody won the tragic event in a Ford. Moody halted an incredible 16-race winning streak for the Carl Kiekhaefer team, whose cars can be seen in the foreground.

1956

November 11 In one of the most peculiar doubleheader days in NASCAR history, Speedy Thompson wins the 100-mile race at Hickory and Marvin Panch wins the same-day event at Lancaster, Calif. Curiously, Thompson's win counts as a 1956 race, while Panch's triumph is considered the opener of the '57 NASCAR Grand National season.

November 18 Buck Baker is declared the winner of the 1956 season finale at Wilson, N.C. Joe Weatherly clearly reaches the checkered flag first, but Baker is the first to pass the scoring stand located near turn one. Baker also wraps up the '56 NASCAR Grand National championship by 704 points over Herb Thomas.

Blackie Pitt's Plymouth kicks up mounds of dirt as he tumbles over the dirt embankment during the July 1 race at Asheville-Weaverville Speedway. Fireball Roberts gets sideways as he fights for control after clipping Pitt's errant car. Bill Bowman guides his Plymouth clear on the inside, escaping the mayhem.

Fireball Roberts and Lee Petty run door-to-door down the backstretch at Asheville-Weaverville Speedway during the 100-miler. Roberts started on the pole in his #22 Ford and led in the early going before a shredded tire put him out of action. Petty went on to win in his Dodge, his first victory of the 1956 season.

CARL KIEKHAEFER

THE ECCENTRIC Carl Kiekhaefer, founder of the Mercury Outboard division, entered NASCAR Grand National racing in 1955 and was a powerful force for the only two seasons that his big white Chryslers and Dodges competed on the tour. A perplexingly complex man, Kiekhaefer demanded excellence from every member of his entourage, whether in the outboard motors business or stock car racing. Every fiber of Kiekhaefer's business life vibrated with passion, and he tackled NASCAR stock car racing like no one else ever had.

Many of his records as a team owner in NASCAR competition still exist and some have been judged to be unbeatable. Perhaps the most sparkling record Kiekhaefer holds is the 16-race stretch in the 1956 season in which his cars won every race. From March 25 through June 3 Kiekhaefer's team went undefeated.

Four different drivers won races in Kiekhaefer cars during the winning streak. Buck Baker won eight times, Speedy Thompson won four races, Herb Thomas bagged three victories, and Tim Flock won once. Six times during the streak, Kiekhaefer cars led the entire distance, and they dominated many of the other races. At Martinsville's Virginia 500, the big white cars led 494 of the 500 laps. At Concord, they collectively led 199 of the 200 laps. After losing the June 10 race at Memphis-Arkansas Speedway, the Kiekhaefer team rebounded to win the next two NASCAR Grand National races, leading 346 of the 400 laps at Charlotte and Rochester.

The final 1956 tabulations showed that the Carl Kiekhaefer team won 30 races in 51 starts, and lead driver Buck Baker laid claim to the national driving title. The year before, Tim Flock drove a Kiekhaefer Chrysler to the '55 NASCAR Grand National championship, winning 18 races and 19 poles. During Flock's dominating performance in 1955, he led every lap from start to finish in 11 races. Kiekhaefer's record sheet for his brief two-year tenure is equally impressive. In 90 NASCAR Grand National races, his cars won 52 times with seven different drivers.

Kiekhaefer's thorough domination caused a rift with competitors and Bill France. Kiekhaefer claimed his cars were the victims of sabotage when they lost, and heightened suspicion when they won. Kiekhaefer's cars were subjected to much postrace scrutiny by NASCAR technical inspectors. Kiekhaefer played within the letter and

Herb Thomas wheels his #92 Chevrolet down the front chute at Raleigh Speedway in the 250-mile NASCAR Grand National event on July 4. Three days earlier, Thomas resigned as driver for the Kiekhaefer team due to a personality clash with the crusty owner. Thomas dusted off his Chevy and ran fourth in the 250-miler on the one-mile banked superspeedway.

Tim Flock latched onto the factory-backed #11 Chevy fielded by three-time Indianapolis 500 winner Mauri Rose in the 250-mile race at Raleigh. Flock started third and finished fourth in one of his infrequent 1956 NASCAR Grand National appearances after quitting the Carl Kiekhaefer team in April.

spirit of the rules, and none of his cars was ever found to be outside of NASCAR's specifications.

During an uncharacteristic skid in the latter half of the 1956 season, Kiekhaefer sent a memo to every member of his multicar team. The memo, in part, said, "If our competition were paying someone within our group to sabotage (Buck) Baker's car, they could not have done better. Since our championship is at stake, it behooves every man to be on the outlook for any careless assembly or purposeful sabotage. A $500 reward is hereby offered for evidence of deliberate sabotage within or without our own crew . . . Loyalty to our team is the first requisite. Without loyalty there can be no teamwork. Without teamwork, we can not win. If we can not win, there is no point in carrying on . . ."

Thereafter, Kiekhaefer's team closed out the 1956 season with five consecutive victories. Baker captured the championship—Kiekhaefer's second in two seasons.

But Kiekhaefer's days in NASCAR were numbered. His entire crew was relentlessly booed, and, in his opinion, hassled by fans and other competitors. Kiekhaefer was unable to philosophically accept the public reaction to his overwhelming success. He was deeply hurt. "What have I done wrong?" he once questioned out loud. "The fans almost riot when they see our cars. I guess they want me to quit."

Kiekhaefer's fate was sealed by a controversial twist in the final stages of the 1956 season. With Baker trailing rival Herb Thomas, a driver who had quit the Kiekhaefer team at midseason, Kiekhaefer leased a track in Shelby, N.C., and arranged for NASCAR's sanction, thus giving Baker another shot to overtake Thomas. In that race, Kiekhaefer driver Speedy Thompson hooked Thomas' rear bumper and sent him into a violent spill. Thomas was critically injured and Baker rode home uncontested as the '56 champion.

Kiekhaefer never appeared at another NASCAR race. Fearing that negative reaction would cause irreparable damage to his Mercury Outboard empire, Kiekhaefer said, "We just cannot afford to have our name further associated with racing."

With that announcement, Carl Kiekhaefer quit NASCAR Grand National racing. His legacy and records remain to this day. Records are made to be broken, but it is unlikely any team in NASCAR racing can match or surpass the marks that Carl Kiekhaefer set in 1955 and '56.

NASCAR Grand National Career Record 1955-1956
Starts: 190 (90 races)
Wins: 51
Top 5s: 116
Top 10s: 138
Poles: 51
Career Winnings: $135,681

1956

The third road course event in NASCAR history was staged on the four-mile course in Elkhart Lake, Wis. The Carl Kiekhaefer crew entered three cars in the 258.3-mile event. The #300 Chrysler was driven by Frank Mundy on race day, starting near the rear of the 26-car field. Mundy qualified Buck Baker's Dodge on the pole in a three-lap qualifying session. It took nearly 10 minutes to complete the time trial. After relinquishing the pole car to Baker, Mundy started 23rd and finished 14th in the #300 Chrysler. Note the truck at the left. Kiekhaefer's team was the first to tow its cars in transporters rather than with tow bars or on open trailers. NASCAR Grand National racing never returned to Road America.

Buck Baker wheels his #502 Dodge into one of the hairpin turns during a practice session for the Aug. 12 NASCAR Grand National at Road America in Elkhart Lake, Wis. Baker started on the pole and finished eighth. Tim Flock won in a Mercury, beating the Kiekhaefer cars in his former boss's backyard.

Young Dink Widenhouse was involved in a multicar collision in the Sept. 3 Southern 500 at Darlington. Widenhouse, who suffered a cut arm in the mishap, started to climb out of his crumpled Ford, but lost consciousness at the sight of his own blood. He got tangled up in the safety belts and was in this alarming position when rescue workers reached him. He was not seriously injured.

Curtis Turner flashes down the front chute at Darlington International Raceway while taking the checkered flag at the Southern 500. The superspeedway triumph was Turner's only NASCAR Grand National win in 1956. He spent most of the season in the new NASCAR Convertible circuit, where he won 22 races. Turner finished 20th in the final points standings.

NASCAR's new Convertible circuit ran 47 races in 17 states and Canada in its inaugural season. Bob Welborn, who drove the #49 Chevrolet, won the championship while winning three races. Hard-charging Curtis Turner won 22 races, but came in a distant second in the points chase.

Buck Baker throttles his #300-B Chrysler in a full four-wheel drift in the corner at Hillsboro's Orange Speedway during the Sept. 30 race. Baker, who finished a close second to winner Fireball Roberts, went on to win the 1956 NASCAR Grand National title, the first of his two championships.

Jack Smith is congratulated by Carl Kiekhaefer after winning at Martinsville on Oct. 28. It was Smith's first ride with the Kiekhaefer team. The race featured both hardtop NASCAR Grand Nationals and Convertibles. NASCAR ran both types of cars in various events through 1959, calling the mixed races "Sweepstakes" races.

1956 NASCAR GRAND NATIONAL POINTS RACE

Rank	Driver	Points	Starts	Wins	Top 5	Top 10	Winnings
1	Buck Baker	9272	48	14	31	39	$34,076.35
2	Speedy Thompson	8788	42	8	24	29	$27,168.62
3	Herb Thomas	8710	48	5	22	36	$19,351.19
4	Lee Petty	8324	47	2	17	28	$15,337.08
5	Jim Paschal	7878	42	1	16	27	$17,203.08
6	Billy Myers	6796	42	2	13	21	$15,829.08
7	Fireball Roberts	5794	33	5	17	22	$14,741.27
8	Ralph Moody	5528	35	4	13	21	$15,492.27
9	Tim Flock	5062	22	4	11	13	$15,768.19
10	Marvin Panch	4680	20	1	12	13	$11,519.40
11	Rex White	4642	24	0	3	14	$5333.27
12	Johnny Allen	4024	32	0	2	11	$4558.19
13	Paul Goldsmith	3788	9	1	4	6	$8568.19
14	Gwyn Staley	3550	22	0	5	13	$5158.19
15	Joe Eubanks	3284	26	0	6	13	$5583.19
16	Joe Weatherly	3084	17	0	6	12	$5250.46
17	Bill Amick	3048	13	0	7	10	$5380.46
18	Jim Reed	2890	11	0	5	5	$5076.46
19	Tiny Lund	2754	21	0	1	8	$2810.46
20	Curtis Turner	2580	13	1	4	5	$14,540.46
21	Jack Smith	2320	15	1	1	6	$3825.00
22	Billy Carden	2108	23	0	0	4	$2175.00
23	Lloyd Dane	2106	10	2	5	9	$4370.00
24	Frank Mundy	1836	9	0	3	5	$3585.00
25	Bobby Johns	1832	9	0	0	3	$1450.00
26	Blackie Pitt	1760	27	0	0	5	$1545.00
27	Harold Hardesty	1724	9	0	2	6	$2380.00
28	Al Watkins	1710	14	0	0	4	$1185.00
29	Chuck Meekins	1656	7	0	3	6	$2815.00
30	Harvey Henderson	1638	18	0	0	4	$1310.00
31	Bill Champion	1632	14	0	0	4	$1570.00
32	Eddie Pagan	1598	8	1	4	4	$4095.00
33	Pat Kirkwood	1540	3	0	1	2	$2025.00
34	Clyde Palmer	1516	11	0	4	6	$2755.00
35	John Kieper	1506	8	1	4	7	$3250.00
36	Johnny Dodson	1488	11	0	0	3	$1450.00
37	Bill Blair	1284	9	0	0	4	$1005.00
38	Junior Johnson	1272	13	0	1	1	$1350.00
39	Ed Cole	1200	12	0	0	1	$950.00
40	Brownie King	1140	15	0	0	0	$925.00
41	Scotty Cain	1124	4	0	1	4	$1235.00
42	Allen Adkins	1104	6	0	2	4	$1465.00
43	Bobby Keck	1076	15	0	0	3	$950.00
44	Gordon Haines	1066	7	0	2	4	$1500.00
	Bob Keefe	1066	7	0	1	2	$1040.00
46	Dick Beaty	1036	15	0	0	3	$910.00
47	Jim Blomgren	992	7	0	0	1	$475.00
48	Ed Negre	952	5	0	2	4	$1255.00
49	Jimmy Massey	950	7	0	3	4	$1545.00
50	Fonty Flock	946	7	1	1	3	$1780.00

A horrendous crash took Herb Thomas out of the championship hunt late in the season, allowing Buck Baker to cruise to the 1956 NASCAR Grand National title. Thomas, leading the points race entering the October race at Shelby, N.C., suffered critical injuries in a multicar crash on the ½-mile dirt track.

Speedy Thompson, Baker's teammate on the Carl Kiekhaefer team, hooked Thomas' bumper in a turn, thus triggering the crash. Controversy flared to epic proportions. Kiekhaefer had leased the track and quickly scheduled a race to give Baker another opportunity to catch up in the points race. Thomas, who quit the Kiekhaefer team at midseason, had taken over the points lead a month earlier.

Thompson drew the wrath of observers and sportswriters for causing the crash that injured Thomas. Team owner Kiekhaefer was also extensively criticized by the media. Baker was exonerated of any alleged "team play" in the race.

Baker won 14 races en route to his first NASCAR championship.

1957

December 30, 1956 Fireball Roberts leads a 1-2-3-4 sweep for Peter DePaolo Fords in the 90-mile NASCAR Grand National race on the Titusville-Cocoa Airport runways in Florida. The DePaolo Engineering team is managed by master mechanic John Holman.

February 17 Cotton Owens drives the Ray Nichels Pontiac to victory in the Daytona Beach NASCAR Grand National event, recording the first NASCAR win for the Pontiac nameplate.

May 19 Buck Baker is declared winner of the Virginia 500 at Martinsville Speedway after a crash halts the event on lap 441 of the scheduled 500-lapper.

June 6 The Automobile Manufacturers Association recommends unanimously that the auto industry divorce itself entirely from all forms of racing, including the NASCAR Grand National series. The factory-supported teams will be disbanded and all machinery will be given to the drivers.

July 4 Paul Goldsmith wheels Smokey Yunick's Chevrolet to victory in the 250-mile NASCAR Grand National race at Raleigh Speedway. Herb Thomas makes his first start of the season after injuries suffered in October 1956.

August 4 Buck Baker wins the 100-mile NASCAR Grand National event on the road course in Watkins Glen, N.Y. Baker dominates the race, leading flag to flag.

September 2 Speedy Thompson wins the Southern 500, averaging 100.094 mph. It is the first Southern 500 to average better than 100 mph. Bobby Myers is fatally injured in a three-car crash on the 28th lap.

October 6 Bob Welborn, with relief help from Possum Jones, wins the Sweepstakes 500 at Martinsville Speedway. Welborn's convertible Chevrolet outruns the 40-car field of sedans and convertibles. It is Welborn's first NASCAR Grand National win.

October 12 Only 900 spectators watch Fireball Roberts wheel his Ford to victory in the 100-mile NASCAR Grand National race at Newberry Speedway in South Carolina. To this day, it remains the smallest trackside attendance in NASCAR history.

Larry Frank loops his #76 Chevy convertible as Curtis Turner slides past during the Feb. 16 NASCAR Convertible race at Daytona. Frank was involved in one of NASCAR's most embarrassing moments two years later. After the final race of the '59 Convertible season, NASCAR declared Frank the winner of the championship following his sixth-place finish at Martinsville. Joe Lee Johnson, who seemingly had wrapped up the title with an eighth-place finish, requested a recount. NASCAR officials discovered that Johnson had earned 20 more points than Frank and reversed the decision. Incorrect basic arithmetic was at the root of the problem.

Paul Goldsmith fishtails in his Smokey Yunick Chevrolet during the Feb. 17 Daytona Beach NASCAR Grand National race. Goldsmith assumed command late in the race, but a blown engine with eight laps to go foiled his victory bid. Five of Goldsmith's nine career NASCAR Grand National wins came in equipment groomed by the capable hands of Yunick, who was regarded as one of the most innovative mechanics in NASCAR.

Curtis Turner whips his #99 Ford through the north turn in the 1957 Daytona Beach NASCAR Grand National. Turner, who was driving for the DePaolo Engineering factory Ford team, came from the 39th starting position to finish seventh.

Number 6 Cotton Owens leads #8 Banjo Matthews and #85 Darel Dieringer in the 1957 Daytona NASCAR Grand National race. Owens drove a Pontiac owned and prepared by Ray Nichels, who was campaigning in his first big NASCAR event. Owens won the race, giving Pontiac its first win in NASCAR Grand National competition.

Number 87 Buck Baker and #47 Jack Smith wheel their Chevrolets around the lapped #154 Ford of Nace Mattingly in the March 17 NASCAR Grand National at Wilson County Fairgrounds in North Carolina. Baker finished second in the race and Thompson came home third. Paul Goldsmith, in the #97 Ford, finished sixth, while Mattingly placed 11th.

Buck Baker, who took an assignment with the #87 Chevrolet factory team when Carl Kiekhaefer disbanded his operation after the 1956 season, enjoyed a successful campaign in '57. Baker won 10 races, won the championship, and only finished out of the top 10 twice in 40 starts. Here, Baker leads #46 Speedy Thompson en route to a win in the March 24 race at Hillsboro's Orange Speedway.

Number 42 Lee Petty and Jim Paschal race in close quarters in the March 24 race at Hillsboro, N.C. Petty and Paschal were close friends throughout their racing careers. Petty provided a ride for Paschal in a number of races during the '60s, and Paschal claimed nine of his 25 NASCAR Grand National career wins piloting Petty equipment.

1957

October 20 Jack Smith edges Lee Petty to win the 100-mile NASCAR Grand National event at North Wilkesboro Speedway.

October 27 Buck Baker wraps up his second straight NASCAR Grand National championship campaign by wheeling his Chevrolet to a win in the 250-lap season finale at Central Carolina Fairground in Greensboro, N.C. Baker beats Marvin Panch by 760 points in the title hunt with his 10th win of the season.

November 27 The first spade of dirt is turned on the tract of land that will become the Daytona International Speedway. After nearly five years, the red tape has been cleared to proceed with the construction of the world's most modern racing facility.

Buck Baker rides under the checkered flag at Hillsboro, his first win of the '57 NASCAR Grand National season. A crowd of about 8000 was on hand to witness the 99-mile event on the 0.9-mile dirt track. The grandstands were situated close to the racing surface on the homestretch. Little protection was in place for spectator safety. Only a chicken-wire fence supported by wooden posts separated the spectators from the track surface.

Number 98 Marvin Panch and #97 Paul Goldsmith slice their way through traffic during the 100-miler at North Wilkesboro Speedway on April 7. Panch and Goldsmith were in Peter DePaolo-owned Fords. Goldsmith finished second as Panch brought his car home fourth.

Firestone Tire & Rubber Company touted its NASCAR success in this national print ad for its new tire the Nylon 500. The ad claimed that 500 miles at Darlington was the equivalent to 50,000 miles on the road. Actually, NASCAR's "oval laboratories," especially paved tracks like Darlington, did help develop tire technology. Still, in the formative years, subpar tires were a limiting factor for NASCAR drivers who wanted to go faster and faster.

Bill France (left) and chief mechanic John Holman shake hands following Fireball Roberts' win in the April 7 event at North Wilkesboro. Team owner Peter DePaolo and Fireball happily look on. DePaolo enjoyed one of the finest days for a team owner in NASCAR history. His cars, driven by Fireball Roberts, Paul Goldsmith, Ralph Moody, and Marvin Panch, swept the top four positions in the 100-mile contest.

Fireball Roberts guns his #22 Ford to the high side in an effort to pass Buck Baker and #17 Jim Paschal in the April 14 race at Langhorne (Pa.) Speedway. Roberts went on to win the 150-miler, leading for 98 of the 150 laps around the circular one-mile track. The Daytona Beach driver hit his stride in 1957, winning eight races and finishing sixth in the points standings.

Paul Goldsmith whips his #3 Smokey Yunick Ford under the checkered flag to win the April 28 250-lap NASCAR Grand National event at Greensboro's Fairgrounds Speedway. The tiny ⅓-mile dirt track hosted three NASCAR Grand Nationals races in the late 1950s. Goldsmith won this 83.25-mile event, beating runner-up Buck Baker by a quarter lap.

Curtis Turner, driving his peach-colored #26 Ford, pairs up with #21 Glen Wood on the front row for the start of the April 22 NASCAR Convertible race at Winston-Salem's Bowman Gray Stadium. Turner prevailed in the race, giving his Peter DePaolo Ford team its eighth win in 11 starts at the outset of the '57 ragtop campaign. A crowd of 7800 packed the grandstands around the flat ¼-mile track to watch the event.

Darlington Raceway added a NASCAR Convertible race to its annual schedule in 1957. The open-top cars were a hit on the superspeedway and remained a fixture on the NASCAR scene until '63. Here, in the inaugural Rebel 300 on May 12, Paul Goldsmith and Roger Baldwin slide through the turn after locking fenders. Joe Weatherly sneaks through in his #12 Ford.

Fireball Roberts salutes to the crowd as he receives the checkered flag in the inaugural Rebel 300-miler at Darlington Raceway. Roberts avoided a nine-car crash on the 30th lap and breezed to a two-lap victory over runner-up Tim Flock. For Roberts, it was the second superspeedway win of his illustrious career. A crowd of 17,000 watched the historic event.

BUCK BAKER

ELZIE WYLIE BAKER, better known as "Buck" in NASCAR racing circles, was one of the toughest and most capable high-speed chauffeurs of the 1950s. A hard-nosed competitor in the rough-and-tumble Modified division, Baker won his share of battles on the racetrack, and compiled an enviable record in postrace fisticuffs.

During the progressive 1950s, Baker was active in all branches of the NASCAR racing tree. He divided his time between the tumultuous short tracks and the popular NASCAR Grand National circuit—and also took time out to win the championship for NASCAR's short-lived open-wheel Speedway Division tour in '52. A driver held in high esteem among team owners, Baker became a sought-after pilot when he wasn't campaigning his own machinery.

In 1955, Carl Kiekhaefer joined the NASCAR touring series and virtually cleaned house. Kiekhaefer's team won 22 of the 39 races, leaving only scraps for the other shade-tree-engineered teams. Kiekhaefer noticed, however, that Baker was giving the Kiekhaefer outfit a good run for the money in his self-owned Oldsmobiles and Buicks. "I saw that Buck was my top competition," Kiekhaefer said at the beginning of the '56 NASCAR Grand National season. "There is only one thing to do with a man like that—hire him!"

Baker won his first start with Kiekhaefer in a 150-miler at Phoenix's dirt track. It set the stage for the remainder of the campaign as Baker won 14 races and captured the 1956 NASCAR Grand National title. He finished in the top five in 30 of his 48 starts.

Kiekhaefer suddenly quit NASCAR after the 1956 season, and Baker found himself in a factory-supported Chevrolet under the direction of Hugh Babb. Baker continued his hot streak, though, winning 10 races and only finishing out of the top 10 twice in his 40 starts. He also racked up his second straight national driving championship. In his title years of '56 and '57, Baker won 24 of his 46 career NASCAR Grand National victories.

In addition to his two championships, Baker won the storied Southern 500 at Darlington three times. The first came

NASCAR Grand National Career Record 1949-1973, 1976
Starts: 636
Wins: 46
Top 5s: 246
Top 10s: 372
Poles: 44
Career Winnings: $362,136

in 1953 in an Oldsmobile owned by T.C. Griffin, when he scampered past a fading Herb Thomas in the closing stages. In '60, he filled in for Jack Smith, who refused to drive at Darlington after he soared out of the speedway in an acrobatic, aerial chiller in the '58 race. As a substitute, Baker wheeled Smith's Pontiac to victory in dramatic fashion. He finished the race on three wheels, throwing up a shower of sparks after blowing a tire with two laps remaining.

Baker's final superspeedway triumph came in 1964 at Darlington, driving a Dodge for master mechanic Ray Fox. It turned out to be the final win of his career, but even at the age of 45, he proved he hadn't lost the edge.

A versatile driver who could hop in unfamiliar machinery and get the most out of it, Baker won races in eight different makes of cars: Hudson, Oldsmobile, Buick, Chrysler, Chevrolet, Ford, Pontiac, and Dodge. He also won for eight different team owners: B.A. Pless, T.C. Griffin, Ernest Woods, Kiekhaefer, Babb, Smith, Fox, and himself.

Not only versatile, but tough as nails, many of Baker's rivals said if they laid a bumper on him during the heat of battle, they could expect a confrontation in the pits afterward. "My dad won his share of races on the track," said Baker's son Buddy years later, "but I don't think he ever lost a battle in the pits."

Baker retired as a full-time driver from NASCAR Grand National competition after the 1968 season and concentrated on the pony league Grand Touring Series, which featured Mustangs and Camaros. He was a front-runner in that series too, winning eight times in four seasons.

After kicking around the short tracks throughout the Carolinas, Baker got restless and wanted to test the big-league waters one final time. In 1976, Baker struck a deal with team owner Junie Donlavey to make his return at Darlington for the April 11 race. After qualifying 13th, Baker went on to finish in sixth place, not bad for a battle-weary 57-year-old veteran.

During his career in NASCAR Grand National racing, Elzie Wylie Baker competed in 636 races, won 46 times, and was the first driver to exceed $300,000 in official career earnings.

Front-row starters Paul Goldsmith and Buck Baker lead the field around the ½-mile Martinsville Speedway on the pace lap of the May 19 Virginia 500. The scheduled 250-miler was cut short when Billy Myers' Mercury sailed off the track on lap 441.

The Petty Engineering pit crew services the #42 Oldsmobile in the Aug. 11 NASCAR Convertible race at Martinsville Speedway. Shirtless Dale Inman trots around the front of the car as Richard Petty helps change a tire on the right-side. Lee Petty, with relief help from Bobby Myers, finished fourth in the 500-lapper on the paved ½-mile track.

Master mechanic Smokey Yunick chats with Paul Goldsmith prior to a practice session for the Southern 500 at Darlington. Yunick entered a pair of Fords for Goldsmith and Curtis Turner, both of which were wiped out in heavy crashes in the race. Yunick, who had a who's who list of top-ranked drivers over the years, always regarded Goldsmith as the best driver to ever buckle a helmet in one of his cars.

Herb Thomas' twisted and deformed Pontiac lays still after a savage crash in the early laps of the Sept. 2 Southern 500. Fonty Flock, who drove the car, spun along the backstretch and stopped broadside at the entrance to the third turn. Paul Goldsmith and Bobby Myers plowed full bore into the idle car. Goldsmith and Flock suffered serious injuries. Myers was killed. Flock announced his retirement from a hospital bed soon thereafter.

1957

Fireball Roberts' #22 Ford slips sideways after a close encounter with Tiny Lund's #55 Pontiac in the Southern 500. Roberts was eliminated from further competition in the ensuing crash. Lund went on to finish 20th in the 50-car field.

Speedy Thompson scored the biggest win of his career in the 1957 Southern 500. Thompson drove his #46 Chevrolet to a three-lap win over Cotton Owens in the grueling 500-miler. The average speed of 100.094 mph was the first Southern 500 to average more than 100 mph. The race enjoyed its third straight sellout. Newspaper reports listed the attendance at 75,000 although the grandstand capacity was a little over 25,000 at the time.

Eddie Pagan's #45 hardtop Ford and Bob Welborn's ragtop Chevrolet pace the field at the start of the Oct. 6 Sweepstakes 500 at Martinsville Speedway. Welborn won the event in his convertible. NASCAR records fail to credit Welborn for the win since he was in a convertible. NASCAR's official record book doesn't credit anyone with the win, creating an unbalanced number of races and winners that still exists today.

NASCAR President Bill France orchestrates a "bury the hatchet" ceremony as Speedy Thompson (left) and Curtis Turner shake hands. The two top-ranked drivers had been engaged in a heated feud for several months. Legend says that at one point, Turner flew over a track where Thompson was competing and dropped a carton of tacks onto the racing surface. Having seen enough of this nonsense, France got the two drivers together and helped settle their differences.

Rookie Ken Rush competed in both the NASCAR Grand National and Convertible circuits in 1957. In 21 Convertible races, he logged 11 top-10 finishes. Rush started 16 NASCAR Grand National races, won one pole, and enjoyed six top-10 finishes. NASCAR named Rush the first official Rookie of the Year. "Ken Rush has been named (1957) NASCAR Rookie of the Year . . . Ken is a man who loves to race, and with his vastly improved driving skill and willingness to work hard at his profession, it seems likely he will quickly develop the promise he shows and take his place among the NASCAR aces in the near future," said a NASCAR press release.

Speedy Thompson limps to the pit area with a flat right front tire in the Oct. 20 race at North Wilkesboro Speedway as Johnny Allen's Plymouth speeds off the fourth turn. Thompson finished fourth despite the unscheduled pit stop. Jack Smith won the 100-miler.

1957 NASCAR GRAND NATIONAL POINTS RACE

Rank	Driver	Points	Starts	Wins	Top 5	Top 10	Winnings
1	Buck Baker	10,716	40	10	30	38	$30,763.40
2	Marvin Panch	9956	42	6	22	27	$24,306.60
3	Speedy Thompson	8560	38	2	16	22	$26,840.58
4	Lee Petty	8528	41	4	20	33	$18,325.28
5	Jack Smith	8464	39	4	17	25	$14,561.10
6	Fireball Roberts	8268	42	8	21	27	$19,828.04
7	Johnny Allen	7068	42	0	4	17	$9814.01
8	L.D. Austin	6532	40	0	1	13	$6484.68
9	Brownie King	5740	36	0	1	16	$5588.68
10	Jim Paschal	5124	35	0	9	17	$7078.68
11	Tiny Lund	4848	32	0	6	15	$6423.68
12	Billy Myers	4640	28	0	4	9	$6565.52
13	Paul Goldsmith	4188	25	4	10	15	$12,733.68
14	Cotton Owens	4032	17	1	3	6	$12,783.68
15	Eddie Pagan	3612	15	3	11	11	$7273.58
16	Bill Amick	3512	21	1	8	12	$8072.44
17	Dick Beaty	3220	20	0	1	7	$3647.44
18	Jim Reed	2836	6	0	2	3	$3407.44
19	Clarence DeZalia	2828	25	0	0	6	$3307.44
20	Frankie Schneider	2516	10	0	3	6	$4587.44
21	Rex White	2508	9	0	4	6	$3870.00
22	Curtis Turner	2356	10	0	2	4	$4830.00
23	George Green	2216	17	0	1	4	$2240.00
24	Whitey Norman	1920	13	0	1	4	$3990.00
25	Lloyd Dane	1852	10	1	7	10	$4985.00
26	Jimmie Lewallen	1796	7	0	0	0	$1030.00
27	Johnny Mackison	1764	5	0	1	2	$1330.00
28	Bobby Keck	1740	16	0	0	2	$1525.00
29	Billy Carden	1600	3	0	0	2	$1675.00
30	Bill Benson	1592	11	0	0	2	$1090.00
31	Dick Getty	1504	10	0	3	8	$1890.00
32	Scotty Cain	1492	11	0	2	6	$1165.00
33	Roy Tyner	1468	10	0	0	2	$1020.00
34	T.A. Toomes	1404	11	0	0	1	$1450.00
35	Possum Jones	1360	6	0	0	4	$2375.00
36	Huck Spaulding	1240	8	0	0	3	$1120.00
37	Ralph Earnhardt	1180	9	0	0	3	$1150.00
38	George Seeger	1108	6	0	5	5	$2740.00
39	Ken Rush	1104	16	0	1	6	$2045.00
40	Peck Peckham	1064	10	0	0	0	$950.00
41	Bill Champion	956	10	0	0	1	$1125.00
42	Chuck Hansen	900	7	0	0	0	$510.00
43	Danny Graves	880	7	1	3	4	$1895.00
44	Marvin Porter	872	6	1	2	3	$1770.00
45	Eddie Skinner	848	4	0	0	0	$605.00
46	Jimmy Thompson	816	2	0	0	0	$325.00
47	Parnelli Jones	812	10	1	1	3	$1625.00
48	Bobby Jones	800	1	0	0	0	$225.00
49	Don Porter	784	6	0	0	4	$810.00
50	Joe Weatherly	776	14	0	5	7	$5240.00

Buck Baker assumed command of the 1957 points race in mid May and easily won his second straight NASCAR Grand National championship. Baker finished 760 points ahead of Marvin Panch, who led the points standings for the first 16 races.

Baker was consistently excellent throughout the season. He began the year with 26 consecutive top-10 finishes and finished the campaign with 38 top-10 efforts in 40 starts. The veteran from Charlotte, N.C., won 10 races along the way in his Chevrolet.

Panch won six races in 42 starts during his first full NASCAR Grand National season, including the opening two events. He led the points standings until the May 19 race at Martinsville, when Baker took the points lead with a victory.

Two-time winner Speedy Thompson wound up third in the points race, followed by Lee Petty and Jack Smith, who both won four events.

1958

February 23 Paul Goldsmith drives Smokey Yunick's Pontiac to victory in the 160-mile NASCAR Grand National race on Daytona's Beach-Road course. The event is the final NASCAR race staged on the picturesque 4.1-mile course on the shore.

March 2 Four days after the race, Lee Petty is declared the winner of the 100-mile NASCAR Grand National at Concord Speedway despite protests from Curtis Turner and Speedy Thompson, the apparent top two finishers. Scorecard data indicates that Petty finishes the 200 laps first although Turner starts on the pole and leads the entire distance.

April 13 Curtis Turner and Joe Weatherly finish first and second in the 100-mile NASCAR Grand National race at Lakewood Speedway in Atlanta. Turner and Weatherly are in potent Fords prepared by John Holman and Ralph Moody, successors of Peter DePaolo on Ford's premier racing team.

May 30 Fireball Roberts drives his Chevrolet to a big win in the 500-mile NASCAR Grand National race at Trenton, N.J. The race is the first 500-miler staged north of Darlington.

June 1 Riverside International Raceway in Southern California opens with three 500-mile races in one weekend. Eddie Gray captures the Crown America 500 for NASCAR Grand National cars in an event that takes more than six hours to complete.

July 4 Fireball Roberts continues his winning spree by taking first place in the 250-mile race at Raleigh Speedway. The Daytona Beach driver outruns a 55-car field on the one-mile banked oval.

July 18 Richard Petty makes his first career NASCAR Grand National start in the 100-lap race at Toronto's Canadian National Exposition Speedway. The 21-year-old Petty finishes 17th in the 19-car field after hitting the fence on the 55th lap.

August 2 Jack Smith wins the 100-mile NASCAR Grand National race at the Bridgehampton road course on Long Island. It is NASCAR's first venture into the New York City area.

Diminutive Rex White grabbed his first NASCAR Grand National victory in the 1958 season opener at Fayetteville, N.C. The 50-mile race on the ⅓-mile track was staged on Nov. 3, 1957. In the first 20 years of NASCAR Grand National racing, NASCAR often began the upcoming season at the tail end of the current year. White won the Fayetteville event in his 34th career start, taking the lead in the final five laps.

Glen Wood, leader of the Wood Brothers clan out of Stuart, Va., enjoyed a successful driving career before hanging up his helmet to concentrate on operating the family team. He divided his time among all of NASCAR's divisions and won at every level. Wood won four NASCAR Grand National events, five Convertible races, and countless Modified contests. He finished sixth in the 1958 Daytona Beach Convertible race on Feb. 22.

Lee Petty slaps the rear quarter panel of Joe Weatherly's Ford in the final lap of the 1958 Daytona Beach ragtop race. Petty shoved Weatherly out of the way and finished second. As Weatherly was attempting to right his path to make it to the finish line, several hundred spectators ran onto the racing surface. Weatherly made it to the finish line in third place without further incidents, but the remaining drivers on the course had to weave their way through the throng at a snail's pace. NASCAR officials quickly restored order before the situation got completely out of control.

The Holman-Moody Ford team bolted a top on Curtis Turner's Ford convertible late Saturday afternoon following the Daytona Beach Convertible race. Turner won the ragtop event, then drove the same car in Sunday's NASCAR Grand National race. NASCAR rules permitted the use of "zipper tops" for teams that wanted to use the same car in different divisions. Turner ran a close second to Paul Goldsmith in the NASCAR Grand National race on the Beach-Road course.

Buck Baker had a new 1958 Chevrolet at the beginning of the '58 NASCAR Grand National campaign. Baker finished seventh at Daytona, fell out early the following week at Concord, N.C., then parked the new model Chevy and returned to driving his trusty '57 Chevy for the remainder of the season. Baker's crew chief was Bud Moore, who later formed his own team and became one of the most accomplished team owners in NASCAR.

Fireball Roberts broadslides through the north turn in the 1958 Daytona Beach NASCAR Grand National race during his ninth-place performance. Roberts was driving a Buick owned by former driver J.C. Van Landingham in the 160-mile contest. With sponsorship from the Fish Carburetor Corp., Roberts was hoping to avenge the '55 Daytona race when his apparent victory in a Fish Carburetor Buick was taken away due to a minor rules infraction. Roberts' car lacked the horsepower needed to run with the leaders and finished two laps off the pace.

In the final lap of the Daytona Beach NASCAR Grand National event, #3 Paul Goldsmith nearly slid over the edge of the north turn. His vision obscured by wet sand and moisture from the ocean spray, Goldsmith found it difficult to negotiate the final turn. Windshield wipers were a standard piece of equipment on cars running the Daytona event, but Goldsmith's were inoperative, having blown back over the roof. Goldsmith's big lead evaporated on the final lap, but he still made it to the finish line just ahead of the hard-charging Curtis Turner.

1958

September 1 Fireball Roberts takes his fourth win of the NASCAR Grand National season at Darlington's Southern 500. Roberts has now won four of his seven starts during the 1958 campaign.

September 28 Joe Eubanks, who recently ended a retirement, drives to his first career victory in the 99-mile NASCAR Grand National contest at Hillsboro's Orange Speedway. Eubanks wins in his fourth start since returning to the speedway battles.

October 26 Junior Johnson edges Fireball Roberts by a whisker to win the NASCAR Grand National season finale at Atlanta's Lakewood Speedway. Lee Petty captures the championship by 644 points over Buck Baker.

▶ Johnny Bruner, Jr., waves the checkered flag for Paul Goldsmith at the finish of the Daytona Beach NASCAR Grand National race. Driving a Smokey Yunick Pontiac, Goldsmith won the final event on the storied course along the shoreline. A week later, Goldsmith quit the NASCAR tour and joined the rival USAC organization so he could get a shot at the Indianapolis 500. Goldsmith competed in five Indy 500s from '58 to '63, twice finishing in the top five. He later returned to NASCAR.

Curtis Turner smiles in victory lane following the second annual Rebel 300 Convertible race at Darlington (S.C) Raceway. Turner won in an epic struggle with Holman-Moody teammate Joe Weatherly. Turner made the decisive pass with 24 laps to go and Weatherly finished second. Turner dominated the Convertible division, winning 38 races in its four-year run. Despite winning twice as many races as anyone else, he never won the Convertible championship.

Lee Petty pits his Oldsmobile during a race at North Wilkesboro (N.C.) Speedway. In the 1950s, pit stops weren't a refined art. Often, changing two tires and filling the fuel tank took more than 40 seconds. Petty won his second NASCAR Grand National championship in 1958, leading the points standings every week with the exception of the season opener. He won seven races and finished among the top 10 in 44 of his 50 starts.

Fireball Roberts cut back his racing schedule after the manufacturers withdrew from active participation in NASCAR Grand National racing in 1957. Rather than operating his own team with the equipment left behind after the factory retreat, Roberts accepted a ride with a Chevy team owned by Frank Strickland. They entered only 10 races in '58, but won six. The 60-percent winning ratio was the high-water mark in NASCAR until David Pearson won 61.1 percent of his starts in '73.

Shorty Rollins was the top NASCAR Grand National rookie in 1958. The Corpus Christi, Texas, hotshot won a NASCAR Grand National event at Busti, N.Y., on July 16. He only finished out of the top 10 seven times during his rookie campaign and wound up an impressive fourth in the final standings. Rollins was named 1958 NASCAR Rookie of the Year, the second year the award was presented.

Clarence DeZalia's #94 Mercury gets entangled in a three-car mishap during a short-track event. DeZalia was one of the many independent drivers of the 1950s. He had no sponsor other than his own garage in Aberdeen, N.C. The crew was limited to DeZalia and a few friends, and they towed their car all over the South to race. DeZalia competed in 27 of the 51 events in '58, scoring six top-10 finishes. He finished 15th in the final standings, and won a shade over $3000.

Bob Welborn (right), winner of the April 20 Virginia 500 at Martinsville, accepts congratulations from Joe Weatherly (left) and Curtis Turner. Welborn led 224 of the 500 laps driving a Chevrolet owned by J.H. (Julian) Petty, brother of NASCAR champion Lee Petty. Cars owned by J.H. Petty finished 1-2 in the race, with Welborn leading teammate Rex White across the finish line.

Jack Smith was one of NASCAR's steadiest and most versatile drivers throughout the 1950s and early '60s. Smith won on short tracks, dirt tracks, superspeedways, and road courses. In late '58, Smith built a new '58 Pontiac, but the car was wiped out at Darlington in a bone-jarring, acrobatic flip over the guardrail. Smith had to borrow a ride in a number of late-season events, but still wound up fifth in the final standings.

1958

Cars barrel into the first turn three abreast at the start of the Sept. 1 Southern 500. Joe Weatherly's #12 Ford surges ahead as pole-sitter #45 Eddie Pagan ducks to the inside. Number 22 Fireball Roberts, #6 (the 6 on the roof faced the crowd) Joe Eubanks, and #26 Curtis Turner follow close behind. The tiny, open-air press box, located outside the turn, gave newspaper reporters a close-up view of the action. Goggles were handed out to occupants to shield their eyes from flying sand, bits of rubber, and other projectiles.

Don Kimberling spins out in his 1958 Chevy in the early laps of the Southern 500. George Dunn, in the #14 Mercury, managed to avoid Kimberling, who was driving in his first NASCAR Grand National race. Kimberling slid backward into the wall and his car erupted in flames. The rookie driver was able to escape the inferno, but never again returned to race in NASCAR's top level of stock car racing.

LEE PETTY

IN NASCAR'S frolicking and carnivorous early days, many of the competitors were hardcore critters who wouldn't think twice about slamming another driver off the track. Not many of the pioneers planned for the future. They were busy running flat out, chasing the checkered flag.

Lee Petty was a refreshing, out of the ordinary member of NASCAR's wild bunch. Petty was never regarded as one of NASCAR's hardest chargers. Instead, he was the great calculator, applying the strategies of a chess player. "I have to finish in the top three cars to make money," Petty said in a 1954 interview. "I have to finish among the first five to break even. After that, I'm going in the red."

Petty drove to finish—and to finish well. An opportunist, Petty ran well enough to become NASCAR's most prolific race winner when he finally hung up his goggles for good in 1964. In his career, he won 54 times, and finished in the top 10 an incredible 332 times in 427 career NASCAR Grand National starts. It is a record of consistency that may never be approached.

Petty won the NASCAR championship three times, in 1954, '58, and '59. During the heavy factory participation in the '50s, Petty's independent team lacked the pure speed of the industry-supported outfits, yet he still racked up more than his share of victories. In '58 and '59, Petty won 18 races and finished second 10 times. He led the NASCAR Grand National points standings virtually all the way for two years running, holding the top spot after 92 of the 95 races—another record that may never fall.

"We were not like some of the others," Petty said several years after his retirement. "Some of the other boys, they drove and took everything out of racing they could. We have put it back. When a sponsor quit, some of the other boys quit. They spent their money for pleasure. We spent ours to build. Everything we've done has been aimed at racing. We started under an ol' reaper shed with no floor in it and we built it up. That was probably what I was most proud of."

Petty was born in Greensboro, N.C., and enjoyed all sports activities. "Played basketball, football, anything competitive," Petty said in a 1970 interview. "That is what I like

Jesse James Taylor climbs the guardrail after spinning out in the Southern 500. Taylor finished second in the '51 Southern 500 when he was a 22-year-old youngster. He was badly injured a few weeks later at Atlanta, which sidelined him from racing for five full years. After making a brief comeback in '56, his start in the '58 Southern 500 represented another brief fling at a comeback. The car was destroyed in the crash, and Taylor didn't return to NASCAR Grand National racing again until '61 when he made one final start.

Eddie Pagan's Ford blasts through the steel guardrail after blowing a tire on the 137th lap of the Southern 500. The car tumbled down the embankment outside the track, but Pagan miraculously escaped injury. Replacing the guardrail was all but impossible, so NASCAR completed the race devoid of proper retaining barriers. Drivers were warned not to drive too close to the gaping hole in the wall.

about racing. It just caught my fancy because it was competitive. I got into it as a hobby first and just stayed with it."

Petty was one of the 33 participants in the inaugural NASCAR late-model event on June 19, 1949. He drove a huge Buick Roadmaster, a car Petty claimed "me and some buddies had gone in on together." In the race, Petty lost control and flipped. The car came to a halt in a battered heap, wheezing steam and oil. Petty climbed out, shaken but uninjured, sat on the track, and peered into the distance dejectedly. In one of racing's grand quotes, Petty recollected his feelings at that moment: "I was just sitting there thinking about having to go back home and explain to my wife where I'd been with the car."

"Pappa" Lee decided that the Buick was too heavy and bulky for the tight corners of most of the short dirt-track speedways. He opted to build a lightweight Plymouth with more user-friendly handling characteristics. He scored his first career win at Heidelberg, Penn., in the 1949 season, and registered at least one win each year in his first 13 seasons of NASCAR Strictly Stock and Grand National competition.

Petty was one of the few pioneer drivers whose career made it to the progressive 1960s. He was able to transition from the dusty bull rings to the lightning-fast

superspeedways. When the Daytona International Speedway opened in '59, Petty drove an Oldsmobile to a two-foot victory over Johnny Beauchamp. With no photo-finish camera in place, NASCAR officials took three days to declare Petty the winner in the thrilling side-by-side finish. Two years later, Petty and Beauchamp hooked bumpers in the closing stages of Daytona's 100-mile qualifying race and both sailed over the wall. Beauchamp was treated at a hospital and released. Petty was gravely injured.

Petty's electric blue Plymouth landed in a smoldering heap outside the Daytona track. His injuries included a punctured lung, multiple fractures of the left chest, a fractured thigh, a broken collarbone, and numerous internal injuries. He was in the hospital from Feb. 26 until June 17.

Petty buckled his helmet for just six more races after his Daytona accident. In his comeback appearance at Martinsville in the Virginia 500 on April 22, 1962, the old master finished an impressive fifth on the ½-mile paved oval. He also had two other top 10 efforts before bowing out for good. "I drove again just to prove I wasn't scared," Petty quipped.

NASCAR Grand National Career Record 1949-1964
Starts: 427
Wins: 54
Top 5s: 231
Top 10s: 332
Poles: 18
Career Winnings: $237,337

A crowd of spectators and safety workers crowd around Jack Smith's Pontiac after it soared over the guardrail during the Southern 500. Smith missed a photographers' stand by inches, and came close to landing in the parking lot. Although unhurt, Smith developed a fear for the cantankerous old raceway and in future years, hired substitute drivers to take the controls in Darlington events.

Fireball Roberts survived the crashfest at Darlington and drove his Chevrolet to a five-lap victory over runner-up Buck Baker. Roberts became the first driver to win three superspeedway races in a single year. He won a 500-miler at Trenton's one-mile paved oval on Memorial Day and also prevailed in the July 4 race at Raleigh Speedway's one-mile paper-clip track. Roberts led nearly half the laps he drove in 1958, and he finished 11th in the final standings despite only competing in 10 of the 51 races.

The 1958 Southern 500 was one of the most brutal races on record. Three cars sailed over the guardrail, including Jack Smith's #47, which is pictured in this sequence. In a 100-mile stretch, Eddie Pagan, Eddie Gray, and Jack Smith plowed through or bounced over the wall. Two other cars nearly cleared the inadequate guardrail. None of the drivers were injured in the spectacular mishaps.

▶ Fireball Roberts flanks pole sitter Glen Wood on the front row at the start of the Martinsville Speedway Sweepstakes race on Oct. 12. The start of the race was delayed for more than an hour while NASCAR officials tried to determine who would participate in the 40-car field. Both NASCAR Grand Nationals and Convertibles were eligible and the entries far exceeded the 40-car limit. NASCAR finally selected 21 hardtops and 19 Convertibles to participate. Darkness curtailed the race after 350 of the 500 laps had been completed. Roberts was a lap ahead of the field when the race was flagged to a halt.

Curtis Turner's Holman-Moody Ford was sponsored by the new Atlanta International Raceway in a number of late-season events. The new 1½-mile track was scheduled to open in early 1959 with a 500-mile NASCAR Grand National event, but construction delays and a shortage of cash postponed the track's opening until July '60.

John Holman and Ralph Moody built a new Ford Thunderbird in preparation for the 1959 season. Previously, the Thunderbird fell into the sports car category and wasn't eligible for the NASCAR Grand Nationals. The Holman-Moody team built the car and submitted it to NASCAR for approval for the '59 season. The T-Bird received NASCAR's blessing and a fleet of cars were built and sold race-ready before the '59 Speedweeks events.

1958 NASCAR GRAND NATIONAL POINTS RACE

Rank	Driver	Points	Starts	Wins	Top 5	Top 10	Winnings
1	Lee Petty	12,232	50	7	28	44	$26,565.00
2	Buck Baker	11,588	44	3	23	35	$25,840.20
3	Speedy Thompson	8792	37	4	18	23	$15,214.56
4	Shorty Rollins	8124	29	1	12	22	$13,398.08
5	Jack Smith	7666	39	2	15	21	$12,633.28
6	L.D. Austin	6972	46	0	0	10	$6245.96
7	Rex White	6552	22	2	13	17	$12,232.40
8	Junior Johnson	6380	27	6	12	16	$13,808.40
9	Eddie Pagan	4910	27	0	11	18	$7471.52
10	Jim Reed	4762	17	4	10	12	$9643.60
11	Fireball Roberts	4420	10	6	8	9	$32,218.20
12	Bobby Keck	4240	30	0	0	8	$3458.20
13	Herman Beam	4224	20	0	0	1	$2598.20
14	Herb Estes	4048	11	0	0	4	$2508.20
15	Clarence DeZalia	3448	27	0	0	6	$3003.20
16	Doug Cox	3736	14	0	3	9	$3403.80
17	Cotton Owens	3716	29	1	8	16	$6578.80
18	Marvin Panch	3424	11	0	5	5	$4113.80
19	Billy Rafter	2916	19	0	1	8	$2798.80
20	Curtis Turner	2856	17	3	8	10	$10,028.80
21	Lloyd Dane	2844	5	0	1	2	$2490.00
22	Bob Duell	2740	7	0	3	6	$2415.00
23	Jimmy Thompson	2540	8	0	2	3	$3275.00
24	Fred Harb	2484	25	0	4	7	$3320.00
25	Tiny Lund	2436	22	0	4	7	$3155.00
26	Bill Poor	2292	24	0	1	7	$3115.00
27	Gene White	2040	9	0	0	2	$1400.00
28	Joe Weatherly	2032	15	1	5	7	$6330.00
29	Johnny Mackison	1680	11	0	2	3	$1255.00
30	Jim Parsley	1488	10	0	0	4	$1135.00
31	Al White	1464	9	0	0	1	$920.00
32	Jimmy Massey	1300	9	0	1	3	$1625.00
33	Parnelli Jones	1140	3	1	1	1	$1010.00
34	Joe Eubanks	1120	7	1	2	3	$2070.00
35	Brownie King	1116	24	0	0	5	$3045.00
36	G.C. Spencer	1040	1	0	0	0	$315.00
37	Richard Petty	1016	9	0	0	1	$760.00
38	Billy Carden	1012	13	0	0	2	$815.00
39	Elmo Langley	980	9	0	1	3	$1090.00
40	Buzz Woodward	964	9	0	0	2	$1195.00
41	Possum Jones	960	11	0	1	3	$1790.00
42	Jim Paschal	928	6	1	2	4	$1670.00
43	Chuck Hansen	916	7	0	0	1	$580.00
44	Eddie Gray	910	3	1	1	1	$3375.00
45	Peck Peckham	868	11	0	0	0	$835.00
46	Lennie Page	836	8	0	0	2	$760.00
47	Bob Keefe	782	2	0	1	2	$925.00
48	R.L. Combs	760	9	0	0	1	$805.00
49	Colney Schulze	680	7	0	0	0	$490.00
50	Dean Layfield	664	7	0	0	0	$370.00

Old pro Lee Petty was a dominant force in 1958 NASCAR Grand National competition, leading the points standings after all but the first race of the season.

The Oldsmobile-driving Petty won seven of his 50 starts and finished 644 points ahead of runner-up Buck Baker. Petty finished out of the top 10 in only six races and held a comfortable margin in the points race nearly the entire season.

Rex White won the season opener at Fayetteville, N.C., to take an early lead in the points standings. Petty took the lead for keeps with a sixth-place finish at Daytona. White didn't make a concerted run at the title, though, competing in only 22 of the 51 races on the schedule.

Fireball Roberts drove in only 10 races, but he won six times and finished 11th in the final points standings. Roberts was also the leading money winner on the tour, pocketing $32,218.20 in the 10 events in which he competed.

1959

February 1 Practice sessions begin on the new Daytona International Speedway in preparation for the inaugural Daytona 500. Shakedown runs are conducted despite the fact that the guardrail isn't completed.

February 22 Johnny Beauchamp is flagged the winner of the first Daytona 500 in a photo finish with Lee Petty. Beauchamp and Petty cross the finish line abreast after 500 miles of green-flag racing. Most observers feel that Petty had reached the finish line first. Bill France announces the results are unofficial and solicits all still photos and film so a decisive winner can be determined.

February 25 Lee Petty is officially declared the winner of the Daytona 500-mile race 61 hours after the checkered flag fell on the historic event. NASCAR president Bill France says photographs and film evidence "substantiated" that Petty won the hard-fought race.

March 29 Junior Johnson wins the 100-miler at Wilson Speedway in North Carolina for his first win of the 1959 season. Less than an hour before the race, the wooden grandstand catches on fire and burns to the ground. No one is injured, but the 8000 spectators have to watch the race while standing along the catch fence.

May 2 Junior Johnson rolls his Ford in practice, but drives the hastily repaired machine to victory in the 100-mile NASCAR Grand National race at Hickory Speedway. Johnson finishes two laps ahead of runner-up Joe Weatherly.

May 17 Tom Pistone, driving a 1959 Ford Thunderbird, scores his first career win in the 100-miler at Trenton Speedway. Rookie Bob Burdick, making his first NASCAR Grand National start, captures the pole.

June 14 Richard Petty finishes first in the 100-miler at Atlanta's Lakewood Speedway, but is protested by the second-place finisher, who happens to be his father Lee. After NASCAR officials study the scorecards, Lee is officially declared the winner with Richard second.

This aerial shot shows the Daytona International Speedway grounds during the early stages of construction. Dirt, extracted from what was to become Lake Lloyd on the inside of the backstretch, was used for the 31-degree banking in the turns. The lake was named after J. Saxton Lloyd, who assisted speedway founder and NASCAR president Bill France through the red tape that delayed construction for more than three years.

Before pavement was laid on the 31-degree banking in the turns, a number of shakedown sessions were conducted by Bill France and several members of the NASCAR community. The banking at Daytona International Speedway was to be the steepest in the country, and it awed many drivers. Modified driver Jimmy Thompson perhaps summed it up best when he said, "There have been other tracks that separated the men from the boys. This is the track that will separate the brave from the weak after the boys are gone."

Teams began arriving at the new Daytona International Speedway in late January 1959. Initial test runs didn't begin until Feb. 1. A crowd of 6500 paid $1 apiece to sit in the new grandstands to watch the practice runs. Fireball Roberts posted the quickest speed in the opening day of practice with a lap of 145.77 mph in his Modified Ford. The quickest time of the day for the NASCAR Grand Nationals was Curtis Turner's 143.12 mph in a new Thunderbird. Practice had to be suspended later in the week so track workers could finish the guardrail on the backstretch.

"There have been other tracks that separated the men from the boys. This is the track that will separate the brave from the weak after the boys are gone."
—Jimmy Thompson

Number 99 Shorty Rollins runs just ahead of #98 Marvin Panch in the 100-mile qualifying race for NASCAR Convertibles. Rollins passed Glen Wood on the final lap and went on to win the first automobile race staged at the new Daytona racing facility. Panch finished second and Lee Petty was third, as Wood, who fell victim to a new phenomenon called "drafting," fell to fourth place. Rollins originally entered a hardtop Ford in the inaugural Daytona 500, but removed the top and competed as a Convertible entrant.

Thirty-eight cars started the NASCAR Grand National 100-mile qualifying race on Friday, Feb. 20. The 40-lap race was a wide-open sprint from the start, with cars running at top speed in a variety of grooves. Bob Welborn held off pesky rookie Fritz Wilson to win the race by a half car length. Welborn's average speed for the 100-miler was 143.198 mph, which just happened to be the exact time of fastest qualifier Cotton Owens.

In perhaps the bravest display of the 1959 Speedweeks festivities, Johnny Bruner, Sr., flagged off the start of the inaugural Daytona 500 from the apron of the track. Bob Welborn and Shorty Rollins were on the front row. Thirty-nine NASCAR Grand Nationals and 20 Convertibles started the inaugural 500-mile grind on Feb. 22. A packed house of 41,921 spectators jammed the grandstands and infield to watch the historic event.

▼ The NASCAR Grand Nationals and Convertibles race through the third turn in the first Daytona 500. Number 41 Curtis Turner, #99 Shorty Rollins, #71 Dick Joslin, #14 Ken Rush, and #11 Junior Johnson whiz through the banking. The lightning-fast speeds at Daytona contributed to the demise of the Convertible division. The open-top cars were unstable in the buffeting winds, and they were about 10 mph slower than their more streamlined counterparts. Only 15 Convertible races were run in 1959, then NASCAR shut the series down.

1959

July 4 Fireball Roberts scores his first win in his hometown by driving a Pontiac to victory in the inaugural Firecracker 250 at Daytona International Speedway. Roberts outruns Joe Weatherly's Convertible Thunderbird in the caution-free event.

July 29 Groundbreaking ceremonies for the new Charlotte Motor Speedway take place on a sultry summer morning. The new speedway will be built by Curtis Turner and Bruton Smith, and the first race is scheduled for May 1960.

August 1 Ned Jarrett records his first NASCAR Grand National win in the 100-miler at Myrtle Beach, S.C. Jarrett had purchased the car only a couple of days earlier with a postdated check that wouldn't clear the bank until the Monday after the race.

September 7 Jim Reed rides his Chevrolet to a big win in the 10th annual Southern 500 at Darlington. Reed gives Goodyear Tire & Rubber Co. its first NASCAR win on a superspeedway. Rookie Bob Burdick finishes second.

October 25 Jack Smith wins the 1959 NASCAR Grand National finale at Concord, N.C., for his fourth win of the season. Rather than accepting a winner's check for $1500, Smith elects to take home a new '60 Ford offered by promoter Bruton Smith. Lee Petty wraps up his third championship by 1830 points over Cotton Owens.

▶ The inaugural Daytona Speedweeks featured a variety of races. The NASCAR Modified-Sportsman race on Saturday had a starting field of 52 cars, ranging from prewar coupes to souped-up models of the mid 1950s. Fireball Roberts, driving the #M-3 Fish Carburetor '55 Ford Modified, led the first 26 laps but was foiled by mechanical problems. Banjo Matthews, in Melvin Joseph's #49 '56 Ford Modified, led the final 30 laps to score the victory. Junior Johnson, in the #47 Chevrolet, finished third but was disqualified for using an oversized fuel tank.

With only a handful of laps remaining, the first Daytona 500 came down to a fight between #42 Lee Petty and #73 Johnny Beauchamp. Number 48 Joe Weatherly was a wildcard in the shuffle, running two laps behind. Without the help of radio communication, Weatherly wasn't sure if he was trailing the leaders. He continued to dice closely with Petty and Beauchamp throughout the final laps.

▼ The cars of Weatherly, Petty, and Beauchamp approach the finish line in a three-abreast cluster. Weatherly was two laps behind and would finish fifth. Petty took the lead with four laps remaining, but Beauchamp caught a good draft in the final turn, seized the opportunity, and pulled alongside Petty at the stripe.

Scottie McCormick greets Johnny Beauchamp in victory lane after the inaugural Daytona 500. Beauchamp was originally declared the winner, but most observers with a clear view of the finish thought Petty had won. NASCAR and Daytona International Speedway president Bill France said the finish would be unofficial until photos and film footage of the finish could be studied.

A bone-tired Bill France, along with Ed Otto and Dick Dolan, studied miles of film footage of the Daytona 500 finish. As more still photographs and film came into NASCAR headquarters, more and more evidence built up to support Lee Petty as the winner. On Wednesday, Feb. 25, film arrived from the *Hearst Metrotone News of the Week*. The footage removed all doubt and Petty was declared the official winner, 61 hours after the inaugural Daytona 500 had ended.

▼ The United States Auto Club Speedway Cars graced the Daytona track in April. George Amick, Rookie of the Year in the 1958 Indy 500, established a new speed record in America with a qualifying speed of 176.887 mph. Jim Rathmann won the 100-miler at an amazing 170.261 mph, an event marred by a nasty crash on the final lap that dealt fatal injuries to Amick.

1959

Bob Welborn wheels his #49 Chevrolet into the first turn at Martinsville Speedway in the May 3 Virginia 500. Rookie Fritz Wilson nips at Welborn's heels in the #114 Ford Thunderbird. Lee Petty outran the field, finishing five laps ahead of runner-up Johnny Beauchamp. Junior Johnson, in the #11 Ford, finished third. Welborn came in sixth, while Wilson fell out with fuel-pump problems after completing 333 of the 500 laps.

Young Bob Burdick (in the Giovannoni Racing T-shirt) entered his first NASCAR Grand National race at Trenton Speedway on May 17. The 22-year-old son of Roy Burdick, who owned the T-Bird that Johnny Beauchamp drove at Daytona, won the pole in his NASCAR Grand National debut. Tiger Tom Pistone (left) drove another T-Bird to victory in the Trenton 150-miler for his first NASCAR triumph.

The 1959 Firecracker 250 was the final race staged at Daytona that contained both NASCAR Grand Nationals and Convertibles. Larry Frank's #76 Chevrolet leads the #43 Plymouth of Richard Petty and Bennie Rakestraw's #20 Mercury in the early stages. The first Firecracker 250 began at 11:00 A.M. so spectators could be back on the beach during the July 4 holiday by early afternoon. Fireball Roberts won the race in a Pontiac NASCAR Grand National car. Joe Weatherly finished second in a Convertible Ford Thunderbird. Richard Petty, who started on the outside of the second row, wound up 26th due to a fuel-pump failure. A disappointing turnout of 12,017 attended the race.

NASCAR star Fireball Roberts and master mechanic Smokey Yunick pose with their Firecracker 250-winning Pontiac. The Roberts-Yunick team only competed in eight NASCAR Grand National events in 1959, limiting their efforts to the big-money races. Officially, the car was owned by Jim Stephens, a Pontiac dealer in Daytona Beach. To disguise their factory participation, the manufacturers often listed one of their factory efforts as a private entity owned by a dealership.

Elmo Langley's #10 Buick Convertible leads the chase off the fourth turn in the Aug. 16 Sweepstakes race at Asheville-Weaverville Speedway. Shep Langdon is behind the wheel of the #64 Ford and Lee Petty is in the familiar #42 Plymouth. Joe Weatherly's Convertible Thunderbird is running the in low groove. Petty finished second, padding his healthy NASCAR Grand National points lead. Petty became the first man to claim three championships in 1959, winning 11 events along the way.

NED JARRETT

AFTER WINNING the NASCAR Sportsman championship in 1957 and '58, Ned Jarrett looked for more lucrative horizons in the world of stock car racing.

A farm boy out of Newton, N.C., Jarrett was unable to convince a front-running car owner to give him a chance. So, with little money, he was forced to improvise. "Paul Spaulding, who owned a Ford that Junior Johnson drove for a year or so, decided he was going to build a new Dodge for late 1959," Jarrett explained. "He had his Ford up for sale with a $2000 price tag.

"I wanted that Ford in the worst way," Jarrett continued. "Only problem was I didn't have $2000. I had known that Junior had won in that car on several occasions and I felt that was the car I needed to make myself known in the Grand Nationals." Prior to 1959, Jarrett had only dabbled in NASCAR Grand National racing, running a total of 10 events. His total winnings amounted to only $530.

The first weekend of August 1959, a pair of NASCAR Grand National events were slated on successive nights in Myrtle Beach and Charlotte. Each 100-miler paid $800 to win, and as NASCAR Sportsman champion, Jarrett was eligible for a $100 appearance fee. "I quickly figured how I could work this thing out," said Jarrett. "I could give Mr. Spaulding a check for the car on Friday after the banks closed, post-date it for the following Monday, and go out and win both of those races. I would have $1800 and I could somehow come up with the other $200 to make the check good. It seemed so simple. I gave Mr. Spaulding a check for $2000 with no money in the bank to cover it."

No one had ever entered the big leagues of NASCAR on such a hair-brained scheme. But Jarrett was a gambler. He was confident. And he was good.

He towed the car to Rambi Speedway in Myrtle Beach, started ninth, and in Cinderella fashion, sped to victory. He pocketed the $900, but it was a costly victory. The steering wheels back in those days were taped up to make them fatter and easier to grip. Normally, they were wrapped from left-to-right so the overlapping edges were smooth. On Jarrett's Ford, the steering wheel was overlapped from right-

**NASCAR
Grand National
Career Record
1953-1966**
Starts: 352
Wins: 50
Top 5s: 185
Top 10s: 239
Poles: 35
Career Winnings:
$348,967

to-left. "On that rough track at Myrtle Beach," said Jarrett, "the edges of the tape cut my hands to the bone. I was in no condition to drive at Charlotte. I could hardly grip the steering wheel with my hands bandaged up. But I had to have another $1100 in the bank Monday morning."

Jarrett started 10th in the Charlotte race, but had to get out of the car early. Joe Weatherly, who was spectating from the pits, relieved Jarrett during the first caution. When Junior Johnson departed on lap 76 with a blown engine, he hopped into Jarrett's car for the balance of the race. "Junior brought the car home first," said Jarrett. "Joe was a little too short to reach the controls. I got paid the $900 and offered some to Junior for helping me out. He didn't accept any payment. And my check was good come Monday morning," chuckled Jarrett. It was the only time in the history of NASCAR Grand National racing that three different drivers ushered a car into victory lane.

Jarrett went on to win 48 more NASCAR Grand National events and two championships along the way. In 1961, he drove Bee Gee Holloway's Chevrolet to the championship while winning only one race. Jarrett won the title again in '65 while driving a factory-backed Ford for Bondy Long. This time he was more dominant, though, winning 13 races during his 1965 championship run.

Following the 1966 season, Jarrett retired while at his peak. "One thing I promised myself is that I would retire while I was at the top. I didn't want to go out while on my way down. It was a tough decision to make," said Jarrett.

Upon his retirement, Jarrett's record of 50 NASCAR Grand National wins was only four shy of Lee Petty's leading win total of 54. "Had I known I was only five wins away from being the all-time victory leader, I would have postponed my retirement. In those days, nobody kept records and no one knew who had the most career wins," said Jarrett.

Jarrett's most decisive win came at the 1965 Southern 500 at Darlington, when he won by 14 laps over runner-up Buck Baker. The margin of victory, 19¼ miles on the then-measured 1⅜-mile Darlington Raceway, remains the greatest in NASCAR history.

Bob Welborn takes the checkered flag to win the Aug. 16 Western North Carolina 500 at Asheville-Weaverville Speedway. It was one of Welborn's nine career NASCAR Grand National wins. The quiet and unassuming driver out of Greensboro, N.C., won the NASCAR Convertible title three years in succession from 1956 to '59. After the ragtop series folded, Welborn scaled back his racing activity and ran a partial schedule until he retired in '64.

Pint-sized Everette "Cotton" Owens drove his #6 Thunderbird to one victory in 1959, the 100-miler at Richmond on Sept. 13. While he managed only one win, Owens string of consistent finishes netted him a second-place finish in the final 1959 NASCAR Grand National points standings.

Richard Petty, shown here in a sleeveless driver's "uniform" that was routine apparel in the late 1950s, was the third recipient of the Rookie of the Year award in 1959. Petty started 21 races and recorded nine top-10 finishes while driving Oldsmobiles and Plymouths from the Petty Enterprises shops. In addition to his NASCAR Grand National activities in '59, Petty competed in a dozen NASCAR Convertible events, winning once and finishing fourth in the points standings.

A special match race between the Petty and Baker families was added to the racing card at Hillsboro's Orange Speedway on Sept. 20. The younger generation of Richard Petty and Buddy Baker started on the front row. Young Buddy, who was at the wheel of Tom Pistone's powerful Ford Thunderbird, won the 10-lap match race on the 0.9-mile dirt track.

Jack Smith's #47 Chevrolet and Richard Petty's Plymouth start on the front row for the 99-mile NASCAR Grand National race at Hillsboro. It was the first career front-row start for the 22-year-old Petty. Smith led in the early stages, but fell out with a broken axle. Petty was running second in the final laps when he, too, broke an axle on the choppy dirt track. He still wound up third despite completing only 100 of the 110 laps.

"Tiger" Tom Pistone spins his T-Bird around during the Sept. 27 Virginia Sweepstakes 500 at Martinsville Speedway. Pistone recovered to finish seventh. A NASCAR rookie in '59, Pistone won two races but wasn't considered in the Rookie of the Year program. Richard Petty won the award. NASCAR officials said Pistone's experience in late-model competition on Midwestern tracks made him ineligible to win the top Rookie award.

1959 NASCAR GRAND NATIONAL POINTS RACE

Rank	Driver	Points	Starts	Wins	Top 5	Top 10	Winnings
1	Lee Petty	11,792	42	11	27	35	$49,219.15
2	Cotton Owens	9962	37	1	13	22	$14,639.35
3	Speedy Thompson	7684	29	0	5	9	$6815.63
4	Herman Beam	7396	30	0	1	12	$6379.48
5	Buck Baker	7170	35	1	14	19	$11,060.04
6	Tom Pistone	7050	22	2	12	18	$12,724.43
7	L. D. Austin	6519	35	0	0	13	$4670.35
8	Jack Smith	6150	21	4	9	12	$13,289.38
9	Jim Reed	5744	14	3	7	9	$23,533.58
10	Rex White	5526	23	5	11	13	$12,359.85
11	Junior Johnson	4864	28	5	14	15	$9674.67
12	Shep Langdon	4768	21	0	0	6	$3525.21
13	G. C. Spencer	4260	28	0	1	5	$3700.21
14	Tommy Irwin	3876	25	0	10	16	$9189.21
15	Richard Petty	3694	21	0	6	9	$8110.21
16	Fireball Roberts	3676	8	1	1	4	$10,660.14
17	Bob Welborn	3588	29	3	10	13	$6490.14
18	Joe Weatherly	3404	17	0	6	10	$9815.14
19	Bobby Johns	2732	8	0	1	2	$5950.14
20	Tiny Lund	2634	27	0	5	10	$4940.14
21	Bob Burdick	2392	6	0	1	3	$10,050.00
22	Larry Frank	2256	15	0	4	9	$5993.00
23	Bobby Keck	2186	18	0	0	0	$1270.00
24	Curtis Turner	2088	10	2	4	4	$3845.00
25	Jim Paschal	1792	6	0	3	4	$2980.00
26	Buddy Baker	1692	12	0	1	5	$1705.00
27	Shorty Rollins	1600	10	0	0	4	$1500.00
28	Elmo Langley	1568	13	0	1	2	$2286.00
29	Jimmy Thompson	1528	5	0	0	1	$1580.00
30	Brownie King	1480	18	0	1	5	$1875.00
31	Tim Flock	1464	2	0	0	1	$850.00
32	Joe Eubanks	1432	13	0	2	7	$2000.00
33	Roy Tyner	1416	28	0	7	14	$5425.00
34	Charlie Cregar	1408	3	0	0	0	$550.00
35	Dick Freeman	1352	3	0	0	0	$475.00
36	Raul Cilloniz	1272	2	0	0	0	$550.00
37	Ned Jarrett	1248	17	2	4	7	$3860.00
38	Dave White	1228	5	0	0	1	$660.00
39	Dick Joslin	1224	4	0	0	0	$485.00
40	Tommy Thompson	1168	3	0	0	0	$510.00
41	Harvey Hege	1152	10	0	0	3	$955.00
42	Eduardo Dibos	1128	3	0	2	2	$1050.00
43	Bill Champion	1120	1	0	0	0	$500.00
44	Joe Caspolich	1040	1	0	0	0	$470.00
45	Jim Austin	1016	5	0	0	0	$440.00
46	Marvin Porter	984	7	0	2	4	$1940.00
47	Jim McGuirk	928	4	0	0	0	$325.00
48	Harlan Richardson	924	10	0	0	2	$1120.00
49	Al White	872	5	0	0	0	$575.00
50	Richard Riley	760	10	0	0	2	$910.00

Lee Petty became the first three-time winner of the NASCAR Grand National championship by dominating the 1959 season. Petty's victory in the inaugural Daytona 500 pushed him atop the standings, a perch he never relinquished. On the strength of 11 victories in 42 starts, Petty finished 1830 points ahead of Cotton Owens in the final tally.

The 45-year-old Petty won major events at Daytona, North Wilkesboro, Martinsville, Atlanta, and Hillsboro along the way to his third title. His 11 race wins more than doubled that of any other driver during the season.

Bob Welborn won the opening two events on the schedule and led the early standings, but the veteran out of Greensboro, N.C., concentrated more heavily on NASCAR's convertible circuit. Welborn competed in 28 NASCAR Grand National races and wound up finishing 17th in the points standings.

Petty established a NASCAR record by leading the points standings after 92 of the 95 races in 1958 and '59.

1960s: Superspeedways & Speedy Muscle Cars

In June 1957, factory representation in NASCAR stock car racing came to an abrupt halt with the resolution adopted by the Automobile Manufacturers Association. Under intense Congressional pressure, the automotive industry unanimously adopted a "hands off" policy toward stock car racing. The gravy train from Detroit to the NASCAR teams was derailed.

Prior to the AMA resolution, factory representation helped NASCAR stock car racing grow by leaps and bounds in the mid-1950s. Many of the top NASCAR teams had immediate and unlimited funding to strengthen their operations, and the sanctioning body received plenty of free advertising in newspapers and magazines, with the manufacturers footing the bill. When Detroit played the "no racing" card, it created a void and a recession in NASCAR stock car racing.

Initially, Ford, General Motors, and Chrysler abided by the spirit of the resolution and drastically reduced their direct involvement in racing. But new showroom cars had to be sold by the auto companies, and NASCAR was a viable selling tool. The old adage of "Win on Sunday, Sell on Monday" certainly worked in the South, and sales executives were well aware of that.

Within a few months, some or most of the factories were conducting racing business under the table. The industry's efforts to conceal their involvement received as much consideration as the development of high-speed equipment. They all had to cover their tracks.

When the Daytona International Speedway opened in 1959, the NASCAR stock car races became major sporting events that drew the attention of the national media. The sport was in a measurable transition as more and more superspeedways were in the planning stages. By '60, work had already begun on new supertracks in Atlanta, Charlotte, and Hanford, Calif.

Also in 1960, NASCAR found its way into the electronic media with CBS Sports' live telecast of three preliminary races during the Daytona Speedweeks. CBS sent a skeleton production crew to Daytona to telecast the Grand National pole position races and compact car races. The pole position races were 10-lap, 25-mile contests and the compact car event was a short distance road race. Both were suitable to the CBS network, which had to insert commercial time into the programming. The telecast was an experiment. CBS didn't attempt to televise the 4½-hour Daytona 500.

With NASCAR races beginning to show up on the tube in American homes, the automobile industry realized the 1957 AMA resolution was hindering their efforts in promotions, sales, and performance.

Factory representation in NASCAR was on a dramatic rise by 1960, although all members of the AMA said publicly that they were still adhering to the original guidelines of the '57 resolution. Ford and General Motors even hired individuals to spy on each other.

According to the Ford spies, General Motors was spending plenty of bucks to win races. In 1960, GM won 20 NASCAR Grand National events, including the Daytona 500, Charlotte's World 600, both races at the new Atlanta International Raceway, and the NASCAR Grand National championship. Ford won 15 times while Chrysler's conservative effort with the Petty Engineering camp scored nine wins.

By 1961, the numbers were more lopsided. General Motors won 41 races, 30 by Pontiac and 11 by Chevrolet. Ford won only seven times. Chrysler managed to win four short-track events. Also in '61, ABC's *Wide World of Sports* began to televise a number of the major superspeedway races in a tape-delayed format. On Saturday afternoon, a half-hour or so of edited highlights of the NASCAR Grand Nationals were beamed into American homes. New Fords, Pontiacs, Chevrolets, and Plymouths were performing on a speedy stage in the living rooms of a car-buying public.

Pontiacs were winning most of the races aired on television. Not surprisingly, Pontiac sales showed a brisk increase. Soon, Pontiac ranked third in automobile sales in the United States, a position that could be directly attributed to lofty results on NASCAR tracks.

Early in the 1962 NASCAR Grand National season, General Motors was racking up impressive numbers in the victory column. GM won 18 of the first 20 races, 12 by Pontiac. Plymouth scored twice and Ford had a big zero. In June '62, Ford Motor Co. president Henry Ford II announced his company was stepping out of the '57 agreement and would actively—and publicly—be involved in NASCAR racing. "We feel that the resolution has come to have neither purpose nor effect," he said. "Accordingly, we have notified the AMA that we feel we can better establish our own standards of conduct with respect to the manner in which the performance of our vehicles is to be promoted and advertised."

Ford didn't pull punches during his announcement. "It is no secret that the racing accomplishments have sharply boosted Pontiac sales," he continued. "We also want to see our cars win races, and auto racing definitely sells cars. For a while other member companies endorsed the soundness of

the principles stated in the resolution. As time passed, however, some car divisions, including our own, interpreted the resolution more and more freely, with the result that increasing emphasis was placed on speed and racing."

Chrysler Corp. indicated it also would act on its own in performance matters, saying that the Ford withdrawal "makes the resolution inoperable." General Motors, on the other hand, declared that it "continues to endorse the soundness of the principles stated in the AMA resolution." That statement drew a series of chuckles at Ford.

NASCAR president Bill France greeted the Ford announcement with enthusiasm and approval. "I think it's a good honest move," said Big Bill. "The resolution was and always has been one which restricted development of safe automobiles. When you consider that these races are put on television with audiences of 15 million, you can see that the factories want to build these cars so the wheels won't fall off."

Veteran driver Buck Baker, who won the 1956 and '57 NASCAR Grand National championships while a member of factory teams, said a full-scale return to racing by the factory teams would mean "a better sport, better equipment, better pay, and a better show. All the top drivers would be bidded for, just like baseball players."

"When I was a member of the factory team," said Baker, who had won only seven times from 1958 to '62 while taking 24 victories in '56 and '57, "I received a monthly salary, promotional appearance money, all expenses paid, and a new car to drive, plus everything I won. With the factories coming back, it'll be better for myself and everyone involved."

The dynamics of high-speed competition on imposing, steeply banked superspeedways ushered in an influx of new faces in the driver ranks. Many of the stalwarts of the 1950s that were short-track icons didn't care for the mind-blowing speeds the superspeedways commanded, and soon new talent was joining the driver ranks. Youthful Fred Lorenzen was hired for Ford's Holman-Moody team in '61. David Pearson joined the Ray Fox Pontiac team. Other newcomers included Cale Yarborough, LeeRoy Yarbrough, Bobby Isaac, and Billy Wade—all striving for a well-funded ride.

By the autumn of 1962, NASCAR had established a set of rules for the '63 campaign that addressed the potential of unlimited engineering by the factories. A 428-cubic-inch limit on engine displacement was in place for '63. By limiting the cid, NASCAR could keep the factories in check and keep the present components from becoming obsolete.

The factories were getting geared up for the 1963 campaign, too. Chrysler kept its Plymouth eggs in the Petty Engineering basket, while Cotton Owens had replaced Bob Osiecki as the top Dodge team. Owens entered a two-car team with David Pearson and rookie Billy Wade as his drivers. Chrysler announced it would begin a full-hearted racing effort, but that it might take time for results to come.

Ford, with Holman-Moody as its undisputed nucleus of racing equipment, had several satellite teams sprouting from the Holman-Moody empire. Ford's "Total Performance" moniker would leave no stone unturned in its efforts within the NASCAR domain. Pontiac and General Motors officials remained mum on racing, but Chevrolet did send a batch of goodies to Daytona Beach for innovative mechanics Smokey Yunick and Ray Fox to share. The new Chevrolet engine would be cloaked in mystery and available to only two teams, and NASCAR would be very lenient to the GM effort so it could have representation from all the manufacturers.

Ford started the 1963 Grand National campaign with a bang, finishing 1-2-3-4-5 in the celebrated Daytona 500. The Pontiacs, under the direction of Ray Nichels, were speedy but encountered problems in the 500. The Chevys danced across the wind-swept banks with amazing agility and quickness, but they too failed to go the distance. Fireball Roberts and Joe Weatherly, who had been the dominant drivers for Pontiac in '61 and '62, simply couldn't keep up with the speedier Fords and Chevys.

Fred Lorenzen, the lead driver for the Holman-Moody team, was racking up big prizes and collecting lots of handsome trophies for his deeds in speed. The "Golden Boy" from Elmhurst, Ill., was well-spoken, colorful, and the darling of the youthful fan base. Accordingly, Ford showroom sales flourished.

By midseason, Fireball Roberts and Joe Weatherly had abandoned the sinking Pontiac ship and joined Ford—Roberts as a teammate with Lorenzen and Weatherly in the Bud Moore Mercury effort. Pontiac also lost Ray Nichels, who switched to Plymouth. Yunick entered his Chevy in seven races with five different drivers: Johnny Rutherford, Banjo Matthews, Buck Baker, Bobby Isaac, and A.J. Foyt. Rutherford prevailed in a 100-mile qualifying race at Daytona, but the Yunick car was hampered with mechanical failures. Fox and Junior Johnson were fast but seldom finished long-distance races.

Ford and Mercury won seven of the 10 races that were 300-miles or more, with Holman-Moody winning five. Johnson won twice in the Ray Fox Chevy and Weatherly won in a Pontiac before his switch to Mercury.

As the curtain lifted on the 1964 NASCAR season, Chrysler was loaded for bear. The Plymouths and Dodges were more streamlined aerodynamically and packed with a bundle of

127

horsepower in the hemispherical engine. Chrysler dusted off an idea from the early 1950s and came up with a "new" engine. Chrysler Corp. bolted hemispherical heads to its 426-cid wedge engine to come up with the 426 Hemi. The hemispherical combustion engine had been in Chrysler's bag of tricks from 1951 to '58, but this new version was a monster.

When the NASCAR stockers began checking into Daytona for the annual Speedweeks carnival, the Hemi-powered Chrysler cars were turning some magic numbers. Richard Petty was running 20 mph faster than he had a year earlier. Speeds were approaching 175 mph, while the Fords were lumbering around in the high 160s. Plymouth swept both 100-mile qualifying races and motored to a 1-2-3 finish in the Daytona 500.

On the ultra-high-speed ovals, the Chryslers were hard to beat. On the short to intermediate tracks, the Ford teams took most of the top honors. Speeds and danger increased in 1964, and the unlimited horsepower race exacted a heavy toll. Joe Weatherly, two-time defending Grand National champion, lost his life in a crash at Riverside in January. NASCAR icon Fireball Roberts suffered burns in Charlotte's World 600 and died in July. Jimmy Pardue crashed to his death at Charlotte in a September tire test.

Following a crash at Daytona, Fred Lorenzen claimed "the speeds are just too fast now." Junior Johnson, regarded as one of the bravest men ever to buckle a helmet, said, "The cars are going too fast for the tracks. We haven't learned enough to keep the cars handling safely at the speeds we can now travel, and the tire companies are having trouble developing tire compounds that will give adequate tire wear."

On Oct. 19, 1964, NASCAR issued new rules for the '65 campaign designed to curb speeds and increase the focus on safety. The engine displacement remained unchanged, but

special limited edition engines were banned. "We are at a crossroads," said France. "The 1965 specifications are designed to provide fair competition among all 1965 standard American size production automobiles."

Richard Petty, the 1964 NASCAR champion, said the effect of the '65 rules "amounts to us going back to 1963 running against 1965 equipment." Dodge team owner Cotton Owens declared the '65 rules "have put the Chrysler teams out of business." Ronney Householder, director of Chrysler's racing effort, took a verbal jab at NASCAR's new regulations. "Regarding Bill France's rule about engines in volume production, I would like to point out that the Chrysler Corporation would like to decide for itself how many engines it is going to build and does not need any instructions from NASCAR. I can't see where people will come out to watch cars run 150 miles per hour when they know there are cars that can go 175. Go fast. That's what racing is all about."

France was hoping the 1965 technical guidelines would pave the way for General Motors to return. "Those who prefer to use General Motors equipment will not be handicapped," declared France.

Having only big luxury cars like the Plymouth Fury to race, with old outdated engines to power them, Chrysler packed up and pulled out of NASCAR. Richard Petty would not defend his championship, and top contenders David Pearson, Paul Goldsmith, Bobby Isaac, Jim Paschal, and LeeRoy Yarbrough were on the sidelines. General Motors executives squelched any rumors that they would return openly to racing. The back door is not only not open, it is being closely guarded," said a high-ranking GM official. "We will not be active in NASCAR racing."

The 1965 Daytona Speedweeks events were filled with plenty of factory-backed Fords and little competition from

other nameplates. Fords scooped up all the marbles in the first half of the '65 season, winning a record 32 straight Grand National races, a mark that still stands today. Ticket sales were lagging with the Ford domination and promoters were taking it on the chin. The dissent in the NASCAR ranks was greater than at any time in history. No one was happy, not even the Ford drivers, who secretly felt their lofty records were tainted by the lack of competition.

In the late spring of 1965, France was actively campaigning for General Motors to put something on the NASCAR tracks. Like the early '60s, when GM supported racing through the guise of dealerships, France carved similar inroads to the NASCAR domain. Only this time, there was no reliable hardware to keep the Chevys running up front. France did permit an illegal Chevy to compete in the World 600 at Charlotte. A few other independent Chevy efforts dotted the starting field. "I hope and pray the Chevys run well at Charlotte," said Lorenzen. "They mean so much to NASCAR racing right now." Fords and Mercurys took the top five positions at Charlotte as the Chevys lagged far behind.

Hope all but vanished for competitive General Motors cars in 1965. With his back against the wall, France permitted the Chrysler teams to return to the short tracks. Petty promptly won four races while David Pearson scored twice. The Hemi engines remained on the sidelines on the superspeedways.

After the close of the 1965 Grand National season, NASCAR was licking its wounds. The Chrysler boycott had produced a box-office disaster. On Monday, Dec. 13, 1965, France toured the Chrysler manufacturing plant to check on volume production. "I saw more Hemi engines made today than Ferrari makes cars in a year," France remarked. When the new '66 guidelines were announced, NASCAR approved

the Hemi engine since it had become a high-volume production item.

Chrysler was back in the fold for 1966. Ford had hoped to introduce a new overhead-cam engine, but it was rejected by NASCAR when Ford failed to prove it was a high-volume item. Chryslers kicked butt in early '66, winning Daytona, Rockingham, and Atlanta. By April, Ford said it was pulling up stakes in NASCAR and began its own walk out.

That left another boycott of major proportions staining the 1966 NASCAR season. Only 7000 spectators paid to watch the Rebel 400 at Darlington, and promoters were counting their losses for a second year in a row. Plymouth and Dodge cleaned house, winning everything save a handful of short track upsets authored by independent Ford drivers Elmo Langley and Tiny Lund. At the end of the year, Ford had returned to the NASCAR battles. Ford had determined that it needed to compete in NASCAR to sell its products. Ford won four of the last five races, without its special overhead-cam engine.

David Pearson won 15 races in his Cotton Owens Dodge and captured the 1966 NASCAR Grand National championship. Chrysler cars had won 34 races while Ford won 12 times and lightly regarded newcomer Bobby Allison scored three short-track wins in his own Chevrolet.

By 1967, the factories were back in NASCAR in full force. Ford had refined its tunnelport 427-cid engine and had bolted it into a fleet of smaller Ford Fairlanes. At Daytona, more than 80 cars filed into the big speedway, and all factory teams were on hand with the exception of General Motors. A record crowd of 94,250 paid to attend the Daytona 500, which exceeded Bill France's most optimistic visions.

Mario Andretti, driving a factory-blessed Holman-Moody Fairlane, outran Fred Lorenzen to win at Daytona. Cale

Yarborough followed with a win in the Atlanta 500 as Ford was off to an impressive start. But during the Darlington race week in May, Fred Lorenzen suddenly retired. When Lorenzen hung up his helmet, he became the third top Ford star to retire in the last six months. Ned Jarrett and Junior Johnson stepped aside at Rockingham in October '66.

Following Lorenzen's retirement, the Ford team hit the skids. Richard Petty began to hit stride, winning nearly everything in sight while flawlessly driving his electric blue Plymouth. During the second half of the 1967 campaign, Petty strung together a 10-race consecutive winning streak. From Aug. 12 through Oct. 1, Petty was undefeated. He won 27 races out of 46 starts, grabbed his second Grand National championship, and earned the nickname "The King."

Ford managed to win the final two races in 1967 in a Fairlane groomed by Lorenzen and driven by emerging star Bobby Allison. At the close of the season, Chrysler had won 36 races while Ford managed only 10 victories.

The company with the "Total Performance" tag had taken its lumps in 1967. Ford went to work quickly to come up with a car to compete with the Petty/Plymouth stampede. The answer was a sleek, slope-backed body for the '68 Ford Torino and Mercury Cyclone models. In preseason testing, the tapered rooflines proved to be a blessing at high speeds. Chrysler, on the other hand, had only made peripheral aerodynamic refinements. The '68 season would pit the sleek Fords against the brute horsepower of Chrysler's Hemi.

General Motors was still on the sidelines, unwilling to reenter a sport that had served the company so well in the early 1960s. Edward M. Cole, president of GM, admitted he was a reluctant party to the corporation's antiracing efforts. Cole indicated that GM would stay out of racing because it feared violating federal safety standards. "It is a very difficult position, the interest the government has in safety," Cole said. "I don't know whether you can equate safety and racing together in the same project."

The Fords and Cale Yarborough's lone Mercury were the top dogs on the superspeedways, while Richard Petty's Plymouth Roadrunner and David Pearson's Holman-Moody Ford racked up wins on the short tracks. Ford scored in nine of the 12 major races on big tracks.

Pearson, whom Ford selected as Lorenzen's replacement on the Holman-Moody team in 1967, captured the '68 NASCAR championship. Dodge's Bobby Isaac won three short-track events and wound up second in the points chase. Petty won 16 times in his Road Runner, but only once on a superspeedway, and ranked third in points.

With full factory representation in place for two years, NASCAR Grand National racing was enjoying an explosion of popularity. A gaggle of new superspeedways were being built in areas outside NASCAR's traditional hotbed of racing. A two-mile oval had opened in Michigan, hosting the USAC Indy Cars. Construction had already broken on new tracks in Dover, Delaware, a one-mile oval with an enclosed grandstand; Texas, a two-miler similar to Michigan; and Talladega, Alabama, a huge 2.66-mile speedway on a nameless patch of property. All would host NASCAR events in 1969.

Ford enhanced its aerodynamic package with a new Torino Talladega, which featured a sloped and narrowed nose. Mercury had the Cyclone Spoiler. And with a new 429-cid "Blue Crescent" engine with semi-hemispherical combustion chambers, the future looked rosy for the Blue Oval.

Richard Petty, who had won 92 races in Plymouths since 1960, was approached by Ford about joining the Ford team for '69. In an earth-shattering development on Nov. 25, 1968, Petty announced he would park his Plymouth and drive Fords in the upcoming season. "Ford has a vast storehouse of racing knowledge," said Petty. "Much more than Chrysler has. The name of the game is money. If I can get a better deal, I'll take it, even if it is working in a supermarket. I want to win as many races as I can and I feel like running a Ford will give me that opportunity."

Ronney Householder, director of Chrysler's racing efforts, was shocked when he got wind of Petty's announcement. "The offer from Ford must have been fantastic," said Householder. "I really didn't think Ford could afford Petty. His leaving creates a big hole in our operation." Chrysler disbanded its Plymouth effort entirely and concentrated on fielding Dodge Chargers.

Ford suffered a mild setback at the beginning of the 1969 season. NASCAR disallowed the use of the new 429-cid engine because the required 500 hadn't been installed in production cars. Even without the new engine, Richard Petty scored an easy win on Riverside's road course and LeeRoy Yarbrough drove a Junior Johnson-prepared Mercury Cyclone Spoiler to victory in the Daytona 500. Yarbrough was in his backup machine at Daytona, having crashed his primary car in practice.

On the superspeedways, Ford and Mercury were virtually unbeatable. On the big tracks hosting races of 300 miles or more, Ford tied together a 13-race winning streak. Fords took the top five spots at Atlanta, the top four at Michigan, and finished first and second in eight of the 13 victories.

Unlike today, NASCAR refrained from tinkering with the rules to maintain a level playing field. The rules were established at the beginning of the season and with rare exceptions, remained unchanged no matter what make of car was winning. Chrysler went back to the drawing board in a meager effort to compete with the Fords.

The response was the needle-nosed, high-winged Dodge Charger Daytona, a product of aerodynamicists Dick LaJoie and Bob Marcell, along with vehicle test engineer John Pointer. The car was introduced in April and 500 had to be in Dodge showrooms across the country by Sept. 1. The Dodge Daytona was scheduled to make its first NASCAR appearance at the inaugural Talladega 500 on Sept. 14, 1969.

Bill France was the mastermind behind the Talladega speedway project, an ultrafast track that would be the fastest closed course on the planet. It was a bit bigger than Daytona, a little bit wider, banked a couple degrees steeper, and much faster than its sister track in Florida. Shakedown runs indicated the 200-mph barrier was within reach.

As the new Alabama International Motor Speedway was nearing completion, a disturbing undercurrent of dissent grew within the driver ranks. NASCAR was in the midst of a popularity explosion with grand new facilities popping up all over the country. The well-financed teams and the independent privateers found expenses rising sharply, yet the posted awards at most of the tracks showed only a minor increase. For instance, at many of the 100-mile Grand Nationals, drivers finishing outside the top 22 didn't win *any* prize money. A driver could drop out early, finish 22nd and win $200. In the same event, a driver could run the entire race and finish in the top 10, yet win only $260.

In August 1969, the drivers held a secret meeting in Ann Arbor, Mich., to discuss a number of concerns. The topics of the discussion included facilities for drivers at the speedways, the lack of prize money, and the alarming speeds at the new Talladega track. The track surface at Talladega also was very bumpy, according to drivers who had conducted tire tests on the new track.

The 11 drivers who were present at the Ann Arbor meeting formed the Professional Drivers Association. Richard Petty was elected president, with Elmo Langley and Cale Yarborough as vice presidents. Drivers actively recruited other PDA members at Darlington, two weeks before the inaugural Talladega 500. Drivers were also being courted from NASCAR's lower divisions. Within a few days,

most of the NASCAR Grand National regulars had paid initiation dues of $200 to become members of the PDA.

When teams arrived at Talladega and began their initial practice runs, it was apparent the tire companies hadn't had enough time to develop a tire to withstand speeds of nearly 200 mph. Tires were shredding apart at speeds over 190.

Members of the PDA approached Bill France, asking him to postpone the 500-miler until suitable tires could be produced. France refused, telling the drivers to slow down and run a more comfortable pace. "It's like flying," said France. "If you run into bad weather, you slow down."

Different tire compounds arrived daily on chartered aircraft. After a series of tests, Firestone packed up and left the speedway. No Firestone tires would be mounted on any car in the Talladega 500. France talked Goodyear into staying, but the tire company said it wouldn't mount tires on any car that qualified above 190 mph.

On late Saturday afternoon, less than 24 hours before the scheduled start of the first Talladega 500, most of the drivers loaded up their cars and went home. The first official drivers boycott in NASCAR history had become a reality.

Sophomore driver Richard Brickhouse was offered a ride in a winged Dodge Charger Daytona owned by Ray Nichels. Brickhouse had become a PDA member at Darlington, but he withdrew from the organization the morning of the Talladega race.

Brickhouse and a dozen other Grand National drivers competed against 23 drivers from the NASCAR Grand Touring pony car division. Several mandated caution flags kept the drivers in check. Brickhouse spent most of the afternoon riding around in the 190-mph range, but did click off a couple of laps at 198 in his late-race spurt. The sandy-haired Brickhouse scampered into the lead 11 laps from the finish and won the controversial Talladega 500, an event that was run without a crash or a spin out. Dodge's first super-speedway win of the season was cloaked in controversy.

In the final months of the 1969 campaign, the PDA drivers returned to the speedway, albeit with considerable tension. Ford drivers Donnie Allison and LeeRoy Yarbrough won at Charlotte and Rockingham as Bobby Isaac won the season finale at the new Texas track in his winged Dodge.

The decade of the 1960s was the most progressive in NASCAR history. The automobiles had advanced from stock production cars to specialized mechanical creations capable of running 200 mph. Crowds had increased and new speedways were built. The entire sport was on a roll, but there were rumblings beneath the surface. Bill France was still harboring ill feelings toward the Professional Drivers Association. Tension was high and despite an encouraging outlook, NASCAR stock car racing was at a crossroads.

1960

January 31 The CBS television network sends a skeleton production crew to Daytona International Speedway to televise the pole position and compact car races during the opening of Speedweeks. Bud Palmer is the anchorman for the first live telecast of NASCAR stock cars.

February 12 Herman Beam becomes the first driver to be black-flagged in a NASCAR event at Daytona International Speedway. Race officials notice that Beam forgot to put on his helmet before the Twin 100-mile qualifying race. NASCAR officials park Beam for the remainder of the race.

February 14 Junior Johnson passes a spinning Bobby Johns with nine laps remaining and hustles to victory in the second annual Daytona 500. Driving a 1959 Chevrolet Impala, Johnson beats a record 68-car field and wins $19,600.

February 28 Young Richard Petty scores the first win of his career in the 100-mile NASCAR Grand National event at the Charlotte Fairgrounds Speedway. The 22-year-old Petty collects $800 for his first win.

March 27 Lee Petty finishes first in the controversial 100-mile race at North Wilkesboro (N.C.) Speedway. Petty bumps his way past Junior Johnson with 14 laps remaining to claim his 49th career NASCAR Grand National win. Petty is pelted with rocks and debris in victory lane. The victory makes Petty the top race winner in NASCAR history, surpassing 48-time-winner Herb Thomas.

June 12 Marvin Porter drives a Ford to victory in the 250-mile race at the new Marchbanks Speedway in Hanford, Calif. Porter leads the final 50 laps on the banked 1.4-mile oval.

June 19 Unheralded Joe Lee Johnson gallops to a four-lap victory in the inaugural World 600 at the new Charlotte Motor Speedway. Jack Smith, who had built a five-lap lead, sees his hopes dashed when a piece of debris slices a hole in his fuel tank. Six drivers, including Lee and Richard Petty, are disqualified for a variety of unapproved pit procedures.

One of the largest crashes in NASCAR history took place on Feb. 13, 1960, just after the start of the Daytona 250-mile Modified-Sportsman race. Near the conclusion of the opening lap, Dick Foley slid sideways through the fourth turn. Foley was able to right his path and continue on, but the field stacked up behind him. Thirty-seven cars became involved and 24 were eliminated. A dozen cars flipped wildly and eight drivers went to the hospital, none injured seriously. The wreck halted the race for nearly an hour, and most of the cars were left sitting in the grassy area off the fourth turn. A total of 73 cars started the race, the largest starting field in Daytona International Speedway history.

Speedy Pontiacs, including #6 Cotton Owens, #47 Jack Smith, #22 Fireball Roberts, and #3 Bobby Johns, dominated time trials and the preliminary races at Daytona in 1960. Roberts turned in the quickest qualifying speed at 151.556 mph, but Cotton Owens started on the pole by virtue of winning a 25-mile pole-position race. In the early years of Daytona International Speedway, a series of preliminary races set the field for the 500, including the front row. In the race, most of the Pontiacs experienced problems. Roberts blew an engine, Owens lost a transmission, Smith had tire problems, and Johns spun while leading on lap 192. Junior Johnson won in a year-old Chevrolet.

Fred Lorenzen, in his self-owned #28 Ford, battles Joe Weatherly's #12 Holman-Moody Ford in the early stages of the Daytona 500. Lorenzen finished eighth, catching the eye of Ralph Moody in the process. A year later, Lorenzen was signed to drive for Holman-Moody, while Weatherly moved to the Bud Moore Pontiac team. Both drivers' careers flourished with Lorenzen becoming NASCAR's superspeedway king and Weatherly winning back-to-back championships in 1962 and '63.

Junior Johnson and crew chief Ray Fox enjoy the spoils of victory lane following their upset win in the Daytona 500. The winning Chevrolet team was owned by Cleveland sportsman John Masoni, who had no idea his '59 Chevy would even be competitive. After paying Johnson, Fox, and the crew, Masoni gave the rest of the winnings to charity. "We're in this racing game for fun, not profit," said Masoni.

A crowd of 7489 witness history from the covered grandstands at Charlotte's Fairgrounds Speedway on Feb. 28. Lined up on the inside of the fourth row is young Richard Petty in a white #43 Plymouth. In his 35th start, Petty, with an assist from his father Lee, scored his first of 200 NASCAR Grand National wins. The elder Petty popped Rex White out of the way in the closing stages, allowing Richard to make the decisive pass. Richard had been flagged in first place in a July 1959 race at Atlanta, but his apparent victory was protested by second place finisher Lee Petty, who claimed he had lapped Richard. After studying the scorecards, NASCAR reversed the decision and awarded the win to Lee.

▼ Number 21 Jimmy Massey and #4 Rex White battle side-by-side on Martinsville's tight ½-mile track during the Virginia 500. Massey got a shot to drive one of the Wood Brothers Fords in the 500-lapper, and the driver from Mebane, N.C., made the most of the opportunity. Massey finished a close second to Richard Petty in the race. Glen Wood came in third in another Wood Brothers Ford. White finished fourth.

Richard Petty's blue Plymouth dashes inside the #29 Chevy of Bob Potter during the April 10 Virginia 500 at Martinsville Speedway. Petty won the 250-miler, his first of 15 wins on the track. Potter finished in 12th place.

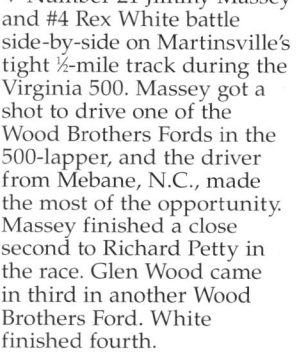

1960

July 4 Jack Smith edges Cotton Owens at the finish line to win the second annual Firecracker 250 at Daytona. Smith becomes the first driver to win on a superspeedway using radio communication with his pit crew. Crew chief Bud Moore keeps Smith abreast of pertinent information during the race.

July 31 Fireball Roberts wheels Smokey Yunick's Pontiac to victory in the Dixie 300 at the new Atlanta International Raceway. Roberts takes the lead with 12 laps to go and out-runs Cotton Owens in the final dash.

September 5 Buck Baker is declared the winner of the tragic Southern 500 at Darlington Raceway. Three men in the pits, including crew chief Paul McDuffie, are killed when Bobby Johns' Pontiac careens into the backstretch pit area. Rex White, who was originally flagged the winner, settles for second after NASCAR officials study the scorecards.

October 16 Speedy Thompson drives the Wood Brothers Ford to a big win in the National 400 at Charlotte Motor Speedway. It is the first big track win for Thompson and the Wood Brothers. Thompson takes the lead 35 laps from the finish when leader Fireball Roberts blows a tire and crashes.

October 30 Bobby Johns drives Cotton Owens' Pontiac to his first career NASCAR Grand National victory in the inaugural Atlanta 500 at Atlanta International Raceway. Rex White finishes fifth and is officially declared the 1960 NASCAR Grand National champion.

◄ Johnny Allen's Chevrolet Convertible blew a tire and sailed off the track on the 149th lap of the May 14 Rebel 300. The airborne car chopped down part of the scoring stand and landed in a mass of twisted metal outside the Darlington Raceway. Miraculously, Allen was uninjured in the horrific spill.

▼ Occupants of the scoring stand are rescued following Johnny Allen's frightful trip over the guardrail at the Rebel 300. The car struck the scoring stand, which was located on the outside of the fourth turn, destroying the steps leading from the ground to the open-air stand. Rescue personnel had to place a ladder for the scorers to use to escape the weakened structure.

▼ Lee Petty and Bobby Johns, wheeling a pair of Petty Plymouths, cut through the fourth turn during the inaugural running of the World 600 on June 19 at Charlotte Motor Speedway. The race was a survival of the fittest, as the new track, paving for which had been completed during qualifying, broke up badly during the race. The Petty Plymouths finished third, fourth, and fifth, but third- and fourth-place finishers Richard and Lee Petty were disqualified for making improper entrances to the pits. They were placed at the rear of the field, losing all money won and all championship points.

Unheralded Joe Lee Johnson, driving the #89 Chevrolet for Paul McDuffie, battles with Curtis Turner in the World 600. Turner, along with Bruton Smith, founded Charlotte Motor Speedway, but Turner's executive position didn't prevent him from continuing his racing career. Turner led for 21 laps before his Ford blew a head gasket. Johnson trailed by five laps at one point, but came back to win the race by four laps.

Charles "Reb" Wickersham campaigned a #33 Oldsmobile on part-time basis in 1960. Throughout his career, Wickersham decorated his cars with the Southern stars and bars—back before it became taboo to do such things. Wickersham is pictured here racing Jim Paschal in the Firecracker 250 at Daytona on July 4. Jack Smith won the race in a Pontiac.

Rex White

DIMINUTIVE REX WHITE, the smallest man (5 feet, 4 inches tall and 135 pounds) to ever wear the NASCAR championship crown, looked more like comedian George Gobel than a race car driver.

He didn't look like a man who could wrestle a speedy automobile around NASCAR's high-banked tracks, nor should he have been one. As a child, White was stricken with polio, but the little guy with the big heart didn't let the one-time crippling disease slow him down.

At the age of 25, he went racing for the first time in the Sportsman division at West Lanham Speedway in Maryland. He was sidelined by engine problems in his initial outing, but from then on, he was a force to be reckoned with. He went on to win the Sportsman championship at the ⅕-mile high-banked oval in his rookie year.

Seemingly a natural on short tracks, White served a two-year apprenticeship on the small ovals near his home in Silver Spring, Md. In 1956, he came south, set up base in Spartanburg, S.C., and began his personal quest to win the NASCAR Grand National title. Rex Allen White started 24 races in '56 and finished in the top 10 on 14 occasions—very impressive stats for a rookie in the big leagues of stock car racing. He also finished second in the final NASCAR Short Track standings, an offspring from the NASCAR Grand Nationals.

In 1959, White missed out on the Short Track championship by just two points to Californian Marvin Porter. It was the closest championship battle in NASCAR late-model history.

In the winter of 1959, White, who ran his own operation, hired Louis Clements to be his chief mechanic and crew chief. "He's the best in the business," White said at the time. "I felt I needed a man like him to win the championship."

NASCAR Grand National Career Record 1956-1964
Starts: 233
Wins: 28
Top 5s: 110
Top 10s: 163
Poles: 36
Career Winnings: $223,514

White offered Clements an unusual deal to keep his motors humming over the long haul of the season. After expenses, White split all the profits 50/50 with Clements. White owned the car and drove it, but paid Clements an amount equal to his own salary to keep it running with the leaders and in tip-top condition.

In 1960, White won six NASCAR Grand National races and claimed the championship. His earnings, after the points fund had been paid, came to a then-record $57,524.85.

The 1961 and 1962 seasons were banner years for White, who won 15 times and finished second and fifth, respectively, in the points standings. In the '62 season finale at Atlanta International Raceway, White won the only superspeedway race of his career. Driving an underpowered Chevrolet in the days when Pontiac and Ford reigned supreme, White kept his chariot in the hunt all afternoon. With just three laps to go, he edged into the lead for the first time. He managed to hold off Joe Weatherly to snare the winner's prize of $10,315.

White's lone big-track win was also the final win of his career. Racing only part-time in 1963, he finished in the top 10 in 14 of 25 starts. White did well enough to finish ninth in the final NASCAR Grand National points standings.

In 1964, while driving a Mercury from the Bud Moore shops, White suddenly retired from NASCAR racing. The reason for his retirement remains a mystery. It is speculated that he was concerned about the escalating speeds and increasing element of danger. Nonetheless, he went out at the top of his game. In his final two starts, he finished third in Charlotte's World 600 and fifth in the Dixie 400 at Atlanta. In his final effort, he was the fastest qualifier at 146.024 mph.

White won 28 NASCAR Grand National races in his 233 career starts and retired while at his prime at age 35.

Number 87 Buck Baker and #16 Dick Joslin pair up on Daytona's high banks in the Firecracker 250. Joslin, a graduate of the Florida Modified battles, competed in the Daytona races for nearly 10 years. His biggest prize was winning the 1954 Sportsman race on the old Daytona Beach-Road course in the rain. During his brief exercise in the NASCAR Grand National ranks, Joslin recorded a pair of top-10 finishes in only 10 career starts.

Fireball Roberts participated in only nine NASCAR Grand National races during the 1960 season, bypassing the short-track events in favor of the high-dollar superspeedway races. The Pontiac driver led every race he entered, but seldom finished due to tire or mechanical failures. His speedy mount held together in the opening event at Atlanta International Raceway on July 31. Roberts rallied late in the Dixie 300, passed Cotton Owens with 12 laps to go, and rode home a winner. Roberts only other win of the year was one of the Twin 100-mile qualifiers at Daytona.

Banjo Matthews wheels his #94 Ford Starliner down the front chute at Asheville-Weaverville Speedway in the Aug. 14 Western North Carolina 500. His day ended early when mechanical problems interrupted a strong run. Matthews was one of the most accomplished Modified drivers in NASCAR history. He was also more than capable on the NASCAR Grand National tour but was constantly hounded by sour luck. He started 51 NASCAR Grand National races, yet only finished 17. He did log 13 top-10 finishes, with a career best second-place effort at Atlanta in 1962.

At the age of 46, "Pappa" Lee Petty was still one of the most prolific winners on NASCAR's Grand National trail. The unrelenting passage of time never eroded Petty's skills. In 1960, Petty won five races and finished sixth in the final NASCAR Grand National points standings. When he hung up his helmet for good in '64, he stood atop the all-time NASCAR victory list.

Bobby Johns' #5 Pontiac lies upside-down after a tragic accident in the backstretch pits during the Sept. 5 Darlington Southern 500. Johns collided with Roy Tyner, and both machines crashed into the open pit area. The crash killed two crew members on Joe Lee Johnson's team, plus one NASCAR official stationed in the pits. Buck Baker drove Jack Smith's Pontiac and won the race on three wheels, having blown a tire with just over a lap to go.

Joe Weatherly leads Rex White into the first turn at Martinsville Speedway during the Sept. 25 Old Dominion 500. Weatherly led most of the way, until White scampered into the lead with nine laps to go. White went on to claim the NASCAR Grand National championship, winning six times in 40 starts. His ascent to the pinnacle of NASCAR racing was meteoric, rising from a lightly regarded independent to a top-ranked pilot in less than two years.

Don O'Dell's Pontiac skids after delivering a solid shot to the door of Lenny Page's Thunderbird (hidden in the dust) in the National 400 at Charlotte Motor Speedway. Page was badly injured in the Oct. 16 crash. Chris Economaki, a photojournalist covering the race for *National Speed Sport News*, was credited with saving Page's life. Economaki administered emergency aid to Page until the ambulance crew arrived on the scene.

The popular Roy Tyner was a fixture on the NASCAR Grand National scene for more than a decade. A hard-working owner, driver, bookkeeper, and repair artist most of his career, Tyner competed in 311 races from 1957 to '70. He finished in the top 10 on 71 occasions. During the latter part of the '60 season, Tyner applied Kennedy-Johnson presidential stickers to his race car, reflecting his political views, not a sponsorship deal.

1960 NASCAR GRAND NATIONAL POINTS RACE

Rank	Driver	Points	Starts	Wins	Top 5	Top 10	Winnings
1	Rex White	21,164	40	6	25	35	$57,524.85
2	Richard Petty	17,228	40	3	16	30	$41,872.95
3	Bobby Johns	14,964	19	1	8	9	$46,114.92
4	Buck Baker	14,674	37	2	15	24	$38,398.31
5	Ned Jarrett	14,660	40	5	20	26	$25,437.38
6	Lee Petty	14,510	39	5	21	30	$31,282.19
7	Junior Johnson	9932	34	3	14	18	$38,989.16
8	Emanuel Zervakis	9720	14	0	2	10	$12,123.97
9	Jim Paschal	8968	10	0	3	7	$15,095.94
10	Banjo Matthews	8458	12	0	0	4	$15,616.99
11	Johnny Beauchamp	8306	11	1	3	5	$17,373.78
12	Herman Beam	7776	26	0	1	6	$5,915.94
13	Joe Lee Johnson	7352	22	1	6	8	$34,518.94
14	Jack Smith	6944	13	3	7	7	$24,720.94
15	Fred Lorenzen	6764	10	0	3	5	$9,135.94
16	Bob Welborn	6732	15	0	6	10	$6,193.96
17	Jimmy Pardue	6682	32	0	1	11	$5,609.96
18	Tom Pistone	6572	20	0	2	8	$6,713.96
19	Johnny Allen	6506	10	0	2	5	$14,788.96
20	Joe Weatherly	6380	24	3	7	11	$20,123.96
21	Doug Yates	6374	24	0	3	18	$5,205.00
22	L.D. Austin	6180	27	0	1	10	$4,785.00
23	David Pearson	5956	22	0	3	7	$5,030.00
24	Gerald Duke	5950	11	0	1	7	$5,930.00
25	Speedy Thompson	5658	9	2	4	5	$18,035.00
26	Marvin Panch	5268	11	0	0	1	$3,225.00
27	Paul Lewis	5212	22	0	0	4	$3,535.00
28	Curtis Crider	4720	24	0	0	2	$3,645.00
29	Fireball Roberts	4700	9	2	2	3	$19,895.00
30	Shorty Rollins	4374	4	0	0	1	$2,120.00
31	Possum Jones	4270	13	0	4	5	$6,330.00
32	Tiny Lund	4124	8	0	0	2	$2,440.00
33	G.C. Spencer	3986	26	0	2	6	$3,910.00
34	Larry Frank	3634	11	0	0	2	$2,440.00
35	Herb Tillman	3504	9	0	0	0	$2,605.00
36	Curtis Turner	3300	9	0	0	1	$3,220.00
37	Bunkie Blackburn	3252	20	0	1	4	$3,400.00
38	Buddy Baker	3070	15	0	0	1	$1,745.00
39	Cotton Owens	3050	14	1	5	5	$14,065.00
40	Charley Griffith	2684	5	0	0	0	$1,300.00
41	Wilbur Rakestraw	2676	12	0	0	1	$2,695.00
42	Jimmy Massey	2662	6	0	2	3	$3,310.00
43	Jimmy Thompson	2472	9	0	0	0	$1,940.00
44	Jim Reed	2340	8	0	1	1	$2,240.00
45	Jim Cook	2178	3	1	1	1	$1,600.00
46	Ernie Gahan	2080	2	0	0	0	$625.00
47	Elmo Henderson	2072	6	0	0	0	$1,425.00
48	Bob Burdick	1970	3	0	0	1	$850.00
49	Roz Howard	1810	3	0	0	2	$1,490.00
50	Bob Potter	1800	3	0	0	1	$640.00

Rex White, a pint-sized driver with a heavy right foot, took the points lead in June and never looked back as he sped to his first NASCAR Grand National championship.

White grabbed first place in the standings following the inaugural World 600 at the new Charlotte Motor Speedway, where he finished sixth. He won six races in 40 starts and finished 3936 points ahead of runner-up Richard Petty.

Petty suffered a major setback in the points race when he was disqualified at Charlotte for making an improper entrance to pit road. Petty had finished fourth in the 600-miler, worth 3520 points, but when NASCAR disqualified him, he lost all of the points he earned that day. Petty won three times during the 1960 season, including his first career win at the old Charlotte Fairgrounds in February.

The points lead changed hands seven times among five different drivers during the 1960 campaign. In addition to White and Petty, Jack Smith, Junior Johnson, and Bobby Johns all took turns leading the NASCAR standings.

1961

February 24 Fireball Roberts and Joe Weatherly share victory lane in Daytona's crash-marred Twin 100-mile qualifying races. Lee Petty is badly injured when he sails over the guardrail in the second event. Richard Petty sprains his ankle after soaring over the rail in the opening 100-miler.

February 26 Marvin Panch takes the lead 13 laps from the finish and wins the third annual Daytona 500. Panch cruises into first place when teammate Fireball Roberts blows his engine while holding a commanding lead.

March 26 Bob Burdick surprises the racing world by winning the Atlanta 500. It is Burdick's first NASCAR Grand National win.

April 9 Former USAC champion Fred Lorenzen racks up his first NASCAR win in the rain-shortened Virginia 500 at Martinsville Speedway. Only 149 of the 500 laps are completed before rain forces cancellation, but NASCAR officials decide to call the race complete and reschedule another 500-lap race at Martinsville later in April.

May 6 Newcomer Fred Lorenzen out-drives Curtis Turner in a frantic last-lap struggle to win the Rebel 300 at Darlington. Lorenzen passes Turner with just over a lap to go to take the win for the Holman-Moody Ford team.

May 28 Sophomore driver David Pearson scores his first career win in the second annual World 600 at Charlotte Motor Speedway. Pearson crosses the finish line on three wheels after blowing a tire with just over a lap to go. Pearson's victory comes in his first start with crew chief Ray Fox.

July 4 David Pearson passes Fred Lorenzen with just over a lap to go and wins Daytona's Firecracker 250. It is Pearson's second win in a row on a superspeedway. The event is taped by the ABC's *Wide World of Sports* and televised a few days later.

July 9 Fred Lorenzen drives his Ford to victory in the Festival 250 at Atlanta International Raceway. The event was added to the NASCAR schedule a week earlier when the USAC drivers pulled out of a scheduled Indy Car race at the eleventh hour.

The newfangled compact cars, America's economy road vehicles, competed in a road-course event at Daytona on Feb. 19. Here, Curtis Turner drives his #62 Ford Falcon just ahead of Ralph Moody's #12 Plymouth Valiant in the contest staged over the 3.1-mile road course. Lee Petty won in a year-old Valiant. Eighteen of the little cars started and 15 were running at the finish.

Daytona's Twin 100-mile qualifying races produced some of the most spectacular crashes in superspeedway history. In the Feb. 24, 1961, 40-lap sprint races, 16 cars were completely demolished and seven drivers were transported to area hospitals. Junior Johnson's new '61 Pontiac was involved in a late crash in the opening Twin 100. When Johnson's car hit the wall head-on, the engine was shoved back into the driver's compartment. Johnson was treated for facial injuries but was able to start a back-up car in the Daytona 500.

Lee Petty and Johnny Beauchamp, principles in the historic photo finish at the end of the inaugural Daytona 500 in 1959, were involved in a horrifying last-lap crash in the second Twin 100-miler in '61. After Beauchamp's #73 Chevrolet snagged the rear bumper of Petty's #42 Plymouth, both cars broke through the guardrail and soared out of the speedway. Petty suffered life-threatening injuries, while Beauchamp sustained less serious head injuries.

The immaculately prepared Petty Plymouths were reduced to shambles after the terrible 1961 Twin 100-mile qualifying crashes. Richard Petty's #43 car went over the wall but remained on all four wheels as it bounced down the dirt embankment. The younger Petty suffered only a cut hand in the crash. Lee Petty's car was thoroughly destroyed when it tumbled outside the speedway. The Petty team was unable to compete in the '61 Daytona 500.

◄ The fourth turn guardrail was destroyed when Petty and Beauchamp sailed out of the Daytona International Speedway. The accident occurred in the final lap of Friday's second Twin 100-mile qualifying race. Speedway crews were able to replace the broken steel barrier in time for the Modified-Sportsman race to take place the following day.

Defending NASCAR Grand National champion Rex White, in the #4 Chevrolet, passes Tim Flock's #83 Ford in the early laps of the Feb. 26 Daytona 500. Flock was driving a Ford owned by Texan Jack Meeks in one of his final NASCAR Grand National starts. Flock finished 24th in the 58-car field, while White ran 12th in his self-owned Chevy.

Ned Jarrett races in close quarters with teammate Johnny Allen in the Daytona 500. Jarrett and Allen, along with "Tiger" Tom Pistone, were all members of the Chevrolet factory team under the guise of Bee Gee Holloway's "independent" operation. Holloway had catchy nicknames for his three teams. Jarrett was in the Dash-Dash-Dash Corp. car, Allen drove the Win-Win-Win Corp. Chevy, and Pistone piloted the Go-Go-Go Corp. car. Jarrett finished seventh in the Daytona 500 and Allen finished eighth for the Chevrolet team. Pistone came in 10th.

Part-time competitor Marvin Panch drove Smokey Yunick's year-old Pontiac in the Daytona 500. The car was fast in 1960 NASCAR Grand National competition but couldn't match the new '61 models. Panch managed to climb to second place in the late stages, running nearly a lap behind Fireball Roberts' '61 Pontiac. Roberts, the lead driver on Yunick's team, blew an engine with 13 laps remaining, allowing Panch to take the lead. Panch went on to score a 16-second win over Joe Weatherly. The win was Panch's first since '57 when he was a member of the Ford factory team.

1961

July 29 Jack Smith and Johnny Allen team up to win the Volunteer 500 at Bristol International Speedway. Allen relieves Smith on the 292nd lap and speeds to victory in the first NASCAR Grand National event on the ½-mile oval.

August 8 Curtis Turner announces that "most of the NASCAR drivers" have joined the Teamsters Union and the Federation of Professional Athletes. NASCAR president Bill France says, "No known union member can compete in a NASCAR race, and I'll use a pistol to enforce it."

August 11 Fireball Roberts withdraws from the Teamsters Union. "The more I thought about it [joining the union], the more I realized that we could possibly accomplish more harm than good for racing." Roberts is reinstated by NASCAR upon his resignation. Rex White and Ned Jarrett also submit resignations and are permitted to resume racing.

August 13 Junior Johnson is declared the winner of the shortened Western North Carolina 500 at Asheville-Weaverville Speedway. The race is halted after 258 laps due to a deteriorating track. About 4000 angry spectators create a mob scene and hold the drivers and team owners hostage in the infield for nearly four hours.

August 15 NASCAR president Bill France bans Curtis Turner and Tim Flock "for life" from all NASCAR racing. Turner and Flock are the only two drivers who refuse to abandon the Teamsters Union project.

September 4 Rookie Nelson Stacy becomes the 19th different winner of the season by passing Marvin Panch with seven laps remaining to win the storied Southern 500 at Darlington.

September 17 David Pearson takes the lead on the final lap and wins his third superspeedway race of the year in the Dixie 400 at Atlanta.

October 29 Joe Weatherly dominates the season finale at Orange Speedway in Hillsboro, N.C., for his ninth win of the season. Ned Jarrett, winner of only one race during the season, is declared the NASCAR Grand National champion. Jarrett beats seven-time winner Rex White by 830 points.

Bobby Johns' Ford slams into the inside guardrail following a spin in the March 26 Atlanta 500. Bob Burdick, in the #53 Pontiac, leads a pack of cars past Johns. Burdick was the surprise winner of the second annual Atlanta 500. He drove an unsponsored Pontiac with a borrowed rear end, used tires, and an inexperienced pit crew.

Most of the NASCAR Grand National teams used flat-bed trailers to haul their cars from track to track in the early 1960s. All of the spare parts of Jimmy Pardue's Chevrolet team were crammed into the back of a conventional pickup truck. With modest sponsorship from Fred Gaddy Leasing Co. in North Wilkesboro, Pardue was able to make 44 races in '61, finishing in the top 10 in 16 events. Pardue finished 11th in the final NASCAR Grand National points standings.

Number 97 Harry Leake, #86 Buck Baker, and #54 Jimmy Pardue race through a turn at Hillsboro's Orange Speedway on April 2. Baker finished third in his Chrysler, while Pardue and Leake placed sixth and 11th, respectively, in their Chevrolets.

Emanuel Zervakis, nicknamed the "Golden Greek," was a stout competitor during the 1961 NASCAR Grand National season. Driving a Chevrolet owned by Monroe Shook, Zervakis won two short-track races and finished third in the final points standings. Here, Zervakis races in close quarters with Glen Wood at Bowman Gray Stadium.

Bowman Gray Stadium's flat ¼-mile paved oval hosted 29 NASCAR Grand National races from 1958 to '71. Rex White stands as the all-time NASCAR Grand National race winner at Bowman Gray with six victories. White won the April 3, 1961, event, beating a field that included #35 E.J. Trivette, #85 Emanuel Zervakis, #11 Ned Jarrett, and Tommy Irwin's white Thunderbird.

NASCAR folded its Convertible division after the 1959 season, but the ragtops continued to perform in Darlington's annual Rebel 300. Here, Curtis Turner leads Fred Lorenzen in the closing laps of the May 6, 1961, Rebel 300. In the final laps, Lorenzen faked a pass to the high-side, then swooped low to steal the win. After the race, Turner hit Lorenzen's bumper in frustration.

Fred Lorenzen joined the Holman-Moody team in 1961 after struggling to make ends meet with his own independent operation. Lorenzen was an instant hit, winning at Martinsville and Darlington in two of his first five starts with the formidable Ford factory team. Joining Lorenzen in Darlington's victory lane following the Rebel 300 are crew chief Herb Nab (to Lorenzen's right) and co-owner Ralph Moody (right). The Rebel 300 win was Lorenzen's first victory on a superspeedway.

Lee Petty was released from a Daytona Beach hospital in time to attend the July 4 Firecracker 250. Petty had been seriously injured in February when his car tumbled over the guardrail. With the aid of an aluminum walker, Petty spoke to the crowd. Pictured with Petty is Bill France (left) and famous bandleader Paul Whiteman.

Number 20 Marvin Panch, #3 David Pearson, and #76 Larry Frank whisk past Daytona's covered Campbell Grandstand during the Firecracker 250. Pearson, the sophomore sensation from Spartanburg, S.C., was taking his second ride in the potent Ray Fox-prepared Pontiac. The 1960 Rookie of the Year won Charlotte's World 600 and followed with a close victory over Fred Lorenzen in Daytona's July 4 event. Panch finished fourth and Frank ran ninth in his Ford.

Curtis Turner and the Teamsters

IN 12 SHORT YEARS, the NASCAR Grand National circuit had become a big healthy boy. From 1949 to '61, Bill France's homespun stock car racing game had grown out of its backwoods image. Gone, or declining in numbers, were the weekend racers who spent Monday through Friday hauling bathtub-brewed joy juice from one hamlet to another. No more driving the family automobile to the track, taping up the headlights, strapping the doors shut, and going racing with all the other rowdies. In the early years, stock car racers were said to be a direct reflection of the failure of the educational system.

NASCAR Grand National racing, with the help of the automotive industry, had become a thriving business, and new modern speedways were being built from Florida to California. One of the new superspeedways, Charlotte Motor Speedway, was built by NASCAR racer Curtis Turner and short-track promoter Bruton Smith.

The Charlotte Motor Speedway project was short on operating funds from the start. Construction costs greatly exceeded estimations. The 1½-mile speedway had to overcome nearly impossible odds. The ramifications of the construction problems carried into the summer of 1961, and produced the biggest challenge Bill France and NASCAR ever had to face—a vicious battle with the Teamsters Union.

Turner and Smith were booted out of the Charlotte Motor Speedway project in June 1961, the victims of a stormy board of directors meeting that left heads rolling in the management offices. Turner, in a last-ditch effort to regain control of the speedway, approached the Teamsters Union for a loan of more than $800,000. In return for the loan, Turner was asked to organize NASCAR-licensed drivers into a union called the Federation of Professional Athletes.

The purpose was to form a union of all professional drivers cutting across NASCAR, USAC, IMCA, and other boundaries. Targeted benefits were, "(1) - better purses;

> "No known Teamster member can compete in a NASCAR race, and I'll use a pistol to enforce it."
> —Bill France

(2) - pension plans; (3) - more adequate insurance coverage; (4) - a scholarship fund for children of deceased members; and (5) - upgraded facilities for drivers at the speedways, including shower areas and lounge facilities." That part of the bargain seemed pretty enticing to most of the drivers, and a majority of NASCAR Grand National joined up. What the Teamsters didn't point out to drivers was their desire to get pari-mutuel gambling approved so America could bet on the results of the races.

On Aug. 8, Turner delivered a prepared announcement: "A majority of the drivers on the Grand National Circuit have signed applications and paid initiation dues of $10 for membership in the Federation of Professional Athletes."

The proverbial mess hit the fan when Big Bill France heard the news.

"No known Teamster member can compete in a NASCAR race," France insisted. "And I'll use a pistol to enforce it." France flew to Winston-Salem, N.C., on Aug. 9 and spoke with the drivers, who were on a midsummer swing of races through the Carolinas. "Gentlemen, before I have this union stuffed down my throat, I will plow up my 2½-mile track in Daytona Beach and plant corn in the infield." France also told the drivers present that Curtis Turner, Tim Flock, and Fireball Roberts, three principle drivers who were recruiting members, "have been suspended for life for conduct detrimental to auto racing."

The NASCAR/Teamsters battle escalated to war within a matter of hours. Turner released a lengthy discourse to the FPA members and the media, detailing the urgent need for the aforementioned concerns, plus some new ones, including a greater awareness of safety precautions. "Bill France knows we are right," Turner said, "and he's already begun to make (the drivers) promises."

France countered with a media power play of his own. "A recent newspaper story suggests that I might be some rootin', hootin', shootin' cuss, waving a pistol and itching to shoot up anyone who might disagree with me," he said. "Honest, I'm nothing like that. But I am an American who believes

A packed house turned out for the inaugural NASCAR Grand National race at Bristol International Speedway on July 29. Fred Lorenzen put his #28 Ford on the pole and was among the front-runners until a rear-end gearing failure sent him to the sidelines. The first Volunteer 500 had 42 cars on the starting grid, including a triple brother act. Sherman, Dub, and Layman Utsman became the first trio of brothers to compete in a NASCAR Grand National race since the famous Flock gang in the mid 1950s.

our constitution and our laws—and that bearing of arms to repel invasion is part of our great American heritage. I am not quite sure yet if it's just plain foolishness or stupidity that makes these boys get associated with movements which can only hurt and degrade our sport and injure the people and organization that helped them grow."

France also continued to strike a chord on the evils of gambling and the havoc it would create. "I do know that organized gambling would be bad for our sport," he said. "It would spill innocent blood on our racetracks. I will fight this to the end. And with the help of all decent auto racing people and their fans, we will lick it."

The first domino tumbled in favor of France on Aug. 11, when Fireball Roberts, the most famous of all NASCAR racers, resigned from the Federation of Professional Athletes. "I drove slowly from Charlotte and took the long way by Lake Lure," said Roberts. "I thought this thing over from all sides. I'm withdrawing my support from the union and am resigning from the Federation of Professional Athletes. It's as simple as that."

"I don't know for sure what the motives of the other FPA officers are," Roberts continued. "I assume they are the same as mine. My motives were clear. I simply wanted to better the positions of race drivers, car owners, myself, and racing in general. I can see now that by affiliating the FPA with the Teamsters, we could possibly accomplish more harm than good for racing. The Teamsters people have implied that to force this issue there might be injunctions and litigations which might disrupt all racing in the South. If that happened, there might be a lot of individuals who would be hurt very badly. Personally, I could live five years without getting behind another wheel, but there are several on the racing circuit who aren't that fortunate. I feel if I do anything to hurt the least man in racing, I will be doing a disservice to my fellow drivers who have been my friends for 15 years. And I will have no part of that." Roberts was reinstated by NASCAR later that same afternoon.

> "I do know that organized gambling would be bad for our sport, it would spill innocent blood on our race tracks."
> —Bill France

Other top-ranked NASCAR drivers followed Roberts in resigning from the FPA. Rex White, the 1960 NASCAR Grand National champion, said, "Drivers have legitimate beefs and we all want a fair deal and more money. I'll admit the union offer of a retirement plan sold me, but from now on, I'll think a week before I sign anything else. We all need to get behind Bill France and decide what's good for racing."

Ned Jarrett, soon to be 1961 NASCAR champion, also resigned from the FPA. "I signed the paper, but didn't consider everything," he remarked. "A lot of us drivers have beefs, but this was going about it in the wrong way."

With virtually all of the drivers back in Bill France's fold, Curtis Turner and Tim Flock, the only two who held their positions in the union effort, weren't forgiven by Big Bill. The "life" suspensions were upheld. Turner and Flock filed a number of lawsuits, including a $300,000 suit for actual and punitive damages, along with a request for a temporary injunction.

Circuit Judge Robert E. Wingfield dismissed the temporary injunction on Jan. 13, 1962. A few days later, Turner was advised by his attorneys to drop all suits against NASCAR. The clincher was that the Teamsters union couldn't have made a loan to a company that they were attempting to organize.

Turner and Bruton Smith lost control of the Charlotte Motor Speedway and it went into bankruptcy. A new board of directors, working closely with the courts, revived and nurtured the speedway back to prosperity. Following the Teamster episode, NASCAR formed a NASCAR Grand National Advisory Board to address the drivers' grievances. The panel was made up of two members each among drivers, NASCAR executives, car owners, and promoters. "The Advisory Board will evaluate the current rule book, race entry regulations, prize money payoffs, and make a comprehensive study of pension plan possibilities, and the overall promotion of racing for the benefit of all concerned," said NASCAR executive manager Pat Purcell.

Big Bill France and NASCAR had prevailed in the ultimate challenge—a battle with the Teamsters Union.

1961

◄ About 4000 fans remain on the grounds after the Aug. 13 Western North Carolina 500 at Asheville-Weaverville Speedway. The scheduled 500-lapper was flagged to a halt after 258 laps due to a disintegrating track surface. Junior Johnson was declared the winner. Nearly half the fans refused to leave, and a handful began rioting. All teams were held hostage in the infield. One person, acting as a mediator between the teams and the mob, was thrown into a lake. Pop Eargle, a giant of a man and Bud Moore crew member, whacked one of the mob leaders over the head with a 2×4. A few minutes later, the teams were permitted to leave and a full-scale riot was averted.

▼ Junior Johnson and Banjo Matthews sit on the front row for the start of the Oct. 1 Wilkes 200 at North Wilkesboro Speedway. Rex White, who started third, drove his Chevrolet to victory, leading the final 201 laps of the 200-mile race. The Bud Moore Pontiacs occupied the third row. Joe Weatherly and Fireball Roberts drove identical cars in the race. Roberts finished second to White, while Weatherly came home eighth. Pole-sitter Johnson led 118 laps and finished fourth.

Wendell Scott's #34 Chevrolet chases Rex White in the Wilkes 200. Scott, a rookie in 1961, finished 13th in the event. Scott should have been NASCAR's Rookie of the Year. The Danville, Va., freshman recorded five top-10 finishes in 23 starts, but the award went to Woodie Wilson, who only started five races and had a single top-10 finish.

Joe Weatherly stands in victory lane following his Oct. 29 win in the 150-mile NASCAR Grand National event at Hillsboro, N.C. To his left is Linda Vaughn, who was Miss Pontiac prior to her role as Miss Hurst Golden Shifter. Weatherly capped a successful first year with team owner Bud Moore (pictured over Weatherly's right shoulder), winning more races than any other team.

Number 8 Joe Weatherly and #4 Rex White started on the front row in the NASCAR Grand National finale at Hillsboro, N.C.'s Orange Speedway. Weatherly, driving Bud Moore's Pontiac, led all but one lap in a dominating performance. White finished second. Weatherly enjoyed a sparkling campaign, winning nine races in just 25 starts and finishing fourth in the points race.

1961 NASCAR GRAND NATIONAL POINTS RACE

Rank	Driver	Points	Starts	Wins	Top 5	Top 10	Winnings
1	Ned Jarrett	27,272	46	1	23	34	$41,055.90
2	Rex White	26,442	47	7	29	38	$56,394.60
3	Emanuel Zervakis	22,312	38	2	19	28	$27,280.65
4	Joe Weatherly	17,894	25	9	14	18	$47,078.36
5	Fireball Roberts	17,600	22	2	13	14	$50,266.09
6	Junior Johnson	17,178	41	7	16	22	$28,540.44
7	Jack Smith	15,186	25	2	10	14	$21,409.81
8	Richard Petty	14,984	42	2	18	23	$25,238.52
9	Jim Paschal	13,922	23	2	12	16	$18,099.91
10	Buck Baker	13,746	42	1	11	15	$13,696.91
11	Jimmy Pardue	13,408	44	0	3	16	$10,561.91
12	Johnny Allen	13,114	22	0	3	11	$13,126.91
13	David Pearson	13,088	19	3	7	8	$51,910.21
14	Bob Welborn	12,570	14	0	3	7	$13,486.91
15	Herman Beam	11,382	41	0	1	14	$9391.91
16	Nelson Stacy	10,436	15	1	4	8	$27,607.94
17	Ralph Earnhardt	10,182	8	0	2	5	$11,472.94
18	Marvin Panch	9392	9	1	3	6	$30,477.94
19	Fred Lorenzen	9316	15	3	6	6	$30,394.94
20	G.C. Spencer	9128	31	0	3	18	$7362.94
21	Curtis Crider	8414	41	0	1	2	$7420.00
22	Cotton Owens	8032	17	4	11	11	$11,560.00
23	Tiny Lund	7740	10	0	0	2	$5545.00
24	Bobby Johns	7590	14	0	1	3	$5010.00
25	L.D. Austin	7306	20	0	0	8	$4530.00
26	Tommy Irwin	7300	26	0	3	8	$7170.00
27	Doug Yates	5878	32	0	2	10	$1090.00
28	Paul Lewis	5712	21	0	0	5	$4095.00
29	Bob Barron	5412	31	0	0	5	$3725.00
30	Elmo Langley	5376	15	0	1	5	$3530.00
31	Banjo Matthews	4924	14	0	1	3	$5560.00
32	Wendell Scott	4726	23	0	0	5	$3240.00
33	Jim Reed	4705	8	0	3	3	$3350.00
34	Fred Harb	4526	27	0	1	8	$3460.00
35	Darel Dieringer	4416	7	0	1	2	$3150.00
36	Bob Burdick	4382	5	1	2	3	$18,750.00
37	Lee Reitzel	4380	17	0	0	3	$2910.00
38	Tom Pistone	3766	4	0	0	3	$1050.00
39	Buddy Baker	3668	14	0	1	3	$4965.00
40	Roscoe Thompson	3602	6	0	0	2	$2535.00
41	Woodie Wilson	3580	5	0	0	1	$2625.00
42	Larry Frank	3162	8	0	0	1	$2380.00
43	Larry Thomas	3140	14	0	0	4	$2015.00
44	Harry Leake	3092	15	0	0	7	$2000.00
45	Paul Goldsmith	2930	2	0	1	2	$6050.00
46	Joe Lee Johnson	2700	9	0	0	3	$2615.00
47	Bill Morgan	2430	5	0	0	1	$1900.00
48	T.C. Hunt	2430	7	0	0	0	$2750.00
49	Marvin Porter	2326	8	0	1	1	$2070.00
50	Joe Eubanks	2320	2	0	0	0	$1475.00

Ned Jarrett won only one race during the 1961 season, a 100-miler at Birmingham in June, but it was good enough to walk away with the NASCAR Grand National championship.

Jarrett and 1960 champion Rex White engaged in a tight duel throughout the summer for top honors. Jarrett took the points lead after the 34th race of the season at Columbia, S.C., and led the rest of the way. Jarrett finished 830 points ahead of White at the conclusion of the 52-race season.

White won seven races and logged 38 top-10 finishes in 47 starts, while Jarrett had 34 top-10 finishes in 46 starts. The points lead changed hands seven times among five drivers during the season.

Emanuel Zervakis placed third in the final standings. Nine-time winner Joe Weatherly was fourth, and two-time winner Fireball Roberts finished fifth. Junior Johnson, who posted seven wins in 40 starts, came in sixth in the final tally.

1962

February 18 Fireball Roberts leads 144 of the 200 laps in his overwhelming triumph in the fourth annual Daytona 500. Roberts caps off a perfect Speedweeks, winning the American Challenge invitational event for winners of 1961 events, the pole position for the 500, the Twin 100-mile qualifier, and the Daytona 500. Richard Petty, who finishes second, protests Roberts' win, claiming the Yunick team used more than six pit crewmen during the race. Roberts' win is upheld three days later.

May 4 Jimmy Pardue rallies in the late stages, passes Rex White, and motors to victory in the 66.7-mile event at Richmond's Southside Speedway. Pardue pockets only $550 for his first NASCAR Grand National victory.

May 27 Nelson Stacy, driving a Ford, overtakes David Pearson with eight laps to go and scores a big victory in the third annual World 600 at Charlotte Motor Speedway. Pearson is headed for his second straight 600 win when the engine in his Pontiac blows in the final laps.

June 11 Ford Motor Co. announces that it will actively support selected NASCAR Grand National racing teams, breaking from the 1957 resolution established by the American Manufacturers Association.

June 16 Veteran driver Johnny Allen scores his first career NASCAR Grand National victory in the 50-mile race at Bowman Gray Stadium in Winston-Salem. Allen edges Rex White by six inches, then crashes over the wall after taking the checkered flag. There is more damage to Allen's Pontiac than the winner's prize of $580 will cover.

July 4 Fireball Roberts continues his mastery of Daytona International Speedway by winning the Firecracker 250. Speedway officials announce the July 1963 race will be lengthened to 400 miles.

July 20 Joe Weatherly captures the 100-mile Grand National at Savannah Speedway. African-American driver Wendell Scott earns his first career pole position in qualifications and finishes eighth.

The father and son team of Lee and Richard Petty pose beside their 1962 Plymouths during Daytona's Speedweeks. Lee had recovered from his nasty spill a year earlier, but decided against competing in the '62 Daytona events. Bunkie Blackburn was given the assignment to drive the #42 Plymouth in the Twin 100-miler and the Daytona 500. Richard finished a surprising second in the 500, while Blackburn brought Lee's car home 13th.

Veteran West Coast racer Bill Amick landed the Wood Brothers ride for the Feb. 18 Daytona 500. The coveted assignment was short-lived as Amick crashed and flipped the car in a practice session. The Wood Brothers didn't have a backup car ready to run, so the formidable team had to forego NASCAR's premier event.

Marvin Panch, winner of the 1961 Daytona 500, hooked up with Dodge team owner Bob Osiecki for the '62 Speedweeks races. The Chrysler effort lagged far behind General Motors and Ford in '62, and Panch's Dodge wasn't capable of running with the leaders. Panch started 37th in the 48-car field and bowed out early with differential problems.

Number 22 Fireball Roberts provides a draft for #43 Richard Petty during the Daytona 500. Petty's Plymouth was no match for Roberts' fleet Pontiac, but he made the most of the suction created by the draft and rode home to a second-place finish. Roberts won easily, leading 144 of the 200 laps. Billy Wade's #01 Ford came home 18th.

Glen "Fireball" Roberts swept all of Daytona's Speedweeks offerings in 1962, winning the Race of Champions, the Pole Position race, the 100-mile qualifier, and the Daytona 500. It was the first Daytona 500 the hometown driver finished. In '59, '60, and '61, Roberts had led but mechanical problems always intervened. Team owner Smokey Yunick parked the winning Pontiac after the 500, and Roberts joined the Banjo Matthews Pontiac effort for the remainder of the season.

Fred Lorenzen whips his #28 Ford around Buck Baker's Chrysler in the April 15 Gwyn Staley Memorial 400 at North Wilkesboro Speedway. Lorenzen finished a close second to Richard Petty. Baker started deep in the field, but a steady drive netted the former NASCAR champion a sixth-place finish.

Number 21 Marvin Panch and #72 Bobby Johns buzz past Maurice Petty's #41 Plymouth during Bristol's Volunteer 500 on April 29. Johns went on to win the 500-lapper, his second NASCAR Grand National victory. Petty made a brief stab at a driving career, running 26 NASCAR Grand National races from 1960 to '64. While he did record 16 top-10 finishes, Petty preferred the role of engine builder and crew chief. He placed 21st in the 500-lapper at Bristol.

1962

August 21 Richard Petty wins the 100-mile race at Spartanburg's Hub City Speedway. It is the sixth consecutive victory for the Petty Enterprises Plymouth team. Teammate Jim Paschal has won two of the races, while Richard Petty has bagged four wins during the streak.

September 3 Larry Frank is declared the winner of the Southern 500 almost five hours after the checkered flag dropped in the Labor Day event. Junior Johnson had been flagged the winner, but after a check of the scorecards, Frank is given credit for his first NASCAR Grand National win.

September 16 Fred Lorenzen drives a Ford owned by 19-year-old Mamie Reynolds to victory in the 100-mile NASCAR Grand National event at Augusta Speedway in Georgia. Reynolds is the daughter of U.S. Senator Robert R. Reynolds, and is the first female car owner to win a race.

September 23 Nelson Stacy steers clear of mechanical mayhem to win the Old Dominion 500 at Martinsville. Fireball Roberts and Fred Lorenzen provided fireworks while battling for the lead in the early stages. Lorenzen had bumped Roberts several times until, finally, Fireball jammed on the brakes. Lorenzen hit Roberts at top speed and retired with a broken radiator.

October 28 Rex White drives his Chevrolet into the lead three laps from the finish and nips Joe Weatherly in a frantic duel to win the Dixie 400 at Atlanta. The win is White's first on a superspeedway. Weatherly wraps up his first NASCAR Grand National championship in the season finale.

The Convertible cars made their final NASCAR appearance at the May 12, 1962, Rebel 300 at Darlington Raceway. Nelson Stacy, driving for the Holman-Moody Ford team, went into the record books as the winner of the final ragtop race. Marvin Panch finished a close second in the #21 Wood Brothers Ford. Stacy was added to the Holman-Moody Ford team in 1961 and immediately clicked off a victory in the Southern 500. In '62, Stacy won three races for Ford as Fred Lorenzen teammate, capturing wins at Darlington, Charlotte, and Martinsville.

The Cliff Stewart Pontiac team practices pit stops as a crowd gathers around to watch the exercise. The team carried sponsorship from Tarheel Speedway in Randleman, N.C., just a stone's throw down the road from the Petty Engineering shops. Jim Paschal won the June 22 race at Richmond's Southside Speedway in the Stewart car. Later in the season, Paschal joined forces with the Petty team.

Banjo Matthews leads Fireball Roberts and Bobby Johns in the early laps of the July 4 Daytona Firecracker 250. A blown engine put Matthews out of the race while leading with 27 laps remaining. Roberts went on to win the 250-miler in a Pontiac owned by Matthews. The 1962 running of the Independence Day event was the final 250 miler. The race only took a shade over 1½ hours to run. Speedway officials tacked on another 150 miles beginning in '63.

Number 3 David Pearson, #28 Fred Lorenzen, and #47 Jack Smith speed past the front-stretch grandstands during the early stages of the Firecracker 250. Pearson, the defending champion of the race, finished in eighth place. Smith finished fourth, and Lorenzen was sidelined in a collision on the 35th lap.

Fireball Roberts, shown with race queen Patti Pennington, chats with Banjo Matthews in Daytona's victory lane after the Firecracker 250. A handheld camera captures the scene. Highlights of the race were aired on ABC's *Wide World of Sports* television program a week later.

Ralph Moody and Fred Lorenzen were at center stage when Ford Motor Co. announced it would actively support Moody's team in NASCAR Grand National racing. The automotive manufacturers officially had been out of racing since the summer of 1957, but NASCAR stock car racing was just too fertile a ground to resist. Ford's announcement of public support kicked off the most progressive period of race car development in NASCAR history.

Number 83 Worth McMillion spins his Pontiac to the inside as a pack of cars scoot past in Bristol's Southeastern 500 on July 29. Joe Weatherly, in the #8 Pontiac, managed to get by without further incident. Weatherly qualified 13th for the 250-mile race. The superstitious Weatherly convinced NASCAR and track officials to list his starting position as 12-A rather than 13th. Later that year, Weatherly balked at signing an entry blank for the 13th annual Southern 500 at Darlington. After promoter Bob Colvin changed the name to the "12th Renewal Southern 500," Weatherly gladly filed his entry.

Number 49 Bob Welborn leads #61 Sherman Utsman and #48 G.C. Spencer off the fourth turn in Bristol's Southeastern 500. Spencer was one of NASCAR's most venerable independent drivers. The Johnson City, Tenn., driver competed in 415 NASCAR Grand National events from 1958 to '77. He never won a race, but came close on many occasions. Spencer finished second seven times, the most runner-up finishes for a driver who never made the trip to victory lane.

Joe Weatherly's Pontiac is serviced by the Bud Moore pit crew in the Southeastern 500. Weatherly finished sixth and maintained his advantage in the NASCAR Grand National points race. The former Motorcycle champion captured the 1962 NASCAR championship on the strength of nine wins in 52 starts. Amazing consistency contributed to Weatherly's title run as he finished out of the top 10 only seven times.

Fireball Roberts

THE INSCRIPTION ON Glenn "Fireball" Roberts' tombstone says it all: "He brought stock car racing a freshness, distinction, a championship quality that surpassed the rewards collected by the checkered flag."

Fireball Roberts was one of NASCAR's most electrifying speed merchants in the 1950s and early '60s. As stock car racing began squeezing its way into the sports mainstream, Roberts was the most recognized name in the rough-and-tumble sport.

His nickname originates from his prowess on the pitcher's mound as a hurler for the Zellwood Mud Hens American Legion semi-pro team. His blazing fastball was more like a fireball, according to most of the hitters who faced him. He applied the same kamikaze attitude whether slinging baseballs or racing stock cars—he was wild, rambunctious, and electrifying.

Roberts began his stock car racing career in 1947. In his first couple of years, he rarely won, but gained notoriety by the way he played the game. As he gained maturity, Roberts became a consistent winner. Inspired and guided by

neighborhood idol Marshall Teague, Roberts had made great progress. A blend of bravery, lightning-quick reflexes, and precise judgment were his signatures.

He scored his first NASCAR Grand National victory on Aug. 13, 1950, at Hillsboro's Occoneechee Speedway. At the tender age of 21, Roberts spanked the field in only his third career start. While he tasted early success in NASCAR's elite stock car racing division, Roberts preferred the appealing Modified division, which had speedier cars with virtually no engine restrictions. When the auto industry shoveled millions of dollars into the NASCAR Grand Nationals, Roberts was a hot commodity.

The factory Ford team added him to its roster in 1956, and he responded with 13 wins over the next two seasons. When the factories retreated in the summer of '57, Roberts finished out the year then sold his equipment. He had no inclinations of being a team owner. For '58, Roberts accepted a ride with Frank Strickland's Chevrolet team, and won six of his 10 starts.

In 1959, Fireball teamed with Pontiac's Smokey Yunick, and the pair became the most feared team in NASCAR. A shining example of excellence, Roberts and Yunick set

LeeRoy Yarbrough spins his Chevrolet in the early stages of Bristol's Southeastern 500. The top-ranked Modified driver made sporadic appearances in the NASCAR Grand National division in 1962, learning the ropes of America's most competitive stock car racing circuit. Yarbrough was a natural talent and by the end of the decade had become one of the most accomplished superspeedway drivers in NASCAR.

Johnny Allen's burned and battered Pontiac lies upside down in a smoldering heap after his spectacular crash in the Sept. 3 Southern 500. Allen popped a tire and skidded into the guardrail. The car lurched up on its side and the fuel tank scraped along the barrier. The car burst into flames and Allen scrambled out unhurt.

dozens of speed records. Roberts was a master in qualifying, taking nine poles in 17 starts in '59 and '60. He won three races, and would have won several more if the tire companies had been able to produce a rubber compound that could've withstood his heavy right foot.

Despite being one of NASCAR's epic risk takers, Roberts possessed an intangible that many other racers lacked—intelligence. A thinking man's racer, Roberts was a master on the high-speed Daytona International Speedway, winning the summer Firecracker 250 and 400-milers three times in five years. He also captured the 1962 Daytona 500 in a Pontiac groomed by Yunick.

During the 1962 Daytona Speedweeks events, Roberts compiled a record that is unsurpassed. He won the American Challenge, an All-Star invitational event open to the previous year's race winners. Roberts beat Joe Weatherly by a half car length in the thrilling contest. Roberts followed by claiming the pole for the Daytona 500, winning his 100-mile qualifying race, and dominating the Daytona 500. He came back in July and bagged the Firecracker 250. His slate for Daytona in '62 was a portrait of perfection.

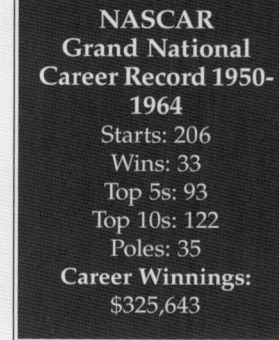

**NASCAR
Grand National
Career Record 1950-
1964**
Starts: 206
Wins: 33
Top 5s: 93
Top 10s: 122
Poles: 35
Career Winnings:
$325,643

Roberts joined the Ford team in 1963 and won four races in 20 starts, including his second triumph in the Southern 500. As a member of the Holman-Moody team, Roberts and teammate Fred Lorenzen ruled the roost.

Roberts was mulling the prospect of retirement in 1964, having just taken a prominent public relations position with the Falstaff Brewing Co. In what was scheduled to be one of his final race appearances, Roberts entered the May 24 Charlotte World 600. He wanted one last crack at Charlotte Motor Speedway, the only superspeedway in the South where he had failed to score a win.

Roberts was running with the leaders on the eighth lap when Junior Johnson and Ned Jarrett hooked bumpers and slid sideways off the second turn. Roberts looped his car to avoid a direct hit but careened into the edge of a concrete wall inside the backstretch. Roberts' Ford burst into flames and tumbled over.

Jarrett climbed out of his burning car and helped pull Roberts to safety. Critically burned, Roberts lay in a Charlotte hospital bed for 39 days before succumbing to his injuries. The life of America's top stock car driver was over at the all-too-early age of 35.

1962

Number 66 Larry Frank runs alongside #20 Emanuel Zervakis during the Southern 500. Frank had one of the quickest cars all day, but the rugged ex-Marine's effort was completely lost in a major scoring breakdown. Officials flagged Junior Johnson in first place. Lee Petty, who was directing the pits for his two-car team, filed a protest of the results. NASCAR officials studied the scorecards and several hours later properly awarded Frank his first NASCAR Grand National win. Johnson was left in second place in the official rundown although it's doubtful he finished there. Midway through the race, Johnson lost several laps after hitting the wall.

Larry Frank poses with Darlington Raceway president Bob Colvin the day after the 1962 Southern 500 Frank wasn't awarded the Southern 500 win until later that night, leaving the next day as the first chance for a photo opportunity. Frank, who drove Ratus Walters' Cafe Burgundy-sponsored Ford in '62, was a dark-horse contender throughout his NASCAR Grand National career. From 1956 to '66, he competed in 102 races at NASCAR's top level, scoring his lone victory at Darlington.

▼ Wendell Scott's well-worn Chevrolet rides in the low groove at North Wilkesboro, giving plenty of room for the faster cars to pass. Scott performed admirably while running on a shoestring budget. On many occasions, he would hop out of his car and help his understaffed pit crew change a tire. In 1962, Scott compiled a remarkable stat sheet, winning a pole at Savannah and finishing in the top 10 on 19 occasions in 41 starts.

Darel Dieringer poses with the #26 Ford built by Holman-Moody and owned by Mamie Reynolds, the 19-year-old daughter of U.S. Senator Robert R. Reynolds. Dieringer crashed the car in the Southern 500. Two weeks later, Fred Lorenzen drove it in a 100-mile NASCAR Grand National race at Augusta, Ga. Lorenzen won the event on the ½-mile dirt track, giving Reynolds a NASCAR Grand National win. Miss Reynolds became the youngest winning team owner and the first female owner to field a winning race car in NASCAR's premier stock car racing series.

Joe Weatherly and Ned Jarrett were two of the title contenders in the 1962 season. Both were on the factory payroll, though General Motors denied any open support of NASCAR stock car racing. Weatherly's car had Gillman Pontiac on the quarter panels, a Pontiac dealership in Houston, Texas. Jarrett's car was "sponsored" by Jim Rathmann Chevrolet in Melbourne, Fla., which was one of the hot spots for the delivery of newly designed racing parts from the Chevrolet factory.

1962 NASCAR GRAND NATIONAL POINTS RACE

Rank	Driver	Points	Starts	Wins	Top 5	Top 10	Winnings
1	Joe Weatherly	30,836	52	9	39	45	$70,742.10
2	Richard Petty	28,440	52	8	31	38	$60,763.30
3	Ned Jarrett	25,336	52	6	19	35	$43,443.12
4	Jack Smith	22,870	51	5	28	36	$34,747.74
5	Rex White	19,424	37	8	18	23	$36,245.36
6	Jim Paschal	18,128	39	4	17	24	$27,347.88
7	Fred Lorenzen	17,554	19	2	11	23	$46,100.00
8	Fireball Roberts	16,380	19	3	9	23	$66,151.22
9	Marvin Panch	15,138	17	0	5	8	$26,745.84
10	David Pearson	14,404	12	0	1	7	$19,031.44
11	Herman Beam	13,650	51	0	0	18	$12,570.94
12	Curtis Crider	13,050	52	0	3	18	$12,015.94
13	Buck Baker	12,838	37	0	6	14	$12,786.44
14	Larry Frank	12,814	19	1	2	8	$32,986.44
15	Bob Welborn	12,368	25	0	5	12	$10,346.44
16	George Green	12,132	46	0	1	15	$9220.96
17	Larry Thomas	11,946	37	0	3	12	$9485.96
18	Thomas Cox	11,688	42	0	3	20	$10,180.96
19	Jimmy Pardue	11,414	29	1	5	15	$12,065.96
20	Junior Johnson	11,140	23	1	7	8	$34,840.96
21	Nelson Stacy	10,934	15	3	5	7	$43,080.00
22	Wendell Scott	9906	41	0	4	19	$7133.00
23	Buddy Baker	9828	31	0	5	10	$7578.00
24	G.C. Spencer	9788	42	0	6	13	$7995.00
25	Bunkie Blackburn	8016	10	0	1	3	$5890.00
26	Johnny Allen	7602	20	1	5	8	$7230.00
27	Emanuel Zervakis	6406	11	0	0	2	$4545.00
28	Bobby Johns	5670	13	1	2	3	$15,863.00
29	Ralph Earnhardt	5472	17	0	2	6	$4545.00
30	Cotton Owens	4984	16	1	7	8	$5905.00
31	Banjo Matthews	4956	5	0	1	2	$11,375.00
32	Sherman Utsman	4896	12	0	1	4	$3580.00
33	Darel Dieringer	4548	14	0	1	3	$4880.00
34	Tiny Lund	4384	10	0	0	0	$2880.00
35	Stick Elliott	4254	21	0	0	2	$3928.00
36	LeeRoy Yarbrough	4240	12	0	1	1	$3285.00
37	Tommy Irwin	3980	20	0	2	9	$3305.00
38	Ed Livingston	3604	13	0	0	0	$2940.00
39	Fred Harb	3430	21	0	0	3	$2220.00
40	Elmo Langley	2556	6	0	0	0	$1795.00
41	Bill Morton	2522	5	0	0	2	$1350.00
42	Speedy Thompson	2522	3	0	0	1	$1400.00
43	Jimmy Thompson	2346	3	0	0	0	$1650.00
44	Red Foote	2274	4	0	0	0	$1600.00
45	Ernie Gahan	2092	3	0	0	1	$725.00
46	Bill Wade	2008	4	0	0	2	$1350.00
47	Jim Cushman	1954	4	0	0	1	$850.00
48	Bill Wimble	1944	2	0	0	0	$675.00
49	Troy Ruttman	1890	1	0	1	1	$1750.00
50	Cale Yarborough	1884	8	0	0	1	$2725.00

Joe Weatherly, in his second year driving Bud Moore's Pontiacs, won the 1962 NASCAR Grand National championship. Weatherly won nine races and posted 31 top-three finishes in 52 starts in his impressive drive to the title.

Weatherly took the points lead following a runner-up finish in Charlotte's World 600 and sprinted to a 2396-point margin over Richard Petty. The Norfolk, Va., veteran won eight races on short tracks and one at Daytona in a 100-mile qualifying race. He only finished out of the top 10 in seven of his 52 starts.

The points lead swapped hands five times among three different drivers. Weatherly held the lead most of the way, relinquishing it briefly to Jack Smith for two races in May.

Petty won eight races, including three in a row, but was no match for Weatherly in the points race. Six-time winner Ned Jarrett placed third in the standings, Jack Smith finished fourth, and Rex White came in sixth.

1963

January 20 Dan Gurney outduels A.J. Foyt to win the 500-mile NASCAR Grand National race on the Riverside, Calif., road course. The race is a grueling affair that takes nearly six hours to complete.

February 22 Johnny Rutherford takes the lead with five laps remaining and wins the second Twin 100-mile qualifying race at Daytona. Rutherford becomes only the sixth driver to win in his first career NASCAR Grand National start.

February 24 DeWayne "Tiny" Lund, filling in for the injured Marvin Panch, drives the Wood Brothers Ford to victory in the Daytona 500. Lund leads a 1-2-3-4-5 sweep for the Ford nameplate. The lead changes hands five times in the final 17 laps.

March 31 Fireball Roberts outruns teammate Fred Lorenzen to win the Southeastern 500 at Bristol. Roberts' victory ride comes in his first start with the Holman-Moody Ford team.

May 11 Joe Weatherly prevails in a confusing, two-part running of the Rebel 300 at Darlington Raceway. The race is run in a doubleheader format, with Weatherly winning the opening 150-miler and Richard Petty taking the second half. A complicated points system is used to determine the race winner. Weatherly edges Fireball Roberts by 6.1 points.

June 2 Fred Lorenzen takes the lead with four laps to go and wins the World 600 at Charlotte Motor Speedway. Junior Johnson's bid for victory is foiled when he blows a tire while holding a narrow lead over Lorenzen.

July 4 Cagey Fireball Roberts swoops under Fred Lorenzen on the final lap and wins the frantic Firecracker 400 at Daytona. Roberts edges Lorenzen and Marvin Panch in a three-car finish. The lead changes hands 39 times among six drivers.

Ten days before the 1963 Daytona 500, Marvin Panch was involved in a fiery crash while testing a Maserati sports car. The car overturned, pinning Panch beneath it. Tiny Lund was one of five bystanders who ran to the aid of Panch and freed the injured driver. Facing a long recovery in a Daytona hospital, Panch asked Glen Wood, owner of the car he was scheduled to drive, to put Lund in the potent Ford for the Daytona 500. Lund responded with a brilliant Cinderella victory.

Versatile Paul Goldsmith, winner of the final NASCAR Grand National race on the old Daytona Beach-Road course, entered the Feb. 24 Daytona 500 with a Ray Nichels-prepared Pontiac. Goldsmith was consistently quick during the Speedweeks activities, finishing second in his Twin 100-mile qualifier and leading the Daytona 500 until mechanical problems set in.

Although Marvin Panch suggested Tiny Lund take his place in the Daytona 500, team owner Glen Wood also had Johnny Allen's name on a short list of candidates. Lund had never won in NASCAR competition, while Allen was a highly capable driver with one victory to his credit. Glen Wood decided to go with Lund after a discussion with his brothers. They were asked the hypothetical question: "If you were in the lead late in the race, who would you rather not see in your rear view mirror?" The Wood Brothers pondered that question and agreed that Lund, known for his tenacity, would be the man other drivers would fear the most.

Stylish Sprint Car driver Johnny Rutherford made his stock car racing debut at Daytona in 1963, driving a finely tuned Smokey Yunick Chevrolet. Rutherford was the quickest qualifier and proceeded to win one of the 100-mile qualifying races. In 1963, championship points were awarded for the qualifying races, so they were counted as official NASCAR Grand National races. Rutherford is the last driver to win in his NASCAR big league debut.

Fred Lorenzen and Tiny Lund get the green flag at the start of the second Twin 100-mile qualifier at Daytona. Lorenzen led in the early stages before Johnny Rutherford took charge in the late stages. Lund, taking his first ride in the Wood Brothers Ford, finished sixth.

Rookie driver #5 Billy Wade and #6 David Pearson formed the Cotton Owens Dodge team in the Daytona 500. Pearson's car was heavily damaged in a consolation race, one of the many preliminary stock car races leading up to the Daytona 500. Back-up cars weren't permitted in 1963, and Pearson only managed to go 12 laps before he had to pull out due to severe handling problems. Wade encountered engine problems in the first 100 miles and was out of the race after 32 laps. The high hopes of the Owens Dodge team were dashed early.

1963

July 13 Glen Wood edges Ned Jarrett to win the 200-lap NASCAR Grand National race at Bowman Gray Stadium in Winston-Salem, N.C. Lee Petty, making his first start since his bad accident at Daytona in 1961, finishes a strong fourth.

July 21 Richard Petty drives his Plymouth to his first career road-course victory in the 100-mile race at Bridgehampton Race Circuit on Long Island. Petty leads all but two laps.

August 16 Junior Johnson leads from start to finish and wins the International 200 at Bowman Gray Stadium. The race is open to foreign cars, but only one makes the field—an MG that Smokey Cook drives to a 17th-place finish.

September 2 Fireball Roberts breezes into the lead in the late stages and wins the Southern 500 at Darlington. Roberts averages a record 129.784 mph in the caution-free event, the only nonstop Southern 500 in history. Third-place finisher Fred Lorenzen tops the $100,000 mark for season earnings, making him the first to reach six digits in winnings.

September 29 Marvin Panch, on the comeback trail after suffering serious injuries at Daytona in February, wheels the Wood Brothers Ford to victory in the Wilkes 250 at North Wilkesboro Speedway. Panch leads the final 49 laps to score his first win since the 1961 Daytona 500.

October 13 Junior Johnson's white #3 Chevrolet spanks the field to win the National 400 at Charlotte Motor Speedway. The victory is the seventh of the season for Johnson and team-owner Ray Fox, who have announced they will move from the Chevrolet camp to Dodge in 1964.

November 3 Darel Dieringer posts a major upset by driving his Bill Stroppe Mercury to victory in the season finale at Riverside, Calif. It is Dieringer's first NASCAR Grand National win. Joe Weatherly, who drives for nine different teams during the course of the season, is declared the NASCAR Grand National champion.

Number 21 Tiny Lund and #11 Ned Jarrett battle in close quarters in the late stages of the Daytona 500. Jarrett was forced to take on fuel with three laps to go, leaving Lund to coast home to an uncontested victory. Lund drove the entire 500 miles on one set of tires, and made one less pit stop than his rivals. The triumph was Lund's first in nine years of competing in the NASCAR Grand Nationals.

Ned Jarrett and Bobby Isaac kick up the dust in the March 10 race at Orange Speedway in Hillsboro, N.C. Jarrett and Isaac were close friends, having grown up near the Catawba River outside of Charlotte. Both drivers began their racing career at the nearby Hickory Speedway and both would eventually become NASCAR champions. Isaac was a rookie in '63, driving a Plymouth owned by Bondy Long. Two years later, Jarrett won the NASCAR Grand National championship as a member of the Long Ford team.

Hollywood starlet Jayne Mansfield attended the Hillsboro NASCAR Grand National event on March 10. She presented the winner's trophy to Junior Johnson after the race. Johnson was almost speechless in the victory lane ceremonies, though he did flash a big smile.

Herman Beam, who looked more like a chemist than a NASCAR race car driver, was nicknamed "The Turtle." Never one to display much speed, Beam relied on a consistent pace to finish races and earn enough prize money to keep his operation above water. Beam established one record that has lived in the NASCAR's record books for more than four decades. From April 30, 1961, through March 10, 1963, Beam was running at the finish in 84 consecutive starts. In the March 17, 1963, race at Atlanta, Beam's engine blew, putting him on the sidelines for the first time in nearly two years.

Number 8 Joe Weatherly leads Paul Goldsmith in the March 17 Atlanta 500. Weatherly began the year with the General Motors team, but car owner Bud Moore switched to Mercury midseason when the factory-blessed bag of GM goodies stopped coming from the Detroit headquarters. Weatherly drove for Moore in the major races, and hitchhiked his way in pick-up rides at the short tracks. Weatherly's championship run in 1963 remains the most unlikely in NASCAR history.

◄ Number 8 Joe Weatherly and #41 Jim Paschal start on the front row for the March 10 NASCAR Grand National race at Hillsboro. Twenty-three cars started the 165-lap race on the 0.9-mile dirt track. Junior Johnson, who started on the outside of the second row, drove his Chevrolet to victory. An estimated crowd of 15,000 jammed the wooden grandstands and packed the spacious infield.

▼ Fireball Roberts took his first ride in the #22 Ford for the Holman-Moody team in the March 31 Bristol Southeastern 500. Roberts claimed the lead with eight laps remaining and edged Fred Lorenzen's #28 Ford by a few car lengths to win. Junior Johnson placed third three laps down in his #3 Chevrolet.

1963

Number 5 Billy Wade leads #43 Richard Petty through the turn at South Boston Speedway as they pass the slower car of E.J. Trivette. Petty won the April 14 400-lap race in the foothills of Virginia. Wade went on to win the 1963 Rookie of the Year honors while driving Dodges for Cotton Owens. In '64, the Houston speedster united with the Bud Moore Mercury team and became the first driver in history to win four consecutive NASCAR Grand National events. Tragically, Wade lost his life in a tire test at Daytona in January 1965.

Junior Johnson's banged up #3 Chevrolet sits in the middle of the track after crashing out of the April 28 Gwyn Staley Memorial 400 at North Wilkesboro. Johnson's engine blew, causing him to lose control. The car took out nearly 20 feet of wooden guardrail upon impact.

Joe Weatherly

OF THE MEN who have won the NASCAR Grand National championship, few if any were more determined than Joe Herbert Weatherly. The stubby Norfolk, Va., leadfoot succeeded in anything he tried, on two wheels or four.

Weatherly's indoctrination into the sport of speed came in motorcycle racing. After becoming one of the sport's top riders, winning the American Motorcycle Association championship twice, he looked to stock cars for his livelihood. "I like having something between my head and the ground when I crash," he reasoned.

Weatherly was the NASCAR Modified champion in 1953 and spent much of the '50s driving souped-up coupes in the bullrings. He dabbled a little in NASCAR Grand National competition while earning a living racing Modifieds. His first NASCAR Grand National start was in a Junie Donlavey-owned Hudson in the '52 Southern 500. Weatherly finished 16th in a field of 66.

From that auspicious beginning, Weatherly was soon to become one of the craftiest drivers in NASCAR. As he became a polished professional, he also became a top-ranked driver in NASCAR's Convertible division, winning a dozen races and finishing among the top five in points for three consecutive years. When the ragtop division folded, Weatherly made the full-time move to the headlining NASCAR Grand Nationals.

In 1961, the 5'7", 140-pound bundle of energy hooked up with team owner Bud Moore. The new unit hit stride immediately in their Pontiac, winning their first start in Daytona's 100-mile qualifying race. Weatherly won nine races in an abbreviated 25-race schedule and finished an amazing fourth in the final points standings. In '62, Moore was prepared to run a full schedule. Again, Weatherly won nine races and walked away with the national driving championship in his first attempt.

When General Motors sliced its racing budget in 1963, Moore was forced to cut back his schedule and forsake the 100-milers on short tracks to concentrate on the big-money superspeedway events. Without a ride for the short tracks, the gritty Weatherly improvised. He spent hours on the phone trying to line up a ride, talking back-markers out of their cars so he could drive for points.

Fireball Roberts' #22 Ford lurches sideways during the May 11 Rebel 300 at Darlington, collecting Bobby Johns' #7A Pontiac. Both drivers recovered, and Roberts went on to finish third. The race was one of the most peculiar in NASCAR history. It was run in two parts—a pair of 150-milers. Roberts finished third in both segments, but was awarded second place. Joe Weatherly was declared the winner based on his first- and second-place finishes.

The Holman-Moody pit crew services Fred Lorenzen's Ford during the June 2 World 600 at Charlotte Motor Speedway. Lorenzen won the 600-miler in the last couple of laps when a tire went flat on Junior Johnson's Chevrolet. The fair-haired Lorenzen became the first driver to win more than $100,000 in single-season winnings in 1963.

Weatherly had to "hitchhike" his way into the starting lineup in 18 races. He drove equipment far below the potential of a champion, but quitting wasn't an option. "Sometimes I would get in a car that I knew couldn't win," said Weatherly. "But I did the best I could and tried to take it easy on the fellow's equipment."

During the course of the season, Weatherly drove for nine different teams, piloting five different makes of cars. Some of the owners who helped Weatherly with a ride included Cliff Stewart, Wade Mounts, Major Melton, Fred Harb, and Pete Stewart, not exactly top-of-the-line NASCAR icons. But Weatherly drove his heart out and, incredibly, won the 1963 championship, beating young Richard Petty in a duel that went down to the final race at Riverside on Nov. 3.

Weatherly took the role of a modest champion. "My luck was better than Richard's," he said. "I had greater luck, rather than greater skill. In the first place, I was lucky to get rides when I needed them. Lots of guys in racing helped me. I don't know how to thank each and every one for their help. I tried to split up the money so they would all be satisfied."

NASCAR Grand National Career Record 1952-1964
Starts: 230
Wins: 25
Top 5s: 105
Top 10s: 153
Poles: 19
Career Winnings: $247,522

Weatherly started the 1964 NASCAR Grand National campaign with consistent finishes and was once again leading the standings when the tour headed for Riverside, Calif., in January for the fifth race of the season. Mechanical problems forced him into the pits early and he lost countless laps while repairs were being made. He was back on the track trying to gather as many points as possible when, on his 232rd mile, he crashed in the "esses" on the twisting road course. As the left front of his Mercury tagged the concrete wall, Weatherly's head flopped out the window and struck the wall. He died instantly.

Weatherly wasn't wearing a shoulder harness in his fatal crash, as NASCAR had yet to make them mandatory. "The thing I fear the most is fire," he once said. "If my car catches on fire, I can get out a lot quicker if I only have my lap belt to unfasten."

The racing fraternity mourned the loss of its two-time NASCAR Grand National champion. During his NASCAR career, Weatherly won 25 races in 230 starts. Only twice did he run the full schedule, and both times he wore the championship crown.

Johnny Allen survived this spectacular tumble outside Atlanta International Raceway in the June 30 Dixie 400. A tire blew on Allen's Ford, sending him over the guardrail. The engine was ripped from the chassis and landed more than 100 feet from the car. Miraculously, Allen only suffered a cut on his nose.

Number 22 Fireball Roberts, #28 Fred Lorenzen, and #21 Marvin Panch treated the trackside audience at Daytona to a thrilling duel in the July 4 Firecracker 400. The lead changed hands nearly every lap as each driver was trying to situate himself in second place for a final-lap slingshot. Roberts executed the strategy, and motored past Lorenzen in the final turn to win by a single car length.

As part of its heavy involvement in NASCAR stock car racing, Ford Motor Co. publicized its lofty on-track records with several full-page advertisements in national magazines. This full-page ad in *Life* magazine featured the Ford sweep in Daytona's Firecracker 400. Pictured are Fireball Roberts and Fred Lorenzen, who ran first and second in the event.

Ford's Total Performance efforts in 1963 gained big rewards on the NASCAR Grand National trail. Fred Lorenzen, Marvin Panch, and other Ford factory team drivers swept most of the season's top honors. Panch made a terrific comeback following his Daytona injuries. He competed in 12 races, winning once and never finishing out of the top 10. It rates as one of the greatest comebacks from serious injury in NASCAR history.

Fred Lorenzen and Richard Petty are on the front row for the July 21 event on the Bridgehampton, N.Y. road course. Petty raced home the winner, his first victory on a road course. Rookie Bobby Isaac had difficulty getting acclimated to the twisting road course. "I was off the track and in the woods so much that the animals were beginning to recognize me," he said.

Fireball Roberts, with mascot Johnny Reb riding the hood, pulls into victory lane following his flawless performance in the Sept. 2 Southern 500. Roberts established a new 500-mile Darlington record with a 129.784 mph triumph, besting the previous top speed of 117.96 mph. The race was run without a caution flag and trackside "experts" judged the winning speed to be unbeatable. Four years later, Richard Petty broke Roberts' record.

Junior Johnson's Ray Fox-prepared #3 Chevrolet was one of the fastest cars on the NASCAR Grand National tour in 1963, but it seldom finished. While he led 21 races in 33 starts and managed to win seven times, the mountain man suffered 21 DNFs. The pieces all held together in Charlotte's National 400 on Oct. 13 as Johnson scampered home first. Marvin Panch, in the #21 Ford, started on the pole and finished third.

1963 NASCAR GRAND NATIONAL POINTS RACE

Rank	Driver	Points	Starts	Wins	Top 5	Top 10	Winnings
1	Joe Weatherly	33,398	53	3	20	35	$74,623.76
2	Richard Petty	31,170	54	14	30	34	$55,964.00
3	Fred Lorenzen	29,684	29	6	21	23	$122,587.28
4	Ned Jarrett	27,214	53	8	32	39	$45,843.29
5	Fireball Roberts	22,642	20	4	11	14	$73,059.30
6	Jimmy Pardue	22,228	52	1	7	20	$20,358.34
7	Darel Dieringer	21,418	20	1	7	15	$29,724.50
8	David Pearson	21,156	41	0	13	19	$24,985.66
9	Rex White	20,976	25	0	5	14	$27,240.76
10	Tiny Lund	19,624	22	1	5	12	$49,396.36
11	Buck Baker	18,114	47	1	16	29	$18,615.61
12	Junior Johnson	17,720	33	7	13	14	$67,350.61
13	Marvin Panch	17,156	12	1	9	12	$39,101.61
14	Nelson Stacy	14,974	12	0	4	9	$18,265.61
15	Wendell Scott	14,814	47	0	1	15	$10,965.61
16	Billy Wade	14,646	31	0	5	15	$15,203.74
17	Curtis Crider	13,996	49	0	2	15	$11,643.74
18	G.C. Spencer	13,744	31	0	4	12	$13,513.74
19	Jim Paschal	13,456	32	5	15	18	$20,978.74
20	Bobby Isaac	12,858	27	0	3	7	$9528.74
21	Bobby Johns	12,652	12	0	3	6	$15915.00
22	Larry Thomas	11,010	32	0	6	12	$8945.00
23	Stick Elliott	9582	28	0	0	7	$6235.00
24	Jack Smith	8218	29	0	3	10	$8645.00
25	Cale Yarborough	8062	18	0	2	7	$5550.00
26	LeeRoy Yarbrough	7872	14	0	1	5	$6680.00
27	Herman Beam	7742	25	0	0	6	$5255.00
28	Larry Frank	7582	11	0	2	2	$5450.00
29	Larry Manning	6952	23	0	1	9	$5405.00
30	Ed Livingston	6818	20	0	0	1	$4930.00
31	Neil Castles	5928	28	0	2	8	$5165.00
32	Tommy Irwin	5176	7	0	2	5	$2655.00
33	Reb Wickersham	4812	14	0	0	1	$3800.00
34	Worth McMillion	4614	15	0	0	4	$3145.00
35	Bob James	4316	10	0	0	0	$3375.00
36	Roy Mayne	4188	20	0	1	4	$3490.00
37	Bob Cooper	4164	9	0	0	0	$3115.00
38	Jimmy Masset	4016	15	0	1	8	$2870.00
39	Elmo Langley	3982	11	0	1	2	$2170.00
40	Bob Welborn	3484	11	0	4	4	$4830.00
41	Fred Harb	3286	16	0	2	7	$2720.00
42	Dave MacDonald	2944	2	0	1	1	$5330.00
43	Major Melton	2806	17	0	0	0	$1910.00
44	Sal Tovella	2570	3	0	0	0	$1300.00
45	Ron Hornaday	2520	2	0	0	1	$1600.00
46	J.D. McDuffie	2498	12	0	0	3	$1620.00
47	Bob Perry	2478	5	0	0	0	$1550.00
48	Bunkie Blackburn	2454	7	0	0	1	$2525.00
49	Bill Foster	2168	10	0	0	2	$1410.00
50	Bud Harless	2156	5	0	0	1	$1550.00

Joe Weatherly authored the most unlikely championship run in NASCAR history in 1963, driving for nine different team owners. Weatherly's primary team, owned by Bud Moore, only entered selected major events, leaving Weatherly without a ride for most of the short-track races. Weatherly showed up at each track and borrowed a car in an effort to accumulate points.

Weatherly won three races in the campaign and finished 2228 points ahead of 14-time winner Richard Petty. He took the lead in the standings for keeps following a fourth-place finish in the Charlotte World 600.

Weatherly's high finishes in superspeedway races were major factors in his championship run. Under NASCAR's points system, more points were available in high-dollar events. Weatherly averaged an eighth-place finish in the 10 races on large tracks while Petty averaged a 17th-place finish.

Fred Lorenzen, the first driver to win over $100,000 in a single season, finished third in points despite missing 26 of the year's 55 races.

1964

December 1, 1963 Following a check of scorecards, Wendell Scott is declared the winner of the 100-mile NASCAR Grand National race at Jacksonville Raceway Park. Scott takes the lead with 25 laps remaining and beats runner-up Buck Baker by two laps. Although staged in December 1963, the race goes into the record books as the fourth event of the '64 season.

January 19 Dan Gurney laps the field and easily wins the Riverside 500. Joe Weatherly, two-time defending NASCAR Grand National champion, loses his life when he crashes into a concrete wall in the late stages.

February 21 Junior Johnson and Bobby Isaac win the Twin 100-mile Daytona qualifying races to kick off Speedweeks. Johnson's win is his first start in a Ray Fox Dodge. Isaac's victory in a three-abreast photo finish is his first NASCAR Grand National win.

February 23 Driving a potent Plymouth with the new Hemi engine, Richard Petty leads 184 of the 200 laps to win the Daytona 500 going away. Plymouths run 1-2-3 at the finish. The triumph is Petty's first on a superspeedway.

March 28 David Pearson wheels his Cotton Owens Dodge to victory in the 100-mile race at Greenville-Pickens Speedway. Dick Hutcherson, making his first NASCAR Grand National start, wins the pole. Hutcherson leads the first 60 laps, but his day is foiled by a wheel problem.

May 1 Hard-charging LeeRoy Yarbrough snares his first NASCAR Grand National win in the 100-mile race at Savannah Speedway. Marvin Panch finishes second as only 12 cars start the race.

May 9 Fred Lorenzen wins his fifth consecutive NASCAR Grand National start in Darlington Raceway's Rebel 300. Lorenzen outruns Holman-Moody teammate Fireball Roberts as Fords finish 1-2-3-4.

Fireball Roberts drives his Ford on Augusta International Speedway's sweeping road course during the Nov. 17, 1963, NASCAR Grand National event. The scheduled 500-miler was shortened to 417 miles because speeds on the three-mile layout were far below expected. The race took still nearly five hours to complete. Roberts led the final 11 laps and scored his 33rd career NASCAR Grand National victory. It turned out to be Roberts' final victory. He lost his life in a crash at Charlotte six months later. In an eerie twist of fate, six of the top seven finishers in the Augusta event would die within 14 months, either in a racing crash or a highway accident.

The third event of the 1964 NASCAR Grand National season took place on Dec. 1, 1963, at Jacksonville's Raceway Park. Jack Smith started on the pole in his #47 Plymouth. A scoring flap marred the 100-mile contest. Buck Baker was flagged the winner, but Wendell Scott, who started 15th, insisted he had won the race. NASCAR studied the scorecards and ruled that Scott was two laps ahead of Baker and had actually run 101 miles. Scott was declared the winner, the only African-American to win a NASCAR Grand National race so far.

Larry Thomas' Dodge lies upside-down after a hard crash in the Jacksonville NASCAR Grand National event. Thomas escaped injury, but the Wade Younts-owned Dodge suffered heavy damage. Total payoffs for short-track races in the 1960s were in the $4000 range. Thomas received only $60 in the Jacksonville race, barely enough to pay for a new tire.

Number 54 Jimmy Pardue and #26 Bobby Isaac joined the factory-backed Chrysler team in 1964. With the new Hemi engine, the Plymouths and Dodges had a clear advantage at Daytona over their Ford rivals. Pardue and Isaac were involved in a photo finish with Richard Petty at the conclusion of their Twin 100-miler. The photo-finish camera malfunctioned, and it took a couple of hours to determine that Isaac had won in the Ray Nichels Dodge.

Jim Paschal's #5 Dodge leads the #00 Ford of A.J. Foyt in the second Twin 100-mile qualifying race at Daytona on Feb. 21. Foyt finished fourth, just ahead of Paschal. Both drivers were involved in ride hopping in the 1964 NASCAR Grand National season. Paschal left the Owens operation to join Petty Enterprises shortly after Daytona, and Foyt accepted a ride with the Ray Nichels Dodge team later in the season.

Number 25 Paul Goldsmith, #43 Richard Petty, and #26 Bobby Isaac battle for the lead in the early laps of the Feb. 23 Daytona 500. Goldsmith won the pole with a record speed of 174.910 mph. Petty qualified nearly 20 mph faster than he did in 1963 when his Plymouth was equipped with a conventional Chrysler engine. Petty drove his Hemi-powered Plymouth to a lopsided victory in the 500, leading 184 of the 200 laps. Goldsmith finished third, while Isaac fell out late and was credited with a 15th-place finish.

While the Chrysler products had their own private battle for top honors in the Daytona 500, the Fords trailed far behind. Only one lap of the race was led by a Ford. Number 28 Fred Lorenzen and #29 Larry Frank drove factory-supported Ford Galaxies, but never challenged for the lead. Lorenzen departed early with an engine failure, while Frank soldiered on and finished eighth, three laps off the pace.

1964

May 24 Jim Paschal wins Charlotte's World 600 to post his first career superspeedway victory. The event is tragic, however, as NASCAR great Fireball Roberts is near death after a fiery pile-up on the eighth lap.

July 2 Fireball Roberts succumbs to burns suffered at Charlotte. It is the same day that qualifying begins for the Daytona Firecracker 400, a race that Roberts won on three occasions.

July 4 A.J. Foyt nips Bobby Isaac at the finish of Daytona's Firecracker 400. Foyt and Isaac are in Dodges prepared by Ray Nichels. Foyt and Isaac swap the lead 16 times in the final 56 laps.

July 19 Billy Wade wheels his Mercury to his fourth straight win in the 150-miler at Watkins Glen. Wade, the 1963 Rookie of the Year, is the first driver to win four consecutive NASCAR Grand National races. Fred Lorenzen won five straight starts earlier in the year, but not in consecutive races.

July 26 Fred Lorenzen, down by three laps with four laps to go, takes advantage of Richard Petty's engine failure to win the Volunteer 500 at Bristol International Speedway. Petty's car creeps to a halt on the final lap, giving Lorenzen his sixth win of the year.

September 14 Team owner Cotton Owens ends his retirement as a driver and wins the Capital City 300 at Richmond, beating his hired driver David Pearson by a full lap.

September 20 Jimmy Pardue, who ranks fourth in the points race, dies in a tire-test crash at Charlotte Motor Speedway. Pardue is the third NASCAR driver to lose his life during the 1964 season.

November 8 Ned Jarrett wins the season finale at Jacksonville, N.C. It is Jarrett's 15th win of the season. Richard Petty wraps up his first NASCAR Grand National championship. The Jacksonville event is the 62nd race of the campaign, the most races ever staged during a single NASCAR season.

Richard Petty and Miss Japan, Akiko Kajima, appear in victory lane following Petty's resounding win in the Daytona 500. Striving to give the annual Speedweeks events an international flavor, NASCAR and Daytona International Speedway president Bill France and invited the beauty queen from Japan to attend the 1964 races.

Sophomore driver Billy Wade, driving Bud Moore's #1 Mercury, runs just ahead of #25 Paul Goldsmith and #43 Richard Petty in the March 22 Southeastern 500 at Bristol International Speedway. While the Fords were spanked on the wind-whipped banks of Daytona, they rebounded nicely on the short ½-mile tracks. Fred Lorenzen won in a Ford, as Ford products took six of the top 10 places. Wade finished 10th, Goldsmith came in third, and Petty was eighth.

Fred Lorenzen scoots past an upside-down Paul Goldsmith on the 56th lap of the April 5 Atlanta 500. Goldsmith led the first 55 laps, but the right front tire on his Plymouth blew as he headed into the third turn. Tire failures plagued the race and crashes were plentiful. Only 10 cars finished. Lorenzen went on to win the race, his third consecutive victory in the spring event at Atlanta.

Number 6 David Pearson and #22 Fireball Roberts collide on the 108th lap of the Atlanta 500. Roberts was making a high-side pass on Pearson at the precise moment the right front tire on Pearson's Dodge blew. Both cars were heavily damaged, but the drivers escaped unharmed.

Richard Petty and Fred Lorenzen battle for first place in the May 9 Darlington Rebel 300. Petty and Lorenzen were the only leaders in the race. An unscheduled pit stop knocked Petty out of contention, leaving Lorenzen to win uncontested. The win was Lorenzen's fifth consecutive in NASCAR Grand National competition. After the race, Lorenzen's crew chief Herb Nab was fired by team owner John Holman for refusing to obey orders. Nab didn't tell Lorenzen to come in for a late pit stop. The strategy worked as Lorenzen won, but Holman didn't like being ignored. Nab was rehired two days later.

The right front tire of Doug Cooper's Ford peels apart on the 44th lap of the June 7 Dixie 400 at Atlanta International Raceway. Cooper ran head-on into the steel guardrail, blowing it apart on impact and tearing 30 posts supporting the rail out of the ground. It took 47 caution laps for safety workers to clean up the debris and patch up the guardrail so green-flag racing could resume.

Mercury drivers #4 Rex White and #16 Darel Dieringer run just ahead of Ned Jarrett's #11 Ford in the late stages of Atlanta's competitive Dixie 400. Twelve drivers swapped the lead 35 times. Jarrett went on to win, his first victory on a superspeedway. Dieringer finished fourth and White fifth. After the race, White, the 1960 NASCAR Grand National champion, suddenly retired.

Ned Jarrett won the Dixie 400 at Atlanta International Raceway in Bondy Long's #11 Ford. Jarrett was the top winner in NASCAR Grand National competition in 1964, winning 15 races, 13 of those coming on short tracks. He finished second to Richard Petty in the final points standings.

1964

"The speeds have gotten out of hand, I'll never run another race at Daytona until they do something about it."

—Fred Lorenzen

Fred Lorenzen's mangled Ford rests in the infield at Daytona International Speedway following a grinding crash in the 50-mile qualifying race for the Firecracker 400. A severed artery in his arm forced Lorenzen to miss the Independence Day 400-miler. From his hospital bed, Lorenzen made a plea to NASCAR officials to develop a set of rules to reduce the speeds. "The speeds have gotten out of hand," said Lorenzen. "I'll never run another race at Daytona until they do something about it."

Number 26 Bobby Isaac leads #47 A. J. Foyt in the final laps of the 1964 Firecracker 400. Following close behind are Paul Goldsmith, driving the #41 Plymouth in relief of Jim Paschal, and Buck Baker's #3 Dodge. Baker and Goldsmith are two laps off the pace, but battling for position. Foyt passed Isaac on the final lap to record his first NASCAR win, and, in the process, gave the Ray Nichels team a 1-2 finish. Baker got around Goldsmith in the last lap to nail down fourth place.

A. J. Foyt sprints toward the finish line just ahead of Bobby Isaac at the end of Daytona's Firecracker 400. Foyt was the most successful auto racer in 1964, winning the Indianapolis 500 and scoring victories in 10 of the 13 USAC Indy Car races he entered. He became the first man to win at Indy and Daytona in the same year.

Richard Petty's Plymouth sits in the pits during the final lap of the Volunteer 500 at Bristol. Petty led 442 of the 500 laps and was running away from the field until his engine blew a half mile short of the finish line. The Petty pit crew is seen looking toward the fourth turn, where Fred Lorenzen appeared moments later. Lorenzen won the race by leading only the final lap.

A near capacity crowd watches the July 26 NASCAR Grand National race at Bristol International Speedway. Neil Castles, in the #88 Chrysler, pulls to the low side to allow passing room for the leaders. Light poles can be seen at the top of the grandstand. The lights were in place for nighttime football games. Racing under the lights didn't appear at Bristol for another 20 years.

Fred Lorenzen

WHEN FRED LORENZEN was 15 years old, he had his first experience in a beefed-up stock car. He and a bunch of his buddies from Elmhurst, Ill., took an old 1937 Plymouth out to an abandoned field and cranked it around in circles. The object of this teenage prank was to see who could flip the automobile first. Lorenzen claimed he was the first to achieve the dubious goal.

The speed game was already under Lorenzen's skin, and within a few years, he was gaining a reputation around short tracks in Illinois. He made a brief stab at NASCAR racing in 1956, but his operating funds ran out after competing in just seven races. Lorenzen went back home broken but undaunted. He graduated up stock car racing's ladder and began running some USAC stock car events in the Midwest. Success came virtually overnight. Lorenzen won the USAC Stock Car championship crown in 1958 and '59. "In my best year, I won $14,000, a trophy, and a gold watch," said Lorenzen. "It was not taking me where I wanted to go."

In 1960, Lorenzen moved south and took up residence in a tiny trailer in a friend's backyard near Charlotte, N.C. He accepted a job with the famous Holman-Moody Ford team as a mechanic, but was restless in that role and quit. "I was bull-headed," said Lorenzen. "That was one of my problems. I thought I could make all the money myself by forming my own team." Lorenzen made 10 NASCAR Grand National starts in 1960, winning $9136. Near the close of the season, Lorenzen sold his car and headed back to Elmhurst. He was out of racing, hungry, disgusted, and discouraged.

On Christmas Eve 1960, Moody phoned Lorenzen and asked him if he was interested in becoming the lead driver on his team. "I was really surprised," said Lorenzen. "I couldn't imagine what I had done to impress them. I'm sure a lot of people thought they were crazy to hire me."

In his second start with the Holman-Moody team at Martinsville in 1961, Lorenzen claimed his first career

NASCAR Grand National Career Record 1956, 1960-67, 1970-72
Starts: 158
Wins: 26
Top 5s: 75
Top 10s: 84
Poles: 33
Career Winnings: $496,574

victory. He followed that up with a highly charged triumph in Darlington's Rebel 300, beating old master Curtis Turner in a late-race duel. Lorenzen went on to win three of his 15 starts in '61, then won twice in 19 races in '62.

By 1963, Ford Motor Co. was back in racing, financing a fleet of cars on the NASCAR Grand National trail. Lorenzen hit stride, winning six races in 29 starts and finishing third in the final points standings, despite starting a shade more than half the races. He amassed winnings that totaled $122,588 and became the first driver to earn more than $100,000 in a single season.

Statistically, Lorenzen's most productive season was 1964 when he won half of his 16 NASCAR Grand National starts. Mechanical problems kept him out of the hunt in the first four races of his abbreviated season. Following the Daytona 500, however, Lorenzen went on a tear, winning five straight starts. He drove his #28 Holman-Moody Ford to consecutive victories at Bristol, Atlanta, North Wilkesboro, Martinsville, and Darlington. Of the 1953 laps during that five-race stretch, Lorenzen led 1679 of them. It remains one of the most dominating performances over seven weeks in the history of NASCAR.

Lorenzen won the Daytona 500 in 1965. He made only five starts in 1967, but after compiling a career record of 26 victories in 129 starts, he suddenly retired from competition, citing ulcers and a loss of weight as reasons for the spur-of-the-moment decision. He played the stock market and remained on the sidelines until May 1970, when the itch returned and he made a comeback attempt. Although he ran up front in a number of races, some of his competitive edge had been lost. By the fall of '72, Lorenzen bowed out for the final time and headed back to Illinois.

Herb Nab, who formed a close working relationship with Lorenzen when he was his crew chief, said Fearless Freddy was one of NASCAR's best drivers ever—if not the very best. "That's the best driver there is," Nab said while pointing to Lorenzen during a lull in the garage area in 1964. "He can drive a race car better than any of the others, including Fireball Roberts. Don't let anyone tell you different."

1964

Darel Dieringer's #16 Mercury gets crossed up in front of Bobby Isaac in the early laps of the Sept. 7 Southern 500 at Darlington. Paul Goldsmith guides his #25 Plymouth to the low side to avoid a collision. Dieringer had a rough day, spinning out four times. Team owner Bud Moore finally flagged Dieringer to the pits and loaded the car on the trailer, calling it quits for the afternoon.

This aerial view shows the neatly manicured Martinsville Speedway during the Sept. 27 Old Dominion 500. Clay Earles' super little speedway has been one of the most fan-friendly facilities throughout NASCAR's history. Back in the 1960s, spectators were permitted to drive their cars into the tiny infield to enjoy the races. Big transporters used by the NASCAR teams today prevent passenger cars from occupying the infield area.

Number 28 Fred Lorenzen leads #43 Richard Petty off the fourth turn in the Old Dominion 500 at Martinsville Speedway. Lorenzen led 493 of the 500 laps and breezed to victory. Petty finished second and clinched the NASCAR Grand National championship with six races remaining. The 1964 season was the most extensive in NASCAR Grand National history, spanning 364 days and featuring 62 races.

Two movie cameras were mounted on Larry Frank's Ford in the Oct. 18 National 400 at Charlotte Motor Speedway. Frank was assigned to gather close-action racing shots for the upcoming feature-length film *Red Line 7000*. Frank had to make repeated pit stops so Paramount Pictures producer Howard Hawkes and his crew could load film into the cameras. Frank finished 122 laps behind winner Fred Lorenzen and earned only $400 for his race effort. However, Paramount paid him well for carrying the camera.

Richard Petty won his first of seven NASCAR championships in 1964. Driving the electric blue Plymouth Belvedere, Petty won nine races in 61 starts and accumulated nearly 5000 more points than runner-up Ned Jarrett. Near the end of the season, NASCAR announced new rules would be in place for '65, including outlawing the Chrysler Hemi engine and the Belvedere model. Petty and most of the other Chrysler factory team cars would withdraw from the '65 NASCAR Grand National tour in protest.

1964 NASCAR GRAND NATIONAL POINTS RACE

Rank	Driver	Points	Starts	Wins	Top 5	Top 10	Winnings
1	Richard Petty	40,252	61	9	37	43	$114,771.45
2	Ned Jarrett	34,950	59	15	40	45	$71,924.05
3	David Pearson	32,146	61	8	29	42	$45,541.65
4	Billy Wade	28,474	35	4	12	25	$36,094.58
5	Jimmy Pardue	26,570	50	0	14	24	$41,597.18
6	Curtis Crider	25,606	59	0	7	30	$22,170.46
7	Jim Paschal	25,450	22	1	10	15	$60,115.68
8	Larry Thomas	22,950	43	0	9	27	$21,225.64
9	Buck Baker	22,366	34	2	15	18	$43,780.88
10	Marvin Panch	21,480	31	3	18	21	$34,835.88
11	Darel Dieringer	19,972	27	1	6	13	$20,684.23
12	Wendell Scott	19,574	56	1	8	25	$16,494.23
13	Fred Lorenzen	18,098	16	8	10	10	$73,859.23
14	Junior Johnson	17,066	29	3	12	15	$26,974.23
15	LeeRoy Yarbrough	16,172	34	2	11	15	$16,629.23
16	Roy Tyner	13,922	46	0	0	17	$11,487.82
17	Neil Castles	13,372	58	0	1	24	$14,317.82
18	Bobby Isaac	13,252	19	1	5	7	$26,732.82
19	Cale Yarborough	12,618	24	0	2	9	$10,377.82
20	Tiny Lund	12,598	22	0	3	9	$9912.82
21	Doug Cooper	11,942	39	0	4	11	$10,445.00
22	Paul Goldsmith	11,700	14	0	3	4	$20,835.00
23	J.T. Putney	10,744	17	0	1	6	$7295.00
24	Larry Frank	10,314	12	0	0	3	$7830.00
25	Jack Anderson	10,040	31	0	1	4	$8510.00
26	G.C. Spencer	10,012	20	0	4	6	$9490.00
27	Fireball Roberts	9900	9	1	5	6	$28,345.00
28	Rex White	8222	6	0	2	3	$12,310.00
29	Dave McDonald	7650	5	0	1	3	$9195.00
30	Worth McMillion	7586	18	0	0	6	$4700.00
31	Buddy Baker	7314	33	0	3	7	$8460.00
32	Bunkie Blackburn	7264	14	0	1	4	$6630.00
33	Bill McMahon	7240	20	0	1	4	$7205.00
34	Buddy Arrington	6364	27	0	2	9	$4715.00
35	Earl Balmer	6170	10	0	2	4	$5795.00
36	Bob Derrington	5896	18	0	0	2	$2755.00
37	Bobby Johns	5436	12	0	0	2	$5700.00
38	E.J. Trivette	5118	26	0	0	3	$5495.00
39	Doug Moore	4970	24	0	0	6	$5175.00
40	Kenny Spikes	4934	6	0	0	1	$3100.00
41	Earl Brooks	4820	28	0	0	8	$3925.00
42	Elmo Langley	4400	14	0	0	5	$3905.00
43	Roy Mayne	4278	13	0	1	2	$4705.00
44	Gene Hobby	4054	18	0	0	3	$2795.00
45	Doug Yates	3778	15	0	3	7	$3290.00
46	Ralph Earnhardt	3720	11	0	1	1	$3290.00
47	Bob Cooper	3602	13	0	0	0	$3360.00
48	Joe Weatherly	3132	5	0	2	3	$5290.00
49	Sam McQuagg	2928	5	0	0	0	$1700.00
50	Bobby Keck	2754	10	0	2	5	$2850.00

Richard Petty posted nine wins, including his first superspeedway victory in the Daytona 500, and ran away with the 1964 NASCAR Grand National championship. Petty finished a staggering 5302 points ahead of runner-up Ned Jarrett, who won 15 races.

Petty took the points lead after the 25th race of the season with a runner-up finish in the World 600 at Charlotte. He continued to pad his lead during the balance of the 62-race season.

Two-time defending champion Joe Weatherly led the standings early in the season. He was the top points man entering the Riverside 500 in January (the '64 season started in November '63), but the beloved champion lost his life in a crash late in the event.

The points lead changed hands six times among four drivers in '64. Marvin Panch led from late February through late May, but fell to 10th in the final tally.

David Pearson made his first concentrated effort for the championship and finished third with eight wins. Sophomore Billy Wade came in fourth and Jimmy Pardue, who was fatally injured in September, still placed fifth in points.

1965

January 1 New NASCAR rules go into effect that eliminate the Chrysler Hemi engine and the Plymouth and Dodge models that were raced in 1964. Chrysler balks at the new rules and announces it will boycott all NASCAR races in 1965.

January 5 Billy Wade is killed during a tire test at Daytona. Wade had replaced the late Joe Weatherly on the Bud Moore Mercury team and had become the first driver to win four NASCAR Grand National events in a row.

January 17 Road-racing expert Dan Gurney wins his second straight 500-miler at Riverside International Raceway. The race is marred by the death of a 20-year-old spectator, who was crushed when a forklift overturned in the infield. Three other spectators were injured.

February 14 Fred Lorenzen wins the rain-shortened Daytona 500, finishing a lap ahead of runner-up Darel Dieringer. Fords and Mercurys take the top 13 positions as the factory Chrysler team continues its boycott.

February 27 Ned Jarrett wins the 100-mile race at Spartanburg by an incredible 22 laps. Only 16 cars start the race. Independent driver G.C. Spencer finishes second despite only completing 178 of the 200 laps.

February 28 Richard Petty loses control of his 1965 Plymouth Barracuda drag car at a dragstrip in Dallas, Ga. The car veers into a group of spectators, killing an eight-year-old boy.

April 17 Talented rookie driver Dick Hutcherson scores his first career win in the 100-mile NASCAR Grand National race at Greenville-Pickens Speedway. Hutcherson leads all but nine of the 200 laps on the ½-mile dirt track.

June 27 Cale Yarborough drives Kenny Myler's Ford to his first career NASCAR Grand National win at Valdosta, Ga. Yarborough takes the lead 18 laps from the finish when engine problems end G.C. Spencer's bid for victory.

Road-racing icon Dan Gurney wheeled the Wood Brothers #121 Ford to a victory in the Jan. 17 season-opening event at Riverside, Calif. Gurney's victory in the Motor Trend 500 was his third-straight win in the annual event on Riverside's twisting 2.7-mile road course. Gurney breezed to an easy win, leading all but 59 of the 185 laps.

Number 28 Fred Lorenzen and #27 Junior Johnson battle side-by-side in the Feb. 12 Twin 100-mile qualifier at Daytona. Lorenzen took the white flag a car length ahead of Johnson, but thought he had seen the checkered flag. He backed off and Johnson sprinted to victory.

▲ Number 27 Junior Johnson leads #28 Fred Lorenzen, #15 Earl Balmer, and #21 Marvin Panch in the early stages of the Feb. 14 Daytona 500. The starting field was comprised mostly of Ford products due to the Chrysler boycott. Nearly half the field was made up of rookies and some of the equipment fell short of first class. Fourteen cars fell out within the first six laps due to mechanical problems. Only 29 cars were still in the race with 485 miles remaining.

◄ Rookie Rod Eulenfeld lost control of his Ford in the opening lap of the Feb. 12 Twin 100-mile qualifying race at Daytona International Speedway and triggered a massive collision. Eulenfeld, who started fifth, broke loose in the fourth turn and shot up the banking into the path of #63 Jimmy Helms. Thirteen cars were demolished. Buck Baker was the only driver injured in the melee, suffering broken ribs and a busted knee cap.

Junior Johnson sprinted to a big early lead in the Daytona 500, but crashed his Ford on the 28th lap when a right front tire blew. Here, rookies #24 Sam McQuagg and #81 Don Tilley, along with sophomore #60 Doug Cooper safely pass Johnson's battered mount.

1965

July 25 Ned Jarrett edges Dick Hutcherson to win Bristol's Volunteer 500. It is the 32nd consecutive victory for Ford, an all-time NASCAR Grand National record. Richard Petty returns to NASCAR Grand National racing as NASCAR relaxes the rules against the Hemi engine on short tracks.

July 31 Following a meeting with concerned promoters, Bill France lifts the lifetime ban on Curtis Turner. Turner plans to enter selected NASCAR Grand National events for the first time since 1961.

August 14 Ned Jarrett scores his 10th win of the season in the 100-mile race at Spartanburg. Curtis Turner gets a ride in a Petty Engineering Plymouth, but crashes in practice and is unable to start.

September 6 Title-bound Ned Jarrett wins the Southern 500 at Darlington. Jarrett crosses the finish line 14 laps (19.25 miles) ahead of runner-up Buck Baker, the largest margin of victory in NASCAR Grand National history. Rookie Buren Skeen is fatally injured in a lap-three crash.

October 17 Fred Lorenzen wins at Charlotte Motor Speedway. Lorenzen outruns Dick Hutcherson, A.J. Foyt, and Curtis Turner in what is regarded as a "race for the ages." Harold Kite, the 1950 Daytona winner who was ending a nine-year retirement, loses his life in a multicar crash on lap two.

October 24 Rookie Dick Hutcherson claims his ninth win of the season at Hillsboro. Hutcherson's feat is the all-time record for race wins during a freshman campaign.

October 31 Curtis Turner returns from exile by winning the inaugural American 500 at the new North Carolina Motor Speedway. Turner wheels his Wood Brothers Ford to a narrow victory over upstart driver Cale Yarborough.

November 7 Ned Jarrett outruns Bobby Isaac to win the 100-mile race at Dog Track Speedway in Moyock, N.C. Jarrett's 13th win of the season helps him wrap up his second championship by 3034 points over Dick Hutcherson.

Neil Castles was among the few independent racers to compete with Chrysler equipment in the 1965 NASCAR Grand National campaign. Driving the #86 Plymouth, Castles competed in 51 of the 55 races and recorded 28 top-10 finishes. Castles, who began his career in 1957, finished eighth in the final NASCAR points standings.

When Chrysler pulled out of NASCAR Grand National racing in a dispute over new rules, 1964 NASCAR Grand National champion Richard Petty drove the #43 Jr. Plymouth Barracuda in drag racing events.

Dick Hutcherson, a veteran International Motorsports Contest Association driver but a rookie in NASCAR competition, joined the Holman-Moody team in 1965. Hutcherson won his first NASCAR Grand National race on April 17 at Greenville, S.C., and proceeded to rack up the most impressive rookie record in NASCAR history. Hutcherson won nine poles and nine races, and finished second to Ned Jarrett in the chase for the championship. Hutcherson's lofty achievements as a rookie haven't been approached since.

Hometown favorite Junior Johnson leads the field up the backstretch in the April 18 Gwyn Staley Memorial 400 at North Wilkesboro Speedway. The backstretch at the ⅝-mile oval contained a prominent incline, and the cars raced downhill on the frontstretch. Johnson won the 250-mile race for his third win of the season. Bobby Johns, trailing in the #7 Ford, finished second.

This aerial shows the four-year-old Bristol International Speedway in the spring of 1965. Slightly fewer than 20,000 spectators turned out for the May 2 Southeastern 500. At the time, it was a near capacity crowd. Today, the ½-mile short track has seating accommodations for nearly 160,000.

Bub Strickler climbs out of his overturned Ford after a crash in the May 8 Rebel 300 at Darlington. Strickler lost control entering the first turn, banged into the guardrail, and flipped over. The car slid on its roof for about 200 yards. One of the many rookies that year, Strickler campaigned his self-owned team on a part-time basis.

Although the Chrysler teams were on the sidelines for most of 1965, LeeRoy Yarbrough made a special run against the clock at Daytona International Speedway. Driving a supercharged Dodge Coronet prepared by Ray Fox, Yarbrough turned a lap of 181.818 mph, establishing a new closed-course record for stock cars.

1965

NASCAR president Bill France tried in vain to get Chevrolet to return to NASCAR Grand National racing in 1965. With the Hemi-powered Chryslers on the sidelines, the ground was fertile for a General Motors return. However, no factory-backed Chevrolets competed on the speedways in '65. Team owner Toy Bolton and driver Ned Setzer campaigned an independent Chevy in a number of superspeedway races. Their best finish was sixth in the May 23 World 600 at Charlotte.

Junior Johnson drove the yellow Holly Farms #27 Ford during the 1965 NASCAR Grand National season and enjoyed perhaps his finest year. He won 13 races and 10 poles in 36 starts, and led 30 races for a total of 3998 laps—all league-leading numbers. Johnson was also featured in the March 1965 issue of *Esquire* magazine, and was nicknamed the "Last American Hero" by author Tom Wolfe.

Turner Returns

IN THE SUMMER of 1961, Curtis Turner, who cofounded Charlotte Motor Speedway only to be deposed by a political power play, attempted to organize the NASCAR drivers into a union affiliated with the Teamsters. Turner's motive was to secure a loan from the Teamsters so he could regain control of his speedway. He recruited most of NASCAR Grand National racing's top drivers, but when NASCAR president Bill France fought the move, only Turner and Tim Flock stuck to their guns.

France then banned Turner and Flock from NASCAR "for life." Turner filed a lawsuit against NASCAR, but the case was thrown out of court.

Curtis Turner in 1963 USAC competition

Within just a few months, members of the motorsports press began an active campaign to get Turner reinstated. Newspapers ran editorial columns and excerpts from fan letters stating the same thing—they wanted Turner back in NASCAR's fold. France refused to budge. Most of the time, he refused to even discuss the matter.

During his suspension from NASCAR, Turner joined the rival United States Auto Club and competed in a handful of stock car events. By 1964, Turner was all but ready to toss in the towel. "I've been waiting and hoping for a long time now," Turner said in a '64 *Charlotte Observer* article. "Running USAC stocks is only costing me money and time. You make more winning one major NASCAR race than all the USAC stocks put together."

The letters in Turner's support continued to pile up on sports editors' desks across the South. Untold numbers were also mailed to NASCAR headquarters in Daytona Beach. France, a proud man, still refused to lift the ban. "The support and encouragement that fans from all over the country have given me has been one of the most gratifying things in my life. They are the only reason I've held on as long as I have," said Turner.

Curiously, the boycott by Chrysler Corp. in 1965 gave Turner one last chance return to NASCAR. With the factory Plymouths and Dodges on the sidelines, Ford drivers plucked all the big prizes. Attendance figures dropped

Curtis Turner, exiled from NASCAR competition for four years, had his lifetime ban lifted by Bill France in the summer of 1965. Turner was a quick fix for sagging attendance figures caused by the Chrysler boycott. Turner made his first start in Darlington's Southern 500 on Sept. 6, driving a big Plymouth Fury owned by Sam Fletcher. Turner qualified eighth, but fell out early with a bad wheel bearing.

Ned Jarrett drove the #11 Bondy Long Ford to the 1965 NASCAR Grand National championship. Jarrett was locked in a season-long points race with rookie Dick Hutcherson, and had to drive most of the season with painful back injuries. Jarrett suffered a severely bruised vertebra and a wrenched back in the June 19 race at Greenville, S.C. With weekly visits to the doctor, Jarrett was able to continue his quest for the title, which he won in a narrow decision over Hutcherson.

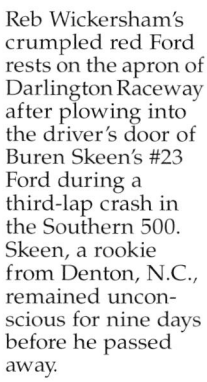

Reb Wickersham's crumpled red Ford rests on the apron of Darlington Raceway after plowing into the driver's door of Buren Skeen's #23 Ford during a third-lap crash in the Southern 500. Skeen, a rookie from Denton, N.C., remained unconscious for nine days before he passed away.

considerably, and speedway promoters weren't making financial ends meet. Atlanta International Raceway promoter Nelson Weaver delivered a message to NASCAR—he would withhold booking any NASCAR events for '66, and, in the meantime, he scheduled a USAC Indy Car race at his superspeedway.

France was in Atlanta in late July to keep an eye on the USAC development. By chance, or maybe not, he met with a group of NASCAR promoters in Atlanta that weekend. Among the heavy-hitting promoters were Richard Howard and A.C. Goines of Charlotte Motor Speedway and Darlington's Bob Colvin. The meeting was electric and tense, and during the discussion, the promoters applied additional pressure to permit Turner's return. The promoters reasoned that Turner would surely attract a good crowd.

A couple hundred miles up the road from Atlanta, Concord Speedway was staging a 100-mile dirt-track race, and Turner was among the participants. Turner was in the infield before the race, relaxing in his air-conditioned, telephone-equipped Lincoln Continental. The phone rang and Colvin delivered the message that Turner had been

NASCAR Grand National Career Record 1949-61, 1965-68
Starts: 184
Wins: 17
Top 5s: 54
Top 10s: 73
Poles: 17
Career Winnings:
$122,155

hoping to hear for four years. Pat Purcell, NASCAR's executive manager spoke briefly with Turner, assuring him that he had been reinstated by NASCAR.

Turner immediately left Concord Speedway before the race started. "This is not a NASCAR track," Turner said to a friend. "From now on, I'm legal."

France issued an official statement from Atlanta: "We feel that Curtis Turner has paid the penalty for his activities by sitting out four years of NASCAR racing. We welcome him back."

Turner's comeback mirrored a Hollywood script. In his seventh start, Turner drove a Wood Brothers Ford to victory in the inaugural American 500 at Rockingham's North Carolina Motor Speedway. Turner led 239 of the 500 laps and outran young gun Cale Yarborough to win. "There's no question about it," said Yarborough, "he can still drive a race car. He proved it out there today."

Turner competed in selected NASCAR Grand National events through 1968, then retired to attend to his timber business full time. Turner lost his life in a private plane crash in 1970 at the age of 46.

1965

"I knew I was in trouble when I saw grass, because I know there ain't no grass on a racetrack."
—Cale Yarborough

Cale Yarborough's Ford sails over the guardrail after tangling with Sam McQuagg's #24 Ford on the 119th lap of the Sept. 6 Southern 500. Yarborough tried to make a daring pass on leader McQuagg, but their fenders touched and Yarborough's Ford went airborne. The car came to rest against a telephone pole outside the track. Yarborough, who was uninjured, said, "I knew I was in trouble when I saw grass, because I know there ain't no grass on a racetrack."

Ned Jarrett takes the checkered flag at Darlington 14 laps and two car lengths ahead of runner-up Buck Baker's #86 Plymouth. Baker's car was manned by relief driver Buddy Baker. Jarrett's 19.25-mile margin of victory is the greatest in NASCAR Grand National history. Jarrett had the only factory-backed car to finish the 500-miler.

▲ This aerial photograph shows Charlotte Motor Speedway's frontstretch during the Oct. 17 National 400. Spectators faced a steep climb up a stairway to reach the grandstands. Charlotte Motor Speedway had gone into bankruptcy a year after it opened, but with new management, the 1½-mile track slowly but steadily rebounded from its financial troubles.

◄ One of the most sensational duels in NASCAR history came in the late laps of the 1965 National 400 at Charlotte Motor Speedway. Number 29 Dick Hutcherson, #28 Fred Lorenzen, and #41 Curtis Turner battled three-abreast for the lead, with A.J. Foyt also in the mix. With six laps to go, Foyt spun as he attempted to overtake Lorenzen for the lead. Hutcherson had to take evasive action and Turner was forced to spin his car to avoid hitting Foyt. Lorenzen scampered home first with Hutcherson close behind. Turner finished third after recovering from the spin.

Number 11 Ned Jarrett and Dick Hutcherson duel for the lead in the Oct. 24 race at Hillsboro's Orange Speedway. Hutcherson went on to win, his ninth victory of his rookie season. Jarrett, one of the top dirt-trackers in NASCAR, said Hutcherson was perhaps the best dirt-track racer he had ever competed against. Hutcherson established numerous rookie records in 1965.

Old pro Curtis Turner appears with Miss Firebird, Winky Louise, following his triumph in the inaugural American 500. Turner's comeback in NASCAR competition after a four-year exile proved he hadn't lost the Midas touch in NASCAR Grand National machinery. Turner took the lead from Cale Yarborough with 27 laps remaining and led the rest of the way.

1965 NASCAR GRAND NATIONAL POINTS RACE

Rank	Driver	Points	Starts	Wins	Top 5	Top 10	Winnings
1	Ned Jarrett	38,824	54	13	42	45	$93,624.40
2	Dick Hutcherson	35,790	52	9	32	37	$57,850.50
3	Darel Dieringer	24,696	35	1	10	15	$52,213.63
4	G. C. Spencer	24,314	47	0	14	25	$29,774.72
5	Marvin Panch	22,798	20	4	12	14	$64,026.29
6	Bob Derrington	21,394	51	0	3	19	$20,119.90
7	J. T. Putney	20,928	40	0	10	24	$22,328.75
8	Neil Castles	20,848	51	0	6	28	$22,328.75
9	Buddy Baker	20,672	42	0	12	17	$26,836.21
10	Cale Yarborough	20,192	46	1	13	21	$26,586.21
11	Wendell Scott	19,902	52	0	4	21	$18,638.93
12	Junior Johnson	18,486	36	13	18	19	$62,215.29
13	Fred Lorenzen	18,448	17	4	5	6	$80,614.61
14	Paul Lewis	18,118	24	0	3	13	$13,246.21
15	E. J. Trivette	13,450	39	0	0	7	$13,247.95
16	Larry Hess	13,148	10	0	0	3	$9259.14
17	Buck Baker	13,136	31	0	3	12	$21,579.14
18	Jimmy Helms	12,996	39	0	0	4	$12,049.14
19	Doug Cooper	12,920	30	0	1	9	$12,379.14
20	Bobby Johns	12,842	13	0	5	5	$24,929.14
21	Tiny Lund	12,820	30	1	8	17	$11,750.00
22	Buddy Arrington	11,744	31	0	6	9	$11,600.00
23	Earl Balmer	11,636	9	0	2	4	$19,045.00
24	Sam McQuagg	11,460	14	0	2	5	$10,555.00
25	Elmo Langley	10,982	34	0	3	9	$10,555.00
26	Henley Gray	9552	38	0	1	7	$8320.00
27	Roy Mayne	8838	14	0	1	5	$9060.00
28	Junior Spencer	8436	21	0	2	7	$9345.00
29	H. B. Bailey	7340	5	0	1	3	$5000.00
30	Wayne Smith	7326	25	0	0	2	$6790.00
31	Donald Tucker	7118	9	0	1	3	$5680.00
32	Tom Pistone	6598	33	0	4	8	$10,050.00
33	Bub Strickler	6540	9	0	0	2	$5275.00
34	Bobby Allison	6152	8	0	0	3	$4780.00
35	Jim Paschal	6046	10	0	4	4	$7805.00
36	Roy Tyner	5882	28	0	1	6	$6505.00
37	LeeRoy Yarbrough	5852	14	0	2	3	$5905.00
38	Richard Petty	5638	14	4	10	10	$16,450.00
39	Curtis Turner	5542	7	1	3	3	$17,440.00
40	David Pearson	5464	14	0	8	11	$8925.00
41	Clyde Lynn	5414	24	0	0	9	$4545.00
42	Gene Black	4970	18	0	0	4	$6080.00
43	Ned Setzer	4828	8	0	0	3	$4805.00
44	Stick Elliott	4332	15	0	2	3	$4985.00
45	Reb Wickersham	4322	7	0	0	2	$4410.00
46	Frank Warren	3814	4	0	0	1	$2880.00
47	Worth McMillion	3794	10	0	0	2	$2590.00
48	Lionel Johnson	3510	8	0	0	2	$3105.00
49	Paul "Bud" Moore	3216	14	0	3	7	$3434.00
50	Sonny Hutchins	3118	10	0	1	2	$3780.00

Veteran Ned Jarrett prevailed in a season-long struggle with rookie driver Dick Hutcherson to capture his second NASCAR Grand National championship. Jarrett and Hutcherson traded the points lead five times during the season.

Jarrett's quest for a second NASCAR title was in jeopardy when he injured his back in a race at Greenville, S.C., in June. With the aid of a back brace, Jarrett continued and managed to overtake Hutcherson in the 34th race of the season at Bristol. Jarrett won 13 races during the season, while Hutcherson set an all-time record for a freshman by winning nine events.

Hutcherson led the standings after 13 races, another rookie record.

The points lead changed hands six times among four drivers during the 55-race campaign. Junior Johnson and Darel Dieringer led briefly during the early stages. Dieringer placed third in the final tally, ahead of G. C. Spencer and Marvin Panch.

1966

February 27 Richard Petty overcomes a two-lap deficit and wins the Daytona 500 in a runaway. Petty is a full lap in front of runner-up Cale Yarborough when a thunderstorm halts the race after 198 of the scheduled 200 laps.

March 20 Sophomore driver Dick Hutcherson steers clear of a rash of crashes and wins the Southeastern 500 at Bristol by four laps. Only seven cars in the starting field of 32 are able to finish the race.

April 7 David Pearson wins the 100-mile race at Columbia, S.C., as Ford announces its factory teams will boycott the NASCAR Grand National season in a dispute over engine rules.

April 30 Richard Petty dominates the Rebel 400 at Darlington, finishing three laps ahead of runner-up Paul Goldsmith. The Ford boycott has a telling effect on the attendance as only 7000 spectators show up, plus 5000 Boy Scouts, who are admitted free.

May 13 Darel Dieringer wins an all-independent 125-mile NASCAR Grand National race at Starlite Speedway in Monroe, N.C. Promoters at the ½-mile dirt track refuse to allow any Chrysler factory entries in the wake of the Ford boycott. A crowd of just 2500 attends the event.

May 22 Marvin Panch quits the Ford camp and drives a Petty Engineering Plymouth to victory in Charlotte's World 600. Only 11 cars in the field of 44 finish the race.

June 4 Independent driver Elmo Langley steers his Ford to victory in the 100-mile NASCAR Grand National race at Spartanburg, S.C. Langley leads the final 40 laps to score his first NASCAR win. Fords lead all 200 laps on the ½-mile dirt track.

July 4 Sophomore Sam McQuagg wheels the Nichels Engineering Dodge Charger to his first career win in the Daytona Firecracker 400. McQuagg's slope-backed Dodge is equipped with a strip of aluminum on the rear deck to make the car more stable. It is the first NASCAR Grand National race to permit cars equipped with "spoilers."

David Pearson developed into one of NASCAR Grand National racing's smoothest road racers. Driving Cotton Owens' #6 Dodge, Pearson won the pole for the Jan. 23 Motor Trend 500 at Riverside International Raceway. Pearson led the race on two occasions and finished second to road-racing expert Dan Gurney.

Bobby Isaac was hired to drive Junior Johnson's #26 Ford at the beginning of the 1966 NASCAR Grand National season. Johnson had announced he was retiring as a driver at the end of the '65 season. In the '66 season opener at Augusta, Ga., Isaac qualified on the pole and finished second. After his successful debut, Isaac ran into a rash of problems, crashing the car in several races. By early summer, Johnson had released Isaac. Toward the end of the year, Johnson ended his retirement and returned to the driver's seat.

Paul Goldsmith and Earl Balmer share victory lane following the Feb. 25 Daytona Twin 100-mile qualifying races. Both Goldsmith and Balmer won their races by making a decisive last-lap pass. Goldsmith holds an edition of the *Daytona Beach Evening News*, which hit the news-stands shortly after the first race. For Balmer, it was his only NASCAR Grand National win.

Number 41 Curtis Turner leads #29 Dick Hutcherson in the early laps of the Feb. 27 Daytona 500. Both of the potent Fords were eliminated from competition with broken windshields. Newly designed tires by Firestone and Goodyear blistered and chunked badly in the 500. The flying rubber broke a number of windshields in the race. "The left rear tire on one damn Hemi Plymouth put three of our Fords out of the race," growled Turner.

◄ David Pearson, in the new slope-backed #6 Dodge Charger, leads #27 Cale Yarborough, #43 Richard Petty, and #99 Paul Goldsmith in the eighth running of the Daytona 500. The new Dodge had sleek aerodynamic features, but was an ill-handling beast on the superfast NASCAR tracks. Pearson managed to keep the car in contention and finished third. Yarborough finished second, behind Petty, who overcame tire problems and posted a one-lap victory.

Jim Paschal motors his #14 Friedkin Enterprises Plymouth under the checkered flag in the April 17 Gwyn Staley Memorial 400 at North Wilkesboro. Paschal, one of NASCAR's steadiest drivers, won by six laps over runner-up G.C. Spencer. Paschal's team, owned by Californian Tom Friedkin, was in its second year on the NASCAR trail. Friedkin and Paschal won two races in 1966.

Number 42 Marvin Panch prepares to lap #34 Wendell Scott in the May 22 World 600 at Charlotte Motor Speedway. Panch, who ignored the Ford boycott and accepted a ride in a Petty Enterprises Plymouth, led 115 of the final 121 laps and scored a two-lap victory. Scott came from the 40th starting spot to nail down a seventh-place finish.

1966

July 12 Bobby Allison wheels his lightly regarded Chevrolet to victory in the 100-mile NASCAR Grand National race at Oxford, Maine. It is Allison's first big NASCAR win and the first for the Chevrolet nameplate since Junior Johnson won at Charlotte Motor Speedway on Oct. 13, 1963.

August 7 Richard Petty edges Buddy Baker to win the Dixie 400 at Atlanta International Raceway, an event marred by controversy. Points-leader David Pearson's Dodge is ruled illegal and doesn't start the race, while the Junior Johnson Ford driven by Fred Lorenzen is permitted to compete despite unapproved aerodynamic enhancements. NASCAR president Bill France admits that "rules were bent at Atlanta," but adds he was hoping the lax rules would lure Ford drivers back into NASCAR racing.

August 18 David Pearson scores his 12th win of the season in the 100-mile race at Columbia, S.C. Curtis Turner finishes third in Junior Johnson's Ford while wearing a three-piece business suit. Turner says sponsor Holly Farms "wanted me to wear a suit, but they didn't specify what kind. So I wore my best."

September 25 Fred Lorenzen is flagged the winner of the Old Dominion 500 at Martinsville, but has his victory stripped due to an oversized fuel tank. Three days later, NASCAR reverses its decision and restores Lorenzen's victory, even though the fuel cell in his Ford held 23.1 gallons of fuel, 1.1 gallons too many. NASCAR announces that since the fuel cell in question was bought directly from a Firestone dealer, the spirit of the rules wasn't encroached.

October 30 Fred Lorenzen outruns a star-studded field to win the American 500 at Rockingham. Ned Jarrett and Junior Johnson, who have both won 50 NASCAR Grand National races, compete in their final race. Jarrett finishes third while Johnson comes home fifth.

Independent campaigner Elmo Langley scored two upset victories on short tracks in the 1966 NASCAR Grand National season. His first win came at Spartanburg, S.C., on June 4, topping a field that consisted mostly of small-budget teams. His second victory came at Manassas, Va., on July 7, a 150-miler that attracted a small trackside crowd of 1459.

Sophomore driver Sam McQuagg drove the #12 Ray Nichels Dodge Charger to an impressive victory in the July 4 Daytona Firecracker 400. The event marked the first appearance of rear deck spoilers. NASCAR permitted each team to place a small aluminum blade on the rear deck to increase stability. McQuagg led all but 34 laps and finished nearly a lap ahead of runner-up Darel Dieringer.

LeeRoy Yarbrough won the pole for the Firecracker 400 in the Jon Thorne-owned Dodge Charger. Thorne, son of Joel Thorne, who owned the 1946 Indianapolis 500-winning automobile driven by George Robson, was a NASCAR rookie team owner in 1966. Yarbrough won two poles and one race in just nine starts in his impressive rookie campaign.

Curtis Turner pits his #13 Smokey Yunick Chevrolet during the Firecracker 400. Turner enjoyed a competitive run, finishing fourth. Yunick gave Turner an ultimatum before the race. "Smokey told me to be in bed by 10:00 the night before the race," said Turner. "Said he'd call just to make sure I wasn't partying. Well, Smokey never called. I wasted a whole evening."

Bobby Allison became an immediate crowd favorite in the summer of 1966 when his little 327-cid Chevrolet started giving the General Motors fans something to cheer about. Allison drove the car to victories at Oxford, Maine; Islip, N.Y.; and Beltsville, Md. Under NASCAR's 1966 power-to-weight ratio rules, Allison's Chevy had to weigh only 3060 pounds. Cars equipped with the 426-cid Hemi engines had to tip the scales at 3997 pounds. On the short tracks, Allison's nimble and well-handling Chevy was able to run circles around most of the heavier cars.

Paul Goldsmith drives his #99 Plymouth under the checkered flag at the July 24 Volunteer 500 at Bristol International Speedway. Goldsmith won three races with the Ray Nichels Plymouth team in 1966, his first NASCAR Grand National victories since the '58 season. The veteran campaigner recorded 11 top-five finishes in 21 starts and finished fifth in the points standings.

> "I ain't never seen anybody who could drive a banana at 150 mile 'n hour."
>
> —Anonymous

Darel Dieringer's #16 Mercury runs just ahead of Fred Lorenzen's creatively modified #26 Ford in the Aug. 7 Dixie 400 at Atlanta International Raceway. With Ford's factory teams sticking to their boycott, NASCAR president Bill France allowed the radically engineered Junior Johnson Ford to compete in the 400-miler despite obvious body enhancements that didn't comply with the rule book. Lorenzen qualified third and led a number of laps before falling out after a bout with the retaining wall.

The Junior Johnson-built #26 Ford, driven by Fred Lorenzen in Atlanta's Dixie 400, was one of the most radical cars to ever compete in NASCAR Grand National competition. The front end of the car sloped downward, the roofline was lowered, the side windows were narrowed, the front windshield was sloped in an aerodynamic position, and the tail was kicked up. Several of rival drivers called the car "The Yellow Banana," "Junior's Joke," and "The Magnafluxed Monster." Despite not adhering to the rules, NASCAR allowed the car to race. Lorenzen crashed while leading in the 139th lap. "No wonder," one wag in the pit area quipped. "I ain't never seen anybody who could drive a banana at 150 mile 'n hour."

1966

Richard Petty leads a pack of cars off the fourth turn at Atlanta International Raceway during the Dixie 400. Petty pushed his Plymouth past Buddy Baker with 36 laps remaining and sped to victory. Petty won eight races and 16 poles in 1966, but his championship hopes were dashed early in the year; a nonracing-related hand injury forced him to miss a couple of races.

Curtis Turner's #47 Chevrolet rests sideways in the turn at Asheville-Weaverville Speedway after the engine blew just three laps into the Aug. 21 Western North Carolina 500. Turner qualified a strong third for the annual summer 250-miler on the ½-mile paved track, but his high hopes were dashed early.

Number 64 Elmo Langley, #1 Paul Lewis, and #49 G.C. Spencer battle through the turn at Asheville-Weaverville Speedway. Spencer finished second in the 250-mile race, even though he was eight laps behind winner Darel Dieringer. Lewis came in seventh, while Langley encountered a lengthy pit stop and placed 22nd. For years, the Asheville-Weaverville Speedway was acknowledged as the fastest ½-mile paved track in the country.

Earl Balmer's Dodge climbs the guardrail on the 189th lap of the Sept. 5 Southern 500. The errant car nearly sailed into the open-scaffold press box located in the first turn, but the inside of the left front tire caught the tip of the guardrail and tossed the car back onto the racing surface. The members of the press were spewed with gasoline and debris. "We were all diving for cover like soldiers seeking the sanctuary of a fox hole," said Tom Higgins, motorsports writer for *The Charlotte Observer*.

Junior Johnson

WHEN WRITER TOM WOLFE dubbed Junior Johnson "The Last American Hero" in the March 1965 issue of *Esquire* magazine, the portly kid from Ingle Hollow, N.C., was already a legend. Growing up on a farm in Wilkes County, Johnson, like many of the pioneers of stock car racing, developed his driving skills running moonshine as a young man. He was one of many drivers who easily transferred his moonshine experience to the highly pitched pavement of the NASCAR superspeedways.

In his first full season, he won five races and finished sixth in the 1955 NASCAR Grand National points standings. If NASCAR had a Rookie of the Year at the time, Johnson surely would have won it. The following year, an unscheduled trip to prison in Chillicothe, Ohio, derailed his racing activities. Johnson was nabbed by federal agents at his father's moonshine still in the Carolina mountains, and served 11 months of a two-year sentence.

Johnson returned to the NASCAR scene in 1958 and picked up where he left off, winning six races. In '59, he won five more NASCAR Grand National races and was regarded as one of the most capable short-track racers in the business.

Johnson was a master in the artistry of dirt-track racing, painting a perfect set of grooves in the tight corners of any dirt canvas. "The two best drivers I've ever competed against on dirt are Junior Johnson and Dick Hutcherson," said two-time NASCAR champion Ned Jarrett.

Fifteen of Johnson's first 16 NASCAR Grand National victories came on dirt tracks. He was regarded as a one-dimensional driver—a prodigious craftsman on dirt, but not well-versed on superspeedways. That all changed in the 1960 Daytona 500 when Johnson drove an outdated and underpowered

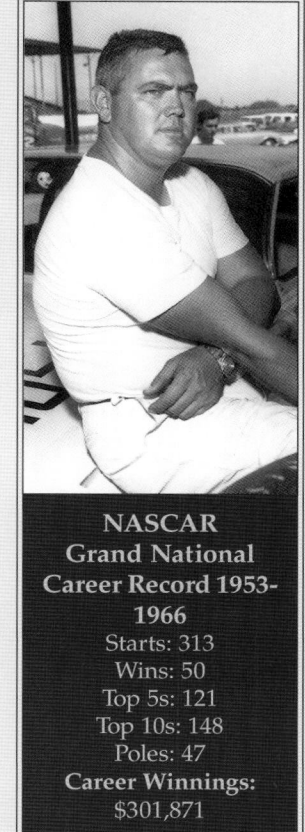

**NASCAR
Grand National
Career Record 1953-
1966**
Starts: 313
Wins: 50
Top 5s: 121
Top 10s: 148
Poles: 47
Career Winnings:
$301,871

Chevrolet to victory in the second running of NASCAR's biggest event. Utilizing the draft for 450 miles, Johnson tagged along behind the speedier Pontiacs, then thrust his way to victory in the final laps. His follow-up wins at Charlotte and Darlington solidified the notion that he could obviously mix more than a little brainpower with his brawn.

Johnson's finest season came in 1965 when he won 13 races while driving Fords for team owner Rex Lovette. He led the NASCAR Grand National brigade by leading 30 races for 3998 laps, both tops for the campaign. He completed 7144 laps in '65 and he led 56 percent of them. If it hadn't been for 19 DNFs, Johnson might have set all sorts of records that year.

When he retired in 1966 at the age of 34, Johnson had accumulated 50 NASCAR Grand National victories, tied for second best on the all-time list. He often said, "I'd rather lead one lap and fall out of the race than stroke it and finish in the money," In 313 starts, Johnson finished among the top three positions 91 times, but he failed to finish 165 events. "Go or blow was always my philosophy in racing," said Junior.

After Johnson hung up his goggles, he established his own racing team, which he ran until 1996. Darel Dieringer, LeeRoy Yarborough, Cale Yarborough, Darrell Waltrip, Neil Bonnett, Terry Labonte, Geoff Bodine, Bill Elliott, and Jimmy Spencer all won races in Johnson-groomed machinery. During his career as a team owner, his cars won 119 races, not including 21 events from 1971 to '74 when he managed a Chevrolet team owned by Richard Howard.

Johnson became one of the most successful team owners in NASCAR's Modern Era. From 1976 to '85, his cars won six NASCAR championships, three each with Yarborough and Waltrip. Yarborough's trifecta in 1976, '77, and '78 marked the first time a driver and owner won three consecutive titles.

Cale Yarborough's #21 Wood Brothers Ford leads Curtis Turner's #26 Junior Johnson Ford in the Southern 500. Yarborough finished 11th and Turner crashed late and placed 14th. Junior Johnson, in his first year as a team owner, had a dreadful season in 1966. In 20 races with five different drivers, the Johnson Ford failed to finish 15 events and crashed eight times.

The right front of Dick Hutcherson's #29 Ford sagged when a tire blew in the Southern 500. An extended pit stop relegated Hutcherson to a seventh-place finish, six laps off the pace. Number 64 Elmo Langley and #12 LeeRoy Yarbrough scoot by safely on the first turn banking. Yarbrough finished eighth and Langley wound up 18th.

Earl Balmer, a lead-footed driver from Floyds Knobs, Ind., was one of the first drivers to campaign Nord Krauskopf's #71 Dodge in NASCAR Grand National competition. Balmer had the reputation of a hard charger, who drove with his foot and not necessarily with his head. One pitside observer had this to say about Balmer's driving style: "He'll jam that car into the corner as deep as it'll go, and if he makes it through the turn, he figures he can jam it in a little deeper the next time around."

Richard Petty's #42 Plymouth rounds the turn at the Richmond Fairgrounds Raceway on Sept. 11. Petty often drove the #42 car rather than his familiar #43 Plymouth in short-track action. Tiny Lund, in the #55 Ford, scored one win in 1966, his first triumph since winning the '63 Daytona 500. Lund won at Beltsville, Md., in a photo finish with rookie James Hylton.

Number 12 LeeRoy Yarbrough duels with #26 Gordon Johncock in the Oct. 16 National 500 at Charlotte Motor Speedway. Yarbrough's Jon Thorne-owned Dodge was the class of the field, leading 301 of the 334 laps and giving Yarbrough his first superspeedway win. Johncock, a USAC Indy Car driver, drove Junior Johnson's Ford to a fourth-place finish.

Veteran G.C. Spencer (left) and rookie James Hylton (right) were two of the most successful independent drivers in 1966. Spencer finished second in three races while running a limited schedule. Hylton finished 33 of his 41 starts in the top 10, including four runner-up efforts, and trailed only David Pearson in the championship race. Hylton was voted the NASCAR Rookie of the Year.

1966 NASCAR GRAND NATIONAL POINTS RACE

Rank	Driver	Points	Starts	Wins	Top 5	Top 10	Winnings
1	David Pearson	35,638	42	15	26	33	$78,193.60
2	James Hylton	33,688	41	0	20	32	$38,722.10
3	Richard Petty	22,952	39	8	20	22	$85,465.11
4	Henley Gray	22,468	45	0	4	18	$21,900.96
5	Paul Goldsmith	22,078	21	3	11	11	$54,608.53
6	Wendell Scott	21,702	45	0	3	17	$23,051.62
7	John Sears	21,432	46	0	11	30	$25,191.35
8	J. T. Putney	21,208	39	0	4	9	$18,652.72
9	Neil Castles	20,446	41	0	7	17	$19,034.09
10	Bobby Allison	19,910	33	3	10	15	$23,419.09
11	Elmo Langley	19,116	47	2	12	20	$22,454.69
12	Darel Dieringer	18,214	25	3	7	9	$52,529.09
13	Ned Jarrett	17,616	21	0	5	8	$23,254.09
14	Jim Paschal	16,404	18	2	6	10	$30,984.09
15	Sam McQuagg	16,068	16	1	4	7	$29,529.09
16	Paul Lewis	15,352	21	1	9	14	$17,826.06
17	Marvin Panch	15,308	14	1	4	6	$38,431.06
18	Cale Yarborough	15,188	14	0	3	3	$24,076.06
19	G. C. Spencer	15,028	20	0	6	9	$26,721.06
20	Clyde Lynn	14,856	40	0	10	15	$13,221.06
21	Buck Baker	14,505	36	0	7	14	$13,860.00
22	Buddy Baker	14,302	41	0	1	7	$21,325.00
23	Fred Lorenzen	12,454	11	2	6	6	$36,310.00
24	Curtis Turner	12,266	21	0	5	6	$16,890.00
25	Roy Mayne	11,074	18	0	1	5	$9940.00
26	LeeRoy Yarbrough	10,528	9	1	2	4	$23,925.00
27	J. D. McDuffie	9572	36	0	1	9	$8545.00
28	Dick Hutcherson	9392	14	3	8	9	$22,985.00
29	Tiny Lund	9332	31	1	5	10	$11,880.00
30	Blackie Watt	8518	20	0	0	9	$7,000.00
31	Frank Warren	8334	11	0	0	1	$6740.00
32	Buddy Arrington	7636	25	0	0	3	$8510.00
33	Wayne Smith	7442	23	0	0	1	$9835.00
34	Jimmy Helms	6530	29	0	0	0	$5815.00
35	Stick Elliott	6358	19	0	1	3	$7335.00
36	Earl Balmer	5794	9	1	2	2	$7935.00
37	Tom Pistone	5788	28	0	6	6	$7765.00
38	Johnny Jack Wynn	5644	21	0	0	5	$4650.00
39	Larry Manning	4964	13	0	1	1	$3920.00
40	Larry Hess	4938	13	0	0	0	$5290.00
41	Roy Tyner	4248	26	0	0	4	$4435.00
42	Hank Thomas	4180	14	0	3	7	$3530.00
43	Bill Seifert	4128	15	0	0	4	$3830.00
44	Bob Derrington	4122	11	0	0	1	$2730.00
45	Joel Davis	4066	21	0	1	3	$4685.00
46	Paul Connors	3986	3	0	0	1	$2820.00
47	Jabe Thomas	3820	13	0	0	0	$3580.00
48	Doug Cooper	3808	20	0	3	4	$5185.00
49	Junior Johnson	3750	7	0	1	1	$3610.00
50	Larry Frank	3738	2	0	0	2	$1575.00

David Pearson took the lead in the 1966 NASCAR Grand National points standings in the second event of the season and sprinted to an easy win over rookie James Hylton. Pearson finished 1950 points ahead of Hylton in the final tally.

Hylton's runner-up effort marked the second straight season a rookie driver finished second in the NASCAR Grand National points race.

Pearson, driving Cotton Owens' Dodge, scored 15 victories during the season. Hylton failed to post any wins, but was able to finish 32 of his 41 starts in the top 10. Pearson survived one close call during the championship chase. His car was ruled out of the 400-miler at Atlanta in August when NASCAR officials determined it didn't conform to specifications. Despite sitting out of the race, Pearson had enough cushion in the points to maintain his lead.

1967

February 24 Fred Lorenzen scores his 26th career victory in the 100-mile qualifying race at Daytona. Lorenzen drives the 100 miles without making a pit stop. LeeRoy Yarbrough wins the other Twin 100-miler.

February 26 USAC star Mario Andretti leads the final 33 laps and wins the Daytona 500. It is Andretti's first NASCAR Grand National win.

April 2 Cale Yarborough dominates the Atlanta 500, leading 301 of the 334 laps to record his first career win on a superspeedway. Curtis Turner, driving the Smokey Yunick Chevrolet, escapes injury in a wild practice crash.

April 16 Darel Dieringer wins the Gwyn Staley Memorial 400 at North Wilkesboro Speedway. Dieringer starts on the pole in Junior Johnson's Ford and is never threatened.

May 13 Richard Petty guides his Plymouth to victory in the Darlington Rebel 400, finishing a lap ahead of David Pearson. It is Petty's 55th career NASCAR Grand National win, putting him first on the all-time victory list. Ford star Fred Lorenzen retires before the race, giving up his seat in the Holman-Moody Ford to Pearson.

June 18 Richard Petty romps to victory in the Carolina 500 at Rockingham for his 11th win of the season. The win pushes Petty atop the NASCAR points standings for the first time.

August 12 Richard Petty hustles his Plymouth to another win in the 250-lapper at Bowman Gray Stadium. The triumph is Petty's 19th of the season, breaking Tim Flock's record of 18 wins during the 1955 campaign.

October 1 With several of the top racing officials from Ford Motor Co. looking on, Richard Petty continues his phenomenal winning streak by taking the Wilkes 400 at North Wilkesboro Speedway. Petty scores his record-shattering 10th consecutive victory.

Mario Andretti's #114 Ford negotiates a tight corner in the Jan. 29 Motor Trend 500 at Riverside International Raceway. Andretti was a teammate of race-winner Parnelli Jones on the Bill Stroppe Ford team. The engine blew in Andretti's Ford after he completed 164 of the 185 laps. He still got credit for finishing ninth. Billy Foster, a USAC driver, was killed in a practice crash.

Don White, top-ranked USAC stock car driver, competed in selected NASCAR Grand National events from 1954 to '72. In the 1967 500-miler at Riverside, White drove the #31 Ray Nichels Dodge Charger to a sparkling fourth-place finish. White drove in 24 NASCAR Grand National races and finished in the top 10 in half of his efforts, including three runner-up finishes.

Curtis Turner became the first driver to surpass 180 mph on an official qualifying run in Daytona 500 time trials. Turner's #13 Smokey Yunick Chevelle was clocked at 180.831 mph, earning the pole position. It was a controversial achievement for two reasons. First, it meant an unsponsored GM car had beaten the Ford and Chrysler factory entries. Second, the car was roughly ⅞ scale. An engine failure in the final 100 miles put Turner out of the Daytona 500.

Fred Lorenzen's 26th and final NASCAR Grand National victory came in the second Twin 100-miler at Daytona on Feb. 24. Lorenzen went the distance without a pit stop, the first driver to run non-stop in the qualifying race. NASCAR tacked on an additional 25 miles in subsequent years so teams would have to pit at least once during the Twin qualifying races.

Jim Paschal, driving for the Friedkin Enterprises Chrysler factory racing team, enjoyed his finest season in 1967, winning four races and finishing sixth in the final points standings. After the season, Chrysler suddenly fired the 40-year-old Paschal, despite his fine effort. Nine different drivers campaigned the Friedkin Enterprises Plymouth in '68, but none came close to winning a race.

Number 97 Henley Gray takes the low groove in the Daytona 500 as #40 Jerry Grant and #11 Mario Andretti fade high to make a pass. Andretti drove his Holman-Moody Ford to a convincing victory in NASCAR's crown jewel event. Grant finished fifth, while Gray took 17th.

Mario Andretti breezes down the short chute at Daytona International Speedway during the Daytona 500. Andretti led 112 of the 200 laps and racked up a win in only his seventh career NASCAR Grand National start. Andretti never came close to winning another NASCAR event.

Bobby Isaac's #71 Dodge and Sam McQuagg's #15 Mercury tour the Atlanta International Raceway on the pace lap of the April 2 Atlanta 500. Isaac, who joined Nord Krauskopf's K&K Insurance team in 1967, finished fifth, just behind the #37 K&K Dodge driven by Charlie Glotzbach. McQuagg finished 18th in the Bud Moore Mercury.

Darel Dieringer and Richard Petty lead the charge into the first turn on the opening lap of the April 23 Virginia 500 at Martinsville Speedway. Dieringer was eliminated in a crash four laps later. Cale Yarborough's #21 Wood Brothers Ford led most of the race, but a late-race gallop netted Petty the victory.

1967

October 15 Buddy Baker grabs his first career NASCAR Grand National win in the Charlotte National 500, halting Richard Petty's 10-race winning streak. It is Baker's 215th start.

October 29 Bobby Allison, driving the retired Fred Lorenzen's Ford, wins the American 500 at Rockingham. Allison gives Ford its first NASCAR Grand National win in nearly three months. Formula One driver Jimmy Clark finishes 30th in his first NASCAR start.

November 5 Bobby Allison prevails in a bumper-grinding shootout with Richard Petty to win the season finale at Asheville-Weaverville Speedway. Petty wraps up the NASCAR Grand National championship by 6028 points over runner-up James Hylton.

A crash at the start of the May 13 Rebel 400 cluttered up the frontstretch at Darlington Raceway. Buck Baker tagged the rear of Friday Hassler's Chevrolet, starting the melee. Six cars were unable to continue. Jabe Thomas' #25 Ford and Roy Mayne's #46 Chevy never had time to get into high gear.

Richard Petty's Plymouth rolls into victory lane following his triumph in Darlington's Rebel 400. Petty, who led 266 of the 291 laps, recorded his 55th career NASCAR Grand National win, moving him into first place on NASCAR's all-time win list. He surpassed his father Lee, who won 54 races.

David Pearson pits the Holman-Moody #17 Ford during the May 28 World 600. Pearson was making his second start with the powerful Holman-Moody team since replacing the retired Fred Lorenzen. Pearson finished second in his first two starts with the factory Ford team, including a close runner-up effort in the 600-miler at Charlotte.

Veteran driver Jim Paschal campaigned the #14 Friedkin Enterprises Plymouth on the NASCAR Grand National trail in 1967. His biggest victory came in the May 28 World 600 at Charlotte. Paschal built a three-lap lead in the 600-miler, but clobbered the wall with 61 laps remaining. His lead disappeared, but he managed to keep the ill-handling car ahead of his rivals in a late-race shoot-out. Paschal beat runner-up David Pearson by five seconds to score his second win in NASCAR's most grueling event.

NASCAR began using templates at the midpoint of the 1967 Grand National season. Some innovative mechanics were getting downsized versions of full-size automobiles through the inspection procedure. Templates measured the body and contour of cars to make sure they conformed to stock guidelines. Here, Armond Holley's Chevrolet goes through the ritual prior to the Firecracker 400. Of the 50 entries for the event, 49 initially failed inspection. Bud Moore's Mercury was the only car to pass the first time.

Number 37 Sam McQuagg, Cale Yarborough, #71 Bobby Isaac, and David Pearson battle two abreast in the July 4 Daytona Firecracker 400. Yarborough won the race, passing Dick Hutcherson on the final lap. Pearson finished fourth, while Isaac took fifth and McQuagg 18th.

Richard Petty

THROUGH THE SECOND week of June 1967, Richard Petty had won 10 of the 24 NASCAR Grand National races. The season was half over and Petty was on a rampage, yet he was trailing winless sophomore driver James Hylton in the points standings. Such is the procedure to determine a NASCAR champion—excellence is not always properly rewarded.

With a victory in the June 18 race at Rockingham, Petty logged his 11th win of the season, but more importantly, he had finally grabbed the NASCAR Grand National points lead. The "Prince of Randleman" (N.C.) wouldn't be threatened in the title chase again, easily recording an overwhelming triumph and racking up his second of seven NASCAR championships.

Petty turned up the heat even higher in the second half of the 1967 season. In the final 24 races, the Plymouth-driving Petty won 17 times, giving him 27 victories in 48 starts—a .563 batting average. He won the championship by 6028 points over Hylton, who parlayed consistency to finish second.

In the unprecedented run of success, Petty won 10 consecutive races, a mind-boggling achievement that just might remain in NASCAR's record books forever. The undefeated string lasted from August into October.

Petty brought himself and NASCAR stock car racing from the small two-paragraph stories at the back of the sports section to front-page headlines. His name, his smile, his mannerisms, and his driving record made every sports page reader below the Mason-Dixon line take notice of the Southern brand of motorsports. Everybody was talking and writing about Richard Petty. In fact, one Carolina daily newspaper reported that Petty had finished second in a 100-mile NASCAR Grand National race at Maryville, Tenn., without noting that Dick Hutcherson had won the event

Petty's achievements earned a write-up in *Newsweek* magazine, the first time the national weekly devoted an article to a stock car driver. He was also featured in *Sports Illustrated*, *Life* magazine, and *True Magazine for Men*. "Richard Petty

For President" bumper stickers and lapel buttons began to appear during the 1967 season.

As Petty's star shined brighter, some members of the media started taking potshots at the new "king" of stock car racing. They said he wasn't deserving of the media attention. One reporter went so far as to say Petty was a snob who didn't care about his fans and supporters. Cheap shots to be sure.

The outrageous remarks didn't sit well with Bill France. The NASCAR president delivered a public plea to end that sort of nonsense. "I know of no other driver in NASCAR history who has brought more recognition to the sport," said France in October 1967. "I can't agree with those who think Richard has gained more than his share. In bringing the spotlight into focus on the Petty team, he is also bringing added recognition to NASCAR. They have worked many years to achieve success. I'm proud he has set his records as a member of NASCAR."

It took King Richard just 10 years to become the number-one driver in NASCAR history. His career began on July 12, 1958, 10 days after his 21st birthday. It was a NASCAR Convertible race at Columbia, S.C., and he finished sixth in an Oldsmobile. "I felt I was ready to race before that," remarked Petty. "But Daddy [Lee Petty] told me that I would have to wait until I was 21." Petty made only nine NASCAR Grand National starts in '58, then became Rookie of the Year in '59.

Petty's first NASCAR Grand National race, oddly, was outside the continental United States. Six days after his baptism in Columbia, "Dick" Petty, as he was called back then, drove the #142 Oldsmobile at the Canadian National Exposition track in Toronto. The fuzzy-cheeked youngster managed to go 55 laps before he "hit the fence." He won a total of $115 for his efforts. "It wasn't much of a race," Petty recalled. "I got in Daddy's way when he was lapping me, so he punted me into the fence. He went on to win, so I reckon it was a good day for the Pettys."

From that inauspicious beginning, Petty became the King of NASCAR racing, winning the championship in 1964, '67, '71, '72, '74, '75, and '79. During his illustrious career, Petty won 200 of his 1184 career starts, scored 712 top-10 finishes, led in 599 events, and traveled 303,662 miles in competition.

NASCAR Winston Cup Career Record 1958-1992

Starts: 1184
Wins: 200
Top 5s: 555
Top 10s: 712
Poles: 126

Career Winnings: $8,541,218

Richard Petty recorded his 19th NASCAR Grand National win of the season in the Aug. 17 event at Columbia Speedway in South Carolina. Petty broke Tim Flock's record of 18 wins in a single season, which had been established in 1955. Flock was among the first to congratulate Petty when he set the record.

Sam McQuagg's Dodge clipped the wall on the 81st lap of the Sept. 4 Southern 500, bounced into the path of Dick Hutcherson, and proceeded to tumble down the frontstretch eight times. McQuagg climbed out of the car without assistance and trotted to the sanctuary of the infield.

Buddy Baker and team owner Ray Fox enjoy the victory celebration after Baker's win in the Oct. 15 National 500 at Charlotte. Baker posted his first NASCAR Grand National victory and snapped Richard Petty's 10-race winning streak. "When I went under the checkered flag," said Baker, "I let out a yell that you could hear in Concord. This is the greatest day of my life. Maybe it will give me a mental boost. Now I know how to win."

Formula One champion Jimmy Clark made one NASCAR Grand National start in his career. Driving a Holman-Moody Ford in the Oct. 29 American 500 at Rockingham, Clark started midpack and completed 144 laps before the engine let go. Having been accustomed to shorter races, Clark had fellow F-1 driver Jochen Rindt standing by as a relief driver. The early engine failure prevented Rindt from getting into the car.

James Hylton's #48 Dodge slams head first into the inside guardrail on the backstretch of North Carolina Motor Speedway in the American 500. The sophomore driver suffered injuries that kept him from competing in the final race of the season. Hylton still managed to place second in the final points standings, thanks to 39 top-10 finishes in his 46 starts.

Number 39 Friday Hassler, #02 Bob Cooper, Dick Hutcherson, #43 Richard Petty, and Cale Yarborough battle in close quarters in the Nov. 5 season finale at Asheville-Weaverville Speedway. Only six cars in the starting field of 30 finished the 500-lap contest on the ½-mile paved oval. Hassler's car fell out with engine problems with 29 laps remaining, but he still got credit for fifth place.

Bobby Allison and Richard Petty engaged in a heated battle in the Western North Carolina 500 at Asheville-Weaverville Speedway. Allison prevailed, beating Petty by a single car length. Recently retired driver Fred Lorenzen was in charge of setting up Allison's Holman-Moody Ford, and the Hueytown, Ala., driver scored back-to-back wins at Rockingham and Weaverville.

Having recorded 14 wins in his four years behind the wheel, Dick Hutcherson retired as a driver after the 1967 NASCAR Grand National season. The Holman-Moody Ford team offered Hutcherson a position as team manager for David Pearson and he accepted the offer. Ford wanted Pearson to make a run for the championship in '68 and Hutcherson was the man to head the operation.

1967 NASCAR GRAND NATIONAL POINTS RACE

Rank	Driver	Points	Starts	Wins	Top 5	Top 10	Winnings
1	Richard Petty	42,472	48	27	38	40	$150,196.10
2	James Hylton	36,444	46	0	26	39	$49,731.50
3	Dick Hutcherson	33,658	33	2	22	25	$85,159.28
4	Bobby Allison	30,812	45	6	21	27	$58,249.64
5	John Sears	29,078	41	0	9	25	$28,936.74
6	Jim Paschal	27,624	45	4	20	25	$60,122.28
7	David Pearson	26,302	22	2	11	13	$72,650.00
8	Neil Castles	23,218	36	0	4	16	$20,682.32
9	Elmo Langley	22,286	45	0	10	24	$23,897.52
10	Wendell Scott	20,700	45	0	0	11	$19,509.76
11	Paul Goldsmith	20,402	21	0	7	8	$38,731.14
12	Darel Dieringer	20,194	19	1	8	9	$34,709.24
13	Clyde Lynn	20,016	44	0	5	22	$19,519.24
14	Bobby Isaac	19,698	12	0	3	5	$24,474.24
15	Buddy Baker	18,600	20	1	7	8	$46,949.24
16	Donnie Allison	18,298	20	0	4	7	$17,613.15
17	Henley Gray	17,502	43	0	0	12	$15,986.16
18	J.T. Putney	16,752	29	0	1	10	$15,686.16
19	Tiny Lund	16,292	19	0	4	5	$17,331.16
20	Cale Yarborough	16,228	16	2	7	8	$57,911.16
21	G.C. Spencer	15,240	29	0	5	10	$20,225.00
22	Bill Seifert	14,676	41	0	0	12	$11,905.00
23	Charlie Glotzbach	11,444	9	0	3	5	$14,790.00
24	Frank Warren	9992	12	0	0	1	$9185.00
25	Earl Brooks	9952	34	0	0	8	$8610.00
26	Buddy Arrington	9768	15	0	1	5	$7720.00
27	Buck Baker	9450	21	0	0	5	$7560.00
28	Wayne Smith	9372	27	0	0	2	$10,225.00
29	Fred Lorenzen	9268	5	1	2	2	$17,875.00
30	Roy Mayne	9262	14	0	0	1	$8830.00
31	Bobby Wawak	9078	14	0	1	3	$8070.00
32	Friday Hassler	8820	21	0	3	9	$10,265.00
33	Paul Lewis	8492	14	0	3	8	$8620.00
34	Sonny Hutchins	8448	7	0	0	2	$6385.00
35	Paul "Bud" Moore	7812	6	0	2	3	$7200.00
36	Sam McQuagg	7400	15	0	3	3	$9845.00
37	LeeRoy Yarbrough	7012	15	1	3	4	$15,325.00
38	Don Biederman	5850	22	0	0	1	$5935.00
39	Ramo Stott	5676	3	0	0	1	$3335.00
40	George Davis	5434	21	0	1	6	$4400.00
41	Jack Harden	5254	10	0	0	0	$4450.00
42	Paul Dean Holt	5006	24	0	0	1	$4220.00
43	Roy Tyner	4936	27	0	0	1	$8170.00
44	Bill Champion	4040	11	0	0	0	$6205.00
45	Dick Johnson	3954	23	0	0	0	$5070.00
46	George Poulos	3780	23	0	0	1	$3040.00
47	Bill Dennis	3730	3	0	0	0	$2335.00
48	Doug Cooper	3666	21	0	2	4	$5665.00
49	Ed Negre	3578	14	0	0	0	$3805.00
50	H.B. Bailey	3482	3	0	0	0	$3850.00

Richard Petty rewrote the record book in 1967, winning 27 races in 46 starts. The newly crowned "king" of stock car racing also won 10 races in a row. The 27 wins and 10-race streak set records that may never be matched.

Despite his thorough domination, Petty didn't grab the points lead until his 11th win of the season at Rockingham in late June. Winless James Hylton held the lead for six months based on consistency. Petty hit stride in the second half of the season, and sprinted to a 6028-point cushion over Hylton by the time the 49-race season ended in November. Dick Hutcherson finished third in points in his final season as a driver. Up-and-coming driver Bobby Allison placed fourth.

Petty became the all-time NASCAR victory leader, passing his father Lee by winning the May 13 400-miler at Darlington. It was the 55th triumph of Petty's career.

1968

November 12, 1967 Bobby Allison wins the 1968 NASCAR Grand National season opener at Middle Georgia Raceway in Macon. An elaborate moonshine operation is discovered beneath the track. Peach County Sheriff Reggie Mullis calls it, "one of the most well-built moonshine stills ever operated."

February 25 Cale Yarborough wins the Daytona 500 by less than a second over LeeRoy Yarbrough. Gordon Johncock's Smokey Yunick-prepared Chevrolet is not permitted to compete when NASCAR officials find a number of rules violations during inspection.

April 21 David Pearson takes the lead in the final 10 laps and wins the Gwyn Staley Memorial at North Wilkesboro Speedway. Seventeen cars are eliminated by engine failures.

May 11 David Pearson scores his first superspeedway victory since 1961 in the Rebel 400 at Darlington Raceway. Pearson's Holman-Moody Ford is powered by a small 396-cid engine, which allows him to run 293 pounds lighter than most of his rivals under the new power-to-weight ratio rules.

June 8 Richard Petty dominates the 100-mile NASCAR Grand National race at Birmingham Speedway. David Pearson finishes third but is disqualified for using improper tires.

June 16 Donnie Allison scores his first career NASCAR Grand National victory in Rockingham's Carolina 500. Rookie Richard Brickhouse, driving in his first Grand National event, finishes fourth.

August 4 LeeRoy Yarbrough snaps a slump by winning the Dixie 500 at Atlanta International Raceway. Bobby Isaac finishes second and takes a one-point lead over David Pearson in the championship race.

August 18 David Pearson wins his third consecutive race in the Western North Carolina 500 at Asheville-Weaverville Speedway. Pearson is the 11th driver to win in the 11 runnings of the event.

Number 16 Cale Yarborough, #27 Bosco Lowe, Charlie Glotzbach, and Richard Petty gun their cars through the turn at Middle Georgia Raceway in the 1968 season opener on Nov. 12, 1967. Petty finished second to Bobby Allison. The other three drivers failed to finish. The 500-lap race on the short track in Macon, Ga., almost didn't run on schedule. Federal authorities discovered a moonshine still beneath the track. Track promoter Lamar H. Brown, Jr., was charged with possession of an apparatus for the distillery of illegal whiskey. He was found not guilty in a trial 13 months later.

Bobby Isaac's #37 Dodge skids off the course during the Jan. 21 Motor Trend 500 at Riverside International Raceway as Dan Gurney passes in the #21 Wood Brothers Ford. Isaac recovered to finish seventh. Gurney went on to win, his fifth win in his last six Grand National starts at the track. It was the first NASCAR Grand National event that included cars with protective screens in the driver's window. The idea came from Charlie Gray of Ford's Vehicles Department. The window screens represented an advancement in safety precautions, but weren't mandated by NASCAR until 1970.

Bud Moore's Dodge lurches sideways in the first turn during the early laps of the Feb. 25 Daytona 500. USAC Stock Car champion Butch Hartman, making his second NASCAR Grand National start, takes his #5 Dodge to the low side to avoid Moore. James Hylton squeezes past in the high groove. Hartman went on to finish 16th. The Twin 125s scheduled for Feb. 23 were rained out, so the starting positions were determined solely by qualifying times.

Former Daytona 500 winners Tiny Lund and Mario Andretti flash down the open straight in the Daytona 500. Lund, who won the race in 1963, carried Bud Moore's #16 Mercury to eighth place. Andretti spun and triggered a multicar collision midway through the race, marking the third straight wreck he was involved in since his '67 win. "That guy takes out one or two contenders every time he races down here [in NASCAR]," grumbled Buddy Baker.

Richard Petty showed up at Daytona with a black vinyl top on his 1968 Plymouth Roadrunner. The ploy was merely a mind game to puzzle other competitors, but it backfired on the Petty Enterprises team in the Daytona 500. The vinyl roof peeled back, forcing Petty to make an unscheduled pit stop for repairs. Petty lost two laps during the pit stop and was relegated to a seventh-place finish, two laps behind the leaders.

Bobby Isaac sits at the end of Daytona's pit road, awaiting the "Go" signal from the NASCAR official to return to the track under caution. Isaac and his K&K Insurance Dodge team made their first attempt at the NASCAR Grand National championship in 1968. Isaac won three short-track races and led the points race from April through July, but finished second to David Pearson in the final tally.

Cale Yarborough pushed his #21 Wood Brothers Mercury around LeeRoy Yarbrough's Junior Johnson Mercury with four laps to go and sped to a close victory in the Daytona 500. Yarborough overcame a two-lap deficit when blown tires intervened early, but scrambled back into contention late in the race. Yarborough gave Ford Motor Co. a victory in the debut of the new slope-backed '68 model cars.

Young Pete Hamilton, the son of a college professor, stands beside the #5 Ford owned by Rocky Hinton before the start of the May 5 Fireball 300. Hamilton qualified 11th and finished 12th after a broken wheel foiled a probable top-five finish. Hamilton drove Hinton's unsponsored car in 10 races in 1968, scoring a runner-up finish at Maryville, Tenn., in his fourth career start. Late in the season, he moved to a Dodge owned by A.J. King. Hamilton won the 1968 Rookie of the Year award in a close decision over Richard Brickhouse.

1968

September 2 Cale Yarborough nips David Pearson by four car lengths and wins the Southern 500 at Darlington. It is Yarborough's record fourth superspeedway win of the season.

September 15 Richard Petty finishes seven laps ahead of the field in the 150-miler at Orange Speedway in Hillsborough, N.C. It is the last NASCAR Grand National race staged at the venerable 0.9-mile dirt oval.

October 20 Sophomore Charlie Glotzbach records his first career win in the National 500 at Charlotte Motor Speedway. Glotzbach edges Paul Goldsmith to give Dodge only its second superspeedway win of the season.

November 3 Cale Yarborough wins the season finale at Jefferson, Ga., as David Pearson is declared the NASCAR Grand National champion. Pearson finishes 126 points ahead of Bobby Isaac to secure his second title.

November 25 Richard Petty announces he will leave Plymouth to drive Fords in the 1969 season. All of Petty's 92 wins have come in Plymouths.

David Pearson's #17 Holman-Moody Ford Torino flashes past the finish line to win the May 5 Fireball 300 at Asheville-Weaverville Speedway. Pearson started on the pole and led 299 of the 300 laps around the ½-mile high-banked paved oval. It was Pearson's fourth win of the season.

Richard Petty's amazing success in 1967 resulted in a publicity machine for '68. This Chrysler Public Relations photo features Richard the family man, with (left to right) daughter Sharon, 6, daughter Lisa, 3, and son Kyle, 7. Chrysler's publicity team noted that Kyle's school notebook was covered with drawings of race cars, all number 43.

Number 29 Bobby Allison, #12 Earl Balmer, #16 Tiny Lund, #3 Buddy Baker, and #17 David Pearson pitch their cars into the first turn at Charlotte Motor Speedway during the May 26 World 600. Baker won in the Ray Fox Dodge when rain halted the event after 255 of the 400 laps had been completed.

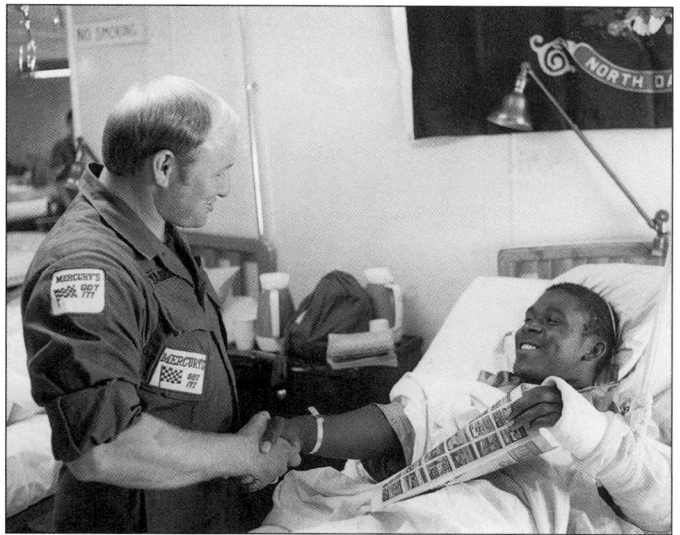

Cale Yarborough, who won four superspeedway races in 1968, went to Vietnam after the close of the season to visit the troops. Yarborough said he was surprised at how many of the American soldiers were aware of NASCAR stock car racing, and that he enjoyed bringing cheer to the wounded military men. Ford named Yarborough its '68 Man of the Year in auto racing, and sponsored his goodwill tour, which ran from Dec. 8 to Dec. 27.

Ford and Plymouth used their NASCAR heritage to sell cars in these two 1968 ads. Ford concentrated on the on-track success of its new fastback models to pitch its Torino, while Plymouth's ad explained how stock car competition inspired the no-nonsense design of its new muscle car, the Road Runner.

A helicopter hovers over Charlotte Motor Speedway as cars sit idle in the early stages of the World 600. Jet dryers, a vital part of any speedway's repertoire today, weren't available in 1968. Low flying helicopters were used to dry wet track surfaces. This practice continued until the early '70s. One helicopter crashed on the backstretch of Michigan International Speedway on a rainy day in '69, elevating concerns about the safety of the antiquated track-drying process.

Richard Brickhouse, a weekend competitor on outlaw dirt tracks in the Carolinas, competed in his first NASCAR Grand National race at Rockingham in the June 16 Carolina 500. Despite never having driven on a paved track, much less a superspeedway, Brickhouse performed admirably in his initial outing. Driving a '67 Plymouth, Brickhouse finished an impressive fourth.

Sophomore driver Charlie Glotzbach joined the Cotton Owens Dodge team in 1968 and the pair enjoyed a successful campaign. Entering selected big-money races, Glotzbach and Owens scored one victory and posted 12 top-10 finishes with their '68 Dodge Charger. Glotzbach placed 19th in the final points standings despite making only 22 starts in the 49-race season.

1968

Cale Yarborough swept both races at Daytona International Speedway in 1968, winning the Daytona 500 in the final laps and romping to an easy win in the Firecracker 400. While the Wood Brothers Mercury team had full Ford factory backing, 60 Minute Cleaners provided additional sponsorship for three years.

Richard Petty sidestepped his familiar electric-blue paint scheme for both Daytona races in 1968. In the Daytona 500, the Petty Enterprises crew attached a black vinyl top to his Plymouth. In July, Petty showed up with a blue-and-white Plymouth. The roof and hood were painted white to deflect the hot summer sun and keep the driver's compartment and the engine a little cooler.

▼ LeeRoy Yarbrough's Ford and the Dodge of Charlie Glotzbach sit on the front row before the start of the July 21 Volunteer 500 at Bristol International Speedway. Thirty-six cars started the 500-lap, 250-mile race, but only 13 finished. David Pearson, who started on the outside of the third row, led most of the way and galloped to victory. Pearson assumed command of the points race with his Bristol triumph.

Ed Negre's #8 Ford is pushed back into the pit area after a collision with Earl Brooks in the Aug. 18 Western North Carolina 500 at Asheville-Weaverville Speedway. The midsummer 500-lap event in the North Carolina mountains always attracted a big crowd, and was considered one of the "major" races on the NASCAR calendar. Spectators filled the wooden grandstands and lined up in the corners and along the backstretch every year.

Earl Brooks' crumpled Ford rests in the pits after blowing a tire on pit road during the Western North Carolina 500. Brooks' Ford darted out of control after the blowout, nearly striking top-ranking NASCAR officials Lin Kuchler and Bill Gazaway. The crash broke through the inside concrete retaining barrier.

The factory-backed drivers from the Ford and Chrysler camps grabbed most of the headlines in NASCAR racing throughout the 1960s, but the backbone of the sport continued to be the small-time operators who campaigned their own outdated machinery every week. (Left to right) Clyde Lynn, Roy Tyner, and Wendell Scott were three of NASCAR's most durable independents. Lynn enjoyed an exceptional season in 1968, finishing fourth in the points standings. Tyner and Scott also placed in the top 10. The money earned in postseason awards enabled many teams to stay in operation.

David Pearson

DAVID PEARSON NEVER had any inclination to drive on NASCAR's Winston Cup Grand National tour. He was quite content on spending most of his free time chasing after $250 top prizes on the short-track Sportsman circuit.

"I used to listen to some of the big races on the radio," said Pearson. "I thought those guys must be crazy running 150 miles per hour at places like Daytona." Pearson, one of the top winners in weekly short-track competition in the 1950s, had a large following of fans, and unbeknownst to him, his legion of supporters was his ticket to the big time.

His fans in and around Spartanburg, S.C., were convinced he could make the grade in big-time NASCAR Grand National competition. So, in late 1959, they began a fund-raising campaign to get Pearson in a NASCAR Grand National car. Pearson's fans donated nearly $1500. Although that was a lot of money in 1959, it was about half the amount needed to buy a good used race car.

"I didn't want anything to do with that idea," said Pearson. "I wanted to give the money back to the people who donated it, but I didn't know where it all came from." Pulling the additional funds needed out of the family bank account, Pearson bought a 1959 Chevrolet from Jack Smith, who had campaigned his own cars quite successfully. Pearson made his plunge into NASCAR Grand National racing at Daytona's 1960 Speedweeks.

He didn't set the world on fire, but did perform admirably. Pearson was awarded the 1960 NASCAR Grand National Rookie of the Year, catching the eye of NASCAR officials with his steady efforts in 22 starts. His best finish was third, and he won one pole position.

In 1961, veteran team owner Ray Fox entered his Pontiac in Charlotte's World 600 without a driver. Pearson's name popped up as a possible chauffeur and Fox signed him to drive in the race. In a storybook ending, Pearson won.

NASCAR Winston Cup Career Record 1960-1986
Starts: 574
Wins: 105
Top 5s: 301
Top 10s: 366
Poles: 113
Career Winnings: $2,836,224

Proving the Charlotte 600 was no fluke, Pearson won the Firecracker 250 at Daytona in a dramatic last-lap duel with Fred Lorenzen. He then topped off the season with a win in the Dixie 400 at Atlanta International Raceway. Pearson's victory at Atlanta was a noteworthy event in NASCAR history. The speedy sophomore passed Bunkie Blackburn, who was driving Junior Johnson's Pontiac in relief, on the final lap. It was the first time in superspeedway history that a race had been decided by a last-lap pass. And it was the only lap Pearson led all afternoon.

Pearson joined the Cotton Owens team in 1963, and went on to win the '66 NASCAR Grand National championship. A year later, he replaced the retired Lorenzen on the famed Holman-Moody team and made two more concentrated attempts to win the championship. In '68 and '69, Pearson won a total of 27 races and finished second 30 times. He won the championship both years, and became only the second driver in NASCAR Grand National history to win three titles.

After winning his third title, Pearson vowed never again to engage in the exhausting exercise of running the full tour. He had actively campaigned for the championship four times, and had won three of them. In 1972, Pearson joined the Wood Brothers Mercury team. The marriage became one of the most successful in history. Pearson won 23 big-track events in the first two and a half years in the Wood Brothers car. In '73, he enjoyed perhaps his finest year. While competing in selected events, Pearson won 10 of his 15 starts on superspeedways and 11 out of 18 for the year. The winning rate of 61.1 percent remains the all-time record for winning percentage in a single season.

Pearson quietly retired in the late 1980s, having competed in 574 NASCAR Winston Cup Grand National races. He won 105 times, which ranks second on the all-time list. It will forever remain a mystery how many races he could have won had he competed full-time.

▲ Number 21 Cale Yarborough and #6 Charlie Glotzbach are on the front row for the start of the Sept. 2 Southern 500 at Darlington Raceway. Glotzbach won the pole, but elected to start on the outside of the front row. Glotzbach finished fourth as Yarborough drove to victory. Yarborough lost two laps due to blistered tires, but roared back to beat David Pearson by a four car lengths. Pearson also lost ground when he tried to pass Yarborough and the two collided. It was very hard to pass on the ancient 1⅜-mile oval.

Cale Yarborough runs just ahead of Buddy Baker in the late stages of the Southern 500. Baker finished third, a remarkable achievement considering he lost his brakes in the first 100 miles. He lost a lot of ground having to shut the engine off while in gear to stop in his designated pit area. Following the 1968 season, the third and fourth turns at Darlington Raceway were revamped to make the grooves wider. The overhaul did widen the lanes, but it didn't change the personality of track coined "The Lady in Black."

Richard Petty leads the field on the pace lap of the Sept. 15 Hillsborough 150 at Orange Speedway in Hillsborough, N.C. It was the last NASCAR Grand National event staged on the 0.9-mile gently banked dirt oval. The new Talladega track in Alabama, under construction in 1968, took Hillsborough's place on the annual NASCAR calendar. Petty won the final appearance at the historic oval, finishing seven laps ahead of runner-up James Hylton.

Number 21 Cale Yarborough, #99 Paul Goldsmith, and #32 Marty Robbins buzz past the frontstretch grandstands during the Oct. 20 National 500 at Charlotte Motor Speedway. Robbins, one of the top Grand Ole Opry stars of Country & Western music, was in his second career NASCAR Grand National start. He finished 12th after starting 32nd. Robbins claimed he was "a racer who can sing, and not a singer who can race."

1968 NASCAR GRAND NATIONAL POINTS RACE

Rank	Driver	Points	Starts	Wins	Top 5	Top 10	Winnings
1	David Pearson	3499	48	16	36	38	$133,064.75
2	Bobby Isaac	3373	49	3	27	35	$60,341.50
3	Richard Petty	3123	49	16	32	35	$99,534.60
4	Clyde Lynn	3041	49	0	2	35	$29,225.55
5	John Sears	3017	49	0	5	24	$29,178.75
6	Elmo Langley	2823	48	0	6	28	$25,831.85
7	James Hylton	2719	41	0	16	27	$32,607.50
8	Jabe Thomas	2687	48	0	1	15	$21,165.70
9	Wendell Scott	2685	48	0	0	10	$20,497.20
10	Roy Tyner	2504	48	0	4	14	$20,246.95
11	Bobby Allison	2454	37	2	16	20	$52,287.95
12	Neil Castles	2330	44	0	4	15	$19,506.35
13	Buddy Baker	2310	38	1	16	18	$56,022.95
14	Bill Seifert	2175	44	0	1	9	$18,402.95
15	Earl Brooks	1957	40	0	0	5	$14,232.95
16	LeRoy Yarbrough	1894	26	2	15	16	$87,919.30
17	Cale Yarborough	1804	21	6	12	12	$138,051.30
18	Paul Dean Holt	1723	40	0	0	0	$8985.30
19	Charlie Glotzbach	1693	22	1	10	12	$43,100.30
20	Henley Gray	1559	30	0	0	6	$12,565.30
21	Darel Dieringer	1525	18	0	5	10	$28,215.00
22	Tiny Lund	1443	17	0	5	10	$17,775.00
23	G. C. Spencer	1401	26	0	1	6	$10,120.00
24	J.D. McDuffie	1370	32	0	0	9	$8335.00
25	Donnie Allison	1307	13	1	5	8	$50,815.00
26	Stan Meserve	1274	31	0	0	1	$7475.00
27	Friday Hassler	1224	20	0	3	8	$12,000.00
28	Bill Champion	1155	18	0	0	2	$10,170.00
29	Paul "Bud" Moore	1086.	16	0	2	9	$12,325.00
30	Paul Goldsmith	1020	15	0	2	4	$24,365.00
31	Ed Negre	928	24	0	0	1	$4985.00
32	Pete Hamilton	919	16	0	3	6	$7920.00
33	Wayne Smith	901	18	0	0	1	$7235.00
34	Dave Marcis	851	10	0	0	2	$7099.00
35	Dr. Don Tarr	827	12	0	0	0	$7510.00
36	E. J. Trivette	821	13	0	0	0	$8295.00
37	Dick Johnson	735	11	0	0	0	$5920.00
38	Bob Cooper	668	14	0	0	1	$4485.00
39	Buck Baker	650	17	0	1	3	$3580.00
40	Walson Gardner	640	14	0	0	2	$4275.00
41	Larry Manning	640	12	0	0	0	$6995.00
42	Frank Warren	611	10	0	0	1	$5365.00
43	Jerry Grant	559	7	0	0	1	$5665.00
44	Harold Fagan	531	12	0	0	1	$3680.00
45	Richard Brickhouse	514	7	0	1	2	$7190.00
46	Jim Hurtubise	504	6	0	0	1	$4490.00
47	Curtis Turner	456	6	0	1	4	$5850.00
48	Bobby Johns	453	7	0	0	0	$5010.00
49	Eddie Yarboro	447	6	0	0	0	$2255.00
50	Red Farmer	407	7	0	1	1	$4810.00

David Pearson and Bobby Isaac engaged in a ferocious duel for the 1968 NASCAR championship before Pearson pulled away in the closing months. It was Pearson's second NASCAR Grand National title.

Pearson won 16 races en route to the championship while Isaac won three times. Pearson took the lead from Isaac in the points race after a victory in the Aug. 8 event at Columbia, S.C. The driver of the Holman-Moody Ford survived two disqualifications, but still won the title by 126 points.

NASCAR instituted a new points system for 1968, with 150 points available to the winner in races of 400 miles or more, 100 points for major short-track events, and 50 points for small short-track races.

Richard Petty, who tied Pearson with the most wins at 16, finished a distant third in the standings. Clyde Lynn, who only posted a pair of top-five finishes, came home fourth. John Sears, with five top-five finishes, rounded out the season's top five.

1969

February 1 In his first start in a Ford, Richard Petty wins the Motor Trend 500 on the Riverside road course. Petty finishes 25 seconds ahead of runner-up A.J. Foyt.

February 23 LeeRoy Yarbrough passes Charlie Glotzbach on the final lap to win the Daytona 500. Yarbrough wins in his back-up car.

March 30 Cale Yarborough dominates the Atlanta 500 in his Mercury, leading 308 of the 334 laps at Atlanta International Raceway. Yarborough's win marks a successful debut for the new Blue Crescent Boss 429-cid engine.

April 27 Richard Petty, with relief help from James Hylton, wins the Virginia 500 at Martinsville Speedway. Petty's Torino Talladega finishes three seconds ahead of runner-up David Pearson.

May 10 LeeRoy Yarbrough drives a battered Mercury to victory in the Rebel 400 at Darlington Raceway. Yarbrough and Bobby Allison tangle while battling for the lead with four laps to go. Allison crashes, while Yarbrough limps to victory.

June 15 Cale Yarborough survives a brush with LeeRoy Yarbrough on the final lap to win in the inaugural Motor State 500 at Michigan International Speedway.

July 6 Richard Petty finishes six laps ahead of the field to win the Mason-Dixon 300 at the new Dover Downs International Speedway. Part-time driver Sonny Hutchins finishes second.

July 20 David Pearson prevails in a wreck-strewn Volunteer 500 at Bristol International Speedway. It is the first event on the ½-mile oval since the turns were redesigned and banked to a staggering 36 degrees.

August 22 Richard Petty drives his Ford to a narrow victory in the 250-lap race at Winston-Salem's Bowman Gray Stadium. It is Petty's 100th NASCAR Grand National victory.

After a 1968 season that produced only one superspeedway win in his Plymouth Roadrunner, Richard Petty requested that Chrysler officials shift him to the more aerodynamic Dodge for the 1969 NASCAR Grand National campaign. Chrysler balked, indicating they wanted to keep him in the Plymouth nameplate. In a shocking decision, Petty bailed out of the Chrysler camp entirely and joined the powerful Ford team. The King of NASCAR racing won his first start in a Ford at Riverside and went on to score eight other wins in the Torino Talladega.

Ford Motor Co. introduced sloped nose extensions on their Ford Torinos and Mercury Cyclones in 1969 in an effort to lengthen their advantage over the Chrysler products. The extensions provided a definite advantage over the conventional Dodge Chargers, particularly on the high-speed ovals. Brothers Donnie and Bobby Allison had factory rides in 1969, Donnie with Ford, and Bobby with Dodge. The new Ford was coined the Torino Talladega while the Mercury special edition was the Cyclone Spoiler. Fords didn't lose on a superspeedway until September, when the shark-nosed and high-winged Dodge Daytonas made their first appearance on NASCAR tracks.

Richard Petty's Ford leads the Dodges of Bobby Isaac and Bobby Allison in the second Twin 125-miler at Daytona on Feb. 20. Isaac won the race, leading the final eight laps. Petty struggled to find the handle of his Ford and finished, a lap off the pace. Allison was leading on the 31st lap when the engine let go in his Mario Rossi Dodge Charger.

Number 17 David Pearson, #48 James Hylton, and #34 Wendell Scott run in three-abreast high-speed formation, just ahead of #96 Ray Elder and #75 George Bauer in the Feb. 22 Daytona 500. Elder, the NASCAR Pacific Coast Late Model champion driver, made a number of appearances at Daytona during his career. Campaigning a family owned Dodge, Elder scored several good finishes at Daytona, including a 10th-place effort in 1969.

LeeRoy Yarbrough erased an 11-second deficit in the final 10 laps of the Daytona 500, stormed past Charlie Glotzbach's Dodge on the final lap, and sprinted to a close victory. Yarbrough was driving a backup #98 Ford out of the Junior Johnson shops, having crashed his primary racer in a practice mishap. Yarbrough's victory was the first Daytona 500 determined by a last-lap pass.

Number 27 Donnie Allison and LeeRoy Yarbrough started on the front row in the May 25 World 600 at Charlotte. Yarbrough went on to win the 600-miler by two laps over runner-up Allison. Yarbrough established a new record in 1969 by winning seven NASCAR Grand National races on superspeedways.

John Sears' #4 Ford flanks Richard Petty on the fourth row at the start of the May 4 Fire-ball 300 at Asheville-Weaverville Speedway. Sears, a burly driver from Ellerbe, N.C., was one of NASCAR's top independent drivers, finishing among the top 10 in the final points standings on four occasions. Sears had a fine run in this 300-lapper at Weaverville, finishing third.

1969

August 24 Bobby Isaac rallies from a five-lap deficit to win the Western North Carolina 500, finishing four laps ahead of runner-up David Pearson. It is Isaac's 11th win of the season.

September 1 LeeRoy Yarbrough passes David Pearson on the final lap to win the rain-shortened Southern 500 at Darlington.

September 14 Unheralded Richard Brickhouse drives a winged Dodge Daytona to victory in the inaugural Talladega 500 at the new Alabama International Motor Speedway. The event is boycotted by virtually all the top NASCAR drivers.

October 26 LeeRoy Yarbrough scores his seventh superspeedway win of the season in the American 500 at Rockingham. Yarbrough loses a lap when a tire blows, sending him into the wall. He scrambles back into contention and takes the lead for keeps with 57 laps remaining.

December 7 Bobby Isaac claims his first career superspeedway victory in the inaugural Texas 500 at the new Texas International Speedway. Cale Yarborough is seriously injured when his Mercury clobbers the wall.

December 17 NASCAR signs a contract with ABC Television, which will televise nine NASCAR Grand National races, including five live broadcasts during the 1970 season.

Cale Yarborough's Mercury leads the Fords of Donnie Allison and David Pearson off the fourth turn at Charlotte Motor Speedway during the World 600. Yarborough led the race early and ran with the leaders until a faulty wheel hub sidelined him after 307 of the 400 laps had been completed. He was relegated to a 23rd-place finish.

Bobby Allison's #22 Dodge and Hoss Ellington's #61 Mercury were involved in a grinding crash on the backstretch of the July 4 Firecracker 400. Cecil Gordon's Ford broke loose and collected Allison, Ellington, and Buddy Arrington. All four cars were knocked out of the race and Arrington was transported to the hospital with injuries. Ellington, a rookie in 1969, hung up his helmet after three races in '70 and went on to become a top-ranked team owner.

Newcomers #03 Richard Brickhouse and #30 Dave Marcis engaged in a spirited duel for sixth place in the Firecracker 400. Marcis won the battle, finishing just ahead of Brickhouse. Marcis drove a Dodge owned by construction magnate Milt Lunda. After the season, Marcis bought the team from Lunda and campaigned his Marcis Auto Racing team for more than 30 years.

Number 13 Joe Leonard, #98 LeeRoy Yarbrough, and #6 Buddy Baker throttle their way through the turn in the Firecracker 400. Leonard's Smokey Yunick Ford retired after an early crash while Yarbrough and Baker went on to fight for the win. Yarbrough edged Baker at the stripe to grab his fourth superspeedway win of the season.

The towering high-banked turns at Alabama International Motor Speedway in Talladega began to take shape in the early summer of 1969. Testing began on the new track in early August, but following initial shakedown runs, most of the drivers felt the track surface was unusually rough. Testing sessions by Ford, Chrysler, and the tire companies were extensive throughout the summer months, but nobody seemed altogether pleased with the abrasive surface of the new track.

LeeRoy Yarbrough continued his winning spree in 1969 by racking up a victory in Atlanta International Raceway's Dixie 500 on Aug. 10. Yarbrough fought back the flu and drove his #98 Junior Johnson Ford to a relatively easy win. The aerodynamically advanced Ford Torino Talladegas swept the top five spots in the 500-miler in another display of raw power with their new Blue Crescent Boss 429-cid engines.

Bobby Isaac's #71 Dodge prepares to lap John Sears' #4 Ford in the Aug. 24 Western North Carolina 500 at Asheville-Weaverville Speedway. Isaac, who once trailed by five laps, stormed back to win going away. Isaac became the 12th different winner in the 12 runnings of the WNC 500 since it joined the NASCAR Grand National schedule in 1958.

1969

Impromptu drivers' meetings took place frequently during the days leading up to the inaugural Talladega 500. Members of the recently formed Professional Drivers Association would often gather to discuss the condition of the new track, the tire problems they were encountering, and the possibility of the massive drivers' boycott that would mar the opening of the Alabama International Motor Speedway.

With threats of an impending drivers' boycott at Talladega, NASCAR president Bill France donned a helmet and took a 1969 Ford out for a practice run. He got up to about 175 mph, which France proudly exclaimed, "is a new world record for a 59-year-old man." France filed an entry for the race, hoping to gain admission to the private meetings of the newly formed Professional Drivers Association. The PDA members prevented France from joining the discussions. Late Saturday afternoon, less than 24 hours before the start of the inaugural Talladega 500, 32 drivers and their cars left the Speedway garage area, pulling out of the race.

David Pearson and Donnie Allison lead the field into the first turn in the Sept. 1 Southern 500 at Darlington Raceway. Both drivers led in the 20th annual running of the granddaddy of all superspeedway events. Pearson led until the final lap, losing the lead to LeeRoy Yarbrough. Heavy rains interrupted the race for several hours, and the event was shortened to 316 miles by impending darkness.

▼ Number 99 Richard Brickhouse and #71 Bobby Isaac drove the only two winged Dodge Daytonas in the Sept. 14 Talladega 500. Jim Vandiver drove Ray Fox's conventional #3 Dodge Charger, replacing Bobby Johns, who joined the Talladega boycott. Brickhouse won the race, passing Vandiver in the final 11 laps. Isaac encountered tire problems and finished fourth, a lap off the pace.

David Pearson's Ford and Cale Yarborough's Mercury line up on the front row before the start of the Sept. 28 Old Dominion 500 at Martinsville Speedway. The annual 500-lapper was run two weeks after the Talladega boycott, and many of the spectators were angered with PDA president Richard Petty for calling the strike. Late in the race, a fan hurled a beer can that struck Petty's windshield. Despite the close call, Petty outran Pearson down the stretch and won the race.

LeeRoy Yarbrough

LONNIE LEEROY YARBROUGH grew up on the rough side of Jacksonville, Fla., and developed an affinity for speed at an early age. When he was 12, Yarbrough put together his first car, a 1934 Ford coupe with a Chrysler engine. He gave the local cops fits when he was a teenager. When he was 19, Yarbrough found his way to a local dirt track to ventilate his lust for speed. Amazingly, Yarbrough won the very first race he ever ran at Jacksonville Speedway in the spring of 1957.

Yarbrough started his racing career in the lower tier Sportsman division. After winning 11 races, Yarbrough moved up to the more powerful Modifieds and won 83 features in a three-year span. "I wanted to be a race car driver ever since I was 12," Yarbrough said in a 1969 interview. "If you think enough about doing something, you should want to be the best. I wanted to be the best race car driver in the world." Unchecked restless behavior became key to his ascent up stock car racing's ladder.

A skillful driver, Yarbrough became an instant success. He won two short-track races in the 1964 NASCAR Grand National season, the first year he competed in more than 14 races. Two years later, Yarbrough scored his first superspeedway win at Charlotte. Driving an unsponsored and lightly regarded Dodge Charger owned by Jon Thorne, Yarbrough dominated the race, leading for 450 of the 500 miles in the Oct. 16 National 500.

Factory-backed rides followed, and Yarbrough responded accordingly. Despite the myriad tribulations that beset his Junior Johnson Ford team early in the 1968 season, LeeRoy rebounded and won at Atlanta and Trenton. Having tasted success, he was energized to tackle the challenge of the '69 NASCAR Grand National season.

Yarbrough had a flair for the dramatic. In the 1969 Daytona 500, Yarbrough found himself trailing Charlie Glotzbach by 11 seconds with 10 laps remaining. He slashed his way through the slower traffic and drew in on the leader. On the final lap, Yarbrough ducked to the low side to make the decisive pass, but a lapped car loomed in his path. In an impressive display of courage and skill, Yarbrough dived to the low side in turn three to clear the lapped car, nearly clipping the apron. He took the lead from Glotzbach and dashed under the checkered flag a car length in front.

The passion he brought to the fight had elevated Yarbrough to the top echelon of his profession. He was the Daytona 500 champion, but he wasn't finished. Next, he won Darlington's Rebel 400 in the final four laps, then won Charlotte's World 600, lapping the entire field at least twice. He also bagged the summer 400-miler at Daytona, prevailing in a tense late-race struggle with Buddy Baker.

NASCAR Grand National Career Record 1960-1972
Starts: 198
Wins: 14
Top 5s: 65
Top 10s: 92
Poles: 10
Career Winnings: $465,771

Yarbrough won the summer race at Atlanta International Raceway despite a 102-degree fever. He captured the Southern 500 by passing David Pearson on the final lap. And he won by a full lap at Rockingham in October, overcoming a lap deficit when a flat tire sent him into the wall. By season's end, Yarbrough had seven wins to his credit.

LeeRoy Yarbrough truly made a name for himself with his outstanding 1969 performance. He won dozens of postseason awards and was voted the best American driver by a panel of experts. Sprinkled with liberal amounts of self-confidence and intelligence, it was his ability that carved a unique niche in the gallery of NASCAR greats.

After his sparkling 1969 season, Yarbrough's performance record tailed off. A victim of the factory withdrawal, Yarbrough had to scramble to locate rides in Grand National events. He won only once in '70, at Charlotte Motor Speedway, and only entered six races in '71. In 1972, he swallowed his pride and accepted a ride in a Ford owned by independent campaigner Bill Seifert. He registered nine top-10 finishes in 18 starts, clearly the finest efforts the Seifert machinery had ever posted.

Yarbrough showed up for Daytona's 1973 Speedweeks, but failed to earn a starting berth for the Daytona 500. He virtually dropped out of sight after that, never again showing up at a NASCAR event.

Number 98 LeeRoy Yarbrough battles #6 Buddy Baker during the Oct. 5 Wilkes 400 at North Wilkesboro Seedway. Yarbrough finished fourth and Baker took fifth in the 250-miler. Richard Petty was seemingly on his way to victory until a late-race caution was thrown to remove a bottle that had been thrown from the grandstands. Petty's big lead was erased and David Pearson came on in the final lap to steal the win.

Richard Petty's #43 Ford zips past the slower #08 car of E.J. Trivette in the Oct. 12 National 500 at Charlotte Motor Speedway. Petty started on the front row, but an engine failure put an end to his victory bid. King Richard won nine races in his Torino and finished second in the points standings. After a single year in Ford products, Petty returned to Plymouth in 1970.

Number 48 James Hylton and #88 Richard Brickhouse, both driving new winged Dodge Daytonas, pass Dr. Don Tarr's #37 1967 Dodge Charger in Charlotte Motor Speedway's National 500. Brickhouse fell out early with mechanical problems and Hylton registered an 11th-place finish. Dr. Tarr, a general practitioner from Miami, ran a strong ninth in his old, outdated Charger.

Bobby Isaac hoists the winner's trophy in victory lane at the new Texas International Speedway following the season finale on Dec. 7. It was Isaac's first super-speedway win after seven years of competing in the NASCAR Grand National series. Isaac took the lead in his winged Dodge Daytona 15 laps from the finish and outran Donnie Allison for the win.

David Pearson won his second straight and third overall NASCAR Grand National championship in 1969. He compiled an envious record, winning 11 races and 14 poles and finishing among the top three 38 times in 51 starts. Counting post-season awards, Pearson also became the first driver to surpass $200,000 in single-season winnings. After the exhausting season, Pearson reduced his schedule and vowed never to take another stab at the championship. During his career, Pearson made four concentrated efforts at the NASCAR title and won three of them.

1969 NASCAR GRAND NATIONAL POINTS RACE

Rank	Driver	Points	Starts	Wins	Top 5	Top 10	Winnings
1	David Pearson	4170	51	11	42	44	$229,760
2	Richard Petty	3813	50	10	31	38	$129,906
3	James Hylton	3750	52	0	27	39	$114,416
4	Neil Castles	3530	51	0	14	30	$54,367
5	Elmo Langley	3383	52	0	13	28	$73,092
6	Bobby Isaac	3301	50	17	29	33	$92,074
7	John Sears	3166	52	0	17	27	$52,281
8	Jabe Thomas	3103	51	0	0	12	$44,989
9	Wendell Scott	3015	51	0	0	11	$47,451
10	Cecil Gordon	3002	51	0	1	8	$39,679
11	E.J. Trivette	2988	49	0	0	15	$35,896
12	Bill Champion	2813	49	0	1	10	$33,656
13	Bill Seifert	2765	50	0	0	15	$44,361
14	J.D. McDuffie	2741	50	0	0	12	$30,861
15	Ben Arnold	2736	48	0	0	8	$33,256
16	LeeRoy Yarbrough	2712	30	7	16	21	$193,211
17	Henley Gray	2517	48	0	0	5	$29,335
18	Earl Brooks	2454	49	0	1	6	$34,793
19	Dave Marcis	2348	37	0	3	11	$32,383
20	Bobby Allison	2055	27	5	13	15	$69,483
21	Dick Brooks	1780	28	0	3	12	$28,187
22	Buddy Baker	1769	18	0	9	11	$62,928
23	Cale Yarborough	1715	19	2	7	8	$74,240
24	Donnie Allison	1662	16	1	10	11	$78,055
25	Richard Brickhouse	1660	24	1	2	9	$45,637
26	G.C. Spencer	1562	26	0	4	8	$21,660
27	Ed Negre	1465	31	0	0	4	$15,160
28	Friday Hassler	1421	18	0	0	7	$17,690
29	Frank Warren	1299	23	0	0	0	$15,677
30	Hoss Ellington	1210	15	0	0	4	$16,552
31	Roy Tyner	1191	21	0	0	1	$12,302
32	Dr. Ed Hessert	1113	16	0	0	7	$17,690
33	Buddy Arrington	1099	16	0	2	6	$12,975
34	Dick Johnson	1055	22	0	0	4	$11,182
35	Buddy Young	981	21	0	1	5	$15,542
36	Dub Simpson	959	20	0	0	0	$12,915
37	Charlies Glotzbach	944	12	0	5	6	$36,090
38	Roy Mayne	924	13	0	0	0	$9875
39	Wayne Smith	922	16	0	0	2	$10,340
40	Paul Goldsmith	892	11	0	4	5	$22,305
41	Dr. Don Tarr	855	12	0	0	3	$13,720
42	Ken Meisenhelder	627	16	0	0	0	$5630
43	Pete Hazelwood	598	16	0	0	1	$4160
44	Sonny Hutchins	535	8	0	2	2	$9552
45	Wayne Gillette	509	16	0	0	0	$5827
46	Paul Dean Holt	485	14	0	0	0	$4442
47	Johnny Halford	465	8	0	0	0	$4200
48	Ray Elder	433	4	0	0	4	$7200
49	John Kennedy	417	9	0	0	0	$6462
50	Dick Polling	408	12	0	0	0	$5467

David Pearson racked up his third NASCAR Grand National championship in 1969, taking the points lead in April and holding it for the remainder of the 54-race season.

With his win in the 250-miler at Richmond on April 13, Pearson took the points lead from Richard Petty, never to relinquish it. Petty's bid for a third championship was derailed in May when he missed two races due to broken ribs suffered in a crash at Asheville-Weaverville Speedway.

Pearson's third NASCAR title came in only his fourth concentrated attempt at the largest plum of the annual NASCAR Grand National campaign. He finished third in 1964 during his first full-season run, and won in '66, '68, and '69.

Bobby Isaac was the most prolific winner in 1969, winning 17 NASCAR Grand National races. He finished sixth in the final standings.

1970s: NASCAR Enters the Modern Era

Auto racing in the United States was billed as "The Sport of the '70s" as the new decade approached. With new, ultra-modern facilities popping up all over the country and millions of dollars being poured into NASCAR stock car racing by the automotive factories, the sport seemed to be on a roll.

Despite the overall rosy appearance, the earth was rumbling a bit within the NASCAR domain. Most of the licensed NASCAR Grand National drivers had formed a union called the Professional Drivers Association, which was an immediate burr under Bill France's saddle. To show their strength as a unit, most of the drivers boycotted the inaugural 1969 Talladega 500 at France's new Alabama International Motor Speedway. The drivers were serious about gaining awareness from NASCAR about conditions at the speedways, including the alarmingly high speeds, the amount of time teams had to spend at a track to prepare for a race, the perceived lack of posted awards, and amenities for the competitors.

The rapid development of the aero cars by the manufacturers was another concern for NASCAR and "Big" Bill France. In two short years, the race cars had gone from stock-appearing highway cars to futuristic vehicles sprouting wings and other aerodynamic complexities. To discourage special-edition high-speed racers, NASCAR adopted a new set of guidelines for 1970. The minimum requirement of 500 units available for public consumption had been in place since the mid '60s, but in '70 the manufacturers were required to build 1000 examples or a total equal to half the number of the make's American dealerships—whichever was greater.

The Plymouth division of Chrysler Corp. was the only manufacturer to produce a limited-edition muscle car for the 1970 NASCAR Grand National season. About 2500 new winged Superbirds were built, primarily to lure Richard Petty back into the MoPar fold after a one-year stint with Ford. Dodge's winged Daytona was still legal, having been introduced in '69 when the required 500 units were in place. Ford introduced a new Ford Torino for '70, but initial track tests indicated the new version was nearly 10 mph slower than the '69 Talladega model. The Dodge and Ford teams would use a year-old model in the '70 season. Plymouth was the only manufacturer to have a 1970 model racing in NASCAR.

During the early days of Daytona's 1970 Speedweeks activities, Ford announced it was drastically cutting back financial backing for NASCAR teams, leaving the Wood Brothers, Junior Johnson, Banjo Matthews, and Holman-Moody with fewer operating funds. Ford's announcement was considered a bombshell, but insiders said it wasn't surprising.

In September 1969, Ford's president, Semon "Bunkie" Knudsen, a friend of NASCAR racing for more than a decade, was fired. The ripple effect didn't surface until February 1970.

On the heels of the announced Ford cutback, the winged Dodges and Plymouths swept 10 of the top 13 positions in the Daytona 500 as Pete Hamilton wheeled a Petty Enterprises Superbird to a narrow victory over David Pearson's Ford Talladega. Hamilton, the 1968 NASCAR Grand National Rookie of the Year, was without a ride in '69. The articulate son of a college professor was content to drive on NASCAR's second-tier Grand Touring Division, which featured Camaros and Mustangs. When the PDA gained momentum in late '69 under the guidance of president Richard Petty, Hamilton was the main recruiter for the PDA within the GT ranks. And when Petty Enterprises returned to Plymouth with a two-car team, Hamilton's PDA recruiting efforts were rewarded with a ride in one of the electric-blue Petty Superbirds.

Hamilton hit stride quickly and drove to a convincing victory in the Alabama 500 at Talladega. Only about 36,000 spectators dotted the massive grandstands for the first spring race at the new track, proving the general public still retained ill feelings about the boycott fiasco seven months earlier. While the grandstands were half empty, the overall audience was well over five million, thanks to NASCAR's new contract with the ABC television network.

In December 1969, Roone Arledge, president of ABC Sports, announced the network would begin live coverage of NASCAR Grand National events. "Auto racing has been one of the mainstays on *ABC's Wide World of Sports*," said Arledge. "It has continued to be one of the best-rated shows. Viewer interest in the sport confirms our belief that the time is ripe for automobile racing's expansion on television. We are confident of the success of our new package."

Bill France knew the electronic media would be a lifeline to NASCAR Grand National racing, but he also had concerns about how the network would squeeze a four-hour race into a 1½-hour time slot. Plans were for the ABC network to pick up the telecast when the races were about half over and show highlights of the early race action. There were no live flag-to-flag telecasts in 1970.

The spring race at Talladega was the first live telecast by ABC Sports' production crew. The exciting early laps were never aired and Hamilton won by nearly a lap over runner-up Bobby Isaac. By Talladega standards, the race was a dud. It was unclear how the initial ABC telecast would serve the sport. One of the individuals who did tune into the telecast

was President Richard Nixon, who felt compelled to write winner Hamilton a congratulatory letter.

Other telecasts included a short-track race at North Wilkesboro, another lackluster race in which Petty led 349 of the 400 laps on his way to victory. Darlington's Rebel 400 was another live effort by ABC, but David Pearson finished three laps ahead of runner-up Dick Brooks. The cameras missed a spectacular tumble by Richard Petty, and the replay tape machine in ABC's trackside production truck wasn't operating properly. No one watching the race on TV ever saw the crash.

Charlotte's World 600 was another runaway race ABC televised. Donnie Allison finished two laps ahead of the field, but some excitement did arise from the return of Fred Lorenzen after a three-year retirement. Lorenzen, Ford's golden boy of the 1960s, had hoped to land a well-financed Ford ride, but given Ford's cutback, he had to accept an offer from Dodge.

The final live telecast of the 1970 season was at Nashville in July, a brutal 420-lapper on the recently refurbished ½-mile track. The turns were steeper than Talladega and the race turned out to be a survival of the fittest contest. Only nine cars finished and Bobby Isaac won by two full laps. Every car running at the finish was in a lap by itself, not exactly high-pitched drama on live television.

Following the Nashville event, ABC abandoned plans to televise any more races live. The remainder of the television schedule returned to the *Wide World of Sports* format with races taped, edited, and aired up to six weeks later, along with log rolling, bobsledding, and wrist-wrestling highlights.

By midsummer, testing sessions for the second annual Talladega 500 revealed that speeds were still hovering around the 200-mph mark. During one shakedown run, David Pearson blew two tires on his Ford and slammed into the concrete retaining barrier. Pearson was uninjured in the mishap, but expressed grave concerns about the conditions for the upcoming race.

Other test sessions also indicated that tires might be a problem, like they had during the inaugural Talladega 500 in 1969. NASCAR had done little to reduce speeds in the first half of the '70 season. Four drivers had suffered injuries, two of them career ending, and one driver had died on the racetrack. With Talladega looming, there were whispers in the garage that some drivers might not run, and another boycott was possible.

From the threats of another boycott came a device that has been cussed and discussed for more than 30 years—the restrictor plate. To curb speeds, NASCAR introduced a restrictive device to limit fuel flow to the carburetor. NASCAR vice president Lin Kuchler said, "Drivers and car owners have told us that they have been on the ragged edge at most of the races this year and have had trouble keeping their equipment together. The introduction of the carburetor plate should provide closer competition and a reduction in speeds."

The Aug. 16 event at Michigan International Speedway went down in history as the first NASCAR Grand National event to be run with restrictor plates. Charlie Glotzbach won the race, which ended under caution. Restrictor plates were in use in all the remaining 1970 NASCAR Grand National races, including short tracks.

Bobby Isaac wound up winning the 1970 NASCAR Grand National championship in a season-long battle with James Hylton and Bobby Allison. In fact, the '70 championship chase remains one of the most diverse in NASCAR history, with 12 lead changes among seven different drivers.

By 1971, Ford had pulled up stakes and withdrawn from NASCAR Grand National racing. Matthew McLaughlin, Ford's vice president of sales, said, "We believe our racing activities have served their purpose, and we propose now to concentrate our promotional efforts on direct merchandising and sale of our products through franchised dealers. Accordingly, effective immediately we are withdrawing from all forms of motorsports competition."

Jaques Passino, Ford's director of racing since 1962, expressed shock with the Ford bailout. "Although Ford has severed its ties with racing," said Passino, "I still feel the racetrack, which has proven to be the real test track for automobile production, will be the same—even more so in the future. A year ago, auto racing drew 53 million spectators and millions more saw it on television. I feel auto racing is on the way to being the number-one sport in the United States and I wanted to be a part of the future. I have considered the other areas offered to me at Ford in manufacturing and merchandising, but I wanted to devote my energies to performance. Effective immediately, I hereby resign from Ford Motor Co."

Chrysler cut back its factory effort too, trimming its potent six-car effort to a pair of cars fielded out of the Petty Enterprises shops. Champion Bobby Isaac, as well as Bobby Allison, Charlie Glotzbach, and Fred Lorenzen got their pink slips. "We had to cut back," said Chrysler's Gayle Porter. "There was no alternative."

The loss of the factory-supported team was a big blow to NASCAR. With the unlimited supply of parts and technical support being reduced to a trickle, the hand-me-down pieces the independent campaigners received were no longer available. Every team in NASCAR in 1971, save Petty Enterprises, felt the pinch of the factory withdrawal.

Originally, the 1971 rules limited engines to 366 cid. However, with purse strings growing tighter, NASCAR waived the rule

and permitted teams to use bigger powerplants. Only a couple of teams could have afforded to develop the smaller engines.

Racing teams were forced to seek outside sponsorship dollars to continue operation. Junior Johnson, who had lost his Ford deal, approached the R.J. Reynolds Tobacco Co. about sponsorship for his team. At the same time, NASCAR was courting the tobacco giant about sponsoring the entire NASCAR Grand National series. Due to a new congressional mandate, the tobacco companies were no longer able to advertise on television. They had huge advertising budgets and a lot of that went to auto racing starting in 1971.

R.J. Reynolds agreed with NASCAR's proposal, and became title sponsor of the entire season. The new name of NASCAR's premier stock car racing tour became the "Winston Cup Grand National Series." The biggest news of the joint venture was a $100,000 points fund. R.J. Reynolds also agreed to sponsor the spring race at Talladega.

The 1971 NASCAR Winston Cup Grand National campaign would be the final year with 40-plus events. The writing was on the wall—the 100- and 125-milers on short tracks were soon to be a thing of the past. Winston increased advertising in the print media when the "major" races of 250 miles or more were in town.

Winston's plunge into NASCAR was one of the few high-water marks in an otherwise troubled year. Many of the top teams were unable to find enough funding to compete, even on a limited schedule. Junior Johnson and Banjo Matthews, two of Ford's top team owners during the height of the factory days, tossed in the towel shortly after the Daytona 500. Cale Yarborough had left NASCAR to join the USAC Indy Car trail, and LeeRoy Yarbrough was on the sidelines with no car to drive. Charlie Glotzbach, a top Dodge pilot in 1970, was out of a ride as well. Team owners Ray Nichels and Cotton Owens found sponsorship for a single season, but their potent Plymouth teams' days were numbered. Mario Rossi fielded a

Dodge as long as his funds held out, but by early summer, he folded his team, too.

The independents also struggled. Without used parts filtering down from the factories, many curtailed their schedule, held on for as long as they could while spending less, or quit altogether. The 1971 season was a bleak time for NASCAR.

The restrictor plates quickly became quite controversial. Different size plates were used for different types of engines. The powerful Chrysler Hemi and Ford Boss 429 engines had the smallest openings, while teams running the more conventional wedge engines were issued bigger plates. Some of the top-contending teams were able to switch back to the old conventional wedge engines, while the independents were forced to use their leftover big engines. The privateers were unable to make the costly engine switch.

In the May 21 short-track event at Asheville Speedway, only 17 cars bothered to show up. Promoter George Ledford paid Richard Petty a $2000 appearance fee to compete in his 100-miler, while the independents didn't receive any appearance money. The independent campaigners who did show up didn't care to be shunned in that manner. Five drivers fell out of the Asheville 100-miler with mechanical problems and seven others simply pulled out in a mini protest. Petty was one of only five cars still running past the halfway point, and he finished four laps ahead of runner-up Elmo Langley.

Car counts were dwindling, ticket sales were off, and the sport was clearly in a deep-rooted recession. Richard Howard, general manager of Charlotte Motor Speedway, became the savior of the 1971 NASCAR Winston Cup Grand National season. Howard was worried about the lack of advance ticket sales for the upcoming World 600, but he had an ace up his sleeve. Howard contacted Junior Johnson and talked him into building a Chevrolet for the 600. Chevrolet

hadn't been seriously competitive since it halted factory support in '63, and with the restrictor plates choking off the beefy Chrysler and Ford engines, the time was ripe for a competitive Chevrolet to return to NASCAR.

Howard wanted Junior to end his five-year retirement and drive the car in the 600. Johnson politely refused Howard's offer and hired Charlie Glotzbach to drive. "I wanted Junior to drive," said Howard. "Junior would bring several thousand spectators if he would have driven. But even as a car builder of a Chevy, he is valuable to our promotion."

Glotzbach put the Chevy on the pole, and presto, a record crowd of 78,000 showed up for the World 600. Glotzbach crashed in the race, but the huge throng had seen the first competitive Chevy since Bobby Allison's efforts of 1966 and '67. The Howard-Johnson-Glotzbach tandem entered selected races for the balance of the '71 season and came away with a win at Bristol's Volunteer 500.

With the dwindling car count, the lower tier NASCAR Grand American Mustangs and Camaros were permitted to compete on the short tracks with the NASCAR Grand Nationals in late summer. Bobby Allison, driving a Mustang, won the first of the "mixed" races on Aug. 6 at Winston-Salem's Bowman Gray Stadium. The lightweight Mustang was much more nimble on the flat ¼-mile track. Tiny Lund won twice in his Camaro—at Hickory and North Wilkesboro. In the Aug. 28 race at Hickory, only 22 cars showed up.

Further dissension surfaced in autumn 1971 within the promoter ranks. Clay Earles, operator of Martinsville Speedway, and Richmond Fairgrounds Raceway's president Paul Sawyer declared they would reject all Grand American entries for their races no matter what the NASCAR rule book dictated. The Grand American teams complained to NASCAR, but Earles and Sawyer prevailed in the end. "We've scheduled a *Grand National* race," said Earles, "and that's what we'll run. I don't think the Grand Americans should intermingle with the larger Grand Nationals."

A total of six "mixed" races were staged in 1971, with the NASCAR Grand Nationals and NASCAR Grand Americans both winning three times. The three wins by Grand American cars created a void in the official NASCAR records. *Nobody* got credit for winning the races at Winston-Salem, Hickory, and North Wilkesboro. According to official NASCAR records, 48 official races were held, but only 45 wins were credited.

By the end of the 1971 season, Chrysler had announced it would withdraw from NASCAR entirely. "We reached a point where we had everything to lose and nothing to gain," said a Chrysler spokesperson. "Ford won virtually all the big races in 1968 and 1969, so we built the car to beat them. We came up with the Plymouth Superbird and the Dodge Daytona. Both were approved by NASCAR for three years. But as soon as the cars won some races, NASCAR changed the rules. They cut the engine size …. We built a 366 cubic-inch engine, but that was outlawed after one race. We built 25 of them, and we have 24 of them left. We had to start all over again." Chrysler left in a huff, and it would be more than a quarter century before the MoPar badge would reappear in NASCAR racing.

NASCAR announced that the 1972 Winston Cup Grand National season would consist of only 31 races. All the short-track 100- and 125-milers were tossed into a short-lived NASCAR *Grand National East* tour, which fizzled out in less than two years.

"We feel the changes in scheduling will benefit the sport in a number of ways," said France. "The new schedule will make it possible for more top-flight drivers and teams to pursue the Winston Cup. Also, sponsorship for teams should be easier to procure with the broader exposure which is sure to become a reality."

But the biggest announcement for 1972 was Bill France stepping down as president of NASCAR. On Jan. 11, Big Bill stepped aside and gave the reins of NASCAR to his son, William Clifton France, better known as Bill France, Jr. "In the past 24 years, NASCAR has grown to be one of the largest and certainly the finest sanctioning body in the world," said the senior France. "Bill, Jr., has lived with NASCAR all his life and he has the foresight and capability to handle the varied and demanding duties of this position."

The forecast for 1972 was uncertain at best. Acquiring sponsorship for the teams proved to be a mighty battle. The STP Corp., which had backed the Ray Nichels and Fred Lorenzen effort in '71, went with Petty Enterprises. Bobby Allison, who had Coca-Cola as an ardent supporter, took the dollars to the Richard Howard and Junior Johnson Chevrolet team. Holman-Moody, Ford's most powerful entity in the '60s, folded its operation. The Wood Brothers had Purolator Filters as a financial backer, and the K&K Insurance team of Bobby Isaac and crew chief Harry Hyde was privately funded and remained intact.

Other than that, quarter-panels on NASCAR Winston Cup Grand National cars were basically empty. Pete Hamilton, Charlie Glotzbach, LeeRoy Yarbrough, Donnie Allison, and Fred Lorenzen were some of the drivers left without regular rides in 1972. A small-scale effort by American Motors stepped into the picture with Roger Penske and Mark Donohue campaigning a boxy AMC Matador.

When the 1972 Daytona Speedweeks rolled around, only five cars were capable of winning. Four of the five encountered problems in the Daytona 500, leaving A.J. Foyt's Wood Brothers Mercury with an easy victory. He was nearly five miles ahead of runner-up Charlie Glotzbach, who took a one-shot deal in Cotton Owens' Dodge. Third-place finisher Jim Vandiver was six full laps behind.

The early part of the 1972 campaign was rather lethargic. Richard Petty lost a cylinder midway through the 250-miler at Martinsville in April, yet still won the race by *seven laps*. Attendance was tapering off, too. Only 12,000 showed up at Richmond, only 16,000 passed through the turnstiles at North Wilkesboro, and a shade over 25,000 turned out at Dover.

A few of the races were televised live by ABC, albeit still under the format that picked up the live telecast when the race was half completed. Whereas ABC had selected noncompelling races to televise in 1970 and '71, they got lucky in March 1972. Bobby Allison drove his Chevrolet to victory in the Atlanta 500, passing Bobby Isaac and A.J. Foyt in the final laps. It was a fantastic three-car finish and Chevrolet's first win on a superspeedway in nearly nine years.

Foyt vacated the Wood Brothers ride to fulfill his USAC Indy Car commitments and David Pearson was tabbed as the full-time driver of the Purolator Mercury. Pearson won his first start with the Wood Brothers at Darlington. Although only seven racers won during the season, the season produced some memorable moments, and three different makes of cars ran up front.

Toward the end of the year, Petty and Allison were battling for the championship. The two headliners had engaged in heated on-track feuds off and on since '66. It had been rekindled in a few late-season events in '71, but throughout the early part of the '72 campaign there was no hint of any ill feelings.

That all changed in September 1972. In the Sept. 10 race at Richmond, Petty and Allison finished eight laps up on the rest of the field. As they were running circles around the rest of the drivers, they were busy running into each other. With just over 100 laps to go, Petty tapped Allison wide in the second turn and made a pass for the lead. As the pair hit the third turn, Allison thrashed Petty's rear bumper. Petty's Plymouth shot toward the railing as Allison steered low. Petty's car climbed on top of the guardrail, and for a moment it appeared to be headed for the grandstands. Amazingly, the car clipped a chain-link fence just beyond the guardrail and bounced back onto the track. To top it off, Petty held onto the lead.

Petty went on to win the race, outrunning Allison in the final laps. "I went completely out of the track and back in," Petty said afterward. "When I hit the fence, it must have throwed me back onto the track. I was surprised the car still had wheels on it. I couldn't believe I was still in the lead."

A memorable race it was, but it was just a teaser of what was to come. Petty and Allison got into another shoving match at Martinsville. Petty again won. Then came North Wilkesboro, which turned out to be one of the most exciting short-track events in NASCAR's 25-year history.

Petty and Allison were four laps ahead of the rest of the field in the final laps of the 400-lapper at North Wilkesboro. The two drivers would swap the lead—and plenty of sheet metal—in the final 39 laps. But the excitement turned into a violent outburst in the final three laps. Petty had taken the lead on lap 389, and repelled all of Allison's efforts to get past. With a shade over two laps remaining, Allison plowed his way into the lead, crowding Petty as they put a lap on rookie Vic Parsons. Petty regained control and a half lap later attempted to pass Allison on the high side. The two cars came together again and Petty bounced off the guardrail as Allison fought to regain control of his car. Allison's Chevy, with right-side tires rubbing sheet metal, began smoking heavily. The entire driver's compartment was filled with smoke as Allison took the white flag three car lengths ahead of Petty.

When Allison got to the first turn, he ran high to miss parts of the front and rear bumper of Petty's Plymouth, which were laying in the middle of the track from the incident a lap earlier. Petty darted under Allison to take the lead and went on to win as the crowd went wild.

The troubled waters of stock car racing had few competitive cars in the 1972 NASCAR Winston Cup Grand National season, but the drama was unsurpassed. Petty took his record-setting fourth NASCAR title as Allison finished second.

For 1973, Allison left the Richard Howard-owned, Junior Johnson-managed Chevrolet team to form his own operation. Petty's two-car team had filtered down to a one-car effort. Pearson was content to drive a limited schedule with the Wood Brothers. Buddy Baker had taken Bobby Isaac's place in the K&K Insurance Dodge. And Cale Yarborough was back in NASCAR's fold after a disappointing two-year stint in USAC. Yarborough joined Junior Johnson with sponsorship from Kar Kare.

Bud Moore, one of NASCAR's top team owners in the mid 1960s, had left to campaign Mustangs on the SCCA Trans-Am tour in '69. He, too, was back in NASCAR with a small 351-cid Ford. NASCAR had not given up hope for the small engines, though the lack of team sponsors prevented the sanctioning body from putting the heavily restricted big engines out to pasture. Restrictor plates were still part of the equation in NASCAR racing, but teams campaigning the small engines were able to run without the plates.

David Pearson enjoyed a record-wrecking year in 1973. Driving the Wood Brothers '71 Mercury, Pearson won 10 of 15 starts on superspeedways and 11 of 18 for the season. The unsponsored team of L.G. DeWitt and Benny Parsons won a single race and took the NASCAR Winston Cup championship trophy in a significant upset. All of the races were won by teams using big engines, except for the season opener at Riverside, which was won by Mark Donohue's 366-cid AMC Matador. Also in '73, Petty resigned as president of the Professional Drivers Association. The PDA had been a quiet force since the infamous Talladega boycott of '69.

In early 1974, NASCAR was confronted with an issue that threatened to shut down the entire sport of auto racing. In late '73, the Organization of the Petroleum Exporting Countries (OPEC) announced a general boycott on oil exports to Europe, Japan, and the United States. Virtually overnight, supplies of crude oil were drying up. To conserve energy, President Nixon told Americans that all gas stations would be closed between 9:00 P.M. Saturday and midnight Sunday.

With motorsports facing a congressional shutdown, the Federal Energy Office was established to monitor the usage of fuel nationwide. The FEO called for citizens to reduce their

Retired NASCAR president Bill France took the bull by the horns. Groomed in politics, Big Bill represented the entire auto-racing fraternity in a meeting with FEO authorities. "While auto racing uses only a minimal amount of fuel in contrast to other leisure-time activities, we are anxious to cooperate in the overall curtailment of the use of fuel," said France. "Auto racing is a highly visible sport and it has a public-relations problem inasmuch as we are very vulnerable. We feel it is important to cooperate with the government's request to exceed the 25-percent cut if possible. I am sure the quality of NASCAR racing for our fans and competitors will be unaffected."

Under France, NASCAR took immediate steps to conserve fuel. The length of all races would be reduced by 10 percent, and a 30-gallon limit of fuel for drivers to use in practice sessions was introduced. Practice days were shortened, and the starting fields at most races were reduced. Following the 1974 Daytona Speedweeks, NASCAR reported that it used 30.1 percent less fuel than it had during the '73 Speedweeks activities. "As far as the government is concerned," said France, "it is looking at all sports with one eye. All sports have agreed to cut energy usage by 25 percent across the board and we will gladly comply with this requirement."

Thanks to Bill France's expert guidance, a full slate of 30 NASCAR Winston Cup Grand National events were run in 1974. Although NASCAR weathered the energy crisis, major problems still existed. Three drivers won 27 of the 30 races, a new points system had reduced the title contenders to two after the Daytona 450, and the move to smaller engines was encouraged by constant rules changes designed to take the final breath of life out of the antiquated big engines.

NASCAR began experimenting with rules changes because it had no testing facilities of its own. Six major rules changes within an eight-week period handcuffed many of the racing teams. The rules were "tweaked" after studying the results of each race. When a rule change was announced, team owners would have to order new parts. In many instances, by the time the newly ordered parts arrived, they were obsolete due to additional changes. Richard Petty felt all the changes were unnecessary. "You have winners and losers every week," said the King. "No matter what the rules are, the same teams are going to win. The only difference is it costs everybody more

Petty and Cale Yarborough each won 10 races in the 1974 campaign, with Petty taking his fifth title. Junior Johnson had taken over sole ownership of his team with the acquisition of sponsor Carling Beer midway through the season. Richard Howard, who got Chevrolet back into racing in '71, resigned as owner of the Johnson-managed team.

By 1975, the transition from big to small engines was complete. All cars were equipped with the same-size engines and the restrictor plates were gone. NASCAR also initiated the Awards and Achievement Plan, a disguise for appearance money. In an effort to offset the costs of the switch to small engines, NASCAR mandated that promoters pay up to $3000 each for top-ranked teams and $500 for independents who competed in all the races.

With the Chrysler Hemi and Ford Boss engines finally laid to rest, General Motors executives began hanging around at more and more NASCAR races. Chevrolet had a vast stock of engines that fit within the NASCAR specifications, and the engineering expertise to make them work. In a mirror image of the 1957 AMA resolution (when the competing automotive manufacturers retreated from NASCAR racing publicly but not privately), traces of General Motors participation could be found, though is wasn't publicly admitted.

With a standard set of rules, stability had gained a foothold within the NASCAR kingdom. However, many of the smaller teams couldn't afford to continue. Finding enough cars to fill the fields was a tough assignment. Only 22 cars showed up at Richmond and only 23 were on hand at Bristol. Rockingham drew only 31 cars. The potent Junior Johnson team ran only selected events, having lost the Carling sponsorship six months after signing a five-year contract.

Despite the small fields, NASCAR Winston Cup Grand National racing was getting more television time. ABC Sports was in its second year of presenting the second half of the Daytona 500 live. The Daytona coverage was up against stiff competition, but it won the time slot handily. NASCAR's big 500-miler drew a 10.7 Neilsen rating, while an NBA game on NBC got an 8.6 and an NHL game on CBS managed a 4.1.

CBS signed a contract with NASCAR to tape-delay coverage of some of the races for which ABC didn't own the rights. The CBS format was similar to ABC's. NASCAR races were taped, edited, and aired later in a package format. Ratings for the *CBS Sports Spectacular* show were always greater when a NASCAR Winston Cup Grand National event was scheduled. "Not only is added televising of NASCAR races a boon to the sport itself," proclaimed Bill France, Jr., "but it will be highly attractive to sponsors and potential sponsors of racing teams at a time when exposure for them is most needed."

By the late 1970s, NASCAR was pulling itself out of the shackles of the post-factory days. Corporate sponsors were jumping on the bandwagon, new team owners found the NASCAR scene appealing, and a few of the surviving independent teams had beefed up their operations. The starting fields were full again, the grandstands were close to capacity, competition was closer, and television ratings were climbing steadily. NASCAR drivers were even invited to the White House by Jimmy and Rosalyn Carter. NASCAR was coming of age.

By February 1978, ABC Sports was preparing for its fifth consecutive live telecast of the second half of the Daytona 500. A couple of executives at CBS were also in Daytona, engaging in discussions with Bill France, Jr., concerning the '79 season. Ken Squier, who handled the public-address chores at Daytona International Speedway, had also been hired by CBS to anchor NASCAR telecasts. Barry Frank, exec-

utive vice president of CBS Sports, and France, Jr., struck a deal that was announced in May 1978. CBS Sports would televise the '79 Daytona 500 live from green to checkered flag.

The Daytona International Speedway had been resurfaced for the first time since it was built in 1959. The new pavement contributed to lightning-fast speeds. Buddy Baker's pole speed of 196.049 mph topped Cale Yarborough's mark of 194.015 mph established nine years earlier during the height of the factory muscle-car era.

The record speeds got plenty of publicity, and a widespread snowstorm blanketed the eastern part of the United States to give the CBS telecast a captive audience. The 21st annual running of the Daytona 500 was spectacular from start to finish. Baker developed mechanical problems right off the bat, and the remaining cars ran in a cluster like never seen before.

Cale Yarborough, Donnie Allison, and Bobby Allison ran for the lead in close quarters during the early going. All three cars spun out and lost at least one lap. Yarborough got bogged down in the wet infield off the backstretch and lost three laps.

With the help of timely caution flags, Cale and Donnie both managed to get back on the lead lap. With just over 50 miles remaining, Allison and Yarborough hooked up in a tight draft and pulled away from the remainder of the field. They took the white flag nearly a half lap ahead of Richard Petty, A.J. Foyt, and Darrell Waltrip.

Donnie Allison led the charge off the backstretch in the final lap. Yarborough whipped his car under Allison in a slingshot maneuver. But Allison, keeping a careful eye in the rearview mirror, swooped low to block Cale's move. Yarborough kept his foot on the throttle, dropped down a lane, and pulled beside Allison. Neither driver lifted as the cars clanged together. Yarborough was suddenly in the infield, his tires churning up grass at 200 mph. Both cars then slid together into the concrete wall, and both were out of the race as Petty, Waltrip, and Foyt flashed by the crash scene. Petty ended a 45-race losing skid with a crowd-pleasing victory.

As Petty made his victory lap, he noticed a commotion inside the third turn. Yarborough and the Allison brothers were scrapping on the ground, throwing punches and kicking each other. Bobby Allison had stopped on the track to check on the condition of his brother and soon got into the fracas.

All of this was captured by the CBS cameras, and about 16 million tuned into the telecast. The Daytona 500 was the top-rated show during each half hour. Overall, the program got a 10.5 national rating, a number that wouldn't be surpassed until 2002. During the final half hour, the ratings jumped to 13.5.

The CBS crew left the production truck with smiles on their faces. "A lot of times you walk out of the truck and you don't know if you did well or not," said producer Michael Pearl. "This time I walked out with a feeling that 'this worked.'"

NASCAR's biggest showcase event turned into a widely viewed "Cale and Donniebrook." Millions of viewers who had never seen a NASCAR car had just witnessed NASCAR Winston Cup racing's finest fracas. The stunning finish made phones ring off the hook in ticket offices at other Winston Cup venues.

The 1979 NASCAR Winston Cup Grand National season was memorable for other reasons beside the electrifying conclusion of the Daytona 500. Freshman driver Dale Earnhardt drove like a savvy veteran, winning at Bristol in his 13th career start. Petty and Waltrip battled down to the wire for the championship, with Petty taking the points lead in the final race and winning by a paper-thin margin of a then-record 12 points. Petty became the NASCAR champion for the seventh time.

By the end of the 1970s, the sport of NASCAR racing regained and, in fact, surpassed the popularity it enjoyed at the start of the decade. It had overcome numerous setbacks, including retreating factory support, thinning fields, competitor unrest, the energy crisis, and weak team sponsorships. The '70s had many bumps along the way, but by the decade's end, NASCAR had emerged as one of the sporting industry's strongest entities.

1970

January 18 A.J. Foyt's Ford nips Roger McCluskey's Plymouth Superbird to win the season opener at Riverside. Five-time Riverside winner Dan Gurney finishes sixth.

February 19 Cale Yarborough and Charlie Glotzbach win the Twin 125-mile qualifiers at Daytona. Rookie Talmadge Prince is fatally injured in a 19th-lap crash in the second qualifier.

February 22 Pete Hamilton, recently signed to drive a Petty Enterprises Plymouth, posts an upset victory in the Daytona 500. Hamilton passes Ford's David Pearson with nine laps to go and wins by three car lengths.

March 1 James Hylton holds off a furious rally by Richard Petty to win the Richmond 500. It is Hylton's first career NASCAR Grand National win and his first start in a Ford after campaigning a Dodge for four years.

March 24 During a Goodyear tire test at Talladega, Buddy Baker becomes the first man to break the 200-mph barrier on a closed course. Baker turns in a lap of 200.447 mph to establish himself as the "Fastest Man on Four Wheels."

April 12 Pete Hamilton cruises to victory in the Alabama 500 at Talladega as ABC Sports televises the second half of the race live to a nationwide audience. The network squeezes the three hour and 17 minute race into a 90-minute time slot.

April 18 Richard Petty breezes to an easy win in the Gwyn Staley Memorial 400 at North Wilkesboro, the second event televised live by ABC Sports. Petty leads 349 of the 400 laps, and is ahead of the pack every lap shown during the live telecast.

May 9 David Pearson scores his first win of the season in the Rebel 400 at Darlington. Richard Petty is injured when his Plymouth flips on the front chute. ABC Sports picks up live coverage a few minutes before Petty's crash.

Following a one-year stint with Ford, Richard Petty was lured back into the Plymouth fold in 1970 with the development of the new winged Plymouth Superbird. Chrysler had to produce more than 1500 of the new models (1920 were built) to gain acceptance from NASCAR to enter Grand National competition. Prior to '70, only 500 factory examples were required to make a car eligible. Chrysler officials determined it was necessary to build the increased number of units to reacquire the services of NASCAR's leading driver.

Dan Gurney jumped from Ford to Plymouth for the Jan. 18 Motor Trend 500 at the Riverside International Raceway road course. Gurney put his #42 Petty Enterprises Plymouth Superbird on the pole, but never led in the race. An extended pit stop for mechanical repairs removed Gurney from contention, but he battled back to finish sixth. Gurney was the acknowledged master of road racing. He won five of the seven races at Riverside from 1963 to '69. In his career, Gurney won five of his 16 NASCAR Grand National starts.

USAC ace Roger McCluskey was added to the Superbird contingent for the Riverside 500-miler. Driving a car owned by Norm Nelson, McCluskey was one of the front runners in the race, but in the end he finished second to A.J. Foyt in a Ford Talladega. Chrysler desperately wanted to win the 1970 season opener at Riverside, but Fords took three of the top four spots.

A.J. Foyt won the 1970 season opener at Riverside, spoiling the debut of the winged Plymouth Roadrunner. During Daytona's Speedweeks, he ran into an assortment of problems in his #11 Jack Bowsher-owned Ford Torino Talladega. Foyt ran a sluggish 14th in the Twin 125-miler and had to start 28th in the Daytona 500. He only went 58 laps before his engine blew. The tough Texan didn't compete in any other Grand National events in '70.

Talmadge Prince, a short-track racer from south Georgia, dreamed of competing in NASCAR's Grand National division. When James Hylton switched from Dodge to Ford in 1970, Prince jumped at the chance to acquire Hylton's Dodge Daytona. The deal was made, and Prince towed the car to Daytona International Speedway and entered the '70 Speedweeks activities. Unfortunately, he would never run in the Daytona 500.

Talmadge Prince's #78 Dodge is towed following a 21st-lap crash in the second Twin 125-mile qualifying race at Daytona on Feb. 19. The rookie driver, competing in his first Grand National race, lost control when the engine blew as he sped into the first turn. The car spun sideways and was hit in the driver's door by Bill Seifert. Prince died upon impact.

Cale Yarborough leads Tiny Lund in a close battle for the lead in the early laps of the Feb. 22 Daytona 500. Cale blew an engine on the 31st lap while leading. Lund encountered overheating problems and finished 13th. In the Twin 125-mile qualifying race three days before the 500, Yarborough won at an average speed of 183.295 mph, an official race speed record that stood for 14 years.

1970

May 24 Donnie Allison finishes two laps ahead of the field to win the Charlotte World 600. Fred Lorenzen ends a three-year retirement with a competitive run, but exits with a blown engine after 378 miles. ABC cameras join the race in progress for the fourth live telecast of the season.

July 25 Bobby Isaac dominates the Nashville 420, finishing two laps ahead of the field. Only nine cars finish the grueling race, which is televised in part by ABC Sports. Third-place finisher Neil Castles finishes 26 laps behind Isaac.

August 16 Restrictor plates make their first appearance in NASCAR racing at Michigan International Speedway. Charlie Glotzbach drives a winged Dodge Daytona to victory under the caution flag.

September 30 The final dirt-track race in NASCAR Grand National history is run at State Fairgrounds Speedway in Raleigh, N.C. Richard Petty wins in a Don Robertson-owned Plymouth.

October 4 Legendary NASCAR driver Curtis Turner perishes in a private plane crash in Pennsylvania. Bobby Isaac finishes first in the 250-miler at North Wilkesboro Speedway.

November 15 Cale Yarborough hustles to victory in the American 500 at Rockingham, and announces from victory lane that he will move to the USAC Indy Car trail in 1971.

November 19 Ford announces that it will cut back its factory effort in 1971. Jacques Passino, director of Ford's racing program, quits the company.

November 22 Bobby Allison captures the season finale at Hampton, Va., as Bobby Isaac is declared the 1970 NASCAR Grand National champion.

December R.J. Reynolds announces its Winston brand of cigarettes will become the title sponsor of NASCAR's premier stock car racing series. The official title will be NASCAR Winston Cup Grand National Series.

Sophomore sensation Dick Brooks had the new Plymouth Superbird sheetmetal and a smattering of support from Chrysler Corp.'s factory-backed NASCAR effort. Brooks, who owned his own team, was running third in the late stages of the Daytona 500, but a blown engine put him out of the race with 19 laps remaining. Later that year, Brooks finished second at Darlington for his best showing of the season.

Buddy Arrington suffered a hard crash on the 89th lap of the Daytona 500. Arrington's Dodge Daytona hit the wall with such force that it snapped the horizontal stabilizer portion of the rear wing. The piece soared into the air and nearly struck John Sears' speeding car. Following this mishap, Chrysler added a cable that ran from the quarter panel into the wing of each race car so the wing wouldn't come apart in a crash. Arrington, who suffered broken ribs in the wreck, never rebuilt his Daytona. He returned with a conventional Dodge Charger.

Pete Hamilton, a dashing youngster from Dedham, Mass., was hired by Petty Enterprises to campaign the #40 Superbird in major NASCAR events. Hamilton was an instant hit, winning the Daytona 500 after a tremendous late-race battle with three-time champion David Pearson. Hamilton was the 1968 NASCAR Grand National Rookie of the Year, but had missed most of the '69 season when he couldn't secure a full-time ride.

In his fifth start since returning to Chrysler's factory-backed NASCAR team, Richard Petty drove a new Superbird to victory in the March 8 Carolina 500. Petty overcame a pair of spin outs in the race. In the early going, he lost control and spun through the first turn. In the late stages, Petty was involved in a pit-road collision with Cale Yarborough. After quick repairs, Petty and Yarborough both got back into competition. Petty won as Yarborough finished second.

On March 24, Buddy Baker took Chrysler's company car, a royal blue Dodge Daytona, to Talladega for a special world record attempt for a closed circuit. In an officially timed run, Baker became the first driver to surpass the magic 200-mph barrier on a closed oval. His best lap was 200.447 mph.

With the driver's boycott of the 1969 Talladega 500 still fresh in the minds of racing fans, a disappointing crowd turned out for the April 12 Alabama 500. Here, #22 Bobby Allison and #6 Buddy Baker race past the massive, sparsely occupied grandstands. The race also marked the first live telecast by ABC Sports, which signed a contract with NASCAR to televise a number of NASCAR Grand National events in '70. Areas within a 100-mile radius of Talladega were blacked out and didn't receive the historic telecast via their ABC affiliate.

Pete Hamilton's #40 Plymouth Superbird passes #34 Wendell Scott and John Sears on the short chute at Alabama International Motor Speedway during the Alabama 500. Hamilton took the lead 18 laps from the finish and recorded his second win of the 1970 season. Hamilton, in his second full season in NASCAR Grand National racing, was the superspeedway sensation in '70, winning the Daytona 500 and both events at Talladega.

Alabama 500 winner Pete Hamilton is congratulated by Alabama Governor George C. Wallace following Hamilton's win in the inaugural spring 500-miler at Talladega. Another key political figure, President Richard M. Nixon, watched the race on television and sent the winner a congratulatory letter a few weeks later.

Number 71 Bobby Isaac, #43 Richard Petty, and #98 LeeRoy Yarbrough battle for the lead in the early stages of the April 18 Gwyn Staley Memorial 400 at North Wilkesboro Speedway. Isaac led the first 51 laps before Petty zoomed into command to stay. Petty lapped the field and recorded an easy victory. ABC Sports picked up the live telecast near the midpoint of the race, but by then, Petty had mounted a huge lead.

The Dodge Daytonas of Bobby Isaac and Bobby Allison are on the front row at the start of the May 24 World 600 at Charlotte. A tall crane behind the frontstretch grandstand was in place to hold cameras for ABC Sports' live telecast of the race. Donnie Allison came from his ninth starting spot to win.

Former Ford star Fred Lorenzen ended his three-year retirement in 1970, but was unable to find an opening on the Ford factory team. He settled for a ride in the #28 Dodge Daytona originally owned by Charlotte Motor Speedway General Manager Richard Howard and later transferred to Ray Fox. The car was sponsored by Piper Trash Can Liners in the July 4 Firecracker 400. Lorenzen competed in seven races in '70, but finished only once. NASCAR rookie Benny Parsons campaigned the L.G. DeWitt #72 Ford and took eighth place in the final points standings.

Dr. Don Tarr authored an historic first in NASCAR competition during the Firecracker 400. Tarr's #36 Superbird was outfitted with a two-way radio so he could communicate with the ABC Sports announcers during caution periods. The experimental gadget worked to perfection, and Tarr delivered some interesting verbiage. Later in the year, Tarr was hired to provide pitside commentary during an ABC telecast at Nashville.

Wendell Scott looks over his crunched #34 Ford after it was destroyed in a practice crash at Trenton Speedway prior to the July 12 Schaefer 300. The end-over-end flip wiped out the only car Scott had in his racing stable. Scott was able to continue racing, however, thanks to the generosity of Don Robertson, who added a car to his team for Scott. The Danville, Va., veteran managed to finish 14th in the 1970 NASCAR Grand National points standings.

Bobby Isaac

BOBBY ISAAC'S JOURNEY to become the 1970 NASCAR Grand National champion is a classic rags-to-riches story. The son of a North Carolina mill worker and one of nine brothers and sisters, Isaac didn't own a pair of shoes until he was 13. Lacking parental supervision, he quit school in the sixth grade, racked balls in a pool hall, and did a lot of aimless hitchhiking.

It wasn't until 1956, when he was 24, that he went racing full time. "I used to race four or five times a week. I raced wherever and whenever I could," he said. During his tenure in the Modified and Sportsman bullrings, Isaac became one of the winningest drivers of the late 1950s and early '60s. He also established new standards for being fined by NASCAR executive manager Pat Purcell. After a heated battle on the track, Isaac would tend to settle "paybacks" with a huge right hand. It took a few years for Purcell to break Isaac of this habit. "He told me that I needed racing a lot more than racing needed me," reflected Isaac. "Racing would do just fine without me, and if I wanted to be a racer, I'd have to get a handle on my temper."

In 1963, a more mature Isaac broke into the NASCAR Grand National ranks driving Ford and Plymouths for Bondy Long. His impressive finishes in equipment regarded as second rate caught the eye of Ray Nichels, who headed a Dodge and Plymouth factory team. Nichels seated Isaac in a Dodge for the '64 season.

Isaac won his very first start for Nichels in the 100-mile qualifying race at Daytona, nosing out Jimmy Pardue and Richard Petty in a three-car photo finish. In 19 starts during the 1964 NASCAR Grand National season, he posted five top-five finishes, including a second in the Atlanta 500.

Boycotts by the automobile manufacturers marred the 1965 and '66 seasons, and Isaac was forced to sit out most of '65 while Chrysler was on the sidelines. He joined the Junior Johnson Ford team in '66 and was again trapped in a corporate dispute. Meanwhile, Nord Krauskopf, owner of the K&K Insurance Co. in Ft. Wayne, Ind., was forming his own NASCAR team. He hired Harry Hyde to turn the wrenches, and, in '67, persuaded Isaac to drive the car. Krauskopf announced a five-year plan to win the NASCAR championship.

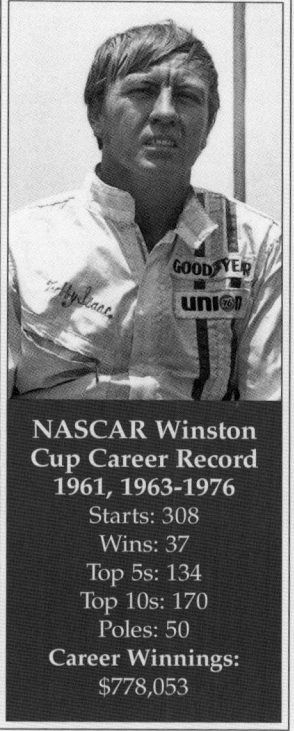

NASCAR Winston Cup Career Record 1961, 1963-1976
Starts: 308
Wins: 37
Top 5s: 134
Top 10s: 170
Poles: 50
Career Winnings: $778,053

Isaac ran a partial 12-race slate in 1967 with a top finish of second at Charlotte. In '68, the K&K Dodge team entered all the races and nearly won the title. With three short-track victories, Isaac finished second to David Pearson in the final standings. "We were basically a new team," said Isaac. "Harry was relatively new to NASCAR and we didn't have any factory help that year. Getting beat by Pearson with all his experience and factory help wasn't too bad."

In 1969, Isaac won 17 races, including his first on a super-speedway at the new Texas track, and earned 20 poles. The 20 poles in a single season remains an all-time NASCAR Cup Series record. "We won a lot of short-track races, but we couldn't pull it all together on the big tracks until the last race of the season at Texas. That win was my biggest moment in racing," said Isaac.

The following year, Isaac and the K&K team jelled into one of stock car racing's most formidable teams. They won 11 races and snared the championship. "Winning the championship gave me personal satisfaction, but I'd rank it second to the Texas win," said Isaac. "The way I look at it, it took me seven years to win a superspeedway race and only three years to win the championship."

Isaac went on to win five more races for Krauskopf's team, never again running a full schedule. In 1972, he suddenly quit the team. He never won another race.

In 1973, he teamed with Bud Moore, who was developing a small engine for future use in NASCAR competition. At the '73 Talladega 500, Isaac called Moore on the radio and told him to get another driver because he was quitting. Isaac brought the car to the pits, climbed out and said he was retiring. The retirement lasted six months. From 1974 to '76, he ran only a few NASCAR Winston Cup Grand National events. During his big league NASCAR career, Isaac won 37 races in 308 starts.

In the twilight of his career, Isaac was back in the saddle of a Sportsman car, competing weekly at his old Hickory Speedway stomping grounds. On the night of Aug. 13, 1977, he suffered a heart attack after getting out of his car during a 200-lapper. He died early the next morning.

Bobby Isaac elevated himself from a world of poverty to one of the most successful stock car racers in the country. He made his own way. Nobody gave him anything.

Charlie Glotzbach campaigned the Dow Chemicals-sponsored Nichels-Goldsmith #99 Dodge Daytona in 1970. Glotzbach won two races, including the Aug. 16 event at Michigan International Speedway. The Michigan race was the first NASCAR Grand National with mandated restrictor plates. Speeds were climbing in 1970, and with the second annual Talladega 500 scheduled a week later, NASCAR introduced the device to control speeds, increase safety, and guard against another drivers' boycott.

Number 8 Ed Negre, #61 Hoss Ellington, and #34 Wendell Scott hustle down the front chute in the Sept. 7 Southern 500 at Darlington. Negre had an unusual sponsor for his self-owned NASCAR Grand National team. Negre's Ford Torino Talladega was sponsored by Pyramid Motors, a small Carolina Chrysler-Plymouth dealership. None of the trio finished in the top 10. Negre experienced engine problems and finished 36th. Ellington placed 18th, and Scott came home 17th.

Number 22 Bobby Allison and #42 Marty Robbins pair up on the banks of Charlotte Motor Speedway during the Oct. 11 National 500. Allison's Mario Rossi team had just landed the Coca-Cola sponsorship, one of the first big nonautomotive firms to back a NASCAR team. Robbins, a country-western singer, was making his first start in two years, having undergone successful heart surgery.

Number 72 Benny Parsons and #98 LeeRoy Yarbrough hook up in a close draft off the fourth turn at Charlotte Motor Speedway. Yarbrough drove his Mercury to victory in the National 500, which turned out to be the final NASCAR Grand National win in his career. Yarbrough was left out of the shuffle for rides when the factories withdrew, and never again drove full time for a top team.

Bobby Isaac drove the K&K Insurance Dodge to the 1970 NASCAR Grand National championship. Team owner Nord Krauskopf started his operation in '66 with a five-year plan to win the NASCAR title. With Isaac driving and Harry Hyde filling the role of crew chief, Krauskopf realized his dream in the allotted time frame. Isaac won 11 races and finished second nine times in 47 starts.

1970 NASCAR GRAND NATIONAL POINTS RACE

Rank	Driver	Points	Starts	Wins	Top 5	Top 10	Winnings
1	Bobby Isaac	3911	47	11	32	38	$199,600
2	Bobby Allison	3860	46	3	30	35	$149,745
3	James Hylton	3788	47	1	22	39	$78,201
4	Richard Petty	3447	40	18	27	31	$151,124
5	Neil Castles	3158	47	0	12	24	$49,746
6	Elmo Langley	3154	47	0	1	19	$45,193
7	Jabe Thomas	3120	46	0	0	23	$42,958
8	Benny Parsons	2993	45	0	12	23	$59,402
9	Dave Marcis	2820	47	0	7	15	$41,111
10	Frank Warren	2697	46	0	0	2	$35,161
11	Cecil Gordon	2514	44	0	2	11	$32,713
12	John Sears	2465	40	0	4	7	$32,675
13	Dick Brooks	2460	34	0	15	18	$53,754
14	Wendell Scott	2425	41	0	0	9	$28,518
15	Bill Champion	2350	38	0	0	6	$30,943
16	J. D. McDuffie	2079	36	0	1	10	$24,905
17	Ben Arnold	1997	29	0	0	3	$25,805
18	Bill Seifert	1962	39	0	1	4	$25,647
19	Henley Gray	1871	34	0	0	2	$23,130
20	Friday Hassler	1831	26	0	1	6	$27,535
21	Pete Hamilton	1819	16	3	10	12	$131,406
22	Joe Frasson	1723	21	0	0	2	$20,172
23	David Pearson	1716	19	1	9	11	$87,118
24	Buddy Baker	1555	18	1	6	8	$63,510
25	Bill Dennis	1432	25	0	0	5	$15,630
26	Ed Negre	1413	31	0	0	1	$14,580
27	G. C. Spencer	1410	20	0	3	9	$17,915
28	Charlie Glotzbach	1358	19	3	7	8	$50,649
29	Roy Mayne	1333	16	0	0	3	$16,910
30	Bill Shirey	1244	29	0	0	1	$12,215
31	Raymond Williams	1204	21	0	0	0	$12,535
32	Larry Baumel	1138	23	0	0	1	$16,645
33	Buddy Arrington	1087	19	0	0	2	$16,845
34	Cale Yarborough	1016	19	3	11	13	$115,875
35	Dr. Don Tarr	995	17	0	0	5	$16,592
36	Johnny Halford	975	25	0	0	0	$15,645
37	Earl Brooks	884	21	0	0	1	$10,340
38	Coo Coo Marlin	876	13	0	0	4	$14,799
39	Ron Keselowski	855	17	0	0	1	$11,985
40	Donnie Allison	841	19	3	10	12	$96,081
41	Ken Meisenhelder	812	19	0	0	2	$7020
42	Roy Tyner	631	14	0	0	3	$5565
43	LeeRoy Yarbrough	625	19	1	7	11	$61,930
44	Dick May	551	16	0	0	0	$4510
45	Jim Vandiver	519	14	0	0	5	$16,080
46	John Kenney	457	11	0	0	0	$4150
47	Dub Simpson	367	6	0	0	1	$4115
48	Leroy Carrigg	355	9	0	0	0	$4130
49	Joe Phipps	325	7	0	0	0	$4090
50	Wayne Smith	300	8	0	0	0	$4505

Bobby Isaac overtook James Hylton in late August and won the 1970 NASCAR Grand National championship. It was the most competitive title chase in NASCAR history. A total of seven drivers swapped the points lead on 12 occasions during the 48-race campaign, a record that still stands.

Isaac moved to the front with a runner-up finish in the Talladega 500 and stayed atop the standings for the final 14 events. Hylton lost his fading hopes for the championship when he crashed in Charlotte's National 500 in October. Bobby Allison surged past Hylton to capture second place in the final standings, 51 points behind Isaac.

For the second straight year, Richard Petty's hopes for a third title were dashed when he missed five races due to an injury suffered at Darlington. The King managed to climb to fourth place in the standings at the end of the season.

The seven drivers who led the points standings at one point in the 1970 season were Isaac, Hylton, Allison, Petty, Dave Marcis, Neil Castles, and LeeRoy Yarbrough.

1971

January 10 West Coast driver Ray Elder surprises the NASCAR touring pros by winning the season-opening Motor Trend 500 at Riverside International Raceway.

February 14 Richard Petty bags his third Daytona 500 win ahead of Buddy Baker, giving Petty Enterprises a 1-2 finish in NASCAR's most celebrated event. Dick Brooks finishes seventh in a winged Dodge Daytona, the final appearance of the exotic aerodynamic wonder in a NASCAR event.

February 28 A.J. Foyt drives the Wood Brothers Mercury to victory in the 500-miler at the new Ontario Motor Speedway. Foyt goes down in the record book as winning the 1000th NASCAR Winston Cup Grand National race.

April 10 Bobby Isaac drives his Dodge to a big win in the 100-mile NASCAR Winston Cup Grand National event at Greenville-Pickens Speedway. The short-track event is televised live flag-to-flag by ABC Sports.

May 9 Sophomore driver Benny Parsons scores his first career NASCAR Winston Cup Grand National win by lapping the field in the 100-mile event at South Boston Speedway in Virginia. Parsons' Ford finishes a lap ahead of runner-up Richard Petty.

May 21 The lightly funded independent drivers stage a mini-boycott of the 100-mile NASCAR Winston Cup Grand National race at Asheville, N.C. Protesting the payoff structure and a lack of any appearance money, seven drivers pull out of the race in the early stages, leaving only five cars running at the finish. Richard Petty wins by four laps over Elmo Langley.

May 30 Bobby and Donnie Allison finish first and second, respectively, in the World 600 at Charlotte Motor Speedway in a pair of Mercurys. Charlie Glotzbach wins the pole in a Chevrolet built by Junior Johnson but crashes on the 234th lap.

Part-time racer and full-time farmer Ray Elder poses with the #96 Dodge he wheeled to victory in the Jan. 10 season opener at Riverside International Raceway. Elder drove past Bobby Allison with 12 laps remaining and scored an upset triumph in the first event under the NASCAR Winston Cup Grand National banner.

With the automotive factories cutting back or completely shutting down their NASCAR participation, Cale Yarborough quit the NASCAR Winston Cup Grand National Series to drive on the USAC Championship Indy Car tour. At Daytona, Yarborough picked up a ride in the #3 Ray Fox Plymouth. Cale finished seventh in the Twin 125-miler, but ran into mechanical problems in the 500 and bowed out early.

Number 71 Bobby Isaac and #22 Dick Brooks battle through the fourth turn in the Feb. 14 Daytona 500. Brooks was driving a winged Dodge Daytona powered by a small 305-cid engine. The aerodynamic wonder had been all but legislated out of business with the new 1971 NASCAR rules. Team owner Mario Rossi, with the blessing of the Chrysler factory, defied the odds and entered the underpowered car in NASCAR's biggest annual event. Brooks finished third in the Twin 125 and seventh in the Daytona 500. Brooks' run marked the Dodge Daytona's final appearance NASCAR Winston Cup Grand National competition.

An engine-compartment fire knocked LeeRoy Yarbrough out of the Daytona 500 on the 46th lap. The safety crew took a long time arriving on the scene, so Yarbrough attempted to put out the blaze himself.

Buddy Baker, who joined the Petty Enterprises team in 1971 as driver of the #11 Dodge, runs just ahead of Pete Hamilton's Plymouth in the Daytona 500. Hamilton, winner of the '70 Daytona 500 as a member of the Petty team, hooked up with team owner Cotton Owens for the '71 NASCAR Winston Cup Grand National campaign. It would be his final full season in NASCAR racing.

Fred Lorenzen, in his second year on the comeback trail, got a full-time assignment in 1971 with the Nichels-Goldsmith Plymouth team and secured STP as sponsor. Lorenzen ran fifth in the Daytona 500, and won the pole for the March 14 race at Rockingham. Lorenzen got credit for a fourth-place finish in the Carolina 500 even though he was involved in a multicar crash with two laps to go.

A.J. Foyt pitches his Wood Brothers Mercury into the first turn in the inaugural 500-miler at Ontario Motor Speedway in Ontario, Calif. Foyt manhandled the 51-car field on the 2.5-mile rectangular course and scored an easy victory. The Feb. 28 race marked the 1000th NASCAR Winston Cup Grand National race in NASCAR history, a noteworthy event that nobody reported.

1971

July 11 Charlie Glotzbach, with relief help from Friday Hassler, scores a big win in the Volunteer 500 at Bristol. The 500-lapper is uninterrupted by a caution flag, the first nonstop NASCAR Winston Cup Grand National race at the ½-mile track. It is Chevrolet's first NASCAR win since 1967.

August 6 Bobby Allison drives a Ford Mustang to victory in the race at Winston-Salem. The event is the first race mixing NASCAR Winston Cup Grand National cars and the ponycars of NASCAR's Grand American division.

November 21 Tiny Lund wheels his Camaro around Charlie Glotzbach with six laps remaining and records a narrow victory in the Wilkes 400 at North Wilkesboro Speedway. Lund's triumph is the third win for the smaller NASCAR Grand American cars since NASCAR permitted them to compete in short-track events.

December 12 Richard Petty roars to his 21st win of the season in the finale at Texas World Speedway. Petty also wraps up his third NASCAR Winston Cup Grand National championship by 364 points over James Hylton.

Reigning NASCAR champion Bobby Isaac intended to defend his title in 1971, but Nord Krauskopf, owner of the #71 K&K Insurance Dodge, drastically reduced the team's schedule following a dispute with NASCAR over restrictor-plate rules. NASCAR used three different size plates in '71, issuing more restrictive plates to teams running bigger engines. Isaac ran about half the races in '71, winning four times.

In the wake of the factory withdrawal, Bobby Allison campaigned his independent Dodge early in the 1971 season. Allison's team was plagued with repeated mechanical problems and was forced to park the car due to a lack of funds. In May, Allison joined the Holman-Moody Mercury team, which parted company with David Pearson after four successful years.

Dave Marcis took the wheel of the #71 K&K Insurance Dodge on the morning of the Talladega Winston 500 when regular driver Bobby Isaac fell ill with kidney stones. Meanwhile, Bobby Allison drove his first race in the #12 Holman-Moody Mercury. Both drivers performed admirably in their new rides. Marcis was leading when the engine blew with seven laps remaining in the May 16 event. Allison went on to finish second behind his brother Donnie. Buddy Baker brought the #11 Petty Dodge home third.

Donnie Allison broke out of a tight three-car battle on the final lap and drove the #21 Wood Brothers Mercury to a big win in the Winston 500. Charlie Roberts was 28 laps behind in his #77 Ford. Allison took over the Wood Brothers ride when A.J. Foyt returned to the USAC Indy Car circuit.

With attendance sagging at most of the NASCAR tracks in 1971, Charlotte Motor Speedway general manager Richard Howard formed a Chevrolet team with Junior Johnson as manager and Charlie Glotzbach at the controls. Howard thought the return of both Chevrolet and Johnson to NASCAR competition would bring back the fans. He was right. Glotzbach won the pole for the May 30 World 600, and the seats were filled to near capacity. Glotzbach led often and ran with the leaders until he crashed just past the midway point.

Restrictor Plates

WITH SPEEDS SPIRALING upward throughout the progressive 1960s, the 200-mph barrier was within reach by late 1969. The tire companies worked at a feverish pace to develop a compound that could withstand the punishment of 200-mph racing. Some of the drivers looked to NASCAR to do something to curb the speeds. Safety issues were being breached, some drivers said, and the sanctioning body needed to address the matter. In the summer of 1970, NASCAR responded by issuing the first carburetor restrictor plates to keep speeds in check.

On NASCAR's speediest high-banked offerings, speeds fell by about 10 mph with the restrictor plates. Unlike today, restrictor plates were used for all tracks and not just the ultrafast Daytona and Talladega venues. The introduction of restrictor plates created immediate controversy among the contestants. The beefy Hemi engines made by Chrysler and Ford were forced to run plates with smaller openings, while the conventional wedge engines were permitted to breath a little more freely with larger openings. The differently sized plates spawned a barrage of complaints from nearly every corner. Top-ranked independent driver James Hylton was perplexed that NASCAR required restrictor plates on small tracks. "Why in the world do we need a restrictor plate at Martinsville?" queried Hylton. "We don't run but 80 miles per hour on that track."

The behemoth engines designed for racing were permitted to compete with a 1¼-inch carburetor opening in all events. In an effort to equalize competition and make racing more affordable to the independents, NASCAR allowed the Ford 427-cid wedge engine to utilize a 1½-inch opening. The Chrysler cars with a less-developed wedge could use a1⅜-inch opening under the 1971 NASCAR rules.

Most of the independent drivers had difficulty gathering enough funds to make the costly switch from the heavily restricted racing engines to the more conventional wedge powerplants. "It's hurting all of us independents," claimed small-time operator Jabe Thomas. "That plate has made finishers out of a lot of those hot dogs. Buddy Baker used to always blow up. Now he's finishing and knocking us poor boys down another notch. And none of us can afford to switch to the wedge engines."

> "The rule was written not to handicap any one manufacturer, but to improve competition by making it possible for the less expensive wedge-type engines to compete..."
> —Lin Kuchler

Richard Petty aired his complaints over the 1971 NASCAR rules. "Everyone's got four tires, a 22-gallon fuel tank, and one four-barrel carburetor," opined Petty. "It's all the same for everybody. So everyone should have the same size plate."

With the different size plates in use, NASCAR became an easy target for complaints. The Chrysler camp complained that Ford's wedge engine had an advantage when Fords started scooping up major wins. When some of the Chrysler teams made the switch to their version of the wedge and won races, the Ford teams cried foul.

"The carburetor rule does not specify brand names of cars," said NASCAR vice president Lin Kuchler. "It goes by the types of engines. The controversy has erupted because of the misunderstanding that one brand is handicapped by the rule more than another. The rule was written not to handicap any one manufacturer, but to improve competition by making it possible for the less-expensive wedge-type engines to compete with the 429 Ford Boss and the 426 Chrysler Hemi. We feel the rule has accomplished our goals."

The 1971 NASCAR season was one of the most chaotic on record. With the loss of factory support, many teams folded leaving top-ranked drivers without rides. Many of the races were one-sided with little competition. In the Dixie 500 at Atlanta International Raceway in August, Petty and Bobby Allison ran circles around the entire field. Third place was nine laps off the pace and the sixth-place Wood Brothers Mercury was 12 laps back. Twenty-one of the 48 races saw the leader finish in a lap by himself, and the Darlington Rebel 400 had a seven lap margin of victory.

By September 1971, the restrictor plates had been replaced by a carburetor "sleeve" in each of the four discharge holes, thus limiting the amount of air and fuel to pass into the carburetor. Again, there were four different sizes of base openings in the new regulations, depending on what type of engine was used.

The controversy subsided very little, and the carburetor plate returned a shade more than a year later. Restrictor plates continued to be part of the NASCAR landscape through the 1974 season. By '75, all of the cars were equipped with smaller engines and all contestants were governed under the same set of rules once again. Restrictor plates were gone for the time being. They wouldn't return to NASCAR until 1988.

Bobby Allison went on a victory tear after taking a seat in the #12 Holman-Moody Mercury. Allison piled up five consecutive wins from May 30 to June. 23. He won at Charlotte, Dover, Michigan, Riverside, and Houston. Allison went on to win 11 races in 1971 in four different models of cars, Mercury Cyclone, Ford Torino and Mustang, and Dodge Charger.

Number 3 Charlie Glotzbach, #43 Richard Petty, #12 Bobby Allison, #99 Fred Lorenzen, and #17 David Pearson battle on the high banks of Daytona in the July 4 Firecracker 400. After leaving the Holman-Moody team in May, Pearson joined the Ray Nichels operation funded by mystery man Chris Vallo, who wanted a competitive Pontiac on the NASCAR tracks. Nichels was snookered by Vallo, and the Pontiac team floundered from the outset. Pearson had to drive a Nichels Plymouth in the Firecracker 400, and he finished eighth.

Charlie Glotzbach and relief driver Friday Hassler piloted the Richard Howard-owned #3 Chevrolet to victory in the July 11 Volunteer 500 at Bristol International Speedway. In the lone win for the new Chevy team, Glotzbach and Hassler scored a three-lap victory in a caution-free event. It remains the only NASCAR Cup Series race in Bristol history without a caution flag.

A shortage of teams in the NASCAR Winston Cup Grand National Series and the lower-ranked Grand American division prompted NASCAR to permit cars from both series to compete in short-track races in 1971. Bobby Allison prevailed in the opening event with the mixed field, driving Melvin Joseph's #49 Mustang in the Aug. 6 race at Winston-Salem's Bowman Gray Stadium.

The entire Holman-Moody pit crew hopped on the winning Mercury that Bobby Allison drove to victory in the Aug. 22 Talladega 500 at Alabama International Motor Speedway. Allison's victory was his eighth over a three-month span. Trackside attendance for the 1971 Talladega races didn't live up to expectations. The loss of the automotive factories and constant squabbling over rules chased many fans away. Only a shade over 40,000 spectators were on hand for the Aug. 22 race.

Number 64 Elmo Langley and #76 Ben Arnold were two of the independent campaigners who managed to keep their teams in operation during the 1971 season. Langley finished fifth in the points standings. The independently funded teams found themselves in a financial pinch in '71, having lost the hand-me-down factory parts that filtered down through the larger teams.

Richard Petty enjoyed a tremendous season in 1971, driving his #43 Plymouth Road Runner to 21 victories in 46 starts. The King became the first driver to surpass $300,000 in single-season winnings, and he also earned the distinction of becoming the first NASCAR driver to top the $1 million mark in career earnings. Petty won his third championship and topped off the year with a visit to the White House, where he met with President Nixon.

1971 NASCAR WINSTON CUP GN POINTS RACE

Rank	Driver	Points	Starts	Wins	Top 5	Top 10	Winnings
1	Richard Petty	4435	46	21	38	41	$351,071
2	James Hylton	4071	46	0	14	37	$90,282
3	Cecil Gordon	3677	46	0	6	21	$69,080
4	Bobby Allison	3636	42	11	27	31	$254,316
5	Elmo Langley	3356	46	0	11	23	$57,037
6	Jabe Thomas	3200	43	0	2	15	$48,241
7	Bill Champion	3058	45	0	3	14	$43,769
8	Frank Warren	2886	47	0	1	10	$40,072
9	J.D. McDuffie	2862	43	0	2	8	$35,578
10	Walter Ballard	2633	41	0	3	11	$30,974
11	Benny Parsons	2611	35	1	13	18	$55,896
12	Ed Negre	2528	43	0	0	2	$29,738
13	Bill Seifert	2403	37	0	0	4	$33,220
14	Henley Gray	2392	39	0	0	4	$31,789
15	Buddy Baker	2358	19	1	13	16	$115,150
16	Friday Hassler	2277	29	0	4	13	$37,305
17	Earl Brooks	2205	35	0	1	3	$25,360
18	Bill Dennis	2181	28	0	4	10	$29,420
19	Wendell Scott	2180	37	0	0	4	$21,701
20	John Sears	2167	37	0	0	3	$26,735
21	Dave Marcis	2049	28	0	8	13	$37,582
22	Neil Castles	2036	38	0	1	10	$22,939
23	Bobby Isaac	1819	25	4	16	17	$106,526
24	Pete Hamilton	1739	22	1	11	12	$60,440
25	Joe Frasson	1619	17	0	1	4	$20,975
26	Ben Arnold	1618	18	0	0	3	$18,491
27	Ron Keselowski	1446	20	0	0	6	$17,680
28	Bill Shirey	1303	27	0	0	2	$9160
29	Donnie Allison	1280	13	1	7	9	$69,995
30	Dean Dalton	1276	19	0	0	1	$13,910
31	Raymond Williams	1270	20	0	0	0	$14,585
32	Dick May	1090	22	0	0	1	$9225
33	Charlie Roberts	1053	19	0	0	2	$12,470
34	G.C. Spencer	1008	17	0	2	6	$11,470
35	Richard Brown	967	13	0	0	2	$11,940
36	Dick Brooks	939	20	0	9	12	$32,921
37	Larry Baumel	904	16	0	0	1	$10,910
38	Maynard Troyer	879	13	0	1	3	$13,115
39	Roy Mayne	852	11	0	0	1	$10,330
40	Ken Meisenhelder	797	15	0	0	1	$5405
41	Tommy Gale	729	9	0	0	1	$8800
42	Charlie Glotzbach	699	20	1	7	10	$38,605
43	Bill Hollar	644	11	0	0	1	$4275
44	Marv Acton	627	11	0	0	0	$8620
45	Fred Lorenzen	611	14	0	7	9	$45,100
46	Richard Childress	601	12	0	0	0	$3855
47	Paul Tyler	561	10	0	0	0	$6360
48	Jim Vandiver	553	7	0	0	3	$13,575
49	Coo Coo Marlin	527	12	0	0	0	$9085
50	Eddie Yarboro	497	7	0	0	0	$3685

Richard Petty won 21 races in 46 starts and breezed to his third NASCAR Winston Cup Grand National championship. The "Randleman Rocket" assumed command of the points chase after the eighth race of the season at Hickory, N.C., in March and never trailed again. He finished 364 points ahead of runner-up James Hylton.

Hylton, Bobby Allison, Benny Parsons, and Bobby Isaac jockeyed the points lead in the early part of the season before Petty set sail. King Richard posted 38 top-five finishes in 46 starts to post a thoroughly dominating performance.

Allison, who joined the Holman-Moody team in May, won 11 races and finished fourth in the standings. He started 42 of the 48 races, but was never was able to challenge Petty for the points lead.

Only two drivers that finished in the top 10 in the points race were able to win races during the 1971 campaign.

1972

January NASCAR announces the 1972 NASCAR Winston Cup Grand National season will be reduced to 30 events. Only races of 250 miles or more will be part of the schedule.

January 11 NASCAR founder Bill France steps down as president and turns the reins over to his son, Bill France, Jr. "I am sure that NASCAR will continue its dynamic leadership in the sport of automobile racing," says the senior France.

February 20 A. J. Foyt blisters the field to win the Daytona 500 by nearly five miles. Foyt leads the final 300 miles in the lackluster event. Third-place driver Jim Vandiver finishes six laps off the pace.

March 5 A. J. Foyt leads most of the way and posts an impressive win in the second annual 500-miler at Ontario Motor Speedway. ABC Sports, which televises the second half of the race live across the nation, reports that the final half hour draws a 12.3 Nielsen rating.

March 26 Bobby Allison drives his Chevrolet to a near photo-finish victory in the Atlanta 500. Allison records the first superspeedway win for Chevrolet since 1963.

April 16 David Pearson slips past Richard Petty with 93 laps to go and speeds to victory in the Rebel 400 at Darlington Raceway. It is Pearson's first start with the famed Wood Brothers Mercury team.

July 4 David Pearson prevails in a three-car finish to win the Daytona Firecracker 400. Pearson beats Richard Petty by four feet as Bobby Allison finishes a close third.

August 6 Independent driver James Hylton enjoys the finest day of his career by taking a narrow victory over Ramo Stott in the Talladega 500. New tires introduced by Goodyear fail to withstand the high-speed punishment and eliminate most of the favorites.

Richard Petty throttles his #43 STP Plymouth down the straightaway at Riverside International Speedway during the Jan. 23 Winston Western 500. Petty was in front of the field when NASCAR officials were forced to red flag the event after 149 of the 191 laps had been completed due to heavy fog conditions. Five days earlier, STP announced it had signed a multiyear pact to sponsor the Petty Enterprises team.

Bill France, Jr., who assumed the presidency of NASCAR in January 1972, makes a point to '70 champion Bobby Isaac (right) and crew chief Harry Hyde (left). Isaac won the pole for the Feb. 20 Daytona 500 with a speed of 186.632 mph, the second time NASCAR's premier race was run with restrictor plates. Isaac also won the first Twin 125-miler three days before the 500. It was the first year that the Twin 125s didn't count as points races.

Versatile road racer Mark Donohue poses with the #16 Roger Penske AMC Matador at Daytona. The lightly regarded American Motors Corporation stepped into NASCAR racing in 1972 with a full factory effort. Donohue's boxy Matador was short on speed during the Daytona festivities, but did manage to finish fifth in one of the Feb. 17 Twin 125-mile qualifiers.

Veteran campaigner Raymond "Friday" Hassler was one of NASCAR's most respected independents. The Chattanooga, Tenn., driver and his red #39 Chevrolet were regular fixtures on the NASCAR Winston Cup Grand National scene for six years. Hassler lost his life in a multicar collision on the 19th lap of the first Twin 125-mile qualifying race at Daytona.

Tough Texan A.J. Foyt was signed to drive the #21 Wood Brothers Purolator Mercury in the early portion of the 1972 NASCAR Winston Cup Grand National season. Foyt dominated the Daytona 500, leading all but 33 laps and finishing nearly five miles ahead of runner-up Charlie Glotzbach. Full factory participation was missing in '72, and prerace experts noted that only five cars had a real shot at winning the race. Third-place Jim Vandiver finished six laps behind the leader and 10th-place Vic Elford was more than 40 miles behind Foyt when the checkered flag fell.

Andy Granatelli's STP Corp. began backing the two-car Petty Enterprises team in 1972. Buddy Baker's #11 Dodge carried the neon red STP colors while Richard Petty's Plymouth had the familiar Petty Blue and STP red colors. Baker's first effort with STP resulted in an early crash in the Daytona 500.

A.J. Foyt relaxes in victory lane following his dominating performance in the Daytona 500. Foyt was unchallenged for the final 300 miles, and he became the second USAC Indy Car driver to pluck NASCAR's sweetest plum in the last six years. No visiting driver from another sanctioning body has won the Daytona 500 since Foyt's victory.

Bobby Allison joined the Richard Howard and Junior Johnson Chevrolet team in 1972. Team owner Howard needed a sponsor to compete on the full schedule and Allison's close ties with the Coca-Cola Company provided the operating funds. The Coca-Cola sponsorship was in the neighborhood of $80,000 for the full season, but team manager Johnson said he needed a minimum of $100,000. Allison had to pay the additional $20,000 to secure the ride.

1972

September 10 Richard Petty emerges victorious after a wild duel with Bobby Allison in the Capital City 500 at Richmond Fairgrounds Speedway. Petty and Allison engage in a heated bumping duel. At one point, Petty's Dodge climbs on top of the guardrail. Incredibly, he returns to the track, retains the lead after the mishap, and motors to victory.

October 1 Richard Petty outruns Bobby Allison in the final laps of an epic slugfest and wins the spine-tingling Wilkes 400 at North Wilkesboro (N.C.) Speedway. Petty and Allison tangle repeatedly during the final laps and both cars are badly crumpled when the checkered flag falls.

October 8 Bobby Allison drives to a two-lap victory in Rockingham's American 500 to record his 10th win of the season. Allison leads in his 39th consecutive race, an all-time record that is acknowledged as stock car racing's "Joe DiMaggio Record."

November 12 Buddy Baker edges A. J. Foyt by a half car length at the finish line to win the season-ending Texas 500 at Texas World Speedway. Richard Petty finishes third and clinches his fourth NASCAR Winston Cup Grand National championship.

David Pearson took over the #21 Wood Brothers/Purolator Mercury after A. J. Foyt left the team to return to the USAC Indy Car tour. In his first race with his new team, Pearson outdueled Richard Petty to win the April 16 Rebel 400 at Darlington Raceway. Many observers felt Pearson was washed up after a lackluster 1971 campaign. "Nothing bothers me as long as I know the truth," remarked Pearson, who went on to win six of his 12 starts with the Wood Brothers team in '72.

Number 21 David Pearson puts a lap on #34 Wendell Scott in the April 30 Virginia 500 at Martinsville Speedway. Scott overcame innumerable odds to compete in the race. The engine in his race car blew up on Saturday, forcing Scott to install the engine that powered his tow truck. His struggles were observed by Charlotte Motor Speedway general manager Richard Howard, who promised to give Scott a ride in a Junior Johnson-prepared car for the upcoming World 600. Scott was lapped 64 times in the Martinsville race, but still managed to finish 16th.

Jimmy Crawford, an Eastern Airlines pilot based near Atlanta, purchased the #3 Ray Fox Plymouth shortly before the May 7 Winston 500 at Talladega. Previously, noncompetitive equipment and a lack of operating funds had plagued Crawford's NASCAR career. In his first ride with his new machine, Crawford was running in the top 10 when he collided with leader Bobby Isaac with just over a lap remaining.

Number 46 Roy Mayne, #14 Coo Coo Marlin, #95 Darrell Waltrip, #31 Jim Vandiver, and #28 Fred Lorenzen battle on the high banks during the Winston 500. Waltrip was making his NASCAR Winston Cup Grand National debut in a self-owned Mercury. A blown engine ended his day after 69 laps. He won a total of $680 for his efforts. Lorenzen finished fifth in his second ride with the Hoss Ellington Ford team.

Number 21 David Pearson leads #71 Bobby Isaac as they lap #47 Raymond Williams during the late stages of the Winston 500. Pearson, taking his third ride in the Wood Brothers Mercury, went on to score his second win of the season. Isaac finished second after a tangle with Jimmy Crawford with just over a lap to go. In the final six laps, Isaac was given the black flag when his crew forgot to secure the gas cap in place during the final pit stop. Isaac said he was fully aware of the black flag, "but quite frankly, I just ignored it," he said. The K&K Insurance Dodge team was fined $1500 for the infraction.

Wendell Scott appears in Charlotte Motor Speedway's victory lane after the May 28 World 600. Scott was awarded the Curtis Turner Memorial award for his contributions to NASCAR racing. He is joined by Turner's widow, Bunny, and Union 76 RaceStopper Royette Tarry. Scott drove a Richard Howard-owned, Junior Johnson-prepared Chevrolet in the 600-miler. Unfortunately, the car was low on horsepower and failed to finish. Buddy Baker won the race.

Allison's Leading Streak

NASCAR'S STATISTICAL DEPARTMENT apparently took a little time off in the early 1970s. The usual points standings updates and race reports were distributed and then safely tucked away, but a number of noteworthy events were completely overlooked. One of these notable events, A.J. Foyt's victory in the 500-miler at the new Ontario Motor Speedway on Feb. 28, 1971, was the 1000th race in the history of NASCAR's top division. The event was televised live by ABC Sports, but no mention was made on the telecast or in any NASCAR press releases about the 1000th race.

Another momentous occasion devoid of publicity was Bobby Allison's incredible streak of leading 39 consecutive NASCAR Cup Series events in 1971 and '72. Often referred to as NASCAR's "Joe DiMaggio Record," Allison led every single NASCAR Cup Series event from Sept. 6, 1971, through Oct. 22, 1972.

Joe DiMaggio's 56-game hitting streak is one of Major League Baseball's most time-honored landmark achievements, and it is well documented in virtually all of baseball's record books. During his amazing hitting streak in 1941, the Yankee Clipper's quest for the record was followed closely in the daily newspapers and radio broadcasts. Thirty years later, Allison's run at a NASCAR equivalent mark in stock car racing went unnoticed. "I certainly didn't know anything about it at the time," said Allison. "I won a race in 1971 at Bowman-Gray Stadium

[in Winston-Salem, N.C.] and I didn't even get credit for it. Nobody got credit for winning the race that I won. So, I guess it's no surprise no one was aware of me leading all those races in a row."

Allison's streak began when he led 329 of the 367 laps during his victory in the 1971 Darlington Southern 500. Driving for the Holman-Moody team during its final season in NASCAR Winston Cup Grand National racing, Allison led at least one lap in each of the final nine races in the '71 season. He took the checkered flag in three of those races.

In 1972, Allison joined the Richard Howard-owned, Junior Johnson-managed Chevrolet team. While making a run for the championship, Allison led each of the first 30 races, winning 10. Toward the end of the season, Allison announced he was leaving the Howard/Johnson team to form his own operation in 1973.

"The last race of the 1972 season was at Texas World Speedway," Allison recalled. "I do remember something being written that I had a chance to be the first driver to lead all the races in a single year, but the report didn't mention anything about those races I led in 1971. Well, I don't think Junior appreciated the fact that I was quitting his team, so I didn't get a real fast car for the Texas race."

Allison started fourth in the Texas 500-miler. He never led the race at any point, and he wound up fourth when the checkered flag fell. The hopes of leading every race in the 1972 campaign had fallen through, and the fabled 39-race streak was over.

Bobby Allison's "Joe DiMaggio" Streak

Race	Date	Location	Laps Led	Finish
1	9/1/71	Darlington, SC	329	Won
2	9/26/71	Martinsville, VA	54	2nd
3	10/10/71	Charlotte, NC	70	Won
4	10/17/71	Dover, DE	394	4th
5	10/24/71	Rockingham, NC	1	3rd
6	11/7/71	Macon, GA	418	Won
7	11/14/71	Richmond, VA	105	2nd
8	11/21/71	North Wilkesboro, NC	11	21st
9	12/12/71	College Station, TX	75	3rd
10	1/23/72	Riverside, CA	102	2nd
11	2/20/72	Daytona Beach, FL	2	16th
12	2/27/72	Richmond, VA	240	2nd
13	3/5/72	Ontario, CA	20	2nd
14	3/12/72	Rockingham, NC	260	27th
15	3/26/72	Atlanta, GA	142	Won
16	4/9/72	Bristol, TN	458	Won
17	4/16/72	Darlington, SC	29	7th
18	4/23/72	North Wilkesboro, NC	79	2nd
19	4/30/72	Martinsville, VA	27	2nd
20	5/7/72	Talladega, AL	14	45th
21	5/28/72	Charlotte, NC	239	2nd
22	6/4/72	Dover, DE	252	Won
23	6/11/72	Brooklyn, MI	10	2nd
24	6/18/72	Riverside, CA	2	6th
25	6/25/72	College Station, TX	10	2nd
26	7/4/72	Daytona Beach, FL	13	3rd
27	7/9/72	Bristol, TN	445	Won
28	7/16/72	Trenton, NJ	53	Won
29	7/23/72	Atlanta, GA	104	Won
30	8/6/72	Talladega, AL	22	3rd
31	8/20/72	Brooklyn, MI	26	2nd
32	8/27/72	Nashville, TN	283	Won
33	9/4/72	Darlington, SC	229	Won
34	9/10/72	Richmond, VA	168	2nd
35	9/17/72	Dover, DE	34	20th
36	9/24/72	Martinsville, VA	432	2nd
37	10/1/72	North Wilkesboro, NC	239	2nd
38	10/8/72	Charlotte, NC	192	Won
39	10/22/72	Rockingham, NC	217	Won

Richard Petty accepts the pole-position trophy prior to the June 25 Lone Star 500 at Texas World Speedway. Petty donned a scraggly straw hat on the incredibly hot Texas afternoon as the race-time temperature exceeded 100 degrees. Petty drove his Plymouth to a convincing win in the race, lapping runner-up Bobby Allison.

A quintet of speedy cars tour the high banks of Daytona in the July 4 Firecracker 400. Bill Champion's #10 Ford ducks to the low side to allow passing room for #14 Coo Coo Marlin, #15 Donnie Allison, #12 Bobby Allison, and #88 Ron Keselowski. Bobby Allison finished third, Marlin fourth, Keselowski seventh, and Donnie Allison eighth. Champion brought his self-owned car home in 18th place. David Pearson prevailed in a three-car shootout with Bobby Allison and Richard Petty.

James Hylton noses out Ramo Stott to win the Aug. 6 Talladega 500. Hylton produced one of the biggest upsets in NASCAR superspeedway history. Hylton and Stott, who battled for the last 150 miles, were five laps ahead of third-place finisher Bobby Allison. The new tires Goodyear had designed for the Talladega race started coming apart in the early laps. Hylton and Stott couldn't afford the new tires, so they mounted the old compound on their cars. It turned out to be the hot trick, and they ran circles around the cars shod with the new tires.

"He could have put me in the boondocks. There's not going to be any more trouble until he hurts me."
—Richard Petty

Vs

"He had to wreck me in order to win, and that's what he did. I had so much smoke in my car I could hardly see"
—Bobby Allison

One of the most thrilling moments in NASCAR history came during the final laps of the Oct. 1 race at North Wilkesboro Speedway. Richard Petty and Bobby Allison rekindled their feud, which dated back to 1967. The final five laps featured an epic slugfest between the two leading drivers. Allison led Petty under the white flag (top photo), but Petty passed Allison after both cars hit the wall on the final lap and Petty won the final sprint to the finish line. Petty was attacked by a drunk fan in victory lane after the race, but order was restored when Richard's brother Maurice smacked the fan on the head with Richard's helmet.

NASCAR ROOKIE DRIVER HANDBOOK prepared by UNION 76-DARLINGTON RECORD CLUB

This handbook has been published to impress new NASCAR drivers with the strenuous physical, mental and technical requirements of the sport and vocation in which they are about to engage. The safety requirements and procedures covered in the handbook are based on the recommendations and experience of successful professional NASCAR champion drivers and veteran race officials. They are intended for the improvement and well-being of all drivers competing at not only Darlington International Raceway, but all speedways.

The Union 76-Darlington Record Club is one of the most exclusive clubs in the sport of stock car racing. To be eligible, a driver must be the fastest qualifier for the Southern 500 for his make of car for that year. Naturally, one man can be the fastest qualifier for a make of car for years, thus limiting the membership of the club. When a driver qualifies and

1ST EDITION   JUNE, 1972

Freshman drivers on NASCAR's Winston Cup Grand National Series were issued the *NASCAR Rookie Driver Handbook* when they checked into Darlington Raceway in preparation for the Sept. 4 Southern 500. The 16-page pocket-size guide offered guidelines on television and radio interviews, a dress code, and sponsor courtesy, stating, "Don't hesitate to mention the company's name if at all possible."

1972 NASCAR WINSTON CUP GN POINTS RACE

Rank	Driver	Points	Starts	Wins	Top 5	Top 10	Winnings
1	Richard Petty	8701.40	31	8	25	28	$339,405
2	Bobby Allison	8573.50	31	10	25	27	$348,939
3	James Hylton	8158.70	31	1	9	23	$126,705
4	Cecil Gordon	7326.05	31	0	4	16	$73,126
5	Benny Parsons	6844.15	31	0	10	19	$102,043
6	Walter Ballard	6781.45	31	0	0	7	$59,745
7	Elmo Langley	6656.25	30	0	1	9	$59,644
8	John Sears	6298.50	28	0	2	7	$51,314
9	Dean Dalton	6295.05	29	0	0	4	$42,299
10	Ben Arnold	6179	26	0	0	7	$44,547
11	Frank Warren	5788.60	30	0	0	2	$45,048
12	Jabe Thomas	5772.55	28	0	0	4	$43,438
13	Bill Champion	5740.70	28	0	0	4	$42,242
14	Raymond Williams	5712.65	28	0	0	5	$37,000
15	Dave Marcis	5459.65	27	0	5	11	$45,012
16	Charlie Roberts	5354.45	26	0	0	1	$32,488
17	Henley Gray	5093.65	28	0	0	2	$38,461
18	J.D. McDuffie	5075.85	27	0	1	2	$36,833
19	Bobby Isaac	5050.85	27	1	10	10	$133,257
20	David Pearson	4718	17	6	12	13	$141,849
21	Ed Negre	4696.90	26	0	0	0	$30,538
22	Buddy Arrington	4555.90	20	0	1	10	$28,700
23	Larry Smith	4173.70	23	0	0	7	$24,215
24	Buddy Baker	3936.70	17	2	8	9	$102,540
25	Coo Coo Marlin	3852.90	20	0	2	5	$28,124
26	David Ray Boggs	3739	24	0	0	0	$19,489
27	Ron Keselowski	3475.60	22	0	1	3	$21,905
28	Joe Frasson	3152.80	16	0	1	4	$21,570
29	Richard Brown	2939	16	0	0	1	$19,283
30	Neil Castles	2789.60	21	0	0	1	$18,760
31	Jim Vandiver	2524.35	16	0	2	3	$27,983
32	Clarence Lovell	2360.30	12	0	0	0	$10,770
33	David Sisco	2310.75	12	0	0	2	$13,700
34	LeeRoy Yarbrough	2157.50	18	0	5	9	$40,705
35	George Altheide	1916.75	11	0	0	0	$10,405
36	Donnie Allison	1849.15	10	0	2	3	$16,826
37	Richard Childress	1521.25	15	0	0	0	$7245
38	Bill Shirey	1468.50	13	0	0	0	$8070
39	Fred Lorenzen	1333.55	8	0	3	4	$19,505
40	Wendell Scott	1317.50	6	0	0	0	$5,830
41	Tommy Gale	1298	6	0	0	0	$7197
42	Bill Dennis	1279.25	11	0	2	2	$9604
43	Pete Hamilton	1238.25	10	0	0	1	$8040
44	Dick May	1229.25	6	0	0	1	$5370
45	Hershel McGriff	1199.75	4	0	2	3	$12,290
46	Les Covey	1128	7	0	0	0	$5070
47	Johnny Halford	1103.75	5	0	0	1	$4955
48	Pete Hamilton	1083.25	5	0	1	1	$8005
49	Dick Brooks	1023.50	14	0	0	1	$14,146
50	Eddie Yarboro	1007.65	6	0	0	0	$3435

Richard Petty drove his Plymouths and Dodges to a record-setting fourth NASCAR Winston Cup Grand National championship, leading the points standings most of the season.

A new points system was introduced, which awarded points per lap completed. This system prevented Petty from taking the points lead until the 11th race of the season at Talladega. Petty had finished higher than James Hylton in nine of the first 10 races, including victories in four events, but Hylton maintained the points lead due to more laps completed. When Hylton was involved in a crash at Talladega, Petty claimed the lead, which he held for the balance of the season.

Petty won eight races and finished 127.9 points in front of runner-up Bobby Allison, who won 10 events. Hylton scored the first superspeedway victory of his career and finished third in the final standings.

Petty, Hylton, and Allison swapped the points lead six times during the season.

1973

January 21 Mark Donohue drives his Roger Penske Matador to a surprising win in the season-opening Winston Western 500 at Riverside. Donohue's first win comes in his fifth NASCAR Winston Cup Grand National start.

February 18 Richard Petty outlasts a speedy Buddy Baker to post his fourth win in the Daytona 500. Pole-sitter Baker leads most of the way but is foiled by an engine failure while running second with six laps to go.

March 25 Cale Yarborough, back in NASCAR's fold after a two-year exile in USAC Indy Cars, drives Junior Johnson's Chevrolet to an overwhelming victory in the Southeastern 500 at Bristol. Yarborough leads all 500 laps.

April 15 David Pearson avoids a late-race crash and drives his Mercury to a 13-lap win in Darlington's Rebel 500. Benny Parsons finishes second.

May 6 David Pearson steers clear of a massive 21-car crash and records an easy win in the Winston 500 at Talladega. Only 17 cars in the 60-car starting field finish.

June 24 David Pearson noses out Buddy Baker in the Motor State 400 at Michigan, the first race staged at the two-mile oval since Roger Penske became owner and promoter. The race is the only NASCAR event at Michigan in 1973. Penske elects to replace the summer NASCAR Winston Cup Grand National event with an Indy Car race.

July 8 Points leader Benny Parsons drives his unsponsored Chevrolet to an impressive win in the Volunteer 500 at Bristol International Speedway. Parsons finishes seven laps ahead of runner-up L. D. Ottinger.

August 12 Dick Brooks posts perhaps the biggest upset win in NASCAR history in the Talladega 500. Brooks is behind the wheel of a Plymouth owned by the Crawford Brothers, a team that has never finished above 16th in a NASCAR Winston Cup Grand National event. Larry Smith, 1972 Rookie of the Year, loses his life in an early crash.

Mark Donohue wheels the #16 Roger Penske American Motors Matador around the twisting Riverside road course en route to an impressive victory in the Jan. 21 season opener. Donohue, regarded as one of the top road racers in the country, lapped the entire field in the 500-miler. The Matador was equipped with four-wheel disc brakes, while the other cars had rear drums. "It made all the difference," said Donohue. "I could carry the car deeper in the corners, and that's what it takes on a road course."

Following a two-year stint in the United States Auto Club Indy Car series with less-than-glowing results, Cale Yarborough returned to NASCAR Winston Cup Grand National racing in 1973. Yarborough replaced Bobby Allison in the Richard Howard-owned, Junior Johnson-managed #11 Chevrolet. Sponsorship came from Kar-Kare, a Carolinas-based auto repair and tune-up service that was partially owned by Howard.

Coo Coo Marlin (left) and Buddy Baker hoist their trophies in victory lane following the Feb. 15 Daytona Twin 125-mile qualifying races. For Marlin, it was his only trip to the winner's circle.

A gaggle of cars run in tight formation in the second Twin 125-miler at Daytona International Speedway. Shown are #77 Charlie Roberts, #61 Clarence Lovell, #8 Ed Negre, #48 James Hylton, #52 Earl Ross, #18 Joe Frasson, and #30 Roy Mayne. Lovell and Roberts failed to qualify for the Daytona 500.

Number 72 Benny Parsons, #95 Darrell Waltrip, and #17 Bill Dennis hustle through the fourth turn in the Feb. 18 Daytona 500. Waltrip, making his first start in the Daytona 500, posted a solid showing, but tangled with Marty Robbins midway through the race and finished 12th. Dennis and Parsons encountered early engine problems and failed to finish. Parsons rebounded from the disappointing Daytona effort to win the NASCAR Winston Cup Grand National championship.

Number 4 John Sears, #28 Gordon Johncock, and #50 A.J. Foyt engage in a speedy three-abreast duel in the Daytona 500. Foyt went on to record a fifth-place finish. Sears, a 10-year veteran of NASCAR Grand National competition, hung up his helmet after the 1973 season. He quit to honor the wishes of his mother, who was fearful of the high speeds attained on the superspeedways.

Bobby Isaac ducks his #15 Ford to the inside of A.J. Foyt in the Daytona 500. Isaac campaigned a Bud Moore Ford with a 351-cid engine. Foyt's big 427-cid engine had a restrictor plate, but Isaac's small block didn't. Under NASCAR rules for 1973, cars with smaller engines could run without the restrictive devices. Isaac finished second.

1973

September 23 Bobby Allison runs down Richard Petty on the final lap to win the Wilkes 400 at North Wilkesboro Speedway. It is Allison's second win of the season.

October 7 Cale Yarborough and Richard Petty lap the field three times as they finish 1-2 in the National 500 at Charlotte Motor Speedway. Controversy flares as NASCAR inspectors find the engines in Yarborough's Chevrolet and Petty's Dodge measure larger than the cubic inch limit. The finish stands with no penalties.

October 9 Bobby Allison, who finished third in the controversial Charlotte race, announces he is quitting NASCAR. "On account of NASCAR's arbitrary and capricious conduct, I find it necessary to withdraw from the remaining races this season."

October 15 Bobby Allison settles his differences with NASCAR in a tense meeting with Bill France, Jr., in Atlanta. NASCAR promises to increase scrutiny in the prerace inspections.

October 21 David Pearson captures his 11th win in 18 starts with a season-ending victory in the American 500 at Rockingham's North Carolina Motor Speedway. Benny Parsons pits for repairs after an early crash. The help of several teams allow him to get back into the race and finish 28th. Parsons holds on to win the NASCAR Winston Cup Grand National championship by 67.15 points over Cale Yarborough.

The 1973 Daytona 500 came down to a battle between the Dodges of Buddy Baker and Richard Petty. Baker won the pole and led most of the way, but the savvy Petty scrambled into contention in the late stages. Petty assumed command with a lightning-fast 8.6-second pit stop with a dozen laps remaining. Baker shortened Petty's lead each lap, but the engine let go with six laps remaining. Petty went on to win his fourth Daytona 500.

With the reduction of the NASCAR Winston Cup Grand National schedule to 30 races, most of the short tracks no longer had a race date. NASCAR inaugurated the Grand National East Series in 1972 to provide races for the short tracks. Two years later, the short-track division for Winston Cup cars folded. Buddy Baker drove his #71 K&K Insurance Dodge to victory in the March 4, 1973, NASCAR Grand National East race at Hickory Speedway. Neil Castles won the '72 championship while Tiny Lund captured the '73 title.

Pete Hamilton poses with the #22 Crawford Brothers Land Harbors of America Plymouth prior to the start of the April 1 Atlanta 500. Hamilton made his final NASCAR Winston Cup Grand National appearance in the 500-miler, bowing out early with engine problems. Hamilton was NASCAR's brightest new star in 1970, winning the Daytona 500 and both races at Talladega. Three short years later, he was off the tour, a victim of the factory withdrawal and a nagging back injury suffered early in his racing career.

Buddy Baker's #71 Dodge and David Pearson's Mercury qualified on the front row in the May 6 Winston 500 at Talladega. Pearson enjoyed a phenomenal season, winning 11 of 18 starts including 10 of 15 on superspeedways. Pearson never wound up lower than third in the races in which he was running at the finish. He lapped the field during his easy win in the Winston 500.

The backstretch of Talladega's Alabama International Motor Speedway is littered with wrecked cars and debris following a 21-car crash in the Winston 500. The accident, which occurred on the 11th lap, took out 19 cars. The caution flag was out for more than 25 laps while safety crews cleaned up the mess. Many of the drivers blamed the huge crash on the 60-car starting field, the most cars to start a NASCAR Winston Cup Grand National race in 13 years. "They wanted to fill up the track with those extra cars," said Bobby Allison. "They filled it up alright—all over the backstretch."

"They wanted to fill up the track with those extra cars. They filled it up alright— all over the backstretch."

—Bobby Allison

The left side of Wendell Scott's new Mercury was sheared off in the incredible 21-car crash at Talladega. Scott escaped with his life, but three broken ribs, lacerations, and a fractured pelvis put him on the mend for most of the season. Scott had worked all season on the new car, and he only went eight laps in the race before the crash.

Billy Scott won the right to drive a Richard Howard-Junior Johnson Chevrolet in the May 27 World 600 at Charlotte Motor Speedway after the "Big Chance Special" voting campaign. Howard, the promoter at Charlotte as well as a team owner, established the contest for fans to vote for a deserving driver to get a shot at NASCAR Winston Cup Grand National competition. Scott, a short-track racer from Union, S.C., received the most votes in the two-month voting period. Scott finished 22nd in the race.

Buddy Baker guns his Dodge down pit road during the World 600. At the time, drivers were allowed to whistle down pit road at any speed. A speed limit was introduced in 1991. Baker took the lead in the final 16 laps and beat David Pearson in a stirring finish. It was Baker's third win in the longest race on the annual NASCAR Winston Cup Grand National calendar.

▲ David Pearson leads Richard Petty in the final laps of the Firecracker 400 at Daytona. Pearson won, nipping Petty at the finish. Although Pearson was on a winning spree, his victory in the July 4 race was termed a "mild upset." The Chevrolets, benefactors of recent rules changes, were fleet in the early laps but fell by the wayside. Pearson and Petty finished four laps ahead of the field after the swift Chevys departed.

◄ David Pearson scored his eighth win of the season in Daytona's Firecracker 400. During a 10-race stretch from March through August 1973, Pearson won nine races and finished second in the other event. Pearson won 14 of his first 22 starts with the Wood Brothers including 13 on superspeedways. It was one of the most dominating performances in NASCAR's modern era.

Larry Smith, the 1972 NASCAR Rookie of the Year, acquired the Carling Black Label sponsorship in his sophomore season. The youngster from Lenoir, N.C., was trying to turn around a miserable season at Talladega. On the 14th lap of the Talladega 500, Smith lost control and slapped the wall. Although the car wasn't badly damaged, Smith was dead upon arrival at the infield medical center. That fatality remains one of the strangest in the annals of NASCAR history.

Benny Parsons

AUGUST 9, 1964. Asheville-Weaverville Speedway in the North Carolina mountains. A 250-mile race for the NASCAR Grand National drivers. The 45th of a record 62 NASCAR Grand National races during the 1964 season.

Ford Motor Co., always on the lookout for a "diamond in the rough," summoned a couple of unheralded youngsters to audition for a factory-backed ride in the Asheville-Weaverville event. The two drivers Ford had their eye on were Cale Yarborough and Benny Parsons. It was a chance of a lifetime in auto racing's lifetime of chance. Both Yarborough and Parsons were strapped into potent '64 Ford Galaxies.

Both qualified in the top 10 in the 36-car field. During the race, Parsons had difficulty getting oriented with the powerful car on the speedy track, and was generally unimpressive in his big chance. Yarborough ran with the leaders at times and drew raves until a broken radiator sent him to the sidelines. "I thought Cale was excellent," said John Holman, head of Ford's racing effort.

While Yarborough's successful audition earned him a factory ride within a year, Parsons went back to the short tracks of the Midwest. "I was just a kid and I didn't perform well," Parsons said years later. "It took me another six years to get into NASCAR racing."

Parsons' skill in stock cars netted him a pair of championships in the Automobile Racing Club of America. Another opportunity in NASCAR didn't come until 1969 and he didn't get a real shot at the big time until '70. Parsons was originally hired by L.G. DeWitt as a substitute driver for Buddy Young, who was injured in the '70 season opener at Riverside. Young's recuperation process took nearly a year. While filling in, Parsons performed admirably, scoring 23 top-10 finishes in 45 starts in his rookie season. At the close of the year, DeWitt elected to keep Parsons on the team's payroll.

Four years later, Parsons wore the crown as NASCAR Winston Cup Grand National champion—and his title run came against nearly impossible odds. The DeWitt team had no sponsorship during the 1973 season. Their racing arsenal contained only three cars while most of the top contenders had a full fleet of machinery at their disposal.

**NASCAR Winston Cup Career Record
1964, 1969-1988**
Starts: 526
Wins: 21
Top 5s: 199
Top 10s: 283
Poles: 20
Career Winnings:
$4,426,287

A unique points system was used in 1973, awarding points for each lap completed in addition to overall finish positions. Parsons only led 374 laps and recorded a single win at Bristol, but he completed 9311 of a possible 10,258 laps. Keeping the car running in most of the races enabled Parsons to build a 194-point lead entering the final race of the year at Rockingham. Under the points system, 371 points would go to the winner of the 500-miler. Five drivers had a shot at the championship.

Parsons qualified a strong fifth. But as the lead pack was lapping the backmarkers in the early laps, Johnny Barnes spun into the wall. Barnes' car bounced into the path of Parsons, who hit him hard. The axle was broken on Parsons' Chevrolet. The entire right side was ripped away. Suspension parts were strewn all over the track. Bluntly, the car was wiped out.

But the racing fraternity rallied around the underdog. Hijacking pieces of a car that had failed to earn a starting spot in the race, hordes of pit crewmen from several teams joined in and reconstructed Parsons' car. Incredibly, Parsons rolled back onto the track 136 laps after the accident and he drove to the championship.

"I was lower than the gutter when I first came back to the pits after the wreck," said Parsons. "We were out of it. Fifth place [in the NASCAR Winston Cup standings] was looking me dead in the eye. But I really got inspired when I saw everyone on our team and so many from the other teams swarming over my car. What they did was a real miracle."

By completing 308 laps, Parsons was able to accumulate enough lap points to win the title by 67.15 points over Cale Yarborough. Parsons wrapped up the title and joined the top echelon of NASCAR Winston Cup racing.

Parsons' NASCAR Winston Cup career continued through the 1988 season. In addition to his title season in '73, he captured NASCAR's biggest event, the Daytona 500, in '75. He logged 21 victories in stock car racing's premier division, and was voted among the top 50 drivers in NASCAR history during the Golden Anniversary in 1998.

After his retirement, Parsons went into television commentary. He served as an analyst for NASCAR NEXTEL Cup broadcasts starting in 1989 and remained a fan favorite until he died of cancer in early 2007.

"I expected it to blow any minute. It wasn't until the last five laps that I realized I could win if the thing held together."

—Dick Brooks

◀ Dick Brooks' #22 Plymouth leads the charge off the fourth turn in the Talladega 500. Brooks took the lead with seven laps remaining and motored home first to produce a stunning upset. Driving the unsponsored Crawford Brothers Plymouth, Brooks overcame a pit-road accident, overheating problems, and long pit stops by a ragtag crew. It was the final NASCAR Winston Cup Grand National victory for the Plymouth nameplate.

▶ Donnie Allison's mangled #88 Chevrolet bounces off the wall at Talladega as Bobby Allison spins his #12 Chevrolet to avoid contact. Rookie Randy Tissot drives safely past in the low groove. The Allison brothers were among the strongest contenders in the Talladega 500 until the accident put them out of the race.

▲ Bart Starr, the Most Valuable Player in Super Bowls I and II, was honored as Grand Marshall of the 1973 Talladega 500. Starr, who played his collegiate career at the University of Alabama, co-owned two Lincoln-Mercury dealerships in Alabama. Starr is pictured with Bill France, the founder of NASCAR and president of the Alabama International Motor Speedway.

NASCAR short-track icon Ralph Earnhardt, the 1956 Sportsman division champion, suffered a heart attack and passed away on Sept. 26 at the age of 45. The elder Earnhardt was still active on short tracks at the time of his death.

Cale Yarborough and Richard Petty battle side by side in the final laps of Charlotte Motor Speedway's National 500 on Oct. 7. Yarborough made the decisive pass 22 laps from the finish. In a postrace inspection, NASCAR technical inspectors discovered disturbing engine readings in Yarborough's Chevrolet and Petty's Dodge. Both cars may have had oversized engines, but both drivers kept their 1-2 finishes without penalty.

Benny Parsons (center) poses with crew chief Travis Carter (left), team owner L.G. DeWitt, and the remains of the Chevrolet that carried the team to an upset victory in the NASCAR Winston Cup Grand National championship. In the final event of the year at Rockingham, Parsons was involved in a thundering collision with Johnny Barnes. The crash ripped the right side of the car away. The DeWitt pit crew, with the help of several other teams, virtually rebuilt the car in a little more than an hour. Parsons got back into the race, finished 28th, and clinched the title.

1973 NASCAR WINSTON CUP GN POINTS RACE

Rank	Driver	Points	Starts	Wins	Top 5	Top 10	Winnings
1	Benny Parsons	7173	28	1	15	21	$182,321
2	Cale Yarborough	7106	28	4	16	19	$267,513
3	Cecil Gordon	7046	28	0	8	18	$102,120
4	James Hylton	6972	28	0	1	11	$82,512
5	Richard Petty	6877	28	6	15	17	$234,389
6	Bobby Baker	6327	27	2	16	20	$190,531
7	Bobby Allison	6272	27	2	15	16	$161,818
8	Walter Ballard	5955	28	0	0	4	$53,875
9	Elmo Langley	5826	27	0	0	4	$49,542
10	J.D. McDuffie	5743	27	0	3	10	$56,140
11	Jabe Thomas	5637	26	0	0	1	$42,955
12	Buddy Arrington	5483	26	0	1	4	$40,877
13	David Pearson	5382	18	11	14	14	$228,408
14	Henley Gray	5215	24	0	0	4	$34,122
15	Richard Childress	5169	25	0	1	2	$37,880
16	Frank Warren	4992	26	0	0	0	$36,551
17	David Sisco	4986	23	0	2	5	$36,205
18	Ed Negre	4942	24	0	1	2	$34,235
19	Dean Dalton	4712	26	0	0	2	$35,954
20	Charlie Roberts	4695	24	0	0	0	$32,144
21	Bill Champion	4447	26	0	0	1	$31,828
22	Coo Coo Marlin	4233	21	0	1	8	$29,997
23	Lennie Pond	4013	23	0	1	9	$25,155
24	Dave Marcis	3973	23	0	3	6	$30,253
25	Raymond Williams	3708	22	0	0	3	$22,728
26	Bobby Isaac	3352	19	0	5	6	$84,550
27	Dick Brooks	3200	14	1	3	9	$55,369
28	Darrell Waltrip	2968	19	0	2	5	$42,466
29	Joe Frasson	2952	14	0	3	4	$25,884
30	Vic Parsons	2929	18	0	0	6	$18,200
31	Jim Vandiver	2508	10	0	0	4	$18,586
32	John Sears	2465	17	0	0	0	$16,890
33	Larry Smith	2367	11	0	0	1	$14,090
34	Rick Newsom	1931	12	0	0	0	$8530
35	Donnie Allison	1755	14	0	2	5	$41,246
36	D.K. Ulrich	1543	11	0	0	0	$3955
37	G.C. Spencer	1503	10	0	0	1	$12,013
38	Mel Larson	1182	10	0	0	0	$8235
39	Johnny Barnes	1174	8	0	0	0	$8585
40	Eddie Bond	1163	6	0	0	0	$6901
41	Earle Canavan	1144	5	0	0	0	$4980
42	Earl Brooks	1075	9	0	0	0	$4880
43	Charlie Glotzbach	903	5	0	0	1	$6451
44	Randy Tissot	887	3	0	0	0	$4245
45	Ron Keselowski	879	5	0	1	1	$6060
46	Jimmy Crawford	846	4	0	0	0	$4059
47	Richard Brown	827	13	0	0	0	$7340
48	Clarence Lovell	813	4	0	1	2	$9175
49	Bill Dennis	809	4	0	0	2	$4225
50	Jim McCoy	793	3	0	1	3	$5270

Benny Parsons, driving the unsponsored L.G. DeWitt Chevrolet, pulled a major upset by winning the 1973 NASCAR Winston Cup Grand National championship despite only winning one race.

Parsons took the points lead with a third-place finish at Talladega in early May and never gave up the lead. He held off a late rally by Cale Yarborough to win by only 67.15 points.

Under NASCAR's points system, in which points per lap completed were factored in, Parsons was unaware of what position he would have to finish in at the finale at Rockingham to seal the championship. Parsons crashed early, but his team was able to make miraculous repairs to get him back into the race. He completed enough laps to wrap up the 1973 title.

Five drivers had a mathematical chance to win the championship entering the final event of the 28-race season. Winless drivers Cecil Gordon and James Hylton finished third and fourth, while six-time winner Richard Petty placed fifth in the final standings.

1974

January 3 In the wake of the crippling energy shortage, NASCAR announces all races will be reduced 10 percent in length to conserve fuel. In addition, NASCAR plans for smaller starting fields and limited practice sessions.

February 17 Richard Petty rallies from a flat tire, takes the lead with 11 laps remaining, and drives to victory in the 450-mile Daytona 500. Speedway officials decide to drop the first 20 laps from the race, and count the first lap as lap 21 to maintain the "500" in the name of NASCAR's most prestigious event.

April 21 Richard Petty wins the Gwyn Staley Memorial 400 at North Wilkesboro Speedway using a small engine in his Dodge. Under NASCAR rules, the small engines can compete without restrictor plates, while the large 426–429-cid engines must run with carburetor-restrictive devices.

May 26 David Pearson racks up his 80th career Winston Cup victory in a thrilling World 600 at Charlotte Motor Speedway. Pearson takes the lead with nine laps remaining and beats Richard Petty by a car length.

July 4 Cagey David Pearson outfoxes Richard Petty to win the Firecracker 400 in a puzzling finish. Pearson leads entering the final lap, but pulls to the low groove to allow Petty to pass. Pearson regains stride, runs Petty down, and makes the decisive pass just before the finish line. Buddy Baker and Cale Yarborough finish in a dead heat for third place.

July 14 Cale Yarborough muscles his way around Buddy Baker on the final lap and squeezes out a narrow win in Bristol's Volunteer 500. It is the seventh win of the season for Yarborough.

August 4 NASCAR makes its first appearance at Pocono International Raceway and Richard Petty prevails in the Purolator 500, which is shortened to 480 miles due to rain. Sprint Car icon Jan Opperman finishes eighth in a Chevrolet.

The DiGard Racing Team, founded by Mike DiProspero and brothers Bill and Jim Gardner, entered NASCAR Winston Cup Grand National racing in 1973. Within a year, an elaborate shop was built in the shadows of Daytona International Speedway. A fleet of DiGard Chevrolets, driven by Donnie Allison, was groomed and prepared in the all-purpose facility.

In his second season on the NASCAR Winston Cup Grand National circuit Darrell Waltrip posted seven top-five and 10 top-10 finishes, serving notice that he would become a force to be reckoned with. His best effort was a second-place finish at Darlington's Southern 500. Waltrip earned $67,774.30 for his efforts and finished 19th in the points race.

Gary Bettenhausen's #16 Penske AMC Matador runs just ahead of #83 Ramo Stott and #2 Dick Brooks in the Feb. 17 Daytona 500. Bettenhausen, driving for Roger Penske's USAC Indy Car team, got the assignment in the redesigned Matador and maintained a pace that kept him in sight of the leaders. Stott had one of his finest runs, finishing third in Norris Reed's Smithville Farms Chevrolet. Brooks finished ninth despite falling out in the final laps when a front wheel collapsed. Bettenhausen finished 12th.

Number 95 Darrell Waltrip leads #31 Jim Vandiver and #90 Bill Dennis on the short chute during the Daytona 500. Waltrip finished seventh. Vandiver, who excelled on NASCAR's ultrafast speedways, finished second in the Twin 125-miler, but radiator troubles put him out of the 450-miler, which had been shortened 50 miles due to the energy crisis. Dennis, NASCAR's 1970 Rookie of the Year, was felled by engine problems in the final 100 miles.

Donnie Allison's DiGard Chevrolet leads Richard Petty's Dodge in the closing stages of the Daytona 500. Petty suffered a flat tire with 19 laps remaining and was forced to make an unscheduled pit stop. Seemingly out of the hunt with 10 laps to go, Petty was nearly a lap behind when Allison ran over a piece of debris, cutting a tire. Allison spun out, allowing Petty to breeze to victory. By the time Allison righted his path, he had fallen to sixth place.

Sophomore driver Lennie Pond wheels his #54 Chevrolet around the ½-mile Richmond Fairgrounds Raceway in the Feb. 24 Richmond 500. Pond, who was named the 1973 NASCAR Winston Cup Grand National Rookie of the Year in a close decision over Darrell Waltrip, started fifth and finished fourth in the race.

◀ Donnie Allison and David Pearson are perched on the front row at the start of the April 7 Rebel 450 at Darlington Raceway. Officials at Darlington elected to make the race 450 miles and call it the Rebel 450 in the wake of the 10-percent reduction mandated by the Federal Energy Office. All other tracks on the NASCAR Winston Cup Grand National Series kept the original name intact and started the first lap as the 51st mile. Pearson won the race in the Wood Brothers Mercury.

1974

August 11 Richard Petty edges David Pearson to win the Talladega 500, an event marred by a mass sabotage in the garage the night before the race. More than two dozen of the top contending cars are tampered with by an unknown assailant during the nighttime hours.

September 29 Canadian rookie Earl Ross outlasts Richard Petty and Cale Yarborough and outruns Buddy Baker in the final laps to win the Old Dominion 500 at Martinsville. Ross becomes the first Canadian driver to win a NASCAR Winston Cup Grand National race.

November 24 Bobby Allison drives a Matador to a surprise victory in the 500-miler at Ontario Motor Speedway. During the customary postrace inspection, NASCAR officials discover the Roger Penske-owned Matador is equipped with illegal roller tappets. The team keeps the win but is fined a record $9100. Richard Petty wins his fifth championship by 567.45 points in a complicated points system used for just one year.

Bobby Allison wheels his #12 Chevrolet Monte Carlo to the inside of #48 James Hylton during the May 26 World 600 at Charlotte Motor Speedway. Allison drove his self-owned car to a third-place finish, but he lagged five laps behind the leaders. Allison dashed around Darrell Waltrip on the final lap.

Buddy Baker, taking his first ride in the Bud Moore Ford, leads Richard Petty and David Pearson in the Charlotte World 600. Baker, who replaced George Follmer in the #15 Ford, led nine times for a total of 94 laps before the engine let go on lap 285. Moore unseated Follmer in his small-engine Ford after early season struggles. Baker was available for the ride when his K&K Insurance Dodge team pulled out of NASCAR due to numerous rules changes, which K&K president Nord Krauskopf said rendered his cars uncompetitive.

◄ Cale Yarborough and David Pearson battle for the lead in the Firecracker 400 at Daytona. The Carling Brewing Co. came on board as primary sponsor of the Richard Howard-Junior Johnson team effective with the July 4 event. When Carling signed the contract, team owner Howard shifted ownership to Johnson, who had served as team manager of the operation since 1971. Pearson won the 400-miler as Yarborough tied for third with Buddy Baker.

▼ Bobby Allison, who became full-time driver for the Roger Penske Matador team at the Firecracker 400, leads #15 Buddy Baker and #88 Donnie Allison in the early laps of the Independence Day event. Allison qualified on the front row and finished fifth. Allison departed with engine problems and Baker finished in a tie for third with Cale Yarborough.

Number 72 Benny Parsons and #2 Dave Marcis ride the high banks during the Aug. 11 Talladega 500. Parsons finished fifth, while Marcis came home 11th. Marcis was one of only five drivers to compete in all 30 races in 1974. He drove for four team owners, usually competing in his own Dodge. Marcis logged six top-five finishes and placed sixth in the points.

Canadian rookie #52 Earl Ross and #28 Bobby Isaac were two strong contenders in the Talladega 500. Isaac, who had suddenly quit in the middle of the Talladega 500 a year earlier, returned in 1974. He drove his Hoss Ellington Chevy to an eighth-place finish. Ross, who joined the Junior Johnson team when the Carling sponsorship materialized, ran 10th at Talladega. Later in the year, he won the Martinsville event. Ross was named Rookie of the Year.

Rookie of the Year

NASCAR BEGAN OFFICIALLY recognizing a Rookie of the Year in 1957. Ken Rush, a young driver from High Point, N.C., received the first official presentation of the top freshman award during the annual victory dinner in Daytona Beach in '58. Rush received a small cash award and a handsome plaque.

Over the years, Rush has been omitted from the official NASCAR Cup Series Rookie of the Year winners list. Shorty Rollins erroneously has been given credit as the first recipient of the Rookie of the Year award in 1958.

From 1957 to '73, NASCAR had no points system for determining the top freshman pilot. NASCAR officials simply huddled near the end of the year and selected a winner. Rookie of the Year candidates were subjective, and not always open to any NASCAR newcomer. In the early years of the award, NASCAR ruled former champions from other sanctioning bodies ineligible. The best example is Dick Hutcherson, who won nine races, claimed nine poles, and finished second in the final points standings as a rookie in 1965. Hutcherson was unable to contend for the Rookie of the Year award since he was a two-time winner of the IMCA Stock Car racing championship.

In 1973, Lennie Pond edged Darrell Waltrip for the Rookie of the Year award, a controversial decision that surprised nearly everyone. With the controversy still in full song,

NASCAR announced that a Rookie points system, separate from the official Winston Cup Grand National points, would be inaugurated for the '74 season.

The points system has curbed controversy but not eliminated it. Twice, in 1976 and '81, the winner of the Rookie of the Year points standings didn't win the award. NASCAR still retains its right to distribute additional points after the close of the season, which can overturn any outcome that was determined on the track. Terry Bivins won the Rookie of the Year points standings in 1976 and Morgan Shepherd won by a wide margin in 1981, yet NASCAR elected to give the nod to Skip Manning and Ron Bouchard, respectively.

Although the Rookie of the Year award first appeared in 1957, there was one earlier unofficial winner. Houston Lawing, NASCAR's first publicity director, unofficially honored Blackie Pitt as "1954 Rookie of the Year" in at least one press release. Pitt was also mentioned as the top '54 rookie in the '55 Daytona Beach Speedweeks souvenir program, which was edited by Lawing.

The accompanying chart details the Rookie of the Year winners from 1957 to 2010. The award has been the launching point for many successful careers. While many top rookies have become household names, some have faded into obscurity. Only time will tell if the recent winners will become the next Jeff Gordon or Dale Earnhardt.

Year	Rookie of the Year	Runner-up	Third Place
1954	Blackie Pitt*		
1957	Ken Rush		
1958	Shorty Rollins		
1959	Richard Petty	Fritz Wilson	Buddy Baker
1960	David Pearson	Gerald Duke	Paul Lewis
1961	Woodie Wilson	Wendell Scott	Lee Reitzel
1962	Thomas Cox	Cale Yarborough	Ed Livingston
1963	Billy Wade	Bobby Isaac	Larry Manning
1964	Doug Cooper	J.T. Putney	Buddy Arrington
1965	Sam McQuagg	Henley Gray	Clyde Lynn
1966	James Hylton	Bill Seifert	Frank Warren
1967	Donnie Allison	Charlie Glotzbach	Paul Dean Holt
1968	Pete Hamilton	Dave Marcis	Dr. Don Tarr
1969	Dick Brooks	Buddy Young	Hoss Ellington
1970	Bill Dennis	Joe Frasson	Jim Vandiver
1971	Walter Ballard	Maynard Troyer	Richard Brown
1972	Larry Smith	David Sisco	Doc Faustina
1973	Lennie Pond	Darrell Waltrip	Johnny Barnes
1974	Earl Ross	Richie Panch	Jackie Rogers
1975	Bruce Hill	Carl Adams	Bruce Jacobi
1976	Skip Manning	Terry Bivins	Neil Bonnett
1977	Ricky Rudd	Sam Sommers	Janet Guthrie
1978	Ronnie Thomas	Roger Hamby	Blackie Wangerin
1979	Dale Earnhardt	Joe Millikan	Terry Labonte
1980	Jody Ridley	Lake Speed	Kyle Petty
1981	Ron Bouchard	Morgan Shepherd	Tim Richmond
1982	Geoff Bodine	Mark Martin	Brad Teague
1983	Sterling Marlin	Trevor Boys	Ronnie Hopkins, Jr.
1984	Rusty Wallace	Phil Parsons	Greg Sacks
1985	Ken Schrader	Eddie Bierschwale	Don Hume
1986	Alan Kulwicki	Michael Waltrip	Chet Fillip
1987	Davey Allison	Dale Jarrett	Steve Christman
1988	Ken Bouchard	Ernie Irvan	Brad Noffsinger
1989	Dick Trickle	Hut Stricklin	Larry Pearson
1990	Rob Moroso	Jack Pennington	Jerry O'Neil
1991	Bobby Hamilton	Ted Musgrave	Stanley Smith
1992	Jimmy Hensley	Andy Belmont	Dave Mader III
1993	Jeff Gordon	Bobby Labonte	Kenny Wallace
1994	Jeff Burton	Steve Grissom	Joe Nemechek
1995	Ricky Craven	Robert Pressley	Randy LaJoie
1996	Johnny Benson, Jr.	Gary Bradberry	Randy MacDonald
1997	Mike Skinner	David Green	Robby Gordon
1998	Kenny Irwin, Jr.	Kevin Lepage	Jerry Nadeau
1999	Tony Stewart	Elliott Sadler	Buckshot Jones
2000	Matt Kenseth	Dale Earnhardt, Jr.	Dave Blaney
2001	Kevin Harvick	Kurt Busch	Casey Atwood
2002	Ryan Newman	Jimmie Johnson	Shawna Robinson
2003	Jamie McMurray	Greg Biffle	Tony Raines
2004	Kasey Kahne	Brendan Gaughan	Brian Vickers
2005	Kyle Busch	Travis Kvapil	
2006	Denny Hamlin	Clint Bowyer	Martin Truex, Jr.
2007	Juan Pablo Montoya	David Ragan	Paul Menard
2008	Regan Smith	Sam Hornish, Jr.	Patrick Carpentier
2009	Joey Logano	Scott Speed	Max Papis
2010	Kevin Conway	Terry Cook	

NASCAR CUP SERIES ROOKIE OF THE YEAR

* Not an official award

1974

"I kept looking back for him [Richard Petty] to challenge me, but evidently he didn't have the muscle."

—David Pearson

Canadian Earl Ross, who hailed from Ailsa Craig, Ontario, was an unheralded freshman when he came to NASCAR Winston Cup Grand National racing in 1974. Having ties with the Carling Brewing Co., Ross was added to the Junior Johnson Chevrolet team at the sponsor's request. Ross became the first Canadian to win a Winston Cup event when he pulled an upset at Martinsville Speedway on Sept. 29. He went on to win the 1974 Rookie of the Year award, then returned to Canadian short tracks when Carling dropped out of racing.

David Pearson's Wood Brothers Mercury leads Richard Petty, Buddy Baker, and Bobby Allison at Michigan International Speedway in the Aug. 25 Yankee 400. The race featured 45 lead changes and Pearson was at the front of the pack when the checkered flag fell. Petty finished second, with Baker fourth and Allison fifth.

Number 11 Cale Yarborough nips at the heels of Richard Petty in the early laps of the Sept. 2 Southern 500 at Darlington. The 26th annual running of NASCAR's oldest superspeedway event was a wreck-marred contest with more than 100 laps run under the caution flag. Only 12 cars finished the race. Yarborough led the final 122 laps and racked up his third triumph in the Labor Day event.

▼ Buddy Baker's #15 Ford slides sideways as Jim Vandiver's #31 Dodge pierces the inside guardrail in a thundering 10-car crash at the outset of the Oct. 6 National 500 at Charlotte Motor Speedway. Baker started at the rear of the 42-car field and charged past 12 cars in less than one lap. In his haste to get to the front, Baker clipped the rear of Dick Brooks' Dodge, triggering the massive pileup.

Dale Earnhardt made his first appearance at Charlotte Motor Speedway in the Oct. 5 300-mile NASCAR Late Model Sportsman event. Driving the #06 Dodge owned by NASCAR Winston Cup Grand National veteran Neil Castles, Earnhardt qualified 12th and finished 13th in the race. He finished five laps behind winner Bobby Allison and earned $1000.

Nord Krauskopf's K&K Insurance Dodge team ended its boycott of NASCAR races in late 1974. In Charlotte's National 500, Dave Marcis and Bobby Isaac both drove the familiar poppy-red machines. Here, Isaac's #17 Dodge leads #5 Harry Gant, who was competing in one of his early NASCAR Winston Cup Grand National events. Mechanical problems forced Isaac and Gant to the sidelines before 100 laps had been completed.

Bobby Allison drove the Roger Penske AMC Matador to a surprising victory in the Nov. 24 season finale at Ontario Motor Speedway. It was only the third race all season won by a driver other than Richard Petty, David Pearson, or Cale Yarborough. After the race, NASCAR technical inspectors discovered illegal roller tappets on the Matador. The victory was upheld, but the Penske team was fined $9100—at the time the largest fine in NASCAR history.

1974 NASCAR WINSTON CUP GN POINTS RACE

Rank	Driver	Points	Starts	Wins	Top 5	Top 10	Winnings
1	Richard Petty	5037.75	30	10	22	23	$432,019.00
2	Cale Yarborough	4470.30	30	10	21	22	$363,781.10
3	David Pearson	2389.25	19	7	15	15	$252,818.92
4	Bobby Allison	2019.19	27	2	17	17	$178,436.90
5	Benny Parsons	1591.50	30	0	11	14	$185,079.72
6	Dave Marcis	1378.20	30	0	6	9	$83,376.01
7	Buddy Baker	1016.88	19	0	11	12	$151,024.62
8	Earl Ross	1009.47	21	1	4	9	$81,198.50
9	Cecil Gordon	1000.65	30	0	1	10	$66,165.32
10	David Sisco	956.20	28	0	2	9	$58,312.32
11	James Hylton	924.95	29	0	1	8	$61,384.32
12	J.D. McDuffie	920.85	30	0	0	7	$59,534.32
13	Bill Champion	820.84	29	0	1	2	$55,778.66
14	Frank Warren	775.44	28	0	2	7	$52,712.32
15	Walter Ballard	748.44	27	0	1	6	$54,038.32
16	Richard Childress	735.44	29	0	0	3	$50,248.30
17	Donnie Allison	728.80	21	0	6	10	$60,314.30
18	Lennie Pond	723.25	22	0	5	11	$55,989.30
19	Darrell Waltrip	609.97	15	0	7	10	$67,774.30
20	Tony Bettenhausen	601.69	27	0	0	1	$38,994.30
21	Jackie Rogers	587.88	23	0	0	6	$32,367.00
22	Coo Coo Marlin	581.67	23	0	1	5	$41,759.00
23	Ed Negre	534.30	26	0	0	0	$24,622.00
24	Bob Burcham	445.50	20	0	1	5	$27,923.00
25	Elmo Langley	433.78	23	0	0	3	$24,722.00
26	Charlie Glotzbach	293.09	14	0	4	5	$33,072.00
27	Dick Brooks	267.52	16	0	0	3	$22,760.00
28	Joe Frasson	240.80	14	0	0	3	$22,629.00
29	George Follmer	230.49	13	0	3	5	$53,780.00
30	Buddy Arrington	221.20	16	0	0	4	$21,510.00
31	Bill Champion	207.72	15	0	0	0	$13,480.00
32	D.K. Ulrich	155.32	15	0	0	0	$11,955.00
33	Bobby Isaac	152.95	11	0	1	5	$23,442.00
34	Travis Tiller	146.44	14	0	0	0	$11,410.00
35	Roy Mayne	141.72	12	0	0	0	$15,284.00
36	Ben Arnold	125.44	14	0	0	0	$12,375.00
37	Neil Castles	123.56	14	0	0	0	$12,479.00
38	G.C. Spencer	96.80	10	0	0	1	$12,985.00
39	Ramo Stott	82.95	6	0	1	4	$23,705.00
40	Jim Vandiver	71.40	7	0	0	1	$15,909.00
41	Dan Daugherty	63.04	8	0	0	1	$12,413.00
42	Jabe Thomas	49.14	9	0	0	1	$7445.00
43	Gary Bettenhausen	49.00	4	0	0	2	$10,350.00
44	A.J. Foyt	41.22	4	0	2	2	$15,560.00
45	Jerry Schild	35.37	5	0	0	1	$8395.00
46	Earle Canavan	34.92	6	0	0	0	$6570.00
47	Dick Trickle	24.78	3	0	0	3	$10,828.00
48	Marty Robbins	23.78	4	0	1	2	$5734.00
49	Alton Jones	20.40	5	0	1	2	$4080.00
50	Herschel McGriff	20.34	5	0	0	1	$8585.00

NASCAR drastically changed its points system for the 1974 season, and it proved to be the most confusing method ever used. Fractions of points were multiplied and remultiplied after each race. The concept was to award points in direct relation to money won.

Under the peculiar system, the 1-2 finishers in the rich Daytona 500 were virtually assured of a 1-2 finish in the final standings. Richard Petty and Cale Yarborough finished first and second at Daytona and ranked 1-2 in the final standings. All drama for the points chase ended in February. Petty and Yarborough had their Daytona points added to their point total after each event, making it virtually impossible for anyone to overtake them.

In the Darlington Southern 500, Petty crashed early and placed 35th, yet still had more points added to his total than Darrell Waltrip, who finished second.

Petty accumulated 5037.75 points, compared to Yarborough's runner-up total of 4470.30. David Pearson finished third with 2389.25 points. Thankfully, the system was changed after only one year.

1975

January NASCAR announces a new points system, the fourth different method of distributing points in the last five years. For the first time in NASCAR history, each race will carry an equal points value throughout the season.

February 16 Benny Parsons takes the lead three laps from the finish and wins the Daytona 500 when leader David Pearson spins on the backstretch. Parsons comes from the 32nd starting position to claim the upset win and the biggest victory of his career.

April 13 Bobby Allison, running two laps behind with 40 laps to go, scrambles back into contention and rides to a narrow victory in the Rebel 500 at Darlington. A crash involving David Pearson and Benny Parsons opens the door for Allison, who edges Darrell Waltrip by a car length at the finish line.

May 4 Buddy Baker ends his two-year drought by winning the Winston 500 at Talladega. Baker's Bud Moore Ford finishes a car length in front of runner-up David Pearson.

May 10 Darrell Waltrip racks up his first career NASCAR Winston Cup Grand National victory with a two-lap triumph in the Music City USA 420 at his hometown Nashville Speedway. Benny Parsons comes home second with Coo Coo Marlin third.

May 25 Richard Petty scores his first victory at Charlotte Motor Speedway since winning a 100-mile qualifying race in 1961 with a resounding win in the World 600. Dale Earnhardt makes his first NASCAR Winston Cup Grand National start, finishing 22nd in a Dodge owned by Ed Negre.

August 16 Buddy Baker noses out Richard Petty in a photo finish to win the Talladega 500, an event marred by the death of DeWayne "Tiny" Lund. Lund is involved in a multicar crash on the seventh lap.

Bobby Allison's Matador snakes its way through the "esses" on Riverside's road course on the way to victory in the Jan. 19 season opening Winston Western 500. Allison was the class of the field in the 500-miler, leading all but 18 of the 191 laps. Richard Petty, seen here chasing Allison, fell out of contention when he backed into the wall on the 33rd lap. Petty lost 19 laps in the pits while repairs were made to his Dodge, but he still managed to finish seventh.

Jim Hurtubise came to Daytona in 1975 without a ride, but found a seat in Rick Newsom's #20 Ford in the Twin 125-miler. Hurtubise finished 10th, securing a berth in the Daytona 500 field. Newsom drove the car in the 500, bowing out early with engine problems. Newsom's career in NASCAR Winston Cup Grand National racing was checkered at best. As a rookie in '73, he was booted off the tour when he failed to obey a black flag in the Twin 125-miler. Later that year, he was reinstated. Newsom attempted to qualify for 159 NASCAR Cup Series races from '72 to '86. He made the field 82 times, but never finished in the top 10. Newsom was killed in a private plane crash in 1988.

Bobby Allison takes the checkered flag at the finish of the first Twin 125-mile qualifying race at Daytona on Feb. 13. Allison blasted out of the starting blocks in 1975, winning the Winston Western 500 and the Twin 125, and finishing second in the Daytona 500. However, team owner Roger Penske decided not to run the full schedule, even with Allison holding the points lead. Allison competed in 19 races in '75, winning three times and finishing 24th in the points standings.

The Petty Enterprises crew works feverishly on a mechanical problem that knocked Richard Petty out of contention in the March 2 Carolina 500 at Rockingham's North Carolina Motor Speedway. Petty led 79 laps before the mechanical gremlins surfaced. Despite losing nine laps on an extended pit stop, Petty still managed to place third behind winner Cale Yarborough and runner-up David Pearson.

Johnny Rutherford (left), the 1974 Indianapolis 500 champion, chats with crew chief Dick Hutcherson before the March 23 Atlanta 500. Rutherford competed in occasional NASCAR Winston Cup Grand National events from '63 to '88. He drove the Norris Reed-owned Chevrolet in the '75 Atlanta 500, qualifying sixth. A crash on the 56th lap took "Lone Star JR" out of the event.

▲ Pole-sitter #88 Donnie Allison takes the green flag at the start of the 17th annual Daytona 500 on Feb. 16, followed closely by David Pearson and Buddy Baker. Allison only led the opening lap and eventually fell out with engine problems. Pearson was headed to victory when he spun off the backstretch with less than three laps remaining. Benny Parsons came from his 32nd starting spot to win NASCAR's crown-jewel event.

▶ Richard Petty whips his Dodge around Lennie Pond on his way to victory in Martinsville Speedway's April 27 Virginia 500. Petty outran Darrell Waltrip in the last 20 laps to secure his 14th career win on the flat ½-mile track. Petty went unchallenged in the NASCAR Winston Cup Grand National championship chase in 1975, winning 13 races and leading the standings after all but the first two races of the year.

1975

September 14 Richard Petty overcomes a six-lap deficit and edges Dick Brooks to win the Delaware 500 at Dover Downs International Speedway. Petty's Dodge snaps a tie rod that requires a lengthy pit stop to repair. Petty gets back onto the lead lap with a late caution and outruns Brooks and Benny Parsons in the final laps.

September 28 Journeyman Dave Marcis drives a Dodge to his first career NASCAR Winston Cup Grand National victory in the Old Dominion 500 at Martinsville Speedway. Marcis passes Benny Parsons with 40 laps to go and scores a three-second victory.

October 12 Darrell Waltrip gives the DiGard Racing team its first NASCAR Winston Cup Grand National win in the 500-lapper at Richmond Fairgrounds Speedway.

November 23 Buddy Baker bags his fourth win of the season with a decisive triumph in the Los Angeles Times 500 at Ontario Motor Speedway. Richard Petty takes his sixth NASCAR championship by a 722-point margin over Dave Marcis.

Buddy Baker put the #15 Bud Moore Ford on the pole for the May 4 Winston 500 at Talladega. After 51 lead changes among 12 drivers, Baker flashed across the finish line just ahead of runner-up David Pearson. For Baker, it ended a two-year winless skid in NASCAR Winston Cup Grand National competition. It was also Bud Moore's first NASCAR win since 1966, and the first for the Ford nameplate since '71.

Marty Robbins spins his #42 Dodge at Talladega after driving through an oil patch dropped by Ramo Stott. Grant Adcox slipped around safely to the high side and continued on to a seventh-place finish. Robbins was gobbled up in a bone-jarring three-car collision. It was the third straight race in which Robbins totaled his Cotton Owens-prepared Dodge.

Richard Petty and Buddy Baker are hooked up in a tight draft during the Winston 500. Petty was in contention until he made an unscheduled pit stop when a wheel bearing caught on fire. Randy Owens, Petty's 20-year-old brother-in-law, was trying to extinguish the fire with a hose attached to a pressurized water tank. The tank exploded, killing Owens instantly.

Flames erupt from the engine of Ramo Stott's #83 Chevrolet as it slides through the turn in the Winston 500. Marty Robbins' Dodge skidded into the side of Stott's car, and, in turn, was hit squarely in the door by the onrushing Chevrolet manned by James Hylton. Miraculously, all three drivers escaped uninjured.

The rear end of Cale Yarborough's #11 Chevrolet kicks out as he chases David Pearson in the World 600 at Charlotte Motor Speedway. Yarborough and team-owner Junior Johnson began the 1975 campaign without a sponsor, having been dropped by Carling Brewing Co. despite a multiyear contract. Johnson was able to secure Holly Farms as a financial backer in the spring, thanks in part to a relationship that dated back to '61.

Benny Parsons (right) gives pointers to rookie driver Randy Bethea prior to Charlotte's May 25 World 600. Bethea, a short-track racer from Johnson City, Tenn., was assigned to drive a Chevrolet owned by D.K. Ulrich in his NASCAR Winston Cup Grand National debut. Bethea barely made it into the starting field, qualifying 39th out of 40. An engine failure relegated him to a 33rd-place finish.

Dale Earnhardt made his NASCAR Winston Cup Grand National debut in the May 25 World 600 at Charlotte Motor Speedway. Driving the #8 Dodge Charger owned and maintained by independent driver Ed Negre, Earnhardt qualified third on the grid. Earnhardt completed 355 of the 400 laps and finished 22nd.

▼ Number 88 Donnie Allison, #15 Buddy Baker, and #17 Darrell Waltrip occupied the front positions at the start of the Firecracker 400. These front-running cars were devoid of major sponsorships in 1975 as corporate America's recession took its toll on NASCAR. Baker's Ford was sponsored by Coppertone sun tan lotion, but it was only a one-shot deal. Despite the lack of solid backing, all three drivers finished strong. Baker was second, Waltrip fourth, and Allison fifth.

▶ Veteran J.D. McDuffie's #70 Chevrolet runs beside rookie Carl Adams in the July 4 Daytona Firecracker 400. McDuffie was injured in a multicar crash in the Daytona 500 and was forced to miss several races while on the mend. McDuffie finished 22nd in the race, while Adams brought his Ford home in the ninth spot.

▲ Elmo Langley guides his #64 Ford to the low side to allow passing room for #72 Benny Parsons, #31 Jim Vandiver, and #35 Darel Dieringer in the Firecracker 400. Dieringer ended a seven-year retirement in 1975, competing in four NASCAR Winston Cup Grand National events. The popular campaigner worked his way into the lead by the 77th lap, but an engine failure four laps later ruined his chances for an upset triumph.

▶ A wobbly but unhurt Dick Brooks is helped from his car following a horrific tumble down the backstretch in the Aug. 17 Talladega 500. Brooks was running in the top five when he scrubbed fenders with Donnie Allison. Brooks' Ford darted off the racing surface, dug into the infield, and flipped numerous times. Unfortunately, a crash on the sixth lap claimed the life of popular NASCAR veteran Tiny Lund.

Bobby Allison clawed his way back into contention in the Sept. 1 Southern 500, rallying from a two-lap deficit to usher Roger Penske's AMC Matador to victory lane. Allison swept both Darlington races in 1975, overcoming a two-lap deficit both times. Team owner Penske campaigned the AMC Matador from '72 to '75, then switched to Mercury products in '76.

Darrell Waltrip's #17 Chevy chases Richard Petty's Dodge in a 1975 NASCAR Winston Cup Grand National event. Waltrip drove his self-owned #17 Chevy Laguna in 17 races before he was signed to drive for the DiGard team in August. Waltrip's first career win came on May 10 at his hometown stomping grounds in Nashville in his own car. It was Waltrip's 50th career NASCAR Winston Cup Grand National start. He ran second at Darlington and Martinsville, and earned a seat in one of the top rides following his impressive outings in his independent machinery.

Richard Petty made one of NASCAR's most memorable comebacks in the Sept. 14 race at Dover Downs. Petty was six laps down at one point, following a long pit stop to repair a mechanical malfunction. With the aid of timely caution flags—and Buddy Arrington—Petty scrambled back into contention and beat Dick Brooks in a close finish. Arrington, who had just purchased a truck from Petty Enterprises, stopped on the track to bring out the final caution flag, thus allowing Petty to get back on the lead lap for the final sprint to the finish line.

The Junie Donlavey pit crew services Dick Brooks' Ford in the 400-lapper at North Wilkesboro Speedway on Sept. 21. Donlavey began fielding cars in NASCAR Winston Cup Grand National racing as early as 1950, and he remained one of the most popular participants in NASCAR history. While driving for Donlavey in '75, Brooks finished 15 of 25 races in the top 10 and managed to score a 10th-place finish in the final points standings.

The NASCAR Points System

THROUGHOUT THE HISTORY of NASCAR Cup Series racing, nearly a dozen different points systems have been used to determine the annual championship. In the early days, NASCAR used a cascading method complete with fractions of points. Only the top finishing positions earned any points at all. Often, over half the field didn't earn a single point.

In the 1950s and '60s, points were awarded on a parallel scale based on total posted awards. For instance, the Daytona 500 usually carried the largest purse, and, in 1967, a total of 6500 points were designated for first place. Richard Petty won the '67 NASCAR championship with a staggering 42,472 points. Under this points system, a part-time driver could rank high in the final tally by winning a major race. Johnny Mantz only entered three races in 1950, yet still finished sixth in the final points standings thanks to a win in the inaugural Southern 500 at Darlington.

To scale down the winner's total and develop a procedure most observers could comprehend, NASCAR changed its points system in 1968. On the superspeedways, the winning driver received 150 points with a drop of three points per position thereafter. Winners at major short tracks received 100 points with a drop of two points throughout the finishing order. Finally, winners in the small 100-mile-or-less races earned 50 points with a drop of one point per finishing position thereafter.

That system lasted only four years. In 1972, NASCAR introduced a method that awarded points for each lap completed. After two years, NASCAR scrapped that system. Entering the final race of the '73 season, no one, including NASCAR statisticians, could figure out where Benny Parsons had to finish to wrap up the title. Even after Parsons had clinched the championship, no one knew for sure. It was a short-lived points structure that simply had to be revamped.

In 1974, NASCAR adopted another points system that again confused everyone, including the most modern computers. Based on posted awards plus multiples determined by the number of starts a driver made, the new points system wreaked havoc for statisticians. No one could understand how Richard Petty could get more points for finishing 35th at Darlington than Darrell Waltrip, who finished second. Thankfully, that points system lasted for only one year as well.

For 1975, NASCAR historian and statistician Bob Latford came up with a more workable solution. For the first time in NASCAR history, all races would carry the same point value, and for the first time, drivers leading laps would get bonus points. The points system was relatively easy to understand: 175 points went to the winner, 170 went to second place, and there was a drop of five points for positions three through six. A four-point drop-off was in place for positions seven through 12. And from 13th place on back, there was a three-point drop-off per position. Five points were awarded to any driver leading a lap, and an additional five points went to the driver leading the most laps. The winner of each race got either 180 or 185 points. Last place in a 43-car field received 34 points.

While the points system was indeed understandable, the results often leave analysts scratching their heads. There was little incentive to run up front, and a single DNF (Did Not Finish) could offset a string of victories. Consistency was the key to winning the NASCAR championship.

NASCAR addressed these issues in subsequent years. Starting with the 2004 season, drivers got an extra five points (180) for a win, and in 2007, NASCAR added another five points for a win, bringing the total to 190 or 195 when leading the most laps.

In 2011, NASCAR simplified the points system in an effort to make it easier to understand. Points are now awarded in one-point increments, with the winner receiving 43 points along with a three-point bonus for winning. The 43rd place finisher receives one point. There are single-point bonuses for leading a lap and for leading the most laps. The maximum amount of points possible for a race is 48.

Darrell Waltrip took over the DiGard Chevrolet ride in August 1975, replacing hard-luck driver Donnie Allison. A short-track wizard, Waltrip gave the DiGard operation its first NASCAR Winston Cup Grand National victory at Richmond on Oct. 12. The flashy Waltrip and DiGard team owner Bill Gardner achieved success during their association, but it was punctuated by a series of stormy public arguments. Here, Waltrip runs at Martinsville on Sept. 28.

Dave Marcis pitches his #71 Dodge into the first turn ahead of Cale Yarborough at Martinsville Speedway. Marcis won the assignment to drive Nord Krauskopf's K&K Insurance Dodge in 1975, and the Wisconsin native racked up his first NASCAR Winston Cup Grand National victory at Martinsville.

Bobby Allison's #16 AMC Matador holds off a challenge from #21 David Pearson as they put a lap on #78 Dr. Dick Skillen during the Oct. 19 race at Rockingham. Allison finished second, while a broken driveshaft put Pearson out after 364 laps. Skillen placed 27th in one of his infrequent NASCAR Winston Cup Grand National appearances.

Buddy Baker enjoyed one of his finest years in 1975, despite not having a full-time sponsor for his Bud Moore-owned #15 Ford. While picking up local sponsorships from race to race, Baker drove the Moore Ford to four superspeedway wins, the most he ever recorded in a single season. Baker closed out the '75 NASCAR Winston Cup Grand National campaign with wins at Atlanta on Nov. 9 and Ontario on Nov. 23.

1975 NASCAR WINSTON CUP GN POINTS RACE

Rank	Driver	Points	Starts	Wins	Top 5	Top 10	Winnings
1	Richard Petty	4783	30	13	21	24	$481,750.80
2	Dave Marcis	4061	30	1	16	18	$240,645.40
3	James Hylton	3914	30	0	2	16	$113,641.86
4	Benny Parsons	3820	30	1	11	17	$214,353.32
5	Richard Childress	3818	30	0	2	15	$96,779.78
6	Cecil Gordon	3702	30	0	7	16	$101,466.24
7	Darrell Waltrip	3462	28	2	11	14	$160,191.35
8	Elmo Langley	3399	29	0	2	7	$67,599.16
9	Cale Yarborough	3295	27	3	13	13	$214,690.62
10	Dick Brooks	3182	25	0	6	15	$93,000.62
11	Walter Ballard	3151	30	0	0	3	$55,695.62
12	Frank Warren	3148	28	0	0	0	$55,670.62
13	David Sisco	3116	28	0	2	7	$62,185.62
14	David Pearson	3057	21	3	13	14	$192,140.62
15	Buddy Baker	3050	23	4	12	13	$236,350.81
16	Bruce Hill	3002	26	0	3	11	$79,427.08
17	Ed Negre	2982	29	0	0	4	$49,628.54
18	J.D. McDuffie	2745	26	0	1	6	$50,936.35
19	Buddy Arrington	2654	25	0	0	3	$45,892.08
20	Coo Coo Marlin	2584	23	0	4	11	$60,012.08
21	Lennie Pond	2540	22	0	6	9	$59,265.00
22	Jabe Thomas	2252	20	0	0	2	$22,390.00
23	Carl Adams	2182	20	0	0	4	$24,865.00
24	Bobby Allison	2181	19	3	10	10	$122,435.00
25	Bruce Jacobi	1732	15	0	0	3	$29,455.00
26	Dean Dalton	1486	15	0	0	3	$19,430.00
27	D.K. Ulrich	1453	16	0	0	1	$16,525.00
28	Donnie Allison	1376	14	0	3	6	$45,595.00
29	Richie Panch	1243	14	0	3	6	$45,595.00
30	Jim Vandiver	1228	13	0	1	4	$24,200.00
31	Bill Champion	1218	13	0	0	0	$11,340.00
32	Earle Canavan	1062	12	0	0	0	$9725.00
33	Grant Adcox	1020	11	0	0	1	$16,540.00
34	Joe Mihalic	957	10	0	0	1	$12,910.00
35	Joe Frasson	939	10	0	0	1	$11,975.00
36	Travis Tiller	922	10	0	0	0	$7780.00
37	Rick Newsom	877	10	0	0	0	$9370.00
38	Ferrel Harris	797	10	0	0	0	$16,165.00
39	Henley Gray	747	8	0	0	1	$8785.00
40	G.C. Spencer	634	9	0	0	1	$14,945.00
41	Dick May	631	8	0	0	1	$11,020.00
42	Earl Brooks	534	7	0	0	0	$4900.00
43	Neil Castles	529	7	0	0	0	$4190.00
44	Jackie Rogers	502	8	0	0	1	$11,000.00
45	Harry Jefferson	455	5	0	0	2	$11,395.00
46	Tommy Gale	437	5	0	0	0	$6570.00
47	Ricky Rudd	431	4	0	0	1	$4345.00
48	Bobby Isaac	405	6	0	0	1	$6695.00
49	Dr. Dick Skillen	389	5	0	0	0	$4865.00
50	Ray Elder	372	3	0	1	1	$8020.00

NASCAR instituted a new points system in 1975. It was the first time in history that every race on the NASCAR Winston Cup Grand National schedule carried an equal point value.

Richard Petty, who won 13 of the 30 races, won his sixth championship by a whopping 722-point margin over Dave Marcis. Petty snatched the points lead from Bobby Allison in the third race of the season and never trailed.

The new points system drew mixed reviews. While it was designed to encourage more teams to commit to running the full schedule, many observers felt a greater amount of points should be awarded at the major superspeedway races than the short tracks. Petty received more points for winning Richmond and leading the most laps than Benny Parsons did for winning the Daytona 500.

NASCAR officials said they approved of the way the points system worked and indicated it would likely remain unchanged for several years to come. It remains in place today.

1976

February 8 NASCAR disallows the speeds of the three fastest qualifiers for the Daytona 500, leaving unheralded Ramo Stott on the pole. A.J. Foyt, Darrell Waltrip, and Dave Marcis have to requalify.

February 15 David Pearson creeps across the finish line at 20 mph to beat Richard Petty in a stunning finish to the Daytona 500. Pearson and Petty swap the lead four times on the final lap and tangle off the fourth turn. Pearson gets his Mercury straightened out and crosses the finish line first.

May 2 Buddy Baker runs away from the field to win Talladega's Winston 500. Averaging a record 169.887 mph, Baker finishes 35 seconds ahead of runner-up Cale Yarborough.

May 30 David Pearson weaves his way through a crash with three laps to go and captures the World 600 for his fifth win of the season. Janet Guthrie makes her NASCAR Winston Cup Grand National debut, finishing 15th.

August 1 Richard Petty takes advantage of David Pearson's flat tire in the final two laps to win the Purolator 500 at Pocono International Raceway. The lead changes hands 48 times among eight different drivers.

August 8 Dave Marcis claims his first win on a superspeedway in the Talladega 500. Marcis finds himself in the catbird seat when Buddy Baker has to pit for fuel with three laps remaining.

September 6 David Pearson leads the final 45 laps and drives to a 2.8-second victory over Richard Petty in the Southern 500 at Darlington. The win gives Pearson a victory in all three crown-jewel events on the NASCAR calendar: the Daytona 500, World 600, and Southern 500.

October 10 Donnie Allison drives to a convincing win in the National 500 at Charlotte and survives a stormy postrace teardown to notch his first NASCAR Winston Cup Grand National victory since 1971.

Qualifying for the 1976 Daytona 500 was perhaps the most interesting in the storied history of Daytona International Speedway. A.J. Foyt, driving Hoss Ellington's #28 Chevrolet, was quickest with a speed of 187.477 mph. Aside from the quick laps turned in by Darrell Waltrip and Dave Marcis, virtually all of the other contenders were 8–10 mph off the pace. The wide discrepancy in speeds led NASCAR to reinspect the quick cars. The times of Foyt, Waltrip, and Marcis were disallowed; Foyt and Waltrip because inspectors found nitrous oxide bottles in their cars, and Marcis for a radiator technicality. With the top three out of the picture, journeyman driver Ramo Stott's #83 Chevy sat on the pole with a speed of 183.456 mph.

Number 71 Dave Marcis and #15 Buddy Baker, principle contenders in the opening Twin 125-mile qualifying race, battled side-by-side for several laps in the preliminary event. Marcis overtook Baker five laps from the finish and recorded a near photo-finish triumph. Marcis and Darrell Waltrip, two drivers who were disqualified on Pole Day, prevailed in the Twin 125s and started the Daytona 500 in the second row.

Number 83 Ramo Stott and rookie Terry Ryan (#61) were the unlikely front-row starters in the Feb. 15 Daytona 500. Ryan, making his NASCAR Winston Cup Grand National debut, became the first rookie to start on the front row in NASCAR's premier event. Stott retired with engine problems shortly after the halfway point, while Ryan finished a strong sixth. Ryan drove in five races in 1976, finishing in the top 10 three times. His William Monaghan-owned team was unable to secure sponsorship to make a concerted run at Rookie of the Year honors.

A ball of flame spits out from the rear of Buddy Baker's Ford after the engine blew on the 84th lap of the Daytona 500. Baker led in the early stages and ran with the leaders until the engine came apart. Baker and team owner Bud Moore acquired sponsorship from Norris Industries in 1976 after winning four races in '75 with no financial backing.

Richard Petty's Dodge hits the retaining barrier as David Pearson's Mercury slides backward in the Daytona 500's heart-stopping last-lap crash. The frantic finish featured four lead changes in the final mile as Petty and Pearson battled for the win. Pearson went on to win one of the most thrilling races in NASCAR history.

A bearded Richard Petty beams from victory lane after his triumph in the Feb. 29 Carolina 500 at North Carolina Motor Speedway. Petty led the final 230 laps and scampered away from the field in a dominating performance. Petty's STP Dodge finished two full laps ahead of runner-up Darrell Waltrip.

David Pearson, joined by Union 76 RaceStoppers Sharon Maitland (left) and Doshia Wall and Miss Winston Jean "Bebop" Hobel (right), enjoy the victory lane ceremonies following the March 21 Atlanta 500. Pearson erased a two-mile deficit and drove the Wood Brothers Mercury home first over runner-up Benny Parsons.

1976

November 7 Dave Marcis outruns David Pearson and Donnie Allison in a three-car shootout to win the Dixie 500 at Atlanta International Raceway. Newcomer Dale Earnhardt survives a wicked tumble with 49 laps to go.

November 21 David Pearson posts his 10th win of the year in the 500-miler at Ontario Motor Speedway. Cale Yarborough claims his first NASCAR Winston Cup Grand National championship by a 195-point margin over Richard Petty.

Bill Champion's #10 Ford rests behind the garage area following his practice crash at Darlington prior to the April 11 Rebel 500. Champion suffered several broken ribs when his car spun and was hit in the driver's door by Jackie Rogers. Champion, a veteran of 289 NASCAR Winston Cup Grand National events from 1951 to '76, announced his retirement from racing shortly after the accident.

Ageless Buck Baker, two-time NASCAR champion in the 1950s, made a NASCAR Winston Cup Grand National comeback in the Rebel 500. The 57-year-old Baker got a ride in Junie Donlavey's Ford and promptly qualified 13th in the field of 36. Baker performed well in the race, finishing sixth with relief help from Dick Brooks.

▼ David Pearson's pit crew does its frenzied dance during the April 25 Virginia 500 at Martinsville Speedway. Pearson finished third in the event, which was won by Darrell Waltrip. Pearson enjoyed a remarkable season in 1976, winning 10 of 22 starts. Despite missing eight of the 30 NASCAR Winston Cup Grand National races, Pearson still finished ninth in the final points standings.

Buddy Baker pushes his #15 Ford under Richard Petty at Talladega during the May 2 Winston 500. Baker held command most of the way, leading for 135 of the 188 laps, including the final 24 trips around the 2.66-mile oval. Baker ran away from the field, finishing 35 seconds ahead of runner-up Cale Yarborough. He averaged 169.887 mph, which at that time was a 500-mile record.

Janet Guthrie, one of America's leading female racers, entered, but never competed in, the Indianapolis 500 in May 1976. She practiced for "The Greatest Spectacle in Racing," but didn't make a qualification attempt. After her Indy efforts fell through, Charlotte Motor Speedway promoter Humpy Wheeler hatched a plan to get Guthrie a ride in the World 600. Lynda Ferreri, vice president of First Union Bank in Charlotte, paid $21,000 via a cashier's check and suddenly became a NASCAR Winston Cup Grand National team owner. Retired mechanic Ralph Moody was hired to organize the team. Guthrie, pictured here with Ferreri and Moody, qualified 27th and finished 15th in the 600-miler.

Fantastic Finish

IT HAS BEEN said that fiction and fantasy are two different things. Fiction is the improbable made possible, while fantasy is the impossible made probable. If you could somehow mesh the two, you just might wind up with the 1976 Daytona 500.

NASCAR's two most revered icons, Richard Petty and David Pearson, were the primary characters in what turned out to be the most stunning finish in NASCAR Winston Cup history. Petty had already won the crown-jewel event five times; no other man had won more than once. Pearson, often a prime contender in the race, appeared on his way to victory in 1975 when Cale Yarborough snagged his rear bumper and spun him out in the final laps.

Petty was at the wheel of his familiar Petty Enterprises Dodge and Pearson was manning the potent Wood Brothers Mercury for the Feb. 15, 1976, event. The duo ranked first and second on the all-time NASCAR Winston Cup Grand National victory list and they had combined to win seven of the nine championships from 1964 to '72. During their illustrious careers, Petty and Pearson had finished first and second in a race 30 times.

Petty and Pearson ran in the lead pack all afternoon. At the 450-mile mark, they had separated themselves from the field and were poised to give the trackside audience of 125,000 another duel to the wire. The ABC Sports cameras were beaming the event into the homes of millions of Americans. Anchorman Bill Flemming and squeaky-voiced Jackie Stewart were calling the action.

The final 22 laps were a green-flag trophy dash. Pearson held the lead until Petty shot past with 13 laps to go. The pair rode nose-to-tail for 12 laps. Pearson, perched on Petty's rear bumper, was biding his time, content to utilize the draft to slingshot his way into the lead on the final lap. Unlike today, the draft was an offensive weapon that was readily used in superspeedway competition, and a driver didn't have to have help from other drivers to make a decisive pass.

On the backstretch of the final lap, Pearson gunned his Mercury to the low side and passed Petty to take the lead. Entering the third turn, Pearson hit the banking and drifted up toward the wall, leaving Petty a slight opening in the low groove. Petty pounced on the opportunity and throttled his Dodge alongside Pearson as the pair whipped through the fourth turn.

In an instant, the two cars slapped together. Pearson and Petty both wobbled, then Pearson's car darted nose first into the outside retaining barrier, clipping Petty's rear bumper in the process. Both cars spun out of control. Pearson twirled around and slid toward the pit road entrance, clipping Joe Frasson's Chevrolet. Pearson had the presence of mind to engage the clutch and keep his engine running. Meanwhile, Petty was performing a wild series of fishtails in an effort to keep his car under control. For an instant, it appeared that Petty had grabbed the handle of his twitching Dodge, but the car dove into the outside wall.

Petty's car spun around and came to a halt less than 100 feet from the finish line. The engine died and Petty frantically tried to get the car restarted. Pearson bumped his car into low gear and inched his way toward the finish line. Driving across the grassy area in the tri-oval, Pearson lumbered past Petty and took the checkered flag at about 20 mph.

Pandemonium ensued as Pearson made his way back around to victory lane. "I'm not sure what happened," said the winner. "He went beneath me and his car broke loose. I got into the wall and came off and hit him. That's what started all the spinning, I think."

Petty accepted blame at first, saying, "My car broke loose. The first time we hit, it was my fault. I told David I was sorry it happened. I didn't want my boys to be mad at him. If there was anybody to blame, it was me."

After reviewing videotape of the crash, Petty wasn't so sure he was entirely to blame for the accident. "You know, I think we were in control when we went through the fourth turn. Then David tapped me and that started all the spinning," he said. "At least me and David did our thing in front of the grandstands so all the people could see it. It must have been quite a finish from their standpoint."

Through all the excitement, both Pearson and Petty kept their cool, underscoring their utmost respect for each other and the professionalism they portrayed throughout their careers. What was supposed to be a 200-mph dash to the finish line became a classic rubdown between the two greatest drivers in NASCAR's domain. A heart-stopping moment became one for the ages. It was a 500-miler cloaked in both fiction and fantasy. But, sometimes, truth can be stranger than fiction and fantasy—and more intriguing.

▲ James Hylton skids through the grass in the final laps of the May 30 World 600 as David Pearson and Benny Parsons scoot past unscathed. Pearson led the final few laps under the caution flag and won the 600-miler, while Parsons finished fifth. It was the sixth win in 10 season starts for Pearson, who successfully rebounded from a disappointing '75 campaign.

▲ Benny Parsons won two races in the 1976 NASCAR Winston Cup Grand National season, the first season he won more than one event. The '73 NASCAR champion made a stout bid for his second title, leading the points standings as late as early August. At the end of the season, Parsons locked down third place in points on the strength of 23 top-10 finishes in 30 races.

Bobby Allison poses with his #2 Roger Penske/Cam2 Motor Oil Mercury that he campaigned in the 1976 NASCAR Winston Cup Grand National season. Allison endured a difficult year, failing to win a single race. In July, he was seriously injured in an independently sanctioned short-track race in Elko, Minn. He drove the rest of the season nursing the injuries. Following the '76 season, Allison quit the Penske Racing team and fielded his own operation.

Rookie Terry Bivins poses with the #30 Chevrolet fielded by Walter Ballard, who won the 1971 NASCAR Rookie of the Year award. Bivins performed admirably with less-than-stellar equipment in 1976, finishing first in the Rookie of the Year points standings. He logged six top-10 finishes in 18 starts, including a fifth-place run at Richmond. Despite outperforming rookie rival Skip Manning, Bivins lost the top freshman award to Manning in a controversial decision.

Donnie Allison holds up his trophy after winning the Oct. 10 National 500 at Charlotte Motor Speedway, his first NASCAR Winston Cup Grand National win in five years, and the first for Hoss Ellington as a team owner. Ellington, who was constantly in and out of trouble with NASCAR's hierarchy due to repeated rules violations, had to sweat out another postrace inspection. As technical inspectors combed over the engine, Ellington assured the media that the car would pass inspection. "This one's legal," claimed Ellington. "We left all our cheater stuff at Darlington."

Sterling Marlin sits in his father Coo Coo's #14 Chevrolet prior to the Aug. 8 Talladega 500. The young Marlin would often practice his dad's car prior to a race, and actually started one NASCAR Winston Cup Grand National event in 1976. Coo Coo ran with the leaders in the '76 Talladega 500, but was robbed of a possible victory when the engine failed on the 57th lap.

Dale Earnhardt's third NASCAR Winston Cup Grand National start came at Atlanta International Raceway on Nov. 7, 1976. Driving the Hy-Gain Chevrolet owned by Johnny Ray, an independent campaigner who was severely injured in the '76 Daytona 500, Earnhardt qualified in 16th position. He ran well until, with 49 laps to go, he ran into the spinning Ford manned by Dick Brooks, and tumbled end over end numerous times. Earnhardt was shaken and bruised in the crash, but wasn't seriously hurt.

Cale Yarborough drove his #11 Junior Johnson/Holly Farms Chevrolet to the 1976 NASCAR Winston Cup Grand National championship. Yarborough won nine races along the way to the first of three consecutive titles. He finished last in the Daytona 500, but assumed command of the points chase in August. Yarborough beat Richard Petty by 195 points. Petty had pulled within 97 points with two races to go, but a 28th-place finish in the next race dashed his championship hopes.

1976 NASCAR WINSTON CUP GN POINTS RACE

Rank	Driver	Points	Starts	Wins	Top 5	Top 10	Winnings
1	Cale Yarborough	4644	30	9	22	23	$453,404.40
2	Richard Petty	4449	30	3	19	22	$374,805.62
3	Benny Parsons	4304	30	2	18	23	$270,042.98
4	Bobby Allison	4097	30	0	15	19	$230,169.72
5	Lennie Pond	3930	30	0	10	19	$159,700.54
6	Dave Marcis	3875	30	3	9	16	$218,249.32
7	Buddy Baker	3745	30	1	16	16	$239,921.10
8	Darrell Waltrip	3505	30	1	10	12	$204,192.88
9	David Pearson	3483	22	10	16	18	$346,889.66
10	Dick Brooks	3447	28	0	3	18	$111,879.66
11	Richard Childress	3428	30	0	0	11	$85,779.66
12	J.D. McDuffie	3400	30	0	1	8	$82,239.66
13	James Hylton	3380	30	0	2	5	$78,704.66
14	D.K. Ulrich	3280	30	0	0	2	$69,434.66
15	Cecil Gordon	3247	30	0	0	5	$73,829.66
16	Frank Warren	3240	30	0	0	3	$67,731.44
17	David Sisco	2994	28	0	0	7	$62,621.44
18	Skip Manning	2931	27	0	0	4	$61,536.44
19	Ed Negre	2709	28	0	0	2	$50,918.22
20	Buddy Arrington	2573	25	0	0	3	$56,646.44
21	Terry Bivins	2099	18	0	1	6	$44,070.00
22	Bobby Wawak	2062	19	0	0	9	$31,415.00
23	Bruce Hill	1995	22	0	0	4	$43,705.00
24	Jimmy Means	1752	19	0	0	0	$20,945.00
25	Dick May	1719	19	0	0	0	$29,425.00
26	Walter Ballard	1554	15	0	0	3	$16,380.00
27	Henley Gray	1425	15	0	0	0	$15,090.00
28	Coo Coo Marlin	1412	12	0	0	6	$39,485.00
29	Gary Myers	1296	15	0	0	0	$11,430.00
30	Jackie Rogers	1173	11	0	0	3	$21,215.00
31	Grant Adcox	1163	11	0	0	2	$25,715.00
32	Neil Bonnett	1130	13	0	1	4	$31,800.00
33	Tommy Gale	1005	12	0	0	0	$18,955.00
34	Donnie Allison	988	9	1	2	5	$48,455.00
35	Joe Mihalic	981	9	0	0	0	$12,925.00
36	Elmo Langley	824	7	0	0	1	$7515.00
37	Travis Tiller	816	9	0	0	0	$6310.00
38	Sonny Easley	772	7	0	0	2	$11,290.00
39	Joe Frasson	707	9	0	0	1	$12,075.00
40	Jabe Thomas	648	6	0	0	0	$6160.00
41	Bill Elliott	635	8	0	0	0	$11,635.00
42	Dean Dalton	633	6	0	0	0	$7,245.00
43	Earle Canavan	610	7	0	0	0	$6035.00
44	Rick Newsom	607	7	0	0	0	$5520.00
45	Tighe Scott	566	6	0	0	1	$15,520.00
46	Terry Ryan	558	5	0	1	3	$24,940.00
47	Darrell Bryant	546	8	0	0	1	$11,925.00
48	Buck Baker	513	8	0	0	1	$12,655.00
49	Chuck Brown	481	5	0	0	0	$5480.00
50	Baxter Price	479	5	0	0	0	$3010.00

Cale Yarborough broke out of a close points race with Benny Parsons at midseason to score his first NASCAR Winston Cup Grand National championship. Yarborough won nine races and finished 195 points in front of runner-up Richard Petty.

Yarborough took the points lead for keeps with a 26th-place finish at Talladega in August. Parsons finished 39th after his engine let go in the early laps. Petty passed Parsons in the points race in September and held on for the runner-up spot.

The points lead changed hands eight times among four drivers. Yarborough, Petty, Parsons, and David Pearson traded first place in a flurry during the early months of the season before it became strictly a three-way battle for top honors. David Pearson won 10 races in 22 starts, but finished ninth in the final standings because he ran a limited schedule.

1977

February 20 Cale Yarborough pulls away from Benny Parsons in the final laps to win in his second Daytona 500.

April 3 Darrell Waltrip wins the race back to the yellow flag to capture the Rebel 500 at Darlington. Waltrip weaves his way through a crash scene in the fourth turn, passing David Pearson, Richard Petty, and Donnie Allison on the final green-flag lap.

May 15 Cale Yarborough roars back from two black flags, a pair of unscheduled pit stops, and a four-lap deficit to win the Mason-Dixon 500 at Dover Downs. It is Yarborough's sixth win of the season.

July 4 Richard Petty wins the Firecracker 400 at Daytona. For the first time since 1949, three women drivers are in the starting field. Janet Guthrie, Christine Beckers, and Lella Lombardi all start the race.

July 16 Scoring problems mar Darrell Waltrip's victory in the Nashville 420 at the Nashville Fairgrounds Speedway. Richard Petty is flagged in second place, but three days later he is dropped to third, two laps off the pace.

August 7 Donnie Allison, with relief help from Darrell Waltrip, outruns Cale Yarborough and Skip Manning to win the Talladega 500.

August 28 Cale Yarborough racks up his eighth win of the year at Bristol's Volunteer 400. Yarborough's Junior Johnson Chevrolet fails the postrace inspection for the second time in a row. Team owner Johnson is fined $500. Janet Guthrie finishes sixth, her best NASCAR Winston Cup Grand National effort.

September 5 Quick pit work nets David Pearson his second straight win in the Southern 500 at Darlington. Darrell Waltrip earns the nickname "Jaws" at the same event. Waltrip, Yarborough, and D. K. Ulrich are involved in a 227th-lap crash. In response to Ulrich's inquiry as to what happened, Yarborough says, "That Jaws ran into you."

Cale Yarborough leads a pack of snarling challengers during the Daytona 500. A. J. Foyt's #51 Chevrolet is seen sniffing the tailpipes of Cale's #11 Chevy. David Pearson and Richard Petty are in hot pursuit. Cale started fourth on the grid, led for more than half the race, and motored to his 41st career NASCAR Winston Cup Grand National victory. Foyt started on the front row, led briefly, and finished sixth.

Cale Yarborough and wife Betty Jo (left) participate in the victory lane ceremonies at the Daytona 500. It was Cale's second of four wins in NASCAR's showcase event. Driving Junior Johnson's Chevrolet, Yarborough shook the draft of a pesky Benny Parsons and motored across the finish line 1.39 seconds ahead of the runner-up. Yarborough collected $63,700 for his 3 hour and 15 minute drive.

The once-powerful K&K Insurance Dodge team, which won the 1970 championship with Bobby Isaac, was in its final year in '77. Owner Nord Krauskopf removed his K&K Insurance logo from the quarter-panels and sought outside sponsorship to keep the team going. Neil Bonnett drove the car in the April 3 Rebel 500 at Darlington with modest sponsorship from the U.S. Army, but the engine blew early. Krauskopf disbanded the team shortly thereafter, ending his 12-year run in NASCAR. The team won 43 races at NASCAR's top level from '66 to '77.

Benny Parsons' #72 Chevrolet hustles past #52 Jimmy Means in the April 3 Rebel 500 at Darlington Raceway. Parsons finished fifth, while Means placed 20th. Means, a short-track veteran from Huntsville, Ala., was in his rookie season. Known for his gritty determination, Means competed in 455 races from 1976 to '93, never finishing in the top five.

Darrell Waltrip's #88 Chevrolet forges ahead of Neil Bonnett on the opening lap of the April 24 Virginia 500 at Martinsville Speedway. Waltrip held his Gatorade/DiGard Racing Chevy up front for most of the early laps, but succumbed to brake failure near the midway point and struggled to finish 21st. Pole-sitter Bonnett drifted to a 12th-place finish.

Rookie Ron Hutcherson's #36 Chevrolet lurches sideways in the May 29 World 600 at Charlotte Motor Speedway as #79 Frank Warren and #2 Dave Marcis pass safely. The younger brother of former NASCAR star Dick Hutcherson recovered from his spin and drove to an 11th-place finish. Marcis, who took over the #2 Roger Penske Mercury in 1977, blew an engine early and placed 36th. Following the '77 season, Penske quit the NASCAR tour after two winless seasons. He wouldn't return to NASCAR full time until '91.

When Nord Krauskopf bowed out of NASCAR Winston Cup Grand National racing halfway through the 1977 season, the mysterious Jim Stacy purchased all of his Dodge equipment. Repainted white and given the number 5, Neil Bonnett drove the car during the latter half of the campaign. Bonnett won the pole for the July 4 Daytona Firecracker 400 in Stacy's maiden voyage into the NASCAR waters.

1977

September 11 Neil Bonnett scores his first career NASCAR Winston Cup Grand National win in the Capital City 400 at Richmond. Bonnett outruns Richard Petty by seven seconds.

November 6 Darrell Waltrip denies David Pearson his 100th victory at Atlanta International Raceway. Waltrip makes a final-lap pass as darkness descends on the track. Unable to see through his tinted windshield, Pearson backs off and accepts second place.

November 20 Neil Bonnett outruns Richard Petty in an epic duel over the final 10 laps to win at Ontario Motor Speedway. Third-place finisher Cale Yarborough takes his second straight NASCAR Winston Cup championship.

For the first time since July 10, 1949, three female drivers competed in a race at NASCAR's highest level when (left to right) Janet Guthrie, Lella Lombardi, and Christine Beckers all drove in the '77 Firecracker 400. All three developed mechanical problems and fell out before the halfway point. The three ladies are joined in this photo by three-time NASCAR champion Lee Petty and Louise Smith, who drove in that '49 race at Daytona's Beach-Road course.

Bobby Allison, who quit the Roger Penske team in 1976, formed his own team in '77, campaigning AMC Matadors on the NASCAR Winston Cup Grand National trail. Allison endured a miserable season in '77, spending nearly as much time in the pits with the hood up as racing on the high-banked speedways. Allison failed to finish 12 races and only posted three top-five finishes. The following year, he joined Bud Moore's team and put his brilliant career back on track.

Skip Manning's #92 Chevrolet runs just ahead of #1 Donnie Allison in the late stages of the Aug. 7 Talladega 500 at Alabama International Motor Speedway. Manning, the 1976 Rookie of the Year, surprised the railbirds with a fantastic run at Talladega, and was poised to win until smoke billowed from his car in the final laps. Allison's Hawaiian Tropic Chevy, with Darrell Waltrip driving in relief, took the lead from Manning with six laps remaining. Allison got credit for the victory, the eighth of his career.

Bobby Isaac, the 1970 NASCAR champion, concentrated on weekly NASCAR Late Model Sportsman action after he left the NASCAR Winston Cup Grand National series in the mid '70s. In a race at his hometown track in Hickory, N.C., on Aug. 13, 1977, Isaac pulled into the pits and requested relief help. Isaac collapsed in the pit area and was rushed to the hospital. Although he was revived briefly at the hospital, a heart attack in the early morning hours proved fatal to the 45-year-old veteran driver.

Janet Guthrie's #68 Chevrolet moves to the low side to make room for #11 Cale Yarborough to pass during the Sept. 6 Southern 500. Guthrie finished 16th, while Yarborough ran fifth despite having a crunched right front fender on his Chevy.

Smoke billows from the #88 Chevrolet of Darrell Waltrip in the closing stages of the Sept. 25 Old Dominion 500 at Martinsville Speedway. Waltrip was running in the top five when the trouble struck. He still managed to finish 10th. Skip Manning slides past in his #92 Chevy. Manning went on to finish 13th.

Consecutive Winning Years

RICHARD PETTY AUTHORED a noteworthy all-time NASCAR record during the 1977 season, an achievement that was largely overlooked. By winning five races in the '77 campaign, Petty ran his consecutive years of winning at least one race to 18. It is a record that may eventually fall, but at the very least, it will remain unchallenged for another five years.

What makes Petty's record even more impressive is the fact that from 1960 to '77, King Richard won at least two races each year, including the '65 campaign when he sat on the sidelines for most of the season due to a dispute between Chrysler Corp. and NASCAR. The chart at the right shows the all-time leaders for consecutive winning years in NASCAR Cup Series competition.

NASCAR Cup Series Consecutive Winning Years

Driver	Winning Years	Consecutive Winning Streak
Richard Petty	18	1960-1977
David Pearson	17	1964-1980
Ricky Rudd	16	1983-1998
Rusty Wallace	16	1986-2001
Darrell Waltrip	15	1975-1989
Dale Earnhardt	15	1982-1996
Jeff Gordon	14	1994-2007
Tony Stewart	14	1999-2012
Lee Petty	13	1949-1961
Cale Yarborough	13	1973-1985
Dale Jarrett	11	1993-2003
Jimmie Johnson	11	2002-2012
Buck Baker	10	1952-1961
Bobby Allison	10	1966-1975
Bill Elliott	10	1983-1992
Tony Stewart	10	1999-2008
Kurt Busch	10	2002-2011
Fireball Roberts	9	1956-1964
Bobby Labonte	9	1995-2003
Junior Johnson	8	1958-1965
Kyle Busch	8	2005-2012
Herb Thomas	7	1950-1956
Jack Smith	7	1956-1962
Ned Jarrett	7	1959-1965
Fred Lorenzen	7	1961-1967
Benny Parsons	7	1975-1981
Terry Labonte	7	1983-1989
Davey Allison	7	1987-1993
Geoff Bodine	7	1988-1994
Mark Martin	7	1989-1995
Dale Earnhardt, Jr.	7	2000-2006
Jimmie Johnson	7	2002-2008
Kurt Busch	7	2002-2008
Denny Hamlin	7	2006-2012
Matt Kenseth	6	2002-2007
Greg Biffle	6	2003-2008

In the summer of 1977, George Elliott purchased the Mercury equipment that Roger Penske had campaigned. Penske was making a switch to Chevrolet, and the Mercury cars were an upgrade for the independent Elliott team. George's son Bill, in his sophomore season, drove the car in the Oct. 9 NAPA National 500 at Charlotte Motor Speedway, finishing a strong 10th.

Dave Marcis powers his #2 Penske Chevrolet Monte Carlo around Richard Childress, who was wheeling the #3 Chevrolet LaGuna in the NAPA National 500. Despite the switch from Mercury to Chevrolet, the Penske team was still hounded with mechanical problems. Marcis departed on lap 237 with a blown engine. Childress started 22nd and finished 16th.

◀ Benny Parsons enjoys the victory lane ceremonies following his big win in the NAPA National 500. Parsons dominated the race, leading 250 of the 334 laps. He did have to overcome a miscalculation late in the race when he ran out of fuel while holding a commanding lead. By the time he coasted around the track, Cale Yarborough had taken the lead. It took Parsons only nine laps to run Yarborough down and reclaim the lead for good.

▼ Number 11 Cale Yarborough leads #1 Donnie Allison and #88 Darrell Waltrip in the Oct. 23 American 500 at North Carolina Motor Speedway. Cale clinched his second straight NASCAR Winston Cup Grand National championship with his fourth-place finish. Allison started the #1 Hoss Ellington Chevy on the pole and went on to win the race, leading the final 72 laps. Waltrip came home third in the DiGard/Gatorade Chevy.

Number 5 Neil Bonnett and Richard Petty line up on the front row before the Nov. 20 Los Angeles Times 500 at Ontario Motor Speedway. Bonnett outran Petty in the 500-miler on the rounded rectangle-shaped track, scoring a win for new team owner Jim Stacy. Bonnett registered the final victory for the Dodge nameplate. Dodge wouldn't win another top-level NASCAR event until the 2001 season.

Cale Yarborough enjoyed a remarkable season in 1977, winning the championship for the second year in a row while driving Junior Johnson's #11 Holly Farms Chevrolet. Yarborough was running at the finish in all 30 races, and he logged 25 top-five finishes. Yarborough racked up 5000 points during the season, which remains a record for a 30-race season under the current points system.

1977 NASCAR WINSTON CUP GN POINTS RACE

Rank	Driver	Points	Starts	Wins	Top 5	Top 10	Winnings
1	Cale Yarborough	5000	30	9	25	27	$561,641.16
2	Richard Petty	4614	30	5	20	23	$406,607.80
3	Benny Parsons	4570	30	4	20	22	$359,340.52
4	Darrell Waltrip	4498	30	6	16	24	$324,813.24
5	Buddy Baker	3961	30	0	9	20	$224,846.96
6	Dick Brooks	3742	29	0	7	20	$151,373.68
7	James Hylton	3476	30	0	0	11	$108,391.40
8	Bobby Allison	3467	30	0	5	15	$94,574.12
9	Richard Childress	3463	30	0	0	11	$97,011.84
10	Cecil Gordon	3294	30	0	0	2	$86,311.84
11	Buddy Arrington	3247	28	0	0	5	$88,886.84
12	J.D. McDuffie	3236	30	0	0	4	$85,226.84
13	David Pearson	3227	22	2	16	18	$221,271.84
14	Skip Manning	3120	28	0	1	8	$111,316.84
15	D.K. Ulrich	2901	30	0	0	0	$69,676.84
16	Frank Warren	2876	29	0	0	1	$67,944.56
17	Ricky Rudd	2810	25	0	1	10	$75,904.56
18	Neil Bonnett	2649	23	2	5	9	$122,614.56
19	Jimmy Means	2640	26	0	0	6	$52,504.56
20	Tighe Scott	2628	26	0	1	1	$63,224.56
21	Sam Sommers	2517	23	0	2	8	$54,525.00
22	Ed Negre	2214	24	0	0	0	$42,665.00
23	Janet Guthrie	2037	19	0	0	4	$37,945.00
24	Donnie Allison	1970	17	2	9	10	$146,435.00
25	Dave Marcis	1931	18	0	5	7	$72,605.00
26	Tommy Gale	1689	18	0	0	0	$39,190.00
27	Dick May	1324	13	0	0	0	$21,690.00
28	Henley Gray	1214	14	0	0	0	$18,610.00
29	Bruce Hill	1213	16	0	0	4	$25,035.00
30	Lennie Pond	1193	14	0	4	6	$49,440.00
31	Butch Hartman	1116	11	0	0	2	$18,615.00
32	Ferrel Harris	1088	11	0	0	0	$19,365.00
33	Baxter Price	1086	12	0	0	0	$10,890.00
34	Coo Coo Marlin	1004	11	0	1	5	$42,450.00
35	Bill Elliott	926	10	0	0	2	$20,075.00
36	Gary Myers	888	10	0	0	0	$10,975.00
37	David Sisco	847	10	0	0	0	$13,920.00
38	Terry Bivins	841	8	0	0	1	$14,920.00
39	G.C. Spencer	785	8	0	0	1	$15,755.00
40	Terry Ryan	702	7	0	0	1	$12,405.00
41	Joe Mihalic	683	8	0	0	0	$7,650.00
42	Elmo Langley	634	7	0	0	0	$5855.00
43	Dean Dalton	620	8	0	0	0	$6255.00
44	Earl Brooks	552	6	0	0	0	$3045.00
45	Bobby Wawak	522	8	0	0	0	$13,455.00
46	Harold Miller	470	6	0	0	0	$8480.00
47	Junior Miller	467	5	0	0	0	$2475.00
48	Ramo Stott	440	5	0	0	0	$10,170.00
49	Grant Adcox	413	6	0	0	0	$8750.00

Cale Yarborough was running at the finish in all 30 NASCAR Winston Cup Grand National races as he dominated the 1977 season to wrap up his second consecutive title. Yarborough won nine races in 30 starts and finished 386 points ahead of runner-up Richard Petty.

Petty captured the points lead briefly at midseason, taking first place after the July 31 race at Pocono. But a runner-up finish the following week at Talladega lifted Yarborough atop the standings again, a lead that he never relinquished.

Benny Parsons finished third in the final standings while winning four races during the season. Six-time winner Darrell Waltrip finished fourth in the NASCAR Winston Cup Grand National standings on the strength of six wins. Buddy Baker rounded out the top five but posted no wins.

1978

January 22 Cale Yarborough drives his Oldsmobile to a close decision over Benny Parsons to win the Winston Western 500 on the road course at Riverside International Raceway. It is the first win for the Oldsmobile nameplate since 1959.

February 19 Bobby Allison ends his 67-race winless skid with a dramatic victory in the Daytona 500. Allison pushes his Bud Moore Ford around Buddy Baker with 11 laps remaining and leads the rest of the way.

March 5 David Pearson rallies from a late spin, passes Benny Parsons, and drives to victory in the Carolina 500 at Rockingham's North Carolina Motor Speedway. It is the 100th win of Pearson's illustrious career.

May 14 Cale Yarborough passes Buddy Baker on the final lap to win the Winston 500 at Talladega. Car owner Harold Miller and driver Keith Davis are suspended for 12 weeks when NASCAR officials discover an illegal bottle of nitrous oxide in the car in prerace inspections.

May 15 Willy T. Ribbs, America's leading African American race driver, fails to appear for two special practice sessions in preparation for the upcoming World 600 at Charlotte. Team owner Will Cronkrite, irked with Ribbs' absence, replaces him with relatively unknown short-track racer Dale Earnhardt.

August 6 Lennie Pond leads the final five laps and staves off challenges from six rivals to post his first career NASCAR Winston Cup Grand National victory in the Talladega 500. Pond averages a record 174.700 mph.

August 20 David Pearson surges past Darrell Waltrip on the final lap to win the Champion Spark Plug 400 at Michigan International Speedway. Richard Petty makes his first start in a Chevrolet, having parked his uncompetitive Dodge Magnum. Petty finishes 14th after a crash sidelines him in the final laps.

Darrell Waltrip skids off turn five at Riverside International Raceway in the Jan. 22 season opener. Waltrip started on the front row and was running in the top five when a transmission failure caused him to lose control of his Gatorade Chevrolet. He finished 23rd in the 35-car field Winston Western 500. Cale Yarborough won the race in an Oldsmobile.

Buddy Baker's #27 Oldsmobile tangled with #15 Bobby Allison in the Feb. 16 Twin 125-miler at Daytona. The qualifying race was run on a foggy day and visibility was a concern for many drivers. The crash forced Baker and Allison to start deep in the field for the Daytona 500, but both became principles in the outcome of the 20th annual running of NASCAR's premier race.

Cruising three-abreast during a caution period in the Feb. 19 Daytona 500 are #27 Buddy Baker, #11 Cale Yarborough, and #51 A.J. Foyt. Baker took the wheel of the M.C. Anderson Oldsmobile team in 1978, replacing rookie driver Sam Sommers. Baker was in contention for the win until his engine let go with four laps remaining. Foyt was sidelined by a bone-jarring tumble on the 68th lap. Yarborough went on to finish second to Bobby Allison.

"I'm so tickled I can't see straight."
—Bobby Allison

Bobby Allison ended a 67-race losing streak with a mild upset win in the Daytona 500, outrunning Cale Yarborough and outlasting Buddy Baker in the final laps. Allison suffered through two winless campaigns in 1976 and '77, and accepted an offer from team owner Bud Moore (upper left) in '78 (a ride that Baker had vacated following a disappointing '77 season). Despite crashing in the Twin 125-miler and having to start 33rd in the 500, Allison emerged in a race that featured wrecks and mechanical failures for many contenders.

David Pearson's #21 Wood Brothers Mercury battles with Richard Petty's STP Dodge Magnum in the early stages of the March 5 Carolina 500 at Rockingham. Temperatures were in the mid 20s at race time, but Pearson blistered the one-mile track to record his 100th career NASCAR Winston Cup Grand National victory. Petty finished fourth in his Magnum, a bulky beast that The King struggled with for most of 1978.

Roland Wlodyka spins his #98 Chevrolet, collecting #5 Neil Bonnett, #54 Lennie Pond, and #11 Cale Yarborough, in the April 2 Southeastern 500 at Bristol International Raceway. The crash took out Wlodyka and Bonnett, but Yarborough and Pond were able to continue. Cale finished fourth, while Pond placed fifth with relief help from Richard Petty.

▼ Buddy Baker's #27 Chevrolet spins down the frontstretch at Darlington Raceway during the April 9 Rebel 500 after being tapped by Dave Marcis. Baker recovered to finish sixth, the first time he was able to complete a race during the 1978 season. The M.C. Anderson team struggled throughout '78 without the aid of a major sponsor. Construction magnate Anderson funded his own operation for three years before acquiring outside funding.

Sophomore driver #22 Ricky Rudd battles with #5 Neil Bonnett and #92 Skip Manning in the Darlington Rebel 500. Rudd was named the 1977 NASCAR Rookie of the Year, but limited funding reduced the family owned team's schedule in '78. Rudd competed in only 13 races, scoring four top-10 finishes. Rudd ran 10th in the Rebel 500. Manning finished eighth, but lost his ride with team owner Billy Hagan later in the season. Bonnett's Dodge Magnum fell victim to a rear-gearing failure and departed in the early laps.

1978

September 4 Cale Yarborough scores his fourth win in the Southern 500. Terry Labonte, making his NASCAR Winston Cup Grand National debut, finishes fourth. D.K. Ulrich is suspended for the remainder of the season after a wreck reveals he has an illegal nitrous oxide bottle in his Chevrolet.

September 17 Bobby Allison bags his third win of the season in the Delaware 500 at Dover. Privateer J.D. McDuffie wins the pole and leads the opening 10 laps, but departs with an engine failure after 80 laps.

November 5 Controversy flares at Atlanta International Raceway as Donnie Allison is declared the winner of the Dixie 500 after the crowd of 40,000 thought Richard Petty had nipped Dave Marcis in a race to the finish. NASCAR scorers failed to notice that Allison had passed both Petty and Marcis with three laps remaining. Rookie Dale Earnhardt finishes fourth in his first start with the Rod Osterlund team.

November 19 Bobby Allison scores his fifth win of the year in the finale at Ontario Motor Speedway. Runner-up Cale Yarborough wins his third consecutive NASCAR Winston Cup Grand National championship by a margin of 474 points over Allison.

Darrell Waltrip hoists a pair of trophies in victory lane after winning the April 23 Virginia 500 at Martinsville Speedway. Waltrip racked up his third win of the season, whipping the field by three full laps. "I laid back in the early going, not wanting to race anybody for the first 100 laps. I knew I needed to save my brakes. When I wanted to go racing, there was nobody left to race with," said Waltrip, who led 310 of the 500 laps.

Lennie Pond spins his #54 Oldsmobile in the May 28 World 600 at Charlotte Motor Speedway. The Charlotte race was a difficult experience for Pond, who got into a public squabble with crew chief Herb Nab. Pond claimed the car was nearly impossible to drive, and it escaped his control in the early going. Nab and the Harry Ranier Racing pit crew made repairs, but Pond refused to get back into the car. Chuck Bown was summoned to drive in relief, but he also crashed later in the race.

Harry Gant, regarded as one of the finest short-track Late Model Sportsman drivers, got an assignment with team owner Kennie Childers for the World 600. Gant qualified fourth and ran with the leaders in the early stages before overheating problems took him out of the race. Team owner Childers was a Virginia coal-mining tycoon who dabbled in NASCAR Winston Cup Grand National racing from 1978 to '81. Ten different drivers drove for Childers in his brief career, including Neil Bonnett, David Pearson, Tim Richmond, Buddy Baker, and Donnie Allison.

▼ Number 21 David Pearson and #88 Darrell Waltrip drive around #70 J.D. McDuffie during the World 600. Pearson crashed into Benny Parsons on the last lap after Parsons tangled with Donnie Allison, leaving Waltrip with clear sailing to his fourth victory of the year. "I don't know what happened behind me," said Waltrip. "All I saw was a lot of smoke."

Ron Hutcherson plows into the side of a spinning Roland Wlodyka during Charlotte's World 600. Ronnie Thomas swings low to avoid the incident. Hutcherson was eliminated in the crash, while Thomas and Wlodyka went on to finish 30th and 21st, respectively. Thomas, a young driver from Christiansburg, Va., won the 1978 NASCAR Rookie of the Year award.

Neil Bonnett poses with his #5 Jim Stacy/Armor All Dodge at Nashville Fairgrounds Raceway prior to the start of the Music City 420 on June 3. Bonnett finished fifth in the race, one of his few impressive outings in the Magnum. Later in the '78 season, team owner Stacy retired the Dodge and made the move to General Motors products.

Dale Earnhardt rides the high line in Will Cronkrite's #96 Cardinal Tractor Ford in Daytona's Firecracker 400. Earnhardt finished a strong seventh in the July 4 event. The Cronkrite Ford was a specially arranged ride for young African American road racer Willy T. Ribbs, who was slated to drive the car at Charlotte in May. Ribbs failed to appear for two practice sessions and was arrested in Charlotte for reckless driving. Cronkrite dumped Ribbs and signed Earnhardt to drive his car for a partial season.

Richard Petty leads David Pearson down the front chute at Pocono International Raceway during the July 30 Coca-Cola 500. Petty fell out with engine problems, while Pearson went on to finish second to Darrell Waltrip. This was one of the final appearances for Petty's Dodge Magnum, a car beset with handling problems. Two weeks later, Petty parked the Dodge and joined the Chevrolet team.

NASCAR's Most Competitive Races

WITH A QUARTER MILE to go in the 2010 Aaron's 499 at Talladega, Jamie McMurray was about to make history. McMurray took the 87th official lead in the race—a NASCAR Cup Series record—with the finish line in sight. But with a final surge, Kevin Harvick slingshotted past McMurray for the 88th lead change, and he prevailed by a mere 0.11 seconds.

That record was tied in 2011, again in the Aaron's 499 at Talladega, when Jimmie Johnson won a hard-fought victory by just .002 second over Clint Bowyer.

Of the 10 most competitive races in NASCAR Cup Series history, in terms of most lead changes, eight have occurred at Talladega. In 1978, Lennie Pond drove his Oldsmobile around Benny Parsons with five laps to go and scored his lone NASCAR Cup Series career victory by a narrow margin. When Pond scooted past Parsons down the backstretch, it was the 67th official lead change during the hotly contested 188-lap, 500-mile event at the world's fastest speedway. Many other "unofficial" lead changes occurred during the race. An official lead change only counts when a new leader crosses the start/finish line.

The 67 lead changes established a NASCAR Cup Series record. The mark finally fell in the May 6, 1984, Winston 500 at Talladega when Cale Yarborough passed Harry Gant on the final lap for the 75th official lead change of the afternoon. The stubby Timmonsville, S.C., driver was in the hunt all day as 13 different drivers swapped first place in the record-setting contest. Seventy-five lead changes remained the record until the first Talladega race of 2010.

Below is a list of the races with the most lead changes in NASCAR Cup Series history through the 2012 season.

Most Competitive NASCAR Cup Series Races*

Date	Location	Lead Changes	Winner
4/25/10	Talladega, AL	88	Kevin Harvick
4/17/11	Talladega, AL	88	Jimmie Johnson
10/31/10	Talladega, AL	87	Clint Bowyer
5/6/84	Talladega, AL	75	Cale Yarborough
2/20/11	Daytona Beach, FL	74	Trevor Bayne
10/23/11	Talladega, AL	72	Clint Bowyer
7/29/84	Talladega, AL	68	Dale Earnhardt
8/6/78	Talladega, AL	67	Lennie Pond
8/16/81	Brooklyn, MI	65	Richard Petty
8/12/73	Talladega, AL	64	Dick Brooks
10/5/08	Talladega, AL	64	Tony Stewart
5/1/77	Talladega, AL	63	Darrell Waltrip
10/8/06	Talladega, AL	63	Brian Vickers
8/17/75	Talladega, AL	60	Buddy Baker
2/17/74	Daytona Beach, FL	60	Richard Petty
5/27/79	Charlotte, NC	59	Darrell Waltrip
8/8/76	Talladega, AL	58	Dave Marcis
2/20/83	Daytona Beach, FL	58	Cale Yarborough
11/1/09	Talladega, AL	58	Jamie McMurray
4/26/09	Talladega, AL	57	Brad Keselowski
7/2/11	Daytona Beach, FL	57	David Ragan
7/30/79	Pocono, PA	56	Cale Yarborough
3/30/06	Talladega, AL	56	Jimmie Johnson
8/22/71	Talladega, AL	54	Bobby Allison
4/18/04	Talladega, AL	54	Jeff Gordon
10/7/12	Talladega, AL	54	Matt Kenseth
5/7/72	Talladega, AL	53	David Pearson
4/27/08	Talladega, AL	52	Kyle Busch
2/14/10	Daytona Beach, FL	52	Jamie McMurray
5/4/75	Talladega, AL	51	Buddy Baker
5/2/82	Talladega, AL	51	Darrell Waltrip

*Based on lead changes

Lennie Pond whips his #54 Oldsmobile under #27 Buddy Baker and #11 Cale Yarborough in the Aug. 6 Talladega 500. Pond grabbed the lead five laps from the finish and held off a quartet of challengers in a near photo finish to snare his first and only NASCAR victory. He averaged a then record 174.700 mph in the event, which featured 67 official lead changes. Pond had already been notified he wouldn't be back as driver for the Harry Ranier-owned team. "I don't want to talk or think about anything except savoring this win," said Pond. "I have gone through a lot of miserable days lately. I'm glad I finally won a big race."

Cale Yarborough flings his #11 Oldsmobile around #96 Dale Earnhardt while keeping a narrow lead over #88 Darrell Waltrip in the Sept. 4 Southern 500 at Darlington. Yarborough drove Junior Johnson's #11 Chevrolet to his fourth win in the famous Labor Day event. Waltrip finished a close second in his DiGard Chevrolet. Earnhardt wound up 16th in his first attempt at Darlington.

Longtime independent campaigner J.D. McDuffie surprisingly won the pole position for the Sept. 17 Delaware 500 at Dover Downs International Speedway. McDuffie's Chevrolet was shod with McCreary tires, which afforded great speed for short periods of time. McDuffie outran the big guns in qualifying and led the first 10 laps. A blown engine put him on the sidelines after just 80 laps, but his quick trip through the timing lights earned McDuffie a starting berth in the inaugural Busch Clash at Daytona in 1979.

Rookie Terry Labonte guns his Chevrolet out of the pits at the Southern 500. Labonte, making his NASCAR Winston Cup Grand National debut on Darlington's wicked track, did a masterful job, finishing fourth. Team owner Billy Hagan discovered the 22-year-old from Corpus Christi, Texas, and seated him in the #92 Chevrolet to replace Skip Manning. Labonte finished in the top 10 in his first three starts.

Richard Petty pits his STP Chevrolet in the Sept. 24 Old Dominion 500 at Martinsville Speedway. It was Petty's sixth start in a Chevrolet after climbing out of his temperamental Dodge Magnum. Petty started on the front row and finished sixth. Petty had a down year in 1978, winning no races and finishing sixth in the points race.

Number 15 Bobby Allison scoots ahead of #5 Neil Bonnett in the early laps of the Oct. 1 Wilkes 400 at North Wilkesboro Speedway. Allison enjoyed a successful season in 1978, winning five races in the Bud Moore Ford and finishing second in the final NASCAR Winston Cup Grand National points standings. The five wins made the '78 campaign sweeter for Allison because he was unable to win a single race in '76 or '77.

This aerial photo of North Wilkesboro Speedway was taken during the Wilkes 400. Cale Yarborough overcame a three-lap deficit to win the 250-miler, taking the lead from Darrell Waltrp with 19 laps remaining. It was Cale's ninth win of the season and it virtually locked up the NASCAR Winston Cup Grand National championship for the cagey veteran.

Dale Earnhardt pokes his #98 Chevrolet under teammate #2 Dave Marcis in the Oct. 7 World Service Life 300 NASCAR Late Model Sportsman race at Charlotte Motor Speedway. The race turned out to be the biggest break of Earnhardt's career. He drove the Rod Osterlund Chevy to a strong runner-up effort in his first ride in competitive machinery, a performance that earned him a permanent assignment with the Osterlund Racing team in 1979. Earnhardt would go on to prove he was worthy of the ride.

Number 11 Cale Yarborough leads the speedy trio of #15 Bobby Allison, #2 Dave Marcis, and #88 Darrell Waltrip in the Oct. 8 NAPA National 500 at Charlotte Motor Speedway. Allison won the 500-miler as Waltrip finished second and Marcis ran third. Yarborough blew an engine on the 206th lap, but his Junior Johnson crew installed a fresh engine in just 13 minutes. NASCAR rules permitted teams to change engines during the running of a race in 1978.

1978 NASCAR WINSTON CUP GN POINTS RACE

Rank	Driver	Points	Starts	Wins	Top 5	Top 10	Winnings
1	Cale Yarborough	4841	30	10	23	24	$623,505.80
2	Bobby Allison	4367	30	5	24	22	$411,516.40
3	Darrell Waltrip	4362	30	6	19	20	$413,907.26
4	Benny Parsons	4350	30	3	15	21	$329,992.12
5	Dave Marcis	4335	30	0	14	24	$205,870.98
6	Richard Petty	3949	30	0	11	17	$242,272.84
7	Lennie Pond	3794	28	1	11	19	$181,095.70
8	Dick Brooks	3769	30	0	5	17	$137,589.99
9	Buddy Arrington	3626	30	0	1	7	$112,959.84
10	Richard Childress	3566	30	0	1	12	$108,701.42
11	J.D. McDuffie	3255	30	0	1	6	$86,856.42
12	Neil Bonnett	3129	30	0	7	12	$162,741.42
13	Tighe Scott	3110	29	0	0	7	$87,911.42
14	Frank Warren	3036	30	0	0	0	$68,172.85
15	Dick May	2936	28	0	0	2	$65,290.71
16	David Pearson	2756	22	4	11	11	$198,774.28
tie	Jimmy Means	2756	27	0	0	2	$61,724.28
18	Ronnie Thomas	2733	27	0	0	2	$75,814.14
19	Cecil Gordon	2641	26	0	0	1	$53,814.14
20	Tommy Gale	2639	26	0	0	0	$60,764.28
21	Roger Hamby	2617	26	0	0	2	$41,315.00
22	D.K. Ulrich	2452	22	0	0	3	$54,550.00
23	Baxter Price	2418	24	0	0	0	$36,560.00
24	Buddy Baker	2130	19	0	4	8	$111,765.00
25	Donnie Allison	1993	17	0	7	8	$127,475.0
26	James Hylton	1965	19	1	0	4	$48,045.00
27	Gary Myers	1915	19	0	0	0	$22,140.00
28	Ed Negre	1857	21	0	0	1	$28,995.00
29	Skip Manning	1802	17	0	1	4	$55,470.00
30	Grant Adcox	1802	14	0	1	3	$37,100.00
31	Ricky Rudd	1260	13	0	0	4	$50,630.00
32	Bruce Hill	1214	14	0	0	2	$25,770.00
33	Bill Elliott	1176	10	0	0	5	$42,215.00
34	Al Holbert	1142	12	0	0	3	$31,075.00
35	Ferrel Harris	1066	14	0	0	5	$39,685.00
36	Coo Coo Marlin	765	9	0	0	2	$19,415.00
37	Blackie Wangerin	760	10	0	0	0	$13,515.00
38	Bobby Wawak	680	8	0	0	0	$5870.00
39	Terry Labonte	659	5	0	1	3	$21,395.00
40	Ralph Jones	634	7	0	0	0	$6305.00
41	Janet Guthrie	592	7	0	0	1	$17,120.00
42	Earle Canavan	559	9	0	0	0	$8740.00
43	Dale Earnhardt	558	5	0	1	2	$20,745.00
44	Roland Wlodyka	549	6	0	0	0	$9910.00
45	Joe Frasson	533	5	0	0	0	$9210.00
46	Nelson Oswald	501	6	0	0	0	$2955.00
47	Joe Mihalic	419	6	0	0	0	$6030.00
48	Jim Thirkettle	389	3	0	0	2	$6850.00
49	Jimmy Insolo	369	3	0	0	2	$8665.00
50	Satch Worley	368	4	0	0	1	$6205.00

Cale Yarborough motored to his record-setting third consecutive NASCAR Winston Cup Grand National championship with another season-long sparkling effort. Yarborough's Junior Johnson team won 10 races and finished a comfortable 474 points ahead of runner-up Bobby Allison. Yarborough clinched the 1978 title at Rockingham in October.

Benny Parsons led the points standings after eight races from March through June, but Yarborough grabbed the lead with a victory at Nashville and never gave it up. Yarborough scored 23 top-five finishes in 30 starts in a near-perfect campaign. Allison won five races, including the Daytona 500.

Darrell Waltrip, a six-time winner, finished third in the NASCAR Winston Cup Grand National standings, while Parsons fell to fourth by the end of the season. Winless Dave Marcis took fifth.

1979

January The CBS Sports television network prepares for its live, flag-to-flag telecast of the Daytona 500. It marks the first time in history that a 500-mile NASCAR Winston Cup Grand National event will be televised by a major network in its entirety.

February 18 Richard Petty hustles past the crashed cars of Cale Yarborough and Donnie Allison to win the Daytona 500, snapping his 45-race winless drought. Yarborough and Allison crash, then fight in the infield following a last-lap incident. The Nielsen ratings for the CBS live telecast are a remarkable 10.5, with the final half hour drawing an amazing 13.5 rating.

March 18 Buddy Baker tames a 40-car field in the Atlanta 500 to notch his first NASCAR Winston Cup Grand National win in nearly three years.

April 1 Outstanding rookie driver Dale Earnhardt scoots around Darrell Waltrip with 27 laps to go and grabs his first career NASCAR Winston Cup Grand National victory in Bristol's Southeastern 500.

April 8 Darrell Waltrip prevails in a last-lap battle with Richard Petty to win the Rebel 500 at Darlington. The two drivers swap the lead four times on the final lap. After the race, legendary David Pearson is released as driver of the Wood Brothers Mercury. A pit mishap is cited as the reason for Pearson's release.

May 20 Neil Bonnett, making his third start for the Wood Brothers, drives around Cale Yarborough with three laps remaining to win the Mason-Dixon 500 at Dover Downs International Speedway.

July 30 Cale Yarborough prevails in a frantic, crash-marred Coca-Cola 500 at Pocono International Raceway for his third win of the year. Rookie driver Dale Earnhardt fractures both collar bones in a hard crash on the 99th lap. The race features 56 lead changes among eight drivers.

Lennie Pond crashes his #54 Oldsmobile into the wall as Geoff Bodine skids into the infield grass during the second Twin 125-mile qualifier at Daytona on Feb. 15. Number 02 Dave Marcis and #05 Dick Brooks scoot through the melee. All four drivers made the Daytona 500 field. Pond was in a one-shot deal with the team owned by Al Rudd, the father of Ricky Rudd. Ricky had taken a ride with the Junie Donlavey Ford team in 1979.

▼ Donnie Allison pushes his #1 Oldsmobile ahead of pole-sitter #28 Buddy Baker at the drop of the green flag on the 16th lap of the Feb. 18 Daytona 500. A wet track surface following an all-night rain forced the first 15 laps to be run under caution. Baker had swept all Speedweeks events he competed in, but the car misfired at the start of the main event. He only managed to run 38 laps before retiring from the race.

▶ Number 1 Donnie Allison runs just ahead of the #11 Oldsmobile of Cale Yarborough in the final laps of the Daytona 500. Allison made up a lap deficit and Yarborough rallied from three laps down to fight for the win. The two cars tangled down the backstretch on the final lap and clobbered the wall in turn three, knocking both out of the race. Richard Petty, more than a mile behind when the white flag waved, stormed through the accident scene to win his sixth Daytona 500.

▲ Richard Petty leads Darrell Waltrip down the backstretch at Daytona during the hectic final lap of the 1979 edition of "The Great American Race." Petty ended a 45-race winless skid with his final-lap heroics, holding off Waltrip and A.J. Foyt in the dash to the finish line.

"For some reason, Cale kept hitting my fist repeatedly with his nose."
—Bobby Allison

After the final-lap crash in the Daytona 500, Cale Yarborough (foreground), Donnie Allison (red), and Bobby Allison (blue) engaged in fisticuffs. Bobby had stopped on the track to check on his brother's condition. Cale approached Bobby and punched him as he sat in the car. Bobby dismounted and wrestled with Cale in the infield as Donnie came over to join the free-for-all. Later, Bobby described the incident with Cale: "For some reason, Cale kept hitting my fist repeatedly with his nose." The finish and the fight made great television, and helped increase the general public's interest in NASCAR.

1979

August 5 Darrell Waltrip finishes comfortably ahead of runner-up David Pearson to win the Talladega 500. Young Kyle Petty makes his NASCAR Winston Cup Grand National debut, finishing an impressive ninth.

September 3 David Pearson, substituting for the injured Dale Earnhardt, leads the final 70 laps to win his third Southern 500 at Darlington Raceway. Upstart third-year driver Bill Elliott finishes second.

November 4 Neil Bonnett edges Dale Earnhardt by about three feet to win the Dixie 500 at Atlanta. Darrell Waltrip carries a narrow two-point lead over Richard Petty into the season finale at Ontario.

November 18 Benny Parsons takes the lead with five laps to go and wins the Los Angeles Times 500 at Ontario Motor Speedway. Fifth-place finisher Richard Petty takes his seventh NASCAR Winston Cup Grand National championship by 11 points over Darrell Waltrip, who finishes eighth.

Rookie driver Dale Earnhardt was tabbed to drive the Osterlund Racing Chevrolets and Oldsmobiles in the 1979 NASCAR campaign, and he responded brilliantly. In the April 1 Southeastern 500 at Bristol, Earnhardt edged Bobby Allison and Darrell Waltrip to post his first NASCAR Winston Cup Grand National victory in only his 16th career start.

Members of the rival Junior Johnson team tend to the disabled #21 Wood Brothers Mercury driven by David Pearson after a pit road mishap in the April CRC Chemicals Rebel 500 at Darlington Raceway. Pearson made a pit stop, and thought the Wood Brothers were going to change only two tires. With the lug nuts loosened all the way around, Pearson sped out of the pits after two tires had been replaced. The loose inside wheels flew off near the end of pit road, ending Pearson's day. A week later, Pearson was released from the Wood Brothers ride, despite scoring 43 wins from 1972 to '78 with the Virginia-based team.

Richard Petty and Darrell Waltrip engaged in one of the most heated and exciting duels in the history of the legendary Darlington Raceway on April 8, 1979. Petty's #43 STP Chevrolet and Waltrip's #88 Gatorade Chevy swapped the lead four times in the four laps before the final lap of the Rebel 500, plus an additional three times on the final lap alone. On that last lap, Waltrip passed Petty in turn one, only to lose the lead in turn three. Waltrip fought back and passed Petty off turn four and won by a car length.

Darrell Waltrip, driving the #88 Chevy, manages to keep #11 Cale Yarborough and #43 Richard Petty at bay during the early laps of the April 22 Virginia 500 at Martinsville Speedway. Waltrip, known as "DW," started on the pole, led the opening 49 laps, and eventually finished third behind Petty and Buddy Baker. An extended pit stop for overheating problems knocked Yarborough down to an 11th-place finish. For Petty, it was his first short-track win since 1975.

NASCAR Goes Live

SUNDAY, MAY 15, 1978, was one of the most pivotal days in NASCAR history. Barry Frank and Bernie Hoffman, top executives at CBS Sports, issued a statement that the Columbia Broadcasting System would televise the 1979 Daytona 500 live from start to finish. "These are the finest stock car drivers in the world," said Hoffman, executive producer at CBS Sports. "It assures CBS of a strong viewing audience. It is the gemstone of our major auto racing package."

Never before had one of the major television networks set aside four hours to televise an entire NASCAR Winston Cup Grand National event. In previous years, networks filmed an event, edited it down to a half hour or 45 minutes and aired the highlights a few weeks later.

CBS also inked contracts to televise races at Michigan and Talladega as part of its auto-racing package.

CBS anchorman Ken Squier served as an important liaison in the discussions. "The sport of NASCAR stock car racing was coming of age," said Squier, an auto-racing wordsmith and enthusiast from Stowe, Vt. "Winston Cup racing represented a down home Americanized sporting event, and many of us felt the time was ripe to introduce live NASCAR racing into the homes across the country."

Squier, who had served as the public-address announcer at Daytona for more than a decade, sold the sport and the idea of an entire live racing telecast to CBS. He also gave the Daytona 500 the nickname "The Great American Race." "Other forms of motorsports had become sprinkled with international flavor," said Squier, "while NASCAR stock car racing reached the nerve of good, solid American sports enthusiasts."

The 1979 Daytona 500 telecast ran more than the four allotted hours. A rainstorm the morning of the race delayed

Broadcaster Ken Squier

the start by more than an hour, but CBS stayed with the event. The race was one of the most exciting in Daytona history and ratings exceeded expectations. Overall, the program netted a 10.5 Nielsen rating. During the final half hour, the rating jumped to 13.5.

The ending of the 1979 Daytona 500 bordered on the unbelievable. Leaders Donnie Allison and Cale Yarborough crashed on the backstretch of the final lap, opening the door for Richard Petty to win and end his 45-race winless skid. After the accident, Yarborough and Donnie and Bobby Allison slugged it out in the infield with the cameras rolling. It was a storybook ending with a good measure of extracurricular activities included.

CBS and NASCAR won the time slot easily. ABC, which was televising the Superstars Olympic-type competition for various well-known sports personalities, drew a 9.4 rating. A golf tournament on NBC got a 5.5.

CBS spokesperson Beano Cook said the network was excited with the high ratings. "We are very, very pleased," said Cook. "For a race that long to get this kind of rating is great. We would have been pleased with a 9.0, but a 10.5 is phenomenal."

The 1979 Daytona 500 was produced by Michael Pearl and directed by Robert Fishman. "A lot of times you walk out of the [production] truck and you don't know if you did well or not," said Pearl. "This time I walked out with a feeling 'this worked.' "

CBS would win a National Academy of Television Arts and Sciences Emmy for the telecast. NASCAR's biggest showcase event had turned into a widely viewed slugfest. Millions of people who had never watched a NASCAR event before had just seen NASCAR's finest perform admirably for 500 miles, and duke it out afterward.

The CBS telecast served as a catalyst to propel NASCAR racing into mainstream America. NASCAR's passed its first test on a live television stage with flying colors.

Dick Brooks loses the grip on his #05 Oldsmobile and plows into the guardrail in an 11th-lap crash during the May 27 World 600 at Charlotte Motor Speedway. Brooks, a capable journeyman driver for most of his NASCAR career, struggled with the Nelson Malloch-owned team in 1979, as wrecks and mechanical problems interrupted several strong runs. Malloch spent two years in NASCAR Winston Cup Grand National racing, fielding cars for Brooks, Ricky Rudd, and Lake Speed.

Number 15 Bobby Allison and #44 Terry Labonte crashed hard on the 91st lap of the July 4 Firecracker 400 at Daytona International Speedway. Labonte was one of the prize rookie drivers of the 1979 season, joining Dale Earnhardt, Harry Gant, and Joe Millikan as stout freshman campaigners. Labonte registered 13 top-10 finishes, earning a 10th place in the final NASCAR Winston Cup Grand National points standings. Earnhardt went on to take seventh in the championship race and earn Rookie of the Year honors.

Kyle Petty poses with his #42 STP Dodge Magnum prior to the Firecracker 400. Petty was hoping to make his NASCAR Winston Cup Grand National debut in the Independence Day classic at Daytona, but crashed in a shakedown run. A similar practice crash derailed his efforts to make the field at Charlotte in May. Kyle was finally able to qualify for the Talladega 500 on Aug. 5, and he handled himself quite nicely, finishing ninth.

Veteran Darrell Waltrip (left) chats with rookie sensation Dale Earnhardt during a lull in the racing action in 1979. Earnhardt was leading the July 30 Coca-Cola 500 at Pocono International Raceway when a tire blew, sending him into the boiler-plate retaining wall. Earnhardt broke both collar bones in the accident and was forced to take six weeks off to recuperate from the painful injuries.

▼ Number 15 Bobby Allison, #2 David Pearson, and #21 Neil Bonnett fan out in three-abreast formation at the frantic start of the Aug. 19 Champion Spark Plug 400 at Michigan International Speedway. Pearson earned the pole in the Osterlund Racing Chevy, substituting for the injured Dale Earnhardt. Bonnett was behind the wheel of the Wood Brothers Mercury, a coveted ride formerly occupied by Pearson. Richard Petty came from his fifth starting slot to win the race, passing Buddy Baker on the final lap. Pearson finished fourth, while Bonnett departed early with ignition problems.

Joe Millikan clobbers the fourth-turn retaining wall in the Sept. 3 Southern 500 at Darlington Raceway. The rookie driver recovered from his shunt with the wall to finish 15th. Millikan, a protégé of Richard Petty, had a superb freshman campaign, scoring 20 top-10 finishes and placing sixth in the final points standings. He was runner-up to Dale Earnhardt in the Rookie of the Year chase.

David Pearson guides the #2 Chevrolet down Darlington's front chute just ahead of #11 Cale Yarborough in the 30th annual Southern 500. Pearson was taking his fourth and final ride in the Osterlund Racing Chevrolet while regular driver Dale Earnhardt recovered from injuries suffered at Pocono. In Cinderella fashion, Pearson won the race on the treacherous old track. It was his third Southern 500 victory.

Cars were once able to run three and four abreast at Dover Downs International Speedway when the turns were pavement rather than the current concrete surface. Here, #08 John Anderson, #11 Cale Yarborough, #64 Tommy Gale, #1 Donnie Allison, #43 Richard Petty, #72 Joe Millikan, and #15 Bobby Allison duel in incredibly tight formation in the Sept. 16 CRC Chemicals 500. Petty is shown driving his patented high-line through the corner, a practice he started at the beginning of his career.

Richard Petty flashes across the finish line just in front of Donnie Allison to win the CRC Chemicals 500 at Dover Downs. The victory, the 189th of Petty's career, marked the beginning of a late-season rally by Petty to catch Darrell Waltrip in the NASCAR Winston Cup Grand National championship battle. Waltrip had a commanding lead at midseason, but the win vaulted Petty to within 83 points of his rival.

Buddy Baker wheels his #28 Chevrolet around Richard Petty in the Sept. 23 Old Dominion 500 at Martinsville Speedway. Baker went on to win the event despite losing his brakes with a shade under 200 laps remaining. Petty finished second. For the big, strapping Baker, it was only the second short-track win of his NASCAR Winston Cup Grand National career.

▼ Pole-sitter Neil Bonnett leads the charge at the start of the Oct. 7 NAPA National 500 at Charlotte Motor Speedway. Bonnett continued an amazing streak of pole positions for the Wood Brothers at the 1½-mile track. The Wood Brothers Purolator Mercury earned the pole position for every NASCAR Winston Cup Grand National race at Charlotte from Oct. 1973 through Oct. 1979—a run of 13 consecutive poles. David Pearson won 11 poles during the streak, and Bonnett took the final two.

▲► Darrell Waltrip skidded into the wall after a tap from Bobby Allison in the Oct. 14 Holly Farms 400 at North Wilkesboro Speedway. Waltrip continued without a front end and finished 13th, while Petty finished third. This incident proved to be a pivotal turn in the tight championship race between Waltrip and Richard Petty. Waltrip's points lead was cut to 17 after the Wilkesboro event, and Petty took the lead the following week at Rockingham. Petty beat Waltrip by 11 points to win the NASCAR Winston Cup Grand National championship.

1979 NASCAR WINSTON CUP GN POINTS RACE

Rank	Driver	Points	Starts	Wins	Top 5	Top 10	Winnings
1	Richard Petty	4830	31	5	23	27	$561,933.20
2	Darrell Waltrip	4819	31	7	19	22	$557,011.60
3	Bobby Allison	4633	31	5	18	22	$428,800.44
4	Cale Yarborough	4604	31	4	19	22	$440,128.28
5	Benny Parsons	4256	31	2	16	21	$264,929.12
6	Joe Millikan	4014	27	1	5	20	$229,712.88
7	Dale Earnhardt	3749	27	1	11	17	$274,809.96
8	Richard Childress	3735	31	0	1	11	$132,921.64
9	Ricky Rudd	3642	28	0	4	17	$150,897.48
10	Terry Labonte	3615	31	0	2	13	$134,652.48
11	Buddy Arrington	3589	31	0	1	7	$131,832.48
12	D.K. Ulrich	3508	31	0	0	5	$113,457.48
13	J.D. McDuffie	3473	31	0	1	7	$113,477.48
14	James Hylton	3405	30	0	0	5	$97,427.48
15	Buddy Baker	3249	26	3	12	15	$342,147.48
16	Frank Warren	3199	31	0	0	3	$94,538.32
17	Ronnie Thomas	2912	30	0	0	3	$100,078.32
18	Tommy Gale	2795	28	0	0	1	$72,808.32
19	Cecil Gordon	2737	28	0	0	0	$66,274.16
20	Dave Marcis	2736	25	0	1	6	$56,433.32
21	Harry Grant	2664	25	0	0	5	$47,185.00
22	Dick Brooks	2622	26	0	1	8	$61,985.00
23	Jimmy Means	2575	27	0	0	1	$55,560.00
24	Donnie Allison	2508	20	0	7	10	$144,770.00
25	Baxter Price	2364	24	0	0	0	$45,165.00
26	Neil Bonnett	2223	21	3	4	6	$151,235.00
27	Tighe Scott	1879	17	0	1	7	$88,010.00
28	Bill Elliott	1548	13	0	1	5	$58,200.00
29	Lennie Pond	1415	15	0	0	2	$42,970.00
30	Dick May	1390	20	0	0	0	$26,345.00
31	Roger Hamby	1231	13	0	0	0	$21,000.00
32	David Pearson	1203	9	1	4	5	$99,180.00
33	Coo Coo Martin	613	7	0	0	0	$27,540.00
34	Bruce Hill	594	7	0	0	0	$17,260.00
35	Blackie Wangerin	571	7	0	0	0	$14,300.00
36	Grant Adcox	560	6	0	0	0	$15,290.00
37	Kyle Petty	559	5	0	0	1	$10,810.00
38	Chuck Bown	523	7	0	0	2	$31,380.00
39	John Anderson	496	4	0	1	1	$11,210.00
40	Ralph Jones	477	6	0	0	0	$12,785.00
41	Earle Canavan	456	7	0	0	0	$6675.00
42	Slick Johnson	431	4	0	0	1	$5360.00
43	Nelson Oswald	431	6	0	0	1	$3610.00
44	Dave Watson	413	4	0	0	1	$7170.00
45	Al Holbert	402	6	0	0	1	$14,710.00
46	Bobby Wawak	376	4	0	0	0	$7295.00
47	Jody Ridley	374	3	0	1	2	$11,245.00
48	Bill Hollar	371	5	0	0	0	$2545.00
49	Rick Newsom	355	4	0	0	0	$5530.00
50	Bill Schmitt	342	3	0	1	1	$11,695.00

Richard Petty won an unprecedented seventh NASCAR Winston Cup Grand National championship as he posted a furious rally late in the 1979 season. Petty trailed Darrell Waltrip by 187 points with just seven races to go. From that point on, Petty never finished lower than sixth.

Waltrip led the points chase most of the season. He assumed command in May and built a healthy lead until his big advantage began to slip away. The lead in the standings changed in each of the last four races. Waltrip led after the 28th race at North Wilkesboro in October. Petty won at Rockingham the following week and took an eight-point lead. Waltrip finished one spot ahead of Petty at Atlanta and carried a two-point lead into the season finale at Ontario Motor Speedway in California.

In the final race, Waltrip spun out while trying to avoid another spinning car and was trapped a lap behind. Unable to make up the lost lap, Waltrip finished eighth, while Petty came home fifth and won the title by 11 points.

1980s: Smaller Cars, Bigger Purses, Grand Exposure

The 1980s began with a refreshing outlook for a sport that had endured a tumultuous trek through peaks and valleys in the preceding 10 years. Through a complex, shifting pano-rama, NASCAR overcame innumerable obstacles in the '70s, from the loss of factory support to the crippling energy crisis and a gripping recession.

The 1980 NASCAR Winston Cup season was to be the final one for the behemoth full-size cars. The writing was on the wall as early as '74 that eventually NASCAR would have to shift to the smaller, more efficient automobiles that were saturating the American marketplace. The huge vehicles that Detroit had produced for two decades were being phased out and NASCAR responded accordingly.

Unpolished sophomore driver Dale Earnhardt, a rugged short-track warrior during his adolescence, had driven his way into the starry world of NASCAR Winston Cup racing with relative ease. He emerged from obscurity to instant fame, fortune, and headlines. Following in the footsteps of his famous father Ralph, one of NASCAR's most rugged short-track specialists, the second-generation Earnhardt possessed the fortitude and supreme self-confidence to make the grade at NASCAR's highest level.

Poor pit strategy robbed Earnhardt of a victory in his first start in the storied Daytona 500 in 1979, but he did walk off with one victory, the Rookie of the Year award and predictions from trackside observers of a promising future.

With a full season under his belt and a strong working relationship with the Rod Osterlund pit crew headed by Jake Elder, Earnhardt blazed his way out of the starting blocks in 1980. A mistake in the pits once again took him out of contention in the Daytona 500, but with second- and fourth-place finishes in the season's first two events, the dazzling driver was atop the NASCAR Winston Cup points standings. Earnhardt scored back-to-back victories at Atlanta and Bristol in March and continued to pad his lead in the standings.

By May, reports circulated of dissension within the Osterlund operation despite their lofty on-track achieve-ments. Crew chief Elder, a talented but temperamental individual who got the most out of men and machinery, was butting heads with team manager Roland Wlodyka. Follow-ing Charlotte's World 600, Elder walked out of one of the most coveted jobs in racing. "Roland could screw up a five-car funeral," huffed Elder. "Dave Marcis [Osterlund's driver in 1978] told me I'd never be able to get along with him and he was exactly right. And since Earnhardt has got some money, he don't know you. He's as cocky as they come now."

The loss of Elder at the peak of the season seemed to spell certain doom for Earnhardt and the Osterlund team. A few days after Elder's abrupt resignation, into the breach stepped 20-year-old Doug Richert, who was promoted into the crew chief's role. A rookie crew chief with a wild-eyed

sophomore driver would certainly fall apart, rivals reasoned.

Showing maturity far beyond his 29 years, Earnhardt never broke stride. In his second start since Richert took over, Earnhardt won at Nashville, expanding his points lead. One by one, challengers fell off the pace. Richard Petty, gunning for an eighth title, suffered injuries in a crash at Pocono and fell out of the picture. Benny Parsons' consistent finishes placed him in the hunt, but a couple of poor efforts left him far behind. Darrell Waltrip and Bobby Allison were blazingly fast, but lost ground in the summer months. Only Cale Yarborough loomed as a title threat.

Earnhardt and Yarborough battled down to the wire in one of the most thrilling championship chases in NASCAR history. Both won twice in the final five races of the year. Heading into the season finale at Ontario Motor Speedway, Earnhardt held a narrow 29-point lead.

Having to finish fifth or better at Ontario to sew up the title, Earnhardt snuggled up to the race leaders while keeping Yarborough in check. On the 71st lap, Earnhardt made a routine green-flag pit stop, only to be trapped a lap behind when the caution came out a few laps after returning to competition. But Earnhardt came roaring back, and with just over 125 miles to go, he passed race leader Yarborough. When the caution came out for oil on the track on the 146th lap, Earnhardt got back onto the lead lap.

Benny Parsons won the race with Yarborough third and Earnhardt fifth. The final margin was 19 points as Earnhardt became the first man to win the Rookie of the Year title and the points championship in back-to-back seasons. Earnhardt led the NASCAR Winston Cup points standings after every race except the season opener.

After the 1980 campaign, the team owners worked feverishly to deal with the new NASCAR guidelines and the smaller race cars. The maximum wheelbase was reduced to 110 inches, down from 115. The '81 assembly line products Detroit was cranking out were boxy and devoid of aerodynamic enhancements. By the time the teams brought the new hardware to Daytona, everyone was back to square one.

After initial practice sessions, virtually every driver expressed concerns that the new cars were twitching frighteningly at high speed. During the 1981 Daytona Speedweeks, cars that got a little sideways suddenly rocketed into airborne acrobatics. John Anderson and Connie Saylor soared wildly out of control in the Twin 125-milers, flipping *backward* as wind currents played tricks with the NASCAR Winston Cup machinery.

"These cars weigh 3700 pounds," said Benny Parsons. "But when those two cars got sideways, they looked like a cardboard box in the wind. It beats anything I've ever seen before." NASCAR addressed the situation by slapping larger spoilers, or stabilizers, onto the rear decks to render the cars manageable.

Steady Richard Petty prevailed in the Daytona 500 after 49 skittish lead changes. The number of lead changes was, at the time, the second most in Daytona 500 history. It served as a sign of what was to come during the remainder of the exciting 1981 campaign. Two weeks after the Daytona 500, the race at Rockingham featured a NASCAR record 36 lead changes. The two Michigan races produced 65 and 47 lead changes—a total of 112 that also established a record. Talladega had a combined 82 lead changes for the two races, and Daytona had 84. Over the course of the 31-race season in '81, fans witnessed 772 lead changes, which set a new standard. Five races were also determined by a last-lap pass, setting yet another NASCAR record.

The Cliff Stewart team (with Morgan Shepherd driving) won at Martinsville in its seventh start. Owners Jack Beebe

(Ron Bouchard) and Junie Donlavey (Jody Ridley) also logged their first career wins during an energized season that no one could predict. In the final analysis, Darrell Waltrip nosed out Bobby Allison for the NASCAR Winston Cup title in a spirited points chase.

Much of the 1981 season was aired on TV. CBS and ABC had produced their usual telecasts, but a new entity was forging its way into the NASCAR empire. The Entertainment Sports Programming Network televised the Nov. 8, 1981, Atlanta Journal 500 live flag to flag. Following the initial production, ESPN knew it had fertile grounds in NASCAR. "We are definitely looking for some [NASCAR Winston Cup] Grand National races," said Rich Canfield, ESPN program planning coordinator. "Atlanta was the first one, and coming from such a big track makes it especially exciting for us. We will be doing more races in the coming year."

ESPN picked up a number of the short-track and super-speedway races from tracks that didn't have a TV contract in place. Rights fees for the races were minimal, some less than $40,000, which pales in comparison to today's billion-dollar deal. But the teams, drivers, tracks, and NASCAR welcomed the addition of the cable sports network since television coverage could only help increase NASCAR's popularity.

The importance of team sponsorship became paramount. Costs were rising sharply, and teams had to perform well to secure and keep sponsorship. Winning races was a prerequisite, and crews often challenged the savvy of the NASCAR technical inspectors in their efforts to gain a "competitive edge." The tradition was as old as stock car racing itself, and was considered part of the game.

In the early part of the 1983 campaign, NASCAR began cracking down on teams that were stepping beyond the specifications. At Darlington, a number of disallowed items were confiscated by the NASCAR cops, including illegal fuel cans, unapproved fuel cells, and other ingenious "modifications." "We are going to get everybody's attention," declared Dick Beaty, NASCAR's technical director. "And the best way to do that is hit them in the pocketbook."

NASCAR was also dealing heavily with teams that used soft left-side tires on the right side of the car in final sprints to the checkered flag. The softer compounds would give better grip and quick lap times for a short period of time before wearing out. NASCAR deemed this practice unsafe and dealt harshly with violators. Tim Richmond was contending for victory in the April 24 race at Martinsville. On a pit stop, his crew put left tires on the right side of Richmond's Pontiac, and NASCAR promptly parked him for five laps in the "penalty box." Richmond finished far down the running order after leading for 58 laps.

Threats failed to curtail the imagination of the sport's top mechanics. Throughout the season, a number of violations were detected and confiscated. Others, perhaps, skirted past the sharp eye of NASCAR's technical inspectors. In October, the NASCAR Winston Cup series was at Charlotte Motor Speedway and several teams were scrambling to line up sponsorship for 1984. Richard Petty had won twice in the '83 season, and both victories came in the early weeks. On more than one occasion, Petty told his brother Maurice, the engine builder for Petty Enterprises, that he needed more horsepower to keep up with the front-running cars.

Petty qualified 20th and spent the entire Charlotte race lagging behind the leaders. During a caution late in the race, Petty made a pit stop for new rubber, and the Petty crew bolted four left-side tires on the STP Pontiac. On the restart, Petty blasted past the competition and drove to a convincing

victory, the 198th of his illustrious career. As Petty went through the routine victory lane proceedings and the post-race interviews, NASCAR inspector Jim Baldwin noticed the number D2881 on all four of Petty's tires. Baldwin knew those were the left-side serial numbers Goodyear used.

"I think we have a problem down here," Baldwin radioed to high-ranking NASCAR officials in the control tower. "I'm going to need some help down here." Word of this development leaked to the press box. One reporter asked Petty about the tires. "All I do is drive the car," said Petty. "I have no idea what tires go on the car."

Petty excused himself from any further interviews in the press box and went to the inspection area, where Dick Beaty and Maurice Petty were huddled in a conference. Maurice braced Beaty for another shock. The engine was too big, he confessed. The engine in Petty's car was measured at 381.983 cid, well above the maximum 358-cid limit. In addition to the improperly mounted tires, Petty was in a heap of trouble.

NASCAR allowed Petty to keep his 198th victory, but stripped him of 104 NASCAR Winston Cup points and fined the team a then-record $35,000. Petty admitted that he had grown "out of touch" with his crew. "I didn't know what was going on. As I get further and further away from the business aspect, I become only the driver. I've been telling the crew I needed more horsepower. I guess they took me at my word. What really upset me was when I found out about the big engine and realized that all them other cats have been passing me on the straights. That makes you wonder what else is going on." The whole embarrassing escapade became knows as "Pettygate."

Bobby Allison went on to record his first NASCAR Winston Cup championship in 1983 after six runner-up finishes. He finally plucked the prize he wanted more than anything in the world. After two painful defeats to Darrell Waltrip in 1981 and 1982, Allison had prevailed and was at the pinnacle of NASCAR Winston Cup racing.

Richard Petty, on the other hand, was deeply hurt by the Charlotte fiasco. At the end of the season, he departed Petty Enterprises. He originally planned to join the RahMoc team headed by Bob Rahilly and Butch Mock, but that deal fell through. Petty had to quickly line up a ride with California music producer Mike Curb, who was forming a team for 1984. Petty took the STP sponsorship with him, leaving the Petty Enterprises team with third-generation driver Kyle Petty to carry the flag.

The 1984 season got off to a shaky start for Richard and Kyle. Both were felled with repeated engine failures. Petty was able to shake off the mechanical gremlins to win race number 199 at Dover in May. After hitting the skids in the early part of the summer, Petty was back in stride for the July 4 Firecracker 400 at Daytona.

Petty and Yarborough were among the quickest cars in the field, and the winner would have a special visitor on the nation's birthday. President Ronald Reagan was scheduled to arrive at the Daytona International Speedway during the running of the race and would greet the winner in victory lane. Petty and Yarborough engaged in a tight battle and the honor of meeting the president. Petty took the lead with 33 laps remaining. Yarborough was perched on his rear bumper, waiting until the final lap to employ the slingshot maneuver. Doug Heveron's spin with three laps to go foiled Yarborough's well-laid plans. The caution flew as the leaders

were on the backstretch. Alerted to the caution flag and knowing the race would end under the yellow, Yarborough made a hastened attempt to pass Petty.

Yarborough moved to the high side and pulled even with Petty. The two raced side by side off the fourth turn. As they approached the caution flag, completing the 158th of 160 laps, the blue smoke spit from the cars as sheetmetal rubbed together. Petty beat Yarborough back to the line by about six inches and won the race under caution. Routine postrace procedures were scrapped. Petty stopped his car at the start-finish line and was escorted to the VIP suites for a meeting with the president and radio interviews. "We all shook hands and then the president and I talked," said Petty in his patented nonchalant manner. "I think it blowed his mind that Cale and I were really running into each other at 200 miles per hour."

Petty had finally won his magical 200th NASCAR Winston Cup victory, and Reagan's presence made it sweeter. The finish awed the president. It was the second and final victory of the 1984 season for the King of NASCAR—and it turned out to be the final win of his career. At season's close, Terry Labonte parlayed consistency to win the championship on the strength of just two wins, but 17 top-five finishes. Petty finished a distant 10th in the final standings.

Bill Elliott emerged as a bona fide superspeedway hero in 1985, clicking off a string of victories on NASCAR's speediest tracks. Elliott led 136 of the 200 laps in the Daytona 500, overcame a costly penalty on pit road, and breezed to an easy win. He followed that with victories at Atlanta and Darlington, then made a miraculous comeback to take Talladega's Winston 500. Elliott dropped off the pace after 48 laps in the Talladega event with a broken oil fitting. After repairs were made, Elliott returned to the track running 26th, nearly two laps behind.

From that point on, nine different drivers took turns leading as Elliott's incredible 205 mph rebound began to unfold. The sellout crowd of 122,000 was awestruck when Elliott zoomed past Yarborough to take the lead on lap 145. He had made up a five-mile deficit without the aid of a caution flag, and he went virtually unchallenged the rest of the way.

The Talladega victory gave Elliott a win in the first two crown-jewel races of 1985, Daytona and Talladega. At the beginning of the season, title sponsor R.J. Reynolds inaugurated "The Winston Million," a million-dollar prize that would go to any driver winning three of the four major races during the campaign. The races selected by R.J. Reynolds were the Daytona 500, the spring Winston 500 at Talladega, Charlotte's World 600, and the Southern 500 at Darlington. Another big-buck plum tossed into the fray was The Winston, NASCAR's version of an all-star race. The Winston would offer $200,000 to the winner, more than even the Daytona 500 winner took home. "We thought we were having evolutionary increases each year," said Gerry Long, president and chief executive officer of R.J. Reynolds, "but we weren't getting much media attention. But this [the 1985 posted bonus awards] is serious money, serious racing, and serious sports. If one driver is good or lucky enough to win three of the four races, we'll make him a millionaire."

The 1985 All-Star race was a big bonus to the drivers and fans of NASCAR Winston Cup racing. The inaugural running of the event, which was open to all drivers who won races in 1984, was staged at Charlotte Motor Speedway on May 25, the day before the World 600. The event was "on the house" for NASCAR enthusiasts, a free event for those who had paid to watch Saturday's 300-mile Late Model Sportsman race.

The media attention during the Charlotte race week was incredible. Elliott was going for $200,000 on Saturday and $1,000,000 on Sunday. After his win at Dover the week before, Elliott commented that he "dreaded" going to Charlotte. The quiet and unassuming boy from the Georgia hills was thrust into the limelight. Distractions were supreme, and it had a telltale effect on the team's performance at Charlotte. Elliott finished a distant seventh in the 12-car field in The Winston as Darrell Waltrip came home first. In the 600, Elliott fell victim to an array of mechanical ills and finished 18th. He also lost the points lead to winless Terry Labonte. Darrell Waltrip established himself as a title contender with a win in the 600.

The Elliott express got back on track following Charlotte. He won twice at Pocono, bagged both Michigan races, and regained a narrow points lead. Heading into Darlington for the Southern 500 and his last shot at winning The Winston Million, Elliott was braced for the onslaught of media attention. This time, Elliott had armed deputies in his garage area, shielding him from the herd of press agents. Interviews were scheduled in advance so Elliott and his team could concentrate on the job at hand.

The Southern 500 was a memorable event. Elliott started on the pole for the 10th time in 20 races. He led the opening 14 laps, but fell off the pace as Cale Yarborough, Dale Earnhardt, and Harry Gant forged to the front. In the middle stages, Elliott was nearly lapped, but a caution flag enabled his pit crew to make a pivotal chassis adjustment. He returned to the track running fourth, but was getting around the age-old track much quicker.

Gant, who had led much of the way, dropped off the pace with engine problems. Then Earnhardt spun out in the second turn to take himself out of contention. Yarborough took the lead with 43 laps remaining with Elliott perched on his rear bumper. Suddenly, Yarborough's Ford threw up a big smoke screen. Elliott, momentarily blinded by the thick smoke, dove to the apron and made a safe pass. What was first thought to be a blown engine on Cale's car was only a power-steering failure. After making a pit stop for quick repairs during the caution period, Yarborough returned to the track on Elliott's bumper for the final dash.

For the final 40 laps, Elliott and Yarborough treated the crowd of 70,000 to a spirited duel. Elliott drove to victory by a couple of car lengths and bagged the million-dollar payoff. Elliott went on to win 11 superspeedway races in 1985, still a single-season record. He gobbled up every laurel and postseason award possible, yet didn't win the NASCAR Winston Cup championship. That honor went to Darrell Waltrip, who won three races. The intricacies of the NASCAR points system rewarded consistency in 1985.

Dale Earnhardt, NASCAR's darling youngster in the early 1980s, rebounded from a few sluggish seasons after his electrifying championship as a sophomore in '80. He went winless while defending his title in 1981, and bounced back and forth with a number of teams. Between 1981 and '84, Earnhardt drove for Rod Osterlund, J.D. Stacy, Richard Childress, Bud Moore, and back to the Childress operation. Childress was one of NASCAR's top independent drivers for 10 years, competing in 285 races before he suddenly hung up his helmet and offered Earnhardt a ride in 1981. Earnhardt finished out the '84 campaign, then took a two-year hiatus from Childress driving Fords for Bud Moore before he returned to the Childress team.

It took a couple of years for the chemistry to mesh, but once they hit stride, Earnhardt's Wrangler Jeans machine ran up front every week. Along the way, Earnhardt ruffled a few feathers, crumpled some sheetmetal, shoved rivals out of the way, and acquired the nickname "The Intimidator." In 1986, Earnhardt won five races and ran away from the field in the NASCAR Winston Cup title race. The following year, the formidable team went for the jugular early, winning six of the first eight races of the season. With a month left in the '87 campaign, Earnhardt locked up the championship, although the outcome was never in doubt after April.

By the end of the 1980s, Earnhardt found himself crowded by Rusty Wallace and Bill Elliott for supremacy in the NASCAR kingdom. Elliott won the '88 NASCAR Winston Cup title, holding off a gallant charge by Wallace. Wallace came back a year later and took the championship, thwarting Earnhardt's sensational late-season rally. The final margin of victory for Wallace was just 12 points.

By the late 1980s, a number of time-honored icons were hanging up their helmets. NASCAR Winston Cup champions Cale Yarborough, David Pearson, Benny Parsons, and Bobby Allison had retired—Allison due to debilitating injuries suffered at Pocono in '88. Tim Richmond, an energized and immensely popular driver who left open-wheel racing to tackle the NASCAR speedways, had electrified the audience with his brazen display of courage only to die prematurely of the AIDS virus in '89. Richmond was Winston Cup racing's top winner in '86, but he had to sit out most of the '87 campaign as he concealed the identity of his illness.

As the 1980s drew to a close, the popularity of NASCAR stock car racing was spiraling upward dramatically. Sponsorship from corporate America was strong, the dynamic heroes behind the wheel were becoming household names, and all of the NASCAR Winston Cup events were being televised live. CBS and ABC provided network coverage of some of the major events while ESPN had the bulk of the races. The TBS cable network was also providing live coverage of several events. Trackside attendance was running at record levels and promoters were adding new grandstands to accommodate the demand for tickets.

The problems during the chaotic 1970s were a distant memory. With adequate financing, superlative public relations, and intelligent leadership, NASCAR Winston Cup racing had rapidly developed into one of the most efficient endeavors in big league sports.

1980

February 17 In his 18th Daytona 500 start, Buddy Baker shakes the monkey off his back with a resounding victory. Baker's Oldsmobile averages a record 177.602 mph. Bobby Allison finishes second.

March 16 Sophomore Dale Earnhardt fends off a pesky Rusty Wallace to score his first superspeedway victory in the Atlanta 500. Earnhardt comes from the 31st starting position to beat Wallace by 9.55 seconds. Wallace was making his NASCAR Winston Cup Grand National debut in a Chevrolet owned by Roger Penske.

April 13 David Pearson, making his first start in the Hoss Ellington Chevrolet, is out front when rain curtails the Rebel 500 at Darlington after 258 miles. It is Pearson's 105th career NASCAR Winston Cup Grand National victory.

April 27 Darrell Waltrip erases a four-lap deficit and storms back to win the Virginia 500 at Martinsville Speedway. Waltrip violates a new rule stating teams aren't permitted to change tires during caution periods.

June 8 Darrell Waltrip passes Neil Bonnett on the final lap to win the 400-kilometer race on Riverside's road course. Waltrip makes the decisive pass in the ninth turn of the last lap and edges Bonnett by a car length.

July 27 Neil Bonnett drives his Mercury to a narrow decision over Buddy Baker to win the Coca-Cola 500 at Pocono. Title contender Richard Petty crashes hard on the 57th lap and suffers a broken neck. Tim Richmond, making his NASCAR Winston Cup Grand National debut, finishes 12th.

September 1 Sophomore driver Terry Labonte scores his first NASCAR Winston Cup Grand National victory in the Southern 500 at Darlington. Labonte comes from fourth to first when a crash wipes out the three leaders in the closing laps.

September 28 Dale Earnhardt leads the final 13 laps to Martinsville's Old Dominion 500, an event marred by 17 cautions. Earnhardt averages less than 70 mph in his fifth career NASCAR Winston Cup Grand National win.

The Rod Osterlund pit crew services Dale Earnhardt's Chevrolet in the NASCAR Winston Cup Grand National season opener at Riverside. Earnhardt started fifth and finished a strong second in the 500-kilometer Winston Western 500. Foul weather played havoc with the race. The event was started on Jan. 13 and completed six days later. A misty rain forced officials to halt the race after 26 laps on the original date, forcing teams to stay in Southern California for an extra week. Today, a postponed race is run on the next clear day.

Dale Earnhardt and future wife Teresa Houston celebrate in victory lane following the second annual Busch Clash at Daytona International Speedway. The sophomore sensation shot past Darrell Waltrip on the final lap and scored a one-car-length victory in the special Speedweeks event for the previous season's pole winners. Earnhardt won $50,000 in the 20-lap, 50-mile dash for cash.

▼ Buddy Baker leads a pack of cars off the fourth turn in the Feb. 17 Daytona 500. The Charlotte native drove his Ranier Racing Oldsmobile to an impressive victory after many years of hard luck in "The Great American Race." It was Baker's 18th Daytona 500 start. He won $102,175, the first time a NASCAR winner took home more than $100,000 in a single event.

Buddy Baker climbs out of his mangled #28 Chevrolet after he bounded of the wall in the late stages of Rockingham's Carolina 500 on March 9. Baker qualified third and led twice for 111 laps in his quest for a second-straight superspeedway win. The crash left him bruised and saddled in 15th-place in the final running order.

Crew members and well wishers push Buddy Baker's #28 Oldsmobile into victory lane after his dominating performance in the Daytona 500. Baker set an all-time 500-mile speed record for the Daytona 500, averaging 177.602 mph, a mark that still stands. Baker led 143 of the 200 laps and was comfortably ahead of runner-up Bobby Allison when a late caution flag came out, forcing the race to end under yellow.

Rusty Wallace, a short-track specialist from St. Louis, was selected by Roger Penske to drive in the March 16 Atlanta 500. For Penske, it was his first NASCAR start since quitting the NASCAR Winston Cup Grand National tour after the 1977 season. For Wallace, it was his NASCAR debut, and he stunned veterans with a runner-up finish to Dale Earnhardt.

Dale Earnhardt wheels his #2 Chevrolet under Buddy Baker during the early laps of the April 13 CRC Chemicals Rebel 500 at Darlington Raceway. Baker crashed early and Earnhardt fell out with engine problems. Earnhardt's Osterlund Racing team picked up sponsorship from Mike Curb Productions in 1980. During his rookie campaign of '79, Earnhardt competed all year without the aid of a sponsor.

David Pearson, who lost his ride with the Wood Brothers in 1979, started his first race of the '80 season in the April 13 Darlington event. Driving the #1 Hoss Ellington/Hawaiian Tropic Chevrolet, Pearson started on the front row, bolted to the lead, and was holding down first place when rain curtailed the event five laps after the halfway point. It was the 105th and final career NASCAR Winston Cup Grand National victory for Pearson.

1980

November 2 Cale Yarborough wins the Atlanta Journal 500 at Atlanta International Raceway to move to within 29 points of Dale Earnhardt in the championship chase. Earnhardt, who has led the standings since the second race of the season, finishes third.

November 15 Benny Parsons wins the season finale at Ontario Motor Speedway as Dale Earnhardt captures his first NASCAR Winston Cup Grand National title. Earnhardt rallies back from a lap deficit to finish fifth. His final margin of victory over Cale Yarborough, who finishes third at Ontario, is 19 points.

Cale Yarborough's #11 Chevrolet runs just ahead of #88 Darrell Waltrip and #27 Benny Parsons in the May 10 Music City USA 420 at the Nashville Fairgrounds Raceway. The two annual events at the .596-mile banked oval were, at that time, the only NASCAR Winston Cup Grand National races run under the lights. Yarborough started on the pole and fended off challenges from Waltrip in the early laps. Cale went on to finish third with Waltrip fourth. Parsons came home second behind winner Richard Petty.

Richard Petty flashes under the checkered flag a car length in front of Benny Parsons to win the Music City 420. Petty was the beneficiary of a new tire rule developed by NASCAR. To save teams money on their tire bills, NASCAR deemed that no team could change tires when the caution flag was out. Cale Yarborough dominated the race, but fell out of contention when a deflating tire couldn't be replaced under the yellow. A subsequent green-flag pit stop put Petty in the catbird seat. It was Petty's 192nd career NASCAR Winston Cup Grand National win.

Dale Earnhardt popped a tire on his #2 Chevrolet and triggered a multicar crash in the May 25 World 600 at Charlotte Motor Speedway. Gobbled up in the 276th-lap incident were #1 David Pearson, #11 Cale Yarborough, and Bobby Allison. Following the 600-miler, Earnhardt's crew chief Jake Elder quit despite the fact that the Osterlund Racing team held the points lead. Elder blamed team manager Roland Wlodyka. "Roland could screw up a five-car funeral," chided Elder.

Darrell Waltrip pushes his #88 Chevrolet alongside #27 Benny Parsons in a stirring duel in the closing laps of the World 600. The two drivers swapped the lead eight times in the final 26 laps, and Parsons went on to prevail by less than a car length. The victory was Parsons' 15th in the NASCAR Winston Cup Grand National Series.

▼ Neil Bonnett and Dale Earnhardt run in close formation in the June 15 400-miler at Michigan International Speedway. Earnhardt was leading with 28 laps remaining when his #2 Chevrolet dropped a cylinder, allowing Benny Parsons to motor home first. Bonnett finished fourth.

►Bobby Allison powers his #15 Bud Moore Ford Thunderbird under the checkered flag to win the July 4 Firecracker 400 at Daytona International Speedway. In victory lane, Allison announced he would be seeking a new ride in 1981. "There are only a few tracks the Ford is competitive on," said Allison. "I'd rather be racing a General Motors car and I feel strong enough to consider a change for next year."

▼ Dale Earnhardt blasts his way past #71 Dave Marcis and Terry Labonte during the late stages of the July 12 Busch Nashville 420 at the Fairgrounds Raceway. Earnhardt went on to win, beating Cale Yarborough in a fender-rubbing duel. Yarborough was making the decisive pass, but found himself bouncing off the wall after Earnhardt crowded him. "I had him," said Cale. "I made a clean pass but he ran me into the wall."

Donnie Allison leans out the window to guide his #12 Oldsmobile back to the pits after an engine failure in the Aug. 3 Talladega 500. Allison was the latest driver to take the controls of the Kennie Childers-owned car. Childers entered NASCAR racing in late 1978 and used seven drivers through the first two years. The others were Harry Gant, Neil Bonnett, Lennie Pond, Jack Ingram, Buck Simmons, and Butch Lindley.

Richard Petty was a threat in the points race until he broke his neck in a crash in the Coca-Cola 500 at Pocono International Raceway on July 27. Petty drove one lap a week later at Talladega before he was relieved by Joe Millikan. On Aug. 17, Petty finished fifth at Michigan, driving the entire distance. He was relieved by Millikan again in four more races, but often drove the distance. Despite his injuries, Petty held on to finish fourth in the final NASCAR Winston Cup Grand National points standings.

Rookie Jody Ridley loops his #90 Ford in the third turn during the Sept. 1 Southern 500 at Darlington. Buddy Arrington and Ralph Jones pass safely to the outside. Ridley competed in NASCAR Winston Cup Grand National racing on a part-time basis from 1973 to '79. In '80, he got a full-time ride with team owner Junie Donlavey and performed admirably, logging 18 top-10 finishes in 31 starts. For his impressive showing, Ridley was named the 1980 NASCAR Rookie of the Year.

Sophomore Terry Labonte waves to the crowd after scoring an upset victory in the 31st Southern 500. Labonte was running a distant fourth with three laps to go when leaders David Pearson, Dale Earnhardt, and Benny Parsons slid through a patch of oil deposited by Frank Warren, who had blown an engine. All three leaders were taken out of contention as Labonte tiptoed his way through the carnage. It was the young Texan's first career NASCAR Winston Cup Grand National win.

Dale Earnhardt

NOV. 5, 1978, was a pivotal day in Dale Earnhardt's stock car racing career. At the age of 27, Earnhardt had spent most of his weekends racing at short tracks for winner's purses of less than $1000. But on this day, the strapping son of the legendary Ralph Earnhardt was seated in a NASCAR Winston Cup Grand National car for only the ninth time. Through the generosity of several track promoters, Earnhardt had managed the occasional ride in NASCAR events. The one-shot deals had come in machinery that wasn't first rate, but the young man from Kannapolis, N.C., seemed to be able to get the most out of the inferior equipment.

On this particular day at Atlanta International Raceway, Earnhardt found himself buckled in the best car he had ever driven, a Chevrolet fielded by Osterlund Racing. The 1978 campaign was team owner Rod Osterlund's first full season in NASCAR Winston Cup Grand National racing. His regular driver, Dave Marcis, had challenged Cale Yarborough for the title earlier in the year. But toward the end of the season, Osterlund and Marcis were at odds. The wealthy sportsman from California made a public announcement that Marcis would be replaced in '79 by "an experienced driver." Obviously, that meant Earnhardt wouldn't get the assignment.

Earnhardt drove the Osterlund car for all it was worth in the 500-miler at Atlanta, finishing fourth after starting 10th. He didn't drive like a rookie. There were few, if any, frayed edges. Earnhardt made bold, crisp moves in traffic. Following the race, Osterlund commented that he was quite pleased with Earnhardt's efforts, but he was still looking for an accomplished veteran to take the controls for the 1979 season.

Over the winter months, Osterlund reconsidered and, against his convictions, hired Earnhardt to be the driver. Earnhardt went on to win the Rookie of the Year award in 1979, a season blessed with standout freshman drivers like Terry Labonte and Harry Gant. Earnhardt nearly won the Daytona 500 for Osterlund, losing due to a botched pit stop and questionable strategy. He still finished eighth. Earnhardt rebounded swiftly to win the Southeastern 500 at Bristol in only his 16th career NASCAR Winston Cup Grand National start. Despite missing four races due to an injury, he finished seventh in the final points standings.

In 1980, Earnhardt made history. He took the lead in the points standings shortly after the Daytona 500 and never relinquished his grip on first place. The young driver bagged his first superspeedway win at Atlanta in March, and scored four other wins during the season. Entering the season finale at Ontario Motor Speedway near Los Angeles, Earnhardt clung to a 29-point lead over hard-charging Cale Yarborough.

Early in the race, Earnhardt fell a lap off the pace when he cut a tire, forcing an unscheduled green-flag pit stop. A caution flag came out shortly after Earnhardt returned to

NASCAR Winston Cup Career Record 1975-2001
Starts: 676
Wins: 76
Top 5: 281
Top 10: 428
Poles: 22
Career Winnings:
$42,203,001

the track, trapping him a full lap behind the leaders. He was in danger of losing the championship in the final race of the year. Undaunted, Earnhardt whipped past his rivals one by one. He swept under them in the low-banked corners and stormed by others on the open straights. He slithered past race-leader Darrell Waltrip, caught a timely caution flag, and was back on the lead lap.

Earnhardt settled for a fifth-place finish as Yarborough came home third. The final margin in the NASCAR Winston Cup Grand National title race was 19 points—at the time the second closest title finish in NASCAR history. No other driver had won the Rookie of the Year award and the championship in back-to-back seasons. The Osterlund Racing team was in its third year of operation, and had captured the title with a sophomore driver and a rookie crew chief.

Earnhardt's meteoric rise to stardom was no flash in the pan. Within a year, he had hooked up with Richard Childress, who gave up the driver's seat to pursue his vision of becoming one of the top team owners in NASCAR. While the unit figuratively stubbed its toes in the beginning, by 1984 Earnhardt and Childress had become a formidable and cohesive unit. They were winning races regularly and always running near the front of the pack.

In 1986, Earnhardt won five races and his second championship. A year later, he thoroughly dominated the NASCAR Winston Cup season, winning 11 times and taking his third title by nearly 500 points. He went on to rack up championships in 1990, '91, '93, and '94, tying Richard Petty with seven titles. Always a hard charger, Earnhardt earned the nickname "The Intimidator" for his aggressive and sometimes bullying driving style.

Earnhardt's quest for a record eighth NASCAR Winston Cup title would never bear fruit. After enduring a bit of a slump in the late 1990s, Earnhardt appeared back at the top of his game by the turn of the century. He finished second in the 2000 NASCAR Winston Cup points standings and was eagerly awaiting the start of the 2001 campaign.

In the final laps of the 2001 Daytona 500, Earnhardt was running third behind Michael Waltrip and Dale Earnhardt, Jr., both of whom were seated in Chevrolets fielded by Dale Earnhardt, Inc. While protecting the third spot, Earnhardt made contact with the nose of Sterling Marlin's Dodge, and lost control. Earnhardt shot up the banking, was hit by Ken Schrader, and delivered a head-on shot into the concrete retaining barrier. While the crash didn't appear to be one of devastating consequences, the angle of the impact was such that it dealt a fatal blow to NASCAR's most popular icon.

The cause of Earnhardt's death sparked controversy, but NASCAR officials responded by tightening safety precautions. They required all competitors to wear the HANS device, a head and neck support collar designed to prevent sudden forward movement of a driver's head in the event of a frontal impact.

1980

The first turn at Martinsville Speedway is a mangled mess as nearly half the field is involved in a crash during the early laps of the Sept. 28 Old Dominion 500. The 500-lapper was punctuated with 17 caution flags—at that time, a NASCAR Winston Cup Grand National record. Dale Earnhardt won the race, taking the lead 12 laps from the finish when a flat tire dashed the hopes of Cale Yarborough.

Lake Speed keeps his #7 Chevrolet Monte Carlo running just ahead of #68 Lennie Pond and #16 Rusty Wallace in the Oct. 5 National 500 at Charlotte Motor Speedway. Speed, a rookie in NASCAR competition, came directly off the go-kart tracks onto the high-speed NASCAR Winston Cup Grand National tour. Speed recorded five top-10 finishes in 19 starts during the season.

Darrell Waltrip gets his #88 Chevy crossed up in front of #27 Benny Parsons in the National 500. Parsons was forced to call it a day after the wreck, while Waltrip was able to continue. Later, Waltrip's engine blew, and he settled for an 18th-place finish.

Number 75 Joe Millikan and #21 Neil Bonnett spin after hitting the wall in the Oct. 19 American 500 at North Carolina Motor Speedway. Neither driver was injured, but both cars were completely wiped out. The duo finished 24th and 25th, respectively, and Millikan went on to relieve Richard Petty, who finished 14th.

Four of the top five finishers in the championship points race were #2 Dale Earnhardt, #11 Cale Yarborough, #43 Richard Petty, and #88 Darrell Waltrip. Earnhardt won the 1979 Rookie of the Year award and followed it up with the coveted championship—the only driver to pull off that incredible feat. Earnhardt took the points lead in the second race of the season and never relinquished first place. He survived a late scare from Yarborough and won by a scant 19 points. Petty finished fourth and Waltrip fifth in the final tally.

1980 NASCAR WINSTON CUP GN POINTS RACE

Rank	Driver	Points	Starts	Wins	Top 5	Top 10	Winnings
1	Dale Earnhardt	4661	31	5	19	24	$671,990.40
2	Cale Yarborough	4642	31	6	19	22	$567,890.20
3	Benny Parsons	4278	31	3	16	21	$411,518.68
4	Richard Petty	4255	31	2	15	19	$397,317.16
5	Darrell Waltrip	4239	31	5	16	17	$405,710.64
6	Bobby Allison	4019	31	4	12	18	$378,969.12
7	Jody Ridley	3972	31	0	2	18	$204,882.60
8	Terry Labonte	3766	31	1	6	16	$222,501.08
9	Dave Marcis	3745	31	0	4	14	$150,164.04
10	Richard Childress	3742	31	0	0	10	$157,419.56
11	Harry Gant	3703	31	0	9	14	$177,149.56
12	Buddy Arrington	3461	31	0	0	7	$120,354.56
13	James Hylton	3449	31	0	0	4	$109,229.56
14	Ronnie Thomas	3066	30	0	0	5	$94,729.56
15	Cecil Gordon	2993	29	0	0	3	$83,299.78
16	J.D. McDuffie	2968	31	0	0	2	$82,401.52
17	Jimmy Means	2947	28	0	0	0	$105,627.60
18	Tommy Gale	2885	29	0	0	0	$84,278.04
19	Neil Bonnett	2865	22	2	10	13	$231,853.04
20	Roger Hamby	2606	26	0	0	0	$51,533.04
21	Buddy Baker	2603	19	2	9	11	$275,200.00
22	Lake Speed	1853	19	0	0	5	$69,670.00
23	Slick Johnson	1851	18	0	0	5	$35,460.00
24	John Anderson	1805	20	0	0	2	$48,265.00
25	Bobby Wawak	1742	19	0	0	1	$21,080.00
26	Donnie Allison	1730	18	0	3	6	$92,640.00
27	Dick Brooks	1698	19	0	2	5	$60,700.00
28	Kyle Petty	1690	15	0	0	6	$36,045.00
29	Baxter Price	1689	18	0	0	0	$26,615.00
30	Lennie Pond	1558	17	0	2	7	$62,265.00
31	Junior Miller	1402	16	0	0	0	$23,420.00
32	Dick May	1323	21	0	0	2	$42,945.00
33	Joe Millikan	1274	12	0	2	6	$74,765.00
34	Bill Elliott	1232	11	0	0	4	$42,545.00
35	Ricky Rudd	1213	13	0	1	3	$50,500.00
36	Bill Ellswick	1053	12	0	0	0	$15,600.00
37	David Pearson	1004	9	1	4	5	$102,730.00
38	D.K. Ulrich	935	11	0	0	1	$23,055.00
39	Tighe Scott	791	10	0	1	2	$21,925.00
40	Frank Warren	559	7	0	0	0	$18,375.00
41	Tim Richmond	527	5	0	0	0	$14,925.00
42	Bill Schmitt	503	4	0	1	1	$21,610.00
43	Buck Simmons	495	6	0	0	0	$6365.00
44	Rick Newsom	483	6	0	0	0	$3830.00
45	Dave Dion	441	4	0	0	1	$5015.00
46	Don Whittington	429	6	0	0	1	$17,610.00
47	Steve Moore	412	4	0	0	0	$9040.00
48	Tommy Houston	396	4	0	0	0	$5020.00
49	Sterling Marlin	387	5	0	0	2	$29,810.00
50	Bruce Hill	348	6	0	0	0	$7540.00

Dale Earnhardt took the championship points lead in the Daytona 500 and staved off challenges by Richard Petty and Cale Yarborough to capture the 1980 NASCAR Winston Cup Grand National title. Earnhardt became the first driver to win Rookie of the Year and championship honors in back-to-back seasons.

Petty was within 48 points of Earnhardt in late July, but he broke his neck in a crash at Pocono. Petty concealed the injury from NASCAR so he could continue racing. Relief drivers assisted Petty but he fell from contention.

Yarborough began his rally in September. He trailed by 173 points following the Richmond event, but then posted a series of top-10 finishes. Going into the season finale at Ontario, Calif., Earnhardt had a narrow 29-point lead.

Earnhardt fell a lap off the pace at Ontario, but muscled his way back onto the lead lap and scrambled to a fifth-place finish. The effort put him 19 points ahead of Yarborough, who took third at Ontario, and gave Earnhardt his first title.

1981

January 17 In light of new guidelines requiring the use of downsized cars (110-inch wheelbase vs. the older 115-inch wheelbase), Richard Petty tests a Dodge Mirada at Daytona. The car is unable to run competitive speeds, so Petty gives up any idea of returning to the Chrysler fold.

February 15 Richard Petty wins his record seventh Daytona 500. Petty's longtime crew chief Dale Inman quits two days later to accept a job with the Rod Osterlund/Dale Earnhardt team.

March 1 Darrell Waltrip drives the Junior Johnson Buick to win Rockingham's Carolina 500. Waltrip has won two of his first four starts with the highly regarded Johnson team.

April 5 Richard Petty outlasts Dave Marcis to score his 15th career win at North Wilkesboro Speedway. Marcis starts on the pole and leads 123 laps, but falls off the pace late when he runs out of tires.

April 26 Rookie Morgan Shepherd drives to an upset win in the Virginia 500 at Martinsville, giving the Pontiac nameplate its first NASCAR Winston Cup Grand National win since 1963.

May 3 Bobby Allison drives a Harry Ranier-owned Buick Regal to victory in the Winston 500 at Talladega for his second win of the season. The Ranier-Allison team was forced to switch from the Pontiac LeMans to the Buick when NASCAR rules changes made the LeMans uncompetitive.

May 17 Jody Ridley drives the Junie Donlavey Ford to a surprise win in the Mason-Dixon 500 at Dover. It is the first NASCAR Winston Cup Grand National win for Ridley and team owner Junie Donlavey, who has been fielding cars since 1950. Controversy erupts due to a "scoring communications difficulty" that may have taken the victory away from Bobby Allison.

June 7 Benny Parsons edges Dale Earnhardt to win at Texas World Speedway. Only 18,000 spectators turn out to watch the race at the financially troubled two-mile track.

Darrell Waltrip, in his first start for the Junior Johnson team, won the pole for the Jan. 11 season opener at Riverside and led the opening three laps in his Mountain Dew Chevrolet. Waltrip skidded off course on the fourth lap, and later had to make an extended pit stop to replace fouled spark plugs. He got back into the running and managed to finish 17th. Bobby Allison won the 500-kilometer event in a 1977 Chevy Monte Carlo to take an early lead in the NASCAR Winston Cup Grand National points standings. The race also marked the final appearance for full-size cars in NASCAR Winston Cup competition.

Buddy Baker, driving Hoss Ellington's #1 Oldsmobile, dices it out with Darrell Waltrip in the second Twin 125-mile qualifying race at Daytona on Feb. 12. Waltrip won the event by passing Benny Parsons on the apron near the finish line. The outcome was controversial because Parsons had to let up and move up the track or risk a multicar crash. Baker finished third. The Twin 125 featured a record 25 official lead changes, a mark that still stands today. There were four unofficial lead changes on the final lap alone.

▼ Bobby Allison and Darrell Waltrip occupy the front row at the start of the Feb. 15 Daytona 500. Allison's Ranier Racing Team brought a sleek Pontiac LeMans to Daytona, which proved to have a considerable aerodynamic advantage over virtually every other make of car in the field. Allison had the best car in the 23rd running of "The Great American Race" but finished second to Richard Petty, who prevailed thanks to superior pit stop strategy.

Richard Petty's #43 Buick chases the fleet #28 Pontiac LeMans of Bobby Allison in the Daytona 500. The King of stock car racing was seemingly out of the hunt late in the race, running a distant fifth with 25 laps remaining. Petty snookered the field, however, by making a splash-and-go stop during his final visit to the pits. Petty got back onto the track ahead of the leaders, all of whom took tires on their final pit stop. Petty, who was able to protect his advantage in the final laps, wheeled his #43 Buick to victory.

Dale Inman (right), a member of the Petty Enterprises team since the late 1950s, guided cousin Richard Petty to 193 NASCAR Winston Cup Grand National victories. Inman made the call that propelled King Richard to his seventh Daytona 500 win, then announced he was quitting the Petty team to join Rod Osterlund's operation with Dale Earnhardt. Inman became Earnhardt's mentor, but the team struggled in '81, failing to win a single race.

Team owner Hal Needham (left), Hollywood film star Burt Reynolds (center), and NASCAR driver Stan Barrett (right) pose with the #33 Skoal Bandit Pontiac prior to the March 15 Atlanta 500. Barrett, a land speed record holder, was tabbed by Needham to drive for the new Mach 1 Racing Team. Barrett finished 10th in the Daytona 500, despite crashing on the final lap, and ran 16th in the 500-miler at Atlanta. However, Barrett had difficulty getting acclimated to the heavy NASCAR Winston Cup Grand National machinery, and Harry Gant would replace him a month later.

Dale Earnhardt pits his Osterlund Racing/Wrangler Jeans Pontiac Grand Prix in the Daytona 500. Earnhardt, the defending NASCAR Winston Cup Grand National champion, ran with the lead pack the entire race and finished fifth. Earnhardt was one of the first to test the new downsized cars in shakedown runs prior to Daytona's Speedweeks. The smaller, boxy cars twitched considerably more than the full-size cars the teams ran in 1980. "I was nervous as hell in those tests," said Earnhardt. "These cars aren't stable enough to run in a pack."

1981

June 21 Bobby Allison rockets from seventh to first on the final green-flag lap to win at Michigan International Speedway. Ten cars were involved in the final dash when Kyle Petty blew an engine, oiling down the second turn. The lead cars spun out, but Allison snaked his way through the carnage.

July 11 Darrell Waltrip dominates the Busch Nashville 420 at the Fairgrounds Raceway. Mark Martin starts on the pole in his third NASCAR Winston Cup Grand National start and finishes 11th.

August 2 Rookie Ron Bouchard passes Darrell Waltrip and Terry Labonte in the final stretch to win the Talladega 500. The lead cars finish three-abreast as Bouchard wins in his 11th career start.

August 16 Richard Petty leads a pack of seven cars to the finish line to win at Michigan. Dale Earnhardt, in his first start with the Richard Childress team, finishes ninth.

September 20 Neil Bonnett wins at Dover as runner-up Darrell Waltrip takes a narrow lead in the championship points chase.

November 22 Bobby Allison wins the season finale at Riverside as Darrell Waltrip's sixth-place finish clinches his first NASCAR Winston Cup Grand National championship.

Darrell Waltrip's #11 Mountain Dew Buick battles with David Pearson's #16 Chevrolet in a 1981 NASCAR Winston Cup Grand National event. Pearson hooked up with a new team owned by wealthy sportsman Joel Halpern for the '81 campaign. Well-funded but lightly sponsored, the Pearson-Halpern team showed flashes of brilliance but inconsistency in the early part of the season. In March, Halpern was fatally injured in a boating accident near New Orleans. The team disbanded shortly thereafter, once again leaving Pearson without a full-time ride.

Bill Elliott sits in his #9 Ford awaiting the start of the April 12 CRC Chemicals Rebel 500 at Darlington. Elliott, a small-time independent with limited funding from Harry Melling, earned his first career pole on the tricky Darlington track. He led the opening 11 laps and finished a strong fourth in the race.

A pack of cars rumble out of Darlington Raceway's second turn and motor down the backstretch during the Rebel 500. Darlington's backstretch grandstands featured an elevated but narrow skybox arrangement, which afforded a splendid view but was eerily unstable in high winds.

Cecil Gordon, the original "Flash Gordon" to drive a #24 on NASCAR's top tour, leads a tightly knit pack of cars through Darlington's treacherous fourth turn. Number 16 David Pearson, #25 Ronnie Thomas, and #67 Buddy Arrington are also pictured. Gordon competed in 450 NASCAR Winston Cup Grand National events from 1968 to '85, logging 111 top-10 finishes. He finished third in the final points standings in '71 and '73.

Darrell Waltrip lounges on the hood of his #11 Mountain Dew Buick after winning the Rebel 500 at Darlington. Waltrip was in his first season with Junior Johnson and the Mountain Dew sponsorship. Waltrip resolved an acrimonious relationship with the DiGard team at the end of the 1980 season by buying out his contract. He signed with Johnson a few days later, saying, driving for Johnson was "a dream come true. When I was a little feller and started following races in the papers and on the radio, Junior was still driving. He was my hero."

Morgan Shepherd, a 39-year-old rookie driver in NASCAR Winston Cup Grand National competition, startled the veterans with an overwhelming triumph in the April 26 Virginia 500 at Martinsville Speedway. The short-track icon, who had set up chassis and done mechanical work for the Cliff Stewart-owned #5 Pontiac, scored his first win in his 16th career big-league start. The victory was also Pontiac's first at NASCAR's highest level since Oct. 27, 1963, when Joe Weatherly won at Hillsboro.

▼ Buddy Baker, in the #1 Oldsmobile, leads #33 Harry Gant, #11 Darrell Waltrip, #50 Bruce Hill, and #27 Cale Yarborough during the May 24 World 600 at Charlotte Motor Speedway. Gant began the '81 season with Roger Hamby, switched to the Race Hill Farms team owned by Jack Beebe, then settled into the seat of the Skoal Bandit ride owned by Hollywood stunt driver and film producer Hal Needham. Gant became one of the most popular pilots in NASCAR, but sour luck hounded him throughout the season.

1981

Richard Petty began the 1981 season with a big victory in the Daytona 500. After the race, he lost crew chief Dale Inman, who was paid a king's ransom to move to Dale Earnhardt's team. With the loss of chemistry provided by Inman, Petty struggled for the remainder of the season. He won three races, a decent number but below The King's expectations, and placed a disappointing eighth in the final points standings. Here, he is shown pitting at Riverside's Warner W. Hodgdon 400 on June 14. He finished third in the race, after being passed by eventual winner Darrell Waltrip with three laps to go.

▼ Tim Richmond, at the wheel of Kennie Childers' #12 Buick, races Richard Petty through a turn during the July 4 Daytona Firecracker 400. Richmond was a whiz in USAC Indy Car competition, winning the Indy 500 Rookie of the Year prize in 1980. Later that year, he made his NASCAR Winston Cup Grand National debut, then became a candidate for Rookie of the Year in '81. In the July 4 Firecracker 400 at Daytona, Richmond finished 15th. Over the course of the year, Richmond logged six top-10 finishes, but finished behind Ron Bouchard and Morgan Shepherd in the Rookie of the Year standings.

Number 28 Bobby Allison pairs up with #27 Cale Yarborough in a frantic battle for the lead in the Firecracker 400. Yarborough went on to win in the M.C. Anderson/Valvoline Buick. Allison, whose Ranier Racing team picked up the Hardee's sponsorship in May, fell victim to engine problems in the 400-miler and finished 28th. By this time, the Ranier team had given up on the Pontiac LeMans, which was made less competitive in March when NASCAR instituted a spoiler height rule for only that make and model of car. Allison had been the only driver piloting a LeMans.

The infield of any NASCAR race has always taken on a lively and interesting culture of its own. Here, fans show their colors during the Aug. 2 Talladega 500 at the rural Alabama International Motor Speedway. A rambunctious trackside audience of 75,000 witnessed a terrific duel between Darrell Waltrip, Terry Labonte, and Ron Bouchard. Unfortunately for this U-Haul contingent, Waltrip lost in a last-lap duel, and Dale Earnhardt finished a disappointing 29th after losing the transmission in his J.D. Stacy-owned #2 Pontiac Grand Prix.

Freshman driver Ron Bouchard snookered Darrell Waltrip and Terry Labonte on the final lap of the Talladega 500 to provide one of NASCAR's biggest upsets in spectacular fashion. Waltrip led entering the final lap and faded high off the fourth turn to deflect Labonte's charge on the high side. Bouchard, making only his 11th NASCAR Winston Cup Grand National start, shot into the open lane to the inside and won by a bumper in a three-abreast finish.

Last-Lap Passes

THE 1981 NASCAR Winston Cup Grand National season produced the most races determined by a last-lap pass in history. Five races were settled by a driver making the decisive pass on the final lap.

In the course of NASCAR Cup Series racing (through 2007), a total of 81 races came down to a battle of nerve and skill in the final lap. Richard Petty was involved in the most last-lap skirmishes, winning six times and losing eight races in which the lead changed while he was the leader entering the final lap. Cale Yarborough owned the best record in last-lap passes during that period, winning seven times while never losing. Other prominent NASCAR heroes who were involved in multiple last-lap decisions include Dale Earnhardt (won four and lost eight), Darrell Waltrip (6-5), David Pearson (3-4), and Buddy Baker (0-5).

The following list details the NASCAR Cup Series events through 2007 in which the winner overtook another driver who was leading entering the final lap.

NASCAR CUP SERIES RACES SETTLED BY A LAST-LAP PASS THROUGH 2007*
* A cumulative win-loss record is provided for each driver in races determined by a last-lap pass.

No.	Date	Site	Miles	Winning Driver	Losing Driver
1	2/15/53	Daytona Beach, Fla.	160	Bill Blair (1-0)	Fonty Flock (0-1)
2	7/26/53	North Platte, Neb.	100	Dick Rathmann (1-0)	Herb Thomas (0-1)
3	9/23/56	Portland, Ore.	125	Lloyd Dane (1-0)	Curley Barker (0-1)
4	11/18/56	Wilson, N.C.	100	Buck Baker (1-0)	Joe Weatherly (0-1)
5	9/15/57	Martinsville, Va.	220.5	Buck Baker (2-0)	Billy Myers (0-1)
6	6/29/57	Spartanburg, S.C.	93.5	Lee Petty (1-0)	Buck Baker (2-1)
7	3/1/59	Hillsboro, N.C.	99	Curtis Turner (1-0)	Bob Welborn (0-1)
8	2/24/61	Daytona Beach, Fla.	100	Joe Weatherly (1-1)	Banjo Matthews (0-1)
9	9/17/61	Atlanta, Ga.	400	David Pearson (1-0)	Junior Johnson (0-1)
10	11/5/61	Concord, N.C.	100	Jack Smith (1-0)	Joe Weatherly (1-2)
11	8/4/63	Darlington, S.C.	151.25	Joe Weatherly (2-2)	Junior Johnson (0-2)
12	7/4/63	Daytona Beach, Fla.	400	Fireball Roberts (1-0)	Fred Lorenzen (0-1)
13	2/21/64	Daytona Beach, Fla.	100	Junior Johnson (1-1)	Buck Baker (2-2)
14	2/21/64	Daytona Beach, Fla.	100	Bobby Isaac (1-0)	Richard Petty (0-1)
15	7/7/64	Daytona Beach, Fla.	400	A.J. Foyt (1-0)	Bobby Isaac (1-1)
16	7/24/64	Bristol, Tenn.	250	Fred Lorenzen (1-1)	Richard Petty (0-2)
17	2/12/65	Daytona Beach, Fla.	100	Junior Johnson (2-2)	Fred Lorenzen (1-2)
18	2/25/66	Daytona Beach, Fla.	100	Paul Goldsmith (1-0)	Richard Petty (0-3)
19	2/25/66	Daytona Beach, Fla.	100	Earl Balmer (1-0)	Dick Hutcherson (0-1)
20	6/12/66	Weaverville, N.C.	150	Richard Petty (1-3)	David Pearson (1-1)
21	7/4/67	Daytona Beach, Fla.	400	Cale Yarborough (1-0)	Dick Hutcherson (0-2)
22	12/8/68	Montgomery, Ala.	100	Bobby Allison (1-0)	Richard Petty (1-4)
23	2/23/69	Daytona Beach, Fla.	500	LeeRoy Yarbrough (1-0)	Charlie Glotzbach (0-1)
24	9/1/69	Darlington, S.C.	316.25	LeeRoy Yarbrough (2-0)	David Pearson (1-2)
25	2/11/71	Daytona Beach, Fla.	125	Pete Hamilton (1-0)	A.J. Foyt (1-1)
26	10/1/72	N.Wilkesboro, N.C.	250	Richard Petty (2-4)	Bobby Allison (1-1)
27	9/23/73	N.Wilkesboro, N.C.	250	Bobby Allison (2-1)	Richard Petty (2-5)
28	7/14/74	Bristol, Tenn.	250	Cale Yarborough (2-0)	Buddy Baker (0-1)
29	8/11/74	Talladega, Ala.	500	Richard Petty (3-5)	David Pearson (1-3)
30	8/24/75	Brooklyn, Mich.	400	Richard Petty (4-5)	David Pearson (1-4)
31	2/15/76	Daytona Beach, Fla.	500	David Pearson (2-4)	Richard Petty (4-6)
32	11/6/77	Atlanta, Ga.	408	Darrell Waltrip (1-0)	Donnie Allison (0-1)
33	5/14/78	Talladega, Ala.	500	Cale Yarborough (3-0)	Buddy Baker (0-2)
34	8/20/78	Brooklyn, Mich.	400	David Pearson (3-4)	Darrell Waltrip (1-1)
35	2/18/79	Daytona Beach, Fla.	500	Richard Petty (5-6)	Donnie Allison (0-2)
36	4/8/79	Darlington, S.C.	500	Darrell Waltrip (2-1)	Richard Petty (5-7)
37	8/19/79	Brooklyn, Mich.	400	Richard Petty (6-7)	Buddy Baker (0-3)
38	6/8/80	Riverside, Calif.	248.9	Darrell Waltrip (3-1)	Neil Bonnett (0-1)
39	5/3/81	Talladega, Ala.	500	Bobby Allison (3-1)	Buddy Baker (0-4)
40	7/4/81	Daytona Beach, Fla.	400	Cale Yarborough (4-0)	Harry Gant (0-1)
41	7/6/81	Pocono, Penn.	500	Darrell Waltrip (4-1)	Richard Petty (6-8)
42	8/2/81	Talladega, Ala.	500	Ron Bouchard (1-0)	Darrell Waltrip (4-2)
43	11/8/81	Atlanta, Ga.	500	Neil Bonnett (1-1)	Darrell Waltrip (4-3)
44	5/2/82	Talladega, Ala.	500	Darrell Waltrip (5-3)	Benny Parsons (0-1)
45	2/20/83	Daytona Beach, Fla.	500	Cale Yarborough (5-0)	Buddy Baker (0-5)
46	7/31/83	Talladega, Ala.	500	Dale Earnhardt (1-0)	Darrell Waltrip (5-4)
47	2/9/84	Daytona Beach, Fla.	500	Cale Yarborough (6-0)	Darrell Waltrip (5-5)
48	5/6/84	Talladega, Ala.	500	Cale Yarborough (7-0)	Harry Gant (0-2)
49	7/29/84	Talladega, Ala.	500	Dale Earnhardt (2-0)	Terry Labonte (0-1)
50	10/21/84	Rockingham, N.C.	500	Bill Elliott (1-0)	Harry Gant (0-3)
51	3/3/85	Rockingham, N.C.	500	Neil Bonnett (2-1)	Harry Gant (0-4)
52	7/20/86	Pocono, Penn.	375	Tim Richmond (1-0)	Geoff Bodine (0-1)
53	3/29/87	Darlington, S.C.	500	Dale Earnhardt (3-0)	Bill Elliott (1-1)
54	9/27/87	Martinsville, Va.	262.5	Darrell Waltrip (6-5)	Dale Earnhardt (3-1)
55	7/31/88	Talladega, Ala.	500	Ken Schrader (1-0)	Dale Earnhardt (3-2)
56	10/15/89	N.Wilkesboro, N.C.	250	Geoff Bodine (1-1)	Dale Earnhardt (3-3)
57	2/18/90	Daytona Beach, Fla.	500	Derrike Cope (1-0)	Dale Earnhardt (3-4)
58	6/9/91	Sears Point, Calif.	186.48	Davey Allison (1-0)	Ricky Rudd (0-1)
59	8/18/91	Brooklyn, Mich.	400	Dale Jarrett (1-0)	Davey Allison (1-1)
60	2/14/93	Daytona Beach, Fla.	500	Dale Jarrett (2-0)	Dale Earnhardt (3-5)
61	5/2/93	Talladega, Ala.	500	Ernie Irvan (1-0)	Dale Earnhardt (3-6)
62	6/12/94	Pocono, Penn.	500	Rusty Wallace (1-0)	Dale Earnhardt (3-7)
63	7/2/94	Daytona Beach, Fla.	400	Jimmy Spencer (1-0)	Ernie Irvan (1-1)
64	4/13/97	Bristol, Tenn.	266.5	Jeff Gordon (1-0)	Rusty Wallace (1-1)
65	8/28/99	Bristol, Tenn.	266.5	Dale Earnhardt (4-7)	Terry Labonte (0-2)
66	6/19/00	Pocono, Penn.	500	Jeremy Mayfield (1-0)	Dale Earnhardt (4-8)
67	7/23/00	Pocono, Penn.	500	Rusty Wallace (2-1)	Jeremy Mayfield (1-1)
68	6/10/01	Brooklyn, Mich.	400	Jeff Gordon (2-0)	Ricky Rudd (0-2)
69	10/21/01	Talladega, Ala.	500	Dale Earnhardt, Jr. (1-0)	Bobby Labonte (0-1)
70	11/18/01	Atlanta, Ga.	500	Bobby Labonte (1-1)	Jerry Nadeau (0-1)
71	3/16/03	Darlington, S.C.	400	Ricky Craven (1-0)	Kurt Busch (0-1)
72	11/16/03	Homestead, Fla.	400	Bobby Labonte (2-1)	Bill Elliott (1-2)
73	3/20/05	Atlanta, Ga.	500	Carl Edwards (1-0)	Jimmie Johnson (0-1)
74	5/29/05	Charlotte, N.C.	600	Jimmie Johnson (1-1)	Bobby Labonte (2-2)
75	10/2/05	Talladega, Ala.	500	Dale Jarrett (3-0)	Tony Stewart (0-1)
76	3/12/06	Las Vegas, Nev.	400	Jimmie Johnson (2-1)	Matt Kenseth (0-1)
77	10/8/06	Talladega, Ala.	500	Brian Vickers (1-0)	Dale Earnhardt, Jr. (1-1)
78	2/18/07	Daytona Beach, Fla.	500	Kevin Harvick (1-0)	Mark Martin (0-1)
79	4/15/07	Fort Worth, Tex.	500	Jeff Burton (1-0)	Matt Kenseth (0-2)
80	7/7/07	Daytona Beach, Fla.	400	Jamie McMurray (1-0)	Kyle Busch (0-1)
81	10/7/07	Talladega, Ala.	500	Jeff Gordon (3-0)	Jimmie Johnson (2-2)

1981

The 1981 season was a tumultuous and stressful campaign for defending NASCAR Winston Cup Grand National champion Dale Earnhardt. Rod Osterlund suddenly sold the team to the mysterious and somewhat shady J.D. Stacy in May, a move that stunned the racing community. By August, Earnhardt had quit Stacy's team and joined the Richard Childress operation. Earnhardt took the Wrangler sponsorship to Childress' #3 Pontiac team, while Joe Ruttman replaced Earnhardt in the J.D. Stacy #2 Pontiac.

Harry Gant powers his #33 Pontiac around #28 Bobby Allison in the middle stages of the Sept. 27 Old Dominion 500 at Martinsville Speedway in Virginia. Gant came close to grabbing his first NASCAR Winston Cup Grand National win, running a close second to winner Darrell Waltrip. Gant was running first and appeared to be headed for victory until a flat tire deflated his bid 30 laps shy of the finish line. Allison finished 10th in the #28 Buick.

Darrell Waltrip and Ricky Rudd battle side-by-side during the Oct. 11 National 500 at Charlotte Motor Speedway. When Waltrip departed the DiGard ride in favor of the coveted Junior Johnson team, Rudd slipped into the controls of the #88 DiGard/Gatorade Chevrolet. Waltrip won 12 times and recorded his first NASCAR Winston Cup Grand National championship, while Rudd finished sixth in the standings.

Tim Richmond's #37 Buick careens down the banking after clobbering the wall in the Nov. 1 American 500 at North Carolina Speedway in Rockingham. Richmond's accident brought out one of the 12 caution flags that consumed 97 of the 492 laps. The caution flag was out so frequently that winner Darrell Waltrip only averaged 107 mph in the 500-miler.

Boyish Ricky Rudd was selected by DiGard president Bill Gardner to replace Darrell Waltrip in the highly regarded #88 DiGard Racing/Gatorade Buick. Rudd only drove for the DiGard team for one season. He was released after the '81 campaign and replaced by Bobby Allison. Rudd went to the Richard Childress team in '82. Rudd failed to record a win in '81, but did manage 17 top-10 finishes in 31 starts.

Bobby Allison drove three different makes of cars in 1981: Buick, Chevrolet, and Pontiac. His Harry Ranier-owned team had a couple of different sponsors before landing the Hardee's fast-food restaurant chain as a major backer. Allison led the points standings most of the year, but was overtaken by Darrell Waltrip late in the season. It was a bitter pill to swallow for Allison, who lost the grip of a once secure 341-point lead.

1981 NASCAR WINSTON CUP GN POINTS RACE

Rank	Driver	Points	Starts	Wins	Top 5	Top 10	Winnings
1	Darrell Waltrip	4880	31	12	21	25	$799,134.00
2	Bobby Allison	4827	31	5	21	26	$680,957.00
3	Harry Gant	4210	31	0	13	18	$280,047.60
4	Terry Labonte	4052	31	0	8	17	$348,702.84
5	Jody Ridley	4002	31	1	3	18	$267,604.80
6	Ricky Rudd	3988	31	0	14	17	$395,684.00
7	Dale Earnhardt	3975	31	0	9	17	$353,971.40
8	Richard Petty	3880	31	3	12	16	$396,071.80
9	Dave Marcis	3507	31	0	4	9	$162,212.60
10	Benny Parsons	3449	31	3	10	12	$311,092.60
11	Buddy Arrington	3381	31	0	0	7	$133,927.60
12	Kyle Petty	3335	31	0	1	10	$117,432.60
13	Morgan Shepherd	3261	29	1	3	10	$170,472.60
14	Jimmy Means	3142	30	0	0	2	$105,627.60
15	Tommy Gale	3140	30	0	0	0	$110,517.60
16	Tim Richmond	3091	29	0	0	6	$96,448.00
17	J. D. McDuffie	2996	28	0	0	1	$105,498.40
18	Lake Speed	2817	27	0	0	0	$94,068.40
19	James Hylton	2753	28	0	0	0	$87,304.20
20	Joe Millikan	2682	23	0	3	10	$148,399.20
21	Ron Bouchard	2594	22	1	5	12	$152,855.00
22	Neil Bonnett	2449	22	3	7	8	$181,670.00
23	Cecil Gordon	2320	25	0	0	0	$55,980.00
24	Cale Yarborough	2201	18	2	6	10	$150,840.00
25	Richard Childress	2144	21	0	1	1	$71,125.00
26	Ronnie Thomas	2138	23	0	0	0	$53,605.00
27	Buddy Baker	1904	16	0	6	9	$115,095.00
28	Joe Ruttman	1851	17	0	2	7	$137,275.00
29	Mike Alexander	1784	19	0	0	3	$34,055.00
30	Bill Elliott	1442	13	0	1	7	$70,320.00
31	Bobby Wawak	1212	14	0	0	1	$21,790.00
32	D. K. Ulrich	1191	15	0	1	1	$38,095.00
33	Johnny Rutherford	1140	12	0	1	2	$38,095.00
34	Lennie Pond	1100	12	0	0	0	$29,045.00
35	Elliott Forbes-Robinson	1020	11	0	0	3	$27,350.00
36	Rick Newsom	768	9	0	0	0	$8625.00
37	Dick May	754	9	0	0	1	$26,380.00
38	Stan Barrett	718	10	0	0	1	$28,540.00
39	Connie Saylor	664	7	0	0	0	$18,780.00
40	Gary Balough	656	10	0	0	1	$34,430.00
41	Rick Wilson	639	8	0	0	0	$15,625.00
42	Mark Martin	615	5	0	1	2	$13,950.00
43	Bruce Hill	596	8	0	0	0	$15,485.00
44	Donnie Allison	527	6	0	1	1	$38,745.00
45	Geoff Bodine	420	5	0	0	1	$15,000.00
46	Joe Fields	418	6	0	0	0	$7750.00
47	Jack Ingram	377	5	0	0	1	$9965.00
48	Randy Ogden	367	4	0	0	0	$3905.00
49	Jim Robinson	351	3	0	0	2	$9505.00
50	Don Waterman	351	3	0	0	0	$8570.00

Darrell Waltrip rallied from a 341-point deficit to bag his first NASCAR Winston Cup Grand National championship in 1981, as Bobby Allison finished second for the fourth time in his career.

Waltrip was seemingly out of the title hunt in early June, but he began to whittle away at Allison's lead with a series of top-five finishes. With six races to go, Waltrip moved into the points lead with a runner-up finish at Dover. In the final six races, Waltrip extended his lead and finished 53 points ahead of Allison.

Waltrip won 12 races during the 1981 season, while Allison won five times. No one else was close in the points race. Harry Gant finished third, 670 points behind Waltrip, and failed to record a single victory. Terry Labonte and Jody Ridley rounded out the top-five finishers.

1982

February 14 Bobby Allison blisters the field to win his second Daytona 500. Allison's #88 DiGard Buick finishes a half-lap ahead of runner-up Cale Yarborough.

February 21 Dave Marcis stays on the track as rain begins to fall at Richmond Fairgrounds Raceway and is the surprise winner when NASCAR officials call the race after 250 of the 400 laps have been run. Marcis is the only driver on the lead lap not to pit during the rain shower.

April 4 Dale Earnhardt ends an 18-month famine with a victory in the Rebel 500 at Darlington Raceway. It is Earnhardt's first career win in a Ford. Cale Yarborough finishes second.

April 25 Harry Gant, a bridesmaid for his entire career, finally hits the jackpot by winning the Virginia National Band 500 at Martinsville. Gant finishes a lap in front of runner-up Butch Lindley to score his first win in his 107th start.

May 2 Darrell Waltrip passes Benny Parsons on the final lap and wins the Winston 500 at Talladega. Parsons starts on the pole with a record 200.176 mph qualifying lap, the first time in history a lap of 200 mph is surpassed in official qualifications.

May 30 Neil Bonnett races around Bill Elliott with 13 laps remaining and scores a narrow victory in Charlotte Motor Speedway's World 600. It is Bonnett's 11th career NASCAR Winston Cup Grand National win.

June 13 Tim Richmond drives a Buick to his first career NASCAR Winston Cup Grand National victory in the 400-kilometer event at Riverside International Raceway.

July 25 Bobby Allison outduels Darrell Waltrip in the final laps of the Mountain Dew 500 at Pocono for his fifth win of the season. Dale Earnhardt survives a tumble on the 136th lap after tangling with Tim Richmond.

Ron Bouchard spins and narrowly avoids clipping the rear of #21 Neil Bonnett during the final lap of the second Twin 125-mile qualifying race at Daytona International Speedway on Feb. 11. Bouchard miraculously came out of the slide unscathed and finished 11th. Bonnett went on to finish seventh.

Pole-sitter #28 Benny Parsons is flanked by #33 Harry Gant at the start of the Feb. 14 Daytona 500. Parsons, taking his first ride with the Ranier Racing Team, earned the pole at 196.317 mph. Parsons never led in the race and was wiped out in a crash on lap 105. Gant finished seventh.

Buddy Arrington whips his #67 Dodge to the high side as he passes rookie #17 Lowell Cowell during the Daytona 500. Arrington, who drove Chrysler products since he came to NASCAR racing in 1964, was one of the last competitors to remain in the MoPar camp in the early '80s. By '82, virtually all of the Chrysler teams had shifted to General Motors products. Arrington finished 15th in the Daytona 500, just behind Cowell, who ran 14th in Roger Hamby's Buick.

Joe Millikan loses the grip on his #50 Pontiac in front of #71 Dave Marcis during the Feb. 21 Richmond 400 at the Richmond Fairgrounds Raceway. Both drivers continued in the race with Marcis scoring a popular upset triumph. Marcis was running sixth when Joe Ruttman's spin brought out a caution flag. With rain clouds hovering close to the ½-mile track, Marcis was the only driver on the lead lap to bypass a pit stop. He was in front when a cloudburst halted the race after 250 of the scheduled 400 laps.

Number 42 Kyle Petty and #71 Dave Marcis spin out after snagging bumpers in the March 28 Carolina 500 at Rockingham. Ron Bouchard sneaks past safely in his #47 Buick. None of the three drivers were running at the finish of the race as half the field departed with mechanical problems or wrecks. Cale Yarborough hung on to post the 72nd win of his career in the slugfest.

Darrell Waltrip cuts his #11 Buick under #2 Tim Richmond in the April 4 CRC Chemicals Rebel 500 at Darlington Raceway. The flamboyant Richmond was making his first start with the J.D. Stacy-owned team after replacing Joe Ruttman. Richmond might have won the race, but lost a lap when a tire went flat. He made up the lap and was running fourth when the race ended. However, Richmond forgot to complete the final lap and dropped to fifth in the final order.

Dale Earnhardt, winless since his sophomore season of 1980, drove Bud Moore's boxy Ford Thunderbird to victory in the spring race at Darlington Raceway. Earnhardt nosed out Cale Yarborough by three feet in a thrilling finish to end a 39-race winless void. Earnhardt settled in with Moore's Ford team in '82, having labored through a winless '81 campaign while driving for three different team owners.

August 1 Darrell Waltrip becomes the first driver to win the Talladega 500 twice. Entering the race, 13 different drivers had won the 13 previous runnings of the midsummer classic at the world's fastest speedway.

September 6 Cale Yarborough edges Richard Petty and Dale Earnhardt to score his record-setting fifth triumph in Darlington's Southern 500. Yarborough has driven four different makes of cars in his Southern 500 wins: Mercury, Chevrolet, Oldsmobile, and Buick.

October 10 Harry Gant gallops past Bill Elliott with five laps to go and racks up his first superspeedway victory in Charlotte's National 500. Bobby Allison's engine failure with 10 laps remaining sets up a late-race dash. Gant finishes 2.93 seconds ahead of Elliott when the checkered flag falls.

October 17 Darrell Waltrip wins the Old Dominion 500 at Martinsville and takes the championship points lead. Bobby Allison suffers an engine failure for the second straight race and trails Waltrip by 37 points in the chase for the NASCAR Winston Cup Grand National title.

November 21 Tim Richmond outruns Ricky Rudd in the final laps to win the season finale at Riverside. Darrell Waltrip finishes third and captures his second straight NASCAR Winston Cup Grand National championship by 72 points over Bobby Allison.

> "Where I came from there were only three choices in life—you could coal mine, moonshine, or move on down the line."
>
> —J.D. Stacy

Harry Melling, a Michigan industrialist, bought the #9 Ford from the Elliott family at the beginning of the 1982 NASCAR Winston Cup Grand National season. The homespun Elliott operation had performed admirably with a shortage of sponsorship, but was facing a shutdown if operating funds couldn't be located. Melling rescued the team and gave Bill Elliott an opportunity to display his talents. Elliott ran a strong third in the April Rebel 500 (shown).

Darrell Waltrip, in the #11 Mountain Dew Buick, prepares to put a lap on #88 Bobby Allison in the April 18 Northwestern Bank 400 at North Wilkesboro Speedway. Waltrip started on the pole and led 345 of the 400 laps in a dominating performance. Allison eventually finished eighth. Harry Gant drove the #33 Buick to a sixth-place finish after starting on the front row.

Number 90 Jody Ridley and #28 Benny Parsons, both sponsored by coal-mining magnate J.D. Stacy, battled #15 Dale Earnhardt and #88 Bobby Allison in the May 2 Winston 500 at Talladega. Stacy sponsored up to seven cars in 1982, including his own team. Parsons pushed the Ranier Racing #28 past 200 mph in qualifying, making him the first man to officially eclipse the 200-mph barrier in time trials for a NASCAR Winston Cup Grand National race. Parsons won the pole at 200.176 mph and led entering the final lap, but finished third after he was passed by Darrell Waltrip and Terry Labonte.

Darrell Waltrip follows the pace car during a caution period in the May 8 Cracker Barrel Country Store 420 at the Nashville Fairgrounds Raceway. Waltrip led 419 of the 420 laps on the banked short track, losing the lead only when he made a routine pit stop. Despite winning four of the first 10 races in the 1982 NASCAR Winston Cup Grand National season, Waltrip trailed winless leader Terry Labonte by 60 points in the title hunt.

◄ Harry Gant drove the #33 Skoal Bandit Buick to his first NASCAR Winston Cup Grand National win in the May 24 Virginia National Bank 500 at Martinsville Speedway. Gant had finished second 10 times before in 106 starts, but never first. After the race, the unassuming Taylorsville, N.C., driver said, "We just got some good luck today. You have to have luck to win a race." Gant was indeed lucky to avoid a major mishap as the race featured nine caution flags. Only 14 of the 31 cars that started were running at the finish.

► Tim Richmond's #2 Buick rests on pit road prior to the start of the May 30 World 600 at Charlotte Motor Speedway. Richmond's car was decorated with mock sponsorship from Clyde Torkle's Chicken Pit for the 1983 film release *Stroker Ace*. Unfortunately, Richmond crashed early, so little footage of the car in action could be used for the film. In the film, which starred Burt Reynolds (right), Loni Anderson (center), Jim Nabors (left), and Ned Beatty, cocky driver Stroker Ace does everything he can to get out of the promotional contract he unknowingly signed with a greedy fried chicken magnate.

▼ The two-mile Michigan International Raceway once produced some of the most spine-tingling excitement ever seen in NASCAR big-league racing. Before radial tires and aerodynamic enhancements, cars could race five-wide on the spacious track. Pictured in this electrifying June 20 battle during the Gabriel 400 are #98 Morgan Shepherd, #27 Cale Yarborough, #2 Tim Richmond, #15 Dale Earnhardt, #33 Harry Gant, #88 Bobby Allison, #11 Darrell Waltrip, #21 Neil Bonnett, and #28 Buddy Baker. Baker was taking his first ride in the Ranier Racing Pontiac.

Terry Labonte keeps his #44 Buick just ahead of #27 Cale Yarborough and #88 Bobby Allison in the Gabriel 400. Labonte entered the race in first place in the championship points standings, but his Billy Hagan-owned team had just lost its sponsorship from J.D. Stacy. Stacy claimed Labonte wasn't aggressive enough. Stacy also yanked sponsorship from Dave Marcis' team two weeks earlier when Marcis played a good samaritan role in pushing a fuel-starved Bobby Allison back to the pits at Pocono.

Number 33 Harry Gant slides into the infield grass as #43 Richard Petty bounces off the wall in a 136th-lap crash during the July 4 Daytona Firecracker 400. The accident was triggered when Tim Richmond tagged the rear of Gant's car, which hit the wall and went airborne. Petty slowed to avoid the incident, but was drop-kicked by rookie Geoff Bodine, a native of New York state. A week or so later, Petty showed up at a race with a bumper sticker that read "Save the South—Teach a Yankee how to drive."

Darrell Waltrip

DARRELL WALTRIP WAS one of short-track racing's flashiest speed artists during his ascent from weekly bullrings to the glamorous stage of NASCAR Winston Cup Grand National racing. Armed with a positive attitude, supreme self-confidence, and some of the finest machinery in the weekly short track wars in the Tennessee-Kentucky area, Waltrip established an enviable portfolio in the late 1960s and early '70s.

Waltrip made a few appearances in the Midwestern-based Automobile Racing Club of America, winning twice. He whipped the invading United States Auto Club headliners in a highly publicized race at Nashville Fairgrounds Raceway in 1972, an event that got plenty of play in national racing publications. Waltrip beat a field that included big names such as Bobby and Al Unser, Gordon Johncock, Butch Hartman, Roger McCluskey, Ramo Stott, and Jack Bowsher. Afterward, Waltrip fired a few verbal jabs at the USAC jet set, reminding everyone that he was headed to the top.

In 1973, Waltrip joined the NASCAR Winston Cup Grand National tour full time and actively campaigned for the Rookie of the Year award. Despite finishing second at Texas

Darrell Waltrip and Junior Johnson

and grabbing a significant number of headlines, NASCAR selected Lennie Pond as its top rookie. Waltrip fired several verbal darts at NASCAR after the controversial decision. It wouldn't be the first time DW would lash out when he felt he was wronged.

In a matter of months, Waltrip gained the reputation of a very capable driver, but an individual who ruffled plenty of feathers. NASCAR racing in the early 1970s was ruled by a small and select number of established veterans—David Pearson, Richard Petty, Cale Yarborough, and the Allison brothers to name a few. Waltrip had all the attributes to become a member of this select group, and he barged into prominence with his mouth running as fast as his race cars.

Waltrip dueled on and off the track with Yarborough, who nicknamed Waltrip "Jaws" after a crash at Darlington. He was scolded on occasion by Petty for aggressive maneuvers on the track. He sparred with rival team owners, too. M.C. Anderson, an energetic owner who at times spoke with an acid tongue declared that no matter how good Waltrip was, Anderson would never consider hiring him as a driver. "I'd fire him quicker than a New York minute," Anderson once said.

Waltrip also earned the wrath of trackside spectators, who

Bobby Allison flashes across the finish line a car length ahead of runner-up Bill Elliott to win the Firecracker 400. For Allison, it was his fourth win of the season and it propelled him to the NASCAR Winston Cup Grand National points lead. Elliott, who was looking for his first top-level NASCAR victory, ran second for the fourth time in his career.

Dale Earnhardt kicks up a cloud of tire smoke as he slides toward the wall in the Aug. 1 Talladega 500. It was the second hard crash in a row for Earnhardt, who flipped violently a week earlier at Pocono, breaking his left knee cap in the incident. Earnhardt's #15 Wrangler Ford was wiped out in this Talladega crash, but the hard-boiled driver was able to hobble away without further injury.

responded with a chorus of boos when he was introduced before a race. The negative reaction bothered the flashy and articulate Waltrip. When he crashed at Charlotte one year, the huge throng cheered. In a radio interview that was played over the track public address system, Waltrip challenged his adversaries in the grandstands to "meet me in the Big K parking lot … and we'll duke it out." After reflecting on the outburst, Waltrip said he was "embarrassed for the sport. It might have indicated the mentality of a race fan. I would hate to think that I could have a kid in the grandstands seeing the way people act. I would never take him back to a race." Those comments simply enhanced the jeers received when he was introduced at future races.

Over the years, Waltrip matured and became a championship-caliber driver. In 1979, Waltrip lost a heartbreaker in the battle for the NASCAR Winston Cup Grand National championship. Leading by more than 200 points at midseason, many had conceded the title to Waltrip. But Richard Petty got his season in gear in the second half and passed Waltrip for the title in the season finale.

In 1981, Waltrip joined forces with Junior Johnson and the new team clicked. Waltrip won his first NASCAR Winston Cup Grand National championship, rallying from a large deficit in the final stretch. In '82, he again scratched and

clawed his way past Bobby Allison to win the championship thanks to a late-season rally. In '85, he won the title for a third time, overtaking Bill Elliott with a late-season charge.

During his championship reign, Waltrip was still one of the most disliked drivers in the NASCAR kingdom. But all that changed on May 21, 1989, at Charlotte Motor Speedway during the running of NASCAR's fifth annual all-star race, The Winston. Waltrip was running first as he approached the white flag, but then second-place driver Rusty Wallace hit the rear of Waltrip's Chevy, spinning him out. Wallace went on to victory and Waltrip publicly stated, "I hope he chokes on that $200,000 [winner's prize]. He drove into me and spun me out. It was pretty flagrant."

In an instant, Waltrip went from disliked bad boy to a popular champion. Waltrip was voted NASCAR's Most Popular Driver in 1989 and 1990 by the NASCAR's fans.

During his storied NASCAR Winston Cup career from 1972 to 2000, Waltrip won 84 races, fourth on the all-time list. Waltrip has further enhanced his public image as an analyst for FOX Sports, adding a touch of Southern charm to the current NASCAR Sprint Cup telecasts. Joining Mike Joy and Larry McReynolds in the broadcast booth, Waltrip is both entertaining and enlightening in his colorful commentary, much like he was as a racer.

> **NASCAR Winston Cup Career Record 1972-2000**
> Starts: 809
> Wins: 84
> Top 5: 276
> Top 10: 390
> Poles: 59
> **Career Winnings:**
> $19,909,271

1982

Bobby Allison motors across the finish line a car length in front of Richard Petty to win the Aug. 22 Champion Spark Plug 400 at Michigan International Speedway. Allison held off a furious rally by Petty to notch his sixth win of the season. Petty erased a 10-second deficit in the final laps, but came up short at the checkered flag. "I caught him on the white-flag lap," said Petty, "but didn't have enough to get around him."

Near midseason, Kyle Petty joined forces with team owner Hoss Ellington. The Petty Enterprises team was having a rough year in 1982, failing to scratch the victory column. The team was also short on cars for its two-car lineup. Ellington was financially strapped, having lost the Hawaiian Tropic sponsorship. Kyle got the ride in the Ellington Chevy and brought along some funding from STP. The 22-year-old Petty finished 14th in the Sept. 6 Southern 500 at Darlington Raceway (shown). By October, Kyle was back in a Petty Enterprises Pontiac, having resigned from the Ellington team.

Number 98 Morgan Shepherd battles with #88 Bobby Allison in the Southern 500. Shepherd was driving a Buick owned by Dr. Ron Benfield, who entered NASCAR Winston Cup Grand National racing in 1981. Benfield acquired the Levi Garrett sponsorship, and his cars proved speedy but seldom reliable over a 500-mile distance. Benfield's cars won five pole positions, but never ran higher than third in a race. By early '85, Benfield tossed in the towel after losing sponsorship funds.

Number 11 Darrell Waltrip prepares to pass a smoking #88 Bobby Allison in the Oct. 3 Holly Farms 400 at North Wilkesboro Speedway. Allison blew his engine after 141 laps, and Waltrip grabbed the lead in the championship points race with his 10th win of the year.

Morgan Shepherd spins his Buick after bouncing off Dale Earnhardt's #15 Ford in the Oct. 17 Old Dominion 500 at Martinsville Speedway. Earnhardt succumbed to brake failure shortly after the incident, having severed his brake line in the mishap. Shepherd continued in the race but was later sidelined by engine failure.

Mark Martin made five appearances on the NASCAR Winston Cup Grand National trail in 1981, winning a couple of poles and finishing in the top 10 three times. Poised for a full-time run in '82, Martin encountered more bumps in the road than he could have imagined. Driving a Buick he leased from team owner Bud Reeder, Martin fell out of 11 races, had his tow rig stolen, and lumbered to a 29th-place finish in the final points standings. He lost a close decision to Geoff Bodine in the Rookie of the Year chase.

Bobby Allison spins coming out of the pits with 42 laps to go as #11 Darrell Waltrip takes the lead in the Oct. 31 Warner W. Hodgdon American 500 at Rockingham. Allison led the most laps in the race and finished second, so both drivers received 180 points for their efforts. It was Waltrip's 12th win of the year, but he failed to improve upon his 37-point lead over Allison. Allison won the next week at Atlanta to trim the lead to 22 points but finished 16th in the finale at Riverside, giving Waltrip the championship by 72 points.

1982 NASCAR WINSTON CUP GN POINTS RACE

Rank	Driver	Points	Starts	Wins	Top 5	Top 10	Winnings
1	Darrell Waltrip	4489	30	12	17	20	$923,150.60
2	Bobby Allison	4417	30	8	14	20	$795,077.80
3	Terry Labonte	4211	30	0	17	21	$398,634.52
4	Harry Gant	3877	30	2	9	16	$337,581.24
5	Richard Petty	3814	30	0	9	16	$465,792.96
6	Dave Marcis	3666	30	1	2	14	$249,026.40
7	Buddy Arrington	3642	30	0	0	8	$178,158.12
8	Ron Bouchard	3545	30	0	3	15	$375,758.12
9	Ricky Rudd	3537	30	0	6	13	$217,139.49
10	Morgan Shepherd	3451	29	0	6	13	$166,029.84
11	Jimmy Means	3423	30	0	0	2	$154,459.84
12	Dale Earnhardt	3402	30	1	7	12	$400,879.84
13	Jody Ridley	3333	30	0	0	10	$308,663.20
14	Mark Martin	3042	30	0	2	8	$142,709.84
15	Kyle Petty	3024	29	0	2	4	$126,284.84
16	Joe Ruttman	3021	29	0	5	7	$191,633.28
17	Neil Bonnett	2966	25	1	7	10	$158,196.56
18	Benny Parsons	2892	23	0	10	13	$252,266.56
19	J.D. McDuffie	2886	30	0	0	1	$112,743.28
20	Lake Speed	2850	30	0	0	5	$118,456.56
21	Tommy Gale	2698	26	0	0	0	$101,485.00
22	Geoff Bodine	2654	25	0	4	10	$247,750.00
23	Buddy Baker	2591	23	0	4	11	$253,675.00
24	D.K. Ulrich	2566	25	0	0	1	$78,120.00
25	Bill Elliott	2558	21	0	8	9	$201,030.00
26	Tim Richmond	2497	26	2	7	12	$175,980.00
27	Cale Yarborough	2022	16	3	8	8	$231,590.00
28	James Hylton	1514	14	0	0	0	$49,130.00
29	Slick Johnson	1261	17	0	0	1	$44,190.00
30	Ronnie Thomas	1093	18	0	0	0	$23,570.00
31	Bobby Wawak	1002	10	0	0	0	$23,660.00
32	Brad Teague	966	9	0	0	0	$14,300.00
33	Lennie Pond	756	13	0	0	2	$45,715.00
34	Rick Wilson	731	8	0	0	2	$33,230.00
35	Rick Newsom	725	8	0	0	0	$12,390.00
36	Joe Millikan	678	8	0	0	2	$56,230.00
37	David Pearson	613	6	0	2	2	$55,945.00
38	Gary Balough	564	6	0	0	1	$35,735.00
39	Lowell Cowell	554	5	0	0	0	$26,215.00
40	Philip Duffie	542	4	0	0	0	$10,910.00
41	H.B. Bailey	462	6	0	0	0	$9455.00
42	Butch Lindley	435	4	0	1	1	$16,695.00
43	Dean Combs	431	5	0	0	0	$7940.00
44	Delma Cowart	410	5	0	0	0	$11,855.00
45	Donnie Allison	406	9	0	0	3	$38,180.00
46	Bobby Hillin, Jr.	379	5	0	0	0	$9830.00
47	Roy Smith	375	3	0	0	2	$26,770.00
48	Randy Ogden	347	5	0	0	0	$9470.00
49	Connie Saylor	335	7	0	0	0	$16,225.00
50	Darryl Sage	324	5	0	0	0	$4970.00

For the second straight season, Darrell Waltrip rallied past Bobby Allison to take the NASCAR Winston Cup Grand National championship. Driving Buicks for Junior Johnson, Waltrip lagged behind in the points race as Terry Labonte and Allison held the top spots most of the summer. With four races remaining, Waltrip seized the points lead with an October victory at Martinsville.

For Allison, it was another frustrating end as he finished second in points for the fifth time in his career. Waltrip's win gave team owner Johnson his fifth NASCAR Winston Cup Grand National championship in the last seven years.

Waltrip won 12 races along the way to his 72-point victory. Allison won eight races. Labonte, who led the standings most of the way through early August despite failing to record a victory, faded to third place, 278 points behind Waltrip.

1983

February 20 Cale Yarborough pushes his Pontiac around Buddy Baker on the final lap to win his third Daytona 500. Yarborough was in a backup car after crashing his Chevrolet in qualifying. Cale topped the 200-mph barrier on his first qualifying lap but flipped and destroyed the car on the second lap.

March 13 Richard Petty ends a 43-race winless streak and nips Bill Elliott by a bumper in the Carolina 500 at Rockingham. The triumph is the 196th of Petty's career.

April 10 Harry Gant slips past a faltering Darrell Waltrip with two laps remaining and wins the TranSouth 500 at Darlington Raceway. Waltrip holds on for second as his Chevrolet belches smoke during the final laps.

May 1 Richard Petty noses out Benny Parsons and Lake Speed in a three-way finish to bag the Winston 500 at Talladega. Phil Parsons' Pontiac flips a dozen times in a 72nd-lap crash that involves 11 cars.

May 15 Bobby Allison takes the points lead with a narrow victory over Darrell Waltrip in the Mason-Dixon 500 at Dover Downs International Speedway. The race finishes under the yellow flag as a torrential downpour hits the one-mile oval.

June 5 Ricky Rudd drives his Richard Childress-owned Chevrolet to victory in the 400-kilometer race at Riverside International Raceway. It is the first NASCAR Winston Cup Grand National triumph for the Rudd/Childress duo.

July 4 Buddy Baker scoots into the lead and wins the Firecracker 400 at Daytona when Terry Labonte runs out of fuel two laps from the finish. It is Baker's 19th career NASCAR Winston Cup Grand National win and his first with the Wood Brothers team.

July 16 Dale Earnhardt drives his Ford to victory in the Nashville 420 for his first short-track win in three years. Earnhardt outruns Darrell Waltrip by more than a half-lap to score his eighth career win.

Cale Yarborough's Chevrolet spirals through the air after bouncing off the wall during qualifications for the Feb. 20 Daytona 500. Yarborough was the first driver to officially top the 200-mph barrier at Daytona, piercing the timing lights at 200.550 mph. On his second qualifying lap, Cale lost control and demolished his mount in this spectacular spill. Yarborough turned in the quickest time on pole day, but the car was withdrawn from the 500, and he lost the pole position. NASCAR rules at the time specified that the car earned a qualifying position, not the driver. So, when the car was withdrawn, the pole speed was removed from the record books.

Ricky Rudd's #3 Piedmont Airlines/Richard Childress Racing Chevrolet inherited the pole position for the Daytona 500 when Cale Yarborough's quick Chevrolet was withdrawn following his bone-jarring crash. Rudd qualified at 198.864 mph, nearly two mph slower than Cale. Rudd led the 500 briefly in the early going and eventually fell out with mechanical problems. Rudd won the pole for the next two races, at Richmond and Rockingham, to become the first driver to ever win the pole for the first three races in a season.

Bobby Allison climbs out of his battered #22 Buick after a fifth-lap crash in the annual Busch Clash at Daytona on Feb. 14. The 1983 campaign got off to a shaky start for Allison as he crashed his backup car the next day in a practice session. The DiGard team had to bring a third car to Daytona for Allison to drive in the Daytona 500. Allison managed to finish ninth after starting 35th.

Dale Earnhardt, wife Teresa, and team owner Bud Moore walk back to the garage area after winning the opening Twin 125-mile qualifying race at Daytona International Speedway. The 1983 Speedweeks events were laced with controversy for the Kannapolis, N.C., throttle stomper. Earnhardt repeatedly ignored a black flag in the Busch Clash and was involved in a multicar crash in the final lap. NASCAR officials fined Earnhardt $10,000, a tariff that later was reduced significantly. Explaining why he ignored the black flag when NASCAR officials noticed smoke seeping from his car, Earnhardt said, "I don't give a (expletive). I listen to Bud Moore, not NASCAR."

Cale Yarborough smiles from victory lane after his win in the frantic final lap of the Daytona 500. Yarborough drove a backup Pontiac in the race after having crashed his primary Chevrolet in qualifying. The car that Cale ushered into victory circle was a show car that was retrieved by his Ranier Racing team following his qualifying crash.

Neil Bonnett leads a pack of challengers, including Lake Speed, Darrell Waltrip, and Mark Martin, in the early stages of the March 13 Warner W. Hodgdon Carolina 500 at Rockingham's North Carolina Motor Speedway. Bonnett drove the #75 RahMoc Chevrolet in 1983 with sponsorship from California sportsman Warner W. Hodgdon. Bonnett won two races and finished sixth in the championship points standings.

Richard Petty grabbed career win number 196 in the Carolina 500. King Richard nosed out Bill Elliott by a half car length to end a winless skid that had mounted to 43 races. Petty started 12th on the grid and didn't lead until the 406th lap. Petty moved into contention when fleet leaders Cale Yarborough and Neil Bonnett crashed, then held off Elliott's bid in a stirring finish.

Tim Richmond (right) and Terry Labonte walk back to the pit area after their opening-lap crash in the April 10 TranSouth 500 at Darlington Raceway. Richmond started on the pole, but blew the engine in his Blue Max Racing Pontiac (seen in background) down the backstretch. Richmond slid back into oncoming traffic and was nailed by Labonte's Chevrolet.

1983

July 31 Dale Earnhardt zips past Darrell Waltrip and scores a dramatic last-lap victory in the Talladega 500. Waltrip finishes second with Tim Richmond coming home third.

September 5 Bobby Allison withstands 97-degree heat and wins the Southern 500 at Darlington for his fourth win in the Labor Day classic. Bill Elliott finishes second for the eighth time in his career.

October 9 Richard Petty scores a controversial win in Charlotte's Miller High Life 500. Petty leads the final 23 laps for his 198th career NASCAR Winston Cup Grand National win, but his team is fined $35,000 and docked 104 points following a postrace inspection. NASCAR officials discover illegal tires on Petty's Pontiac and an oversized engine.

November 18 Richard Petty announces he will leave Petty Enterprises at the end of the 1983 season after 26 years. Petty's announcement comes in wake of the controversial Charlotte race, known as "Pettygate."

November 20 Bill Elliott scores his first career win in the season finale at Riverside. Elliott passes Benny Parsons with five laps remaining to seal the victory. Bobby Allison finishes ninth and wraps up his first NASCAR Winston Cup Grand National championship.

Terry Labonte's #44 Budweiser Chevrolet leads a group of cars down the front chute during North Wilkesboro Speedway's April 17 Northwestern Bank 400. Labonte finished sixth and maintained his high ranking in the points standings. Labonte's smooth and steady approach to racing often placed him in or near the points lead in the annual NASCAR Winston Cup Grand National championship chase. He led briefly in 1983 and finished fifth in the final tally.

Darrell Waltrip takes the low groove as Richard Petty rides the high line during the May 7 Marty Robbins 420 at Nashville's Fairgrounds Raceway. The race was named in honor of former country singer and NASCAR driver Marty Robbins, who had died of a heart attack the previous December. Waltrip put a licking on the field, leading for all but 38 laps in the Saturday-night affair. After the race, runner-up Bobby Allison said, "Darrell has too much of something. No one can beat him on the short tracks with that set up. A lot of us would like to know what it is he has."

Number 22 Bobby Allison, #18 Slick Johnson, and #17 Sterling Marlin slide off the fourth turn in a pivotal crash that affected the outcome of the May 29 World 600 at Charlotte Motor Speedway. A blown tire on rookie Marlin's Chevrolet triggered the wreck. Allison and Bill Elliott, who were running first and second, got involved, opening the door for Neil Bonnett to hustle to victory. Marlin went on to be named NASCAR's Rookie of the Year.

Bobby Allison wheels his #22 Buick around the lapped car of #08 Rick McCray in the Budweiser 400 at Riverside International Raceway on June 5. Although he finished 22nd in the Riverside road race, Allison maintained his NASCAR Winston Cup Grand National points lead. The Hueytown, Ala., veteran finally cashed in on NASCAR's most elusive prize in 1983 by winning the championship. Allison took the lead in the standings in May and held on the rest of the way, fending off Darrell Waltrip's late-season charge.

Bobby Allison

ON JULY 12, 1966, a newcomer by the name of Bobby Allison won a NASCAR Grand National race at Oxford Plains Speedway in Oxford, Maine. The 28-year-old Allison outdueled Tiny Lund to win the 300-lapper on the ⅓-mile paved oval.

The spectators in attendance cheered Allison's arrival, who drove a self-groomed Chevrolet. It was the first win for the Chevrolet nameplate in NASCAR's premier series since Dec. 1, 1963, when Wendell Scott won at Jacksonville, Fla. The drought had spanned 155 races.

In an era when General Motors cars were rendered noncompetitive in the face of the big-buck Ford and Chrysler factory efforts, Allison became a leader of the "little guys" and the unheralded "bowtie brigade." The Hueytown, Ala., driver won three times in 1966, then started attracting offers from top-ranked teams. During his career, Allison won races for a dozen different team owners and drove eight different makes of cars into victory lane.

A brilliant driver for more than two decades, Allison became one of NASCAR's most prolific race winners. During his career, which lasted until 1988, Allison won 85 races, third in all-time rankings. His greatest desire, however, was to win the elusive NASCAR Winston Cup Grand National championship.

Allison came close on a number of occasions. In 1970, he finished second to Bobby Isaac in the final points standings. He might have won, but missing an early season race at Richmond left him with a deficit he was unable to overcome. While driving for Mario Rossi's factory-supported Dodge team, which entered only major events, Allison had to build his own short-track car to run the smaller 100-milers that made up the bulk of the 1970 season. The car wasn't complete by the Richmond race in March, so he was forced to forego the event. If Allison had competed at Richmond, he would have only had to finish 24th or better to win the championship.

Allison won 10 races and 12 poles in 1972, but finished a close second to Richard Petty. Allison led virtually every category in '72. He had the most wins, won more poles than any other driver, led more than twice as many laps as any other driver, and led more races. He finished first or second

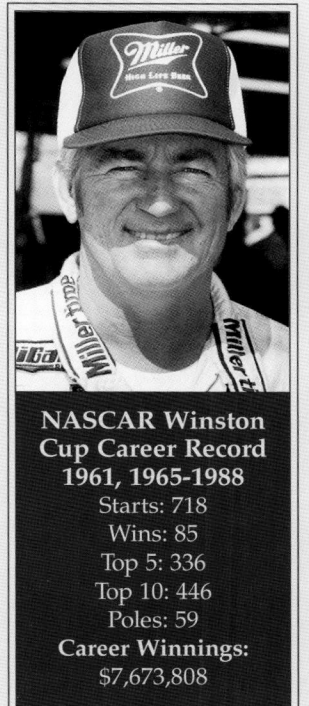

NASCAR Winston Cup Career Record 1961, 1965-1988
Starts: 718
Wins: 85
Top 5: 336
Top 10: 446
Poles: 59
Career Winnings: $7,673,808

in 22 of the 31 races. A season laced with excellence rewarded Allison with everything except that which he most wanted, the coveted driver's championship.

Three other runner-up finishes in the championship standings in 1978, '81, and '82 were bitter pills to swallow, especially in '81 and '82. In both years, Allison had built up big points leads only to see Darrell Waltrip rally in the closing stages to snatch the title. "I've come so close so many times," said a discouraged Allison in '82. "Maybe I'm never going to win a Winston Cup championship."

In 1983, while driving Buicks for the Charlotte-based DiGard Racing team, Allison again was a prime contender for NASCAR's highest honor. By May, Allison had climbed atop the standings and in a mirror image of the previous two seasons, he had a commanding lead by midsummer. But once again, Waltrip began his patented late-season charge and closed within 41 points heading into September.

This time, Allison was up to the challenge. He clicked off three consecutive victories at Darlington, Richmond, and Dover. A brief stumble at Rockingham allowed Waltrip to get within striking distance, but in the final two events of 1983, Allison finished third and ninth to wrap up the title. "I've worked hard for a long, long time," said Allison after locking up the championship. "My wife Judy has worked with me, and so many people have supported me over the years. This is something I have wanted for my entire career and today I'm going to celebrate it. I just thank God for it."

Allison won the Daytona 500 three times with three different team owners—Bud Moore, DiGard, and the Stavola Brothers. His win in the 1988 Daytona 500 was the 85th and final victory of his career, an event in which he finished just ahead of his son Davey in a stirring finish. Later that year, Allison's driving career ended when he was seriously injured in an opening-lap crash at Pocono. A flat tire sent his Buick into a spin and Jocko Maggiacomo plowed into his driver's door. After a long recovery, Allison eventually returned to the NASCAR stage as a team owner.

Bobby Allison remains one of the greatest drivers to ever strap on a racing helmet, not only in NASCAR, but in any racing series. The fans adored his warm smile, his amiable attitude and, most of all, his irrepressible spirit.

Number 22 Bobby Allison and #21 Buddy Baker hook up in a tight draft during the June 19 Gabriel 400 at Michigan International Speedway. Allison finished second, while Baker placed seventh. Baker took over the controls of the Wood Brothers Ford in 1983 and was able to score one victory during the campaign. Allison posted six wins in the DiGard Racing Buick.

Dick Brooks' #90 Ford spins wildly in a three-car entanglement with Richard Petty and Bobby Allison in the July 4 Firecracker 400 at Daytona International Speedway. Brooks and Petty were eliminated in the 79th-lap crash, while Allison recovered and salvaged a 14th-place finish. Journeyman driver Brooks was seated in the Junie Donlavey Ford in 1983. He had several impressive efforts, finishing in the top 10 six times. Brooks placed 15th in the final points standings.

Buddy Baker drives his Wood Brothers Ford under the checkered flag to win the Firecracker 400. For Baker, it was his first NASCAR Winston Cup Grand National win since 1980. The strapping driver from Charlotte sped into the lead with just over a lap to go when leader Terry Labonte ran out of fuel. Baker finished a whopping 29 seconds in front of runner-up Morgan Shepherd.

Dale Earnhardt drove Bud Moore's sleek #15 Wrangler Ford to a pair of victories in 1983, including the July 31 Talladega 500. Earnhardt placed eighth in the final NASCAR Winston Cup Grand National points standings as 13 DNFs prevented him from challenging for the championship. Earnhardt drove for Moore for two seasons, then reunited with Richard Childress in '84.

Tim Richmond seems a bit perplexed after winning the pole for the Oct. 9 race at Charlotte Motor Speedway. In a public-relations nightmare, Richmond won the Busch Pole for the Miller High Life 500 in an Old Milwaukee-sponsored car. He received the keys to a Ford Thunderbird passenger car after driving his Pontiac Grand Prix to a quick 163.073-mph lap in time trials. Richmond led 99 laps in the race and finished fifth.

Richard Petty moves to the high side of Darrell Waltrip in the final laps of the Miller High Life 500. Petty labored deep in the field for most of the race, then bolted past a slew of challengers in the final laps. As Petty was going through the customary postrace celebrations, NASCAR officials noticed left side tires mounted on the right side of his Pontiac, a clear violation of the rules. Further investigation revealed the engine far exceeded the 358-cid maximum. Petty was fined a record $35,000 and docked 104 points for the infractions, but he kept his 198th career NASCAR Winston Cup Grand National win.

Number 44 Terry Labonte and Tim Richmond battle in the closing stages of the Oct. 30 Warner W. Hodgdon American 500 at North Carolina Motor Speedway. Labonte and Richmond raced side-by-side for five laps before Labonte inched his way out front. Labonte crossed the finish line .68-second ahead of Richmond to grab his second career NASCAR Winston Cup Grand National win.

Bill Elliott ran the full schedule for the first time in 1983, and performed well. Driving Harry Melling's #9 Ford Thunderbird, Elliott scored his first NASCAR Winston Cup Grand National win in the season finale at Riverside. The lanky Dawsonville, Ga., driver also finished an impressive third in the final points standings on the strength of 22 top-10 finishes in 30 starts.

1983 NASCAR WINSTON CUP GN POINTS RACE

Rank	Driver	Points	Starts	Wins	Top 5	Top 10	Winnings
1	Bobby Allison	4667	30	6	18	25	$883,009.40
2	Darrell Waltrip	4620	30	6	22	25	$865,184.47
3	Bill Elliott	4279	30	1	12	22	$514,029.22
4	Richard Petty	4042	30	3	9	21	$508,883.76
5	Terry Labonte	4004	30	1	11	20	$388,418.62
6	Neil Bonnett	3842	30	2	10	17	$453,585.09
7	Harry Gant	3790	30	1	10	16	$414,352.36
8	Dale Earnhardt	3732	30	2	9	14	$465,202.88
9	Ricky Rudd	3693	30	2	7	14	$275,399.14
10	Tim Richmond	3612	30	1	10	15	$262,138.14
11	Dave Marcis	3361	30	0	0	7	$306,354.86
12	Joe Ruttman	3342	30	0	4	10	$223,808.32
13	Kyle Petty	3261	30	0	0	2	$163,847.76
14	Dick Brooks	3230	30	0	2	6	$180,555.22
15	Buddy Arrington	3158	30	0	0	2	$138,428.28
16	Ron Bouchard	3113	28	0	1	7	$159,172.12
17	Geoff Bodine	3019	28	0	5	9	$209,610.58
18	Jimmy Means	2983	28	0	0	3	$132,914.04
19	Sterling Marlin	2980	30	0	0	1	$148,252.48
20	Morgan Shepherd	2733	25	0	3	13	$287,325.40
21	Buddy Baker	2621	21	1	6	12	$216,355.00
22	Ronnie Thomas	2515	26	0	0	0	$47,190.00
23	Tommy Gale	2507	28	0	0	1	$88,305.00
24	D.K. Ulrich	2400	22	0	0	2	$85,245.00
25	Trevor Boys	2293	23	0	0	1	$87,555.00
26	J.D. McDuffie	2197	25	0	0	0	$73,425.00
27	Lake Speed	2114	18	0	2	5	$78,220.00
28	Cale Yarborough	1960	16	4	4	8	$265,035.00
29	Benny Parsons	1657	16	0	4	5	$129,760.00
30	Mark Martin	1627	16	0	1	3	$99,055.00
31	Ronnie Hopkins	1147	13	0	0	0	$26,455.00
32	Jody Ridley	1050	10	0	0	3	$45,710.00
33	David Pearson	943	10	0	1	4	$71,720.00
34	Lennie Pond	887	10	0	0	2	$41,530.00
35	Ken Ragan	836	8	0	0	0	$27,905.00
36	Bobby Wawak	825	9	0	0	0	$19,130.00
37	Bobby Hillin, Jr.	737	12	0	0	0	$30,275.00
38	Slick Johnson	705	10	0	0	0	$13,665.00
39	Mike Potter	662	11	0	0	0	$20,375.00
40	Cecil Gordon	649	8	0	0	0	$17,340.00
41	Rick Newsom	573	6	0	0	0	$14,445.00
42	Dean Combs	500	5	0	0	1	$21,370.00
43	Phil Parsons	458	5	0	0	0	$23,850.00
44	Bob Senneker	436	5	0	0	0	$11,355.00
45	Jerry Bowman	419	5	0	0	0	$8610.00
46	Clark Dwyer	411	5	0	0	1	$14,570.00
47	Greg Sacks	359	5	0	0	0	$8060.00
48	Rick McCray	313	4	0	0	0	$3710.00
49	Delma Cowart	277	4	0	0	0	$7750.00
50	Philip Duffie	265	4	0	0	0	$6480.00

Bobby Allison held off another patented rally by Darrell Waltrip to secure his first NASCAR Winston Cup Grand National championship in 1983. Allison held a comfortable 170-point lead in late July, but Waltrip shaved the margin down to 41 points by September. Allison responded with three straight wins at Darlington, Richmond, and Dover, and held off a last-ditch surge by Waltrip to win by 47 points.

During the course of the season, the points lead changed hands six times among six drivers. In the early weeks of the campaign, Cale Yarborough, Joe Ruttman, Harry Gant, Bill Elliott, and Neil Bonnett traded the lead. Allison took the lead at Dover in May and held it to the end of the season.

Allison and Waltrip each won six races. Elliott, making his first attempt at the championship, won one race and finished third in the final NASCAR Winston Cup Grand National points standings.

1984

February 19 Cale Yarborough wins his fourth Daytona 500. Yarborough passes Darrell Waltrip on the final lap and outruns Dale Earnhardt off the final turn to preserve the victory.

February 26 Ricky Rudd posts a heart-warming victory in the 400-lapper at Richmond Fairgrounds Raceway. Rudd was battered and bruised after a crash in Daytona's Busch Clash invitational race two weeks earlier. Rudd's Bud Moore Ford finishes 3.2 seconds ahead of runner-up Darrell Waltrip.

March 18 Benny Parsons outruns Dale Earnhardt and Cale Yarborough in a spirited late-race duel to win the Coca-Cola 500 at Atlanta International Raceway. It is Parsons' 21st NASCAR Winston Cup Grand National win.

April 1 Darrell Waltrip cruises to victory in the Valleydale 500 at Bristol, giving team owner Junior Johnson his eighth straight victory at the steeply banked ½-mile track. Terry Labonte finishes second.

April 29 Geoff Bodine runs away from Ron Bouchard in the final laps and scores his first career NASCAR Winston Cup Grand National win in Martinsville's Sovran Bank 500. The triumph also gives team owner Rick Hendrick his first NASCAR win in the team's eighth career start.

May 6 Cale Yarborough passes Harry Gant on the final lap to win the Winston 500 at Talladega. Yarborough's Chevrolet nips Gant at the finish line in the most competitive race in NASCAR history. Thirteen drivers swap the lead a record 75 times in the 188-lap race.

May 12 Neil Bonnett finishes first, but Darrell Waltrip is declared the winner of the controversial Nashville 420. Waltrip leads as the caution flag comes out with two laps to go. Although the field is given the yellow flag, Bonnett continues to race and passes Waltrip. NASCAR reverses the decision the following day.

Dale Earnhardt took the Wrangler sponsorship to the Richard Childress operation for the 1984 NASCAR Winston Cup Grand National campaign. Earnhardt drove briefly for Childress in the latter part of the '81 season, then departed for a two-year stint with Bud Moore's Ford team. Earnhardt started the '84 season smoothly with a runner-up finish in the Daytona 500.

Pole-sitter Cale Yarborough jumps out to an early lead at the start of the Feb. 19 Daytona 500. Yarborough was in the hunt all day, playing a game of patience until the final lap. Perched on the rear bumper of Darrell Waltrip for 38 laps, Yarborough applied the spurs to his #28 Chevrolet and motored past his rival in the final mile. It was the sixth time Yarborough won a NASCAR Winston Cup Grand National race with a last-lap pass.

Ricky Rudd pushes his #15 Ford past #3 Dale Earnhardt in the Feb. 26 Miller High Life 400 at Richmond Fairgrounds Raceway. Rudd took the lead with 20 laps remaining and scampered to victory. The Chesapeake, Va., driver was banged up in a spill in Daytona's Busch Clash two weeks earlier. With his swollen eyes taped open so he could see, Rudd finished a credible eighth in the Daytona 500, then won a week later at Richmond while making his second start with the Bud Moore team.

The Wrangler Jeans company had a unique NASCAR sponsorship package for the 1984 season. Long associated with Dale Earnhardt, Wrangler moved to the Richard Childress team when Earnhardt took the saddle of the #3 Chevrolet. But Wrangler also enjoyed a fine relationship with team owner Bud Moore, for whom Earnhardt drove in '82 and '83. Given that relationship, Wrangler continued to sponsor Moore's #15 Ford, now driven by Ricky Rudd. The unique arrangement meant that two different teams had the same sponsor.

Neil Bonnett hops out of his car after an ignition fire ended his day at the March 4 Warner W. Hodgdon Carolina 500 at Rockingham. Driving for the Junior Johnson team, Bonnett failed to win in 1984, but posted seven top-five and 14 top-10 finishes, and placed eighth in the final championship points race.

Number 55 Benny Parsons runs just ahead of #3 Dale Earnhardt and #28 Cale Yarborough on the final lap of the March 18 Atlanta 500. Parsons, often regarded as NASCAR's Mr. Nice Guy, had to scrap like a badger to fend off aggressive challenges from Earnhardt and Yarborough to nail down his 21st career victory. It was the first win for Parsons in nearly three years, and it turned out to be his final NASCAR Winston Cup Grand National triumph.

Darrell Waltrip powers his #11 Budweiser Chevrolet under teammate #12 Neil Bonnett en route to an impressive win in the April 1 Valleydale 500 at Bristol International Speedway. Waltrip's victory gave team owner Junior Johnson his eighth straight win on the paved oval. Bonnett struggled most of the way and finished a disappointing 11th.

North Wilkesboro Speedway always attracted an enthusiastic audience for its two annual NASCAR Winston Cup Grand National races. The ⅝-mile oval, which had an uphill backstretch and a downhill front chute, was NASCAR's second-oldest track, having staged races since the inaugural 1949 season. Tim Richmond won the April 8 Northwestern Bank 400, passing Ricky Rudd in the final 28 laps to score the victory. The final NASCAR Winston Cup race at North Wilkesboro was run in 1996.

1984

May 20 Richard Petty drives his Mike Curb-owned Pontiac to victory in the Budweiser 500 at Dover for his 199th career NASCAR Winston Cup Grand National triumph. Petty outruns Tim Richmond by four seconds.

June 10 Bill Elliott dashes past Terry Labonte with eight laps remaining and hustles to victory in the 400-miler at Michigan International Speedway. It is Elliott's first win on a superspeedway.

July 4 With President Ronald Reagan in attendance on the nation's birthday, Richard Petty wheels his Pontiac to victory in the Pepsi Firecracker 400 at Daytona. It is Petty's 200th NASCAR Winston Cup Grand National victory, a milestone that will likely live in NASCAR's record books forever.

July 29 Dale Earnhardt keeps his Chevrolet ahead of a snarling 10-car pack to win the frantic Talladega 500. Earnhardt passes Terry Labonte on the final lap, which is the 68th lead change of the race.

August 25 Terry Labonte battles back from two crashes and wins the Busch 500 at Bristol International Raceway. Dale Earnhardt taps Labonte into a spin in the early stages, and Labonte survives a scrape with Neil Bonnett with 50 laps to go. Labonte also takes the championship points lead.

October 21 Bill Elliott passes Harry Gant on the final lap to win the American 500 at Rockingham in a photo finish. Gant and Elliott swap the lead three times in the final three laps.

November 11 Dale Earnhardt edges Bill Elliott in the Atlanta Journal 500 at Atlanta International Raceway. Rookie driver Terry Schoonover, in his second career NASCAR Winston Cup Grand National race, is fatally injured in a single-car crash on the 129th lap.

November 18 Geoff Bodine takes the lead in the final four laps and wins the season finale at Riverside International Raceway. Terry Labonte finishes third and wins the 1984 NASCAR Winston Cup Grand National championship by a 65-point margin over Harry Gant.

The pit area at Darlington Raceway is a crowded scene during a caution flag in the April 15 TranSouth 500 as Bobby Allison's bent and broken Buick (bottom right) prepares to chug back onto the track. Allison finished 37 laps off the pace, but was able to salvage a 20th-place finish. Other cars shown in the pits are #9 Bill Elliott, the team Junior Johnson cars of #11 Darrell Waltrip and #12 Neil Bonnett, and #44 Terry Labonte. Waltrip won the race as Labonte finished second and Elliott third.

D.K. Ulrich's #6 Chevrolet lurches high into the air during a multicar scramble in the April 15 race at Darlington Raceway. Other cars involved include #88 Rusty Wallace, #5 Geoff Bodine, #51 Greg Sacks, and Dick Brooks. Incredibly, Ulrich was able to continue in the race following the crash, but eventually fell out with steering problems.

Number 28 Cale Yarborough runs just ahead of #43 Richard Petty and #12 Neil Bonnett in the May 6 Winston 500 at the Alabama International Motor Speedway. The 188-lap contest around Talladega's massive 2.66-mile tri-oval featured the most official lead changes in the history of NASCAR Winston Cup Grand National racing. Thirteen drivers swapped the lead 75 times in the race, with Yarborough pulling off the last lead change when he passed Harry Gant on the final lap for the win.

Terry Labonte drives his Piedmont Airlines Chevrolet down the front chute during the June 3 Budweiser 400 on Riverside's twisting road course. The young Corpus Christi, Texas, driver withstood a fender-bending duel with Tim Richmond to win the race. In the 1980s, Labonte was regarded as one of NASCAR's finest road racers. The Riverside win placed Labonte solidly in the hunt for the championship, which he eventually won in a close decision over Harry Gant.

Terry Labonte

IN THE SUMMER of 1978, Terry Labonte was driving Sportsman cars on the short tracks in and around his hometown of Corpus Christi, Texas. In August, NASCAR team owner Billy Hagan, who had just released 1976 Rookie of the Year Skip Manning, decided to give the 22-year-old kid a shot at the big time.

Darlington's Southern 500 was the next race on the annual NASCAR Winston Cup Grand National calendar. Eerie Darlington, with a personality akin to an angry pit bull, was hardly the place for a green rookie to attempt his first big-league start. "I had never even seen Darlington before I went there in 1978," said Labonte. While taking a maiden voyage at Darlington could be considered suicidal, Labonte was up to the task. Driving the Hagan Chevrolet, Labonte was smooth, steady, and fast. Most importantly, he didn't flinch in the face of Darlington's fearsome reputation. The Texas hotshot finished an amazing fourth.

Two years later, Labonte was back at Darlington for the 1980 Southern 500. Starting 10th on the grid, Labonte again quietly and effectively drove into contention. Throughout the 500-miler, Labonte managed to keep his car on the lead lap. Near the end of the race, David Pearson, Dale Earnhardt, and Benny Parsons were engaged in a dogfight for the lead. With three laps to go, a slower car driven by Frank Warren blew an engine entering the first turn. NASCAR spotters on the scene said there didn't appear to be any oil deposited on the racing surface, so the green flag stayed out.

As the leaders charged into the turn, oil on the track sent the cars lurching sideways. Tires smoked, metal crunched,

NASCAR NEXTEL Cup Career Record 1978-2006
Starts: 848
Wins: 22
Top 5: 182
Top 10: 361
Poles: 27
Career Winnings:
$36,472,512

and the three leaders suddenly found themselves in a battle for survival instead of victory.

Pearson overcame a spin and, with tires smoking, headed off the fourth turn toward the yellow flag. Labonte, running at full stride, dove low and passed Pearson a couple of feet before the stripe. He beat Pearson back to the caution flag by less than two feet to secure his first NASCAR Winston Cup Grand National victory as the race ended under the yellow.

With his signature steady driving, Labonte became a contender for the championship by his third full season. He finished fourth in 1981, third in '82, and fifth in '83. In 1984, Labonte overtook Dale Earnhardt for the points lead in August and drove to his first NASCAR Winston Cup Grand National title. He won two races during the run.

A dozen years later, Labonte drove to his second NASCAR championship as a member of the Hendrick Motorsports team. He and teammate Jeff Gordon engaged in a stirring points battle during the final stretch of the 1996 season. With three races remaining, Labonte overtook Gordon and edged his stablemate by a mere 37 points.

Labonte set another mark in 1996. With his April 21 start at Martinsville, Labonte broke Richard Petty's record of 513 consecutive starts. The streak extended into the 2000 season when he made his 655th consecutive NASCAR Winston Cup start at Daytona in July. A wreck at that race forced him to miss the Aug. 5 race at Indianapolis. Labonte's streak, which started in 1979, was surpassed by Ricky Rudd in 2002.

Labonte decided to hang it up after running a part-time schedule in the 2006 season. Consistency and an "iron man" mentality made Labonte one of NASCAR's top drivers for almost three decades.

1984

"It's just another number, but it's a big one. I figured I'd eventually get there, but as hard as they've gotten to be, I didn't know when."

—Richard Petty on his 200th win

Richard Petty races mere inches ahead of Cale Yarborough back to the yellow flag in the final three laps of the July 4 Firecracker 400 at Daytona International Speedway. Doug Heveron's spin brought out the caution flag and both Petty and Yarborough were aware that whoever got back to the caution flag first would win the race. Petty prevailed by the width of a bumper to score his much-awaited 200th career NASCAR Winston Cup Grand National win. President Ronald Reagan (inset) witnessed the milestone from the broadcast booth. Motor Racing Network's Ned Jarrett (shown next to the President) interviewed Reagan on MRN's radio broadcast of the race. It marked the first time a sitting President attended a NASCAR Winston Cup Grand National event.

◄ Dale Earnhardt and wife Teresa share the victory lane accolades following Earnhardt's last-lap victory in the July 29 Talladega 500. Earnhardt throttled his way past Terry Labonte in the final mile and edged Buddy Baker to win what many observers said at the time was the greatest NASCAR race in history. A total of 16 drivers traded the lead 68 times and 10 cars were involved in the frantic finish. Six of the top-10 finish positions had to be determined by a high-speed electronic camera. Transponders didn't grace the NASCAR landscape until more than a decade later.

Harry Gant #33 leads the #15 Ford of Ricky Rudd in the Sept. 2 Southern 500 at Darlington Raceway. The race marked the first time the famed event was held on a Sunday rather than the traditional Labor Day. Gant thoroughly dominated the race, leading for 277 of the 367 laps. "This is the best race I've ever driven," said Gant. "Travis [Carter, crew chief] and the crew have gotten me about 45 extra horsepower and it showed today."

Dale Earnhardt runs side-by-side with rival Geoff Bodine in the Sept. 9 Wrangler Sanfor-Set 400 at Richmond Fairgrounds Raceway. Bodine drove the #5 Chevrolet for Hendrick Motorsports in Rick Hendrick's first year fielding a NASCAR Winston Cup Grand National team. Bodine won three races for the freshman team and finished ninth in the points race. Earnhardt won twice and ranked fourth in the final tally.

Harry Gant guns his #33 Chevrolet across the finish line to win the Sept. 16 Delaware 500 at Dover Downs International Speedway. Trevor Boys, in the #48 Chevrolet, posted a 10th-place finish, nine laps behind Gant's fleet Chevy. Gant put on a late-season charge and challenged Terry Labonte for the championship. Gant placed second in the final tally, 65 points behind.

Terry Labonte drove Billy Hagan's #44 Piedmont Airlines Chevrolet to the 1984 NASCAR Winston Cup Grand National championship. Labonte won a short-track event at Bristol and prevailed on Riverside's road course along the way to the title. Labonte was the first NASCAR champion to win the title without a victory on a superspeedway since '73.

1984 NASCAR WINSTON CUP GN POINTS RACE

Rank	Driver	Points	Starts	Wins	Top 5	Top 10	Winnings
1	Terry Labonte	4508	30	2	17	24	$767,715.94
2	Harry Gant	4443	30	3	15	23	$673,059.48
3	Bill Elliott	4377	30	3	13	24	$680,343.82
4	Dale Earnhardt	4265	30	2	12	22	$634,670.18
5	Darrell Waltrip	4230	30	7	13	20	$731,022.54
6	Bobby Allison	4094	30	2	13	20	$641,048.88
7	Ricky Rudd	3918	30	1	7	16	$497,778.24
8	Neil Bonnett	3802	30	0	7	14	$282,532.58
9	Geoff Bodine	3734	30	3	7	14	$413,747.26
10	Richard Petty	3643	30	2	5	13	$257,931.94
11	Ron Bouchard	3609	30	0	5	10	$246,509.88
12	Tim Richmond	3505	30	1	6	11	$345,847.82
13	Dave Marcis	3416	30	0	3	9	$330,765.37
14	Rusty Wallace	3316	30	0	2	4	$201,738.68
15	Dick Brooks	3265	30	0	1	5	$192,406.62
16	Kyle Petty	3159	30	0	1	6	$329,919.56
17	Trevor Boys	3040	30	0	0	1	$165,375.50
18	Joe Ruttman	2945	29	0	0	8	$168,432.48
19	Greg Sacks	2545	29	0	0	1	$75,183.18
20	Buddy Arrington	2504	26	0	0	0	$128,801.92
21	Buddy Baker	2477	21	0	4	12	$151,635.00
22	Cale Yarborough	2448	16	3	10	10	$403,853.00
23	Clark Dwyer	2374	26	0	0	0	$114,335.00
24	Phil Parsons	2290	23	0	0	3	$90,700.00
25	Jimmy Means	2218	22	0	0	0	$105,105.00
26	Lake Speed	2023	19	0	2	7	$98,320.00
27	Benny Parsons	1865	14	1	7	10	$241,665.00
28	Mike Alexander	1862	19	0	0	1	$94,820.00
29	Morgan Shepherd	1811	20	0	0	1	$59,670.00
30	Ronnie Thomas	1775	21	0	0	0	$79,325.00
31	Tommy Ellis	1738	20	0	0	1	$44,315.00
32	Bobby Hillin, Jr.	1477	16	0	0	0	$45,020.00
33	Tommy Gale	1426	16	0	0	0	$69,385.00
34	J.D. McDuffie	1366	16	0	0	0	$50,320.00
35	Jody Ridley	1288	14	0	0	3	$64,135.00
36	Doug Heveron	1265	16	0	0	0	$39,950.00
37	Sterling Marlin	1207	14	0	0	2	$54,355.00
38	Lennie Pond	923	12	0	0	2	$54,200.00
39	Dean Combs	903	12	0	0	0	$22,385.00
40	Ken Ragan	873	10	0	0	0	$37,045.00
41	David Pearson	812	11	0	0	3	$54,125.00
42	D.K. Ulrich	810	9	0	0	0	$31,040.00
43	Connie Saylor	367	8	0	0	0	$19,675.00
44	Jerry Bowman	362	5	0	0	0	$6265.00
45	Elliott Forbes-Robinson	349	5	0	0	0	$11,335.00
46	Jeff Hooker	322	4	0	0	0	$4495.00
47	Bobby Wawak	307	4	0	0	0	$8575.00
48	Dick May	300	3	0	0	0	$5325.00
49	Dean Roper	294	3	0	0	0	$19,150.00
50	Bobby Gerhart	262	4	0	0	0	$7585.00

Terry Labonte overtook Dale Earnhardt with 10 races to go and held off a late charge by Harry Gant to win the 1984 NASCAR Winston Cup Grand National championship. Labonte moved into the lead with a victory at Bristol in August.

Gant, who trailed by 131 points in mid August, pulled to within 42 points of Labonte in the season's closing weeks. Labonte ran third in the season finale on the Riverside, Calif., road course to seal his first title by 65 points over Gant.

Labonte won two races, one short track event and one on a road course. He became the first driver since 1973 to win the NASCAR Winston Cup Grand National championship without posting a superspeedway victory.

Bill Elliott won three races and finished third, 131 points behind Labonte. Dale Earnhardt placed fourth with two wins, and Darrell Waltrip, who won a season high seven races, rounded out the top five.

1985

February 17 Bill Elliott leads 136 of the 200 laps in dominating the Daytona 500. Elliott dominates Daytona's Speedweeks, winning the pole at more than 205 mph and nearly lapping the field in the Twin 125-mile qualifier.

March 17 Driving with a broken leg suffered in a crash at Rockingham, Bill Elliott outruns Geoff Bodine by 2.64 seconds to win the Coca-Cola 500 at Atlanta. Elliott wins two of the first four races, but ranks a distant fifth in the points standings.

April 6 Dale Earnhardt manhandles his Chevrolet and comes out on top of the Valleydale 500 at Bristol. The power-steering unit in Earnhardt's Chevrolet fails in the first 50 miles, but he never lets it slow him down.

May 5 In one of the most miraculous comebacks in NASCAR history, Bill Elliott rallies from a five-mile deficit without the aid of a caution flag and wins the Winston 500 at Talladega. A broken oil fitting had knocked Elliott nearly two laps off the pace early.

May 25, 26 Darrell Waltrip passes Harry Gant with two laps to go and wins the inaugural The Winston NASCAR all-star race at Charlotte Motor Speedway. Waltrip captures the World 600 the next day and pockets $290,733 for his back-to-back wins.

June 16 Bill Elliott wins his seventh superspeedway race in nine starts, taking the checkered flag in Michigan's Miller 400. Darrell Waltrip finishes a distant second and trails Elliott by 86 points in championship race.

July 4 Unheralded Greg Sacks stuns the favorites by winning the Pepsi Firecracker 400 at Daytona. Sacks drives an unsponsored car to a 23.5-second triumph over runner-up Bill Elliott. It is not only Sacks' first NASCAR Winston Cup Grand National victory, but also his first top-five finish.

July 28 Cale Yarborough nabs his first win of the season, winning the Talladega 500. Yarborough nips Neil Bonnett and Ron Bouchard in the final laps.

Bill Elliott makes a quick pit stop in the Feb. 17 Daytona 500, an event the Dawsonville, Ga., driver dominated from start to finish. Elliott led 136 of the 200 laps, overcame a penalty on pit road, and thrashed the competition in an electrifying performance. Elliott had a memorable Speedweeks. In addition to his Daytona 500 performance, he won the pole at a record 205.114 mph and nearly lapped the field in the Twin 125-miler.

Lake Speed, a journeyman driver from Jackson, Miss., took the controls of the #75 RahMoc Pontiac in 1985. The team failed to secure a sponsor until the day before the Daytona 500. Despite the undecorated car, Speed made a miraculous run in "The Great American Race" and drove to a well-earned second-place finish.

After a bumper-grinding battle with Tim Richmond, Dale Earnhardt drove the #3 Wrangler Jeans Chevrolet to victory in the Feb. 24 Miller High Life 400 at Richmond's Fairgrounds Raceway. A collision with Richmond with 14 laps remaining crumpled the right front of Earnhardt's car, but he scampered to an easy victory as Richmond fell to ninth place.

Dick Brooks pulls the #1 Petty Enterprises Ford Thunderbird into the pits during the March 3 Carolina 500 at Rockingham. Richard Petty had left Petty Enterprises in late 1983 to drive for Mike Curb's new team. When Kyle Petty went to drive for the Wood Brothers in '85, Maurice Petty had to scrape to keep the team going. Brooks drove the car in three races and Morgan Shepherd took over for one event. By mid April, Maurice was forced to fold the operation. Petty Enterprises remained defunct until King Richard returned in '86.

Bill Elliott signs an autograph during the March 17 Coca-Cola 500 festivities at Atlanta International Raceway. Elliott shook off the effects of a broken leg suffered two weeks earlier at Rockingham and notched his second win of the '85 campaign. Despite winning two of the first four races, Elliott only ranked fifth in the NASCAR Winston Cup Grand National points standings.

Lake Speed spins his #75 Pontiac in the turn at Bristol during the April 6 Valleydale 500. Speed recovered to finish seventh. Number 3 Dale Earnhardt avoided the crash and won the race despite a power-steering failure. Speed, who leaped from go-kart racing directly into NASCAR Winston Cup competition in 1980, led the points standings briefly in the '85 campaign. The Jackson, Miss., driver eventually finished 10th in the championship race with 14 top-10 finishes in 28 starts.

David Pearson pits his #21 Hoss Ellington Chevrolet after a bout with the wall during the April 14 TranSouth 500 at Darlington Raceway. Pearson, near the end of his racing career, was running a limited schedule. Pearson drove in 12 races in 1985 with one top-10 finish. He still holds the distinction of the all-time Darlington race winner with 10 victories.

Geoff Bodine drives his #5 Hendrick Motorsports Chevrolet Monte Carlo past the spinning #11 Chevy of Darrell Waltrip in the April 28 Sovran Bank 500 at Martinsville Speedway. Waltrip started on the pole and led in the early stages, but engine failure eventually put him on the sidelines. Bodine qualified second and motored home to a third-place finish.

1985

September 1 Bill Elliott grabs his 10th win of the season and pockets the inaugural offering of the Winston Million $1 million bonus in Darlington's Southern 500. Elliott leads the championship chase by 206 points.

September 29 Harry Gant dominates the field to win the Holly Farms 400 at North Wilkesboro Speedway as Darrell Waltrip takes the points lead. Bill Elliott finishes out of the top 10 for the fourth consecutive race.

November 3 Bill Elliott rebounds with a victory in the Atlanta Journal 500 for his record-setting 11th superspeedway win of the season. Elliott tops David Pearson's 1973 record of 10 superspeedway wins in a season.

November 17 Ricky Rudd wins the season finale at Riverside as Darrell Waltrip finishes seventh and wraps up his third NASCAR Winston Cup Grand National championship. Bill Elliott experiences transmission problems early, erasing his title hopes.

Front-row starters Bill Elliott and Cale Yarborough lead the field at the start of the May 5 Winston 500 at Talladega's Alabama International Motor Speedway. The field was the smallest in Talladega's history, but there was no shortage of entries. Greg Sacks qualified for the race, but pulled out due to an engine problem. No other driver was permitted to take Sacks' place in the field, so only 39 cars started.

Smoke erupts from the #9 Coors Ford of Bill Elliott in the Winston 500. Elliott was holding a solid lead when a broken oil fitting required him to limp into the pits for repairs. Elliott returned to the track running 26th, 2.03 seconds from going two laps down. At that point, Elliott began one of the most memorable comebacks in NASCAR history. Without the aid of a caution flag, he rallied from the five-mile deficit and zoomed into the lead 97 laps later. He went on to score his fourth win of the season.

Bill Elliott had a shot at the Winston Million bonus at Charlotte's May 26 Coca-Cola 600, but a variety of problems relegated him to an 18th-place finish. During one pit stop, the #9 Ford had no brakes and Bobby Allison's Miller crew had to help push the car back into the proper pit stall. Elliott would get a second chance to pocket the $1 million offered by R.J. Reynolds at Darlington, and he nabbed the prize in the first year it was offered.

Darrell Waltrip beams from Charlotte's victory lane after a big win in the Coca-Cola 600. Waltrip won back-to-back races on Saturday and Sunday, including the first The Winston all-star race. Waltrip also moved into contention for the NASCAR Winston Cup Grand National championship with his first win of the year.

▶ Greg Sacks authored one of the most unlikely upsets in NASCAR Winston Cup Grand National racing history in the July 4 Pepsi Firecracker 400 at Daytona. Driving the unsponsored #10 Chevrolet with a part-time, rag-tag pit crew, Sacks wheeled his DiGard Racing research and development car to an overwhelming victory. Sacks outran runner-up Bill Elliott by 23.5 seconds to register the lone NASCAR Winston Cup Grand National triumph of his career.

Harry Gant leads Darrell Waltrip through the sweeping ninth turn at Riverside International Raceway in the June 2 Budweiser 400. Never a top-ranked road racer, Gant managed to finish second to Terry Labonte in the 400-kilometer California event. Waltrip started on the pole and finished eighth.

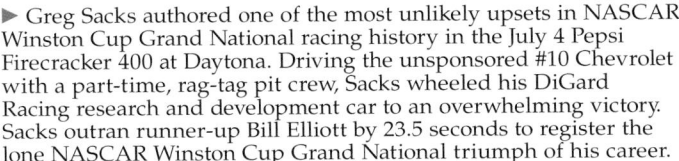

Cale Yarborough and his Ranier Racing team switched from GM products to Fords in 1985. Although regarded as one of the most formidable teams on the tour, Yarborough struggled with his new mount. He went winless until the July 28 Talladega 500. Yarborough took the lead when Bill Elliott's smooth-running Ford developed problems in the final laps. It was only the fourth race all year that Yarborough was able to finish.

Bill Elliott made national headlines by nabbing the Winston Million $1 million bonus with a win in the Sept. 1 Southern 500 at Darlington Raceway. R.J. Reynolds had offered the bonus to any driver who could win three of NASCAR's four crown-jewel events: the Daytona 500, Talladega's Winston 500, Charlotte's Coca-Cola 600, and the Southern 500. Elliott failed at Charlotte, but won in his final chance at Darlington.

Number 8 Bobby Hillin, Jr., feels pressure from #32 Alan Kulwicki and #52 Jimmy Means in the Sept. 8 Wrangler Sanfor-Set 400 at Richmond Fairgrounds Raceway. Kulwicki, driving Bill Terry's #32 Ford, was making his first appearance on NASCAR's Winston Cup Grand National tour. He qualified 25th and finished 19th, eight laps behind winner Darrell Waltrip. Hillin came in 21st and Means finished 23rd.

Bobby Allison delivers a solid blow to the wall in the September race at Richmond. Allison began the season driving for the DiGard operation, but quit in July to form his own team. The Hueytown, Ala., veteran failed to scratch victory circle in 1985 and finished outside the top 10 in points for the first time since '75.

Geoff Bodine spins his #5 Chevrolet into the infield grass in Richmond's Wrangler Sanfor-Set 400 as Ron Bouchard loops his #47 Buick in the middle of the track. Rusty Wallace sneaks through the narrow opening in his #2 Pontiac. Bodine recovered from the spin to nail down a seventh-place finish.

Bill Elliott's sterling season began to unravel after his $1 million victory in the Southern 500. He held a commanding 204-point lead entering September, but the lead had all but evaporated three weeks later. In Martinsville's Sept. 22 Goody's 500, Elliott clobbered the wall (shown) and finished 17th. When the points were tabulated following the event, Elliott held a narrow 23-point lead over Darrell Waltrip.

Number 11 Darrell Waltrip spins in the Goody's 500 at Martinsville. Waltrip recovered from the incident to finish a close second to Dale Earnhardt, who posted his fourth win of the season. Waltrip had begun his charge to the NASCAR Winston Cup Grand National title with a victory in Richmond's Wrangler Sanfor-Set 400 two weeks earlier. Trailing by 204 points after Darlington's Southern 500, it took Waltrip only four races to gobble up the deficit and take the points lead for keeps.

NASCAR All-Star Race

DURING THE 1984 NASCAR Winston Cup Grand National awards ceremony at New York's Waldorf-Astoria Hotel, R.J. Reynolds president Gerald H. Long announced that beginning in 1985, a special all-star event would join the annual schedule. The invitational race, called The Winston, would be a nonpoints race, with the previous-season race winners jostling for $500,000 in posted awards. The inaugural The Winston was held on May 25, 1985, at Charlotte Motor Speedway. Originally, the all-star event was intended to be held at a different track each year. The '86 race took place at Atlanta International Raceway, but a pathetic crowd sent the event back to Charlotte, where it has remained ever since.

"R.J. Reynolds is committed to ensuring that Winston Cup racing has no rival when it comes to being first in motorsports," said Long. "The series is already first worldwide in attendance and prestige. This is another big leap forward. The Winston will be the richest per-mile race in the world."

The NASCAR all-star event rekindled an idea Bill France had in the early 1960s. During the Speedweeks events in February, France staged a special race for drivers who had won in the previous NASCAR Grand National season. Three races were run in 1961, '62, and '63. France called his all-star event the American Challenge, then changed the name to the Race of Champions. Joe Weatherly, Fireball Roberts, and Fred Lorenzen won the first three all-star races

The "Dashing Dozen" participants of the inaugural The Winston: (left to right) Cale Yarborough, Harry Gant, Darrell Waltrip, Bill Elliott, Terry Labonte, Richard Petty, Ricky Rudd, Tim Richmond, Dale Earnhardt, Benny Parsons, Geoff Bodine, and Bobby Allison.

at Daytona. The race was dropped after '63, when only seven teams accepted the invitation to compete for the proposed '64 event. The winner's share for the first three all-star events was only $1000.

The Winston of 1985 featured the 12 race winners from '84, and all of them prepared cars to compete in the 105-mile contest. The race was run as part of a doubleheader on Saturday, and essentially was a free show for the spectators who purchased tickets for the NASCAR Late Model Sportsman race the day before the World 600. A crowd of 110,000 was on hand for the highly publicized event.

Darrell Waltrip passed Harry Gant with just over a lap remaining to nail down the first-place prize of $200,000. As Waltrip took the checkered flag, his engine blew to pieces. "Junior [team owner Junior Johnson] said he put a motor in the car that would run 105 miles," said Waltrip. "He had it figured pretty close."

In 1986, The Winston was moved to Atlanta on Mother's Day weekend—a weekend without a scheduled NASCAR Winston Cup event. Bill Elliott won the 1986 race in a runaway.

Over the years, the format of The Winston changed, race procedures were tweaked, and the length varied. In 1992, the race was staged under the lights for the first time. In 2004, the name changed to the NASCAR NEXTEL All-Star Challenge, and changed again in 2008 to the NASCAR Sprint All-Star Race. One thing has remained the same: The race always features close and exciting action.

NASCAR All-Star Race Winners

Year	Track	Race Winner	Car	Miles
1961	Daytona International Speedway	Joe Weatherly	Pontiac	25
1962	Daytona International Speedway	Fireball Roberts	Pontiac	25
1963	Daytona International Speedway	Fred Lorenzen	Ford	25
1985	Charlotte Motor Speedway	Darrell Waltrip	Chevrolet	105
1986	Atlanta International Raceway	Bill Elliott	Ford	126.326
1987	Charlotte Motor Speedway	Dale Earnhardt	Chevrolet	202.5
1988	Charlotte Motor Speedway	Terry Labonte	Chevrolet	202.5
1989	Charlotte Motor Speedway	Rusty Wallace	Pontiac	202.5
1990	Charlotte Motor Speedway	Dale Earnhardt	Chevrolet	105
1991	Charlotte Motor Speedway	Davey Allison	Ford	105
1992	Charlotte Motor Speedway	Davey Allison	Ford	105
1993	Charlotte Motor Speedway	Dale Earnhardt	Chevrolet	105
1994	Charlotte Motor Speedway	Geoff Bodine	Ford	105
1995	Charlotte Motor Speedway	Jeff Gordon	Chevrolet	105
1996	Charlotte Motor Speedway	Michael Waltrip	Ford	105
1997	Charlotte Motor Speedway	Jeff Gordon	Chevrolet	105
1998	Charlotte Motor Speedway	Mark Martin	Ford	105
1999	Lowe's Motor Speedway	Terry Labonte	Chevrolet	105
2000	Lowe's Motor Speedway	Dale Earnhardt, Jr.	Chevrolet	105
2001	Lowe's Motor Speedway	Dale Jarrett	Ford	105
2002	Lowe's Motor Speedway	Ryan Newman	Ford	135
2003	Lowe's Motor Speedway	Jimmie Johnson	Chevrolet	135
2004	Lowe's Motor Speedway	Matt Kenseth	Ford	135
2005	Lowe's Motor Speedway	Mark Martin	Ford	135
2006	Lowe's Motor Speedway	Jimmie Johnson	Chevrolet	135
2007	Lowe's Motor Speedway	Kevin Harvick	Chevrolet	120
2008	Lowe's Motor Speedway	Kasey Kahne	Dodge	150
2009	Lowe's Motor Speedway	Tony Stewart	Chevrolet	150
2010	Charlotte Motor Speedway	Kurt Busch	Dodge	150
2011	Charlotte Motor Speedway	Carl Edwards	Ford	150
2012	Charlotte Motor Speedway	Jimmie Johnson	Chevrolet	135

1985

The Blue Max Racing pit crew works under the hood of Tim Richmond's #27 Pontiac during the Sept. 29 Holly Farms 400 at North Wilkesboro Speedway. Richard and team owner Raymond Beadle struggled throughout the 1985 campaign, failing to scratch the victory column and only posting three top-five finishes. In the North Wilkesboro race, Richmond rallied from the extended pit stop to finish seventh.

▶ Bill Elliott leads Geoff Bodine into the first turn in the Oct. 6 Miller High Life 500 at Charlotte Motor Speedway. After a string of mechanical ills and wrecks, Elliott finally experienced a trouble-free race and ran a close second to Cale Yarborough. Bodine drove his Chevrolet to a third-place finish.

▼ American patriotism made the quarter-panels of Mike Alexander's #95 Chevrolet in the Oct. 6 race at Charlotte Motor Speedway. The youngster from Tennessee, whose Sadler Brothers Chevy was adorned with the "Share The Pride" colors, finished 18th after starting 32nd. Buddy Baker, seen nosing ahead of Alexander, went on to finish eighth in the 500-miler.

▶ Ricky Rudd powers his Bud Moore Ford around turn nine at Riverside International Raceway in the Nov. 17 Winston Western 500 season finale. Rudd drove past Terry Labonte with 24 laps remaining and grabbed his only win of the season. Title contender Darrell Waltrip, leading Bill Elliott by 20 points entering the race, wrapped up the championship with a seventh-place finish. Elliott's title hopes were dashed early when a transmission bolt sheared on the sixth lap. Lengthy repairs caused Elliott to finish 31st in the race and a disappointing second in points despite 11 wins.

Bill Elliott enjoyed a record-wrecking year in 1985 behind the wheel of the #9 Harry Melling/Coors Ford Thunderbird. He won 11 races on superspeedways, an accomplishment still unchallenged in NASCAR's record books. Despite the overwhelming success on NASCAR's speediest offerings, Elliott failed to win the NASCAR Winston Cup Grand National title. Three-time winner Darrell Waltrip took advantage of NASCAR's points system and claimed his third championship.

1985 NASCAR WINSTON CUP GN POINTS RACE

Rank	Driver	Points	Starts	Wins	Top 5	Top 10	Winnings
1	Darrell Waltrip	4292	28	3	18	21	$1,318,374.60
2	Bill Elliott	4191	28	11	16	18	$2,433,186.30
3	Harry Gant	4033	28	3	14	19	$804,286.48
4	Neil Bonnett	3902	28	2	11	18	$530,144.64
5	Geoff Bodine	3862	28	0	10	14	$565,867.82
6	Ricky Rudd	3857	28	1	13	19	$512,440.98
7	Terry Labonte	3683	28	1	8	17	$694,509.16
8	Dale Earnhardt	3561	28	4	10	16	$546,595.32
9	Kyle Petty	3528	28	0	7	12	$296,366.40
10	Lake Speed	3507	28	0	2	14	$300,325.50
11	Tim Richmond	3413	28	0	3	13	$290,283.30
12	Bobby Allison	3312	28	0	7	11	$272,535.56
13	Ron Bouchard	3267	28	0	5	12	$240,303.94
14	Richard Petty	3140	28	0	1	13	$306,141.76
15	Bobby Hillin, Jr.	3091	28	0	0	5	$145,069.58
16	Ken Schrader	3024	28	0	0	3	$211,522.40
17	Buddy Baker	2986	28	0	2	7	$235,479.11
18	Dave Marcis	2871	28	0	0	5	$173,466.93
19	Rusty Wallace	2867	28	0	2	8	$233,669.74
20	Buddy Arrington	2780	28	0	0	1	$153,221.92
21	Phil Parsons	2740	28	0	0	4	$104,840.00
22	Clark Dwyer	2641	28	0	0	0	$128,710.00
23	Jimmy Means	2548	28	0	0	0	$132,130.00
24	Eddie Bierschwale	2396	26	0	0	0	$102,650.00
25	Greg Sacks	1944	20	1	1	0	$234,141.00
26	Cale Yarborough	1861	16	2	6	5	$310,465.00
27	J.D. McDuffie	1853	23	0	0	7	$84,965.00
28	Trevor Boys	1461	20	0	0	0	$76,325.00
29	Benny Parsons	1427	14	0	1	0	$94,450.00
30	Joe Ruttman	1410	16	0	1	6	$81,425.00
31	Morgan Shepherd	1406	16	0	1	4	$55,985.00
32	Bobby Wawak	1226	14	0	0	2	$42,165.00
33	Lennie Pond	1107	12	0	0	0	$70,640.00
34	Tommy Ellis	1100	14	0	0	0	$27,695.00
35	Mike Alexander	1046	11	0	0	1	$43,765.00
36	David Pearson	879	12	0	0	0	$55,625.00
37	Sterling Marlin	645	8	0	0	1	$31,155.00
38	Don Hume	637	7	0	0	0	$22,230.00
39	Ronnie Thomas	631	7	0	0	0	$10,505.00
40	Alan Kulwicki	509	5	0	0	0	$10,290.00
41	Rick Newsom	450	6	0	0	0	$8690.00
42	Mike Potter	443	6	0	0	0	$10,855.00
43	Jerry Bowman	434	5	0	0	0	$8665.00
44	Bobby Gerhart	422	5	0	0	0	$7400.00
45	A.J. Foyt	410	7	0	1	1	$29,750.00
46	Phil Good	406	4	0	0	0	$6870.00
47	Ken Ragan	356	7	0	0	0	$35,995.00
48	Slick Johnson	343	6	0	0	0	$24,995.00
49	Connie Saylor	296	5	0	0	0	$8915.00
50	Jim Sauter	267	3	0	0	0	$15,465.00

The NASCAR Winston Cup Grand National points system came under fire in 1985 as Bill Elliott, who won a record 11 superspeedway races, was blown away in the points race by three-time winner Darrell Waltrip.

Waltrip, who won the title for the third time, also questioned the points system. "There's not enough incentive for winning the race," said Waltrip. "This year I was the beneficiary of the points system. I've been on the other end of it, too. I will be the first to admit that with the year Bill had, he deserved to be the champion."

Elliott led virtually every category, but lost the championship to Waltrip by 101 points. It was the biggest margin of victory since 1978.

Elliott squandered a 206-point lead in the final two months of the season. Waltrip took a commanding lead by finishing 14th at North Wilkesboro in late September. He was never threatened during the final four races.

The points lead changed hands 10 times among five drivers. Lake Speed, Terry Labonte, and Geoff Bodine also enjoyed brief stints atop the standings.

1986

January Following an announcement in late 1985, NASCAR changes the names of its premier stock car racing series and its second-ranked division. "Grand National" has been dropped from the Winston Cup Series and shifted to the old Late Model Sportsman division. "We feel our friends at Winston deserve a name of their own," says NASCAR president Bill France, Jr. The official titles of NASCAR's two leading stock car racing series become NASCAR Winston Cup and NASCAR Busch Grand National.

February 16 Geoff Bodine outlasts Dale Earnhardt to win the Daytona 500. Earnhardt is poised to slingshot around Bodine for the win, but runs out of fuel with three laps remaining.

February 23 Kyle Petty comes from fifth to first when the top four cars are wiped out in a crash and wins the Miller High Life 400 at Richmond Fairgrounds Raceway. Dale Earnhardt triggers a massive pileup in the final laps when he hooks Darrell Waltrip's rear bumper.

March 16 Morgan Shepherd, driving Jack Beebe's unsponsored Buick, holds Dale Earnhardt at bay in the final laps to win the Motorcraft 500 at Atlanta. The victory is the second of Shepherd's NASCAR Winston Cup career.

April 6 Rusty Wallace leads the final 101 laps at Bristol to score the first NASCAR Winston Cup win of his career. Wallace outruns runner-up Ricky Rudd by 10.69 seconds.

May 4 Bobby Allison fends off Dale Earnhardt in a dramatic last-lap duel in the Winston 500 at Talladega. Allison ends a two-year drought with the victory.

June 15 Bill Elliott outruns Harry Gant to win the Miller American 400 at Michigan. Gant makes a miraculous comeback from serious injuries, including a bruised heart, suffered in a crash a week earlier at Pocono. The race is billed as Richard Petty's 1000th career start, although it is only his 999th career NASCAR Winston Cup race.

Richard Petty returned to the Petty Enterprises family operation in 1986 following two seasons with Californian Mike Curb. Pontiac unveiled a new slope-backed Grand Prix 2+2 in '86, but instead of cutting the air smoothly, the car turned out to be an ill-handling beast. Petty failed to win a race for the second year in a row, and he led in only seven of the 29 events.

Neil Bonnett's #12 Chevrolet dives down to the apron as Joe Ruttman's #26 Buick darts toward the outside wall in the Feb. 16 Daytona 500. A broken wheel on Bonnett's car triggered the massive pileup. No drivers were injured in the melee. Numerous crashes brought out 120 miles worth of caution flags, depleting the field for the 28th edition of "The Great American Race." Geoff Bodine won the race without a challenge after Dale Earnhardt, who was running a close second, ran out of gas with three laps to go.

Number 8 Bobby Hillin, Jr., fends off the hard-charging #27 Pontiac of Rusty Wallace in the Feb. 23 Miller High Life 400 at Richmond's Fairgrounds Raceway. Hillin finished sixth and Wallace 10th. Each of the young drivers would score his first NASCAR Winston Cup victory in the 1986 season—Wallace at Bristol and Hillin at Talladega.

Kyle Petty is greeted by wife Pattie in victory lane following Kyle's first career NASCAR Winston Cup victory in the Miller High Life 400. Petty, laboring in fifth place with little hope of winning, scooted into the lead with three laps to go when Dale Earnhardt hooked Darrell Waltrip and triggered a crash that took out the top four runners. Petty weaved his way through the accident unharmed, and drove to victory under the caution flag.

Tim Richmond keeps his #25 Chevy ahead of a thundering herd of challengers in the March 16 Motorcraft 500 at Atlanta International Raceway. Following closely are #44 Terry Labonte, #3 Dale Earnhardt, and a side-by-side trio of #55 Benny Parsons, #5 Geoff Bodine, and #22 Bobby Allison. Earnhardt finished second to Morgan Shepherd, who drove an unsponsored Buick to an upset win. Richmond placed seventh.

Bill Elliott slings his #9 Ford into the high-banked turn at Bristol International Raceway ahead of #43 Richard Petty, #33 Harry Gant, and #5 Geoff Bodine during the April 6 Valleydale 500. Elliott, not known for his short-track prowess, had one of his finest runs at Bristol, finishing fifth.

Dale Earnhardt spins his #3 Chevrolet in the Valleydale 500. Earnhardt backed into the concrete barrier while running with the leaders. He recovered with only cosmetic damage, and went on to finish 10th. Rusty Wallace, a 29-year-old St. Louis native, recorded his first career NASCAR Winston Cup victory in the 500-lap race.

Bobby Hillin, Jr.'s #8 Miller Buick slaps the concrete wall at Darlington Raceway after spinning out in the April 13 TranSouth 500. Rusty Wallace's #27 Pontiac scoots safely past to the low side. Wallace went on to finish sixth, but he was three full laps behind winner Dale Earnhardt. Earnhardt, who manhandled the field, was never passed under green-flag conditions.

1986

July 27 Bobby Hillin, Jr., a 22-year-old Texan, holds off Tim Richmond in a last-lap battle to win the Talladega 500. Hillin, Jr., becomes the third youngest driver to win a NASCAR Winston Cup race.

August 10 The NASCAR Winston Cup Series makes its first visit to Watkins Glen since 1965, and Tim Richmond wins the 219-mile event. Richmond's Chevy beats Darrell Waltrip by 1.45-seconds on the twisting road course.

September 14 Ricky Rudd scores his first career superspeedway victory in the Delaware 500 at Dover Downs. Rudd beats runner-up Neil Bonnett by 5.08 seconds.

October 5 Dale Earnhardt romps to victory in Charlotte's Oakwood Homes 500. Tire problems force Earnhardt to make two unscheduled pit stops early, dropping him two laps and more than four miles behind the leaders. Timely caution flags help Earnhardt make up the laps and sprint to the win.

November 16 Tim Richmond wins his seventh race of the season as Dale Earnhardt captures his second NASCAR Winston Cup championship. Earnhardt places second and finishes 288 points in front of Darrell Waltrip for the title.

Joe Ruttman's #26 Buick is knocked sideways after a tap from #3 Dale Earnhardt during the middle stages of the April 20 First Union 400 at North Wilkesboro Speedway. Ruttman was in contention for the win until the mishap, but he recovered to finish fifth. Earnhardt went on to outrun Ricky Rudd by two car lengths for the win, and from victory lane, made a public apology for spinning Ruttman.

Bill Elliott's red Ford spits a plume of smoke in the early laps of the April 27 Sovran Bank 500 at Martinsville Speedway. Elliott's engine expired after only 42 laps, leaving him with a last-place finish. Kyle Petty drove the #7 Wood Brothers Ford to a fourth-place showing.

Willy T. Ribbs became the fifth African American driver to compete at NASCAR's top level in the April 20 First Union 400. Ribbs, driving a car prepared by the once-powerful DiGard team, spun out twice and salvaged a 22nd-place finish. Ribbs was first offered a NASCAR Winston Cup Grand National ride in 1978, but he failed to show up for two practice sessions and was dumped by team owner Will Cronkrite. A kid by the name of Dale Earnhardt took Ribbs' place. Eight years later, Ribbs finally received a second chance at the NASCAR Winston Cup Series.

► Ricky Rudd drives the #15 Bud Moore/Motorcraft Ford Thunderbird under the checkered flag to win the Sovran Bank 500. Rudd had a free ride in the late stages of the event as virtually every other contender fell out of the race. The drivers that finished second through 16th never led, and Rudd finished a full lap ahead of the field.

Number 25 Tim Richmond hugs the low line as he battles with #43 Richard Petty, #22 Bobby Allison, and #3 Dale Earnhardt in the May 4 Winston 500 at Talladega. Allison and Earnhardt treated the sellout audience to a terrific last-lap duel. The two determined drivers swapped the lead three times on the final lap before Allison forged ahead at the finish line. Allison's triumph gave the Stavola Brothers their first NASCAR Winston Cup win.

Rookie Michael Waltrip skids into the infield dirt after his solo crash in the Winston 500. Driving a Pontiac for Bob Bahre, the young Waltrip made a stab at the 1986 Rookie of the Year honors. He competed in 28 races, but didn't crack the top 10 in the championship points race. Waltrip wound up second in the rookie chase to Alan Kulwicki.

D.K. Ulrich talks with Richard Petty on the day before the May 25 Coca-Cola World 600 at Charlotte Motor Speedway. Petty crashed his familiar #43 Pontiac in a practice session two days before the race, suffering a concussion and a bruised leg. NASCAR officials didn't allow Petty to bring in a backup car. On the verge of having to sit out the race, Petty was offered a seat in Ulrich's #6 Chevrolet. Petty accepted and the lime-green car was dressed with STP decals for the 600. Petty departed the race early with mechanical problems.

Tim Richmond and Dale Earnhardt share victory lane after Earnhardt's win in the Coca-Cola 600 at Charlotte Motor Speedway. Earnhardt struggled deep in the field for most of the day and was only a couple of car lengths from going a lap down. He rallied in the final stages and took the lead for keeps with 16 laps remaining. Richmond finished second.

Greg Sacks' Chevrolet lurches sideways during the Pepsi Firecracker 400 at Daytona. Sacks, the defending champion of the July 4 event, struggled throughout the 1986 NASCAR Winston Cup campaign as the once-powerful DiGard Racing team fell on hard times. The DiGard team could only secure an associate sponsorship package from TRW in '86. A year later, the DiGard team folded.

Rick Wilson skids off the banking at Daytona International Speedway during the Pepsi Firecracker 400. Wilson was able to continue in the race and motor to a 21st-place finish. Wilson was driving the #4 Kodak Film Oldsmobile fielded by the Morgan-McClure team, which was in its fourth year of operation. The 1986 campaign marked the first year of Kodak's long association with Larry McClure's formidable unit.

Bobby Allison (right) gives some pointers to his young son Davey during the July 27 Talladega 500 weekend. The 25-year-old Davey was appointed to drive Junior Johnson's Chevrolet in place of Neil Bonnett, who had to sit out the race due to injuries suffered in a crash at Pocono. Allison responded brilliantly, finishing seventh after leading for 13 laps. Bobby placed 10th, the victim of a last-lap crash while running in the top five.

Tim Richmond wrestles his #25 Chevrolet around the Watkins Glen road course in the Aug. 10 The Budweiser at the Glen. The historic road course in the Finger Lake region of upstate New York returned to the annual NASCAR tour after a 15-year void. Richmond drove past Darrell Waltrip with 12 laps remaining and sped to victory. Richmond developed into one of NASCAR's brightest stars in 1986, posting short-track, superspeedway, and road-course wins in his first year driving for team owner Rick Hendrick.

Number 3 Dale Earnhardt surges past #28 Cale Yarborough, #27 Rusty Wallace, #15 Ricky Rudd, and #55 Benny Parsons during the Aug. 17 Champion Spark Plug 400 at Michigan International Speedway. Earnhardt finished fourth and held on to his commanding lead in the NASCAR Winston Cup points standings. Earnhardt took the points lead in early May and never relinquished it along the way to his second championship.

Richard Petty runs ahead of Dale Earnhardt in the Sept. 7 Wrangler Jeans Indigo 400 at Richmond's tight ½-mile oval. Petty had one of his finer runs of the season at Richmond, finishing fourth. Earnhardt came home second. Earnhardt had knocked Petty out of the Southern 500 the previous week. Afterward, Petty said of Earnhardt, "his mind goes out of gear when he flips on the switch to turn on the motor."

200-mph Qualifying Runs

ON MARCH 24, 1970, Buddy Baker became the first man to eclipse 200 mph in a special speed run at Talladega. Driving a winged Dodge Daytona in a series of speed runs, Baker's first lap over 200 was measured at 200.096 mph. He surpassed the 200-mph barrier on two additional laps, the quickest being 200.447 mph.

Restrictor plates made their first appearance five months after Baker's record run, and no more 200-mph laps were seen until 12 years later.

Benny Parsons became the first NASCAR driver to top 200 mph in an official qualifying run. Driving a Pontiac out of the Harry Ranier Racing shops, Parsons won the pole for the May 2, 1982, Talladega Winston 500 at 200.176 mph.

By 1986, qualifying laps in excess of 200 mph were fairly routine. Bill Elliott, nicknamed "The Fastest Man Alive," was zipping through the electric timing lights at alarming speeds. In time trials for the '86 Winston 500 at Talladega, Elliott's Ford won the pole at a 212.229-mph clip. The following year, in the last race at Talladega without carburetor restrictor plates, Elliott turned in an all-time NASCAR Cup Series qualifying record of 212.809 mph.

By the summer of 1987, NASCAR had imposed a smaller carburetor on all cars. At the beginning of the '88 season, carburetor restrictor plates had returned for all races at Daytona and Talladega. That immediately brought down qualifying speeds below 200 mph, and it wasn't until 2012, on the newly repaved Michigan International Speedway, that a 200+ mph qualifying speed was once again posted.

Through 2012, a total of 77 NASCAR Cup Series drivers have turned in official qualifying laps above the 200-mph barrier. Topping the list with the most 200+ mph qualifying laps is Cale Yarborough, with 15.

Top 30 Qualifying Speeds in NASCAR NEXTEL Cup History

Rank	Driver	Qualifying Speed	Race	Track
1	Bill Elliott	212.809	1987 Winston 500	Talladega
2	Bill Elliott	212.229	1986 Winston 500	Talladega
3	Bobby Allison	211.797	1987 Winston 500	Talladega
4	Davey Allison	210.610	1987 Winston 500	Talladega
5	Darrell Waltrip	210.471	1987 Winston 500	Talladega
6	Bill Elliott	210.364	1987 Daytona 500	Daytona
7	Dale Earnhardt	210.360	1987 Winston 500	Talladega
8	Kyle Petty	210.346	1987 Winston 500	Talladega
9	Sterling Marlin	210.194	1987 Winston 500	Talladega
10	Terry Labonte	210.101	1987 Winston 500	Talladega
11	Phil Parsons	209.963	1987 Winston 500	Talladega
	Lake Speed	209.963	1987 Winston 500	Talladega
13	Geoff Bodine	209.710	1987 Winston 500	Talladega
14	Buddy Baker	209.701	1987 Winston 500	Talladega
15	Bill Elliott	209.398	1985 Winston 500	Talladega
16	Bobby Allison	209.274	1986 Winston 500	Talladega
17	Davey Allison	209.084	1987 Daytona 500	Daytona
18	Bill Elliott	209.005	1986 Talladega 500	Talladega
19	Ron Bouchard	208.910	1987 Winston 500	Talladega
20	Rusty Wallace	208.251	1987 Winston 500	Talladega
21	Ken Schrader	208.227	1987 Daytona 500	Daytona
22	Geoff Bodine	208.169	1986 Winston 500	Talladega
23	Ken Schrader	208.160	1987 Winston 500	Talladega
24	Bobby Hillin, Jr.	208.142	1987 Winston 500	Talladega
25	Ricky Rudd	208.138	1987 Winston 500	Talladega
26	Cale Yarborough	208.092	1986 Winston 500	Talladega
	Cale Yarborough	208.092	1987 Winston 500	Talladega
28	Dale Earnhardt	208.052	1986 Talladega 500	Talladega
29	Morgan Shepherd	207.831	1987 Winston 500	Talladega
30	Bobby Allison	207.795	1987 Daytona 500	Daytona

1986

Alan Kulwicki guides his #35 Quincy's Steak House Ford through a turn at Richmond en route to a 15th-place finish. Kulwicki's freshman season in NASCAR Winston Cup racing was quite remarkable. He bought the car from team owner Bill Terry in spring and tackled the NASCAR Winston Cup tour with his one-and-only car. Driving the car on short tracks, superspeedways, and road courses, Kulwicki managed to log four top-10 finishes. For his determined efforts with a short-handed crew and a single-car operation, Kulwicki was voted 1986 Rookie of the Year.

Number 3 Dale Earnhardt and #25 Tim Richmond battle side-by-side in the Oct. 5 Oakwood Homes 500 at Charlotte Motor Speedway. Earnhardt rallied from a two-lap deficit early in the event. Two cut tires dropped him four miles off the pace, but with the aid of a rash of caution flags, he was able to scramble back onto the lead lap in just 20 laps. Once back in contention, Earnhardt easily disposed of the field, lapping all rivals except runner-up Harry Gant. The win gave Earnhardt a comfortable 159-point lead in the title chase with just three races to go.

Sophomore Ken Schrader, driving Junie Donlavey's #90 Ford, battles with #22 Bobby Allison, #11 Darrell Waltrip, and #27 Rusty Wallace in the Oct. 19 Nationwise 500 at North Carolina Motor Speedway. A product of Midwestern open-wheel racing, Schrader enjoyed a moderately successful campaign in 1986. He landed in the top 10 in four races and placed 16th in the final NASCAR Winston Cup points standings.

When Rick Hendrick hired Tim Richmond in 1986, veteran crew chief Harry Hyde (left) took on the task of tutoring and nurturing the thirty-year-old driver. Despite predictions to the contrary due to their opposite personalities, the two men immediately developed a cohesive chemistry and enjoyed a highly successful season. Following his seven-win season, Richmond announced that he would be unable to begin the '87 NASCAR Winston Cup campaign due to a mysterious illness. Richmond would eventually die of complications caused by the AIDS virus on Aug. 13, 1989.

1986 NASCAR WINSTON CUP POINTS RACE

Rank	Driver	Points	Starts	Wins	Top 5	Top 10	Winnings
1	Dale Earnhardt	4468	29	5	15	23	$1,768,879.80
2	Darrell Waltrip	4180	29	3	21	22	$1,099,734.90
3	Tim Richmond	4174	29	7	13	17	$973,220.92
4	Bill Elliott	3844	29	2	8	16	$1,049,141.92
5	Ricky Rudd	3823	29	2	11	17	$671,547.74
6	Rusty Wallace	3762	29	2	4	16	$557,353.94
7	Bobby Allison	3698	29	1	6	15	$503,094.96
8	Geoff Bodine	3678	29	2	10	15	$795,110.96
9	Bobby Hillin, Jr.	3546	29	1	4	14	$448,451.46
10	Kyle Petty	3537	29	1	4	14	$403,241.98
11	Harry Gant	3498	29	0	9	13	$583,023.63
12	Terry Labonte	3473	29	1	5	10	$522,234.73
13	Neil Bonnett	3369	28	1	6	12	$485,929.18
14	Richard Petty	3314	29	0	4	11	$280,656.38
15	Joe Ruttman	3295	29	0	5	14	$259,262.48
16	Ken Schrader	3052	29	0	0	4	$235,903.58
17	Dave Marcis	2912	20	0	1	4	$220,460.21
18	Morgan Shepherd	2896	27	1	4	8	$244,145.21
19	Michael Waltrip	2853	28	0	0	0	$108,766.86
20	Buddy Arrington	2776	26	0	0	0	$186,587.96
21	Alan Kulwicki	2705	23	0	1	4	$94,450.00
22	Jimmy Means	2495	26	0	0	0	$157,940.00
23	Tommy Ellis	2393	24	0	0	3	$78,310.00
24	Buddy Baker	1924	17	0	6	6	$138,600.00
25	Eddie Bierschwale	1860	24	0	0	0	$98,110.00
26	J.D. McDuffie	1825	20	0	0	0	$106,115.00
27	Phil Parsons	1742	17	0	1	5	$84,680.00
28	Rick Wilson	1698	17	0	0	4	$88,820.00
29	Cale Yarborough	1642	16	0	2	5	$137,010.00
30	Benny Parsons	1555	16	0	2	4	$176,985.00
31	Ron Bouchard	1553	17	0	0	2	$106,835.00
32	Chet Fillip	1433	17	0	0	0	$36,110.00
33	Jody Ridley	1213	12	0	0	1	$84,380.00
34	Trevor Boys	1064	14	0	0	0	$74,645.00
35	Doug Heveron	1052	13	0	0	0	$74,030.00
36	Sterling Marlin	989	10	0	2	4	$113,070.00
37	D.K. Ulrich	804	10	0	0	0	$47,795.00
38	Pancho Carter	706	9	0	0	0	$56,366.00
39	Ken Ragan	627	7	0	0	0	$33,890.00
40	Lake Speed	608	5	0	0	2	$82,800.00
41	Greg Sacks	579	8	0	0	1	$64,810.00
42	Ronnie Thomas	504	6	0	0	0	$25,215.00
43	Bobby Wawak	480	6	0	0	0	$10,155.00
44	Rodney Combs	421	5	0	0	0	$12,180.00
45	Derrike Cope	400	5	0	0	1	$8025.00
46	James Hylton	386	5	0	0	0	$22,090.00
47	Davey Allison	364	5	0	0	1	$24,190.00
48	Mark Martin	364	5	0	0	0	$20,515.00
49	Jim Sauter	361	8	0	0	0	$52,020.00
50	A.J. Foyt	355	5	0	0	0	$24,135.00

Dale Earnhardt grabbed his second NASCAR Winston Cup championship in 1986, finishing a comfortable 288 points ahead of runner-up Darrell Waltrip.

Earnhardt grabbed the points lead in early May with a runner-up finish in Talladega's Winston 500. The determined Richard Childress Chevrolet driver never let anybody challenge his healthy advantage for the remainder of the season. He held a lead of at least 100 points the entire second half of the season.

Tim Richmond compiled the biggest numbers during the season, winning seven races and eight poles. But Richmond's slow start to the season made it impossible for him to overtake Earnhardt. Waltrip won three races and edged Richmond for second place by only six points. Bill Elliott and Ricky Rudd rounded out the top five.

1987

January 8 Tim Richmond announces he will miss the first part of the 1987 NASCAR Winston Cup season with an illness he says is "double pneumonia." Team owner Rick Hendrick announces Benny Parsons will replace Richmond until he can return.

February 15 Geoff Bodine runs out of fuel with three laps to go, allowing Bill Elliott to score his second win in the Daytona 500. Benny Parsons finishes second in his first assignment since replacing Tim Richmond.

March 8 Dale Earnhardt crashes in practice, but drives a repaired Chevrolet to his 22nd career victory in the Miller High Life 400 at Richmond Fairgrounds Raceway.

April 12 Dale Earnhardt bangs Sterling Marlin out of the lead near the midway point and speeds to victory in the Valleydale 500 at Bristol. Richard Petty finishes a close second.

May 3 Bill Elliott wins the pole for the Winston 500 at Talladega with a record run of 212.809 mph. Rookie Davey Allison wins the race in his 14th career NASCAR Winston Cup start. The event is marred by a scary crash when Bobby Allison blows a tire and sails into the catch fence. The race is halted for three hours while the fence is repaired.

May 24 Kyle Petty survives a day of heavy attrition and captures Charlotte's Coca-Cola 600 for his first superspeedway win. Driving the Wood Brothers Ford, Petty gives the Stuart, Va., team its 70th superspeedway win.

June 14 Tim Richmond makes his first start of the season and wins the Miller High Life 500 at Pocono. The seriously ill Richmond finishes just in front of runner-up Bill Elliott.

July 4 Bobby Allison blasts out of the middle of the pack, roars past Ken Schrader with two laps to go, and wins the Pepsi Firecracker 400 at Daytona. Allison is running 13th with five laps to go, but makes up the deficit and drives to an impressive triumph.

Bill Elliott won the pole for the Feb. 15 Daytona 500 with a record speed of 210.364 mph. His time trial came in an era before NASCAR mandated restrictive devices for the ultrafast speedways in Daytona and Talladega. In May, Elliott qualified at an all-time record 212.809 mph at Talladega. That mark will likely live in the record books forever because NASCAR officials take measures to ensure that the 200-mph barrier will never be topped again.

Davey Allison pokes his unsponsored #28 Ford under #35 Benny Parsons in the Feb. 12 Twin 125-miler at Daytona. Allison, a rookie, hooked up with team owner Harry Ranier in 1987, and promptly earned a front-row starting position for the Daytona 500. Parsons was in his first assignment with the Hendrick Motorsports team, replacing the AIDS stricken Tim Richmond. Parsons won the Twin 125 as Allison finished sixth.

Bill Elliott and Davey Allison lead the charge to the green flag for the 29th running of the Daytona 500. Elliott led more than half the race and won his second Daytona 500 in a three-year span. Allison ran with the leaders in the early going, but lost 17 laps on an extended pit stop when a wheel dislodged from his car following a routine stop. Allison made up one lap, but still finished 16 laps down in 27th place. His impressive showing at Speedweeks was rewarded shortly thereafter as the Ranier team picked up sponsorship from Texaco.

Rusty Wallace drove the slope-backed #27 Kodiak Pontiac in 1987, winning twice. The victories came on the road courses at Watkins Glen and Riverside. Wallace was also a stout contender on the short tracks and many of the superspeedways. Wallace finished fifth in the final NASCAR Winston Cup points standings on the strength of 16 top-10 efforts.

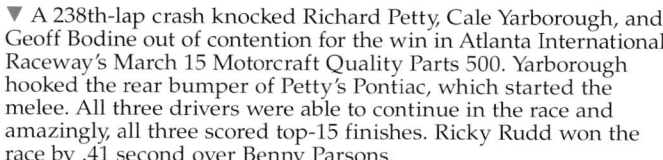

▼ A 238th-lap crash knocked Richard Petty, Cale Yarborough, and Geoff Bodine out of contention for the win in Atlanta International Raceway's March 15 Motorcraft Quality Parts 500. Yarborough hooked the rear bumper of Petty's Pontiac, which started the melee. All three drivers were able to continue in the race and amazingly, all three scored top-15 finishes. Ricky Rudd won the race by .41 second over Benny Parsons.

Dale Earnhardt's #3 Chevrolet leads #35 Benny Parsons and #88 Buddy Baker in the Daytona 500. All three drivers enjoyed strong performances in "The Great American Race." Parsons finished second, while Baker was fourth and Earnhardt fifth. Baker was in his third year of driving his own car, which he co-owned with Danny Schiff. "I never knew how much it costs to run a team until I had to pay the bills Monday after the race," said Baker.

Number 9 Bill Elliott runs just ahead of #3 Dale Earnhardt and #90 Ken Schrader in the March 29 Darlington TranSouth 500. Schrader recorded his first career pole in Junie Donlavey's Ford, tripping the timing lights at 158.367 mph. Schrader went on to finish fifth. Earnhardt won the race when leader Elliott ran out of fuel on the final lap.

Number 3 Dale Earnhardt took a bite out of #44 Sterling Marlin's rear bumper, sending him into the wall on the 252nd lap of the April 12 Valleydale 500 at Bristol. Marlin was leading when Earnhardt's bump sent him tail-first into the concrete retaining wall. Marlin and several other drivers complained about Earnhardt's rough driving in the Bristol race. "He's gotta learn to try to pass other cars and not spin them out," said Marlin. Earnhardt went on to win easily, leading all but one of the final 122 laps.

August 16 Bill Elliott passes Dale Earnhardt with three laps remaining and wins the Champion Spark Plug 400 at Michigan International Speedway. Tim Richmond, driving in his final NASCAR Winston Cup event, finishes 29th.

September 27 Darrell Waltrip barges through Dale Earnhardt and Terry Labonte on the final lap to score his first win with Hendrick Motorsports in the wild Goody's 500 at Martinsville Speedway. Labonte and Earnhardt spin in the third turn as Waltrip shoots the gap to score the win.

October 25 Bill Elliott wins the AC Delco 500 at Rockingham as Dale Earnhardt clinches his third NASCAR Winston Cup championship. Earnhardt finishes second and has a 515-point lead in the championship standings with two races left in the season.

November 22 Bill Elliott leads 162 of the 328 laps at Atlanta and easily wins the season finale. Newly crowned NASCAR champion Dale Earnhardt finishes second.

Morgan Shepherd wheels his creased #26 Buick around Martinsville Speedway during the April 26 Sovran Bank 500. Shepherd won the pole in Kenny Bernstein's Buick and led the opening 34 laps, but he got mixed up in one of the 11 incidents that brought out the caution flag. Shepherd finished 17th after his engine expired in the late stages.

Dale Earnhardt whizzes past the frontstretch grandstands in the April 26 race at Martinsville. The Intimidator grabbed the lead 17 laps from the finish when leader Geoff Bodine spun out. It was the fourth consecutive victory for Earnhardt, who also won six of the first eight races of the season. He led the points standings all year long with the exception of the first two races.

Davey Allison celebrates his first career NASCAR Winston Cup victory in Talladega's victory lane. Allison drove past Dale Earnhardt with 10 laps remaining in the May 3 Winston 500 and led the rest of the way. The race was the final event at Talladega without carburetor restrictor plates. Smaller carburetors were in place for the summer event at Talladega and by '88, restrictor plates were issued to all teams. Bobby Allison's frightening 21st-lap crash, in which he nearly sailed into the grandstands, prompted NASCAR to slow the cars down for future races at Talladega and Daytona.

Tim Richmond, the flashy NASCAR star afflicted with the AIDS virus, made his return to competitive racing in the May 17 The Winston all-star race. The driver from Ashland, Ohio, finished third behind Dale Earnhardt and Terry Labonte. Richmond made his return in an official NASCAR Winston Cup points race in June and immediately posted back-to-back victories at Pocono and Riverside. He competed in eight races over the next nine weeks before his failing health forced him to sit out for the remainder of the year. Richmond never got back into a race car and eventually passed away on Aug. 13, 1989.

Neil Bonnett's #75 Pontiac whacks the wall hard in the late stages of Charlotte Motor Speedway's May 24 Coca-Cola 600. Bonnett's crash resulted in one of the 12 caution flags in the wreck-strewn event. Only 17 of the 42 starters were able to finish. Bonnett, who was uninjured in the hard crash, placed 13th even though he sat on the sidelines for the final 21 laps. Kyle Petty posted his second career victory in the race.

The Pass in the Grass

THE THIRD ANNUAL running of The Winston, NASCAR's all-star race, featured a 20-car starting field comprised of NASCAR Winston Cup racing's most recent winners. It was indeed an all-star cast, with such luminaries as Dale Earnhardt, Bill Elliott, Tim Richmond, Richard Petty, Cale Yarborough, Davey Allison, Darrell Waltrip, Harry Gant, and a host of other top-ranked drivers.

NASCAR's all-star shootout in 1987 was a spine-tingling episode that still ranks as one of stock car racing's most memorable finishes. The three-part event was staged on May 17, 1987, at Charlotte Motor Speedway. The race has been unofficially christened "The Pass in the Grass," although events that transpired on that afternoon never featured a pass in the grass.

Earnhardt was at center stage during the 1987 NASCAR Winston Cup campaign. By May, he had already virtually locked up the championship. He had a huge cushion in the points race and he would remain unchallenged for the remainder of the year. As Earnhardt's star rose, he acquired the nickname "The Intimidator," which he would proudly carry the rest of his career. Many of Earnhardt's adversaries claimed his aggressive driving style led to unnecessary incidents—and there was plenty of damaged sheetmetal along the way.

Early in the year, Harry Gant claimed Earnhardt was "blind as a bat" following an incident at Richmond. After a tap from behind, Gant slugged the wall. At Bristol a few weeks later, Sterling Marlin complained loudly about Earnhardt's antics following a hard crash Marlin felt was caused by Earnhardt. "He needs to start trying to pass people instead of knocking them into the wall," Marlin fumed.

The fireworks were really lit in The Winston at Charlotte. Bill Elliott led virtually all the way in the first two segments of the three-part special event. At the start of the final 10-lap dash, Geoff Bodine got the jump on the field and led the speedy parade into the first turn. Earnhardt thrust his Chevrolet to the outside, moved beside Elliott, and pinched his Ford rival onto the apron. Elliott's car wobbled and

snagged Bodine's rear bumper as he came back onto the banking. Bodine spun out, carrying Elliott to the high side. Earnhardt bolted to the low groove and took the lead.

When the green flag came out, Earnhardt led Elliott by a narrow margin, and the two put on a suspenseful show for the trackside audience. The rear bumper of Earnhardt's Chevrolet moved out wider each lap, and all of Elliott's attempts to take the lead were foiled. Elliott faked to the high side exiting the fourth turn and swept down low. Earnhardt blocked both moves, but fenders made contact. Earnhardt angled across the racing surface and into the grass in the tri-oval. Miraculously, he came back onto the track still in the lead. It was one of racing's most memorable moments, and it thus it became known as "The Pass in the Grass."

On the backstretch, Elliott made one final attempt at a pass on the high side. As the pair sped into the turn, Earnhardt guided his car up and nearly forced Elliott into the wall. Two laps later, Elliott blew a tire and fell off the pace. Elliott placed 14th as Earnhardt sped to victory. After the race ended, Elliott weaved his Ford through traffic and popped Earnhardt's rear bumper with a solid lick.

"Earnhardt turned left into me and tried to push me into the grass," Elliott said. "Then he tried to run me into the wall. It's pretty obvious what he did. If a man has to run over you, it's time to stop. I'm sick of it. Everybody knows his style."

Bodine agreed, saying, "I guess we have to blame this on Earnhardt. It seems he's been doing a lot of that lately. It isn't safe and it isn't racing when you have to knock people out of the way to win a race." Earnhardt defended his actions and pointed his finger at Elliott. "Elliott clipped me and turned me sideways," steamed Earnhardt. "I guarantee if I had turned someone sideways like that, I'd be hanging from the flag pole right now. After the race, he ran into me." Earnhardt, Elliott, and Bodine were all fined and placed on probation after the fracas. For the most part, cooler heads prevailed for the remainder of the year.

The Winston of 1987 is still regarded as one of the most energized and spectacular thrill shows in NASCAR Cup Series history.

1987

Ken Schrader's Ford barrel rolls down the short chute at Daytona International Speedway on the last lap of the July 4 Pepsi Firecracker 400. Schrader was battling for second place when he lost control of his car and darted into the high-speed groove. The errant Ford slid upside down across the finish line and Schrader still got credit for finishing seventh.

Bobby Allison smiles from victory lane after his unexpected win in the July 4 Pepsi Firecracker 400. Allison was a lap behind with nine laps to go, but regained the lap with the aid of a late caution period. Lined up 13th on the restart with five laps to go, Allison mounted an incredible charge. He slashed his way through the field and swept into the lead with a little over a lap remaining. Radio, television, and track announcers had no idea Allison was even on the lead lap when he drove across the finish line first.

Darrell Waltrip steers his #17 Tide Chevrolet through a tight corner at Martinsville during the Sept. 27 Goody's 500. Waltrip barged his way through leaders Dale Earnhardt and Terry Labonte in the third turn of the final lap. "I shot into Terry, he shot into Dale, and I shot into the lead," explained Waltrip. In his first year with Hendrick Motorsports, Waltrip struggled with the #17 Tide Chevrolet team for most of the '87 campaign, managing only to win at Martinsville.

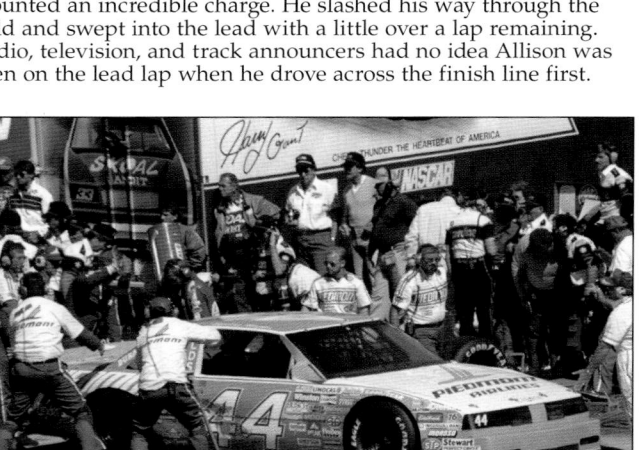 

Terry Labonte's Junior Johnson pit crew services the #44 Oldsmobile during the Oct. 4 Holly Farms 400 at North Wilkesboro Speedway. Labonte's day was almost over early when a blown tire caused him to graze the wall. Labonte parked the car on the track, bringing out a caution flag. He then drove into the pits to have the tire fixed. A quick late-race pit stop helped Labonte to a car-length lead over Dale Earnhardt, which he parlayed into his first victory with the Junior Johnson team.

Team owner Richard Childress drives a Chevrolet with the black Goodwrench colors prior to the start of the Oct. 25 AC Delco 500 at Rockingham's North Carolina Motor Speedway. After a successful seven-year relationship with Wrangler Jeans, Childress and driver Dale Earnhardt announced that GM Goodwrench would begin sponsoring the #3 Chevy in 1988.

Bill Elliott won three of the final four races of the year, taking the checkered flag at Charlotte, Rockingham, and Atlanta. His late-season spurt earned him second place in the final points standings and gave him momentum heading into the 1988 campaign. Driving the Harry Melling/Coors Ford, Elliott won six races and logged 20 top-10 finishes in '87.

Dale Earnhardt wrapped up the NASCAR Winston Cup championship by simply starting the AC Delco 500 on Oct. 25. Earnhardt piled up an insurmountable points lead early in the year and coasted to his third NASCAR title. Earnhardt enjoyed his most productive season in 1987. He won 11 races, the most of his career. Earnhardt was virtually unchallenged for the championship by early summer and finished 489 points in front of runner-up Bill Elliott. He finished in the top five in 24 of his 29 starts.

1987 NASCAR WINSTON CUP POINTS RACE

Rank	Driver	Points	Starts	Wins	Top 5	Top 10	Winnings
1	Dale Earnhardt	4696	29	11	21	24	$2,069,243
2	Bill Elliott	4207	29	6	16	20	$1,599,210
3	Terry Labonte	4007	27	1	13	20	$805,054
4	Darrell Waltrip	3911	29	1	6	16	$511,768
5	Rusty Wallace	3818	29	2	9	16	$690,652
6	Ricky Rudd	3742	29	2	10	13	$653,508
7	Kyle Petty	3737	29	1	6	14	$544,437
8	Richard Petty	3708	27	0	9	13	$445,227
9	Bobby Allison	3530	29	1	4	13	$515,894
10	Ken Schrader	3405	29	0	1	10	$375,918
11	Sterling Marlin	3381	29	0	4	8	$306,412
12	Neil Bonnett	3352	26	0	5	15	$401,541
13	Geoff Bodine	3328	29	0	3	10	$449,816
14	Phil Parsons	3327	29	0	1	7	$180,261
15	Alan Kulwicki	3238	29	0	3	9	$369,889
16	Benny Parsons	3215	29	0	6	9	$566,484
17	Morgan Shepherd	3099	29	0	7	11	$317,034
18	Dave Marcis	3080	29	0	2	7	$256,354
19	Bobby Hillin, Jr.	3027	29	0	1	4	$346,735
20	Michael Waltrip	2840	29	0	0	1	$205,370
21	Davey Allison	2824	22	2	9	10	$361,060
22	Harry Gant	2725	29	0	0	4	$197,645
23	Jimmy Means	2483	28	0	0	1	$154,055
24	Buddy Baker	2373	20	0	3	10	$255,320
25	Buddy Arrington	1885	20	0	0	0	$115,300
26	Dale Jarrett	1840	24	0	0	2	$143,405
27	Steve Christman	1727	20	0	0	0	$54,965
28	Rick Wilson	1723	19	0	0	1	$65,935
29	Cale Yarborough	1450	16	0	2	4	$111,025
30	J.D. McDuffie	1361	17	0	0	0	$45,555
31	Lake Speed	1345	13	0	1	5	$110,810
32	Brett Bodine	1271	16	0	0	2	$71,460
33	Greg Sacks	1200	16	0	0	0	$54,815
34	Eddie Bierschwale	1162	14	0	0	0	$66,790
35	Rodney Combs	1098	14	0	0	0	$90,990
36	Tim Richmond	1063	8	2	3	4	$151,850
37	Derrike Cope	797	12	0	0	0	$33,750
38	Mark Stahl	687	9	0	0	0	$32,850
39	Bobby Wawak	638	8	0	0	0	$22,505
40	D.K. Ulrich	625	7	0	0	0	$30,915
41	Ken Ragan	549	6	0	0	0	$30,575
42	Connie Saylor	486	10	0	0	0	$59,455
43	Jerry Cranmer	482	5	0	0	0	$20,660
44	Trevor Boys	460	10	0	0	0	$59,240
45	Mike Potter	456	6	0	0	0	$13,290
46	Slick Johnson	444	8	0	0	0	$40,630
47	Ron Bouchard	440	5	0	0	1	$24,105
48	H.B. Bailey	428	5	0	0	0	$18,885
49	A.J. Foyt	409	6	0	0	0	$21,075
50	Larry Pearson	401	4	0	0	1	$18,555

Dale Earnhardt blasted out of the starting blocks by winning six of the first eight races in the 1987 NASCAR Winston Cup season and coasted to his third championship. By September, Earnhardt had built up a hefty 608-point lead.

On the strength of 11 victories in his 29 starts, Earnhardt finished 489 points in front of runner-up Bill Elliott, who won six races. Earnhardt finished out of the top five in only eight races. The outcome of the championship was never in doubt past April.

Elliott led the points standings after the first two races, but Earnhardt charged into the lead with a victory at Richmond on March 8. By the sixth race of the year, Earnhardt held a lead of more than 100 points. He clinched the championship after the 27th race of the season at Rockingham.

Besides Earnhardt and Elliott, no other driver won more than two races.

1988

February 14 It is "Allison Wonderland" in the 30th running of the Daytona 500 as Bobby and Davey Allison finish first and second in NASCAR's most prestigious event. Richard Petty survives a wild tumble just past the halfway point. NASCAR's "tire wars" begin as 10 teams use Hoosier tires at Daytona.

March 6 Neil Bonnett comes from the 30th starting spot to win the Goodwrench 500 at Rockingham's North Carolina Motor Speedway for his second win in a row. Bonnett edges Lake Speed by less than a second. The first four finishers are running Hoosier tires.

March 20 Lake Speed speeds to his first NASCAR Winston Cup triumph in Darlington Raceway's TranSouth 500. Speed's Oldsmobile finishes a half-lap in front of runner-up Alan Kulwicki.

April 10 Bill Elliott overcomes a late spinout and rallies past Geoff Bodine to score his first career short-track win in the Valleydale 500 at Bristol. Bodine taps Elliott into a spin with nine laps to go, but Elliott roars back to take the lead with three laps remaining.

May 1 Phil Parsons takes the lead with 15 laps remaining and drives to his first career NASCAR Winston Cup victory in Talladega's Winston 500. Driving the #55 Oldsmobile, Parsons finishes a car length in front of Bobby Allison to notch his first win, which comes in his 111th start.

June 12 Rusty Wallace, one of NASCAR's finest road racers, tames the field to win the Budweiser 400 at Riverside International Raceway. The event is the final NASCAR Winston Cup race staged at the venerable Southern California road course.

June 19 Geoff Bodine scampers to an eight-second victory over Michael Waltrip after Bobby Allison is critically injured in an opening-lap crash in Pocono's Miller High Life 500. Allison's Buick suffers a flat tire and spins in the "tunnel turn," then is hit in the driver's door by Jocko Maggiacomo.

Richard Petty's spectacular crash on the 106th lap of the Feb. 14 Daytona 500 spewed parts all over the frontstretch at Daytona International Speedway. Petty brushed bumpers with Phil Barkdoll, then was hit by A.J. Foyt. Petty's Pontiac went airborne and tumbled for a couple hundred yards before being hit by Brett Bodine. The King was shaken up, but not seriously injured in the incident.

▲ Bobby Allison's #12 Buick crosses the finish line two car lengths ahead of runner-up Davey Allison's #28 Ford at the conclusion of the Daytona 500. The 1-2 finish by father and son was the first in NASCAR history since Lee and Richard Petty ran 1-2 in a race a Heidelberg, Penn., on July 10, 1960. The victory was the 85th of Allison's storied career.

Ken Schrader, who won the pole for the March 27 Darlington TranSouth 500 in his #25 Chevrolet, tried to squeeze back into a line of bumper-to-bumper traffic on the 16th lap and triggered a massive pileup. The incident gobbled up #4 Rick Wilson, Terry Labonte, Darrell Waltrip, Brett Bodine, Morgan Shepherd, and Harry Gant. "I tore up a bunch of good race cars and I shouldn't have," admitted Schrader after the accident. Lake Speed, a privateer who built and maintained his own #83 Oldsmobile, avoided the crash and recorded an upset win. It would be the first and only NASCAR Winston Cup win for the Jackson, Miss., driver.

Bill Elliott's #9 Ford spins wildly after a tap from Geoff Bodine knocked him out of the lead in the waning laps of the April 10 Valleydale 500 at Bristol International Raceway. The incident occurred with nine laps remaining. Elliott made a quick trip to the pits to replace the flat-spotted tires, and resumed the chase. It took Elliott only three laps to run down Bodine and pass him for the lead. Elliott went on to notch the first short-track victory of his NASCAR Winston Cup career.

▼ Dale Earnhardt rattles the bumper of #26 Ricky Rudd in the early stages of the April 24 Pannill Sweatshirts 500 at Martinsville Speedway. Rudd started on the pole and led the first 37 laps, but a blown engine eventually put him out of the race. Earnhardt went on to win, leading the final 182 laps. For Earnhardt, it was his seventh win in his last 12 short-track races.

1988

July 31 Ken Schrader comes from fourth place to first in the final lap and bags his first NASCAR Winston Cup win in the Talladega DieHard 500. Schrader prevails in a terrific 10-car scramble to the checkered flag. The race is Buddy Baker's last, as he is forced to retire when a blood clot is discovered in his brain.

August 27 Dale Earnhardt holds off Bill Elliott to win the Busch 500 at Bristol. Elliott takes a 16-point lead over Rusty Wallace in the championship chase.

October 23 Rusty Wallace rallies from a three-lap deficit caused by a cut tire to win Rockingham's AC Delco 500. Wallace outruns runner-up Ricky Rudd by 13.5 seconds to score his fifth win of the season.

November 6 Alan Kulwicki wins at Phoenix International Raceway for his first career NASCAR Winston Cup win. It is the first NASCAR Winston Cup event on the one-mile track.

November 20 Bill Elliott's 11th-place finish seals his first NASCAR Winston Cup championship as Rusty Wallace wins the season finale at Atlanta. Elliott finishes 24 points ahead of Wallace in the title chase. For Cale Yarborough and Benny Parsons, it is the last race of their careers.

Phil Parsons runs inches ahead of Ken Schrader and Darrell Waltrip in the May 1 Winston 500 at Talladega. The #55 Richard Jackson-owned Oldsmobile was the class of the field. Parsons overcame nearly a lap deficit when he ran out of fuel on the 48th lap. Parsons ran down the pack, and led the final 15 laps. The win was the first and only in Parsons' NASCAR Winston Cup career.

Bobby Allison began the 1988 NASCAR Winston Cup season with a victory in the storied Daytona 500. In the June 19 Miller High Life 500 at Pocono, the Hueytown, Ala., veteran nearly lost his life in a grinding crash on the opening lap. Allison's #12 Buick spun sideways after a tire went flat and Jocko Maggiacomo hit him squarely in the door. Allison was airlifted to LeHigh Valley Hospital in Allentown with multiple critical injuries. Allison, who lapsed into a coma for a few weeks, would never race again.

Dale Earnhardt pits during the June 26 Miller High Life 400 at Michigan International Speedway. Earnhardt was again a factor in the chase for the NASCAR Winston Cup title, leading the points from March into early June. The Intimidator won three races and finished third in the final points standings. Rusty Wallace, who posted his first career superspeedway victory in the Miller High Life 400, would go on to finish second in the championship hunt.

After bouncing from team to team from 1981 to '87, Mark Martin found stability by signing with the Jack Roush team in '88. His first campaign with Roush was punctuated with the usual indoctrination period—10 DNFs in 29 races, peppered with flashes of brilliance. Martin finished 15th in the points standings and cracked the top five in three events. With a full year under their belts, Martin and Roush looked forward to the '89 campaign and perhaps Martin's first NASCAR Winston Cup victory.

Ken Schrader celebrates his first NASCAR Winston Cup victory in Talladega's victory lane after a stunning come-from-behind gallop in the July 31 DieHard 500. Schrader, with astute coaching from team manager Harry Hyde via radio, came from fourth place to first on the final lap to record a narrow victory. Schrader zipped past Dale Earnhardt entering the third turn and crossed the finish line two car lengths ahead of teammate Geoff Bodine.

▲ Davey Allison limps to the pits with sparks flying off his #28 Ford in the Aug. 27 Busch 500 at Bristol International Raceway as #75 Neil Bonnett and #2 Ernie Irvan drive past. Allison was in the hunt for victory until he lost a wheel. He was able to get back into the race and scampered to a fourth-place finish.

Neil Bonnett pokes his #75 Pontiac under Terry Labonte's #11 Chevrolet during the Sept. 4 Southern 500 at Darlington Raceway. Labonte took the controls of Junior Johnson's Budweiser machine in 1987 and won four races during his three-year stint with the team. Bonnett won two of the first three races in '88, then tapered off to finish 16th in the points race. Both teams fielded GM cars, but the cars were very different. Pontiac had introduced the new, downsized, front-wheel-drive Grand Prix for the 1988 model year, and NASCAR teams used it (albeit with rear-wheel drive). Chevy teams, however, were still using the rear-wheel-drive Monte Carlo. Olds and Buick teams also ran downsized, front-drive cars.

Independent campaigner Jimmy Means (left) chats with Richard Petty prior to the start of the Sept. 25 Goody's 500 at Martinsville. Means was one of NASCAR's most popular small-time racers during his career. From 1976 to '93, he started 455 NASCAR Winston Cup races and finished among the top 10 in 17 events. In 1988, the Huntsville, Ala., driver led four races, the most he ever led in a single season.

1988

Number 28 Davey Allison chases #7 Alan Kulwicki into the turn at Martinsville Speedway in the Goody's 500. Kulwicki was in position to win the race, but was blackflagged by NASCAR officials late in the going for having a loose lug nut on his Ford. By the time he returned to the track, he trailed leader Darrell Waltrip by 8.2 seconds. He whittled the lead down to 2.9 seconds, but shot too fast into a corner and lost momentum. He recovered to finish second but couldn't challenge for the win.

NASCAR's Greatest Upsets

LAKE SPEED and Phil Parsons authored major upset victories during the 1988 NASCAR Winston Cup season. Speed drove his self-owned Oldsmobile to victory in the March 27 TranSouth 500 at Darlington for his lone win at NASCAR's highest level. Scarcely a month later, Parsons wheeled the Richard Jackson Oldsmobile to a close win in Talladega's Winston 500. It, too, was Parsons' only win in NASCAR's elite stock car racing series.

There have been many feel-good upsets in NASCAR Cup Series superspeedway history. It is always a wonderful human interest story when a driver scores that elusive first victory, whether it is a rookie or a journeyman veteran.

The following are some of the other more remarkable upsets in NASCAR Cup Series history:

March 26, 1961, Atlanta Part-time competitor Bob Burdick, drives a family owned Pontiac with used tires and a borrowed rear-gearing unit. Serviced by a rag-tag rookie pit crew, Burdick led the final 43 laps to win the Atlanta 500 at Atlanta International Raceway. The 24-year-old driver from Omaha, Neb., recorded his only win in his 11th career start. Burdick only competed in 15 races during his brief career. With operating funds running low, Burdick headed back to Omaha having driven his final NASCAR race at the age of 25.

September 3, 1962, Darlington A massive scoring break-down nearly kept Larry Frank from getting credit for his lone NASCAR Grand National victory in the Southern 500 at Darlington Raceway. Frank, an ex-Marine who had never tasted the fruits of victory in a major league NASCAR event, was flagged in fourth place in the Labor Day 500-miler at the venerable speedway. Hours later, NASCAR officials determined that Frank led the final 85 laps and had handily beaten Junior Johnson, who was originally flagged the winner. It was perhaps NASCAR's most embarrassing scoring flap. Frank was driving

an independent Ford for Ratus Walters, whose cars had never led a single lap before Frank's disputed victory. Frank's victory came in his 64th career start.

February 22, 1970, Daytona Young whipper-snapper Pete Hamilton gunned his Plymouth Superbird around David Pearson in the final laps to score a shocking upset in the Daytona 500. Hamilton, who had been out of a ride for most of the '69 season, was taking his first ride with the Petty Enterprises team. Although teamed with a proven winner, observers felt that immediate success for the Massachusetts driver was out of the question. Pitted against three-time NASCAR champion Pearson, Hamilton rose to the occasion. He took the lead with nine laps remaining and staved off the champion's last ditch effort with just over a lap to go. Hamilton's first victory came in his 21st career NASCAR Grand National start. The Daytona 500 victory propelled Hamilton to a successful 1970 campaign as he went on to sweep both 500-milers at Talladega.

August 12, 1973, Talladega Dick Brooks drove the unsponsored and outdated Crawford Brothers Plymouth to his lone NASCAR Winston Cup Grand National victory in the Talladega 500, perhaps the biggest upset in NASCAR history. Prior to the race, the Crawford Brothers' team had never finished above 16th place in a race at NASCAR's highest level. The Crawford Brothers team never finished better than 16th after Brooks' unlikely victory.

August 2, 1981, Talladega Freshman driver Ron Bouchard outfoxed two of the foxiest NASCAR Winston Cup Grand National drivers to record his only career victory in the Talladega 500 at Alabama International Motor Speedway. Bouchard, driving Jack Beebe's unsponsored Buick, snookered Darrell Waltrip and Terry Labonte in the final mile and prevailed in a three-abreast photo finish. Bouchard's win came in only his 11th start.

July 4, 1985, Daytona Greg Sacks, behind the wheel of a

Cale Yarborough drives his #29 Oldsmobile Cutlass through a banked corner at Charlotte Motor Speedway in the Oct. 8 Oakwood Homes 500. The three-time NASCAR Winston Cup champion was near the close of his illustrious career. He retired after the 1988 season with 83 career wins, which still ranks fifth on the all-time list. Yarborough made only 10 starts in '88, posting three top-10 finishes.

Ricky Rudd guns his #26 Buick to the low side of #3 Dale Earnhardt in the Oct. 16 Holly Farms 400 at North Wilkesboro Speedway. Rudd and Earnhardt engaged in a bumping feud during the race. Rudd bumped Earnhardt out of the groove to take the lead on the 459th lap. Earnhardt retaliated and knocked Rudd into a spin one lap later. Both drivers had to visit NASCAR's "Big Red Truck" to be disciplined for their extracurricular activities.

research and development Chevrolet out of the DiGard racing shops, ran away from the field in the final laps to win the Pepsi Firecracker 400 at Daytona International Speedway. Sacks was making his first start with the experimental DiGard car and it was the first top-five finish of his career, which began in 1983. Sacks' pit crew consisted of a gang of part timers, most of whom didn't even know each other. After a sluggish green-flag pit stop, Sacks returned to the track trailing leader Bill Elliott by seven seconds. Without the air of a drafting partner, Sacks erased the deficit quickly. He eventually finished 23.5 seconds ahead of Elliott.

July 27, 1986, Talladega Young Bobby Hillin, Jr. motored into the lead nine laps from the finish and kept his Buick ahead of a snarling pack to win the Talladega 500 at Alabama International Motor Speedway. The 22-year-old Texan became the youngest driver to win on a superspeedway and the third youngest winner in NASCAR Cup Series history. The race featured 49 lead changes among a record 26 different drivers as two-thirds of the cars remained in contention until a series of wrecks depleted the field. Hillin, Jr., edged Tim Richmond by a couple car lengths when the checkered flag fell.

February 19, 1990, Daytona Lightly regarded Derrike Cope took advantage of a blown tire on Dale Earnhardt's Chevrolet in the final lap and stormed to a huge upset victory in the Daytona 500. Cope tagged the heels of the lead pack, but was no match for Earnhardt's powerful mount. With Earnhardt seemingly on his way to an easy win, the right rear tire blew when he ran over a piece of debris on the backstretch. The tire came apart in the third turn. Cope gunned his Chevy to the low side and beat runner-up Terry Labonte by two car lengths. It was Cope's first-ever top-five finish.

October 13, 2002, Charlotte Unheralded Jamie McMurray, making his second career NASCAR Winston Cup start,

stunned observers by driving to victory in the UAW-GM Quality 500 at Lowe's Motor Speedway. McMurray, who enjoyed only limited success in the NASCAR Busch Series, was tapped to drive the Chip Ganassi Dodge in place of the injured Sterling Marlin. McMurray's victory was the quickest in NASCAR's elite series since Johnny Rutherford won his inaugural start in a 100-mile qualifying race at Daytona International Speedway in 1963.

April 26, 2009, Talladega Brad Keselowski started the day by making his fifth NASCAR Sprint Cup start and his first start in Phoenix Racing's #09 Chevrolet. At the end of the afternoon, he and his team had scored their first Cup Series win. Keselowski had an average finish of 25th place in his first four starts, and Phoenix Racing had run 104 Cup Series races since 1990 with only a pair of top-five finishes to show for it. Talladega Superspeedway and the draft have always been great equalizers, and they combined to enable Keselowski to hook up with Carl Edwards and make a run for the finish. Coming through the tri-oval on the last lap with Edwards leading, contact was made between the two and Edwards' Ford spun and lifted into the outside catch fence, allowing Keselowski to cruise to an upset victory.

February 20, 2011, Daytona When 20-year-old Trevor Bayne went to Daytona in February, he was simply wanting to make his second NASCAR Sprint Cup Series start. When he left, he was a Daytona 500 champion. Bayne had been fast all week in the Wood Brothers #21 Ford and adapted quickly to the tandem draft. During the 500, he ran with Jeff Gordon and kept out of trouble while others had problems. On a late restart, he got the lead when leader David Ragan was black flagged for changing lanes too early. On the last restart, Bayne and Bobby Labonte hooked up and stayed in the lead until turn four on the last lap. Bayne threw a clean block on a hard-charging Carl Edwards and took the win. With that, he became the youngest Daytona 500 winner up to that time.

1988

Infield spectators cheer wildly as #27 Rusty Wallace punches #5 Geoff Bodine into a near spin on the final lap of the Oct. 16 Holly Farms 400. Bodine scrubbed past Wallace in the first turn to take the lead, and Wallace delivered a shot to the back bumper of Bodine a half-lap later. Wallace went on to win. Phil Parsons grabbed second place as Bodine fought to bring his car back under control and slipped to third.

Rusty Wallace and Raymond Beadle celebrate in victory lane following Wallace's brilliant drive in the Oct. 23 AC Delco 500 at Rockingham's North Carolina Motor Speedway. Wallace overcame a three-lap deficit to pull out the win. Wallace went on a late-season charge, winning four of the final five races. His rally came up just short in the chase for the NASCAR Winston Cup championship as he finished 24 points behind Bill Elliott.

Alan Kulwicki steered his #7 Ford into the lead 16 laps from the finish and racked up his first career NASCAR Winston Cup win in the inaugural Checker 500 at Phoenix International Raceway on Nov. 6. After receiving the checkered flag, Kulwicki took a celebratory victory lap around the track in the opposite direction. "That was my Polish victory lap," said Kulwicki. "I had been planning that for a long time."

Bill Elliott drove his #9 Harry Melling/Coors Ford Thunderbird to the 1988 NASCAR Winston Cup championship, winning six races along the way. Elliott had dominated the '85 season with 11 wins, but lost the title to Darrell Waltrip, who won three times. Both Elliott and Rusty Wallace won six races during the course of the season, but Wallace had more top-five and top-10 efforts. With more consistency, Elliott took the title much the same way he had lost it to Waltrip three years earlier.

1988 NASCAR WINSTON CUP POINTS RACE

Rank	Driver	Points	Starts	Wins	Top 5	Top 10	Winnings
1	Bill Elliott	4488	29	6	15	22	$1,554,639
2	Rusty Wallace	4464	29	6	19	23	$1,411,567
3	Dale Earnhardt	4256	29	3	13	19	$1,214,089
4	Terry Labonte	4007	29	1	11	18	$950,781
5	Ken Schrader	3858	29	1	4	17	$631,544
6	Geoff Bodine	3799	29	1	10	16	$570,643
7	Darrell Waltrip	3764	29	2	10	14	$731,659
8	Davey Allison	3631	29	2	12	16	$844,532
9	Phil Parsons	3630	29	1	6	15	$532,043
10	Sterling Marlin	3621	29	0	6	13	$521,464
11	Ricky Rudd	3547	29	1	6	11	$410,954
12	Bobby Hillin, Jr.	3446	29	0	1	7	$330,217
13	Kyle Petty	3296	29	0	2	8	$377,092
14	Alan Kulwicki	3176	29	1	7	9	$448,547
15	Mark Martin	3142	29	0	3	10	$223,630
16	Neil Bonnett	3040	27	2	3	7	$440,139
tie	Lake Speed	2984	29	1	4	7	$260,500
18	Michael Waltrip	2949	29	0	1	3	$240,400
19	Dave Marcis	2854	29	0	0	2	$212,485
20	Brett Bodine	2828	29	0	2	5	$433,658
21	Rick Wilson	2762	28	0	2	5	$209,925
22	Richard Petty	2644	29	0	1	5	$190,155
23	Dale Jarrett	2622	29	0	0	1	$118,640
24	Benny Parsons	2559	27	0	0	1	$210,755
25	Ken Bouchard	2378	24	0	0	1	$109,410
26	Ernie Irvan	2319	25	0	0	0	$96,370
27	Harry Gant	2266	24	0	0	3	$173,325
28	Morgan Shepherd	2193	23	0	2	6	$197,425
29	Buddy Baker	2056	17	0	0	7	$184,200
30	Jimmy Means	2045	27	0	0	0	$139,290
31	Derrike Cope	1985	26	0	0	0	$132,835
32	Mike Alexander	1931	16	0	2	6	$200,709
33	Bobby Allison	1654	13	1	3	6	$409,295
34	Eddie Bierschwale	1481	20	0	0	0	$59,355
35	Rodney Combs	1468	19	0	0	0	$54,150
36	Brad Noffsinger	1316	17	0	0	0	$54,645
37	Greg Sacks	1237	15	0	0	3	$105,579
38	Cale Yarborough	940	10	0	0	3	$66,065
39	Joe Ruttman	803	12	0	0	1	$46,455
40	Brad Teague	802	13	0	0	0	$53,105
41	Jimmy Horton	647	8	0	0	0	$23,575
42	A.J. Foyt	523	7	0	0	0	$29,660
43	H.B. Bailey	478	7	0	0	0	$15,775
44	Jim Sauter	463	9	0	0	0	$35,040
45	Chad Little	405	4	0	0	0	$14,225
46	Buddy Arrington	352	4	0	0	0	$22,165
47	Ken Ragan	314	5	0	0	0	$15,775
48	Dana Patten	313	4	0	0	0	$9595
49	Rick Jeffrey	307	4	0	0	0	$25,535
50	Mickey Gibbs	283	5	0	0	0	$12,850

Bill Elliott overcame challenges by Rusty Wallace and Dale Earnhardt to win the 1988 NASCAR Winston Cup championship. After leading the standings from June until late August, Wallace stumbled in September and was 124 points behind with five races remaining.

Wallace won four of the final five races, but Elliott performed well enough in those events to wrap up his first title. He finished 24 points ahead of Wallace. Earnhardt led the standings from March through early June, but fell off the pace in the second half of the season and placed third, 232 points behind Elliott.

For Elliott, it was sweet redemption for his bitter defeat in the 1985 NASCAR Winston Cup title chase.

Aside from the top three, no other driver seriously contended for the title or won more than two races.

1989

February 19 In his 17th Daytona 500 start, Darrell Waltrip prevails in an economy run. Waltrip runs the final 132.5 miles without a pit stop and coasts across the finish line 7.64 seconds ahead of runner-up Ken Schrader. Most of the field runs on Hoosier tires as Goodyear pulls out of the race due to safety concerns with its new radial tire.

April 2 Harry Gant ends a 90-race winless drought in Darlington's TranSouth 500. Gant leads the final 20 laps and beats Davey Allison to claim his 10th career NASCAR Winston Cup victory.

April 16 Dale Earnhardt runs away from Alan Kulwicki to win the First Union 400 at North Wilkesboro Speedway as the new Goodyear radial tire makes its NASCAR Winston Cup debut. "The more I drove on them, the better I liked the radials," said the winner.

May 7 Davey Allison leads a 1-2-3 Ford sweep in the Winston 500 at Talladega. Allison outruns Terry Labonte and Mark Martin to score his fifth career NASCAR Winston Cup win.

May 8 Bob Newton, president of Hoosier Tire Co., announces he will withdraw from NASCAR competition following the 1989 season. Newton's 18-employee Indiana-based company began making tires for NASCAR Winston Cup cars in '88. Hoosier stood toe-to-toe with corporate giant Goodyear for two seasons, and registered more than a dozen victories. Facing impossible odds, Newton finally tossed in the towel. "Even though we are considered to be the world's smallest tire manufacturer, we compete with the world's largest to demonstrate that the small guy can also be a winner," said Newton.

June 11 Ricky Rudd bumps and blocks Rusty Wallace to score a close decision in the first NASCAR Winston Cup race at Sears Point International Raceway in Sonoma, Calif. Wallace's bid to take the lead with three laps to go is foiled by Rudd, who pushes his rival into the sandy runoff area on the scenic road course.

After Davey Allison was clipped by Geoff Bodine on the 23rd lap of the Feb. 19 Daytona 500, his #28 Ford slid into the backstretch infield, then flipped over when it skidded into the protective dirt embankment. The Robert Yates pit crew patched the car with reams of duct tape, and Allison got back into the running. He eventually finished 25th in the battered machine, seven laps off the pace.

Darrell Waltrip drove his #17 Hendrick Motorsports/Tide Chevrolet into the lead four laps from the finish and went on to win the Daytona 500. Waltrip, making his 17th start in "The Great American Race," crossed the finish line with a near-empty fuel tank. Hendrick Motorsports cars finished first and second in the race, with Waltrip beating Ken Schrader by 7.64 seconds.

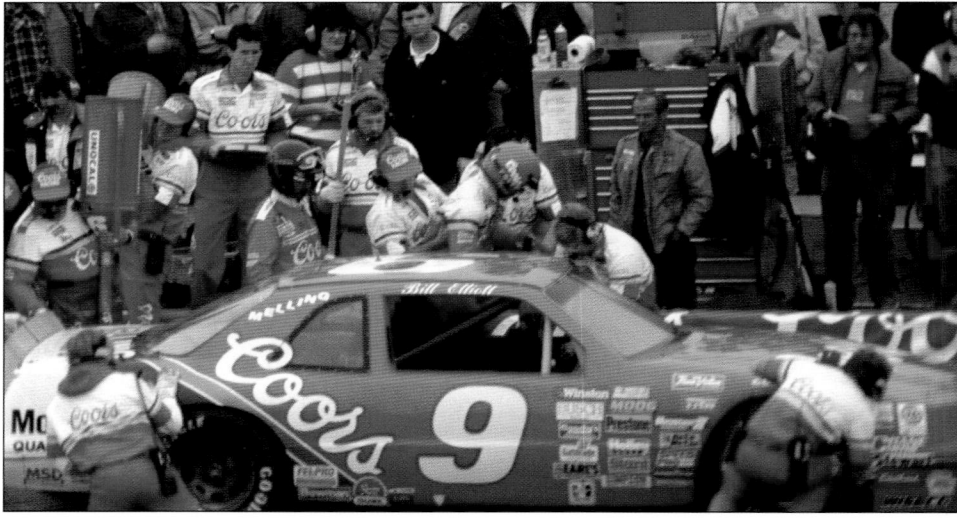

Bill Elliott climbs out of his #9 Ford and turns the wheel over to relief driver Jody Ridley in Rockingham's March 5 Goodwrench 500. Elliott broke his wrist in a practice crash at Daytona and was still unable to crank the steering wheel without severe pain. Ridley carried Elliott's car to a 19th-place finish.

Phil Parsons, driving the #55 Jackson Brothers Oldsmobile, dove a little too deep into Darlington's third turn during the April 2 TranSouth 500, and slid into the path of onrushing Darrell Waltrip. Parsons' car was knocked out of action, but Waltrip was able to get back into the running after missing nearly 100 laps for repair work.

Harry Gant throttles his #33 Oldsmobile under #5 Geoff Bodine in the late stages of the TranSouth 500. Gant ended a 90-race drought with a win. His most recent victory had come at North Wilkesboro in 1985. "The Bandit is back," said a cheerful Gant in victory lane. "I was confident before the race that we had the car to beat."

Ken Schrader tags the wall with his #25 Chevrolet in the early laps of the April 9 Valleydale 500 at Bristol International Raceway. Schrader fell on hard times after his fine showing in Daytona's Speedweeks. The Bristol crash was his third in his last five races. He would go on to finish fifth in the finals points standings.

The steeply banked track at Bristol affords some of the closest racing in NASCAR Cup Series racing. Here, #5 Geoff Bodine, #28 Davey Allison, and #84 Dick Trickle battle in close quarters in the Valleydale 500. Bodine ran third in the 500-lapper, followed by Allison and Trickle. Trickle took the controls of the Stavola Brothers Buick when Mike Alexander pulled himself off the tour due to injuries suffered in a crash in an independent short-track race the previous December.

Brothers Michael and Darrell Waltrip zip through the fourth turn at North Wilkesboro Speedway in the early stages of the April 16 First Union 400. Michael drove Chuck Rider's #30 Pontiac from 1988 to '95 in one of the longest owner/driver relationships in NASCAR Winston Cup racing. Michael fell out early in the North Wilkesboro event, while Darrell wfinished eighth.

July 23 Bill Elliott recovers from an unscheduled pit stop in the opening laps, hustles back into contention, and wins the AC Spark Plug 500 at Pocono International Raceway.

July 30 By pocketing $47,965 for his second-place finish in the Talladega 500, Darrell Waltrip becomes NASCAR's first $10 million winner.

August 20 Rusty Wallace grabs his fifth win of the season at Michigan and has his sights set on Dale Earnhardt's precarious points lead. Wallace finishes comfortably in front of runner-up Morgan Shepherd as Earnhardt struggles and finishes 17th.

October 8 Ken Schrader runs down Mark Martin in the final laps to win the All Pro Auto Parts 500 at Charlotte as Rusty Wallace takes the points lead with an eighth-place finish. A broken crankshaft on the 13th lap relegates Dale Earnhardt to a last-place finish and causes him to lose the points lead.

October 15 Geoff Bodine passes the spinning cars of Dale Earnhardt and Ricky Rudd on the final lap and scores an unlikely triumph in the Holly Farms 400 at North Wilkesboro. Earnhardt attempts to shut the door on Rudd's bid to pass in the last lap, but the cars collide and both spin out.

October 22 Mark Martin survives a rash of caution flags and notches his first career NASCAR Winston Cup win in the AC Delco 500 at Rockingham. Championship contenders Rusty Wallace and Dale Earnhardt tangle midway through the race, causing major damage to Earnhardt's Chevrolet. Wallace now has a 109-point lead over Earnhardt in the standings.

November 19 Dale Earnhardt romps to an overwhelming victory in the season-ending Atlanta Journal 500 as Rusty Wallace wraps up his first NASCAR Winston Cup title with a 15th-place finish. Wallace nips Earnhardt by 12 points in the final tally. Veteran driver Grant Adcox is killed in a 202nd-lap crash.

Rusty Wallace's keeps his #27 Pontiac ahead of #3 Dale Earnhardt in the opening laps of the April 17 First Union 400. Wallace qualified on the pole, but had conventional bias-ply Goodyears on his car. Earnhardt's Richard Childress team mounted the new radial tires on his #3 Chevy, which proved better on long runs. Earnhardt went on to win the race, while Wallace ran ninth.

Rusty Wallace fends off a challenge by #3 Dale Earnhardt in an exciting duel during the April 23 Pannill Sweatshirts 500 at Virginia's Martinsville Speedway. Wallace led three times for 64 laps and was leading when his engine went sour. Earnhardt picked up the lead and was headed for victory until an air wrench broke on his final pit stop. He still finished second to Darrell Waltrip, despite missing two lug nuts on the left rear tire. NASCAR levied no points penalty, but fined the RCR Enterprises team $300 for the infraction.

The Hendrick Motorsports crew pushes Darrell Waltrip's #17 Chevrolet Lumina toward victory lane after the May 28 Coca-Cola 600 at Charlotte Motor Speedway. Waltrip was in the new Lumina that Chevrolet introduced in the spring of '89 as a '90 model. The car took the place of the highly successful Monte Carlo model starting with the May 7 Winston 500 at Talladega. Waltrip, ever the jokester, remarked, "I about flipped when they told me I had to park my Monte Carlo in favor of some new aluminum car GM had come up with."

▲ Mark Martin's #6 Stroh's Light Ford slides through the tri-oval area of Daytona International Speedway after a 55th-lap incident in the July 1 Pepsi 400. Dale Earnhardt and Geoff Bodine collided while battling in tight formation, sending Bodine's car into the rear of Martin's Ford. Martin recovered and battled back to the front, but ran out of fuel while leading with five laps remaining.

Davey Allison took the lead in the final six laps and motored his #28 Robert Yates Racing/Havoline Ford to victory in the Pepsi 400. Allison held off underdog hopefuls Morgan Shepherd and Phil Parsons to score his second win of the year. A series of crashes eliminated 13 cars from the race.

Terry Labonte's #11 Budweiser Ford and Darrell Waltrip's #17 Tide Chevrolet were two of the strongest performers on the big speedways in Daytona and Talladega. Waltrip won the Daytona 500 and Labonte captured the July 30 Talladega DieHard 500. Labonte and team owner Junior Johnson switched to Ford products in 1989, ending a long association with Chevrolet. Labonte won twice and finished 10th in the NASCAR Winston Cup points standings.

Rusty Wallace powers his #27 Blue Max Racing/Kodiak Pontiac through the rounded front chute at Michigan International Speedway during the Aug. 20 Champion Spark Plug 400. Wallace drove to his fifth win of the season and crept to within 82 points of NASCAR Winston Cup leader Dale Earnhardt. Wallace mounted a memorable charge in the last half of the season to nail down the championship by a mere 12 points.

1989

▶ Front-row starters Bill Elliott and Ken Schrader lead the charge off the fourth turn at the start of the Oct. 8 All Pro Auto Parts 500 at Charlotte Motor Speedway. Schrader took the lead 15 laps from the finish when a deflating tire foiled Mark Martin's quest for his first NASCAR Winston Cup win. Elliott finished fourth.

▼ Kyle and Richard Petty sit in the pits at North Wilkesboro during the Oct. 15 Holly Farms 400. A crash relegated Richard's #43 STP Pontiac to last place in the 32-car field, while #42 SabCo Racing/Peak Pontiac finished just one spot ahead when mechanical problems forced Kyle to retire after completing 124 laps.

> "My life is fulfilled. My goal in life has been to win a Winston Cup race."
> —Mark Martin

In his second season with the Jack Roush team, Mark Martin had a sparkling campaign. He finally cracked the victory column at Rockingham in October, and consistent strong finishes netted him third place in the final NASCAR Winston Cup points standings. Martin won six poles and recorded 12 finishes of third or better. "My life is fulfilled," said Martin after winning the Oct. 22 AC Delco 500. "My goal in life has been to win a Winston Cup race."

▲ Ricky Rudd attempted to duck under Dale Earnhardt's #3 Goodwrench Chevy in the first turn of the final lap in the Holly Farms 400. As Rudd pulled his #26 Quaker State Buick down low, Earnhardt swept down to block the move. With Rudd already having established his position, the two cars collided, and both spun into the wall. Geoff Bodine seized on the opportunity and drove the #5 Levi Garrett Chevy to victory, leading only the final lap. Rudd and Earnhardt recovered from the spin and finished ninth and 10th, respectively.

362

After the conclusion of the electrifying Holly Farms 400 at North Wilkesboro, last-lap combatants Ricky Rudd and Dale Earnhardt parked their cars on pit road. The crews got together to "discuss" the incident that had taken both cars out of victory contention. When interviewed by the ESPN television reporters, Earnhardt unleashed a profanity-laced verbal barrage at Rudd, claiming Rudd "should be suspended for the rest of the season." Rudd kept his tongue in check, but didn't mince his words. "I got under him cleanly and he pinched me off and wrecked me. I guess he didn't want to give up the lead."

Rusty Wallace and Dale Earnhardt staged one of the best championship races in NASCAR Winston Cup history. Wallace took the points lead from Earnhardt on Oct. 8 and led by 78 points entering the final race at Atlanta. Wallace needed to finish within 19 positions of Earnhardt in the Nov. 19 Atlanta Journal 500 to claim the title. Earnhardt won the race, but Wallace overcame several minor problems to place 15th and claim the championship. Wallace and the Blue Max Racing team also overcame internal strife in '89. Wallace filed a lawsuit in July to get out of the remaining year of his contract, but had agreed to stay one more year by the end of the season.

1989 NASCAR WINSTON CUP POINTS RACE

Rank	Driver	Points	Starts	Wins	Top 5	Top 10	Winnings
1	Rusty Wallace	4176	29	6	13	20	$2,237,950
2	Dale Earnhardt	4164	29	5	14	19	$1,432,230
3	Mark Martin	4053	29	1	14	18	$1,016,850
4	Darrell Waltrip	3971	29	6	14	18	$1,312,479
5	Ken Schrader	3876	29	1	10	14	$1,037,941
6	Bill Elliott	3774	29	3	8	14	$849,370
7	Harry Gant	3610	29	1	9	14	$639,792
8	Ricky Rudd	3608	29	1	7	15	$533,624
9	Geoff Bodine	3600	29	1	9	11	$619,494
10	Terry Labonte	3569	29	2	9	11	$703,806
11	Davey Allison	3481	29	2	7	13	$640,956
12	Sterling Marlin	3422	29	0	4	13	$473,267
13	Morgan Shepherd	3403	29	0	5	13	$544,255
14	Alan Kulwicki	3236	29	0	5	9	$501,295
15	Dick Trickle	3203	28	0	6	9	$343,728
16	Bobby Hillin, Jr.	3139	28	0	1	7	$283,181
17	Rick Wilson	3119	29	0	2	7	$312,402
18	Michael Waltrip	3057	29	0	0	5	$249,233
19	Brett Bodine	3051	29	0	1	6	$281,274
20	Neil Bonnett	2995	26	0	0	11	$271,628
21	Phil Parsons	2933	29	0	2	3	$285,012
22	Ernie Irvan	2919	29	0	0	4	$155,329
23	Larry Pearson	2860	29	0	0	2	$156,060
24	Dale Jarrett	2789	29	0	2	5	$232,317
25	Dave Marcis	2715	27	0	0	1	$196,161
26	Hut Stricklin	2705	27	0	1	4	$152,504
27	Lake Speed	2550	24	0	1	5	$201,977
28	Derrike Cope	2180	23	0	0	4	$125,630
29	Richard Petty	2148	25	0	0	0	$133,050
30	Kyle Petty	2099	19	0	1	5	$117,027
31	Jimmy Means	1698	22	0	0	0	$65,005
32	Greg Sacks	1565	20	0	0	2	$113,535
33	Jim Sauter	1510	17	0	0	2	$73,832
34	Jimmy Spencer	1445	17	0	0	3	$121,065
35	Rick Mast	1315	13	0	0	1	$128,102
36	Eddie Bierschwale	1306	16	0	0	1	$82,695
37	Ben Hess	921	9	0	0	0	$48,490
38	Chad Little	602	8	0	0	0	$44,690
39	Butch Miller	576	9	0	0	0	$22,520
40	A.J. Foyt	527	7	0	0	0	$31,995
41	Mickey Gibbs	508	7	0	0	0	$27,040
42	Rodney Combs	470	9	0	0	0	$36,090
43	Joe Ruttman	469	9	0	0	1	$64,645
44	J.D. McDuffie	457	7	0	0	0	$27,720
45	Phil Barkdoll	378	4	0	0	0	$29,050
46	Jimmy Horton	377	5	0	0	0	$19,232
47	Dick Johnson	322	4	0	0	0	$11,515
48	Ken Bouchard	313	4	0	0	0	$33,930
49	Terry Byers	306	3	0	0	0	$15,400
50	Darin Brassfield	306	3	0	0	0	$10,852

Rusty Wallace took the lead from Dale Earnhardt with five races remaining to win the 1989 NASCAR Winston Cup championship.

Wallace and Earnhardt engaged in a hard-fought battle for supremacy during the season. While racing side-by-side at Rockingham in the 27th race of the 29-race campaign, Wallace slid into Earnhardt, forcing him into a spin. Earnhardt left Rockingham trailing by 109 points, but he staged a furious rally in the final two events.

Needing only to finish 18th in the season finale at Atlanta, Rusty nursed his Pontiac to a 15th-place finish as Earnhardt dominated the race. Wallace squeaked out a narrow 12-point decision over Earnhardt to take his first NASCAR Winston Cup title.

Wallace won six times during his championship season, while Earnhardt took five victories. Mark Martin, who scored his first career win at Rockingham, finished third in points, 123 points behind Wallace.

The 1990s arrived with NASCAR's wheels churning progressively forward. Several motivated, energetic, youthful drivers were pressing the seasoned veterans for membership in the elite status of NASCAR Winston Cup racing. A number of the old warriors were conceding to Father Time as they fell further and further behind the newcomers.

The 32nd annual running of the Daytona 500 kicked off the 1990s with its usual flair. With three NASCAR Winston Cup titles already under his belt, Dale Earnhardt was intent on regaining the championship. Earnhardt had come agonizingly close to winning the championship again in '89, losing a close decision to Rusty Wallace.

Earnhardt and the Richard Childress team were sharply focused on ending the Daytona 500 void that had plagued them. Late-race misfortune had snatched NASCAR's most important race from Earnhardt's grasp on several occasions.

During the shakedown runs for the 1990 Daytona 500, Earnhardt was near the top of the chart every session. He qualified on the front row for the first time, and the black Goodwrench Chevrolet was the odds-on favorite to finally take the Daytona 500 trophy.

Earnhardt was a formidable force during the 1990 Speedweeks. He easily won the Twin 125-miler and Saturday's NASCAR Busch Series event. In the Daytona 500, no driver in the field could keep up with him. Earnhardt motored away from all rivals, leading for 155 of the 200 laps. No driver had passed Earnhardt under green-flag conditions for the entire race. "The only way anybody will beat Earnhardt today is if someone shoots his tires out," said Harold Elliott, engine builder for Rusty Wallace's team.

Nobody shot Earnhardt's tires out, but the results were the same. A late caution flag erased a 27-second lead and put a pack of cars within striking distance. Still, it was a minor inconvenience for Earnhardt, until the final lap.

While running first, Earnhardt ran over a piece of metal on the backstretch. Going into the third turn, the #3 Lumina darted toward the wall and only an impeccable craftsman like Earnhardt could keep the car under control. Unheralded Derrike Cope, who had never finished in the top five of a NASCAR Winston Cup race, grabbed the lead and scored a huge upset in NASCAR's most celebrated event.

The hand of fate had dealt Earnhardt another evil card at Daytona, but fate can also shuffle the deck. The following week, Mark Martin won at Richmond, but NASCAR technical inspectors discovered that the carburetor in Martin's Ford was mounted on the intake manifold with an aluminum-block spacer ½-inch thicker than the two inches allowed. NASCAR upheld Martin's victory, but fined the team $40,000 for the infraction. More importantly, Martin was docked 46 championship points.

Earnhardt led the NASCAR Winston Cup points chase through May, but by early summer, Martin had rebounded from the penalty and began challenging for the lead. For the next six months, Earnhardt and Martin battled ferociously for the title. Martin gained the upper hand toward the end of the season, and was on the doorstep of the championship.

But Earnhardt didn't flinch in the heat of battle. Over the years, he had developed patience to compliment his undiminished aggression. Having once lived on raw natural ability, by 1990 Earnhardt was using his head to channel his talents more effectively.

Entering the Nov. 4 race at Phoenix, the next-to-last stop of the season, Earnhardt trailed Martin by 45 points. Knowing he had to put pressure on Martin, Earnhardt flashed his aura of invincibility. He took the lead on the 50th mile and drove to a lopsided victory. Martin managed to finish in the

top 10, but lost the lead in the standings and now trailed by six points. Earnhardt cruised to a third-place finish in the season finale at Atlanta, sewing up his fourth title by 26 points over Martin, who finished sixth. "This championship was the toughest of all," said Earnhardt. "They made us sweat for it. To come from behind and race them all the way to the end made the championship worth that much more."

For Martin and his Jack Roush team, the 46-point penalty at Richmond in February was the deciding factor. The runner-up took the defeat graciously and refused to speculate on the points penalty. "There are 29 races that make up the Winston Cup schedule, not just one," he remarked. "We put Richmond behind us long ago. We got beat by the best," said Martin. "We pushed 'em, and we pushed 'em hard."

Earnhardt added another championship to his sparkling portfolio in 1991, taking the points lead in early May and never giving up the top spot. Earnhardt won four times and finished a comfortable 195 points ahead of runner-up Ricky Rudd. Earnhardt wrapped up the title by merely starting his car at Atlanta's season-ending event. Under NASCAR rules, the event officially gets underway when the drivers roll onto the pace lap. With a 165-point cushion in the points race, Earnhardt officially won his fifth NASCAR Winston Cup championship when his engine came to life on pit road, giving him a minimum of 43 points.

As Earnhardt galloped to an easy championship run, 51-year-old Harry Gant was drawing the most attention. During the month of September, the mild-mannered Gant went undefeated in NASCAR Winston Cup competition and won a couple of NASCAR Busch Series races for good measure. Gant wheeled his Richard Jackson-owned Oldsmobile to consecutive wins at Darlington, Richmond, Dover, and Martinsville, earning him the nickname "Mr. September."

The Martinsville victory was one to provoke wonder. Gant was once again running away with the race, leading for 111 straight laps when Rusty Wallace tapped him into a spin. Morgan Shepherd hit the spinning Gant, inflicting severe damage to the #33 Oldsmobile. "It bent the front wheel out a whole lot and that really affected the car going into the corner," Gant said afterward. "We had a lot of stuff knocked loose that we had to get off the car. The main thing was my crew couldn't do anything in the time we had as far as resetting the front end. We just had to leave it like it was. We also had an oil cooler that was almost jammed into the wheel," Gant continued. "We had a brake duct knocked loose. It took a lot of time to get that off the car. We knew we couldn't go back on the track dragging it or NASCAR would have black-flagged us."

Gant restarted in 12th place, having remained on the lead lap during the yellow flag. Nobody thought he had a shot to keep his winning streak alive. But the ageless wonder began picking off his rivals one by one. In less than 50 miles, Gant scrubbed past Brett Bodine and led the rest of the way.

Earnhardt halted Gant's winning streak at North Wilkesboro, but only by a stroke of luck. Gant led for 350 of the 400 laps but fell victim to brake failure, which allowed Earnhardt to make the decisive pass in the final nine laps.

The Earnhardt, Martin, and Gant headlines dominated the 1991 season, but the campaign was also marred by the death of a longtime regular. J.D. McDuffie was a homespun racer and a fixture on the NASCAR scene for nearly 30 years. In the early laps of the road race at Watkins Glen, McDuffie's Pontiac shot off the course and smashed into a steel guardrail. The 52-year-old driver died in what was his 653rd start.

Also in 1991, NASCAR Winston Cup racing attracted a new television network. The Nashville Network (TNN) snatched five events from cable rival ESPN—two each at Dover and Rockingham, along with the lone Phoenix race. The television contracts were handled in an independent manner in the early '90s, with networks cutting deals with individual tracks. In

addition to the NASCAR Winston Cup telecasts, TNN gobbled up NASCAR Busch Series races that didn't have a TV deal.

The 1992 NASCAR Winston Cup season was most memorable, but was tainted by the unfortunate loss of NASCAR founder Bill France. On the morning of June 7, William Henry Getty France died in his sleep in Ormond Beach, Fla. He was 82. France, who founded NASCAR in 1948 and guided the sport into the progressive modern age, had been in declining health for eight years as he suffered from Alzheimer's disease.

The 1992 NASCAR Winston Cup championship chase was one of the closest in years. It featured an array of challengers. Surprisingly, Dale Earnhardt wasn't among them. Shackled by ill fortune and a car that was a shade off the pace, Earnhardt won only once and finished outside of the top 10 in championship points for the first time in 10 years.

On the other hand, Alan Kulwicki was in the hunt during most of the season. Kulwicki was one of the new breed to hit the NASCAR trail in the late 1980s. A self-styled loner who left Wisconsin in 1986 to tackle NASCAR Winston Cup racing, Kulwicki set up his own skeleton racing operation with little more than passion and a far-fetched dream to carry him to stock car racing's highest level.

An accomplished short-track racer, Kulwicki methodically approached obstacles that loomed in his path. Calm and devoid of flair, Kulwicki's face was expressionless and his speech quiet and measured. His desire, however, was unsurpassed. Kulwicki was no pink-cheeked prima donna waving a padded checkbook and flaunting fast-lane connections. Against overwhelming and perhaps impossible odds, Kulwicki took on the giants of the sport with his home-grown, lightly regarded team.

During his early years, Kulwicki struggled to gain a foothold in NASCAR Winston Cup racing. Still, he was able to win the 1986 Rookie of the Year award while using an arsenal of just two cars. Most teams had more than a dozen finely groomed machines at their disposal. Kulwicki attracted the attention of several top-ranked team owners, including Junior Johnson. On at least two occasions, Johnson offered Kulwicki a ride with his established and well-funded team. Kulwicki politely turned down the offers. His decision jolted nearly everyone in the sport.

"Junior's offer was a helluva opportunity," said Kulwicki. "If anybody would have told me three years ago that I would pass up an opportunity to drive for him for the kind of money available, I would have told them they were crazy and go on down the road. Maybe now people will think I'm crazy for not accepting the offer. But I had to work hard for all these years to get where I'm at and now I'm used to working hard and I don't mind it. And I believe in the people I have with me now. Sure, things have been bad for us lately, but now I don't get down or as frustrated as I used to. The thinking on my team right now is, 'We have a problem, so let's go fix it.' And then we fix it. Time will tell if my decision is right or wrong. But I have never been a quitter in my life. Even as things have been lately, if I joined another team, I would feel like I never stuck it out with what I have now. Down the road, I would never be able to say to myself that I gave it my best shot. I would have always second-guessed myself. I made my decision solely in principle."

Kulwicki managed to keep the leaders within sight during the first half of the 1992 points chase. Bill Elliott, who left Harry Melling's team to join the Junior Johnson ride in '92, shot out of the starting blocks and won four of the first five races. Curiously, Elliott never led the standings during his winning spree, casting another dose of light onto the NASCAR points system. While Elliott was winning races, he

trailed in the points standings, but from April through October, he went winless and built a hefty points lead.

Elliott had things well in hand going into late September. At that point, the wheels came off the Elliott-Johnson chariot. Uncharacteristic mechanical problems and unforeseen gremlins erased the comfortable cushion and invited five other drivers to battle for top honors in the season finale at Atlanta. The wrap-up at Atlanta had many story lines, including the tight points race, the final hurrah of King Richard Petty, and the maiden voyage into NASCAR Winston Cup racing by youngster Jeff Gordon.

Petty had announced in late 1991 that the '92 NASCAR Winston Cup campaign would be his 34th and final one. Petty would call it his "Fan Appreciation Tour." "It's not a farewell tour or anything like that," said the adored King. "Heck, I ain't going nowhere. This will be our way of telling the fans how much we appreciate their support over the last 34 years. Without the fans, I wouldn't have had a job."

Petty was in the twilight of his career and his performance had slipped in recent seasons. He hadn't won a race since July 1984, and he hadn't registered a top-five finish since '88. "Not winning races, not finishing races, not doing the things I am capable of doing. It all adds up," said Petty. "God might have given me 25 years of good luck and I might be trying to stretch it to 35. Maybe He's trying to tell me something, like, 'Hey, you'd better get out of this thing before something happens to you and I can't look out for you no more.'"

Petty had been harboring thoughts of retirement since late 1990, but didn't air his convictions until a year later. He told his family first, in a private moment at his home in Level Cross, N.C. "They had mixed emotions at first," reflected Petty. "They all wanted me to quit, but they know how I love it so much that they hurt for me because they know I'm going to have to get out of it. It was pretty emotional around there for about 10 minutes."

While NASCAR and Atlanta Motor Speedway promoters were preparing for a snazzy send-off for Petty, the championship contenders were getting suited up for the epic 500-mile battle. Davey Allison, who survived many trials and tribulations during the season, saw his hopes dashed when Ernie Irvan spun out of control, taking Allison with him. Mark Martin's hopes went up in smoke with an early engine failure, and Kyle Petty fell victim to the same ailment. In the final laps, Elliott and Kulwicki were running first and second and the outcome was very much in doubt.

Both drivers had been up front the entire way, and both had led approximately the same number of laps. In the end, Elliott motored to victory, his first since his four-race winning streak in the early spring, while Kulwicki took second. Kulwicki prevailed by the narrowest margin in championship history, a mere 10 points. Credit the lone-wolf Kulwicki, whose team carefully calculated the number of laps he needed to lead to clinch the lap-leader bonus. Kulwicki led a single lap more than Elliott, which was the difference in winning the championship and finishing second.

By 1992, diecast collectible-car manufacturers were taking notice of NASCAR and offering well-detailed replicas of cars from the top teams. The new products were well received by the public. Prior to the '90s, a few major toy companies dabbled with occasional NASCAR-related products, and their efforts were met with passive interest. But interest was growing in the early '90s. Diecast cars and collector cards were starting to become sales sensations.

The 1993 NASCAR Winston Cup season was more tragic than any in nearly 30 years. Kulwicki perished in a private plane crash on April 1, and Davey Allison died in a July 13

helicopter crash at Talladega. Two of NASCAR's brightest young stars were gone, leaving a void for years to come.

Rusty Wallace hit his stride in 1993, winning 10 races including five of the last eight. But he was no match for the consistent Earnhardt, who took his sixth NASCAR Winston Cup championship and his fifth in the last eight years. Earnhardt stepped into Richard Petty's shadows, only one championship away from the seven Petty won during his career.

By 1994, Jeff Gordon, a 21-year-old starry-eyed youngster, had become a polished and skillful driver. In his first start at Daytona in '93, he shockingly won the Twin 125-miler, becoming the youngest driver to ever win in NASCAR Winston Cup machinery at Daytona International Speedway. Gordon was flashy and spectacular as a rookie, but he just missed earning a trip to victory lane.

Team owner Rick Hendrick hired Gordon in 1992 after watching him closely during his two-year tenure in the NASCAR Busch Series. "I had watched him at Atlanta," said Hendrick. "He was smoking his tires, he was so loose in the corners. I nudged a guy who was standing with me and I told him, 'Watch, he's going to bust his tail on the next lap.' I said that for about 20 laps. Finally, I said, 'I can't believe this.' You can see a lot of raw talent when a guy can handle a car when it's that loose. As young as he was and with the lack of experience he had, I was kind of blown away." Although Gordon was under Ford Motor Company's wing early in his fledgling career, Hendrick inquired about his contractual status. "When I found out he wasn't under contract, I signed him within five days," Hendrick said.

While Gordon was getting acquainted with NASCAR Winston Cup racing in 1994, Dale Earnhardt and Rusty Wallace were engaged in their customary battle for the championship. Wallace won twice as many races as Earnhardt, eight-to-four, but was no match in the points race. Earnhardt's tactical awareness, savvy, and intelligence were unsurpassed. He knew how and when to apply the spurs to his steed, but he was also the best at coaxing his car to a decent finish when problems intervened.

Earnhardt ran away with the championship in 1994, finishing 444 points ahead of Mark Martin, who won twice during the season. For Earnhardt, the joys of the championship season were tempered by the death of close friend Neil Bonnett, who lost his life in a practice crash at

Daytona. Bonnett had been out of action since a 1990 accident at Darlington that left him with amnesia. He attempted a brief comeback in '93, starting two races as Earnhardt's teammate. Bonnett had announced he was going to run selected races for team owner James Finch in '94.

Trackside attendance for NASCAR races was figuratively going through the roof by the end of 1994. Bolstered by the addition of the Brickyard 400 at the hallowed Indianapolis Motor Speedway, NASCAR Winston Cup races drew 4,896,000 spectators for the 31 events, an increase of more than one million from '93. Many track owners and promoters were forced to add grandstands at their facilities to accommodate public demand. Television ratings were also showing a significant increase.

While the sport was experiencing tremendous growth in corporate headquarters, Earnhardt's on-track prowess remained at its peak in 1995. Earnhardt clearly ruled the NASCAR Winston Cup roost in the early '90s, but he was starting to get company at the top in the form of Jeff Gordon. Gordon had charisma, an articulate manner, and Hollywood good looks. A blend of bravery, computerized reflexes, and infallible judgment aided his ascent to NASCAR's elite. He won three of the first six races in the '95 season. Although that didn't put him atop the points, he was poised to make a run at his first NASCAR Winston Cup title.

The crafty and wise Earnhardt and the new golden boy Gordon traded the points lead in the early weeks. By early July, Gordon had assumed command, and tightened his grip with a string of success through mid September. Following the Sept. 19 event at Dover, Gordon led Earnhardt by 309 points. Only a case of late-season jitters by Gordon and a relentless rally by Earnhardt made the race close. Earnhardt sliced the deficit over the last six races and came within a whisker of recording his eighth championship. Gordon prevailed by a mere 34 points in only his third full season.

The 1995 season was immensely successful, and NASCAR public relations officers claimed "1995 marked the year the NASCAR lifestyle became a national phenomenon" with cover stories in *Forbes* magazine and *Sports Illustrated* featuring NASCAR's colorful and dynamic appeal. Attendance at NASCAR Winston Cup events surpassed five million for

the first time in history. Teams began unveiling new paint schemes for many of the major events, giving the diecast car industry additional gimmicks to sell collectible toys. In late '95, NASCAR found a new way to reach fans by developing its own site on the World Wide Web.

In 1996, NASCAR expanded to New York City, establishing an office devoted to further developing and servicing corporate marketing and sponsorship relationships.

As NASCAR was going full speed ahead off the track, Jeff Gordon was grabbing headlines on the track. He enjoyed his finest year in 1996, winning 10 NASCAR Winston Cup races and recording 17 top-three finishes in 31 starts. Terry Labonte, a revitalized warrior who joined the Hendrick Motorsports operation in '94, won twice and somehow squeezed Gordon off the championship throne. Both Chevrolet drivers had the same number of top-five and top-10 finishes, but the similarities in the record sheet ended there. Gordon led 2314 laps to Labonte's 973. However, when the final tallies were tabulated, Labonte prevailed by 39 points.

Gordon began the 1997 season with a victory in the Daytona 500, leading a 1-2-3 sweep for Hendrick Motor-sports machinery. It represented the first step of a two-year onslaught by Gordon. With his image and skills buffed to a high gloss, Gordon clearly became the most accomplished star along the NASCAR Winston Cup trail. He won at all of NASCAR's offerings, from short tracks to intermediate ovals to road courses to the blindingly fast superspeedways. Gordon won 10 races in '97 and claimed the championship by a mere 14 points over a rejuvenated Dale Jarrett. A year later, Gordon won 13 races, tying Richard Petty for the most single-season wins in the "Modern Era" (1972 and later). He took the lead at the midpoint of the '98 season and sprinted to his third championship. By the time Gordon was 27 years old, he had already nailed down three championships.

The 1998 season was the 50th anniversary for NASCAR, and a promotional bonanza was already in high gear by the time Daytona's Speedweeks rolled around. Dale Earnhardt was going through the usual Daytona rituals, cleaning house in the preliminary events, and focusing on winning the Daytona 500, the race that had escaped his grasp on so many occasions. "The car is runnin' good and our team is ready for the challenge," said Earnhardt. "Maybe this will be the year we finally come through."

The seven-time NASCAR champion earned a second-row starting position for the Daytona 500 by winning his Twin 125-mile qualifying event. It was Earnhardt's ninth straight win in the Thursday preliminary and his 11th overall. He made it look easy, leading all 50 laps.

He was just as dominant in the 500, taking the lead for the first time on the 17th lap. Earnhardt kept his black Chevrolet ahead of the pack for most of the race, leading for a total of 107 laps, including the final 61. Several challengers made repeated attempts to get by, but even with drafting help, no one was able to deny Earnhardt on this day.

In the 40th annual running of the Daytona 500, Earnhardt whisked away years of frustration by winning NASCAR's crown-jewel event in his 20th try. After finishing the 500 miles, Earnhardt wheeled his car down pit road. In a moving display of honor and respect, virtually every crewmember from every team lined up on the edge of pit road and offered a congratulatory high five as Earnhardt slowly drove past. "I knew some of the teams would come out," said Earnhardt, "but to see all those guys out there was pretty cool. I couldn't go too fast or I would have torn my arm off. These are memories that will last forever."

Earnhardt's victory came on the heels of a winless 1997 campaign, a season laced with more frustration than he had experienced since '81. Earnhardt held a gaggle of challengers at bay to win the race he cherished more than any other.

The decade of the 1990s closed with Dale Jarrett securing his first NASCAR Winston Cup championship in '99 after a season-long battle with Bobby Labonte and Mark Martin. A new fleet of youthful talent had made their way to the NASCAR scene, with freshman Tony Stewart leading the way. Stewart won three races in his freshman campaign, the most races won by a rookie since Dick Hutcherson's all-time record of 10 victories in his 1965 rookie campaign.

As NASCAR prepared for the new millennium, television ratings on the major networks and cable systems were at an all-time high. The sport had stepped over into the mainstream in convincing fashion. With increasing exposure and the high demand for tickets, promoters were again building additional grandstands to accommodate the overflow crowds. NASCAR stock car racing had become the second most popular professional sport in America, ranking ahead of everything except the National Football League.

1990

February 18 Dale Earnhardt cuts a tire on the final lap, allowing for Derrike Cope to post his first NASCAR Winston Cup win in the Daytona 500. Cope edges Terry Labonte by two car lengths.

February 25 Mark Martin finishes first at Richmond, leading the final 16 laps of the Pontiac Excitement 400. Martin's Roush Racing Ford is docked 46 points and crew chief Robin Pemberton is fined $40,000 when NASCAR officials find an unapproved carburetor spacer plate. Martin is allowed to keep the win.

March 4 Kyle Petty wins the GM Goodwrench 500 at North Carolina Motor Speedway and pockets $284,550. The total includes $220,400 in Unocal 76 money that goes to a driver who wins the pole and the race.

April 1 Dale Earnhardt edges Mark Martin to win the TranSouth 500 at Darlington, an event in which veteran Neil Bonnett is injured after a 212th-lap crash. Bonnett suffers a concussion and amnesia.

April 8 Davey Allison noses out Mark Martin in a photo finish to win the Valleydale Meats 500 at Bristol International Raceway. The margin of victory is listed as eight inches.

April 22 Brett Bodine drives Kenny Bernstein's Buick to his first career NASCAR Winston Cup win in the First Union 400 at North Wilkesboro.

June 10 Rusty Wallace tames the field on the twisting road course in Sonoma, Calif., for his fifth win in his last seven starts on road courses. Mark Martin finishes second as the race ends under the yellow flag.

July 7 A 24-car crash on the second lap depletes the Pepsi 400 field and Dale Earnhardt breezes to an easy win at Daytona International Speedway.

August 25 Ernie Irvan passes Dale Earnhardt in the final 50 miles and speeds to his first NASCAR Winston Cup victory in Bristol's Busch 500.

Greg Sacks takes the #46 Chevrolet to the high side in a battle with #25 Ken Schrader in the 1990 Daytona Twin 125-miler. Sacks was driving one of the special cars prepared by Hendrick Motorsports for the upcoming feature-length film *Days of Thunder*. To get authentic racing scenes from in-car cameras, NASCAR permitted a handful of the movie cars to run a few laps in the Twin 125-milers and the early laps of the Daytona 500. Despite the cooperative efforts of the sanctioning body, Hendrick Motorsports, and several expert consultants, *Days of Thunder* turned out to be another dreadful Hollywood film about NASCAR.

◄ ▲ Jerry Bruckheimer and Don Simpson produced *Days of Thunder* for Paramount Pictures. The film starred Tom Cruise as Cole Trickle, a brash, cocky, and talented young driver fresh off the Sprint Car circuit. Nicole Kidman costarred as Dr. Claire Lewicki, a neurosurgeon who falls in love with Trickle. Robert Duval played Harry Hogge, a Harry Hyde-like crew chief who has to harness Trickle's talent. Despite several scenes from NASCAR lore (Trickle's crew eating ice cream in the pits, a fender-rubbing rental car duel, Trickle ramming winner Rowdy Burns' car after a race), the formulaic movie fell short with most NASCAR fans.

Number 3 Dale Earnhardt and #10 Derrike Cope race side-by-side in the Feb. 18 Daytona 500. Earnhardt clearly had the car to beat, leading for 155 of the 200 laps. He was seemingly on his way to an easy victory when a tire blew in the final turn of the final lap, opening the door for Cope to steal his first NASCAR Winston Cup victory. Cope's Daytona 500 triumph was also his first career top-five finish.

Mark Martin and team owner Jack Roush were all smiles after winning the Feb. 25 Pontiac Excitement 400 at Richmond International Raceway. Martin finished comfortably ahead of runner-up Dale Earnhardt. In a postrace inspection, NASCAR officials determined that Martin's Ford used an unapproved carburetor spacer plate. While NASCAR allowed Martin to keep the victory, the Roush team was penalized 46 points for the infraction. It was a penalty that would decide the outcome of the 1990 NASCAR Winston Cup championship.

Kyle Petty stomped the field to win the March 4 Goodwrench 500 at North Carolina Motor Speedway, pocketing $284,450. Petty led 433 of the 492 laps and scooted across the finish line a few car lengths ahead of runner-up Geoff Bodine. Petty's hefty winner's share was sweetened by a $220,400 bonus from Unocal, which posted the extra money to any driver who won a NASCAR Winston Cup race from the pole. The money rolled over week to week, and it had been a year since any driver had pulled off the feat.

Dale Earnhardt and Rusty Wallace lead the field off pit road during the pace lap for the March 18 Motorcraft Quality Parts 500 at Atlanta International Raceway. Earnhardt won the race with a nifty three-abreast pass on Morgan Shepherd with two laps remaining. Earnhardt manhandled the field, leading for 216 of the 328 laps, but he needed a rally at the finish to overtake Shepherd and nab his 40th career NASCAR Winston Cup victory.

Ricky Rudd's #5 Chevrolet lurches sideways as #42 Kyle Petty slaps the wall in the April 1 Darlington TranSouth 500. Rusty Wallace, in the #27 Pontiac, finds his line blocked as he arrives on the scene. All three drivers got back into the race after repairs. Petty finished 13th, Wallace came home 18th, and Rudd placed 24th. Another crash left Neil Bonnett with a concussion and amnesia, causing him to give up his ride in the Wood Brothers Ford to Dale Jarrett. Dale Earnhardt won the race and Mark Martin came in a close second.

1990

September 30 Mark Martin wins the Tyson Holly Farms 400 at North Wilkesboro Speedway, and rookie driver Rob Moroso finishes 21st. A few hours after the race, Moroso and another motorist are killed in a highway accident.

November 4 Dale Earnhardt leads all but the first 50 laps as he dominates the 312-mile Checker 500 at Phoenix. Earnhardt takes the points lead as leading contender Mark Martin struggles to finish 10th.

November 18 Morgan Shepherd wins the season finale at Atlanta as Dale Earnhardt finishes third and captures his fourth NASCAR Winston Cup title. Mike Ritch, a crewman for Bill Elliott's team, is fatally injured when he is hit on pit road.

Davey Allison keeps his #28 Ford just ahead of #6 Mark Martin in a frantic last-lap duel in the Valleydale Meats 500 at Bristol Motor Speedway. The two cars crossed the finish line in a near dead heat with Allison prevailing by a margin of no more than eight inches. Before promoters at Bristol laid down the concrete surface in 1993, the asphalt track afforded quite a bit of side-by-side action. Allison's victory over Martin was the closest in Bristol history.

Brett Bodine wheels his #26 Buick down pit road after winning the April 22 First Union 400 at North Wilkesboro Speedway. For Bodine, it was his first NASCAR Winston Cup victory. He was credited with leading the final 83 laps and finished less than one second in front of runner-up Darrell Waltrip.

Darrell Waltrip failed to score a NASCAR Winston Cup victory in the 1990 season for the first time since 1974. The three-time champion was injured in a practice accident in July at Daytona, forcing him to miss six races. His best finish was a runner-up effort at North Wilkesboro's April 22 First Union 400. He logged 11 other top-10 finishes in his abbreviated campaign.

372

The Wood Brothers #21 Ford sits on pit road during the spring Talladega race week with Dale Jarrett at the wheel. Neil Bonnett, who had to give up the ride when he was injured at Darlington in April, made his trackside return at Talladega. Greeting him was Bobby Allison, who suffered near fatal head injuries two years earlier. Bonnett broke the ice in the press conference when he described his first conversation with Allison. "Me and Bobby were sitting there on the couch," said Bonnett. "Between Bobby trying to say what he was thinking and me trying to remember what he was saying, it was a helluva conversation." Bonnett then told reporters he would not attempt to compete in NASCAR Winston Cup racing again in 1990.

Dale Earnhardt battles with a pesky Greg Sacks in the late stages of the May 6 Winston 500 at Talladega Superspeedway. Sacks was driving a car fielded by Hendrick Motorsports and new associate Paul Newman. Despite starting 17th, Sacks raced into contention early and dogged Earnhardt for most of the race. Earnhardt beat Sacks to the finished line by two car lengths.

"Between Bobby trying to say what he was thinking and me trying to remember what he was saying, it was a helluva conversation."
—Neil Bonnett

Dale Earnhardt's #3 Chevrolet lies in a smoldering heap after clobbering the wall during a 103rd-lap crash in the May 27 Coca-Cola 600 at Charlotte Motor Speedway. A tire popped on Earnhardt's car, causing him to lose control. Repairs were made, and Earnhardt salvaged a 30th-place finish. The efforts of the Richard Childress Racing team allowed Earnhardt to pick up an additional 24 points in the NASCAR Winston Cup championship chase. Quite often, NASCAR championships are won when a team can get a title contender back into a race to improve his finish position.

Rusty Wallace thoroughly dominated the Coca-Cola 600 at Charlotte Motor Speedway. Driving Raymond Beadle's #27 Miller Genuine Draft Pontiac, Wallace led the final 91 laps and easily disposed of the 42-car field. Wallace had already announced he would break his association with Beadle's team in 1991.

Derrike Cope proved his Daytona 500 victory was no fluke by steering the #10 Purolator Chevrolet to a convincing win in the June 3 Budweiser 500 at Dover Downs International Speedway. Cope ran down Rusty Wallace with 55 laps remaining and drove to his second career NASCAR Winston Cup win. Dale Earnhardt's engine blew just 23 laps into the race, relegating him to a 31st-place finish. Earnhardt's troubles allowed Morgan Shepherd, who finished sixth, to take the championship points lead.

Number 27 Rusty Wallace leads #26 Brett Bodine, #21 Morgan Shepherd, and a hungry pack off Pocono's flat third turn during the June 17 Miller Genuine Draft 500. Harry Gant, pictured at the rear of this shot, stormed through the field, nabbed Wallace with 12 laps to go, and scored a popular victory. Gant's victory ended a personal 14-month winless skid and made him the oldest driver to win a NASCAR Cup Series race at the age of 50 years, 158 days.

"We ought to go over there and work that boy's head with a hammer."
—Bud Moore

Jimmy Spencer's #57 Pontiac slid down the backstretch on its roof, then rolled back onto its wheels after tangling with Ken Schrader on the final lap of the July 29 Talladega 500. Spencer managed to finish 24th. Schrader was unable to continue, but his 186 laps completed netted him a 16th-place finish. Dale Earnhardt won the race, placing him just one point behind Mark Martin in the NASCAR Winston Cup points race.

Ken Schrader bumps the wall in his #25 Chevrolet as #15 Morgan Shepherd and #42 Kyle Petty tiptoe past during the 41st annual running of Darlington's Southern 500 on Sept. 2. Schrader, who tried to make a high-side pass, felt that Shepherd had squeezed him into the wall, causing the 25th-lap accident. Schrader's car had to be towed to the pits where the Hendrick Motorsports crew began repairs.

Following 40 minutes of repairs after a mishap with Morgan Shepherd in the Southern 500, Ken Schrader brought his #25 back onto the track. Within moments, Schrader steered into the side of Shepherd, causing both to crash. Bud Moore, owner of Shepherd's #15 Ford, went ballistic, charging that Schrader deliberately trashed both cars. "We ought to go over there and work that boy's [Schrader] head with a hammer," growled Moore.

Chuck Bown, a top-ranked NASCAR Busch Series driver, landed a ride with team owner Tex Powell in the Oct. 7 Mello Yello 500 at Charlotte Motor Speedway. Bown spun the car into the grass in the middle stages of the event, but recovered and finished 24th. Bown went on to win the 1990 Busch Series championship, and dabbled a bit in NASCAR Winston Cup racing.

Daytona's Twin Qualifiers

DALE EARNHARDT WON the second Twin 125-mile qualifier in 1990, beginning an incredible 10-year winning streak in the hotly contested preliminary events leading up to the annual Daytona 500. Earnhardt was clearly the master of Daytona International Speedway, winning 34 races on the high-banked 2.5-mile track. Twelve of the 34 wins came in the Twin sprint races that determine the starting order for NASCAR's crown-jewel event.

From 1959 to '71, the Twin qualifiers counted as official NASCAR Grand National races. Championship points were awarded, and wins counted as official victories for the drivers.

In '72, the events were reduced to qualifying races. They no longer carried points and were no longer official NASCAR Winston Cup Grand National events.

The doubleheader races have been regarded among the most spectacular events on NASCAR's schedule. To secure a starting berth in the Daytona 500, drivers often race as hard as they can.

After Fred Lorenzen went the entire 100 miles without a pit stop in '67, NASCAR added 25 miles to ensure at least one pit stop. By '89, drivers were routinely running the 125 miles without a pit stop. In 2005, the races were lengthened to 150 miles, thus requiring drivers to pit for gas.

Winners of the Twin Qualifiers at Daytona

Year	Winning Driver	Car	Speed	Year	Winning Driver	Car	Speed
1959	Shorty Rollins	Ford	129.500	1986	Dale Earnhardt	Chevrolet	153.270
1959	Bob Welborn	Chevrolet	143.198	1987	Ken Schrader	Ford	130.397
1960	Fireball Roberts	Pontiac	137.614	1987	Benny Parsons	Chevrolet	182.778
1960	Jack Smith	Pontiac	146.520	1988	Bobby Allison	Buick	130.966
1961	Fireball Roberts	Pontiac	133.037	1988	Darrell Waltrip	Chevrolet	133.889
1961	Joe Weatherly	Pontiac	152.607	1989	Ken Schrader	Chevrolet	147.203
1962	Fireball Roberts	Pontiac	156.999	1989	Terry Labonte	Ford	189.554
1962	Joe Weatherly	Pontiac	145.396	1990	Geoff Bodine	Ford	187.110
1963	Junior Johnson	Chevrolet	164.083	1990	Dale Earnhardt	Chevrolet	157.233
1963	Johnny Rutherford	Chevrolet	162.969	1991	Davey Allison	Ford	165.380
1964	Junior Johnson	Dodge	170.777	1991	Dale Earnhardt	Chevrolet	156.794
1964	Bobby Isaac	Dodge	169.811	1992	Dale Earnhardt	Chevrolet	116.430
1965	Darel Dieringer	Mercury	165.669	1992	Bill Elliott	Ford	169.811
1965	Junior Johnson	Ford	111.076	1993	Jeff Gordon	Chevrolet	153.270
1966	Paul Goldsmith	Plymouth	160.427	1993	Dale Earnhardt	Chevrolet	157.288
1966	Earl Balmer	Dodge	153.191	1994	Ernie Irvan	Ford	156.304
1967	LeeRoy Yarbrough	Dodge	163.694	1994	Dale Earnhardt	Chevrolet	146.771
1967	Fred Lorenzen	Ford	174.583	1995	Sterling Marlin	Chevrolet	150.050
1968	Rained Out			1995	Dale Earnhardt	Chevrolet	131.887
1969	David Pearson	Ford	152.181	1996	Dale Earnhardt	Chevrolet	143.039
1969	Bobby Isaac	Dodge	151.668	1996	Ernie Irvan	Ford	186.027
1970	Cale Yarborough	Mercury	183.015	1997	Dale Jarrett	Ford	166.113
1970	Charlie Glotzbach	Dodge	147.734	1997	Dale Earnhardt	Chevrolet	162.749
1971	Pete Hamilton	Plymouth	175.029	1998	Sterling Marlin	Chevrolet	139.925
1971	David Pearson	Mercury	168.728	1998	Dale Earnhardt	Chevrolet	147.203
1972	Bobby Isaac	Dodge	127.118	1999	Bobby Labonte	Pontiac	163.517
1972	Bobby Allison	Chevrolet	178.217	1999	Dale Earnhardt	Chevrolet	155.280
1973	Buddy Baker	Dodge	173.611	2000	Bill Elliott	Ford	188.758
1973	Coo Coo Marlin	Chevrolet	157.177	2000	Ricky Rudd	Ford	188.048
1974	Bobby Isaac	Chevrolet	123.212	2001	Mike Skinner	Chevrolet	162.338
1974	Cale Yarborough	Chevrolet	129.724	2001	Sterling Marlin	Dodge	147.493
1975	Bobby Allison	Matador	156.685	2002	Jeff Gordon	Chevrolet	183.647
1975	David Pearson	Mercury	156.958	2002	Michael Waltrip	Chevrolet	131.965
1976	Dave Marcis	Dodge	119.458	2003	Robby Gordon	Chevrolet	181.140
1976	Darrell Waltrip	Chevrolet	156.250	2003	Dale Earnhardt, Jr.	Chevrolet	180.845
1977	Richard Petty	Dodge	179.856	2004	Dale Earnhardt, Jr.	Chevrolet	156.087
1977	Cale Yarborough	Chevrolet	171.429	2004	Elliott Sadler	Ford	182.334
1978	A.J. Foyt	Buick	123.018	2005	Michael Waltrip	Chevrolet	140.492
1978	Darrell Waltrip	Chevrolet	169.683	2005	Tony Stewart	Chevrolet	145.161
1979	Buddy Baker	Oldsmobile	167.598	2006	Elliot Sadler	Ford	140.625
1979	Darrell Waltrip	Oldsmobile	153.009	2006	Jeff Gordon	Chevrolet	146.490
1980	Neil Bonnett	Mercury	138.250	2007	Tony Stewart	Chevrolet	113.490
1980	Donnie Allison	Oldsmobile	165.441	2007	Jeff Gordon	Chevrolet	154.955
1981	Bobby Allison	Pontiac	150.125	2008	Dale Earnhardt, Jr.	Chevrolet	160.810
1981	Darrell Waltrip	Buick	152.905	2008	Denny Hamlin	Toyota	128.428
1982	Cale Yarborough	Buick	135.298	2009	Jeff Gordon	Chevrolet	139.436
1982	Buddy Baker	Buick	144.509	2009	Kyle Busch	Toyota	157.251
1983	Dale Earnhardt	Ford	157.746	2010	Jimmie Johnson	Chevrolet	146.461
1983	Neil Bonnett	Chevrolet	122.183	2010	Kasey Kahne	Ford	174.644
1984	Cale Yarborough	Chevrolet	129.459	2011	Kurt Busch	Dodge	159.794
1984	Bobby Allison	Buick	139.578	2011	Jeff Burton	Chevrolet	136.571
1985	Bill Elliott	Ford	179.784	2012	Tony Stewart	Chevrolet	159.104
1985	Cale Yarborough	Ford	155.387	2012	Matt Kenseth	Ford	194.175
1986	Bill Elliott	Ford	153.636				

Dale Earnhardt loops his #3 Chevrolet on the 115th lap of the Oct. 7 Mello Yello 500 at Charlotte Motor Speedway as rookie Jack Pennington squeezes past. Earnhardt's mishap knocked him down to 25th in the final rundown, leaving him 49 points behind Mark Martin in the NASCAR Winston Cup championship chase. Pennington, a product of dirt late-model racing, was impressive as a freshman in NASCAR Winston Cup competition. He finished second to Rob Moroso in the Rookie of the Year voting.

Davey Allison salutes the crowd with a wave as he crosses the finish line to win the Mello Yello 500. Allison muscled his way around Michael Waltrip with 12 laps to go and drove to a 2.59-second victory over runner-up Morgan Shepherd. For Allison, it was his eighth career NASCAR Winston Cup victory.

Alan Kulwicki earned a trip to victory lane by winning the Oct. 21 AC Delco 500 at Rockingham's North Carolina Motor Speedway. Kulwicki led the final 55 laps and was comfortably in front of runner-up Bill Elliott when the race concluded. For Kulwicki, it was his second career victory and his first in nearly two years.

Dale Earnhardt finished third in the 1990 season finale at Atlanta Motor Speedway, enabling him to wrap up the NASCAR Winston Cup championship by a narrow 26-point margin over Mark Martin. Earnhardt won nine races during the season and led 2438 laps, while Martin won three times and led 451 laps. Despite the lopsided numbers, Earnhardt had to rally in the championship chase, taking command in the next-to-last race of the season.

Mark Martin is consoled by wife Arlene after losing the NASCAR Winston Cup championship race to Dale Earnhardt. Martin led the points standings from early June through October, but Earnhardt charged past to capture his fourth championship. Martin actually scored more points than Earnhardt, but the loss of 46 points after his disputed Richmond victory in February proved to be the difference. Martin became only the second driver to lose the title on a penalty. Lee Petty lost the 1950 NASCAR Grand National championship when Bill France docked him 849 points at midseason.

1990 NASCAR WINSTON CUP POINTS RACE

Rank	Driver	Points	Starts	Wins	Top 5	Top 10	Winnings
1	Dale Earnhardt	4430	29	9	18	23	$3,308,056
2	Mark Martin	4404	29	3	16	23	$1,302,958
3	Geoff Bodine	4017	29	3	11	19	$1,131,222
4	Bill Elliott	3999	29	1	12	16	$1,090,730
5	Morgan Shepherd	3689	29	1	7	16	$666,915
6	Rusty Wallace	3676	29	2	9	16	$954,129
7	Ricky Rudd	3601	29	1	8	15	$573,650
8	Alan Kulwicki	3599	29	1	5	13	$550,936
9	Ernie Irvan	3593	29	1	6	13	$535,280
10	Ken Schrader	3572	29	0	7	14	$769,934
11	Kyle Petty	3501	29	1	2	14	$746,326
12	Brett Bodine	3440	29	1	5	9	$442,681
13	Davey Allison	3423	29	2	5	10	$640,684
14	Sterling Marlin	3387	29	0	5	10	$369,167
15	Terry Labonte	3371	29	0	4	9	$450,230
16	Michael Waltrip	3251	29	0	5	10	$395,507
17	Harry Gant	3182	28	1	6	9	$522,519
18	Derrike Cope	3140	29	2	2	6	$569,451
19	Bobby Hillin, Jr.	3048	29	0	1	4	$339,366
20	Darrell Waltrip	3013	20	0	5	12	$520,420
21	Dave Marcis	2944	29	0	0	0	$242,724
22	Dick Trickle	2863	29	0	2	4	$350,990
23	Rick Wilson	2666	29	0	1	3	$242,067
24	Jimmy Spencer	2579	26	0	0	2	$219,775
25	Dale Jarrett	2558	24	0	1	7	$214,495
26	Richard Petty	2556	29	0	0	1	$169,465
27	Butch Miller	2377	23	0	0	1	$151,941
28	Hut Stricklin	2316	24	0	0	2	$169,199
29	Jimmy Means	2271	27	0	0	0	$135,165
30	Rob Moroso	2184	25	0	0	1	$162,002
31	Rick Mast	1719	20	0	0	1	$112,875
32	Greg Sacks	1663	16	0	2	4	$216,148
33	Chad Little	1632	18	0	0	0	$80,140
34	Jack Pennington	1278	14	0	0	0	$95,860
35	Larry Pearson	822	9	0	0	0	$72,305
36	Jimmy Horton	756	9	0	0	0	$72,375
37	Mickey Gibbs	755	9	0	0	0	$38,665
38	Mike Alexander	682	7	0	0	0	$41,080
39	Phil Parsons	632	9	0	0	0	$90,010
40	J. D. McDuffie	557	8	0	0	0	$26,170
41	Buddy Baker	498	8	0	0	0	$40,085
42	Lake Speed	479	6	0	0	0	$75,537
43	Neil Bonnett	455	5	0	0	0	$62,600
44	Mark Stahl	371	5	0	0	0	$18,470
45	Bill Venturini	349	4	0	0	0	$22,970
46	Rodney Combs	323	5	0	0	0	$23,365
47	Irv Hoerr	281	2	0	0	2	$14,775
48	Tommy Kendall	281	3	0	0	1	$14,120
49	Ted Musgrave	280	4	0	0	0	$17,190
50	Chuck Brown	276	3	0	0	0	$10,150

Dale Earnhardt and Mark Martin battled down to the wire for the 1990 NASCAR Winston Cup championship, and Earnhardt took his fourth title in the final two races of the season.

Martin led the standings from June through October, but Earnhardt rallied with a win at Phoenix and a third-place effort in the finale at Atlanta, and prevailed by 26 points over Martin.

Martin's loss was bitter for his Jack Roush team. Martin won at Richmond in February, but NASCAR officials discovered that his carburetor spacer was ½ inch too thick. The team was fined $40,000 and stripped of 46 points.

In October, Earnhardt left the pits at Charlotte with the left-side wheels unattached, and they flew off in the first turn. His pit crew ran out to the car and secured the tires in place, ignoring a NASCAR official's command to stay away from the car. Rules state that a pit crew can't work on a car when it is on the racing surface. Earnhardt rejoined the race without losing much time. NASCAR considered imposing a penalty, but none was given, and Earnhardt went on to win the title.

1991

After losing sponsorship from Zerex, Alan Kulwicki faced the prospect of competing in the 1991 season without financial backing. For the Daytona 500, Kulwicki was blessed with Army sponsorship, which was actually funded by title sponsor Winston and R.J. Reynolds. In a public display of unity during the Gulf War crisis, Winston also lined up sponsorship from the Marines, Coast Guard, Air Force, and Navy for other unsponsored drivers. Kulwicki came from his 27th starting spot to finish seventh in the Feb. 19 Daytona 500.

Ernie Irvan crosses under the checkered flag to win the Daytona 500 while running on the apron of Daytona International Speedway. Irvan snatched the lead from Dale Earnhardt with six laps remaining. Earnhardt crashed a lap later, resulting in the ninth caution period of the day. Irvan, who was low on fuel, tooled around the last couple of laps on the flat part of the track to conserve fuel. Sterling Marlin finished second in the #22 Ford.

Dale Jarrett's #21 Ford goes airborne after ramming the concrete retaining barrier in the April 7 TranSouth 500 at Darlington Raceway. The accident occurred on the 31st lap when rookie Bill Measell pinched #33 Harry Gant into a spin in the third turn. Gant darted into Jarrett, sending both on a harrowing 150-mph slide. Gant continued in the race, but Jarrett was sidelined.

Michael Waltrip drove the finest race of his young career in the TranSouth 500 at Darlington Raceway, leading for 208 of the 367 laps. His #30 Pennzoil Pontiac was the class of the field and was headed for victory until a jammed air hose on his final pit stop knocked him out of the hunt. The pit stop took 37.4 seconds, and relegated Waltrip to a third-place finish. Waltrip would have to wait another 10 years before he would post his first victory.

Ricky Rudd and his Hendrick Motorsports team carefully calculated fuel mileage in Darlington's 1991 spring race, and it paid off handsomely. Rudd made one less pit stop than his front-running rivals and crossed the finish line 11.2 seconds ahead of runner-up Davey Allison. Despite winning only one race and recording nine top-five finishes, Rudd remained in contention for the NASCAR Winston Cup championship for the entire campaign.

Ken Schrader's #25 Chevrolet spins in a tight clump of traffic during the April 14 Valleydale Meats 500 at Bristol International Raceway. Number 7 Alan Kulwicki and #98 Jimmy Spencer skim past as #1 Rick Mast and #26 Brett Bodine look for an opening. Spencer went on to finish eighth.

Darrell Waltrip, in the #17 Chevrolet, runs just ahead of Dale Earnhardt in the final laps of the First Union 400. Waltrip went on to edge Earnhardt at the stripe by less than one second. It marked the first win for Waltrip in a car that he owned since the 1975 NASCAR Winston Cup Grand National season.

Geoff Bodine spins his #11 Ford in the early stages of the April 21 First Union 400 at North Wilkesboro Speedway. Bodine had a long afternoon on the demanding short track. Later in the race, he tangled with Davey Allison, causing him to spin again. He grabbed low gear and popped Allison as both cars were facing the wrong way. "Aw, we were both just trying to get out of each other's way," Bodine said tongue in cheek. NASCAR officials parked Bodine for the remainder of the race.

"Aw, we were both just trying to get out of each other's way."
—Geoff Bodine

1991

July 28 Dale Earnhardt leads the final 28 laps and thwarts a gaggle of foes on the final lap to win the DieHard 500 at Talladega.

August 11 Ernie Irvan leads most of the way to win the 218.52-mile race at Watkins Glen, a tragic affair that takes the life of veteran campaigner J.D. McDuffie. The 52-year-old McDuffie dies instantly when he slides off the track and hits a steel retaining barrier.

August 18 Dale Jarrett prevails in a photo finish over Davey Allison to win his first NASCAR Winston Cup event in the Champion Spark Plug 400. Jarrett edges Allison by 10 inches in the closest finish in Michigan International Speedway history.

September 1 Harry Gant steers his Oldsmobile to an easy victory in Darlington's Southern 500. Kyle Petty makes his first start since being injured at Talladega in April.

September 22 Harry Gant, the new "Mr. September," grabs his fourth consecutive win at Martinsville Speedway, overcoming a crash late in the race that knocks him a lap off the pace.

September 29 Harry Gant's late-race brake failure opens the door for Dale Earnhardt to win the Tyson Holly Farms 400 at North Wilkesboro. Gant was attempting to become the first driver to win five straight races since 1971.

October 6 Geoff Bodine's extraordinary fuel mileage nets him a win in Charlotte's Mello Yello 500. Bodine goes the final 114 miles without a pit stop.

November 3 Davey Allison leads the final 60 laps and wins the Pyroil 500 at Phoenix. Rusty, Mike, and Kenny Wallace all compete in the race, the first triple brother act in NASCAR Winston Cup racing since 1961.

November 17 Mark Martin scores his first win of the season in the finale at Atlanta. Dale Earnhardt clinches his fifth NASCAR Winston Cup championship by simply starting the race.

Davey Allison chats with crew chief Larry McReynolds before the start of the April 28 Hanes 500 at Martinsville Speedway. Allison was in position to take his first win of the season, leading with 45 laps remaining when a tire blew. The ensuing pit stop knocked him a lap off the pace and he eventually finished eighth. Allison's misfortune opened the door for Dale Earnhardt to post his second win of the season.

" I don't like getting upside down, and I was fixin' to."
—Mark Martin

◄▲ Mark Martin's #6 Ford flies down the backstretch of Talladega Superspeedway during a multicar collision on the 71st lap of the May 6 Winston 500. Prior to the advent of roof flaps, NASCAR Winston Cup machinery often went airborne on NASCAR's speediest tracks. Martin's car came down on all four wheels without flipping over. "I don't like getting upside down, and I was fixin' to," said Martin. "I closed my eyes when I went into the air."

Harry Gant's #33 Oldsmobile takes the checkered flag ahead of teammate Rick Mast in the Winston 500. Gant shocked all pitsiders by running 149 miles on one tank of fuel. He finally ran out of gas on the final lap and Mast bumped him a couple of times to keep him chugging along. While NASCAR prohibits any car from assisting another on the final lap, Gant kept the victory and wasn't penalized.

Number 90 Dick Brooks and #14 Coo Coo Marlin head into the first turn of the special Winston Legends event staged at Charlotte Motor Speedway on May 19. Winston invited 22 of NASCAR's legendary heroes to compete in a race on the flat ¼-mile speedway located between the front-stretch and pit road. The 30-lap event was the biggest hit of Charlotte's May Speedweek, and the retired racers put on one whale of a show. Elmo Langley came from the 16th starting position to win, passing Cale Yarborough on the final lap.

Alan Kulwicki's #7 Ford slides down the embankment at Charlotte Motor Speedway after an engine failure sent him into the wall during the May 26 Coca-Cola 600. Kulwicki landed sponsorship from an Atlanta restaurant chain called Hooters in March after winning the pole for the March 18 race in Atlanta, but he was continually hounded by engine troubles and sour luck in the early part of the year. The Kulwicki-Hooters relationship would prove beneficial to both parties in the future.

Darrell Waltrip blazes down the front chute at Pocono International Raceway en route to a win in the June 16 Champion Spark Plug 500. Waltrip slipped past Dale Earnhardt with 18 laps remaining and went on to record his second win of the year. "Winning races at this point in my career, in my own car, and coming back from the [1990] injury to put this whole thing together, has been special," said Waltrip. Waltrip had suffered leg injuries in a practice crash before the Pepsi 400 at Daytona in '90.

Bill Elliott drove the blue #9 Coors Light Ford during the 1991 NASCAR Winston Cup season. In what was destined to be his final year driving for team owner Harry Melling, Elliott scored one win—at the July 6 Pepsi 400. Following the disappointing 1991 season, in which Elliott finished 11th in the final points standings, he left to join the Junior Johnson operation.

Dale Earnhardt survived a late-race surge from several Ford drivers to win in the July 28 DieHard 500 at Talladega. The Ford drivers' hopes were dashed when Bill Elliott pulled out of their draft, leaving contender Davey Allison to fall back to ninth without the aid of the draft. Allison, who broke his hand by punching the wall of his transporter after the race, said, "All we needed was four more inches to clear Earnhardt.... If you trust another Ford driver, then they leave you hung out to dry, that's pitiful."

Longtime NASCAR independent campaigner J.D. McDuffie was bucking heavy odds by 1991. With corporate sponsorship financing most of the teams, McDuffie's homespun operation was only able to qualify for a few NASCAR Winston Cup events. McDuffie attempted to qualify 14 times in '91, but only made the field for five events. In the Aug. 11 race on the Watkins Glen road course, McDuffie lost a wheel and slammed into a retaining barrier. Tragically, he died in the accident. McDuffie competed in 653 races from 1963 to '91, logging 106 top-10 finishes.

Ernie Irvan wheels his #4 Chevrolet through a series of turns at Watkins Glen en route to a big win in the Budweiser at the Glen event in picturesque upstate New York. Irvan withstood a challenge from Mark Martin on the final lap to record his first road-course win. Irvan won twice for the Morgan-McClure team in 1991 and finished fifth in the final points standings.

Manufacturers Points

THE CHEVROLET BOWTIE brigade captured its record ninth consecutive manufacturers championship in 1991, a postseason award that has been in place since '52. NASCAR awarded no manufacturers championship during the '49 NASCAR Strictly Stock campaign or the NASCAR Grand National seasons of '50 and '51.

While there have been a number of different procedures to determine a winner among nameplates, the method most used is an "International Point System" that awards points to the top six positions on a 9-6-4-3-2-1 breakdown.

Currently, all manufacturers earn points in every race, even if they don't place in the top six finishing positions.

The most puzzling manufacturers points race occurred in 1967 when Plymouth won 31 times while Ford racked up 10 victories. Ford won by nearly 300 points due to more entries. The manufacturer points system was changed the following year such that only the highest finishing car earned points for its make.

In 1952, a record 15 different makes of cars earned manufacturers points, meaning 15 different brands recorded top-10 finishes.

NASCAR Cup Series Manufacturers Rankings 1952-2010

Year	Champion	Runner-up	Third	Fourth	Fifth
1952	Hudson	Plymouth	Oldsmobile	Ford	Chrysler
1953	Hudson	Oldsmobile	Dodge	Plymouth	Nash
1954	Hudson	Oldsmobile	Dodge	Chrysler	Mercury
1955	Oldsmobile	Chrysler	Chevrolet	Hudson	Buick
1956	Ford	Chevrolet	Dodge	Chrysler	Mercury
1957	Ford	Chevrolet	Oldsmobile	Mercury	Pontiac
1958	Chevrolet	Ford	Oldsmobile	Pontiac	Mercury
1959	Chevrolet	Ford	Ford T-Bird*	Plymouth	Oldsmobile
1960	Chevrolet	Ford	Plymouth	Pontiac	Ford T-Bird*
1961	Chevrolet	Pontiac	Ford	Plymouth	Chrysler
1962	Pontiac	Chevrolet	Plymouth	Ford	Chrysler
1963	Ford	Pontiac	Plymouth	Chevrolet	Dodge
1964	Ford	Plymouth	Dodge	Mercury	Chevrolet
1965	Ford	Plymouth	Dodge	Plymouth	Mercury
1966	Ford	Plymouth	Dodge	Chevrolet	Oldsmobile
1967	Ford	Plymouth	Dodge	Chevrolet	Mercury
1968	Ford	Plymouth	Dodge	Mercury	Chevrolet
1969	Ford	Dodge	Plymouth	Mercury	Chevrolet
1970	Dodge	Plymouth	Ford	Mercury	Chevrolet
1971	Plymouth	Dodge	Mercury	Ford	Chevrolet
1972	Chevrolet	Dodge	Mercury	Plymouth	Ford
1973	Chevrolet	Dodge	Mercury	Ford	Plymouth
1974	Chevrolet	Dodge	Mercury	Ford	Matador
1975	Dodge	Chevrolet	Ford	Mercury	Matador
1976	Chevrolet	Mercury	Dodge	Ford	None
1977	Chevrolet	Dodge	Mercury	Ford	Matador
1978	Chevrolet	Oldsmobile	Ford	Mercury	Dodge
1979	Chevrolet	Ford	Oldsmobile	Mercury	Buick
1980	Chevrolet	Mercury	Ford	Oldsmobile	Buick
1981	Buick	Pontiac	Ford	Chevrolet	Oldsmobile
1982	Buick	Pontiac	Ford	Chevrolet	Chrysler
1983	Chevrolet	Buick	Ford	Pontiac	None
1984	Chevrolet	Ford	Pontiac	Buick	None
1985	Chevrolet	Ford	Buick	Pontiac	Oldsmobile
1986	Chevrolet	Ford	Buick	Pontiac	Oldsmobile
1987	Chevrolet	Ford	Pontiac	Buick	Oldsmobile
1988	Chevrolet	Ford	Pontiac	Oldsmobile	Buick
1989	Chevrolet	Ford	Pontiac	Buick	Oldsmobile
1990	Chevrolet	Ford	Pontiac	Oldsmobile	Buick
1991	Chevrolet	Ford	Oldsmobile	Pontiac	Buick
1992	Ford	Chevrolet	Pontiac	Olds	None
1993	Chevrolet	Ford	Pontiac	None	None
1994	Ford	Oldsmobile	Pontiac	None	None
1995	Chevrolet	Ford	Pontiac	None	None
1996	Chevrolet	Ford	Pontiac	None	None
1997	Ford	Chevrolet	Pontiac	None	None
1998	Chevrolet	Ford	Pontiac	None	None
1999	Ford	Chevrolet	Pontiac	None	None
2000	Ford	Pontiac	Chevrolet	None	None
2001	Chevrolet	Ford	Pontiac	Dodge	None
2002	Ford	Chevrolet	Dodge	Pontiac	None
2003	Chevrolet	Dodge	Ford	Pontiac	None
2004	Chevrolet	Ford	Dodge	None	None
2005	Chevrolet	Ford	Dodge	None	None
2006	Chevrolet	Dodge	Ford	None	None
2007	Chevrolet	Ford	Dodge	Toyota	None
2008	Chevrolet	Ford	Toyota	Dodge	None
2009	Chevrolet	Toyota	Ford	Dodge	None
2010	Chevrolet	Toyota	Ford	Dodge	None
2011	Chevrolet	Ford	Toyota	Dodge	None
2012	Chevrolet	Toyota	Ford	Dodge	None

*Ford Thunderbird was classified as a different car make than Ford in 1959 and '60.

Crafty veteran Harry Gant keeps his #33 Oldsmobile ahead of Davey Allison's #28 Ford in the 42nd edition of Darlington's Southern 500 on Sept. 1. Gant passed Allison with 70 laps remaining and scampered to a 10-second victory over runner-up Ernie Irvan. Gant pocketed a $100,000 bonus from NASCAR title sponsor R.J. Reynolds for winning two of the four events included in the Winston Million promotion.

Harry Gant runs ahead of #26 Brett Bodine and #28 Davey Allison in the Sept. 22 Goody's 500 at Martinsville Speedway. Gant posted his fourth straight win in the 500-lapper despite getting knocked into the wall in the late stages by Rusty Wallace. Gant sliced through the field following the wreck and nabbed first place from Bodine with 47 laps remaining. Gant's late-season winning streak earned him the nickname "Mr. September."

Richard Petty's #43 Pontiac lifts into the air after a collision with Chad Little in the early stages of the Sept. 29 Tyson Holly Farms 400 at North Wilkesboro Speedway. Both drivers recovered and coninued in the event. Petty finished 19th, while Little brought his Ford home 21st.

Dale Earnhardt nips at the heels of Harry Gant's fleet Oldsmobile in the closing stages of the Tyson Holly Farms 400. Gant was on his way to his fifth consecutive NASCAR Winston Cup victory when a malfunctioning O-ring caused a brake failure. The 10-cent part cost Gant $170,000 when Earnhardt passed Gant with nine laps to go and drove to victory.

Geoff Bodine pushes his #11 Ford around Dale Earnhardt in the middle stages of the Oct. 6 Mello Yello 500 at Charlotte Motor Speedway. Bodine went on to win the race, making a fuel-mileage run that baffled virtually every crew chief on pit road. Bodine ran the final 114 miles on one tank of fuel and cruised to an easy victory. Rival teams flatly stated no car can go 114 miles on 22 gallons of fuel. "The furthest we can go is 97½ miles," said Larry McReynolds, crew chief on the runner-up car driven by Davey Allison. "He can't run that far on 22 gallons. No way."

Dale Earnhardt runs in the high groove as his #3 Chevrolet spews smoke in the Nov. 3 Pyroil 500 at Phoenix International Raceway. The smoke was apparently caused by a loose oil fitting. With the championship in their sites, Earnhardt's crew prepared a car that was more bulletproof than fleet. Earnhardt's ninth-place finish at Phoenix assured him of the 1991 championship by simply starting the finale at Atlanta. It was The Intimidator's fifth NASCAR Winston Cup title.

1991 NASCAR WINSTON CUP POINTS RACE

Rank	Driver	Points	Starts	Wins	Top 5	Top 10	Winnings
1	Dale Earnhardt	4287	29	4	14	21	$2,416,685
2	Ricky Rudd	4092	29	1	9	17	$1,093,765
3	Davey Allison	4088	29	5	12	16	$1,712,924
4	Harry Gant	3985	29	5	15	17	$1,194,033
5	Ernie Irvan	3925	29	2	11	19	$1,079,017
6	Mark Martin	3914	29	1	14	17	$1,039,991
7	Sterling Marlin	3839	29	0	7	16	$633,690
8	Darrell Waltrip	3711	29	2	5	17	$604,854
9	Ken Schrader	3690	29	2	10	18	$772,434
10	Rusty Wallace	3582	29	2	9	14	$502,073
11	Bill Elliott	3535	29	1	6	12	$705,605
12	Morgan Shepherd	3438	29	0	4	14	$521,147
13	Alan Kulwicki	3354	29	1	4	11	$595,614
14	Geoff Bodine	3277	27	1	6	12	$625,256
15	Michael Waltrip	3254	29	0	4	12	$440,812
16	Hut Stricklin	3199	29	0	3	7	$426,254
17	Dale Jarrett	3124	29	1	3	8	$444,256
18	Terry Labonte	3024	29	0	1	7	$348,898
19	Brett Bodine	2980	29	0	2	6	$376,220
20	Joe Ruttman	2938	29	0	1	4	$361,661
21	Rick Mast	2918	29	0	1	3	$344,020
22	Bobby Hamilton	2915	28	0	0	4	$259,105
23	Ted Musgrave	2841	29	0	0	0	$200,910
24	Richard Petty	2817	29	0	0	1	$268,035
25	Jimmy Spencer	2790	29	0	1	6	$283,620
26	Rick Wilson	2723	29	0	0	0	$241,375
27	Chad Little	2678	28	0	0	1	$184,190
28	Derrike Cope	2516	28	0	1	2	$419,380
29	Dave Marcis	2374	27	0	0	1	$219,760
30	Bobby Hillin, Jr.	2317	22	0	0	1	$251,645
31	Kyle Petty	2078	18	1	2	4	$413,727
32	Lake Speed	1742	20	0	0	0	$149,300
33	Jimmy Means	1562	20	0	0	0	$111,210
34	Mickey Gibbs	1401	15	0	0	0	$100,360
35	Dick Trickle	1258	14	0	0	1	$129,125
36	Stanley Smith	893	12	0	0	0	$56,915
37	Larry Pearson	848	11	0	0	0	$56,570
38	Wally Dallenbach, Jr.	803	11	0	0	0	$54,020
39	Greg Sacks	791	11	0	0	0	$84,215
40	Buddy Baker	552	6	0	0	0	$58,060
41	Jimmy Hensley	488	4	0	0	1	$32,125
42	Eddie Bierschwale	431	5	0	0	0	$55,025
43	Jim Sauter	423	6	0	0	0	$47,395
44	Kenny Wallace	412	5	0	0	0	$58,325
45	Jeff Purvis	399	6	0	0	0	$42,910
46	Phil Barkdoll	364	4	0	0	0	$41,655
47	Mike Chase	356	5	0	0	0	$22,700
48	J.D. McDuffie	335	5	0	0	0	$19,795
49	Bill Sedgwick	324	3	0	0	0	$15,150
50	Randy LaJoie	304	4	0	0	0	$23,875

Dale Earnhardt claimed his fifth NASCAR Winston Cup championship in 1991, finishing comfortably ahead of runner-up Ricky Rudd. Earnhardt won four races along the way to the title and finished 195 points ahead of Rudd in the final point tally.

Earnhardt assumed command of the points race in early May and never trailed again. Rudd managed to cling to second place in the points standings despite only one win and nine top-five finishes in the 29-race season.

Ageless Harry Gant provided the most fireworks during the season, winning four races in a row during the month of September. The 51-year-old Gant won five races for the year and had six more top-five finishes than Rudd, but finished a distant fourth in the title race, more than 100 points behind runner-up Rudd.

Davey Allison finished third in the points on the strength of five victories and Ernie Irvan rounded out the top five with two wins.

1992

February 16 Davey Allison dodges several wrecks and finishes a car length ahead of Morgan Shepherd to win the Daytona 500. A 14-car crash cripples or takes out nine of the 16 cars running on the lead lap.

March 29 Bill Elliott breezes to his fourth consecutive NASCAR Winston Cup triumph with a big win in Darlington's TranSouth 500. Elliott has now won four of the first five NASCAR Winston Cup races, but doesn't lead the points standings.

April 5 Alan Kulwicki hustles past Dale Jarrett with 27 laps remaining and scores a narrow victory in the Food City 500 at Bristol International Raceway. It is the fourth win of Kulwicki's NASCAR Winston Cup career.

May 3 Davey Allison keeps a firm grip on the championship points lead with a victory in the Winston 500 at Talladega. Allison nips Bill Elliott at the finish line to give Ford a victory in all nine races thus far in the 1992 NASCAR Winston Cup season.

May 24 Dale Earnhardt avoids the watchful eye of NASCAR officials as he exceeds the 55-mph speed limit down pit road for his final stop, then outruns Ernie Irvan to win the Coca-Cola 600 at Charlotte. Earnhardt trails by more than three seconds entering the pit stop, but returns to the track 1.27 seconds ahead of his closest rival. Other contenders howl in protest after the race.

June 7 NASCAR founder William Henry Getty France passes away in an Ormond Beach, Fla., hospital at the age of 82. Ernie Irvan wins the race at Sears Point as flags fly at half-staff.

July 4 Ernie Irvan squeezes past Sterling Marlin to register a two car-length victory in the Pepsi 400 at Daytona. President George Bush accompanies Richard Petty in prerace ceremonies, commemorating The King's final race at Daytona International Speedway.

Alan Kulwicki pokes his #7 Hooters Ford under #10 Derrike Cope during the Feb. 16 Daytona 500. Kulwicki barely made it into the field for the 34th running of "The Great American Race," having earned one of the two provisional starting sports. Kulwicki marched his way through the field and landed in fourth place when the checkered flag fell. Cope placed 34th, having departed on lap 120 with a cracked radiator. Kulwicki's sparkling effort in the Daytona 500 kicked off an unlikely championship run.

Davey Allison noses out Morgan Shepherd to win the Daytona 500. After a 92nd-lap crash eliminated or crippled nine of the 16 cars that were on the lead lap, Allison and Shepherd emerged as prime contenders for the most sought after prize in NASCAR. Allison kept the #28 Robert Yates Racing/Havoline Ford on the point for the final 30 laps and prevailed by a car length.

Davey Allison runs side-by-side with Bill Elliott in the March 8 Pontiac Excitement 400 at Richmond International Raceway. Elliott, in his third effort with the powerful Junior Johnson team, dominated the race, leading 348 of the 400 laps. Elliott racked up his second of four consecutive wins. Prior to 1992, Elliott hadn't won in anything but Harry Melling-owned machinery. Allison finished fourth to retain the lead in the NASCAR Winston Cup title chase.

Jeff Gordon sits in his Ford Thunderbird prior to the March 14 NASCAR Busch Series race at Atlanta Motor Speedway. Gordon dazzled the huge trackside throng, as well as NASCAR Winston Cup team owner Rick Hendrick with his dominating win from the pole. Although Gordon was being groomed by Ford Motor Co. for a splash into the NASCAR Winston Cup Series in 1993, Hendrick snapped up the 21-year-old with a lucrative long-term contract to drive his Chevrolets.

Dale Earnhardt's #3 Chevrolet slaps the wall as #18 Dale Jarrett takes evasive action during the April 5 Food City 500 at Bristol International Raceway. Earnhardt ran into a series of problems in the event and finished 18th, 29 laps behind winner Alan Kulwicki. Jarrett finished second. Earnhardt got off to a slow start in the 1992 NASCAR Winston Cup season, scoring only one top-five finish in the first eight races.

Davey Allison and Rusty Wallace engaged in a terrific duel in the April 12 First Union 400 at North Wilkesboro Speedway. Allison motored past Wallace on the 313th lap and staved off Wallace's late-race challenge to prevail by two car lengths. Allison shook off the effects of a painful shoulder, which he injured in a crash at Bristol a week earlier.

Rusty Wallace's #2 Pontiac gets sideways after a tap from #26 Brett Bodine near the midpoint of the March 29 TranSouth 500 at Darlington Raceway. Wallace avoided the retaining wall and recovered to finish 12th. Bodine was involved in two skirmishes in the race, but managed to bring his car home sixth. Geoff Bodine, in the #15 Ford, placed eighth.

Dale Jarrett enjoyed his finest run of 1992 during Bristol's spring 500-lapper. Driving the #18 Chevrolet, Jarrett led until the 474th lap when Alan Kulwicki made the decisive pass. Kulwicki edged Jarrett at the finish line by .72 seconds to record his fourth career NASCAR Winston Cup victory.

July 19 Darrell Waltrip outruns the field to win the Miller Genuine Draft 500 at Pocono as Davey Allison survives a scary tumble with 50 laps to go.

August 16 Harry Gant bags Michigan's Champion Spark Plug 400 with a perfectly planned fuel-economy run to score his 18th career victory. Clifford Allison, younger brother of Davey, loses his life in a practice crash for the NASCAR Busch Series event three days before the race.

August 29 Darrell Waltrip scampers to victory in the Bud 500 at Bristol, the first race at the facility since the track was resurfaced with concrete.

September 20 Ricky Rudd holds off Bill Elliott to win the Peak AntiFreeze 500 at Dover Downs International Speedway. Alan Kulwicki is eliminated in an early crash, leaving him 278 points behind in the title chase. Kulwicki says, "This probably finishes us off in the championship deal."

October 11 Mark Martin edges Alan Kulwicki to win Charlotte's Mello Yello 500 for his second win of the season. Points leader Bill Elliott departs with mechanical problems, leaving six drivers within 114 points in what has suddenly become a wide-open championship race.

November 1 Davey Allison snatches the lead in the NASCAR Winston Cup title chase with a win in the Pyroil 500 at Phoenix. Allison leads Alan Kulwicki by 30 points and Elliott by 40 points heading into the finale at Atlanta.

November 15 Bill Elliott and Alan Kulwicki engage in an epic struggle, with Elliott scoring a narrow victory in the season-ending Hooters 500 at Atlanta. Points leader Davey Allison is knocked out of the title hunt by an early crash. Elliott wins the race but fails to pick up points on Kulwicki, who clings to a 10-point margin in the final standings. It sets a record for the closest title race in NASCAR history. Jeff Gordon makes his first NASCAR Winston Cup start as Richard Petty competes in his final event.

Kyle Petty climbs out of his burning Pontiac after clobbering the backstretch wall during the final laps of the April 26 Hanes 500 at Martinsville Speedway. "I ran out of brakes," said Petty. "I tore down the walls and tore up my race car." Petty got credit for an 18th-place finish.

Mark Martin guides his #6 Roush Racing/Valvoline Ford down the frontstretch en route to victory in the Hanes 500. Martin outran Sterling Marlin and outlasted a host of rivals to capture the 500-lap event on the flat, paper-clip-shaped ½-mile oval. Broken axles foiled many contenders, including Dale Earnhardt, Alan Kulwicki, and Ernie Irvan. Most NASCAR teams were experimenting with cambered rear ends—slightly bending the rear axle inward to give the tires a wider "footprint." While cornering speeds were greatly enhanced, the stress on the axles proved to be a noteworthy risk.

Sterling Marlin's #22 Ford leads a pack of cars during Talladega's Winston 500 on May 3. Marlin led five times for 58 laps in Junior Johnson's Maxwell House Ford, but was unable to fend off the pursuit of Davey Allison's #28 Ford. Allison finished two car lengths ahead of runner-up Bill Elliott, who drove the #11 Ford. Dale Earnhardt rode home third in the #3 Chevrolet, while Marlin was fourth and #7 Alan Kulwicki sixth.

Davey Allison crashes into the concrete retaining barrier after tangling with Kyle Petty at the finish of the May 16 The Winston race at Charlotte Motor Speedway. The annual NASCAR all-star event was presented under the lights for the first time, attracting a sell-out crowd. Allison and Petty slapped quarter-panels in the dash to the checkered flag, causing Allison's Ford to dart out of control. Allison crossed the finish line first, albeit backward. The young Alabama driver was transported to the hospital with minor injuries. Victory lane ceremonies went on as scheduled—even though the winning driver wasn't present.

Dick Trickle spins his #8 Ford to the apron of Charlotte Motor Speedway as cars tangle in the fourth turn during the May 24 Coca-Cola 600. Trickle recovered and finished 10th in the Stavola Brothers/ Snickers machine. Dale Earnhardt snaked his #3 Chevrolet through the mess and went on to score his only win of the 1992 NASCAR Winston Cup season.

▼ Richard Petty made his final competitive appearance at Daytona International Speedway in the July 4 Pepsi 400. Petty qualified his STP Pontiac on the front row for the first time since 1986. With President George Bush in attendance, King Richard led the opening five laps as the holiday crowd cheered wildly. Petty became fatigued in the oppressive heat and had to call it quits after running 84 of the 160 laps. The seven-time Daytona 500 champion had to settle for 36th place.

Clifford Allison, the 27-year-old younger brother of Davey Allison, was making strides and honing his talents in NASCAR's Busch Series in 1992. However, in a practice session at Michigan International Speedway on Aug. 13, Allison was fatally injured in a single-car accident. The loss was devastating to the NASCAR community and the Allison family.

Darrell Waltrip's #17 Chevrolet hooks up in a tight battle with Ricky Rudd's #5 Tide Chevrolet in the Aug. 29 Bud 500 on Bristol International Raceway's new concrete surface. Raceway officials put down the low-maintenance concrete slats after repeated incidents when the asphalt surface peeled apart under the heavy NASCAR artillery. Waltrip made the decisive pass on Rudd in the Bud 500 with 33 laps remaining. It was one of three races Waltrip won in 1992 driving his self-owned Western Auto Chevrolet.

Davey Allison's #28 Havoline Ford runs a car length ahead of #83 Lake Speed in the Oct. 11 Mello Yello 500 at Charlotte Motor Speedway. Speed competed in a handful of NASCAR Winston Cup races in 1992 while driving his own Purex Detergent-sponsored Ford. Allison led the points standings most of the season, but his performance slipped in the latter half of the campaign. He was lapped five times in the Mello Yello 500 and finished a disappointing 19th. Speed fell victim to clutch trouble in the closing laps, which robbed him of a top-10 finish. He placed 26th.

Alan Kulwicki

ALAN KULWICKI, an underdog from the Greenfield, Wis., produced NASCAR's most unlikely championship run in the 1992 NASCAR Winston Cup season. He overcame the greatest late-season deficit in championship history, and, along the way, gave hope to every small-time operator in NASCAR.

Kulwicki began the 1992 NASCAR Winston Cup season as one of the dozens of drivers with seemingly no realistic shot at NASCAR's most elusive prize. As an owner, driver, bookkeeper, and strategist, Kulwicki faced an uphill battle against the heavily funded and established teams.

But Kulwicki had a habit of doing things his way. Twice, the Wisconsin engineering graduate turned down offers to drive for legendary team owner Junior Johnson. Kulwicki thought he had the Maxwell House sponsorship tucked safely away in 1991, only to lose the big-buck sponsor to the Johnson team. Against all odds, Kulwicki still insisted on running his own operation.

Kulwicki barely made the field for 1992's season-opening Daytona 500, having to accept a provisional starting spot on the last row. He rallied from 41st to finish a credible fourth in NASCAR's most celebrated event. But three finishes out of the top 15 in the next seven NASCAR Winston Cup events left Kulwicki far behind the points leaders.

On the strength of consistent finishes and a couple of victories during the spring and summer, Kulwicki clambered back into contention, though still with slim hopes for the championship. In the September race at Dover, Kulwicki crashed early after rubbing fenders with a lapped car. When the points were tallied following the event, Kulwicki trailed Bill Elliott by 278 points with just six races remaining.

"Realistically, this probably finishes us off in the championship deal," Kulwicki said after the Dover crash. "I don't like to give up, but I know it will be hard to come back now." Kulwicki was aware of the intricacies of NASCAR's points system. It is impossible to catch up unless the points leader falls victim to a major dose of trouble. But Elliott and his Junior Johnson team stumbled down the stretch, encountering repeated mechanical problems that allowed the other contenders, including Kulwicki, back in the points race.

Entering the season finale at Atlanta, six drivers had a shot at the championship. Kulwicki was only 30 points behind points leader Davey Allison and 10 points ahead of Elliott. One of the most dynamic duels in the history of the title chase unfolded that afternoon at Atlanta Motor Speedway.

Allison's title hopes were dashed when he hit a spinning Ernie Irvan midway through the race. With Allison out of the

Mark Martin's #6 Ford leads #66 Jimmy Hensley, #7 Alan Kulwicki, and #94 Terry Labonte during the Mello Yello 500 at Charlotte. Martin wrestled the lead away from Kulwicki with 32 laps remaining and sprinted to a 1.88-second triumph. For Martin, it was his seventh career NASCAR Winston Cup victory. Hensley won the 1992 Rookie of the Year honors in the #66 Ford owned by NASCAR legend Cale Yarborough.

▶ Pole-sitter Rusty Wallace gets the jump on the field at the start of the Nov. 1 Pyroil 500 at Phoenix International Raceway. Wallace led 161 of the first 203 laps and appeared to be on his way to an easy win when the battery soured in his Penske Racing Pontiac. "There was no way anybody could touch us," Wallace said. "We had it won, hands down. That's the third time this has happened to me this year. This year is just trash. Really frustrating." Wallace logged only five top-five finishes in 1992 and finished 13th in the NASCAR Winston Cup points standings.

hunt, the championship race took an interesting twist. There was a distinct possibility that for the first time in history, a tiebreaker would be used to determine the NASCAR Winston Cup champion.

Elliott, by virtue of leading Kulwicki 4-2 in race wins, held the tiebreaker. Both drivers led laps in the early going, and Elliott and Kulwicki were vying not only for the Atlanta win, but also for the most laps led. If Elliott could lead the most laps, he would pick up five additional bonus points. With Elliott and Kulwicki running first and second, if the finish stayed the same, Elliott could win the title on the tiebreaker.

During the final laps of the race, Elliott and Kulwicki had separated themselves from the other contenders. Paul Andrews, Kulwicki's crew chief, was keeping tabs of the number of laps each driver had led. He knew it was going to be close. Andrews was in constant communication with his driver and told him that if he could lead until the 310th lap, he would only need to finish second to wrap up the title. He would no longer have to beat Elliott to win.

Kulwicki stretched his fuel and made his final pit stop on the 311th lap. Elliott went on to win the race, beating Kulwicki by 8.06 seconds. But Kulwicki finished second and beat Elliott by 10 points for the championship. "I thank God for the fortune to be here and to be an American and compete in the Winston Cup circuit," said a gracious Kulwicki in his

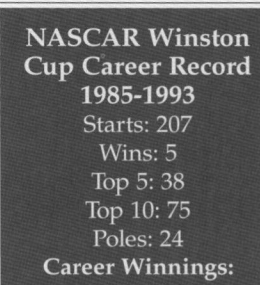

NASCAR Winston Cup Career Record 1985-1993
Starts: 207
Wins: 5
Top 5: 38
Top 10: 75
Poles: 24
Career Winnings: $5,059,052

impromptu acceptance speech. "When I moved down South [in 1986], this was my dream. I came here in a pickup truck and a trailer. I nicknamed this Ford the 'Underbird' because we were going into this race as the underdog. If you were to bet money back in '86 that I'd be where I am today, the odds were slim. When you consider everything it took to get here from there, you'd say it couldn't be done. But you can't look at it that way. I didn't. Obstacles are what you see when you take your eyes off the goal line," said the new NASCAR Winston Cup champ.

Kulwicki's title run in 1992 was one for the ages. It proved that with determination, hard work, intelligence, and a little luck, a small-time operator could rise to the pinnacle of his profession.

In 1993, Kulwicki had begun his title defense in solid fashion, scoring three top-10 finishes in the first five events of the NASCAR Winston Cup campaign and holding down ninth in the points standings. Following an appearance for sponsor Hooters Restaurants in Knoxville, Tenn., on April 1, Kulwicki was aboard the company plane to Bristol for the Food City 500. The twin-engine Merlin Fairchild 300 disappeared from radar six miles short of reaching the Tri-Cities Regional Airport and crashed into a meadow near Blountville, Tenn. The lives of Kulwicki, Mark Brooks, Dan Duncan, and pilot Charlie Campbell were lost. The champion wouldn't have the chance to defend his title.

Alan Kulwicki scampers past Darrell Waltrip during the Nov. 1 Pyroil 500 at Phoenix International Raceway along the way to a fourth-place finish. Kulwicki made a miraculous comeback in the season's final weeks, rallying from a 278-point deficit in mid September to challenge for the NASCAR Winston Cup title. Following the Phoenix event, Kulwicki trailed points leader Davey Allison by 30 points heading into the season finale at Atlanta.

Joe Gibbs, who coached the NFL's Washington Redskins to three Super Bowl titles, completed his first NASCAR campaign as a team owner in 1992. With financial backing from Interstate Batteries, Gibbs hired Dale Jarrett to campaign the #18 Chevrolet Lumina. "I had to get a good quarterback," said Gibbs, "and I think Dale is the obvious choice." Jarrett scored a pair of top-five finishes and placed 19th in the final NASCAR Winston Cup points standings. Although a trip to victory lane wasn't in the mix, solid groundwork was laid for long-term success.

◀ NASCAR icon Dale Earnhardt passes newcomer Jeff Gordon in the early laps of the Nov. 15 Hooters 500 at Atlanta Motor Speedway. Driving the #24 Hendrick Motorsports/DuPont Chevrolet, Gordon qualified 21st and placed 31st, falling victim to a crash after completing 164 laps. Earnhardt closed out a disappointing year by finishing 26th. Earnhardt won only one race and posted just six top-five finishes, placing him 12th in the final points standings. It was the first time Earnhardt had finished out of the top 10 in points since 1982.

"It caught on fire. I figured I'd better find me a fire truck, so I drove down the track until I found one."
—Richard Petty

Richard Petty's #43 Pontiac erupts in flames following a crash on the 95th lap of the Hooters 500. The King of NASCAR was competing in his 1184th and final NASCAR Winston Cup event. He got mixed up in the accident while trying to miss several spinning cars. "It broke the oil line and oil got on the headers," explained Petty. "It caught on fire. I figured I'd better find me a fire truck, so I drove down the track until I found one." Petty got back into the race and finished 35th in the field of 41.

▲▶ The 1992 season finale at Atlanta Motor Speedway became an instant classic. Davey Allison needed only to finish fifth to wrap up the NASCAR Winston Cup championship. Things fell apart when Ernie Irvan spun out on lap 254, blocking Allison's path. Extensive repairs relegated Allison to a 27th-place finish. That left Bill Elliott and Alan Kulwicki to duel for top honors in both the race and the championship chase. Elliott drove his #11 Budweiser Ford to victory as Kulwicki finished second in the #7 Ford "Underbird." Kulwicki and crew chief Paul Andrews calculated the laps led during the race for both warriors, and Kulwicki grabbed the five-point lap-leader bonus when he led the 310th lap. Kulwicki edged Elliott by 10 points to win the title, but the outcome would have been reversed if Elliott had led one more lap. Both drivers led the same number of green-flag laps, but Kulwicki led one more lap under caution. Allison settled for third in the final standings.

1992 NASCAR WINSTON CUP POINTS RACE

Rank	Driver	Points	Starts	Wins	Top 5	Top 10	Winnings
1	Alan Kulwicki	4078	29	2	11	17	$2,322,561
2	Bill Elliott	4068	29	5	14	17	$1,692,381
3	Davey Allison	4015	29	5	15	17	$1,955,628
4	Harry Gant	3955	29	2	10	15	$1,122,776
5	Kyle Petty	3945	29	2	8	17	$1,107,063
6	Mark Martin	3887	29	2	10	17	$1,000,571
7	Ricky Rudd	3735	29	1	9	18	$793,903
8	Terry Labonte	3674	29	0	4	16	$600,381
9	Darrell Waltrip	3659	29	3	10	13	$876,492
10	Sterling Marlin	3603	29	0	6	13	$649,048
11	Ernie Irvan	3580	29	3	9	11	$996,885
12	Dale Earnhardt	3574	29	1	6	15	$915,463
13	Rusty Wallace	3556	29	1	5	12	$657,925
14	Morgan Shepherd	3549	29	0	3	11	$634,222
15	Brett Bodine	3491	29	0	2	13	$495,224
16	Geoff Bodine	3437	29	2	7	11	$716,583
17	Ken Schrader	3404	29	0	4	11	$639,679
18	Ted Musgrave	3315	29	0	1	7	$449,121
19	Dale Jarrett	3251	29	0	2	8	$418,648
20	Dick Trickle	3097	29	0	3	9	$429,521
21	Derrike Cope	3033	29	0	0	3	$277,215
22	Rick Mast	2830	29	0	0	1	$350,740
23	Michael Waltrip	2825	29	0	1	2	$410,545
24	Wally Dallenbach, Jr.	2799	29	0	1	1	$220,245
25	Bobby Hamilton	2787	29	0	0	2	$367,065
26	Richard Petty	2731	29	0	0	0	$348,870
27	Hut Stricklin	2689	28	0	0	4	$336,965
28	Jimmy Hensley	2410	22	0	0	4	$247,660
29	Dave Marcis	2348	29	0	0	0	$218,045
30	Greg Sacks	1759	20	0	0	0	$178,120
31	Chad Little	1669	19	0	0	1	$145,805
32	Jimmy Means	1531	22	0	0	0	$133,160
33	Jimmy Spencer	1284	12	0	3	3	$183,585
34	Bobby Hillin, Jr.	1135	13	0	0	0	$102,160
35	Stanley Smith	959	14	0	0	0	$89,650
36	Mike Potter	806	11	0	0	0	$74,710
37	Jim Sauter	729	9	0	0	0	$56,045
38	Lake Speed	726	9	0	0	0	$49,545
39	Jimmy Horton	660	9	0	0	0	$50,125
40	Bob Schacht	611	9	0	0	0	$58,815
41	Charlie Glotzbach	592	7	0	0	0	$48,060
42	James Hylton	476	8	0	0	0	$37,910
43	Andy Belmont	467	8	0	0	0	$39,820
44	Jeff Purvis	453	6	0	0	0	$45,545
45	Dave Mader III	436	5	0	0	0	$69,635
46	Jerry O'Neil	429	6	0	0	0	$32,370
47	Eddie Bierschwale	277	4	0	0	0	$25,995
48	Buddy Baker	255	3	0	0	0	$49,500
49	Rich Bickle	252	3	0	0	0	$13,370
50	Mike Wallace	249	3	0	0	0	$17,415

Alan Kulwicki made a miraculous comeback to win the 1992 NASCAR Winston Cup championship by the closest margin in the history of the sport.

Kulwicki trailed Bill Elliott by 278 points with only six races remaining. It was a daunting task to get back into contention, but Elliott's Junior Johnson team ran into a flurry of mechanical problems that allowed several contenders back into the hunt. Elliott led the standings from August through October, but a mechanical failure at Phoenix gave the points lead to Davey Allison going into the season finale.

Allison, who took a 30-point lead into the season-ending Hooters 500 at Atlanta, was eliminated in an early crash, leaving Elliott and Kulwicki to battle it out.

Elliott took the lead with 13 laps to go and won the race. But Kulwicki led the most laps and earned the five-point bonus that goes to the lap leader of each race. Kulwicki edged Elliott by 10 points in the final analysis, and maintaining the lead for a single caution-flag lap was all the difference.

1993

February 14 Dale Jarrett muscles his way past Dale Earnhardt on the final lap and records a one car-length victory in the Daytona 500. Jarrett's last-lap heroics thwart Earnhardt's 15th bid for a win in NASCAR's most prestigious event.

March 7 Davey Allison leads all but four of the final 157 laps and throttles his Ford to an easy win in the Pontiac Excitement 400 at Richmond International Raceway.

March 20 Morgan Shepherd takes the lead with 12 laps remaining to win the Motorcraft Quality Parts 500 at Atlanta, an event postponed six days due to a blizzard. It is Shepherd's fourth career NASCAR Winston Cup win, three of which have come at Atlanta Motor Speedway.

March 28 Dale Earnhardt scrambles back from a one-lap deficit to win the TranSouth 500 at Darlington Raceway. Earnhardt's victory ends a personal 10-month losing skid. Alan Kulwicki finishes sixth in what is destined to be his final race.

April 1 Reigning NASCAR Winston Cup champion Alan Kulwicki perishes in a private plane crash en route to Bristol for the Food City 500. Rusty Wallace wins the race three days later and honors Kulwicki with a ceremonial opposite-direction "Polish victory lap."

May 2 Ernie Irvan prevails in an intense two-lap shootout to win Talladega's Winston 500. Rusty Wallace, who has won four of the nine races in the 1993 campaign, flips across the finish line after a tap from Dale Earnhardt. Wallace finishes sixth and retains his points lead, but suffers multiple injuries in a nasty crash.

May 30 Dale Earnhardt overcomes three penalties, one for rough driving, to win the Coca-Cola 600 at Charlotte Motor Speedway. Earnhardt takes a 129-point lead in the championship chase over Rusty Wallace, who races despite injuries suffered at Talladega.

Pole-sitter #42 Kyle Petty and #18 Dale Jarrett lead the pack at the start of the Feb. 14 "Daytona 500 by STP" at Daytona International Speedway. Petty earned his seventh career pole and was in contention until a late crash put him out of the race. Jarrett went on to win the race, giving team owner Joe Gibbs his first career NASCAR Winston Cup victory.

Rusty Wallace's #2 Pontiac goes airborne in a horrific tumble down the backstretch on the 169th lap of the Daytona 500. Wallace was running in the lead pack when #30 Michael Waltrip and #98 Derrike Cope rubbed together. Cope spun and clipped the rear of Wallace's car, sending him into a series of rollovers. The veteran campaigner suffered only a cut chin in the spectacular mishap. Wallace credited his full-face helmet for preventing major head injuries.

Dale Jarrett holds the winner's trophy after capturing the Daytona 500 in a last-lap duel with Dale Earnhardt. Miss Winston Brooke Sealy, the future Mrs. Jeff Gordon, joins Jarrett after the event. Jarrett caught Earnhardt at the drop of the white flag and made the decisive pass entering the first turn of the final lap. He was able to stave off Earnhardt the rest of the way and rack up his first Daytona 500 victory. The moment was made more special by Dale Jarrett's father, Ned, who was calling the race for the CBS Sports live telecast. Ned took over the call on the last lap, rooting his son on to victory.

Team owner Robert Yates and Davey Allison celebrate their March 7 victory in the Pontiac Excitement 400 at Richmond International Raceway. Allison led all but four of the final 157 laps on the ¾-mile oval and beat runner-up Rusty Wallace by 4.28 seconds. It was Allison's 19th career NASCAR Winston Cup victory. The win was the last for Allison, who lost his life on July 13, a day after the helicopter he was piloting crashed at Talladega Superspeedway.

Rookie Jeff Gordon engages in close combat with #3 Dale Earnhardt in the March 20 Motorcraft Quality Parts 500 at Atlanta Motor Speedway. Gordon nearly won in his fifth career NASCAR Winston Cup start. He was leading with 13 laps to go, but a late pit stop for fuel put him out of the hunt. He still managed to finish fourth as Earnhardt brought his car home 11th. Morgan Shepherd overcame a tire failure with 69 laps to go and parlayed good fuel mileage into a victory. Three of Shepherd's four career NASCAR Winston Cup wins came at Atlanta.

Kyle Petty and Alan Kulwicki run together in the early stages of the March 28 TranSouth 500 at Darlington Raceway. Petty finished seventh, while Kulwicki's sixth-place finish put him ninth in the NASCAR Winston Cup points standings. The 500-miler turned out to be the final event in Kulwicki's career. Tragically, he lost his life in a plane crash four days later while traveling to Bristol.

Dale Earnhardt zips his #3 Goodwrench Chevrolet past Mark Martin's #6 Valvoline Ford in the stretch duel at Darlington. Earnhardt led all but one of the final 149 laps and posted his 54th career NASCAR Winston Cup victory, which tied him with Lee Petty on the all-time win list. The victory ended a personal 10-month winless skid for the popular NASCAR hero.

1993

June 13 Kyle Petty runs away from his rivals and dodges a spectator who runs onto the track during green-flag conditions to win the Champion Spark Plug 500 at Pocono. Sixth-place finisher Davey Allison radios to his crew when he notices the dazed spectator on the speedway surface, "Guys, you ain't gonna believe this. There is some nut standing out here on the racetrack."

July 11 Rusty Wallace chases down Davey Allison in the final laps to win the first NASCAR Winston Cup race staged at the New Hampshire International Speedway. The following day, Allison is gravely injured in a helicopter crash on the grounds of Talladega Superspeedway. Allison passes away the following morning.

July 18 Dale Earnhardt holds off Rusty Wallace on the final lap to win the Miller Genuine Draft 500 at Pocono International Raceway. After the race, Earnhardt and the RCR Enterprises crew pay tribute to the late Davey Allison in a moving prayer service.

July 25 Dale Earnhardt beats Ernie Irvan by an eyelash to win the DieHard 500 at Talladega. In one of the closest finishes on record, Earnhardt's margin of victory is a scant .005 second.

September 5 Mark Martin racks up his fourth straight victory with a win in the rain-delayed Mountain Dew Southern 500 at Darlington Raceway. Martin is 1.51 seconds in front of Brett Bodine when the race ends 16 laps short of its scheduled distance due to darkness.

September 26 Ernie Irvan wins the Goody's 500 at Martinsville in his fourth start with the Robert Yates team. Irvan is wearing a Davey Allison T-shirt under his uniform in honor of the late driver he replaced on the Yates Ford team.

November 14 Rusty Wallace nails down his 10th win of the season at Atlanta Motor Speedway. Despite posting the most wins, as well as the most top-five and top-10 finishes, Wallace falls 80 points shy of winning the championship. Dale Earnhardt takes his sixth NASCAR Winston Cup title.

Dale Jarrett backs his #18 Chevrolet into the wall as cars skid in all directions behind him during the April 4 Food City 500 at Bristol International Raceway. Jarrett blamed Bobby Hillin, Jr., for triggering the crash, and threw his helmet at Hillin, Jr., when he passed by under caution. Number 11 Bill Elliott and #33 Harry Gant suffered heavy damage in the crash, which brought out one of the day's 17 caution flags. Jimmy Spencer took his #12 Ford to the low side and missed the melee. He eventually finished fourth. Wally Dallenbach, Jr,. avoided the crash in his #16 Ford and went on to finish 11th.

Rusty Wallace drove his #2 Pontiac to victory in the 500-mile slugfest at Bristol. After the race ended, Wallace took a slow trip around Bristol's high banks in a clockwise manner, saluting fallen NASCAR champion Alan Kulwicki with a ceremonial "Polish victory lap."

Dale Earnhardt and Rusty Wallace hooked up in a crowd-pleasing duel in the April 25 Hanes 500 at Martinsville Speedway. Wallace clearly had the upper hand most of the day, leading 409 of the 500 laps. Earnhardt eventually fell victim to engine problems and failed to finish. Wallace rode home with an easy win, his fourth in the season's eight races.

Rusty Wallace's Pontiac crosses the finish line airborne after a spectacular last-lap spin in the May 2 Winston 500 at Talladega. Wallace and Dale Earnhardt were battling for fourth place in a frantic scramble when Earnhardt flicked Wallace's rear bumper. Air got under Wallace's car and he soared across the finish line in sixth place. Earnhardt finished third. Wallace suffered a broken wrist, a concussion, facial cuts, and a chipped tooth in the incredible flip.

Jeff Gordon

BY THE TIME Jeffrey Michael Gordon was 10 years old, he had already won two national championships. Having raced Quarter Midgets since the age of five, Gordon racked up a pair of titles in 1979 and '81, beating competition as old as 17. Before he was old enough to drive on public streets, Gordon attained four championships in go-karts and had won races in the All Star Circuit of Champions Sprint Car series. "When I was five years old," reflected Gordon, who was born in Vallejo, Calif., "it was just something my dad did to keep me out of my mom's way and give me something to do in the field near our house. For most of my life, racing was what we did for fun on weekends."

The climb to racing's major leagues was planned by stepfather John Bickford. When Gordon was 15, Bickford moved the family to the Indianapolis suburbs of Pittsboro so the young driver could get more experience in open-wheel racing. Gordon made an immediate impact in Sprint Cars built by Bickford. At 16, he became the youngest recipient of a United States Auto Club competitor's license. In 1989, Gordon won races in three USAC open-wheel divisions, graduated from high school with a B average, and became a full-time race car driver.

In 1990, at age 19, Gordon won nine of 21 starts in USAC's rugged Midget division, and became its youngest champion. He also dabbled in World of Outlaws Sprint Car competition, the nation's leading organization for the free-wheeling Sprints. By '91, Gordon had won USAC's Silver Crown title, winning major events at Phoenix and at Indianapolis' one-mile dirt track.

After completing a course at the Buck Baker Driving School for stock cars, Gordon landed a ride with Bill Davis' NASCAR Busch Series team. "My focus for the future is NASCAR racing," Gordon said at the time. "I'm in stock cars

NASCAR Cup Series Career Record 1992-2012*
Starts: 689
Wins: 87
Top 5s: 298
Top 10s: 414
Poles: 72

*still active

to stay. For me, NASCAR racing holds the greatest promise and potential."

Gordon made the most of his opportunity. He won three NASCAR Busch Series superspeedway events in 1992, captured 11 poles, and finished fourth in the final points standings. Gordon's knack for high-speed superspeedway racing caught the eye of NASCAR Winston Cup team owner Rick Hendrick, who quickly signed him to a multiyear contract.

In his second ride in a NASCAR Winston Cup car, Gordon won the 1993 Twin 125-mile qualifier at Daytona. The remainder of his rookie campaign was characterized by speedy runs but plenty of crashes. By '94, the frayed edges had been polished with experience and maturity, and Gordon won his first two NASCAR Winston Cup points races, Charlotte's Coca-Cola 600 and the inaugural Brickyard 400 at Indianapolis Motor Speedway.

In 1995, Gordon snared his first NASCAR Winston Cup championship at the age of 24, becoming the second youngest man to ever cop NASCAR's most cherished crown. "Realistically, we were hoping for a top-five finish in the points," said Gordon. "You always start a season with the championship in mind, but in 1995, we didn't think it was possible." Gordon built a solid points lead by late summer, but had to hold off a furious rally by cagey veteran Dale Earnhardt to secure his first title.

Gordon won the NASCAR Winston Cup championship again in 1997 and '98, and lost the '96 title by a narrow margin after winning 10 races. His fourth championship came in 2001, at which time he became the third person to win more than three titles at NASCAR's top level of competition.

Time will tell if Jeff Gordon is able to match or surpass the record of seven championships jointly held by Richard Petty and Dale Earnhardt. This much is certain, though. Jeff Gordon shines brightly among NASCAR's biggest stars.

Jimmy Hensley's #7 Ford skids through the fourth turn at Charlotte Motor Speedway during the May 22 The Winston all-star race. Hensley was driving the car formerly campaigned by the late Alan Kulwicki. Geoff Bodine purchased Kulwicki's NASCAR equipment from his estate and seated Hensley in the #7 Ford for most of the 1993 NASCAR Winston Cup season. Dale Earnhardt bolted past leader Mark Martin on a restart with two laps to go to win the race. Earnhardt never led until the final two laps.

Neil Bonnett's #31 Richard Childress Racing Chevrolet lifts into the air during a frightening crash on the 132nd lap of the July 25 DieHard 500. Bonnett, making his first NASCAR Winston Cup start in 2½ years, slipped sideways while battling Ted Musgrave and Dick Trickle. Bonnett's car crashed into the protective catch fence along the main grandstands, but Bonnett escaped injury.

Bobby Labonte drove the #22 Bill Davis/Maxwell House Ford during the 1993 campaign. After a sluggish start, Labonte began running well by midsummer. In the Talladega DieHard 500, Labonte was perched in third place with one lap remaining. Poised to make a run for his first victory, Labonte ran out of fuel on the final lap. He coasted across the finish line in 15th place.

Jimmy Spencer's #12 Bobby Allison Racing/Meineke Ford runs ahead of the pack in the Oct. 10 Mello Yello 500 at Charlotte Motor Speedway. Spencer scored 10 top-10 finishes during the 1993 NASCAR Winston Cup season, including a strong sixth in Charlotte's fall 500-miler.

Ernie Irvan assumed the full-time driving chores for the Robert Yates #28 Ford in September, replacing the late Davey Allison. Irvan dominated the Mello Yello 500 at Charlotte Motor Speedway, leading all but six of the 334 laps. After taking the checkered flag, Irvan gave a fitting tribute to his fallen comrade by touring the track in a reverse-lap salute. Jeff Gordon, who earned his first career pole at the race, lost the lead early and finished fifth.

Rusty Wallace racked up his 10th victory of the season in the Nov. 10 Hooters 500, and Dale Earnhardt clinched his sixth NASCAR Winston Cup Championship with a 10th-place finish. After the race, Wallace and Earnhardt carried flags bearing the numbers 28 and 7 to honor Davey Allison and Alan Kulwicki. The moving Polish victory lap tribute put an end to an exciting but tragic 1993 campaign.

1993 NASCAR WINSTON CUP POINTS RACE

Rank	Driver	Points	Starts	Wins	Top 5	Top 10	Winnings
1	Dale Earnhardt	4526	30	6	17	21	$3,353,789
2	Rusty Wallace	4446	30	10	19	21	$1,702,154
3	Mark Martin	4150	30	5	12	19	$1,657,662
4	Dale Jarrett	4000	30	1	13	18	$1,242,394
5	Kyle Petty	3860	30	1	9	15	$914,662
6	Ernie Irvan	3834	30	3	12	14	$1,400,468
7	Morgan Shepherd	3807	30	1	3	15	$782,523
8	Bill Elliott	3774	30	0	6	15	$955,859
9	Ken Schrader	3715	30	0	9	15	$952,748
10	Ricky Rudd	3644	30	1	9	14	$752,562
11	Harry Gant	3524	30	0	4	12	$772,832
12	Jimmy Spencer	3496	30	0	5	10	$686,026
13	Darrell Waltrip	3479	30	0	4	10	$746,646
14	Jeff Gordon	3447	30	0	7	11	$765,168
15	Sterling Marlin	3355	30	0	1	8	$628,835
16	Geoff Bodine	3338	30	1	2	9	$783,762
17	Michael Waltrip	3291	30	0	0	5	$529,923
18	Terry Labonte	3280	30	0	0	10	$531,717
19	Bobby Labonte	3221	30	0	0	6	$395,660
20	Brett Bodine	3183	29	0	3	9	$582,014
21	Rick Mast	3001	30	0	1	5	$568,095
22	Wally Dallenbach, Jr.	2978	30	0	1	4	$474,340
23	Kenny Wallace	2893	30	0	0	3	$330,325
24	Hut Stricklin	2866	30	0	1	2	$494,600
25	Ted Musgrave	2853	29	0	2	5	$458,615
26	Derrike Cope	2787	30	0	0	1	$402,515
27	Bobby Hillin, Jr.	2717	30	0	0	0	$263,540
28	Rick Wilson	2647	29	0	0	1	$299,725
29	Phil Parsons	2454	26	0	0	2	$293,725
30	Dick Trickle	2224	26	0	1	2	$244,065
31	Davey Allison	2104	16	1	6	8	$513,585
32	Jimmy Hensley	2001	21	0	0	2	$368,150
33	Dave Marcis	1970	23	0	0	0	$202,305
34	Lake Speed	1956	21	0	0	1	$319,800
35	Greg Sacks	1730	19	0	0	1	$168,055
36	Jimmy Means	1471	18	0	0	0	$148,205
37	Bobby Hamilton	1348	15	0	0	1	$142,740
38	Jimmy Horton	841	13	0	0	0	$115,105
39	Jeff Purvis	774	8	0	0	0	$106,045
40	Todd Bodine	715	10	0	0	0	$63,245
41	Alan Kulwicki	625	5	0	2	3	$165,470
42	P. J. Jones	498	6	0	0	1	$53,370
43	Joe Ruttman	417	5	0	1	1	$70,700
44	Joe Nemechek	389	5	0	0	0	$56,580
45	Loy Allen, Jr.	362	5	0	0	0	$34,695
46	Mike Wallace	343	4	0	0	0	$30,125
47	Jimmy Sauter	295	4	0	0	0	$48,860
48	Rich Bickle	292	5	0	0	0	$36,095
49	Rick Carelli	258	3	0	0	0	$19,650
50	John Andretti	250	4	0	0	0	$24,915

Dale Earnhardt built a big points lead early in the season and cruised to his sixth NASCAR Winston Cup championship in 1993. Earnhardt took the points lead in mid May and paced the standings for the rest of the 30-race campaign.

Rusty Wallace trailed by more than 300-points at one point during the season, but he strung together a flurry of wins and top-five finishes, and gradually worked his way back into contention. Wallace won five of the last eight races in the season and finished 80 points behind Earnhardt in the final tally.

Earnhardt won six races as Wallace took the checkered flag 10 times. Wallace had more top-five finishes than Earnhardt and an equal number of top-10 finishes, but couldn't overtake his rival in the points chase.

Five-time winner Mark Martin placed third in the final points standings with five wins.

1994

February 11 Veteran driver Neil Bonnett loses his life in a practice crash at Daytona International Speedway in preparation for the upcoming Daytona 500. Bonnett's Chevrolet breaks loose in the fourth turn and slaps the wall nearly head-on.

February 20 Sterling Marlin holds Ernie Irvan at bay in the final laps to record his first career NASCAR Winston Cup victory in the Daytona 500. Marlin's first triumph comes in his 279th start, the longest it has ever taken a driver to post his first win.

February 27 In Rusty Wallace's second start in a Ford, he rides to victory in the Goodwrench 500 at Rockingham. Wallace and the Roger Penske team switched from Pontiacs to Fords during the off-season.

March 27 Dale Earnhardt enjoys a resounding victory in Darlington's TranSouth 400. The 7.4-second triumph over runner-up Mark Martin is Earnhardt's ninth career win on the venerable Darlington track, one shy of David Pearson's all-time mark of 10 wins on the 1.366-mile oval.

May 1 Dale Earnhardt gallops past Jimmy Spencer with five laps to go and racks up his seventh career win at Talladega Superspeedway. Earnhardt's Chevrolet finishes .06 second ahead of runner-up Ernie Irvan, who currently holds the championship points lead.

May 29 Youthful Jeff Gordon hustles past Ricky Rudd with nine laps to go and goes on to win the Coca-Cola 600. It is the first career NASCAR Winston Cup win for the 22-year-old.

June 12 Rusty Wallace charges past Dale Earnhardt on the final lap and holds on to win at Pocono. A late caution flag sets up the final one-lap dash.

July 2 Jimmy Spencer nabs Ernie Irvan a few feet short of the finish line and prevails in a photo finish, scoring the first NASCAR Winston Cup win of his career in the Pepsi 400 at Daytona. Spencer leads only the final lap and beats Irvan by .08 second.

Sterling Marlin outruns Ernie Irvan by two car lengths to win the Feb. 20 Daytona 500. The Marlin-Irvan 1-2 finish is dipped in irony. Irvan won the 1991 Daytona 500 in the #4 Morgan-McClure/Kodak Chevrolet and enjoyed a successful three-year run with the Virginia-based team. In late '93, Irvan left Larry McClure's team to join forces with Robert Yates' Ford team. Marlin drove the Kodak Chevrolet to his first career victory in "The Great American Race." It was Marlin's 279th career start in 18 years of NASCAR Winston Cup competition.

Rival pit crews stand at the edge of pit road to congratulate Sterling Marlin after his first career NASCAR Winston Cup win in the 1994 Daytona 500. Marlin took the lead 21 laps from the finish and kept runner-up Ernie Irvan at bay for the final 50 miles. It was the final win for the Chevrolet Lumina model in NASCAR's biggest annual event. The popular Monte Carlo would return in '95.

Bobby Hamilton, Dale Earnhardt, Ernie Irvan, and Ward Burton speed down the frontstretch at Bristol International Raceway during the April 10 Food City 500. Earnhardt came from the 24th starting position to easily outdistance the 37-car field. Earnhardt led the final 183 laps to record his first short-track victory since October 1991. Irvan ran strong in the early going but departed with a blown engine after completing 167 laps.

Jimmy Spencer's #27 Ford cranks sideways after a shot in the rear from #25 Ken Schrader in the April 17 First Union 400 at North Wilkesboro Speedway. The two drivers were battling for second place when Schrader swatted Spencer out of his way on the 209th lap. The NASCAR veterans got into a heated bumping duel during the ensuing caution flag.

Jimmy Spencer drills the rear bumper of Ken Schrader during a yellow-flag lap following an on-track confrontation in the First Union 400. Schrader had bumped Spencer into a spin, and Spencer retaliated. NASCAR officials ordered Spencer to the penalty box for a five-lap cool-off period. Schrader went on to finish ninth, despite significant body damage on his #25 Chevrolet.

As Dale Earnhardt and Mark Martin raced into the third turn on the 190th lap of the May 29 Coca-Cola 600 at Charlotte Motor Speedway, Martin's #6 Valvoline Ford spun into the high groove. With a pack of cars breathing down his neck, Martin found himself in the middle of a 14-car crash. Number 31 Ward Burton and #32 Dick Trickle were eliminated, but most of the other damaged cars continued in the event.

Jeff Gordon took the lead from Ricky Rudd 19 laps from the finish and sped to his first NASCAR Winston Cup victory in the 1994 Coca-Cola 600. On the final round of green-flag pit stops, virtually all of Gordon's challengers took on four tires and fuel. When Gordon pitted on lap 381, crew chief Ray Evernham ordered only a two-tire stop. The quick pit stop gave Gordon a lead that he never relinquished.

Todd Bodine's #75 Ford slams hard into the concrete retaining wall on the 132nd lap of the June 19 Miller Genuine Draft 400 at Michigan International Speedway. Bodine was groggy after the mishap, but otherwise uninjured. Bodine got the ride with team owner Butch Mock on a full-time basis in late 1993. While he proved he could get the most out of his machinery, Bodine got caught up in more than his fair share of crashes.

July 10 Ricky Rudd, in his first season as owner/driver, runs down Dale Earnhardt and scores a close win in the Slick 50 300 at New Hampshire International Speedway. It is Rudd's 15th career victory, marking the 12th consecutive season he has won at least one race.

August 6 Sophomore Jeff Gordon leads the final five laps and holds off Brett Bodine to win the inaugural Brickyard 400 at Indianapolis Motor Speedway. More than 340,000 trackside spectators watch Gordon claim his second career victory.

August 21 Geoff Bodine starts on the pole and dominates the Champion Spark Plug 400 at Michigan International Speedway. Ernie Irvan is critically hurt in a practice crash the day before the race.

September 4 Bill Elliott ends a 52-race winless skid with a victory in Darlington's Mountain Dew Southern 500. Elliott overcomes heating problems to score his 40th career victory.

September 25 Rusty Wallace scores a one-car-length victory over Dale Earnhardt at Martinsville. Despite eight wins to Earnhardt's three, Wallace trails by 222 points and is effectively out of the championship hunt.

October 23 With a narrow victory over Rick Mast in the 500-miler at Rockingham, Dale Earnhardt locks up a record-tying seventh NASCAR Winston Cup championship.

Jimmy Spencer noses his McDonald's Ford ahead of Ernie Irvan a few feet before the finish line in the July 2 Pepsi 400 at Daytona Inernational Speedway. For Spencer, it was his first career NASCAR Winston Cup victory. Spencer dogged Irvan's heels in the final 50 miles and nudged his way in front on the final lap. Irvan led for more than half the race, but Spencer refused to be denied as he gave team owner Junior Johnson his first win of the season.

Dale Earnhardt rattled the back bumper of Derrike Cope, causing Cope to lose control in the July 10 Slick 50 300 at New Hampshire International Speedway. Earnhardt glanced off Cope and maintained his momentum. Earnhardt went on to finish a close second to Ricky Rudd in the 300-lapper and took a narrow four-point lead over Ernie Irvan in the NASCAR Winston Cup championship chase.

Dale Earnhardt runs a car length ahead of rookie Jeff Burton in the early stages of the Slick 50 300. Burton signed up with Bill and Mickey Stavola's Ford team in 1994, and the freshman driver performed remarkably. He recorded a pair of top-five finishes and won the Raybestos Rookie of the Year award despite formidable competition from brother Ward Burton, Joe Nemechek, and Steve Grissom.

Ernie Irvan pits his #28 Ford during the July 10 race at New Hampshire. Irvan won the pole, but got mixed up in a crash that left him with a 30th-place finish. Irvan had held first place in the NASCAR Winston Cup points standings for all but two weeks since early March. He lost the lead at New Hampshire, then regained it at Talladega. A late tire failure robbed him of a win at Indianapolis, and he fell further behind points leader Dale Earnhardt. In a practice session at Michigan International Speedway on Aug. 20, Irvan was gravely injured in a crash. His injuries would keep him out of a race car for more than a year.

Geoff Bodine drove his self-owned #7 Ford to an overwhelming victory in the July 17 Miller Genuine Draft 500 at the triangular Pocono International Raceway. Shod with Hoosier tires, Bodine had little trouble disposing of the field, leading 156 of the 200 laps. Hoosier Tire Co. made a brief return to NASCAR Winston Cup racing in 1994, but had difficulty signing up top drivers. Bodine was the horse of the Hoosier-contracted teams, winning three races and five poles during the season.

Ted Musgrave spins his #16 Family Channel Ford Thunderbird in tandem with John Andretti on the 23rd lap of the July 24 DieHard 500 at Talladega Superspeedway. Both cars were damaged in the off-track excursion and finished far down in the order. Andretti was in his rookie season with team owner Billy Hagan. A month later, Andretti joined the Petty Enterprises team as Hagan's team ran low on operating funds and pulled out of the NASCAR Winston Cup tour.

Pole-sitter Rick Mast duels with Dale Earnhardt at the start of the inaugural Brickyard 400 at Indianapolis Motor Speedway. The biggest trackside audience in NASCAR history, about 340,000, watched Mast become the first driver to lead a lap at Indy in a NASCAR stock car. Indianapolis Motor Speedway was built in 1909 and its first competitive event was a balloon race. Originally constructed of crushed stone and dirt, the track was paved with bricks in late '09, acquiring its nickname "The Brickyard."

Geoff Bodine's #7 Ford leads #4 Sterling Marlin and Jeff Gordon as they put a lap on #50 A.J. Foyt and #44 Bobby Hillin, Jr., in the Aug. 6 Brickyard 400. Bodine led twice in the race and was leading when he and younger brother Brett tangled on lap 100. Geoff spun out of the race, opening the door for Gordon, who had lived in Indiana, to win the historic event.

Mark Martin cruised to an easy win in the Aug. 14 Budweiser At The Glen on the famous road course in upstate New York. Martin put the Roush Racing #6 Ford on the pole and led 75 of the 90 laps. He held off Ernie Irvan and Dale Earnhardt after a late caution flag bunched up the field to record his first win of the season.

Rusty Wallace fended off a late-race surge by Dale Earnhardt to win a narrow decision in the Sept. 25 Goody's 500 at Martinsville Speedway. For Wallace, it was his eighth win of the season, but he still trailed three-race winner Earnhardt by 222 points in the NASCAR Winston Cup championship standings.

Geoff Bodine's #7 Ford rounds a turn in the Oct. 2 Tyson Holly Farms 400 at North Wilkesboro Speedway. Despite starting in the 18th position, Bodine marched through the field and dominated the event, leading 335 of the 400 laps. He finished a lap in front of Terry Labonte. It marked the last time a driver has lapped the field in a NASCAR Cup Series event.

▶ Bobby Labonte's #22 Pontiac broke loose on the fifth lap of the Oct. 9 Mello Yello 500 at Charlotte Motor Speedway. Incredibly, the trailing pack of cars managed to miss Labonte's spinning, fire-engulfed car. Labonte bailed out unhurt, but his car was wiped out. Dale Jarrett won the race after he failed to qualify for the previous race at North Wilkesboro.

Mark Martin wrestled the lead from Todd Bodine with 27 laps remaining and sped to his second victory of the year in the Nov. 13 season finale Hooters 500 at Atlanta Motor Speedway. Martin overtook Rusty Wallace for second place in the final NASCAR Winston Cup points standings, marking the second time he finished runner-up to Dale Earnhardt in the race for the national driving title.

Dale Earnhardt won his record-tying seventh NASCAR Winston Cup championship in 1994, a feat matched only by Richard Petty. Earnhardt wrapped up the title by winning the third-to-last race of the season at Rockingham. Six of Earnhardt's seven titles came with the Richard Childress-owned RCR Enterprises team; the other was with Rod Osterlund in 1980. Here, Petty joins Earnhardt at the postseason awards banquet in New York.

1994 NASCAR WINSTON CUP POINTS RACE

Rank	Driver	Points	Starts	Wins	Top 5	Top 10	Winnings
1	Dale Earnhardt	4694	31	4	20	25	$3,300,733
2	Mark Martin	4250	31	2	15	20	$1,628,906
3	Rusty Wallace	4207	31	8	17	20	$1,914,072
4	Ken Schrader	4060	31	0	9	18	$1,171,062
5	Ricky Rudd	4050	31	1	6	15	$1,044,441
6	Morgan Shepherd	4029	31	0	9	16	$1,089,038
7	Terry Labonte	3876	31	3	6	14	$1,125,921
8	Jeff Gordon	3776	31	2	7	14	$1,779,523
9	Darrell Waltrip	3688	31	0	4	13	$835,680
10	Bill Elliott	3617	31	1	6	12	$936,779
11	Lake Speed	3565	31	0	4	9	$832,463
12	Michael Waltrip	3512	31	0	2	10	$706,426
13	Ted Musgrave	3477	31	0	1	8	$656,187
14	Sterling Marlin	3443	31	1	5	11	$1,127,683
15	Kyle Petty	3339	31	0	2	7	$806,332
16	Dale Jarrett	3298	30	1	4	9	$881,754
17	Geoff Bodine	3297	31	3	7	10	$1,276,126
18	Rick Mast	3238	31	0	4	10	$722,361
19	Brett Bodine	3159	31	0	1	6	$791,444
20	Todd Bodine	3048	30	0	2	7	$494,316
21	Bobby Labonte	3038	31	0	1	2	$550,305
22	Ernie Irvan	3026	20	3	13	15	$1,311,522
23	Bobby Hamilton	2749	30	0	0	1	$514,520
24	Jeff Burton	2726	30	0	2	3	$594,700
25	Harry Gant	2720	30	0	0	7	$556,020
26	Hut Stricklin	2711	29	0	0	1	$333,495
27	Joe Nemechek	2673	29	0	1	3	$386,315
28	Steve Grissom	2660	28	0	0	3	$300,915
29	Jimmy Spencer	2613	29	2	3	4	$479,235
30	Derrike Cope	2612	30	0	0	2	$398,436
31	Greg Sacks	2593	31	0	0	3	$411,728
32	John Andretti	2299	29	0	0	0	$391,920
33	Mike Wallace	2191	22	0	1	1	$265,115
34	Dick Trickle	2019	25	0	0	1	$244,806
35	Ward Burton	1971	26	0	1	2	$302,950
36	Dave Marcis	1910	23	0	0	1	$261,650
37	Jeremy Mayfield	1673	20	0	0	0	$226,265
38	Wally Dallenbach, Jr.	1493	14	0	1	3	$241,492
39	Loy Allen, Jr.	1468	19	0	0	0	$216,751
40	Kenny Wallace	1413	12	0	1	3	$235,005
41	Jimmy Hensley	1394	17	0	0	0	$203,520
42	Chuck Bown	1211	13	0	0	1	$225,260
43	Rich Bickle	849	12	0	0	0	$115,575
44	Bobby Hillin, Jr.	749	9	0	0	0	$125,340
45	Brad Teague	548	8	0	0	0	$59,990
46	Jeff Purvis	484	7	0	0	0	$78,755
47	Billy Standridge	404	8	0	0	0	$56,405
48	Randy LaJoie	312	3	0	0	0	$30,565
49	Rick Carelli	283	4	0	0	0	$31,975
50	Phil Parsons	243	3	0	0	0	$21,415

Entering the Aug. 21 race at Michigan, Ernie Irvan and Dale Earnhardt were locked in a tight battle for supremacy in the 1994 NASCAR Winston Cup championship race. However, Irvan suffered near-fatal injuries in a practice crash before the GM Goodwrench Dealers 400, leaving Earnhardt uncontested for the title.

Earnhardt finished 444 points ahead of runner-up Mark Martin to record his record-tying seventh NASCAR championship. Irvan led the standings after 12 of the first 18 races and appeared to be up to the challenge until his unfortunate crash took him out of the chase.

Earnhardt won four races during the campaign while Martin won twice. Rusty Wallace was again the season's top winner with eight wins, but he finished a distant third in the points. At one point in the season, Wallace won three of five races and never finished below seventh, yet he lost points to Earnhardt during the streak.

1995

February 5 NASCAR launches the Craftsman Truck Series with an 80-lap race at Phoenix International Speedway. Mike Skinner becomes the series' first winner after qualifying 16th.

February 19 Sterling Marlin holds off Dale Earnhardt to score his second straight victory in the Daytona 500. Earnhardt is running 14th with 11 laps remaining, but charges to second and is edged by Marlin by .61 second.

April 2 Jeff Gordon posts his third win in the season's first six races with a victory in the Food City 500 at Bristol. Despite batting .500 in the early part of the season, Gordon ranks only fourth in the points standings.

April 30 Mark Martin edges Jeff Gordon at the flag to take his first win of the season. Dale Earnhardt spins out on the final lap after a tap from Morgan Shepherd and winds up 21st. Gordon and Earnhardt are tied for the championship points lead.

May 7 Dale Earnhardt forges past Mark Martin with two laps to go and records his first career win on a road course with a victory at Sears Point International Raceway. It is Earnhardt's 36th career start on a road course.

May 28 Bobby Labonte motors to his first career win in Charlotte's Coca-Cola 600. Terry Labonte finishes second, marking the first time brothers have finished 1-2 in a NASCAR Winston Cup race since 1971, when Bobby and Donnie Allison did it at Charlotte.

June 4 Kyle Petty comes from his 37th starting position to win the Miller Genuine Draft 500 at Dover Downs for his first NASCAR Winston Cup win in 60 races. Petty finishes a car length in front of runner-up Bobby Labonte.

July 16 Dale Jarrett scores his first win with the Robert Yates Ford team, beating Jeff Gordon in a classic duel at Pocono. The lead changes hands 37 times among 13 drivers in the highly competitive event.

After running four exhibition races starting in July 1994, the NASCAR Super Truck Series made its official debut on Feb. 5, 1995, at Phoenix International Raceway. Mike Skinner won the series' inaugural race, and went on to claim the championship with eight wins and 17 top-five finishes in 20 starts. Skinner won $428,096 for his sterling season. Four pioneering off-road team owners—Dick Landfield, Jimmy Smith, Jim Venable, and Frank Vessels—convinced Bill France, Jr., in 1993 that trucks would be a popular racing attraction. "In only 18 months, this series has risen to a level that took the NASCAR Winston Cup Series 20 years to reach," noted France at the first postseason awards banquet. The Super Truck series became the NASCAR Craftsman Truck tour in 1996, when it acquired backing from Sears' popular tools brand.

Sterling Marlin peels his #4 Chevrolet out of the pits just ahead of #3 Dale Earnhardt in the Feb. 19 Daytona 500. Number 25 Ken Schrader completes his pit stop and chases the leaders back onto the track. Marlin led the final 20 laps to become only the third driver to win back-to-back Daytona 500s, but he had to stave off a late challenge by Earnhardt. Marlin's victory marked a triumphant return to NASCAR Winston Cup racing for the Chevrolet Monte Carlo, which replaced the Lumina that ran from 1989 to '94.

Rookie Robert Pressley, driving the #33 Chevrolet, runs just ahead of #3 Dale Earnhardt and #32 Chuck Bown in the April 2 Food City 500 at Bristol International Raceway. Pressley, a standout in the NASCAR Busch Series, recorded his first top-10 finish at Bristol. Earnhardt and Bown struggled in the 500-lapper, finishing 25th and 31st, respectively.

Terry Labonte's #5 Chevrolet leaps over Morgan Shepherd's #21 Ford as #3 Dale Earnhardt gets crowded into the wall in a bone-jarring crash on the fifth la of the April 23 Hanes 500 at Martinsville Speedway. Labonte was unable to get back into the race, while Earnhardt and Shepherd eventually returned, finishing 29th and 31st, respectively. Rusty Wallace led 172 of the 356 laps to win the scheduled 500-lapper, which was delayed by rain and shortened by darkness.

Dale Earnhardt's #3 Goodwrench Chevrolet spins off the second turn after a tap from #21 Morgan Shepherd on the final lap of the April 30 Winston Select 500 at Talladega Superspeedway. Earnhardt and Shepherd were battling for second place when they locked horns with a little over a mile remaining. Shepherd went on to finish third, while Earnhardt limped home 21st. Mark Martin won the race. Earnhardt's spin left him tied with runner-up Jeff Gordon for the NASCAR Winston Cup points lead.

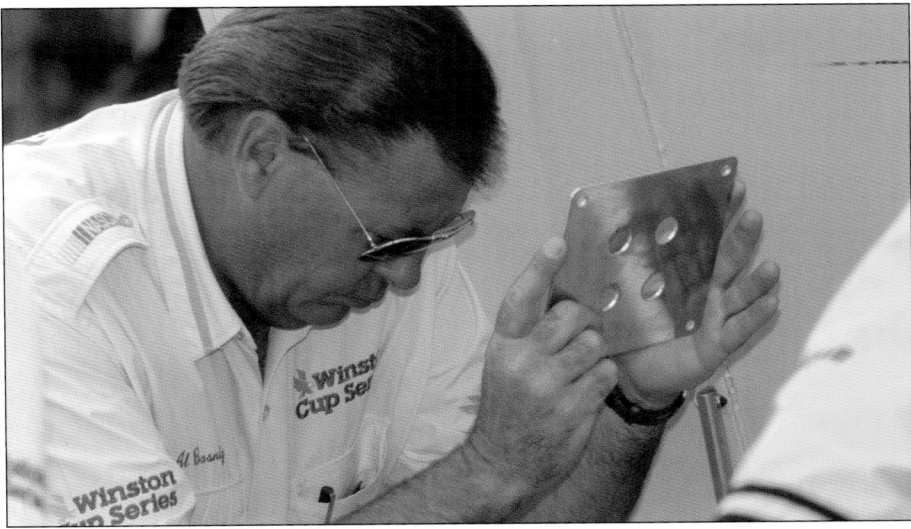

NASCAR technical inspector Al Basnig examines a restrictor plate during the Talladega race weekend. A restrictor plate restricts the amount of air and fuel flow into the carburetor, thus slowing the NASCAR Winston Cup machinery considerably. Restrictor plates originally became a source of controversy when they were introduced in 1970 for use on all tracks. They were no longer required after the '74 season, but returned for NASCAR's two fastest tracks, Daytona and Talladega, in '88 after 210+ mph speeds prompted safety concerns.

Bobby Labonte hoists the winner's trophy in victory lane ceremonies following his first career NASCAR Winston Cup win in the May 28 Coca-Cola 600 at Charlotte Motor Speedway. Driving the Joe Gibbs Racing Chevrolet, Labonte grabbed the lead with 43 laps remaining and outran older brother Terry to the finish line. The 1-2 finish by brothers marked the first time two NASCAR siblings claimed the top spots since Bobby and Donnie Allison ran 1-2 in the 1971 World 600 at Charlotte.

◄ Kyle Petty drives to victory at Dover Downs International Speedway in the hotly contested June 4 Miller Genuine Draft 500. Petty ended a two-year void with the dramatic victory over Bobby Labonte and Ted Musgrave on Dover's "Monster Mile" concrete oval. Petty was trapped in traffic in the final lap, allowing the challengers to close in. Petty prevailed by a half car length to record his eighth career NASCAR Winston Cup win.

August 5 Dale Earnhardt bides his time in the early going, then hustles into the lead in the closing stages to win the second annual Brickyard 400 at Indianapolis Motor Speedway.

August 13 Mark Martin posts his third straight victory on the road course at Watkins Glen. Jeff Gordon finishes third and increases his points lead over Dale Earnhardt to 197.

August 26 Terry Labonte slides across the finish line just ahead of Dale Earnhardt to win the Goody's 500 at Bristol. Earnhardt slaps Labonte sideways on the final lap in a bid to win. Labonte's Chevrolet crashes into the concrete barrier just after taking the checkered flag.

September 17 Jeff Gordon leads 400 of the 500 miles at Dover to nail down an easy triumph in the MBNA 500. Gordon takes a hefty 309-point lead in the NASCAR Winston Cup standings.

October 1 Mark Martin holds off Rusty Wallace to win the Tyson Holly Farms 400 at North Wilkesboro. Ernie Irvan, making his first NASCAR Winston Cup start since his terrible accident in August 1994 at Michigan, leads 31 laps and finishes seventh.

October 22 Ward Burton scores his first NASCAR Winston Cup victory in the AC Delco 400 at Rockingham. Points leader Jeff Gordon finishes 20th, but still clings to a 162-point lead over Dale Earnhardt.

October 29 Ricky Rudd scores his first win of the season in the Dura Lube 500 at Phoenix International Raceway. Rudd starts 29th. It is the first time in NASCAR Winston Cup history that a driver has come from 29th to win a race.

November 12 Dale Earnhardt storms to victory in the season-ending NAPA 500 at Atlanta as Jeff Gordon captures his first NASCAR Winston Cup title after finishing 32nd. Gordon holds off Earnhardt's furious rally and wins the title by 34 points.

Jeff Gordon speeds toward the checkered flag at the finish of the July 1 Pepsi 400 at Daytona International Speedway. The first 12 cars finished within a second of each other. Behind Gordon in order are #4 Sterling Marlin, #3 Dale Earnhardt, #6 Mark Martin, #16 Ted Musgrave, #25 Ken Schrader, #42 Kyle Petty, #10 Ricky Rudd, #23 Jimmy Spencer, #94 Bill Elliott, #33 Robert Pressley, and #15 Dick Trickle.

Jeff Gordon tapped teammate Ken Schrader's #25 Chevrolet into a wild flip in the July 23 DieHard 500 at Talladega Superspeedway. The incident occurred on the 139th lap and gobbled up nine other cars. Schrader was able to free himself from the mangled mess under his own power. Gordon, who led the most laps until the crash, went on to finish eighth. Sterling Marlin went on to win the race from the pole.

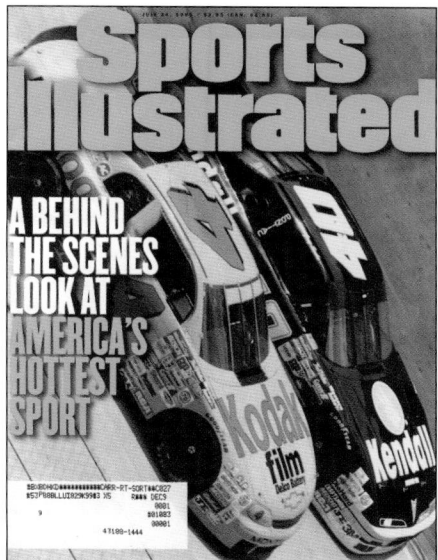

The cover story of the July 24, 1995, issue of *Sports Illustrated* put NASCAR Winston Cup racing on the map with America's other major sports—NFL football, Major League Baseball, NBA basketball, and NHL hockey. *SI* writer Michael Silver credited NASCAR for its down home attitude, stating, "In a sports world tarnished by a widening gap between performer and consumer, NASCAR is a grand exception, an unspoiled bastion of Americana, a traveling road show in which even the biggest stars are taught to regard themselves as commoners." NASCAR was growing, and the *SI* article helped introduce the sport to ball sports fans who hadn't previously been exposed to it.

Dale Earnhardt gets quick pit service during the Aug. 5 Brickyard 400 at Indianapolis Motor Speedway. Earnhardt started 13th and kept the leaders in sight for most of the race. After the final round of pit stops, the RCR Enterprises crew got Earnhardt back on the track first. He was able to keep his rivals at bay over the final 28 laps to score a $565,600 victory in the 400-miler. It was the richest event on the 1995 NASCAR calendar.

▶ Brothers #22 Ward Burton and #8 Jeff Burton battle on the concrete banks of Bristol International Raceway in the Aug. 26 Goody's 500. Ward replaced Randy LaJoie in the Bill Davis Pontiac at midseason. Ward was eliminated in an early crash, while younger brother Jeff motored home to a ninth-place finish. Dale Earnhardt rallied from a penalty after spinning Rusty Wallace in the middle stages of the event. At the finish, Earnhardt tagged Terry Labonte into a spin, but Labonte slid across the finish line first to win the race.

Bill Elliott's McDonald's Ford Thunderbird spins sideways in thick traffic during Darlington's Sept. 3 Mountain Dew Southern 500. Bobby Hamilton runs inches ahead of the mishap, while #30 Michael Waltrip, #5 Terry Labonte, and Jimmy Spencer look for an opening. Waltrip skirted around Elliott and went on to score an impressive fifth-place finish in the 46th running of NASCAR's oldest superspeedway event. Jeff Gordon nabbed his sixth win of the season at Darlington, increasing his NASCAR Winston Cup points lead to 217 over Sterling Marlin.

Terry Labonte guides his #5 Kellogg's Chevrolet through a turn at Richmond International Raceway in the Sept. 9 Miller Genuine Draft 400. The autumn event under the lights is one of the most popular fan attractions of any NASCAR Winston Cup season. Labonte finished second in the 300-miler after starting 23rd. Rusty Wallace grabbed his 41st career win at Richmond, fending off the challenges of Labonte and Dale Earnhardt.

Number 9 Lake Speed and #16 Ted Musgrave race in close quarters in the Sept. 17 MBNA 500 at Dover Downs. Speed took over the driving chores for the Harry Melling-owned team in 1995, and also served as the team manager. Melling's operation was at the pinnacle of success in the mid-to-late '80s when Bill Elliott was at the controls. After Elliott departed, the Melling operation had several drivers behind the wheel of the #9 Ford. From 1992 to '95, a total of 12 different drivers were seated in Melling's car. Jeff Gordon thoroughly dominated the MBNA 500, leading 400 of the 500 laps. With his victory, Gordon's points lead over Dale Earnhardt grew to 309 with six races remaining.

Ricky Rudd's #10 Tide Ford leads Derrike Cope's #12 Ford down the front chute at Martinsville Speedway during the Sept. 24 Goody's 500. Dale Earnhardt began his late-season charge by winning at Martinsville. Earnhardt closed to within 275 points of NASCAR Winston Cup points leader Jeff Gordon, who finished seventh. Rudd was in his second season as owner of his team. With a win at Phoenix in late October, Rudd posted at least one win for the 13th straight year. Cope, driving Bobby Allison's Ford, finished a close second to Rudd at Phoenix, his best effort since winning at Dover in 1990.

Bobby Hamilton hooked up with Petty Enterprises in 1995, driving the famed #43 Pontiac on the NASCAR Winston Cup tour. Hamilton recorded four top-five finishes in '95, including a strong fourth at Martinsville's Goody's 500. The veteran from Nashville has always been regarded as a chassis specialist, and his expertise helped Petty Enterprises improve their on-track performance.

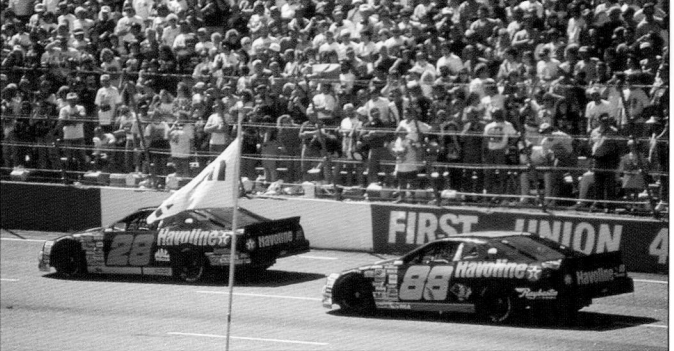

Teammates on the formidable Robert Yates Racing operation, #28 Dale Jarrett and #88 Ernie Irvan, battle nose-to-tail in the Oct. 1 Tyson Holly Farms 400 at North Wilkesboro Speedway. Irvan was making his competitive return to NASCAR Winston Cup racing for the first time since his bad spill at Michigan in August 1994. Irvan performed admirably, leading for 31 laps and finishing sixth. Jarrett followed Irvan across the finish line in seventh. Mark Martin outran Rusty Wallace to win the race. All 36 cars were running at the finish—the first time the whole field finished a NASCAR Winston Cup race since 1959.

Sophomore driver Ward Burton gave himself and team owner Bill Davis their first NASCAR Winston Cup win in the Oct. 22 AC Delco 400 at North Carolina Motor Speedway. Burton, who took over the #22 MBNA Pontiac at midseason, had a comfortable lead, but it was wiped out with a controversial caution flag. Dale Earnhardt had been blackflagged to the pits for a missing lug nut after his final pit stop. The Richard Childress crew said they securely replaced all lug nuts. In an unprecedented move, NASCAR threw out a yellow flag to check Earnhardt's tires, which were indeed secured in place by all five lug nuts. The late caution nearly cost Burton his first career win, but he was able to hold off Rusty Wallace in a stirring shootout over the final nine laps.

One Hot Crash-Filled Night

BRISTOL MOTOR SPEEDWAY'S high-banked bowl of concrete has been one of NASCAR's most popular venues. The 500-lapper under the lights in late August is considered the toughest ticket to find in NASCAR NEXTEL Cup stock car racing. Fender-bending action and sustained excitement all add up to a thrilling three-hour exercise in speed, hard knocks, and close racing.

Bristol Motor Speedway opened in 1961 as a gently banked ½-mile paved track. The wide, sweeping turns were able to accommodate three-abreast racing, and it soon became one of the most popular tracks among the contestants.

In 1969, however, the banking in the turns was elevated to a staggering 36 degrees. The trend toward higher-banked tracks all across NASCAR's landscape filtered down to the short tracks. The inaugural race on the high banks at Bristol drew an array of complaints from the drivers, who said the increased banking was the cause of many accidents. The number of caution flags was relatively low in races staged on the low banks, but the incidents increased dramatically once the banking was elevated.

In the summer of 1992, the pavement was replaced with slabs of concrete. The heavy NASCAR Winston Cup cars and the newfangled radial tires were shaving off the top of the pavement, creating a minefield of debris and loose asphalt in the corners. The concrete surface alleviated that problem, but on the flip side, it narrowed the groove and made passing difficult.

In the Aug. 26, 1995, Goody's 500, 15 caution flags consumed 106 laps. While it was a crashfest from the drop of the green flag, the electric finish remains one of NASCAR's most memorable.

Dale Earnhardt, The Intimidator, provided many of

> "That's the first time I've ever won a race going backwards. I'm not mad, but if I had lost the race, I probably would be mad."
> —Terry Labonte

the fireworks in the action-packed race. Driving like a proverbial bull through a china shop, Earnhardt disposed of many of his rivals in the old-fashioned manner of thumping rear bumpers. Lake Speed, Derrike Cope, and Rusty Wallace fell victim to the famous "Earnhardt Tap." The incident with Wallace triggered some extracurricular activities in the pit area following the race. After angrily dismounting his car at the conclusion of the event, Wallace slung a water bottle at Earnhardt. The bottle bounced off the roof of Earnhardt's car and appeared to hit Earnhardt in the head. "I ain't forgetting Talladega, and I ain't forgetting tonight," growled Wallace. "I'll see you at Darlington. You were all over me. You'd better watch that front bumper."

Earnhardt managed to stay in contention all evening. In the final laps, he was chasing leader Terry Labonte, who had carefully steered clear of the mechanical mayhem. In the final 10 laps, Labonte held the advantage as he attempted to tiptoe past clusters of battle-scarred and lapped cars. Earnhardt, with a fresh set of tires, put on one of his patented charges, slashing his way closer to Labonte every lap.

On the final lap, Labonte was momentarily slowed by three lapped cars, which allowed Earnhardt to draw close. Coming off the fourth turn, Earnhardt drilled the rear of Labonte's car, sending it careening out of control. Labonte bounced off the side of Greg Sacks' car, spun across the track, and plowed head-first into the retaining barrier as he crossed the finish line.

"That was some finish, wasn't it?" said Labonte, who drove his crumpled car into victory lane. "Dale gave me a shot in the back, but I just stayed on the gas and got across the finish line. That's the first time I've ever won a race going backwards. I'm not mad, but if I had lost the race, I probably would be mad."

Earnhardt, who finished a close second, said in his customary manner, "That's racing. I got jammed up behind all those slow cars and got into him."

Indy Car star John Andretti made the move to NASCAR Winston Cup racing in 1993, driving a partial schedule for team owner Billy Hagan. By '95, the diminutive speedster was assigned to drive the #37 Ford owned by former Ford racing boss Michael Kranefuss. Andretti blossomed into a respected stock car racer in '95, scoring five top-10 finishes, earning his first pole in the Sept. 3 Mountain Dew Southern 500 at Darlington, and placing 18th in the final points standings.

▼ Dale Earnhardt tucks his #3 Chevrolet under the #88 Ford of Ernie Irvan in the Oct. 29 Dura Lube 500 at Phoenix International Raceway. Irvan was the class of the field in his second start since his 1994 injuries, leading for 111 laps before engine failure put him out of the race. Earnhardt went on to finish third. Ricky Rudd passed Derrike Cope with 23 laps remaining to win the race, making him the first driver in NASCAR history to win after starting 29th. The win also kept Rudd's streak intact for winning at least one NASCAR Winston Cup race every year since 1983.

Mark Martin and Ernie Irvan relax in the garage before the start of the season finale at Atlanta Motor Speedway. Irvan had another splendid run in the Nov. 12 NAPA 500, finishing seventh. Martin was three laps off the pace in 17th place. Irvan's return to racing in 1995 was miraculous, considering the head injuries he suffered at Michigan the year before. The California native competed in three races in '95, and recorded a pair of top-10 finishes.

Bobby Hamilton guns his #43 Pontiac ahead of #16 Ted Musgrave, #1 Rick Mast, and #12 Derrike Cope during the Nov. 12 NAPA 500 at Atlanta Motor Speedway. Hamilton qualified third and led a handful of laps in the early going before sliding back to finish 25th. Dale Earnhardt dominated the race, but Jeff Gordon wrapped up his first NASCAR Winston Cup championship with a 32nd-place finish.

Jeff Gordon drove the #24 Hendrick Motorsports Chevrolet to the NASCAR Winston Cup championship in 1995. The 24-year-old Gordon became the youngest winner of the NASCAR crown since 23-year-old Bill Rexford took the title in 1950. Gordon led virtually every category in '95, winning the most races (seven), the most poles (eight), leading the most races (29 of 31), and leading the most laps (2600). He edged Dale Earnhardt by 34 points.

1995 NASCAR WINSTON CUP POINTS RACE

Rank	Driver	Points	Starts	Wins	Top 5	Top 10	Winnings
1	Jeff Gordon	4614	31	7	17	23	$4,347,343
2	Dale Earnhardt	4580	31	5	19	23	$3,154,241
3	Sterling Marlin	4361	31	3	9	22	$2,253,502
4	Mark Martin	4320	31	4	13	22	$1,893,519
5	Rusty Wallace	4240	31	2	15	19	$1,642,837
6	Terry Labonte	4146	31	3	14	17	$1,558,659
7	Ted Musgrave	3949	31	0	7	13	$1,147,445
8	Bill Elliott	3746	31	0	4	11	$996,816
9	Ricky Rudd	3734	31	1	10	16	$1,337,703
10	Bobby Labonte	3718	31	3	7	14	$1,413,682
11	Morgan Shepherd	3618	31	0	4	10	$966,374
12	Michael Waltrip	3601	31	0	2	8	$898,338
13	Dale Jarrett	3584	31	1	9	14	$1,363,158
14	Bobby Hamilton	3576	31	0	4	10	$804,505
15	Derrike Cope	3384	31	0	2	8	$683,075
16	Geoff Bodine	3357	31	0	1	4	$1,011,090
17	Ken Schrader	3221	31	0	2	10	$886,566
18	John Andretti	3140	31	0	1	5	$593,542
19	Darrell Waltrip	3078	31	0	4	8	$850,632
20	Brett Bodine	2988	31	0	0	2	$893,029
21	Rick Mast	2984	31	0	0	3	$749,550
22	Ward Burton	2926	29	1	3	6	$634,655
23	Lake Speed	2921	31	0	0	2	$529,435
24	Ricky Craven	2883	31	0	0	4	$597,054
25	Dick Trickle	2875	31	0	0	1	$694,920
26	Jimmy Spencer	2809	29	0	0	4	$507,210
27	Steve Grissom	2757	29	0	1	4	$428,925
29	Robert Pressley	2663	31	0	0	1	$698,425
30	Kyle Petty	2638	30	1	1	5	$698,875
31	Jeremy Mayfield	2637	27	0	0	1	$436,805
32	Jeff Burton	2556	29	0	1	2	$630,770
33	Todd Bodine	2372	28	0	1	3	$664,620
34	Mike Wallace	2178	26	0	0	1	$428,006
35	Dave Marcis	2126	28	0	0	0	$337,853
36	Hut Stricklin	2082	24	0	2	5	$486,065
37	Bobby Hillin, Jr.	1686	18	0	0	1	$244,270
38	Elton Sawyer	1499	20	0	0	0	$416,490
39	Greg Sacks	1349	20	0	0	0	$323,720
40	Randy LaJoie	1133	14	0	0	0	$281,945
41	Loy Allen, Jr.	890	11	0	0	1	$186,670
42	Kenny Wallace	878	11	0	0	0	$151,700
43	Chuck Bown	618	9	0	0	0	$99,995
44	Jimmy Hensley	558	9	0	0	0	$161,025
45	Rich Bickle	538	8	0	0	0	$153,250
46	Davy Jones	520	7	0	0	0	$109,925
47	Jeff Purvis	391	7	0	0	0	$93,875
48	Ernie Irvan	354	3	0	0	2	$54,875
49	Steve Kinser	287	5	0	0	0	$105,224
50	Wally Dallenbach, Jr.	221	2	0	1	1	$63,900

Young Jeff Gordon took the points lead in the 16th race of the season at Loudon, N.H., in July and held off a gallant rally by Dale Earnhardt to win the 1995 NASCAR Winston Cup championship. The 24-year-old Gordon became the second-youngest winner of NASCAR's crown.

With six races remaining, Gordon led Earnhardt by a hefty 309-point margin. With a strong late-season charge, The Intimidator sliced the deficit by large chunks each week. When the checkered flag fell on the season, Earnhardt was only 34 points behind.

Gordon won seven races during his championship run. Earnhardt won five events, including two of the final six, as he made a stab to overtake the emerging NASCAR star. Daytona 500 winner Sterling Marlin finished third in the final tally with three victories to his credit.

1996

February 18 Dale Jarrett passes Dale Earnhardt with 24 laps remaining and scores his second win in the Daytona 500. Jarrett blocks Earnhardt's final-lap moves to post a .12-second victory.

February 25 Dale Earnhardt swats erstwhile leader Bobby Hamilton out of the way with 50 miles to go and sprints to a controversial win in the Goodwrench 400 at Rockingham.

April 14 Terry Labonte ties Richard Petty's streak of 513 consecutive NASCAR Winston Cup starts, capping a perfect weekend by winning the First Union 400 from the pole. Chevrolets finish 1-2-3-4-5 in the race.

April 28 Sterling Marlin holds on for a narrow victory in the Winston Select 500 at Talladega, an event that sends Ricky Craven and Bill Elliott to the hospital. Craven is only bruised, but Elliott suffers a broken leg in a single-car crash.

May 26 Dale Jarrett starts deep in the field but runs away for an easy triumph in Charlotte's Coca-Cola 600.

June 16 Jeff Gordon rolls to his fifth win of the season at Pocono. Dale Earnhardt finishes 32nd, but still leads the championship race by 52 points over Terry Labonte.

July 14 Ernie Irvan caps his miraculous comeback from life-threatening injuries by winning the Jiffy Lube 300 at New Hampshire International Speedway.

July 28 Jeff Gordon surges past a thinned-out field to win the shortened DieHard 500 at Talladega for his sixth win of the season. Dale Earnhardt escapes with a broken sternum and a fractured collarbone after a 20-car crash.

August 3 Dale Jarrett passes Ernie Irvan with seven laps to go and wins the Brickyard 400. Rookie Johnny Benson, Jr., leads the most laps but drops back in a pit-stop shuffle and finishes eighth.

August 11 Geoff Bodine ends a two-year drought by winning on his hometown track in Watkins Glen, N.Y. Dale Earnhardt, driving with painful injuries, wins the pole and finishes sixth.

Ernie Irvan, still on the comeback trail after his 1994 Michigan crash, nipped a quartet of pesky challengers to win the Feb. 15 Gatorade Twin 125-mile qualifying race at Daytona International Speedway. Irvan's #28 Havoline Ford beat runner-up Ken Schrader by a fender length. John Andretti, Jeff Gordon, and Ricky Rudd rounded out the top five.

Sterling Marlin, trying to become the first man in history to post a three-peat in "The Great American Race," forged to the front in his #4 Kodak Chevrolet on the 77th lap of the Feb. 18 Daytona 500. After biding his time through the first 190 miles, Marlin seemed poised to etch his name into the history books. But three laps after he took the lead, his engine soured, leaving him with a disappointing 40th-place finish.

John Andretti's #37 Ford twitched a little as he exited turn two on the 130th lap of the Daytona 500. The car darted to the inside, then shot back across the track and delivered a head-on blow to the concrete retaining barrier. Andretti's car nearly tipped over as it bounced off the wall. Many trackside observers said it was one of the most violent single-car accidents ever at Daytona.

Dale Jarrett's #88 Quality Care Ford crosses the finish line two car lengths ahead of runner-up Dale Earnhardt to capture the 39th annual running of the celebrated Daytona 500. Jarrett pushed his mount to the front with 24 laps to go and deflected repeated efforts from runner-up Earnhardt to post his second win in NASCAR's most prestigious event. For Earnhardt, it was his third runner-up effort in the last three years.

In the late stages of the Feb. 25 Goodwrench 400 at Rockingham, Bobby Hamilton appeared to be a shoo-in for his first NASCAR Winston Cup victory, and the first for the Petty Enterprises team since 1983. Hamilton was pulling away from the field when a caution flag interrupted his bid for a convincing win. On the restart, Hamilton quickly dashed to the front, passing #3 Dale Earnhardt. But as Hamilton assumed command, Earnhardt flicked the quarter panel of Hamilton's Pontiac, sending it out of control and into the wall. Hamilton blew a tire and crashed two laps later as Earnhardt drove to a controversial victory.

Dale Earnhardt leads Terry Labonte in the late stages of the March 10 Purolator 500 at Atlanta Motor Speedway. Earnhardt led 136 of the 328 laps, including the final 28 trips around the high-banked 1.522-mile oval, to snag his second win of the season. The triumph was Earnhardt's eighth at Atlanta, placing him first on the all-time list of race winners at the speedway.

Mike Skinner's #31 Chevrolet runs inches ahead of #24 Jeff Gordon in an early duel at Bristol's March 31 Food City 500. Skinner, making his first start for the Richard Childress-owned RCR Enterprises team, led 10 laps after qualifying sixth. Skinner later went out in a crash, and Gordon drove his Hendrick Motorsports Chevrolet to victory over teammate Terry Labonte.

Terry Labonte held off Jeff Gordon's last-lap efforts to capture the April 14 First Union 400 at North Wilkesboro Speedway. The silver paint scheme on Labonte's #5 Kellogg's Chevrolet commemorated his "iron man" streak. By starting the race, he tied Richard Petty's record string of 513 consecutive NASCAR Winston Cup starts. Labonte started on the pole and recorded his 17th career victory.

1996

September 1 Jeff Gordon scores his third straight victory at Darlington and seventh of the season, thwarting Hut Stricklin's upset bid. Stricklin leads the most laps, but overheating problems knock him off the pace in the final laps.

September 29 Jeff Gordon racks up his 10th win of the year in the Tyson Holly Farms 400 at North Wilkesboro Speedway. It is the final event in the colorful history of the ⅝-mile oval. New owners Bruton Smith and Bob Bahre will move future North Wilkesboro race dates to Texas and New Hampshire, respectively.

October 6 Terry Labonte moves to within one point of NASCAR Winston Cup standings leader Jeff Gordon with a win at Charlotte. Gordon has won 10 races to Labonte's two, but the points race is the closest in NASCAR history.

October 27 Bobby Hamilton drives the Petty Enterprises Pontiac to victory in the Dura Lube 500 at Phoenix International Raceway. It is the first NASCAR Winston Cup victory for Petty Enterprises since 1983.

November 10 Bobby Labonte holds off Dale Jarrett in a spirited duel to win the season finale at Atlanta, as his brother Terry finishes fifth and wraps up his second NASCAR Winston Cup championship. The elder Labonte finishes 37 points ahead of Jeff Gordon to nail down the title.

John Andretti's #37 Ford runs three-abreast with #94 Bill Elliott and #12 Derrike Cope through the tight corners at Martinsville Speedway during the April 21 Goody's Headache Powder 500. The tiny Martinsville track has hosted NASCAR's premier stock car racing series since 1949, and the '96 500-lapper was the 95th NASCAR Winston Cup event to be staged on the ½-mile oval. Rusty Wallace won the race, passing Jeff Gordon with 12 laps remaining. Andretti came from 21st to finish sixth, while Elliott ran 13th and Cope 28th.

Bill Elliott's #94 Ford slides off the second turn in the 78th lap of the April 28 Winston Select 500 at Talladega Superspeedway, and soars down the backstretch. The car lifted high into the air and crashed back down to the ground without turning over. Elliott suffered a broken leg in the incident, which sidelined him until July.

▲▶ The speedy three-abreast formation often seen at Talladega can go awry in an instant. On the 130th lap of the Winston Select 500, one little twitch sent cars flying in all directions. Ricky Craven's #41 Chevrolet climbed over another car and sailed into the catch fence. Craven's car was ripped apart in the multicar accident, but the driver from Newburgh, Maine, climbed out with only bruises—proof that NASCAR machinery can protect a pilot in the most dire situations.

Sterling Marlin keeps his yellow Kodak Chevrolet Monte Carlo at the head of the line in the waning laps of Talladega's spring 500-miler. Marlin led the final 22 laps and sped to his fifth career NASCAR Winston Cup win. He beat runner-up Dale Jarrett by .22 second.

Joe Nemechek's Chevrolet plows into the tire-enforced barrier in the early laps of the May 5 Save Mart Supermarkets 300 at Sears Point Raceway. Nemechek lost control in one of the tight, switchback corners on the twisting 2.52-mile California road course. The Florida native got back into the race after the mishap and finished in 41st place. Rusty Wallace raced around Jeff Gordon with six laps remaining and hustled to victory. It was Wallace's sixth career win on a road course.

Mark Martin's #6 Ford leads the potent Hendrick Motorsports Chevrolet team of #5 Terry Labonte and #24 Jeff Gordon in the May 26 Coca-Cola 600 at Charlotte Motor Speedway. The 600-miler began in late daylight and ended under the lights. Dale Jarrett dominated the race and won in a runaway. Labonte finished third, Gordon fourth, and Martin seventh. Labonte and Gordon emerged as primary championship contenders later in the season and finished 1-2 in the NASCAR Winston Cup standings.

Johnny Benson, Jr.'s #30 Pennzoil Pontiac sheds sheetmetal after a late crash in Charlotte's Coca-Cola 600. The talented rookie driver got mixed up in a three-car entanglement off turn two. The car was demolished, but Benson emerged relatively unscathed.

Number 5 Terry Labonte and #43 Bobby Hamilton battle side-by-side on Dover Downs' "Monster Mile" during the June 2 Miller Genuine Draft 500. Labonte finished second to teammate Jeff Gordon and maintained second place in the NASCAR Winston Cup standings. Labonte trailed Dale Earnhardt by 136 points at the time, but the tough Texan began a summer charge that would put him atop the standings by July.

The #30 Pontiac manned by freshman Johnny Benson, Jr., spins wildly in the early stages of the June 23 Miller Genuine Draft 400 at Michigan International Speedway. Derrike Cope's #12 Ford scoots to the outside and #4 Sterling Marlin dips to the low groove to miss Benson, Jr. Marlin finished third, behind Rusty Wallace and Terry Labonte. Benson went on to win Rookie of the Year honors on the strength of six top-10 finishes and one pole.

Ernie Irvan, who lost the inaugural Brickyard 400 in 1994 due to a tire failure in the final laps, was seeking redemption in the Aug. 3, 1996, race at Indianapolis Motor Speedway. Irvan had his #28 Havoline Ford up front with less than 10 laps to go, but teammate Dale Jarrett squeezed past and went on to a narrow victory. Irvan finished second, swallowing another bitter loss.

Rusty Wallace jams his #2 Ford into the tire barrier during the Aug. 11 The Bud At The Glen. Wallace, a road-racing master, got side swiped by another car and slid off the scenic course in Watkins Glen, N.Y. Damage sustained in the crash relegated Wallace to 33rd place. Geoff Bodine, from nearby Chemung, came from his 13th starting spot to score his 18th career win.

Ernie Irvan's #28 Ford hustles down the front chute at Michigan International Speedway, flanked by #24 Jeff Gordon and #88 Dale Jarrett, in the Aug. 18 GM Goodwrench Dealers 400. Jarrett racked up his fourth win of the NASCAR Winston Cup season. Irvan and Gordon recorded sterling efforts too, finishing fourth and fifth, respectively.

Rusty Wallace steers his #2 Roger Penske/Miller Ford under #9 Lake Speed in the Aug. 24 Goody's Headache Powder 500 at Bristol Motor Speedway. Wallace trounced the field and scored his fifth win of the '96 campaign. The race was the first since Bruton Smith took over management of the popular ½-mile concrete oval. Smith changed the name of the track from Bristol International Raceway to Bristol Motor Speedway.

Dale Jarrett

ONE OF DALE JARRETT'S first assignments in auto racing came at Hickory Speedway in the early 1970s. The tiny .363-mile oval, managed by Dale's father Ned, hosted weekly NASCAR Sportsman races. As a teenager, the younger Jarrett was responsible for chores that included mowing the grass. Possessed of an innovative mind, Jarrett conjured up an idea to reduce his labor at a small cost. He traded a golf club for two goats and stationed the hungry critters in a grass parking lot, which contained the remains of jalopies wrecked in races and demolition contests. "All they would eat was the upholstery in the cars and the vinyl tops," Jarrett said years later. "They wouldn't eat grass if you put it in their mouths."

A short time later, Jarrett found his way onto Hickory Speedway's racing surface. Driving in the entry-level stock car racing classes, Jarrett only enjoyed moderate success. After five years kicking around Hickory and other weekly tracks, Jarrett moved to NASCAR's Late Model Sportsman division, now known as the NASCAR Busch Series. It took him five years to win a race.

Jarrett got a few one-shot deals in NASCAR Winston Cup racing beginning in 1984 and landed a full-time assignment by '87. Success was slow to come, though. Jarrett only recorded a pair of top-five finishes in his first 110 NASCAR Winston Cup starts from '84 to '90.

Driving for the Wood Brothers Ford team in 1991, Jarrett's lengthy apprenticeship began to reap rewards. He scored his first NASCAR Winston Cup victory at Michigan, nosing out Davey Allison in a photo finish. He accepted a ride with the new Joe Gibbs team in '92 and was competitive, although he failed to record a victory. In '93, Jarrett rallied past

**NASCAR Cup Series
Career Record
1984-2008**
Starts: 668
Wins: 32
Top 5s: 163
Top 10s: 260
Poles: 16
Career Winnings:
$51,247,439

Dale Earnhardt on the final lap and won his first Daytona 500. The win was made more special by his father, retired NASCAR Grand National champion Ned Jarrett. Ned, color commentating for CBS Sports, became more of a proud papa than an impartial journalist as he rooted for his son to win. The call made great TV, and became one of NASCAR's most memorable moments.

After three years with the Gibbs operation, Jarrett moved over to the Robert Yates camp in 1995. He won once in '95 and then captured his second Daytona 500 prize in the '96 season opener. He also drove home first in the Brickyard 400, plucking the two biggest races of the annual NASCAR calendar.

Jarrett was a serious championship contender in 1996, finishing third on the strength of four victories. He finished a close second to Jeff Gordon in the '97 points race, took third in '98, and finally grabbed the crown after a sparkling season in '99. Jarrett nabbed the points lead after the 11th race of the season in May and never looked back. "The championship is my greatest accomplishment. I'm prouder of that than anything else."

In capturing NASCAR's most cherished prize, the Jarrett racing family became only the second father and son to win the NASCAR championship.

Jarrett's prowess continued into the 21st century. He contended for the title in 2000 and '01, finishing in the top five in points both years before slipping to ninth in the final standings in '02. Jarrett won at least one race every season from 1993 to 2003. Known as a Ford driver, Jarrett was one of the first to switch to Toyota for the 2007 season. His versatility and steadiness helped Toyota mount a serious threat. After amassing 32 NASCAR Cup Series victories, Jarrett retired in mid-2008.

Dale Jarrett guns his #88 Ford into the lead at the outset of the Sept. 1 Mountain Dew Southern 500 at Darlington Raceway. Jarrett had a shot at the Winston Million bonus, having won at Daytona and Charlotte earlier in the season. Jarrett was holding down first place when a blown tire sent his car into the wall. He lost a couple of laps in the pits, then returned to the race and finished 14th. Jeff Gordon, who started second, went on to win.

Terry Labonte cuts a quick lap on Charlotte Motor Speedway's front chute in the Oct. 6 UAW-GM Quality Parts 500. Labonte entered the race trailing NASCAR Winston Cup standings leader Jeff Gordon by 111 points, but shaved that deficit down to a single point with a resounding triumph in the 500-miler. Gordon stumbled, finishing 31st, which put Labonte and Gordon in a virtual dead heat for the championship with three events remaining.

Ricky Rudd keeps his #10 Tide Ford just ahead of #88 Dale Jarrett in the Oct. 20 AC Delco 400 at Rockingham's North Carolina Motor Speedway. Rudd drove away from Jarrett in the final laps to record his first win of the season. The triumph marked the 14th consecutive year Rudd had won a NASCAR Winston Cup race, four years short of the all-time record of 18 set by Richard Petty from 1960 to '77. Terry Labonte took over the points lead with a third-place finish.

Bobby Labonte heads the field through the turn at Phoenix International Raceway during the Oct. 27 Dura Lube 500. Labonte won the pole and led early before drifting back to a ninth-place finish. Bobby Hamilton won the 312-mile, 500 kilometer event, the first of his career and the first for the Petty Enterprises team in 13 seasons. Terry Labonte ran third in the race, then placed fifth in the season finale the next week at Atlanta to wrap up the NASCAR Winston Cup championship.

1996 NASCAR WINSTON CUP POINTS RACE

Rank	Driver	Points	Starts	Wins	Top 5	Top 10	Winnings
1	Terry Labonte	4657	31	2	21	24	$4,030,648
2	Jeff Gordon	4620	31	10	21	24	$3,428,485
3	Dale Jarrett	4568	31	4	17	21	$2,985,418
4	Dale Earnhardt	4327	31	2	13	17	$2,285,926
5	Mark Martin	4278	31	0	14	23	$1,887,396
6	Ricky Rudd	3845	31	1	5	16	$1,503,025
7	Rusty Wallace	3717	31	5	8	18	$1,665,315
8	Sterling Marlin	3682	31	2	5	10	$1,588,425
9	Bobby Hamilton	3639	31	1	3	11	$1,151,235
10	Ernie Irvan	3632	31	2	12	16	$1,683,313
11	Bobby Labonte	3590	31	1	5	14	$1,475,196
12	Ken Schrader	3540	31	0	3	10	$1,089,603
13	Jeff Burton	3538	31	0	6	12	$884,303
14	Michael Waltrip	3535	30	0	1	11	$1,182,811
15	Jimmy Spencer	3476	31	0	2	9	$1,090,876
16	Ted Musgrave	3466	31	0	2	7	$961,512
17	Geoff Bodine	3218	31	1	2	6	$1,031,762
18	Rick Mast	3190	31	0	1	5	$924,559
19	Morgan Shepherd	3133	31	0	1	5	$719,059
20	Ricky Craven	3078	31	0	3	5	$941,959
21	Johnny Benson	3004	30	0	1	6	$947,080
22	Hut Stricklin	2854	31	0	1	1	$631,055
23	Lake Speed	2834	31	0	0	2	$817,175
24	Brett Bodine	2814	30	0	0	1	$767,716
25	Wally Dallenbach, Jr.	2786	30	0	1	3	$837,001
26	Jeremy Mayfield	2721	30	0	2	2	$592,853
27	Kyle Petty	2696	28	0	0	2	$689,041
28	Kenny Wallace	2694	30	0	0	2	$457,665
29	Darrell Waltrip	2657	31	0	0	2	$740,185
30	Bill Elliott	2627	24	0	0	6	$716,506
31	John Andretti	2621	30	0	2	3	$688,511
32	Robert Pressley	2485	30	0	2	3	$690,465
33	Ward Burton	2411	27	0	0	4	$873,619
34	Joe Nemechek	2391	29	0	0	2	$666,247
35	Derrike Cope	2374	29	0	0	3	$675,781
36	Dick Trickle	2131	26	0	0	1	$404,927
37	Bobby Hillin, Jr.	2128	26	0	0	0	$395,224
38	Dave Marcis	2047	27	0	0	0	$435,177
39	Steve Grissom	1188	13	0	1	2	$314,983
40	Todd Bodine	991	10	0	0	1	$198,525
41	Mike Wallace	799	11	0	0	0	$169,082
42	Greg Sacks	710	9	0	0	0	$207,755
43	Elton Sawyer	705	9	0	0	0	$129,618
44	Chad Little	627	9	0	0	0	$164,752
45	Loy Allen, Jr.	603	9	0	0	0	$130,667
46	Gary Bradberry	591	9	0	0	0	$155,785
47	Mike Skinner	529	5	0	0	0	$65,850
48	Jeff Purvis	328	4	0	0	0	$91,127
49	Jeff Green	247	4	0	0	0	$46,875
50	Randy MacDonald	228	3	0	0	0	$33,910

Hendrick Motorsports teammates Terry Labonte and Jeff Gordon battled for the 1996 NASCAR Winston Cup championship, and Labonte parlayed consistency to win his second title.

Labonte took the lead in the standings with a third-place finish at Rockingham in late October. Top-five finishes in the final two events were enough to capture the title by 37 points over Gordon.

Gordon won 10 races, while Labonte won twice. Both Chevrolet drivers had 21 top-five finishes and 24 top-10 efforts. Gordon led 2314 laps as Labonte led 973 laps. Gordon seemed to have a better year, but Labonte was able to come out on top of the points race thanks to fewer DNFs.

Four-time winner Dale Jarrett placed fourth in the NASCAR Winston Cup standings and two-time winner Dale Earnhardt finished fourth.

1997

February 16 Jeff Gordon drives past Bill Elliott with six laps remaining and leads a 1-2-3 sweep for the Hendrick Motorsports team in the 39th running of the Daytona 500. Gordon, Terry Labonte, and Ricky Craven gang up on Elliott in the stretch drive and take the top three spots in NASCAR's most celebrated event.

March 9 Dale Jarrett leads the final 59 laps and breezes to victory in the Primestar 500 at Atlanta Motor Speedway for his first win of the season. Ernie Irvan finishes second, giving the Robert Yates team a 1-2 finish. Steve Grissom survives a tumble on the backstretch late in the race without serious injury.

April 6 Jeff Burton comes on strong in the final 100 miles and racks up his first career NASCAR Winston Cup victory as Texas Motor Speedway stages its inaugural race, the Interstate Batteries 500. The race is punctuated by several crashes, which contribute to 10 caution flags for a total of 73 laps run under the yellow flag.

April 13 Jeff Gordon nudges past Rusty Wallace on the final lap to win the Food City 500 at Bristol Motor Speedway. Twenty caution flags fly and 132 laps are run in single-file formation.

May 10 Mark Martin prevails in the nonstop Winston 500 at Talladega Superspeedway and holds off Dale Earnhardt to win in record time. Martin averages a staggering 188.354 mph in the caution-free event. It is Martin's first NASCAR Winston Cup victory since the 1995 season.

June 8 Jeff Gordon passes Ted Musgrave with 16 laps remaining and sprints to a narrow victory over Jeff Burton, registering his sixth triumph of the season in the Pocono 500 in Pennsylvania. With the win, Gordon ties winless Terry Labonte for the lead in the NASCAR Winston Cup points standings.

Petty Enterprises and the STP Corp. unveiled a new Silver Anniversary paint scheme for the 1997 NASCAR Winston Cup season. Commemorating the 25th consecutive season STP had sponsored the Petty camp, the #43 Pontiac driven by Bobby Hamilton would be decorated with a number of nostalgic paint schemes during the course of the year. Hamilton finished 15th in the Feb. 16 Daytona 500 in the silver STP Pontiac.

Dale Earnhardt's #3 Chevrolet begins a wild upside-down ride down the backstretch on the 189th lap of the Feb. 16 Daytona 500. Earnhardt had just been passed by Jeff Gordon for second place when the Goodwrench Chevy glanced off the wall. Dale Jarrett, Ernie Irvan, and Terry Labonte got stacked up behind Earnhardt in a chain reaction. Earnhardt's car tumbled over and landed in its wheels. While sitting in the ambulance awaiting the mandatory trip to the infield care center, Earnhardt said he "noticed the wheels were still on the car. I got out of the ambulance and asked the guy in my car to crank it. When it fired, I told him to give me my car back." Earnhardt drove the remaining laps and salvaged a 31st-place finish. "My chances of winning the Daytona 500 were over," said Earnhardt, "but I can still win an eighth Winston Cup championship."

A rash of late-race crashes forced the Daytona 500 to end under caution, with Jeff Gordon running first, Terry Labonte second, and Ricky Craven third. The trio crossed the finish line in three-wide formation, giving team owner Rick Hendrick a 1-2-3 finish in "The Great American Race." The three stablemates from the Hendrick Motorsports team ganged up on leader Bill Elliott with six laps remaining and made the decisive pass in unison. It was the first time that teammates ran 1-2-3 in NASCAR's biggest event.

A happy Jeff Gordon pumps his fists in celebration in Daytona's victory lane following his win in the 39th annual running of the Daytona 500 as CBS Sports reporter Mike Joy waits to interview the winner. At 25 years of age, Gordon became the youngest winner of the Daytona 500. Richard Petty, who was 26 when he won his first Daytona 500 in 1964, held the distinction for 33 years.

Rusty Wallace spins his #2 Miller Lite Ford in front of #10 Ricky Rudd during the March 2 Pontiac Excitement 400 at Richmond International Raceway. Wallace and Rudd recovered from the shunt and continued in the race. Wallace galloped past Dale Jarrett with three laps remaining to win the race. Rudd came home sixth.

Mark Martin ended a 42-race winless skid with a resounding triumph in the May 4 Save Mart Supermarkets 300 at Sears Point Raceway. Martin started on the pole in his #6 Jack Roush Ford, led the most laps, and nosed out Jeff Gordon in a close finish.

Pole-sitter #88 Dale Jarrett and #24 Jeff Gordon lead the field to the green flag at the start of the April 6 Interstate Batteries 500 at the new Texas Motor Speedway. The inaugural race at the new 1½-mile facility was the first NASCAR Winston Cup event held in Texas since 1981. Jeff Burton dodged several accidents to take the win. Jarrett finished second, while Gordon was eliminated in a crash with Ernie Irvan and Greg Sacks.

Mark Martin drove his #6 Valvoline/Roush Racing Ford to victory in the caution-free May 10 Winston 500 at Talladega Superspeedway. Martin started midpack and drove into contention in the early stages. He led the final 31 laps and edged Dale Earnhardt at the finish line. The 500-miler was rained out twice in April and held on a Saturday in May. Martin averaged 188.354 mph, a record for a 500-mile NASCAR Winston Cup race.

Cars snake through an early accident in the May 25 Coca-Cola 600 at Charlotte Motor Speedway. Todd Bodine drove the #7 Ford as a substitute for injured brother Geoff, who suffered a concussion in a practice crash four days earlier. Bodine's engine failure triggered the crash, and Todd finished last in the 43-car field. Jeff Gordon won the 600-miler to bag the second jewel of NASCAR racing's Winston Million bonus program.

June 15 In a crowd-pleasing late-race spurt, Ernie Irvan drives to victory in the Miller 400 at Michigan International Speedway, claiming a win at the track that nearly took his life in August 1994. Irvan leads the final 21 laps and beats runner-up Bill Elliott by 2.9 seconds.

June 22 Jeff Gordon christens the new California Speedway with a win in the California 500, the inaugural event on the two-mile oval. Terry Labonte takes second, giving Hendrick Motorsports another 1-2 finish.

July 5 John Andretti holds off Terry Labonte on the final lap to score his first career NASCAR Winston Cup victory in the Pepsi 400 at Daytona. Andretti's win gives Cale Yarborough his first win as a NASCAR team owner.

August 4 Owner/driver Ricky Rudd gambles on fuel mileage and it pays off with a $571,000 triumph in the Brickyard 400 at Indianapolis. Rudd leads the final 14 laps and finishes a scant .18 second in front of runner-up Bobby Labonte.

August 31 Jeff Gordon prevails in a fender-rubbing final-lap skirmish with Jeff Burton to win Darlington's Mountain Dew Southern 500 and the Winston Million bonus. Gordon is the first driver to pocket the $1 million bonus since Bill Elliott won in the inaugural offering in 1985.

October 12 Terry Labonte takes the lead in the final two laps and edges his younger brother Bobby at the finish line in the DieHard 500 at Talladega Superspeedway. It is the 19th career win for the two-time NASCAR Winston Cup champion.

November 16 Bobby Labonte throttles his way into the lead in the final 11 laps and speeds to victory in the NAPA 500 at Atlanta Motor Speedway. Dale Jarrett finishes second, but he falls 14 points short of Jeff Gordon's point total in the NASCAR Winston Cup standings. Gordon finishes 17th, and becomes the youngest driver to capture two championships.

Following the close of the Riverside road course in 1987, southern California hadn't hosted a NASCAR Winston Cup race in more than 10 years. The magnificent new two-mile California Speedway filled a void within the NASCAR domain. The inaugural California 500 on June 22 opened to a packed house. The race featured 21 lead changes among a dozen different drivers. Jeff Gordon passed Mark Martin with 11 laps remaining and sped to victory.

▼ RCR Enterprises teammates Mike Skinner and Dale Earnhardt occupy the front row moments before the start of the July 5 Pepsi 400 at Daytona International Speedway. Skinner won the pole and led the first two laps, but was caught up in a big crash on lap 33.

John Andretti's 100th career NASCAR Winston Cup start was a memorable one. Driving Cale Yarborough's #98 RCA Ford in the Pepsi 400 at Daytona, Andretti was in contention the entire race. By the 137th lap, Andretti had motored his way into the lead. He held off Terry Labonte, Sterling Marlin, and Dale Earnhardt to post his first career win. It was the first and only win for Yarborough as a team owner.

Jeff Gordon runs out front in the early stages of the July 13 Jiffy Lube 300 at New Hampshire International Speedway as #3 Dale Earnhardt and #7 Geoff Bodine close in. Gordon struggled to finish 23rd and lost the NASCAR Winston Cup points lead to Hendrick Motorsports partner Terry Labonte. Earnhardt went on to finish second behind winner Jeff Burton, and Bodine ran 10th in his self-owned Ford.

Irvan Exorcises Ghosts at Michigan

ERNIE IRVAN EMERGED from a last round of green-flag pit stops with a lead that he maintained for the final 20 laps to win the June 17, 1997, Miller 400 at Michigan International Speedway. Irvan's heartwarming victory came three years after a crash in the second turn of the two-mile superspeedway that nearly took his life.

Rewind to 1994. Irvan, who had led the NASCAR Winston Cup points standings for most of the season, was shaking down his Ford in an Aug. 20 practice session. As he sped through the turn, a tire deflated, sending him crashing into the concrete retaining barrier. The mangled car slid to a halt and medical attendants were on the scene immediately. The quick attention by the first-class Michigan International Speedway medical crew was responsible for his surviving the first traumatic moments after the crash. Irvan was airlifted to a hospital in Ypsilanti, Mich., in critical condition. He spent months in the hospital recovering from severe head injuries.

Initially, Irvan was given no better than a 10-percent chance of surviving the horrible injuries. Dr. Errol Erlandson and his staff tended to Irvan and overcame heavy odds. After a 13-month recovery period, Irvan returned to compete in NASCAR's premier stock car racing division in late 1995.

Irvan's win in the 1997 Miller 400 laid to rest the ghosts of Michigan past. "I got a little teary-eyed in the last 10 laps," admitted Irvan, who drove Robert Yates' Ford to a most satisfying triumph. "I kept going through turn two thinking, 'Man, this is where the wreck happened.' It started playing with my mind. That wasn't too good because

NASCAR Winston Cup Career Record 1987-1999
Starts: 313
Wins: 15
Top 5s: 68
Top 10s: 124
Poles: 22
Career Winnings:
$11,624,617

it's hard to drive with tears in your eyes."

The crash in 1994 removed Irvan from a possible championship run, and sidelined him for more than a year. His recovery was slow, but he never gave up hopes of returning to the NASCAR Winston Cup tour. "I still don't remember any of the wreck," said Irvan, "and the only film I ever saw was after the wreck. No one ever had any film that actually showed me hitting the wall. I'm glad there wasn't any. I don't really care to see it."

Prior to Irvan's Michigan win, the 1997 NASCAR Winston Cup season had been laced with frustration. Late-race problems robbed him of the chance to win several races. "We should have won two or three races this year only to have something happen in the last few laps. We were in position to win the Daytona 500, but Dale [Earnhardt] rolled over on our roof. We should have won at Dover, too," said Irvan.

Irvan wasn't regarded as a top-ranked contender in the 400-miler at Michigan. He started in 20th position and didn't lead until the final 75 miles. But with the help of a lightning-fast pit stop and a strong-running car, Irvan scrambled to the top of the leader board. He outran Bill Elliott in the final laps to post his 15th career NASCAR Winston Cup victory. "I am real happy for the guys on this team that we were able to pull this one off. It was pretty good for Ernie Irvan, too."

Irvan left the Robert Yates team following the conclusion of the 1997 season and joined a new operation headed by Nelson Bowers. In practice for the Aug. 22, 1999, race at Michigan, Irvan was again involved in a hard practice crash. He announced his retirement a week later. After he parted ways with the Yates team, Irvan never again finished in the top five in a NASCAR Winston Cup event.

Ricky Rudd's #10 Tide Ford runs just ahead of #9 Lake Speed in the Aug. 4 Brickyard 400 at Indianapolis Motor Speedway. Rudd started fourth, took the lead 14 laps from the finish, stretched his dwindling fuel supply, and won in an upset. Speed came from 27th to finish a strong 12th. Rudd had formed his own NASCAR Winston Cup team in '94. With the financial support of Tide, Rudd never broke stride and continued his streak of winning at least one race every year since 1983. The Brickyard 400 win was Rudd's second victory of the '97 season, marking the first time he had won more than once in 10 years.

Dick Trickle pokes his #90 Ford under #33 Ken Schrader in the late laps of the Aug. 23 Goody's 500 at Bristol Motor Speedway. Trickle had a splendid run in Junie Donlavey's Ford, finishing a strong third, ahead of many of the heavy hitters. Dale Jarrett and Mark Martin ran 1-2 in the event in heavily financed Ford machinery. Schrader placed sixth.

Dale Earnhardt drifts into the upper groove in the opening laps of the Aug. 31 Mountain Dew Southern 500 at Darlington as #1 Lance Hooper, #17 Darrell Waltrip, and #43 Bobby Hamilton steer clear. Earnhardt suffered a mysterious lapse of consciousness on the opening lap and grazed the wall. Team owner Richard Childress told the seven-time champion via radio to bring the car to pit road. Two laps later, Earnhardt drove into the pits, where he was replaced by Mike Dillon, who took the car to a 30th-place finish. Earnhardt was examined by a team of doctors, but the cause for the momentary blackout went unresolved. "We were told [by doctors] they found no medical reason he couldn't race," said a NASCAR spokesperson. "That was good enough for us." Earnhardt competed at Richmond six days later.

Effective with the 1997 Mountain Dew Southern 500, the straightaways at Darlington Raceway were flip-flopped. What was once the backstretch became the frontstretch. Raceway officials sited more land area for expansion on the old backstretch as the main reason the switch was made. Jeff Gordon nosed out Jeff Burton by a car length to win the 500-miler and become only the second driver to capture the Winston Million bonus. Gordon won three of NASCAR's three crown-jewel events: the Daytona 500, the Charlotte 600, and Darlington's Southern 500.

Jeff Burton gets his #99 Ford alongside leader Jeff Gordon on the final lap of the Mountain Dew Southern 500. Although he was poised to make the decisive last-lap pass and prevent Gordon from taking home the $1 million bonus from Winston, Burton backed off when the two reached the tight first turn. In the driver's meeting before the race, all drivers were cautioned to avoid crowding Gordon in his quest to take home the bonus money. After finishing second to Gordon, Burton claimed, "I tried to put him in the wall and missed." The widely circulated quote kept Burton's reputation as a strong racer intact, while his actions on the track kept him in the good graces of NASCAR officials.

Terry Labonte flashes across the finish line a couple car lengths ahead of #18 Bobby Labonte at the conclusion of the Oct. 12 DieHard 500 at Talladega Superspeedway. The Labonte siblings teamed up and whisked around leader Ken Schrader with two laps remaining. "You have to have help to pass somebody in these restrictor plate races," said the winner. "I was glad to see Bobby behind me." Terry recorded the 11th win for Chevrolet during the '97 NASCAR Winston Cup season, but it was the first for any driver other than Jeff Gordon.

Kenny Irwin, Jr., making his second career NASCAR Winston Cup start, holds his #27 Ford just ahead of #28 Ernie Irvan in the Sept. 28 Hanes 500. Irwin, Jr., who would be hired by team owner Robert Yates to replace Irvan in the #28 Havoline Ford in 1998, qualified third and ran strong until a fuel-pump failure knocked him out after 257 laps. Irvan qualified 30th and finished 10th.

Jeff Green, driving the #29 Chevrolet, nipped the rear bumper of Jeremy Mayfield, sending the #37 Ford spinning in the Sept. 28 Hanes 500 at Martinsville. Both drivers recovered, but neither was a threat to win the event. Jeff Burton won the race, which was dipped in controversy. NASCAR blackflagged leader Rusty Wallace for jumping a restart with 22 laps remaining. Burton held off a hard-charging Dale Earnhardt to secure the triumph.

Rusty Wallace won the third race of the 1997 season at Richmond, but failed to scratch victory lane for the remainder of the year. However, he was able to keep intact his string of winning at least one race in 12 consecutive seasons. An unusually high nine DNFs relegated Wallace to a ninth-place finish in the 1997 NASCAR Winston Cup points standings.

Rusty Wallace holds the low line in his #2 Ford in a three-abreast battle with #28 Ernie Irvan and #24 Jeff Gordon in the Oct. 5 UAW-GM Quality 500 at Charlotte Motor Speedway. Gordon, who went on to finish fifth behind race winner Dale Jarrett, maintained a healthy 125-point lead over Mark Martin in the NASCAR Winston Cup championship chase. Wallace managed to finish 12th, while Irvan struggled and placed 18th.

A sold-out grandstand and a packed hillside audience watched Dale Jarrett beat Rusty Wallace in the Nov. 2 Dura Lube 500 at Phoenix International Raceway. The one-mile oval in the Arizona desert is one of the most picturesque tracks on the annual NASCAR schedule. The Phoenix track, as well as those at Pocono, Michigan, and Indianapolis, were designed specifically for Indy Car racing. With NASCAR's emergence as America's most popular motorsport, virtually every speedway promoter began lobbying for a NASCAR Winston Cup race date.

Brett Bodine spins his #11 Ford after a shove from #00 Buckshot Jones during the early laps of the Nov. 16 NAPA 500 at Atlanta Motor Speedway. Jones, making his first NASCAR Winston Cup start, finished last in the 43-car field due to the crash. Bobby Labonte went on to win the 500-miler.

Jeff Gordon drove his #24 DuPont Chevrolet to the 1997 NASCAR Winston Cup championship. Gordon racked up his second consecutive 10-win season, edging Dale Jarrett by 14 points to secure his second NASCAR title. At the age of 26, Gordon became NASCAR's youngest two-time champion.

1997 NASCAR WINSTON CUP POINTS RACE

Rank	Driver	Points	Starts	Wins	Top 5	Top 10	Winnings
1	Jeff Gordon	4710	32	10	22	23	$6,375,658
2	Dale Jarrett	4696	32	7	20	23	$3,240,542
3	Mark Martin	4681	32	4	16	24	$2,532,484
4	Jeff Burton	4285	32	3	13	18	$2,296,614
5	Dale Earnhardt	4216	32	0	7	16	$2,151,909
6	Terry Labonte	4177	32	1	8	20	$2,270,144
7	Bobby Labonte	4101	32	1	9	18	$2,217,999
8	Bill Elliott	3836	32	0	5	14	$1,607,827
9	Rusty Wallace	3598	32	1	8	12	$1,705,625
10	Ken Schrader	3576	32	0	2	8	$1,355,292
11	Johnny Benson, Jr.	3575	32	0	0	8	$1,256,457
12	Ted Musgrave	3556	32	0	5	8	$1,256,680
13	Jeremy Mayfield	3547	32	0	3	8	$1,067,203
14	Ernie Irvan	3534	32	1	5	13	$1,614,281
15	Kyle Petty	3455	32	0	2	9	$984,314
16	Bobby Hamilton	3450	32	1	6	8	$1,478,843
17	Ricky Rudd	3330	32	2	6	11	$1,975,981
18	Michael Waltrip	3173	32	0	0	6	$1,138,599
19	Ricky Craven	3108	30	0	4	7	$1,259,550
20	Jimmy Spencer	3079	32	0	1	4	$1,073,779
21	Steve Grissom	3061	31	0	3	6	$1,074,374
22	Geoff Bodine	3046	29	0	3	10	$1,092,734
23	John Andretti	3019	32	1	3	3	$1,143,725
24	Ward Burton	2987	31	0	0	7	$1,004,944
25	Sterling Marlin	2954	32	0	2	6	$1,301,370
26	Darrell Waltrip	2942	31	0	1	4	$958,679
27	Derrike Cope	2901	31	0	1	2	$707,404
28	Joe Nemechek	2754	30	0	0	3	$732,194
29	Brett Bodine	2716	31	0	0	2	$936,694
30	Mike Skinner	2669	31	0	0	3	$900,569
31	Dick Trickle	2629	28	0	2	2	$656,189
32	Rick Mast	2569	29	0	0	2	$829,339
33	Kenny Wallace	2462	31	0	0	2	$939,001
34	Hut Stricklin	2423	29	0	0	1	$802,904
35	Lake Speed	2301	25	0	0	0	$715,074
36	Chad Little	2081	27	0	0	1	$555,914
37	David Green	2038	26	0	0	0	$512,583
38	Morgan Shepherd	2033	23	0	1	3	$662,999
39	Jeff Green	1624	20	0	1	2	$434,685
40	Robby Gordon	1495	20	0	1	1	$622,439
41	Wally Dallenbach, Jr.	1475	22	0	0	1	$471,479
42	Dave Marcis	1405	19	0	0	0	$427,364
43	Robert Pressley	984	14	0	0	0	$252,478
44	Gary Bradberry	868	16	0	0	0	$251,930
45	Greg Sacks	778	12	0	0	0	$320,714
46	Mike Wallace	541	7	0	0	0	$159,303
47	Bobby Hillin, Jr.	511	10	0	0	0	$211,978
48	Lance Hooper	402	6	0	0	0	$145,000
49	Kenny Irwin	390	4	0	0	1	$71,730
50	Billy Standridge	366	6	0	0	0	$149,824

Jeff Gordon prevailed in a three-way showdown with Dale Jarrett and Mark Martin to win the 1997 NASCAR Winston Cup championship.

Gordon took the points lead with a September victory in Darlington's Mountain Dew Southern 500 and maintained the narrow advantage over his rivals for the rest of the season. Gordon posted his second NASCAR Winston Cup championship by a close 14 points over runner-up Jarrett. Martin was only 29 points behind in the closest three-way title chase in NASCAR Winston Cup history.

The points lead changed hands seven times among four drivers. Gordon led most of the season, but Jarrett, Martin, and Terry Labonte enjoyed brief stints atop the points standings.

Gordon racked up 10 wins during the season, while Jarrett won seven events and Martin grabbed four victories.

1998

February 15 With the Thunderbird no longer available, Ford introduces the Taurus for competition in NASCAR's 50th Anniversary season. Dale Earnhardt ends two decades of frustration at the Daytona 500. Earnhardt, making his 20th start in NASCAR's annual "Super Bowl," leads the final 61 laps and edges Bobby Labonte at the finish. It is the 71st win of Earnhardt's career and it snaps a victory drought that dates back to 1996.

March 1 Mark Martin drives his Ford Taurus to victory in the inaugural NASCAR Winston Cup event at Las Vegas Motor Speedway. Martin finishes 1.6 seconds ahead of teammate Jeff Burton as the Jack Roush team posts a 1-2 showing.

April 5 Mark Martin passes Chad Little with 30 laps remaining and motors to a close victory in the Texas 500 at Texas Motor Speedway. Little and third-place finisher Robert Pressley enjoy the best finishes of their careers. A 13-car crash on the opening lap takes out many of the top contenders.

April 20 Bobby Hamilton's dominating performance nets an overwhelming victory in the Goody's 500 at Martinsville Speedway. Hamilton finishes 6.3 seconds ahead of runner-up Ted Musgrave to score his third career NASCAR Winston Cup victory.

May 24 Jeff Gordon runs down Rusty Wallace with 10 laps to go and hustles to victory in the Coca-Cola 600 at Charlotte Motor Speedway. With his late-race pass, Gordon denies Wallace a shot at the Winston No Bull 5 $1 million bonus. Gordon also takes the points lead for the first time in the 1998 campaign.

June 6 Terry Labonte bumps his way past Dale Jarrett with three laps remaining and notches his first win of the season in the Pontiac 400 at Richmond International Raceway. Jeff Gordon's victory bid is derailed when Rusty Wallace knocks him into the wall with 28 laps remaining.

Dale Earnhardt rides under the checkered flag to win the Feb. 12 Gatorade Twin 125-mile qualifying race at Daytona International Speedway. The narrow victory over the new Ford Tauruses of Dale Jarrett and Jeremy Mayfield was the ninth win in a row for Earnhardt in the preliminary sprint races. After using the Thunderbird as its model of preference in NASCAR Winston Cup racing, Ford brought the Taurus to NASCAR for the first time in 1998, making it the first four-door car to be approved for NASCAR's top series.

Dale Earnhardt leads a pack of cars down the front chute as they approach the white flag of the Feb. 15 Daytona 500. Using the lapped car of #75 Rick Mast to prevent Jeremy Mayfield and Bobby Labonte from passing him, Earnhardt won the race back to the caution flag. The final lap was run under caution due to an accident involving John Andretti and Lake Speed. Earnhardt finally prevailed in NASCAR's crown-jewel event after 20 years of trying. He also halted a career-long 59-race winless streak that stretched back to 1996.

After the conclusion of the 40th annual Daytona 500, which kicked off NASCAR's 50th Anniversary celebration, winner Dale Earnhardt was congratulated by a reception line that included crews of virtually every other team. "To see all those guys come out [on pit road] was pretty impressive," said Earnhardt, who led the final 61 laps in a dominating performance. Earnhardt earned $1,059,805 for the win.

Jeff Gordon rides the high side around #21 Michael Waltrip in the Feb. 22 GM Goodwrench Service Plus 400 at North Carolina Speedway. Gordon overcame handling problems and rallied from deep in the field to win going away. After Gordon fell to 31st in the first 100 miles, crew chief Ray Evernham adjusted the car on each pit stop. Near the end of the race, Gordon's #24 Chevrolet was untouchable. It was the 30th career NASCAR Winston Cup win for Gordon and his second straight at Rockingham.

Veteran Mark Martin drove his Roush Racing Ford to victory in the inaugural NASCAR Winston Cup event at Las Vegas Motor Speedway on March 1. Martin drove past Geoff Bodine with 23 laps remaining and banked $313,900 for winning the first annual Las Vegas 400. Along with the cash prize, Martin also had the privilege to share the victory lane celebration with a couple of Las Vegas lovelies.

Rusty Wallace, driving the #2 Ford, battles with #99 Jeff Burton and #12 Jeremy Mayfield during the March 22 TranSouth Financial 400 at Darlington Raceway. The trio engaged in a duel for third place on the final lap. Wallace nabbed the position, just ahead of his Penske Racing teammate Mayfield. Burton placed fifth. Burton led the most laps, but Dale Jarrett prevailed in a late-race rally.

Ted Musgrave's #16 Ford climbs on top of Todd Bodine's #35 Pontiac in the early laps of the March 29 Food City 500 at Bristol Motor Speedway. Incredibly, Musgrave recovered from the mishap to finish eighth. The crash was one of 14 incidents that brought out the caution flag. Jeff Gordon went on to win his fourth consecutive spring race on the steeply banked Bristol track.

Darrell Waltrip donned his Pennzoil uniform to drive in the April 20 Goody's 500 at Martinsville Speedway, his third effort with the DEI team in a replacement role for injured Steve Park. Park, a promising rookie, was injured in a practice crash at Atlanta in March. Team owner Dale Earnhardt seated the three-time NASCAR Winston Cup champion in the car. Waltrip got mixed up in a crash in the opening laps and retired at the midpoint of the race. When Waltrip landed the DEI ride, he sold all of his racing equipment and got out of the owner/driver business.

Jerry Nadeau limps around the inside of Martinsville Speedway during the Goody's 500. One of the promising freshman drivers on the NASCAR tour in 1998, Nadeau hooked up with team owner Bill Elliott and sponsor First Plus Financial, whose public relations spokesperson was then-Miami Dolphins quarterback Dan Marino (who wore number 13). The new team struggled early in the '98 season and Nadeau lost his ride at midseason. The former road racer from Connecticut moved over to the Harry Melling team to finish out the season.

1998

June 21 Jeremy Mayfield holds off Jeff Gordon and Dale Jarrett in a stirring finish to bag his first career NASCAR Winston Cup win in the Pocono 500. Mayfield leads 122 of the 200 laps on the triangular 2.5-mile speedway and the win comes in his 125th career start.

July 4 Raging forest fires in the state of Florida force Daytona International Speedway officials to postpone the Pepsi 400 until October. Wildfires burn more than 300,000 acres in the Sunshine State. It is the first time the holiday NASCAR classic is postponed since the track was built in 1959.

August 16 Title-bound Jeff Gordon racks up his fourth consecutive victory in the Pepsi 400 at Michigan Speedway, rallying from a two-mile deficit in the final 22 laps. A timely caution flag bunches up the field and Gordon takes the lead with nine laps remaining.

September 6 Jeff Gordon bags his sixth victory in the last seven races and wins another Winston No Bull 5 $1 million bonus with a win in the Pepsi Southern 500 at Darlington. Gordon pads his lead in the NASCAR Winston Cup standings to 199 points over Mark Martin.

September 27 Ricky Rudd overcomes 100-degree heat to win the NAPA Autocare 500 at Martinsville, giving him a victory in 16 consecutive NASCAR Winston Cup seasons. Rudd's feat leaves him two years shy of NASCAR's all-time record of 18 set by Richard Petty.

October 17 Jeff Gordon passes Kenny Irwin, Jr., with 38 laps remaining and hustles to victory in the rescheduled Pepsi 400 at Daytona International Speedway. For the first time, a race is staged under the lights at Daytona. Gordon wins for the 11th time in the 1998 season and is virtually assured of winning his third championship.

November 8 After nearly a seven-hour rain delay, Jeff Gordon wins the finale at Atlanta for his 13th win of the season. Gordon finishes 364 points ahead of runner-up Mark Martin in the final NASCAR Winston Cup standings.

Bobby Hamilton's #4 Chevrolet battles fiercely with John Andretti's #43 STP Pontiac in the late stages of Martinsville's Goody's 500. Hamilton led 378 of the 500 laps and racked up his third career win in his first season driving for team owner Larry McClure. Andretti's bid was foiled when he ran out of fuel with six laps to go. The heartbreaking experience dropped Andretti from second to 18th in the final rundown.

The battered cars of #42 Joe Nemechek, #43 John Andretti, and #4 Bobby Hamilton tool around Talladega Superspeedway at reduced speed after a 20-car crash in the April 26 DieHard 500. NASCAR's points system encourages teams to rebuild wrecked cars to get back into the race. With an increase of three points per position from 13th place on back to last in each race, NASCAR Cup Series championships are often won by picking up points in a rebuilt race car. Hamilton accumulated an additional 30 points by advancing from 40th to 30th place in the DieHard 500.

Number 50 Randy LaJoie and #3 Dale Earnhardt tangled on the 338th lap of the May 24 Coca-Cola 600 at Charlotte Motor Speedway, knocking both cars out of the race. Earnhardt, who suffered a rib injury in a similar crash a week earlier in The Winston all-star race, climbed from his car holding his side. He refused to take the NASCAR-mandated trip to the care center in the ambulance, saying he could heal better on his own. Jeff Gordon beat Rusty Wallace in the final laps to win the 600-miler.

Dale Earnhardt and crew chief Larry McReynolds hooked up before the 1997 NASCAR Winston Cup season. McReynolds was hired by team owner Richard Childress when Andy Petree left to form his own team. McReynolds, one of the finest crew chiefs in the racing game, struggled to find chemistry with the seven-time champion. The pair won once in 45 races as a team. In June, Childress paired McReynolds with Mike Skinner, and shifted Kevin Hamlin to the Earnhardt team. Both Earnhardt and Skinner had more productive outings after the switch.

Jeff Gordon sails down the frontstretch at Indianapolis Motor Speedway en route to victory in the Brickyard 400. Gordon started third, motored into the lead on the 19th lap, and put his #24 DuPont Chevrolet on the point for most of the race. He outran runner-up Mark Martin to become the first driver to win the Brickyard 400 twice and to claim the Winston No Bull 5 $1 million bonus.

Jeff Gordon swept both road-course events on the 1998 NASCAR Winston Cup slate, prevailing at Sears Point in June and Watkins Glen in August. In the Aug. 9 The Bud At The Glen, Gordon overcame a slow pit stop, rallied from an 11-second deficit, and raced past leader Mike Skinner with four laps remaining. The victory gave Gordon an 82-point lead in the championship chase and put him in position to capture his third title in four years.

Jeff Gordon continued his hot streak in the Sept. 6 Pepsi Southern 500 at Darlington Raceway, scoring his seventh win in the last nine races. Gordon charged past Jeff Burton with 27 laps remaining and scooted away from the pack to win easily. Gordon bagged another Winston No Bull 5 $1 million bonus with his late victory gallop, and the triumph gave him a comfortable 199-point lead in the NASCAR Winston Cup standings.

Jeff Gordon rides around Darlington Raceway following a Loomis, Fargo & Co. armored car spewing million dollar bills with Gordon's likeness on them. The No Bull 5 bonus replaced the Winston Million, which had only been won twice since it debuted in 1985. The bonus was offered in five different races at five different tracks each year from 1998 to 2002. The top-five finishers at the previous designated No Bull race qualified for the next $1 million opportunity. Six drivers won the Winston No Bull 5 bonus 13 out of the 25 times it was offered, and a lucky fan also won a million dollars each time.

Short-track master Bobby Hamilton loses the grip on his #4 Chevrolet in the Sept. 27 NAPA Autocare 500 at Martinsville Speedway. Hamilton recovered from the spin and finished 14th. Ricky Rudd won the race, which was run on a terribly hot day with temperatures pushing 100 degrees. For Rudd, 1998 was the 16th consecutive season in which he had won at least one NASCAR Winston Cup event. He would not win the following season.

▲ Restrictor-plate master Dale Earnhardt runs three abreast with #4 Bobby Hamilton and #12 Jeremy Mayfield during the Oct. 11 Winston 500 at Talladega Superspeedway. Earnhardt suffered mechanical problems that relegated him to 32nd place. Hamilton finished 15th, while Mayfield placed fifth. Mayfield led the NASCAR Winston Cup points standings for four races in late spring, but a rash of mechanical problems and foul luck dropped him to seventh in the final tally.

For the first time in history, Daytona International Speedway's Pepsi 400, traditionally a midsummer classic, was run in October. The event was postponed to Oct. 17 when wildfires swept through the central Florida region. The 400-miler was also the first race presented under the new lighting system at Daytona. Jeff Gordon prevailed in a frantic three-lap shootout following a 37-minute red flag due to rain. Gordon outran Bobby Labonte to rack up his 11th win of the season. Gordon's points lead grew to 358, virtually assuring him of his third championship.

Dale Earnhardt passes #1 Steve Park in the Oct. 25 Dura Lube/Kmart 500 at Phoenix International Raceway. Park was on the sidelines for five months recuperating from a hard crash at Atlanta in March. By August, he was back behind the wheel of the #1 Pennzoil Chevrolet owned by his mentor, Dale Earnhardt. Earnhardt finished third behind winner Rusty Wallace at Phoenix as Park came home 24th.

Sterling Marlin slides his #40 Chevrolet in front of #26 Johnny Benson, Jr., during the Nov. 1 AC Delco 400 at North Carolina Speedway. Marlin recovered and finished a credible 13th. Jeff Gordon continued his winning spree at Rockingham, scoring his 12th win of the season and clinching the 1998 NASCAR Winston Cup championship.

Jeff Gordon won the rain-shortened Nov. 8 NAPA 500 at Atlanta Motor Speedway, claiming his 13th win of the year. Gordon's 13 wins were the most in a season since Richard Petty bagged 13 races in 1975. Gordon sailed to the NASCAR Winston Cup championship, finishing 362 points ahead of Mark Martin, and became the youngest three-time champion in NASCAR history.

1998 NASCAR WINSTON CUP POINTS RACE

Rank	Driver	Points	Starts	Wins	Top 5	Top 10	Winnings
1	Jeff Gordon	5328	33	13	26	28	$9,306,584
2	Mark Martin	4964	33	7	22	26	$4,309,006
3	Dale Jarrett	4619	33	3	19	22	$4,019,657
4	Rusty Wallace	4501	33	1	15	21	$2,667,889
5	Jeff Burton	4415	33	2	18	23	$2,626,987
6	Bobby Labonte	4180	33	2	11	18	$2,980,052
7	Jeremy Mayfield	4157	33	1	12	16	$2,332,034
8	Dale Earnhardt	3928	33	1	5	13	$2,990,749
9	Terry Labonte	3901	33	1	5	15	$2,054,163
10	Bobby Hamilton	3786	33	1	3	8	$2,089,566
11	John Andretti	3682	33	0	3	10	$1,838,379
12	Ken Schrader	3675	33	0	3	11	$1,887,399
13	Sterling Marlin	3530	32	0	0	6	$1,350,161
14	Jimmy Spencer	3464	31	0	3	8	$1,741,012
15	Chad Little	3423	32	0	1	7	$1,449,659
16	Ward Burton	3352	33	0	1	5	$1,516,183
17	Michael Waltrip	3340	32	0	0	5	$1,508,680
18	Bill Elliott	3305	32	0	0	5	$1,618,421
19	Ernie Irvan	3262	30	0	0	11	$1,600,452
20	Johnny Benson	3160	32	0	3	10	$1,360,335
21	Mike Skinner	3153	30	0	4	9	$1,518,901
22	Ricky Rudd	3131	33	1	1	5	$1,602,895
23	Ted Musgrave	3124	32	0	2	5	$1,253,626
24	Darrell Waltrip	2957	33	0	1	2	$1,056,475
25	Brett Bodine	2907	33	0	0	0	$1,281,673
26	Joe Nemechek	2897	32	0	1	4	$1,343,991
27	Geoff Bodine	2864	32	0	1	5	$1,247,255
28	Kenny Irwin	2760	32	0	1	4	$1,459,967
29	Dick Trickle	2678	32	0	0	1	$1,208,771
30	Kyle Petty	2675	33	0	0	2	$1,287,731
31	Kenny Wallace	2615	31	0	0	7	$1,019,861
32	Robert Pressley	2388	30	0	1	1	$996,721
33	Rick Mast	2296	30	0	0	1	$894,327
34	Steve Grissom	2215	27	0	0	2	$1,030,041
35	Kevin Lepage	2196	27	0	0	2	$852,721
36	Jerry Nadeau	2121	30	0	0	0	$804,867
37	Derrike Cope	2065	28	0	0	0	$956,980
38	Wally Dallenbach, Jr.	1832	23	0	0	3	$807,856
39	Rich Bickle	1773	21	0	1	1	$682,255
40	Jeff Green	1687	22	0	0	0	$589,841
41	Todd Bodine	1322	14	0	1	2	$378,766
42	Steve Park	1322	17	0	0	0	$487,265
43	Lake Speed	1297	16	0	0	0	$552,521
44	David Green	1014	15	0	0	0	$441,121
45	Dave Marcis	949	13	0	0	0	$444,946
46	Ricky Craven	907	11	0	0	1	$527,875
47	Morgan Shepherd	843	12	0	0	0	$364,541
48	Gary Bradberry	787	13	0	0	0	$341,307
49	Randy LaJoie	768	9	0	1	3	$336,905
50	Hut Stricklin	700	13	0	0	0	$337,106

Jeff Gordon moved past Jeremy Mayfield in late June to take the NASCAR Winston Cup points lead and left all rivals to battle over the leftovers. Gordon motored to a 364-point win to capture his third championship during the NASCAR's 50th anniversary celebration.

Gordon won 13 races, tying a modern-era mark established by Richard Petty in 1975. Mark Martin finished a distant second to Gordon, marking his third runner-up finish.

Over the course of the season, the points lead changed hands five times among four drivers before Gordon set sail. Rusty Wallace, Dale Earnhardt, and Mayfield traded the lead before Gordon assumed command.

Third-place finisher Dale Jarrett won three races during the year, but his title hopes were dashed with poor finishes at Martinsville and Charlotte in the fall.

1999

February 14 Jeff Gordon assumes command with 11 laps remaining and staves off a charge by Dale Earnhardt to win his second Daytona 500. Gordon makes the decisive pass around Rusty Wallace on the apron of the speedway.

March 7 Jeff Burton passes his brother Ward with 10 laps remaining and captures the Las Vegas 400. The siblings battle side-by-side for five full laps before Jeff is able to forge ahead. Mike Skinner takes the lead in the NASCAR Winston Cup points standings with a fourth-place finish.

March 21 Jeff Burton's crumpled Ford lies in a smoking heap on the front-stretch at Darlington Raceway as rain begins to fall, securing his victory in one of the zaniest finishes in NASCAR history. Burton is involved in a crash on lap 163, but manages to keep his car rolling until heavy rains curtail the scheduled 400-miler.

April 18 John Andretti overcomes a spinout and a lap deficit to win the Goody's 500 at Martinsville Speedway. Andretti, driving for Petty Enterprises, finishes 1.06 seconds in front of runner-up Jeff Burton to grab his second career NASCAR Winston Cup victory.

April 25 Dale Earnhardt sprints past Dale Jarrett on the final lap and racks up his eighth win at Talladega in the DieHard 500. Another of his patented late-race kicks takes Earnhardt from 16th to first in the final 50 laps.

May 30 Jeff Burton rallies past Bobby Labonte in the final 17 laps and wins the Coca-Cola 600 at Lowe's Motor Speedway. Tony Stewart makes history, finishing ninth in the Indianapolis 500 and fourth in the NASCAR 600-miler on the same day.

June 13 Dale Jarrett leads 150 of the 200 laps in the Kmart 400 at Michigan Speedway. Jarrett's 20th career win goes uninterrupted by a single caution flag. It is the first caution-free NASCAR Winston Cup event since 1997.

After scrubbing fenders with teammate Kenny Irwin, Jr., Dale Jarrett's #88 Ford lurched out of control on the 135th lap of the Feb. 14 Daytona 500. The ensuing collision involved more than a dozen cars, sidelining six, including Jarrett. Irwin, Jr., driving Robert Yates' #28 Ford, went on to finish third—his best career effort in the NASCAR Winston Cup Series.

There was plenty of three-abreast driving in the 41st running of "The Great American Race," particularly near the end. Here, #24 Jeff Gordon battles with #3 Dale Earnhardt and #99 Jeff Burton. In the closing laps, the top 12 cars were separated by less than a half second. Gordon took a risky dive to the apron to swing pst Rusty Wallace, nearly clipping the car of Ricky Rudd, who was accelerating slowly after a pit stop. The daring move propelled Gordon into the lead, which he never gave up. Earnhardt finished a close second. "You've gotta do what you've gotta do to win the Daytona 500," said Gordon, who won the event for a second time.

Jeff Gordon's #24 Chevrolet pairs up with Bobby Labonte's #18 Pontiac, while the duo of #6 Mark Martin and #88 Dale Jarrett look for an opening at Rockingham's Feb. 21 Dura Lube/Kmart 400. Martin won the 400-miler, leading the final 36 laps. Jarrett placed second with Labonte third. Gordon departed with an engine failure in the final 100 miles.

Rookie Tony Stewart's battered #20 Pontiac and Robert Pressley's #77 Ford rest on the apron of Bristol Motor Speedway after a multicar entanglement in the April 11 Food City 500. Number 58 Ricky Craven and #71 Dave Marcis pass safely to the high side, as #24 Jeff Gordon attempts to resume the chase. Gordon managed to rebound to finish sixth, while Stewart slipped to 15th. Rusty Wallace started on the pole and won the race.

Kenny Irwin, Jr.'s #28 Ford climbs the pit wall after colliding with Jimmy Spencer and Tony Stewart in the April 18 Goody's Body Pain 500 at Martinsville Speedway. Irwin, Jr., slid in front of Spencer, triggering the crash, but he was able to get back into the race to finish 36th. A gifted driver with an open-wheel background, Irwin, Jr., had flashes of brilliance in his second season with the Robert Yates team but never produced the lofty numbers the team expected. He was released the following season.

John Andretti and The King, Richard Petty, enjoy the victory lane ceremonies following Andretti's come-from-behind win at Martinsville. Andretti spun out in the early laps, but battled back from a one-lap deficit. Driving the Petty Enterprises Pontiac, Andretti raced past Jeff Burton with four laps remaining to record the win. It was Andretti's second career NASCAR Winston Cup victory, and it came at the track where team owner Petty had won 15 times in his illustrious career.

Dale Earnhardt leads Jeff Gordon in the early stages of the April 25 DieHard 500 at Talladega Superspeedway. Earnhardt drove his familiar #3 Goodwrench Chevrolet to victory to end a 14-month winless stretch. Gordon was involved in a 49th-lap incident on the backstretch when Mike Skinner crowded Tony Stewart off the track, triggering a huge pileup. Gordon brushed Skinner and slid across the track. For Earnhardt, it was his 72nd career NASCAR Winston Cup triumph.

Dale Earnhardt leads his son Dale Earnhardt, Jr., in the May 30 Coca-Cola 600 at Lowe's Motor Speedway. The younger Earnhardt, a third-generation NASCAR driver, was making his first start in stock car racing's elite series. He performed well, qualifying eighth and finishing 16th. The elder Earnhardt started 15th and finished sixth. Jeff Burton won the race, nosing out runner-up Bobby Labonte. In a blockbuster move, Bruton Smith, chairman of Charlotte Motor Speedway, changed the name of his 1½-mile track to Lowe's Motor Speedway prior to the 1999 season, making it the first NASCAR facility to take on a corporate sponsor's name.

1999

August 7 Title-bound Dale Jarrett enjoys a trouble-free ride in the Brickyard 400 at Indianapolis Motor Speedway and pockets $712,240 for his fourth win of the season. Jarrett's victory puts him 274 points ahead of Mark Martin in the NASCAR Winston Cup championship chase.

August 28 Dale Earnhardt knocks leader Terry Labonte into a spin on the final lap and wins the Goody's 500 at Bristol. It is Earnhardt's second win of the season.

September 11 Rookie Tony Stewart leads 333 of the 400 laps and dominates the Exide Batteries 400 at Richmond International Raceway. It is the first NASCAR Winston Cup win for the talented freshman driver. Bobby Labonte, Stewart's stablemate on the Joe Gibbs team, finishes second.

September 19 Joe Nemechek pulls a shocking upset by winning the Dura Lube/Kmart 300 at New Hampshire International Speedway. It is Nemechek's first career NASCAR Winston Cup win and the first victory for team owner Felix Sabates since 1995.

October 17 Dale Earnhardt comes from the 27th starting spot to win the Winston 500 at Talladega Superspeedway in the final laps. Earnhardt squeezes past Dale Jarrett with four laps remaining and nabs his 74th career NASCAR Winston Cup triumph.

November 14 Tony Stewart breezes to an easy 5.2-second victory over Bobby Labonte in the first NASCAR Winston Cup event at Homestead-Miami Speedway. It is Stewart's third win of the season, the most victories for a rookie driver since 1965 when Dick Hutcherson won nine times.

November 21 Bobby Labonte comes from a provisional starting spot to win the season-ending NAPA 500 at Atlanta Motor Speedway. Dale Jarrett finishes second and wraps up his first NASCAR Winston Cup championship by a 201-point margin over Labonte.

Bill Elliott pushes his #94 Ford down the frontstretch at Dover Downs International Speedway in the June 6 MBNA Platinum 400. Elliott campaigned his self-owned Ford since 1995 with only moderate success. e failed to post a single victory driving his own machinery, but was a contender in several events. Elliott ran 12th at Dover, a race that was won by Bobby Labonte. The lack of success didn't sour his fans. Elliott was still named NASCAR's most popular driver every year from 1991 to 2000.

▲ Number 88 Dale Jarrett puts a lap on Yates Racing stablemate #28 Kenny Irwin, Jr., in the June 13 Kmart 400 at Michigan Speedway. Jarrett romped to an easy victory. The NASCAR points leader assumed command on the 53rd lap and never relinquished the lead. Jarrett took the NASCAR Winston Cup points lead in mid May and never gave up the top spot. He went on to capture his first championship by 201 points over Bobby Labonte.

◀ Dale Jarrett hugs the low line at Indianapolis Motor Speedway during the sixth annual running of the Brickyard 400. The Aug. 7 event was another notch in Jarrett's holster. He dominated the 400-miler, leading 116 of the final 121 laps on the rectangular 2½-mile track. It was Jarrett's second win in the midsummer classic, and it padded his NASCAR Winston Cup lead to 274 points. Bobby Labonte ran second in the Brickyard 400, followed by Jeff Gordon and Mark Martin.

Jeremy Mayfield's #12 Ford runs just ahead of #3 Dale Earnhardt and Michael Waltrip in the middle stages of the Brickyard 400. Earnhardt, winner of the event in 1995, started 18th and climbed to 10th when the checkered flag fell. Mayfield dropped a lap off the pace and wound up 29th. Waltrip qualified a strong fifth, but drifted back to a 27th-place finish.

▶ Mark Martin drives onto the slick racing surface during a practice session at Watkins Glen International prior to the Aug. 15 Frontier At The Glen. Goodyear had developed a special treaded rain tire for use on a road course in inclement weather. Racing in the rain is impossible on high-speed ovals but makes for an interesting possibility on a road course. The competitors used the rain tires in practice, but NASCAR chose to cancel qualifying and start the field in order of points earned.

Sibling Rivalries

JEFF AND WARD BURTON finished first and second in three NASCAR Winston Cup events in 1999. Each time, Jeff led his older brother Ward across the finish line—at Las Vegas, Darlington, and Rockingham.

Sibling rivalry has been present in NASCAR's premier stock car racing series since the pioneer days. The first time brothers finished first and second occurred in the 10th NASCAR Grand National event ever run. On April 2, 1950, Tim Flock finished first in a 100-miler at the old Charlotte

Speedway, just ahead of runner-up Bob Flock. In the history of NASCAR, brothers have taken the first two positions 25 times. Tim and Fonty Flock were the top two in eight of those races.

NASCAR has never witnessed a 1-2-3 finish for brothers, but it almost happened on Aug. 25, 1951. In a 100-mile NASCAR Grand National race at Greenville-Pickens Speedway, Bob Flock won with Tim in hot pursuit. Fonty came in fourth. Only third-place finisher Buck Baker interrupted the flock of Flocks from taking the first three spots. No family has come close again.

Brothers Finishing First and Second

No.	Date	Site	Track	Winner	Second
1	4/2/50	Charlotte, N.C.	Charlotte Speedway	Tim Flock	Bob Flock
2	4/8/51	Mobile, Ala.	Lakeview Speedway	Tim Flock	Fonty Flock
3	4/29/51	North Wilkesboro, N.C.	North Wilkesboro Speedway	Fonty Flock	Tim Flock
4	8/25/51	Greenville, S.C.	Greenville-Pickens Speedway	Bob Flock	Tim Flock
5	9/30/51	Wilson, N.C.	Wilson County Speedway	Fonty Flock	Bob Flock
6	11/11/51	Atlanta, Ga.	Lakewood Speedway	Tim Flock	Bob Flock
7	6/8/52	Hillsboro, N.C.	Occoneechee Speedway	Tim Flock	Fonty Flock
8	8/17/52	Weaverville, N.C.	Asheville-Weaverville Speedway	Bob Flock	Tim Flock
9	4/18/54	Hillsboro, N.C.	Orange Speedway	Herb Thomas	Donald Thomas
10	5/2/55	Richmond, Va.	Richmond Fairgrounds Raceway	Tim Flock	Fonty Flock
11	6/17/55	Rochester, N.Y.	Monroe County Speedway	Tim Flock	Fonty Flock
12	7/6/55	Spartanburg, S.C.	Piedmont Interstate Fairgrounds	Tim Flock	Fonty Flock
13	7/10/55	Weaverville, N.C.	Asheville-Weaverville Speedway	Tim Flock	Fonty Flock
14	11/20/55	Charlotte, N.C.	Charlotte Speedway	Fonty Flock	Tim Flock
15	6/16/68	Rockingham, N.C.	North Carolina Motor Speedway	Donnie Allison	Bobby Allison
16	10/12/69	Charlotte, N.C.	Charlotte Motor Speedway	Donnie Allison	Bobby Allison
17	4/5/70	Bristol, Tenn.	Bristol International Speedway	Donnie Allison	Bobby Allison
18	5/16/71	Talladega, Ala.	Alabama International Motor Speedway	Donnie Allison	Bobby Allison
19	5/30/71	Charlotte, N.C.	Charlotte Motor Speedway	Bobby Allison	Donnie Allison
20	5/28/95	Charlotte, N.C.	Charlotte Motor Speedway	Bobby Labonte	Terry Labonte
21	8/20/95	Brooklyn, Mich.	Michigan International Speedway	Bobby Labonte	Terry Labonte
22	10/12/97	Talladega, Ala.	Talladega Superspeedway	Terry Labonte	Bobby Labonte
23	3/7/99	Las Vegas, Nev.	Las Vegas Motor Speedway	Jeff Burton	Ward Burton
24	9/5/99	Darlington, S.C.	Darlington Raceway	Jeff Burton	Ward Burton
25	10/24/99	Rockingham, N.C.	North Carolina Speedway	Jeff Burton	Ward Burton

Johnny Benson, Jr., spins his #26 Ford in the inner loop at Watkins Glen International. The spin knocked Benson, Jr., out of contention, and he eventually finished 38th. Jeff Gordon won the race, his record fifth in a row on a road course. Ron Fellows, a road-racing specialist making an infrequent NASCAR appearance, finished second.

▲ Bobby Labonte leads Jeff Gordon to the finish line before a packed house in Michigan Speedway's Aug. 22 Pepsi 400 Presented by Meijer. Labonte snatched the lead from Dale Earnhardt with 17 laps remaining and outran Gordon by less than a second to post his fourth win of the season. Labonte's pass was daring, as he scampered around Earnhardt and Gordon on the high side in one fell swoop to grab the lead for keeps.

Dale Earnhardt zeroes in on the rear bumper of Terry Labonte in the waning laps of the Aug. 28 Goody's Headache Powder 500 at Bristol Motor Speedway. Labonte raced past Earnhardt just before the white flag and took a high line through the first and second turns, staying as far away from Earnhardt as possible. Earnhardt darted into Labonte's rear bumper anyway, spinning him out. Earnhardt went on to win his second race of the season. "I wasn't trying to wreck him. I just wanted to rattle his cage," Earnhardt said as he was loudly booed during the winner's interview.

Talented rookie driver Tony Stewart pumps his fist out the window after scoring his first career NASCAR Winston Cup victory in the Sept. 11 Exide NASCAR Select Batteries 400 at Richmond International Raceway. Stewart led 333 of the 400 laps and held off a late challenge by Bobby Labonte to post his first victory in his 25th career start.

Tony Stewart and Kenny Irwin, Jr., tangled three times during the Oct. 3 NAPA Auto-care 500 at Martinsville Speedway. Stewart finally spun when Irwin, Jr., rapped his rear bumper. After exiting his car, Stewart tossed his heel pads at Irwin and tried to climb inside the rolling #28 Ford to further "discuss" the incident. Stewart settled for 41st in the final order. Jeff Gordon won the race in his first start with new crew chief Brian Whitesell. Ray Evernham left the successful Hendrick Motorsports operation to form his own team for the Dodge factory effort that would debut in 2001.

Dale Earnhardt, Jr., won his second straight NASCAR Busch Series championship in 1999, and had his eyes focused on entering NASCAR Winston Cup racing on a full-time basis in 2000. The third-generation driver competed in five NASCAR Winston Cup events in '99 with one top-10 finish. Having signed a long-term contract with Budweiser, Earnhardt, Jr., would race a #8 Chevrolet for DEI Racing in 2000.

1999 NASCAR WINSTON CUP POINTS RACE

Rank	Driver	Points	Starts	Wins	Top 5	Top 10	Winnings
1	Dale Jarrett	5262	34	4	24	29	$6,649,596
2	Bobby Labonte	5061	34	5	23	26	$4,763,615
3	Mark Martin	4943	34	2	19	26	$3,509,744
4	Tony Stewart	4774	34	3	12	21	$3,190,149
5	Jeff Burton	4733	34	6	18	23	$5,725,399
6	Jeff Gordon	4620	34	7	18	21	$5,858,633
7	Dale Earnhardt	4492	34	3	7	21	$3,048,236
8	Rusty Wallace	4155	34	1	7	16	$2,454,050
9	Ward Burton	4062	34	0	6	16	$2,405,913
10	Mike Skinner	4003	34	0	5	14	$2,499,877
11	Jeremy Mayfield	3743	34	0	5	12	$2,125,227
12	Terry Labonte	3580	34	1	1	7	$2,475,365
13	Bobby Hamilton	3564	34	0	1	10	$2,019,255
14	Steve Park	3481	34	0	0	5	$1,767,690
15	Ken Schrader	3479	34	0	0	6	$1,939,147
16	Sterling Marlin	3397	34	2	2	5	$1,797,416
17	John Andretti	3394	34	1	3	10	$2,001,832
18	Wally Dallenbach, Jr.	3367	34	0	1	6	$1,741,176
19	Kenny Irwin, Jr.	3338	34	0	2	6	$2,125,810
20	Jimmy Spencer	3312	34	0	2	4	$1,752,299
21	Bill Elliott	3246	34	0	1	2	$1,624,101
22	Kenny Wallace	3210	34	0	3	5	$1,416,208
23	Chad Little	3193	34	0	0	5	$1,623,976
24	Elliott Sadler	3191	34	0	0	1	$1,589,221
25	Kevin Lepage	3185	34	0	1	2	$1,587,841
26	Kyle Petty	3103	32	0	0	9	$1,278,953
27	Geoff Bodine	3053	34	0	1	2	$1,257,494
28	Johnny Benson	3012	34	0	0	2	$1,567,668
29	Michael Waltrip	2974	34	0	1	3	$1,701,160
30	Joe Nemechek	2956	34	1	1	3	$1,634,946
31	Ricky Rudd	2922	34	0	3	5	$1,632,011
32	Rick Mast	2845	34	0	0	2	$1,290,143
33	Ted Musgrave	2689	32	0	0	2	$1,162,403
34	Jerry Nadeau	2686	34	0	1	2	$1,370,229
35	Brett Bodine	2351	32	0	0	0	$1,321,396
36	David Green	2320	32	0	0	0	$1,079,536
37	Darrell Waltrip	2158	27	0	0	0	$973,133
38	Rich Bickle	2149	24	0	0	2	$892,456
39	Robert Pressley	2050	28	0	0	0	$1,033,223
40	Ernie Irvan	1915	21	0	0	5	$1,073,775
41	Ricky Craven	1513	24	0	0	0	$853,835
42	Dave Marcis	1324	20	0	0	0	$731,221
43	Hut Stricklin	918	10	0	0	1	$378,942
44	Derrike Cope	915	15	0	0	0	$617,976
45	Buckshot Jones	676	10	0	0	0	$345,128
46	Todd Bodine	529	7	0	0	0	$208,382
47	Dick Trickle	528	9	0	0	0	$275,364
48	Dale Earnhardt, Jr.	500	5	0	0	1	$162,095
49	Matt Kenseth	434	5	0	1	1	$143,561
50	Steve Grissom	336	6	0	0	0	$193,529

Dale Jarrett moved into the NASCAR Winston Cup points lead in May with a victory at Richmond and never gave a backward glance as he stormed to his first championship. Jarrett won four races during the 34-race campaign and finished 201 points ahead of runner-up Bobby Labonte.

Jarrett became the second second-generation driver to reach the pinnacle of NASCAR Winston Cup stock car racing. He and his father Ned joined Lee and Richard Petty as the only father-son combinations to wear the championship crown.

Labonte won five races en route to the runner-up spot in the championship chase. Two-time winner Mark Martin came in third. Jeff Gordon won the most races, with seven, but finished sixth in the final tally.

Jarrett gave team owner Robert Yates his first career NASCAR Winston Cup championship.

2000s: The New Millennium

NASCAR Winston Cup Series racing experienced tremendous growth throughout the 1990s with record attendance and increased television ratings. The new millennium promised continued interest of epic proportions. *Sports Illustrated*, once considered strictly a stick-and-ball sports weekly, began to issue a number of annual special editions focused entirely on NASCAR stock car racing. NASCAR also made the covers of several publications that you would least expect, including *Forbes* and *The Wall Street Journal*. Clearly, NASCAR was America's hottest sport.

Strong and steady administration guided NASCAR's development. By the end of 1999, negotiations were under way to revamp the entire television package. Incumbents CBS, ABC, ESPN, and TNN would have to dole out millions, perhaps even billions, to retain rights to keep their networks firmly planted in NASCAR's landscape.

From the time television networks developed an interest in NASCAR, each track sold its own television rights for each race, a scattershot process that resulted in NASCAR races being aired on several different networks and cable systems. In the negotiations, NASCAR required that, starting with the 2001 season, it would have a unified television package with the sanctioning body as the nucleus and more events aired on the major networks.

On Nov. 11, 1999, NASCAR announced that FOX and NBC had landed the multibillion-dollar television package, with a number of races to be televised on the TNT cable system and FOX cable affiliates. Under the new pact, NASCAR would distribute television revenues on an individual event basis, with 65 percent of the funds going to the tracks, 25 percent to race purses, and 10 percent to NASCAR. The agreement, which went into effect in 2001, offered nearly a 500-percent increase in revenue compared to the old method. "The important thing is that this process elevates NASCAR as a true professional sport against other professional sports," said NASCAR president Mike Helton. "This tells the world what our fans have believed for a long time."

Left out were incumbents, CBS, ABC, and ESPN, along with CBS' cable outlet TNN, but each would continue to honor their agreements through the 2000 season as lame-duck networks. CBS and ABC had been NASCAR's flagship networks since the early 1960s. FOX had never aired a live NASCAR race and NBC hadn't been in the picture since tape-delayed coverage in '85. "It is unfortunate we couldn't figure out how to include everybody going forward," added Helton, "but we think we did the right package for everybody, the fans in particular, the promoters, and the competitors."

The opening events of the 2000 season at Daytona showed that side-by-side competition and the thrill-a-minute exploits on the track were no longer what they used to be. The enhanced aerodynamic packages that NASCAR premier series

teams used and the new, dreaded term "aero-push" (the turbulence that affects trailing cars, causing them to push up the track in turns) had made passing difficult. Neither Twin 125 featured a single lead change, and the Daytona 500 recorded only nine lead changes—a far cry from the 50-60 lead changes seen a quarter century earlier. In the Daytona 500, only four on-track lead changes occurred under green-flag conditions. Dale Jarrett scored his second Daytona 500 win, passing Johnny Benson, Jr., with four laps remaining. Once passed, Benson was a sitting duck outside the train of cars following Jarrett, and he drifted to a 12th-place finish.

The lack of door-to-door competition in NASCAR's premier event underscored a disturbing trend. From 1997 to 2000, there were only 14 lead changes in the Daytona 500. By contrast, in '74, 21 lead changes took place in the first 100 miles. In the return trip to Daytona in July 2000, the lead changed hands only 10 times, six of them occurring during pit stops. With the multibillion-dollar contract with the new television networks just a few months away, NASCAR officials knew they needed to address the issue.

In an effort to increase on-track competition, NASCAR issued a new set of rules for the Oct. 15, 2000, Talladega race. A small blade was attached to the roofs of all the cars, creating "dirty air" that flowed over the top of the vehicles. The blade made the cars less stable, thus reacquainting drivers with the nervy and tedious aspects of superspeedway racing known to drivers years earlier.

The 500-miler at Talladega turned out to be the most exciting event of the 2000 campaign. Dale Earnhardt, who started 20th, whipped his Chevrolet into the lead by the 15th lap. The lead swapped hands throughout the race. In the closing laps, more than half of the starting field was in contention for victory.

With less than 10 laps to go, Earnhardt got shuffled back to the rear of the lead pack. He was barely running in the top 20 and seemed hopelessly out of the hunt. Faced with insurmountable odds, Earnhardt slashed his way through the field, taking a center line in the three-abreast formation, and blasted to the lead with two laps to go. Earnhardt kept the gaggle of challengers at bay and rode under the checkered flag as spectators cheered wildly. Earnhardt's high-speed, flawless drive became an instant magical moment in NASCAR's glorious history. The race had 49 official lead changes, the most in a NASCAR premier series race in 11 years. The drivers still voiced their displeasure with restrictor-plate racing, but the Talladega race was one for the ages.

Aerodynamic rules identical to Talladega remained in place for the 2001 Daytona 500. Joining the Ford, Chevrolet, and Pontiac contingent was a fleet of Dodge Intrepids, the first time the Dodge nameplate had been active in NASCAR Winston Cup Series racing since 1985. Ray Evernham, who had served as Jeff Gordon's tutor and crew chief during his

ascent to the elite of NASCAR racing, was the fulcrum of Dodge's development program, which was announced in March 2000. Testing began in the summer, and by the time Speedweeks 2001 got under way, five teams and 10 Dodges were sprinkled throughout the Daytona 500 field.

Dodges swept the front row in qualifying as Bill Elliott and Stacy Compton turned in the quickest time-trial runs. Sterling Marlin won the opening Twin 125-mile qualifying race in his Dodge, passing Dale Earnhardt on the final lap. The testing program had proven successful for the MoPar teams, and their on-track performance showed they would have to be reckoned with in the upcoming season.

With the new television deal in place, FOX Sports covered virtually every aspect of Daytona's Speedweeks. Practice sessions, qualifying, preliminary events for a variety of divisions, and the NASCAR Winston Cup events were all televised. Nearly 40 hours of TV coverage marked a successful debut for FOX. The Twin 125-mile qualifiers were aired live for the first time ever. The qualifying races produced 21 lead changes, the most since 1982.

In the Daytona 500, swarms of cars battled throughout the race. In one of the most spectacular 500s in memory, the lead changed hands 49 times, the most in 20 years. On the 174th lap, Robby Gordon snagged the rear bumper of Ward Burton, triggering a massive 19-car crash on the backstretch. Tony Stewart went airborne, but escaped injury. The red flag came out while workers cleared the debris off the track.

When the race resumed, Michael Waltrip, never a winner in his 462-race career, was battling Dale Earnhardt, Jr., and Dale Earnhardt for the lead. Waltrip and the younger Earnhardt were driving cars fielded by Dale Earnhardt, Inc. Sterling Marlin, whose Dodge dropped almost a lap behind due to an unscheduled pit stop, found himself back in the hunt following the big crash. Marlin was a real threat, and the elder Earnhardt kept Marlin busy with a personal battle as the two DEI cars scampered away from the field.

Entering the final lap, Waltrip led Earnhardt, Jr., off the fourth turn. Then, pandemonium broke loose behind them. The cars were battling three-abreast and Earnhardt squeezed a tad low while battling Marlin for third place. The two touched and Earnhardt's Chevrolet darted toward the outside retaining wall, collecting Ken Schrader's Pontiac in the process. Earnhardt clobbered the wall nearly head-on. Waltrip bolted under the checkered flag as Earnhardt's skidding car came to a halt inside the fourth turn.

Waltrip, whose career had been revitalized when Earnhardt signed him in late 2000, finally removed the goose egg from his personal victory column with the Daytona 500 victory. Earnhardt, Jr., finished second, giving the DEI cars the first two positions. It was supposed to be a joyous occasion, but something had gone terribly wrong in that final-lap crash.

Emergency workers cut the top off Earnhardt's car and administered aid to the stricken driver. He was transported to the hospital and was pronounced dead at 5:16 P.M. The life of NASCAR's most dynamic hero had passed. The official announcement came nearly two hours later when NASCAR president Mike Helton, who had taken over the position in the off-season, uttered the words nobody wanted to hear: "Today . . . we lost Dale Earnhardt."

Earnhardt's death was the fourth in a nine-month period in NASCAR's top three racing divisions. Adam Petty lost his life in a NASCAR Busch Series practice crash at New Hampshire in May 2000. Kenny Irwin, Jr., died in NASCAR Winston Cup practice at the same track in July. Tony Roper was killed in a NASCAR Craftsman Truck Series race at Texas in October. All four drivers died of basal skull fractures, and safety issues immediately became paramount. Within several weeks, all drivers were required to wear the HANS device, a safety collar designed to prevent the head from snapping forward in a head-on accident. Other safety-awareness programs followed as NASCAR reacted to the death of its top star.

The Daytona 500 television viewership was fantastic, drawing a 10.0 Nielsen rating and easily winning its time slot. The 10.0 rating was the highest since the 1979 Daytona 500 televised by CBS, which topped the all-time NASCAR charts with a 10.5. Much of the success was attributed to the heavy advertising aired during other FOX Sports shows.

Following Earnhardt's tragic demise, team owner Richard Childress hired NASCAR Busch Series driver Kevin Harvick to take the wheel of the Goodwrench Chevrolet. Driving the #29 Chevy, Harvick nosed out Jeff Gordon in a thriller in Atlanta in just his third career NASCAR premier series start. The ghost of Dale Earnhardt remained prominent. "There was somebody in the car making it go a lot better than I was," declared Harvick.

Waltrip and Harvick provided two fresh faces in victory lane in the season's first four races. Elliott Sadler scored his first career win at Bristol in the sixth event of the 2001 campaign, giving the Wood Brothers their first NASCAR premier series win since 1993. Ricky Craven completed a successful comeback from injuries with his first win at Martinsville in autumn. And Robby Gordon nabbed his first win in the season finale at New Hampshire. Overall, the 2001 season featured five first-time winners, the most since 1966.

Sterling Marlin ushered in Dodge's first NASCAR premier series win since 1977 when he took the checkered flag at Michigan in August. Two new magnificent speed fortresses joined the growing list of venues in 2001. Harvick won the inaugural event at the Chicagoland Speedway south of Chicago and Jeff Gordon christened victory lane in the first NASCAR premier series race at Kansas Speedway.

During the year's first half, FOX telecasts recorded the highest ratings in the history of NASCAR coverage. For all NASCAR Winston Cup races televised in the first half of the 2001 season, FOX Sports and its cable affiliate FX combined to average a 5.3 rating, a hefty 29-percent increase over the same races a year earlier. In its inaugural season, NASCAR and FOX race telecasts reached an average of 19.9 million viewers, more than a million more than in 2000.

NBC picked up the television coverage in July and the ratings bonanza continued. Despite rain delays and rainouts, NBC's average ratings for the second half of the season were 3.9, 34 percent higher than the 2001 telecasts. "The 2001 campaign was certainly a breakthrough year for NASCAR," said Paul Brooks, president of NASCAR Media Group/senior vice president for NASCAR. "Looking back, it was the first time in our history that our broadcast partners treated us like a national franchise and the results were significant. Our broadcast partners brought incredible production values to showcase our sport in the way we had never seen before. Lower camera angles, new sound technology, and global positioning technology brought the fans closer to the action. Most importantly, FOX/FX and NBC/TNT were able to serve our core fans while attracting a generation of new fans."

Thirty-year-old Jeff Gordon won his fourth NASCAR premier series title in 2001, making him the youngest four-time champion in NASCAR history. A record 44 drivers topped the million-dollar earnings mark during the year, with Gordon pocketing $10,879,757 in winnings. Nineteen different drivers won races, matching an all-time standard in professional stock car racing.

The 2002 season dawned with promise. The television agreement signed in late 1999 stipulated that FOX and NBC would alternate covering the Daytona 500. So, NBC televised "The Great American Race" for the first time. The aero package that was used in 2001 was no longer in place, having been scrapped due to safety concerns in the wake of the Earnhardt crash.

Despite the new rules, the Daytona 500 was a thrilling event, although it was punctuated by crashes that sidelined eight cars and crippled at least 25 others. The first big accident occurred on the 149th lap when second-place

Harvick attempted to squeeze back in line and clipped the front of Jeff Gordon's car. The crash gobbled up 20 cars, most of which were in contention. Another scramble in the closing laps took Gordon out of the lead, when he spun after trying to shut the door on Sterling Marlin. When the two lead cars touched, the front fender of Marlin's Dodge was pressed onto the right front tire. NASCAR officials brought the field to a halt to ensure a green-flag finish.

When the cars crept to a halt on the backstretch with five laps to go, leader Marlin got out of his car and pried the fender off the tire, a violation of NASCAR rules that prohibit any work from being done on a car during a red flag. He was black-flagged upon the restart and was lucky to charge back into the top 10 during the final four-lap dash to the finish.

Ward Burton, who missed being involved in both collisions by paper-thin margins, took the lead when Marlin was flagged to the pits, then held off a surge by Elliott Sadler to win the Daytona 500. It was the first win for Dodge in the premier NASCAR event since 1974. "The pivotal point was missing the first big crash," said Burton. "I knew Harvick was going to slide up the track, so I cut hard left and got sideways. The back of his car missed the nose of mine by about a foot. I was lucky to get my car under control." NBC's ratings for the annual Speedweeks finale were an all-time record of 10.9.

NASCAR's new breed of rookie drivers dominated many of the headlines during the early months of 2002. Jimmie Johnson, who joined the formidable Hendrick Motorsports Chevrolet team after a NASCAR Busch Series tenure with only spotted success, won the pole for the Daytona 500. In April, Johnson's 13th NASCAR premier series start netted him a victory at California Speedway.

Ryan Newman, a rookie on the Roger Penske team, was also making a name for himself. A noted quick qualifier, Newman was knocking on the door nearly every outing. His perseverance paid off with a win in NASCAR's all-star race in May. Newman held off Dale Earnhardt, Jr., in a stirring finish that underscored his destiny as one of NASCAR's future lead drivers.

The chase for the 2002 NASCAR Winston Cup crown was one of the tightest in years. Sterling Marlin led the standings from February through late September, but in the closing weeks, any driver in the top 10 had a legitimate shot at the championship. Tony Stewart, on probation for a series of incidents off the track, rallied from a big deficit to loom as a title threat. Marlin, Mark Martin, Jeff Gordon, Matt Kenseth, sophomore Kurt Busch, and rookies Johnson and Newman provided a cluster of contenders in the final weeks.

Marlin's hopes were dashed by hard licks at Richmond and Kansas. He was forced to sit out the final events to recuperate from a neck injury. Chip Ganassi tapped Jamie McMurray, a NASCAR Busch Series regular, to replace Marlin in his #40 Dodge. McMurray finished 26th in his NASCAR premier series debut at Talladega as Stewart took the points lead with a runner-up finish. A week later, the 26-year-old McMurray stunned onlookers with a triumph at Lowe's Motor Speedway. It was McMurray's second career start, and he became the quickest winner at NASCAR's top level since Johnny Rutherford won his first start at Daytona in 1963.

Kurt Busch, a natural behind the wheel who came to NASCAR Winston Cup racing after a single season in the NASCAR Craftsman Truck Series, won three of the final five races. In the season finale at Homestead, Fla., Busch won by passing Newman in the final 11 laps, and Stewart won the championship by lumbering to an 18th-place finish. Stewart edged Mark Martin by 38 points. Youthful exuberance had the upper hand on crafty veterans as the season closed. Network ratings were solid, though they fell just short of the record levels of 2001.

The 2003 NASCAR campaign was marked by change. R.J. Reynolds, title sponsor of the NASCAR Winston Cup Series since 1971, announced it would bow out after 33 years if NASCAR could find a proper suitor. In June, Nextel Communications signed a pact with NASCAR to become the title sponsor beginning with the 2004 season. Winston had helped guide the sport to the lofty status it enjoys today, but increasing pressure on tobacco companies to halt racing sponsorships led R.J. Reynolds to sever ties with NASCAR. Nextel, a young, aggressive company, was viewed as a company with the marketing expertise to take NASCAR deeper into the nation's mainstream.

In October 2003, NASCAR chairman Bill France, Jr., turned over the reins of the sport to his 41-year-old son Brian. There was even talk of changing the points system for the first time in nearly 30 years. Also in October, Pontiac announced it wouldn't return in 2004, leaving Chevrolet as the lone GM marque on the tour. NASCAR also announced the beginning of its scheduling realignment effective in 2004, with California Speedway taking the traditional Labor Day weekend Southern 500 from Darlington after 54 years.

Meanwhile, the action on the speedways was hot and heavy. Michael Waltrip dodged a couple of big accidents to prevail in the rain-shortened season-opening Daytona 500. In the next eight races, eight different drivers racked up victories, including Ricky Craven, who nosed out Kurt Busch in Darlington's spring 400-miler. Craven, driver of the #32 PPI car owned by Cal Wells III, was a single-car team. Given little chance against the heavily funded multicar teams, Craven's triumph at Darlington was a shot in the arm for the little guys.

Craven and Busch swapped the lead four times in the final three laps. As the pair whipped off the fourth turn on the final lap, Craven's Pontiac and Busch's Ford fused together. The cars rubbed against each other the length of the frontstretch—even after the checkered flag had fallen. Craven prevailed by 0.002 second—about two inches—in

what was the closest finish on record since NASCAR began using electronic transponders in 1993.

By late March, Matt Kenseth had parlayed consistency into a healthy points lead. In 2002, Kenseth won more races than any other driver, but finished a distant eighth in the final points standings. The capable Wisconsin driver adjusted his plan of attack in '03. While winning only once, the smooth-and-steady Kenseth was remarkably consistent, clicking off top-10 finishes in bundles. By July, Kenseth's lead was more than 200 points.

With Kenseth in control, sophomore Ryan Newman was giving new meaning to the old slogan "the thrill of victory and the agony of defeat." Newman began the 2003 campaign with a wicked tumble in the Daytona 500, then performed a bone-jarring encore at Talladega in April and was involved in a fiery, noncontact incident at Michigan in June. The crashes left Newman hopelessly behind in the points race.

But Newman hit stride by summer, winning six races in a 13-event stretch. The former USAC open-wheel icon won twice as many races as any other driver on the 2003 NASCAR Winston Cup tour. Newman seemingly dominated, but he was a nonplayer in the title chase. Meanwhile, Kenseth's consistency became impossible to overcome. His points lead grew to 436 in mid September by clicking off one top-10 finish after another. It turned out to be a cushion Kenseth would need to secure the title. In the final eight races of the year, Kenseth suffered a pair of DNFs and crashed at Kansas. His final margin of victory was 90 points over sophomore Jimmie Johnson, who was white-hot during the final stretch.

The 2004 NASCAR campaign was punctuated by an additional flurry of radical changes. Under the direction of new chairman Brian Z. France, NASCAR's movement from the Southeast to the West hit full stride. Rockingham's North Carolina Speedway hosted its final race and the venerable Darlington Raceway staged the final Southern 500. Meanwhile, the Phoenix and Texas tracks each acquired a second race date for the '05 season.

NASCAR's most high-profile change for 2004 was the "Chase for the NASCAR NEXTEL Cup," which called for the top 10 drivers after the season's first 26 races to compete in a final 10-race "Chase." The Chase worked according to NASCAR's plan, with the championship coming down to the final lap of the season. Kurt Busch's eight-point margin of victory over Jimmie Johnson was the closest in NASCAR's 56-year history. Near the end of the Chase, television ratings surged upward nearly 30 percent from 2003.

The Chase didn't go exactly as hoped in 2005, as two of NASCAR's biggest stars, Jeff Gordon and Dale Earnhardt, Jr., failed to qualify. Nonetheless, the competition for the title was exciting. Tony Stewart trailed a game Jimmie Johnson early in the season, then poured it on midyear, winning five of seven races during a particularly dominant stretch. The title wasn't decided until the final race, though. Stewart held on for a 15th-place finish in the last race of the year at Homestead-Miami Speedway, placing just 35 points ahead of Greg Biffle and Carl Edwards for the title.

While Stewart drove for Joe Gibbs Racing, all five of Roush Racing's full-time teams qualified for the Chase. Roush's dominance didn't sit well with NASCAR, and by the end of the year, the sanctioning body had announced that no owner would be allowed to field more than four full-time teams starting in 2006. Roush would be grandfathered for the remainder of existing sponsor contracts, but after that, four would be the limit.

The team limit was the second team-related rule within a year. After the 2004 season, NASCAR announced that the top 35 teams in the points standings would be guaranteed a spot in the starting lineup for each '05 race, no matter how they qualified. This franchise-style system protects the NASCAR NEXTEL Cup Series' regular competitors while making inroads for part-timers increasingly difficult. The aggressive changes, Brian France claimed, allow NASCAR to keep abreast with other major league sporting organizations, particularly the NFL.

The 2005 season witnessed the end of one of NASCAR's most successful careers. Rusty Wallace, NASCAR's eighth winningest driver, retired after qualifying for the Chase and finishing eighth overall. The photogenic Wallace went on to become an analyst for ESPN.

Perhaps the biggest off-the-track news of 2005 was NASCAR's new TV deal that would take affect for the 2007 season. The eight-year, $4.48 billion deal was announced on Dec. 7 and involved five networks. Under the terms of the agreement, FOX would broadcast the season's first 13

races, TNT would get races 14 to 19, ABC and ESPN would televise the final 17 races, and all of the races of the Chase would appear on ABC. In addition, FOX subsidiary SPEED Channel would show the NASCAR NEXTEL All-Star Challenge and qualifying for the Daytona 500, ESPN and ESPN2 would split the NASCAR Busch Series telecasts, and SPEED Channel would show NASCAR Craftsman Truck races. The rights fees, which were set at about $555 million per year, came in at 40 percent higher than the last television deal. Major League Baseball and the NBA still brought in more money annually (in the neighborhood of $200 million more), but those sports also had many more events to broadcast. The deal trailed the NFL by a considerable margin, as the NFL brought in about $3.7 billion annually at the time.

NASCAR turned its eye toward other means of expansion during the 2005 season. In addition to giving more races to

California Speedway and Texas Motor Speedway, NASCAR's International Speedway Corporation was trying to make inroads into New York and Washington state. The company even bought land on Staten Island and in Kitsap County, just south of Seattle. NASCAR also opened the bidding for a host city for the NASCAR Hall of Fame. It would be announced in March 2006 that Charlotte, N.C., home to numerous NASCAR teams, was the winner. The NASCAR Hall of Fame would be operational by 2010.

Even more changes were in store for 2006. Toyota stirred things up early in the year with the announcement that it would compete with the Camry in NASCAR NEXTEL Cup competition starting in 2007. As the season went on, established names started to climb aboard the Toyota train, Michael Waltrip the first among them. He was followed by Dale Jarrett, Jeremy Mayfield, Mike Skinner, and Brian Vickers. Even promising rookie AJ Allmendinger signed with Toyota.

The seven-year "new car design" project, led by NASCAR vice president for research and development Gary Nelson, also started to bear fruit. NASCAR unveiled the car during the Speedweeks activities that led up to the Daytona 500. Nelson and his crew designed the new car with safety and cost reduction in mind. To lessen the reliance on aerodynamics and slow the cars down, they made the car four inches wider and two inches taller than the current model, set the windshield at a more upright angle, and added a boxier front bumper. To increase protection in side impacts, they shifted the roll cage three inches to the rear and four inches to the right. Instead of a blade-type spoiler, the car had a larger attached wing. The wing could be easily changed to allow one car to be used on more tracks. This would reduce costs because teams wouldn't have to build as many different cars for different types of tracks. After some discussion with the teams, NASCAR said the new car would be run in 16 races in 2007, 26 races in 2008, and all of the races in 2009.

On the track, the racing in 2006 was exciting. Jimmie Johnson, the 31-year-old golden boy who had been successful since his first season in 2002, finally put it all together. Despite the suspension of crew chief Chad Knaus, Johnson won the season-opening Daytona 500. He would go on to win at Indianapolis and claim five wins. Johnson swapped the points lead with Matt Kenseth early in the season. He was second going into the Chase for the NASCAR NEXTEL Cup, but he struggled early in the Chase. A win in the fifth race of the Chase at Martinsville put him back into contention, and he took the lead for good with a second-place finish at Texas with two races left on the schedule. Going into the finale at Homestead-Miami Speedway, Johnson needed only to finish 12th or better to secure his first NASCAR NEXTEL Cup championship. Johnson placed a comfortable ninth in the race, giving team owner Rick Hendrick his sixth championship and Jeff Gordon his first as a co-owner.

Defending champion Tony Stewart met some bad luck during the season and failed to make the Chase. He put on a hard charge, though, and won three Chase races. Perhaps it was Stewart missing the Chase or maybe it was the fact that television ratings were down for the first time in a long time, but NASCAR decided to make some changes to the Chase format after the season. In January 2007, NASCAR announced it was increasing the number of drivers to qualify for the Chase from 10 to 12 and was adding five more points for wins. The rule that allowed any driver within 400 points of the lead to qualify for the Chase was eliminated. Under the new system, each driver that qualifies for the Chase was given 5000 points at the start of the Chase, plus an additional 10 for each win.

Along with the changes in the points system for 2007, there were also changes for the teams. During the year, Dale Earnhardt, Jr., announced he would be leaving the DEI team his father had built—and was now run by his stepmother, Teresa—and move to Hendrick Motorsports for the 2008 season, where he would join four-time NASCAR Sprint Cup Series champion Jeff Gordon and two-time champion Jimmie Johnson. Since Earnhardt, Jr.'s, traditional #8 wasn't released by DEI, he adopted the #88 made available to him by Robert Yates Racing.

Adding Earnhardt, Jr., forced Hendrick Motorsports to release Kyle Busch, who signed with Joe Gibbs Racing for the 2008 season to partner with two-time champion Tony Stewart and newcomer Denny Hamlin. Halfway through 2007, the team announced it would be switching from Chevrolets to Toyotas in 2008, becoming the eighth and most promising team to run for the foreign manufacturer.

The new car made its long-awaited debut at Bristol in March 2007. Kyle Busch won the race, but still voiced concern that the new design needed further development. As the year progressed, teams got a better handle on the new car, and NASCAR later announced that instead of phasing in the new car over three seasons as originally planned, it would be run full-time starting in 2008 rather than 2009.

Due to the cost savings of the new car, that turned out to be a fortuitous decision. With the nation's economy in a downturn, teams were scrambling to find enough sponsorship support to survive. A few found salvation in mergers. Ginn Motorsports had joined with Dale Earnhardt, Inc., in 2007, and DEI merged with Ganassi Motorsports at the end of 2008. The new team was called Earnhardt Ganassi Racing.

Some others weren't so lucky. Bill Davis Racing, which won the 2002 Daytona 500, failed to find a partner and the team was sold at the end of 2008. The famed Wood Brothers team ran only a partial schedule due to lack of a full-season sponsor. Petty Enterprises, which had fielded cars since 1949, lost sponsorship for both of its cars, including the legendary #43, and majority interest in the team was sold to an investment group, Boston Ventures. Before the 2009 season opened, the team merged with Gillett-Evernham Motorsports to become Richard Petty Motorsports with George Gillett having controlling interest in the four-car Dodge team.

Tony Stewart took a leap of faith after the end of the 2008 season and left Joe Gibbs Racing after 10 years and two NASCAR Sprint Cup Series championships. He took an offer from team owner Gene Haas and became part owner of the two-car organization now called Stewart-Haas Racing. Stewart became an owner-driver and hired Ryan Newman away from Penske Racing to drive the team's second car. Using cars and engines supplied by Hendrick Motorsports, Stewart had four wins in 2009 and both cars made the Chase.

Perhaps more than at any other time in NASCAR history, the team landscape is changing, and those that manage to hang on are facing a challenging future. And although stock-car racing remains the number-two sport in the country, NASCAR itself is facing similar challenges. There is little doubt, however, that the NASCAR Sprint Cup Series will carry on, and continue to offer fans America's most exciting form of motorsport.

2000

February 20 Dale Jarrett exercises patience to grab his third victory in the Daytona 500. After following Johnny Benson, Jr., for 50 miles, Jarrett makes the decisive pass with four laps to go to beat Jeff Burton.

March 12 Dale Earnhardt and Bobby Labonte engage in a terrific late-race duel at Atlanta Motor Speedway. Earnhardt leads the final 20 laps and nips Labonte at the finish line by a bumper to score his 75th career NASCAR Winston Cup victory.

March 19 Ward Burton ends a five-year victory famine with a win in the mall.com 400 at Darlington Raceway. Burton leads the final 37 laps and finishes 1.4 seconds ahead of Dale Jarrett to take his second career win.

April 2 Third-generation driver Dale Earnhardt, Jr., is the class of the field, winning the 500-miler at Texas Motor Speedway for his first NASCAR Winston Cup victory. Earnhardt, Jr., wins comfortably over Jeff Burton.

April 16 Jeff Gordon comes from the 36th starting position, takes the lead six laps from the finish, and wins the DieHard 500 at Talladega for his 50th career victory.

May 28 Rookie driver Matt Kenseth outruns Dale Earnhardt, Jr., in the final laps and wins the Coca-Cola 600 at Lowe's Motor Speedway. Kenseth, who leads the final 26 laps, is the 11th different winner in the first 12 races on the 2000 calendar.

June 19 Jeremy Mayfield rubs Dale Earnhardt out of the way on the final lap and speeds to victory in the Pocono 500. It is Mayfield's third career NASCAR Winston Cup win.

July 9 Tony Stewart outruns Joe Nemechek in the final laps and is declared the winner at New Hampshire when a thunderstorm shortens the scheduled 300-lapper to 273 laps. Kenny Irwin, Jr., a promising young star, is killed in a practice crash.

Dale Earnhardt, sporting an orange paint scheme on his #3 Chevrolet, races with his son Dale, Jr., in the early laps of the Feb. 20 Daytona 500. The elder Earnhardt, regarded as the master of the Daytona International Speedway, uncharacteristically sloshed through the 500 in the middle of the pack. He never led the race and finished a disappointing 21st. "Little E," competing in his first Daytona 500, finished 13th.

Dale Jarrett crosses the finish line with #99 Jeff Burton riding his bumper as the 2000 Daytona 500 concludes under a caution flag. Jarrett powered his way past Johnny Benson, Jr., with four laps remaining and was in front when a Jimmy Spencer crash brought out the yellow flag for the final two laps. The win earned Jarrett a king's ransom, as he banked $2,277,975, which included the $1 million Winston No Bull 5 bonus.

Unseasonably cool and wet weather hampered the March 5 carsdirect.com 400 at Las Vegas Motor Speedway. Temperatures were in the 40s, but the NASCAR Winston Cup drivers put on a heated show at the 1½-mile track until rain curtailed the event after 222 of the 400 miles had been run. The cars of #7 Michael Waltrip, #32 Scott Pruett, and #24 Jeff Gordon all qualified in the top 10, but all three ran into problems during the race, which was won by Jeff Burton. Pruett started on the front row but was knocked into a spin early and finished 42nd. Waltrip placed 33rd and Gordon struggled to take 28th.

Sterling Marlin spins his #40 Chevrolet to the apron as Ken Schrader and #33 Joe Nemechek whack the wall in the March 19 mall.com 400 at Darlington Raceway. Marlin was able to right his path and soldier on to a 21st-place finish. Ward Burton won the race, scoring his second career victory. "Anybody who can win at Darlington ought to change his uniform in a telephone booth and leap tall buildings in a single bound," claimed Marlin, citing the wicked and complex personality of the 50-year-old Darlington oval. Burton's win ended a 132-race drought that dated back to October 1995.

"Anybody who can win at Darlington ought to change his uniform in a telephone booth and leap tall buildings in a single bound."
—Sterling Marlin

Flashy rookies Dale Earnhardt, Jr., and Matt Kenseth battle in the April 2 DirecTV 500 at Texas Motor Speedway. Earnhardt, Jr., in only his 12th NASCAR Winston Cup start, drove his #8 Chevrolet to his first career victory. He led the most laps and drove away from all challengers down the stretch. Kenseth was in contention until a cut tire forced him into the wall on the 290th lap.

Jeff Gordon started 36th in the April 16 DieHard 500 at Talladega Superspeedway, one of the worst qualifying efforts of his career. After the halfway point, Gordon flexed his muscles and slashed his way into contention. Here, he dives under #99 Jeff Burton and #40 Sterling Marlin on his way to the front. Gordon drove past Mark Martin and led the final six laps to score the victory. Marlin finished eighth, while Burton placed 12th. Ten drivers exchanged the lead 27 times in the hotly contested affair.

Jeremy Mayfield is doused with water by cheerful team members following his triumph in the NAPA Auto Parts 500 at California Speedway. Mayfield's second career NASCAR Winston Cup victory was shrouded in controversy when officials determined the roof of his car was lower than the 51-inch minimum. "I jumped on top of the car in victory lane like everyone else does," said Mayfield. "I guess in knocked the roof in a little." NASCAR upheld Mayfield's victory but fined the Penske-Kranefuss team $25,000.

2000

July 23 Rusty Wallace takes advantage of Jeremy Mayfield's misfortune and wins the Pennsylvania 500, taking the lead on the final lap. Mayfield's victory bid is thwarted when he suffers a flat tire, allowing Wallace to take his second win of the season.

August 13 Steve Park wins in an upset at Watkins Glen for his first victory on the NASCAR Winston Cup Series. Top road racers Tony Stewart and Jeff Gordon tangle on the first lap, effectively removing both from contention.

September 3 Bobby Labonte, who fails to lead a single green-flag lap, wins the rain-shortened Pepsi Southern 500 at Darlington Raceway. After starting 37th, Labonte grabs the lead with a quick caution-flag pit stop and is out front when a thunderstorm brings the race to a halt.

September 17 Jeff Burton leads all 300 laps in his win at New Hampshire International Speedway. Burton becomes the first driver to lead every lap in a superspeedway event since Fireball Roberts did it at Hanford, Calif., in 1961.

October 15 Seven-time champion Dale Earnhardt makes a miraculous comeback to win the Winston 500 at Talladega Superspeedway. Earnhardt comes from 18th to first in the final five laps and edges Kenny Wallace.

November 20 Jerry Nadeau holds off Dale Earnhardt to post his first career victory in the season finale at Atlanta Motor Speedway. Bobby Labonte finishes fifth and takes the NASCAR Winston Cup championship by 261 points over Jeff Burton. Darrell Waltrip uses a champion's provisional to enter the race and finishes 34th, seven laps off the pace. It is the final race of Waltrip's illustrious career.

November 28 Mike Helton succeeds Bill France, Jr., as NASCAR president. "Mike is well-suited to carry on the tradition of strong leadership at NASCAR. Not only within our offices, but for the entire industry," notes France, Jr.

Dale Earnhardt, in the multicolored #3 Good-wrench Chevrolet, battles with Dale Earnhardt, Jr., in the May 28 Coca-Cola 600 at Lowe's Motor Speedway. Special paint schemes were growing more popular in the late 1990s and early 2000s, giving the diecast car industry a financial kick. The elder Earnhardt finished a strong third in the Charlotte 600-miler, while Earnhardt, Jr., fell to fourth in the final laps after leading almost half the race.

Rookie Matt Kenseth rides down pit road in his #17 Ford after winning Charlotte's Coca-Cola 600. Kenseth took the lead with 26 laps remaining and held off Bobby Labonte in a final-lap shootout to record his first NASCAR Winston Cup victory. Kenseth was the 11th different winner in the first 12 races of the 2000 season. Kenseth and fellow freshman Dale Earnhardt, Jr., became the first pair of rookies to win since 1981 when Morgan Shepherd and Ron Bouchard accomplished the feat.

Tony Stewart blazes down the front chute at Dover Downs International Speedway during the June 4 MBNA Platinum 400. Stewart authored a decisive romp in the 400-miler on Dover's "Monster Mile," leading 242 of the 400 laps. The sophomore sensation drove aggressively as most of his rivals took a conservative approach due to heavy tire wear. Stewart wore the competition down and scampered to an easy victory over rookie Matt Kenseth.

Dale Earnhardt took command of the June 19 Pocono 500 with 16 laps remaining and held a narrow advantage entering the final lap. Coming across the treacherous "tunnel turn," Jeremy Mayfield popped Earnhardt sideways and slipped past to record his third career win. "I was just rattling his cage a little," said Mayfield, who was met with a mixed chorus of boos and cheers as he motored across the finish line. Earnhardt regained the handle of his car, but dropped to fourth in the final mile.

▲ Dark storm clouds gather over Michigan Speedway in the late stages of the June 11 Kmart 400 as Dale Earnhardt, Jr., makes a pit stop. Earnhardt, Jr., finished 13th, a lap off the leader. Tony Stewart claimed his second straight NASCAR Winston Cup victory when a cloudburst curtailed the event six laps short of its scheduled distance.

▶ Jeff Gordon runs through one of the tight corners at Sears Point Raceway during the June 25 Save Mart/Kragen 300. Gordon pulled off one of racing's most astonishing feats by winning his sixth consecutive NASCAR Winston Cup event on a road course. Gordon led the final 27 laps on the 1.949-mile California track and drove to a comfortable win over runner-up Sterling Marlin. Marlin, not known for his finesse on road courses, remarked, "Road racing is like having a friend with a mean dog. If you're going to spend time with the friend, you've gotta learn to love the dog."

Road Courses

NASCAR VENTURED into road racing for the first time in 1954. The runways at the Linden, N.J., airport served as the first road course for NASCAR's top division. The inaugural road-racing event was open to both foreign and domestic vehicles, and Al Keller drove a lightweight Jaguar to victory. It was the first NASCAR Cup Series event won by a foreign manufacturer.

Ten different road courses have presented NASCAR Cup Series races. Along with the Linden course, which was used just once, other road course sites have included Lancaster, Calif.; Elkhart Lake, Wis.; Titusville, Fla.; Bremerton, Wash.; Bridgehampton, N.Y.; Augusta, Ga.; Riverside, Calif.; and the two in operation today, Sonoma, Calif., and Watkins Glen, N.Y. From 1967 to '85, Riverside's twisting course in Southern California served as the only road course for NASCAR's premier level of stock car racing.

Fireball Roberts, noted for his expertise on high-banked superspeedways, was the first driver to win twice on road courses. Roberts won at Titusville in December 1956, and Augusta in November '63. Both courses were used only once, and Roberts' win at Augusta was his 33rd and final trip to Victory Lane.

Jeff Gordon, one of the most versatile athletes in NASCAR Cup Series racing, holds many of the records. He has the most victories with nine, and on June 25, 2000, Gordon racked up his record-setting fifth consecutive road-course win. Gordon's seventh road-course win, at Watkins Glen in

2001, broke him out of a tie for the most road-course wins. Bobby Allison, Richard Petty, Rusty Wallace, and Ricky Rudd all won six events on tracks requiring right- and left-hand turns.

The magnificent four-mile road course in Elkhart Lake hosted NASCAR's stock car tour on Aug. 12, 1956. Despite rainy conditions, the race went on as scheduled. Tires with grooved treads were used on all the vehicles in the race, enabling the drivers to negotiate the turns without sliding off the course. Tires without tread weren't used in NASCAR until 1970. The race at Elkhart Lake remains the only top-level NASCAR event to be run in the rain.

The following drivers have won more than one race on a road course. The number of wins is listed in parentheses.

Jeff Gordon (9)	Geoff Bodine (3)
Tony Stewart (7)	Ernie Irvan (3)
Bobby Allison (6)	Fireball Roberts (2)
Richard Petty (6)	Parnelli Jones (2)
Rusty Wallace (6)	Marvin Panch (2)
Ricky Rudd (6)	Billy Wade (2)
Dan Gurney (5)	Ray Elder (2)
Tim Richmond (5)	Terry Labonte (2)
Darrell Waltrip (5)	Robby Gordon (2)
David Pearson (4)	Kyle Busch (2)
Mark Martin (4)	Juan Pablo Montoya (2)
Cale Yarborough (3)	Marcos Ambrose (2)

Tony Stewart kneels in victory lane after winning the rain-shortened thatlook.com 300 at New Hampshire International Speedway. It was Stewart's second win in less than a month in a rain-shortened NASCAR Winston Cup event. During the damp victory lane rituals, Stewart dedicated the win to Kenny Irwin, Jr., who had lost his life in a practice crash two days before the 300-lap event on the 1.058-mile flat oval.

Bobby Labonte stalked Rusty Wallace nearly the whole way in the Aug. 5 Brickyard 400 before making a bold charge with 14 laps to go. Labonte wheeled his Pontiac around Wallace and pulled away to win by 4.229 seconds. The talented Texan assumed command in the NASCAR Winston Cup title chase in early May and kept his advantage until the end of the season. Labonte would join his older brother Terry as NASCAR Winston Cup champion, making them the first siblings to hold NASCAR's highest honor.

Steve Park, who cut his teeth on the short tracks of NASCAR's New England Modified Tour, pulled off a shocker on Watkins Glen's twisty road course in the Aug. 13 Global Crossing @ The Glen. Park guided his #1 Pennzoil/DEI Chevrolet around Ricky Rudd with 27 laps remaining and staved off Mark Martin to rack up his first career NASCAR Winston Cup victory.

A three-car collision knocked #88 Dale Jarrett, #01 Ted Musgrave, and #24 Jeff Gordon out of contention in the Oct. 8 UAW-GM Quality 500 at Lowe's Motor Speedway. The crash relegated Jarrett to a 40th-place finish and effectively ended his bid for a second NASCAR Winston Cup championship. Bobby Labonte won the race, building his lead to 252 points with five races remaining.

Dale Earnhardt leads a pack of 27 cars separated by less than one second late in the Oct. 15 Winston 500 at Talladega Superspeedway. Earnhardt put on a monumental charge in the closing laps. Mired in 18th place with five laps remaining, Earnhardt galloped past the field in just three laps, forging to the front as the trackside audience went wild. Earnhardt led the final two laps and won his 76th and final NASCAR Winston Cup race. The lead changed hands 49 times among 21 drivers in the highly competitive affair.

Michael Waltrip's #7 Chevrolet delivers a solid shot to the retaining barrier during a 129th-lap accident in the Nov. 20 NAPA 500 at Atlanta Motor Speedway. Waltrip, who was shaken but uninjured in the wreck, was taking his final ride with the Jim Smith-owned team. Having struggled throughout the 2000 NASCAR Winston Cup season with only one top-10 finish, Waltrip announced he would drive for Dale Earnhardt, Inc. in the 2001 campaign. The decision would net the veteran his first career victory.

After finishing second in the 1999 NASCAR Winston Cup points chase, Bobby Labonte was a model of efficiency in the race for the 2000 championship. He stalked the points leaders early in the season, then grabbed first place in late April. For the remainder of the year, Labonte stayed atop the points standings and thwarted a rally from Dale Earnhardt in early autumn. He sealed the first title for himself and the Joe Gibbs operation with a fourth-place finish in the next-to-last race of the year, the Pennzoil 400 at Homestead-Miami Speedway. Labonte won four races and amassed a 265-point margin over Earnhardt, who was going for his record-setting eighth NASCAR championship.

In a show of respect, Dale Earnhardt points to #25 Jerry Nadeau moments after Nadeau beat him to the finish line in the Nov. 20 season finale at Atlanta Motor Speedway. Nadeau led the final seven laps of the NAPA 500 and nipped Earnhardt at the checkered flag for his first career NASCAR Winston Cup victory. Nadeau became the 14th different winner of the season, and was one of four drivers to score his first career win in 2000.

2000 NASCAR WINSTON CUP POINTS RACE

Rank	Driver	Points	Starts	Wins	Top 5	Top 10	Winnings
1	Bobby Labonte	5130	34	4	19	24	$7,361,386
2	Dale Earnhardt	4865	34	2	13	24	$4,918,886
3	Jeff Burton	4836	34	4	15	22	$5,959,439
4	Dale Jarrett	4684	34	2	15	24	$5,984,475
5	Ricky Rudd	4575	34	0	12	19	$2,974,970
6	Tony Stewart	4570	34	6	12	23	$3,642,348
7	Rusty Wallace	4544	34	4	12	20	$3,621,468
8	Mark Martin	4410	34	1	13	20	$3,098,874
9	Jeff Gordon	4361	34	3	11	22	$3,001,144
10	Ward Burton	4152	34	1	4	17	$2,699,604
11	Steve Park	3934	34	1	6	13	$2,283,629
12	Mike Skinner	3898	33	0	1	11	$2,205,320
13	Johnny Benson	3716	34	0	3	7	$1,841,324
14	Matt Kenseth	3711	34	1	4	11	$2,408,138
15	Joe Nemechek	3534	34	0	3	9	$2,105,041
16	Dale Earnhardt, Jr.	3516	32	2	3	5	$2,801,880
17	Terry Labonte	3433	34	0	3	6	$2,239,716
18	Ken Schrader	3398	34	0	0	2	$1,711,476
19	Sterling Marlin	3363	34	0	1	7	$1,992,301
20	Jerry Nadeau	3273	32	1	3	5	$2,164,778
21	Bill Elliott	3267	34	0	3	7	$2,580,823
22	Jimmy Spencer	3188	34	0	2	5	$1,936,762
23	John Andretti	3169	34	0	0	2	$2,035,902
24	Jeremy Mayfield	3156	32	2	6	12	$2,169,251
25	Robert Pressley	3055	34	0	1	1	$1,460,317
26	Kenny Wallace	2874	34	0	1	1	$1,723,966
27	Michael Waltrip	2797	34	0	1	1	$1,689,421
28	Kevin Lepage	2795	32	0	1	3	$1,679,186
29	Elliott Sadler	2762	33	0	0	1	$1,578,356
30	Bobby Hamilton	2715	34	0	0	2	$1,619,775
31	David Blaney	2656	33	0	0	2	$1,272,689
32	Chad Little	2634	27	0	0	1	$1,418,884
33	Rick Mast	2366	29	0	0	2	$1,156,427
34	Wally Dallenbach, Jr.	2344	30	0	0	1	$1,169,069
35	Brett Bodine	2145	29	0	0	0	$1,020,659
36	Darrell Waltrip	1981	29	0	0	0	$1,246,280
37	Scott Pruett	1879	28	0	0	1	$1,135,854
38	Stacy Compton	1857	27	0	0	0	$1,069,649
39	Mike Bliss	1748	25	0	0	1	$953,948
40	Ted Musgrave	1614	18	0	0	0	$827,216
41	Kyle Petty	1441	19	0	0	1	$894,911
42	Kenny Irwin	1440	17	0	1	1	$949,436
43	Robby Gordon	1309	17	0	1	2	$620,781
44	Ricky Craven	1175	16	0	0	0	$636,562
45	Geoff Bodine	1039	14	0	0	0	$704,981
46	Dave Marcis	723	11	0	0	0	$405,572
47	Ed Berrier	628	10	0	0	0	$417,144
48	Kurt Busch	613	7	0	0	0	$311,915
49	Todd Bodine	456	5	0	0	1	$234,065
50	Hut Stricklin	436	7	0	0	0	$255,200

Bobby Labonte gave team owner Joe Gibbs his first NASCAR Winston Cup championship to go with the former Washington Redskins coach's three Super Bowl rings in 2000. Labonte took the points lead with a runner-up finish at California Speedway in April and held on to record his first career championship.

Labonte posted four victories and held off a mild late-season rally by Dale Earnhardt to win the title by 265 points. Earnhardt won twice, including a dramatic win at Talladega in October when he came from 18th place to first in the final five laps to win a thrilling 500-mile race.

Four-time race winner Jeff Burton finished third in the NASCAR Winston Cup standings, 29 points behind Earnhardt. Super sophomore Tony Stewart racked up the most wins with six, including the first of his career, and finished sixth in the championship points race.

2001

February 18 Michael Waltrip nips Dale Earnhardt, Jr., at the finish line to win the Daytona 500, a tragic affair in which NASCAR icon Dale Earnhardt is fatally injured in a last-lap crash. Waltrip's first NASCAR Winston Cup victory turns from a joyous occasion to despair after the loss of NASCAR's most dynamic competitor.

March 11 Kevin Harvick, replacement driver for the late Dale Earnhardt, stunningly wins the Cracker Barrel Old Country Store 500 at Atlanta Motor Speedway in only his third career NASCAR Winston Cup start.

March 25 Elliott Sadler becomes the third first-time winner in the first six races of the season with a triumph in Bristol's Food City 500. Sadler comes from his 38th starting position to nip John Andretti at the finish. It is the Wood Brothers' first win since 1993.

April 22 Bobby Hamilton gives team owner Andy Petree his first career NASCAR Winston Cup victory in the Talladega 500. Hamilton wins the caution-free race at a sizzling average speed of 184.003 mph.

May 27 Jeff Burton ends a personal slump with a big victory in the Coca-Cola 600 at Lowe's Motor Speedway. Tony Stewart finishes third after his sixth-place effort in the Indianapolis 500 on the same day. Stewart completes all 1100 miles of racing in a heroic doubleheader effort.

June 17 Ricky Rudd outruns Jeff Gordon in the final laps to win the Pocono 500. It is Rudd's first victory in three years and his first with the powerful Robert Yates Ford team.

June 24 Tony Stewart scoots past Robby Gordon with 11 laps remaining and scores a victory in the Dodge/Save Mart 350 at the renamed Infineon Raceway in Sonoma, Calif. Gordon is poised to grab his first NASCAR Winston Cup victory until the lapped car of Kevin Harvick pushes him out of the way.

Evernham Motorsports
2001 NASCAR Winston Cup Series

Dodge ⏣ Different.

Dodge division of Chrysler Corp. announced it would return to NASCAR Cup Series racing for the first time since the late 1970s, and assembled a formidable team for the 2001 season. Ray Evernham, who left the Hendrick Motorsports Chevrolet operation in '99, was hired by MoPar to direct Dodge's effort. Evernham was in charge of Dodge's two-car flagship team with drivers Casey Atwood and Bill Elliott. Other Dodge teams included Bill Davis Racing, Felix Sabates, Melling Racing, and Petty Enterprises, which returned to the Chrysler fold for the first time since '78.

The Feb. 18 Daytona 500 was the most competitive since 1974 with 49 official lead changes among 14 different drivers. NASCAR-mandated rules requiring a strip of aluminum on each car's roof enhanced the on-track action, but concerns about a big crash still remained. On the 174th lap, Robby Gordon's #4 Chevrolet tapped #22 Ward Burton into a spin, triggering a 19-car collision on the backstretch. In the mishap, Tony Stewart's #20 Pontiac soared high into the air. Stewart was shaken but uninjured in the spectacular accident.

Dale Earnhardt's #3 Chevrolet hugs the rear bumper of the #96 Ford driven by rookie Andy Houston. Cal Wells III, owner of Houston's car, came over from the CART Champ Car series to NASCAR in 2000 with Indy Car veteran Scott Pruett. Ricky Craven replaced Pruett in 2001 and Houston was added to the lineup. Houston's team disbanded shortly after the halfway point of the season, leaving the promising rookie without a ride.

Michael Waltrip's #15 NAPA Chevrolet leads teammate #8 Dale Earnhardt, Jr., across the finish line at the conclusion of the 2001 Daytona 500. Waltrip, taking his first ride with the DEI team, scored his first victory in his 463rd NASCAR Winston Cup Series start. While the DEI cars ran 1-2, it was a tragic day for the entire NASCAR community. NASCAR legend Dale Earnhardt lost his life in an accident on the final turn of the final lap. It was the first death to occur in the history of the Daytona 500.

The NASCAR community paid its respects to its fallen icon Dale Earnhardt throughout the 2001 NASCAR Winston Cup season. All telecasts of NASCAR Winston Cup races honored Earnhardt with a silent third lap, special tribute hats were handed out at many speedways, prerace tributes were included at virtually all the events, and pit crews would often have their own way of honoring the late Earnhardt. At Rockingham a week after Earnhardt's death, teams held up Earnhardt banners before the race.

Steve Park drives his #1 Chevrolet off the final corner just ahead of #18 Bobby Labonte in the Feb. 26 Dura Lube 400 at North Carolina Speedway. Park nipped Labonte at the finish line by an eyelash to pocket his second career NASCAR Winston Cup victory. After the race, Park drove around the track in a reverse victory lap holding a Dale Earnhardt hat out the window.

Rookie Kevin Harvick, replacement for the late Dale Earnhardt, made his third career NASCAR Winston Cup start in the March 11 Cracker Barrel Old Country Store 500 at Atlanta Motor Speedway. Harvick performed like a veteran. On the final lap, Harvick's #29 Goodwrench Chevy washed out to the high side, leaving the door open for #24 Jeff Gordon to challenge for first place. Harvick got back on the throttle and nipped Gordon at the finish line by .006 second in one of the closest finishes in NASCAR history. After the race, Harvick drove around the track in reverse direction showing three fingers in honor of the fallen Dale Earnhardt.

Elliott Sadler pulled a major upset in the March 25 Food City 500 at Bristol Motor Speedway. Coming from his 38th starting position, Sadler stayed on the lead lap throughout the first half of the race as cautions kept the field bunched up. He took the lead with 70 laps to go when #29 Kevin Harvick encountered tire problems, and led the rest of the way. The win was the first for the Wood Brothers team since 1993 and the first of Sadler's NASCAR Winston Cup career.

July 15 Rookie Kevin Harvick holds off Robert Pressley to win the inaugural race at Chicagoland Speedway. The victory is Harvick's second of the season. Jeff Gordon and Dale Jarrett are locked in a tie for the lead in the championship points race.

August 19 Sterling Marlin drives a Dodge to victory in the Pepsi 400 at Michigan Speedway for his first win of the season. Marlin breaks the ice in Dodge's return to NASCAR racing. It is the first win for Dodge since Neil Bonnett won at Ontario in 1977.

September 8 Ricky Rudd prevails in a game of bumper-tag with Kevin Harvick and wins the Chevrolet 400 at Richmond International Speedway. Harvick punches Rudd out of the lead with 18 laps remaining, but Rudd returns the favor 12 laps later.

September 30 Jeff Gordon scores a narrow victory over Ryan Newman to win the Protection One 400 at the new Kansas Speedway. Gordon's sixth victory of the season gives him a 222-point lead over Ricky Rudd in the championship race.

October 15 Underdog Ricky Craven takes the lead in the closing stages of the Old Dominion 500 when Kevin Harvick spins Bobby Hamilton. Craven holds off a late charge by Dale Jarrett to claim his first career NASCAR Winston Cup win. It is also team owner Cal Wells' first trip to victory lane.

November 11 Bill Elliott passes Dodge teammate Casey Atwood with five laps remaining to end a personal seven-year winless streak with a victory at Homestead-Miami Speedway. Elliott gives Ray Evernham his first win as a NASCAR Winston Cup team owner.

November 23 Robby Gordon speeds to his first NASCAR Winston Cup win in the season finale at New Hampshire International Speedway. The race was postponed from Sept. 16 after the Sept. 11 terrorist attacks. Jeff Gordon nabs his fourth NASCAR Winston Cup title by 349 points over Tony Stewart.

Jerry Nadeau loses the handle of his #25 Chevrolet in tight traffic during the April 1 Harrah's 500 at Texas Motor Speedway. Terry Labonte runs just ahead of the mishap, while #97 Kurt Busch sweeps low to get past unscathed. Robert Pressley's #77 would get tangled up with Nadeau and be eliminated from further competition. Nadeau went to the pits for repairs and returned to finish 29th. Dale Jarrett won the 500-miler in a close decision over runner-up Steve Park.

Bobby Hamilton's #55 Chevrolet leads a pack of snarling cars in the final laps of the April 22 Talladega 500. The 500-miler on the 2.66-mile high-banked track was uninterrupted by a single caution flag. Drivers ran flat out the entire way, and 26 different drivers swap the lead 37 times. Hamilton blasted out of the pack in the final stages, grabbed the lead with two laps to go, and won the race. For Hamilton, it was his fourth career NASCAR Winston Cup victory, and it gave team owner Andy Petree his first trip to victory lane.

Rusty Wallace keeps his #2 Ford just ahead of #24 Jeff Gordon in the decisive last lap of the April 29 NAPA Auto Parts 500 at California Speedway. Wallace snagged his 54th career NASCAR Cup Series victory by holding off Gordon's late surge. The triumph gave Wallace a win in 16 consecutive seasons, two years short of Richard Petty's all-time record.

Ryan Newman, in his third career NASCAR Winston Cup start, shocked onlookers by winning the pole position for the May 27 Coca-Cola 600 at Lowe's Motor Speedway. The open-wheel veteran and newcomer to stock cars led the opening 10 laps before he lost control of his #02 Ford a lap later. The car slugged the wall and spun to the bottom of the track. Newman was uninjured in the mishap. Jeff Burton went on to win the race.

Mike Skinner's #31 Chevrolet erupts in flames after plowing into the wall during the early laps of the July 15 Tropicana 400 at the new Chicagoland Speedway. Skinner was able to get out of the car without suffering any burns, a testament to the quality of the fire-retardant uniform that NASCAR mandates. Skinner was badly shaken in the accident and would miss much of the remainder of the 2001 NASCAR Winston Cup season.

Rookie Kevin Harvick keeps his #29 Chevrolet ahead of #97 Kurt Busch in the inaugural NASCAR Winston Cup race at the ultramodern Chicagoland Speedway in central Illinois. Harvick took the lead 26 laps from the finish and held off the challenge of runner-up Robert Pressley to win his second race of the year. Pressley's effort netted him the best finish of his career. Busch, another freshman driver, finished eighth after starting 31st.

Bill Elliott's #9 Dodge fades to the upper groove as #40 Sterling Marlin charges past in the late stages of the Aug. 5 Brickyard 400 at Indianapolis Motor Speedway. Marlin led the race with 25 laps to go, but was unable to fend off the high-speed exploits of Jeff Gordon, who went on to win his third event at the Indianapolis Motor Speedway. Elliott started on the front row and finished eighth in Ray Evernham's Dodge.

Boris Said, an accomplished road racer, was one of the "hired guns" to compete in the Aug. 12 Global Crossing At The Glen on the historic Watkins Glen road course. Driving the #77 Jasper Engines Ford, Said wrestled the car around the 2.45-mile track to an eighth-place finish. That's Jerry Nadeau in the background doing a little agricultural racing through the track's inner loop.

Number 1 Steve Park, #8 Dale Earnhardt, Jr., and #15 Michael Waltrip, all in Dale Earnhardt, Inc. Chevrolets, battle for position in the Aug. 25 Sharpie 500 at Bristol Motor Speedway. Park enjoyed a fine run, coming from 37th to finish seventh. Earnhardt, Jr., came home 14th, while Waltrip encountered problems and finished 39th. Tony Stewart won the race ahead of Kevin Harvick and Jeff Gordon.

The new Kansas Speedway hosted its first NASCAR Winston Cup race on Sept. 30. The Protection One 400 attracted an enthusiastic wall-to-wall crowd, who watched Jeff Gordon motor to his sixth win of the '01 season. Rookie Ryan Newman nearly pulled off a colossal upset, finishing a strong second. The Kansas Speedway is one of the best-designed facilities in America, and can handle large crowds with few traffic tie-ups.

Freshman driver Jason Leffler's #01 Dodge gets tangled up with #75 Stuart Kirby in a 46th-lap accident in the Oct. 7 UAW-GM Quality 500 at Lowe's Motor Speedway. Number 32 Ricky Craven and #4 Bobby Hamilton, Jr., squeeze past to the low side. All four drivers finished far down in the final order as Sterling Marlin drove his Dodge to victory, beating runner-up Tony Stewart.

Jason Leffler won his first career pole for the 400-miler at Kansas Speedway and led the first eight laps. The former open-wheel short-track star was having his best run of the season in the #01 Monte Carlo when a tire problem caused him to punch the wall in the closing laps. The misfortune knocked Leffler down to a 29th-place finish. At the conclusion of the '01 season, team owner Chip Ganassi released the talented but unproven driver. Jeff Gordon's win at Kansas put him 222 points ahead of Ricky Rudd, leaving him in prime position to capture his fourth championship.

Bobby Hamilton seemed to have the Oct. 15 Old Dominion 500 at Martinsville well in hand until the closing laps. Number 29 Kevin Harvick drilled Hamilton's rear bumper, sending the #55 Chevy spinning and dropping Hamilton to 13th in the final order. Harvick was penalized a lap for rough driving and finished 22nd. Kevin Lepage, who placed 21st, talked about the short tempers usually found at Martinsville. "Martinsville is not an anger management seminar," said Lepage. "In fact, it might do you some good to attend one of those before the race."

"Martinsville is not an anger management seminar. In fact, it might do you some good to attend one of those before the race."
—Kevin Lepage

Early Winners

KEVIN HARVICK, replacement driver on the Richard Childress-owned RCR Enterprises team for the late Dale Earnhardt, recorded a major upset in the 2001 500-miler at Atlanta Motor Speedway. In just his third career NASCAR Cup Series start, Harvick took the lead with 26 laps to go and held off Jeff Gordon to win by .006 seconds. It was one of the closest finishes in NASCAR history.

Harvick became the sixth driver to win a top-level NASCAR event in his third career start. Six drivers won in their maiden voyage into big-time NASCAR racing.

Virtually all of the instant winners occurred in NASCAR's formative wildcat years when unknown racers could seemingly come out of the woodwork to be competitive right off the bat. In the modern era (since 1972), it is a highly unusual occurrence for newcomers to catch a falling star and win without the aid of big-league experience.

A list of the drivers who won early in their NASCAR careers:

Start	Driver	Date	Track	Location
1st	Jim Roper	6/19/49	Charlotte Speedway	Charlotte, N.C.
1st	Jack White	9/18/49	Hamburg Speedway	Hamburg, N.Y.
1st	Harold Kite	2/5/50	Daytona's Beach-Road Course	Daytona Beach, Fla.
1st	Leon Sales	9/24/50	North Wilkesboro Speedway	North Wilkesboro, N.C.
1st	Marvin Burke	10/14/51	Oakland Stadium	Oakland, Calif.
1st	Johnny Rutherford	2/22/63	Daytona International Speedway	Daytona Beach, Fla.
2nd	Red Byron	7/10/49	Daytona's Beach-Road Course	Daytona Beach, Fla.
2nd	Norm Nelson	10/16/55	Las Vegas Park Speedway	Las Vegas, Nev.
2nd	Chuck Stevenson	11/20/55	Willow Springs Speedway	Lancaster, Calif.
2nd	John Rostek	4/3/60	Arizona State Fairgrounds Speedway	Phoenix, Ariz.
2nd	Jamie McMurray	10/13/02	Charlotte Motor Speedway	Harrisburg, N.C.
2nd	Trevor Bayne	2/20/11	Daytona International Speedway	Daytona Beach, Fla.
3rd	Bob Flock	8/7/49	Occoneechee Speedway	Hillsboro, N.C.
3rd	Fireball Roberts	8/13/50	Occoneechee Speedway	Hillsboro, N.C.
3rd	Johnny Mantz	9/4/50	Darlington International Raceway	Darlington, S.C.
3rd	Bill Norton	11/11/51	Carrell Speedway	Gardena, Calif.
3rd	Dan Gurney	1/20/63	Riverside International Raceway	Riverside, Calif.
3rd	Kevin Harvick	3/11/01	Atlanta Motor Speedway	Hampton, Ga.
4th	Curtis Turner	9/11/49	Langhorne Speedway	Langhorne, Penn.
4th	Jimmy Florian	6/25/50	Dayton Speedway	Daytona, Ohio
5th	Lee Petty	10/2/49	Heidelberg Speedway	Pittsburgh, Penn.
5th	Marshall Teague	2/11/51	Daytona's Beach-Road Course	Daytona Beach, Fla.
5th	Tommy Thompson	2/11/51	Michigan State Fairgrounds Speedway	Detroit, Mich.
5th	Danny Weinberg	10/28/51	Hanford Motor Speedway	Hanford, Calif.
5th	John Soares	5/30/54	Carrell Speedway	Gardena, Calif.
5th	Mark Donohue	1/21/73	Riverside International Raceway	Riverside, Calif.
5th	Brad Keselowski	4/26/09	Talladega Superspeedway	Talladega, Ala.

Ricky Craven flashes his #32 Ford across the finish line, beating Dale Jarrett by less than a second to post his first career NASCAR Winston Cup win in Martinsville's Oct. 14 Old Dominion 500. For Craven, it was sweet redemption in a career with plenty of peaks and valleys. Having been injured at Texas in 1997, Craven lost his ride and his recuperation was lengthy. With his Martinsville triumph, he filled a void in the victory column—and also became the first driver to ever win in a car bearing the number 32.

A last-lap scramble in the Oct. 21 EA Sports 500 at Talladega Superspeedway decided the finish. In an effort to protect his lead, Bobby Labonte squeezed into Bobby Hamilton in turn two. Fenders snagged and Labonte's #18 Pontiac toppled over in the midst of a pack of cars. Sixteen cars were involved in the crash. Dale Earnhardt, Jr., took the lead on the final lap and stormed to victory.

Joe Nemechek drove his #33 Chevrolet to a runaway victory in the Nov. 4 Pop Secret Microwave Popcorn 400 at North Carolina Speedway. Nemechek was a lame-duck driver with the Andy Petree-owned team, which was losing sponsor Oakwood Homes at the end of the season. Nemechek, who had announced he was leaving Petree's outfit, beat runner-up Kenny Wallace by 6.2 seconds.

The Ray Evernham Motorsports Dodges of Bill Elliott and Casey Atwood lead the pace lap of the Nov. 11 Pennzoil Freedom 400 at Homestead-Miami Speedway. Elliott scampered around Atwood with five laps remaining to record his first win since 1994—a span of 227 races. It was his 41st career NASCAR Cup Series win.

Bobby Labonte's #18 Pontiac runs side-by-side with Dale Earnhardt, Jr.'s #8 Chevy in the Nov. 18 NAPA 500 at Atlanta Motor Speedway. Labonte came from his 39th starting position to win, taking advantage of Jerry Nadeau's fuel-starved car on the final lap. Labonte's second win of the year enabled the 2000 NASCAR Winston Cup champion to finish sixth in the '01 final points standings. Jeff Gordon's sixth-place finish assured him of his fourth championship. It was the fourth consecutive year that the championship was decided with one race remaining.

2001 NASCAR WINSTON CUP POINTS RACE

Rank	Driver	Points	Starts	Wins	Top 5	Top 10	Winnings
1	Jeff Gordon	5112	36	6	18	24	$10,879,757
2	Tony Stewart	4763	36	3	15	22	$4,941,463
3	Sterling Marlin	4741	36	2	12	20	$4,517,634
4	Ricky Rudd	4706	36	2	14	22	$4,878,027
5	Dale Jarrett	4612	36	4	12	19	$5,377,742
6	Bobby Labonte	4561	36	2	9	20	$4,786,779
7	Rusty Wallace	4481	36	1	8	14	$4,788,652
8	Dale Earnhardt, Jr.	4460	36	3	9	15	$5,827,542
9	Kevin Harvick	4406	35	2	6	16	$4,302,202
10	Jeff Burton	4394	36	2	8	16	$4,230,737
11	Johnny Benson	4152	36	0	6	14	$2,894,903
12	Mark Martin	4095	36	0	3	15	$3,797,006
13	Matt Kenseth	3982	36	0	4	9	$2,565,579
14	Ward Burton	3846	36	1	6	10	$3,583,692
15	Bill Elliott	3824	36	1	5	9	$3,618,017
16	Jimmy Spencer	3782	36	0	3	8	$2,669,638
17	Jerry Nadeau	3675	36	0	4	10	$2,507,827
18	Bobby Hamilton	3575	36	1	3	7	$2,527,310
19	Ken Schrader	3480	36	0	0	5	$2,418,181
20	Elliott Sadler	3471	36	1	2	2	$2,683,225
21	Ricky Craven	3379	36	1	4	7	$1,996,981
22	Dave Blaney	3303	36	0	0	6	$1,827,896
23	Terry Labonte	3280	36	0	1	3	$3,011,901
24	Michael Waltrip	3159	36	1	3	3	$3,411,644
25	Robert Pressley	3156	34	0	1	5	$2,171,520
26	Casey Atwood	3132	35	0	1	3	$1,797,111
27	Kurt Busch	3081	35	0	3	6	$2,170,629
28	Joe Nemechek	2994	31	1	1	4	$2,510,723
29	Todd Bodine	2960	35	0	2	2	$1,740,315
30	Brett Bodine	2948	36	0	0	2	$1,740,526
31	John Andretti	2943	35	0	1	2	$2,873,184
32	Steve Park	2859	24	1	5	12	$2,385,971
33	Stacy Compton	2752	34	0	0	1	$1,704,962
34	Mike Wallace	2693	29	0	1	6	$2,075,044
35	Jeremy Mayfield	2651	28	0	5	7	$2,682,603
36	Kevin Lepage	2461	29	0	0	1	$1,424,852
37	Jason Leffler	2413	30	0	0	1	$1,724,692
38	Ron Hornaday	2305	32	0	0	1	$1,435,857
39	Kenny Wallace	2054	24	0	1	2	$1,507,922
40	Mike Skinner	2029	23	0	0	1	$1,921,186
41	Buckshot Jones	1939	30	0	0	0	$1,631,488
42	Hut Stricklin	1770	22	0	0	1	$1,006,021
43	Kyle Petty	1673	24	0	0	0	$1,008,919
44	Robby Gordon	1552	17	1	2	3	$1,371,900
45	Rick Mast	1187	17	0	0	0	$680,321
46	Andy Houston	1123	17	0	0	0	$865,263
47	Bobby Hamilton	748	10	0	0	0	$546,847
48	Jeff Green	539	8	0	0	1	$441,449
49	Ryan Newman	497	7	0	2	2	$465,276
50	Boris Said	272	2	0	0	1	$124,340

Jeff Gordon took the NASCAR Winston Cup points lead with an eighth-place finish at Pocono in July, then romped to his fourth championship with ease. After being locked in a tight battle during the first half of the season, Gordon left all challengers in the dust as he won by a 349-point cushion over runner-up Tony Stewart.

The points lead changed hands seven times among five different drivers as several contenders jockeyed for points early in the year. By late summer, it was a one-horse race with Gordon leading by more than 300 points in August.

Gordon won six races along the way to his fourth title. Stewart overcame a sluggish start to finish second on the strength of three victories. Two-time winner Sterling Marlin finished third in the points chase with two wins. Ricky Rudd and Dale Jarrett rounded out the top five. Jarrett posted the second most wins of the season with four.

2002

February 17 Ward Burton leads only the final five laps and scores an upset win in the Daytona 500. Sterling Marlin is penalized by NASCAR when he pulls a fender off his right front tire during a late red flag. NASCAR rules prohibit work from being done to a car during a red-flag situation.

March 17 Sterling Marlin wheels his Dodge to victory in the Carolina Dodge Dealers 400 at Darlington Raceway. Steve Park, returning after a six-month layoff due to injury, crashes while leading early. Tony Stewart is shaken up while leading in the late stages when he is involved in a multi-car collision.

March 24 Sophomore Kurt Busch rattles his way past Jimmy Spencer in the final 30 miles and sprints to his first career NASCAR Winston Cup victory at Bristol. Busch and Spencer battle ferociously in the closing laps.

April 28 Rookie Jimmie Johnson surges into the lead with 13 laps remaining and outruns Kurt Busch to win the California 500. Johnson's first NASCAR Winston Cup victory comes in his 13th career start.

May 26 Mark Martin slices his way through lapped traffic and holds off teammate Matt Kenseth in a stirring finish to win the Coca-Cola 600 at Lowe's Motor Speedway. Martin's victory ends a 25-month famine in NASCAR Winston Cup competition.

June 23 Jerry Nadeau's rear-gearing failure in the final three laps opens the door for Ricky Rudd to win the 224-mile race at Infineon Raceway in Sonoma, Calif. The win is Rudd's first on a road course since 1990.

August 4 Bill Elliott runs down Rusty Wallace in the final 12 laps and scores a popular win in the Brickyard 400 at Indianapolis Motor Speedway. Elliott finishes 1.2 seconds ahead of Wallace to nail down his 43rd career NASCAR Cup Series victory.

During a red flag five laps from the finish of the Feb. 17 Daytona 500, Sterling Marlin climbed from his #40 Dodge on the backstretch and pulled a bent fender away from his right front tire. Marlin, who was leading at the time, had crumpled the fender in a skirmish with Jeff Gordon. NASCAR rules prohibit any work from being done to a car during a red flag, and Marlin was flagged to the pits when the race continued. Marlin resumed the chase in 14th place, but battled back to finish eighth.

Ward Burton, who took the lead for the first time with five laps remaining in the 2002 Daytona 500, wheeled his #22 Dodge to a narrow victory over Elliott Sadler. Burton snaked his way through nine caution flags and a pair of big accidents to put himself in position to win NASCAR's crown-jewel event. Burton held the lead after Sterling Marlin's red-flag miscue and gave Dodge its first win in "The Great American Race" since 1974.

Matt Kenseth gunned his #17 Ford around Mark Martin with seven laps remaining to win the Feb. 24 Subway 400 at North Carolina Speedway in Rockingham. Kenseth started 25th on the grid and methodically worked his way through the pack. It was the second NASCAR Winston Cup win of his career, and it ended a 59-race winless drought dating back to May 2000.

Sterling Marlin hoists the winner's trophy in Las Vegas Motor Speedway's victory lane after topping the field in the March 3 UAW-Daimler Chrysler 400. Marlin zipped past Jeremy Mayfield with 17 laps left and sprinted to a 1.1-second victory. Marlin led the NASCAR Winston Cup points standings from February through early September, but lost hopes of capturing his first title when injuries suffered at Richmond and Kansas put him on the sidelines for the final seven races.

Kurt Busch celebrates his initial NASCAR Winston Cup victory in the winner's circle at Bristol Motor Speedway following his thrilling duel with Jimmy Spencer. Busch's ascent to the top echelon of NASCAR racing was meteoric. Team owner Jack Roush plucked him off the western short tracks and placed him in the NASCAR Craftsman Truck Series in 2000. Later that year, Roush seated him in a Winston Cup car, bypassing the NASCAR Busch Series entirely. "The kid has a knack about this sport, and he'll be very successful," said Roush.

Tony Stewart's #20 Pontiac leads #8 Dale Earnhardt, Jr., and rookie sensation #48 Jimmie Johnson in the final laps of the March 10 MBNA 500 at Atlanta Motor Speedway. Stewart nailed down his first win of the season with a close decision over "Little E" and Johnson. The victory enabled Stewart to leap to fifth in the NASCAR Winston Cup points standings despite a last-place finish in the season opener at Daytona.

Jimmy Spencer, in the #41 Dodge, and #97 Kurt Busch battled ferociously in the final laps of the March 24 Food City 500 at Bristol Motor Speedway. Spencer and Busch swapped the lead before a packed house that exceeded 150,000. Busch scrubbed his way past Spencer for the final time on lap 445 and sped to his first NASCAR Winston Cup victory.

Dale Earnhardt, Jr., plants a bumper on the rear of Tony Stewart's car during the April 14 Virginia 500 at Martinsville. Rattling the rear bumper of a rival is a driving technique that has been in stock car racing since the beginning. A craftsman like Earnhardt, Jr., can swat a competitor just enough to make him wobble out of the groove and leave room for a critical pass. Bobby Labonte won the 2002 Virginia 500.

August 24 Jeff Gordon nudges his way past Rusty Wallace with three laps to go and ends a 31-race losing streak with a triumph in the Sharpie 500 at Bristol. Fifteen caution flags dot the crash-marred contest.

September 15 Freshman driver Ryan Newman holds off a late-race gallop by Kurt Busch to win the rain-shortened event at New Hampshire International Speedway. Newman leads the final 41 laps and is only a car length ahead of Busch when rain curtails the event after 207 of the scheduled 300 laps have been run.

October 13 Jamie McMurray, making his second start since replacing the injured Sterling Marlin, leads the final 31 laps and authors a stunning upset in Charlotte's UAW-GM Quality 500. McMurray becomes the quickest winner in NASCAR Cup Series history since Johnny Rutherford won in his first start at Daytona in 1963.

November 3 Johnny Benson, Jr., posts his first NASCAR Winston Cup victory in his 227th start by staving off Mark Martin's late surge at Rockingham. Benson leads the final 28 laps and gives the Read Morton-owned team its first NASCAR Winston Cup win.

November 17 Kurt Busch wins his fourth race of the year at Homestead-Miami Speedway and Tony Stewart coasts to an 18th-place finish to put the lid on his championship campaign. Stewart beats runner-up Mark Martin by 38 points to capture the NASCAR Winston Cup title.

Robby Gordon, in the #31 Chevrolet, and #18 Bobby Labonte find themselves in the middle of a massive accident on Talladega Superspeedway's backstretch during the April 21 Aaron's 499. Tony Stewart got squeezed into the wall, setting off the wild melee. No drivers were injured, but the crash depleted the field considerably as 24 cars were involved. Dale Earnhardt, Jr., driving like his legendary father on the restrictor-plate tracks, scored the win in the 500-miler, beating Michael Waltrip and Kurt Busch.

Two of NASCAR's top-ranked young guns, #48 Jimmie Johnson and #97 Kurt Busch, battle side-by-side in the April 28 NAPA Auto Parts 500 at California Speedway. Busch dominated the race until the late stages when Johnson galloped into the lead 14 laps from the finish. Johnson scored his first NASCAR Winston Cup victory as Busch ran second.

Roush Racing teammates #17 Matt Kenseth and #6 Mark Martin battled down to the wire in the May 26 Coca-Cola 600 at Lowe's Motor Speedway. Martin, riding a 73-race losing streak into the Charlotte race, grabbed the lead with 40 laps to go and held off Kenseth's dynamic efforts in the final laps. Martin collected the $1 million Winston No Bull 5 bonus in his 33rd career NASCAR Winston Cup triumph.

Dale Jarrett rounds the corner at Pocono Raceway along the way to his first win of the season in the June 9 Pocono 500. Jarrett took advantage of teammate Ricky Rudd's late-race misfortune. Rudd fell back when a tire went soft, and Jarrett drove his #88 Ford into the lead six laps from the finish. The victory ended a 30-race winless drought for the former champion. "You get into a little bit of a slump and you honestly wonder when and if another win is going to come," said the exhausted Jarrett.

Matt Kenseth's pit crew, headed by crew chief Robbie Reiser, services the #17 DeWalt Ford on a splash-and-go stop during the June 16 Sirius Satellite Radio 400 at Michigan International Speedway. The lightning-fast pit stop, which took barely three seconds, enabled Kenseth to race home first for his third win of the season.

Ricky Rudd won the June 23 Dodge SaveMart 350 at Infineon Raceway in Sears Point, Calif., nipping runner-up #20 Tony Stewart to score his first win of the season. Rudd got past Stewart to take second place in the final 10 laps, then found himself in the catbird seat when leader Jerry Nadeau ran into mechanical problems within sight of the checkered flag. Rudd motored past the idle Nadeau and held off Stewart to post the win.

Kevin Harvick ended a disappointing start to the 2002 season with a resounding victory in the July 14 Tropicana 400 at Chicagoland Speedway. Harvick, the '01 rookie sensation, had been shut out of victory lane the first half of the '02 campaign, and was parked by NASCAR officials for one race for rough driving. Harvick overcame a spinout at Chicago, grabbed the lead with 25 laps remaining, and outran Jeff Gordon for his third career win.

Number 20 Tony Stewart battles with #97 Kurt Busch in the July 21 New England 300 at New Hampshire International Speedway. Stewart departed early in the race and his 39th-place finish dropped him to seventh in the NASCAR Winston Cup points standings. Stewart trailed Sterling Marlin by 227 points following the 19th race of the season, but he began a midsummer charge that would eventually earn him the championship.

Bill Elliott drove his #9 Dodge to a pair of back-to-back victories at Pocono and Indianapolis in the summer, serving notice that the Georgia veteran was back in top form. Elliott won a rain-shortened event at Pocono, then bagged the ninth annual Brickyard 400 on Aug. 4 (shown) with a crisp pass of leader Rusty Wallace with 12 laps remaining. Elliott stalked Wallace for a dozen laps before making his final charge. The Indy win was his 43rd career NASCAR Cup Series victory.

Ward Burton provided the night's most notable display of anger during the Aug. 24 Sharpie 500 at Bristol Motor Speedway. Dale Earnhardt, Jr., bumped Burton into a spin and crash in the final 50 miles. As Junior drove past under the caution flag, Burton threw the heat shields of his driving shoes at the #8 car. Burton was saddled with a 37th-place finish, while Earnhardt finished third.

Jeff Gordon makes the decisive final pass on Rusty Wallace with three laps remaining in Bristol's Sharpie 500. Both Gordon and Wallace had failed to post a victory in first six months of the 2002 season. The race under Bristol's lights was a typical barnburner. Gordon popped Wallace's rear bumper and shot the gap to come out on top, ending a personal a 31-race victory drought.

Rusty Wallace's #2 Ford climbs on top of Kyle Petty's #45 Dodge in an early entanglement during the Sept. 15 New Hampshire 300 at New Hampshire International Speedway. Wallace was doing everything in his power to log a win in '02 so he could keep his 16-year streak of winning at least one NASCAR Winston Cup race intact. Although he came close on many occasions, a victory wasn't in the cards, and Wallace's streak was halted two years short of Richard Petty's all-time record of 18 consecutive winning seasons.

Rookie Ryan Newman, who had posted four runner-up finishes in his freshman campaign, finally broke through with his first career NASCAR Winston Cup victory in the New Hampshire 300. Newman held his #12 Dodge in front of a tenacious Kurt Busch over the final 41 laps. Rain curtailed the event after 207 of the 300 laps had been completed. Newman went on to win the Rookie of the Year award in a close decision over Jimmie Johnson.

Jeff Gordon and #12 Ryan Newman battle side-by-side in the closing stages of the Sept. 29 Protection One 400 at Kansas Speedway. Gordon nabbed his third win of the season, while Newman posted his fifth runner-up finish. With the victory, Gordon placed himself in solid contention for a fifth NASCAR Winston Cup championship. He was in fifth place, but only 109 points out of the lead.

Most Popular Drivers

BILL ELLIOTT WON the NASCAR Winston Cup Most Popular Driver award for the 16th time in 2002, giving him a win in 11 of the last 12 popularity polls. Since 1991, the only year Elliott didn't win the award was in 2001 when he removed his name from the ballot so the late Dale Earnhardt could officially win an award he always deserved.

The Most Popular Driver award began in 1949, during NASCAR's first season for what is now the NASCAR Sprint Cup Series. Flamboyant Curtis Turner won the popularity vote, which was conducted at the racetracks. No MPD award was given in '50 and '51.

The popularity vote was reinstated in 1952, shortly after NASCAR began publishing its twice-monthly *NASCAR Newsletter*. Ballots appeared in the newsletter and NASCAR members were obliged to cast their vote. After Lee Petty won the award from '52 to '54, NASCAR said that beginning in '55, any previous winner would be ineligible to win again. That rule was rescinded in the early '60s.

In 1958, the Most Popular Driver award ended in a tie with Jack Smith and Junior Johnson. NASCAR mailed follow-up ballots with just the names of Smith and Johnson to voting members. Smith won the runoff.

Today, the Most Popular Driver award is open to anyone. Ballots may be cast by mail, on the internet, or at the speedways. Elliott's fan club was largely responsible for his dominance in the annual Most Popular Driver award voting, but Dale Earnhardt, Jr., has been the fan favorite for the past few years. Below is a list of winners over the years.

Year	Most Popular Driver	Year	Most Popular Driver	Year	Most Popular Driver
1949	Curtis Turner	1972	Bobby Allison	1993	Bill Elliott
1952	Lee Petty	1973	Bobby Allison	1994	Bill Elliott
1953	Lee Petty	1974	Richard Petty	1995	Bill Elliott
1954	Lee Petty	1975	Richard Petty	1996	Bill Elliott
1955	Tim Flock	1976	Richard Petty	1997	Bill Elliott
1956	Curtis Turner	1977	Richard Petty	1998	Bill Elliott
1957	Fireball Roberts	1978	Richard Petty	1999	Bill Elliott
1958	Jack Smith*	1979	David Pearson	2000	Bill Elliott
1959	Glen Wood	1980	David Pearson	2001	Dale Earnhardt
1960	Rex White	1981	Bobby Allison	2002	Bill Elliott
1961	Joe Weatherly	1982	Bobby Allison	2003	Dale Earnhardt, Jr.
1962	Richard Petty	1983	Bobby Allison	2004	Dale Earnhardt, Jr.
1963	Fred Lorenzen	1984	Bill Elliott	2005	Dale Earnhardt, Jr.
1964	Richard Petty	1985	Bill Elliott	2006	Dale Earnhardt, Jr.
1965	Fred Lorenzen	1986	Bill Elliott	2007	Dale Earnhardt, Jr.
1966	Darel Dieringer	1987	Bill Elliott	2008	Dale Earnhardt, Jr.
1967	Cale Yarborough	1988	Bill Elliott	2009	Dale Earnhardt, Jr.
1968	Richard Petty	1989	Darrell Waltrip	2010	Dale Earnhardt, Jr.
1969	Bobby Isaac	1990	Darrell Waltrip	2011	Dale Earnhardt, Jr.
1970	Richard Petty	1991	Bill Elliott	2012	Dale Earnhardt, Jr.
1971	Bobby Allison	1992	Bill Elliott		

*Jack Smith and Junior Johnson tied for the 1958 Most Popular Driver Award. Smith prevailed in a runoff.

Todd Bodine's Ford darts out of control in Talladega Superspeedway's tri-oval during the Oct. 6 EA Sports 500. Miraculously, Bodine kept the car from spinning, thus averting a big pileup. Bodine had run among the leaders most of the race, but fell a lap off the pace late and could only salvage a 23rd-place finish.

Dale Earnhardt, Jr., pushes his #8 Chevrolet across the finish line two car lengths ahead of #20 Tony Stewart to win Talladega's EA Sports 500. Earnhardt, Jr., won his third-straight race on the steeply banked 2.66-mile tri-oval as Stewart claimed the lead in the 2002 NASCAR Winston Cup points standings.

Jamie McMurray, a rookie who replaced the injured Sterling Marlin in the #40 Dodge, stunned the NASCAR community by winning the Oct. 13 UAW-GM Quality 500 at Lowe's Motor Speedway in only his second career start. Joining him in victory lane is team owner Chip Ganassi. McMurray stormed into the lead with 31 laps to go and kept Bobby Labonte at bay in the final shootout.

Johnny Benson, Jr., pushes his #10 Pontiac to the high side during a stretch battle with #6 Mark Martin in the Nov. 3 Pop Secret Microwave Popcorn 400 at Rockingham, N.C. Benson held off Martin in the furious final laps to record his first NASCAR Winston Cup victory. Benson finally pulled off his first win in his 226th career start.

Tony Stewart gave team owner Joe Gibbs his second NASCAR Winston Cup title in the last three years with a come-from-behind victory in the championship chase of 2002. The season got off to a rocky start for the versatile Stewart, having finished last in the Feb. 17 Daytona 500. He clawed his way into contention by late summer, and moved to the top of the heap in early October. Stewart won three races during the year and beat runner-up Mark Martin by 38 points.

2002 NASCAR WINSTON CUP POINTS RACE

Rank	Driver	Points	Starts	Wins	Top 5	Top 10	Winnings
1	Tony Stewart	4800	36	3	15	21	$9,163,761
2	Mark Martin	4762	36	1	12	22	$7,004,893
3	Kurt Busch	4641	36	4	12	20	$5,105,394
4	Jeff Gordon	4607	36	3	13	20	$6,154,475
5	Jimmie Johnson	4600	36	3	6	21	$3,788,268
6	Ryan Newman	4593	36	1	14	22	$5,346,651
7	Rusty Wallace	4574	36	0	7	17	$4,785,134
8	Matt Kenseth	4432	36	5	11	19	$4,514,203
9	Dale Jarrett	4415	36	2	10	18	$4,421,951
10	Ricky Rudd	4323	36	1	8	12	$4,444,614
11	Dale Earnhardt Jr.	4270	36	2	11	16	$4,970,034
12	Jeff Burton	4259	36	0	5	14	$4,244,856
13	Bill Elliott	4158	36	2	6	13	$4,122,699
14	Michael Waltrip	3985	36	1	4	10	$3,185,969
15	Ricky Craven	3888	36	0	3	9	$2,838,087
16	Bobby Labonte	3810	36	1	5	7	$4,183,715
17	Jeff Green	3704	36	0	4	6	$2,531,339
18	Sterling Marlin	3703	29	2	8	14	$4,228,889
19	Dave Blaney	3670	36	0	0	5	$2,978,593
20	Robby Gordon	3632	36	0	1	5	$3,342,703
21	Kevin Harvick	3501	35	1	5	8	$3,849,216
22	Kyle Petty	3501	36	0	0	1	$2,198,073
23	Elliott Sadler	3418	36	0	2	7	$3,491,694
24	Terry Labonte	3417	36	0	1	4	$3,244,240
25	Ward Burton	3362	36	2	3	8	$4,899,884
26	Jeremy Mayfield	3309	36	0	2	4	$2,494,583
27	Jimmy Spencer	3187	34	0	2	6	$2,136,792
28	John Andretti	3161	36	0	0	1	$2,954,229
29	Johnny Benson	3132	31	1	3	7	$2,791,879
30	Ken Schrader	2954	36	0	0	0	$2,460,140
31	Mike Skinner	2886	36	0	0	1	$2,094,232
32	Bobby Hamilton	2832	31	0	0	3	$2,196,956
33	Steve Park	2694	32	0	0	2	$2,681,594
34	Joe Nemechek	2682	33	0	3	3	$2,454,482
35	Casey Atwood	2621	35	0	0	0	$1,988,254
36	Brett Bodine	2276	32	0	0	0	$1,766,820
37	Jerry Nadeau	2250	28	0	0	1	$1,806,133
38	Todd Bodine	1987	24	0	1	4	$1,879,767
39	Kenny Wallace	1868	21	0	0	1	$1,379,803
40	Hut Stricklin	1781	22	0	0	0	$1,313,548
41	Mike Wallace	1551	21	0	0	1	$1,274,703
42	Stacy Compton	1527	21	0	0	0	$1,185,709
43	Geoff Bodine	803	10	0	1	2	$1,224,501
44	Steve Grissom	769	10	0	0	1	$529,781
45	Hermie Sadler	698	10	0	0	0	$473,290
46	Jamie McMurray	679	6	1	1	2	$717,942
47	Rick Mast	576	9	0	0	0	$469,843
48	Greg Biffle	570	7	0	0	0	$394,773
49	Buckshot Jones	559	7	0	0	0	$394,223
50	Ted Musgrave	452	5	0	0	0	$283,770

Bad-boy Tony Stewart rallied from a last-place finish in the season-opening Daytona 500, scrambled back into contention, and delivered a late-season kick to capture the 2002 NASCAR Winston Cup championship.

Stewart took the lead in the points standings with a runner-up finish at Talladega in the 30th event of the 36-race campaign. Rookie Jimmie Johnson led going into the Talladega event, becoming the first rookie to lead the NASCAR standings since Dick Hutcherson in 1965.

Sterling Marlin led the points race from February through late September, but his season ended when he injured his neck at Kansas Speedway. Mark Martin, Johnson, and Stewart all led the standings in the final stretch.

Stewart cruised to an 18th-place finish in the season finale at Homestead-Miami Speedway to seal his first title. He finished 38 points ahead of runner-up Martin, who finished second in the NASCAR Winston Cup points chase for the fourth time in his career.

2003

February Tobacco company R.J. Reynolds confirms it has offered to step away from its Winston Cup sponsorship of NASCAR's premier stock car racing series.

February 16 Michael Waltrip wins the rain-shortened Daytona 500. Waltrip's Chevrolet is out front when the race is called after 272.5 miles and 109 laps.

March 2 Matt Kenseth scampers away from the field in the final laps and finishes nine seconds in front of runner-up Dale Earnhardt, Jr., to win the UAW-Daimler Chrysler 400 at Las Vegas Motor Speedway. It will be Kenseth's lone triumph in 2003.

March 16 Ricky Craven edges out Kurt Busch to win the Carolina Dodge Dealers 400 at Darlington Raceway. The official margin of victory is 0.002 second, the closest finish since NASCAR began using electronic timing systems in 1993.

April 6 Dale Earnhardt, Jr., makes a decisive pass with a controversial dip below the out-of-bounds line and wins the Aaron's 499 at Talladega. NASCAR officials rule that Earnhardt, Jr., completed the pass on Matt Kenseth and Jimmie Johnson before he crossed below the line.

June 19 NASCAR announces Nextel Communications will become the title sponsor of its top racing series in 2004. Nextel will replace Winston, which has provided sponsorship since 1971.

July 5 Rookie Greg Biffle pulls off an upset win in the Pepsi 400 at Daytona International Speedway. Pit strategy puts Biffle out front, and he coasts home when Bobby Labonte runs out of fuel on the final lap.

August 10 Road-racing specialists Robby Gordon and Scott Pruett run 1-2 in the Sirius @ The Glen. Gordon leads the final 30 laps to sweep both 2003 road-course events.

August 15 NASCAR announces that Sunoco will replace longtime sponsor Unocal as the Official Fuel of NASCAR beginning in 2004. Unocal and its predecessor Pure Oil and Union 76 have supported NASCAR since 1952.

In the 56th lap of the 45th annual running of the Daytona 500 on Feb. 16, Ken Schrader's #49 Dodge was clipped by Ward Burton, triggering a pileup. Schrader's car veered into the path of Ryan Newman, whose #12 Dodge went airborne and flipped violently into the infield grass along the front chute. Newman's car disintegrated into a million pieces, but, fortunately, the talented sophomore escaped unharmed.

Michael Waltrip dashed around leader Jimmie Johnson on the 106th lap of the Daytona 500, and was leading when a downpour, the second of the day, halted NASCAR's most-celebrated event after 109 laps had been completed. Waltrip's DEI Chevrolet was only in the lead for about three minutes on the track, but his #15 sat atop the scoreboard for nearly two hours in the rain before NASCAR was forced to call the race official. Waltrip's celebration didn't come from behind the wheel, but from a damp pit lane when the announcement was made.

▲ Matt Kenseth in the #17 Ford takes the checkered flag at Las Vegas Motor Speedway. Kenseth led the final 32 laps in the March 2 UAW-DaimlerChrysler 400 for his first win of the young season. The win propelled Kenseth to within three points of the NASCAR Winston Cup points lead. A week later, Kenseth took command in the points race and never trailed again even though he never again cracked victory lane in the 2003 campaign.

▶ With smoke spitting off their cars, #32 Ricky Craven and Kurt Busch grind toward the finish line in the thrilling conclusion to the March 16 Carolina Dodge Dealers 400 at Darlington Raceway. Craven nipped Busch by 0.002 second, the closest finish in NASCAR Cup Series history. Craven's triumph was the only one for the Pontiac nameplate in 2003 and may be its last victory in NASCAR. In October, Pontiac announced it was withdrawing from NASCAR's elite level of stock car racing.

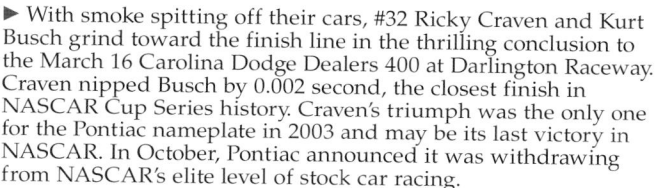

◀ A massive crash occurred on the fourth lap of the April 6 Aaron's 499 at Talladega Superspeedway. Ryan Newman's Dodge peeled a rear tire, sending his car head-first into the concrete retaining barrier. The ensuing collision took out seven cars and crippled a dozen others. Dale Earnhardt, Jr.'s #8 Chevrolet suffered cosmetic damage in the crash, but he was able to scramble back into contention and drive to his first victory of the season.

▶ Jimmie Johnson's #48 Chevrolet leads #17 Matt Kenseth and #8 Dale Earnhardt, Jr., in the latter stages of the Aaron's 499 at Talladega. This trio became the principles in a controversial late-race pass. As Kenseth was battling Johnson for the lead, Earnhardt, Jr., swept low to overtake both rivals, making the decisive pass while his left tires were below the yellow "out of bounds" line. NASCAR ruled that Earnhardt, Jr., had completed the pass before he drove below the line, a decision that outraged many of the other competitors. Number 29 Kevin Harvick chased Earnhardt, Jr., across the finish line to come home second, while Kenseth drifted to ninth and Johnson drifted all the way to 15th.

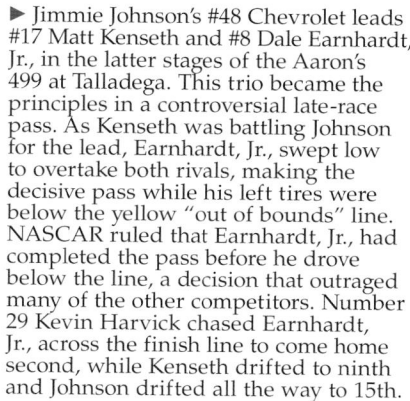

August 17 Ryan Newman wins the Michigan 400 at Michigan International Speedway. Jimmy Spencer and Kurt Busch fight in the garage after the race. NASCAR suspends Spencer for one week for punching Busch.

August 31 Terry Labonte wins last Labor Day weekend Southern 500 at Darlington Raceway. NASCAR has announced that beginning in 2004, the race date will be moved from NASCAR's original superspeedway to California Speedway.

September 13 Bill France, Jr., steps down as chairman and chief executive officer of NASCAR and names his 41-year-old son Brian as his successor.

September 21 Ryan Newman makes up a two-lap deficit to win the MBNA 400 at Dover International Speedway. For the race, NASCAR implemented a rule that prohibits racing back to the caution flag, and gives a lap back to drivers who aren't on the lead lap. The new rule was announced in the wake of drivers narrowly avoiding a collision with Dale Jarrett's crashed car a week earlier at New Hampshire.

October 28 Pontiac announces it is withdrawing from NASCAR competition, leaving Chevrolet as the lone General Motors make for 2004.

November 9 With a fourth-place finish in the Pop Secret 400 at Rockingham's North Carolina Speedway, Matt Kenseth wraps up his first NASCAR Winston Cup Championship. Bill Elliott scores his first win of the season in what will be Rockingham's final autumn race.

November 16 Bill Elliott pops a tire on the final lap allowing Bobby Labonte to win the Ford 400 at Homestead-Miami Speedway. Elliott, in his final full season as a competitor, had dominated the race until fate dealt him a harsh card with less than a mile remaining.

December Reports indicate NASCAR will adopt a new points procedure to determine the 2004 NASCAR Nextel Cup champion. NASCAR will adjust the points awarded to race winners, and develop a 10-race Chase for the Nextel Cup. The top 10 in the points standings after the 26th race qualify for the final 10-race chase.

Steve Park's twisted #1 Chevrolet rests facing traffic after he clobbered the wall in the early laps of the May 3 Pontiac Excitement 400 at Richmond International Raceway. A rash of accidents plagued Park during the 2003 NASCAR Winston Cup campaign and the Richmond event was his final ride with the DEI racing team. Joe Nemechek won after starting 22nd.

Jimmie Johnson shoves his #48 Chevrolet under Jeff Gordon to make the decisive pass in the May 17 The Winston NASCAR all-star race at Charlotte's Lowe's Motor Speedway. Johnson led the final 16 laps to pocket the million-dollar prize in what turned out to be the final all-star race sponsored by R.J. Reynolds and Winston. Johnson came back to Charlotte the following week and scampered to victory in the rain-shorted Coca-Cola 600.

Dale Earnhardt, Jr.'s #8 Budweiser Chevrolet slaps the wall on the 222nd lap of the Coca-Cola 600 at Charlotte as #1 Jeff Green ducks under safely. Green was taking his first ride in the DEI #1 Chevy in place of Steve Park, who had been beset with a series of crashes. Green finished 19th and Earnhardt, Jr., got credit for 41st in the final order. Earnhardt, Jr., found himself with a 160-point deficit to points leader Matt Kenseth after the Charlotte mishap.

Kurt Busch crosses the finish line first to win the June 15 Sirius 400 at Michigan International Speedway. With the win, Busch moved into the top five in points and became the season's first three-time winner. Busch finished with four wins for the season, which ranked second behind only Ryan Newman. Nonetheless, Busch was unable to crack the top 10 in the final points standings.

Rookie Greg Biffle flashes under the checkered flag to score an upset win in the July 5 Pepsi 400 at Daytona International Speedway. Biffle led the final 21 laps and won the race on fuel mileage. The underpowered Ford cars took an unlikely 1-2-3 sweep in the race under the lights. Biffle's triumph also halted a seven-race winning streak for DEI team cars in restrictor-plate races.

▲ Matt Kenseth's #17 DeWalt Ford runs just ahead of the #12 Dodge manned by Ryan Newman in the early stages of the July 27 Pennsylvania 500 at Pocono Raceway. Newman went on to rack up his fourth win of the season, which moved him into the top 10 in the NASCAR Winston Cup points standings for the first time in 2003. Kenseth drifted to a 13th-place finish, but still held a commanding 232-point lead in the lopsided chase for the championship.

Kevin Harvick cranks out a smoky burnout after his dramatic Aug. 3 win in the 10th annual Brickyard 400 at Indianapolis Motor Speedway. Harvick drove around Jamie McMurray with 16 laps to go and held on to win the celebrated race. Harvick finished 2.758 seconds ahead of runner-up Matt Kenseth, who was trapped in lapped traffic in the final laps. McMurray finished third.

One of the rituals of the Brickyard 400 is "Kissing of the Bricks." The honor goes to the winning team in the midsummer classic at Indianapolis Motor Speedway. Kevin Harvick, wife DeLana, team owner Richard Childress, and the entire GM Goodwrench team knelt down in unison to perform the joyous celebration. The Brickyard 400 victory was Harvick's first of the 2003 season.

Robby Gordon pushed his #31 RCR Enterprises Chevrolet to a big lead in the Aug. 10 Sirius @ The Glen event on the historic Watkins Glen road course. Gordon led the final 30 laps and outran hired-gun and road-racing specialist Scott Pruett to rack up his second straight road-course win. Gordon also prevailed in the June 22 race at Sonoma, Calif., giving him a sweep of the '03 road races.

Kurt Busch and Jimmy Spencer ran in close quarters quite often during the 2003 NASCAR Winston Cup season. During the Aug. 17 Michigan 400 at Michigan International Speedway, Busch and Spencer got into a bumping match near the end of the race. Busch admittedly put a "slide job" on Spencer, who registered his complaints immediately after the race with a couple of short jabs to Busch's nose. Spencer was reprimanded by NASCAR for his extracurricular activity in the garage area and had to sit out the following week's race at Bristol. Ryan Newman won the Michigan event when Busch ran out of fuel in the final four miles.

The battered cars of #2 Rusty Wallace and Michael Waltrip rest in a smoking heap after a bone-jarring collision in the Aug. 23 Sharpie 500 at Bristol Motor Speedway. Waltrip's car spun into the wall and bounced into the path of Wallace, who hit him squarely. Both drivers were shaken but not injured. Wallace suffered through his second straight winless season in '03 after winning at least one race for 16 consecutive years from 1986 to 2001.

Number 24 Jeff Gordon pops Ryan Newman's #12 Dodge into a sideways ride through the corner during the Sharpie 500. Newman and Gordon got into a couple of fender-bending grudge matches in the latter half of the 2003 campaign. Newman recovered from this shunt to finish sixth at Bristol, while Gordon was involved in a late-race wreck that left him with a 28th-place finish. Kurt Busch scored his third win in four races on the high banks of Bristol Motor Speedway.

Terry Labonte authored a heartwarming triumph in the Aug. 31 Southern 500 at Darlington Raceway. In a season dominated by the "young guns," the Texas veteran's late-race gallop to his 22nd career victory was perhaps *the* "feel good" story of 2003. The 54th annual running of the Labor Day weekend race at Darlington was a bittersweet affair for NASCAR traditionalists. Earlier in the year, NASCAR had announced that California Speedway would assume Darlington's holiday race date beginning in 2004.

▲ Elliott Sadler's Ford gyrates through the air in a wild tumble with six laps remaining in the Oct. 28 EA Sports 500 at Talladega Superspeedway. Sadler won the pole position in qualifying and was among the front-runners when the accident occurred. Dale Earnhardt, Jr., made a move to the inside of a pack of cars and Sadler flinched. Sadler made contact with Kurt Busch, spinning backward and high into the air. Fortunately, Sadler escaped the season's most spectacular wreck unharmed.

◄ Michael Waltrip pops through the roof of his #15 Chevrolet after a dramatic win in Talladega's EA Sports 500. Waltrip staved off a last-lap challenge from Dale Earnhardt, Jr., to score his second win of the season. Waltrip's Dale Earnhardt Inc. team was among the first to experiment with the roof hatch as an emergency escape device late in the 2003 season.

▼ Tony Stewart smokes up the frontstretch of Lowe's Motor Speedway after his victory in the Oct. 11 UAW-GM Quality 500. Stewart, the 2002 NASCAR Winston Cup champion, outran Ryan Newman for his second win of the season and celebrated with a lively burnout. In recent years, burnouts have become a customary procedure.

The Phoenix International Raceway is often referred to as the "Desert Jewel." Located in the Arizona desert 18 miles west of Phoenix, the picturesque one-mile track has hosted NASCAR's Cup Series since 1988. Many spectators opt to view the race from the hillside overlooking turns three and four. Dale Earnhardt, Jr., recorded his second and final win of the 2003 season with a triumph in the Nov. 2 Checker Auto Parts 500 presented by Havoline.

Near the end of the season, 49-year-old Bill Elliott hinted that he may cut back on his racing schedule in 2004. While the 1988 NASCAR Winston Cup champion was pondering his future, his on-track performance took a dramatic upswing toward the end of the year. In the Nov. 9 Pop Secret Microwave Popcorn 400 at Rockingham's North Carolina Speedway, Elliott spanked the field, leading five times for 141 laps. Elliott finished comfortably ahead of runner-up Jimmie Johnson to record his 44th career victory.

Matt Kenseth hoists the 2003 NASCAR Winston Cup championship trophy in victory lane following the Pop Secret Microwave Popcorn 400. Kenseth finished in fourth place behind winner Bill Elliott and wrapped up the title after 35 of the 36 races. Kenseth won only once in his title campaign, becoming only the fourth driver to take the championship with only one victory. By contrast, Kenseth won more races than any driver in 2002, yet only ranked eighth in the final standings. Kenseth proved consistency wins championships.

Jamie McMurray, one of the many high-profile young guns to hit the NASCAR Winston Cup tour in recent seasons, campaigned the #42 Chip Ganassi Dodge in 2003. The 27-year-old driver from Joplin, Miss., competed in all 36 events in the '03 season, logging five top-five finishes and 13 top-10 efforts. McMurray won the '03 Rookie of the Year award, finishing 27 points ahead of runner-up Greg Biffle. McMurray's best efforts were a pair of third-place finishes at Indy and Bristol, both in August.

"It's kind of like breaking through a plate-glass window not knowing what's on the other side.... It has been really tough emotionally to think about the four times we were so close with Mark [Martin] and came up just short."

—Jack Roush on his first championship

▶ Jack Roush, affectionately nicknamed the "Cat in the Hat," realized a lifelong dream by winning the 2003 NASCAR Winston Cup title. Since joining the NASCAR tour in 1988, Roush's cars had finished second four times, but had never won. In 1990, his championship quest was foiled by a 46-point penalty that cost Mark Martin the title. Matt Kenseth's incredibly consistent season in '03 finally gave the crusty mechanical genius from Livonia, Mich., a much-deserved championship ring.

NASCAR Winston Cup champion Matt Kenseth and his Jack Roush team pose in their black-tie best for photographers outside the Waldorf=Astoria Hotel in New York City. Shots like these are taken annually during the December NASCAR Awards Banquet, and the 2003 edition saw blizzard conditions play havoc with the normally festive ceremonies. The show went on as usual, though, as the Roush Racing team members discarded their heavy coats and shivered to allow photographers to record the wintry scene.

2003 NASCAR WINSTON CUP POINTS RACE

Rank	Driver	Points	Starts	Wins	Top 5	Top 10	Winnings
1	Matt Kenseth	5022	36	1	11	25	$9,422,764
2	Jimmie Johnson	4932	36	3	14	20	$7,745,530
3	Dale Earnhardt, Jr.	4815	36	2	13	21	$6,880,807
4	Jeff Gordon	4758	36	3	15	20	$6,622,002
5	Kevin Harvick	4770	36	1	11	18	$6,237,119
6	Ryan Newman	4711	36	8	17	22	$6,100,877
7	Tony Stewart	4549	36	2	12	18	$6,136,633
8	Bobby Labonte	4377	36	2	12	17	$5,505,018
9	Bill Elliott	4303	36	1	9	12	$5,008,530
10	Terry Labonte	4162	36	1	4	9	$4,283,625
11	Kurt Busch	4150	36	4	9	14	$5,587,384
12	Jeff Burton	4109	36	0	3	11	$4,384,752
13	Jamie McMurray	3965	36	0	5	13	$3,258,806
14	Rusty Wallace	3850	36	0	2	12	$4,246,547
15	Michael Waltrip	3934	36	2	8	11	$4,929,620
16	Robby Gordon	3856	36	2	4	10	$4,157,064
17	Mark Martin	3769	36	0	5	10	$4,486,560
18	Sterling Marlin	3745	36	0	0	11	$4,384,491
19	Jeremy Mayfield	3736	36	0	4	12	$3,371,879
20	Greg Biffle	3696	36	1	3	6	$2,805,673
21	Ward Burton	3550	36	0	0	4	$3,628,600
22	Elliott Sadler	3525	36	0	2	9	$3,795,174
23	Ricky Rudd	3521	36	0	4	5	$3,240,614
24	Johnny Benson, Jr.	3448	36	0	2	4	$3,544,793
25	Joe Nemechek	3426	36	1	2	6	$2,626,484
26	Dale Jarrett	3358	36	1	1	7	$4,121,487
27	Ricky Craven	3334	36	0	1	4	$3,216,211
28	Dave Blaney	3194	36	0	1	4	$2,828,692
29	Jimmy Spencer	3147	35	0	1	4	$2,565,803
30	Kenny Wallace	3061	36	0	0	1	$2,480,492
31	Todd Bodine	2976	35	0	0	1	$2,521,724
32	Steve Park	2923	35	0	1	3	$2,686,915
33	Tony Raines	2772	35	0	0	1	$2,122,739
34	Jeff Green	2656	31	0	0	1	$2,693,533
35	Casey Mears	2638	36	0	0	0	$2,639,178
36	Ken Schrader	2451	32	0	0	2	$2,007,424
37	Kyle Petty	2414	33	0	0	0	$2,293,222
38	John Andretti	2379	29	0	0	1	$2,577,616
39	Mike Skinner	1960	26	0	0	0	$1,782,804
40	Jack Sprague	1284	18	0	0	0	$1,187,834
41	Larry Foyt	1228	20	0	0	0	$1,180,994
42	Mike Wallace	1189	14	0	0	2	$1,031,103
43	Kevin Lepage	877	11	0	0	0	$742,077
44	Christian Fittipaldi	857	15	0	0	0	$1,265,835
45	Jerry Nadeau	844	10	0	1	1	$861,628
46	Derrike Cope	822	18	0	0	0	$1,030,691
47	Jason Leffler	764	10	0	0	0	$594,500
48	Scott Wimmer	599	6	0	0	1	$487,060
49	Brian Vickers	379	5	0	0	0	$263,484
50	Hermie Sadler	373	10	0	0	0	$552,741

Matt Kenseth dominated the 2003 season with amazing consistency. The Cambridge, Wisc., native only won one race but held the points lead for most of the year. With a fourth-place finish in the March 9 Bass Pro Shops MBNA 500 at Atlanta, Kenseth moved atop the points standings and never trailed again. He had only two DNFs the entire year.

Kenseth coasted home 90 points in front of runner-up Jimmie Johnson, and became the fourth driver to capture the title with only one win.

Kenseth led the points after 33 of the 36 races, the most dominating performance since Dale Earnhardt led all but two races in 1987. He also led the points standings more than any driver since Richard Petty led after 41 of 48 races in '71.

Kenseth, who gave owner Jack Roush his first title, was also the final champion crowned by series sponsor Winston. Effective in 2004, Nextel Communications became the title sponsor for NASCAR's top stock car racing series.

2004

January 20 NASCAR chairman and CEO Brian Z. France announces radical changes to the method used to determine the annual champion in 2004. Officially called the "Chase for the NASCAR NEXTEL Cup," the new points structure calls the top 10 drivers in the points standings through the first 26 races compete for the title over the final 10 races.

February 15 Dale Earnhardt, Jr., becomes the third son of a former Daytona 500 winner to capture the checkered flag at "The Great American Race." The previous father-son winners were Lee and Richard Petty and Bobby and Davey Allison.

February 22 Matt Kenseth nips rookie Kasey Kahne to win the Subway 400 at Rockingham. The thrilling contest is the final NASCAR Cup Series event at North Carolina Motor Speedway; the race will be moved to Phoenix.

April 25 Jeff Gordon wins the controversial Aaron's 499 at Talladega when a caution flag freezes the field as Dale Earnhardt, Jr., attempts a decisive pass for the lead. Rules implemented in late 2003 prohibit "racing back to the flag" during a caution period.

May 14 NASCAR announces that North Carolina Speedway in Rockingham will no longer host a NASCAR NEXTEL Cup event in 2005, and Darlington Raceway, the nation's first superspeedway, will host only one race in '05. NASCAR also announces that the Phoenix and Texas tracks will each host a second race in '05.

June 6 Mark Martin ends a two-year drought with a come-from-behind win in the MBNA 400 "A Salute to Heroes" at Dover International Speedway.

July 18 Dale Earnhardt, Jr., holding down second place in the NASCAR NEXTEL Cup points standings, suffers serious burns during practice for an American Le Mans Series race at Infineon Raceway in Sonoma, Calif.

September 5 Elliott Sadler wins the inaugural Pop Secret 500 at California Speedway. It is the first year for the event, which had been the traditional Labor Day Southern 500 at Darlington Raceway since 1950.

Dale Earnhardt, Jr., drives his #8 Chevrolet Monte Carlo across the finish line three car lengths in front of #20 Tony Stewart to win the 46th running of the Daytona 500 on Feb. 15. Earnhardt, Jr., charged past his friendly rival with 20 laps to go and maintained his narrow advantage for the final 50 miles to post his first win in "The Great American Race."

Small-time independent racer Carl Long tumbles down the backstretch on lap 264 of the Feb. 22 Subway 400 at Rockingham's North Carolina Speedway. A privateer with no sponsorship funding, Long demolished his only car in the mishap. Long was clipped from behind and darted into the wall before rolling over several times. Fortunately, he escaped injury.

North Carolina Speedway has been one of NASCAR's most competitive tracks since it opened in 1965. The finish of the 2004 Subway 400 enhanced that reputation as #17 Matt Kenseth held off a frantic late-race charge by rookie #9 Kasey Kahne to score a photo-finish victory. Kahne, a graduate from the rugged Midwestern Sprint Car circuit, was making only his second start in the NASCAR Nextel Cup Series. The 400-miler was the final race at Rockingham. Its race date was moved to Phoenix for 2005.

Tony Stewart passes a spinning #80 Andy Hillenburg during the March 21 Carolina Dodge Dealers 400 at Darlington Raceway. Hillenburg drifted into Stewart's path and made contact, spinning the #80 Ford into Jeff Gordon's race line. Gordon hit Hillenburg in the side, causing his #24 DuPont Chevrolet to start on fire. Both Gordon and Hillenburg were shaken but uninjured. Gordon's teammate, Jimmie Johnson, won the race.

A jubilant Kurt Busch pumps his fists in victory lane following his win in the March 28 Food City 500 at Bristol Motor Speedway. Busch led the final 119 laps on the high-banked concrete oval and beat runner-up Rusty Wallace by less than a half-second. With the win, Busch joined Darrell Waltrip, Cale Yarborough, and Fred Lorenzen as the only drivers to win three in a row at Bristol.

Elliott Sadler guns his #38 Ford across the finish line a half car length in front of #9 Kasey Kahne to score a victory in the April 4 Samsung/Radio Shack 500 at Texas Motor Speedway. The triumph was Sadler's first in three years. Kahne finished second for the third time in the first seven races of his rookie season.

Rusty Wallace whips his #2 Dodge through the fourth turn at Martinsville Speedway on his way to victory in the April 18 Advance Auto Parts 500. The narrow triumph over Bobby Labonte ended a three-year void for the former NASCAR champion, who last won at California Speedway in 2001. Wallace led the final 45 laps to secure his 55th career NASCAR Cup Series win.

Jeff Gordon inspects damage to the front of his DuPont Chevrolet during a red-flag stop at Martinsville Speedway. A chunk of concrete dislodged from the third turn on lap 290 and struck the front of Gordon's car as he was attempting to pass Dale Earnhardt, Jr., for the lead. The red flag was out for one hour and 17 minutes while workmen patched the track. The incident foiled Gordon's efforts to win a third consecutive Martinsville race from the pole. He finished sixth.

September 11 Jeremy Mayfield wins the Chevy Rock & Roll 400 at Richmond International Raceway. Mayfield ends a winless skid dating back to June 2000. He also grabs one of the coveted spots in the "Chase for the NASCAR NEXTEL Cup."

September 19 Kurt Busch scores a lopsided victory in the Sylvania 300 at New Hampshire International Raceway, site of the first race of the new Chase for the NASCAR NEXTEL Cup. Busch and Dale Earnhardt, Jr., are tied for the points lead with nine races left.

October 3 Dale Earnhardt, Jr., takes the lead in the title chase with a win in the EA Sports 500 at Talladega Superspeedway. During the television interview in victory lane, Junior's response to a question includes an expletive. Following a precedent set earlier in the year, NASCAR docks Earnhardt $10,000 and 25 points, dropping him from first to second in the standings.

October 24 Tragedy strikes when the Hendrick Motorsports company plane crashes into a foggy mountainside minutes before the Subway 500 at Martinsville Speedway. None of the 10 people onboard survive. Hendrick Motorsports driver Jimmie Johnson wins, and is informed of the tragic incident after the race.

November 10 NASCAR president Mike Helton lifts the long-standing ban on sponsorship from hard liquor companies effective with the 2005 season. NASCAR teams can now recruit sponsorship dollars from corporations that manufacture "spirits."

November 14 Jimmie Johnson, counted out of the "Chase" a month ago, racks up his fourth win in the last five races in the final Mountain Dew Southern 500 at Darlington Raceway. Johnson has rallied from a 247-point deficit and ninth place in the standings to 18 points behind leader Kurt Busch with one race remaining.

November 21 Roush Racing hits the jackpot as Greg Biffle wins the Ford 400 at Homestead-Miami Speedway and Kurt Busch finishes fifth to claim the 2004 "Chase for the NASCAR NEXTEL Cup" championship. Bush's eight-point margin over Jimmie Johnson is the closest finish in the 56 years of NASCAR Cup Series racing.

Kerry Earnhardt's #33 Chevrolet lurches sideways after a tap from #15 Michael Waltrip during the April 25 Aaron's 499 at Talladega Superspeedway. Earnhardt started 36th, but made a spectacular run to the front and climbed to seventh before the lap-113 shunt with Waltrip ended his day. Earnhardt made only three NASCAR NEXTEL Cup starts in 2004.

Jeff Gordon cruises along Talladega Superspeedway's littered frontstretch during the final laps of the Aaron's 499. Dale Earnhardt, Jr., was in the process of passing Gordon for the lead with five laps remaining, but Gordon's teammate Brian Vickers spun out, bringing out the caution flag. NASCAR officials elected to let the race end under the yellow, inciting the wrath of the huge trackside throng of 155,000. A rule enacted in autumn 2003 that prevents drivers from racing back to the flag when a yellow comes out froze the field and gave Gordon a controversial win. Spectators tossed beverage cans and other debris onto the track. The race was the slowest in the history of the Talladega Superspeedway, featuring a record 11 caution flags that consumed nearly 150 miles.

Jimmie Johnson pushed his #48 Chevrolet around Jamie McMurray's #42 Dodge with 17 laps remaining, and charged to victory in the May 30 Coca-Cola 600 at Charlotte's Lowe's Motor Speedway. Johnson thoroughly dominated the race. He led 334 of the 400 laps, and was never passed under green-flag conditions. Johnson finished one lap shy of Jim Paschal's record of 335 laps led in the 1967 World 600.

Jimmie Johnson coasts under the checkered and yellow flags just ahead of runner-up #19 Jeremy Mayfield to win the June 13 Pocono 500 at Pocono Raceway. Johnson overcame an officiating oversight that kept him off pit road while many competitors were allowed to pit under yellow. The 500-miler was plagued by a record number of caution laps. In fact, including the Pocono event, four of the last six races in the '04 season set records for the slowest average speed in each track's history.

Mark Martin ended a 72-race winless drought with a surprising victory in the June 6 MBNA 400 "A Salute To Heroes" at Dover International Speedway. Martin was the beneficiary of the "lucky dog" rule late in the race. The rule, which was instituted in late 2003, allows the first car running a lap down to get his lap back when a caution flag comes out. Martin was given the lucky dog freebie at Dover even though Dave Blaney was actually the first driver a lap down. Given renewed life by the error, Martin came on strong toward the end, leading the final 19 laps to score his 34th career NASCAR Cup Series win.

Ryan Newman sailed past Dale Jarrett with 17 laps remaining to take the lead in the June 20 DHL 400 at Michigan International Speedway. Newman went on to record his first victory of the 2004 season. Newman, who had won eight races in 2003 and finish sixth in the points standings, would win only one more time in '04 and finish seventh in points. Jarrett finished third in the DHL 400 after starting 37th.

Tony Stewart drives his #20 Chevrolet under Kasey Kahne during the July 11 Tropicana 400 at Chicagoland Speedway. Stewart and Kahne were the principles in a lap-128 crash that triggered a pit road free-for-all among the respective pit crews. Stewart slapped the rear bumper of Kahne on a green-flag restart, sending Kahne's Dodge into the wall. Members of Kahne's Evernham Racing pit crew took their complaints to the Stewart/Joe Gibbs Racing pits, and a scuffle ensued. NASCAR officials quickly got the situation under control. Stewart went on to score his first victory of the year.

July 17-18 was one of the very few free weekends on the crowded NASCAR NEXTEL Cup schedule. Without a NASCAR commitment, Dale Earnhardt, Jr., planned to compete in an American Le Mans Series race at Infineon Speedway in Sonoma, Calif. Driving a Chevrolet Corvette C5-R, Earnhardt, Jr., crashed on the opening lap of a July 18 morning practice session and the car burst into flames. Earnhardt, Jr., was able to climb out of the burning vehicle with burns to his legs and back. Earnhardt missed no NASCAR NEXTEL Cup races due to his injuries, but he did need help from relief drivers in the next two races.

The Roush Racing pit crew hurriedly services Greg Biffle's Ford during a stop in the Aug. 22 GFS Marketplace 400 at Michigan International Speedway. One crewman strips a piece of film off the windshield as other pit-crew members refuel the car and change tires. NASCAR NEXTEL Cup cars have several layers of the plastic film on their windshields. Layers can be removed if the windshield gets dirty or pitted during a race. Biffle went on to win the race for his second career NASCAR Cup Series victory.

Casey Mears and Ward Burton follow the pace car prior to the start of the Aug. 8 Brickyard 400 at Indianapolis Motor Speedway. Mears earned his first career pole and kept alive a Mears family tradition by taking the pole at Indianapolis. His uncle Rick Mears won six poles for the famed Indianapolis 500. Mears finished 26th. Jeff Gordon won the event for the fourth time in 11 tries.

A pack of cars speeds past the frontstretch grandstands as darkness descends upon the California Speedway during the Sept. 5 Pop Secret 500. The two-mile track became home to the Labor Day NASCAR NEXTEL Cup race as the historic Darlington Raceway lost its traditional holiday weekend event. Elliott Sadler scored his third career win in the 500-miler.

Dale Earnhardt, Jr., squeezes his #8 Budweiser Chevrolet past #48 Jimmie Johnson during the middle stages of the Aug. 28 Sharpie 500 at Bristol Motor Speedway. Earnhardt, Jr., started in 30th position, but easily scrambled his way through the field in dominating fashion. Junior led 295 of the 500 laps and finished comfortably ahead of runner-up Ryan Newman. Johnson finished third.

▶ Jeremy Mayfield and his Evernham Racing crew celebrate after the Sept. 11 Chevy Rock & Roll 400 at Richmond International Raceway. Mayfield prevailed in the 26th and final "regular season" NASCAR NEXTEL Cup race, earning his way into the final 10-race chase. Mayfield took the lead seven laps from the finish when leader Kurt Busch ran out of fuel. The win put Mayfield ninth in the ten-man "Chase for the NASCAR NEXTEL Cup." Mayfield's Evernham Motorsports teammate Kasey Kahne fell out of the top 10 with a 24th-place finish.

In the first ever race in the Chase for the NASCAR NEXTEL Cup was the Sept. 19 Sylvania 300 at New Hampshire International Speedway. Controversy flared when #31 Robby Gordon knocked Greg Biffle into a spin, also collecting #19 Jeremy Mayfield and Tony Stewart, who was running just behind the incident. Gordon admittedly took out Biffle, but he was unaware that the crash would also scoop up two of the playoff contenders and take them out of the title hunt. Kurt Busch won the race and leaped from seventh to a first-place tie in the points standings.

Elliott Sadler's #38 Ford breaks loose in the tri-oval area of Talladega Superspeedway on the final lap of the Oct. 3 EA Sports 500. Dale Earnhardt, Jr., took the checkered flag as Sadler's car sailed through the air and landed on all four wheels near the finish line. Sadler got credit for a 23rd-place finish, losing 10 positions during his 190-mph pirouette.

The Chase for the NASCAR NEXTEL Cup

IN NASCAR'S STORIED HISTORY, a number of points systems have determined the annual championship. Starting in 1975, all races offered an equal number of points.

From 1975 to 2003, this is how it worked: 175 points were awarded to the winner of each race, with 170 for second, and a drop of five points for positions three through six. Positions seven through 12 each had a four-point reduction, and from 13th through 43rd, points dropped three for each position. In addition, five bonus points were awarded to any driver who officially led a lap, and another five points were earned by the driver leading the most laps. The most points a driver could win in a race was 185, and 43rd position netted 34 points.

With the goal of garnering better TV ratings against the NFL, NASCAR introduced a new way to determine its top dog for the 2004 season.

The new system would would use the same points structure, but award another five points to the winner of each race. More importantly it would sidestep the season-long accumulation of points to determine a champion. Instead, the season's first 26 races would determine the qualifiers for the final 10-race chase. The top 10 drivers, and any other driver within 400 points of the leader, would compete for the title. NASCAR called the new system the "Chase for the NEXTEL Cup."

Traditionalists balked at the idea, saying the first 26 events would merely serve as qualifying races. However, NASCAR chairman and CEO Brian Z. France was confident that the new system would add excitement to the final championship stretch and create a host of contenders over the final 10 races.

The 10 qualifiers for the 2004 "Chase for the NASCAR NEXTEL Cup" (from left to right): Dale Earnhardt, Jr., Jeff Gordon, Matt Kenseth, Tony Stewart, Jimmie Johnson, Elliott Sadler, Jeremy Mayfield, Kurt Busch, Ryan Newman, and Mark Martin.

The 10 qualifiers for the final "Chase" had their points adjusted after the 26th event. The finalists were separated by no more than 45 points entering the final 10-race stretch. "If more drivers have an opportunity to win a championship," France said, "that's a great thing."

In retrospect, the first Chase for the NASCAR NEXTEL Cup lived up to its billing. The 2004 title came down to a frantic battle among Kurt Busch, Jimmie Johnson, and Jeff Gordon. Dale Earnhardt, Jr., and Mark Martin also had a mathematical chance entering the final race at Homestead, Fla. That last race provided a lap-by-lap struggle like the sport hadn't seen since 1992 when Alan Kulwicki edged Bill Elliott by 10 points for the title. The outcome in '04 wasn't determined until the last lap when Busch finished fifth to beat Johnson by a scant eight points. It was the closest title chase in NASCAR history.

Busch would have finished a distant fourth in the customary points system and Jeff Gordon would have won his fifth championship. Under the new system, Busch snatched the title with a spirited run in the all-important 10-race Chase.

But NASCAR wasn't satisfied to rest on its laurels. After fan favorites Dale Earnhardt, Jr., and Jeff Gordon failed to make The Chase in 2005 and defending champion Tony Stewart failed to qualify in 2006, NASCAR amended the rules to include 12 drivers in the annual 10-race Chase. The points standings entering The Chase were also changed. Each driver was given 5000 points plus 10 extra points for each win. The rule stating that any driver within 400 points of the leader would also qualify was eliminated. This system was retained when the name was changed to the Chase for the NASCAR Sprint Cup in 2008.

2004

Dale Earnhardt, Jr., is interviewed by the NBC television network following his dramatic victory in the 500-miler at Talladega. In the heat of the celebration, Junior said of his victory, "It don't mean s--- right now. Daddy's won here 10 times" to NBC reporter Matt Yocum. Earnhardt, Jr.'s victory moved him atop the NASCAR NEXTEL Cup points standings, but NASCAR docked him 25 points and $10,000 the next day for cursing on network television, moving him 12 points behind new leader Kurt Busch.

Jeff Gordon's ill-handling #24 Chevrolet cuts across the front of Rusty Wallace's #2 Dodge on lap 76 of the Oct. 16 UAW-GM Quality 500 at Lowe's Motor Speedway. Gordon fell a lap off the pace and was in danger of losing considerable ground in the championship hunt. But after the halfway mark, Gordon was the recipient of the controversial "lucky dog" rule and got back on the lead lap. A tremendous rally in the late stages netted Gordon a second-place finish behind teammate Jimmie Johnson.

Dale Earnhardt, Jr., wrestles his battered Chevrolet down pit road after a bout with the inside retaining wall during the final stages of the Oct. 31 Bass Pro Shops/MBNA 500 at Atlanta Motor Speedway. The mishap occurred when Junior was running in third place. He wound up finishing 33rd, which cost him more than 100 valuable points in the "Chase for the NASCAR NEXTEL Cup."

The Hendrick Motorsports pit crew services Jimmie Johnson's Chevrolet during the 500-miler at Atlanta. A message reading "Always In Our Hearts" was placed on the hood of Johnson's car in tribute to the 10 members of the Hendrick Motorsports family that perished in a private plane crash near Martinsville on Oct. 24. Johnson won the Atlanta race to rack up his third straight victory.

The sun sets over the Darlington Raceway during the late stages of the Nov. 14 Mountain Dew Southern 500. This photo serves as a portrait of the present and future of stock car racing's oldest superspeedway, and the demise of the famed Southern 500. The rich tradition of the Southern 500 was effectively ended with this, the final running of the 54-year-old event at the 1.366-mile speedway. Jimmie Johnson won the race. It was his fourth victory in his last five starts, and his eighth of the 2004 season.

The winner, the champ, and he who would be king: Greg Biffle leads Kurt Busch and Jeff Gordon at Homestead-Miami Speedway in the Nov. 21 Ford 400. Biffle drove to victory in the season finale as Busch wrapped up the NASCAR NEXTEL Cup Championship with a hard-fought fifth-place finish. Busch overcame a broken wheel and several unscheduled pit stops to finish in the top five and win the title by eight points over Jimmie Johnson, who finished second. Gordon finished third, and also wound up third in the final points standings.

2004 NASCAR NEXTEL CUP POINTS RACE

Rank	Driver	Points	Starts	Wins	Top 5	Top 10	Winnings
1	Kurt Busch	6506	36	3	10	21	$9,677,543
2	Jimmie Johnson	6498	36	8	20	23	$8,275,721
3	Jeff Gordon	6490	36	5	16	25	$8,439,382
4	Mark Martin	6399	36	1	10	15	$5,479,004
5	Dale Earnhardt, Jr.	6368	36	6	16	21	$8,913,510
6	Tony Stewart	6326	36	2	10	19	$7,830,807
7	Ryan Newman	6180	36	2	11	14	$6,354,256
8	Matt Kenseth	6069	36	2	8	16	$7,405,309
9	Elliott Sadler	6024	36	2	8	14	$6,244,954
10	Jeremy Mayfield	6000	36	1	5	13	$4,919,342
11	Jamie McMurray	4597	36	0	9	23	$4,676,311
12	Bobby Labonte	4277	36	0	5	11	$5,201,397
13	Kasey Kahne	4274	36	0	13	14	$5,415,611
14	Kevin Harvick	4228	36	0	5	14	$5,321,337
15	Dale Jarrett	4214	36	0	6	14	$5,097,396
16	Rusty Wallace	3960	36	1	3	11	$4,981,100
17	Greg Biffle	3902	36	2	4	8	$4,092,877
18	Jeff Burton	3902	36	0	2	6	$4,054,310
19	Joe Nemechek	3878	36	1	3	9	$4,345,554
20	Michael Waltrip	3878	36	0	2	9	$4,694,564
21	Sterling Marlin	3857	36	0	3	7	$4,457,443
22	Casey Mears	3690	36	0	1	9	$3,462,623
23	Robby Gordon	3646	36	0	2	6	$4,225,719
24	Ricky Rudd	3615	36	0	1	3	$3,905,141
25	Brian Vickers	3521	36	0	0	4	$3,135,886
26	Terry Labonte	3519	36	0	0	6	$3,745,242
27	Scott Wimmer	3198	35	0	1	2	$3,675,879
28	Brendan Gaughan	3165	36	0	1	4	$2,929,396
29	Scott Riggs	3090	35	0	1	2	$3,443,345
30	Jeff Green	3054	36	0	0	1	$3,483,436
31	Ken Schrader	3032	36	0	0	1	$2,666,592
32	Ward Burton	2929	34	0	0	3	$2,471,941
33	Kyle Petty	2811	35	0	0	0	$2,780,131
34	Ricky Craven	2086	26	0	0	0	$2,337,417
35	Jimmy Spencer	1969	26	0	0	0	$1,985,121
36	Johnny Sauter	1430	16	0	0	0	$1,333,521
37	Carl Edwards	1424	13	0	1	5	$1,410,571
38	Dave Blaney	1347	16	0	0	0	$1,461,638
39	Bobby Hamilton, Jr.	1271	17	0	0	0	$1,259,213
40	Derrike Cope	1058	18	0	0	0	$1,349,621
41	Todd Bodine	986	21	0	0	0	$1,275,532
42	Morgan Shepherd	925	19	0	0	0	$1,133,618
43	Kevin Lepage	915	17	0	0	0	$1,217,519
44	Hermie Sadler	852	16	0	0	0	$945,459
45	John Andretti	818	9	0	0	0	$752,386
46	Mike Wallace	764	10	0	0	1	$624,850
47	Kirk Shelmerdine	723	18	0	0	0	$1,095,040
48	Bill Elliott	595	6	0	0	1	$567,900
49	Mike Bliss	407	4	0	1	2	$284,405
50	Kenny Wallace	365	5	0	0	0	$366,155

The first "Chase for the NASCAR NEXTEL Cup" produced a thrilling conclusion to the 2004 NASCAR season. Five drivers had a shot to win the title entering the season finale. Kurt Busch claimed top honors by a scant eight points over runner-up Jimmie Johnson. Jeff Gordon placed third, only 16 points behind.

Busch overcame numerous problems on his road to the title. Twice during the final 10-race chase, Busch spun in heavy traffic but escaped unscathed. Constantly battling back from deep in the pack, Busch logged nine top-10 finishes in the final 10 races to win the closest points race in NASCAR history.

Busch was the most consistent driver during the important 10-race "chase," with an average finish position of 8.9. Johnson averaged a 10.2 position.

Under the previous points system, Jeff Gordon would have edged teammate Johnson by 47 points. Busch would have placed a distant fourth, 247 points out of first place.

All told, the points lead changed hands eight times among five drivers.

2005

February 20 Jeff Gordon squeaks past Tony Stewart in the waning laps and wins the first Daytona 500 in history to go into overtime. The race is also the first for the new Dodge Charger, which replaces the Intrepid.

February 27 Greg Biffle wins the Auto Club 500 at California Speedway. Traditionally the race date for Rockingham's North Carolina Speedway, the weekend is now a second race date for California. Unlike previous events at California, this one is not a sellout.

April 17 Greg Biffle leads 219 of 334 laps in the Samsung/Radioshack 500 at Texas Motor Speedway in his back-up car and goes on to win. Biffle crashed his main car in practice and had to move from fifth to the back of the field. It is the Roush Racing driver's second win of the season and it puts him in second in the points race.

April 23 Defending champion Kurt Busch wins the Subway Fresh 500, the first night race at Phoenix International Raceway. It is also the first spring date for Phoenix, in addition to its usual late-season race.

May 7 Greg Biffle wins the first night race at Darlington Raceway. The race goes into overtime when a yellow flag comes out after Mark Martin spins with four laps to go. The caution erases Ryan Newman's four-second lead. It is Biffle's third win of the season and the fifth win in 10 races for Roush Racing.

May 14 After six career second-place finishes, Kasey Kahne scores his first career NASCAR NEXTEL Cup victory in the Chevy American Revolution 400 at Richmond International Raceway.

June 12 Carl Edwards drives to victory in the Pocono 500 at Pocono Raceway. The win is bittersweet because it causes Edwards to miss a rain-delayed NASCAR Busch Series race at Nashville and thus lose his points lead in NASCAR's second highest series.

July 14 Ford unveils the NASCAR version of its new 2006 Fusion midsize sedan. The car is set to make its racing debut at the February 2006 Daytona 500, marking the first time in 38 years that Ford has introduced a brand-new model and raced it in the same year.

Jeff Gordon celebrates with a burnout after winning the Feb. 20 Daytona 500. Gordon posted his third victory in "The Great American Race" with a late spurt, passing Tony Stewart in the first overtime race in the history of the Daytona 500. Stewart led for more than half of the race, but got juked by Jimmie Johnson and wound up in seventh place. Kurt Busch finished second with Dale Earnhardt, Jr., third.

Jimmie Johnson strikes a pose wearing a championship-boxing style belt after winning the March 13 UAW-DaimlerChrysler 400 at Las Vegas Motor Speedway. In the postrace inspection, NASCAR officials found the roof to be too low. The win was allowed to stand, but Johnson was docked 25 driver points and crew chief Chad Knaus was suspended for two races (the suspension was lifted on appeal). Nineteen-year old rookie and hometown boy Kyle Busch finished second at Las Vegas, one spot ahead of older brother Kurt.

Carl Edwards performs what would become his trademark backflip after winning the March 20 Golden Corral 500 at Atlanta Motor Speedway. Edwards passed Jimmie Johnson at the finish line to win by a scant .028 second. It was the first career win for the Roush Racing driver in only his 17th start, and it came a day after he won his first NASCAR Busch Series race. Edwards would go on to post four wins in his first full season on the NASCAR NEXTEL Cup circuit.

Bristol Motor Speedway's fast half mile is known for mayhem, but it's often single-car wrecks. Lap 333 of the April 3 Food City 500 included a pileup the likes of which are usually reserved for restrictor-plate racing at Talladega. The incident started when Bobby Hamilton tapped Ken Schrader, sending him into the wall in turn three. Fourteen cars were collected in the crash, which brought out a red flag to clear the track that lasted almost 14 minutes. Number 97 Kurt Busch survived the accident, only to experience a harder crash 30 laps later when he hit a spinning Jeff Burton. No drivers were hurt in the two incidents.

Kevin Harvick takes the checkered flag to win the Food City 500. For Harvick, it was his fourth win in NASCAR NEXTEL Cup competition. After five races in the 2005 season, Harvick's win was the first by a team other than Roush Racing or Hendrick Motorsports. The two powerhouse teams would go on to win 19 of the season's 36 races.

Greg Biffle drives his #16 Ford Taurus under the checkered flag in the Samsung/Radioshack 500 at Texas Motor Speedway. Biffle led 219 of the 334 laps in the April 17 event, even though he was driving his backup car. Biffle had crashed his primary car in practice on Saturday, moving him from fifth in the starting lineup to the back of the field. The win was Biffle's second in seven 2005 starts, and it left him comfortably in second in the points race.

The red flag waves signaling a temporary halt in the action after a lap 133 crash in the May 1 Aaron's 499 at Talladega Superspeedway. A total of 25 cars were involved in the incident that started when Jimmie Johnson tapped Mike Wallace in turn one. Eighteen cars went to the garage for repairs and 10 drivers were treated in the infield care center, but none were seriously hurt. Jeff Gordon steered clear of trouble and won the race.

August 7 Indiana-native Tony Stewart calls winning the Allstate 400 at the Brickyard "The greatest day of my life." It is Stewart's fourth of five wins in a seven-race span.

September 4 Kyle Busch, 20, becomes the youngest driver ever to win a NASCAR Cup Series race when he outduels Greg Biffle in the Sony HD 500 at California Speedway.

September 10 Ryan Newman benefits from Jamie McMurray's lap 362 crash to claim the final spot in the Chase for the NASCAR NEXTEL Cup. Fan favorites Jeff Gordon and Dale Earnhardt, Jr., fail to qualify for The Chase.

October 15 NASCAR mandates minimum tire pressures and institutes competition cautions to check pressures during the UAW-GM Quality 500 at Lowe's Motor Speedway. Twenty-two cautions had flown at the track in the May race, and 15 more followed in the fall, many due to blown tires. The track was scheduled to be repaved prior to the 2006 events. Jimmie Johnson recovers from a blown tire to win his fourth straight race at Lowe's.

November 10 NASCAR announces owners will be limited to fielding four teams during the 2006 campaign. The ruling will most affect Roush Racing, which has qualified all five of its teams for the 10-car Chase for the NASCAR NEXTEL Cup. Roush will be allowed to field five teams for the duration of existing sponsor contracts, and teams that field developmental drivers on a part-time basis will be allowed to exceed the limit.

November 20 Ricky Rudd finishes 37th in the Ford 400 at Homestead-Miami Raceway, then retires. The race marked Rudd's 788th consecutive start, a NASCAR NEXTEL Cup record that may never be broken. The streak started in 1981.

November 20 Tony Stewart holds on for a 15th place finish to wrap up the 2005 NASCAR NEXTEL Cup title. Greg Biffle edges out Mark Martin at the finish line and moves from fourth to second in the final standings.

December 7 NASCAR announces it has signed an eight-year, $4.48 billion television contract with ABC, ESPN, FOX, and TNT that will be effective starting with the 2007 season.

Kasey Kahne holds the trophy after winning the May 14 Chevy American Revolution 500 at Richmond International Raceway. It was the 25-year-old's first career NASCAR NEXTEL Cup win, after six second-place finishes in 47 starts.

Bill Elliott's #91 Dodge Charger lurches sideways in the May 29 Coca-Cola 600 at Lowe's Motor Speedway, one of 22 caution flags for 103 laps in the 5¼-hour marathon. Ryan Newman won the pole at nearly 193 mph, but the average speed for the 600 miles was only 114 mph. It was the most caution flags ever in a NASCAR NEXTEL Cup race.

Jimmie Johnson pushes his #48 Chevrolet past Bobby Labonte on the last lap of the Coca-Cola 600. The late-race heroics gave Johnson his third straight win at Lowe's, this one by only .027 seconds. Fred Lorenzen is the only other driver to win three straight at the Charlotte, N.C., track.

Tony Stewart pilots his #20 Chevrolet Monte Carlo during the June 26 Dodge/Save Mart 350 at Infineon Raceway. Stewart passed Ricky Rudd with 10 laps to go and went on to win by 2.2 seconds over the veteran Rudd, who hung on to finish second. For Stewart, it was his first win of the season and his fourth in 13 starts on a road course.

Dale Earnhardt, Jr., and #22 Scott Wimmer duke it out during the July 10 USG Sheetrock 400 at Chicago Speedway. The race was the highlight of Earnhardt's disappointing season. A win at Chicago boosted Earnhardt from 16th to 13th in the standings with eight races left to qualify for the Chase for the NASCAR NEXTEL Cup. Seventeenth entering The Chase, Earnhardt failed to qualify and he would drop to 19th in the final standings.

Tony Stewart and his entire crew scale the fence at Indianapolis Motor Speedway following the Aug. 7 Allstate 400 at the Brickyard. Though new to NASCAR, the spiderlike celebration was made popular by Indy Racing League driver Helio Castroneves. Stewart started 22nd but ran down the favorites to win his second consecutive race in a flourish that would see him win five out of seven NASCAR NEXTEL Cup events.

Rusty Wallace waves to his fans during a parade lap prior to the Sharpie 500 at Bristol Motor Speedway. Though he posted no wins, Wallace had a successful campaign for Penske Racing South, qualifying for the Chase for the NASCAR NEXTEL Cup and finishing eighth overall. The 1989 champion went out as the eighth winningest driver in NASCAR history, visiting victory lane 55 times during his 26-year career.

A member of Ryan Newman's pit crew examines his wrecked #12 Dodge after a lap 317 crash caused by Dale Jarrett. Jarrett was retaliating for a tap on lap 301 by Newman that sent him spinning. Kevin Harvick was also collected in the incident, which threatened the Chase for the NASCAR NEXTEL Cup hopes of all three drivers. NASCAR penalized Jarrett by instructing him to park his car for two laps. Jarrett and Harvick would fail to make The Chase, but Newman managed to hang on for the last spot.

Rookie Kyle Busch celebrates his first career win after the Sept. 4 Sony HD 500 at California Speedway. Busch became the youngest winner in NASCAR history, topping the 53-year-old standard set by Donald Thomas. Busch was 20 years old when he won at California Speedway, four days younger than Thomas was when he won at Atlanta's Lakewood Speedway on Nov. 16, 1952.

Mark Martin, #24 Jeff Gordon, and #12 Ryan Newman dice it out in close quarters during the Sept. 10 Chevy Rock & Roll 400 at Richmond International Raceway. It was the 26th and final run to see who graduated into the Chase for the NASCAR NEXTEL Cup, and two of them made it. Martin was solidly in The Chase and Newman took advantage of Jamie McMurray's misfortune to claim the last spot. Gordon finished 30th at Richmond, leaving him 12th overall and out of The Chase. Dale Earnhardt, Jr., another fan favorite, missed The Chase as well.

Ryan Newman buries the start/finish line under a cloud of smoke after kicking off the Chase for the NASCAR NEXTEL Cup with a win in the Sept. 18 Sylvania 300 at New Hampshire International Speedway. Newman passed Tony Stewart on the second-to-last lap, and moved from 10th to third in the points race. A tussle with Scott Riggs left reigning champion Kurt Busch with a 35th-place finish and struck a blow to his title defense.

Jimmie Johnson pushes his #48 Chevrolet under the checkered flag ahead of Kyle Busch to win the Sept. 25 MBNA RacePoints 400 at Dover International Raceway. Johnson held off Kyle Busch in an overtime two-lap shootout. The win boosted Johnson from sixth to first in the points race. After the first two races in the Chase for the NASCAR NEXTEL Cup, six of the 10 Chase qualifiers were within 23 points of first place.

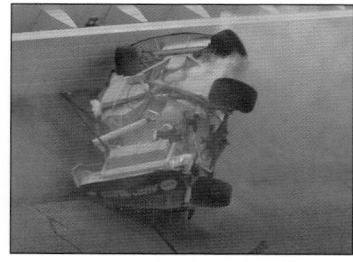

Number 15 Michael Waltrip, #00 Mike Skinner, and #6 Mark Martin were three of the seven drivers involved in a spectacular lap 20 crash in the Oct. 2 UAW-Ford 500 at Talladega Superspeedway. None of the drivers were seriously hurt in the incident, but that didn't stop them from voicing their concerns. "When you have 230-mile-an-hour race cars running around at 185, this is what you're going to get," Martin said after the race. Another crash late in the race took out eight drivers.

Dale Jarrett does a reverse victory lap after winning the UAW-Ford 500. The 48-year-old driver ended a 98-race winless streak that stretched back to 2003 with a last-lap pass of Tony Stewart. Stewart finished second and claimed first in the Chase for the NASCAR NEXTEL cup standings with seven races left.

Mark Martin and team owner Jack Roush celebrate in victory lane after Martin won the Oct. 9 Banquet 400 at Kansas Speedway. At the start of the 2005 campaign, Martin said it would be his last. But when Roush lost the services of Jamie McMurray and Kurt Busch, he asked Martin to come back for 2006 and Martin agreed. The 46-year-old had a fine season, winning the NEXTEL All-Star Challenge at Lowe's Motor Speedway in May, qualifying for the Chase for the NASCAR NEXTEL Cup, and finishing fourth overall.

Tony Stewart

TONY STEWART'S ROOKIE season in 1999 was one of the most eventful in the history of NASCAR racing. The 27-year-old from Rushville, Ind., finished fourth overall in the championship chase on the strength of three wins (all in the season's second half), 12 top-five finishes, and 21 top-10 showings. On May 30, he raced in two events on the same day, finishing ninth in the Indy Racing League's Indianapolis 500 and fourth in NASCAR's Coca-Cola 600 at Lowe's Motor Speedway. He reprised this jaw-dropping feat in 2001, bettering his 1999 showing by finishing sixth in the Indy 500 and third in the 600-miler.

In 2002, Stewart rallied from a last-place finish in the season-opening Daytona 500 to scramble back into contention. He delivered a late-season kick to capture the 2002 NASCAR Winston Cup championship. He nabbed the title again in 2005 after racking up five wins, as well as 17 top-five and 25 top-10 finishes. Even in 2006, when a bit of bad luck kept him out of the Chase for the NASCAR NEXTEL Cup, Stewart managed to post five victories, including three during The Chase when the focus was on the 10 Chase drivers. At the start of the 2007 NASCAR NEXTEL Cup season, just eight years into his stock car racing career, Stewart has an impressive 29 wins to his credit.

Stewart's quick success in NASCAR's Premier Series is not surprising, given his racing history. He cut his teeth on

NASCAR Cup Series Career Record 1999-2012*

Starts: 500
Wins: 47
Top 5s: 174
Top 10s: 282
Poles: 14

*still active

go-kart racing at a young age, snagging his first championship title when he was eight years old. He moved up the open-wheel ranks of three-quarter midgets and then on to the USAC (United States Auto Club) series. In 1995, he became the first driver to sweep the USAC Midget, Sprint Car, and Silver Crown championships. In 1996, Stewart entered the newly formed IRL (Indy Racing League), where he claimed the Rookie of the Year title and followed that up with the IRL championship the following year. Stewart hooked up with Joe Gibbs Racing in 1997, running in NASCAR's Busch series before moving with Gibbs to NASCAR's Premier Series.

Stewart's NASCAR career has been undeniably successful but also volatile, with a notable number of scuffles with other drivers and trackside photographers. This hot-tempered personality has earned Stewart a bit of a "bad boy" reputation, as well as some punitive fines from NASCAR officials. Stewart's positive emotions are equally unrestrained. Stewart brought a new level of boisterous showmanship to the traditional NASCAR victory celebration, with such antics as smoke-billowing burnouts and fence climbing.

In addition to a grueling racing schedule, Stewart maintained an incredibly hectic lifestyle, busying himself with such diverse ventures as his own dirt track (Eldora Speedway in Rossburg, Ohio), his own World of Outlaws sprint car team, the Tony Stewart Foundation charity organization, even his own line of "Smoke"-branded merchandise. On the track or off, Tony Stewart's life has been nothing if not eventful.

Sparks fly as Jimmie Johnson loses a tire during the Oct. 15 UAW-GM Quality 500 at Lowe's Motor Speedway. Johnson recovered to win his fourth straight race at Lowe's. After 22 caution flags flew at the Coca-Cola 600 in May, the fall race had 15 more, many caused by blown tires. To counter the problem, NASCAR mandated minimum tire pressures and instituted competition cautions to check pressures. The track was scheduled to be repaved prior to the 2006 events. The win put Johnson atop the points standings, tied with Tony Stewart, who finished 25th due to one of the many tire failures.

Tony Stewart powers away as Mike Bliss' Chevrolet sends Sterling Marlin's Dodge into the air in the Oct. 23 Subway 500 at Martinsville Speedway. Jeff Gordon went on to win the race, and Stewart took second, leaving him with a slight 15-point lead over Jimmie Johnson with four races remaining.

Rookie Kyle Busch talks to the media following his win in the Nov. 13 Checker Auto Parts 500 at Phoenix International Raceway. Busch didn't want to answer questions about his older brother Kurt, who had been suspended for the season's final two races by team owner Jack Roush for a run-in with Phoenix-area police. For the younger Busch, it was the second win of his career. The older Busch would finish 10th in the final standings.

Ricky Rudd, a veteran of 31 seasons, made his record 788th consecutive NASCAR NEXTEL Cup start in the Nov. 20 Ford 400 at Homestead-Miami Speedway. Rudd finished 37th in the season finale, and retired after the race. Rudd was the runner-up for the championship in 1991. Rudd would fill in for Tony Stewart in one race in 2006, then return to competition in 2007.

The last lap of the season-ending Ford 400 at Homestead-Miami Speedway was a dramatic door-to-door showdown between Greg Biffle and #6 Mark Martin. The two Roush Racing drivers crossed the finish line neck and neck, with Biffle winning the race. It was Biffle's sixth win, the most by any driver, and it moved him up two spots to second in the final standings.

Greg Zipadelli and Tony Stewart are all smiles following the Ford 500. Stewart finished 15th in the race but claimed the season title by 35 points over Greg Biffle. Stewart set a record for winnings in NASCAR NEXTEL Cup Series competition, bagging $13,578,168. "I'm so happy that I could get Zippy his championship and do it the right way for him instead of with the hell I put this team through in 2002," said an elated Stewart.

2005 NASCAR NEXTEL CUP POINTS RACE

Rank	Driver	Points	Starts	Wins	Top 5	Top 10	Winnings
1	Tony Stewart	6533	36	5	17	25	$13,578,168
2	Greg Biffle	6498	36	6	15	21	$8,354,052
2	Carl Edwards	6498	36	4	13	18	$6,893,157
4	Mark Martin	6428	36	1	12	19	$7,731,468
5	Jimmie Johnson	6406	36	4	13	22	$8,336,712
6	Ryan Newman	6359	36	1	8	16	$7,259,518
7	Matt Kenseth	6352	36	1	12	17	$7,034,134
8	Rusty Wallace	6140	36	0	8	17	$6,070,826
9	Jeremy Mayfield	6073	36	1	4	9	$5,741,989
10	Kurt Busch	5974	36	3	9	18	$7,930,830
11	Jeff Gordon	4174	36	4	8	14	$6,855,440
12	Jamie McMurray	4130	36	0	4	10	$3,923,970
13	Elliott Sadler	4084	36	0	1	12	$5,024,120
14	Kevin Harvick	4072	36	1	3	10	$4,970,050
15	Dale Jarrett	3960	36	1	4	7	$4,705,440
16	Joe Nemechek	3953	36	0	2	9	$4,223,380
17	Brian Vickers	3847	36	0	5	10	$3,982,130
18	Jeff Burton	3803	36	0	3	6	$4,265,670
19	Dale Earnhardt, Jr.	3780	36	1	7	13	$5,761,830
20	Kyle Busch	3753	36	2	9	13	$4,185,240
21	Ricky Rudd	3667	36	0	2	9	$4,300,410
22	Casey Mears	3637	36	0	3	9	$4,234,170
23	Kasey Kahne	3611	36	1	5	8	$4,874,840
24	Bobby Labonte	3488	36	0	4	7	$4,627,400
25	Michael Waltrip	3452	36	0	3	7	$4,375,090
26	Dave Blaney	3289	36	0	0	2	$3,342,290
27	Kyle Petty	3288	36	0	0	2	$3,465,690
28	Mike Bliss	3262	36	0	0	2	$3,091,110
29	Jeff Green	3241	36	0	0	0	$4,040,430
30	Sterling Marlin	3183	35	0	1	5	$4,080,120
31	Ken Schrader	3159	36	0	0	3	$3,057,530
32	Scott Wimmer	3122	36	0	0	0	$3,682,980
33	Travis Kvapil	3077	36	0	0	2	$3,293,450
34	Scott Riggs	2965	36	0	2	4	$4,030,680
35	Mike Wallace	2269	28	0	0	1	$2,325,740
36	Bobby Hamilton, Jr.	2183	33	0	0	0	$2,898,090
37	Robby Gordon	2117	29	0	1	2	$2,271,310
38	Jason Leffler	1538	19	0	0	0	$1,663,870
39	Kevin Lepage	1460	21	0	0	1	$1,774,790
40	Terry Labonte	1071	14	0	0	1	$1,202,520
41	Denny Hamlin	806	7	0	0	3	$610,030
42	Boris Said	791	9	0	1	1	$1,006,680
43	Johnny Sauter	722	10	0	0	1	$749,453
44	Hermie Sadler	717	12	0	0	0	$943,248
45	Bill Elliott	695	9	0	0	0	$809,013
46	Jimmy Spencer	667	11	0	0	0	$808,985
47	Martin Truex, Jr.	589	7	0	0	1	$929,028
48	Mike Garvey	491	9	0	0	0	$595,642
49	Mike Skinner	487	10	0	0	0	$969,109
50	Tony Raines	419	6	0	0	0	$420,500

Once Tony Stewart grabbed the lead in the points standings in June, he was only out of first place a total of two weeks. He spent the early part of the season chasing Jimmie Johnson, who set the early pace, then hit stride and assumed command.

Stewart won five of seven races during the midpoint of the campaign, and took a five-point lead into the Chase for the NASCAR NEXTEL Cup. The reduced Chase points format was a mere inconvenience for Stewart as he held first place for eight of the final 10 weeks. His final margin of victory was 35 points over Jack Roush drivers Greg Biffle and Carl Edwards.

Five of the 10 players in The Chase were Roush competitors, which prompted a rules change limiting the number of teams one owner could field. Johnson, Stewart's biggest threat for the title, fell from second to fifth in the final race. Defending champion Kurt Busch was suspended for the final two races following a run-in with police in Phoenix, and fell to 10th place in the final standings.

2006

January 12 After three years in the NASCAR Craftsman Truck Series, Toyota announces it will field Camrys in NASCAR NEXTEL Cup competition in 2007. Bill Davis Racing, Team Red Bull, and Michael Waltrip Racing are the first to sign with Toyota.

January 23 NASCAR announces that the "Car of Tomorrow" will be run at 16 races in 2007, 26 races in 2008, and the full schedule in 2009. The schedule could move forward if the teams agree that they want to switch to the new car exclusively.

February 19 Jimmie Johnson wins the Daytona 500 six days after his crew chief Chad Knaus is suspended by NASCAR for a rear-window violation detected after qualifying.

March 6 NASCAR Chairman Brian France announces that Charlotte, N.C., has won the bidding to be the host city for a new NASCAR Hall of Fame. Construction is due to be completed no later than spring 2010. (It officially opened on May 11, 2010.)

March 17 NASCAR NEXTEL Cup driver Bobby Hamilton announces he has been diagnosed with cancer, causing him to bow out of the 2006 season. The 2004 NASCAR Craftsman Truck Series champion would lose his battle with the disease on January 7, 2007, at age 49.

March 20 Bill Lester becomes the first African American to start a race at NASCAR's top level since Willy T. Ribbs in 1986. Lester qualifies for the Golden Corral 500 at Atlanta Motor Speedway and finishes 38th.

June 4 Despite retiring after the 2005 season, Ricky Rudd fills in for the injured Tony Stewart in the Neighborhood Excellence 400 at Dover International Raceway. Stewart broke his shoulder the previous week at Charlotte.

June 11 Rookie Denny Hamlin wins the Pocono 500 at Pocono Raceway. It is the rookie's first career NASCAR NEXTEL Cup victory, and it comes in his 21st start.

Brett Bodine, NASCAR's director of cost research, tests a Dodge version of NASCAR's "Car of Tomorrow" before the Daytona 500. The Car of Tomorrow was a seven-year project led by NASCAR vice president of research and development Gary Nelson. It was designed to improve safety and performance and reduce costs. Four inches wider and two inches taller than the outgoing cars, it also had an open front bumper designed to catch more air. These features, among others, increase drag, thus lessening aerodynamics to keep speeds in check. The roll cage was moved three inches back and four inches to the right to increase protection in driver's side impacts. One consistent body, frame, and roll cage, and an adjustable rear wing instead of a spoiler, would let the car be used on all types of tracks, eliminating the need for cars tuned to specific tracks and reducing costs for the teams. NASCAR announced plans to run the COT in 16 events during 2007, 26 in 2008, and full-time in 2009.

Number 20 Tony Stewart and #17 Matt Kenseth tangled three times in the Feb. 20 Daytona 500. After saying before the race that bump drafting could cause someone to get hurt, Stewart pushed Kenseth off the backstretch on lap 107. Stewart felt Kenseth had crowded him during a pass earlier in the race. Stewart was sent to the back of the longest line on the restart from the yellow flag. When Kenseth pulled alongside Stewart exiting the pits to give him a piece of his mind, NASCAR made him pass through pit road under green, and added a lap penalty when Kenseth was slow in responding to the first penalty. Kenseth lost valuable position and finished 15th, while Stewart rallied to place fifth.

Jimmie Johnson's winning #48 Chevrolet is watched over by NASCAR inspectors after the Daytona 500. Johnson's Chevy didn't pass inspection earlier in the week. His car was found to have a device that raised the rear window during qualifying, thus giving it an aerodynamic advantage. NASCAR suspended Johnson's crew chief Chad Knaus for the Daytona 500 and three additional races. Johnson took the lead in the race with 17 laps to go and held off Ryan Newman to earn the sixth Daytona 500 victory for Hendrick Motorsports.

Number 48 Jimmie Johnson beats #17 Matt Kenseth to the finish line in the March 12 UAW-DaimlerChrysler 400 at Las Vegas Motor Speedway. Johnson hadn't led all day, but a caution flag two laps from the finish bunched up the field for a one final green-white flag lap. Johnson managed to pass Kenseth on the outside on turn four of the last lap and hold on to win by .045 second.

Bill Lester, a 45-year-old former road racer who had run in the NASCAR Craftsman Truck Series since 2002, started the March 20 Golden Corral 500 at Atlanta Motor Speedway. In doing so, he became the first African American driver to compete in NASCAR's top series since Willy T. Ribbs in 1986. Lester drove his #23 Bill Davis Racing Dodge to a 38th-place finish and started again at Michigan in June, where he finished 32nd. Lester gave up a lucrative tech career at Hewlett-Packard to pursue his NASCAR dream.

Matt Kenseth was leading the March 26 Food City 500 at Bristol Motor Speedway with five laps to go when he received the "bump and run" treatment from #2 Kurt Busch. Busch, in only his fifth start for Penske Racing South, used the move to take the checkered flag. Kenseth proceeded to punt Jeff Gordon into the wall on the final lap and held on to finish third. An irate Gordon, who was relegated to a 21st-place finish, greeted Kenseth in the pits after the race and pushed him in the chest. The two were called to the NASCAR trailer for a little talk, and Gordon was fined $10,000 and placed on probation until Aug. 30. Kenseth was not penalized.

Kasey Kahne celebrates in victory lane following the April 9 Samsung/Radioshack 500 at Texas Motor Speedway. Kahne breezed to victory, leading the last 40 laps and finishing 5.2 seconds ahead of runner-up Matt Kenseth. The win was Kahne's second of the season and it pushed him to third place in the points standings.

Hendrick Racing teammates #48 Jimmie Johnson and #25 Brian Vickers jockey for position late in the May 1 Aaron's 499 at Talladega Superspeedway. Johnson shot past Vickers early on the final lap to take the win. It was Johnson's third win in nine 2006 races, and it solidified his lead in the points standings. Vickers, looking for his first career victory, finished third.

2006

July 9 Jeff Gordon drives to his 75th career win in the USG Sheetrock 500 at Chicagoland Speedway. Gordon is now one win behind Dale Earnhardt for sixth on the all-time list. On the same day, Chip Ganassi Racing announces that it has signed Formula One driver and former CART champion Juan Pablo Montoya for the 2007 NASCAR NEXTEL Cup season.

July 26 Popular broadcaster and former NASCAR champion Benny Parsons begins treatments for lung cancer. Parsons would succumb to the disease less than six months later on January 16, 2007. He was 65.

September 9 Kasey Kahne finishes third in the Chevy Rock & Roll 400 at Richmond International Raceway to claim the last spot in the annual Chase for the NASCAR NEXTEL Cup. Defending champ Tony Stewart is out of the top 10 after finishing 18th.

September 24 Jeff Burton posts his first victory in five years in the Dover 400 to take the points lead in the Chase for the NASCAR NEXTEL Cup.

October 8 Brian Vickers taps teammate Jimmie Johnson on the last lap of the UAW-GM 500 at Talladega Superspeedway, sending Johnson and Dale Earnhardt, Jr., spinning. Vickers goes on to win, while Johnson finishes 24th, leaving him mired in eighth in points with six races remaining.

October 21 NASCAR announces that NASCAR NEXTEL Cup cars will switch from leaded to unleaded fuel for all 2007 races except the Daytona 500.

November 5 Tony Stewart wins the Dickies 500 at Texas Motor Speedway. It is Stewart's third win in the last six races, all during the Chase for the NASCAR NEXTEL Cup. Jimmie Johnson places second and takes the points lead.

November 19 Mark Martin's start in the Ford 400 at Homestead-Miami Speedway marks his final race with Jack Roush. Martin ran 19 years with Roush Racing, posting 35 NASCAR Nextel Cup wins. The 47-year-old Martin plans to run a limited schedule for owner Bobby Ginn in 2007. Jimmie Johnson wraps up his first NASCAR NEXTEL Cup title with an 11th-place finish.

Dale Earnhardt, Jr., paid tribute to his late father with a familiar silver and black paint scheme on his #8 Chevrolet in the Aaron's 499. The day would prove to be a bad one for Earnhardt, who spun on lap 88, lost his engine on lap 151, and finished 31st. The poor showing dropped Earnhardt one spot to eighth in the season's points standings.

▲ Dale Earnhardt, Jr., pilots his #8 Chevrolet under the checkered flag in the May 6 Crown Royal 400 at Richmond International Raceway. Earnhardt outlasted rookie Denny Hamlin to take the win. Kevin Harvick led 272 of the 400 laps, but pit strategy left him with older tires and he lost his lead on lap 329 and finished third.

◄ Jimmie Johnson gets a champagne shower from crew chief Chad Knaus after winning the May 20 NASCAR NEXTEL All-Star Challenge at Lowe's Motor Speedway. Johnson survived the brutal race that saw 10 of the 20 cars fail to finish due to accidents. The win, which paid a cool $1 million, was Johnson's seventh at Lowe's in his last 10 NASCAR NEXTEL starts there.

Second in points entering the May 28 Coca-Cola 600 at Lowe's Motor Speedway, Tony Stewart experienced a setback when a blown tire caused him to crash on lap 33. Stewart left with a broken shoulder, and his 42nd-place finish dropped him to fourth in the overall standings. Ricky Rudd replaced Stewart in the #20 Chevrolet the next week at Dover on lap 37 and finished 25th, earning valuable points for Stewart. Stewart returned to full-time duty on June 11 at Pocono, where he finished third.

Kasey Kahne celebrates with the crowd after winning the Coca-Cola 600. It was the third win of the season for the third-year driver, already making it his best season yet. The win also gave Kahne's Evernham Motorsports team more wins in 2006 than in any season since the team started in 2001.

Matt Kenseth pilots his #17 DeWalt Ford across the finish line to win the Neighborhood Excellence 400 at Dover International Speedway on June 4. The win was one of four for Kenseth in his tumultuous season, and it kept him solidly in second in points after 13 races.

Denny Hamlin takes the checkered flag at the June 11 Pocono 500 at Pocono Raceway. The 25-year-old rookie, driving for Joe Gibbs Racing, won in his 21st start. Hamlin had also won the Budweiser Shootout in February—a nonpoints race—and his Pocono win proved that he belonged at NASCAR's top level. He went on to win the July race at Pocono, qualify for the Chase for the NASCAR NEXTEL Cup, finish third in the final season standings, and claim Raybestos Rookie of the Year honors.

Terry Labonte chases Jeff Gordon in the June 25 Dodge/Save Mart 350 at Sonoma, California's Infineon Raceway. Gordon went on to post his eighth career road course victory, the most ever. The win snapped a 19-race winless streak for Gordon and vaulted him into eighth in the points standings. Labonte was in his final season and driving part-time for the Hall of Fame Racing team owned by former Dallas Cowboy greats Roger Staubach and Troy Aikman. He led for 17 laps and placed an impressive third.

Noted road course driver Boris Said leads the pack late in the July 1 Pepsi 400 at Daytona International Speedway. Said surprised the NASCAR world when he put his #60 Ford on the pole, then followed up with a strong fourth-place finish. Tony Stewart pushed his #20 Chevrolet past Said on lap 158 of 160 and went on to take the win, his second of the season. The win bumped Stewart from seventh to fifth in the points race.

Two NASCAR-themed motion pictures were released in the summer of 2006. *Cars*, an animated blockbuster from Disney Pixar, featured Owen Wilson as Lightning McQueen, a brash young Piston Cup car that learns a life lesson from a small southwestern town and a race lesson from a 1951 Hudson Hornet stock car voiced by Paul Newman. *Talladega Nights: The Ballad of Ricky Bobby* was a comedy starring Will Ferrell (shown) as a cocky NASCAR driver who learns the hard way that a "win at all costs" attitude can be too costly.

Jimmie Johnson kisses the bricks on the start/finish line after winning the Aug. 6 Allstate 400 at the Brickyard. Johnson recovered from a flat tire on lap 40 that dropped him to 39th to take the lead on lap 117. He reclaimed the lead for good with 10 laps to go and posted his fourth win of the season. With the win, Johnson increased his lead in the points race to 107 over Matt Kenseth.

In what could be construed as payback for an incident at Bristol in March, #24 Jeff Gordon bumped Matt Kenseth with seven laps to go in the July 9 USG Sheetrock 400 at Chicagoland Speedway. The bump sent Kenseth into a spin. Gordon passed him and went on to win the race while Kenseth was relegated to a 22nd-place finish. The win was Gordon's 75th, placing him seventh all time and just one win behind Dale Earnhardt. Earlier in the day, Chip Ganassi announced that former CART champion and Formula One driver Juan Pablo Montoya would race for him next season.

The 10 qualifiers for the Chase for the NASCAR NEXTEL Cup pose after the Sept. 9 Chevy Rock & Roll 400 at Richmond International Raceway. Despite his five wins on the season, it took two outstanding finishes, a first at California the prior weekend and a third at Richmond, for Kasey Kahne to move into the top 10 and make The Chase. Defending NASCAR NEXTEL Cup champion Tony Stewart was ninth entering the event, but a practice crash relegated him to a backup car that he could pilot to no better than an 18th-place finish. The mediocre showing pushed Stewart to 11th-place overall, 16 points and one spot out of The Chase.

"If I couldn't win, honestly, there's nobody else I'd rather see win the race. Jeff Burton is a great guy."
—Matt Kenseth on former Roush Racing teammate Jeff Burton after the Dover 400

Matt Kenseth congratulates #31 Jeff Burton after the Sept. 24 Dover 400 at Dover International Speedway. The pair raced side-by-side for 25 of the last 31 laps, but Burton passed Kenseth with six laps to go and held on for the win. The performance snapped a 175-race winless streak for Burton and moved him from fifth into first place in the Chase for the NASCAR NEXTEL Cup. Kenseth ran out of gas heading to the white flag and finished 10th.

Tony Stewart coasts to a win in the Oct. 1 Banquet 400 at Kansas Speedway. Stewart ran out of gas in the second turn of the last lap but had such a large lead that he was able to coast across the finish line and take the checkered flag. Not in the Chase for the NASCAR NEXTEL Cup, Stewart was able to gamble on pit strategy and it paid off. Mark Martin was the highest Chase finisher, placing third and moving from sixth to third in the overall standings. A 14th-place finish left Jimmie Johnson mired in eighth among the 10 title contenders.

Brian Vickers' #25 Chevrolet is showered with beer cans after the Oct. 8 UAW-Ford 500 at Talladega Superspeedway. The race ended in controversy when Vickers, running third on the final lap, knocked Hendrick Motorsports teammate Jimmie Johnson into race leader Dale Earnhardt, Jr. Vickers went on to claim his first career win, while Earnhardt finished 23rd and Johnson placed 24th. Vickers was not one of the 10 qualifiers for the Chase for the NASCAR NEXTEL Cup but the other two drivers were. It was already known that Vickers would not be back with Hendrick in 2007.

Jeff Gordon's chances for his fifth NASCAR Premier Series championship took a hard hit when he got caught up in a 13-car wreck on lap 138 of the UAW-Ford 500. Gordon finished 36th, leaving him seventh in the standings. Matt Kenseth's fourth-place showing put him in second overall, just six points behind Chase leader Jeff Burton. The race featured 63 lead changes, the most since July 1984 when there were 68 at Talladega.

◄ Jimmie Johnson began his hard charge for the title with a win in the Oct. 22 Subway 500 at Martinsville Speedway. The win vaulted Johnson from seventh to third in the points standings with four races remaining. Matt Kenseth finished 11th and claimed the points lead.

Tony Stewart celebrates in victory lane after his win in the Dickies 500. The win was Stewart's third in the first eight races of the Chase for the NASCAR NEXTEL Cup. Unfortunately, Stewart had failed to qualify for the ten-driver Chase. Jimmie Johnson, who had been the number-two qualifier, drove to a second-place finish at Texas that earned him the points lead with two races left.

The Nov. 5 Dickies 500 at Texas Motor Speedway marked the final NASCAR NEXTEL Cup race for 49-year-old Terry Labonte. To commemorate the event, Labonte's son Justin drove his father's old #44 Chevrolet Monte Carlo during the parade lap prior to the race. It was the same car that Terry drove to his first career victory in 1980 at Darlington Raceway. Labonte finished his career with 22 wins and two NASCAR titles.

Mark Martin's start in the Nov. 19 Ford 400 at Homestead-Miami Speedway marked his final race with Jack Roush. Martin ran 19 years with Roush Racing, posting 35 NASCAR NEXTEL Cup wins. The 47-year-old Martin, who planned to run a limited schedule for owner Bobby Ginn in 2007, finished 18th at Homestead and ninth in the overall standings.

Juan Pablo Montoya made his first career NASCAR NEXTEL Cup start in the 2006 Ford 400. Montoya brought an impressive résumé to the Chip Ganassi Racing with Felix Sabates team. The Bogata, Columbia, native was the 1999 CART champ, he won the 2000 Indianapolis 500, and he raced in Formula One from 2001 to 2006, posting seven wins. Montoya crashed on lap 252 at Homestead and finished 34th.

(Left to right) Jimmie Johnson, team owner Rick Hendrick, and crew chief Chad Knaus celebrate after claiming the 2006 NASCAR NEXTEL Cup championship. Johnson needed to finish 12th or better in the Ford 400 to secure the title. Johnson overcame misfortune early in the race when debris flew through his grille on lap 15. The title was the first for the popular 31-year-old driver and the sixth for the Hendrick Motorsports team.

2006 NASCAR NEXTEL CUP POINTS RACE

Rank	Driver	Points	Starts	Wins	Top 5	Top 10	Winnings
1	Jimmie Johnson	6475	36	5	13	24	$15,875,125
2	Matt Kenseth	6419	36	4	15	21	$9,544,966
3	Denny Hamlin	6407	36	2	8	20	$6,607,932
4	Kevin Harvick	6397	36	5	15	20	$8,231,406
5	Dale Earnhardt, Jr.	6328	36	1	10	17	$7,111,739
6	Jeff Gordon	6256	36	2	14	18	$7,471,447
7	Jeff Burton	6228	36	4	17	20	$6,439,995
8	Kasey Kahne	6183	36	6	12	19	$7,721,378
9	Mark Martin	6168	36	0	7	15	$5,568,748
10	Kyle Busch	6027	36	1	10	18	$6,077,337
11	Tony Stewart	4727	36	5	15	19	$8,801,569
12	Carl Edwards	4428	36	0	10	20	$5,353,629
13	Greg Biffle	4075	36	2	8	15	$5,347,623
14	Casey Mears	3914	36	0	2	8	$6,128,449
15	Brian Vickers	3906	36	1	5	9	$4,602,990
16	Kurt Busch	3900	36	1	7	12	$5,681,655
17	Clint Bowyer	3833	36	0	4	11	$4,550,134
18	Ryan Newman	3748	36	0	2	7	$5,960,473
19	Martin Truex, Jr.	3673	36	0	2	5	$4,759,248
20	Scott Riggs	3619	35	0	1	8	$3,773,674
21	Bobby Labonte	3567	36	0	3	8	$4,949,058
22	Elliott Sadler	3469	36	0	1	7	$4,852,654
23	Dale Jarrett	3438	36	0	1	4	$4,739,491
24	Reed Sorenson	3434	36	0	1	5	$3,702,767
25	Jamie McMurray	3405	36	0	3	7	$5,241,224
26	Dave Blaney	3259	36	0	1	2	$3,479,643
27	Joe Nemechek	3255	36	0	0	2	$4,099,914
28	Jeff Green	3253	36	0	0	2	$3,767,754
29	J.J. Yeley	3220	36	0	0	3	$4,336,547
30	Robby Gordon	3113	36	0	1	3	$3,143,787
31	Ken Schrader	3049	36	0	0	2	$4,130,883
32	Kyle Petty	2928	36	0	0	2	$3,655,539
33	David Stremme	2865	34	0	0	0	$3,456,113
34	Sterling Marlin	2854	36	0	0	1	$3,248,034
35	Tony Raines	2609	29	0	0	1	$2,358,230
36	Travis Kvapil	2451	31	0	0	0	$2,867,087
37	Michael Waltrip	2350	33	0	0	0	$2,971,978
38	Scott Wimmer	1812	24	0	0	0	$1,904,783
39	Jeremy Mayfield	1684	22	0	0	0	$2,641,732
40	Kevin Lepage	1346	22	0	0	0	$1,823,351
41	Terry Labonte	1278	17	0	1	1	$1,547,359
42	David Gilliland	1178	15	0	0	0	$1,564,901
43	Kenny Wallace	984	17	0	0	0	$1,386,818
44	Bill Elliott	765	10	0	0	0	$1,056,131
45	Paul Menard	669	7	0	0	1	$546,993
46	Chad Chaffin	553	10	0	0	0	$819,218
47	Boris Said	415	4	0	1	2	$429,000
48	Mike Bliss	387	6	0	0	0	$471,458
49	Brent Sherman	372	6	0	0	0	$637,056
50	Mike Wallace	355	4	0	0	0	$519,218

Jimmie Johnson overcame bad luck in the first four races of the Chase for the NASCAR NEXTEL Cup to claim his first championship. It marked the sixth title for co-owner Rick Hendrick and the first for Jeff Gordon as a co-owner. Gordon also qualified for The Chase and finished sixth in the overall standings.

Five drivers had a shot to win the title entering the season finale. In the end, however, Johnson claimed the top honors by 56 points over runner-up Matt Kenseth. Rookie Denny Hamlin was third, Kevin Harvick fourth, and Dale Earnhardt, Jr., fifth.

Johnson got off to a quick start with a win in the season-opening Daytona 500. In addition to Daytona, Johnson won the Allstate 400 at the Brickyard, making him the only driver to ever win the big races at Daytona and Indianapolis as well as the championship in the same season. Johnson posted five wins in points races, plus a victory at the NASCAR NEXTEL All-Star Challenge.

All told, the points lead changed hands nine times among Johnson, Kenseth, and Jeff Burton.

2007

January 22 NASCAR announces changes to the NASCAR Sprint Cup Series points system. Race winners get an additional five points for winning a race. The Chase for the NASCAR Sprint Cup field increases from the top 10 drivers in points after the 26th race to the top 12. All Chase drivers start with 5000 points plus 10 bonus points for each race win from the regular season.

February 14 Roush Racing announces that 50 percent of the team has been sold to Fenway Sports Group to create Roush Fenway Racing.

February 18 Kevin Harvick beats Mark Martin to the finish line as cars crash behind them at the end of the Daytona 500. Harvick won by .020 second, the closest finish in the 500 since electronic scoring began in 1993. Clint Bowyer finishes 18th while on his roof.

March 25 After seven years of development, NASCAR's new car design races for the first time at the Food City 500 in Bristol TN. When Kyle Busch's Chevrolet Impala takes the checkered flag, it marks the first time a winged NASCAR Sprint Cup car would head to Victory Lane since Richard Petty won at Dover on September 20, 1970, in a Plymouth Superbird.

May 10 Dale Earnhardt, Jr., announces he is leaving Dale Earnhardt, Inc., the team founded by his father in 1996 and now owned by Teresa Earnhardt.

May 22 NASCAR announces that the new car will be used full time in 2008. The original plan was to use the new car in 16 races in 2007, 26 races in 2008, and the full 36-race schedule in 2009.

June 4 Bill France, Jr., dies in Florida at the age of 74. France, Jr., took over the presidency of NASCAR in 1972 and led until November 2000. He remained chairman of the board of NASCAR until 2003.

June 13 Dale Earnhardt, Jr., and Hendrick Motorsports announce a five-year deal for Earnhardt, Jr., to drive for the team starting in 2008.

At the end of 2006, Dale Jarrett left Robert Yates Racing and Ford Motor Company after 10 years, 29 wins, and the 1999 NASCAR Sprint Cup Series championship. In 2007, he and sponsor UPS moved to the new Toyota team of Michael Waltrip Racing with Jarrett driving the #44 Toyota Camry. The move proved to be less than successful, with Jarrett failing to qualify for 12 of the 36 events and netting a best finish of 17th. By the end of the year, he announced he was retiring from driving after the first five races of 2008. Jarrett plans to follow in his dad Ned Jarrett's footsteps and cover races from the ESPN TV booth.

In 2007, Mark Martin and Regan Smith began the season sharing the driving duties of the Ginn Racing #01 U.S. Army Chevrolets. Martin was lured to Ginn Racing after 19 years at Roush Fenway Racing by the prospects of a limited 22-race NASCAR Nextel Cup schedule and a chance to tutor young development drivers for the organization. For Smith, it was a chance to step into a top-flight car to begin his Nextel Cup career. By midyear, however, Ginn Racing was no more, being merged with Dale Earnhardt, Inc. While Martin continued his planned schedule at DEI, Smith got only two more starts after the merger, with Aric Almirola getting the other five.

Michael Waltrip takes a moment during a press conference at Daytona while responding to questions about a rules infraction found with his #55 NAPA Toyota during qualifying for the Daytona 500. A foreign substance was found in the intake manifold, and Waltrip's car was disqualified. The team was fined 100 points and $100,000. Waltrip took a teammate's backup car and qualified it through one of the Gatorade Duel qualifying races to make the Daytona 500 field. Waltrip's trouble continued into the rest of the season. He failed to make the field in 19 more races in 2007 but did have two top-10 finishes and a pole at Talladega in the 14 races in which he competed.

Tony Stewart in the #20 Chevrolet and Kurt Busch in the #2 Dodge crash late in the Daytona 500. Stewart and Busch had combined to lead 130 of the 153 laps completed at the time of the incident. Later in the season, the two would once again tangle, this time at Dover during the Autism Speaks 400 in June.

Kevin Harvick in the #29 Chevrolet noses out Mark Martin in the #01 Chevrolet at the finish line for his first Daytona 500 victory. The green-white-checkered finish was set up with a strong outside run by Harvick, a push from Matt Kenseth, and a wreck behind them. Martin was ahead of Harvick coming off turn four on the final lap when the crash started behind them, but with no caution thrown, Harvick was able to beat Martin to the line. This would be Harvick's only points-paying victory of the season, though he did win the NASCAR Sprint All-Star Race at Lowe's Motor Speedway in May.

The #07 Chevrolet of Clint Bowyer finishes 18th while upside down, just ahead of Juan Pablo Montoya who finished 19th in the Daytona 500. Bowyer was part of a wreck on the last lap that jumbled the finishing order of the race. Later in the year, Bowyer, in just his second season, would surprise everyone by making the Chase for the NASCAR Sprint Cup and winning his first Sprint Cup race at Loudon. He moved into third place in the Chase standings after the third race of the Chase at Kansas, and stayed there the rest of the season to be the highest-placing Richard Childress Racing driver in the season points standings.

July 7 Officials with Sprint-Nextel and NASCAR announce that the NASCAR Nextel Cup Series will be renamed the NASCAR Sprint Cup Series in 2008. Nextel was acquired by Sprint in late 2004.

July 29 ESPN returns after six seasons away from broadcasting NASCAR Sprint Cup events. The Allstate 400 at the Brickyard in Indianapolis is the first NASCAR Sprint Cup race on ESPN since the NAPA 500 in Atlanta on November 19, 2000. ESPN is credited with bringing NASCAR to the masses in the 1980s with live broadcasts of NASCAR Sprint Cup races in an era of tape-delayed highlights.

August 12 Tony Stewart and Jeff Gordon trade spins in the Centurion Boats at the Glen race at Watkins Glen, NY, with Stewart coming out on top. On lap 45, Stewart spins in turn one, and Gordon passes him to take the lead. With two laps to go, Gordon spins in the same location, allowing Stewart to pass and win the event.

August 14 Hendrick Motorsports announces it has been unable to obtain Dale Earnhardt, Jr.'s, traditional number 8 from Dale Earnhardt, Inc. for use on Earnhardt, Jr.'s, car.

September 16 All 43 cars finish the Sylvania 300 at Loudon, NH, the first time all starters completed a race since the series adopted the 43-car field in 1998.

September 19 At a press conference in Dallas, TX, Dale Earnhardt, Jr., announces his Hendrick Motorsports Chevrolet will wear number 88, which became available after Robert Yates agreed to release the number.

November 2 Bruton Smith buys New Hampshire Motor Speedway in Loudon, NH. The purchase gives Smith's Speedway Motorsports, Inc., seven tracks and 12 NASCAR Sprint Cup dates.

November 18 Matt Kenseth won the race, Jimmie Johnson won the championship, and Juan Pablo Montoya won the Raybestsos Rookie of the Year after the Ford 400 at Homestead-Miami Speedway. Johnson became the first back-to-back NASCAR Sprint Cup Champion since Jeff Gordon in 1997-98. The Ford 400 was the last race for the old car that had been in use since 1981.

Dale Earnhardt, Jr., and Kasey Kahne share a moment before qualifying starts for the Auto Club 500 at Auto Club Speedway. Before the year was over, Kahne would be announced as the new face of Budweiser in NASCAR. When Earnhardt, Jr., signed with Hendrick Motorsports in June, a sponsor conflict prevented Budweiser from going there with him. Budweiser's search for a new face led to Kahne and the Gillett Evernham Motorsports #9 Dodge.

Kyle Busch stands on his #5 Chevrolet after winning the Food City 500 at Bristol. This was the first race for the new car, which had been in development for several years. The new car was designed to be safer than the old car, and, with its rear wing and front splitter, intended to make racing more competitive. Indeed, the finish of the Food City 500 was exciting, with Busch and Jeff Burton finishing side-by-side. Tony Stewart had led 257 laps before a fuel pump problem put him several laps down. His Gibbs teammate Denny Hamlin led 177 laps, including 109 consecutive laps, before a fuel pick-up problem late in the race cost him positions. Kyle Busch's victory was the 600th in NASCAR Sprint Cup Series racing for Chevrolet.

Kyle Busch poses with the trophy from his victory in the Food City 500 in March at Bristol. This was his only win in 2007, but he still had an eventful season. Busch finished the year fifth in points with 11 top-five finishes and 20 top tens and was still released by Hendrick Motorsports at the end of the season. When Dale Earnhardt, Jr., made the decision to leave DEI at midseason, it set off a ripple effect that ended with Earnhardt, Jr., at Hendrick Motorsports, Busch at Joe Gibbs Racing, and J.J. Yeley at Hall of Fame Racing. Busch would see more changes other than a team swap. Joe Gibbs Racing became the lead Toyota team after a deal was reached in midseason, putting Busch in a Camry for 2008.

Hendrick Motorsports teammates Jimmie Johnson in the #48 Chevrolet and Jeff Gordon in the #24 Chevrolet cross the finish line after waging a fender-banging battle for the win at Martinsville during the Goody's Cool Orange 500. During the last 50 laps, Gordon repeatedly beat on the rear bumper of Johnson in an effort to move him out of the way, but Johnson didn't give an inch. The victory gave Johnson three wins out of six races run thus far in the 2007 season while Gordon had yet to score a win. By the end of the year, however, the Johnson-Gordon combination would have 16 wins, 10 by Johnson and six by Gordon, and first and second place in the final points standings.

Jeff Burton climbs from his #31 Chevrolet after beating Matt Kenseth in a late-race duel in the Samsung 500 at Texas Motor Speedway. Burton only led the last lap to become the first two-time NASCAR Sprint Cup winner at Texas.

Jeff Gordon carries a #3 flag in honor of the late Dale Earnhardt after winning the Subway Fresh Fit 500 at Phoenix. The team had been carrying the flag for some time and planned to honor the late champion after Gordon's 75th victory at Chicago in July 2006. This victory tied Gordon and Earnhardt at 76 wins and sixth overall on the all-time win list. This was also Gordon's first win at Phoenix after 22 tries. He needed wins at only Texas and Home-stead to claim victories at all of the currently active NASCAR Sprint Cup Series tracks.

Ken Schrader drives the famed #21 Wood Brothers Ford through the garage at Talladega Superspeedway during the Aaron's 499 weekend. Schrader's was one of nine cars that failed to qualify for the event. This was the first race the Wood Brothers had missed in seven years, dating back to this same event in 2000. Schrader also missed the next race at Richmond, but Bill Elliott qualified the car at Charlotte and the team made the remainder of the events in 2007. The Wood Brothers used four different drivers during the year with Elliott starting 20 races, Schrader 13, and Jon Wood and Boris Said one each.

Jeff Gordon celebrates after winning the one-day rain-delayed Dodge Avenger 500 at Darlington Raceway on Mother's Day. The #24 Chevrolet was visibly overheating for the last 20 or so laps, but it held together and Gordon had his ninth top-five finish in the first 11 races of the season, and a 231-point lead over teammate Jimmie Johnson in the standings.

Casey Mears celebrates his first NASCAR Sprint Cup win in the Coca-Cola 600 at Lowe's Motor Speedway. J.J. Yeley, Kyle Petty, Reed Sorenson, and Brian Vickers finished second through fifth. Yeley's second-place finish was a career best while Petty's third place was his first top-five since 1997. Sorenson's fourth-place finish was a career high, and Vicker's fifth place was the first top-five for a Toyota in NASCAR Sprint Cup competition. Mears finished the year with five top-five finishes, 10 top-10 finishes, and placed 15th overall in the NASCAR Sprint Cup points standings.

Juan Pablo Montoya celebrates atop his #42 Dodge at Infineon Raceway after the Toyota/Save Mart 350. Montoya's first NASCAR Sprint Cup win came in his 17th start, and he became the first driver from a Spanish-speaking country to win a NASCAR Sprint Cup race. The former Formula 1 and IndyCar driver started 32nd in the field and didn't lead the race until the final six laps. Montoya had two other top-five finishes in his first season—both on ovals—at Atlanta and Indianapolis. A 20th-place finish in the series points standings helped Montoya win the Raybestos Rookie of the Year title, and his success led several other open-wheel drivers to join the NASCAR Sprint Cup Series in 2008.

Martin Truex, Jr., wins his first NASCAR Sprint Cup race at Dover in the Autism Speaks 400 presented by Visa. Truex led 216 of the 400 laps and gave DEI its first win of the year in the one-day rain-delayed event. The #1 Chevrolet team jumped from 16th to 12th in points after the win and rode that into the Chase for the NASCAR Sprint Cup, where Truex had four top-10 finishes in the 10 races and finished 11th in the Chase. With Dale Earnhardt, Jr., leaving DEI after the 2007 season, Truex was poised to be the team's number-one driver.

The three Richard Childress Racing Chevrolets speed down the backstretch at Michigan during the Citizens Bank 400. RCR put all three cars in the 2007 Chase for the NASCAR Sprint Cup with Clint Bowyer in the #07 finishing third in points, Jeff Burton in the #31 eighth, and Kevin Harvick in the #29 10th. The teammates combined for 108 starts, three wins, 18 top five's and 50 top-10 finishes for the season. RCR had plans to expand to a four-car team in 2008, but Childress said he couldn't find the right situation that would benefit his established teams and delayed the expansion.

Jamie McMurray in the #26 Ford edges out Kyle Busch in the #5 Chevrolet in the Coke Zero 400 at Daytona. The lead changed hands five times in the last six laps, and McMurray hit the wall after winning by .005 second. This finish is tied for the second closest margin of victory in NASCAR Sprint Cup history. This was the last restrictor-plate race for the conventional style car with the new car being phased in for the last 2007 plate race at Talladega in October.

With crew chief Greg Zipadelli watching from the pit box, the Home Depot crew bangs out a pit stop on the #20 Chevrolet at Chicagoland Speedway. Driver Tony Stewart, in typical fashion, waited until midyear to win his first race of the season here in the USG Sheetrock 400. Stewart, a notorious slow starter, came on strong in the second half of the season with a stretch of three wins in four races and easily made the Chase for the NASCAR Sprint Cup. He finished sixth in the season points standings, and after a manufacturer change at Joe Gibbs Racing, began preparing to drive a Toyota for the 2008 season.

Dale Earnhardt, Jr., in the #8 Chevrolet leads Denny Hamlin in the #11 Chevrolet and Jeff Gordon in the #24 Chevrolet during the Allstate 400 at the Brickyard at the Indianapolis Motor Speedway. Earnhardt, Jr., led 13 laps, but an engine problem left him 34th at the end of the race. After contract negotiations broke down for him at Dale Earnhardt, Inc., Earnhardt, Jr., talked to several different teams. These included Richard Childress Racing, where his father drove for more than 18 years, but he eventually signed with Hendrick Motorsports. Earnhardt, Jr.'s, switch resulted in changes at six other NASCAR Sprint Cup teams, either through driver changes or sponsor moves.

Tony Stewart, in the #20 Chevrolet takes the checkered flag for his second Allstate 400 at the Brickyard victory. The Indiana native led 65 of the 160 laps. Reed Sorenson in the #41 Dodge won his first career pole at Indy and led the first sixteen laps finishing fifth in the race. Juan Pablo Montoya finished second and became the only person to run a NASCAR Sprint Cup race, an Indianapolis 500, and a Formula 1 race at the famed Indianapolis Motor Speedway.

Kenny Wallace waits for the crew to get the #88 Ford ready for practice during the Chevy Rock & Roll 400 weekend at Richmond. Wallace filled in for four races for an injured Ricky Rudd in the Robert Yates Racing Taurus. Since 2000, Wallace has been the driver to go to in the NASCAR Sprint Cup Series when a substitute is needed. He has driven for Roush Racing, Dale Earnhardt, Inc., Andy Petree Racing, Richard Childress Racing, Petty Enterprises, and Michael Waltrip Racing, among others.

Carl Edwards does his traditional backflip after winning the Dodge Dealers 400 at Dover International Speedway. It was Edwards' third win of the season and the seventh of his career, and he finished ninth in the Chase for the NASCAR Sprint Cup. After winning four times in his first 46 NASCAR Sprint Cup Series races, it took Edwards 52 more events to get win number five at Michigan in June.

Greg Biffle celebrates in the tri-oval grass after a strange day at Kansas Speedway, where he won the Lifelock 400. The race was stopped twice for rain that kept the red flag out for more than two hours. Many teams thought the event would be called after the second red flag because the race was past the halfway point, but the track was dried and the cars sent back out. Due to impending darkness, NASCAR cut the race length first by 42 laps, then by another 15 due to a caution flag, and canceled the green-white-checkered finish rule. Biffle took the lead on lap 174 of the now-210-lap event and stretched his fuel to the end. A blown tire brought out the final caution of the day, and as Biffle was coming to the checkered flag under yellow, he shut off his car and coasted. Several cars passed him and got to the finish line before he did, but NASCAR ruled that Biffle had maintained a cautious pace and was declared the winner.

The UAW-Ford 500 at Talladega was the first superspeedway event for the new race car. Uncertainty over how the car would handle on the 2.66-mile track led to a unique strategy for most of the NASCAR Sprint Cup drivers. Much of the event featured a single-file line of cars just patiently waiting until the end of the race to make a move. Eventual winner Jeff Gordon adopted that strategy himself after starting 34th. Gordon averaged a 28th position for the race, and the only lap he led was the last one. The win allowed Gordon to take back first place in the Chase for the NASCAR Sprint Cup from teammate Jimmie Johnson.

Jimmie Johnson in the #48 Lowe's Chevrolet and Matt Kenseth in the #17 USG Sheetrock Ford waged a stirring battle for the win at Texas in the Dickies 500. The two Chase contenders swapped the lead four times in the last seven laps, with Johnson taking the lead with two laps to go. With both drivers in the Chase for the NASCAR Sprint Cup, they let it all hang out in what Johnson descibed as "a full-blown brawl." While both drivers got sideways in the pursuit of victory, they ran a clean race. Johnson's victory at Texas was his third of four in a row during the Chase, and it enabled him to take the points lead away from teammate Jeff Gordon, who finished seventh in the event.

Matt Kenseth and crew chief Robbie Reiser celebrate in Victory Lane after winning the season-ending Ford 400 at Homestead-Miami Speedway. The victory was Kenseth's second win of the season, and it moved the #17 DeWalt team from sixth to fourth in the final standings. This was Reiser's last race as crew chief for Kenseth, as the duo was split up due to Reiser's promotion to General Manager at Roush Fenway Racing. The nine-year partnership resulted in 15 NASCAR Sprint Cup Series wins and 142 top-10 finishes out of 291 races run, along with the 2003 NASCAR Sprint Cup Championship.

Ricky Rudd and Robert Yates, along with the whole #88 Snickers team, pose for a group photo before the start of the Ford 400 at Homestead. This was the final NASCAR Sprint Cup Series race for the Rudd/Yates duo. Rudd, after 32 years at the NASCAR Sprint Cup level, retired with 906 starts, 29 poles, and 23 wins. Robert Yates transferred ownership of his team to his son, Doug, after 18 years, 57 wins, and the 1999 NASCAR Sprint Cup championship. The new team, called Yates Racing, aligned with Roush Fenway Racing, with which it would share information and technology.

2007 NASCAR SPRINT CUP SERIES POINTS RACE

Rank	Driver	Points	Starts	Wins	Top 5	Top 10
1	Jimmie Johnson	6723	36	10	20	24
2	Jeff Gordon	6646	36	6	21	30
3	Clint Bowyer	6377	36	1	5	17
4	Matt Kenseth	6298	36	2	13	22
5	Kyle Busch	6293	36	1	11	20
6	Tony Stewart	6242	36	3	11	23
7	Kurt Busch	6231	36	2	6	14
8	Jeff Burton	6231	36	1	9	18
9	Carl Edwards	6222	36	3	11	15
10	Kevin Harvick	6199	36	1	4	15
11	Martin Truex, Jr.	6164	36	1	7	14
12	Denny Hamlin	6143	36	1	12	18
13	Ryan Newman	4046	36	0	7	15
14	Greg Biffle	3991	36	1	5	11
15	Casey Mears	3949	36	1	5	10
16	Dale Earnhardt, Jr.	3929	36	0	7	12
17	Jamie McMurray	3556	36	1	3	9
18	Bobby Labonte	3517	36	0	0	3
19	Kasey Kahne	3489	36	0	1	8
20	Juan Pablo Montoya	3487	36	1	3	6
21	J.J. Yeley	3456	36	0	1	3
22	Reed Sorenson	3275	36	0	3	6
23	David Ragan	3251	36	0	2	3
24	David Stremme	3163	36	0	0	3
25	Elliott Sadler	3140	36	0	0	2
26	Robby Gordon	3014	35	0	1	2
27	Mark Martin	2960	24	0	5	11
28	David Gilliland	2924	36	0	1	2
29	Tony Raines	2920	34	0	0	1
30	Johnny Sauter	2875	35	0	1	2
31	Dave Blaney	2781	33	0	1	4
32	Jeff Green	2704	32	0	0	3
33	Ricky Rudd	2622	31	0	0	1
34	Paul Menard	2496	30	0	0	0
35	Kyle Petty	2312	29	0	1	1
36	Scott Riggs	2135	27	0	0	1
37	Joe Nemechek	2117	28	0	0	1
38	Brian Vickers	2065	23	0	1	5
39	David Reutimann	1878	26	0	0	0
40	Sterling Marlin	1752	21	0	0	0
41	Dale Jarrett	1584	24	0	0	0
42	Bill Elliott	1579	20	0	0	0
43	A.J. Allmendinger	1165	17	0	0	0
44	Michael Waltrip	1149	14	0	0	2
45	Jeremy Mayfield	1126	17	0	0	0
46	Kenny Wallace	1066	15	0	0	0
47	Ward Burton	939	16	0	0	0
48	John Andretti	932	15	0	0	0
49	Ken Schrader	932	13	0	0	0
50	Regan Smith	516	7	0	0	0

Jimmie Johnson started off the season with a disappointing 39th-place finish in the Daytona 500 and never led the points standings until after the first Chase for the NASCAR Sprint Cup event at Loudon. He remained between first and third in the standings until taking the points lead from his teammate Jeff Gordon after a win at Texas with two races to go. In the end, Johnson won the title by just 77 points. His victory came despite some midyear misfortune. In May, at Infineon Raceway, crew chief Chad Knaus was suspended for six weeks and the team fined $100,000 and 100 points for having altered fenders on the #48 Chevrolet. Car chief Ron Malec took over crew chief duties until Knaus returned from the suspension. The 2007 NASCAR Sprint Cup title was the second in a row for Johnson, who had 10 wins in the season along with 20 top-five finishes. This was also Rick Hendrick's seventh NASCAR Sprint Cup Series owner's title, which put him in second place behind Petty Enterprises in the team owner championship standings.

2008

January 11 Larry McClure announces that due to lack of sponsorship, Morgan-McClure Motorsports is shutting down. The team formed in 1983 and had three Daytona 500 victories and 14 total NASCAR Sprint Cup Series wins.

January 21 NASCAR says it will begin donating fine money collected from teams and drivers to the NASCAR Foundation, which supports charities, instead of adding it to the season-ending point fund.

February 17 Ryan Newman wins the Daytona 500 driving for Roger Penske. It's the first restrictor-plate win for Penske Racing.

March 9 Kyle Busch wins the first NASCAR Sprint Cup Series race for Toyota. It's the 40th start in a points race for the manufacturer.

March 16 Richard Childress Racing drivers Jeff Burton, Kevin Harvick, and Clint Bowyer finish 1-2-3 in the Food City 500 at Bristol.

April 5 Newcomer Michael McDowell crashes his #00 Aaron's Toyota in qualifying at Texas. The car rolled numerous times and forced the replacement of 28 feet of SAFER barrier. McDowell escaped injury.

May 3 Kyle Busch spins Dale Earnhardt Jr. out of the lead with two laps to go and enrages a sell-out crowd at Richmond in the Crown Royal 400.

May 17 Kasey Kahne wins the NASCAR Sprint All-Star Race at Lowe's Motor Speedway. He is the first driver in the history of the event to win after being voted in by the fans.

May 21 Humpy Wheeler, president and promoter of Lowe's Motor Speedway, announces he is retiring from the speedway after 33 years. It was Wheeler's idea to light a superspeedway for night races.

June 13 Petty Enterprises sells majority interest in the family-owned race team to Boston Ventures, a private equity firm.

Rick Hendrick and Dale Earnhardt, Jr., celebrate in Victory Lane after the Budweiser Shootout at Daytona. This was the first race for Earnhardt, Jr., in the #88 Chevrolet for Hendrick Motorsports. After winning again in his Gatorade Duel qualifying race, many people expected a big season for NASCAR's most popular driver.

◄ Dario Franchitti waves to the crowd during driver introductions for the Daytona 500. Franchitti was one of several open-wheel drivers who came to NASCAR after seeing the success enjoyed by Juan Pablo Montoya in 2007. Franchitti, who won the 2007 IndyCar series and the 2007 Indy 500, signed with Chip Ganassi Racing to run a full 2008 NASCAR Sprint Cup Series schedule. However, after missing five NASCAR Sprint Cup Series races due to injuries, Franchitti's team was shut down in early July.

▼ Car owner Roger Penske sprays his driver, Ryan Newman, with champagne after Newman gave Penske Racing its first Daytona 500 victory. Newman broke an 81-race winless streak to finally give Penske a Daytona 500 win after 24 attempts. The victory came after the two Penske Racing Dodges driven by Newman and Kurt Busch hooked up in a draft on the last lap to go around Toyota teammates Tony Stewart and Kyle Busch.

As part of the celebration commemorating the 50th running of the Daytona 500 in 2008, many former winners of the event were invited to take part in pre-race activities. Marvin Panch (right) finished 17th in the first Daytona 500 run in 1959 and won the event in 1961. The inaugural 500 finish was so close that officials had to wait to review photographs before declaring Lee Petty the winner. T. Taylor Warren (left) took the picture that determined the outcome. Warren was still an active racing photographer during the 2008 Speedweeks at Daytona.

Carl Edwards does his signature backflip after winning the UAW-Dodge 400 at Las Vegas Motor Speedway. This was Edwards' second win in a row after a victory the previous Monday in the rain-delayed Auto Club 500 at Fontana. During post-race inspection, it was discovered that the lid on the oil-tank reservoir of the #99 Ford was loose. The team was penalized 100 points, and crew chief Bob Osborne was fined $100,000 and suspended for six weeks. Edwards was also not awarded the 10 bonus points for winning a race that is used in the Chase for the NASCAR Sprint Cup seeding.

▲ Toyota's first win in NASCAR Sprint Cup Series competition came at the hands of Kyle Busch in the Kobalt Tools 500 at Atlanta Motor Speedway. This was the 40th points-paying race for Toyota, and only the fourth race in which Joe Gibbs Racing had fielded a Camry. Busch led 173 of the 325 laps and finished more than two seconds ahead of teammate Tony Stewart. It was the first victory for a foreign car at the NASCAR Sprint Cup Series level since 1954, when Al Keller won with a Jaguar in NASCAR's first road-course race in Linden, NJ.

▲ Fire follows the #84 Toyota of Mike Skinner during the Food City 500 at Bristol. A broken oil line caused the fire, and after repairs, Skinner completed 441 of the 500 laps and finished 40th. The #84 Red Bull car had four different drivers in 2008. A.J. Allmendinger started the season, followed after three races by Skinner, who piloted it for five events. Then it was Allmendinger again, then former F-1 driver Scott Speed. Finally, Red Bull teammate Brian Vickers drove it in the last race of the season at Homestead.

▶ Local hero Denny Hamlin (center) enjoys Victory Lane with friends after the Goody's Cool Orange 500 at Martinsville. On a misty, overcast day, Hamlin led three different times and beat Jeff Gordon by several car lengths for his first win in his home state of Virginia. This would be Hamlin's only victory in 2008, though he had eleven other top-five finishes and made the Chase for the third time in his three full-time seasons. He went on to finish eighth in the final points standings.

2008

July 10 Tony Stewart announces he is leaving Joe Gibbs Racing and will be driver and co-owner of Stewart-Haas Racing.

July 14 Ryan Newman says he will leave Penske Racing at the end of the 2008 season. Newman has won 43 poles and 13 NASCAR Sprint Cup Series races for Penske.

August 15 Tony Stewart introduces Ryan Newman as his teammate at Stewart-Haas Racing.

September 23 NASCAR announces a new random drug-testing policy. Also, all drivers, officials, and over-the-wall crew members will be tested in the preseason.

October 5 Carl Edwards sparks a 12-car crash during the Amp Energy 500 at Talladega that involves half of the Chase field.

November 9 TV network ABC cuts away from the last 22 laps of the Checker Auto Parts 500 at Phoenix and moves it to a cable channel, forcing many to miss the end of the race.

November 12 Dale Earnhardt, Inc., and Chip Ganassi Racing merge to become Earnhardt-Ganassi Racing, to be based in the Ganassi shops.

November 16 Jimmie Johnson wins his third consecutive NASCAR Sprint Cup Series title, tying Cale Yarborough for that record. Regan Smith wins Raybestos Rookie of the Year.

More than half the field runs three wide during the Aaron's 499 at Talladega Superspeedway. There were 52 lead changes over 188 laps, with Kyle Busch in the #18 Toyota winning his second NASCAR Sprint Cup Series race of the year. Juan Pablo Montoya finished second behind Busch, and had a shot at a win until a caution came out on the final lap.

With two laps to go in the Crown Royal Presents the Dan Lowry 400 at Richmond International Raceway, Kyle Busch in the #18 Toyota tagged Dale Earnhardt, Jr., in the #88 Chevrolet while racing for the lead. Earnhardt, Jr., went from a possible win to a 15th-place finish with a battered car. Busch came back to finish second to Clint Bowyer, who slipped past the two and led the final 12 laps after the race was extended by 10 laps to accommodate NASCAR's green-white-checkered rule. Denny Hamlin had won the pole and led 381 of the first 382 laps, until a flat tire with eight laps to go along with a NASCAR penalty for stopping on the track left him with a 24th-place finish.

◄ An emotional Dale Jarrett prepares to get behind the wheel of a NASCAR Sprint Cup Series car for the last time in the NASCAR Sprint All-Star Race at Lowe's Motor Speedway. His final points race was at Bristol in the Food City 500 in March. Jarrett amassed 32 wins—including three Daytona 500s—in 668 starts and was the 1999 NASCAR Sprint Cup champion. He announced plans to cover NASCAR races as a TV commentator for ESPN starting in 2009.

► Roush Racing teammates Greg Biffle (#16), Carl Edwards (#99), and David Ragan (#6) race their Fords through the tri-oval at Lowe's Motor Speedway during the Coca-Cola 600. Biffle finished second in the race to Kasey Kahne, Edwards came in ninth, and Ragan finished 12th. Both Biffle and Edwards made the Chase for the NASCAR Sprint Cup while Ragan finished 13th in the final points standings.

The field rolls into turn four at Infineon Raceway during the Toyota/Save Mart 350. Kyle Busch in the #18 Toyota won by almost two seconds to garner his fifth victory of the season. David Gilliland in the #38 Ford came in second for his career-best finish in NASCAR Sprint Cup Series competition. Australian Marcos Ambrose, in his first NASCAR Sprint Cup Series race, ran as high as second in the Wood Brothers #21 Ford before transmission problems knocked him out on lap 83.

► A seven-car crash in turn one on the final lap of the Coke Zero 400 Powered by Coca-Cola at Daytona (shown) brought out the yellow flag and prompted a green-white-checkered finish. Leader Kyle Busch brought the field to the green flag at a slow pace. As the field accelerated, second-place Jeff Gordon tried to jump under Busch in turn one but was clipped by Carl Edwards who was making a move of his own. Gordon spun to the inside of turn one but was far enough off the track that the race stayed green. On the last lap, as Edwards was making a move on Kyle Busch, Sam Hornish got turned around and shot back up the track, collecting six other cars and bringing out the last caution. NASCAR determined that Busch was ahead of Edwards at the time of the yellow, giving Busch his sixth NASCAR Sprint Cup win of the season.

Jimmie Johnson kisses the bricks after winning the Allstate 400 at the Brickyard in Indianapolis. Due to tire problems at the track, NASCAR inserted competition cautions that allowed teams to change tires at regular intervals. Johnson took the lead after the last pit stop of the day on lap 151, and led the last seven laps to beat Carl Edwards to the checkered flag by less than half a second.

▲ Regan Smith in the #01 Chevrolet beats Tony Stewart in the #20 Toyota to the finish line in the Amp Energy 500 at Talladega. While Smith finished first, he completed the pass below the yellow out-of-bounds line and NASCAR awarded the victory to Stewart. Smith was put back to the last car on the lead lap and was credited with an 18th-place finish. It marked the first time a NASCAR Sprint Cup Series win was taken away since 1991 at Infineon Raceway, when Ricky Rudd had a victory overturned due to rough driving.

Crew members ready Carl Edwards' #99 Ford for the Bank of America 500 at Lowe's Motor Speedway. Edwards came into the race in second place in the Chase for the Sprint Cup, 72 points behind Jimmie Johnson. Fifty laps into the race, both of the ignition systems in Edwards' Ford failed. The Roush Racing crew fixed the problem but lost 17 laps doing repairs, and Edwards finished 33rd. He fell to fourth in the Chase, 168 points behind Johnson, while Jeff Burton won the race and moved into second place with five races to go.

The Roush Racing Fords of Greg Biffle (#16) and Matt Kenseth (#17) lead the two Hendrick Motorsports Chevrolets of #48 Jimmie Johnson and #88 Dale Earnhardt, Jr., at Martinsville near the end of the Tums QuickPak 500. Biffle finished 12th in the event and moved to second in the Chase, 149 points behind Johnson. Kenseth finished 8th and moved up to 10th place in the Chase. Johnson and Earnhardt, Jr., finished 1st and 2nd while fellow Hendrick drivers Jeff Gordon and Casey Mears finished 4th and 6th, respectively, putting all four team cars in the top six.

▶ Jamie McMurray's #26 Ford gets serviced on pit road at Texas Motor Speedway during the Dickies 500. After a slow start to the season and rumors of his departure from the Roush Fenway Racing team, McMurray came on strong in the last third of the season and ended the year with three straight third-place finishes and five top-seven finishes in his last six races.

Carl Edwards celebrates his season-leading ninth NASCAR Sprint Cup win in the 2008 Ford 400 finale at Homestead–Miami Speedway. Edwards finished the year second in NASCAR Sprint Cup points, 69 behind Jimmie Johnson. Edwards had a stellar year in 2008. In addition to his nine victories, he accrued 19 top-fives and 27 top-10s, leading the series in all three statistics.

2008 NASCAR SPRINT CUP SERIES POINTS RACE

Rank	Driver	Points	Starts	Wins	Top 5	Top 10
1	Jimmie Johnson	6684	36	7	15	22
2	Carl Edwards	6615	36	9	19	27
3	Greg Biffle	6467	36	9	19	27
4	Kevin Harvick	6408	36	0	7	19
5	Clint Bowyer	6381	36	1	7	17
6	Jeff Burton	6335	36	2	7	18
7	Jeff Gordon	6316	36	0	13	19
8	Denny Hamlin	6214	36	1	12	18
9	Tony Stewart	6202	36	1	10	16
10	Kyle Busch	6186	36	8	17	21
11	Matt Kenseth	6184	36	0	9	20
12	Dale Earnhardt, Jr.	6127	36	1	10	16
13	David Ragan	4299	36	0	6	14
14	Kasey Kahne	4085	36	2	4	14
15	Martin Truex, Jr.	3839	36	0	3	11
16	Jamie McMurray	3809	36	0	4	11
17	Ryan Newman	3735	36	1	2	8
18	Kurt Busch	3635	36	1	5	10
19	Brian Vickers	3580	36	0	3	6
20	Casey Mears	3527	36	0	1	6
21	Bobby Labonte	3448	36	0	0	2
22	David Reutimann	3397	36	0	0	4
23	Travis Kvapil	3384	36	0	0	4
24	Elliott Sadler	3364	36	0	2	8
25	Juan Pablo Montoya	3329	36	0	2	3
26	Paul Menard	3151	36	0	1	1
27	David Gilliland	3064	36	0	1	2
28	Mark Martin	3022	24	0	4	11
29	Michael Waltrip	2889	36	0	1	2
30	Dave Blaney	2851	35	0	0	2
31	Scott Riggs	2797	34	0	0	1
32	Reed Sorenson	2795	35	0	1	2
33	Robby Gordon	2770	36	0	0	3
34	Regan Smith	2672	34	0	0	0
35	Sam Hornish, Jr.	2523	34	0	0	0
36	A.J. Allmendinger	2436	27	0	0	2
37	Joe Nemechek	1989	32	0	0	0
38	Patrick Carpentier	1794	24	0	0	0
39	Bill Elliott	1528	20	0	0	0
40	Michael McDowell	1466	20	0	0	0
41	J.J. Yeley	1263	17	0	1	1
42	Aric Almirola	1075	12	0	0	1
43	Ken Schrader	1040	15	0	0	0
44	Kyle Petty	879	15	0	0	0
45	Marcos Ambrose	844	11	0	1	1
46	Terry Labonte	811	10	0	0	0
47	Tony Raines	800	11	0	0	0
48	Mike Skinner	734	11	0	0	0
49	Dario Franchitti	606	10	0	0	0
50	Jeremy Mayfield	578	8	0	0	0

Jimmie Johnson etched his name in the NASCAR record books in 2008. The 2006/2007 NASCAR Sprint Cup Series champion added his third consecutive title, a feat matched only by the legendary Cale Yarborough, who won three in a row in 1976-78. Johnson also garnered another win at Indianapolis with his second Allstate 400 at the Brickyard victory in July. All this came after a disappointing start, as the #48 Lowe's team didn't score a win until the eighth race at Phoenix, and remained in the shadows while Kyle Busch and Carl Edwards dominated for most of the season. With two races to go before the beginning of the Chase, Johnson and the team stepped up and won both regular-season races and entered the Chase third behind Busch and Edwards. Johnson ran steadily in the Chase with three wins, and never finished worse than 15th. At the NASCAR Awards Banquet in New York, 69-year-old Cale Yarborough awarded the 2008 championship ring to Johnson, who, at 33 years of age, could be a serious contender to Richard Petty and Dale Earnhardt's record of seven titles.

2009

February 8 Martin Truex, Jr. and Mark Martin take the front row for the 2009 Daytona 500. This is Truex's first start for the new Earnhardt Ganassi Racing and Martin's first start for Hendrick Motorsports.

April 23 NASCAR announces that the NASCAR Sprint Cup Series Awards Ceremony will move to Las Vegas after 28 years in New York.

May 2 Kyle Busch wins the Crown Royal 400 at Richmond International Raceway on his 24th birthday. Cale Yarborough is the only other driver to win a NASCAR Sprint Cup race on their birthday.

May 6 Hendrick Motorsports announces that Mark Martin will drive another full schedule in 2010. Martin was initially going to drive part-time in 2010, sharing the ride with Brad Keselowski, but after the win in Phoenix on April 18, Martin agreed to another full season.

May 31 Tony Stewart's second-place finish in the Autism Speaks 400 at Dover International Speedway moves him into the NASCAR Sprint Cup points lead. It's the first time since Alan Kulwicki in November 1992 that an owner-driver has led the series points.

June 5 NASCAR implements double-file restarts for NASCAR Sprint Cup races. The first event to use the new procedure will be the June 7 Pocono 500. All of the lead-lap cars will line up side-by-side at the front of the field with the leader able to pick whether to start at the front of the inside or outside line.

June 7 Tony Stewart wins the Pocono 500 at Pocono, Penn. He becomes the first owner-driver to go to Victory Lane since Ricky Rudd won at Martinsville in 1998.

Matt Kenseth and crew celebrate an unexpected win in the February 15 Daytona 500. Kenseth's timing for taking the lead couldn't have been better. With rain in the area and a storm on the radar, Kenseth drove his #17 DeWALT Ford Fusion around Elliott Sadler's Dodge on Lap 146, and half a lap later, the caution came out due to rain, stopping the race. After a short wait, NASCAR called the event official and Kenseth was declared the winner. This was Kenseth's first restrictor-plate win as well as Roush Fenway Racing's first Daytona 500 victory after 21 years of effort.

2009 Raybestos Rookie of the Year contenders Joey Logano in the #20 Home Depot Toyota and Scott Speed in the #82 Red Bull Toyota race together at Daytona in February. Logano won the Rookie of the Year title over Speed; Lagano was the highest-finishing rookie 26 times while Speed was highest finisher eight times. Logano made his mark by becoming the youngest Rookie of the Year winner in series history.

Hometown hero Kyle Busch kisses the start-finish line after winning the March 1 Shelby 427 at Las Vegas Motor Speedway. As a kid, Busch watched the track being built while he raced at a short track located near the new superspeedway. After moving up to the NASCAR Sprint Cup Series, Busch badly wanted to win a race at "home." He got his wish when, with 17 laps to go, he passed Clint Bowyer for the lead and took the checkered flag.

Eleven of the 12 participating drivers in Bristol Motor Speedway's "Saturday Night Special" exhibition race on March 21 pose for pictures before the event. Pictured from left to right are: David Green, Terry Labonte, Jack Ingram, Harry Gant, Rusty Wallace, Phil Parsons, former race queen Linda Vaughn, Larry Pearson, Cale Yarborough, L.D. Ottinger, Jimmy Spencer, and Sterling Marlin. Junior Johnson was not present for the photo. The race was open to past NASCAR Nationwide and NASCAR Sprint Cup winners at the speedway. The drivers used late-model stock cars painted to resemble their old rides to run a 35-lap race before the afternoon NASCAR Nationwide event. Marlin started from the pole and beat Wallace and a fast-charging Ottinger for the win. The event was so popular that it was scheduled to be run again in 2010.

Jimmie Johnson moves past Denny Hamlin with 16 laps remaining to take the lead in the March 29 Goody's Fast Relief 500 at Martinsville. Johnson went on to score his first win of the year and his sixth at the half-mile speedway. This race marked the 25th anniversary of Hendrick Motorsports' first victory. "It was in my mind that it would be awfully special to win for Rick (Hendrick) here," Johnson said afterward. Former Hendrick driver Geoffrey Bodine was a special guest of Rick Hendrick for this race. Bodine had won the first NASCAR Sprint Cup race for Hendrick Motorsports here on April 29, 1984.

Jeff Gordon fires the six-shooters after winning the April 5 Samsung 500, making it his first career victory at Texas Motor Speedway. The four-time NASCAR Sprint Cup champion was riding a 47-race winless streak dating back to October 2007, and this was to be Gordon's only victory of the 2009 season. Nevertheless, Gordon maintained a presence in the top 10 in the points standings all year, and finished third behind Hendrick teammates Jimmie Johnson and Mark Martin.

June 21 Kasey Kahne wins the Save Mart 350 at Infineon Raceway to give Richard Petty his first win as a car owner since April 1999 at Martinsville.

June 28 Nineteen-year-old Joey Logano becomes the youngest NASCAR Sprint Cup winner after victory in the rain-shortened Lenox Tools 301 at New Hampshire Motor Speedway. The win came in his 20th series start.

August 16 Brian Vickers' win at Michigan in the CarFax 400 gives Red Bull Racing its first victory after almost three years in the NASCAR Sprint Cup Series.

September 18 Mark Martin announces he will drive full-time through the 2011 NASCAR Sprint Cup season when he will be 52 years old.

October 10 Restrictor-plate size is reduced for the upcoming Amp Energy 500 at Talladega Superspeedway. The reduction in size is expected to slow the cars 3 to 5 mph in qualifying.

October 14 The first five inductees of the new NASCAR Hall of Fame are announced in Charlotte, N.C. Richard Petty, Dale Earnhardt, Junior Johnson, Bill France, and Bill France, Jr., will be inducted as the inaugural class in May 2010.

November 22 Jimmie Johnson rides to a fifth-place finish in the Ford 400 at Homestead-Miami Speedway and takes his record-setting fourth consecutive NASCAR Sprint Cup title. Hendrick Motorsports teammates Mark Martin and Jeff Gordon finish second and third, respectively.

November 23 Joey Logano is named the 2009 Raybestos Rookie of the Year. Logano is the youngest driver to win the award.

Brad Keselowski in the #09 Chevrolet heads toward the finish line while Carl Edwards in the #99 Ford heads toward the fence at the end of the April 26 Aaron's 499 at Talladega Superspeedway. The incident was set up when Edwards and Keselowski used a two-car push draft to pass Ryan Newman and Dale Earnhardt, Jr., at the white flag. Coming toward the finish line, second-place Keselowski darted low, and Edwards came down to block his move. Contact was made and Edwards' Ford spun and lifted off the track. Newman hit the airborne car and tossed it into the frontstretch catchfence. Keselowski went on to win, marking his first NASCAR Sprint Cup victory in only his fifth start, and also giving long-time independent car owner James Finch his first series victory. Edwards' battered car failed to cross the finish line and he finished 24th.

Mark Martin takes a victory lap after winning the May 9 Southern 500 at Darlington, S.C. The 50-year-old took the lead late in the race and won the 4-hour-11-minute event by 1.5 seconds over teammate Jimmie Johnson. Martin was running in the top 10 just before the halfway point of the race when a slow pit stop put him near the end of the lead-lap cars. A call by crew chief Alan Gustafson not to pit for tires put Martin in the lead with 46 laps to go and he led the remainder of the event. The win moved Martin into the top 12 in the points standings. At least 19 of the 43 starters had contact with either the unforgiving Darlington wall or another competitor.

Jeremy Mayfield walks to his car before his qualifying run for the May 9 Southern 500 at Darlington Raceway. Mayfield failed to make the field for the race, but bigger problems were to come the next day. During the pre-race entertainment, a press conference was held in the infield media center where it was announced that Mayfield had tested positive for a banned substance the previous week at Richmond. Per NASCAR's drug-testing procedures, when Mayfield's first test came back positive, a second test was done to confirm or refute the initial test. When the second test returned positive, Mayfield was suspended indefinitely. While several crew members had tested positive in the past, Mayfield was the first NASCAR Sprint Cup driver to fail a random drug test. Mayfield had begun the season as a feel-good story after starting his own team in the off-season, but by the end of July, Mayfield's team had shut down and was sold.

The Chevrolet of Dale Earnhardt, Jr., trails smoke after a crash on Lap 343 at Darlington Raceway during the May 9 Southern 500. Smoke, bent sheet metal, and mistakes typified Earnhardt's 2009 effort. During the season opener at Daytona, two pit-road mistakes and a crash put Earnhardt well back in the field. The next week at the Auto Club 500, a blown engine left him in 39th place in the race and 35th in the points standings. The next five races were not bad for Earnhardt, but a run-in with Casey Mears in the Subway Fresh Fit 500 at Phoenix put him in 31st place and on probation for six weeks. Later in the season, Earnhardt's long-time crew chief, Tony Eury, Jr., was relieved and replaced by Lance McGrew, but the change didn't help, and Earnhardt finished the year 25th in the points standings.

Ryan Newman tries to cool off after the May 9 Southern 500 at Darlington Raceway. Newman had been sick all day, but toughed out the longest race of the year—which clocked in at 4 hours and 11 minutes—to finish fourth, one spot behind car owner Tony Stewart. Newman came to Stewart-Haas Racing after nine seasons at Penske Racing to join his fellow sprint-car alumni, Stewart, in Stewart's new career as a NASCAR Sprint Cup car owner. Expectations for the new team were low, and the year didn't start off well. But beginning at Talladega in April, Newman reeled off six straight top-10 finishes—including five top-fives—to move up to fourth in the points standings. He rode the momentum of that streak into the Chase for the NASCAR Sprint Cup. He scored three top-10s in the Chase and finished ninth in the points standings.

Tony Stewart celebrates with a burnout after winning the 25th NASCAR Sprint All-Star Race on May 16 at Lowe's Motor Speedway. The win in the non-points-paying event was Stewart's first as a NASCAR Sprint Cup owner/driver and paid a cool $1 million-plus to the Stewart-Haas team. The 2009 running of the event featured four segments consisting of one 50-lap contest, a pair of 20-lap races, and a final 10-lap "dash for the cash." Jimmie Johnson led the entire 50-lap segment while Kyle Busch led all 20 laps in the second segment. Jeff Gordon and Kyle Busch each led 10 laps apiece of the third segment. In the final 10-lap shoot-out, there were five different leaders with Stewart leading only the last two laps to take the win. Sam Hornish won the Sprint Showdown earlier in the evening and Jeff Burton's pit crew won the NASCAR Sprint Pit Crew Challenge presented by Craftsman.

Car owner Michael Waltrip (right) and driver David Reutimann wait out the rain on pit road during the May 25 running of the Coca-Cola 600. The race was rained out on Sunday and rescheduled for Monday the 25th, which was Memorial Day. Rain halted the race several times, but Reutimann, running 14th, stayed out on the track when everyone in front of him pitted during a caution, giving him the lead. Heavy rain soon brought out the red flag, and the race was called with Reutimann declared the winner. It was Reutimann's first NASCAR Sprint Cup win and also the first series victory for Michael Waltrip Racing. In honor of Memorial Day, a caution flag was thrown at 3 P.M. and the field brought to a halt on the frontstretch. Pit crews lined up on pit road and engines were shut off in a moment of silence.

Richard Petty and Kasey Kahne share Victory Lane after Kahne won the June 21 Toyota/Save Mart 350 at Infineon Raceway. The victory was the first since April 18, 1999, for a Petty-owned team. In early 2008, Petty sold controlling interest of the team to Boston Ventures, and later that year, moved his shop from its long-time home in Level Cross, N.C., to Mooresville, N.C. In January 2009, the team merged with Gillett Evernham Motorsports to become Richard Petty Motorsports, fielding a four-car Dodge effort with drivers Kahne, Elliott Sadler, Reed Sorenson, and AJ Allmendinger. By the end of 2009, RPM announced a merger with Yates Racing to become a four-car Ford team running Roush cars and engines.

◀ Rookie Joey Logano holds up part of the hardware he received as winner of the June 28 Lenox 301 at New Hampshire Motor Speedway. His victory in the rain-shortened event made Logano the youngest winner ever in NASCAR Sprint Cup competition; at 19 years and 35 days old, he replaced Kyle Busch at 20 years 125 days old in the record book. He is also the youngest winner in the NASCAR Nationwide Series. Logano was a non-factor in the event until the rains came. He inherited the lead during green-flag pit stops four laps before the final caution for rain. Before that he had spun once and twice received the free pass awarded to lap-down cars. The win was the first top-five finish in his 20-race NASCAR Sprint Cup career.

▼ Kyle Busch in the #18 Toyota edges out the #9 Dodge of Kasey Kahne for 14th place at the end of the July 4 Coke Zero 400 at Daytona International Speedway. Busch was leading the event with a few hundred yards to go when contact with eventual winner Tony Stewart sent Busch into the outside wall. Busch bounced back into traffic and was hit twice more, first by Kahne and then by teammate Joey Logano. This was the second straight restrictor-plate race where the leader spun within sight of the finish line. After Regan Smith had a win taken from him at the end of 2008 at Talladega for passing below the yellow line, drivers were not giving an inch at the end of plate races and the result was contact and crashes. After the race, Stewart said "It's nobody's fault. It's just racing. It's a product of the environment."

The new NASCAR Hall of Fame takes shape in downtown Charlotte, N.C. Construction on the hall, which has an opening date of May 11, 2010, started January 25, 2007, on a five-acre piece of property adjoining the Charlotte Convention Center. The hall itself will be more than 150,000 square feet in size and will contain a 275-seat theater, a 40,000-square-foot ballroom, and the NASCAR Media Group broadcast studios. Next to the property is a 19-story office tower and a parking deck. While there are several other racing Hall of Fame sites around the country—most notably the National Motorsports Hall of Fame in Darlington, S.C., and the International Motorsports Hall of Fame at Talladega Superspeedway—this one is dedicated to NASCAR. On October 14, 2009, the first five inductees to the hall were announced. "Big Bill" France and his son and successor Bill France, Jr., are part of the first class as the founder and leaders of the sport. Seven-time champions Richard Petty and Dale Earnhardt are also part of the inaugural class, as is Junior Johnson, who rode with the sport from its moonshine beginnings as a driver to the company boardrooms as a car owner.

The #42 Chevrolet of Juan Pablo Montoya leads the field in the July 26 Brickyard 400 at Indianapolis Motor Speedway. Montoya led 116 of the first 124 laps in the 160-lap event until he was caught speeding after a green-flag pit stop. The resulting pass-through penalty moved Montoya back to 12th place in the field, and he only made up one position by the end of the race. The mistake by Montoya allowed Jimmie Johnson and Hendrick teammate and event pole-sitter Mark Martin to race for the win. On the last restart, Johnson beat Martin to turn one and led the remaining 24 laps. The Brickyard win moved Johnson to second in the points standings behind Tony Stewart.

Kyle Busch in the #18 M&M's Toyota and Mark Martin in the #5 Carquest Chevrolet race for the win at the end of the August 22 Sharpie 500 at Bristol Motor Speedway. Both drivers were racing for more than just a victory, as with only two races left before the start of the Chase for the NASCAR Sprint Cup, they each needed points. Martin entered the race 12th in points while Busch entered in 15th; only the top 12 drivers make the Chase. Busch led the final 68 laps of the race but Martin was on him the whole time, with both drivers racing each other respectfully on the high-banked half-mile bullring. "It's such an honor to race with him," said Busch of Martin. "He didn't let me win the race, but he certainly didn't take it from us." With his win at Bristol, Busch moved to within 34 points of getting into the Chase while Martin's second-place run moved him into 10th place with a 60-point cushion over Busch.

The Chase for the NASCAR Sprint Cup class of 2009 poses for a group photo after the September 12 Chevy Rock & Roll 400 at Richmond International Raceway. Four drivers—Tony Stewart, Jeff Gordon, Jimmie Johnson, and Denny Hamlin—were locked in before even getting to Richmond, while 11 others had a chance to take one of the last eight positions available. Carl Edwards, Kasey Kahne, Kurt Busch, Juan Pablo Montoya, Ryan Newman, Mark Martin, and Greg Biffle all maintained their spots in the top 12 while Brian Vickers raced his way into the Chase, bumping Matt Kenseth out in the process. For Vickers and Montoya, this was their first time in the Chase; for Kenseth, it was the first time he had missed the Chase. Johnson was the only driver to make the Chase in the first six seasons it had been used.

Bobby Labonte in the #96 Ask.com Ford and Elliott Sadler in the #19 Stanley Dodge go pink in the October 17 NASCAR Banking 500 at Charlotte Motor Speedway. October is National Breast Cancer Awareness Month and five NASCAR Sprint Cup teams ran pink cars at Lowe's to help the Susan G. Komen for the Cure foundation bring attention to the disease. Bill Elliott in the #21 Wood Brothers Ford, Michael Waltrip in the #55 NAPA Toyota, and Kyle Busch in the #18 M&M's Toyota also ran pink paint schemes. Among the five sponsors, the Komen foundation was guaranteed a minimum of $350,000 through donations and sales of merchandise. Busch was the highest finisher of the group with an eighth-place finish.

Carl Edwards spent the first part of the Chase on crutches after breaking his right foot while playing Frisbee with his friends in the off-week between Bristol and Atlanta. Edwards didn't miss any races because of the injury. After winning nine races and finishing second in the 2008 standings, Edwards was expected to contend for the title in 2009. But even before the broken foot, Edwards' season had been a major disappointment. In 2009, Carl managed only 13 top-10 finishes in his 36 starts with no wins. He finished 11th in points, his worst showing since the 2006 season when he finished 12th.

David Reutimann gives Brad Keselowski a shove during the November 1 Amp Energy 500 at Talladega Superspeedway. Talladega's two NASCAR Sprint Cup events were the most talked-about races during the 2009 season. Both the Aaron's 499 in April and the Amp Energy 500 in November featured typical Talladega slam-bam action.

Jimmie Johnson came into the November 8 Dickies 500 at Texas Motor Speedway with a 184-point lead in the NASCAR Sprint Cup standings with only three races to go. With a maximum swing of 161 points in a race, Johnson had more than a full-race lead over second-place Mark Martin. But on just the third lap of the Dickies 500, Johnson got involved in a crash started by contact between David Reutimann and Sam Hornish. After 113 laps worth of repairs that included replacing the front and rear sheetmetal of his car with unpainted pieces, Johnson returned to the track. Without the repairs, Johnson would have finished 43rd, but thanks to the hard work of crew chief Chad Knaus and the Lowe's crew, he got the #48 Chevrolet back on the track and completed 205 laps of the 334-lap race. That earned him a 38th-place finish and an extra 15 points. Johnson left Texas with a 73-point lead with two races to go.

Jimmie Johnson leads Kurt Busch during the late stages of the November 15 Checker O'Reilly Auto Parts 500 at Phoenix International Raceway. The two drivers led a combined 307 of the race's 312 laps. Johnson beat second-place-finisher Jeff Burton by more than a second while Busch fell back and finished sixth. Johnson's win gave him a 108-point lead over Mark Martin going into the final race at Homestead-Miami Speedway. Busch's sixth-place finish put him fourth in points with a chance to move up and break Hendrick Motorsports' hold on the top three positions in the series standings.

Denny Hamlin burns 'em down after winning the November 22 season-finale Ford 400 at Homestead-Miami Speedway. The victory topped off Hamlin's best year to date in the NASCAR Sprint Cup Series, with four wins and 15 top-five finishes. He ended the season in impressive fashion, finishing second, third, and first in the last three races, leaving him fifth in points at the end of the Chase.

Jimmie Johnson poses with his four NASCAR Sprint Cup Series championship trophies. The 34-year-old earned a place in the NASCAR record books by winning his fourth consecutive title, something no other NASCAR Sprint Cup driver has ever accomplished. Furthermore, he became just the fourth driver to win four or more NASCAR Sprint Cup titles, joining seven-time champs Richard Petty and Dale Earnhardt, along with four-time champion Jeff Gordon in that elite group.

Las Vegas welcomed NASCAR and four-time NASCAR Sprint Cup champion Jimmie Johnson to the city for three days of celebration on December 2-4. Prior to the move to Las Vegas, the NASCAR Sprint Cup Series Awards Ceremony had been held in New York since 1981.

Jimmie Johnson does a burnout on Las Vegas Boulevard in front of the Wynn Hotel as part of the NASCAR Sprint Cup Series Victory Lap. The city of Las Vegas closed the boulevard and allowed the top-10 drivers in the points standings to cruise "The Strip" in their cars. The parade traveled the city street from the MGM Grand to the Wynn and back to the MGM Grand. The parade was part of Champions Week, which ended with the NASCAR Sprint Cup Series Awards Ceremony on December 4.

2009 NASCAR SPRINT CUP SERIES POINTS RACE

Rank	Driver	Points	Starts	Wins	Top 5	Top 10
1	Jimmie Johnson	6652	36	7	16	24
2	Mark Martin	6511	36	5	14	21
3	Jeff Gordon	6473	36	1	16	25
4	Kurt Busch	6446	36	2	10	21
5	Denny Hamlin	6335	36	4	15	20
6	Tony Stewart	6309	36	4	15	23
7	Greg Biffle	6292	36	0	10	16
8	Juan Pablo Montoya	6252	36	0	7	18
9	Ryan Newman	6175	36	0	5	15
10	Kasey Kahne	6128	36	2	7	14
11	Carl Edwards	6118	36	0	7	14
12	Brian Vickers	5929	36	1	4	13
13	Kyle Busch	4457	36	4	9	13
14	Matt Kenseth	4389	36	2	7	12
15	Clint Bowyer	4359	36	0	4	16
16	David Reutimann	4221	36	1	5	10
17	Jeff Burton	4022	36	0	5	10
18	Marcos Ambrose	3830	36	0	4	7
19	Kevin Harvick	3796	36	0	5	9
20	Joey Logano	3791	36	1	3	7
21	Casey Mears	3759	36	0	0	4
22	Jamie McMurray	3604	36	1	1	5
23	Martin Truex, Jr.	3503	36	0	1	6
24	A.J. Allmendinger	3476	36	0	1	6
25	Dale Earnhardt, Jr.	3422	36	0	2	5
26	Elliott Sadler	3350	36	0	1	5
27	David Ragan	3252	36	0	0	2
28	Sam Hornish, Jr.	3203	36	0	2	7
29	Reed Sorenson	3147	36	0	0	1
30	Bobby Labonte	3128	36	0	1	2
31	Paul Menard	2979	36	0	0	0
32	David Stremme	2919	33	0	0	0
33	Michael Waltrip	2839	34	0	0	2
34	Robby Gordon	2699	35	0	1	1
35	Scott Speed	2690	35	0	1	1
36	John Andretti	2597	34	0	0	0
37	David Gilliland	1928	31	0	0	0
38	Brad Keselowski	1528	15	1	1	4
39	Regan Smith	1440	18	0	0	0
40	Joe Nemechek	1342	30	0	0	0
41	Dave Blaney	1204	30	0	0	0
42	Bill Elliott	1095	12	0	0	0
43	Max Papis	1047	15	0	0	1
44	Mike Bliss	577	13	0	0	0
45	Tony Raines	528	13	0	0	0
46	Aric Almirola	527	8	0	0	0
47	Erik Darnell	472	7	0	0	0
48	Scott Riggs	448	8	0	0	0
49	Travis Kvapil	378	6	0	0	0
50	Patrick Carpentier	351	6	0	0	0

After tying Cale Yarborough's record of three successive championships in 2008, Johnson set his own record in 2009 by winning his fourth consecutive championship. In typical Jimmie Johnson fashion, he didn't lead the standings until after the 30th race of the year. With victories at Martinsville in March, Dover in May, and Indianapolis in July, Johnson entered the Chase tied with Tony Stewart for second, 10 points behind leader Mark Martin. Then Johnson went on a tear, winning four of the 10 Chase races. He took the points lead after a win in the October 11 Pepsi 500 and never looked back. Johnson finished 141 points ahead of second-place teammate Martin and 179 points ahead of third-place teammate Jeff Gordon, giving team owner Rick Hendrick a 1-2-3 finish. In eight full NASCAR Sprint Cup seasons, Johnson had amassed 47 wins, 117 top-five and 180 top-10 finishes in 291 starts. Add in his more than $81 million in winnings, and Johnson had numbers on a level with the best of all time—with a lot of years left to compete.

2010s: Changing with the Times

Going into the second decade of the new millennium, NASCAR instituted several changes intended to increase competition and give fans a closer connection to the sport. These changes affected the cars, the rules, and the points system.

After extensive testing at high-speed tracks early in the 2010 racing season, NASCAR announced that the rear wing, which had been phased in during 2007, would be replaced by a spoiler starting at the March 28th race at Martinsville. This was done largely to restore the look of the more-traditional NASCAR Sprint Cup Series cars.

Competition changes for 2010 included doing away with the "no bump-draft" rule that had been in place at Talladega and Daytona, a rule that had been difficult to enforce. This change in policy came in the form of a comment from Vice President of Competition and Racing Development Robin Pemberton. "The bump drafting as we know it at Daytona and Talladega over the past few years will be totally eliminated. We will put it back in the hands of the drivers and we will say 'Boys, have at it and have a good time', that's all I can say," he said. This comment was reduced to "Boys, have at it" by some press and competitors and became the unofficial policy for the sport.

Elimination of the "no bump-draft" rule created a whole new style of racing at Daytona and Talladega. In the 2010 Daytona 500, the drivers generally continued to bump-draft on the straightaway, which kept them in the large packs. By the time the series got to Talladega in April, the drivers had started to experiment with tandem drafting, where two cars would stay attached nose-to-tail for an extended period of time. The drivers learned quickly what would work and what wouldn't. There were a record 88 lead changes with a record 29 different drivers

leading the race. There were also five cautions for multi-car crashes as the result of tandem drafting gone bad.

Shortly before the start of the 2010 Daytona 500 in February, NASCAR announced that the Green-White-Checker rule that had been in place since July 2004 was being modified to allow for up to three attempts at a G-W-C finish. As it turned out, the rule change affected the outcome of the Daytona 500, as it took a second attempt at a green-flag finish after a three-car crash in the first try. Jamie McMurray won his first Daytona 500 while another multi-car crash occurred behind the leaders. NASCAR allowed the race to finish under green. The race will also be remembered for the pothole that opened up in the racing groove just after the halfway point. There were two red-flag periods to repair the hole that pushed the total time of running the race to more than six hours. The two G-W-C attempts also made the race the longest Daytona 500, with the extra eight laps adding 20 miles to the race distance. The track was completely repaved prior to the opening of the 2011 season.

Competition was at an all-time high in 2010. There was an average of 25.4 lead changes per race, which broke a record set in 1981. There was also an average of 11.4 leaders per race, breaking a record set in the 2006 season. Out of the 75 drivers who took a green flag in the 2010 NASCAR Sprint Cup season, 55 of them led at least one lap during the year. The points championship came down to the last race of the year at Homestead, with Jimmie Johnson coming from 15 points down to beat Denny Hamlin. It was Johnson's fifth straight championship, and the first time a driver had come from behind to win the title since Alan Kulwicki in 1992.

When the teams came to Daytona to start the 2011 season, the

NASCAR Sprint Cup Series cars had a different look. The wing had been removed from the back of the car in early 2010. Now the front of the car was different. The open front splitter braces and gap under the front bumper were replaced with a smooth front fascia, which gave the cars a more stock-looking appearance. The bodies were still aero-matched, with only nose and tail decals giving the appearance of Ford, Chevrolet, Dodge, or Toyota.

There was a new track for the NASCAR Sprint Cup Series competitors in 2011. Kentucky Speedway joined the series, running its first NASCAR Sprint Cup Series race on July 9. Also that year, Auto Club Speedway lost one of its NASCAR Sprint Cup weekends, as did Atlanta Motor Speedway. Kentucky received one of the dates, while Kansas Speedway got a second NASCAR Sprint Cup Series weekend.

Starting with the 2011 season, NASCAR and official fuel supplier Sunoco brought Sunoco Green E-15 high-performance fuel to the NASCAR Sprint Cup Series. E-15 is a blend of gasoline and 15 percent ethanol made from corn grown in the U.S. The fuel burns the same as gasoline, but reduces emissions by 20 percent.

Another change for the teams was the implementation of the self-venting fuel can. It had been used successfully in the NASCAR Camping World Truck Series in 2010 and was now being brought to the NASCAR Sprint Cup Series. It is essentially a closed-loop system where the fuel empties and vents into the same container. The new fuel can eliminated the need for a catch-can man, and NASCAR changed pit-road rules to allow only six crewmembers over the wall, which removed 43 people from pit road for safety.

There were also several changes to the NASCAR Sprint Cup Series points system and the way that drivers would become eligible for the Chase for the NASCAR Sprint Cup. The entire points system was revamped to make it simpler and easier to understand. The new system awarded points in one-point increments, with last place getting one point and the winner receiving 43 points. A win brought a three-point bonus, while single-point bonuses were awarded for leading a lap and leading the most laps. The race winner could thus receive a maximum of 48 points. The Chase for the NASCAR Sprint Cup was changed by having the final two Chase spots in the 12-driver field be wild-card positions, based on wins in the first 26 races if the drivers were in the top 20 in points. If there were no drivers with wins outside the top 10, the spots would go to the 11th- and 12th-place drivers in points. The top 10 positions in the Chase itself were set by wins in the regular season, with the driver with the most wins seeded first and the two wild-card positions seeded 11th and 12th.

Starting in 2011, drivers also had to choose a series in which to score points. Drivers choosing the NASCAR Sprint Cup Series could still run NASCAR Nationwide Series and NASCAR Camping World Truck Series events, but they would not score any driver points for those series.

The qualifying procedures were also changed for 2011, with the qualifying order now set based on speeds in the first practice session of the weekend in order of slowest to fastest. Previously the order was set by blind draw.

The tandem draft had become the norm at the two restrictor-plate tracks by 2011, and NASCAR made rule changes during the season in an attempt to break up the two-car drafts. Since the only thing that would keep the cars apart was overheating (the car in back couldn't get air through the radiator to cool it off) NASCAR seized on that vulnerability. First, teams had to remove air hoses under the hood that were being used to bring fresh air in from a source other than the grill opening. Second, the size of the grille opening was reduced. Third, the pressure allowed on the cooling system was lowered to 33 pounds, which in turn lowered the

boiling point of the coolant. Later in the year, cooling-system pressure was reduced further, and teams were prohibited from greasing the rear bumpers on their cars, which was done to let the two drafting cars slide a bit when they touched.

An offshoot of the tandem draft was that drivers were talking to each other during the race. Visibility for the pushing car was non-existent, so the front driver could radio the rear driver and let him know what he was planning. Some drivers just had teammates on their radios, but some had as many as 12 different drivers dialed up.

Off the track, the TV ratings for the 2011 season improved over 2010. FOX saw a 9 percent increase for its 13 races in the first part of the season. TNT saw a 3 percent increase for the six races it broadcast in the summer. ABC/ESPN had a 6 percent increase for its 17-race schedule and a whopping 14.8 percent increase for its 10-race Chase for the NASCAR Sprint Cup coverage.

Statistically, 2011 was one of the most competitive years ever. A record average 27.1 lead changes per race broke the record set in 2010. The average number of leaders was 12.8, which also broke the record that was set in 2010. The NASCAR Sprint Cup Series championship had to be determined by a tie-breaker when Tony Stewart and Carl Edwards finished the season tied. Stewart won the title by having five wins in the season while Edwards had only one.

Also newsworthy was that there were five first-time winners in 2011, and they won in some of the biggest races. Trevor Bayne won the Daytona 500 in only his second NASCAR Sprint Cup Series start. Regan Smith won at Darlington in the SHOW TIME Southern 500. David Ragan took the win in the July Coke Zero 400 Powered by Coca-Cola at Daytona. Paul Menard scored an emotional victory for the Menard family in the Brickyard 400 Presented by Big Machine Records at Indianapolis, and Marcos Ambrose won at the historic Watkins Glen road course. There were 18 different winners in 2011, one short of the all-time record.

A historic mechanical change was instituted for the 2012 season, though it was completely invisible to the fans. After extensive development and testing, electronic fuel injection (EFI) made its debut on NASCAR Sprint Cup Series cars. Gone were the old carburetors and distributors; the new setup consisted of a throttle body (mounted where the carburetor used to sit) along with a fuel injector and coil pack for each cylinder.

When former open-wheel race-car driver Danica Patrick took the green flag for the 2012 Daytona 500, she became the first woman since 2002 to run in the NASCAR Sprint Cup Series. Shawna Robinson had seven starts in 2002, but since then, no women had made the step up to the NASCAR Sprint Cup Series. Stewart-Hass Racing, with whom Patrick was under contract, made a deal with Tommy Baldwin Racing to field Patrick's car using points earned by Baldwin's #36 team in 2011. This guaranteed that Danica was locked into the Daytona 500, which would be her first NASCAR Sprint Cup Series start. Patrick made 10 starts in 2012 as a precursor to a full 2013 schedule. She had a best finish of 17th in her last race of the year in November at Phoenix.

Two years after the "Boys, have at it" policy was adopted, NASCAR Vice President of Competition and Racing

Development Robin Pemberton said, "There were times that it got out of hand, and we're going to discuss what 'out of hand' really is moving forward."

Since 2010, there had been several on-track paybacks and face-to-face confrontations after events. While some drivers and owners had been fined, NASCAR had generally allowed the participants to work it out amongst themselves.

Three race tracks had new pavement for the 2012 season, and one track was slightly reconfigured. Michigan International Speedway, Pocono Raceway, and Kansas Speedway had all been repaved in the off-season, and all were smooth and fast. Marcos Ambrose qualified at more than 203 mph at Michigan, nine mph faster than the previous record, and 19 drivers posted speeds over 200 mph. At Pocono, Joey Logano set a new track record of 179.598 mph, and the top 36 qualifiers all broke the old track record. Kansas Speedway was repaved and reconfigured with variable banking between its April and October events. On the old configuration, the track record was 180.856 set in 2005. The new track was faster, with Kasey Kahne sitting on the pole with a speed of more than 191 mph. Meanwhile, Bristol Motor Speedway had its upper groove ground down after the spring race in March. Track owner Bruton Smith was determined to bring back the old style of racing at Bristol, which usually involved lots of on-track contact. If the August race was any indication, he succeeded. There were 13 cautions on the night, 11 of them for crashes.

Early in 2012, Penske Racing announced that it was leaving Dodge and would run Ford products beginning with the 2013 season. The two-car Penske team was Dodge's only factory-

supported entry in the NASCAR Sprint Cup Series. In August 2012, Dodge announced it was leaving NASCAR, with hopes to return in the future. Ironically, the Penske team ended up giving Dodge its first NASCAR Sprint Cup Series championship since 1975, and only its fifth in the series' history. Since returning to the series in 2001, Dodge had 57 NASCAR Sprint Cup Series wins.

Off the track, the FOX network and NASCAR agreed to an eight-year extension of its TV contract. The new deal begins in 2015 and extends through 2022. FOX will get the first 13 NASCAR Sprint Cup Series races each season, along with the complete NASCAR Camping World Truck Series schedule. ESPN/ABC and TNT Sports have the rights to the remainder of the NASCAR Sprint Cup Series schedule, and their contracts run through 2014. In January 2012, NASCAR bought back its digital rights from Turner Sports and will take control of NASCAR.com beginning in January 2013. This will allow NASCAR control over all of its interactive, digital and social media rights including technical operations and infrastructure of all NASCAR digital platforms. Turner had acquired the digital rights in 2000 when NASCAR negotiated its first TV deal.

In June, Twitter and NASCAR teamed up to give fans a live,

behind-the-scenes experience with the Twitter.com/#NASCAR page. The #NASCAR page gave fans the opportunity to see tweets and photos from drivers, pit crew members, and other insiders in one location. Most NASCAR drivers have Twitter accounts, as it allows them to interact instantly with fans and each other. In September, NASCAR, Turner Sports, and Sprint released the NASCAR Sprint Cup Mobile App. This app allows users to keep in touch with the sport from their handheld devices.

On August 7, 2012, a new NASCAR Sprint Cup Series car took to the track at Martinsville. This was just a Goodyear tire test, but it was also the first official run for the NASCAR Gen-6 car. Carl Edwards, Martin Truex, Jr., Jimmie Johnson, and Kevin Harvick all took part in getting information for Goodyear, as well as shaking down the new car. Further testing took place at Talladega, Texas, Phoenix, and Charlotte before the end of the year. The Gen-6 car replaces the Gen-5 that came on the circuit in 2007. Ford will campaign its Fusion, while Toyota will race its Camry. Chevrolet will introduce a new street car as well as its race car as a Chevrolet SS.

In the early part of the decade, it was clear that the times were changing. But it was equally clear that NASCAR was ready and willing to change with them.

2010

February 6 At age 51, Mark Martin becomes the oldest pole sitter for the Daytona 500, and Dale Earnhardt, Jr., starts second for a Hendrick Motorsports sweep of the front row.

February 11 After the Budweiser Shootout ended under caution at Daytona the previous weekend, NASCAR announces that they will make up to three attempts at a green-white-checkered finish to try to end races under green.

April 10 Ryan Newman breaks a 77-race winless streak with a victory at the Subway Fresh Fit 600 in Phoenix. It is his first win for Stewart-Hass Racing and the first win for a car carrying the #39 in NASCAR Sprint Cup Series history.

May 23 Richard Petty, Dale Earnhardt, Junior Johnson, Bill France, Sr., and Bill France, Jr., become the first five members inducted into the NASCAR Hall of Fame in Charlotte, N.C.

June 9 Steve Lane, the crew chief of the #38 NASCAR Sprint Cup team of Travis Kvapil, is penalized $100,000 and suspended for 12 races for using bleeder valve stems on the car at Pocono.

June 20 After shutting his car off to save fuel while leading under caution in the last seven laps of the Toyota/Save Mart 350 at Sonoma, Marcos Ambrose has trouble restarting and falls to seventh place before it fires, giving Jimmie Johnson the lead and the win.

July 3 Kevin Harvick wins the Coke Zero 400 Powered by Coca-Cola at Daytona while six multi-car crashes in the last half of the race—including a 19-car pileup on lap 147—leave many challengers in the garage.

On January 21 at the NASCAR Research and Development Center, NASCAR officials announced several rule changes for the 2010 NASCAR Sprint Cup Series season. For the restrictor-plate tracks at Daytona and Talladega, the size of the openings in the plate were allowed to be enlarged in an effort to give drivers more throttle response and "allow the drivers to drive." Also, the rule against bump drafting was being rescinded to try and make the racing better at the two superspeedways. In addition, it was announced that sometime in March, the wing on the back of the NASCAR Sprint Cup cars would be replaced with a traditional blade spoiler. On the scheduling side, it was announced that most of the races would begin at either 1 P.M., 3 P.M. or 7:30 P.M. to standardize starting times. Robin Pemberton, NASCAR's vice president of competition said all of this was done in an effort to put the racing back in the hands of the drivers and allow them to "Have at it."

Jamie McMurray in the #1 Chevrolet crosses the finish line just ahead of the #88 Chevrolet of Dale Earnhardt, Jr., at the end of the Daytona 500 on February 14. It was McMurray's first Daytona 500 victory and his second NASCAR Sprint Cup win at Daytona. There were 52 lead changes with 21 different drivers leading laps. The race was red-flagged twice to repair a hole in the track that opened up in the second turn. Greg Biffle was leading the race when the caution flag came out just before he took the white flag. With NASCAR's new use of multiple green-white-checkered attempts to finish races under green, another restart was in order. On the first G-W-C attempt, Kevin Harvick had taken the lead from Biffle when another caution came out before he could take the white flag. On the second G-W-C attempt, McMurray powered by Harvick and led the final two laps.

Brad Keselowski's #12 Dodge takes flight after being hit by Carl Edwards' Ford in the March 7 Kobalt Tools 500 at Atlanta Motor Speedway. Edwards turned Keselowski with two laps to go in retaliation for earlier contact the two had on lap 40 that sent the #99 Ford to the garage for repairs. After Edwards returned to the track, he ran down Keselowski but missed on his first attempt to crash him. One lap later he succeeded. Keselowski's car became airborne and hit the outside retaining wall, then landed on its wheels and slid to a stop. Keselowski climbed unhurt from the vehicle. Edwards was immediately parked by NASCAR officials for the rest of the event, and later put on probation for the next three races.

Jimmie Johnson in the #48 Chevrolet and Kurt Busch in the #2 Dodge race wheel-to-wheel late in the March 21 Food City 500 at Bristol. Busch led a race-high 278 laps but wound up third after a caution with 16 laps to go changed the outcome. All of the leaders pitted, but four teams elected to change only two tires while Busch and Johnson changed four and restarted fifth and sixth, respectively. After the lap 491 restart, it took Johnson only three laps to get to the front, and he led to the end for his first win at Bristol. This was Johnson's 50th NASCAR Sprint Cup victory, tying him with Junior Johnson and Ned Jarrett for 10th place on the all-time win list. The race was the last in which cars used a rear wing; thereafter they ran a conventional rear spoiler.

Matt Kenseth in the #17 Ford heads toward the outside wall after contact with the #24 Chevrolet of Jeff Gordon while Denny Hamlin races to the inside and takes the win at the March 29 Goody's Fast Pain Relief 500 at Martinsville. The race was rain-delayed until Monday, but the fans who returned were treated to a good-old-fashioned short-track race. Eight different drivers led the event with Hamlin leading the most at 172 laps. A late caution led to a green-white-checkered restart with Gordon in the lead and Hamlin in fourth. A skirmish between Gordon and Kenseth allowed Hamlin and Joey Logano to go by on the inside, and they finished first and second. Jimmie Johnson finished ninth but took the points lead for the first time in the 2010 season.

Kevin Harvick in the #29 Chevrolet noses out Jamie McMurray in the #1 Chevrolet for the win at the April 25 Aaron's 499 at Talladega Superspeedway. It broke a 115-race winless streak for Harvick that dated back to the 2007 Daytona 500. Harvick led only two laps and took the win on the third attempt at a green-white-checkered finish. The race set records for the most lead changes, at 88, and for different leaders, at 29. Seven of the top 10 drivers in the points standings were involved in crashes, which allowed Harvick to jump to second place in NASCAR Sprint Cup points.

August 1 Greg Biffle breaks a 64-race winless streak with a victory in the Sunoco Red Cross Pennsylvania 500 at Pocono. It is also the first win for a Ford since the October 2009 race at Talladega. Elliott Sadler escapes injury in a crash that tears the engine out of his car.

August 18 NASCAR announces its 2011 NASCAR Sprint Cup schedule. Kansas gets a second race, Kentucky gets a NASCAR Sprint Cup race, and Auto Club and Atlanta each lose a race.

September 11 Denny Hamlin takes the win in the Air Guard 400 at Richmond and becomes the top seed in the Chase for the NASCAR Sprint Cup.

October 10 Tony Stewart wins at Auto Club Speedway as chase contenders Kyle Busch, Kurt Busch, Greg Biffle, Matt Kenseth, and Carl Edwards all have problems.

October 13 The second class of NASCAR Hall of Fame members is announced. Bobby Allison, David Pearson, Ned Jarrett, Bud Moore, and Lee Petty will be inducted in May 2011.

October 16 NASCAR announces that the top three touring series will begin using 15-percent-ethanol fuel starting in 2011.

November 21 Kevin Conway is named 2010 Raybestos Rookie of the Year in the NASCAR Sprint Cup Series.

November 22 Richard Petty Motorsports cuts back from four race teams to two. Elliott Sadler, Aric Almirola, and Paul Menard leave while Marcos Ambrose arrives and A.J. Allmendinger stays.

November 23 Hendrick Motorsports changes three of its four NASCAR Sprint Cup Series teams' crew chiefs. Steve Letarte moves from Jeff Gordon to Dale Earnhardt, Jr., Alan Gustafson moves from Mark Martin to Jeff Gordon, and Lance McGrew moves from Dale Earnhardt, Jr., to Mark Martin.

◄ Kevin Harvick celebrates his first victory of the year in the Aaron's 499 at Talladega on April 25. After a dismal 2009 season, it appeared Harvick would be leaving the Richard Childress Racing team when his contract expired at the end of 2010. Furthermore, it was determined that primary sponsor Shell Oil would not be returning, either. But a strong start to the season found the team leading the points after the second race, and, in April, Budweiser signed a three-year sponsor deal. Harvick went on to win two more races and qualify for the Chase, finishing the season in third, just two points behind Denny Hamlin.

▼ Kyle Busch in the #18 Toyota leads the May 8 Southern 500 at Darlington as teammate #11 Denny Hamlin closes in. Busch started 39th in a back-up car after crashing in practice and led 29 laps before finishing seventh. Hamlin stayed out of trouble during the almost four-hour event, taking the lead from Jeff Burton when Burton was penalized on pit road for running over an air hose and sent to the tail end of the lead lap. Hamlin lead the final 24 laps to take his third win of 2010.

In a lighthearted but serious press conference the morning of the NASCAR Sprint All-Star Race on May 22 at Charlotte Motor Speedway, Brian Vickers (center) and Team Red Bull general manager Jay Frye (right) explain that Vickers will not compete for the remainder of the 2010 season. Vickers missed the previous week's event at Dover after having chest pains while in Washington, D.C. A trip to the emergency room revealed blood clots in his left leg and both lungs. After being examined by Dr. Steven Limentani (left), his regular physician, Vickers was placed on blood thinners to treat the clots. "I can race on blood thinners, I just can't crash," Vickers said with a laugh. In July, Vickers underwent surgery to repair a hole in his heart and had a stent placed in his leg.

Kurt Busch enters Victory Lane backwards in his battered #2 Dodge after winning the May 22 NASCAR Sprint All-Star Race at Charlotte Motor Speedway. Busch started from the pole, which he gained in a blind draw when qualifying was rained out, and won the first 50-lap segment. Jimmie Johnson took the lead at the start of the second segment that consisted of 20 laps and led through that and the third 20-lap segment as well. The final 10-lap run for the big money didn't get through the first lap before an eight-car crash eliminated five drivers. Three laps after the restart, Joe Gibbs Racing teammates Denny Hamlin and Kyle Busch tangled while racing for the lead, allowing Kurt Busch to pass both and go on for the win.

▶ David Reutimann tears up the infield grass after winning the Lifelock.com 400 on July 10 at Chicagoland Speedway. This was Reutimann's second career win and also the second NASCAR Sprint Cup victory for Michael Waltrip Racing. Reutimann's first win had come in the rain-shortened Coca-Cola 600 at Charlotte in May 2009. The #00 Toyota inherited the lead due to the timing of pit stops; Reutimann never made a pass for the lead on the track.

▲ Jamie McMurray does a burnout across the Yard of Bricks at the finish line after winning the Brickyard 400 on July 25. McMurray's teammate Juan Pablo Montoya dominated the event for the second straight year only to have problems late in the race. While pitting during a caution for debris on lap 139 of 160, Montoya took four tires on the stop and restarted seventh; McMurray and several others took only two tires and restarted at the front of the pack. Montoya crashed while trying to get back to the front. On the race's final restart, McMurray got past leader Kevin Harvick and led the final 11 laps to win his first Brickyard 400. The win gave team owner Chip Ganassi victories in the same year in three of the biggest races in the U.S.: The Daytona 500 and Brickyard 400 with McMurray, and the Indy 500 with Dario Franchitti.

Juan Pablo Montoya in the #42 Chevrolet leads Marcos Ambrose in the #47 Toyota through a turn on his way to victory in the August 8 Heluva Good! Sour Cream Dips at the Glen in Watkins Glen, N.Y. Montoya led 74 of the 90 laps to score his second NASCAR Sprint Cup win and broke a 113-race winless streak dating back to 2007. Both of Montoya's NASCAR Sprint Cup wins have been on road courses.

Tony Stewart does a victory burnout after winning his first race of the year on September 5 in the Emory Healthcare 500 at Atlanta Motor Speedway. He won again five races later at Auto Club Speedway in Fontana. Stewart was in and out of the top 10 in points throughout the season before finally getting into the top 10 for good after the 16th race of the year at Sonoma. He started the Chase seeded sixth and finished the season in seventh. Old Spice, which was the primary sponsor for Stewart in 14 races in 2010, announced midseason that it would be leaving Stewart-Hass Racing at the end of the season. Mobil 1 signed on for 2011 to sponsor the #14 Chevrolet for eleven races.

Kyle Busch holds the broom in Victory Lane on August 21 after sweeping all three major NASCAR touring races at Bristol. On Wednesday night in the O'Reilly 200 NASCAR Camping World Truck Series race, Busch won the pole but had to start in the rear after an unapproved adjustment to his truck. It took him 91 laps to get to the front and he held on through a green-white-checkered finish. On Friday night in the Food City 250 NASCAR Nationwide Series race, Busch scored his 10th series win of 2010. On Saturday night, Busch led 283 of 500 laps to win the Irwin Tools Night Race. It was the first time a driver had won all three events in a single weekend.

Clint Bowyer races down the backstretch during the September 19 Sylvania 300 at New Hampshire Motor Speedway. He led 177 of the 300 laps and took his first victory of the year after he outlasted Tony Stewart in a gamble on fuel. The win moved Bowyer up from 12th to second in the Chase for the NASCAR Sprint Cup. However, during post-race inspection, it was found that the body mounting points of Bowyer's Chevrolet were not correct, causing the rear of the car to be too high. The team was ultimately fined 150 owner and driver points, and crew chief Shane Wilson was fined $150,000 and suspended for six races. The points penalty moved Bowyer from second place to 12th in the standings.

Kurt Busch spins early in the race during the October 16 Bank of America 500 at Charlotte Motor Speedway. Though he didn't hit anything and continued the race, he finished a disappointing 30th and fell from sixth to ninth in the points standings. Busch had an up-and-down season. He scored two victories and won the NASCAR Sprint All-Star Race, but also had seven finishes of 30th or worse. He finished 11th in the season points standings. With the new "Boys, have at it" edict from NASCAR, Busch had several run-ins during the season. Jimmie Johnson and Busch traded bumps at Loudon in the spring with Johnson coming out ahead with the win. At Sonoma, Jeff Gordon spun Busch late in the race and sent him back to a 32nd-place finish. Busch got his payback on Gordon at the fall Martinsville race, when, after being pushed aside by Gordon in a classic "bump and run," Busch retaliated by putting Jeff into the frontstretch wall.

Denny Hamlin had the best season of his six-year NASCAR Sprint Cup career with a series-leading eight wins. He probably also had his biggest disappointment with his second-place finish in the points standings. He started the year by tearing the ACL in his left knee two weeks before the season started at Daytona. He didn't miss any races and actually won the Samsung Mobile 500 at Texas Motor Speedway less than three weeks after the surgery. He made the Chase and was leading the points race with a 15-point advantage over Jimmie Johnson going into the season finale at Homestead. But an early race spin by Hamlin and a strong run by Johnson led to a 54-point swing that left Hamlin as the first driver in 18 years to lose the NASCAR Sprint Cup championship in the final race of the season.

When NASCAR's vice president of competition Robin Pemberton said "Boys, have at it" in January, nobody knew what would happen. As the season progressed, competitors found out what he meant. While fines and suspensions were levied for a few flagrant actions, several on- and off-track occurrences that raised some eyebrows and would probably have drawn penalties in earlier years were ignored. In what was probably the most unexpected "Boys, have at it" moment of the year, veterans Jeff Gordon and Jeff Burton got into a shoving match on the backstretch at Texas Motor Speedway during the AAA Texas 500 after Burton crashed Gordon under caution. There were no penalties from NASCAR. In another incident, after the Carfax 400 at Michigan, Joey Logano and Ryan Newman had a face-to-face confrontation in the garage, with Logano pushing Newman before the two were separated. NASCAR Sprint Cup Series director John Darby dismissed the confrontation by saying "I've seen more pushing to get into a Walmart."

Joe Gibbs, Denny Hamlin, and J.D. Gibbs (left to right) enjoy Victory Lane at Martinsville on October 24 after Hamlin's third straight win at the Virginia short track, his seventh win of the season. Hamlin was far from dominant on the day, leading only 40 laps—the first 10 and the last 30. Short-track tempers flared when Jeff Burton and teammate Kevin Harvick had a tiff during the event, Harvick being critical of the way Burton was racing him. Jeff Gordon bumped Kurt Busch on lap 386 and Busch retaliated by putting Gordon into the frontstretch wall. Hamlin's win, along with Jimmie Johnson's fifth-place finish, allowed Hamlin to move to within six points of Johnson in the Chase for the NASCAR Sprint Cup with only four races remaining.

The three Penske Racing Dodge Chargers jockey for position at Martinsville Speedway in the TUM's Fast Relief 500 on October 24. Penske had the only factory-supported Dodge team in 2010, with several other smaller teams running a Dodge on occasion. Dodge finished fourth in the Manufacturers points standings with Kurt Busch being the most successful of the Dodge boys with two wins and an 11th-place finish in the points standings. Brad Keselowski finished 25th, while Sam Hornish Jr. ended the year in 29th place. Kurt Busch signed a multiyear extension with Penske that will move him from the #2 Miller Lite car to the #22 Shell/Pennzoil sponsored Dodge; Keselowski will take over the #2 Dodge. Sam Hornish Jr. in the #77 will lose sponsor Mobil 1, possibly leaving him without a NASCAR Sprint Cup Series ride for 2011.

A frustrated Jeff Burton kicks his battered Chevrolet after crashing out of the October 31 AMP Energy Juice 500 at Talladega. Contact from Dale Earnhardt, Jr., put the #31 in the turn-three wall on lap 134 of the 188-lap race. Burton had strong cars in the four restrictor-plate races in 2010. In the Daytona 500, he ran up front all day and finished 11th. He led the most laps in the spring Talladega race but was involved in a multicar crash and finished 32nd. In the summer Daytona race, he led 11 laps and finished fifth. Richard Childress Racing had a strong plate program with Harvick winning two of the four races and Clint Bowyer winning another. The Earnhardt-Childress Racing engine group also had the win in the Daytona 500 with Jamie McMurray giving them a perfect record in the 2010 restrictor-plate races.

Kurt Busch in the #2 Dodge is swarmed by three Chevrolets at Talladega on October 31. Chevrolet won all four restrictor-plate events, half of the season's 36 races, and the 2010 NASCAR Manufacturers Championship. This was the 34th title for Chevrolet and its eighth title in a row. Toyota finished second with 12 wins, while Ford was third with four wins, and Dodge was fourth with two wins.

2010

A.J. Allmendinger's run at the AMP Energy Juice 500 at Talladega Speedway on October 31 ended a lap early when he got caught up in a five-car crash on the last lap and flipped several times. He was credited with a 32nd-place finish, one lap down. The crash caused the last caution of the day, with two of Richard Childress's cars side-by-side for the lead at the time. It took NASCAR officials several minutes to study time-stamped video tape to determine who was leading at the moment the yellow flag came out. Clint Bowyer was determined to be ahead of Kevin Harvick and was declared the winner. The race was relatively clean for a restrictor-plate race with only four crashes on the day, with 31 cars on the lead lap at the end.

The AAA Texas 500 on November 7 at Texas was probably the strangest NASCAR Sprint Cup race of 2010. While one driver dominated but failed to win, another driver took himself out of contention with his finger, two unlikely veterans sparred on the backstretch, and a championship-contending team changed pit crews in midrace. Greg Biffle led 224 of the 334 laps, but late-race transmission issues left him finishing fifth. After Kyle Busch was hit with a penalty for speeding on pit road, he had two laps added for "saluting" officials with an obscene gesture. On lap 191, Jeff Gordon and Jeff Burton played tag and both crashed. When the two met to discuss the matter, Gordon shoved Burton and started swinging. The two drivers were separated by officials but then placed in the same ambulance for the ride to the infield care center. During the ensuing caution period, Jimmie Johnson's pit crew turned in another sub-par pit stop, and Chad Knaus called in Gordon's pit crew to service Johnson's car for the remainder of the event.

Trevor Bayne made his NASCAR Sprint Cup Series debut in the AAA Texas 500 on November 7 at Texas Motor Speedway. The 19-year old qualified the Wood Brothers #21 Ford 28th and stayed on the lead lap all day to finish 17th. Bayne is one of the young drivers coming up through the NASCAR feeder system. He started in the NASCAR K&N Pro Series East in 2008 where he had one win. He ran his first NASCAR Nationwide Series race at Bristol in March of 2009. In 2010, Bayne started the NASCAR Nationwide Series season with Diamond-Waltrip Racing, but when the team could not find sponsorship for the upcoming 2011 season, Bayne signed with Roush Fenway Racing and ran the last seven NASCAR Nationwide Series races of 2010 for them. He is set for a full 2011 NASCAR Nationwide Series schedule with the possibility of seven NASCAR Sprint Cup Series starts.

Carl Edwards heads into the grandstands to celebrate with fans after winning the Kobalt Tools 500 on November 14 in Phoenix. Edwards broke a 70-race winless streak that dated back to the 2008 season-ending event at Homestead. Denny Hamlin dominated the race by leading 190 of the 312 laps, but he pitted for fuel with 15 laps to go while many other drivers stayed out, and he finished 12th. Of the teams that gambled on fuel mileage, the biggest risk-taker was Jimmie Johnson. With 19 cars on the lead lap, Johnson could have lost a lot of points if he'd run out of gas. But the #48 Chevrolet made it to the end and cut Hamlin's point lead in half going into the last race at Homestead. Edwards stretched his fuel to win, but Juan Pablo Montoya ran out while running second and fell to 16th.

The Team Red Bull crew services the #83 Toyota of Kasey Kahne during the November 21 Ford 400 at Homestead-Miami Speedway. Kahne started the year with Richard Petty Motorsports, which was a distant incarnation of the Evernham Motorsports team where Kahne started his NASCAR Sprint Cup career in 2004. A crash in the season-opening Daytona 500 put Kahne in the hole points-wise, and he never recovered, only getting as high as 16th during the year. With his contract at RPM ending at the end of 2010, Rick Hendrick signed Kahne to drive for Hendrick Motorsports starting with the 2012 season when Hendrick would have an open seat in the #5 car. A deal was reached for Kahne to drive the 2011 season for Team Red Bull. As it turned out, he ran the last five races of 2010 with Red Bull after being released early from RPM.

2010 NASCAR Sprint Cup champion Jimmie Johnson and Ford 400 winner Carl Edwards both celebrate on the frontstretch on November 21 at Homestead-Miami Speedway. Johnson finished second in the race behind Edwards to overcome a 15-point deficit and become a five-time champion. Denny Hamlin came into the race with the points lead while Kevin Harvick was third, 46 points back, and both drivers had a chance to leave Homestead with the title. Hamlin and Harvick qualified back in the field while Johnson started sixth, and he was the only driver of the three to lead a lap on the day. Hamlin spun on lap 25 and finished 14th. Harvick was caught speeding on pit road and was only able to get back to third place.

2010 NASCAR SPRINT CUP SERIES POINTS RACE

Rank	Driver	Points	Starts	Wins	Top 5	Top 10
1	Jimmie Johnson	6622	36	6	17	23
2	Denny Hamlin	6583	36	8	14	18
3	Kevin Harvick	6581	36	3	16	26
4	Carl Edwards	6393	36	2	9	19
5	Matt Kenseth	6294	36	0	6	15
6	Greg Biffle	6247	36	2	9	19
7	Tony Stewart	6221	36	2	9	17
8	Kyle Busch	6182	36	3	10	18
9	Jeff Gordon	6176	36	0	11	17
10	Clint Bowyer	6155	36	2	7	18
11	Kurt Busch	6142	36	2	9	17
12	Jeff Burton	6033	36	0	6	15
13	Mark Martin	4364	36	0	7	11
14	Jamie McMurray	4325	36	3	9	12
15	Ryan Newman	4302	36	1	4	14
16	Joey Logano	4185	36	0	7	16
17	Juan Pablo Montoya	4118	36	1	6	14
18	David Reutimann	4024	36	1	6	9
19	A.J. Allmendinger	3998	36	0	2	8
20	Kasey Kahne	3961	36	0	7	10
21	Dale Earnhardt, Jr.	3953	36	0	3	8
22	Martin Truex, Jr.	3916	36	0	1	7
23	Paul Menard	3776	36	0	1	6
24	David Ragan	3599	36	0	0	3
25	Brad Keselowski	3485	36	0	0	2
26	Marcos Ambrose	3422	36	0	2	5
27	Elliott Sadler	3234	36	0	0	1
28	Regan Smith	3229	36	0	0	0
29	Sam Hornish, Jr.	3214	36	0	0	1
30	Scott Speed	3178	36	0	0	2
31	Bobby Labonte	2583	36	0	0	0
32	David Gilliland	2445	32	0	0	0
33	Travis Kvapil	2426	34	0	0	0
34	Robby Gordon	2028	27	0	1	1
35	Kevin Conway	1830	28	0	0	0
36	Casey Mears	1573	21	0	0	0
37	Dave Blaney	1416	29	0	0	0
38	Joe Nemechek	1361	31	0	0	0
39	Reed Sorenson	1355	16	0	0	1
40	Brian Vickers	1158	11	0	0	3
41	Bill Elliott	1107	13	0	0	0
42	Mike Bliss	1050	17	0	0	2
43	Max Papis	907	18	0	0	0
44	J.J. Yeley	891	17	0	0	0
45	Michael McDowell	879	24	0	0	0
46	David Stremme	825	11	0	0	0
47	Landon Cassill	717	16	0	0	0
48	Aric Almirola	704	9	0	1	1
49	Tony Raines	534	9	0	0	0
50	Patrick Carpentier	474	6	0	0	0

With 53 wins and five consecutive titles already to his credit, it's not hard to imagine 35-year-old Jimmy Johnson one day being compared to the likes of Richard Petty and Dale Earnhardt. By winning his fourth straight NASCAR Sprint Cup title in 2009, Johnson did what no other NASCAR Sprint Cup Series driver had ever done. His fifth consecutive win in 2010—only his ninth full season of Sprint Cup competition—just spread icing on the cake. After dropping out of the Daytona 500 with an axle problem that put him 35th in points, Johnson ran hot and cold during the season. But he was in seventh going into the Chase for the NASCAR Sprint Cup and seeded second after the points were reset. Going into the last race of the season at Homestead, Johnson was in second, 15 points behind Denny Hamlin. Johnson finished second in the race while a spinout caused Hamlin to finish 14th, giving Johnson his fifth consecutive NASCAR Sprint Cup title.

2011

January 26 NASCAR announces changes in the points systems for all three national touring series for 2011. There will be two "wild card" spots available in the Chase for the NASCAR Sprint Cup. Also, qualifying order will be set by practice speeds, with slowest going out first. NASCAR Sprint Cup Series teams will only be allowed five sets of tires for practice and qualifying instead of the six previously used. A closed-loop fueling system will be used in all three touring series.

February 2-11 NASCAR announces that starting in 2012, the NASCAR Sprint Cup Series will run fuel-injection systems. Robin Pemberton, NASCAR's vice president of competition, said the change "will provide greater fuel efficiency and a greener footprint while maintaining the same great competition."

February 12 Kurt Busch wins the Budweiser Shootout after Denny Hamlin's late move is disallowed for passing below the yellow line. Hamlin was put back to the tail end of the lead lap and finished 12th.

March 23 *National Speed Sport News* shuts down after 76 years of publication. The newspaper was first published as *National Auto Racing News* on August 16, 1934, and printed its last issue, dated March 23, 2011. Chris Economaki was the long-time owner, publisher, and editor of the paper.

April 16 Hendrick Motorsports takes the first four starting spots for the Aaron's 499 at Talladega Superspeedway. Jeff Gordon, Jimmie Johnson, Mark Martin, and Dale Earnhardt, Jr., qualify first through fourth. It's only the third time in NASCAR Sprint Cup Series history that a team has swept the top four starting positions. Gordon's pole-winning speed of 178.248 mph is the slowest pole-winning speed ever at Talladega.

April 26 The last part of the late Smokey Yunick's "Best Damn Garage in Town" burns to the ground in Daytona Beach, Florida. The winners of the 1961 and 1963 Daytona 500s were built in the shop.

On January 26, during the annual media tour, NASCAR Chairman Brian France (left) announced changes to the points system for the NASCAR Sprint Cup Series. Starting in 2011, points would be awarded in one-point increments with first place earning 43 points, last place earning one point. Three bonus points would go to the winning driver, one point to a race leader, and one point to the driver leading the most laps, for a maximum of 48 points per race. For the Chase for the NASCAR Sprint Cup, two wild-card spots were added for the two highest non-top-10-ranked drivers with the most wins, as long as they'd ranked in the top 20 in points. Also announced was that drivers who competed in multiple series would have to choose just one in which they could accumulate points toward the driver championship.

▼ Trevor Bayne, in the Wood Brothers #21 Ford, leads #99 Carl Edwards and #34 David Gilliland across the finish line in the February 20 Daytona 500. The 20-year-old Bayne stunned the stock car world by winning the Daytona 500 in only his second NASCAR Sprint Cup Series start, and in doing so, set a record for being the youngest driver to ever win the race. The race itself also set a couple of records. There was an event-record 74 lead changes among 22 drivers and a record 16 cautions for 60 laps. The race on the newly repaved speedway was an event of tandem drafting with pairs of cars hooking up and making runs to the front. Bayne never led until lap 203 of 208 after his teammate David Ragan was black-flagged from the lead after changing lanes on a restart before crossing the start/finish line. The win also marked Ford's 600th NASCAR Sprint Cup Series victory.

Jeff Gordon celebrates after winning the February 27 SUBWAY Fresh Fit 500 at Phoenix International Raceway. After dodging some early mayhem in which 23 cars were involved in accidents, Gordon ran down Kyle Busch and passed him with a bump and run with eight laps to go. The victory broke a 66-race winless streak for Gordon that dated back to April 2009. It was also his 83rd career win, which tied him for fifth with Cale Yarborough on the all-time win list. The race was the last on the old Phoenix layout. The track is due to be completely repaved and get a wider frontstretch, a reconfigured backstretch, and variable banking in the turns.

◀ The crowd at Martinsville Speedway enjoys a great short-track finish when, for the second week in a row, Kevin Harvick saves the best for last as he wins the April 3 Goody's Fast Relief 500. Harvick passed Dale Earnhardt, Jr., with just four laps to go for the win. Earnhardt barely held off Kyle Busch at the line to finish second. There were a track-record 31 lead changes among 12 drivers with Kyle Busch leading 151 laps and taking the series points lead from Carl Edwards.

▲ Matt Kenseth leads the way at Texas Motor Speedway in the April 9 Samsung Mobile 500. Kenseth led 169 of the 334 laps and won by more than eight seconds over Clint Bowyer. The victory broke a 76-race winless streak for Kenseth going back to when he won the first two races of the 2009 season. Roush Fenway Racing had a good night at Texas with all four team drivers finishing in the top seven. For the second week in a row, Martin Truex took a hard hit but walked away unhurt. Carl Edwards regained the points lead from Kyle Busch, who finished a lap down.

The top eight finishers cross the line at Talladega Superspeedway in the April 17 running of the Aaron's 499. The #48 of Jimmie Johnson won by .002 seconds over the #33 of Clint Bowyer, which tied it for the closest finish since electronic timing began being used in 1993. The tandem drafting at the plate tracks has allowed pairs of cars to move through the field at will, and there were 88 lead changes among 26 drivers. Dale Earnhardt, Jr., committed to pushing Johnson, and the pair came from 5th place to 1st between the fourth turn and the finish line. The speed-enhancing effect of tandem drafting is clearly shown by the fact that Jeff Gordon sat on the pole with a qualifying speed of 178.248 mph, but while tandem drafting during the race, Clint Bowyer ran a lap of more than 195 mph.

Kyle Busch takes the checkered flag in the Crown Royal Presents the Matthew & Daniel Hansen 400 at Richmond International Raceway on April 30. It was Busch's second of four wins in 2011. Although he finished the season 12th in the final points standings, Busch had a great year from a competition standpoint. He led the most laps, the most miles, and in the most races (26), and according to NASCAR statistics, he also had the highest average running position for the year and passed more cars than anyone in the 2011 season.

Regan Smith celebrates his first NASCAR Sprint Cup Series win on May 7 at the Southern 500 at Darlington Raceway. This victory came in Smith's 105th start and was his first top-5 finish as well. He ran in the top 10 most of the night, and when a caution came out with 10 laps to go, he stayed on the track while most of the other lead lap cars pitted. Another caution came out with two laps to go and on the green-white-checkered finish, Smith held off Carl Edwards and Brad Keselowski for the win. Almost overshadowing the winner was a post-race pit-road encounter between Kyle Busch and Kevin Harvick. Busch and Harvick tangled late in the event, and after the race, Harvick approached Busch, who was still in his car. Busch used his car to push Harvick's into the pit wall and drove away. Both drivers were later placed on a four-race probation and fined $25,000 each.

2011

May 17 ESPN announces that the network's coverage of the Chase for the NASCAR Sprint Cup events will include "NASCAR NonStop," which will be a split-screen format with commercials and race coverage sharing the screen during the last half of the events.

May 23 David Pearson, Lee Petty, Bobby Allison, Ned Jarrett, and Bud Moore are inducted as the second class of the NASCAR Hall of Fame in Charlotte, North Carolina.

August 10 Pocono Raceway announces it will cut its races from 500 miles to 400 miles starting in 2012.

August 25 Danica Patrick says she will run 8-10 NASCAR Sprint Cup Series races for Stewart-Hass Racing in 2012, starting with the Daytona 500.

September 1 Hendrick Motorsports and Dale Earnhardt, Jr., sign a five-year contract extension that will keep Earnhardt, Jr., in the #88 through 2017.

October 7 Michael Waltrip Racing announces a three-year deal for Clint Bowyer to drive the team's #15 Toyota with 5-Hour Energy as primary sponsor.

November 4 Michael Waltrip Racing signs Mark Martin to replace David Reutimann in the #00 Aaron's Toyota. Martin will run 25 races a year, Waltrip will run five, and other drivers will fill the remainder of the schedule.

November 21 A day after leading Tony Stewart to the 2011 NASCAR Sprint Cup Series title, crew chief Darian Grubb reveals that he was told six weeks earlier that he would not be back at Stewart-Hass Racing.

November 28 Steve Addington becomes crew chief for Tony Stewart after leaving the #22 Penske Racing team of Kurt Busch.

December 2 Sprint CEO Dan Hesse announces that the company will remain the title sponsor of the NASCAR Sprint Cup Series through 2016.

December 8 Red Bull Racing shuts down after five seasons. The team had 284 NASCAR Sprint Cup Series starts with ten different drivers and won two races, in 2009 with Brian Vickers and in 2011 with Kasey Kahne.

Carl Edwards' #99 Aflac Ford is towed away after winning the May 21 NASCAR Sprint All-Star Race at Charlotte Motor Speedway. While taking a post-race celebratory slide through the tri-oval grass, he hit a high spot with the nose of the car and destroyed the front end. Only four drivers led in the 100-lap event with Greg Biffle leading the most laps at 46 and winning the first 50-lap segment. Edwards won the second and third segments, both 20 laps in length. In the final 10-lap segment, Edwards jumped out to the lead and was never pressured. David Ragan won the Sprint Showdown with Brad Keselowski finishing second. Both transferred to the NASCAR Sprint All-Star Race where Ragan finished eighth and Keselowski finished 18th.

Trevor Bayne (right) and Ricky Stenhouse, Jr., share a moment before the May 29 Coca-Cola 600 at Charlotte Motor Speedway. Stenhouse, Jr., was filling in for Bayne in the race, as Bayne was showing effects from an insect bite suffered the week of the April 9 Texas race. It was later determined he had Lyme disease. Roush Fenway Racing driver Stenhouse, Jr., was brought in to substitute for Bayne at Charlotte. Stenhouse, Jr., qualified ninth in his first NASCAR Sprint Cup Series start, ran well all night, and finished 11th. Bayne returned to the car in its next scheduled start at Michigan International Speedway in June and ran the remainder of the events. Stenhouse, Jr., went on to win the NASCAR Nationwide Series championship and will possibly drive some NASCAR Sprint Cup Series races in 2012 in the #21 Ford.

Kevin Harvick in the #29 Budweiser Chevrolet passes the coasting Dale Earnhardt, Jr., for the lead off turn four on the last lap of the May 29 Coca-Cola 600 at Charlotte Motor Speedway. The 4-hour, 33-minute marathon became a fuel-mileage race after a caution on lap 344 put the teams at the very edge of making it on fuel. When Jimmie Johnson blew an engine on lap 395 and the caution flew, it put several teams over the edge. Leader Greg Biffle had to pit before the green came out and gave the lead to Kasey Kahne. On the restart, Kahne ran out of gas before reaching the first turn and backed up the field as Earnhardt, Jr., slipped by for the lead. With cars banging and spinning behind him and no caution flag in sight, Earnhardt, Jr., pulled away and led at the white flag. Coming off the fourth turn and coming to the checkered flag, the #88 National Guard/AMP Energy Chevrolet ran out of gas. As he coasted to the line, Harvick passed him for the win. Earnhardt, Jr., fell from first to seventh in less than a quarter mile.

Jeff Gordon pits early in the June 12 5-Hour Energy 500 at Pocono Raceway. Gordon went on to rack up his 84th NASCAR Sprint Cup Series victory, tying him with Darrell Waltrip and Bobby Allison for third on the all-time wins list. Points leader Carl Edwards came into the event with a 40-point lead in the standings, but a blown engine left him 37th in the final rundown and with only a six-point lead leaving Pocono. Kyle Busch's third-place car failed post-race inspection for being too low on the left front, and the team was penalized $25,000 and six driver and owner points.

Kurt Busch leads the field in the Toyota/Save Mart 350 on June 26 at Sonoma Raceway in California. Busch led 76 of the 110 laps and finished more than two and a half seconds ahead of Jeff Gordon. It marked Busch's first NASCAR Sprint Cup Series win on a road course. Beating Gordon here was a bonus after the previous year's event in which Gordon spun Busch late in the race. This was also Busch's first win since the Coca-Cola 600 in May 2010. The two road-course races on the schedule (the other being Watkins Glen) have become some of the roughest events of the season with lots of bumping and banging.

▶ David Ragan celebrates his first NASCAR Sprint Cup Series win at the July 2 Coke Zero 400 Powered by Coca-Cola at Daytona International Speedway. The victory was a bit of redemption for Ragan after a mistake while leading in the closing laps of the Daytona 500 cost him a chance at that victory. The tandem drafting on the restrictor-plate tracks led to another exciting and competitive event. The race featured a track-record 25 different leaders and an event-record 57 lead changes. As with the previous two restrictor-plate races this year, you needed a partner to run fast and Ragan and Roush Fenway Racing teammate Matt Kenseth had a plan from the start. The two ran together most of the night, with Kenseth pushing. The pair dodged three multi-car crashes in the last twelve laps to finish first and second.

▼ Kyle Busch leads the field at the start of the first NASCAR Sprint Cup Series race at Kentucky Speedway. The Quaker State 400 on July 9th was 11 years in the making at the track that opened in 2000 and had been pushing for a NASCAR Sprint Cup Series race ever since. When Bruton Smith bought the track in early 2009, he used the NASCAR practice of "realignment" of race dates from his other tracks to open up a date for Kentucky. Qualifying was rained out on Friday after half the field had gone out, and the starting lineup was set by practice speeds. On race day, Kyle Busch made it a perfect weekend by starting first, turning the fastest lap during the race, leading the most laps, and winning.

Paul Menard takes the checkered flag at the Indianapolis Motor Speedway to win the July 31 Brickyard 400. This was Menard's first NASCAR Sprint Cup Series win, and it came in one of the biggest races of the year. The Menard family had been coming to Indy since the early 1980s. Paul's father, John, sponsored—and then eventually owned—open-wheeled racers in an attempt to win the Indianapolis 500, but only got as close as a third-place finish in 1992. In his 167th NASCAR Sprint Cup Series start, Paul made the family proud by stretching his fuel and holding off a hard-charging Jeff Gordon to win by less than a second. Of the season's four "Big" races, three of them had first-time winners: Trevor Bayne won the Daytona 500, Regan Smith won the Southern 500 at Darlington, veteran Kevin Harvick won the Coca-Cola 600 at Charlotte, and Paul Menard won the Brickyard 400 at Indianapolis.

Marcos Ambrose finally gets to celebrate a NASCAR Sprint Cup Series win at the August 14 Heluva Good! Sour Cream Dips At the Glen race at Watkins Glen, New York. Ambrose had been close to a NASCAR Sprint Cup Series win several times at the series' two road-course events, coming closest in 2010 at Infineon Raceway where he basically gave away the victory while under caution late in the race. This year, Ambrose had a fifth at Infineon and came into the Watkins Glen race as a favorite. Rain pushed back the race to Monday and Kyle Busch led the most laps, but in the end, it was Ambrose going three wide into turn one on the last restart to get the win. In doing so, he became the fifth first-time winner of the 2011 season.

▶ Jeff Gordon holds up a poster signifying his 85th NASCAR Sprint Cup Series win while in Victory Lane following the September 6 AdvoCare 500 at Atlanta Motor Speedway. Gordon won the two-day rain-delayed race by beating teammate Jimmie Johnson in a 15-lap dash at the end. The win moved Gordon into third place on the all-time wins list behind Richard Petty with 200 wins and David Pearson with 105 wins. Gordon's first career NASCAR Sprint Cup Series start was in 1992 at Atlanta where car owner Rick Hendrick had first noticed his future superstar during a NASCAR Nationwide Series race. By the end of the 2011 season, Gordon had 653 NASCAR Sprint Cup starts with 85 wins, 287 top fives, and 396 top tens.

Brad Keselowski celebrates his third win of the year at the August 27 Irwin Tools Night Race at Bristol Motor Speedway. Keselowski came into the 2011 season after a disappointing first full year of NASCAR Sprint Cup Series racing in 2010 when he had a best finish of tenth. Penske Racing promoted Keselowski's NASCAR Nationwide Series crew chief Paul Wolfe to lead the #2 Miller Lite NASCAR Sprint Cup Series team, and midway into the season, the team clicked. A fuel-mileage win at Kansas in June showed the team had potential. Then, during an August 3 test session at Road Atlanta, Keselowski crashed hard and broke his left ankle. He arrived at the next race at Pocono in obvious pain but drove the #2 Dodge to its second win of the year. It was the beginning of a remarkable four-race stretch of two wins, a second, and a third that helped put Keselowski into the Chase for the NASCAR Sprint Cup. Keselowski finished fifth in the Chase, 84 points behind Tony Stewart.

The Chase for the NASCAR Sprint Cup class of 2012 poses for the traditional group shot after the running of the September 10 Wonderful Pistachios 400 at Richmond international Raceway. Nine of the drivers were locked in before the race started. Jimmie Johnson, Kurt and Kyle Busch, Carl Edwards, Matt Kenseth, Jeff Gordon, Kevin Harvick, and Ryan Newman were all in on points. Dale Earnhardt, Jr., only needed to finish better than 20th to lock in, and he finished 16th. Tony Stewart needed a finish of 18th or better to advance, and he finished 7th. Brad Keselowski was guaranteed a wild-card spot with his three wins, and Denny Hamlin's win at Michigan and his 12th place in points gave him the final spot.

Darian Grubb and Tony Stewart pose in Victory Lane after Stewart's victory in the September 19 Geico 400 at Chicagoland Speedway. After making the Chase for the NASCAR Sprint Cup with no wins, Stewart got his first victory of the year in the first Chase race. The event was delayed for a day until Monday because of rain, and as it wound to its conclusion, it became a fuel-mileage race. The last restart came with 50 laps to go and all of the teams were at their limits on fuel. Stewart made it to the end but Chase contenders Jeff Gordon, Jimmie Johnson, Kyle Busch, and Matt Kenseth ran out of fuel on the last lap. Johnson coasted across the finish line 10th, while Gordon fell to 24th and Kyle Busch fell to 22nd. Matt Kenseth coasted across the finish line 8th, but J.J. Yeley pushed him on the last lap. NASCAR rules stipulate that cars may not be assisted on the final lap, so Kenseth was not credited with the last lap and finished 21st after the penalty.

Lynn Evans, widow of racing great Richie Evans, looks over the #36 NASCAR Sprint Cup Series Chevrolet painted like her husband's modifieds at the September 25 Sylvania 300 at New Hampshire International Speedway. Richie was chosen in the third class of inductees to go into the NASCAR Hall of Fame along with drivers Darrell Waltrip and Cale Yarborough, Petty Enterprises crew chief Dale Inman, and car owner Glen Wood. Evans was a nine-time NASCAR Modified Tour champion who died as a result of a practice crash in 1985 at the age of 44.

▶ Coming to the finish line with two laps to go, Tony Stewart in the #14 Mobil 1 Chevrolet passes Clint Bowyer as Bowyer runs out of fuel in the September 25 Sylvania 300 at New Hampshire Motor Speedway. This race was a perfect example of turnabout being fair play. In this same event last year, Stewart ran out of gas with two laps to go allowing Bowyer to win that race. For the second week in a row, fuel mileage played a big part in the finish with two Chase for the NASCAR Sprint Cup contenders paying the price. Denny Hamlin ran out of fuel with three laps to go and finished 29th. Jeff Gordon, who led the most laps, had to slow down to stretch his fuel and finished 4th. Stewart's win moved him to the top of the Chase standings, while Hamlin's finish put him 32 points behind 11th place in the standings after only two Chase races.

Brian Vickers in the #83 Red Bull Toyota heads for the wall off the front of Matt Kenseth's Ford during the October 30 TUMS Fast Relief 500 at Martinsville Speedway. Kenseth said that he had gotten tired of Vickers beating on his door, so he dumped him. On the following restart, Kenseth was involved in another incident that left him 23 laps down and 31st in the finishing order, dropping him from 2nd to 5th in the Chase. Vickers had several run-ins during the season and pushed the limits of "Boys, have at it." He and Tony Stewart traded blows at Sonoma in June. At Richmond in September, he had a run-in with Marcos Ambrose, and in Phoenix in November, he punted Kenseth into the wall again.

◄ Kasey Kahne celebrates his victory in the November 13 Kobalt Tools 500 at Phoenix International Raceway. This was his first win since September 2009, an 81-race winless streak. Kahne was driving only one season for the Red Bull Racing Team while he waited for his ride at Hendrick Motorsports to open up starting with the 2012 season. In June, Red Bull announced that it was ending its NASCAR Sprint Cup Series program at the end of the 2011 season.

► Greg Biffle gets fuel during the November 20 Ford 400 at Homestead-Miami Speedway. Missing from the over-the-wall crew is the catch-can man. For 2011, the NASCAR Sprint Cup Series began using a closed-loop fueling system in which the fuel can would self-vent, eliminating the catch-can man's position. Some teams had problems with the new fuel can, which needs to be fully seated to operate properly, and long pit stops were common early in the season before the kinks were worked out of the system. Fuel mileage was also a big issue in 2011. The outcome of at least seven races was directly related to fuel mileage, with teams staying on track to maintain position because passing had become more difficult.

Carl Edwards and Tony Stewart came into the season's final race at Homestead-Miami Speedway with only each other to worry about. Edwards had a three-point lead over Stewart, but all of the other Chase for the NASCAR Sprint Cup contenders were too far back to be a threat. Edwards started the weekend by winning the pole for the Ford 400 while Stewart qualified 15th. After pitting twice to get problems fixed, Stewart found himself at the back of the field. Yet by lap 232, he had fought his way into the lead. Four laps later, Edwards moved up to second. Edwards chased Stewart for the final 31 laps but could never get close to him, and Stewart won the race by 1.3 seconds. In the end, both Edwards and Stewart had amassed 2403 points. According to NASCAR rules, the first tiebreaker is the number of wins during the season. Since Edwards had one and Stewart had five, the title went to Stewart.

The Busch brothers battled each other at Bristol Motor Speedway in March, but the siblings had plenty of other conflicts during the 2011 season, both on track and off. Kurt had racing run-ins with Jimmie Johnson at Pocono Raceway and Richmond International Raceway, as well as confrontations with two different reporters at the September Richmond event. At the final event of the year at Homestead-Miami Speedway, Kurt broke a transmission on the third lap of the race and had to go to the garage for repairs. While waiting to be interviewed for live TV, Kurt launched into a profanity-filled rant at the reporter, which was caught on video by a fan. After the race, the video was posted on YouTube, and NASCAR fined Kurt $50,000. Three weeks later, Penske Racing and Kurt Busch agreed to part ways. Kyle Busch had a run-in on pit road with Kevin Harvick at Darlington Raceway that cost him $25,000. A little more than two weeks later, Kyle was caught doing 128 mph in a 45-mph zone on a North Carolina highway and he lost his drivers license for 45 days. Kyle's biggest problem, however, came during the November 4 NASCAR Camping World Truck Series race at Texas. Early in the event, Kyle and championship contender Ron Hornaday had an on-track run-in and during the ensuing caution, Kyle crashed Hornaday. NASCAR parked Kyle for the remainder of the weekend, forcing him to miss the NASCAR Nationwide Series and NASCAR Sprint Cup Series races. He was fined $50,000. His primary sponsor, M&M's, then pulled its support for the rest of the 2011 season.

2011 NASCAR SPRINT CUP SERIES POINTS RACE

Rank	Driver	Points	Starts	Wins	Top 5	Top 10
1	Tony Stewart	2403	36	5	9	19
2	Carl Edwards	2403	36	1	19	26
3	Kevin Harvick	2345	36	4	9	19
4	Matt Kenseth	2330	36	3	12	20
5	Brad Keselowski	2319	36	3	10	14
6	Jimmie Johnson	2304	36	2	14	21
7	Dale Earnhardt, Jr.	2290	36	0	4	12
8	Jeff Gordon	2287	36	3	13	18
9	Denny Hamlin	2284	36	1	5	14
10	Ryan Newman	2284	36	1	9	17
11	Kurt Busch	2262	36	2	8	16
12	Kyle Busch	2246	35	4	14	18
13	Clint Bowyer	1047	36	1	4	16
14	Kasey Kahne	1041	36	1	8	15
15	AJ Allmendinger	1013	36	0	1	10
16	Greg Biffle	997	36	0	3	10
17	Paul Menard	947	36	1	4	8
18	Martin Truex, Jr.	937	36	0	3	12
19	Marcos Ambrose	936	36	1	5	12
20	Jeff Burton	935	36	0	2	5
21	Juan Pablo Montoya	932	36	0	2	8
22	Mark Martin	930	36	0	2	10
23	David Ragan	906	36	1	4	8
24	Joey Logano	902	36	0	4	6
25	Brian Vickers	846	36	0	3	7
26	Regan Smith	820	36	1	2	5
27	Jamie McMurray	795	36	0	2	4
28	David Reutimann	757	36	0	1	3
29	Bobby Labonte	670	36	0	1	2
30	David Gilliland	572	36	0	1	2
31	Casey Mears	541	35	0	0	0
32	Dave Blaney	508	35	0	1	1
33	Andy Lally	398	30	0	0	0
34	Robby Gordon	268	25	0	0	0
35	J.J. Yeley	192	31	0	0	0
36	Michael McDowell	139	32	0	0	0
37	Tony Raines	129	12	0	0	0
38	Ken Schrader	110	7	0	0	0
39	Terry Labonte	102	8	0	0	0
40	Bill Elliott	100	5	0	0	0
41	David Stremme	80	18	0	0	0
42	Michael Waltrip	56	3	0	0	1
43	Boris Said	38	2	0	0	0
44	Geoffrey Bodine	33	4	0	0	0
45	T.J. Bell	29	5	0	0	0
46	Stephen Leicht	20	1	0	0	0
47	Andy Pilgrim	18	1	0	0	0
48	Chris Cook	17	1	0	0	0
49	Brian Simo	11	1	0	0	0
50	Brian Keselowski	3	1	0	0	0

It didn't start out looking like a stellar season for Tony Stewart, but it sure ended up that way. Aside from a second-place finish at the Kobalt Tools 400 in March and another at the Lennox Industrial Tools 301 in July, Stewart had a decidedly lackluster first half. But he qualified for the Chase for the NASCAR Sprint Cup in 9th place, and won the first race—the Geico 400—in Chicago. He also won the following race at New Hampshire Motor Speedway, giving him the points lead. Stewart then started a roller-coaster ride that saw some bad finishes but also two more wins, and he entered the final event at Homestead-Miami in second place, three points behind Carl Edwards. At the end of the day, it became a 32-lap duel for the title with Stewart leading the race and Edwards following in second. When the checkered flag fell, Stewart was ahead by 1.3 seconds. Both drivers finished the season with 2403 points, so the championship came down to the tiebreaker of most wins. Edwards had one victory while Stewart had five, and that gave Stewart his third NASCAR Sprint Cup Series championship.

2012

January 26 NASCAR announces that it will no longer issue fines to its competitors without making the fines public. Several drivers had been fined in the past, but the infractions were not released to the public.

February 18 Kyle Busch wins the Budweiser Shootout despite being spun out coming to the white flag. The ensuing caution forced a green-white-checkered finish, and Busch rallied to beat Tony Stewart by 0.013 second.

February 29 NASCAR suspends Jimmie Johnson's crew chief Chad Knaus and car chief Ron Malec for six weeks for unapproved car body modifications found during inspection on February 17 at Daytona. Knaus was also fined $100,000, and the team was penalized 25 driver and owner points. Hendrick Motorsports immediately appealed.

March 1 Penske Racing announces it will switch manufacturers from Dodge to Ford starting with the 2013 season. Penske had been with Dodge since 2003.

March 20 The NASCAR Chief Appellate Officer rescinds almost all of the penalties levied against Hendrick Motorsports at Daytona. All suspensions and points penalties against the team and crew chief Chad Knaus are overturned with only the $100,000 fine against Knaus left in place.

May 18 NASCAR and Twitter announce a partnership to enhance the live event experience at the track through Twitter. The "Twitter.com/#NASCAR" link will show relevant tweets from NASCAR drivers and personalities.

May 19 Jimmie Johnson wins the NASCAR Sprint All-Star Race at Charlotte Motor Speedway. It is his third victory in the all star event, tying him with Dale Earnhardt and Jeff Gordon for most wins.

Starting in 2012, electronic fuel injection finally made its way to NASCAR. The EFI package consists of a throttle body, eight injectors, an engine control unit made by Freescale/McLaren, and several different sensors. Fuel is injected directly into the intake runners, and only air passes through the throttle body where the carburetor used to sit. On restrictor plate tracks, the plate is placed between the throttle body and intake manifold to reduce airflow and cut horsepower. Early in the 2012 season, there were several issues with the new technology, among them relay problems and keeping enough electrical power to the system. By midseason, these had all been worked out.

Matt Kenseth takes the checkered flag in his #17 Ford for the Monday night running of the 2012 Daytona 500. Kenseth led the final 38 laps and held off a fast-charging Dale Earnhardt, Jr., to win by .021 of a second. Heavy rains pushed the race from Sunday to Monday, and it was the first time in 53 years that the Daytona 500 had been postponed. The race itself had something for everyone. There were 25 lead changes and five multi-car crashes, including one on the final lap. An extended red-flag period resulted after Juan Pablo Montoya crashed into a jet dyer on the track while under caution, resulting in an explosion and fire. While no one was hurt, it took safety and repair crews more than two hours to clean up and fix the melted upper surface of the newly repaved speedway. The race didn't end until after midnight.

Denny Hamlin raced away from the field to win the March 4 Subway Fresh Fit 500 at Phoenix International Raceway by more than seven seconds. Hamlin took the lead from Kevin Harvick on lap 253 of 312 and led the rest of the way. Harvick made a run at Hamlin with three laps to go, but fuel issues made him back off of his challenge in order to finish the race. The win was Hamlin's 18th career NASCAR Sprint Cup Series victory and his first with new crew chief Darian Grubb, who was released from Stewart-Hass Racing after taking Tony Stewart to the 2011 NASCAR Sprint Cup title. It was also Hamlin's first NASCAR Sprint Cup win with a crew chief other than Mike Ford. The race had 25 lead changes, the same as the previous week's race at Daytona.

Brad Keselowski in the #2 Dodge avoids the spinning #5 Chevrolet of Kasey Kahne on lap 25 of the Food City 500 at Bristol Motor Speedway. The smooth move allowed Keselowski to escape with minimal damage and go on to lead 232 of the 500 laps and claim his first NASCAR Sprint Cup Series win of 2012. Michael Waltrip Racing put all three of its cars in the top five. Martin Truex, Jr., finished third, Clint Bowyer finished fourth, and Brian Vickers finished fifth after signing a six-race deal with MWR. Dale Earnhardt, Jr., got into Hendrick Motorsports teammate Jeff Gordon on lap 360 and cut a tire on Gordon's Chevrolet, causing Gordon to spin into the third-turn wall. Polesitter Greg Biffle came into the race with three straight top-three finishes and led the first 41 laps, but fell back and finished 13th. He remained the early season points leader over Kevin Harvick.

The top three go spinning at Martinsville in the Goody's Fast Relief 500 after contact between the #15 Toyota of Clint Bowyer and the #24 Chevrolet of Jeff Gordon on a late-race restart. Gordon was leading with two laps to go when David Reutimann, who had been running off the pace for several laps, stopped on the track. On the first green-white-checkered restart, Bowyer dove inside leader Gordon going into turn one. He pushed up the track into Gordon, who in turn got into Jimmie Johnson; all three spun while Ryan Newman went into the lead. On the next G-W-C restart, Newman held off AJ Allmendinger for the win. Gordon, who had led 329 laps on the day, ran out of gas and finished 14th, one lap down.

▲ On April 15, 36 drivers brought NASCAR racing back to Rockingham Speedway in the Good Sam Roadside Assistance 200 NASCAR Camping World Truck Series race. The race track had run NASCAR Sprint Cup Series and NASCAR Nationwide Series events from 1965 through 2004. After the 2004 NASCAR Sprint Cup race, track owners moved the race date to another speedway and the track sat unused. When Andy Hillenburg bought the track at auction in 2007, his goal was to bring some form of NASCAR racing back to the North Carolina speedway. Several ARCA series and late-model races were run at the speedway starting in 2008, and after SAFER barriers were installed in 2011, NASCAR agreed to return to the speedway with the truck series. A crowd of more than 20,000 saw Kasey Kahne start from the rear of the field to take the win after leading the final 46 laps.

◄ Kyle Busch celebrates in Victory Lane with his wife Samantha after winning the Capital City 400 Presented by Virginia is for Lovers at Richmond International Raceway on April 28. Although this would prove to be Busch's only NASCAR Sprint Cup Series win in 2012, he was competitive throughout the season. He led more than 13 percent of all laps run in the NASCAR Sprint Cup season, second only to Jimmie Johnson's 16.7 percent, and had four second-place finishes to go with the Richmond win. On the downside, he ranked 21st in laps completed and had six finishes of 30th place or worse, enough to keep him out of the Chase for the NASCAR Sprint Cup.

Brad Keselowski celebrates with his crew in Victory Lane after winning the Aarons 499 at Talladega Superspeedway. Keselowski and Kyle Busch teamed up in a tandem draft on a late-race restart to pass the Roush Fenway Racing pair of Matt Kenseth and Greg Biffle, and the unlikely duo pulled away to settle the race among themselves. Entering turn three on the last lap, Keselowski suddenly went up high on the banking, broke Busch's momentum, and beat him back to the finish line. Keselowski told reporters later that he had planned the move ahead of time and just waited for an opportunity to use it. He became the first driver in the last five NASCAR Sprint Cup Series Talladega races to win after leading with one lap to go. The victory was the first for a Dodge at the track since August 1976.

May 23 Buck Baker, Cotton Owens, Herb Thomas, Leonard Wood, and Rusty Wallace are announced as the 2013 NASCAR Hall of Fame inductees. The five will be formally inducted in ceremonies on February 8, 2013.

June 7 Recently announced NASCAR Hall of Fame inductee Cotton Owens dies. He won nine times as a driver and 38 times as a car owner. David Pearson won one of his three NASCAR Sprint Cup Series titles driving cars owned by Owens.

July 7 Bill Elliott makes what could be his last NASCAR Sprint Cup Series start in the Coke Zero 400 Powered by Coca-Cola at Daytona. Elliott started sixth and finished 37th. After qualifying, Elliott was asked if he would race again. "Right now, I don't have anything planned," was his response.

August 7 Dodge announces that it will leave NASCAR competition at the end of the 2012 season.

October 15 NASCAR and FOX network sign an eight-year contract extension that will keep NASCAR Sprint Cup Series racing on the network through 2022. The contract also includes the full NASCAR Camping World Truck Series calendar.

October 16 NASCAR officials tell teams that there will be changes in qualifying starting with the 2013 season. The rule that locked in the top 35 teams in points will go away and be replaced with the fastest 36 cars making the field, with the remaining seven positions being set by points.

Rick Hendrick poses with his four current drivers and their teams after Jimmie Johnson's win in the May 12 Bojangles' Southern 500 at Darlington Raceway. The win was the 200th NASCAR Sprint Cup Series win for Hendrick Motorsports since the inception of the team in 1984. The first win was with Geoff Bodine at Martinsville on April 29, 1984, in only the team's eighth race. At the time of the 200th win, HMS had 2,995 NASCAR Sprint Cup Series starts with 41 different drivers, including Hendrick, who made two starts in the late '80s at the road course in Riverside, California. Only the defunct Petty Enterprises has more NASCAR Sprint Cup Series wins than HMS, at 268.

Kasey Kahne in the #5 Chevrolet and Greg Biffle in the #16 Ford swap the lead late in the Coca-Cola 600 at Charlotte Motor Speedway. These two drivers accounted for 15 of the 31 lead changes and led 300 of the 400 laps. At the end of the night, Kahne came out on top and got his first victory for Hendrick Motorsports and his third Coca-Cola 600 win overall. Biffle faded late to a fourth-place finish, but he maintained his NASCAR Sprint Cup Series points lead over teammate Matt Kenseth. The 2012 edition of the Coca-Cola 600 was the fastest ever run, clocking in at 3 hours and 51 minutes with only five caution periods and 23 yellow-flag laps.

Jimmie Johnson shows his fun side while in Victory Lane after winning the June 3 FedEx 400 benefiting Autism Speaks at Dover International Speedway. Johnson's Lowes Chevrolet was co-sponsored by the movie *Madagascar 3*, in which one of the characters wears a multicolored wig. Some of the wigs made their way to the speedway, and they popped up after the race. Johnson dominated the event, leading 289 of the 400 laps, and won his seventh NASCAR Sprint Cup Series race at Dover. That victory tied him with Richard Petty and Bobby Allison for all-time wins at the Speedway. Tony Stewart touched off a 12-car crash on the 10th lap that brought out an almost-20-minute red-flag delay to clean up the mess on Dover's backstretch. After repairs to his car, Stewart finished 69 laps down in 25th place.

Joey Logano breaks in the new pavement with a victory burnout at Pocono Raceway after taking his second career NASCAR Sprint Cup Series win in the June 10 Pocono 400. Logano's first win came in 2009 at Loudon, NH, 104 races before. The entire speedway was repaved for the first time since 1995, and the track speed record was broken by the top 36 drivers in qualifying, with Logano winning the pole at 179.598 mph. This was also the first 400-mile race at the speedway, as the event was shortened by 40 laps. On the final restart, with seven laps to go, Mark Martin, Logano's early career mentor, took the lead from the 22-year-old Joe Gibbs driver and pulled away. Logano caught him with four laps to go and pulled a "bump and run" on the 53-year-old veteran driver and won by almost one second. The NASCAR Sprint Cup Series win and nine NASCAR Nationwide Series wins in 2012 were not enough for Logano to keep his ride at Joe Gibbs Racing, and his contract was allowed to expire at the end of the season.

Junior Nation's 143-race wait finally ends as Dale Earnhardt, Jr., takes the checkered flag in the June 17 Quicken Loans 400 at Michigan International Speedway. Unlike Earnhardt, Jr.'s last win here in 2008, which was on fuel mileage, this win was on speed. He led 95 of the 200 laps, and after beating Tony Stewart off of pit road on lap 171, he pulled away for a five-second margin of victory. For the second week in a row, the circuit went to a newly paved speedway, and for the second week in a row, the speeds were fast. Marcos Ambrose put his Richard Petty Motorsports Ford on the pole with a speed of 203.241 mph, which marked the first 200-mph-plus qualifying lap on a track outside of Talladega and Daytona, and the 11th-fastest qualifying speed ever in the NASCAR Sprint Cup Series.

Clint Bowyer in the #15 Toyota leads #14 Tony Stewart and #51 Kurt Busch through turn 11 on the way to his first 2012 win in the Toyota/Save Mart 350 at Sonoma, CA. This was his first road-course win and his first win for Michael Waltrip Racing. Bower had always run well at Sonoma, with four top 10s in six starts, and he led the last 39 laps of this race. But it wasn't an easy win. Kurt Busch in the unsponsored James Finch-owned Chevrolet pressured Bowyer over the last 20 laps. Busch might have made a race of it at the end, but with eight laps to go, he bounced the car off a tire wall and damaged the rear suspension. Nevertheless, Busch held on for third place, his best finish of the season.

Brad Keselowski leads the field in his #2 Miller Lite Dodge early in the Quaker State 400 at Kentucky Speedway. The lead was short lived as defending race champion Kyle Busch went to the front and led 116 of the first 129 laps. Contact with the outside wall broke a shock mount on Busch's Toyota that sent him to pit road for repairs. He came back to finish 10th. Keselowski had two incidents in practice with Juan Pablo Montoya that sent the Penske team to a back-up car for the race. A fired-up Keselowski vowed he would "not be pushed around," and he and the team made a statement during the race by being fast on pit road and on the track. Keselowski took the lead on lap 212 and pulled away for a four-second margin of victory over Kasey Kahne at the end of the 267-lap race.

AJ Allmendinger had his best opportunity so far in his NASCAR Sprint Cup Series career when he replaced Kurt Busch in the #22 Shell Pennzoil Dodge at Penske Racing for the 2012 season. He had a second-place finish at Martinsville in April and was coming off two straight top 10s at the end of June, when about two hours before the start of the July 7 Coke Zero 400 Powered by Coca-Cola at Daytona, he was suspended by NASCAR for failing a random drug test from the week before. Sam Hornish, Jr., filled in for Allmendinger while the team waited for his second sample to be tested. On July 24, the second sample came back positive, and Penske Racing fired Allmendinger on August 1. Allmendinger enrolled in NASCAR's Road to Recovery program and was reinstated on September 18, driving four races for Phoenix Racing before the season ended.

2012

Greg Biffle in the #16 Ford spins as Tony Stewart (tail end of car shown at far left), Matt Kenseth in the #17 Ford, and Jeff Burton in the #31 Chevrolet slip past the fourth and final multicar crash of the Coke Zero 400 Powered by Coca-Cola at Daytona. Stewart never led until the 131st lap of the 160-lap race, in part due to having started 42nd after his qualifying time was disallowed because he had an open cooling hose in the car. Roush Fenway Racing teammates Matt Kenseth and Greg Biffle dominated the night leading 124 laps between them while tandem drafting. A last-lap move by Stewart busted up the pair, and Biffle got loose in traffic and spun off turn four, collecting 14 other cars. Stewart was leading when the caution came out and got his third win of the season. Thirty-two cars were listed as being involved in crashes on the night, and several were in more than one accident.

Brad Keselowski in the #2 Dodge and Marcos Ambrose in the #9 Ford put on one of the best races of the year at the end of the Finger Lakes 355 at the Glen in Watkins Glen, NY. Kyle Busch, Brad Keselowski, and Marcos Ambrose each led on the final lap with Busch leading at the white flag. Bobby Labonte's car had dropped oil on the track, and as Busch led the field into turn one, he hit the oil and got loose. Keselowski caught him and got into his right rear and spun him in the esses. Keselowski got in the oil coming out of turn five and Ambrose drilled him, but Keselowski didn't spin. The two raced side by side through turn six and bumped before Ambrose shot ahead off turn seven to win by just .571 of a second. It was his second consecutive NASCAR Sprint Cup Series win at Watkins Glen. Keselowski finished second while Kyle Busch recovered from his spin to finish seventh.

On August 19, during the running of the Pure Michigan 400 at Michigan International Speedway, Mark Martin got lucky. After starting on the pole and leading 54 of the first 64 laps, Martin, who was leading at the time, was involved in a spin with two other cars. Martin's #55 Toyota slid down pit road and through an opening that leads to the garage area. The driver's side of the car speared the end of the wall just behind the drivers seat, and the impact sent crew members scattering on pit road. No one was hurt in the incident. Martin drove a partial schedule in 2012 in the NASCAR Sprint Cup Series for Michael Waltrip Racing, sharing the car with Brian Vickers and Michael Waltrip. The three drivers put the #55 car 15th in the owners points standings.

Danica Patrick finally came to NASCAR full time in 2012, and it was not an easy ride. This crash in the August 25 IRWIN Tools Night Race at Bristol left her with a bent car and a bad finish. Patrick started 10 NASCAR Sprint Cup Series races in 2012. Her best finish was 17th in her final race of the year at Phoenix, and she ended the year with an average finish of 28.3. Patrick will move to the NASCAR Sprint Cup Series full time in 2013 with hopes of improving her luck as she runs for Sunoco Rookie of the Year honors.

Denny Hamlin does a victory burnout after winning his first Bristol NASCAR Sprint Cup Series event in the IRWIN Tools Night Race on August 25. This was the 200th win for a car bearing the number 11. After repaving the speedway in 2007, owner Bruton Smith had the upper part of the banking ground down following the 2012 spring race. The result was a one-groove track that brought back the beating and banging that had made Bristol famous. The race was competitive with 13 different drivers taking a turn up front. Matt Kenseth and Tony Stewart tangled while racing for second, with Stewart throwing his helmet and hitting Kenseth's car.

Clint Bowyer leads the field late into the night during the September 8 Federated Auto Parts 400 at Richmond International Raceway. The start of the event was delayed by rain, and the race was stopped short of halfway by another shower. NASCAR made every effort to get the complete race run since so much was on the line for setting up the Chase for the NASCAR Sprint Cup. The event didn't end until well into Sunday morning. Bowyer went the final 122 laps without a pit stop and took the win, while Jeff Gordon finished second and bumped Kyle Busch from the Chase field. Denny Hamlin led more than half the race, but fuel-mileage issues while running second forced him to pit road with eight laps to go, and he finished 18th, one lap down.

▲ The #17 Ford of Matt Kenseth scoots away from a last-lap 25-car crash at the end of the October 7 Good Sam Roadside Assistance 500 at Talladega Superspeedway. Tony Stewart, who last season vowed to crash anyone who blocked him, cut down to block a run by Michael Waltrip and Casey Mears, which started the crash. Kenseth was one of the few lead-lap cars to escape, and he won his second restrictor-plate race of the season. Stewart was leading at the time of his move but fell to 22nd place after failing to complete the last lap. David Ragan, driving the #34 Ford that is in the middle of the crash up against the wall, managed to keep moving and finished 4th. In 2011, when tandem drafting was in full swing, there were 291 lead changes in the four restrictor-plate races. In 2012, with NASCAR making rules to end the tandem draft, there were 124 lead changes at the plate tracks.

◀ A NASCAR official tells Kurt Busch to park his car during the October 7 Good Sam Roadside Assistance 500 at Talladega Superspeedway. Busch had run out of gas coming off turn two, was hit by Jamie McMurray, and spun into the inside wall. After realizing the car was not badly damaged, Busch restarted the car to bring it to the garage for repairs. The speedway safety crews had started to help him, and Busch drove away with a bag of equipment sitting on top of the car, which fell onto the track. The race team and NASCAR radioed Busch to stop the car, but he had his helmet off. The car stopped again before he got to the garage, and Busch was informed he was done for the day. In June, Busch was suspended by NASCAR for one race after verbally abusing a reporter, and in April, he was fined $50,000 at Darlington for speeding through Ryan Newman's pit stall. Busch left Phoenix Racing and moved to Furniture Row Racing for the 2013 season.

▲ In 2012, social media took off in the NASCAR world. When Brad Keselowski tweeted pictures of the jet-dryer fire at Daytona from his car while the race was stopped under a red flag, he picked up more than 150,000 Twitter followers. While Keselowski became the leader in social media, almost everyone else was involved, also. Even Mark Martin, at the age of 54, used Twitter to keep in touch with his fans. Breaking stories were usually found first on someone's Facebook or Twitter account, and even driver insults showed up.

Regan Smith is all smiles before the start of the October 13 Bank Of America 500 at Charlotte Motor Speedway. Smith was tapped to fill in for Dale Earnhardt, Jr., in the #88 Amp Energy Drink/National Guard Chevrolet after Earnhardt, Jr., stepped out because of a concussion sustained in the previous week's crash at Talladega. Smith lost his ride in the #78 Furniture Row Chevrolet when the team decided to put Kurt Busch in the car for the remainder of the 2012 season to get ready for a full 2013 together. The Charlotte race was a disappointment when Smith's engine failed after 61 of the 334 laps. Smith filled in again at Kansas the next weekend and finished 7th. Earnhardt, Jr., hired Smith to drive his #5 NASCAR Nationwide Series car for the full schedule in 2013 in hopes of bringing an NNS championship to JR Motorsports.

2012

► The year 2012 certainly had its ups and downs for Dale Earnhardt, Jr. On the upside, Earnhardt, Jr., broke a 143-race winless streak and led the NASCAR Sprint Cup Series points standings for the first time since 2004. On the downside, he had to sit out two races after suffering two concussions in a six-week period. During a tire test at Kansas Speedway on August 29, Earnhardt, Jr.'s car blew a right-front tire, and he hit the wall hard but walked away from the infield care center on his own. He said later that he felt the symptoms of a concussion then, but decided to work through it. At Talladega on October 7, he was involved in the 25-car last-lap crash and appeared to be fine afterward, but when headaches didn't go away later in the week, he met with neurosurgeon Dr. Jerry Petty. The doctor would not clear him to race. Earnhardt, Jr., missed races at Charlotte and Kansas before returning at Martinsville. He then ran the last four events of the season. Many drivers, both active and retired, spoke highly of Earnhardt, Jr.'s decision to step up and take the break in order to properly heal.

◄ Michael Waltrip takes his own Victory Lane pictures of the #15 Clint Bowyer-led team after winning the Bank of America 500 at Charlotte Motor Speedway on October 13. This was Bowyer's third win of the 2012 season, and it kept him within striking distance of the NASCAR Sprint Cup Series points title. The year 2012 was the high-water mark for Michael Waltrip Racing since the team started running in the NASCAR Sprint Cup Series full time in 2007. In the first five full-time years, MWR had two wins and 17 top-five finishes. In 2012 alone, the teams had three wins and 24 top-fives. The team put two drivers, Bowyer and Martin Truex, Jr., in the Chase for the NASCAR Sprint Cup in 2012. Bowyer's three wins along with his second-place finish in the NASCAR Sprint Cup Series points standings gave MWR its most productive season so far.

When Jimmie Johnson spun and backed into the fourth-turn wall on lap 135 of the Hollywood Casino 400 at Kansas Speedway, the first reaction of crew chief Chad Knaus was to take the car to the garage. The rear bumper cover was torn off, the decklid was pushed up into the back window, and both rear quarter panels were damaged. As Johnson came down pit road, Knaus changed his mind. The Lowes crew beat, banged, and taped the #48 Chevrolet back together and kept it on the lead lap even through multiple pit stops. Johnson raced the damaged car hard for over 100 laps and finished ninth out of 22 cars on the lead lap, remaining second in the NASCAR Sprint Cup Series standings.

In the November 11 AdvoCare 500 at Phoenix International Raceway, Jeff Gordon decided that enough was enough after contact with Clint Bowyer, and he crashed Bowyer in turn four coming to the white flag. On lap 305 of the scheduled 312-lap race, Gordon and Bowyer made contact, with Gordon hitting the wall in turn four. Gordon rode slowly around on the apron of the track and waited for Bowyer. Coming to the white flag, Gordon turned into NASCAR Sprint Cup Series championship contender Bowyer, who was running fifth at the time, and put him head-on into the wall. Also collected in the crash were Joey Logano and Aric Almirola. Two days later, Gordon was fined $100,000 and 25 points for actions detrimental to stock car racing.

The 2012 NASCAR Sprint Cup Series champion Brad Keselowski in the #2 Dodge and Ford EcoBoost 400 winner Jeff Gordon celebrate on the frontstretch at Homestead-Miami Speedway. Keselowski came into the race with a 20-point lead over five-time champion Jimmie Johnson, and needed to finish 15th or better to take the title outright. The two title contenders used different race strategies, with Johnson running up front while Keselowski ran patiently just outside the top 10. With 55 laps to go, Johnson came to pit road leading the race and not having to stop again for fuel. However, a lug nut was left off and he had to come back in, and the extra stop left him a lap down. With 40 laps to go, Johnson was again on pit road, this time with rear gear failure. He never returned to the track. Keselowski had to pit for fuel with 19 laps to go, and he finished one lap down in 15th place. Clint Bowyer finished second in the race and moved past Johnson to finish second in the NASCAR Sprint Cup standings.

2012 NASCAR SPRINT CUP SERIES POINTS RACE

Rank	Driver	Points	Starts	Wins	Top 5	Top 10
1	Brad Keselowski	2400	36	5	13	23
2	Clint Bowyer	2361	36	3	10	23
3	Jimmie Johnson	2360	36	5	18	24
4	Kasey Kahne	2345	36	2	12	19
5	Greg Biffle	2332	36	2	12	21
6	Denny Hamlin	2329	36	5	14	17
7	Matt Kenseth	2324	36	3	13	19
8	Kevin Harvick	2321	36	1	5	14
9	Tony Stewart	2311	36	3	12	16
10	Jeff Gordon	2303	36	2	11	18
11	Martin Truex, Jr.	2299	36	0	7	19
12	Dale Earnhardt, Jr.	2245	34	1	10	20
13	Kyle Busch	1133	36	1	13	20
14	Ryan Newman	1051	36	1	6	14
15	Carl Edwards	1030	36	0	3	13
16	Paul Menard	1006	36	0	1	9
17	Joey Logano	965	36	1	2	12
18	Marcos Ambrose	950	36	1	3	8
19	Jeff Burton	883	36	0	2	6
20	Aric Almirola	868	36	0	1	4
21	Jamie McMurray	868	36	0	0	3
22	Juan Pablo Montoya	810	36	0	0	2
23	Bobby Labonte	772	36	0	0	3
24	Regan Smith	747	34	0	1	4
25	Kurt Busch	735	35	0	1	5
26	Mark Martin	701	24	0	4	10
27	Travis Kvapil	638	35	0	0	1
28	David Ragan	622	36	0	1	2
29	Casey Mears	612	36	0	0	0
30	David Gilliland	605	36	0	0	0
31	Landon Cassill	598	36	0	0	0
32	AJ Allmendinger	453	21	0	1	3
33	Dave Blaney	417	34	0	0	0
34	David Reutimann	388	25	0	0	0
35	Brian Vickers	250	8	0	3	5
36	David Stremme	236	28	0	0	0
37	Michael McDowell	187	30	0	0	0
38	J.J. Yeley	166	24	0	0	0
39	Josh Wise	147	30	0	0	0
40	Ken Schrader	146	13	0	0	0
41	Stephen Leicht	126	15	0	0	0
42	Scott Speed	124	17	0	0	0
43	Michael Waltrip	94	4	0	0	1
44	Terry Labonte	94	4	0	0	0
45	Tony Raines	71	7	0	0	0
46	Scott Riggs	56	20	0	0	0
47	Brendan Gaughan	50	4	0	0	0
48	Boris Said	34	2	0	0	0
49	Bill Elliott	14	2	0	0	0
50	Hermie Sadler	13	1	0	0	0

Brad Keselowski surprised many people when he won the 2012 NASCAR Sprint Cup Series championship. There was no doubt that he could win races and run up front–he had proven that in 2011–but he lacked the consistency needed to win a title. In 2012, Keselowski and crew chief Paul Wolfe found that consistency. With three wins and ten top-fives in the first 26 races, the #2 Miller Lite team entered the Chase for the NASCAR Sprint Cup as the fourth-seeded team. In the first Chase race at Chicago, Keselowski and his Miller Lite team beat Jimmie Johnson and the five-time championship Hendrick Motorsports team to take the points lead. During the next several races, the two drivers swapped the lead back and forth, with Keselowski 20 points ahead going into the final race at Homestead. Johnson ran up front until a bad pit stop put him a lap down, and rear-gear trouble later in the race put him out. That left the door wide open for Keselowski, who finished 15th, netting him and team owner Roger Penske their first NASCAR Sprint Cup Series title.

2013

January 11 During testing of the new Gen-6 cars at Daytona, Dale Earnhardt, Jr. sets off a crash that involves 12 of the 18 cars there. Several teams go home early because they do not have backup cars available.

March 5 FOX Sports Media group announces that SPEED will be rebranded as FOX Sports 1 on August 17th. The new channel will continue to cover motorsports events but will cover other sports as well.

March 7 Denny Hamlin is fined $25,000 for a comment he made following the March 3rd NASCAR Sprint Cup Series race at Phoenix. Hamlin said that the new Gen-6 car did not race as well as the old Gen-5 car. A NASCAR statement said the fine was issued because, "The sactioning body will not tolerate publicly made comments by its drivers that denigrate the racing product."

May 22 Tim Flock, Maurice Petty, Dale Jarrett, Jack Ingram and Fireball Roberts are announced as the newest members of the NASCAR Hall of Fame.

July 23 NASCAR and NBC Sports Group announce that NBC has bought the rights to the final 20 races in the NASCAR Sprint Cup Series, which includes the Chase for the NASCAR Sprint Cup, starting with the 2015 season. NBC will replace ESPN and TNT as a broadcasting partner with NASCAR.

September 7 In the closing laps of the Federated Auto Parts 400 at Richmond, Clint Bowyer spins his car, causing a caution flag. A few laps later, both Bowyer and teammate Brian Vickers pit under the green flag. These actions allow fellow Michael Waltrip Racing teammate Martin Truex, Jr. to qualify for the Chase for the NASCAR Sprint Cup, while knocking Ryan Newman and Jeff Gordon out of contention. Questions arise as to whether the spin and pit stops were part of a team strategy to put Truex into the Chase.

◄ The 2013 NASCAR Sprint Cup Series season saw the introduction of the new "Gen-6" race car. The new race cars that race on the track feature a body that more closely resembles their street counterparts. The new design has a longer hood and shorter rear deck than the Gen-5 car. It has a carbon-fiber hood and deck lid to reduce topside weight, and all makes have the same "greenhouse" area from the top of the door to the top of the roof. Also new for 2013 was allowing the teams to put a single sponsor logo on the roof and having the driver's last name and car manufacturer logo at the top of the windshield. The Gen-6 car was certainly fast in its first year. In 32 qualifying sessions out of 36 (four were rained out), 19 track records were broken, including a 203.949 mph lap by Joey Logano at Michigan International Raceway in August. This was the ninth-fastest qualifying lap in NASCAR Sprint Cup Series history.

▶ Jimmie Johnson celebrates after his victory in the February 24th Daytona 500. This was Johnson's second win in the Daytona 500 but it was crew chief Chad Knaus' first. When Johnson won in 2006, Knaus was at home after being suspended for a rules infraction before that year's Daytona 500. Johnson was a low-key figure this year during the week leading up to the race. Kevin Harvick won the February 16th Saturday night running of the Sprint Unlimited race. Johnson's Hendrick Motorsports teammate Danica Patrick grabbed the headlines early in the week when she became the first female to win a NASCAR Sprint Cup Series Coors Light Pole Award. On Thursday, Harvick and Kyle Busch won

their Budweiser Duel races while Johnson ran a quiet fourth in the first race. In the Daytona 500 itself, Matt Kenseth, Jeff Gordon, and Denny Hamlin led most of the laps, but Kenseth broke a motor while leading with 51 laps to go, and Hamlin and Gordon got shuffled toward the back at the end of the race. At that point, Brad Keselowski became Johnson's primary competitor. The two swapped the lead five times in the last 15 laps. A caution for debris on lap 193 bunched the field for a final restart. Johnson took the lead on the restart with six laps to go and led the rest of the way. Dale Earnhardt, Jr., and Mark Martin made a charge on the last lap but came up short and finished second and third respectively.

▲ Carl Edwards does his signature backflip after winning the Subway Fresh Fit 500 at Phoenix. It had been 70 races since Edwards' last NASCAR Sprint Cup Series win, which came in the spring of 2011. Edwards' season started out rough after he was involved in five different crashes during Speedweeks at Daytona. He came to Phoenix looking to turn his bad luck around, and he did so by leading 122 of the 316 laps. Edwards started the 2013 season with his third crew chief since the beginning of 2012. Veteran crew chief Jimmy Fennig took over the #99 Roush Fenway Racing Ford in the offseason, and the change worked. In 2012, the team had no wins and failed to make the Chase for the NASCAR Sprint Cup. In 2013, Carl won at Phoenix and again at Richmond in the fall, and he stayed in the top five in points for most of the season. Entering the Chase for the NASCAR Sprint Cup as the fifth-seeded driver, and after having good runs at Chicago and Loudon, he moved up to fourth place. At Dover, a rear-wheel hub went bad late in the race, and he finished 35th in the race and fell to 11th in the points standings and never recovered. A 13th-place finish in the points was not an accurate measurement of Edwards' 2013 season.

◄ Kasey Kahne leads the field in his #5 Great Clips Chevrolet on the way to victory in the March 17th Food City 500 at Bristol Motor Speedway. Kahne took the lead on a restart with 40 laps to go and led the rest of the way. While Kahne had been up front all day, he had a little help when, on lap 391, then-leader Jeff Gordon blew a right-front tire that put him and second-place runner Matt Kenseth into the wall and out for the day. Brad Keselowski and Kahne were the only cars to lead after that. The biggest excitement on the day was an on- and off-track confrontation between former Joe Gibbs racing teammates Joey Logano and Denny Hamlin. On lap 348 of the 500 lapper, Hamlin tried a bump and run on Logano that put the #22 Ford of Logano into the wall. After the race, Logano approached Hamlin, who was still in his car, to talk about the situation. Hamlin's crew tried to pull Logano away, and both teams had a little shoving match, but no punches were thrown.

◄ As the rest of the field crosses the finish line, Denny Hamlin's battered #11 FedEx Express Toyota sits on pit road at the end of the March 24th Auto Club 400 at Fontana. Hamlin and Joey Logano were racing for the win on the last lap, and after trading bumps, Hamlin wound up running into the inside wall off of turn 4. He suffered a fracture of his L1 vertebra that forced him to miss the next four races. Mark Martin and Brian Vickers substituted for Hamlin until he returned for the Aaron's 499 at Talladega, a race in which he started, but turned the car over to Vickers at the first caution on lap 24. After returning full time to the #11 Toyota, Hamlin could have still qualified for the Chase for the NASCAR Sprint Cup in a Wild Card spot if he could win some races and move into the top 20 in the standings. He finished second and fourth in his next two starts, and it appeared that he would be up for the task. But he only scored one more top-10 finish before the final regular season race at Richmond, and fell short. Hamlin did win the season-ending Ford EcoBoost 400 at Homestead to extend his streak of winning at least one NASCAR Sprint Cup Series race in each of the eight years he has competed full time.

▲ David Ragan is one of two Davids who helped slay the Goliaths at the May 5th Aaron's 499 at Talladega Superspeedway. Front Row Motorsports teammates Ragan and David Gilliland hooked up on the last lap to finish first and second. The superspeedways at Daytona and Talladega have always been big equalizers, where everyone feels like they have a shot to win. Team owner Bob Jenkins formed Front Row Motorsports in 2005 and started running a full NASCAR Sprint Cup Series schedule in 2009. While underfunded compared to other top teams, Front Row puts good equipment on the track. Ragan came to the team in 2012 after leaving Roush Fenway Racing and had a fourth-place finish for the team at Talladega that year. The 2013 Aaron's 499 came down to a two-lap shoot-out where Ragan restarted tenth. In turn one on the last lap, teammate David Gilliland came up and gave Ragan a push down the backstretch to help him clear then-leader Carl Edwards. Gilliland then beat Edwards to the line for second place, giving Front Row Motorsports the 1-2 sweep. In the October 20th return trip to Talladega, Ragan finished sixth for his only other top-10 finish of the season.

▲ Matt Kenseth in the #20 Toyota passes Joe Gibbs Racing teammate Kyle Busch (#18) for the win with 13 laps to go in the May 11th running of the Bojangles' Southern 500 at Darlington. The race was run at a record pace with only five cautions for 25 laps and only four leaders and nine lead changes over the 501-mile distance. Kyle Busch led for 265 of the 367 laps, but a deflating right-rear tire pushed him back to sixth place at the end. Kenseth came into the race with two wins already in the 2013 season, but he lost crew chief Jason Ratcliff for this race due to a penalty from NASCAR for a rules violation at Kansas. Substituting as crew chief for this race was Wally Brown, who worked at the Joe Gibbs complex. Kenseth started seventh and never ran lower than eighth all night. Kyle Busch was leading at the last restart with 30 laps to go while Kenseth restarted fourth. As Busch's tire slowly went down, Kenseth caught and passed him for the win. Denny Hamlin made his full-time return to the #11 SportClips Toyota after recovering from his back injury. He finished second.

September 7 Kurt Busch and the Furniture Row Racing team become the first single-car team to qualify for the Chase for the NASCAR Sprint Cup. While the team receives support from Richard Childress Racing, the team is based in Colorado.

September 14 In a meeting at Chicagoland Speedway, NASCAR chairman and CEO Brian France calls for all teams and drivers to "Give 100 percent effort, their best effort, to complete a race and race as hard as they possibly can." France also said, "Any competitor who takes action with the intent to artificially alter the finishing positions of the event or encourages, persuades, or induces others to artificially alter the finishing position of the event shall be subject to a penalty from NASCAR." The statement was in response to the controversy of the previous week at Richmond.

October 24 Beginning with the 2014 season, all of NASCAR's national touring series drivers will be required to have a preseason baseline concussion test. This will give doctors a baseline to compare to a post-concussion test and help determine if a driver is healthy enough to return to action.

November 17 Ricky Stenhouse Jr. wins the Sunoco Rookie of the Year honors. He had a third-place run at Talladega for his best finish of the season.

December 12 Richard Childress Racing announces that Austin Dillon will drive the #3 Chevrolet full-time in the NASCAR Sprint Cup Series beginning in 2014. It will mark the first time the #3 has been used in the NASCAR Sprint Cup Series since the 2001 Daytona 500.

▲ Kevin Harvick in the #29 Budweiser Folds of Honor Chevrolet and Kasey Kahne in the #5 Time Warner Cable Chevrolet lead the field into turn one on the last restart of the May 26th Coca-Cola 600 at Charlotte Motor Speedway. The 2013 running of the annual Memorial Day weekend 600-mile marathon had more twists and turns this year than usual. Denny Hamlin started from the pole, led the first six laps and, though he never led again, still finished fourth. On lap 123, a cable from the network covering the race fell on the track and caused two red flags, damaging several cars including that of then-leader Kyle Busch. Sunoco Rookie of the Year contender Ricky Stenhouse, Jr. was involved in a crash with his girlfriend and fellow Sunoco Rookie of the Year contender Danica Patrick on lap 320. The wreck also took out defending NASCAR Sprint Cup Series champion Brad Keselowski. A seven-car crash among the leaders on lap 327 brought out the third red flag of the night. Points leader Jimmie Johnson spun and crashed on lap 335 and took Matt Kenseth with him. When the last caution of the night came out with 14 laps to go, leader Kasey Kahne stayed out while everyone else pitted. Kevin Harvick took only two tires and was the first off pit road. On the restart, he quickly passed Kahne and led the final 11 laps.

◄ After running 10 NASCAR Sprint Cup Series races in 2012, Danica Patrick ran her first full NASCAR Sprint Cup Series season in 2013. She competed against Timmy Hill and Ricky Stenhouse, Jr. for Sunoco Rookie of the Year honors, where she finished second to Stenhouse. Patrick started the season by winning the pole for the Daytona 500, making her the first woman to win a NASCAR Sprint Cup Series pole. She led the race twice and ran up front most of the day. She was third with one lap to go when she got shuffled on the last lap and finished eighth. It was her only top 10 of the year. Patrick also had a good run at the spring race at Martinsville where she finished 12th. Another highlight was being voted into the NASCAR Sprint All-Star Race at Charlotte. She had on-track run-ins with David Gilliland and Travis Kvapil during the mid-part of the season. She crashed on the first lap of the fall Kansas race and finished last. On August 24th at Bristol, she broke Janet Guthrie's record of most starts by a female. Patrick finished the season 27th in points.

▶ Martin Truex, Jr. leads Juan Pablo Montoya (#42) during the June 23rd Toyota/Save Mart 350 at Sonoma Raceway. When Truex came to Sonoma, he was riding a 218-race winless streak. It had been since the spring Dover race in 2007 when he won his first and only NASCAR Sprint Cup Series event. Truex qualified 14th for the 352-kilometer road-course race where group qualifying was used for the first time at the NASCAR Sprint Cup Series level. He didn't lead until lap 41, but he led 51 of the remaining 69 laps. Road-course race strategy is based on fuel mileage: be the first to pit for the last time. Truex's crew chief, Chad Johnston, made the right calls to put the #56 NAPA Toyota in

front at the right times. Montoya ran strong all day and was second to Truex at the white flag, but Montoya ran out of gas on the last lap and finished 34th, the last car on the lead lap. This was Truex's second career NASCAR Sprint Cup Series win and his first for Michael Waltrip Racing, for whom he started driving in 2010. Truex was also the ninth consecutive different winner at Sonoma Raceway.

◄ Pictured are the ninth- through fifteenth-place finishers in the July 6th Coke Zero 400 at Daytona International Speedway. It was the second wreck on the last lap of the race that was won by Jimmie Johnson. Going into turn one on the final lap, Carl Edwards got turned around and took several cars with him. Race officials held the yellow flag to allow the race to finish under green, as the crash was far enough into the turn that there was room for the remaining cars to slow down after the finish. Coming to the finish line, Danica Patrick, who was running ninth, got turned and collected at least 10 other cars in the aftermath. Jimmie Johnson made it a season sweep by winning both races at Daytona in 2013. He became the fifth driver to do so, the last being Bobby Allison in 1982. Johnson led 94 of the 161 laps run, including the last 31.

◄ Morgan Shepherd holds an award given to him by the New Hampshire Motor Speedway on July 14th for being the oldest driver to start a NASCAR Sprint Cup Series race. Shepherd was 71 years old when he cranked up the #52 Brian Keselowski Motorsports Toyota to start the Camping World RV Sales 301. He ran 92 of the 302 laps before falling out with a vibration problem. Shepherd ran his first of 515 NASCAR Sprint Cup Series races in 1970 in Hickory, N.C., and has four wins with four different car owners. He finished fifth in the 1990 NASCAR Sprint Cup Series points standings. Along with his NASCAR Sprint Cup Series career, Shepherd has 351 starts and 15 wins in the NASCAR Nationwide Series, and 56 starts in the NASCAR Camping World Truck Series. He was the 1980 NASCAR Late Model Sportsman Division champion. Morgan started the Morgan Shepherd Charitable Fund in 1986, and every year in December, he leads a charity drive to deliver gifts to people in need.

► A jubilant Brian Vickers celebrates with fans after winning the Camping World RV Sales 301 at New Hampshire Motor Speedway on July 14th. It had been 75 starts and four years since his last win at Michigan in 2009. After that victory and making the Chase for the NASCAR Sprint Cup in 2009 while driving for Red Bull Racing, Vickers had to sit out most of the 2010 season with health problems that threatened his career. He returned in 2011 with Red Bull, but the team shut down at the end of the year leaving Vickers without a ride. When Mark Martin went to Michael Waltrip Racing in 2012, he didn't want to run the full schedule, and Vickers was asked to drive eight races. In those eight races, Vickers had three top fives and five top-10 finishes. In 2013, he was scheduled to run nine races for MWR, but when Denny Hamlin got hurt, he was allowed to drive the #11 FedEx Toyota until Hamlin could return. On August 13th, MWR announced that Brian Vickers would race the #55 Aaron's Toyota full time in 2014. Tony Stewart was hurt in a sprint car crash in early August, and Mark Martin was allowed to leave MWR to substitute for him. That allowed Vickers the chance to finish the season in the #55 Aaron's Toyota. After the October 12th race at Charlotte, Vickers was diagnosed again with a blood clot and missed the final five races of the season.

◄ Austin Dillon (#39) leads Kyle Larson (#30) in NASCAR's return to dirt-track racing in the July 24th Mudsummer Classic at Eldora Speedway in Rossburg, Ohio. The last time a major NASCAR race was run on dirt was September 30, 1970, in Raleigh, N.C., and Richard Petty won that race. Eldora track owner Tony Stewart bought the speedway in 2003 and worked for years to convince NASCAR to bring the NASCAR Camping World Truck Series to the half-mile dirt track. The race was announced on January 5th, and by January 29th, the last grandstand ticket was sold. Ken Schrader made history by becoming NASCAR's oldest pole winner at 58, and he also led the first 15 laps of the main event. Thirty trucks started the main event, but Kyle Larson and Austin Dillon were the class of the field leading 115 of the 153 laps. Larson was leading late in the race when he got hung up in lap traffic, and that allowed Dillon to get around. Dillon led the remainder of the event.

▲ Kyle Busch (#18) leads Brad Keselowski (#2) in the August 11th Cheez-It 355 at The Glen. Busch won his second NASCAR Sprint Cup Series race at Watkins Glen International and has had an impressive eight consecutive top 10s out of the nine NASCAR Sprint Cup Series races he has run there. Marcos Ambrose was the man to beat on this day. He won the pole with a new track record speed and jumped to the front at the start of the race, leading the first 28 laps. After a cycle of pit stops, he regained the lead on lap 39 and led for another 23 laps. A caution during the middle of the next pit stop cycle put Ambrose back into the middle of the pack and brought Kyle and Kurt Busch, Keselowski, Clint Bowyer, and Martin Truex, Jr. to the front of the field. On lap 82, a wild crash in the high-speed esses involved Dale Earnhardt, Jr., Kasey Kahne, and Matt Kenseth, among others. While trying to get back to the front, Ambrose was involved in a crash on lap 86 with Brian Vickers and Max Papis that ended Ambrose's day. On the final restart, with two laps to go, Brad Keselowski stayed after Busch and even gave him a shot to the rear bumper on the last corner, but he couldn't rattle him. It was the second straight year Keselowski had finished second at the Glen.

▲ Kurt Busch in the #78 Chevrolet and Joey Logano in the #22 Ford started up front and ended up front in the August 18th Pure Michigan 400 at Michigan International Speedway. Logano sat on the pole with a track record speed of 203.949 miles per hour, which is the ninth-fastest qualifying speed in NASCAR Sprint Cup Series history. Busch qualified second, and he was also faster than the old track record. Logano and Busch led 94 of the 200 laps, with Logano winning and Busch finishing third. This was Logano's third career win and his first for Roger Penske. The win was important to Logano's chances for making the Chase for the NASCAR Sprint Cup. He moved from 16th to 13th in the points standings, and the victory put him in contention for one of the two Wild Card spots. The third-place finish for Busch moved him from 11th to 9th in the points standings and into a Chase spot with only three races left before the regular-season finale at Richmond.

◀ A NASCAR official waits to give Ryan Newman the checkered flag after the Crown Royal Presents the Samuel Deeds 400 at the Brickyard Powered by BigMachineRecords.com at Indianapolis Motor Speedway on July 28th. Newman found out two weeks earlier that he would not be coming back to Stewart-Haas Racing at the end of the season, as he was being replaced by Kevin Harvick. Newman was offered a one-year contract at the end of 2012 to run the 2013 season, and when Harvick became available, Newman was out of a ride. He came to Indy wanting to impress several different car owners in an attempt to set up a deal for the next year. In qualifying, Newman was the last driver out, and he knocked Jimmie Johnson off the pole with a track record speed. On race day, Johnson was the class of the field, leading 73 of the 160 laps. But on the last pit-stop sequence with less than 30 laps to go, Newman's pit crew beat Johnson's on pit road, and that gave Newman a big lead on track. Johnson could not catch Newman, who won by more than two-and-a-half seconds. On September 9th, Newman was introduced as the replacement driver for Jeff Burton at Richard Childress Racing.

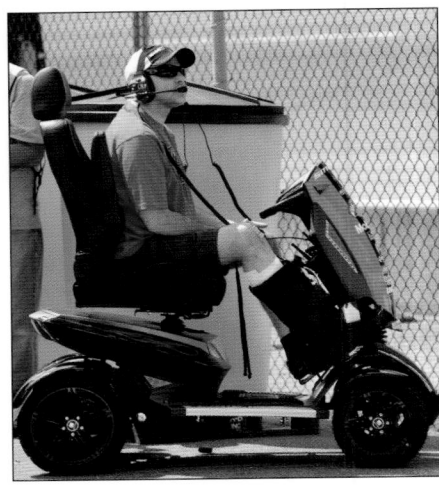

▲ Tony Stewart sits in his custom-made wheelchair during practice for the Federated Auto Parts 400 at Richmond in September. Stewart broke his right leg in a sprint car crash at Southern Iowa Speedway on August 5th. He was leading the race with five laps to go when he collided with a lapped car. Stewart suffered a grade 2 compound fracture of both his tibia and fibula that required two different operations to repair. A titanium rod was inserted in his leg on the second operation to stabilize the leg. Stewart missed the remainder of the 2013 NASCAR Sprint Cup Series season. He had started 521 consecutive NASCAR Sprint Cup Series races dating back to the 1999 Daytona 500. Several different drivers filled in for Stewart in the #14 Chevrolet, with Max Papis, Austin Dillon, and Mark Martin all taking turns. They kept the car 18th in owner points. On October 7th, Stewart underwent a third surgery on his right shin to clean up an infection. Before his accident, Stewart won a NASCAR Sprint Cup Series race at Dover to continue a 15-year streak of winning at least one race each season. That is the longest active winning streak in the NASCAR Sprint Cup Series.

▲ With seven laps to go in the September 7th Federated Auto Parts 400 at Richmond International Raceway, Clint Bowyer spun by himself coming off turn four. The single-car incident looked innocent enough at the time, but after the race was over, fingers began to point at a conspiracy inside the Michael Waltrip Racing team. At the time of the spin, Ryan Newman was leading the race, and that would have put him in the Chase for the NASCAR Sprint Cup and bumped Bowyer's teammate, Martin Truex, Jr., out. When the race restarted, Newman could only get to third place by the finish, and as a result, he would not make the Chase. On the restart with three laps to go, Jeff Gordon and Joey Logano seemed to be in position to qualify for the Chase, but MWR teammates Brian Vickers and Bowyer both pitted when the green flag came out and lost laps. That allowed Logano to move ahead of Gordon in points, which bumped Gordon from the Chase and allowed Truex back in.

▲ NASCAR President Mike Helton and NASCAR Chairman and CEO Brian France address the media on September 13th at Chicagoland Speedway. In the days after the previous week's Federated Auto Parts 400 at Richmond, NASCAR studied video and audio tapes that convinced them that the Michael Waltrip Racing team had intentionally manipulated the finishing order of the race, and as a result, the championship race as well. NASCAR fined MWR $300,000, suspended general manager Ty Norris, and penalized each of the three MWR teams 50 points. The points penalty bumped Martin Truex, Jr., from the Chase for the NASCAR Sprint Cup and moved Ryan Newman back in. NASCAR also added Jeff Gordon to the Chase because, according to Brian France, "We've decided that due to the totality of the events that were outside of Jeff Gordon's — his issues — we're going to add a 13th position to the field, and Jeff Gordon will qualify for the championship this year, the Sprint Cup championship."

◀ Kevin Harvick starts to roll out of pit stall #1 after a two-tire change during the running of the Hollywood Casino 400 at Kansas Speedway on October 6th. He went on to score his third victory of the 2013 season. The Richard Childress Racing team was able to choose stall #1 because Harvick won the pole at Kansas, his first pole in 254 races. The last time he qualified on the pole, back in 2006, he also won. The race saw a track record 15 cautions and 71 caution-flag laps. Kyle Busch crashed once in practice and twice during the race and finished 34th. As a result, he fell from third to fifth in the Chase for the NASCAR Sprint Cup standings. Ryan Newman was involved in a crash and fell from 7th to 12th in the standings. Jimmie Johnson finished 6th with a sick motor, while Matt Kenseth finished 11th and lost five more points to Johnson. With six races to go, there were only three points between them.

▲ Matt Kenseth celebrates after his victory in his 500th career NASCAR Sprint Cup Series start in the September 22nd running of the Sylvania 300 at New Hampshire Motor Speedway. This was Kenseth's second win in a row after winning the opening race of the Chase for the NASCAR Sprint Cup the previous week at Chicagoland Speedway. The two victories gave Kenseth a 14-point lead over Joe Gibbs Racing teammate Kyle Busch, and an 18-point lead over Jimmie Johnson. A general rule of thumb in the Chase is that you can have one bad finish and still have a chance at the championship. Dale Earnhardt, Jr., Joey Logano, and Kasey Kahne got their bad finishes early. Both Earnhardt and Logano had engine issues at Chicagoland that left them more than 50 points back after the first Chase race. Both had decent finishes at Loudon but were still more than 60 points back after the two races. Kahne crashed with 47 laps to go at Loudon, and he joined the pair at the back of the Chase pack, 71 points off the lead.

◀ Kurt Busch started 2013 driving for his third different team in three years. At the end of 2011, he lost his ride with Team Penske and started 2012 with Phoenix Racing. Before the 2012 season was over, he moved to Furniture Row Racing. FRR had a win in 2011 with Regan Smith but not much consistency at running up front. In 120 races with Smith driving, the team had one win, two other top fives, and eight top tens. Busch drove 42 races for FRR and had 11 top fives and 19 top tens, and he put the team into the Chase for the NASCAR Sprint Cup. Gene Haas, part owner of Stewart-Haas Racing, hired Busch away from FRR and teamed him with Tony Stewart, Kevin Harvick, and Danica Patrick for 2014.

► Defending NASCAR Sprint Cup Series champion Brad Keselowski gets doused with victory champagne after winning the October 12th Bank of America 500 at Charlotte Motor Speedway. This would be Keselowski's only win of 2013 in a disappointing follow-up to his 2012 championship. He started the year strong with four consecutive top fives in the first four races and seven top 10s in the first eight races. A NASCAR penalty of 25 points after the spring Texas race slowed the #2 Miller Lite team down, but Keselowski maintained a position in the top 10 in the NASCAR Sprint Cup Series standings. A crash in Kentucky resulted in a 33rd-place finish, and Keselowski fell to 13th in the standings. The team struggled to climb out of the hole and briefly moved back into the top 10 until another crash at the fall Bristol race effectively ended any chance of making the Chase for the NASCAR Sprint Cup. In October, it was announced that Keselowski and sponsor Miller Lite had both signed multi-year extensions to remain with Team Penske.

◄ Jamie McMurray carries the checkered flag to Victory Lane following his win in the October 20th Camping World RV Sales 500 at Talladega Superspeedway. The victory broke a 108-race winless streak for McMurray, who last won in 2010. When racing at restrictor-plate tracks, teams and fans are always waiting for multi-car accidents, but this time at Talladega, a large one never came. There were only three cautions for 10 laps, with the most spectacular coming on the last lap. Austin Dillon, driving Tony Stewart's #14 Chevrolet, spun off of turn two while running third and was hit from behind by Casey Mears. That shot the rear of Dillon's car high in the air. The race finished under caution, and that prevented Dale Earnhardt, Jr., who was running second, from trying to make a move on McMurray. NASCAR Sprint Cup Series points leader Matt Kenseth finished 20th while Jimmie Johnson finished 13th, and that enabled Johnson to take the points lead for the first time in the Chase for the NASCAR Sprint Cup.

► Darrell Wallace, Jr., stands next to the grandfather clock trophy after his historic win in the October 26th Kroger 200 NASCAR Camping World Truck Series race at Martinsville Speedway. The 20-year-old became the first African-American to win a NASCAR national series event since Wendell Scott won a NASCAR Sprint Cup Series race in Jacksonville, Florida, in 1963. Wallace has been racing since he was nine years old, moving up from Legends cars to late models and then to the NASCAR K&N Pro Series East in 2010. He ran 36 races in three years in that series and had six wins and 16 top fives. In 2013, he signed with Kyle Busch Motorsports to drive fulltime in the NASCAR Camping World Truck Series. He ran all 22 events in the 2013 season and had five top fives and 12 top-10 finishes along with a pole at Dover. Wallace is signed with Joe Gibbs Racing as one of their development drivers.

Jeff Gordon celebrates his only win of 2013 at the October 27th Goody's Headache Relief Shot 500 Powered by Kroger at Martinsville. Gordon's win moved him up to third place in the Chase for the NASCAR Sprint Cup standings. Gordon's 2013 season was not typical for the four-time NASCAR Sprint Cup Series champion. He had seven finishes of 30th or worse and only made the Chase because of a ruling by NASCAR that made him a 13th participant after the Richmond controversy. In the AAA Texas 500 the week after Martinsville, Gordon cut a tire and hit the wall early in the event and finished 38th. He fell back to sixth in the Chase standings, 69 points behind the leader.

Kevin Harvick celebrates in Victory Lane with wife DeLana and son Keelan on November 10th at Phoenix International Raceway. The victory in the AdvoCare 500 was Harvick's fourth of the 2013 season. In January 2013, it was announced that Harvick would be leaving Richard Childress Racing at the end of the year after 13 seasons of driving the #29 Chevrolet. Harvick won four races, including two Chase for the NASCAR Sprint Cup events, and finished third in the standings.

Matt Kenseth leads three of the Rick Hendrick Motorsports cars late in the November 17th Ford EcoBoost 400 at Homestead-Miami Speedway. Coming to Homestead for the last race of the season, Jimmie Johnson needed only a 23rd-place or better finish to take his sixth NASCAR Sprint Cup Series title. Kenseth led seven different times for a race-high 144 laps and finished second to Joe Gibbs Racing teammate Denny Hamlin. Johnson never led, but he ran in the top 10 most of the day, and finished ninth to take the NASCAR Sprint Cup Series championship by 19 points. There were several "lasts" at Homestead. Jeff Burton drove the last of his 338 starts over nine seasons for Richard Childress Racing. Ryan Newman left Stewart-Haas Racing after five seasons. Kevin Harvick finished his 13th year at RCR to move on to Stewart-Haas Racing. After four seasons, Martin Truex, Jr., ran his last race for Michael Waltrip Racing. Kurt Busch left Furniture Row Racing after one season. And Juan Pablo Montoya finished his seven-year tenure at Earnhardt-Ganassi Racing.

2013 NASCAR SPRINT CUP SERIES POINTS RACE

Rank	Driver	Points	Starts	Wins	Top 5	Top 10
1	Jimmie Johnson	2,419	36	6	16	24
2	Matt Kenseth	2,400	36	7	12	20
3	Kevin Harvick	2,385	36	4	9	21
4	Kyle Busch	2,364	36	4	16	22
5	Dale Earnhardt, Jr.	2,363	36	0	10	22
6	Jeff Gordon	2,337	36	1	8	17
7	Clint Bowyer	2,336	36	0	10	19
8	Joey Logano	2,323	36	1	11	19
9	Greg Biffle	2,321	36	1	4	13
10	Kurt Busch	2,309	36	0	11	16
11	Ryan Newman	2,286	36	1	6	18
12	Kasey Kahne	2,283	36	2	11	14
13	Carl Edwards	2,282	36	2	9	16
14	Brad Keselowski	1,041	36	1	9	16
15	Jamie McMurray	1,007	36	1	4	9
16	Martin Truex, Jr.	998	36	1	7	15
17	Paul Menard	949	36	0	3	9
18	Aric Almirola	913	36	0	1	6
19	Ricky Stenhouse, Jr.	909	36	0	1	3
20	Jeff Burton	906	36	0	2	6
21	Juan Pablo Montoya	894	36	0	4	8
22	Marcos Ambrose	872	36	0	0	6
23	Denny Hamlin	753	32	1	4	8
24	Casey Mears	719	36	0	0	1
25	Mark Martin	649	28	0	1	5
26	David Gilliland	648	36	0	1	2
27	Danica Patrick	646	36	0	0	1
28	David Ragan	633	36	1	1	2
29	Tony Stewart	594	21	1	5	8
30	Dave Blaney	526	35	0	0	0
31	Travis Kvapil	496	36	0	0	0
32	J.J. Yeley	472	35	0	0	1
33	David Reutimann	465	36	0	0	0
34	Bobby Labonte	412	28	0	0	0
35	AJ Allmendinger	410	18	0	0	1
36	David Stremme	362	25	0	0	0
37	Michael McDowell	210	33	0	0	1
38	Timmy Hill	190	19	0	0	0
39	Ken Schrader	118	10	0	0	0
40	Michael Waltrip	114	4	0	2	2
41	Scott Speed	99	12	0	0	1
42	Terry Labonte	87	5	0	0	0
43	Boris Said	48	2	0	0	0
44	Ron Fellows	31	2	0	0	0
45	Alex Kennedy	21	3	0	0	0
46	Justin Marks	14	1	0	0	0
47	Scott Riggs	11	7	0	0	0
48	Victor Gonzalez, Jr.	10	2	0	0	0
49	Brian Keselowski	9	2	0	0	0
50	Tomy Drissi	8	2	0	0	0

Jimmie Johnson hoists the NASCAR Sprint Cup Series champion's trophy for the sixth time in eight years after the end of the Ford EcoBoost 400 at Homestead. Fellow driver Denny Hamlin said, "We're racing in the Jimmie Johnson era." Johnson became the youngest driver to win six championships and accomplished it the fastest. Only Richard Petty and Dale Earnhardt have more NASCAR Sprint Cup Series titles with seven each. Johnson started the year with his second Daytona 500 win and added five more victories during the season. He also won his fourth NASCAR Sprint All-Star Race. Along with his six wins, he had 16 top-five finishes and 24 top 10s out of the 36 points-paying races, and he led more laps on the season than anyone else. Johnson never fell lower than third place in points at any time during the 2013 season.

2014

January 26 Doctors clear Tony Stewart to race but tell him not to drive until February 14, the first day of practice at Daytona. Stewart missed the last half of the 2013 NASCAR Sprint Cup Series season after breaking his leg in a race outside of NASCAR.

February 16 Austin Dillon puts the #3 Richard Childress Racing Chevrolet on the pole for the Daytona 500. It's the first time a #3 NASCAR Sprint Cup Series car has been on track since Dale Earnhardt died from injuries suffered in the 2001 Daytona 500. Dillon finishes ninth.

March 16 After a two-hour start delay and three-hour red-flag stoppage in the Food City 500 at Bristol, the flagman accidentally trips the caution-light switch in the flag stand with two laps to go. Before the race can be restarted, the rain returns. Carl Edwards wins under caution.

March 25 Lynda Petty—wife of Richard Petty, mother of Kyle Petty, and grandmother of Adam Petty—dies at the age of 72 after a long illness.

June 28 While celebrating his win in the Quaker State 400 at Kentucky Speedway, Brad Keselowski cuts his hand in Victory Lane while trying to break open a champagne bottle. He has to have stitches to close the wound.

July 6 Barney Hall, the longtime play-by-play announcer for radio's Motor Racing Network, calls his last race. After over 50 years in the booth, the 82-year-old steps away from race coverage but will still do special projects for the network.

July 13 Turner Sports airs its last NASCAR Sprint Cup Series race. The network began showing NASCAR events in 1983. NBC and FOX will broadcast the series starting in 2015.

On January 30, 2014, NASCAR announced a change in the format of the Chase for the NASCAR Sprint Cup Championship eligibility. The Chase grid will consist of 16 drivers. The top 15 drivers with wins after the 26th race automatically transfer to the Chase grid. The 16th spot is for the points leader, if that driver does not already have a win. If there are fewer than 15 winners, the Chase grid will be filled with the winless drivers highest in points. The Chase will consist of four rounds: Challenger, Contender, Eliminator, and then the Championship at Homestead. A win in any round automatically advances a driver to the next round. After each of the first three rounds, the three lowest-ranked drivers will be eliminated, leaving four drivers to compete for the NASCAR Sprint Cup Series Championship in the final round.

Dale Earnhardt, Jr. celebrates after winning the rain-delayed 2014 Daytona 500. The victory broke a 55-race dry spell for Earnhardt, Jr. and was his second Daytona 500 win. Earnhardt, Jr. led the most laps at 54 laps. This was the eighth Daytona 500 win for team owner Rick Hendrick. The race was red flagged for over 6 hours after storms moved into the area. After the race resumed, the next 100 laps were run caution free. On lap 146 of 200, there was the first of four multicar accidents. There were 25 different cars involved in the four crashes—Austin Dillon was in three of them. Despite the crashes, 20 cars finished on the lead lap.

In 2014, the NASCAR Sprint Cup Series moved to group qualifying instead of single-car runs. Starting with the second race of the year at Phoenix, qualifying was held in rounds. Tracks of 1.25 miles in length or longer have three rounds of qualifying. All cars have 25 minutes to turn laps. The fastest 24 advance to the next round. The fastest 12 cars in the second round advance to the final round. The fastest in the final round is the pole sitter. Tracks under 1.25 miles and road courses have only two rounds. Teams were allowed to make basic adjustments on pit road but could not open the hood or jack up the car, and at first, cars were going back on the track at reduced speed to cool the engines. This created an on-track safety issue, so NASCAR allowed teams to plug cool-down units in under the cowl flaps.

Team Penske's NASCAR Sprint Cup Series teams showed remarkable improvement in 2014 versus 2013. In 2013, Joey Logano and Brad Keselowski had a combined two wins, 20 top fives, and 35 top 10s, and only Logano made the Chase for the NASCAR Sprint Cup. In 2014, their second season in Fords, both drivers started strong at Daytona and ran well all season. Both drivers made the Chase for the NASCAR Sprint Cup and Logano made it all the way to Homestead. The two drivers combined for 11 wins, six pole positions, 37 top-five finishes, and 42 top-10 finishes.

Kurt Busch sweetened his comeback with a win in the March 30 STP 500 at Martinsville Speedway. Busch parted ways with Penske Racing at the end of the 2011 season and spent 2012 struggling with James Finch's underfunded team. Busch moved to Furniture Row Racing for 2013 and put them in the Chase for the NASCAR Sprint Cup. Gene Haas wanted Busch for Stewart-Haas Racing and sponsored Busch's car himself. The team was sometimes strong in 2014 but lacked consistency and missed a chance to race for the NASCAR Sprint Cup Series Championship.

▲ Brad Keselowski's #2 Miller Lite Ford blows past coasting Dale Earnhardt, Jr. on the backstretch during the last lap of the March 9 Kobalt 400 at Las Vegas Motor Speedway. After his Daytona 500 win virtually guaranteed #88 a spot in the Chase for the NASCAR Sprint Cup, Earnhardt, Jr.'s team took a gamble on fuel in the Kobalt 400. Crew chief Steve Letarte brought Earnhardt Jr. down pit road for four tires and fuel under green on lap 212. When a caution waved on lap 222, Earnhardt, Jr. stayed out and took the lead, which he held until his fuel cell went dry with half a lap to go. Earnhardt, Jr. held on for second place.

◄ Kevin Harvick's #4 Budweiser Chevrolet passes Dale Earnhardt, Jr.'s #88 National Guard Chevrolet in the Bojangles' Southern 500 at Darlington Raceway. Harvick led 238 of the 374 laps but he had to run down Earnhardt, Jr. and Jimmie Johnson at the end. A caution with nine laps to go brought leader Harvick and others to pit road. Harvick changed four tires, while Earnhardt, Jr., Johnson, Matt Kenseth, and Jeff Gordon each changed two tires. Harvick worked his way up from fifth over two more cautions and restarts, passing Earnhardt, Jr. on the outside and winning by over half a second.

August 17 Jeff Gordon wins the pole for the Pure Michigan 400 at Michigan International Speedway with a speed of 206.558 mph. It is the seventh-fastest qualifying speed ever in the NASCAR Sprint Cup Series and the fastest since the 1987 advent of restrictor plates.

September 20 16-year-old Cole Custer becomes the youngest winner in a NASCAR national touring series race when he wins the NASCAR Camping World Truck Series UNOH 175 race at New Hampshire Motor Speedway.

September 23 NASCAR releases the rules package for the 2015 season, including a two-inch reduction in rear spoiler height, reduced horsepower using a tapered spacer, and prohibition on private testing at any track.

December 15 Brian Vickers announces that he will miss the first part of the 2015 NASCAR Sprint Cup Series season due to health issues. Vickers missed 25 races in 2010 and 4 races at the end of 2013 with health issues.

December 16 Sprint informs NASCAR that it will not renew its title sponsorship of the NASCAR Sprint Cup Series when the current contract expires at the end of the 2016 season.

Bill Elliott and Rex White share a moment during a press conference with the 2015 inductees for the NASCAR Hall of Fame. Along with Elliott and White, Fred Lorenzen, Wendell Scott, and Joe Weatherly were honored. Elliott won the 1988 Cup title and 44 Cup races in his career. White was the 1960 Cup champion and had 28 wins in the nine years he competed. Lorenzen won 26 Cup races in only 158 starts and was one of the sport's first superstars from outside the South. Weatherly won back-to-back Cup championships in 1962 and 1963 but died in a crash in 1964 as defending champion. Scott was the first African-American to race full time in the Cup Series. He won a Cup race in Jacksonville, Florida in 1963 and made 495 starts.

▶ Denny Hamlin celebrates his win in the May 4 Aaron's 499 at Talladega Superspeedway. This was his only win of the 2014 NASCAR Sprint Cup Series but qualified him for the Chase for the NASCAR Sprint Cup. Hamlin advanced through Chase elimination by racing conservatively while others had problems and fell from contention. In the finale at Homestead, Hamlin led 50 laps. Under caution with 20 laps to go, the #11 team elected to stay on track while the other title contenders came to pit road. The track position gave Hamlin the lead, but with another caution later, he couldn't compete with others on fresher tires. Hamlin fell to seventh by the end of the race and finished third in the standings.

◀ Second-generation driver Chase Elliott poses in Darlington Raceway's Victory Lane with mother Cindy and father Bill after winning the Help a Hero 200 NASCAR Nationwide Series (NNWS) race. Chase Elliott finished his first NNWS season with three wins, 16 top fives, and 26 top 10s in 33 starts. When he won the 2014 NNWS title, he became the youngest ever NASCAR national series champion. He was also the 2014 Rookie of the Year and Most Popular Driver. The 18-year-old Elliott's driving talent and poise has impressed many racing insiders who predict great things for the son of the 1988 NASCAR Sprint Cup Series Champion. His performance and affiliation with Hendrick Motorsports will guarantee him a chance in a quality NASCAR Sprint Cup Series car in the future.

Jimmie Johnson takes a victory lap in reverse after winning the May 25 Coca-Cola 600 at Charlotte Motor Speedway. Johnson led 164 of the 400 laps and beat Kevin Harvick by 1.2 seconds in the four-hour event. This was Johnson's first win of the 2014 season and his first pole of the year. Kevin Harvick was his toughest competition early in the event. They swapped the lead seven times in the first half of the race. Jeff Gordon and Matt Kenseth later made runs at the six-time NASCAR Sprint Cup Series Champion but Johnson passed Kenseth with nine laps to go. Harvick rallied and beat Kenseth for a second-place finish.

Kurt Busch waits between races for his May 25 double-header. The Indy 500 was Busch's first Verizon IndyCar Series race and Michael Andretti Motorsports gave Busch a strong car. He qualified 12th, finished sixth, and won Rookie of the Year. Busch then flew 550 miles to Charlotte for the Coca-Cola 600. He had to start at the back of the field because he missed the drivers meeting. He ran as high as fifth in the 600 before the engine in his Stewart-Haas Chevrolet broke after 271 of the 400 laps. He finished 40th at Charlotte.

In 2014, Joey Logano had his breakout year in the NASCAR Sprint Cup Series, with career-best five wins, 16 top five, and 22 top 10s. He also made the Chase for the NASCAR Sprint Cup for the second year in a row. Logano won at Texas, Richmond, Bristol, Loudon, and Kansas. He entered the final race of the season at Homestead with a shot at the NASCAR Sprint Cup Series Championship. Logano never led the race but was in contention until a pit stop went bad with 20 laps to go. Logano came to pit road running sixth but the car fell off the jack and Logano fell to 21st. He only made it back to 16th before the race ended and finished fourth in the final point standings.

The 2014 NASCAR Sprint Cup Series introduced two strong rookies from well funded teams. Kyle Larson landed the #42 Target Chevrolet of Ganassi Racing and Austin Dillon brought back the #3 Chevrolet of Richard Childress Racing. Larson had the stronger season of the two: a pole at Richmond, eight top-five finishes, 17 top-10 finishes, and an average finish of 14.2. Dillon had one top-five and four top-10 finishes and a finishing average of 17.5, but he also finished more laps than anyone in the series except Jeff Gordon. Following the season finale at Homestead, Larson was announced as the 2014 Sprint Cup Series Rookie of the Year.

On August 22, 2004, Carl Edwards ran his first NASCAR Sprint Cup Series race for Roush Fenway Racing, replacing Jeff Burton in the #99 Ford. He finished 10th that afternoon at Michigan. Edwards ran his last NASCAR Sprint Cup Series race for Roush, 373 races and 23 wins later, in the 2014 season finale at Homestead. It was rumored since 2011 that Joe Gibbs Racing wanted to grab Edwards away from Roush Fenway and that Ford Motor Company created incentives to keep Edwards. On July 27, 2014, Roush Fenway Racing announced its 2015 NASCAR Sprint Cup Series driver lineup and Edwards was not part of it. On August 19, it was finally announced that Edwards was joining Joe Gibbs Racing and driving the #19 Toyota Camry in 2015.

▲ In 2013, Toyota won 14 NASCAR Sprint Cup Series races with five different drivers. In 2014, Kyle Busch and Denny Hamlin accounted for Toyota's only two victories. Throughout the 2014 season, Toyota Racing Development flagbearers Joe Gibbs Racing and Michael Waltrip Racing appeared to have fewer horsepower than other Sprint Cup series manufacturers. Despite that, all three Joe Gibbs Racing cars made the Chase for the Sprint Cup, but Busch and Matt Kenseth were eliminated before the final race at Homestead and poor pit strategy cost Hamlin the title.

Crew chief Trent Owens (right) and driver Aric Almirola enjoy their win in the rain-delayed and shortened Coke Zero 400 at Daytona International Speedway. This was the first Sprint Cup Series win for each. Almirola took over the seat of the #43 Richard Petty car at the start of 2012 and Owens became his crew chief in 2014. Owens is team owner Richard Petty's nephew. The win came 30 years and two days after Richard Petty won his final Sprint Cup Series race—also at Daytona. The win put Almirola and the #43 team in the Chase for the Sprint Cup, but he was eliminated after the first round.

◄ On August 29 at Atlanta Motor Speedway, Tony Stewart spoke to the press for the first time since a fatal sprint-car accident at Canandaigua Motorsports Park in upstate New York. On the night of August 9, local driver Kevin Ward Jr.'s car spun and came to a stop against the outside wall, where he exited the vehicle and walked onto the track's surface to confront Stewart. As Stewart came around, Ward Jr. was struck by the right rear tire of Stewart's car and died of blunt force trauma. Stewart cooperated fully with the investigation and was cleared of any wrongdoing on September 24. Stewart sat out three NASCAR Sprint Cup Series races while he dealt with the tragedy.

▲ AJ Allmendinger celebrates his first NASCAR Sprint Cup Series win in the August 10 Cheez-It 355 at Watkins Glen International Raceway. The victory was sweet for once-troubled Allmendinger. In 2012, Allmendinger landed a top ride in the #22 Pennzoil Dodge of Penske Racing. Seventeen races into that season, he lost the ride and was suspended from NASCAR for failing a random drug test. Allmendinger returned after completing NASCAR's Road to Recovery program. In 2013, Roger Penske put Allmendinger in a NASCAR Nationwide Series car for two road-course events and he won both. JTG Daugherty Racing hired Allmendinger to drive their #47 Chevrolet for the 2014 season. The win at Watkins Glen put the team in the Chase for the NASCAR Sprint Cup where the team finished 13th in the final point standings—the highest ranking for the team in its six-year history.

Jeff Gordon wins the September 28 AAA 400 at Dover International Speedway. Gordon's victory moved him into the second round of the Chase for the NASCAR Sprint Cup. While Gordon celebrated in Victory Lane, Aric Almirola, Greg Biffle, Kurt Busch and AJ Allmendinger found out that they had been eliminated from championship contention. Almirola's chances were first threatened at Chicago when a blown engine led him to a 41st-place finish. Biffle ran poorly in all three races and finished of 23rd, 16th, and 21st in the challenger round. Busch finished 8th at Chicago but cut a tire at Loudon and finished 36th. He entered Dover eight points out of a transfer spot but finished 18th and missed the cut. Allmendinger had finishes of 22nd, 13th, and 23rd in three races and only missed transferring by two points.

Jimmie Johnson's #48 Lowe's Chevrolet bounces off the wall late in the November 9 Quicken Loans Race for Heroes 500 at Phoenix International Raceway. He finished 39th. Johnson's 2014 season was not typical for the six-time champion. While he had four wins on the season, he had the worst average finish of his career at 15.3 and his worst finishing position, 11th, in the NASCAR Sprint Cup Series point standings. There was enough evident tension between Johnson and crew chief Chad Knaus that each made a statement saying they were staying together. Johnson made it past the challenger round in the Chase for the NASCAR Sprint Cup but was eliminated after the contender round at Talladega.

Brad Keselowski leaves the NASCAR hauler after an official discussion about a post-race brawl with Matt Kenseth following the October 11 Bank of America 500 at Charlotte Motor Speedway. With the new postseason format, tension among drivers and teams was at an all-time high. At Charlotte, Kenseth and Denny Hamlin didn't like the way Keselowski raced them on a late restart and confronted him after the race. Keselowski was fined $50,000 as a "behavioral penalty." At Texas three weeks later, Keselowski and Jeff Gordon and their crews had a full-blown brawl after Keselowski made contact with Gordon on the track. After the Richmond NASCAR Sprint Cup Series race in April, Marcos Ambrose punched Casey Mears in the face while having a post-race discussion about on-track contact. Ambrose was fined $25,000 and Mears $15,000.

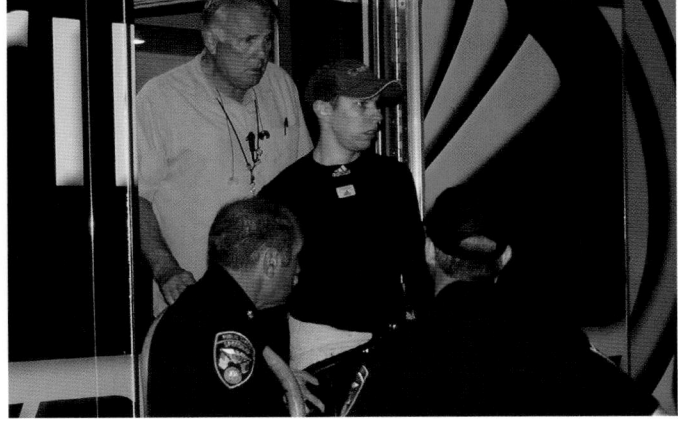

Jimmy Fennig steps off the pit box as crew chief for the last time after the November 16 Ford 400 at Homestead. He called his first race as crew chief in the 1986 Daytona 500 with driver Mark Martin. He won the 1988 Daytona 500 with Bobby Allison. Fennig was crew chief for 889 Sprint Cup Series races over 29 years. Fennig worked with 16 different drivers— including Jamie McMurray, Dick Trickle and Jimmy Spencer— and won races with Bobby Allison, Mark Martin, Kurt Busch, Matt Kenseth, and Carl Edwards. In 2004, Fennig led young, hard-driving Kurt Busch to a Sprint Cup Series Championship.

◄ Terry Labonte poses with his wife Kim before the October 19 GEICO 500 at Talladega Superspeedway. Fifty-eight-year-old Labonte said that this would be his 890th and last NASCAR Sprint Cup Series race. He previously "retired" in 2006 but ran 42 more races over the next eight years. For the last four years he drove Frank Stoddard's GoFAS Racing Chevrolet, primarily at the restrictor-plate tracks. Labonte started his NASCAR Sprint Cup Series career in 1978 with three straight top-10 finishes and won his first race in 1980. He was the 1984 and 1996 NASCAR Sprint Cup Series Champion.

▲ Jeff Gordon's 2014 season was one of his best in recent years. Gordon was competitive all year after a mediocre 2013. In 2014 he won more races, had more top-five and top-10 finishes, led more laps, and had a better average finish than he did in 2013. He led the NASCAR Sprint Cup Series standings for 20 weeks. Gordon won his fifth NASCAR Sprint Cup Series race at the Indianapolis Motor Speedway along with wins at Kansas, Michigan and Dover. In February, Gordon made the comment that if he won the 2014 NASCAR Spring Cup Series Championship he would retire. "If that happened, that would be all the reasons I need to say, 'This is it, I'm done.' Go out on a high note," Gordon said. When asked again in December about retirement, Gordon responded, "I don't believe in retirement, number one, but I know that I won't always be a full-time Cup driver. That time is coming."

▲ Brad Keselowski leads the pack to the finish line in the October 19 GEICO 500 at Talladega Superspeedway. This was a must-win situation for Keselowski to advance to the next round of the Chase for the NASCAR Sprint Cup. A cut tire at Kansas two weeks earlier left Keselowski with a 36th place finish, and he needed to win at Charlotte or Talladega. A 16th place finish at Charlotte meant that the only way Keselowski could advance was to win at Talladega. Keselowski started at the back but was leading by the 26th lap. On a green-white-checkered finish, Keselowski held off a hard-charging Ryan Newman and Matt Kenseth to take the win and advance to the elimination round.

▲ Jimmie Johnson leads the pack during the GEICO 500 on October 19th at Talladega Superspeedway. This was the second elimination race in the Chase for the NASCAR Sprint Cup, and four more drivers were removed from contention. Johnson led the most laps while trying to win and advance to the next round. While running up front on the last restart, Johnson tangled with Trevor Bayne and finished 24th. Dale Earnhardt, Jr. was involved in a late-race crash and finished 31st. Kyle Busch crashed on lap 104 and finished 40th. Kasey Kahne finished 12th and would have advanced by points, but Brad Keselowski's win automatically advanced him and pushed Kahne out of the next round.

▲ Jeff Gordon talks with reporters after the Quicken Loans Help for Heroes 500 at Phoenix International Raceway. A 29th-place finish at Texas doomed his chance to advance to the championship round unless he won one of the three elimination-round races of the Chase for the NASCAR Sprint Cup. Though Gordon finished second in two of the three races, the new format means one bad finish can end a title run. Matt Kenseth had a sixth-, third-, and 25th-place finish in the three elimination-round races and failed to transfer. Brad Keselowski had two top fives but a 31st-place finish kept him from racing for the championship at Homestead. Carl Edwards had finishes of 20th, 9th, and 15th and dashed his championship hopes at Phoenix.

▲ Kevin Harvick exits his #4 Budweiser Chevrolet after dominating the November 9 Quicken Loans Race for Heroes 500 at Phoenix International Raceway. Harvick had to win here to race for the NASCAR Sprint Cup Series Championship the following week at Homestead. Harvick has a handle on the one-mile Phoenix track. He has won four of the last five NASCAR Sprint Cup Series races here, including the last three in a row, and led a combined 488 of the 624 laps at the track in 2014 NASCAR Sprint Cup Series races.

RYAN NEWMA

Ryan Newman has always been an intense competitor, but in 2014, his first year at Richard Childress Racing, it was quiet consistency that put him in contention for the NASCAR Sprint Cup Series title. He had five top-five finishes and 16 top-10 finishes but no wins and no poles. He made the Chase for the NASCAR Sprint Cup on points and advanced each round by being consistent. At Phoenix in the final elimination race, Newman roughed up rookie Kyle Larson on the final turn of the final lap to advance to the championship round at Homestead. He moved eleven places into the top 10 in the first third of the final race. Newman restarted second late in the race but could not get around Kevin Harvick for the win.

2014 NASCAR SPRINT CUP SERIES POINTS RACE

Rank	Driver	Points	Starts	Wins	Top five	Top 10
1	Kevin Harvick	5043	36	5	14	20
2	Ryan Newman	5042	36	0	5	16
3	Denny Hamlin	5037	35	1	7	18
4	Joey Logano	5028	36	5	16	22
5	Brad Keselowski	2361	36	6	17	20
6	Jeff Gordon	2348	36	4	14	23
7	Matt Kenseth	2334	36	0	13	22
8	Dale Earnhardt, Jr.	2301	36	4	12	20
9	Carl Edwards	2288	36	2	7	14
10	Kyle Busch	2285	36	1	9	15
11	Jimmie Johnson	2274	36	4	11	20
12	Kurt Busch	2263	36	1	6	11
13	AJ Allmendinger	2260	36	1	2	5
14	Greg Biffle	2247	36	0	3	11
15	Kasey Kahne	2234	36	1	3	11
16	Aric Almirola	2195	36	1	2	7
17	Kyle Larson	1080	36	0	8	17
18	Jamie McMurray	1014	36	0	7	13
19	Clint Bowyer	979	36	0	5	15
20	Austin Dillon	958	36	0	1	4
21	Paul Menard	944	36	0	5	13
22	Brian Vickers	921	36	0	3	9
23	Marcos Ambrose	870	36	0	3	7
24	Martin Truex, Jr.	857	36	0	1	5
25	Tony Stewart	799	33	0	3	7
26	Casey Mears	782	36	0	1	3
27	Ricky Stenhouse, Jr.	757	35	0	1	5
28	Danica Patrick	735	36	0	0	3
29	Justin Allgaier	636	35	0	0	0
30	David Gilliland	554	36	0	0	0
31	Cole Whitt	532	36	0	0	0
32	David Ragan	531	36	0	0	1
33	Michael Annett	531	36	0	0	0
34	Reed Sorenson	516	36	0	0	0
35	Alex Bowman	412	36	0	0	0
36	Josh Wise	405	35	0	0	0
37	Michael McDowell	255	19	0	0	1
38	Travis Kvapil	214	21	0	0	1
39	Ryan Truex	193	23	0	0	0
40	Terry Labonte	88	4	0	0	0
41	Jeff Burton	87	4	0	0	0
42	Michael Waltrip	76	4	0	0	0
43	David Stremme	75	10	0	0	0
44	Timmy Hill	62	11	0	0	0
45	Brett Moffitt	60	7	0	0	0
46	Bobby Labonte	54	3	0	0	0
47	Parker Kligerman	54	8	0	0	0
48	Juan Pablo Montoya	47	2	0	0	0
49	Alex Kennedy	47	5	0	0	0
50	Dave Blaney	46	7	0	0	0

Kevin Harvick left Richard Childress Racing for Stewart-Haas Racing after 13 seasons because he wanted to win a championship. In their first year together the new partners accomplished that goal. The #4 Budweiser Racing team was strong right out of the box at Daytona and they dominated and won the second race of the season at Phoenix. Other wins came at Darlington and the fall Charlotte race. There should have been more wins, but bad luck at the Atlanta race and the fall Dover event cost the team possible victories. Harvick, who is know as "the closer," finished the season with a second-place finish at Texas and back-to-back wins at Phoenix and Homestead. Harvick led the most laps and miles in 2014 by large margins and won the most poles with eight. The 2014 season with five wins was his best since he won five times in 2006.

2015

February 15 Jeff Gordon wins the pole for his final Daytona 500. It was the 23rd consecutive year that Gordon had won a pole position. It is the all-time Sprint Cup series record for pole positions.

February 27 At the QuikTrip 500 at Atlanta, 13 Sprint Cup series teams do not get a chance to post qualifying. Among them were Jeff Gordon, Jimmie Johnson, Tony Stewart and Matt Kenseth. Multiple cars failed first inspection and the line to be reinspected backed up. NASCAR delayed qualifying for 15 minutes but there was not enough time to get all the cars through inspection.

March 29 Kyle Larson misses the STP 500 at Martinsville. He passed out the day before during an autograph session. He was taken to two different hospitals for tests and while nothing was found wrong with him, doctors felt like he should not race. Regan Smith filled in for Larson.

March 31 Richard Childress Racing's #31 team of Ryan Newman is penalized for manipulating the wheels or tires of the car at the March 22nd Sprint Cup race at Auto Club Speedway. Crew chief Luke Lambert is fined $125,000 and suspended for six races. The team is also penalized 75 driver and car owner points. The exact infraction is not disclosed but it involved bleeding pressure from the tires as they heated up during the race.

April 29 Go Daddy Inc. announces they are leaving NASCAR at the end of the 2015 season. The company had been associated with Danica Patrick since 2007 and became her primary sponsor in 2010.

▲ In 2015, 45 cameras like those pictured were mounted high above each speedway and will replace around 14 NASCAR officials on pit road. The system was tested near the end of the 2014 season and implemented for the 2015 season. Each camera will monitor two pit stalls and send the video back to a command truck where computer software will analyze the stop and flag any infractions such as driving through too many stalls, crewmembers over the wall too soon, uncontrolled tires, and more. When the computer flags a stop, one of eight officials in the command truck will review the footage and confirm that a violation took place or determine that an infraction didn't take place. Teams will be informed of any penalties after they leave pit road. The pit camera system and electronic measurement of pit road speed enables NASCAR to accurately police pit road infractions.

▲ Kyle Busch impacts the wall during the February 21, 2015 "Alert Today Florida 300" Xfinity Series race at Daytona International Speedway. Busch suffered a compound fracture of his right lower leg and a mid-foot fracture of his left foot. Electronics in the car showed that the car took a 90g hit and an impact speed of 90 mph. Busch said later that he knew instantly that both legs were broken and that both his helmet and chest hit the steering wheel. He missed the first 11 races of the 2015 Sprint Cup Series and required a waiver from NASCAR to be eligible to compete for the Sprint Cup Series championship. After Busch's crash, the section that he hit was redesigned and a SAFER barrier was installed.

▲ Joey Logano celebrates the biggest victory of his career, so far, in the 2015 Daytona 500. Logano took the lead with nine laps to go and held it through one red flag period and a green-white-checkered finish. Jeff Gordon, driving in his final Daytona 500, started from the pole and led the most laps but finished 33rd after being involved in a last lap crash that forced the race to end under caution. The event had 27 lead changes between 12 different drivers. On the last restart, Logano jumped out to a lead with help from Clint Bowyer, but Kevin Harvick and Dale Earnhardt Jr. hooked up and were trying to make a run on Logano when the caution came out that ended the race. They finished second and third while Denny Hamlin finished fourth and Jimmy Johnson rounded out the top five.

▲ David Ragan started the 2015 Sprint Cup season in what was to be his fourth year with the underfunded Front Row Motorsports team. When Kyle Busch was hurt in the season opening Xfinity Series race at Daytona, Joe Gibbs Racing knew they would need a long term relief driver. Front Row Motorsports made a deal to loan Ragan out to drive the 18 JGR Toyota until Busch was able to return. He ran nine races for the team with a best finish of fifth at Martinsville. Meanwhile at Michael Waltrip Racing, Brian Vickers was forced from the 55 Aaron's Toyota because of medical issues and they needed a driver to run the final 26 races of the 2015 season. Ragan stepped into the 55 starting at Kansas in May. His best finish was a 12th at Daytona in July. He had hoped that this could lead to a full time job driving the MWR 55 in the future, but when the team shut down at the end of 2015, Ragan was without a ride.

▲ Brad Keselowski and girlfriend Paige White celebrate in victory lane after the March 22nd Auto Club 400 in Fontana, CA. He only led the last lap of the race and this would be his only Sprint Cup series win of the year. The victory qualified Keselowski for the Chase for the Sprint cup. Keselowski had a career high 25 top ten finishes in 2015 but fell short of being able to crack the top five in races and only had 9 top fives. He pointed his way through the Challenger and Contender rounds of the Chase but a 32nd place finish at Martinsville in the first race of the Eliminator round put him 24 points out of a spot in the Championship round. He had finishes of second and ninth in the next two races, but fell 13 points short of transferring to the Championship round at Homestead.

May 30 Several Sprint Cup series drivers, selected by vote among all drivers, meet formally with NASCAR officials to discuss the sport. Competition, safety and rules were some of the topics. The drivers council hopes to meet with NASCAR at least several times a year in an effort to improve communication.

August 2 Matt Kenseth wins the Windows 10 400 at Pocono after both Joey Logano and Kyle Busch run out of gas while leading in the last two laps. Logano ran out with two laps to go and Busch took the lead. Busch ran out after taking the white flag.

August 10 Former NASCAR driver and TV commentator Buddy Baker dies of lung cancer at the age of 74. Baker won 19 times in the Sprint Cup series and was a Superspeedway specialist. He won the Daytona 500 in 1980 and was a four time winner at both Talladega and Charlotte.

September 27 Furniture Row Racing announces it will switch from Chevrolet to Toyota starting with the 2016 season. The team also forms an alliance with Joe Gibbs Racing that will provide FRR with cars and technical information.

September 29 Tony Stewart announces that he will retire at the end of the 2016 season. "This is a moment every driver eventually comes to terms with, and I know this is the right decision for me," said Stewart. Clint Bowyer will replace Stewart in the #14 starting with the 2017 season.

December 31 Marvin Panch, the 1961 Daytona 500 winner, dies at the age of 89. Panch won 17 Sprint Cup series races in a 15 year career. He won races while driving for Smokey Yunick, Herb Thomas, Petty Enterprises and the Wood Brothers.

▲ David Ragan in the 18 Snickers Toyota and Kevin Harvick in the 4 Jimmy Johns Chevrolet crash during the April 19th Food City 500 at Bristol Motor Speedway. The lap 312 accident was one of 11 cautions in the day long marathon. The start of the race was delayed for an hour because of rain, and the race was stopped three more times for rain: on lap 23 for 3 hours and 58 minutes; on lap 273 for 13 minutes; and the final time before the green-white-checkered finish. The 11 cautions led to 117 laps, almost one quarter of the total distance of the race, being run under the yellow flag. While the actual race time was just over 3:37 minutes, it took 8:08 total time from the start engine command to the checkered flag to run the full event. Matt Kenseth won the race, his first victory of 2015. Brad Keselowski, Joey Logano, Martin Truex Jr, Kurt Busch, Carl Edwards and Kasey Kahne were all involved in accidents. Second place finisher Jimmie Johnson was part of two accidents.

▲ Joey Logano climbs from his crashed Ford after contact with Matt Kenseth near the end of the November 1st Goody's Headache Relief Shot 500 at Martinsville Speedway. The drivers had been feuding since contact between the pair two races earlier at Kansas. After Logano spun Kenseth from the lead late at Kansas and then brake checked him the following week at Talladega, Kenseth was in no mood to play at Martinsville. On lap 435, while racing for the lead, Brad Keselowski clipped Kenseth and put him in the inside wall on the backstretch. Kenseth lost nine laps making repairs and, when he returned to the track, he was looking for Logano. On lap 454 he found him going into turn one. Kenseth drove Logano, who was leading at the time, into the outside wall. Both cars were heavily damaged and Kenseth's crew was informed by NASCAR that he was parked for the day. Two days later, Kenseth was suspended by NASCAR for two races. All appeals by Joe Gibbs Racing were denied and Kenseth missed his first cup race since the start of the 2000 season.

◄ One of the standouts among the group of young drivers coming up through the NASCAR ranks is Erik Jones. He started driving ASA Late Models when he was 14 and started racing in the ARCA series at 15. In 2012 he beat Kyle Busch in the annual Snowball Derby late model race, so in March of 2013 Busch signed the kid to drive his NASCAR Camping World series truck. With NASCAR's age restrictions, Jones could only drive on tracks of one mile or shorter. He ran five NCWTS races in 2013, won at Phoenix and finished in the top ten in all five. In 2014 he made three Xfinity Series starts for Joe Gibbs Racing and finished in the top 10 in all three. He also ran 12 more Camping World truck series races for Kyle Busch Motorsports and won three of those 12 starts. The first year that Jones was old enough to run a full NASCAR touring series schedule was in 2015. KBM ran him for the truck series championship, and he delivered. Jones again won three races and became the youngest Champion in truck series history. He also made 23 Xfinity Series starts for JGR and won twice. On May 9th at Kansas Speedway at the age of 18, he made his first Sprint Cup series start, subbing for JGR teammate Kyle Busch. He led early but crashed while running in fourth place and finished 40th. He ran two more Sprint Cup races late in the year, filling in for JGR teammate Matt Kenseth after Kenseth was suspended for two events.

▲ Dale Earnhardt Jr. leads the field during the May 3rd Geico 500 at Talladega Superspeedway. Earnhardt Jr. led 67 of the 188 laps, the most of any driver, as he won his sixth race at the 2.66 mile track. He led the last 25 laps as the top ten ran single file until one lap to go. On the final lap, Carl Edwards spun alone in turn one while running in eighth place. Several other drivers spun coming off of turn two but no caution was thrown and that allowed the race to finish under green. Jeff Gordon won the pole for the race and led 47 laps himself but was caught speeding on pit road during the last green-flag pit stops and had to restart at the back of the field. Gordon was unable to get back to the front of the field and was involved in the last lap crash, finishing 31st.

◄ Carl Edwards heads toward victory lane after winning the May 24th Coca-Cola 600 at Charlotte Motor Speedway. This was Edwards's first win of 2015 and his first for Joe Gibbs Racing. The victory also earned Edwards a spot in the Chase for the Sprint Cup. The leaders pitted on lap 338 of the 400 lap race and Edwards was the only one able to go the distance from there. He took the lead with 20 laps to go after Martin Truex Jr. had to pit for fuel. Truex Jr. lead the most laps on the night but fell to fifth at the finish. It was the second consecutive race in which he led the most laps but did not win. Kyle Busch returned to the Sprint Cup series in the 600 after breaking his leg in a crash at Daytona in February. He finished 11th. There were 22 lead changes between nine different drivers in the race that took over four hours to run.

◄ The future of the NASCAR Sprint Cup series runs together during the May 24th Coca-Cola 600 at Charlotte Motor Speedway. Ryan Blaney in the #21 Ford Fusion, Chase Elliott in the #25 Chevrolet SS and Kyle Larson in the #42 Chevrolet SS appear to be the next generation of superstar drivers. Blaney, the 21-year-old son of sprint car legend Dave Blaney, was signed by Penske Racing who set him up with a Sprint Cup series ride in the Wood Brothers Fords. Elliott is the 19-year-old son of NASCAR legend Bill Elliott. He was chosen by Hendrick Motorsports to replace Jeff Gordon in the #24 Sprint Cup Series car. In 2014, 22-year-old Kyle Larson came to the Sprint Cup series full time. Chip Ganassi Racing signed him to replace Juan Montoya in the #42 car. All of these young drivers were already winners in the NASCAR Xfinity series and each of them have the potential to be Sprint Cup series champions.

►Martin Truex Jr. celebrates his win in the June 7th Axalta "We Paint Winners" 400 at Pocono Raceway. This was his first Sprint Cup Series win since 2013 and his third career series win overall. The win locked Truex Jr. and Furniture Row Racing in the Chase for the Sprint Cup. The team had a miserable 2014 season and led only one lap all year. A new crew chief, Cole Pearn, helped turn the team around for 2015. The team started the season with 14 top ten finishes in the first 15 races, including the Pocono win. While the team didn't win again, they made it to the Championship round at Homestead. Truex Jr. qualified 11th at Homestead and led three laps just past the halfway point, but the team was a bit off and Truex Jr. finished the race 12th, and fourth in the Sprint Cup standings. It was the highest career points finish for the team and driver.

▼ David Ragan and Clint Bowyer race together in their Michael Waltrip Racing Toyotas. MWR was formed in 1994 and started operations behind Michael Waltrip's house. In its early years, it ran Xfinity Series races with many different drivers. MWR ran its first Sprint Cup series race in 2002 and in 2007 it became Toyota's lead team at the Cup level. The 2007 season was so bad for the MWR team that Waltrip took on Robert Kauffman as a 50% partner in October of that year. On August 19, 2015, Kauffman announced that MWR would shut down at the end of 2015. He bought interest in Chip Ganassi Racing before the end of the year. Clint Bowyer was named as Tony Stewart's replacement at Stewart-Hass Racing but he won't drive the car until after the 2016 season. MWR ran 782 Sprint Cup races and won seven times.

◄ Crew members rush to the aid of Austin Dillon after he was involved in a massive crash at the end of the July 5th Coke Zero 400 at Daytona. On a green-white-checkered finish, the pack of at least 29 cars raced to the finish line with Dale Earnhardt Jr. winning. Just before the finish line Denny Hamlin, who was running second, got turned and the pack behind him scattered. Dillon was spun from the bottom lane across the track. His car rode up over another into the front stretch catch fence and hit a fence post nose first. The car stopped and fell back onto the track upside down. Several seconds later, Brad Keselowski's out-of-control car slammed into the remains of Dillon's car. Crew members from several teams rushed to the car to help and Dillon emerged quickly without serious injury and waved to the cheering fans. The impact was so severe that the engine was torn from the car. The catch fence did its job and kept the car and large parts out of the grandstands but five people did receive treatment for minor injuries.

▼ Kyle Busch celebrates his win in the July 26th Jeff Kyle 400 at the Indianapolis Motor Speedway. Busch pulled off a weekend sweep at Indianapolis by winning the Xfinity race on Saturday and the Sprint Cup race on Sunday. The race was the first event run with a high-drag, high-downforce aero package that NASCAR hoped would improve the quality of racing at the speedway. The cars ran a 9-inch-tall rear spoiler along with several other aero features that were different here than at other tracks. There were 16 lead changes among six drivers which was about average for this track. Kevin Harvick led the most laps but finished third. Busch held off Joey Logano on a green-white-checkered restart and gave Toyota its first Sprint Cup series win at Indy. It was also Busch's 3rd straight win and fourth win in his last five races.

▲ Kyle Busch takes a bow after his victory in the July 11th Quaker State 400 at Kentucky Speedway. This was the first of two races in 2015 to feature a reduced downforce package, the other being Darlington in September. Many hope this package will lead to more competitive racing. The package features a 3½-inch-tall rear spoiler instead of the standard 6 inch. The front splitter is shorter and the radiator pan under the car is smaller. All of the changes were estimated to reduce downforce in the cars by 25%. NASCAR had scheduled two days of testing at Kentucky the week of the race, but both days were rained out. The results of the new rules were a doubling of green flag passes in the field from the 2014 event, and a track record of 22 green-flag passes for the lead. The racing was visibly better and the drivers all praised the package.

◄ Kyle Busch leads older brother Kurt on the way to his first Sprint Cup series win of 2015 in the June 28th Toyota/Save-Mart 350 on the road course at Sonoma Raceway. Kurt finished second. It was the first 1-2 finish for the brothers in Sprint Cup competition. This was Kyle Busch's fifth Sprint Cup series race after missing the first 11 races of the year with leg injuries suffered at Daytona in February. The win was the first step towards Kyle Busch qualifying for the Chase for the Sprint Cup. Both Busch brothers missed races in 2015. Kurt missed three races and Kyle missed 11. Both drivers were granted waivers and allowed to compete for the Sprint Cup championship. Kurt would win two races and finish eighth in the final point standings while Kyle would win five races and the 2015 Sprint Cup Championship.

◄ Clint Bowyer and Aric Almirola race together during the September 6th Southern 500 at Darlington Raceway. Clint Bowyer is driving the #15 Toyota painted as Buddy Baker's mid 1970's era car and Aric Almirola is driving the #43 Ford painted in 1972 STP colors. When it was announced in August of 2014 that Darlington Raceway was getting its Labor Day race back, traditionalists applauded the decision. The speedway made a decision to embrace its past with a throwback weekend where they invited past Sprint Cup champions to the track and encouraged current teams to paint their cars in older paint schemes. The idea steamrolled into one of the most talked about races of the year. More than 30 Sprint Cup teams and several Xfinity series teams showed up with vintage paint schemes. NBC brought retired broadcasters Ken Squire and Ned Jarrett into the booth and they called part of the race for the TV audience. For a pre-race concert the speedway brought in Grand Funk Railroad. Tanya Tucker sang the national anthem. The track's concession stands offered food items that were sold at the speedway "back in the day." The weekend was so successful that Darlington Raceway won the 2015 NMPA Myers Brothers award that is given for outstanding contributions to the sport.

◄ Kevin Harvick leads the field during the October 4th AAA 400 at Dover. This was the final race of the Challenger round of the Chase for the Sprint Cup. Harvick was one of four drivers that needed to win to advance to the Contender round. He led 355 of the 400 laps and advanced to the next round. Jimmie Johnson needed to finish 25th or better to advance, but an axle seal failed early in the race and he finished 41st and was eliminated. Clint Bowyer and Paul Menard had to win to advance and neither did and they were also eliminated. Johnson's problems gave Dale Earnhardt Jr. and Jamie McMurray a chance to advance. Earnhardt Jr. finished third in the race while McMurray finished fourth which had the pair tied in points. The tiebreaker was who had the highest finish in the Challenger round and that went to Earnhardt Jr. with his third place finish in this race.

▲ Restarts have always been a dark art in NASCAR racing. Some drivers are good at it, others are good at working the rules of it. Throughout the year, drivers had been penalized, or thought someone else should have been, for jumping the restart. In September, NASCAR placed a camera on the restart zone and assigned an official to monitor the area. In the first two weeks of use, the system cleared Jeff Gordon of jumping at Chicago and penalized Brad Keselowski for jumping at Loudon. Earlier in the year, Denny Hamlin and Jeff Gordon both said they thought the restart zone was too short. In October, NASCAR doubled the size of the restart zones. The length of the zone is determined by the pit road speed at each track. The pit road speed is multiplied by two and that will determine the length of the zone. At Charlotte, pictured above, pit road speed is 45 mph so the restart zone is 90 feet long.

▼ Joey Logano takes the checkered and caution flags in the October 25th CampingWorld.com 500 at Talladega Superspeedway. The race ended under caution after a multi-car crash while coming to the green flag for a green-white-checkered finish. Joey Logano and Dale Earnhardt Jr. were side by side when the caution came out. NASCAR officials had to study video to determine who was leading and Logano was a nose ahead. It was Logano's third straight Sprint Cup series win and he swept all the races in the Contender round of the Chase. Earnhardt Jr. was one of two drivers that had to win in order to advance into the Eliminator round of the Chase, the other being Matt Kenseth. Those two, along with Denny Hamlin and Ryan Newman, failed to advance. Kevin Harvick managed to finish the race with a sour engine. On the previous restart he failed to come up to speed but a quick caution saved his position. On the last restart he collided with Trevor Bayne and the ensuing crash brought out the race ending caution. If the race had finished under the green flag, Harvick would not have had enough points to advance to the next round of the Chase.

▲ Carl Edwards celebrates his second win of 2015 in the September 6th Bojangles' Southern 500 at Darlington. It was a throwback weekend with vintage paint schemes on the cars and many retired drivers present at the second oldest track on the current Sprint Cup schedule. The race was also the second test of the low-downforce package that NASCAR is considering for use starting in future seasons. The race set a track record for cautions with the yellow flag waving 18 times and a track record for most cars on the lead lap at 28. Edwards beat Brad Keselowski off pit after the final round of pit stops with 12 laps to go and led the rest of the way. At one point in the race, Edwards had been two laps down. The low-downforce package helped contribute to 24 green-flag passes for the lead and all the drivers loved the new package.

◄ Joey Logano spins Matt Kenseth with five laps to go in the October 18th Hollywood Casino 400 at Kansas Speedway. Kenseth had led the most laps of the day, 153 of 269, and was leading when the contact with Logano occurred. Logano had chased Kenseth down and made an attempt to pass him but was blocked. Going into turn one with five laps to go and in lapped traffic, Logano went inside of Kenseth and made slight contact with the #20 Dollar General Toyota. It was enough to spin Kenseth from the lead. On the restart, Logano pulled away for the win. Logano had won the previous week at Charlotte and was guaranteed to advance to the next round of the Chase for the Sprint Cup, while Kenseth needed a win or good finish to advance after a 42nd place finish at Charlotte. Kenseth finished 14th here at Kansas and 26th the next week at Talladega and failed to advance in the Chase.

◄ Joey Logano takes a selfie with his winner's trophy from the October 11th Bank Of America 500 at Charlotte Motor Speedway. The win in the one-day-rain-delayed race automatically moved Logano into the Eliminator round in the Chase for the Sprint Cup. This was Logano's fourth win of the 2015 season and his first at Charlotte. He took the lead for good on lap 300 after green flag pit stops and led a total of 227 of the 334 laps. Pole sitter Matt Kenseth led 72 laps but had multiple issues that finally put him out of the race. He finished 42nd and was put in a must win situation to be able to transfer into the next round of the Chase. Kyle Busch and Kyle Larson were involved in a collision at the entrance to pit road while under caution. Both were able to continue after repairs. Logano was the only finisher in the top five to lead a lap.

◄ Jeff Gordon, Kevin Harvick, Martin Truex Jr. and Kyle Busch pose prior to the season ending Ford Ecoboost 400 at Homestead-Miami Speedway with the Sprint Cup Series championship trophy that one of them would take home at the end of the day. Under the Chase for the Sprint Cup system, the driver that finished in the highest position of the four would be the champion. Martin Truex Jr. started 11th and led once for three laps and finshed 12th. Jeff Gordon started fifth and led one time for nine laps and finished sixth. Kevin Harvick started farthest back of the four but got to the front and led one time for 46 laps and finished second. Kyle Busch started third and raced up front all day, led six different times for 41 laps and won the race and the Sprint Cup Championship. Brad Keselowski was leading with 12 laps to go when a caution came out. Kyle Busch was third at the time. After pit stops, Busch restarted second with seven laps to go, powered around leader Keselowski coming off turn two and led the rest of the way.

◄ Jeff Gordon celebrates after his victory in the November 1st Goody's Headache Relief Shot 500 at Martinsville Speedway. This was Gordon's first and only victory of 2015 and the last of his Sprint Cup career. The win qualified Gordon to race for the Sprint Cup championship at Homestead. Gordon was running second with 47 laps to go when leader Joey Logano was crashed out by Matt Kenseth. Logano had won the previous three races and appeared to be on his way to a fourth straight win until the contact with Kenseth. Denny Hamlin and AJ Allmendinger stayed out under the caution and restarted first and second while Gordon pitted and restarted third with four new tires. Allmendinger took the lead from Hamlin on the restart and led the next 18 laps until Gordon got past him with 21 laps to go. It had been 39 races since Gordon's last win and with only three more races left in his Sprint Cup career, Gordon enjoyed every minute of this victory.

▲ On November 15, 1992, at Atlanta Motor Speedway, 21-year-old Jeff Gordon ran his first Sprint Cup Series race. He started 21st and finished 31st after a crash. He made $6,285 that day. On November 22, 2015, at Homestead-Miami Speedway at the age of 44, he ran his last Cup series race. He started 5th and finished 6th and made $153,801. In his 24-year Sprint Cup Series career, Gordon ran 797 consecutive races (which is a record) finished in the top five 325 times and was running at the finish of 698 races. He won 93 times, placing him third on the all time win list behind just Richard Petty and David Pearson. Gordon has career Sprint Cup earnings of almost $154 million dollars and spent his entire Cup career at Hendrick Motorsports. By coming from open wheel spring and midget cars, Gordon opened the door for many drivers to come to NASCAR. Tony Stewart, Kasey Kahne, Steve Kinser, Danny Sullivan, Ryan Newman, Mike Bliss and Dave Blaney, to name just a few. Gordon is not leaving the sport. Starting in 2016, he moves into the Fox Sports broadcast booth as an analyst.

► Kevin Harvick came into 2015 as the defending Sprint Cup champion. He finished 2014 with two straight wins and the title. Harvick continued on his hot streak in 2015 with finishes of first or second in the first five races of the year. He finished in the top 10 in 28 of the 36 races and finished in the top five a remarkable 23 times. On top of his three wins, Harvick also finished second 13 times in 2015. He led the point standings for 23 weeks with his consistency. Even with two bad finishes in the first round of the Chase, he won at Dover and advanced to the next round. In the second round of the Chase, he had finishes of second at Charlotte and 16th at Kansas. At Talladega in the final race of the Contender round, Harvick had an engine problem late in the race and if not for a timely caution on the only green-white-checkered restart, he would not have advanced. In the three Eliminator round races, Harvick finished eighth, third and second and advanced to the Championship round at Homestead. Harvick finished second to Kyle Busch in the race and the Sprint Cup championship.

Rank	Driver	Points	Starts	Wins	Top five	Top 10
1	Kyle Busch	5043	25	5	12	16
2	Kevin Harvick	5042	36	3	23	28
3	Jeff Gordon	5038	36	1	5	21
4	Martin Truex Jr	5032	36	1	8	22
5	Carl Edwards	2368	36	2	7	15
6	Joey Logano	2360	36	6	22	28
7	Brad Keselowski	2347	36	1	9	25
8	Kurt Busch	2333	33	2	10	21
9	Denny Hamlin	2327	36	2	14	20
10	Jimmie Johnson	2315	36	5	14	22
11	Ryan Newman	2314	36	0	5	15
12	Dale Earnhardt Jr	2310	36	3	16	22
13	Jamie McMurray	2295	36	0	4	10
14	Paul Menard	2262	36	0	2	5
15	Matt Kenseth	2234	34	5	12	20
16	Clint Bowyer	2175	36	0	2	12
17	Aric Almirola	940	36	0	3	6
18	Kasey Kahne	939	36	0	3	10
19	Kyle Larson	872	35	0	2	10
20	Greg Biffle	869	36	0	3	4
21	Austin Dillon	832	36	0	1	5
22	AJ Allmendinger	758	36	0	0	3
23	Casey Mears	754	36	0	0	1
24	Danica Patrick	716	36	0	0	2
25	Ricky Stenhouse Jr	712	36	0	1	3
26	Sam Hornish Jr	709	36	0	0	3
27	David Ragan	701	36	0	1	1
28	Tony Stewart	695	36	0	0	3
29	Trevor Bayne	655	36	0	0	2
30	Justin Allgaier	588	36	0	0	1
31	Cole Whitt	553	36	0	0	0
32	David Gilliland	533	36	0	0	0
33	Alex Bowman	437	35	0	0	0
34	Brett Moffitt	422	31	0	0	1
35	Matt DiBenedetto	399	33	0	0	0
36	Michael Annett	398	35	0	0	0
37	Josh Wise	254	24	0	0	1
38	Jeb Burton	216	28	0	0	0
39	Michael McDowell	213	16	0	0	0
40	Alex Kennedy	120	13	0	0	0
41	Reed Sorenson	74	9	0	0	0
42	Bobby Labonte	60	4	0	0	0
43	Michael Waltrip	58	3	0	0	0
44	Ryan Preece	35	5	0	0	0
45	Brian Vickers	32	2	0	0	0
46	Will Kimmel III	11	2	0	0	0
47	Mike Wallace	8	1	0	0	0
48	T.J. Bell	7	1	0	0	0
49	Eddie MacDonald	7	1	0	0	0
50	Kyle Fowler	3	1	0	0	0

Kyle Busch won his first Sprint Cup Championship in 2015. It took him 11 full-time seasons to earn the title. He and his brother Kurt became the second set of brothers, after Terry and Bobby Labonte, to both win Sprint Cup titles. Kyle broke his right leg and left foot in the Daytona Xfinity series race and missed the first 11 races of the Sprint Cup season. NASCAR granted Busch a waiver to qualify for the Chase for the Sprint Cup, provided he would win a race and finish the regular season in the top 30 in points. He made his return to the series in May. It took him five races to get a win — at Sears Point in June — and just 11 races to move into the top 30 in points. In the first two rounds of the Chase, Busch advanced by slim margins. But with three top 5's in the third round, Busch easily advanced to the Championship round where his victory at Homestead assured him of his Championship. He became the first Sprint Cup champion since Richard Petty in 1971 to miss a race and still win the title.

2016

February 14 NASCAR ends posting race winnings in the Sprint Cup Series. With the new Charter system in place, posting race winnings is "not contemporary" with the new system.

February 24 Ford and Stewart-Haas Racing announce the team will switch to Ford beginning with the 2017 season. The team will build their own cars and use Roush-Yates motors.

March 13 Kevin Harvick beats Carl Edwards in a photo finish at Phoenix. The margin of victory is .010 seconds.

April 21 Tony Stewart is fined $35,000 for comments about NASCAR not requiring teams to have five lug nuts on each wheel. Four days later NASCAR issued a memo to teams that they would now be required to have all five lug nuts mounted in a safe and secure manner.

April 24 Tony Stewart returns to his Sprint Cup car after missing the first eight races of the year due to a back injury suffered in the off season.

May 1 During the Geico 500 at Talladega, Dale Earnhardt Jr.'s steering wheel come off. He kept the car from hitting the wall. Hendrick Motorsports teammate Jimmie Johnson had the same issue during qualifying earlier in the year at Phoenix and he did hit the wall.

May 19 Amid rumors of him leaving Stewart-Haas Racing for Hendrick Motorsports, Kevin Harvick announces he has re-signed with SHR for multiple years.

▲ On February 9th NASCAR announced that it would introduce a Charter system for the Sprint Cup Series. The initial 36 Charters are granted to Cup Series teams that attempted to qualify for every race over the past three years. A team with a Charter will be guaranteed a starting position in every Sprint Cup Series race. The agreement is for nine years. The value of a Charter to a team is that it can guarantee a sponsor, or potential sponsor, that it will be in every Sprint Cup Series race. It also has a guaranteed revenue stream from NASCAR. If a team with a Charter does not field a car, it will lose its Charter. There is also a performance clause where if a Charter team finishes in the bottom three positions in points among the Chartered teams for three consecutive years, the Charter can be revoked by NASCAR. A Charter is also a commodity that a team owner can lease to another team or sell on the open market. As part of the new system, the starting fields will be reduced from 43 cars to 40. With 36 cars locked into the field with Charters, the remaining four starting positions will be available for the fastest qualifying teams that don't have Charters. At the beginning of the 2016 season, there were four teams that planned to run all the races that did not qualify for Charters: the 19 Carl Edwards/Joe Gibbs Racing team, the 21 Ryan Blaney/Wood Brothers Racing team, the 41 Kurt Busch/Stewart-Haas Racing team, and the 46 Michael Annett/HScott Motorsports team. Joe Gibbs Racing and Stewart-Haas Racing each bought a Charter from the recently closed Michael Waltrip Racing team. HScott Motorsports leased a Charter from Premium Motorsports. The Wood Brothers elected not to pursue a Charter. It was reported that the Michael Waltrip Racing Charters sold for $5 million each, but the exact price was never revealed. Forbes estimates that a Charter on the open market could bring $15 to $17 million.

▲ Any race fan over the age of 50 who grew up listening to NASCAR races on the radio knew the voice of this man, Barney Hall. Hall passed away on January 26, 2016, at the age of 83. The native of Elkin, NC, began his racing broadcasting career in 1960, working the Daytona 500, and in 1961, he became the public address announcer for the new race track in Bristol, TN. When Bill France formed the Motor Racing Network in 1970, Barney Hall got the call. He started as a turn announcer, but soon advanced to the booth as lead anchor of the radio broadcasts. For 44 years, race fans were painted a picture of the action on the track through his words. On July 6, 2014, he called his last race, the Coke Zero 400 at Daytona. In 2007, he was inducted into the National Motorsports Hall of Fame, and in 2012, the NASCAR Hall of Fame announced the creation of the Squier-Hall Award for Media Excellence, named for longtime broadcasters Ken Squier and Hall.

▲ Martin Truex, Jr., in the 78 Furniture Row Toyota, races with nominal teammates Denny Hamlin (11) and Matt Kenseth (20) in the Joe Gibbs Racing Toyotas. In late 2015, Furniture Row Racing announced that it was switching from Chevrolet to Toyota starting with the 2016 season and the team would get technical help, as well as cars and engines, from JGR. The results were immediate, with Truex, Jr. finishing a close second to Hamlin in the Daytona 500. Throughout the year, the 78 Toyota was fast, with Truex, Jr. winning four times and leading more laps than any other driver in the 2016 season. The performance led part-time sponsor Bass Pro Shops to increase its primary sponsorship role on the car from 12 races in 2016 to 16 races in 2017. On August 7th, the team announced a one-year deal to field a second Cup Series car for Joe Gibbs Racing development driver Erik Jones in the 2017 season.

▲ Alex Bowman's 88 Hendrick Motorsports Chevrolet goes under "the claw" at Charlotte Motor Speedway. The claw, as it is called, is a one-piece template that fits over the entire car to ensure that no illegal body modifications have been done. In an effort to make the on-track racing better, NASCAR made many changes to the Cup Series cars for the 2016 season. For all tracks except Talladega and Daytona, the rear spoiler height was reduced from six inches to three and a half. The radiator pan under the car was reduced from 38 inches wide to 33, and the front splitter's leading edge was reduced from being extended two inches back to only one quarter inch. All of this was done to reduce downforce in the cars and make on-track passing easier. A digital dashboard was also required starting in 2016.

▲ With the checkered flag already in the air and just a few feet to go, Denny Hamlin, in the FedEx Toyota, eases ahead of Martin Truex, Jr., at the finish of the 2016 Daytona 500. The margin of victory was 0.01 seconds, the closest Daytona 500 finish ever. Hamlin led 95 of the 200 laps, the most of any driver. Rookie Chase Elliott started from the pole and led the first three laps but crashed on lap 19 and finished 37th. Matt Kenseth was leading in turn three on the last lap, but he went high to block when he saw Hamlin coming on the outside. As Hamlin turned under him in turn four, Kenseth's car got loose, made slight contact with Hamlin's car, and fell back as he lost momentum. He finished 14th. Dale Earnhardt Jr. led 15 laps but crashed while running fourth with 29 laps to go.

May 25 The 2017 class of inductees for the NASCAR Hall of Fame is announced. Richard Childress, Rick Hendrick, Mark Martin, Raymond Parks and Clay Earles will be enshrined in January of 2017.

June 26 Tony Stewart and Denny Hamlin bang doors on the last lap of the Toyota/Save Mart 350 at Sonoma Raceway. Stewart wins as Hamlin clips the wall trying to get back by.

August 29 Betty Jane France dies at the age of 78. She was the executive vice president and assistant treasurer of NASCAR. She was the wife of Bill France, Jr.

September 10 Hurricane Matthew forces a Xfinity-Sprint Cup double header at Charlotte Motor Speedway. This was the second weekend in a row where the two series ran both races on the same day. The previous weekend at Dover also had weather issues.

September 26 NASCAR announces it will limit Sprint Cup Series drivers with five or more years of full time experience to only ten Xfinity Series starts and seven Camping World Truck Series starts beginning in 2017.

November 10 Just three weeks after a career best second place finish in the Hellmann's 500 Sprint Cup race at Talladega, 29-year-old Brian Scott announces that he is retiring from racing.

▲ Matt DiBenedetto has fun during the lively driver introductions for the April 17th Food City 500 at Bristol Motor Speedway. The 24-year-old from Grass Valley, California, would later that day go on to a surprising sixth place finish in the race. Driving for the underfunded BK Racing team, DiBenedetto came from a lap down late in the race and passed Kevin Harvick with four laps to go for his best finish in 41 Cup Series starts. This was also BK Racing's best finish since the team was formed in 2012. When race winner Carl Edwards was later told where DiBenedetto had finished, he replied, "Man, that's unbelievable. That's probably tougher than what we did." Later in the year, while driving an Xfinity Series race at Texas, DiBenedetto crashed hard and suffered concussion-like symptoms that kept him out of the next day's Sprint Cup Series event. He was medically cleared in time for the next week's race at Phoenix. At the end of the season, he left BK Racing to drive a full 2017 Cup Series schedule for Go Fas Racing.

▲ Joey Logano celebrates his victory in the May 21st Sprint All-Star Race at Charlotte Motor Speedway. Logano didn't win his first points-paying event until June at Michigan, and that qualified him for the Chase for the Sprint Cup. Logano entered the Chase ranked ninth with his one win and had finishes of 2nd, 11th, and 6th in the first round to point his way into the Round of 12. After second round finishes of 36th at Charlotte and 3rd at Kansas, Logano went into the elimination race at Talladega at the bottom of the cutoff line. He won at Talladega and transferred to the Round of 8. His victory at Phoenix in that round advanced him to the Championship race at Homestead. Logano qualified 13th at Homestead and led only six laps but was in contention for the title at the end. On a late-race restart with the Sprint Cup championship in sight, Logano made contact with fellow championship contender Carl Edwards and crashed him out of contention. Logano pitted after the contact and had to restart eighth with five laps to go. He finished fourth in the race and second in the 2016 Sprint Cup championship.

◄ Carl Edwards congratulates race winner Martin Truex, Jr. after his dominating win in the May 29th Coca-Cola 600 at Charlotte Motor Speedway. Truex, Jr. started from the pole and led 392 of the 400 laps in the Sprint Cup Series' longest race. Truex, Jr. set records for most laps led in a race, most miles led in a race (588) and fastest time for a 600-mile race at 3 hours 44 minutes. Jimmie Johnson, Joey Logano, and Paul Menard were the only other lap leaders, mostly during pit stop cycles. Truex, Jr. was only passed on the track once, during the last restart on lap 344 by Jimmie Johnson, but Truex, Jr. took the lead back on the next lap and led to the end. This was Truex, Jr.'s first win of 2016, and it guaranteed him and the Furniture Row team a spot in the Chase for the Sprint Cup.

▲ Ryan Newman, in the 31 Chevrolet, and Austin Dillon, in the 3 Chevrolet, along with Paul Menard, were Richard Childress Racing's 2016 team lineup. This was Dillon's third full season in the Sprint Cup Series, and it was his best. Dillon had four top-five finishes, with a best of third at Talladega in the spring, and 13 top-tens, along with two pole positions. He was the only RCR driver to make the Chase for the Sprint Cup, in which he finished 14th. 2016 was also Newman's third year with RCR, but it was his worst with the organization, with only two top-fives, ten top-tens, and no poles. He finished 18th in the point standings. Menard is the senior driver at RCR, with six seasons under his belt. His 2016 season consisted of only three top-ten finishes and a 25th place finish in the point standings. Between the three teams, they led only 61 laps combined. Richard Childress Racing has not had a Sprint Cup Series win since the 2013 season, when Kevin Harvick won four times.

▶ Even with NASCAR working to reduce downforce on cars in an effort to promote more passing on track, the easiest way to make up, or lose positions, is on pit road. Kevin Harvick, in the Stewart-Haas Racing 4, was especially critical of his pit crew during the 2016 season. At the Southern 500 in Darlington, Harvick led 214 of the 367 laps but lost a total of 17 spots on pit road during the race, including 12 positions on one stop when an air gun broke, and felt it cost him the win. Denny Hamlin's pit road pain was self-inflicted. He was penalized 10 times during the season for speeding on pit road. Martin Truex, Jr., on the other hand, benefited on pit road, with his crew gaining him the lead at Darlington late in the race, and again at Chicagoland, where they got him out ahead of leader Chase Elliott. Each time, Truex, Jr. won the race.

► Greg Biffle leads Roush Fenway Racing teammate Trevor Bayne during the March 6th Kobalt 400 at Las Vegas Motor Speedway. The 46-year-old Biffle ran 19 seasons for RFR, including 15 seasons in the Cup Series. He brought Jack Roush his first NASCAR championship in 2000 when he won the Camping World Truck Series title, but after several dismal seasons at RFR and no relief in sight, Biffle left the team. The entire Roush Fenway organization had a lackluster 2016. The three teams of Biffle, Trevor Bayne, and Ricky Stenhouse, Jr. had only seven top five finishes combined and led only 82 laps between them. Carl Edwards won the last Sprint Cup Series race for the organization back in 2014. With Biffle leaving, the team leased the 16 team Charter and development driver Chris Buescher to JTG Daugherty Racing for the 2017 season. RFR will run only two Cup Series cars in 2017, with Bayne and Stenhouse, Jr. driving.

◄ Kyle Larson celebrates his first Sprint Cup Series win in his 99th series start in the August 28th Pure Michigan 400 at Michigan International Speedway. Many thought the 24-year-old would have won before now. When Larson came to the Cup Series in 2014, he was "the next big thing," and while he showed promise and ran strong, he just couldn't break through with a victory. Larson's win made him eligible for the Chase for the Sprint Cup, but with finishes of 18th at Chicago, 10th at Loudon, and 25th at Dover during the Round of 16, he failed to transfer to the next round. After being eliminated from the Chase, Larson finished in the top 10 in four of the remaining seven races. At the season finale at Homestead, Larson led 132 of the 268 laps and was leading at the final restart with two laps to go but lost the lead, and the race, to Jimmie Johnson.

► Carl Edwards does his traditional victory backflip after his win in the April 24th Toyota Owners 400 at Richmond International Raceway. Edwards led 151 of the 400 laps, the most of any driver, but the win didn't come easy. Joe Gibbs Racing teammate Kyle Busch was leading with one lap to go with Edwards close behind. Going into turn one, Edwards looked inside Busch but couldn't make the move. In the middle of turns three and four, Edwards got into the back of Busch and moved him just enough to get by for the win. After the race, when Edwards was asked about the contact, he said he told himself, "Man, I'm going to give him a little nudge." Kyle Busch said, "It was just racing, I guess." Edwards' win was his second in a row after his victory the week before at Bristol.

◄ During a September 4 press conference at Darlington Raceway, Dale Earnhardt Jr., car owner Rick Hendrick, and Dr. Micky Collins discussed Earnhardt Jr.'s medical condition. Two days earlier, it was announced that Earnhardt Jr. would miss the remainder of the 2016 NASCAR season after he sat out the previous six races with concussion-like symptoms. After a crash in the June 12 Michigan Sprint Cup Series race, Earnhardt Jr. didn't feel well but continued to race. He later met with a neurological specialist who felt that he shouldn't be in a race car. After several evaluations over a period of weeks, it was determined that he would not be cleared to race for the rest of the year. Earnhardt Jr. missed two races in 2012 with a concussion as well. In an ironic twist, in April he had announced that he was donating his brain to science for concussion research. In December, Earnhardt Jr. ran 185 laps in a test at Darlington and afterward was cleared to return to action for the 2017 season. He missed 18 races.

► Tony Stewart, in the 14 Mobil 1 Chevrolet, leads his replacement driver, Clint Bowyer, at Charlotte Motor Speedway. In September of 2015, Stewart announced that he would retire from Sprint Cup competition at the end of the 2016 season and that Clint Bowyer would replace him in the Stewart-Haas Racing flagship car. With Bowyer's 2015 team, Michael Waltrip Racing, shutting down at the end of that season, a deal was made with HScott Motorsports for Bowyer to race the 2016 season in their 15 Chevrolet while Stewart ran his final season at SHR. Bowyer's season at HScott was frustrating, to say the least, with only three top-10 finishes and only three laps led. By mid-season, Bowyer's sponsor of five years, 5-Hour Energy, had announced that they were leaving him at the end of 2016 to go to the new 77 Furniture Row team of Eric Jones for the 2017 season.

▲ Kyle Busch appears to have found the secret to the Indianapolis Motor Speedway. He has won the last four NASCAR races at the historic speedway, the Xfinity and Sprint Cup races in both 2015 and 2016. In 2016, he started both races from the pole; he led 62 of the 63 laps of the Lilly Diabetes 250 Xfinity Series race and then led 149 of the 170-lap Combat Wounded Coalition 400 Sprint Cup Series event the next day. It was the first time a driver had swept both pole positions and races on a weekend. The reduced downforce rules used in 2016 were expected to help the racing at the speedway, where green flag lead changes have been scarce, but there were only four lead changes among three drivers, with Busch leading the final 109 laps. After the race, Indiana native Tony Stewart and Indiana transplant Jeff Gordon took their Sprint Cup cars for a lap around the speedway together in what will probably be their last competitive event at Indy.

▲ Chris Buescher, on right, and crew chief Bob Osborne hoist the trophy for their win in the rain-delayed and rain-shortened Pennsylvania 400 at Pocono Raceway. With rain in the area and his team off-sequence from the others, the veteran crew chief kept Buescher on the race track when all the front-runners had to pit. Six laps later, the rain came, and then heavy fog forced the race to end 22 laps short. The unexpected win by the underfunded Front Row Racing team gave the team a chance to qualify for the Chase for the Sprint Cup. One of the eligibility requirements for a team with a victory to make the Chase is to be in the top 30 in points. After the win, with five races to go before the cutoff, the team was six points out. A fifth place finish at Bristol two races later moved them into the 30th position, and they were able to maintain the spot and make the Chase. In the Round of 16, the team had finishes of 28th at Chicago, 30th at Louden, and 23rd at Dover, and they failed to advance to the Round of 8.

◄ Alex Bowman talks with Dale Earnhardt Jr. prior to the October 9th running of the Bank of America 500 at Charlotte Motor Speedway. When the 2016 NASCAR season started, the 23-year-old Bowman only had nine Xfinity Series races on his schedule, after running the full Sprint Cup Series schedule the previous two seasons. All of that changed on July 14th when it was announced that Dale Earnhardt Jr. would have to sit out the July 17th New Hampshire 301 at New Hampshire Motor Speedway due to concussion-like symptoms. Bowman was already at the track to race Earnhardt Jr.'s JR Motorsports Xfinity Series car and was quickly set up to substitute in the Cup car. Bowman qualified the 88 car 20th and ran in the top 10 late in the race until a cut tire put him into the wall and he finished 26th. Bowman would eventually run 10 races in his substitute role, and he had three top 10 finishes, with a best of sixth at Phoenix, where he also won the pole and led 194 of the 324 laps. When the 2016 season ended, so did Bowman's ride. At Dale Earnhardt Jr.'s urging, Hendrick Motorsports is allowing Bowman to drive the 88 car in the 2017 Clash at Daytona for the previous season's pole winners, even though Earnhardt Jr. himself was eligible to run the non-points-paying event.

▼ Clint Bowyer in the 15 5-Hour Energy Chevrolet and Michael Annett in the 46 Pilot Chevrolet race together during the October 9th Bank of America 500 at Charlotte Motor Speedway. The two cars were run out of the HScott Motorsports shop, which was formed when James Finch sold his Phoenix Racing team to Harry Scott, Jr. in the middle of the 2013 season. Bowyer came to the team in 2016 with sponsor 5-Hour Energy because he needed a place to run a single season while waiting for Tony Stewart to exit the 14 Stewart-Haas ride that he would take over in 2017. Annett brought Pilot Flying J truck stops with him in 2015 and ran two seasons with the organization. When the Charter system began at the start of 2016, HScott Motorsports owned one Charter for the 15 team and leased another for the 46 car to guarantee it would make every race. Bowyer's season with the team was disappointing, to say the least, with only three top-ten finishes and a best finish of 7th in the May 1st Geico 500 at Talladega. In Annett's two seasons with the team, he had a best finish of 13th in his first start with the team in the 2015 Daytona 500. By the middle of September, there were already whispers that with Bowyer and his sponsor leaving and the Pilot sponsorship a year-to-year deal, HScott Motorsports was in trouble. In November, it was announced that Annett and Pilot were leaving for Dale Earnhardt Jr.'s Xfinity Series team. The leased Charter was returned to its team, the HScott Motorsports Charter was sold to Premium Motorsports, and the team suspended operations.

▲ Hendrick Motorsports team owner Rick Hendrick and drivers Chase Elliott and Jeff Gordon share a moment at the Indianapolis Motor Speedway in July. Elliott replaced Gordon in the 24 Chevrolet in 2016, and he ran his first full season in Sprint Cup competition. Many expected Elliott to win in his first season, and while he was very competitive, he never got to victory lane. He started the season by winning the pole for the Daytona 500 and led laps early but crashed and finished 37th. The next week at Atlanta, he scored his first top-ten finish. Elliott had a strong first half of the season and scored 11 top-ten finishes in the first 15 races of the season. In the middle part of the season, Elliott had a period of eight races in which his best finish was 15th, but a second place at Michigan in August helped put the team back on track. Even with no wins, Elliott made the Chase for the Sprint Cup based on points. He advanced to the Round of 12 of the Chase, but finishes of 33rd, 31st, and 12th in the second round kept him from advancing to the Round of 8. Elliott finished the season with 10 top-five finishes and 17 top-10's in 36 starts and a 10th place finish in the Sprint Cup point standings, along with being named the 2016 Rookie of the Year.

▲ At the end of 2015, Jeff Gordon retired from the Sprint Cup Series, but when Hendrick Motorsports teammate Dale Earnhardt Jr. had to step out of his 88 Chevrolet, Gordon answered the call from team owner Rick Hendrick and filled in. Gordon put the fire suit back on and ran eight races, including Indy, Watkins Glen, and Darlington. Gordon's time back in a Cup Series car was steady, but not spectacular. He finished on the lead lap in all of the races except Dover, where he was only one lap down, and he had a best finish of sixth at Martinsville. After finishing his last scheduled substitution race at Martinsville, Gordon was asked again if this was his last Cup Series race. "Never say never is all I know what to say," he replied.

▲ For the second consecutive year, Darlington Raceway had its "Throwback Weekend" for the Southern 500 race weekend. These crew members for Tony Stewart's team dressed the part in pit uniforms with the vintage look of the early 1970's Coca-Cola-sponsored race teams. At least 35 of the 40 Cup Series cars sported throwback paint schemes, and almost half the field for the Xfinity race also participated. With a year's notice for this year's weekend, many teams, drivers, and even media personnel took advantage of the time and acquired vintage clothing and other items of the era to bring to the track. Jimmie Johnson, who was driving a Dale Earnhardt, Sr. Lowe's throwback scheme, even went as far as to ask Dale Earnhardt Jr. if he could borrow one of his dad's old uniforms to wear for driver introductions. He got to borrow a vintage hat instead. Leonard Wood brought one of the old pit boards that was used when David Pearson drove the Wood Brothers cars in the early 1970's and used it for current driver Ryan Blaney. Blaney went just a bit too far and practiced his car without wearing safety gloves. "I wanted to go out there with no gloves. They didn't have gloves in the '70s, you know," said Blaney. NASCAR fined Blaney $1,000 for improper equipment. The speedway brought in the band Kansas for a pre-race concert, and Barry Williams of the 1970's TV show *The Brady Bunch* sang the national anthem.

◄ The Sprint Cup Series wheel pictured here has one broken wheel stud and two missing lugs. In late 2014, NASCAR stepped away from policing lug nuts in the top three touring series: Sprint Cup, Xfinity, and Camping World Truck. Previously, an inspector on pit road would check each wheel during a pit stop to make sure there were five lug nuts installed. If not, the car could not leave pit road or would be called back in if it had already pulled away. When the new pit road camera system came online in 2015, there would not be inspectors in each pit to confirm if five lugs were on the wheel, so the rule was abolished. Now it would be up to the teams to gamble on how many lugs they wanted the tire changers to install. By midseason, teams were only gluing up four lugs per wheel and, on late stops, some teams were only putting two lugs on the left side wheels. After a rash of loose wheels during 2015 and the early part of the 2016 season, NASCAR issued a memo on April 25th that stated that "lug nuts must be 'installed in a safe and secure manner' or have the driver risk being called back into the pits during the race. If the infraction is found after the race, a crew chief will receive a minimum $20,000 fine and a one-race suspension." By September, five crew chiefs had been suspended for missing lug nuts. NASCAR amended the rule in mid-September that only one missing lug nut would not result in a crew chief suspension, but the fine remained in place.

▲ The hood goes up on Jamie McMurray's Chevrolet during the October 2nd Citizen Soldier 400 at Dover International Speedway. McMurray and Chip Ganassi Racing teammate Kyle Larson came into the event basically needing to win to advance into the next round of the Chase for the Sprint Cup. McMurray's troubles were terminal, and he finished last in the 40-car field, while Larson had electrical issues and finished six laps down in 25th. Both failed to advance into the Round of 12. Tony Stewart and Chris Buescher were in the same situation as the Ganassi drivers; they needed a win to advance. Stewart finished 13th, one lap down, and Buescher was 23rd, six laps down, and they also failed to advance. Martin Truex, Jr. won the race, his second victory in the three-race Round of 16, while Kevin Harvick broke a track bar early in the race and finished 37th . Harvick's win the week before at Louden guaranteed advancement into the Round of 12 for the Chase.

◄ Joe Gibbs Racing teammates Carl Edwards (19), Matt Kenseth (20), and Kyle Busch (18) draft together during the October 23rd running of the Hellmann's 500 at Talladega Superspeedway. The event was the cutoff race for the Round of 12 of the Chase, and coming into the race, only Jimmie Johnson and Kevin Harvick were guaranteed to advance. The three JGR drivers were in good shape to advance to the Round of 8 on points and elected to fall to the rear of the field before the start and ride at the back to avoid trouble. All three, along with teammate Denny Hamlin, advanced. Other Chase drivers were not in comfortable enough positions to coast into the next round. Chase Elliott needed a win but finished 12th and failed to advance. Brad Keselowski was another driver who needed a win to guarantee advancement, and he ran at the front all day, leading 90 laps, but his engine failed and he finished 38th and did not advance. Martin Truex, Jr. and Austin Dillon were the other two drivers who did not move into the next round, while Joey Logano won the race to transfer and Kurt Busch made it on points into the Round of 8.

► Matt Kenseth's battered Joe Gibbs Racing Toyota limps down pit road at the end of the November 13th Can-Am 500 at Phoenix International Raceway. For the second year in a row, a crash derailed Kenseth's chances to advance in the Chase for the Sprint Cup. In 2015, A crash in the second round of the Chase at Kansas while leading with five laps to go severely hurt his chance to advance. This year, Kenseth was leading at Phoenix on a green-white-checkered restart when he was hit by Alex Bowman in the 88 Chevrolet going into turn one; Kenseth spun backwards into the outside wall. He finished 21st. A win would have advanced Kenseth into the Championship round at Homestead. Joe Gibbs Racing teammate Denny Hamlin was also eliminated from the Chase at Phoenix, as were Stewart-Haas Racing's Kevin Harvick and Kurt Busch.

▲ Car owner Tommy Baldwin and driver Regan Smith pose with the team's crew and Chevrolet SS at the 2016 Sprint Cup season finale at Miami -Homestead Speedway. Baldwin became a Sprint Cup Series crew chief in 1997, working with Junie Donlavey. In 1998, he moved to Bill Davis Racing, where over the next four years he won four races with driver Ward Burton, including the 2002 Daytona 500. He formed Tommy Baldwin Racing in 2001 as an Xfinity Series team, and in 2009, TBR began fielding a Sprint Cup Series car. The Sprint Cup Series team ran a total of 392 races over eight seasons, at times running two cars. The team had a best finish of third, once in 2011 at Talladega with Dave Blaney and again in 2016 with Smith at Pocono. When the NASCAR Charter system was formed at the beginning of 2016, TBR received a charter and was guaranteed a spot in every race. Before the season-ending race at Homestead, Baldwin announced that he had sold his charter and would shut down the team.

◄ Tony Stewart takes a lap around the Homestead-Miami Speedway prior to the November 20th Ford EcoBoost 400. The 45-year-old native of Columbus, Indiana, retired from NASCAR competition after 18 years and 618 races in the Sprint Cup Series. Stewart is a three-time Cup champion (2002, 2005, 2011) and has 49 wins, which ranks him 13th on the all-time win list. With his 1997 Indy Racing League series championship, Stewart is the only driver ever to win titles in both series. In his last four Sprint Cup seasons, he ran the full schedule of events only one year, 2015. Injuries and other issues kept him off the track in the other seasons, and in a September interview, he admitted that frustration with the sport played a part in his getting out of the car. Stewart will continue to be a Sprint Cup Series car owner, and he said he planned to run 40 to 50 races in 2017 in his own open wheel sprint car.

◄ A dejected Carl Edwards walks down pit road after a late-race crash that ended his hopes for the 2016 Sprint Cup Series championship. Edwards had a very competitive 2016 season, with three victories and six pole positions in the 19 Joe Gibbs Racing Toyota. He won back-to-back races early in the season at Bristol and Richmond and then won at Texas in November to advance to the Championship Round of the Chase for the Sprint Cup at Homestead-Miami Speedway. He qualified 10th for the Ford EcoBoost 400 and led the race eight different times for 47 laps. On a restart with 10 laps to go, Edwards restarted on the inside front row and had to block fellow Championship contender Joey Logano, who had a run on him. Contact was made and Edwards hit the inside and outside walls and was out of the race. He finished 34th in the race and fourth in the Sprint Cup standings. On January 11, 2017, Edwards stunned the NASCAR world by announcing that he was stepping away from driving full-time in the Cup Series. His reasons given were that he was satisfied with his career, he wanted to do things outside the sport, and that he was still healthy.

► In the middle of December 2014, Sprint announced it was not renewing its sponsorship of the NASCAR Cup Series. The company came on board with NASCAR in 2004 under the Nextel brand when it signed a 10-year deal to sponsor the Cup Series, replacing Winston cigarettes. Nextel and Sprint merged in 2006, and in 2008, the series was rebranded from Nextel Cup to the Sprint Cup Series. Before the original 10-year deal expired, NASCAR and Sprint agreed to an additional three years that would take the partnership to the end of 2016. When Sprint announced it was not renewing the deal, many different companies were mentioned as possible replacements, including Coca-Cola, Pepsi, Subway, and Panasonic, to name but a few. The price tag for such a deal was hefty, with Sprint reportedly spending between 50 to 70 million dollars a year. On December 1, 2016, NASCAR introduced a Coca-Cola-owned company, Monster Energy Drink, as the new series sponsor. The Cup Series will be known as the Monster Energy NASCAR Cup Series.

2016 NASCAR SPRINT Cup Series POINTS RACE

Rank	Driver	Points	Starts	Wins	Top five	Top 10
1	Jimmie Johnson	5040	36	5	11	16
2	Joey Logano	5037	36	3	16	26
3	Kyle Busch	5035	36	4	17	25
4	Carl Edwards	5007	36	3	9	18
5	Matt Kenseth	2330	36	2	8	19
6	Denny Hamlin	2320	36	3	12	22
7	Kurt Busch	2296	36	1	9	21
8	Kevin Harvick	2289	36	4	17	27
9	Kyle Larson	2288	36	1	10	15
10	Chase Elliott	2285	36	0	10	17
11	Martin Truex, Jr.	2271	36	4	8	17
12	Brad Keselowski	2267	36	4	16	22
13	Jamie McMurray	2231	36	0	2	12
14	Austin Dillon	2223	36	0	4	13
15	Tony Stewart	2211	28	1	5	8
16	Chris Buescher	2169	36	1	2	2
17	Kasey Kahne	898	36	0	3	13
18	Ryan Newman	895	36	0	2	10
19	AJ Allmendinger	830	36	0	2	9
20	Ryan Blaney	812	36	0	3	9
21	Ricky Stenhouse, Jr.	772	36	0	4	6
22	Trevor Bayne	762	36	0	2	5
23	Greg Biffle	691	36	0	1	3
24	Danica Patrick	689	36	0	0	0
25	Paul Menard	678	36	0	0	3
26	Aric Almirola	638	36	0	0	1
27	Clint Bowyer	628	36	0	0	3
28	Casey Mears	556	36	0	0	0
29	Landon Cassill	530	36	0	0	0
30	Michael McDowell	500	31	0	0	2
31	Brian Scott	481	36	0	1	1
32	Dale Earnhardt Jr.	461	18	0	5	6
33	David Ragan	455	36	0	0	0
34	Regan Smith	452	35	0	1	2
35	Matt DiBenedetto	386	35	0	0	1
36	Michael Annett	328	35	0	0	0
37	Cole Whitt	276	26	0	0	0
38	Jeff Gordon	218	8	0	0	2
39	Reed Sorenson	198	28	0	0	0
40	Josh Wise	168	29	0	0	0
41	Jeffrey Earnhardt	159	22	0	0	0
42	Brian Vickers	86	5	0	0	1
43	Bobby Labonte	61	4	0	0	0
44	David Gilliland	46	2	0	0	0
45	Michael Waltrip	42	2	0	0	0
46	Boris Said	17	1	0	0	0
47	Patrick Carpentier	11	2	0	0	0
48	Gray Gaulding	6	3	0	0	0
49	Eddie MacDonald	5	1	0	0	0
50	Alex Kennedy	5	1	0	0	0

2016 was a season of records for Jimmie Johnson. In winning his seventh Sprint Cup championship, he joined Richard Petty and Dale Earnhardt as the only seven-time Cup Series champions. With his five victories this year, he raised his total to 80 Cup Series wins and passed Earnhardt, who has 76 wins, for seventh on the all-time Sprint Cup win list. Since Johnson is only 41 years old, he has an excellent chance to set himself apart from the other "7-timers". Johnson's seventh title didn't come through domination like some of his others. While he did win two races early at Atlanta and Fontana, the mid part of the season was a struggle, with Johnson going 24 races without a win, the longest winless streak of his 15-year Sprint Cup career. Rumors of a break-up of the Johnson-Knaus pairing circulated during that period, and after the season, team owner Rick Hendrick acknowledged that he had indeed considered splitting them up. By the time the Chase for the Sprint Cup started, Johnson was out of his slump. He advanced into the Round of 12 on points and then won the first race of that round at Charlotte to lock in advancement to the Round of 8. Then the series came to Martinsville, where Johnson had won eight times previously. He didn't lead until after the 400-lap mark, but he led the last 92 laps to win and advance to the Championship round at Homestead. Before the start of the title-determining Ford EcoBoost 400 race, the 48 team was forced to start at the back of the field because of an illegal body modification made to the car after inspection. Johnson moved up quickly from the back of the field but never led the race until the last restart, when he passed leader Kyle Larson and led the last three laps to win the race and his seventh Sprint Cup title.

Appendix

The following pages detail every top-level NASCAR race in the history of the sanctioning body, including the winner of each race. The numbers for 1948 reflect the NASCAR Championship Modified season, the only series run that year. NASCAR introduced late-model stock car racing in 1949 in the form of the NASCAR Strictly Stock Circuit. The name of that series changed to the NASCAR Grand National Circuit in 1950. It retained that name until 1971, when it became the NASCAR Winston Cup Grand National Series. The name changed to the NASCAR Winston Cup Series in 1986. In 2004, it became the NASCAR NEXTEL Cup, and in 2008, the NASCAR Sprint Cup.

1948 NASCAR Championship Modified Season

No.	Date	Site	Race Winner	Car	Speed	Lead Chgs	Ldrs	Caut.	C.Laps	Pole Winner	Speed*	Winner Started
1	2/15/48	Daytona Beach, FL	Red Byron	Ford	75.747	4	3	0	0	No Time Trials	NTT	2nd
2	2/24/48	Jacksonville, FL	Fonty Flock	Ford	n/a	n/a	n/a	n/a	n/a	Bill Snowden	Heat Race	2nd
3	3/27/48	Atlanta, GA	Fonty Flock	Ford	n/a	n/a	n/a	n/a	n/a	n/a	n/a	n/a
4	3/04/48	Macon, GA	Fonty Flock	Ford	n/a	n/a	n/a	n/a	n/a	Fonty Flock	Heat Race	Pole
5	4/11/48	Augusta, GA	Bob Flock	Ford	n/a	n/a	n/a	n/a	n/a	Fonty Flock	Heat Race	4th
6	4/18/48	Jacksonville, FL	Skimp Hersey	Ford	56.524	n/a	n/a	3	n/a	Roscoe Thompson	Heat Race	4th
7	4/18/48	Greensboro, NC	Fonty Flock	Ford	n/a	0	1	1	15	Fonty Flock	Heat Race	Pole
8	4/25/48	N.Wilkesboro, NC	Red Byron	Ford	n/a	n/a	n/a	n/a	n/a	Swayne Pritchett	Heat Race	4th
9	5/02/48	Lexington, NC	Red Byron	Ford	n/a	n/a	n/a	n/a	n/a	Red Byron	Heat Race	Pole
10	5/09/48	Wadesboro, NC	Red Byron	Ford	n/a	n/a	n/a	n/a	n/a	Speedy Thompson	Heat Race	3rd
11	5/16/48	Richmond, VA	Red Byron	Ford	n/a	n/a	n/a	n/a	n/a	Buddy Shuman	Heat Race	7th
12	5/23/48	Macon, GA	Gober Sosebee	Ford	n/a	n/a	n/a	n/a	n/a	Ed Samples	Heat Race	4th
13	5/23/48	Danville, VA	Bill Blair	Ford	n/a	0	1	n/a	n/a	Buck Baker	Heat Race	7th
14	5/23/48	Dover, NJ	Johnny Rogers	Ford	n/a	n/a	n/a	n/a	n/a	Johnny Rogers	Heat Race	Pole
15	5/29/48	Greensboro, NC	Bob Flock	Ford	n/a	n/a	n/a	n/a	n/a	Marshall Teague	Heat Race	7th
16	5/30/48	N.Wilkesboro, NC	Marshall Teague	Ford	n/a	n/a	n/a	n/a	n/a	Speedy Thompson	Heat Race	7th
17	5/30/48	Jacksonville, FL	Paul Pappy	Ford	n/a	n/a	n/a	n/a	n/a	L.B. Michaels	Heat Race	4th
18	6/04/48	Danville, VA	Bob Flock	Ford	n/a	n/a	n/a	n/a	n/a	Fonty Flock	Heat Race	4th
19	6/05/48	Greensboro, NC	Red Byron	Ford	n/a	n/a	n/a	n/a	n/a	Speedy Thompson	Heat Race	7th
20	6/06/48	Lexington, NC	Bob Flock	Ford	n/a	n/a	n/a	n/a	n/a	P.E. Godfrey	Heat Race	6th
21	6/13/48	Wadesboro, NC	Fonty Flock	Ford	n/a	n/a	n/a	n/a	n/a	Ike Keiser	Heat Race	5th
22	6/20/48	Birmingham, AL	Fonty Flock	Ford	n/a	n/a	n/a	n/a	n/a	Billy Carden	Heat Race	4th
23	6/20/48	Columbus, GA	Bob Flock	Ford	n/a	n/a	n/a	n/a	n/a	Doug Cox	Heat Race	2nd
24	6/20/48	Greensboro, NC	Tim Flock	Ford	n/a	n/a	n/a	n/a	n/a	Johnny Grubb	Heat Race	4th
25	6/27/48	Hillsboro, NC	Fonty Flock	Ford	n/a	n/a	n/a	n/a	n/a	Marshall Teague	Heat Race	9th
26	7/04/48	Martinsville, VA	Fonty Flock	Ford	n/a	n/a	n/a	n/a	n/a	Tim Flock	Heat Race	2nd
27	7/11/48	Charlotte, NC	Red Byron	Ford	n/a	n/a	n/a	2	n/a	Jack Smith	Heat Race	n/a
28	7/18/48	N.Wilkesboro, NC	Curtis Turner	Ford	n/a	n/a	n/a	n/a	n/a	Jack Smith	Heat Race	3rd
29	7/25/48	Greensboro, NC	Curtis Turner	Ford	n/a	n/a	n/a	n/a	n/a	Curtis Turner	Heat Race	Pole
30	7/25/48	Columbus, GA	Billy Carden	Ford	n/a	n/a	n/a	n/a	n/a	Ed Samples	Heat Race	4th
31	8/01/48	Lexington, NC	Curtis Turner	Ford	n/a	n/a	n/a	n/a	n/a	Fonty Flock	Heat Race	6th
32	8/08/48	Daytona Beach, FL	Fonty Flock	Ford	n/a	2	1	0	0	Joe Allen	77.155	3rd
33	8/15/48	Langhorne, PA	Al Keller	Ford	60.883	9	6	n/a	n/a	Tommy Coates	n/a	n/a
34	9/05/48	Columbus, GA	Gober Sosebee	Ford	n/a	n/a	n/a	n/a	n/a	Gober Sosebee	n/a	Pole
35	9/05/48	N.Wilkesboro, NC	Curtis Turner	Ford	n/a	0	1	0	0	Curtis Turner	Heat Race	Pole
36	9/05/48	N.Wilkesboro, NC	Curtis Turner	Ford	n/a	n/a	n/a	0	0	Jimmy Ingram	Inverted Start	14th
37	9/12/48	Charlotte, NC	Curtis Turner	Ford	n/a	n/a	n/a	n/a	n/a	Curtis Turner	Heat Race	Pole
38	9/12/48	Charlotte, NC	Buddy Shuman	Ford	n/a	n/a	n/a	n/a	n/a	Bob Smith	Inverted Start	4th
39	9/19/48	Hillsboro, NC	Fonty Flock	Ford	n/a	n/a	n/a	n/a	n/a	Fonty Flock	Heat Race	Pole
40	9/19/48	Hillsboro, NC	Fonty Flock	Ford	n/a	n/a	n/a	n/a	n/a	Buck Baker	Inverted Start	14th
41	9/26/48	Lexington, NC	Fonty Flock	Ford	n/a	n/a	n/a	n/a	n/a	Curtis Turner	Heat Race	2nd
42	9/26/48	Lexington, NC	Gober Sosebee	Ford	n/a	n/a	n/a	n/a	n/a	Lou Perry	Inverted Start	2nd
43	10/03/48	Elkin, NC	Buddy Shuman	Ford	n/a	n/a	n/a	n/a	n/a	Buddy Shuman	Heat Race	Pole
44	10/03/48	Elkin, NC	Curtis Turner	Ford	n/a	n/a	n/a	n/a	n/a	n/a	n/a	n/a
45	10/03/48	Macon, GA	Billy Carden	Ford	n/a	n/a	n/a	n/a	n/a	Red Byron	Heat Race	7th
46	10/03/48	Macon, GA	Red Byron	Ford	n/a	n/a	n/a	n/a	n/a	Charles Rush	Inverted Start	10th
47	10/10/48	Greensboro, NC	Fonty Flock	Ford	n/a	n/a	n/a	n/a	n/a	n/a	n/a	n/a
48	10/16/48	Greensboro, NC	Fonty Flock	Ford	n/a	n/a	n/a	n/a	n/a	n/a	n/a	n/a
49	10/17/48	N.Wilkesboro, NC	Red Byron	Ford	n/a	n/a	n/a	n/a	n/a	n/a	n/a	n/a
50	10/24/48	Charlotte, NC	Red Byron	Ford	n/a	n/a	n/a	n/a	n/a	Buck Baker	Heat Race	4th
51	10/31/48	Winston-Salem, NC	Fonty Flock	Ford	n/a	n/a	n/a	n/a	n/a	n/a	n/a	n/a
52	11/14/48	Columbus, GA	Red Byron	Ford	n/a	n/a	n/a	n/a	n/a	Red Byron	Heat Race	Pole

*Pole winner for most events was determined by Heat races, not qualifying speed.

1949 NASCAR Strictly Stock Circuit Season

No.	Date	Site	Race Winner	Car	Speed	Lead Chgs	Ldrs	Caut.	C.Laps	Pole Winner	Speed	Winner Started
1	6/19/49	Charlotte, NC	Jim Roper	Lincoln	n/a	2	3	n/a	n/a	Bob Flock	67.958	12th
2	7/10/49	Daytona Beach, FL	Red Byron	Olds	80.883	1	2	0	0	Gober Sosebee	n/a	2nd
3	8/07/49	Hillsboro, NC	Bob Flock	Olds	76.800	n/a	n/a	n/a	n/a	n/a	n/a	n/a
4	9/01/49	Langhorne, PA	Curtis Turner	Olds	69.403	n/a	n/a	n/a	n/a	Red Byron	77.482	11th
5	9/18/49	Hamburg, NY	Jack White	Lincoln	n/a	n/a	n/a	n/a	n/a	n/a	n/a	n/a
6	9/25/49	Martinsville, VA	Red Byron	Olds	n/a	2	3	n/a	n/a	Curtis Turner	n/a	3rd
7	10/02/49	Pittsburgh, PA	Lee Petty	Plymouth	57.458	n/a	n/a	n/a	n/a	Al Bonnell	61.475	n/a
8	10/16/49	N.Wilkesboro, NC	Bob Flock	Olds	53.364	2	2	n/a	n/a	Ken Wagner	57.563	n/a

1950 NASCAR Grand National Circuit Season

No.	Date	Site	Race Winner	Car	Speed	Lead Chgs	Ldrs	Caut.	C.Laps	Pole Winner	Speed	Winner Started
1	2/05/50	Daytona Beach, FL	Harold Kite	Lincoln	89.894	3	2	0	0	Joe Littlejohn	98.840	3rd
2	4/02/50	Charlotte, NC	Tim Flock	Lincoln	n/a	3	3	1	n/a	Red Byron	67.839	5th
3	4/16/50	Langhorne, PA	Curtis Turner	Olds	69.399	7	5	n/a	n/a	Tim Flock	n/a	n/a
4	5/21/50	Martinsville, VA	Curtis Turner	Olds	n/a	1	2	n/a	n/a	Buck Baker	n/a	n/a
5	5/30/50	Canfield, OH	Bill Rexford	Olds	n/a	2	2	n/a	n/a	Jimmy Forian	n/a	n/a
6	6/18/50	Vernon, NY	Bill Blair	Mercury	n/a	2	3	n/a	n/a	Chuck Mahoney	n/a	n/a
7	6/25/50	Dayton, OH	Jimmy Florian	Ford	63.351	6	4	n/a	n/a	Dick Linder	66.543	n/a
8	7/02/50	Rochester, NY	Curtis Turner	Olds	50.614	0	1	3	7	Curtis Turner	54.794	Pole
9	7/23/50	Charlotte, NC	Curtis Turner	Olds	n/a	0	1	n/a	n/a	Curtis Turner	n/a	Pole

No.	Date	Site	Race Winner	Car	Speed	Lead Chgs	Ldrs	Caut.	C.Laps	Pole Winner	Speed	Winner Started
10	8/13/50	Hillsboro, NC	Fireball Roberts	Olds	n/a	3	3	1	n/a	Dick Linder	n/a	15th
11	8/20/50	Dayton, OH	Dick Linder	Olds	n/a	3	3	n/a	n/a	Curtis Turner	n/a	2nd
12	8/27/50	Hamburg, NY	Dick Linder	Olds	50.747	4	3	1	n/a	Dick Linder	53.113	Pole
13	9/04/50	Darlington, SC	Johnny Mantz	Plymouth	75.250	4	4	2	13	Curtis Turner	82.034	43rd
14	9/17/50	Langhorne, PA	Fonty Flock	Olds	72.801	4	3	n/a	n/a	Wally Campbell	77.104	n/a
15	9/24/50	N.Wilkesboro, NC	Leon Sales	Plymouth	n/a	5	4	n/a	n/a	Fireball Roberts	73.266	11th
16	10/01/50	Vernon, NY	Dick Linder	Olds	n/a	2	2	n/a	n/a	Dick Linder	n/a	Pole
17	10/15/50	Martinsville, VA	Herb Thomas	Plymouth	n/a	2	3	n/a	n/a	Fonty Flock	54.761	19th
18	10/15/50	Winchester, IN	Lloyd Moore	Mercury	63.875	2	3	n/a	n/a	Dick Linder	68.834	n/a
19	10/29/50	Hillsboro, NC	Lee Petty	Plymouth	n/a	5	3	1	n/a	Fonty Flock	85.898	15th

1951 NASCAR Grand National Circuit Season

No.	Date	Site	Race Winner	Car	Speed	Lead Chgs	Ldrs	Caut.	C.Laps	Pole Winner	Speed	Winner Started
1	2/11/51	Daytona Beach, FL	Marshall Teague	Hudson	82.238	1	2	0	0	Tim Flock	102.200	6th
2	4/01/51	Charlotte, NC	Curtis Turner	Nash	70.545	1	2	n/a	n/a	Fonty Flock	68.337	7th
3	4/08/51	Mobile, AL	Tim Flock	Olds	50.260	3	2	n/a	n/a	No Time Trials	NTT	2nd
4	4/08/51	Gardena, CA	Marshall Teague	Hudson	61.047	1	1	1	n/a	Andy Pierce	62.959	2nd
5	4/15/51	Hillsboro, NC	Fonty Flock	Olds	80.889	0	1	1	7	Fonty Flock	88.287	Pole
6	4/22/51	Phoenix, AZ	Marshall Teague	Hudson	60.153	3	2	n/a	n/a	Fonty Flock	70.936	n/a
7	4/29/51	N.Wilkesboro, NC	Fonty Flock	Olds	n/a	0	1	n/a	n/a	Fonty Flock	72.184	Pole
8	5/06/51	Martinsville, VA	Curtis Turner	Olds	n/a	7	4	n/a	n/a	Tim Flock	55.062	7th
9	5/30/51	Canfield, OH	Marshall Teague	Hudson	49.308	n/a	n/a	n/a	n/a	Bill Rexford	54.233	1st
10	6/10/51	Columbus, OH	Tim Flock	Olds	n/a	1	1	4	n/a	Gober Sosebee	57.766	2nd
11	6/15/51	Columbia, SC	Frank Mundy	Stude	50.683	3	2	n/a	n/a	Frank Mundy	57.563	Pole
12	6/24/51	Dayton, OH	Curtis Turner	Olds	n/a	1	2	n/a	n/a	Tim Flock	70.838	n/a
13	6/30/51	Gardena, CA	Lou Figaro	Hudson	n/a	0	1	1	n/a	Lou Figaro	76.988	Pole
14	7/01/51	Grand Rapids, MI	Marshall Teague	Hudson	n/a	1	2	n/a	n/a	Tim Flock	n/a	Pole
15	7/08/51	Bainbridge, OH	Fonty Flock	Olds	65.753	0	1	n/a	n/a	Fonty Flock	n/a	Pole
16	7/15/51	Pittsburgh, PA	Herb Thomas	Olds	n/a	1	2	n/a	n/a	Fonty Flock	61.983	n/a
17	7/29/51	Weaverville, NC	Fonty Flock	Olds	n/a	0	1	n/a	n/a	Billy Carden	64.608	Pole
18	7/31/51	Rochester, NY	Lee Petty	Plymouth	n/a	1	2	n/a	n/a	Fonty Flock	n/a	n/a
19	8/01/51	Altamont, NY	Fonty Flock	Olds	n/a	0	1	n/a	n/a	Fonty Flock	n/a	Pole
20	8/12/51	Detroit, MI	Tommy Thompson	Chrysler	57.588	12	6	5	n/a	Marshall Teague	69.131	5th
21	8/19/51	Toledo, OH	Tim Flock	Olds	50.847	3	3	2	n/a	Fonty Flock	55.521	4th
22	8/24/51	Morristown, NJ	Tim Flock	Olds	n/a	2	2	n/a	n/a	Tim Flock	58.670	Pole
23	8/25/51	Greenville, SC	Bob Flock	Olds	n/a	n/a	n/a	n/a	n/a	n/a	n/a	n/a
24	9/03/51	Darlington, SC	Herb Thomas	Hudson	76.906	6	5	4	26	Frank Mundy	84.173	2nd
25	9/07/51	Columbia, SC	Tim Flock	Olds	n/a	2	1	2	25	Tim Flock	58.843	Pole
26	9/08/51	Macon, GA	Herb Thomas	Plymouth	53.222	2	3	n/a	n/a	Bob Flock	54.266	6th
27	9/15/51	Langhorne, PA	Herb Thomas	Hudson	71.043	2	3	n/a	n/a	Fonty Flock	81.733	3rd
28	9/23/51	Charlotte, NC	Herb Thomas	Hudson	n/a	5	3	n/a	n/a	Billy Carden	66.914	n/a
29	9/23/51	Dayton, OH	Fonty Flock	Olds	n/a	0	1	2	n/a	Fonty Flock	n/a	Pole
30	9/30/51	Wilson, NC	Fonty Flock	Olds	n/a	n/a	n/a	n/a	n/a	Fonty Flock	n/a	Pole
31	10/07/51	Hillsboro, NC	Herb Thomas	Hudson	72.454	2	2	n/a	n/a	Herb Thomas	79.628	Pole
32	10/12/51	Thompson, CT	Neil Cole	Olds	n/a	4	4	1	3	Neil Cole	59.269	Pole
33	10/14/51	Shippenville, PA	Tim Flock	Olds	n/a	n/a	n/a	n/a	n/a	n/a	n/a	n/a
34	10/14/51	Martinsville, VA	Frank Mundy	Olds	n/a	4	5	1	n/a	Herb Thomas	56.109	3rd
35	10/14/51	Oakland, CA	Marvin Burke	Mercury	78.748	n/a	n/a	n/a	n/a	n/a	n/a	4th
36	10/21/51	N.Wilkesboro, NC	Fonty Flock	Olds	67.791	1	2	n/a	n/a	Herb Thomas	68.828	4th
37	10/28/51	Hanford, CA	Danny Weinberg	Stude	n/a	n/a	n/a	n/a	n/a	n/a	n/a	n/a
38	11/04/51	Jacksonville, FL	Herb Thomas	Hudson	53.412	n/a	n/a	n/a	n/a	Herb Thomas	64.818	Pole
39	11/11/51	Atlanta, GA	Tim Flock	Hudson	59.960	2	3	n/a	n/a	Frank Mundy	74.013	4th
40	11/11/51	Gardena, CA	Bill Norton	Mercury	n/a	5	4	n/a	n/a	Fonty Flock	n/a	10th
41	11/25/51	Mobile, AL	Frank Mundy	Stude	n/a	0	1	2	9	Frank Mundy	61.113	Pole

1952 NASCAR Grand National Circuit Season

No.	Date	Site	Race Winner	Car	Speed	Lead Chgs	Ldrs	Caut.	C.Laps	Pole Winner	Speed	Winner Started
1	1/20/52	W.Palm Beach, FL	Tim Flock	Hudson	n/a	0	1	2	n/a	Tim Flock	64.794	Pole
2	2/10/52	Daytona Beach, FL	Marshall Teague	Hudson	85.612	2	2	0	0	Pat Kirkwood	110.970	11th
3	3/16/52	Jacsonoville, FL	Marshall Teague	Hudson	55.197	0	1	1	4	Marshall Teague	60.100	Pole
4	3/30/52	N.Wilkesboro, NC	Herb Thomas	Hudson	58.597	0	1	n/a	n/a	Herb Thomas	75.075	Pole
5	4/06/52	Martinsville, VA	Dick Rathmann	Hudson	42.862	7	5	5	n/a	Buck Baker	54.945	9th
6	4/12/52	Columbia, SC	Buck Baker	Hudson	53.460	3	3	n/a	n/a	Buck Baker	n/a	Pole
7	4/20/52	Atlanta, GA	Bill Blair	Olds	66.877	3	4	n/a	n/a	Tim Flock	n/a	7th
8	4/27/52	Macon, GA	Herb Thomas	Hudson	53.853	1	2	n/a	n/a	Jack Smith	54.429	4th
9	5/04/52	Langhorne, PA	Dick Rathmann	Hudson	67.669	1	1	n/a	n/a	Herb Thomas	76.045	2nd
10	5/10/52	Darlington, SC	Dick Rathmann	Hudson	83.818	7	5	n/a	n/a	No Time Trials	NTT	4th
11	5/18/52	Dayton, OH	Dick Rathmann	Hudson	65.526	2	2	1	n/a	Fonty Flock	71.884	3rd
12	5/30/52	Canfield, OH	Herb Thomas	Hudson	48.057	2	2	4	n/a	Dick Rathmann	58.102	4th
13	6/01/52	Augusta, GA	Gober Sosebee	Chrysler	n/a	1	1	n/a	n/a	Tommy Moon	51.561	2nd
14	6/01/52	Toledo, OH	Tim Flock	Hudson	47.175	1	2	n/a	n/a	Fonty Flock	57.034	4th
15	6/08/52	Hillsboro, NC	Tim Flock	Hudson	81.008	n/a	n/a	n/a	n/a	Fonty Flock	91.977	2nd
16	6/15/52	Charlotte, NC	Herb Thomas	Hudson	64.820	1	2	3	n/a	Fonty Flock	70.038	2nd
17	6/29/52	Detroit, MI	Tim Flock	Hudson	59.908	4	4	n/a	n/a	Dick Rathmann	70.230	16th
18	7/01/52	Niagara Falls, ONT	Buddy Shuman	Hudson	45.610	1	2	3	n/a	Herb Thomas	52.401	8th
19	7/04/52	Owego, NY	Tim Flock	Hudson	56.603	n/a	n/a	n/a	n/a	Tim Flock	67.699	Pole
20	7/06/52	Monroe, MI	Tim Flock	Hudson	44.499	n/a	n/a	n/a	n/a	Tim Fock	57.600	Pole
21	7/11/52	Morristown, NJ	Lee Petty	Plymouth	59.661	2	3	n/a	n/a	Herb Thomas	60.996	3rd
22	7/20/52	South Bend, IN	Tim Flock	Hudson	41.889	1	2	n/a	n/a	Herb Thomas	58.120	2nd
23	8/15/52	Rochester, NY	Tim Flock	Hudson	n/a	3	3	n/a	n/a	No Time Trials	NTT	22nd
24	8/17/52	Weaverville, NC	Bob Flock	Hudson	57.288	n/a	n/a	n/a	n/a	Herb Thomas	64.888	6th
25	9/01/52	Darlington, SC	Fonty Flock	Olds	74.512	6	4	7	40	Fonty Flock	88.550	Pole
26	9/07/52	Macon, GA	Lee Petty	Plymouth	48.404	3	4	n/a	n/a	Fonty Flock	59.113	8th
27	9/14/52	Langhorne, PA	Lee Petty	Plymouth	72.463	5	5	n/a	n/a	Herb Thomas	85.287	24th
28	9/21/52	Dayton, OH	Dick Rathmann	Hudson	61.643	3	3	n/a	n/a	Fonty Flock	71.741	3rd
29	9/28/52	Wilson, NC	Herb Thomas	Hudson	35.398	n/a	n/a	n/a	n/a	Herb Thomas	55.883	Pole
30	10/12/52	Hillsboro, NC	Fonty Flock	Olds	73.489	2	1	2	n/a	Bill Blair	75.901	4th
31	10/19/52	Martinsville, VA	Herb Thomas	Hudson	47.566	7	3	n/a	n/a	Perk Brown	55.333	2nd
32	10/26/52	N.Wilkesboro, NC	Herb Thomas	Hudson	67.044	2	1	3	12	Herb Thomas	76.013	Pole

| 33 | 11/16/52 | Atlanta, GA | Donald Thomas | Hudson | 64.853 | 6 | 4 | 3 | n/a | Donald Thomas | 72.874 | Pole |
| 34 | 11/30/52 | W.Palm Beach, FL | Herb Thomas | Hudson | 58.008 | 0 | 1 | n/a | n/a | Herb Thomas | 63.716 | Pole |

1953 NASCAR Grand National Circuit Season

No.	Date	Site	Race Winner	Car	Speed	Lead Chgs	Ldrs	Caut.	C.Laps	Pole Winner	Speed	Winner Started
1	2/01/53	W.Palm Beach, FL	Lee Petty	Dodge	60.220	2	3	n/a	n/a	Dick Rathmann	65.023	7th
2	2/15/53	Daytona Beach, FL	Bill Blair	Olds	89.789	2	2	0	0	Bob Pronger	115.770	6th
3	3/08/53	Spring Lake, NC	Herb Thomas	Hudson	48.826	0	1	n/a	n/a	Herb Thomas	51.918	Pole
4	3/29/53	N.Wilkesboro, NC	Herb Thomas	Hudson	71.907	6	5	n/a	n/a	Herb Thomas	78.424	Pole
5	4/05/53	Charlotte, NC	Dick Passwater	Olds	n/a	16	6	n/a	n/a	Tim Flock	71.108	9th
6	4/19/53	Richmond, VA	Lee Petty	Dodge	45.535	n/a	n/a	n/a	n/a	Buck Baker	48.565	n/a
7	4/26/53	Macon, GA	Dick Rathmann	Hudson	56.417	2	3	n/a	n/a	n/a	n/a	n/a
8	5/03/53	Langhorne, PA	Buck Baker	Olds	72.743	5	4	n/a	n/a	No Time Trials	NTT	25th
9	5/09/53	Columbia, SC	Buck Baker	Olds	53.707	n/a	n/a	n/a	n/a	Herb Thomas	58.67	3rd
10	5/16/53	Hickory, NC	Tim Flock	Hudson	n/a	n/a	n/a	n/a	n/a	n/a	n/a	n/a
11	5/17/53	Martinsville, VA	Lee Petty	Dodge	n/a	3	3	n/a	n/a	n/a	n/a	n/a
12	5/24/53	Columbus, OH	Herb Thomas	Hudson	56.127	n/a	n/a	n/a	n/a	Fonty Flock	59.288	2nd
13	5/30/53	Raleigh, NC	Fonty Flock	Hudson	70.629	6	6	n/a	n/a	Slick Smith	76.230	43rd
14	6/07/53	Shreveport, LA	Lee Petty	Dodge	53.199	n/a	n/a	n/a	n/a	Herb Thomas	58.727	n/a
15	6/14/53	Pensacola, FL	Herb Thomas	Hudson	63.316	n/a	n/a	n/a	n/a	Dick Rathmann	n/a	n/a
16	6/21/53	Langhorne, PA	Dick Rathmann	Hudson	64.434	1	1	4	n/a	Lloyd Shaw	82.200	2nd
17	6/23/53	High Point, NC	Herb Thomas	Hudson	58.186	n/a	n/a	n/a	n/a	Herb Thomas	66.152	Pole
18	6/28/53	Wilson, NC	Fonty Flock	Hudson	53.803	n/a	n/a	n/a	n/a	n/a	n/a	n/a
19	7/03/53	Rochester, NY	Herb Thomas	Hudson	56.939	1	2	n/a	n/a	No Time Trials	NTT	n/a
20	7/04/53	Spartanburg, SC	Lee Petty	Dodge	56.934	n/a	n/a	n/a	n/a	Buck Baker	58.027	n/a
21	7/10/53	Morristown, NJ	Dick Rathmann	Hudson	69.417	5	2	n/a	n/a	Herb Thomas	61.061	2nd
22	7/12/53	Atlanta, GA	Herb Thomas	Hudson	70.685	2	2	n/a	n/a	Herb Thomas	72.756	Pole
23	7/22/53	Rapid City, SD	Herb Thomas	Hudson	57.270	n/a	n/a	n/a	n/a	Herb Thomas	55.727	Pole
24	7/26/53	North Platte, NE	Dick Rathmann	Hudson	54.380	n/a	n/a	n/a	n/a	Herb Thomas	54.397	n/a
25	8/02/53	Davenport, IA	Herb Thomas	Hudson	62.500	n/a	n/a	n/a	n/a	Buck Baker	54.397	n/a
26	8/09/53	Hillsboro, NC	Curtis Turner	Olds	75.125	0	1	2	n/a	Curtis Turner	89.078	Pole
27	8/16/53	Weaverville, NC	Fonty Flock	Hudson	62.434	n/a	n/a	n/a	n/a	Curtis Turner	n/a	n/a
28	8/23/53	Norfolk, VA	Herb Thomas	Hudson	51.040	n/a	n/a	n/a	n/a	Curtis Turner	54.200	n/a
29	8/29/53	Hickory, NC	Fonty Flock	Hudson	n/a	1	2	n/a	n/a	Tim Flock	79.362	2nd
30	9/07/53	Darlington, SC	Buck Baker	Olds	92.881	35	4	4	17	Fonty Flock	107.983	7th
31	9/13/53	Macon, GA	Speedy Thompson	Olds	55.172	7	5	n/a	n/a	Joe Eubanks	60.811	n/a
32	9/20/53	Langhorne, PA	Dick Rathmann	Hudson	67.046	4	3	4	n/a	Herb Thomas	n/a	n/a
33	10/03/53	Bloomsburg, PA	Herb Thomas	Hudson	n/a	n/a	n/a	n/a	n/a	Jim Paschal	55.935	n/a
34	10/04/53	Wilson, NC	Herb Thomas	Hudson	56.022	0	1	n/a	n/a	Herb Thomas	56.962	Pole
35	10/11/53	N.Wilkesboro, NC	Speedy Thompson	Olds	71.202	13	4	3	16	Buck Baker	78.288	n/a
36	10/18/53	Martinsville, VA	Jim Paschal	Dodge	56.013	2	2	n/a	n/a	Fonty Flock	58.958	n/a
37	11/01/53	Atlanta, GA	Buck Baker	Olds	63.18	3	4	n/a	n/a	Tim Flock	73.58	n/a

1954 NASCAR Grand National Circuit Season

No.	Date	Site	Race Winner	Car	Speed	Lead Chgs	Ldrs	Caut.	C.Laps	Pole Winner	Speed	Winner Started
1	2/07/54	W.Palm Beach, FL	Herb Thomas	Hudson	58.958	5	4	1	2	Dick Rathmann	66.371	3rd
2	2/21/54	Daytona Beach, FL	Lee Petty	Chrysler	89.108	2	2	0	0	Lee Petty	123.410	Pole
3	3/07/54	Jacksonville, FL	Herb Thomas	Hudson	56.461	4	3	n/a	n/a	Curtis Turner	63.581	2nd
4	3/21/54	Atlanta, GA	Herb Thomas	Hudson	60.494	2	2	2	n/a	Herb Thomas	75.514	Pole
5	3/28/54	Savannah, GA	Al Keller	Hudson	59.820	1	2	n/a	n/a	Herb Thomas	63.202	3rd
6	3/28/54	Oakland, CA	Dick Rathmann	Hudson	50.692	n/a	n/a	n/a	n/a	Hershel McGriff	55.624	26th
7	4/04/54	N. Wilkesboro, NC	Dick Rathmann	Hudson	68.545	3	2	n/a	n/a	Gober Sosebee	78.698	2nd
8	4/18/54	Hillsboro, NC	Herb Thoas	Hudson	77.386	2	3	1	n/a	Buck Baker	86.767	4th
9	4/25/54	Macon, GA	Gober Sosebee	Olds	55.410	6	4	n/a	n/a	Dick Rathmann	57.859	7th
10	5/02/54	Langhorne, PA	Herb Thomas	Hudson	74.883	1	2	1	n/a	Lee Petty	87.217	2nd
11	5/09/54	Wilson, NC	Buck Baker	Olds	52.279	5	3	n/a	n/a	Jim Paschal	55.469	5th
12	5/16/54	Martinsville, VA	Jim Paschal	Olds	46.153	2	2	3	n/a	No Time Trials	NTT	n/a
13	5/23/54	Sharon, PA	Lee Petty	Chrysler	n/a	2	3	n/a	n/a	Dick Rathmann	62.090	n/a
14	5/29/54	Raleigh, NC	Herb Thomas	Hudson	73.909	7	4	0	0	Herb Thomas	76.660	Pole
15	5/30/54	Charlotte, NC	Buck Baker	Olds	49.805	3	2	2	26	Al Keller	68.947	2nd
16	5/30/54	Gardena, CA	John Soares	Dodge	53.438	2	3	n/a	n/a	Danny Letner	62.849	17th
17	6/06/54	Columbia, SC	Curtis Turner	Olds	56.719	n/a	n/a	n/a	n/a	Buck Baker	62.240	10th
18	6/13/54	Linden, NJ	Al Keller	Jaguar	77.569	4	3	4	n/a	Buck Baker	80.536	7th
19	6/19/54	Hickory, NC	Herb Thomas	Hudson	82.872	0	1	n/a	n/a	Herb Thomas	81.669	Pole
20	6/25/54	Rochester, NY	Lee Petty	Chrysler	52.455	1	2	n/a	n/a	Herb Thomas	60.422	n/a
21	6/17/54	Mechanicsburg, PA	Herb Thomas	Hudson	51.085	5	2	n/a	n/a	Dick Rathmann	54.945	n/a
22	7/03/54	Spartanburg, SC	Herb Thomas	Hudson	59.181	n/a	n/a	n/a	n/a	Hershel McGriff	58.120	n/a
23	7/04/54	Weaverville, NC	Herb Thomas	Hudson	61.318	n/a	n/a	n/a	n/a	Herb Thomas	67.771	Pole
24	7/10/54	Willow Springs, IL	Dick Rathmann	Hudson	72.216	1	2	n/a	n/a	Buck Baker	75.662	5th
25	7/11/54	Grand Rapids, MI	Lee Petty	Chrysler	52.090	2	3	n/a	n/a	Herb Thomas	59.055	n/a
26	7/30/54	Morristown, NJ	Buck Baker	Olds	58.968	2	2	n/a	n/a	Buck Baker	66.666	Pole
27	8/01/54	Oakland, CA	Danny Petner	Hudson	53.045	n/a	n/a	n/a	n/a	Marvin Panch	55.248	n/a
28	8/13/54	Charlotte, NC	Lee Petty	Chrysler	51.362	n/a	n/a	n/a	n/a	Buck Baker	57.270	n/a
29	8/22/54	San Mateo, CA	Hershel McGriff	Olds	64.710	n/a	n/a	n/a	n/a	Hershel McGriff	75.566	Pole
30	8/09/54	Corbin, KY	Lee Petty	Chrysler	63.080	n/a	n/a	n/a	n/a	Jim Paschal	65.789	n/a
31	9/06/54	Darlington, SC	Herb Thomas	Hudson	95.026	12	6	2	4	Buck Baker	108.261	23rd
32	9/12/54	Macon, GA	Hershel McGriff	Olds	50.527	1	2	n/a	n/a	Tim Flock	56.907	n/a
33	9/24/54	Charlotte, NC	Hershel McGriff	Olds	53.167	n/a	n/a	n/a	n/a	Hershel McGriff	54.054	Pole
34	9/26/54	Langhorne, PA	Herb Thomas	Hudson	71.186	8	4	6	25	Herb Thomas	89.418	Pole
35	10/10/54	LeHi, AR	Buck Baker	Olds	89.013	2	2	n/a	n/a	Junior Johnson	n/a	n/a
36	10/17/54	Martinsville, VA	Lee Petty	Chrysler	44.547	4	2	3	n/a	Lee Petty	53.191	Pole
37	10/24/54	N.Wilkesboro, NC	Hershel McGriff	Olds	65.175	4	2	4	n/a	Hershel McGriff	77.612	Pole

1955 NASCAR Grand National Circuit Season

No.	Date	Site	Race Winner	Car	Speed	Lead Chgs	Ldrs	Caut.	C.Laps	Pole Winner	Speed	Winner Started
1	11/07/54	High Point, NC	Lee Petty	Chrysler	62.882	2	2	n/a	n/a	Herb Thomas	71.942	3rd
2	2/06/55	W.Palm Beach, FL	Herb Thomas	Hudson	56.013	11	2	n/a	n/a	Dick Rathmann	65.454	2nd
3	2/13/55	Jacksonville, FL	Lee Petty	Chrysler	69.031	8	3	n/a	n/a	Dick Rathmann	63.514	2nd
4	2/27/55	Daytona Beach, FL	Tim Flock	Chrysler	91.999	0	1	0	0	Tim Flock	130.293	Pole
5	2/06/55	Savannah, GA	Lee Petty	Chrysler	60.150	1	2	n/a	n/a	Dick Rathmann	62.805	6th
6	3/26/55	Columbia, SC	Fonty Flock	Chevrolet	n/a	1	2	n/a	n/a	Tim Flock	n/a	n/a
7	3/27/55	Hillsboro, NC	Jim Paschal	Olds	82.304	1	2	1	n/a	Tim Flock	91.696	3rd
8	4/03/55	N.Wilkesboro, NC	Buck Baker	Olds	73.126	0	1	n/a	n/a	Dink Widenhouse	77.720	2nd
9	4/17/55	Montgomery, AL	Tim Flock	Chrysler	60.872	3	3	n/a	n/a	Jim Paschal	64.290	5th
10	4/24/55	Langhorne, PA	Tim Flock	Chrysler	72.893	0	1	3	n/a	Tim Flock	86.699	Pole
11	5/01/55	Charlotte, NC	Buck Baker	Buick	52.630	2	2	2	18	Herb Thomas	70.184	16th
12	5/07/55	Hickory, NC	Junior Johnson	Olds	58.823	5	4	6	32	Tim Flock	64.478	2nd
13	5/08/55	Phoenix, AZ	Tim Flock	Chrysler	71.485	1	1	n/a	n/a	Bill Amick	75.519	2nd
14	5/15/55	Tucson, AZ	Danny Letner	Olds	51.428	7	5	n/a	n/a	Bill Amick	56.179	3rd
15	5/15/55	Martinsville, VA	Tim Flock	Chrysler	52.554	2	2	2	n/a	Jim Paschal	58.823	4th
16	5/22/55	Richmond, VA	Tim Flock	Chrysler	54.298	4	3	n/a	n/a	No Time Trials	NTT	22nd
17	5/28/55	Raleigh, NC	Junior Johnson	Olds	50.522	1	2	6	20	Tim Flock	58.612	3rd
18	5/29/55	Winston-Salem, NC	Lee Petty	Chrysler	50.583	2	3	8	n/a	Fonty Flock	56.710	9th
19	6/10/55	New Oxford, PA	Junior Johnson	Olds	65.371	3	3	n/a	n/a	Junior Johnson	75.853	Pole
20	6/17/55	Rochester, NY	Tim Flock	Chrysler	57.170	1	1	2	8	Buck Baker	61.141	3rd
21	6/18/55	Fonda, NY	Junior Johnson	Olds	58.413	1	2	1	4	Fonty Flock	61.770	9th
22	6/19/55	Plattsburg, NY	Lee Petty	Chrysler	59.074	2	2	0	0	Lee Petty	55.744	Pole
23	6/24/55	Charlotte, NC	Tim Flock	Chrysler	51.289	0	1	n/a	n/a	Tim Flock	57.915	Pole
24	7/06/55	Spartanburg, SC	Tim Flock	Chrysler	49.106	0	1	6	n/a	Tim Flock	58.517	Pole
25	7/09/55	Columbia, SC	Jim Paschal	Olds	55.469	n/a	n/a	n/a	n/a	Jimmie Lewallen	59.741	5th
26	7/10/55	Weaverville, NC	Tim Fock	Chryser	62.739	0	1	n/a	n/a	Tim Flock	69.310	Pole
27	7/15/55	Morristown, NJ	Tim Flock	Chrysler	58.092	2	2	1	n/a	Tim Flock	63.649	Pole
28	7/29/55	Altamont, NY	Junior Johnson	Olds	n/a	4	3	n/a	n/a	Tim Flock	56.603	7th
29	7/30/55	Syracuse, NY	Tim Flock	Chrysler	76.522	0	1	0	0	Tim Flock	78.311	Pole
30	7/31/55	San Mateo, CA	Tim Flock	Chrysler	68.571	4	3	n/a	n/a	Fonty Flock	79.330	Pole
31	8/05/55	Charlotte, NC	Jim Paschal	Olds	48.806	1	2	n/a	n/a	Tim Flock	57.859	3rd
32	8/07/55	Winston-Salem, NC	Lee Petty	Dodge	50.111	1	2	n/a	n/a	Tim Flock	59.016	3rd
33	8/14/55	LeHi, AR	Fonty Flock	Chrysler	89.892	2	2	0	0	Fonty Flock	99.944	Pole
34	8/20/55	Raleigh, NC	Herb Thoams	Buick	76.400	4	3	0	0	Tim Flock	78.722	3rd
35	9/05/55	Darlington, SC	Herb Thomas	Chevrolet	92.281	10	7	8	51	Fireball Roberts	110.682	8th
36	9/11/55	Montgomery, AL	Tim Flock	Chrysler	63.733	0	1	n/a	n/a	Tim Flock	68.728	Pole
37	9/18/55	Langhorne, PA	Tim Fock	Chrysler	77.888	4	3	3	n/a	Tim Flock	92.095	Pole
38	9/30/55	Raleigh, NC	Fonty Flock	Chrysler	73.289	4	3	3	n/a	Fonty Flock	82.098	Pole
39	10/06/55	Greenville, SC	Tim Flock	Chrysler	57.942	1	1	1	n/a	Bob Welborn	58.037	2nd
40	10/09/55	LeHi, AR	Speedy Thompson	Ford	83.948	2	2	n/a	n/a	Fonty Flock	100.390	10th
41	10/15/55	Columbia, SC	Tim Flock	Chrysler	55.393	3	2	n/a	n/a	Junior Johnson	61.728	2nd
42	10/16/55	Martinsville, VA	Speedy Thompson	Chrysler	59.210	7	5	3	n/a	No Time Trials	NTT	17th
43	10/16/55	Las Vegas, NV	Norm Nelson	Chrysler	44.449	2	2	n/a	n/a	Norm Nelson	74.518	Pole
44	10/23/55	N.Wilkesboro, NC	Buck Baker	Ford	72.347	0	1	3	n/a	Buck Baker	79.815	Pole
45	10/30/55	Hillsboro, NC	Tim Flock	Chrysler	70.465	0	1	3	n/a	Tim Flock	81.673	Pole

1956 NASCAR Grand National Circuit Season

No.	Date	Site	Race Winner	Car	Speed	Lead Chgs	Ldrs	Caut.	C.Laps	Pole Winner	Speed	Winner Started
1	11/13/55	Hickory, NC	Tim Flock	Chrysler	56.962	2	2	4	23	Tim Flock	n/a	Pole
2	11/20/55	Charlotte, NC	Fonty Flock	Chrysler	61.825	0	1	2	7	Fonty Flock	70.496	Pole
3	11/20/55	Lancaster, CA	Chuck Stevenson	Ford	66.512	7	2	0	0	Jim Reed	76.556	2nd
4	12/11/55	W.Palm Beach, FL	Herb Thomas	Chevrolet	65.009	1	2	n/a	n/a	Fonty Flock	78.912	3rd
5	1/22/56	Phoenix, AZ	Buck Baker	Chrysler	64.408	n/a	n/a	n/a	n/a	Joe Weatherly	71.315	12th
6	2/26/56	Daytona Beach, FL	Tim Flock	Chrysler	90.657	2	2	2	2	Tim Flock	135.747	Pole
7	3/04/56	W.Palm Beach, FL	Billy Myers	Mercury	68.990	2	3	1	3	Buck Baker	81.081	2nd
8	3/18/56	Wilson, NC	Herb Thomas	Chevrolet	46.287	n/a	n/a	n/a	n/a	Herb Thomas	57.197	Pole
9	3/25/56	Atlanta, GA	Buck Baker	Chrysler	70.643	1	1	n/a	n/a	Tim Flock	82.154	23rd
10	4/08/56	N.Wilkesboro, NC	Tim Flock	Chrysler	71.034	2	3	n/a	n/a	Tim Flock	78.370	Pole
11	4/22/56	Langhorne, PA	Buck Baker	Chrysler	75.928	2	2	n/a	n/a	Buck Baker	104.590	Pole
12	4/29/56	Richmond, VA	Buck Baker	Dodge	56.232	2	2	n/a	n/a	Buck Baker	67.091	Pole
13	5/05/56	Columbia, SC	Speedy Thompson	Dodge	54.545	3	3	2	n/a	Buck Baker	63.274	2nd
14	5/06/56	Concord, NC	Speedy Thompson	Chrysler	61.633	2	2	1	3	Speedy Thompson	65.241	Pole
15	5/10/56	Greenvville, SC	Buck Baker	Dodge	60.362	n/a	n/a	n/a	n/a	Rex White	61.100	2nd
16	5/12/56	Hickory, NC	Speedy Thompson	Chrysler	59.442	0	1	6	n/a	Speedy Thompson	67.447	Pole
17	5/13/56	Hillsboro, NC	Buck Baker	Chrysler	83.720	2	2	n/a	n/a	Buck Baker	89.305	Pole
18	5/20/56	Martinsville, VA	Buck Baker	Dodge	60.824	5	3	7	20	Buck Baker	66.103	Pole
19	5/25/56	Abottstown, PA	Buck Baker	Dodge	69.619	3	3	n/a	n/a	Speedy Thompson	n/a	5th
20	5/27/56	Charlotte, NC	Speedy Thompson	Chrysler	64.866	6	2	3	9	Speedy Thompson	76.966	Pole
21	5/27/56	Portland, OR	Herb Thomas	Chrysler	63.815	n/a	n/a	n/a	n/a	John Kieper	67.230	18th
22	5/30/56	Eureka, CA	Herb Thomas	Chrysler	38.814	n/a	n/a	n/a	n/a	John Kieper	66.040	6th
23	5/30/56	Syracuse, NY	Buck Baker	Chrysler	86.179	2	2	1	3	Buck Baker	83.975	Pole
24	6/03/56	Merced, CA	Herb Thomas	Chrysler	47.325	n/a	n/a	n/a	n/a	Herb Thomas	58.234	Pole
25	6/10/56	LeHi, AR	Ralph Moody	Ford	74.313	5	4	5	n/a	Buck Baker	98.504	23rd
26	6/15/56	Charlotte, NC	Speedy Thompson	Chrysler	56.022	3	2	2	6	Fireball Roberts	59.661	2nd
27	6/22/56	Rochester, NY	Speedy Thompson	Chrysler	57.288	3	3	1	7	Jim Paschal	57.434	11th
28	6/24/56	Portland, OR	John Kieper	Olds	62.586	4	3	n/a	n/a	Herb Thomas	65.934	12th
29	7/01/56	Weaverville, NC	Lee Petty	Dodge	56.435	n/a	n/a	n/a	n/a	Fireball Roberts	72.260	11th
30	7/04/56	Raleigh, NC	Fireball Roberts	Ford	79.822	8	6	1	n/a	Lee Petty	82.587	32nd
31	7/07/56	Spartanburg, SC	Lee Petty	Dodge	50.483	n/a	n/a	n/a	n/a	Fireball Roberts	58.900	8th
32	7/08/56	Sacramento, CA	Lloyd Dane	Mercury	74.074	3	4	n/a	n/a	Eddie Pagan	76.612	15th
33	7/21/56	Chicago, IL	Fireball Roberts	Ford	61.037	n/a	n/a	n/a	n/a	Billy Myers	n/a	3rd
34	7/27/56	Shelby, NC	Speedy Thompson	Dodge	53.699	n/a	n/a	n/a	n/a	Ralph Moody	55.658	2nd
35	7/29/56	Montgomery, AL	Marvin Panch	Ford	67.252	n/a	n/a	n/a	n/a	Marvin Panch	69.444	Pole
36	8/03/56	Oklahoma City, OK	Jim Paschal	Mercury	60.100	2	3	0	0	Speedy Thompson	64.655	8th
37	8/12/56	Elkhart Lake, WI	Tim Flock	Mercury	73.858	4	4	0	0	Frank Mundy	n/a	6th
38	8/17/56	Old Bridge, NJ	Ralph Moody	Ford	65.170	1	2	n/a	n/a	Jim Reed	72.028	n/a
39	8/19/56	San Mateo, CA	Eddie Pagan	Ford	68.161	n/a	n/a	n/a	n/a	Eddie Pagan	81.614	Pole

40	8/22/56	Norfolk, VA	Billy Myers	Mercury	56.408	n/a	n/a	n/a	n/a	Ralph Moody	58.631	9th
41	8/23/56	Spartanburg, SC	Ralph Moody	Ford	54.372	2	2	n/a	n/a	Ralph Moody	61.433	Pole
42	8/25/56	Myrtle Beach, SC	Fireball Roberts	Ford	50.576	n/a	n/a	n/a	n/a	Ralph Moody	58.346	3rd
43	8/26/56	Portland, OR	Royce Hagerty	Dodge	63.429	3	3	0	0	John Kieper	65.861	8th
44	9/03/56	Darlington, SC	Curtis Turner	Ford	95.167	14	6	7	68	Speedy Thompson	118.683	11th
45	9/09/56	Montgomery, AL	Buck Baker	Chrysler	60.893	3	4	n/a	n/a	Tim Flock	64.864	14th
46	9/12/56	Charlotte, NC	Ralph Moody	Ford	52.847	2	2	n/a	n/a	Joe Eubanks	59.464	11th
47	9/23/56	Langhorne, PA	Paul Goldsmith	Chevrolet	70.615	10	5	9	n/a	Buck Baker	93.628	2nd
48	9/23/56	Portland, OR	Lloyd Dane	Ford	n/a	5	3	n/a	n/a	Royce Hagerty	n/a	n/a
49	9/29/56	Columbia SC	Buck Baker	Dodge	61.193	4	3	n/a	n/a	Tim Flock	61.940	6th
50	9/30/56	Hillsboro, NC	Fireball Roberts	Ford	72.734	6	3	4	n/a	Speedy Thompson	88.067	6th
51	10/07/56	Newport, TN	Fireball Roberts	Ford	61.475	2	2	0	0	Joe Eubanks	65.597	14th
52	10/17/56	Charlotte, NC	Buck Baker	Chrysler	72.268	3	3	0	0	Ralph Moody	75.041	2nd
53	10/23/56	Shelby, NC	Buck Baker	Chrysler	54.054	n/a	n/a	2	n/a	Doug Cox	58.479	5th
54	10/28/56	Martinsville, VA	Jack Smith	Dodge	61.136	7	6	4	n/a	Buck Baker	67.643	23rd
55	11/11/56	Hickory, NC	Speedy Thompson	Chrysler	66.420	4	4	n/a	n/a	Ralph Earnhardt	68.278	9th
56	11/18/56	Wilson, NC	Buck Baker	Chrysler	50.597	3	3	n/a	n/a	Buck Baker	60.160	Pole

1957 NASCAR Grand National Circuit Season

No.	Date	Site	Race Winner	Car	Speed	Lead Chgs	Ldrs	Caut.	C.Laps	Pole Winner	Speed	Winner Started
1	11/11/56	Lancaster, PA	Marvin Panch	Ford	78.648	2	2	0	0	Marvin Panch	78.596	Pole
2	12/02/56	Concord, NC	Marvin Panch	Ford	55.883	1	2	n/a	n/a	Curtis Turner	62.586	3rd
3	12/30/56	Titusville, FL	Fireball Roberts	Ford	n/a	1	2	0	0	Paul Goldsmith	69.106	2nd
4	2/17/57	Daytona Beach, FL	Cotton Owens	Pontiac	101.541	5	2	1	1	Banjo Matthews	134.382	3rd
5	3/03/57	Concord, NC	Jack Smith	Chevrolet	59.860	5	3	1	n/a	Mel Larson	62.225	9th
6	3/17/57	Wilson, NC	Ralph Moody	Ford	55.079	1	2	n/a	n/a	Fireball Roberts	59.269	4th
7	3/24/57	Hillsboro, NC	Buck Baker	Chevrolet	82.233	5	3	n/a	n/a	Fireball Roberts	87.828	3rd
8	3/31/57	Weaverville, NC	Buck Baker	Chevrolet	65.693	2	3	n/a	n/a	Marvin Panch	73.649	3rd
9	4/07/56	N.Wilkesboro, NC	Fireball Roberts	Ford	75.015	0	1	2	5	Fireball Roberts	81.500	Pole
10	4/14/57	Langhorne, PA	Fireball Roberts	Ford	85.850	5	3	1	3	Paul Goldsmith	93.701	2nd
11	4/19/57	Charlotte, NC	Fireball Roberts	Ford	52.083	3	3	3	n/a	Marvin Panch	60.060	4th
12	4/27/57	Spartanburg, SC	Marvin Panch	Ford	55.130	n/a	n/a	n/a	n/a	Speedy Thompson	61.538	5th
13	4/28/57	Greensboro, NC	Paul Goldsmith	Ford	49.905	3	2	4	n/a	Buck Baker	50.120	2nd
14	4/28/57	Portland, OR	Art Watts	Ford	64.754	0	1	0	0	Art Watts	65.813	Pole
15	5/04/57	Shelby, NC	Fireball Roberts	Ford	54.861	5	4	2	n/a	Tiny Lund	57.544	2nd
16	5/05/57	Richmond, VA	Paul Goldsmith	Ford	62.445	2	2	n/a	n/a	Russ Hepler	64.239	7th
17	5/19/57	Martinsville, VA	Buck Baker	Chevrolet	57.318	5	4	3	51	Paul Goldsmith	65.693	14th
18	5/26/57	Portland, OR	Eddie Pagan	Ford	64.732	n/a	n/a	n/a	n/a	Art Watts	66.732	6th
19	5/30/57	Eureka, CA	Lloyd Dane	Ford	55.957	n/a	n/a	n/a	n/a	Parnelli Jones	63.92	5th
20	5/30/57	New Oxford, PA	Buck Baker	Chevrolet	76.126	n/a	n/a	1	n/a	Marvin Panch	78.238	2nd
21	6/01/57	Lancaster, SC	Paul Goldsmith	Ford	61.622	n/a	n/a	n/a	n/a	Buck Baker	67.365	7th
22	6/08/57	Los Angeles, CA	Eddie Pagan	Ford	n/a	n/a	n/a	n/a	n/a	Eddie Pagan	67.290	Pole
23	6/15/57	Newport, TN	Fireball Roberts	Ford	60.687	n/a	n/a	0	0	Speedy Thompson	61.813	5th
24	6/20/57	Columbia, SC	Jack Smith	Chevrolet	58.045	n/a	n/a	n/a	n/a	Buck Baker	64.585	3rd
25	6/22/57	Sacramento, CA	Bill Amick	Ford	59.580	n/a	n/a	n/a	n/a	Art Watts	69.337	3rd
26	6/29/57	Spartanburg, SC	Lee Petty	Olds	46.287	1	2	3	n/a	Lee Petty	59.642	Pole
27	7/30/57	Jacksonville, NC	Buck Baker	Chevrolet	55.342	n/a	n/a	n/a	n/a	Lee Petty	61.328	3rd
28	7/04/57	Raleigh, NC	Paul Goldsmith	Ford	75.693	8	3	2	14	Frankie Schneider	83.371	7th
29	7/12/57	Charlotte, NC	Marvin Panch	Ford	56.302	6	4	4	12	Tiny Lund	60.913	7th
30	7/14/57	LeHi, AR	Marvin Panch	Pontiac	67.167	4	4	2	34	Speedy Thompson	98.991	10th
31	7/14/57	Portland, OR	Eddie Pagan	Ford	64.539	n/a	n/a	n/a	n/a	Art Watts	66.396	2nd
32	7/20/57	Hickory, NC	Jack Smith	Chevrolet	58.737	8	6	n/a	n/a	Gwyn Staley	66.085	3rd
33	7/24/57	Norfolk, VA	Buck Baker	Chevrolet	47.987	n/a	n/a	n/a	n/a	Bill Amick	56.338	8th
34	7/30/57	Lancaster, SC	Speedy Thompson	Chevrolet	66.543	0	1	0	0	Speedy Thompson	67.694	Pole
35	8/04/57	Watkins Glen, NY	Buck Baker	Chevrolet	83.064	0	1	0	0	Buck Baker	87.071	Pole
36	8/04/57	Bremerton, WA	Parnelli Jones	Ford	38.959	n/a	n/a	n/a	n/a	Art Watts	62.657	3rd
37	8/10/57	New Oxford, PA	Marvin Panch	Ford	77.569	n/a	n/a	n/a	n/a	Tiny Lund	80.971	6th
38	8/16/57	Old Bridge, NJ	Lee Petty	Olds	65.813	4	3	1	4	Rex White	71.599	3rd
39	8/26/57	Myrtle Beach, SC	Gwyn Staley	Chevrolet	50.782	n/a	n/a	n/a	n/a	Johnny Allen	58.139	3rd
40	9/02/57	Darlington, SC	Speedy Thompson	Chevrolet	100.094	13	8	6	23	Cotton Owens	117.416	7th
41	9/05/57	Syracuse, NY	Gwyn Staley	Chevrolet	80.591	2	2	n/a	n/a	Gwyn Staley	83.045	Pole
42	9/08/57	Weaverville, NC	Lee Petty	Olds	67.950	5	4	1	10	Bill Amick	77.687	2nd
43	9/08/57	Sacramento, CA	Danny Graves	Chevrolet	68.663	n/a	n/a	n/a	n/a	Danny Graves	78.007	Pole
44	9/15/57	San Jose, CA	Marvin Porter	Ford	n/a	n/a	n/a	n/a	n/a	Lloyd Dane	n/a	12th
45	9/15/57	Langhorne, PA	Gwyn Staley	Chevrolet	72.759	n/a	n/a	n/a	n/a	Paul Goldsmith	92.072	25th
46	9/19/57	Columbia, SC	Buck Baker	Chevrolet	60.514	n/a	n/a	n/a	n/a	Buck Baker	63.649	Pole
47	9/21/57	Shelby, NC	Buck Baker	Chevrolet	53.699	6	4	4	19	Buck Baker	58.177	Pole
48	10/05/57	Charlotte, NC	Lee Petty	Olds	51.583	n/a	n/a	n/a	n/a	Lee Petty	60.585	Pole
49	10/06/57	Martinsville, VA	Bob Welborn	Chevrolet	63.025	6	4	4	14	Eddie Pagan	65.837	2nd
50	10/12/57	Newberry, SC	Fireball Roberts	Ford	50.398	3	4	n/a	n/a	Jack Smith	56.514	10th
51	10/13/57	Concord, NC	Fireball Roberts	Ford	59.553	6	4	5	n/a	Jack Smith	65.052	5th
52	10/20/57	N.Wilkesboro, NC	Jack Smith	Chevrolet	69.902	5	3	2	n/a	Fireball Roberts	81.640	4th
53	10/27/57	Greensboro, NC	Buck Baker	Chevrolet	38.927	4	2	n/a	n/a	Ken Rush	48.358	n/a

1958 NASCAR Grand National Circuit Season

No.	Date	Site	Race Winner	Car	Speed	Lead Chgs	Ldrs	Caut.	C.Laps	Pole Winner	Speed	Winner Started
1	11/03/57	Fayetteville, NC	Rex White	Chevrolet	59.170	3	3	0	0	Jack Smith	62.655	5th
2	2/23/58	Daytona Beach, FL	Paul Goldsmith	Pontiac	101.113	0	1	0	0	Paul Goldsmith	140.570	Pole
3	3/02/58	Concord, NC	Lee Petty	Olds	58.555	2	2	1	n/a	Speedy Thompson	n/a	n/a
4	3/15/58	Fayetteville, NC	Curtis Turner	Ford	56.141	3	3	1	n/a	Lee Petty	62.600	n/a
5	3/16/58	Wilson, NC	Lee Petty	Olds	48.459	4	3	n/a	n/a	Marvin Panch	58.901	6th
6	3/23/58	Hillsboro, NC	Buck Baker	Chevrolet	78.502	2	2	1	n/a	Buck Baker	83.076	Pole
7	4/05/58	Fayetteville, NC	Bob Welborn	Chevrolet	50.229	2	3	2	n/a	Lee Petty	60.576	2nd
8	4/10/58	Columbia, SC	Speedy Thompson	Chevrolet	n/a	n/a	n/a	n/a	n/a	Possum Jones	66.201	7th
9	4/12/58	Spartanburg, SC	Speedy Thompson	Chevrolet	56.613	n/a	n/a	n/a	n/a	Speedy Thompson	61.412	Pole
10	4/13/58	Atlanta, GA	Curtis Turner	Ford	79.016	3	2	0	0	Joe Weatherly	81.577	2nd

No.	Date	Site	Race Winner	Car	Speed	Lead Chgs	Ldrs	Caut.	C.Laps	Pole Winner	Speed	Winner Started
11	4/18/58	Charlotte, NC	Curtis Turner	Ford	53.254	0	1	3	8	Curtis Turner	57.471	Pole
12	4/20/58	Martinsville, VA	Bob Welborn	Chevrolet	66.166	5	4	4	n/a	Buck Baker	66.007	20th
13	4/25/58	Manassas, VA	Frankie Schneider	Chevrolet	67.590	n/a	n/a	n/a	n/a	Eddie Pagan	69.018	4th
14	4/27/58	Old Bridge, NJ	Jim Reed	Ford	68.438	0	1	n/a	n/a	Jim Reed	71.371	Pole
15	5/03/58	Greenville, SC	Jack Smith	Chevrolet	62.295	n/a	n/a	n/a	n/a	Jack Smith	60.484	Pole
16	5/01/58	Greensboro, NC	Bob Welborn	Chevrolet	45.628	2	2	n/a	n/a	Bob Welborn	46.250	Pole
17	5/15/58	Roanoke, VA	Jim Reed	Ford	49.504	0	1	n/a	n/a	Jim Reed	51.963	Pole
18	5/18/58	N.Wilkesboro, NC	Junior Johnson	Ford	78.636	3	3	n/a	n/a	Jack Smith	82.056	3rd
19	5/24/58	Winston-Salem, NC	Bob Welborn	Chevrolet	40.407	1	2	n/a	n/a	Rex White	46.851	10th
20	5/30/58	Trenton, NJ	Fireball Roberts	Chevrolet	84.522	3	4	3	15	Marvin Panch	89.020	17th
21	6/01/58	Riverside, CA	Eddie Gray	Ford	79.481	1	2	n/a	n/a	Parnelli Jones	85.569	6th
22	6/05/58	Columbia, SC	Junior Johnson	Ford	54.752	2	3	8	n/a	Buck Baker	64.308	6th
23	6/12/58	Bradford, PA	Junior Johnson	Ford	59.840	n/a	n/a	n/a	n/a	Bob Duell	65.831	6th
24	6/15/58	Reading, PA	Junior Johnson	Ford	53.763	5	4	n/a	n/a	Speedy Thompson	60.687	2nd
25	6/25/58	New Oxford, PA	Lee Petty	Olds	69.726	n/a	n/a	n/a	n/a	Ken Rush	82.796	2nd
26	6/28/58	Hickory, NC	Lee Petty	Olds	62.413	n/a	n/a	3	11	Speedy Thompson	68.768	9th
27	6/29/58	Weaverville, NC	Rex White	Chevrolet	73.892	4	2	n/a	n/a	Rex White	76.857	Pole
28	7/04/58	Raleigh, NC	Fireball Roberts	Chevrolet	73.691	8	7	8	32	Cotton Owens	83.896	3rd
29	7/12/58	Asheville, NC	Jim Paschal	Chevrolet	46.440	0	1	n/a	n/a	Jim Paschal	50.336	Pole
30	7/16/58	Busti, NY	Shorty Rollins	Ford	47.110	n/a	n/a	n/a	n/a	Lee Petty	n/a	3rd
31	7/18/58	Toronto, ONT	Lee Petty	Olds	43.184	1	2	n/a	n/a	Rex White	51.406	3rd
32	7/19/58	Buffalo, NY	Jim Reed	Ford	46.972	1	2	0	0	Rex White	38.593	3rd
33	7/25/58	Rochester, NY	Cotton Owens	Pontiac	59.900	5	3	n/a	n/a	Rex White	62.871	3rd
34	7/26/58	Belmar, NJ	Jim Reed	Ford	65.395	1	1	1	5	Rex White	68.936	2nd
35	8/02/58	Bridgehampton, NY	Jack Smith	Chevrolet	80.696	0	1	0	0	Jack Smith	82.001	Pole
36	8/07/58	Columbia, SC	Speedy Thompson	Chevrolet	54.820	n/a	n/a	n/a	n/a	Speedy Thompson	64.240	Pole
37	8/10/58	Nashville, TN	Joe Weatherly	Ford	59.269	1	2	5	n/a	Rex White	71.315	8th
38	8/17/58	Weaverville, NC	Fireball Roberts	Chevrolet	66.780	n/a	n/a	n/a	n/a	Jimmy Massey	76.596	2nd
39	8/22/58	Winston-Salem, NC	Lee Petty	Olds	39.258	3	3	n/a	n/a	George Dunn	46.680	2nd
40	8/23/58	Myrtle Beach, SC	Bob Welborn	Chevrolet	60.443	n/a	n/a	n/a	n/a	Speedy Thompson	66.667	8th
41	9/01/58	Darlington, SC	Fireball Roberts	Chevrolet	102.585	8	6	6	28	Eddie Pagan	116.952	2nd
42	9/05/58	Charlotte, NC	Buck Baker	Chevrolet	52.280	3	4	n/a	n/a	Lee Petty	57.897	7th
43	9/07/58	Birmingham, AL	Fireball Roberts	Chevrolet	60.678	n/a	n/a	n/a	n/a	Cotton Owens	64.034	3rd
44	9/07/58	Sacramento, CA	Parnelli Jones	Ford	65.550	n/a	n/a	n/a	n/a	Parnelli Jones	77.922	Pole
45	7/12/58	Gastonia, NC	Buck Baker	Chevrolet	47.856	n/a	n/a	n/a	n/a	Tiny Lund	51.650	2nd
46	9/14/58	Richmond, VA	Speedy Thompson	Chevrolet	57.878	4	3	n/a	n/a	Speedy Thompsom	62.915	Pole
47	9/28/58	Hillsboro, NC	Joe Eubanks	Pontiac	72.439	4	4	4	19	Tiny Lund	87.308	7th
48	10/05/58	Salisbury, NC	Lee Petty	Olds	58.271	n/a	n/a	n/a	n/a	Gober Sosebee	72.162	n/a
49	10/12/58	Martinsville, VA	Fireball Roberts	Chevrolet	64.344	1	2	n/a	n/a	Glen Wood	67.950	4th
50	10/19/58	N.Wilkesboro, NC	Junior Johnson	Ford	84.906	n/a	n/a	0	0	Glen Wood	86.805	2nd
51	10/26/58	Atlanta, GA	Junior Johnson	Ford	69.570	n/a	n/a	n/a	n/a	Glen Wood	81.522	4th

1959 NASCAR Grand National Circuit Season

No.	Date	Site	Race Winner	Car	Speed	Lead Chgs	Ldrs	Caut.	C.Laps	Pole Winner	Speed	Winner Started
1	11/09/58	Fayetteville, NC	Bob Welborn	Chevrolet	56.001	2	2	n/a	n/a	Bob Welborn	61.985	Pole
2	2/20/59	Daytona Beach, FL	Bob Welborn	Chevrolet	143.198	10	4	0	0	Fireball Roberts	140.581	7th
3	2/22/59	Daytona Beach, FL	Lee Petty	Olds	135.521	33	7	0	0	Bob Welborn	140.121	15th
4	3/01/59	Hillsboro, NC	Curtis Turner	T-Bird	81.612	7	3	2	n/a	Curtis Turner	87.544	Pole
5	3/08/59	Concord, NC	Curtis Turner	T-Bird	59.239	2	3	2	n/a	Buck Baker	66.420	4th
6	3/22/59	Atlanta, GA	Johnny Beauchamp	T-Bird	75.172	0	1	n/a	n/a	Buck Baker	77.888	2nd
7	3/29/59	Wilson, NC	Junior Johnson	Ford	50.300	4	4	n/a	n/a	No Time Trials	NTT	22nd
8	3/30/59	Winston-Salem, NC	Jim Reed	Ford	43.562	n/a	n/a	n/a	n/a	Rex White	46.296	20th
9	4/04/59	Columbia, SC	Jack Smith	Chevrolet	57.343	n/a	n/a	n/a	n/a	Jack Smith	60.730	Pole
10	4/05/59	N.Wilkesboro, NC	Lee Petty	Olds	71.985	2	3	4	9	Speedy Thompson	85.746	4th
11	4/26/59	Reading, PA	Junior Johnson	Ford	53.011	2	2	1	12	No Time Trials	NTT	n/a
12	5/02/59	Hickory, NC	Junior Johnson	Ford	62.165	5	4	4	n/a	Junior Johnson	68.900	Pole
13	5/03/59	Martinsville, VA	Lee Petty	Olds	59.512	4	4	3	n/a	Bobby Johns	66.030	24th
14	5/17/59	Trenton, NJ	Tom Pistone	T-Bird	87.350	4	3	n/a	n/a	Bob Burdick	88.950	3rd
15	5/22/59	Charlotte, NC	Lee Petty	Olds	55.300	4	4	3	12	Bob Welborn	57.950	4th
16	5/24/59	Nashville, TN	Rex White	Chevrolet	71.006	5	4	0	0	Rex White	70.890	Pole
17	5/30/59	Los Angeles, CA	Parnelli Jones	Ford	50.982	n/a	n/a	n/a	n/a	Jim Reed	53.590	4th
18	6/05/59	Spartanburg, SC	Jack Smith	Chevrolet	55.547	n/a	n/a	n/a	n/a	Cotton Owens	63.180	9th
19	6/13/59	Greenville, SC	Junior Johnson	Ford	51.480	n/a	n/a	n/a	n/a	Jack Smith	65.838	11th
20	6/14/59	Atlanta, GA	Lee Petty	Plymouth	58.499	n/a	n/a	n/a	n/a	No Time Trials	NTT	37th
21	6/18/59	Columbia, SC	Lee Petty	Plymouth	58.726	5	3	n/a	n/a	Bob Burdick	64.865	3rd
22	6/20/59	Wilson, NC	Junior Johnson	Ford	58.065	n/a	n/a	n/a	n/a	No Time Trials	NTT	18th
23	6/21/59	Richmond, VA	Tom Pistone	T-Bird	56.881	n/a	n/a	n/a	n/a	Buck Baker	66.420	12th
24	6/27/59	Winton-Salem, NC	Rex White	Chevrolet	41.228	1	1	n/a	n/a	Lee Petty	47.071	2nd
25	6/28/59	Weaverville, NC	Rex White	Chevrolet	72.934	n/a	n/a	n/a	n/a	Glen Wood	76.820	4th
26	7/04/59	Daytona Beach, FL	Fireball Roberts	Pontiac	140.581	7	4	0	0	Fireball Roberts	144.997	Pole
27	7/21/59	Pittsburgh, PA	Jim Reed	Chevrolet	45.000	3	4	1	4	Dick Bailey	47.970	6th
28	7/26/59	Charlotte, NC	Jack Smith	Chevrolet	49.533	n/a	n/a	9	22	Buck Baker	63.070	5th
29	8/01/59	Myrtle Beach, SC	Ned Jarrett	Ford	52.941	n/a	n/a	n/a	n/a	Bob Welborn	66.470	9th
30	8/02/59	Charlotte, NC	Ned Jarrett	Ford	52.794	n/a	n/a	n/a	n/a	Bob Welorn	62.540	10th
31	8/09/59	Nashville, TN	Joe Lee Johnson	Chevrolet	63.343	n/a	n/a	n/a	n/a	Rex White	74.044	2nd
32	8/16/59	Weaverville, NC	Bob Welborn	Chevrolet	71.833	n/a	n/a	n/a	n/a	Rex White	77.687	4th
33	8/21/59	Winston-Salem, NC	Rex White	Chevrolet	44.085	0	1	2	n/a	Rex White	47.433	Pole
34	8/22/59	Greenville, SC	Buck Baker	Chevrolet	58.055	n/a	n/a	n/a	n/a	Lee Petty	63.313	4th
35	8/29/59	Columbia, SC	Lee Petty	Plymouth	48.264	n/a	n/a	n/a	n/a	No Time Trials	NTT	9th
36	9/07/59	Darlington, SC	Jim Reed	Chevrolet	111.836	11	8	2	12	Fireball Roberts	123.734	14th
37	9/11/59	Hickory, NC	Lee Petty	Plymouth	63.380	n/a	n/a	n/a	n/a	No Time Trials	NTT	13th
38	9/13/59	Richmond, VA	Cotton Owens	T-Bird	60.382	n/a	n/a	n/a	n/a	Cotton Owens	62.674	Pole
39	9/123/59	Sacramento, CA	Eddie Gray	Ford	54.753	n/a	n/a	n/a	n/a	No Time Trials	NTT	19th
40	9/20/59	Hillsboro, NC	Lee Petty	Plymouth	77.868	2	3	n/a	n/a	Jack Smith	85.533	7th
41	9/27/59	Martinsville, VA	Rex White	Chevrolet	60.500	6	5	7	n/a	Glen Wood	69.471	14th
42	10/11/59	Weaverville, NC	Lee Petty	Plymouth	76.433	n/a	n/a	n/a	n/a	Tommy Irwin	78.568	4th
43	10/18/59	N.Wilkesboro, NC	Lee Petty	Plymouth	74.829	1	1	3	n/a	Glen Wood	86.606	2nd
44	10/25/59	Concord, NC	Jack Smith	Chevrolet	54.005	2	2	2	n/a	No Time Trials	NTT	18th

Appendix

1960 NASCAR Grand National Circuit Season

No.	Date	Site	Race Winner	Car	Speed	Lead Chgs	Ldrs	Caut.	C.Laps	Pole Winner	Speed	Winner Started
1	11/08/59	Charlotte, NC	Jack Smith	Chevrolet	52.409	6	4	8	n/a	Buck Baker	64.103	3rd
2	11/26/59	Columbia, SC	Ned Jarrett	Ford	55.071	n/a	n/a	n/a	n/a	Junior Johnson	65.217	3rd
3	2/12/60	Daytona Beach, FL	Fireball Roberts	Pontiac	137.614	1	1	2	5	Cotton Owens	149.892	2nd
4	2/12/60	Daytona Beach, FL	Jack Smith	Pontiac	146.520	0	1	2	2	Jack Smith	148.157	Pole
5	2/14/60	Daytona Beach, FL	Junior Johnson	Chevrolet	124.740	13	8	4	32	Cotton Owens	149.892	9th
6	2/28/60	Charlotte, NC	Richard Petty	Plymouth	53.404	n/a	n/a	n/a	n/a	Lee Petty	62.110	7th
7	2/27/60	N.Wilkesboro, NC	Lee Petty	Plymouth	66.347	3	3	6	n/a	Junior Johnson	83.860	8th
8	4/03/60	Phoenix, AZ	John Rostek	Ford	71.899	4	4	n/a	n/a	Mel Larson	78.930	n/a
9	4/05/60	Columbia, SC	Rex White	Chevrolet	50.697	n/a	n/a	n/a	n/a	Doug Yates	66.030	3rd
10	4/10/60	Martinsville, VA	Richard Petty	Plymouth	63.943	8	6	8	n/a	Glen Wood	69.150	4th
11	4/15/60	Hickory, NC	Joe Weatherly	Ford	66.347	n/a	n/a	n/a	n/a	Rex White	71.080	2nd
12	4/17/60	Wilson, NC	Joe Weatherly	Ford	55.113	n/a	n/a	n/a	n/a	Emanuel Zervakis	60.500	5th
13	4/18/60	Winston-Salem, NC	Glen Wood	Ford	43.082	0	1	n/a	n/a	Glen Wood	47.240	Pole
14	4/23/60	Greenville, SC	Ned Jarrett	Ford	62.337	2	3	0	0	Curtis Turner	64.720	5th
15	4/24/60	Weaverville, NC	Lee Petty	Plymouth	63.368	4	4	n/a	n/a	Junior Johnson	78.090	8th
16	5/14/60	Darlington, SC	Joe Weatherly	Ford	102.640	7	4	4	n/a	Fireball Roberts	127.750	2nd
17	5/08/60	Spartanburg, SC	Ned Jarrett	Ford	51.843	n/a	n/a	n/a	n/a	Jack Smith	64.220	16th
18	5/29/60	Hillsboro, NC	Lee Petty	Plymouth	83.583	0	1	1	6	Richard Petty	88.190	2nd
19	6/05/60	Richmond, VA	Lee Petty	Plymouth	62.251	7	6	1	6	Ned Jarrett	64.560	10th
20	6/12/60	Hanford, CA	Marvin Porter	Ford	88.032	4	5	n/a	n/a	Frank Secrist	93.040	8th
21	6/19/60	Charlotte, NC	Joe Lee Johnson	Chevrolet	107.735	11	6	8	45	Fireball Roberts	133.904	20th
22	6/26/60	Winston-Salem, NC	Glen Wood	Ford	45.872	1	1	n/a	n/a	Lee Petty	47.850	3rd
23	7/04/60	Daytona Beach, FL	Jack Smith	Pontiac	146.842	10	3	0	0	Jack Smith	152.129	Pole
24	7/10/60	Pittsburgh, PA	Lee Petty	Plymouth	67.450	2	2	n/a	n/a	Lee Petty	71.970	Pole
25	7/17/60	Montgomery, AL	Rex White	Chevrolet	88.626	6	4	1	n/a	John Rostek	91.650	3rd
26	7/23/60	Myrtle Beach, SC	Buck Baker	Chevrolet	60.985	n/a	n/a	n/a	n/a	Ned Jarrett	64.610	11th
27	7/31/60	Atlanta, GA	Fireball Roberts	Pontiac	112.652	12	6	n/a	n/a	Fireball Roberts	133.870	Pole
28	7/03/60	Birmingham, AL	Ned Jarrett	Ford	54.463	0	1	0	0	Ned Jarrett	55.866	Pole
29	8/07/60	Nashville, TN	Johnny Beauchamp	Chevrolet	56.966	n/a	n/a	n/a	n/a	Rex White	74.810	2nd
30	8/14/60	Weaverville, NC	Rex White	Chevrolet	65.024	8	6	n/a	n/a	Jack Smith	77.850	2nd
31	8/16/60	Spartanburg, SC	Cotton Owens	Pontiac	59.681	n/a	n/a	n/a	n/a	Cotton Owens	63.250	Pole
32	8/18/60	Columbia, SC	Rex White	Chevrolet	54.265	n/a	n/a	n/a	n/a	Tommy Irwin	60.360	7th
33	8/20/60	S.Boston, VA	Junior Johnson	Chevrolet	50.732	12	n/a	n/a	n/a	Ned Jarrett	51.903	2nd
34	8/23/60	Winston-Salem, NC	Glen Wood	Ford	44.389	0	1	1	3	Glen Wood	46.970	Pole
35	9/05/60	Darlington, SC	Buck Baker	Pontiac	105.901	14	7	5	61	Fireball Roberts	125.459	2nd
36	9/09/60	Hickory, NC	Junior Johnson	Chevrolet	69.998	n/a	n/a	n/a	n/a	Buck Baker	71.180	2nd
37	9/01/60	Sacramento, CA	Jim Cook	Dodge	70.629	n/a	n/a	n/a	n/a	Jim Cook	78.45	Pole
38	9/15/60	Sumter, SC	Ned Jarrett	Ford	41.208	n/a	n/a	n/a	n/a	David Pearson	45.070	2nd
39	9/18/60	Hillsboro, NC	Richard Petty	Plymouth	80.161	0	1	1	3	Richard Petty	82.285	Pole
40	9/25/60	Martinsville, VA	Rex White	Chevrolet	60.439	n/a	n/a	n/a	n/a	Glen Wood	68.440	2nd
41	10/02/60	N.Wilkesboro, NC	Rex White	Chevrolet	77.444	n/a	n/a	5	n/a	Rex White	93.399	Pole
42	10/16/60	Charlotte, NC	Speedy Thompson	Ford	112.905	8	5	7	34	Fireball Roberts	133.465	3rd
43	10/23/60	Richmond, VA	Speedy Thompson	Ford	63.739	3	3	n/a	n/a	Ned Jarrett	64.410	3rd
44	10/30/60	Atlanta, GA	Bobby Johns	Pontiac	108.408	7	4	n/a	n/a	Fireball Roberts	134.596	5th

1961 NASCAR Grand National Circuit Season

No.	Date	Site	Race Winner	Car	Speed	Lead Chgs	Ldrs	Caut.	C.Laps	Pole Winner	Speed	Winner Started
1	11/06/60	Charlotte, NC	Joe Weatherly	Ford	59.435	4	3	4	n/a	Lee Petty	63.581	11th
2	11/20/60	Jacksonville, FL	Lee Petty	Plymouth	64.400	4	4	n/a	n/a	Junior Johnson	68.623	13th
3	2/24/61	Daytona Beach, FL	Fireball Roberts	Pontiac	129.711	n/a	3	5	10	Fireball Roberts	155.709	Pole
4	2/24/61	Daytona Beach, FL	Joe Weatherly	Pontiac	152.671	8	3	n/a	n/a	Joe Weatherly	154.122	Pole
5	2/26/61	Daytona Beach, FL	Marvin Panch	Pontiac	49.601	9	5	0	0	Fireball Roberts	155.709	4th
6	3/04/61	Spartanburg, SC	Cotton Owens	Pontiac	59.152	4	2	3	n/a	Ned Jarrett	63.920	4th
7	3/05/61	Weaverville, NC	Rex White	Chevrolet	72.420	0	1	2	n/a	Rex White	79.295	Pole
8	3/12/61	Hanford, CA	Fireball Roberts	Pontiac	95.621	1	1	n/a	n/a	Bob Ross	98.370	2nd
9	3/26/61	Atlanta, GA	Bob Burdick	Pontiac	124.172	n/a	6	2	n/a	Marvin Panch	135.755	7th
10	4/01/61	Greenville, SC	Emanuel Zervakis	Chevrolet	52.189	2	3	4	20	Junior Johnson	62.090	2nd
11	4/02/61	Hillsboro, NC	Cotton Owens	Pontiac	84.695	3	3	n/a	n/a	Ned Jarrett	91.836	3rd
12	4/03/61	Winston-Salem, NC	Rex White	Chevrolet	45.500	n/a	n/a	n/a	n/a	Glen Wood	48.700	2nd
13	4/09/61	Martinsville, VA	Fred Lorenzen	Ford	63.366	1	2	2	n/a	Rex White	70.280	2nd
14	4/16/61	N.Wilkesboro, NC	Rex White	Chevrolet	83.248	4	4	6	33	Junior Johnson	95.660	2nd
15	4/20/61	Columbia, SC	Cotton Owens	Pontiac	51.940	1	2	n/.a	n/a	Ned Jarrett	64.380	2nd
16	4/22/61	Hickory, NC	Junior Johnson	Pontiac	66.654	4	3	4	19	Junior Johnson	74.074	Pole
17	4/23/61	Richmond, VA	Richard Petty	Plymouth	62.456	2	2	n/a	n/a	Richard Petty	66.667	Pole
18	4/30/61	Martinsville, VA	Junior Johnson	Pontiac	66.278	2	3	1	6	Rex White	71.320	17th
19	5/06/61	Darlington, SC	Fred Lorenzen	Ford	119.520	16	8	1	n/a	Fred Lorenzen	128.965	Pole
20	5/21/61	Charotte, NC	Richard Petty	Plymouth	133.554	22	3	0	0	Fred Lorenzen	137.480	7th
21	5/21/61	Charlotte, NC	Joe Weatherly	Pontiac	115.591	3	3	2	14	Junior Johnson	136.951	3rd
22	5/21/61	Riverside, CA	Lloyd Dane	Chevrolet	82.512	n/a	n/a	0	0	Eddie Gray	82.512	2nd
23	5/27/61	Los Angeles, CA	Eddie Gray	Ford	68.833	n/a	n/a	n/a	n/a	Danny Weinberg	71.940	2nd
24	5/28/61	Charlotte, NC	David Pearson	Pontiac	111.633	17	7	7	57	Richard Petty	131.611	3rd
25	6/02/61	Spartanburg, SC	Jim Paschal	Pontiac	55.495	n/a	n/a	n/a	n/a	Joe Weatherly	61.250	11th
26	6/4/611	Birmingham, AL	Ned Jarrett	Chevrolet	61.068	n/a	n/a	n/a	n/a	Johnny Allen	65.910	4th
27	6/08/61	Greenville, SC	Jack Smith	Pontiac	58.441	1	2	n/a	n/a	Ned Jarrett	65.480	7th
28	6/10/61	Winston-Salem, NC	Rex White	Chevrolet	42.714	n/a	n/a	1	5	Junior Johnson	47.720	4th
29	6/17/61	Norwood, MA	Emanuel Zervakis	Chevrolet	53.827	3	3	1	n/a	Rex White	55.870	3rd
30	6/23/61	Hartsville, SC	Buck Baker	Chrysler	46.234	n/a	n/a	n/a	n/a	Emanuel Zervakis	54.970	3rd
31	6/24/61	Roanoke, VA	Junior Johnson	Pontiac	49.907	n/a	n/a	n/a	n/a	Rex White	53.700	2nd
32	7/04/61	Daytona Beach, FL	David Pearson	Pontiac	154.294	12	6	0	0	Fireball Roberts	157.150	2nd
33	7/09/61	Atlanta, GA	Fred Lorenzen	Ford	118.067	n/a	7	1	12	Fireball Roberts	136.088	5th
34	7/20/61	Columbia, SC	Cotton Owens	Pontiac	62.198	3	3	n/a	n/a	Cotton Owens	67.650	Pole
35	7/22/61	Myrtle Beach, SC	Joe Weatherly	Pontiac	57.655	0	1	n/a	n/a	Joe Weatherly	66.690	Pole
36	7/30/61	Bristol, TN	Jack Smith	Pontiac	68.373	7	5	8	n/a	Fred Lorenzen	79.225	12th
37	8/06/61	Nashville, TN	Jim Paschal	Pontiac	56.455	2	2	3	172	Rex White	76.69	10th

No.	Date	Site	Race Winner	Car	Speed	Lead Chgs	Ldrs	Caut.	C.Laps	Pole Winner	Speed	Winner Started
38	8/09/61	Winston-Salem, NC	Rex White	Chevrolet	42.452	2	2	n/a	n/a	Junior Johnson	48.050	3rd
39	8/13/61	Weaverville, NC	Junior Johnson	Pontiac	65.704	1	1	n/a	n/a	Jim Paschal	80.430	2nd
40	8/18/61	Richmond, VA	Junior Johnson	Pontiac	51.605	0	1	1	8	Junior Johnson	58.860	Pole
41	8/27/61	S.Boston, VA	Junior Johnson	Pontiac	48.348	2	2	n/a	n/a	Cotton Owens	52.630	3rd
42	9/04/61	Darlington, SC	Nelson Stacy	Ford	117.787	19	6	6	21	Fireball Roberts	128.680	3rd
43	9/08/61	Hickory, NC	Rex White	Chevrolet	67.529	6	3	2	n/a	Rex White	72.290	Pole
44	9/10/61	Richmond, VA	Joe Weatherly	Pontiac	61.677	n/a	n/a	n/a	n/a	Junior Johnson	65.010	7th
45	9/10/61	Sacramento, CA	Eddie Gray	Ford	n/a	1	2	n/a	n/a	Bill Amick	79.260	n/a
46	9/17/61	Atlanta, GA	David Pearson	Pontiac	125.384	7	5	n/a	n/a	Fireball Roberts	136.294	5th
47	9/24/61	Martinsville, VA	Joe Weatherly	Pontiac	62.586	9	6	7	n/a	Fred Lorenzen	70.730	4th
48	10/01/61	N.Wilkesboro, NC	Rex White	Chevrolet	84.675	3	3	4	23	Junior Johnson	94.540	3rd
49	10/15/06	Charlotte, NC	Joe Weatherly	Pontiac	119.950	13	5	3	18	David Pearson	138.577	6th
50	10/22/61	Bristol, TN	Joe Weatherly	Pontiac	72.452	6	5	3	n/a	Bobby Johns	80.645	2nd
51	10/28/61	Greenville, SC	Junior Johnson	Pontiac	63.346	3	3	n/a	n/a	Buck Baker	66.667	3rd
52	10/29/61	Hillsboro, NC	Joe Weatherly	Pontiac	85.249	2	2	n/a	n/a	Joe Weatherly	95.154	Pole

1962 NASCAR Grand National Circuit Season

No.	Date	Site	Race Winner	Car	Speed	Lead Chgs	Ldrs	Caut.	C.Laps	Pole Winner	Speed	Winner Started
1	11/05/61	Concord, NC	Jack Smith	Pontiac	59.405	n/a	n/a	n/a	n/a	Joe Weatherly	68.543	2nd
2	11/12/61	Weaverville, NC	Rex White	Chevrolet	68.467	5	4	3	14	Joe Weatherly	81.743	5th
3	2/16/62	Daytona Beach, FL	Fireball Roberts	Pontiac	156.999	2	2	0	0	Fireball Roberts	158.744	Pole
4	2/16/62	Daytona Beach, FL	Joe Weatherly	Pontiac	145.395	2	2	1	n/a	Darel Dieringer	155.086	3rd
5	2/18/62	Daytona Beach, FL	Fireball Roberts	Pontiac	152.529	22	5	1	3	Fireball Roberts	158.744	Pole
6	2/25/62	Concord, NC	Joe Weatherly	Pontiac	53.161	0	1	n/a	n/a	Joe Weatherly	n/a	Pole
7	3/04/62	Weaverville, NC	Joe Weatherly	Pontiac	75.471	3	3	1	n/a	Rex White	80.460	3rd
8	3/17/62	Savannah, GA	Jack Smith	Pontiac	58.775	4	4	3	n/a	Rex White	70.588	4th
9	3/18/62	Hillsboro, NC	Rex White	Chevrolet	86.948	4	2	n/a	n/a	Joe Weatherly	96.285	3rd
10	4/01/62	Richmond, VA	Rex White	Chevrolet	51.363	7	6	5	32	No Time Trials	NTT	20th
11	4/13/62	Columbia, SC	Ned Jarrett	Chevrolet	56.710	n/a	n/a	n/a	n/a	Joe Weatherly	64.423	7th
12	4/15/62	N.Wilkesboro, NC	Richard Petty	Plymouth	84.737	5	5	5	n/a	Junior Johnson	94.142	15th
13	4/19/62	Greenville, SC	Ned Jarrett	Chevrolet	57.480	n/a	n/a	n/a	n/a	Ned Jarrett	66.568	Pole
14	4/21/62	Myrtle Beach, SC	Jack Smith	Pontiac	63.036	n/a	n/a	n/a	n/a	Ned Jarrett	68.939	3rd
15	4/22/62	Martinsville, VA	Richard Petty	Plymouth	66.425	6	6	2	n/a	Fred Lorenzen	71.287	7th
16	4/23/62	Winston-Salem, NC	Rex White	Chevrolet	43.392	n/a	n/a	n/a	n/a	Rex White	48.417	Pole
17	4/29/62	Bristol, TN	Bobby Johns	Pontiac	73.397	5	3	4	37	Fireball Roberts	81.374	6th
18	5/04/62	Richmond, VA	Jimmy Pardue	Pontiac	67.747	1	2	n/a	n/a	Rex White	71.145	12th
19	5/05/62	Hickory, NC	Jack Smith	Pontiac	71.216	0	1	1	5	Jack Smith	74.074	Pole
20	5/06/62	Concord, NC	Joe Weatherly	Pontiac	57.052	1	2	n/a	n/a	No Time Trials	NTT	7th
21	5/12/62	Darlington, SC	Nelson Stacy	Ford	117.429	9	7	6	n/a	Fred Lorenzen	129.810	3rd
22	5/19/62	Spartanburg, SC	Ned Jarrett	Chevrolet	60.080	n/a	n/a	n/a	n/a	Cotton Owens	64.423	2nd
23	5/27/62	Charlotte, NC	Nelson Stacy	Ford	125.552	18	7	2	14	Fireball Roberts	140.150	18th
24	6/10/62	Atlanta, GA	Fred Lorenzen	Ford	101.983	23	7	3	61	Banjo Matthews	137.640	7th
25	6/16/62	Winston-Salem, NC	Johnny Allen	Pontiac	45.466	1	2	n/a	n/a	Rex White	48.179	2nd
26	6/19/62	Augusta, GA	Joe Weatherly	Pontiac	59.850	0	1	n/a	n/a	Joe Weatherly	63.069	Pole
27	6/22/62	Richmond, VA	Jim Paschal	Pontiac	66.293	2	3	1	n/a	Rex White	70.435	3rd
28	6/23/62	S.Boston, VA	Rex White	Chevrolet	72.540	1	2	n/a	n/a	Jack Smith	79.458	2nd
29	7/04/62	Daytona Beach, FL	Fireball Roberts	Pontiac	153.688	14	3	2	7	Banjo Matthews	160.499	4th
30	7/07/62	Columbia, SC	Rex White	Chevrolet	62.370	n/a	n/a	n/a	n/a	Jack Smith	66.667	4th
31	7/13/62	Asheville, NC	Jack Smith	Pontiac	78.294	2	2	0	0	Rex White	82.285	3rd
32	7/14/62	Greenville, SC	Richard Petty	Plymouth	62.219	n/a	n/a	n/a	n/a	Rex White	66.055	4th
33	7/17/62	Augusta, GA	Joe Weatherly	Pontiac	55.104	n/a	n/a	n/a	n/a	Jack Smith	65.885	4th
34	7/20/62	Savannah, GA	Joe Weatherly	Pontiac	67.239	n/a	n/a	n/a	n/a	Wendell Scott	71.627	6th
35	7/21/62	Myrtle Beach, SC	Ned Jarrett	Chevrolet	64.171	2	2	n/a	n/a	Ned Jarrett	68.467	Pole
36	7/29/62	Bristol, TN	Jim Paschal	Plymouth	75.276	12	6	4	21	Fireball Roberts	80.321	12th
37	8/03/62	Chattanooga, TN	Joe Weatherly	Pontiac	71.145	3	3	0	0	Richard Petty	73.365	5th
38	8/05/62	Nashville, TN	Jim Paschal	Plymouth	64.469	5	4	3	108	Johnny Allen	77.854	3rd
39	8/08/62	Huntsville, AL	Richard Petty	Plymouth	54.644	0	1	0	0	Richard Petty	54.086	Pole
40	8/12/62	Weaverville, NC	Jim Paschal	Plymouth	77.492	1	2	2	n/a	Jack Smith	82.720	2nd
41	8/15/62	Roanoke, VA	Richard Petty	Plymouth	51.165	n/a	n/a	n/a	n/a	Jack Smith	54.086	2nd
42	8/18/62	Winston-Salem, NC	Richard Petty	Plymouth	46.875	3	2	0	0	Jack Smith	48.102	3rd
43	8/21/62	Spartanburg, SC	Richard Petty	Plymouth	59.870	n/a	n/a	n/a	n/a	Richard Petty	61.590	Pole
44	8/25/62	Valdosta, GA	Ned Jarrett	Chevrolet	61.454	n/a	n/a	n/a	n/a	Richard Petty	59.386	5th
45	9/03/62	Darlington, SC	Larry Frank	Ford	117.965	9	7	4	27	Fireball Roberts	130.246	10th
46	9/07/62	Hickory, NC	Rex White	Chevrolet	70.574	1	2	0	0	Junior Johnson	71.357	3rd
47	9/09/62	Richmond, VA	Joe Weatherly	Pontiac	64.981	8	4	1	9	Rex White	66.127	2nd
48	9/11/62	Moyock, NC	Ned Jarrett	Chevrolet	43.078	0	1	n/a	n/a	Ned Jarrett	45.569	Pole
49	9/13/62	Augusta, GA	Fred Lorenzen	Ford	60.759	2	2	n/a	n/a	Joe Weatherly	65.241	4th
50	9/23/62	Martinsville, VA	Nelson Stacy	Ford	66.874	4	3	2	n/a	Fireball Roberts	71.513	3rd
51	9/30/62	N.Wilkesboro, NC	Richard Petty	Plymouth	86.186	2	3	3	n/a	Fred Lorenzen	94.657	5th
52	10/14/62	Charlotte, NC	Junior Johnson	Pontiac	132.085	10	4	1	6	Fireball Roberts	140.287	3rd
53	10/28/62	Atlanta, GA	Rex White	Chevrolet	124.740	16	6	3	n/a	Fireball Roberts	138.978	5th

1963 NASCAR Grand National Circuit Season

No.	Date	Site	Race Winner	Car	Speed	Lead Chgs	Ldrs	Caut.	C.Laps	Pole Winner	Speed	Winner Started
1	11/04/62	Birmingham, AL	Jim Paschal	Plymouth	68.350	2	2	1	4	Jim Paschal	73.952	Pole
2	11/11/62	Tampa, FL	Richard Petty	Plymouth	57.167	3	3	2	n/a	Rex White	60.090	5th
3	11/22/62	Randleman, NC	Jim Paschal	Plymouth	47.544	1	2	0	0	Glen Wood	51.933	2nd
4	1/20/63	Riverside, CA	Dan Gurney	Ford	84.965	9	6	6	n/a	Paul Goldsmith	98.809	11th
5	2/22/63	Daytona Beach, FL	Junior Johnson	Chevrolet	164.083	n/a	n/a	0	0	Fireball Roberts	160.943	2nd
6	2/22/63	Daytona Beach, FL	Johnny Rutherford	Chevrolet	162.969	4	3	0	0	Fred Lorenzen	161.870	9th
7	2/24/63	Daytona Beach, FL	Tiny Lund	Ford	151.566	29	10	2	10	Fireball Roberts	160.943	12th
8	3/02/63	Spartanburg, SC	Richard Petty	Plymouth	55.598	2	3	2	n/a	Junior Johnson	64.470	2nd
9	3/03/63	Weaverville, NC	Richard Petty	Plymouth	76.664	n/a	n/a	n/a	n/a	Junior Johnson	82.750	3rd
10	3/10/63	Hillsboro, NC	Junior Johnson	Chevrolet	83.129	5	3	3	n/a	Joe Weatherly	95.716	4th
11	3/17/63	Atanta, GA	Fred Lorenzen	Ford	130.582	12	8	n/a	n/a	Junior Johnson	141.038	2nd
12	3/24/63	Hickory, NC	Junior Johnson	Chevrolet	67.950	2	2	2	n/a	Junior Johnson	75.235	Pole
13	3/31/63	Bristol, TN	Fireball Roberts	Ford	76.910	8	5	1	9	Fred Lorenzen	80.681	3rd

No.	Date	Site	Race Winner	Car	Speed	Lead Chgs	Ldrs	Caut.	C.Laps	Pole Winner	Speed	Winner Started
14	4/04/63	Augusta, GA	Ned Jarrett	Ford	60.089	1	2	n/a	n/a	LeeRoy Yarbrough	64.610	3rd
15	4/07/63	Richmond, VA	Joe Weatherly	Pontiac	58.624	11	4	6	37	Rex White	69.151	3rd
16	4/13/63	Greenville, SC	Buck Baker	Pontiac	54.853	6	5	7	n/a	Jimmy Pardue	66.270	9th
17	4/14/63	S.Boston, VA	Richard Petty	Plymouth	75.229	1	2	0	0	Ned Jarrett	78.720	2nd
18	4/15/63	Winston-Salem, NC	Jim Paschal	Plymouth	46.814	n/a	n/a	n/a	n/a	Richard Petty	48.280	3rd
19	4/21/63	Martinsville, VA	Richard Petty	Plymouth	64.823	3	3	5	n/a	Rex White	72.000	8th
20	4/28/63	N.Wilkesboro, NC	Richard Petty	Plymouth	83.301	4	4	n/a	n/a	Fred Lorenzen	96.150	7th
21	5/02/63	Columbia, SC	Richard Petty	Plymouth	51.650	n/a	n/a	13	n/a	Richard Petty	68.080	Pole
22	5/05/63	Randleman, NC	Jim Paschal	Plymouth	48.605	1	2	0	0	Ned Jarrett	50.856	3rd
23	5/11/63	Darlington, SC	Joe Weatherly	Pontiac	122.745	9	6	3	14	Fred Lorenzen	131.718	6th
24	5/18/63	Manassas, VA	Richard Petty	Plymouth	70.275	2	2	0	0	Richard Petty	71.580	Pole
25	5/19/63	Richmond, VA	Ned Jarrett	Ford	65.052	4	2	1	6	Ned Jarrett	70.642	Pole
26	6/02/63	Charlotte, NC	Fred Lorenzen	Ford	132.417	15	6	2	14	Junior Johnson	141.148	2nd
27	6/09/63	Birmingham, AL	Richard Petty	Plymouth	68.195	2	2	1	3	Jack Smith	71.146	2nd
28	6/30/63	Atlanta, GA	Junior Johnson	Chevrolet	121.139	18	6	2	32	Marvin Panch	140.753	2nd
29	7/04/63	Daytona Beach, FL	Fireball Roberts	Ford	150.927	39	6	3	19	Junior Johnson	166.005	3rd
30	7/07/63	Myrtle Beach, SC	Ned Jarrett	Ford	60.996	2	3	n/a	n/a	Richard Petty	68.700	3rd
31	7/10/63	Savannah, GA	Ned Jarrett	Ford	59.622	1	2	2	n/a	Richard Petty	71.340	2nd
32	7/11/63	Moyock, NC	Jimmy Pardue	Ford	45.464	2	2	1	n/a	Junior Johnson	47.120	6th
33	7/13/63	Winston-Salem, NC	Glen Wood	Ford	44.390	3	3	3	n/a	Glen Wood	48.387	Pole
34	7/14/63	Asheville, NC	Ned Jarrett	Ford	63.384	5	4	n/a	n/a	David Pearson	67.235	5th
35	7/19/63	Old Bridge, NJ	Fireball Roberts	Ford	73.022	1	2	4	n/a	Joe Weatherly	75.850	5th
36	7/21/63	Bridgehampton, NY	Richard Petty	Plymouth	86.047	2	2	0	0	Richard Petty	86.301	Pole
37	7/28/63	Bristol, TN	Fred Lorenzen	Ford	74.844	6	4	7	36	Fred Lorenzen	82.229	Pole
38	7/30/63	Greenville, SC	Richard Petty	Plymouth	62.456	3	3	2	n/a	Ned Jarrett	65.526	7th
39	8/04/63	Nashville, TN	Jim Paschal	Plymouth	60.126	n/a	n/a	n/a	98	Richard Petty	78.878	3rd
40	8/08/63	Columbia, SC	Richard Petty	Plymouth	55.598	2	1	n/a	n/a	Richard Petty	69.014	Pole
41	8/11/63	Weaverville, NC	Fred Lorenzen	Ford	77.673	3	3	2	n/a	No Time Trials	NTT	2nd
42	8/14/63	Spartanburg, SC	Ned Jarrett	Ford	52.424	4	4	n/a	n/a	Joe Weatherly	64.958	2nd
43	8/16/63	Winston-Salem, NC	Junior Johnson	Chevrolet	46.320	0	1	1	4	Junior Johnson	49.806	Pole
44	8/18/63	Huntington, WV	Fred Lorenzen	Ford	59.340	4	4	7	30	Fred Lorenzen	66.568	Pole
45	9/02/63	Darlington, SC	Fireball Roberts	Ford	129.784	9	4	0	0	Fred Lorenzen	133.648	10th
46	9/06/63	Hickory, NC	Junior Johnson	Chevrolet	62.926	8	4	3	16	David Pearson	72.471	7th
47	9/08/63	Richmond, VA	Ned Jarrett	Ford	66.339	4	3	n/a	n/a	Joe Weatherly	68.104	7th
48	9/22/63	Martinsville, VA	Fred Lorenzen	Ford	67.486	3	2	5	18	Junior Johnson	73.379	2nd
49	9/24/63	Moyock, NC	Ned Jarrett	Ford	43.000	n/a	2	n/a	n/a	Joe Weatherly	45.988	2nd
50	9/29/63	N.Wilkesboro, NC	Marvin Panch	Ford	89.428	9	4	2	17	Fred Lorenzen	96.566	3rd
51	10/05/63	Randleman, NC	Richard Petty	Plymouth	46.001	1	2	n/a	n/a	Fred Lorenzen	51.724	2nd
52	10/13/63	Charlotte, NC	Junior Johnson	Chevrolet	132.105	13	5	3	12	Marvin Panch	142.461	2nd
53	10/20/63	S.Boston, VA	Richard Petty	Plymouth	76.325	4	4	0	0	Jack Smith	81.081	4th
54	10/27/63	Hillsboro, NC	Joe Weatherly	Pontiac	85.559	3	3	2	14	Joe Weatherly	93.156	Pole
55	11/03/63	Riverside, CA	Darel Dieringer	Mercury	91.465	7	3	1	n/a	Dan Gurney	101.050	3rd

1964 NASCAR Grand National Circuit Season

No.	Date	Site	Race Winner	Car	Speed	Lead Chgs	Ldrs	Caut.	C.Laps	Pole Winner	Speed	Winner Started
1	11/10/63	Concord, NC	Ned Jarrett	Ford	56.897	5	4	n/a	n/a	David Pearson	69.257	3rd
2	11/17/63	Augusta, GA	Fireball Roberts	Ford	86.320	10	5	0	0	Fred Lorenzen	88.590	2nd
3	12/01/63	Jacksonville, FL	Wendell Scott	Chevrolet	58.252	3	4	5	24	Jack Smith	70.921	15th
4	12/29/63	Savannah, GA	Richard Petty	Plymouth	68.143	1	2	3	n/a	Ned Jarrett	73.529	5th
5	1/19/64	Riverside, CA	Dan Gurney	Ford	91.245	5	4	2	n/a	Fred Lorenzen	102.433	4th
6	2/21/64	Daytona Beach, FL	Junior Johnson	Dodge	170.777	4	3	0	0	Paul Goldsmith	174.910	2nd
7	2/21/64	Daytona Beach, FL	Bobby Isaac	Dodge	169.811	1	2	0	0	Richard Petty	174.418	4th
8	2/23/64	Daytona Beach, FL	Richard Petty	Plymouth	154.334	6	4	3	19	Paul Goldsmith	174.910	2nd
9	3/10/64	Richmond, VA	David Pearson	Dodge	60.233	5	4	2	n/a	Ned Jarrett	69.070	10th
10	3/22/64	Bristol, TN	Fred Lorenzen	Ford	72.196	1	2	4	54	Marvin Panch	80.640	2nd
11	3/28/64	Greenville, SC	David Pearson	Dodge	57.554	5	4	4	n/a	Dick Hutcherson	66.740	9th
12	3/30/64	Winston-Salem, NC	Marvin Panch	Ford	47.796	0	1	0	0	Marvin Panch	49.830	Pole
13	4/05/64	Atlanta, GA	Fred Lorenzen	Ford	134.137	11	6	4	19	Fred Lorenzen	146.470	Pole
14	4/11/64	Weaverville, NC	Marvin Panch	Ford	81.669	0	1	0	0	Marvin Panch	84.905	Pole
15	4/12/64	Hillsboro, NC	David Pearson	Dodge	83.319	2	1	n/a	n/a	David Pearson	99.784	Pole
16	4/14/64	Spartanburg, SC	Ned Jarrett	Ford	58.852	2	3	3	n/a	Dick Hutcherson	69.044	4th
17	4/16/64	Columbia, SC	Ned Jarrett	Ford	64.412	5	5	6	14	David Pearson	71.485	2nd
18	4/19/64	N.Wilkesboro, NC	Fred Lorenzen	Ford	81.930	5	4	7	35	Fred Lorenzen	94.024	Pole
19	4/26/64	Martinsville, VA	Fred Lorenzen	Ford	70.098	5	3	2	14	Fred Lorenzen	74.472	Pole
20	5/01/64	Savannah, GA	LeeRoy Yarbrough	Plymouth	70.326	1	2	n/a	n/a	Jimmy Pardue	73.111	4th
21	5/09/64	Darlington, SC	Fred Lorenzen	Ford	130.013	10	2	1	5	Fred Lorenzen	135.727	Pole
22	5/15/64	Hampton, VA	Ned Jarrett	Ford	65.300	1	2	0	0	David Pearson	67.542	4th
23	5/16/64	Hickory, NC	Ned Jarrett	Ford	69.364	5	3	3	19	Junior Johnson	76.882	2nd
24	5/17/64	S.Boston, VA	Richard Petty	Plymouth	71.957	5	4	3	14	Marvin Panch	80.023	7th
25	5/24/64	Charlotte, NC	Jim Paschal	Plymouth	125.772	14	8	7	48	Jimmy Pardue	144.346	12th
26	5/30/64	Greenville, SC	LeeRoy Yarbrough	Plymouth	56.559	1	2	n/a	n/a	Marvin Panch	68.050	8th
27	5/31/64	Asheville, NC	Ned Jarrett	Ford	66.538	3	2	n/a	n/a	Richard Petty	69.889	2nd
28	6/07/64	Atlanta, GA	Ned Jarrett	Ford	112.535	35	13	3	63	Junior Johnson	145.906	17th
29	6/11/64	Concord, NC	Richard Petty	Plymouth	66.352	4	3	1	n/a	Richard Petty	68.233	Pole
30	6/14/64	Nashville, TN	Richard Petty	Plymouth	76.498	3	2	n/a	n/a	David Pearson	80.142	2nd
31	6/19/64	Chattanooga, TN	David Pearson	Dodge	70.051	3	2	n/a	n/a	Richard Petty	75.235	2nd
32	6/21/64	Birmingham, AL	Ned Jarrett	Ford	67.643	1	1	n/a	n/a	David Pearson	72.115	2nd
33	6/23/64	Valdosta, GA	Buck Baker	Dodge	61.328	3	3	n/a	n/a	Ned Jarrett	65.146	2nd
34	6/26/64	Spartanburg, SC	Richard Petty	Plymouth	58.233	7	4	3	n/aa	David Pearson	66.939	2nd
35	7/04/64	Daytona Beach, FL	A.J. Foyt	Dodge	151.451	19	4	5	25	Darel Dieringer	172.678	19th
36	7/08/64	Manassas, VA	Ned Jarrett	Ford	67.652	2	2	n/a	n/a	Ned Jarrett	73.609	Pole
37	7/10/64	Old Bridge, NJ	Billy Wade	Mercury	73.891	4	3	0	0	Billy Wade	76.66	Pole
38	7/12/64	Bridgehampton, NJ	Billy Wade	Mercury	87.707	8	4	n/a	n/a	Richard Petty	90.600	3rd
39	7/15/64	Islip, NY	Billy Wade	Mercury	46.252	2	2	1	n/a	Billy Wade	51.100	Pole
40	7/19/64	Watkins Glen, NY	Billy Wade	Mercury	97.988	5	3	n/a	n/a	Billy Wade	102.222	Pole
41	7/21/64	New Oxford, PA	David Pearson	Dodge	82.568	2	2	n/a	n/a	David Pearson	86.289	Pole
42	7/26/64	Bristol, TN	Fred Lorenzen	Ford	78.044	5	4	1	14	Richard Petty	82.910	8th
43	8/02/64	Nashville, TN	Richard Petty	Plymouth	73.208	0	1	3	26	Richard Petty	80.826	Pole
44	8/07/64	Myrtle Beach, SC	David Pearson	Dodge	61.750	2	2	n/a	n/a	David Pearson	69.659	Pole

No.	Date	Site	Race Winner	Car	Speed	Lead Chgs	Ldrs	Caut.	C.Laps	Pole Winner	Speed	Winner Started
45	8/09/64	Weaverville, NC	Ned Jarrett	Ford	77.600	5	3	2	n/a	Junior Johnson	84.626	4th
46	8/13/64	Moyock, NC	Ned Jarrett	Ford	63.965	2	2	n/a	n/a	Ned Jarrett	67.643	Pole
47	8/16/64	Huntington, WV	Richard Petty	Plymouth	70.488	4	4	6	36	Billy Wade	79.505	3rd
48	8/21/64	Columbia, SC	David Pearson	Dodge	61.697	5	5	5	n/a	Ned Jarrett	69.150	9th
49	8/22/64	Winston-Salem, NC	Junior Johnson	Ford	46.192	0	1	1	4	Junior Johnson	49.846	Pole
50	8/23/64	Roanoke, VA	Junior Johnson	Ford	49.847	1	2	n/a	n/a	Glen Wood	55.970	3rd
51	9/07/64	Darlington, SC	Buck Baker	Dodge	117.757	12	7	7	50	Richard Petty	136.815	6th
52	9/11/64	Hickory, NC	David Pearson	Dodge	67.797	2	2	5	n/a	David Pearson	74.418	Pole
53	9/14/64	Richmond, VA	Cotton Owens	Dodge	61.955	7	3	5	23	Ned Jarrett	66.890	3rd
54	9/18/64	Manassas, VA	Ned Jarrett	Ford	68.842	4	3	n/a	n/a	David Pearson	74.626	3rd
55	9/20/64	Hillsboro, NC	Ned Jarrett	Ford	86.725	4	3	n/a	n/a	David Pearson	89.280	6th
56	9/27/64	Martinsville, VA	Fred Lorenzen	Ford	67.320	6	4	6	28	Fred Lorenzen	74.196	Pole
57	10/09/64	Savannah, GA	Ned Jarrett	Ford	68.663	0	1	0	0	Ned Jarrett	68.886	Pole
58	10/11/64	N.Wilkesboro, NC	Marvin Panch	Ford	91.398	9	4	2	28	Junior Johnson	100.761	5th
59	10/18/64	Charlotte, NC	Fred Lorenzen	Ford	134.475	10	4	4	21	Richard Petty	150.711	3rd
60	10/25/64	Harris, NC	Richard Petty	Plymouth	59.009	2	3	3	16	Billy Wade	64.787	4th
61	11/01/64	Augusta, GA	Darel Dieringer	Mercury	68.641	7	4	6	45	Ned Jarrett	82.455	5th
62	11/08/64	Jacksonville, NC	Ned Jarrett	Ford	57.535	4	4	4	22	Doug Yates	64.285	2nd

1965 NASCAR Grand National Circuit Season

No.	Date	Site	Race Winner	Car	Speed	Lead Chgs	Ldrs	Caut.	C.Laps	Pole Winner	Speed	Winner Started
1	1/17/65	Riverside, CA	Dan Gurney	Ford	87.708	7	4	2	n/a	Junior Johnson	102.846	11th
2	2/12/65	Daytona Beach, FL	Darel Dieringer	Mercury	165.669	3	3	0	0	Junior Johnson	171.151	Pole
3	2/12/65	Daytona Beach, FL	Junior Johnson	Ford	111.076	9	3	1	13	Darel Dieringer	168.444	Pole
4	2/14/65	Daytona Beach, FL	Fred Lorenzen	Ford	141.539	7	4	3	43	Darel Dieringer	171.151	4th
5	2/27/65	Spartanburg, SC	Ned Jarrett	Ford	66.367	5	3	0	0	Dick Hutcherson	70.644	5th
6	2/28/65	Weaverville, NC	Ned Jarrett	Ford	75.678	2	2	2	n/a	Ned Jarrett	84.230	Pole
7	3/07/65	Richmond, VA	Junior Johnson	Ford	61.416	5	4	8	45	Junior Johnson	67.847	Pole
8	3/14/65	Hillsboro, NC	Ned Jarrett	Ford	90.663	1	2	1	4	Junior Johnson	98.570	4th
9	4/11/65	Atlanta, GA	Marvin Panch	Ford	129.410	8	5	5	26	Marvin Panch	145.581	Pole
10	4/17/65	Greenville, SC	Dick Hutcherson	Ford	56.899	3	2	3	n/a	Bud Moore	67.695	2nd
11	4/18/65	N.Wilkesboro, NC	Junior Johnson	Ford	95.047	5	3	3	9	Junior Johnson	101.033	Pole
12	4/25/65	Martinsville, VA	Fred Lorenzen	Ford	66.765	6	3	5	49	Junior Johnson	74.503	2nd
13	4/28/65	Columbia, SC	Tiny Lund	Ford	55.591	6	4	6	n/a	Ned Jarrett	71.061	4th
14	5/02/65	Bristol, TN	Junior Johnson	Ford	74.937	8	4	7	39	Marvin Panch	84.626	3rd
15	5/08/65	Darlington, SC	Junior Johnson	Ford	111.849	11	7	6	50	Fred Lorenzen	138.133	3rd
16	5/14/65	Hampton, VA	Ned Jarrett	Ford	57.815	1	2	1	18	Dick Hutcherson	66.790	2nd
17	5/15/65	Winston-Salem, NC	Junior Johnson	Ford	47.911	0	1	0	0	Junior Johnson	49.261	Pole
18	5/16/65	Hickory, NC	Junior Johnson	Ford	72.130	6	3	2	9	G.C. Spencer	76.312	5th
19	5/23/65	Charlotte, NC	Fred Lorenzen	Ford	121.722	22	6	11	80	Fred Lorenzen	145.268	Pole
20	5/27/65	Shelby, NC	Ned Jarrett	Ford	63.909	1	2	n/a	n/a	Dick Hutcherson	65.862	3rd
21	5/29/65	Asheville, NC	Junior Johnson	Ford	66.293	0	1	n/a	n/a	Junior Johnson	70.601	Pole
22	5/30/65	Harris, NC	Ned Jarrett	Ford	56.851	2	2	n/a	n/a	Paul Lewis	61.644	5th
23	6/03/65	Nashville, TN	Dick Hutcherson	Ford	71.386	1	1	n/a	n/a	Tom Pistone	79.155	2nd
24	6/06/65	Birmingham, AL	Ned Jarrett	Ford	56.364	0	1	1	33	Ned Jarrett	71.575	Pole
25	6/13/65	Atlanta, GA	Marvin Panch	Ford	110.120	17	7	8	98	Fred Lorenzen	143.407	2nd
26	6/19/65	Greenville, SC	Dick Hutcherson	Ford	55.274	2	3	4	n/a	Ned Jarrett	65.574	2nd
27	6/24/65	Myrtle Beach, SC	Dick Hutcherson	Ford	59.701	3	3	n/a	n/a	Dick Hutcherson	66.421	Pole
28	6/27/65	Valdosta, GA	Cale Yarborough	Ford	58.862	2	3	n/a	n/a	Dick Hutcherson	64.540	5th
29	7/04/65	Daytona Beach, FL	A.J. Foyt	Ford	150.046	19	7	3	20	Marvin Panch	171.510	11th
30	7/08/65	Manassas, VA	Junior Johnson	Ford	68.165	1	2	1	8	Ned Jarrett	73.569	2nd
31	7/09/65	Old Bridge, PA	Junior Johnson	Ford	72.087	4	3	2	16	Marvin Panch	77.286	2nd
32	7/14/65	Islip, NY	Marvin Panch	Ford	43.828	0	1	n/a	n/a	Marvin Panch	51.246	Pole
33	7/18/65	Watkins Glen, NY	Marvin Panch	Ford	98.182	3	3	0	0	No Time Trials	NTT	3rd
34	7/25/65	Bristol, TN	Ned Jarrett	Ford	61.826	9	4	8	167	Fred Lorenzen	84.348	6th
35	7/31/65	Nashville, TN	Richard Petty	Plymouth	72.383	2	1	1	13	Richard Petty	82.117	Pole
36	8/05/65	Shelby, NC	Ned Jarrett	Ford	64.748	1	2	2	5	David Pearson	67.797	3rd
37	8/08/65	Weaverville, NC	Richard Petty	Plymouth	74.343	8	4	5	n/a	Richard Petty	86.455	Pole
38	8/13/65	Maryville, TN	Dick Hutcherson	Ford	65.455	2	2	n/a	n/a	Ned Jarrett	77.620	3rd
39	8/14/65	Spartanburg, SC	Ned Jarrett	Ford	56.926	2	2	n/a	n/a	Dick Hutcherson	66.890	5th
40	8/15/65	Augusta, GA	Dick Hutcherson	Ford	71.499	1	2	2	12	Ned Jarrett	81.118	2nd
41	8/19/65	Columbia, SC	David Pearson	Dodge	57.361	5	3	4	38	Dick Hutcherson	71.343	6th
42	8/24/65	Moyock, NC	Dick Hutcherson	Ford	63.047	1	2	n/a	n/a	Richard Petty	68.493	3rd
43	8/25/65	Beltsville, MD	Ned Jarrett	Ford	74.165	0	1	n/a	n/a	Ned Jarrett	79.260	Pole
44	8/28/65	Winston-Salem NC	Junior Johnson	Ford	46.632	1	2	n/a	n/a	Richard Petty	50.195	2nd
45	9/06/65	Darlington, SC	Ned Jarrett	Ford	115.878	23	8	7	44	Junior Johnson	137.571	10th
46	9/10/65	Hickory, NC	Richard Petty	Plymouth	74.365	7	4	0	0	Junior Johnson	74.766	5th
47	9/14/65	New Oxford, PA	Dick Hutcherson	Ford	82.607	1	2	n/a	n/a	Richard Petty	86.705	2nd
48	9/17/65	Manassas, VA	Richard Petty	Plymouth	67.890	2	3	n/a	n/a	Ned Jarrett	73.851	2nd
49	9/18/65	Richmond, VA	David Pearson	Dodge	60.983	10	5	n/a	n/a	Dick Hutcherson	67.340	2nd
50	9/26/65	Martinsville, VA	Junior Johnson	Ford	67.056	5	2	3	19	Richard Petty	74.503	3rd
51	10/03/65	N.Wilkesboro, NC	Junior Johnson	Ford	88.801	3	3	5	36	Fred Lorenzen	101.580	5th
52	10/17/65	Charlotte, NC	Fred Lorenzen	Ford	119.117	28	9	6	47	Fred Lorenzen	147.773	Pole
53	10/24/65	Hillsborough, NC	Dick Hutcherson	Ford	87.462	3	3	3	14	Dick Hutcherson	98.810	Pole
54	10/31/65	Rockingham, NC	Curtis Turner	Ford	101.942	16	6	8	55	Richard Petty	116.620	6th
55	11/07/65	Moyock, NC	Ned Jarrett	Ford	63.773	7	3	n/a	n/a	Bobby Isaac	68.143	2nd

1966 NASCAR Grand National Circuit Season

No.	Date	Site	Race Winner	Car	Speed	Lead Chgs	Ldrs	Caut.	C.Laps	Pole Winner	Speed	Winner Started
1	11/14/65	Augusta, GA	Richard Petty	Plymouth	73.569	6	4	3	22	Richard Petty	82.987	Pole
2	1/23/66	Riverside, CA	Dan Gurney	Ford	97.952	9	3	2	n/a	David Pearson	106.078	2nd
3	2/25/66	Daytona Beach, FL	Paul Goldsmith	Plymouth	160.427	5	3	1	3	Richard Petty	175.165	8th
4	2/25/66	Daytona Beach, FL	Earl Balmer	Dodge	153.191	5	5	1	7	Dick Hutcherson	174.317	6th
5	2/27/66	Daytona Beach, FL	Richard Petty	Plymouth	160.927	14	6	4	22	Richard Petty	175.165	Pole
6	3/13/66	Rockingham, NC	Paul Goldsmith	Plymouth	100.027	26	10	10	70	Paul Goldsmith	116.684	Pole
7	3/20/66	Bristol, TN	Dick Hutcherson	Ford	69.952	7	4	7	92	David Pearson	86.248	6th
8	3/27/66	Atlanta, GA	Jim Hurtubise	Plymouth	131.247	23	9	5	31	Richard Petty	147.742	5th
9	4/03/66	Hickory, NC	David Pearson	Dodge	68.428	7	5	6	29	Elmo Langley	75.117	4th
10	4/07/66	Columbia, SC	David Pearson	Dodge	65.574	4	4	8	19	Tom Pistone	72.202	6th

No.	Date	Site	Race Winner	Car	Speed	Lead Chgs	Ldrs	Caut.	C.Laps	Pole Winner	Speed	Winner Started
11	4/09/66	Greenville, SC	David Pearson	Dodge	65.850	3	2	3	11	Tiny Lund	68.208	2nd
12	4/11/66	Winston-Salem, NC	David Pearson	Dodge	51.341	2	2	11	4	David Pearson	54.479	Pole
13	4/17/66	N.Wilkesboro, NC	Jim Paschal	Plymouth	89.045	6	2	8	48	Jim Paschal	102.693	Pole
14	4/24/66	Martinsville, VA	Jim Paschal	Plymouth	69.156	6	4	1	6	Jim Paschal	76.345	Pole
15	4/30/66	Darlington, SC	Richard Petty	Plymouth	131.933	6	5	1	5	Richard Petty	140.815	Pole
16	5/07/66	Hampton, VA	Richard Petty	Plymouth	60.616	2	2	n/a	n/a	Richard Petty	66.821	Pole
17	5/10/66	Macon, GA	Richard Petty	Plymouth	82.023	4	3	0	0	Richard Petty	85.026	Pole
18	5/13/66	Monroe, NC	Darel Dieringer	Ford	60.140	4	4	3	n/a	James Hylton	65.099	20th
19	5/15/66	Richmond, VA	David Pearson	Dodge	66.539	5	4	2	14	Tom Pistone	70.978	4th
20	5/22/66	Charlotte, NC	Marvin Panch	Plymouth	135.042	14	8	5	18	Richard Petty	148.637	7th
21	5/29/66	Moyock, NC	David Pearson	Dodge	61.913	1	2	n/a	n/a	Richard Petty	69.164	2nd
22	6/02/66	Asheville, NC	David Pearson	Dodge	64.917	1	2	n/a	n/a	Richard Petty	72.964	2nd
23	6/04/66	Spartanburg, SC	Elmo Langley	Ford	60.050	2	2	n/a	n/a	David Pearson	68.027	6th
24	6/09/66	Maryville, TN	David Pearson	Dodge	71.986	1	2	2	7	Tom Pistone	78.947	4th
25	6/12/66	Weaverville, NC	Richard Petty	Plymouth	81.423	4	2	0	0	Richard Petty	86.455	Pole
26	6/15/66	Beltsville, MD	Tiny Lund	Ford	73.409	1	2	n/a	n/a	Richard Petty	80.250	7th
27	6/25/66	Greenville, SC	David Pearson	Dodge	66.286	0	1	1	n/a	David Pearson	69.364	Pole
28	7/04/66	Daytona Beach, FL	Sam McQuagg	Dodge	153.813	17	6	4	23	LeeRoy Yarbrough	176.660	4th
29	7/07/66	Manassas, VA	Elmo Langley	Ford	68.079	5	4	2	n/a	Bobby Allison	73.973	2nd
30	7/10/66	Bridgehampton, NY	David Pearson	Dodge	86.949	2	2	0	0	David Pearson	Qual Race	Pole
31	7/12/66	Oxford, ME	Bobby Allison	Chevrolet	56.782	2	2	4	25	Bobby Allison	65.681	Pole
32	7/14/66	Fonda, NY	David Pearson	Dodge	61.010	8	4	n/a	n/a	Richard Petty	71.514	12th
33	7/16/66	Islip, NY	Bobby Allison	Chevrolet	47.285	2	3	n/a	n/a	Tom Pistone	55.919	7th
34	7/24/66	Bristol, TN	Paul Goldsmith	Plymouth	77.963	3	3	2	24	Curtis Turner	84.309	4th
35	7/28/66	Maryville, NC	Paul Lewis	Plymouth	69.822	4	3	n/a	n/a	Buddy Baker	77.821	27th
36	7/30/66	Nashville, TN	Richard Petty	Plymouth	71.770	0	1	4	41	Richard Petty	82.493	Pole
37	8/07/66	Atlanta, GA	Richard Petty	Plymouth	130.244	18	7	6	37	Curtis Turner	148.331	5th
38	8/18/66	Columbia, SC	David Pearson	Dodge	66.128	4	4	2	n/a	Bobby Allison	73.469	4th
39	8/21/66	Weaverville, NC	Darel Dieringer	Mercury	76.700	8	4	3	23	Junior Johnson	86.831	2nd
40	8/24/66	Beltsville, MD	Bobby Allison	Chevrolet	68.899	2	2	n/a	n/a	Bobby Allison	79.330	Pole
41	8/27/66	Winston-Salem, NC	David Pearson	Dodge	45.928	4	3	3	16	Richard Petty	54.348	2nd
42	9/05/66	Darlington, SC	Darel Dieringer	Mercury	114.830	28	10	8	80	LeeRoy Yarbrough	140.058	3rd
43	9/09/66	Hickory, NC	David Pearson	Dodge	70.533	3	2	5	14	Richard Petty	76.923	2nd
44	9/01/66	Richmond, VA	David Pearson	Dodge	62.886	4	3	5	29	David Pearson	70.644	Pole
45	9/18/66	Hillsborough, NC	Dick Hutcherson	Ford	90.603	2	1	0	0	Dick Hutcherson	95.716	Pole
46	9/25/66	Martinsville, VA	Fred Lorenzen	Ford	69.177	6	4	4	26	Junior Johnson	75.598	2nd
47	20/02/66	N.Wilkesboro, NC	Dick Hutcherson	Ford	89.012	4	3	5	52	Junior Johnson	103.069	4th
48	10/16/66	Charlotte, NC	LeeRoy Yarbrough	Dodge	130.576	14	6	6	46	Fred Lorenzen	150.533	17th
49	10/30/66	Rockingham, NC	Fred Lorenzen	Ford	104.348	20	2	4	35	Fred Lorenzen	115.988	Pole

1967 NASCAR Grand National Circuit Season

No.	Date	Site	Race Winner	Car	Speed	Lead Chgs	Ldrs	Caut.	C.Laps	Pole Winner	Speed	Winner Started
1	11/13/66	Augusta, GA	Richard Petty	Plymouth	71.809	1	2	2	n/a	Dick Hutcherson	84.112	3rd
2	1/22,29/67	Riverside, CA	Parnelli Jones	Ford	91.080	10	7	n/a	n/a	Dick Hutcherson	106.951	6th
3	2/24/67	Daytona Beach, FL	LeeRoy Yarbrough	Dodge	163.934	14	4	1	n/a	Curtis Turner	180.831	3rd
4	2/24/67	Daytona Beach, FL	Frad Lorenzen	Ford	174.587	15	6	0	0	Richard Petty	179.068	6th
5	2/26/67	Daytona Beach, FL	Mario Andretti	Ford	146.926	36	9	6	54	Curtis Turner	180.831	12th
6	3/05/67	Weaverville, NC	Richard Petty	Plymouth	83.360	6	3	1	5	Darel Dieringer	88.626	2nd
7	3/19/67	Bristol, TN	David Pearson	Dodge	75.937	13	6	6	59	Darel Dieringer	87.124	14th
8	3/25/67	Greenville, SC	David Pearson	Dodge	61.824	3	2	n/a	n/a	Dick Hutcherson	70.313	2nd
9	3/27/67	Winston-Salem, NC	Bobby Allison	Chevrolet	49.248	3	3	1	8	Bobby Allison	53.476	Pole
10	4/02/67	Atlanta, GA	Cale Yarborough	Ford	131.238	9	5	6	39	Cale Yarborough	148.996	Pole
11	4/06/67	Columbia, SC	Richard Petty	Plymouth	65.455	7	2	n/a	n/a	Dick Hutcherson	74.166	2nd
12	4/09/67	Hickory, NC	Richard Petty	Plymouth	69.699	10	6	5	22	Richard Petty	79.120	Pole
13	4/16/67	N.Wilkesboro, NC	Darel Dieringer	Ford	93.594	0	1	6	33	Darel Dieringer	104.603	Pole
14	4/23/67	Martinsville, VA	Richard Petty	Plymouth	67.446	11	4	8	57	Darel Dieringer	77.319	2nd
15	4/28/67	Savannah, GA	Bobby Allison	Chevrolet	66.802	3	4	n/a	n/a	John Sears	72.173	5th
16	4/30/67	Richmond, VA	Richard Petty	Plymouth	65.982	6	3	6	32	Richard Petty	70.038	Pole
17	5/13/67	Darlington, SC	Richard Petty	Plymouth	125.738	12	6	5	31	David Pearson	144.536	2nd
18	5/19/67	Beltsville, MD	Jim Paschal	Plymouth	71.036	3	2	3	n/a	Richard Petty	80.286	3rd
19	5/20/67	Hampton, VA	Richard Petty	Plymouth	66.704	4	3	0	0	Richard Petty	68.214	Pole
20	5/28/67	Charlotte, NC	Jim Paschal	Plymouth	135.832	11	7	5	32	Cale Yarborough	154.385	10th
21	6/02/67	Asheville, NC	Jim Paschal	Plymouth	63.080	5	4	n/a	n/a	Richard Petty	73.710	5th
22	6/06/67	Macon, GA	Richard Petty	Plymouth	80.321	2	2	1	3	Richard Petty	88.538	Pole
23	6/08/67	Maryville, TN	Richard Petty	Plymouth	72.919	4	2	n/a	n/a	Jim Hunter	79.051	6th
24	6/10/67	Birmingham, AL	Bobby Allison	Dodge	88.999	1	2	n/a	n/a	Jim Paschal	94.142	4th
25	6/18/67	Rockingham, NC	Richard Petty	Plymouth	104.682	20	5	9	45	Dick Hutcherson	116.486	2nd
26	6/24/67	Greenville, SC	Richard Petty	Plymouth	61.781	2	2	2	n/a	Richard Petty	69.498	Pole
27	6/27/67	Montgomery, AL	Jim Paschal	Plymouth	72.435	1	2	n/a	n/a	Richard Petty	77.088	3rd
28	7/04/67	Daytona Beach, FL	Cale Yarborough	Ford	143.583	41	8	4	43	Darel Dieringer	179.802	2nd
29	7/09/67	Trenton, NJ	Richard Petty	Plymouth	95.322	8	3	4	n/a	Richard Petty	101.208	Pole
30	7/11/67	Oxford, ME	Bobby Allison	Chevrolet	61.697	8	4	2	4	James Hylton	66.043	2nd
31	7/13/67	Fonda, NY	Richard Petty	Plymouth	65.826	4	3	5	20	Richard Petty	72.173	Pole
32	7/15/67	Islip, NY	Richard Petty	Plymouth	42.428	5	4	5	29	Richard Petty	51.136	Pole
33	7/23/67	Bristol, TN	Richard Petty	Plymouth	78.705	11	3	6	42	Richard Petty	86.621	Pole
34	7/27/67	Maryville, TN	Dick Hutcherson	Ford	65.765	2	2	n/a	n/a	Dick Hutcherson	79.540	Pole
35	7/29/67	Nashville, TN	Richard Petty	Plymouth	70.866	7	5	8	50	Dick Hutcherson	84.260	2nd
36	8/06/67	Atlanta, GA	Dick Hutcherson	Ford	132.286	13	6	6	38	Darel Dieringer	150.669	8th
37	8/12/67	Winston-Salem, NC	Richard Petty	Plymouth	50.893	0	1	0	0	Richard Petty	53.16	Pole
38	8/17/67	Columbia, SC	Richard Petty	Plymouth	64.274	4	2	5	n/a	Richard Petty	74.968	Pole
39	8/25/67	Savannah, GA	Richard Petty	Plymouth	65.041	0	1	n/a	n/a	Richard Petty	71.942	Pole
40	9/04/67	Darlington, SC	Richard Petty	Plymouth	130.423	6	4	3	25	Richard Petty	143.486	Pole
41	9/08/67	Hickory, NC	Richard Petty	Plymouth	71.414	9	4	6	44	Dick Hutcherson	86.538	2nd
42	9/10/67	Richmond, VA	Richard Petty	Plymouth	57.631	7	6	10	71	No Time Trials	NTT	2nd
43	9/15/67	Beltsville, MD	Richard Petty	Plymouth	76.563	6	2	n/a	n/a	Richard Petty	81.044	Pole
44	9/17/67	Hillsborough, NC	Richard Petty	Plymouth	81.574	3	3	3	33	Richard Petty	94.159	Pole
45	9/24/67	Martinsville, VA	Richard Petty	Plymouth	69.605	3	3	7	43	Cale Yarborough	77.386	5th
46	10/01/67	N.Wilkesboro, NC	Richard Petty	Plymouth	94.837	6	5	3	20	Dick Hutcherson	104.312	5th
47	10/15/67	Charlotte, NC	Buddy Baker	Dodge	130.317	22	7	9	64	Cale Yarborough	154.872	4th
48	10/29/67	Rockingham, NC	Bobby Allison	Ford	98.420	26	11	9	81	David Pearson	117.120	3rd
49	11/05/67	Weaverville, NC	Bobby Allison	Ford	76.291	21	4	10	73	Bobby Allison	90.407	Pole

1968 NASCAR Grand National Circuit Season

No.	Date	Site	Race Winner	Car	Speed	Lead Chgs	Ldrs	Caut.	C.Laps	Pole Winner	Speed	Winner Started
1	11/12/67	Macon, GA	Bobby Allison	Ford	81.001	7	4	6	n/a	LeeRoy Yarbrough	94.323	2nd
2	11/26/67	Montgomery, AL	Richard Petty	Plymouth	70.644	2	2	4	20	Richard Petty	79.964	Pole
3	1/21/68	Riverside, CA	Dan Gurney	Ford	100.598	16	4	n/a	n/a	Dan Gurney	110.971	Pole
4	2/25/68	Daytona Beach, FL	Cale Yarborough	Mercury	143.251	21	9	11	60	Cale Yarborough	189.222	Pole
5	3/17/68	Bristol, VA	David Pearson	Ford	77.247	18	4	11	81	Richard Petty	88.582	2nd
6	3/24/68	Richmond, VA	David Pearson	Ford	65.217	7	3	n/a	n/a	Bobby Isaac	67.822	16th
7	3/31/68	Atlanta, GA	Cale Yarborough	Mercury	125.564	15	6	11	73	LeeRoy Yarbrough	155.646	4th
8	4/07/68	Hickory, NC	Richard Petty	Plymouth	79.435	4	3	2	19	David Pearson	86.975	4th
9	4/13/68	Greenville, SC	Richard Petty	Plymouth	63.347	5	3	6	n/a	David Pearson	67.848	3rd
10	4/18/68	Columbia, SC	Bobby Isaac	Dodge	71.358	1	2	4	n/a	Richard Petty	75.282	6th
11	4/21/68	N.Wilkesboro, NC	David Pearson	Ford	90.425	13	6	10	67	David Pearson	104.993	Pole
12	4/28/68	Martinsville, VA	Cale Yarborough	Mercury	66.686	9	5	10	72	David Pearson	78.230	3rd
13	5/03/68	Augusta, GA	Bobby Isaac	Dodge	73.099	2	2	n/a	n/a	Bobby Isaac	83.877	Pole
14	5/05/68	Weaverville, NC	David Pearson	Ford	75.167	2	2	6	45	David Pearson	89.708	Pole
15	5/11/68	Darlington, SC	David Pearson	Ford	132.699	13	7	4	23	LeeRoy Yarbrough	148.850	2nd
16	5/17/68	Beltsville, MD	David Pearson	Ford	74.844	3	3	n/a	n/a	Richard Petty	83.604	2nd
17	5/18/68	Hampton, VA	David Pearson	Ford	71.457	7	3	n/a	25	Richard Petty	80.801	2nd
18	5/26/68	Charlotte, NC	Buddy Baker	Dodge	104.207	16	8	6	110	Donnie Allison	159.223	12th
19	5/31/68	Asheville, NC	Richard Petty	Plymouth	65.741	0	1	n/a	n/a	Richard Petty	74.349	Pole
20	6/02/68	Macon, GA	David Pearson	Ford	79.342	n/a	n/a	1	10	David Pearson	86.873	Pole
21	6/06/68	Maryville, TN	Richard Petty	Plymouth	76.743	2	23	n/a	n/a	David Pearson	88.583	Pole
22	6/08/68	Birmingham, AL	Richard Petty	Plymouth	89.153	3	2	2	n/a	David Pearson	97.784	2nd
23	6/16/68	Rockingham, NC	Donnie Allison	Ford	99.338	20	5	8	74	LeeRoy Yarbrough	118.644	7th
24	6/22/68	Greenville, SC	Richard Petty	Plymouth	64.609	3	3	6	18	David Pearson	68.834	2nd
25	7/04/68	Daytona Beach, FL	Cale Yarborough	Mercury	167.247	9	4	2	14	Charlie Glotzbach	185.156	4th
26	7/07/68	Islip, NY	Bobby Allison	Chevrolet	48.561	3	4	1	3	Buddy Baker	51.873	5th
27	7/09/68	Oxford, ME	Richard Petty	Plymouth	63.717	3	3	0	0	Buddy Baker	67.835	2nd
28	7/11/68	Fonda, NY	Richard Petty	Plymouth	64.935	1	2	3	19	David Pearson	73.800	2nd
29	7/14/68	Trenton, NJ	LeeRoy Yarbrough	Ford	89.079	11	4	5	28	LeeRoy Yarbrough	103.717	Pole
30	7/21/68	Bristol, TN	David Pearson	Ford	76.310	8	5	13	92	LeeRoy Yarbrough	87.421	6th
31	7/25/68	Maryville, TN	Richard Petty	Plymouth	71.513	1	2	n/a	39	Bobby Isaac	86.538	2nd
32	7/27/68	Nashville, TN	David Pearson	Ford	72.980	3	2	6	42	Richard Petty	85.066	3rd
33	8/04/68	Atlanta, GA	LeeRoy Yarbrough	Mercury	127.068	29	9	11	67	Buddy Baker	153.361	5th
34	8/08/68	Columbia, SC	David Pearson	Ford	67.039	4	4	n/a	n/a	Buddy Baker	74.196	10th
35	8/10/68	Winston-Salem, NC	David Pearson	Ford	42.940	1	2	5	34	Richard Petty	53.828	2nd
36	8/18/68	Weaverville, NC	David Pearson	Ford	73.686	7	4	7	90	Darel Dieringer	88.409	2nd
37	8/23/68	S.Boston, VA	Richard Petty	Plymouth	75.916	2	2	n/a	n/a	Richard Petty	84.428	Pole
38	8/24/68	Hampton, VA	David Pearson	Ford	75.582	0	1	0	0	David Pearson	78.007	Pole
39	9/02/68	Darlington, SC	Cale Yarborough	Mercury	126.132	13	6	7	65	Charlie Glotzbach	144.830	2nd
40	9/06/68	Hickory, NC	David Pearson	Ford	80.357	2	3	n/a	n/a	Richard Petty	85.868	2nd
41	9/08/68	Richmond, VA	Richard Petty	Plymouth	85.659	13	5	10	52	Richard Petty	103.178	Pole
42	9/13/68	Beltsville, MD	Bobby Isaac	Dodge	71.033	1	2	n/a	n/a	Cale Yarborough	81.311	3rd
43	9/15/68	Hillsborough, NC	Richard Petty	Plymouth	87.681	3	2	1	4	Richard Petty	93.225	Pole
44	9/22/68	Martinsville, VA	Richard Petty	Plymouth	65.808	11	5	7	60	Cale Yarborough	77.279	6th
45	9/29/68	N.Wilkesboro, NC	Richard Petty	Plymouth	94.103	8	4	3	25	Bobby Allison	104.525	3rd
46	10/05/68	Augusta, GA	David Pearson	Ford	75.821	1	2	1	n/a	Bobby Allison	84.822	3rd
47	10/20/68	Charlotte, NC	Charlie Glotzbach	Dodge	135.234	26	9	6	49	Charlie Glotzbach	156.060	Pole
48	10/27/68	Rockingham, NC	Richard Petty	Plymouth	105.060	18	7	6	46	Cale Yarborough	118.717	4th
49	11/03/68	Jefferson, GA	Cale Yarborough	Mercury	77.737	4	3	n/a	n/a	David Pearson	90.694	3rd

1969 NASCAR Grand National Circuit Season

No.	Date	Site	Race Winner	Car	Speed	Lead Chgs	Ldrs	Caut.	C.Laps	Pole Winner	Speed	Winner Started
1	11/17/68	Macon, GA	Richard Petty	Plymouth	85.121	12	4	2	16	David Pearson	95.472	5th
2	11/08/68	Montgomery, AL	Bobby Allison	Plymouth	73.200	7	3	2	11	Richard Petty	80.899	3rd
3	2/01/69	Riverside, CA	Richard Petty	Ford	105.498	9	4	0	0	A.J. Foyt	110.323	4th
4	2/20/69	Daytona Beach, FL	David Pearson	Ford	152.181	5	5	2	17	Buddy Baker	188.901	15th
5	2/20/69	Daytona Beach, FL	Bobby Isaac	Dodge	151.668	9	5	1	15	Bobby Isaac	188.726	Pole
6	2/23/69	Daytona Beach, FL	LeeRoy Yarbrough	Ford	157.950	17	8	5	38	Buddy Baker	188.901	19th
7	3/09/69	Rockingham, NC	David Pearson	Ford	102.569	23	7	10	82	David Pearson	119.619	Pole
8	3/16/69	Augusta, GA	David Pearson	Ford	77.586	1	2	1	10	Bobby Isaac	86.901	3rd
9	3/23/69	Bristol, TN	Bobby Allison	Dodge	81.455	9	3	4	32	Bobby Isaac	88.669	4th
10	3/30/69	Atlanta, GA	Cale Yarborough	Mercury	132.191	10	4	5	53	David Pearson	156.794	5th
11	4/03/69	Columbia, SC	Bobby Isaac	Dodge	68.558	7	5	4	21	Bobby Isaac	73.806	Pole
12	4/06/69	Hickory, NC	Bobby Isaac	Dodge	79.086	0	1	4	19	Bobby Isaac	85.612	Pole
13	4/08/69	Greenville, SC	Bobby Isaac	Dodge	64.389	10	5	5	27	David Pearson	70.539	2nd
14	4/13/69	Richmond, VA	David Pearson	Ford	73.752	6	4	6	40	David Pearson	82.538	Pole
15	4/20/69	N.Wilkesboro, NC	Bobby Allison	Dodge	95.268	11	4	4	30	Bobby Isaac	106.731	11th
16	4/27/69	Martinsville, VA	Richard Petty	Ford	64.405	11	5	8	61	Bobby Allison	78.260	6th
17	5/04/69	Weaverville, NC	Bobby Isaac	Dodge	72.581	2	2	3	34	Bobby Isaac	90.361	Pole
18	5/10/69	Darlington, SC	LeeRoy Yarbrough	Mercury	131.572	11	6	4	24	Cale Yarborough	152.293	4th
19	5/16/69	Beltsville, MD	Bobby Isaac	Dodge	73.059	0	1	3	29	Bobby Isaac	83.329	Pole
20	5/17/69	Hampton, VA	David Pearson	Ford	75.789	4	2	1	5	David Pearson	80.236	Pole
21	5/25/69	Charlotte, NC	LeeRoy Yarbrough	Mercury	134.361	13	7	5	45	Donnie Allison	159.296	2nd
22	6/01/69	Macon, GA	Bobby Isaac	Dodge	73.717	3	2	2	28	David Pearson	87.946	2nd
23	6/05/69	Maryville, TN	Bobby Isaac	Dodge	81.706	3	2	1	8	David Pearson	87.976	3rd
24	6/15/69	Brooklyn, MI	Cale Yarborough	Mercury	139.254	26	12	7	35	Donnie Allison	160.135	4th
25	6/19/69	Kingsport, TN	Richard Petty	Ford	73.619	3	3	5	35	Bobby Isaac	90.112	3rd
26	6/21/69	Greenville, SC	Bobby Isaac	Dodge	61.813	4	2	5	29	Bobby Isaac	66.030	Pole
27	6/26/69	Raleigh, NC	David Pearson	Ford	65.418	3	2	4	12	Bobby Isaac	72.942	2nd
28	7/04/69	Daytona Beach, FL	LeeRoy Yarbrough	Ford	160.875	16	7	2	27	Cale Yarborough	190.706	9th
29	7/06/69	Dover, DE	Richard Petty	Ford	115.772	7	3	4	27	David Pearson	130.430	3rd
30	7/10/69	Thompson, CT	David Pearson	Ford	89.498	4	3	2	13	David Pearson	99.800	Pole
31	7/13/69	Trenton, NJ	David Pearson	Ford	121.008	8	4	2	10	Bobby Isaac	132.668	2nd
32	7/15/69	Beltsville, MD	Richard Petty	Ford	77.253	8	4	2	9	Richard Petty	82.094	Pole
33	7/20/69	Bristol, VA	David Pearson	Ford	79.737	9	7	8	58	Cale Yarborough	103.432	3rd
34	7/26/69	Nashville, TN	Richard Petty	Ford	78.740	2	2	5	18	Richard Petty	84.918	Pole

No.	Date	Site	Race Winner	Car	Speed	Lead Chgs	Ldrs	Caut.	C.Laps	Pole Winner	Speed	Winner Started
35	7/27/69	Maryville, TN	Richard Petty	Ford	82.417	4	3	1	7	David Pearson	87.434	3rd
36	8/10/69	Atlanta, GA	LeeRoy Yarbrough	Ford	133.001	19	7	3	31	Cale Yarborough	155.413	2nd
37	8/17/69	Brooklyn, MI	David Pearson	Ford	115.508	26	12	7	78	David Pearson	161.714	Pole
38	8/21/69	S.Boston, VA	Bobby Isaac	Dodge	76.906	3	2	2	13	Bobby Isaac	84.959	Pole
39	8/22/69	Winston-Salem, NC	Richard Petty	Ford	47.458	2	2	3	17	Richard Petty	54.253	Pole
40	8/24/69	Weaverville, NC	Bobby Isaac	Dodge	80.450	7	3	4	17	Bobby Isaac	89.000	Pole
41	9/01/69	Darlington, SC	LeeRoy Yarbrough	Ford	105.612	20	8	7	85	Cale Yarborough	151.985	4th
42	9/05/69	Hickory, NC	Bobby Isaac	Dodge	80.519	4	3	3	11	Bobby Isaac	86.212	Pole
43	9/07/69	Richmond, VA	Bobby Allison	Dodge	76.388	3	2	6	39	Richard Petty	91.257	25th
44	9/14/69	Talladega, AL	Richard Brickhouse	Dodge	153.778	35	7	7	38	Bobby Isaac	196.386	9th
45	9/18/69	Columbia, SC	Bobby Isaac	Dodge	70.230	3	2	2	15	Richard Petty	73.108	2nd
46	9/28/69	Martinsville, VA	Richard Petty	Ford	63.127	11	6	11	61	David Pearson	83.197	6th
47	10/05/69	N.Wilkesboro, NC	David Pearson	Ford	93.429	6	4	3	23	Bobby Isaac	106.032	2nd
48	10/12/69	Charlotte, NC	Donnie Allison	Ford	131.271	28	6	9	50	Cale Yarborough	162.162	3rd
49	10/17/69	Savannah, GA	Bobby Isaac	Dodge	78.482	2	2	2	11	Bobby Isaac	86.095	Pole
50	10/19/69	Augusta, GA	Bobby Isaac	Dodge	78.740	2	2	0	0	Bobby Isaac	85.689	Pole
51	10/26/69	Rockingham, NC	LeeRoy Yarbrough	Ford	111.938	25	7	7	66	Charlie Glotzbach	136.972	9th
52	11/02/69	Jefferson, GA	Bobby Isaac	Dodge	85.106	1	2	1	4	David Pearson	89.565	2nd
53	11/09/69	Macon, GA	Bobby Allison	Dodge	81.079	14	4	10	58	Bobby Isaac	98.148	5th
54	12/07/69	College Station, TX	Bobby Isaac	Dodge	144.277	35	6	3	29	Buddy Baker	176.284	7th

1970 NASCAR Grand National Circuit Season

No.	Date	Site	Race Winner	Car	Speed	Lead Chgs	Ldrs	Caut.	C.Laps	Pole Winner	Speed	Winner Started
1	1/18/70	Riverside, CA	A.J. Foyt	Ford	97.450	20	7	6	31	Dan Gurney	112.060	3rd
2	2/19/70	Daytona Beach, FL	Cale Yarborough	Mercury	183.295	4	4	0	0	Cale Yarborough	194.015	Pole
3	2/19/70	Daytona Beach, FL	Charlie Glotzbach	Dodge	147.734	4	3	1	13	Buddy Baker	192.624	2nd
4	2/22/70	Daytona Beach, FL	Pete Hamilton	Plymouth	149.601	24	10	6	45	Cale Yarborough	194.015	9th
5	3/01/70	Richmond, VA	James Hylton	Ford	82.044	2	3	1	7	Richard Petty	89.137	3rd
6	3/08/70	Rockingham, NC	Richard Petty	Plymouth	116.117	24	7	9	67	Bobby Allison	139.048	8th
7	3/15/70	Savannah, GA	Richard Petty	Plymouth	82.418	2	2	1	4	Richard Petty	85.874	Pole
8	3/29/70	Atlanta, GA	Bobby Allison	Dodge	139.554	20	8	4	23	Cale Yarborough	159.929	9th
9	4/05/70	Bristol, TN	Donnie Allison	Ford	87.543	10	6	6	58	David Pearson	107.079	2nd
10	4/12/70	Talladega, AL	Pete Hamilton	Plymouth	152.321	32	8	6	42	Bobby Isaac	199.658	6th
11	4/18/70	N.Wilkesboro, NC	Richard Petty	Plymouth	94.246	1	2	3	21	Bobby Isaac	107.041	16th
12	4/30/70	Columbia, SC	Richard Petty	Plymouth	62.685	5	4	6	30	Larry Baumel	72.239	7th
13	5/09/70	Darlington, SC	David Pearson	Ford	129.668	20	7	4	37	Charlie Glotzbach	153.822	3rd
14	5/15/70	Beltsville, MD	Bobby Isaac	Dodge	76.370	5	4	1	10	James Hylton	83.128	3rd
15	5/18/70	Hampton, VA	Bobby Isaac	Dodge	72.245	3	3	2	11	Bobby Isaac	79.659	Pole
16	5/24/70	Charlotte, NC	Donnie Allison	Ford	129.680	28	11	10	66	Bobby Isaac	159.277	9th
17	5/28/70	Maryville, TN	Bobby Isaac	Dodge	82.558	1	1	2	15	Bobby Allison	92.094	2nd
18	5/31/70	Martinsville, VA	Bobby Isaac	Dodge	68.584	4	3	7	46	Donnie Allison	82.609	2nd
19	6/07/70	Brooklyn, MI	Cale Yarborough	Mercury	138.302	15	6	3	28	Pete Hamilton	162.737	4th
20	6/14/70	Riverside, CA	Richard Petty	Plymouth	101.120	3	2	3	13	Bobby Allison	111.621	2nd
21	6/20/70	Hickory, NC	Bobby Isaac	Dodge	68.011	0	1	2	14	Bobby Isaac	79.596	Pole
22	6/26/70	Kingsport, TN	Richard Petty	Plymouth	68.583	2	2	2	14	Richard Petty	75.056	Pole
23	6/27/70	Greenville, SC	Bobby Isaac	Dodge	75.345	3	3	2	10	Bobby Isaac	82.327	Pole
24	7/04/70	Daytona Beach, FL	Donnie Allison	Ford	162.235	32	10	3	17	Cale Yarborough	191.640	15th
25	7/07/70	Malta, NY	Richard Petty	Plymouth	68.589	3	3	1	4	Bobby Isaac	73.213	2nd
26	7/09/70	Thompson, CT	Bobby Isaac	Dodge	80.296	3	3	1	7	Bobby Isaac	87.029	Pole
27	7/12/70	Trenton, NJ	Richard Petty	Plymouth	120.724	12	6	3	13	Bobby Isaac	131.749	4th
28	7/19/70	Bristol, TN	Bobby Allison	Dodge	84.880	9	2	8	54	Cale Yarborough	107.375	10th
29	7/24/70	Maryville, TN	Richard Petty	Plymouth	84.956	3	3	2	7	Richard Petty	91.264	Pole
30	7/25/70	Nashville, TN	Bobby Isaac	Dodge	87.943	5	4	4	39	LeeRoy Yarbrough	114.115	2nd
31	8/02/70	Atlanta, GA	Richard Petty	Plymouth	142.712	10	4	1	10	Fred Lorenzen	157.625	6th
32	8/06/70	Columbia, SC	Bobby Isaac	Dodge	67.101	1	2	3	22	Richard Petty	72.695	7th
33	8/11/70	Ona, WV	Richard Petty	Plymouth	78.358	4	3	1	2	Bobby Allison	83.970	3rd
34	8/16/70	Brooklyn, MI	Charlie Glotzbach	Dodge	147.571	18	8	1	9	Charlie Glotzbach	157.363	Pole
35	8/23/70	Talladega, AL	Pete Hamilton	Plymouth	158.517	23	9	4	30	Bobby Isaac	186.834	4th
36	8/28/70	Winston-Salem, NC	Richard Petty	Plymouth	51.527	2	2	0	0	Richard Petty	54.533	Pole
37	8/29/70	S.Boston, VA	Richard Petty	Plymouth	73.060	2	2	1	10	Richard Petty	81.187	Pole
38	9/07/70	Darlington, SC	Buddy Baker	Dodge	128.817	19	8	9	50	David Pearson	150.555	2nd
39	9/11/70	Hickory, NC	Bobby Isaac	Dodge	73.365	4	2	1	5	Bobby Isaac	78.411	Pole
40	9/13/70	Richmond, VA	Richard Petty	Plymouth	81.476	2	2	2	9	Richard Petty	87.014	Pole
41	9/20/70	Dover, DE	Richard Petty	Plymouth	112.103	9	3	4	27	Bobby Isaac	129.538	2nd
42	9/30/70	Raleigh, NC	Richard Petty	Plymouth	68.376	2	3	1	4	John Sears	71.380	6th
43	10/04/70	N.Wilkesboro, NC	Bobby Isaac	Dodge	90.162	12	3	4	32	Bobby Isaac	105.406	Pole
44	10/11/70	Charlotte, NC	LeeRoy Yarbrough	Ford	123.246	23	8	8	63	Charlie Glotzbach	157.273	5th
45	10/18/70	Martinsville, VA	Richard Petty	Plymouth	72.235	5	4	5	32	Bobby Allison	82.167	4th
46	11/08/70	Macon, GA	Richard Petty	Plymouth	82.284	12	4	5	35	Richard Petty	94.064	Pole
47	11/15/70	Rockingham, NC	Cale Yarborough	Mercury	117.811	13	5	7	46	Charlie Glotzbach	136.498	2nd
48	11/22/70	Hampton, VA	Bobby Allison	Dodge	69.584	3	3	2	10	Benny Parsons	78.239	4th

1971 NASCAR Winston Cup Grand National Series Season

No.	Date	Site	Race Winner	Car	Speed	Lead Chgs	Ldrs	Caut.	C.Laps	Pole Winner	Speed	Winner Started
1	1/10/71	Riverside, CA	Ray Elder	Dodge	100.783	10	4	1	9	Richard Petty	107.084	3rd
2	2/11/71	Daytona Beach, FL	Pete Hamilton	Plymouth	175.029	9	5	0	0	A.J. Foyt	182.744	2nd
3	2/11/71	Daytona Beach, FL	David Pearson	Mercury	168.728	20	4	1	3	Bobby Isaac	180.050	4th
4	2/14/71	Daytona Beach, FL	Richard Petty	Plymouth	144.462	48	11	7	44	A.J. Foyt	182.744	5th
5	2/28/71	Ontario, CA	A.J. Foyt	Mercury	134.168	28	7	5	21	A.J. Foyt	151.711	Pole
6	3/07/71	Richmond, VA	Richard Petty	Plymouth	79.836	6	4	3	18	Dave Marcis	87.178	30th
7	3/14/71	Rockingham, NC	Richard Petty	Plymouth	118.696	19	7	7	36	Fred Lorenzen	133.892	2nd
8	3/21/71	Hickory, NC	Richard Petty	Plymouth	67.700	4	5	3	22	Bobby Allison	79.001	4th
9	3/28/71	Bristol, TN	David Pearson	Ford	91.704	9	5	5	45	David Pearson	105.525	Pole
10	4/04/71	Atlanta, GA	A.J. Foyt	Mercury	131.375	23	6	4	31	A.J. Foyt	155.152	Pole
11	4/08/71	Columbia, SC	Richard Petty	Plymouth	76.514	6	4	2	10	James Hylton	84.229	4th
12	4/10/71	Greenville, SC	Bobby Isaac	Dodge	78.159	1	2	1	5	David Pearson	82.557	2nd
13	4/15/71	Maryville, TN	Richard Petty	Plymouth	88.697	3	4	1	3	Friday Hassler	91.464	2nd

No.	Date	Site	Race Winner	Car	Speed	Lead Chgs	Ldrs	Caut.	C.Laps	Pole Winner	Speed	Winner Started
14	4/18/71	N.Wilkesboro, NC	Richard Petty	Plymouth	98.479	6	4	0	0	Bobby Isaac	106.217	3rd
15	4/25/71	Martinsville, VA	Richard Petty	Plymouth	77.707	10	4	1	3	Donnie Allison	82.529	3rd
16	5/02/71	Darlington, SC	Buddy Baker	Dodge	130.678	14	3	5	30	Donnie Allison	149.826	5th
17	5/09/71	S.Boston, VA	Benny Parsons	Ford	72.271	4	3	2	14	Bobby Isaac	81.548	2nd
18	5/16/71	Talladega, AL	Donnie Allison	Mercury	147.419	45	4	7	45	Donnie Allison	185.869	Pole
19	5/21/71	Asheville, NC	Richard Petty	Plymouth	71.231	4	2	0	0	Richard Petty	79.598	Pole
20	5/23/71	Kingsport, TN	Bobby Isaac	Dodge	63.242	2	2	6	35	Bobby Isaac	75.167	Pole
21	5/30/71	Charlotte, NC	Bobby Allison	Mercury	140.422	13	5	3	24	Charlie Glotzbach	157.788	2nd
22	6/06/71	Dover, DE	Bobby Allison	Ford	123.119	21	6	0	0	Richard Petty	129.486	2nd
23	6/13/71	Brooklyn, MI	Bobby Allison	Mercury	149.567	32	5	3	13	Bobby Allison	161.190	Pole
24	6/20/71	Riverside, CA	Bobby Allison	Dodge	93.427	12	5	6	32	Bobby Allison	107.315	Pole
25	6/23/71	Houston, TX	Bobby Allison	Dodge	73.489	6	3	0	0	Bobby Allison	78.226	Pole
26	6/26/71	Greenville, SC	Richard Petty	Plymouth	74.297	7	4	3	15	Bobby Allison	81.555	2nd
27	7/04/71	Daytona Beach, FL	Bobby Isaac	Dodge	161.947	34	8	2	11	Donnie Allison	183.228	21st
28	7/11/07	Bristol, TN	Charlie Glotzbach	Chevrolet	101.074	7	3	0	0	Richard Petty	104.589	2nd
29	7/14/71	Malta, NY	Richard Petty	Plymouth	66.748	7	4	2	10	Richard Petty	74.896	Pole
30	7/15/71	Islip, NY	Richard Petty	Plymouth	49.925	0	1	0	0	Richard Petty	46.133	Pole
31	7/18/71	Trenton, NJ	Richard Petty	Plymouth	120.347	13	5	3	12	Friday Hassler	129.134	2nd
32	7/24/71	Nashville, TN	Richard Petty	Plymouth	89.667	2	2	4	46	Richard Petty	114.628	Pole
33	8/01/71	Atlanta, GA	Richard Petty	Plymouth	129.061	27	4	5	48	Buddy Baker	155.796	3rd
34	8/06/71	Winston-Salem, NC	Bobby Allison	Mustang	44.792	1	2	6	36	Richard Petty	55.283	2nd
35	8/08/71	Ona, WV	Richard Petty	Plymouth	83.805	13	3	5	38	Bobby Allison	84.053	2nd
36	8/15/71	Brooklyn, MI	Bobby Allison	Mercury	149.862	29	5	2	12	Pete Hamilton	161.901	2nd
37	8/22/71	Talladega, AL	Bobby Allison	Mercury	145.945	54	6	5	43	Donnie Allison	187.323	2nd
38	8/27/71	Columbia, SC	Richard Petty	Plymouth	64.831	6	4	6	41	Richard Petty	85.137	Pole
39	8/28/71	Hickory, NC	Tiny Lund	Camaro	72.937	1	2	2	7	Dave Marcis	80.147	3rd
40	9/06/71	Darlington, SC	Bobby Allison	Mercury	131.398	14	3	5	32	Bobby Allison	147.912	Pole
41	9/26/71	Martinsville, VA	Bobby Isaac	Dodge	73.681	10	3	3	33	Bobby Allison	83.635	Pole
42	10/10/71	Charlotte, NC	Bobby Allison	Mercury	126.140	10	5	6	37	Charlie Glotzbach	157.085	3rd
43	10/17/71	Dover, DE	Richard Petty	Plymouth	123.254	3	3	2	9	Bobby Allison	132.811	4th
44	10/24/71	Rockingham, NC	Richard Petty	Plymouth	113.405	14	5	9	58	Charlie Glotzbach	135.167	5th
45	11/07/71	Macon, GA	Bobby Allison	Ford	80.859	8	4	7	44	Bobby Allison	95.334	Pole
46	11/14/71	Richmond, VA	Richard Petty	Plymouth	80.025	9	4	4	24	Bill Dennis	n/a	11th
47	11/21/71	N.Wilkesboro, NC	Tiny Lund	Camaro	96.174	8	4	3	19	Charlie Glotzbach	107.558	6th
48	12/12/71	College Station, TX	Richard Petty	Plymouth	144.000	22	4	3	28	Pete Hamilton	170.830	3rd

1972 NASCAR Winston Cup Grand National Series Season

No.	Date	Site	Race Winner	Car	Speed	Lead Chgs	Ldrs	Caut.	C.Laps	Pole Winner	Speed	Winner Started
1	1/23/72	Riverside, CA	Richard Petty	Plymouth	104.016	8	3	3	7	A.J. Foyt	110.033	2nd
2	2/20/72	Daytona Beach, FL	A.J. Foyt	Mercury	161.550	13	3	3	17	Bobby Isaac	186.632	2nd
3	2/27/72	Richmond, VA	Richard Petty	Plymouth	76.258	13	3	3	46	Bobby Allison	90.573	3rd
4	3/05/72	Ontario, CA	A.J. Foyt	Mercury	127.082	35	7	4	31	A.J. Foyt	153.217	Pole
5	3/12/72	Rockingham, NC	Bobby Isaac	Dodge	113.895	13	4	8	57	Bobby Allison	137.539	Pole*
6	3/26/72	Atlanta, GA	Bobby Allison	Chevrolet	128.214	18	6	6	47	Bobby Allison	156.245	Pole
7	4/09/72	Bristol, TN	Bobby Allison	Chevrolet	92.826	6	4	2	25	Bobby Allison	106.875	Pole
8	4/16/72	Darlington, SC	David Pearson	Mercury	124.406	14	7	5	37	David Pearson	148.209	Pole
9	4/23/72	N.Wilkesboro, NC	Richard Petty	Plymouth	86.381	17	3	5	45	Bobby Isaac	107.506	3rd
10	4/30/72	Martinsville, VA	Richard Petty	Plymouth	72.657	15	5	4	24	Bobby Allison	84.163	3rd
11	5/07/72	Talladega, AL	David Pearson	Mercury	134.400	53	7	9	62	Bobby Isaac	192.428	2nd
12	5/28/72	Charlotte, NC	Buddy Baker	Dodge	142.255	22	4	3	24	Bobby Allison	158.162	6th
13	6/04/72	Dover, DE	Bobby Allison	Chevrolet	118.019	13	4	3	25	Bobby Isaac	130.809	2nd
14	6/11/72	Brooklyn, MI	David Pearson	Mercury	146.639	20	6	2	12	Bobby Allison	160.764	3rd
15	6/18/72	Riverside, CA	Ray Elder	Dodge	98.761	12	5	3	11	Richard Petty	108.688	7th
16	6/25/72	College Station, TX	Richard Petty	Plymouth	144.185	16	4	3	26	Richard Petty	169.412	Pole
17	7/04/72	Daytona Beach, FL	David Pearson	Mercury	160.821	23	6	2	14	Bobby Isaac	186.277	2nd
18	7/09/72	Bristol, TN	Bobby Allison	Chevrolet	92.735	4	3	5	30	Bobby Allison	107.279	Pole
19	7/16/72	Trenton, NJ	Bobby Allison	Chevrolet	114.030	9	5	5	21	Bobby Isaac	133.126	2nd
20	7/23/72	Atlanta, GA	Bobby Allison	Chevrolet	131.295	24	9	5	40	David Pearson	158.353	3rd
21	8/06/72	Talladega, AL	James Hylton	Mercury	148.728	30	9	5	37	Bobby Isaac	190.677	22nd
22	8/20/72	Brooklyn, MI	David Pearson	Mercury	134.416	19	7	3	26	Richard Petty	157.607	4th
23	8/27/72	Nashville, TN	Bobby Allison	Chevrolet	92.578	7	3	3	53	Bobby Allison	16.932	Pole
24	9/04/72	Darlington, SC	Bobby Allison	Chevrolet	128.124	30	7	5	43	Bobby Allison	152.228	Pole
25	9/10/72	Richmond, VA	Richard Petty	Plymouth	75.899	18	4	8	57	Bobby Allison	89.669	3rd
26	9/17/72	Dover, DE	David Pearson	Mercury	120.506	14	4	2	22	Bobby Allison	133.323	2nd
27	9/24/72	Martinsville, VA	Richard Petty	Plymouth	69.989	13	3	8	58	Bobby Allison	85.890	4th
28	10/01/72	N.Wikesboro, NC	Richard Petty	Plymouth	95.816	16	3	1	12	Buddy Baker	105.922	3rd
29	10/08/72	Charlotte, NC	Bobby Allison	Chevrolet	133.234	21	6	6	40	David Pearson	158.539	4th
30	10/22/72	Rockingham, NC	Bobby Allison	Chevrolet	118.275	20	8	4	35	David Pearson	137.528	5th
31	11/12/72	College Station, TX	Buddy Baker	Dodge	147.059	23	3	5	29	A.J. Foyt	170.273	2nd

1973 NASCAR Winston Cup Grand National Series Season

No.	Date	Site	Race Winner	Car	Speed	Lead Chgs	Ldrs	Caut.	C.Laps	Pole Winner	Speed	Winner Started
1	1/21/73	Riverside, CA	Mark Donohue	Matador	104.055	10	3	3	10	David Pearson	110.856	4th
2	2/18/73	Daytona Beach, FL	Richard Petty	Dodge	157.205	20	5	4	28	Buddy Baker	185.662	7th
3	2/25/73	Richmond, VA	Richard Petty	Dodge	74.764	19	7	8	78	Bobby Allison	90.952	8th
4	3/18/73	Rockingham, NC	David Pearson	Mercury	118.649	2	2	7	47	David Pearson	134.021	Pole
5	3/25/73	Bristol, TN	Cale Yarborough	Chevrolet	88.952	0	1	7	56	Cale Yarborough	107.608	Pole
6	4/01/73	Atlanta, GA	David Pearson	Mercury	139.351	23	4	4	31	No Time Trials	NTT	9th
7	4/08/73	N.Wilkesboro, NC	Richard Petty	Dodge	97.224	5	3	1	9	Bobby Allison	106.750	2nd
8	4/15/73	Darlington, SC	David Pearson	Mercury	122.655	21	5	11	71	David Pearson	153.463	Pole
9	4/29/73	Martinsville, VA	David Pearson	Mercury	70.251	11	3	7	49	David Pearson	86.369	Pole
10	5/06/73	Talladega, AL	David Pearson	Mercury	131.956	14	10	4	54	Buddy Baker	193.435	2nd
11	5/12/73	Nashville, TN	Cale Yarborough	Chevrolet	98.419	3	3	2	6	Cale Yarborough	105.741	Pole
12	5/27/73	Charlotte, NC	Buddy Baker	Dodge	134.890	23	6	6	48	Buddy Baker	158.051	Pole
13	6/03/73	Dover, DE	David Pearson	Mercury	119.745	13	4	3	22	David Pearson	133.111	Pole
14	6/10/73	College Station, TX	Richard Petty	Dodge	142.114	28	5	5	38	Buddy Baker	169.248	2nd
15	6/17/73	Riverside, CA	Bobby Allison	Chevrolet	100.215	12	3	4	22	Richard Petty	110.027	2nd
16	6/24/73	Brooklyn, MI	David Pearson	Mercury	153.485	25	5	0	0	Buddy Baker	158.273	2nd
17	7/04/73	Daytona Beach, FL	David Pearson	Mercury	158.468	25	5	2	17	Bobby Allison	179.619	6th

No.	Date	Site	Race Winner	Car	Speed	Lead Chgs	Ldrs	Caut.	C.Laps	Pole Winner	Speed	Winner Started
18	7/08/73	Bristol, TN	Benny Parsons	Chevrolet	91.342	5	3	5	33	Cale Yarborough	106.472	2nd
19	7/22/73	Atlanta, GA	David Pearson	Mercury	130.211	14	5	6	47	Richard Petty	157.163	5th
20	8/12/73	Talladega, AL	Dick Brooks	Plymouth	145.454	64	15	7	52	Bobby Allison	187.064	24th
21	8/25/73	Nashville, TN	Buddy Baker	Dodge	89.310	5	4	3	28	Cale Yarborough	103.024	7th
22	9/03/73	Darlington, SC	Cale Yarborough	Chevrolet	134.033	25	5	7	38	David Pearson	150.366	8th
23	9/09/73	Richmond, VA	Richard Petty	Dodge	63.215	6	3	5	123	Bobby Allison	90.245	5th
24	9/16/73	Dover, DE	David Pearson	Mercury	112.852	23	5	7	56	David Pearson	124.649	Pole
25	9/23/73	N.Wilkesboro	Bobby Allison	Chevrolet	95.130	12	4	2	9	Bobby Allison	105.619	Pole
26	9/30/73	Martinsville, VA	Richard Petty	Dodge	68.831	6	3	6	69	Cale Yarborough	85.922	6th
27	10/07/73	Charlotte, NC	Cale Yarborough	Chevrolet	145.240	12	7	2	16	David Pearson	158.315	2nd
28	10/21/73	Rockingham, NC	David Pearson	Mercury	117.749	20	6	5	36	Richard Petty	135.748	2nd

1974 NASCAR Winston Cup Grand National Series Season

No.	Date	Site	Race Winner	Car	Speed	Lead Chgs	Ldrs	Caut.	C.Laps	Pole Winner	Speed	Winner Started
1	1/20,26/74	Riverside, CA	Cale Yarborough	Chevrolet	101.140	15	5	2	12	David Pearson	110.098	2nd
2	2/17/74	Daytona Beach, FL	Richard Petty	Dodge	140.894	60	16	10	53	David Pearson	185.817	2nd
3	2/24/74	Richmond, VA	Bobby Allison	Chevrolet	80.095	11	4	3	16	Bobby Allison	90.353	Pole
4	3/04/74	Rockingham, NC	Richard Petty	Dodge	121.622	9	3	2	15	Cale Yarborough	134.868	2nd
5	3/17/74	Bristol, TN	Cale Yarborough	Chevrolet	64.533	5	5	3	28	Donnie Allison	107.785	3rd
6	3/24/74	Atlanta, GA	Cale Yarborough	Chevrolet	136.910	12	7	3	24	David Pearson	159.242	9th
7	4/07/74	Darlington, SC	David Pearson	Mercury	117.543	29	8	7	66	Donnie Allison	150.689	2nd
8	4/21/74	N.Wilkesboro, NC	Richard Petty	Dodge	96.200	3	3	2	11	Bobby Allison	105.669	4th
9	4/28/74	Martinsville, VA	Cale Yarborough	Chevrolet	70.427	5	3	12	70	Cale Yarborough	84.362	Pole
10	5/05/74	Talladega, AL	David Pearson	Mercury	130.320	52	13	6	60	David Pearson	186.086	Pole
11	5/11-12/74	Nashville, TN	Richard Petty	Dodge	82.240	10	6	8	96	Bobby Allison	100.088	2nd
12	5/19/74	Dover, DE	Cale Yarborough	Chevrolet	115.057	9	3	3	25	David Pearson	134.403	3rd
13	5/26/74	Charlotte, NC	David Pearson	Mercury	135.720	37	5	8	48	David Pearson	157.498	2nd
14	6/09/74	Riverside, CA	Cale Yarborough	Chevrolet	102.489	5	4	2	5	George Follmer	109.093	3rd
15	6/16/74	Brooklyn, MI	Richard Petty	Dodge	127.098	50	9	6	40	David Pearson	156.426	4th
16	7/04/74	Daytona Beach, FL	David Pearson	Mercury	138.310	48	9	6	41	David Pearson	180.759	Pole
17	7/14/74	Bristol, TN	Cale Yarborough	Chevrolet	75.430	22	5	9	105	Richard Petty	107.351	3rd
18	7/20/74	Nashville, TN	Cale Yarborough	Chevrolet	76.368	13	6	4	57	Darrell Waltrip	101.274	2nd
19	7/28/74	Atlanta, GA	Richard Petty	Dodge	131.651	23	7	5	38	Cale Yarborough	156.750	2nd
20	8/04/74	Pocono, PA	Richard Petty	Dodge	115.593	20	5	4	42	Buddy Baker	144.122	3rd
21	8/11/74	Talladega, AL	Richard Petty	Dodge	148.637	34	11	6	40	David Pearson	184.926	3rd
22	8/25/74	Brooklyn, MI	David Pearson	Mercury	133.045	45	8	5	30	David Pearson	157.946	Pole
23	9/02/74	Darlington, SC	Cale Yarborough	Chevrolet	111.075	26	13	11	101	Richard Petty	150.132	4th
24	9/08/74	Richmond, VA	Richard Petty	Dodge	64.430	6	4	13	123	Richard Petty	88.852	Pole
25	9/15/74	Dover, DE	Richard Petty	Dodge	113.640	6	6	7	55	Buddy Baker	133.640	2nd
26	9/22/74	N.Wilkesboro, NC	Cale Yarborough	Chevrolet	80.782	11	4	6	71	Richard Petty	105.087	2nd
27	9/29/74	Martinsville, VA	Earl Ross	Chevrolet	66.232	11	7	10	78	Richard Petty	84.119	11th
28	10/06/74	Charlotte, NC	David Pearson	Mercury	119.911	47	11	9	79	David Pearson	158.749	Pole
29	10/20/74	Rockingham, NC	David Pearson	Mercury	118.493	23	5	4	37	Richard Petty	135.297	3rd
30	11/24/74	Ontario, CA	Bobby Allison	Matador	134.963	39	5	3	17	Richard Petty	149.940	4th

1975 NASCAR Winston Cup Grand National Series Season

No.	Date	Site	Race Winner	Car	Speed	Lead Chgs	Ldrs	Caut.	C.Laps	Pole Winner	Speed	Winner Started
1	1/19/75	Riverside, CA	Bobby Allison	Matador	98.627	13	5	5	29	Bobby Allison	110.382	Pole
2	2/16/75	Daytona Beach, FL	Benny Parsons	Chevrolet	153.649	19	7	3	21	Donnie Allison	185.827	32nd
3	2/23/75	Richmond, VA	Richard Petty	Dodge	74.913	2	2	7	89	Richard Petty	93.340	Pole
4	3/02/75	Rockingham, NC	Cale Yarborough	Chevrolet	117.588	15	5	4	34	Buddy Baker	137.611	7th
5	3/16/75	Bristol, TN	Richard Petty	Dodge	97.053	6	4	2	27	Buddy Baker	110.951	2nd
6	3/23/75	Atlanta, GA	Richard Petty	Dodge	133.496	22	7	5	43	Richard Petty	159.029	Pole
7	4/06/75	N.Wilkesboro, NC	Richard Petty	Dodge	90.009	15	7	4	36	Darrell Waltrip	105.520	2nd
8	4/13/75	Darlington, SC	Bobby Allison	Matador	117.597	22	10	11	79	David Pearson	155.433	5th
9	4/27/75	Martinsville, VA	Richard Petty	Dodge	69.282	18	7	4	58	Benny Parsons	85.789	6th
10	5/04/75	Talladega, AL	Buddy Baker	Ford	144.948	51	12	5	45	Buddy Baker	189.947	Pole
11	5/10/75	Nashville, TN	Darrell Waltrip	Chevrolet	94.107	2	2	1	8	Darrell Waltrip	103.793	Pole
12	5/18-19/75	Dover, DE	David Pearson	Mercury	100.820	20	5	8	103	David Pearson	136.612	2nd
13	5/25/75	Charlotte, NC	Richard Petty	Dodge	145.327	17	5	3	12	David Pearson	159.353	3rd
14	6/08/75	Riverside, CA	Richard Petty	Dodge	101.028	9	3	3	17	Bobby Allison	110.353	2nd
15	6/15/75	Brooklyn, MI	David Pearson	Mercury	131.398	44	9	5	36	Cale Yarborough	158.541	3rd
16	7/04/75	Daytona Beach, FL	Richard Petty	Dodge	158.381	16	6	3	17	Donnie Allison	188.737	13th
17	7/20/75	Nasville, TN	Cale Yarborough	Chevrolet	89.792	5	4	2	19	Benny Parsons	103.247	3rd
18	8/03/75	Pocono, PA	David Pearson	Mercury	111.179	44	6	5	47	Bobby Allison	146.491	2nd
19	8/17/75	Talladega, AL	Buddy Baker	Ford	130.892	60	17	8	61	Dave Marcis	191.340	2nd
20	8/24/75	Brooklyn, MI	Richard Petty	Dodge	107.583	25	13	6	63	David Pearson	159.798	4th
21	9/01/75	Darlington, SC	Bobby Allison	Matador	116.825	20	8	10	72	David Pearson	153.401	3rd
22	9/14/75	Dover, DE	Richard Petty	Dodge	111.372	18	7	5	41	Dave Marcis	133.953	3rd
23	9/21/75	N.Wilkesboro, NC	Richard Petty	Dodge	88.986	11	3	7	34	Richard Petty	105.500	Pole
24	9/28/75	Martinsville, VA	Dave Marcis	Dodge	75.819	19	7	7	40	Cale Yarborough	86.199	7th
25	10/05/75	Charlotte, NC	Richard Petty	Dodge	132.209	29	13	7	53	David Pearson	161.701	9th
26	10/12/75	Richmond, VA	Darrell Waltrip	Chevrolet	81.886	10	4	4	23	Benny Parsons	91.071	2nd
27	10/19/75	Rockingham, NC	Cale Yarborough	Chevrolet	120.129	15	4	4	23	Dave Marcis	132.021	4th
28	11/02/75	Bristol, TN	Richard Petty	Dodge	97.016	12	5	5	28	Cale Yarborough	110.162	4th
29	11/09/75	Atlanta, GA	Buddy Baker	Ford	130.990	19	8	2	40	Dave Marcis	160.662	3rd
30	11/32/75	Ontario, CA	Buddy Baker	Ford	140.712	20	6	1	9	David Pearson	153.525	2nd

1976 NASCAR Winston Cup Grand National Series Season

No.	Date	Site	Race Winner	Car	Speed	Lead Chgs	Ldrs	Caut.	C.Laps	Pole Winner	Speed	Winner Started
1	1/18/76	Riverside, CA	David Pearson	Mercury	99.180	17	9	5	20	Bobby Allison	112.416	2nd
2	2/15/76	Daytona Beach, FL	David Pearson	Mercury	152.181	19	7	7	35	Ramo Stott	183.456	7th
3	2/29/76	Rockingham, NC	Richard Petty	Dodge	113.665	13	5	5	45	Dave Marcis	138.287	3rd
4	3/07/76	Richmond, VA	Dave Marcis	Dodge	72.792	19	5	7	66	Bobby Allison	92.715	2nd
5	3/14/76	Bristol, TN	Cale Yarborough	Chevrolet	87.377	16	7	6	79	Buddy Baker	110.720	3rd

No.	Date	Site	Race Winner	Car	Speed	Lead Chgs	Ldrs	Caut.	C.Laps	Pole Winner	Speed	Winner Started
6	3/21/76	Atlanta, GA	David Pearson	Mercury	128.904	33	10	8	47	Dave Marcis	160.709	2nd
7	4/04/76	N.Wilkesboro, NC	Cale Yarborough	Chevrolet	96.858	8	3	2	8	Dave Marcis	108.585	5th
8	4/11/76	Darlington, SC	David Pearson	Mercury	122.973	32	10	8	54	David Pearson	154.171	Pole
9	4/25/76	Martinsville, VA	Darrell Waltrip	Chevrolet	71.759	11	4	6	47	Dave Marcis	86.286	4th
10	5/02/76	Talladega, AL	Buddy Baker	Ford	169.887	24	8	3	14	Dave Marcis	189.197	12th
11	5/08/76	Nashville, TN	Cale Yarborough	Chevrolet	84.512	16	7	5	33	Benny Parsons	104.328	2nd
12	5/16/76	Dover, DE	Benny Parsons	Chevrolet	115.436	17	5	6	38	Dave Marcis	136.013	7th
13	5/30/76	Charlotte, NC	David Pearson	Mercury	137.352	37	5	7	38	David Pearson	159.132	Pole
14	6/13/76	Riverside, CA	David Pearson	Mercury	106.279	7	3	1	4	David Pearson	111.437	Pole
15	6/20/76	Brooklyn, MI	David Pearson	Mercury	141.148	17	7	3	20	Richard Petty	158.569	8th
16	7/04/76	Daytona Beach, FL	Cale Yarborough	Chevrolet	160.966	41	8	2	14	A.J. Foyt	183.090	2nd
17	7/17/76	Nashville, TN	Benny Parsons	Chevrolet	86.908	9	5	3	21	Neil Bonnett	103.049	6th
18	8/01/76	Pocono, PA	Richard Petty	Dodge	115.875	48	8	7	38	Cale Yarborough	147.865	5th
19	8/08/76	Talladega, AL	Dave Marcis	Dodge	157.547	58	8	3	25	Dave Marcis	190.651	Pole
20	8/22/76	Brooklyn, MI	David Pearson	Mercury	140.078	34	10	4	20	David Pearson	160.875	Pole
21	8/02/76	Bristol, TN	Cale Yarborough	Chevrolet	99.175	1	2	2	13	Darrell Waltrip	110.300	2nd
22	9/06/76	Darlington, SC	David Pearson	Mercury	120.534	31	10	8	65	David Pearson	154.699	Pole
23	9/12/76	Richmond, VA	Cale Yarborough	Chevrolet	77.993	12	5	2	37	Benny Parsons	92.460	6th
24	9/19/76	Dover, DE	Cale Yarborough	Chevrolet	115.740	21	6	2	27	Cale Yarborough	133.377	Pole
25	9/26/76	Martinsville, VA	Cale Yarborough	Chevrolet	75.370	7	2	3	27	Darrell Waltrip	88.484	4th
26	10/03/76	N.Wilkesboro, NC	Cale Yarborough	Chevrolet	96.380	5	5	2	9	Darrell Waltrip	107.449	4th
27	10/10/76	Charlotte, NC	Donnie Allison	Chevrolet	141.226	26	7	3	18	David Pearson	161.223	15th
28	10/24/76	Rockingham, NC	Richard Petty	Dodge	117.718	15	5	6	35	David Pearson	139.117	4th
29	11/07/76	Atlanta, GA	Dave Marcis	Dodge	127.396	17	5	4	41	Buddy Baker	161.652	2nd
30	11/21/76	Ontario, CA	David Pearson	Mercury	137.101	4	3	2	19	David Pearson	153.964	Pole

1977 NASCAR Winston Cup Grand National Series Season

No.	Date	Site	Race Winner	Car	Speed	Lead Chgs	Ldrs	Caut.	C.Laps	Pole Winner	Speed	Winner Started
1	1/16/77	Riverside, CA	David Pearson	Mercury	107.038	3	2	0	0	Cale Yarborough	112.686	2nd
2	2/20/77	Daytona Beach, FL	Cale Yarborough	Chevrolet	153.218	30	10	6	37	Donnie Allison	188.048	4th
3	2/27/77	Richmond, VA	Cale Yarborough	Chevrolet	73.084	9	7	4	35	Neil Bonnett	93.632	7th
4	3/13/77	Rockingham, NC	Richard Petty	Dodge	97.860	30	10	11	118	Donnie Allison	135.387	2nd
5	3/20/77	Atlanta, GA	Richard Petty	Dodge	144.093	15	3	2	11	Richard Petty	162.501	Pole
6	3/27/77	N.Wilkesboro, NC	Cale Yarborough	Chevrolet	88.950	12	6	6	42	Neil Bonnett	107.537	2nd
7	4/03/77	Darlington, SC	Darrell Waltrip	Chevrolet	128.817	28	7	6	39	David Pearson	151.269	4th
8	4/17/77	Bristol, TN	Cale Yarborough	Chevrolet	100.989	6	4	2	9	Cale Yarborough	110.168	Pole
9	4/24/77	Martinsville, VA	Cale Yarborough	Chevrolet	77.405	8	5	3	22	Neil Bonnett	88.923	5th
10	5/01/77	Talladega, AL	Darrell Waltrip	Chevrolet	164.877	63	11	6	27	A.J. Foyt	192.424	11th
11	5/07/77	Nashville, TN	Benny Parsons	Chevrolet	87.490	3	4	3	27	Darrell Waltrip	103.643	2nd
12	5/15/77	Dover, DE	Cale Yarborough	Chevrolet	123.327	11	5	2	10	Richard Petty	136.033	6th
13	5/29/77	Charlotte, NC	Richard Petty	Dodge	137.676	25	8	6	31	David Pearson	161.435	2nd
14	6/12/77	Riverside, CA	Richard Petty	Dodge	105.021	5	4	1	5	Richard Petty	112.432	Pole
15	6/19/77	Brooklyn, MI	Cale Yarborough	Chevrolet	135.033	19	8	4	25	David Pearson	159.175	4th
16	7/04/77	Daytona Beach, FL	Richard Petty	Dodge	142.716	34	8	2	26	Neil Bonnett	187.191	5th
17	7/16/77	Nashville, TN	Darrell Waltrip	Chevrolet	78.999	7	6	10	54	Benny Parsons	104.210	6th
18	7/31/77	Pocono, PA	Benny Parsons	Chevrolet	128.379	47	6	4	22	Darrell Waltrip	147.591	4th
19	8/07/77	Talladega, AL	Donnie Allison	Chevrolet	162.524	49	9	5	27	Benny Parsons	192.684	2nd
20	8/22/77	Brooklyn, MI	Darrell Waltrip	Chevrolet	137.944	31	6	5	24	David Pearson	160.346	3rd
21	8/28/77	Bristol, TN	Cale Yarborough	Chevrolet	79.726	14	6	6	42	Cale Yarborough	109.746	Pole
22	9/05/77	Darlington, SC	David Pearson	Mercury	106.797	32	7	6	93	Darrell Waltrip	153.493	5th
23	9/11/77	Richmond, VA	Neil Bonnett	Dodge	80.644	12	6	5	30	Benny Parsons	92.281	2nd
24	9/18/77	Dover, DE	Benny Parsons	Chevrolet	114.708	9	4	3	25	Neil Bonnett	134.233	7th
25	9/25/77	Martinsville, VA	Cale Yarborough	Chevrolet	73.447	13	5	9	57	Neil Bonnett	87.637	3rd
26	10/02/77	N.Wilkesboro, NC	Darrell Waltrip	Chevrolet	86.713	10	4	3	32	Richard Petty	108.350	3rd
27	10/09/77	Charlotte, NC	Benny Parsons	Chevrolet	142.780	18	7	4	18	David Pearson	160.892	8th
28	10/23/77	Rockingham, NC	Donnie Allison	Chevrolet	113.584	24	5	9	75	Donnie Allison	138.685	Pole
29	11/06/77	Atlanta, GA	Darrell Waltrip	Chevrolet	110.052	12	6	5	22	Sam Sommers	160.229	8th
30	11/20/77	Ontario, CA	Neil Bonnett	Dodge	128.296	37	11	5	22	Richard Petty	154.905	2nd

1978 NASCAR Winston Cup Grand National Series Season

No.	Date	Site	Race Winner	Car	Speed	Lead Chgs	Ldrs	Caut.	C.Laps	Pole Winner	Speed	Winner Started
1	1/22/78	Riverside, CA	Cale Yarborough	Olds	102.269	12	4	4	17	David Pearson	113.204	4th
2	2/19/78	Daytona Beach, FL	Bobby Allison	Ford	159.730	37	6	5	24	Cale Yarborough	187.536	33rd
3	2/26/78	Richmond, VA	Benny Parsons	Chevrolet	80.304	10	6	5	33	Neil Bonnett	93.382	3rd
4	3/05/78	Rockingham, NC	David Pearson	Mercury	116.681	24	9	8	62	Neil Bonnett	141.940	9th
5	3/19/78	Atlanta, GA	Bobby Allison	Ford	142.520	9	6	4	16	Cale Yarborough	162.006	4th
6	3/02/78	Bristol, TN	Darrell Waltrip	Chevrolet	92.401	13	3	4	40	Neil Bonnett	110.409	7th
7	4/09/78	Darlington, SC	Benny Parsons	Chevrolet	127.544	24	9	7	44	Bobby Allison	151.862	8th
8	4/16/78	N.Wilkeboro, NC	Darrell Waltrip	Chevrolet	92.345	18	7	4	25	Benny Parsons	108.510	2nd
9	4/23/78	Martinsville, VA	Darrell Waltrip	Chevrolet	77.971	6	3	4	27	Lennie Pond	88.637	3rd
10	5/14/78	Talladega, AL	Cale Yarborough	Olds	155.699	44	8	5	30	Cale Yarborough	191.904	Pole
11	5/21/78	Dover, DE	David Pearson	Mercury	114.664	18	9	6	37	Buddy Baker	135.452	3rd
12	5/28/78	Charlotte, NC	Darrell Waltrip	Chevrolet	138.355	43	6	6	32	David Pearson	160.551	17th
13	6/03/78	Nashville, TN	Cale Yarborough	Olds	87.541	1	1	2	22	Lennie Pond	105.094	2nd
14	6/11/78	Riverside, CA	Benny Parsons	Chevrolet	104.311	10	6	1	4	David Pearson	112.882	4th
15	6/18/78	Brooklyn, MI	Cale Yarborough	Olds	149.563	25	7	1	8	David Pearson	163.936	3rd
16	7/04/78	Daytona Beach, FL	David Pearson	Mercury	154.340	29	10	4	21	Cale Yarborough	186.803	3rd
17	7/15/78	Nashville, TN	Cale Yarborough	Olds	88.924	5	4	3	15	Lennie Pond	104.257	2nd
18	7/30/78	Pocono, PA	Darrell Waltrip	Chevrolet	142.540	37	4	1	3	Benny Parsons	149.236	4th
19	8/06/78	Talladega, AL	Lennie Pond	Olds	174.700	67	9	4	17	Cale Yarborough	192.917	5th
20	8/20/78	Brooklyn, MI	David Pearson	Mercury	129.566	34	10	7	35	David Pearson	164.073	Pole
21	8/26/78	Bristol, TN	Cale Yarborough	Olds	88.628	16	7	10	59	Lennie Pond	110.958	4th
22	9/04/78	Darlington, SC	Cale Yarborough	Olds	116.828	21	10	9	72	David Pearson	153.685	6th
23	9/10/78	Richmond, VA	Darrell Waltrip	Chevrolet	79.568	15	6	5	27	Darrell Waltrip	91.964	Pole
24	9/17/78	Dover, DE	Bobby Allison	Ford	119.323	7	5	3	18	J.D. McDuffie	135.480	2nd
25	9/24/78	Martinsville, VA	Cale Yarborough	Olds	79.185	6	4	4	19	Lennie Pond	86.558	6th
26	10/01/78	N.Wilkesboro, NC	Cale Yarborough	Olds	97.847	1	2	1	4	Darrell Waltrip	109.397	3rd
27	10/08/78	Charlotte, NC	Bobby Allison	Ford	141.826	40	9	4	21	David Pearson	161.355	8th
28	10/22/78	Rockingham, NC	Cale Yarborough	Olds	117.288	19	13	5	52	Cale Yarborough	142.067	Pole

No.	Date	Site	Race Winner	Car	Speed	Lead Chgs	Ldrs	Caut.	C.Laps	Pole Winner	Speed	Winner Started
29	11/05/78	Atlanta, GA	Donnie Allison	Chevrolet	124.312	25	8	7	63	Cale Yarborough	168.425	13th
30	11/19/78	Ontario, CA	Bobby Allison	Ford	137.783	30	9	4	17	Cale Yarborough	156.190	2nd

1979 NASCAR Winston Cup Grand National Series Season

No.	Date	Site	Race Winner	Car	Speed	Lead Chgs	Ldrs	Caut.	C.Laps	Pole Winner	Speed	Winner Started
1	1/14/79	Riverside, CA	Darrell Waltrip	Chevrolet	107.820	13	5	0	0	David Pearson	113.659	4th
2	2/18/79	Daytona Beach, FL	Richard Petty	Olds	143.977	36	13	7	57	Buddy Baker	196.049	13th
3	3/04/78	Rockingham, NC	Bobby Allison	Ford	122.727	13	5	7	39	Bobby Allison	136.790	Pole
4	3/11/79	Richmond, VA	Cale Yarborough	Olds	83.608	3	2	2	8	Bobby Allison	92.957	9th
5	3/18/79	Atlanta, GA	Buddy Baker	Olds	135.136	29	6	5	42	Buddy Baker	165.951	Pole
6	3/25/79	N.Wilkesboro, NC	Bobby Allison	Ford	88.400	20	11	4	32	Benny Parsons	108.136	3rd
7	4/01/79	Bristol, TN	Dale Earnhardt	Chevrolet	91.033	8	6	6	44	Buddy Baker	111.668	9th
8	4/08/79	Darlington, SC	Darrell Waltrip	Chevrolet	121.721	25	8	6	53	Donnie Allison	154.797	2nd
9	4/22/79	Martinsville, VA	Richard Petty	Chevrolet	78.562	11	5	5	32	Darrell Waltrip	87.383	2nd
10	5/06/79	Talladega, AL	Bobby Allison	Ford	154.770	21	8	4	30	Darrell Waltrip	195.644	12th
11	5/12/79	Nashville, TN	Cale Yarborough	Olds	88.652	9	5	3	27	Joe Millikan	104.155	4th
12	5/20/79	Dover, DE	Neil Bonnett	Mercury	111.269	26	8	6	48	Darrell Waltrip	136.103	5th
13	5/27/79	Charlotte, NC	Darrell Waltrip	Chevrolet	136.674	59	10	9	48	Neil Bonnett	160.125	3rd
14	6/03/79	College Station, TX	Darrell Waltrip	Chevrolet	156.216	22	4	1	5	Buddy Baker	167.903	4th
15	6/10/79	Riverside, CA	Bobby Allison	Ford	103.732	5	4	2	6	Dale Earnhardt	113.089	4th
16	6/17/79	Brooklyn, MI	Buddy Baker	Chevrolet	135.798	47	12	6	33	Neil Bonnett	162.371	3rd
17	7/04/79	Daytona Beach, FL	Neil Bonnett	Mercury	172.890	28	8	2	11	Buddy Baker	193.196	2nd
18	7/14/79	Nashville, TN	Darrell Waltrip	Chevrolet	92.227	2	2	3	19	Darrell Waltrip	105.430	Pole
19	7/30/79	Pocono, PA	Cale Yarborough	Chevrolet	115.207	56	8	7	46	Harry Gant	148.711	2nd
20	8/05/79	Talladega, AL	Darrell Waltrip	Olds	161.229	34	8	5	28	David Pearson	193.600	8th
21	8/19/79	Brooklyn, MI	Richard Petty	Chevrolet	130.376	21	8	5	35	David Pearson	162.922	5th
22	8/25/79	Bristol, TN	Darrell Waltrip	Chevrolet	91.493	18	6	6	60	Richard Petty	120.524	5th
23	9/03/79	Darlington, SC	David Pearson	Chevrolet	126.259	18	7	9	52	Bobby Allison	154.880	5th
24	9/09/79	Richmond, VA	Bobby Allison	Ford	80.604	6	4	2	20	Dale Earnhardt	92.605	2nd
25	9/16/79	Dover, DE	Richard Petty	Chevrolet	114.366	27	7	11	49	Dale Earnhardt	135.726	4th
26	9/23/79	Martinsville, VA	Buddy Baker	Chevrolet	75.119	12	5	10	54	Darrell Waltrip	88.265	7th
27	10/07/79	Charlotte, NC	Cale Yarborough	Chevrolet	134.266	28	14	8	40	Neil Bonnett	164.304	4th
28	10/14/79	N.Wilkesboro, NC	Benny Parsons	Chevrolet	91.454	12	5	9	48	Dale Earnhardt	112.783	5th
29	10/21/79	Rockingham, NC	Richard Petty	Chevrolet	108.356	20	11	4	32	Buddy Baker	141.315	7th
30	11/04/79	Atlanta, GA	Neil Bonnett	Mercury	140.120	25	7	5	29	Buddy Baker	164.813	4th
31	11/18/79	Ontario, CA	Benny Parsons	Chevrolet	132.822	35	9	6	26	Cale Yarborough	154.902	2nd

1980 NASCAR Winston Cup Grand National Series Season

No.	Date	Site	Race Winner	Car	Speed	Lead Chgs	Ldrs	Caut.	C.Laps	Pole Winner	Speed	Winner Started
1	1/13,19/80	Riverside, CA	Darrell Waltrip	Chevrolet	94.974	5	4	2	30	Darrell Waltrip	113.404	Pole
2	2/17/80	Daytona Beach, FL	Buddy Baker	Olds	177.602	29	7	9	72	Buddy Baker	194.009	Pole
3	2/24/80	Richmond, VA	Darrell Waltrip	Chevrolet	67.703	19	7	9	72	Darrell Waltrip	93.695	Pole
4	3/09/80	Rockingham, NC	Cale Yarborough	Olds	108.735	18	6	12	93	Darrell Waltrip	136.765	21st
5	3/16/80	Atlanta, GA	Dale Earnhardt	Chevrolet	134.808	27	11	7	45	Buddy Baker	166.212	31st
6	3/30/80	Bristol, TN	Dale Earnhardt	Chevrolet	96.977	15	6	3	14	Cale Yarborough	111.688	4th
7	4/13/80	Darlington, SC	David Pearson	Chevrolet	112.397	12	7	7	47	Benny Parsons	155.866	2nd
8	4/20/80	N.Wilkesboro, NC	Richard Petty	Chevrolet	95.501	9	4	5	32	Bobby Allison	113.797	7th
9	4/27/80	Martinsville, VA	Darrell Waltrip	Chevrolet	69.049	5	5	8	91	Darrell Waltrip	88.566	Pole
10	5/04/80	Talladega, AL	Buddy Baker	Olds	170.481	40	12	6	28	David Pearson	197.704	2nd
11	5/10/80	Nashville, TN	Richard Petty	Chevrolet	89.471	11	4	4	29	Cale Yarborough	106.591	6th
12	5/18/80	Dover, DE	Bobby Alison	Ford	113.866	17	6	9	67	Cale Yarborough	138.814	8th
13	5/25/80	Charlotte, NC	Benny Parsons	Chevrolet	119.265	47	12	14	113	Cale Yarborough	165.194	6th
14	6/01/80	College Station, TX	Cale Yarborough	Chevrolet	159.046	9	4	0	0	Cale Yarborough	170.709	Pole
15	6/08/80	Riverside, CA	Darrell Waltrip	Chevrolet	101.846	20	8	5	15	Cale Yarborough	113.792	2nd
16	6/15/80	Brooklyn, MI	Benny Parsons	Chevrolet	131.808	25	5	7	43	Benny Parsons	163.662	Pole
17	7/04/80	Daytona Beach, FL	Bobby Alison	Ford	173.473	40	8	3	11	Cale Yarborough	194.670	14th
18	7/12/80	Nashville, TN	Dale Earnhardt	Chevrolet	93.821	10	5	1	4	Cale Yarborough	104.817	7th
19	7/27/80	Pocono, PA	Neil Bonnett	Mercury	124.392	49	11	5	26	Cale Yarborough	151.469	2nd
20	8/03/80	Talladega, AL	Neil Bonnett	Mercury	166.894	36	11	5	25	Buddy Baker	198.545	2nd
21	8/17/80	Brooklyn, MI	Cale Yarborough	Chevrolet	145.352	31	9	4	17	Buddy Baker	162.693	2nd
22	8/23/80	Bristol, TN	Cale Yarborough	Chevrolet	86.973	19	8	10	57	Cale Yarorough	110.990	Pole
23	9/01/80	Darlington, SC	Terry Labonte	Chevrolet	115.210	27	12	14	79	Darrell Waltrip	153.838	10th
24	9/07/80	Richmond, VA	Bobby Allison	Ford	79.722	18	8	7	31	Cale Yarborough	93.466	2nd
25	9/14/80	Dover, DE	Darrell Waltrip	Chevrolet	116.024	29	11	8	39	Cale Yarborough	137.583	Pole
26	9/21/80	N.Wilkesboro, NC	Bobby Allison	Ford	75.510	14	5	8	113	Cale Yarborough	111.996	2nd
27	9/28/80	Martinsville, VA	Dale Earnhardt	Chevrolet	69.654	25	9	17	79	Buddy Baker	88.500	7th
28	10/05/80	Charlotte, NC	Dale Earnhardt	Chevrolet	135.243	43	11	8	44	Buddy Baker	165.634	4th
29	10/19/80	Rockingham, NC	Cale Yarborough	Chevrolet	114.159	35	12	9	61	Donnie Allison	142.648	2nd
30	11/02/80	Atlanta, GA	Cale Yarborough	Chevrolet	131.190	28	13	6	49	Bobby Allison	165.620	12th
31	11/15/80	Ontario, CA	Benny Parsons	Chevrolet	129.441	25	7	6	30	Cale Yarborough	155.499	4th

1981 NASCAR Winston Cup Grand National Series Season

No.	Date	Site	Race Winner	Car	Speed	Lead Chgs	Ldrs	Caut.	C.Laps	Pole Winner	Speed	Winner Started
1	1/11/81	Riverside, CA	Bobby Allison	Chevrolet	95.263	15	9	6	31	Darrell Waltrip	114.711	2nd
2	2/15/81	Daytona Beach, FL	Richard Petty	Buick	169.651	49	9	4	18	Bobby Allison	194.624	8th
3	2/22/81	Richmond, VA	Darrell Waltrip	Buick	76.570	6	4	7	50	Morgan Shepherd	92.821	7th
4	3/01/81	Rockingham, NC	Darrell Waltrip	Buick	114.594	36	10	14	75	Cale Yarborough	140.448	4th
5	3/15/81	Atlanta, GA	Cale Yarborough	Buick	133.619	23	9	5	39	Terry Labonte	162.940	17th
6	3/29/81	Bristol, TN	Darrell Waltrip	Buick	89.530	21	11	8	44	Darrell Waltrip	112.125	Pole
7	4/05/81	N.Wilkesboro, NC	Richard Petty	Buick	85.381	12	4	10	87	Dave Marcis	114.647	13th
8	4/12/81	Darlington, SC	Darrell Waltrip	Buick	126.703	20	5	6	40	Bill Elliott	153.896	3rd
9	4/26/81	Martinsville, VA	Morgan Shepherd	Pontiac	75.019	13	6	5	38	Ricky Rudd	89.056	12th
10	5/03/81	Talladega, AL	Bobby Allison	Buick	149.376	43	10	7	44	Bobby Allison	195.864	Pole
11	5/09/81	Nashville, TN	Benny Parsons	Ford	89.756	5	3	5	23	Ricky Rudd	104.409	3rd
12	5/17/81	Dover, DE	Jody Ridley	Ford	116.595	12	5	2	24	David Pearson	138.425	11th

No.	Date	Site	Race Winner	Car	Speed	Lead Chgs	Ldrs	Caut.	C.Laps	Pole Winner	Speed	Winner Started
13	5/24/81	Charlotte, NC	Bobby Allison	Buick	129.326	32	7	7	50	Neil Bonnett	158.115	7th
14	6/07/81	College Station, TX	Benny Parsons	Ford	132.475	35	9	5	31	Terry Labonte	167.543	4th
15	6/14/81	Riverside, CA	Darrell Waltrip	Buick	93.597	15	8	6	21	Darrell Waltrip	114.378	Pole
16	6/21/81	Brooklyn, MI	Bobby Allison	Buick	130.589	47	11	7	36	Darrell Waltrip	160.471	4th
17	7/04/81	Daytona Beach, FL	Cale Yarborough	Buick	142.588	35	10	6	37	Cale Yarborough	192.852	Pole
18	7/11/81	Nashville, TN	Darrell Waltrip	Buick	90.052	14	5	3	15	Mark Martin	104.353	4th
19	7/26/81	Pocono, PA	Darrell Waltrip	Buick	119.111	27	10	6	39	Darrell Waltrip	150.148	Pole
20	8/02/81	Talladega, AL	Ron Bouchard	Buick	156.737	39	10	8	36	Harry Gant	195.897	10th
21	8/16/81	Brooklyn, MI	Richard Petty	Buick	123.457	65	14	9	51	Ron Bouchard	161.501	7th
22	8/22/81	Bristol, TN	Darrell Waltrip	Buick	84.723	11	5	7	52	Darrell Waltrip	110.818	Pole
23	9/07/81	Darlington, SC	Neil Bonnett	Ford	126.410	23	9	8	45	Harry Gant	152.693	3rd
24	9/13/81	Richmond, VA	Benny Parsons	Ford	69.998	18	8	9	63	Mark Martin	93.435	4th
25	9/20/81	Dover, DE	Neil Bonnett	Ford	119.561	17	9	4	22	Ricky Rudd	136.757	3rd
26	9/27/81	Martinsville, VA	Darrell Waltrip	Buick	70.089	14	9	11	72	Darrell Waltrip	89.014	Pole
27	10/04/81	N.Wilkesboro, NC	Darrell Waltrip	Buick	93.091	10	5	8	49	Darrell Waltrip	114.065	Pole
28	10/11/81	Charlotte, NC	Darrell Waltrip	Buick	117.483	27	13	12	78	Darrell Waltrip	162.744	Pole
29	11/01/81	Rockingham, NC	Darrell Waltrip	Buick	107.399	33	11	12	97	Darrell Waltrip	138.164	Pole
30	11/08/81	Atlanta, GA	Neil Bonnett	Ford	130.391	36	11	7	50	Harry Gant	163.266	5th
31	11/22/81	Riverside, CA	Bobby Allison	Buick	95.288	19	9	7	33	Darrell Waltrip	114.981	5th

1982 NASCAR Winston Cup Grand National Series Season

No.	Date	Site	Race Winner	Car	Speed	Lead Chgs	Ldrs	Caut.	C.Laps	Pole Winner	Speed	Winner Started
1	2/14/82	Daytona Beach, FL	Bobby Allison	Buick	153.991	31	10	5	34	Benny Parsons	196.317	7th
2	2/21/82	Richmond, VA	Dave Marcis	Chevrolet	72.914	11	7	6	33	Darrell Waltrip	93.256	6th
3	3/14/82	Bristol, TN	Darrell Waltrip	Buick	94.025	10	6	3	25	Darrell Waltrip	111.068	Pole
4	3/21/82	Atlanta, GA	Darrell Waltrip	Buick	124.824	31	8	7	47	Dale Earnhardt	163.774	14th
5	3/28/82	Rockingham, NC	Cale Yarborough	Buick	108.992	31	12	9	86	Benny Parsons	141.577	11th
6	4/04/82	Darlington, SC	Dale Earnhardt	Ford	123.554	30	11	8	53	Buddy Baker	153.979	5th
7	4/18/82	N.Wilkesboro, NC	Darrell Waltrip	Buick	97.646	9	5	6	34	Darrell Waltrip	114.801	Pole
8	4/25/82	Martinsville, VA	Harry Gant	Buick	75.073	14	7	9	46	Terry Labonte	89.988	3rd
9	5/02/82	Talladega, AL	Darrell Waltrip	Buick	156.657	51	13	8	39	Benny Parsons	200.176	2nd
10	5/08/82	Nashville, TN	Darrell Waltrip	Buick	83.502	2	2	5	39	Darrell Waltrip	102.773	Pole
11	5/16/82	Dover, DE	Bobby Allison	Chevrolet	120.136	9	3	6	32	Darrell Waltrip	139.308	3rd
12	5/30/82	Charlotte, NC	Neil Bonnett	Ford	130.058	47	12	10	62	David Pearson	162.511	13th
13	6/06/82	Pocono, PA	Bobby Allison	Buick	113.579	45	11	7	51	No Time Trials	NTT	3rd
14	6/13/82	Riverside, CA	Tim Richmond	Buick	103.816	10	5	1	7	Terry Labonte	114.352	4th
15	6/20/82	Brooklyn, MI	Cale Yarborough	Buick	118.101	24	15	3	42	Ron Bouchard	162.404	4th
16	7/04/82	Daytona Beach, FL	Bobby Allison	Buick	163.099	28	8	5	25	Geoff Bodine	194.721	9th
17	7/10/82	Nashville, TN	Darrell Waltrip	Buick	86.524	3	3	5	24	Morgan Shepherd	103.959	3rd
18	7/25/82	Pocono, PA	Bobby Allison	Buick	115.496	46	11	6	43	Cale Yarborough	150.764	4th
19	8/01/82	Talladega, AL	Darrell Waltrip	Buick	168.157	38	11	5	25	Geoff Bodine	199.400	2nd
20	8/22/82	Brooklyn, MI	Bobby Allison	Buick	136.454	31	12	5	29	Bill Elliott	162.995	10th
21	8/28/82	Bristol, TN	Darrell Waltrip	Buick	94.318	15	8	3	15	Tim Richmond	112.507	8th
22	9/06/82	Darlington, SC	Cale Yarborough	Buick	115.224	41	17	14	87	David Pearson	155.739	9th
23	9/12/82	Richmond, VA	Bobby Allison	Chevrolet	82.800	6	4	2	12	Bobby Allison	93.435	Pole
24	9/19/82	Dover, DE	Darrell Waltrip	Buick	107.642	26	11	9	67	Ricky Rudd	139.384	3rd
25	10/03/82	N.Wilkesboro, NC	Darrell Waltrip	Buick	98.071	4	2	4	26	Darrell Waltrip	113.860	Pole
26	10/10/82	Charlotte, NC	Harry Gant	Buick	137.208	12	6	6	34	Harry Gant	164.694	Pole
27	10/17/82	Martinsville, VA	Darrell Waltrip	Buick	71.315	23	11	10	70	Ricky Rudd	89.132	3rd
28	10/31/82	Rockingham, NC	Darrell Waltrip	Buick	115.122	33	10	8	55	Cale Yarborough	143.220	4th
29	11/07/82	Atlanta, GA	Bobby Allison	Buick	130.884	45	14	10	56	Morgan Shepherd	166.779	9th
30	11/21/82	Riverside, CA	Tim Richmond	Buick	99.823	14	9	3	16	Darrell Waltrip	114.995	4th

1983 NASCAR Winston Cup Grand National Series Season

No.	Date	Site	Race Winner	Car	Speed	Lead Chgs	Ldrs	Caut.	C.Laps	Pole Winner	Speed	Winner Started
1	2/20/83	Daytona Beach, FL	Cale Yarborough	Pontiac	155.979	58	11	6	36	Ricky Rudd	198.864	8th
2	2/27/83	Richmond, VA	Bobby Allison	Chevrolet	79.584	15	8	5	25	Ricky Rudd	93.439	6th
3	3/6 & 13/83	Rockingham, NC	Richard Petty	Pontiac	113.055	30	11	10	94	Ricky Rudd	143.413	12th
4	3/27/83	Atlanta, GA	Cale Yarborough	Chevrolet	124.055	21	10	7	62	Geoff Bodine	167.703	22nd
5	4/10/83	Darlington, SC	Harry Gant	Buick	130.406	20	8	5	37	Tim Richmond	157.818	5th
6	4/17/83	N.Wilkesboro, NC	Darrell Waltrip	Chevrolet	91.436	12	7	7	49	Neil Bonnett	112.332	10th
7	4/24/83	Martinsville, VA	Darrell Waltrip	Chevrolet	66.460	13	7	9	105	Ricky Rudd	89.910	3rd
8	4/01/83	Talladega, AL	Richard Petty	Pontiac	153.936	27	13	7	42	Cale Yarborough	202.650	15th
9	5/07/83	Nashville, TN	Darrell Waltrip	Chevrolet	70.717	2	2	5	52	Darrell Waltrip	103.119	Pole
10	5/15/83	Dover, DE	Bobby Allison	Buick	114.847	28	9	9	53	Joe Ruttman	139.616	10th
11	5/22/83	Bristol, TN	Darrell Waltrip	Chevrolet	93.445	12	5	4	22	Darrell Waltrip	110.409	Pole
12	5/28/83	Charlotte, NC	Neil Bonnett	Chevrolet	140.707	23	9	5	28	Buddy Baker	162.841	5th
13	6/05/83	Riverside, CA	Ricky Rudd	Chevrolet	88.063	11	8	5	35	Darrell Waltrip	116.421	4th
14	6/12/83	Pocono, PA	Bobby Allison	Buick	128.636	22	11	6	25	Darrell Waltrip	152.315	7th
15	6/19/83	Brooklyn, MI	Cale Yarborough	Chevrolet	138.728	15	6	5	22	Terry Labonte	161.965	9th
16	7/04/83	Daytona Beach, FL	Bbuddy Baker	Ford	167.442	39	11	3	16	Cale Yarborough	196.635	8th
17	7/16/83	Nashville, TN	Dale Earnhardt	Ford	85.726	12	5	4	25	Ron Bouchard	103.020	3rd
18	7/24/83	Pocono, PA	Tim Richmond	Pontiac	114.818	41	11	5	52	Tim Richmond	151.981	Pole
19	7/31/83	Talladega, AL	Dale Earnhardt	Ford	170.611	46	10	2	16	Cale Yarborough	201.744	4th
20	8/21/83	Brooklyn, MI	Cale Yarborough	Chevrolet	147.511	27	11	2	7	Terry Labonte	162.437	7th
21	8/27/83	Bristol, TN	Darrell Waltrip	Chevrolet	89.430	12	6	5	31	Joe Ruttman	111.923	2nd
22	9/05/83	Darlington, SC	Bobby Allison	Buick	123.343	17	9	9	60	Neil Bonnett	157.187	14th
23	9/11/83	Richmond, VA	Bobby Allison	Buick	79.381	6	4	4	22	Darrell Waltrip	96.069	6th
24	9/18/83	Dover, DE	Bobby Allison	Buick	116.077	21	8	7	51	Terry Labonte	139.573	7th
25	9/25/83	Martinsville, VA	Ricky Rudd	Chevrolet	76.134	6	5	6	37	Darrell Waltrip	89.342	2nd
26	10/02/83	N.Wilkesboro, NC	Darrell Waltrip	Chevrolet	100.716	8	5	1	4	Darrell Waltrip	114.539	Pole
27	10/09/83	Charlotte, NC	Richard Petty	Pontiac	139.998	31	13	8	35	Tim Richmond	163.073	20th
28	10/30/83	Rockingham, NC	Terry Labonte	Chevrolet	119.324	36	10	0	63	Neil Bonnett	143.876	3rd
29	11/06/83	Atlanta, GA	Neil Bonnett	Chevrolet	137.643	28	8	6	39	Tim Richmond	168.151	15th
30	11/20/83	Riverside, CA	Bill Elliott	Ford	95.859	13	8	5	26	Darrell Waltrip	116.782	10th

Appendix

1984 NASCAR Winston Cup Grand National Series Season

No.	Date	Site	Race Winner	Car	Speed	Lead Chgs	Ldrs	Caut.	C.Laps	Pole Winner	Speed	Winner Started
1	2/19/84	Daytona Beach, FL	Cale Yarborough	Chevrolet	150.994	34	9	7	39	Cale Yarborough	201.848	Pole
2	2/26/84	Richmond, VA	Ricky Rudd	Ford	76.736	11	4	9	40	Ricky Rudd	93.439	6th
3	3/04/84	Rockingham, NC	Bobby Allison	Buick	122.931	23	6	6	42	Harry Gant	145.084	15th
4	3/18/84	Atlanta, GA	Benny Parsons	Chevrolet	144.945	20	4	3	17	Buddy Baker	166.642	8th
5	4/01/84	Bristol, TN	Darrell Waltrip	Chevrolet	93.967	17	7	4	19	Ricky Rudd	111.390	3rd
6	4/08/84	N.Wilkesboro, NC	Tim Richmond	Pontiac	97.830	13	7	5	23	Ricky Rudd	113.487	17th
7	4/15/84	Darlington, SC	Darrell Waltrip	Chevrolet	119.925	19	11	9	65	Benny Parsons	156.328	9th
8	4/29/84	Martinsville, VA	Geoff Bodine	Chevrolet	73.264	13	6	11	54	Joe Ruttman	89.426	6th
9	5/06/84	Talladega, AL	Cale Yarborough	Chevrolet	172.988	75	13	4	17	Cale Yarborough	202.692	Pole
10	5/12/84	Nashville, TN	Darrell Waltrip	Chevrolet	85.702	13	6	7	32	Darrell Waltrip	104.439	Pole
11	5/20/84	Dover, DE	Richard Petty	Pontiac	118.717	26	7	6	40	Ricky Rudd	140.807	5th
12	5/27/84	Charlotte, NC	Bobby Allison	Buick	129.233	22	6	5	48	Harry Gant	162.496	16th
13	6/03/84	Riverside, CA	Terry Labonte	Chevrolet	102.910	10	6	4	12	Terry Labonte	115.921	Pole
14	6/10/84	Pocono, PA	Cale Yarborough	Chevrolet	138.164	33	12	3	12	David Pearson	150.921	12th
15	6/17/84	Brooklyn, MI	Bill Elliott	Ford	134.705	20	10	6	28	Bill Elliott	164.339	Pole
16	7/04/84	Daytona Beach, FL	Richard Petty	Pontiac	171.204	29	8	3	15	Cale Yarborough	199.743	6th
17	7/14/84	Nashville, TN	Goeff Bodine	Chevrolet	80.908	14	7	3	24	Ricky Rudd	104.120	5th
18	7/22/84	Pocono, PA	Harry Gant	Chevrolet	121.351	27	11	9	41	Bill Elliott	152.184	3rd
19	7/29/84	Talladega, AL	Dale Earnhardt	Chevrolet	155.485	68	16	7	37	Cale Yarborough	202.474	3rd
20	8/12/84	Brooklyn, MI	Darrell Waltrip	Chevrolet	153.863	7	5	0	0	Bill Elliott	165.217	7th
21	8/25/84	Bristol, TN	Terry Labonte	Chevrolet	85.365	12	6	12	66	Geoff Bodine	111.734	6th
22	9/02/84	Darlington, SC	Harry Gant	Chevrolet	128.270	17	9	8	51	Harry Gant	155.502	Pole
23	9/09/84	Richmond, VA	Darrell Waltrip	Chevrolet	74.780	9	5	9	42	Darrell Waltrip	92.518	Pole
24	9/16/84	Dover, DE	Harry Gant	Chevrolet	111.856	20	9	10	73	No Time Trials	NTT	3rd
25	9/23/84	Martinsville, VA	Darrell Waltrip	Chevrolet	75.532	11	8	8	39	Geoff Bodine	89.523	3rd
26	10/07/84	Charlotte, NC	Bill Elliott	Ford	148.861	22	7	3	15	Benny Parsons	165.579	2nd
27	10/14/84	N.Wilkesboro, NC	Darrell Waltrip	Chevrolet	90.525	7	5	7	35	Darrell Waltrip	113.304	Pole
28	10/21/84	Rockingham, NC	Bill Elliott	Ford	112.617	28	12	10	91	Geoff Bodine	144.415	2nd
29	11/11/84	Atlanta, GA	Dale Earnhardt	Chevrolet	134.610	26	11	7	44	Bill Elliott	170.198	10th
30	11/18/84	Riverside, CA	Geoff Bodine	Chevrolet	98.448	12	7	4	20	Terry Labonte	116.714	12th

1985 NASCAR Winston Cup Grand National Series Season

No.	Date	Site	Race Winner	Car	Speed	Lead Chgs	Ldrs	Caut.	C.Laps	Pole Winner	Speed	Winner Started
1	2/17/85	Daytona Beach, FL	Bill Elliott	Ford	172.265	22	9	5	18	Bill Elliott	205.114	Pole
2	2/24/85	Richmond, VA	Dale Earnhardt	Chevrolet	67.945	9	6	10	74	Darrell Waltrip	95.218	4th
3	3/03/85	Rockingham, NC	Neil Bonnett	Chevrolet	114.953	29	6	10	76	Terry Labonte	145.067	4th
4	3/17/85	Atlanta, GA	Bill Elliott	Ford	140.273	17	10	6	31	Neil Bonnett	170.278	3rd
5	4/06/85	Bristol, TN	Dale Earnhardt	Chevrolet	81.790	18	10	14	90	Harry Gant	112.778	12th
6	4/14/85	Darlington, SC	Bill Elliott	Ford	126.295	22	9	7	51	Bill Elliott	157.454	Pole
7	4/21/85	N.Wilkesboro, NC	Neil Bonnett	Chevrolet	93.818	10	6	6	36	Darrell Waltrip	111.899	5th
8	4/28/85	Martinsville, VA	Harry Gant	Chevrolet	73.022	12	7	10	57	Darrell Waltrip	90.279	13th
9	5/05/85	Talladega, AL	Bill Elliott	Ford	186.288	28	10	2	8	Bill Elliott	209.398	Pole
10	5/19/85	Dover, DE	Bill Elliott	Ford	123.094	7	4	5	37	Terry Labonte	138.106	4th
11	5/26/85	Charlotte, NC	Darrell Waltrip	Chevrolet	141.807	29	8	7	34	Bill Elliott	164.703	4th
12	6/02/85	Riverside, CA	Terry Labonte	Chevrolet	104.276	10	8	3	9	Darrell Waltrip	115.533	2nd
13	6/09/85	Pocono, PA	Bill Elliott	Ford	138.974	13	4	3	10	Bill Elliott	152.563	Pole
14	6/16/85	Brooklyn, MI	Bill Elliott	Ford	144.724	20	9	2	15	No Time Trials	NTT	Pole
15	7/04/85	Daytona Beach, FL	Greg Sacks	Chevrolet	158.730	19	10	6	26	Bill Elliott	201.523	9th
16	7/21/85	Pocono, PA	Bill Elliott	Ford	134.008	37	12	6	24	Bill Elliott	151.973	2nd*
17	7/28/85	Talladega, AL	Cale Yarborough	Ford	148.772	30	12	7	44	Bill Elliott	207.578	2nd
18	8/11/85	Brooklyn, MI	Bill Elliott	Ford	137.430	14	7	5	28	Bill Elliott	165.479	Pole
19	8/24/85	Bristol, TN	Dale Earnhardt	Chevrolet	81.388	18	8	11	82	Dale Earnhardt	113.586	Pole
20	9/01/85	Darlington, SC	Bill Elliott	Ford	121.254	20	9	114	70	Bill Elliott	156.641	Pole
21	9/08/85	Richmond, VA	Darrell Waltrip	Chevrolet	72.508	14	7	7	65	Geoff Bodine	94.535	22nd
22	9/15/85	Dover, DE	Harry Gant	Chevrolet	120.538	16	6	6	45	Bill Elliott	141.543	4th
23	9/22/85	Martinsville, VA	Dale Earnhardt	Chevrolet	70.694	11	7	12	65	Geoff Bodine	90.521	11th
24	9/29/85	N.Wilkesboro, NC	Harry Gant	Chevrolet	95.077	10	5	6	31	Goeff Bodine	113.967	11th
25	10/06/85	Charlotte, NC	Cale Yarborough	Ford	136.761	15	6	6	41	Harry Gant	166.139	7th
26	10/20/85	Rockingham, NC	Darrell Waltrip	Chevrolet	118.344	27	9	10	64	Terry Labonte	141.841	20th
27	11/03/85	Atlanta, GA	Bill Elliott	Ford	139.597	12	4	6	39	Harry Gant	67.940	3rd
28	11/17/85	Riverside, CA	Ricky Rudd	Ford	105.065	14	8	3	10	Terry Labonte	116.938	4th

*Darrell Waltrip won the pole and started first, but his pole time was disallowed 2 weeks later.

1986 NASCAR Winston Cup Series Season

No.	Date	Site	Race Winner	Car	Speed	Lead Chgs	Ldrs	Caut.	C.Laps	Pole Winner	Speed	Winner Started
1	2/16/86	Daytona Beach, FL	Geoff Bodine	Chevrolet	148.124	28	10	8	46	Bill Elliott	205.039	2nd
2	2/23/86	Richmond, VA	Kyle Petty	Ford	71.078	12	8	8	63	No Time Trials	NTT	12th
3	3/02/86	Rockingham, NC	Terry Labonte	Chevrolet	120.488	22	10	9	50	Terry Labonte	146.348	Pole
4	3/16/86	Atlanta, GA	Morgan Shepherd	Buick	132.126	18	7	9	56	Dale Earnhardt	170.713	3rd
5	4/06/86	Bristol, TN	Rusty Wallace	Pontiac	89.747	14	8	7	56	Geoff Bodine	114.850	14th
6	4/13/86	Darlington, SC	Dale Earnhardt	Chevrolet	128.994	17	8	11	54	Geoff Bodine	159.197	4th
7	4/20/86	N.Wilkesboro, NC	Dale Earnhardt	Chevrolet	88.408	10	6	8	70	Geoff Bodine	112.419	5th
8	4/27/86	Martinsville, VA	Ricky Rudd	Ford	76.882	15	8	7	33	Tim Richmond	90.716	4th
9	5/04/86	Talladega, AL	Bobby Allison	Buick	157.698	24	9	9	41	Bill Elliott	212.219	2nd
10	5/18/86	Dover, DE	Geoff Bodine	Chevrolet	115.009	29	10	8	67	Ricky Rudd	138.217	3rd
11	5/25/86	Charlotte, NC	Dale Earnhardt	Chevrolet	140.406	38	15	6	32	Geoff Bodine	164.511	3rd
12	6/01/86	Riverside, CA	Darrell Waltrip	Chevrolet	105.083	14	5	3	8	Darrell Waltrip	117.006	Pole
13	6/08/86	Pocono, PA	Tim Richmond	Chevrolet	113.279	18	11	9	53	Geoff Bodine	153.625	3rd
14	6/15/86	Brooklyn, MI	Bill Elliott	Ford	138.851	34	12	8	39	Tim Richmond	172.031	8th
15	7/04/86	Daytona Beach, FL	Tim Richmond	Chevrolet	131.916	31	14	8	58	Cale Yarborough	203.519	9th
16	7/20/86	Pocono, PA	Tim Richmond	Chevrolet	124.218	20	6	8	33	Harry Gant	154.392	5th
17	7/27/86	Talladega, AL	Bobby Hillin, Jr.	Buick	151.522	49	26	9	44	Bill Elliott	209.005	13th
18	8/10/86	Watkins Glen, NY	Tim Richmond	Chevrolet	90.463	11	5	4	16	Tim Richmond	117.563	Pole
19	8/17/86	Brooklyn, MI	Bill Elliott	Ford	135.376	23	10	5	38	Benny Parsons	171.924	3rd

20	8/23/86	Bristol, TN	Darrell Waltrip	Chevrolet	86.934	15	9	6	56	Geoff Bodine	114.665	10th
21	8/31/86	Darlington, SC	Tim Richmond	Chevrolet	121.068	16	9	12	79	Tim Richmond	158.489	Pole
22	9/07/86	Richmond, VA	Tim Richmond	Chevrolet	70.161	15	12	12	75	Harry Gant	93.966	4th
23	9/14/86	Dover, DE	Ricky Rudd	Ford	114.329	27	11	13	88	Geoff Bodine	146.205	11th
24	9/21/86	Martinsville, VA	Rusty Wallace	Pontiac	73.191	15	9	12	54	Geoff Bodine	90.599	8th
25	9/28/86	N.Wilkesboro, NC	Darrell Waltrip	Chevrolet	95.612	15	9	4	22	Tim Richmond	113.447	4th
26	10/05/86	Charlotte, NC	Dale Earnhardt	Chevrolet	132.403	26	9	6	44	Tim Richmond	167.078	3rd
27	10/19/86	Rockingham, NC	Neil Bonnett	Chevrolet	126.381	22	8	6	29	Tim Richmond	146.948	6th
28	11/02/86	Atlanta, GA	Dale Earnhardt	Chevrolet	152.523	19	8	2	7	Bill Elliott	172.905	4th
29	11/16/86	Riverside, CA	Tim Richmond	Chevrolet	101.246	12	8	7	25	Tim Richmond	118.247	Pole

1987 NASCAR Winston Cup Series Season

No.	Date	Site	Race Winner	Car	Speed	Lead Chgs	Ldrs	Caut.	C.Laps	Pole Winner	Speed	Winner Started
1	2/15/87	Daytona Beach, FL	Bill Elliott	Ford	176.263	28	10	4	15	Bill Elliott	210.364	Pole
2	3/01/87	Rockingham, NC	Dale Earnhardt	Chevrolet	117.566	26	10	10	55	Davey Allison	146.989	14th
3	3/08/87	Richmond, VA	Dale Earnhardt	Chevrolet	95.153	12	8	6	35	Alan Kulwicki	95.153	3rd
4	3/15/87	Atlanta, GA	Ricky Rudd	Ford	133.689	32	10	9	51	Dale Earnhardt	175.497	6th
5	3/29/87	Darlington, SC	Dale Earnhardt	Chevrolet	122.540	27	11	10	71	Ken Schrader	158.387	2nd
6	4/05/87	N.Wilkesboro, NC	Dale Earnhardt	Chevrolet	94.103	11	7	8	49	Bill Elliott	116.003	3rd
7	4/12/87	Bristol, TN	Dale Earnhardt	Chevrolet	75.621	19	11	13	125	Harry Gant	115.674	3rd
8	4/26/87	Martinsville, VA	Dale Earnhardt	Chevrolet	72.808	14	7	11	65	Morgan Shepherd	92.355	4th
9	5/03/87	Talladega, AL	Davey Allison	Ford	154.228	18	10	9	39	Bill Elliott	212.809	3rd
10	5/24/87	Charlotte, NC	Kyle Petty	Ford	131.483	23	10	12	68	Bill Elliott	170.901	7th
11	5/31/87	Dover, DE	Davey Allison	Ford	112.958	18	8	9	59	Bill Elliott	145.056	2nd
12	6/14/87	Pocono, PA	Tim Richmond	Chevrolet	122.166	17	9	9	45	Terry Labonte	155.502	3rd
13	6/21/87	Riverside, CA	Tim Richmond	Chevrolet	102.183	9	5	4	14	Terry Labonte	117.541	5th
14	6/28/87	Brooklyn, MI	Dale Earnhardt	Chevrolet	148.454	13	7	5	18	Rusty Wallace	170.746	5th
15	7/04/87	Daytona Beach, FL	Bobby Allison	Buick	161.074	28	10	4	20	Davey Allison	198.085	11th
16	7/19/87	Pocono, PA	Dale Earnhardt	Chevrolet	121.745	35	15	9	46	Tim Richmond	155.979	16th
17	7/26/87	Talladega, AL	Bill Elliott	Ford	171.293	18	10	4	18	Bill Elliott	203.827	Pole
18	8/10/87	Watkins Glen, NY	Rusty Wallace	Pontiac	90.682	7	5	5	15	Terry Labonte	117.956	2nd
19	8/16/87	Brooklyn, MI	Bill Elliott	Ford	138.648	16	9	5	25	Davey Allison	170.705	3rd
20	8/22/87	Bristol, TN	Dale Earnhardt	Chevrolet	90.373	12	7	8	49	Terry Labonte	115.758	6th
21	9/06/87	Darlington, SC	Dale Earnhardt	Chevrolet	115.520	13	6	5	50	Davey Allison	157.232	5th
22	9/13/87	Richmond, VA	Dale Earnhardt	Chevrolet	67.074	13	7	12	82	Alan Kulwicki	94.052	8th
23	9/20/87	Dover,, DE	Ricky Rudd	Ford	124.706	19	7	6	31	Alan Kulwicki	145.826	13th
24	9/27/87	Martinsville, VA	Darrell Waltrip	Chevrolet	76.410	13	6	8	35	Geoff Bodine	91.218	14th
25	10/04/87	N.Wilkesboro, NC	Terry Labonte	Chevrolet	96.051	5	5	4	24	Bill Elliott	115.196	4th
26	10/11/87	Charlotte, NC	Bill Elliott	Ford	128.443	29	17	7	59	Bobby Allison	171.636	7th
27	10/25/87	Rockingham, NC	Bill Elliott	Ford	118.258	31	11	8	46	Davey Allison	145.609	3rd
28	11/08/87	Riverside, CA	Rusty Wallace	Pontiac	98.035	10	6	4	21	Geoff Bodine	117.934	3rd
29	11/22/87	Atlanta, GA	Bill Elliott	Ford	139.047	12	8	5	33	Bill Elliott	174.341	Pole

1988 NASCAR Winston Cup Series Season

No.	Date	Site	Race Winner	Car	Speed	Lead Chgs	Ldrs	Caut.	C.Laps	Pole Winner	Speed	Winner Started
1	2/14/88	Daytona Beach, FL	Bobby Allison	Buick	137.531	26	12	7	42	Ken Schrader	198.823	3rd
2	2/21/88	Richmond, VA	Neil Bonnett	Pontiac	66.401	11	6	14	83	Morgan Shepherd	94.645	3rd
3	3/06/88	Rockingham, NC	Neil Bonnett	Pontiac	120.159	23	9	7	40	Bill Elliott	146.612	20th
4	3/20/88	Atlanta, GA	Dale Earnhardt	Chevrolet	137.588	19	10	7	40	Geoff Bodine	176.623	2nd
5	3/27/88	Darlington, SC	Lake Speed	Olds	131.284	18	11	8	42	Ken Schrader	162.657	8th
6	4/10/88	Bristol, TN	Bill Elliott	Ford	83.115	11	8	12	70	Rick Wilson	117.552	13th
7	4/17/88	N.Wilkesboro, NC	Terry Labonte	Chevrolet	99.075	12	5	5	20	Terry Labonte	117.332	Pole
8	4/24/88	Martinsville, VA	Dale Earnhardt	Chevrolet	74.740	10	7	7	46	Ricky Rudd	91.328	14th
9	5/01/88	Talladega, AL	Phil Parsons	Olds	156.547	23	9	7	29	Davey Allison	198.969	3rd
10	5/29/88	Charlotte, NC	Darrell Waltrip	Chevrolet	124.460	43	18	13	89	Davey Allison	173.594	5th
11	6/05/88	Dover, DE	Bill Elliott	Ford	118.726	25	11	7	45	Alan Kulwicki	146.681	17th
12	6/13/88	Riverside, CA	Rusty Wallace	Pontiac	88.341	14	9	7	27	Ricky Rudd	118.484	2nd
13	6/19/88	Pocono, PA	Geoff Bodine	Chevrolet	126.147	17	7	6	31	Alan Kulwicki	158.806	3rd
14	6/26/88	Brooklyn, MI	Rusty Wallace	Pontiac	153.551	13	9	4	15	Bill Elliott	172.687	5th
15	7/02/88	Daytona Beach, FL	Bill Elliott	Ford	163.302	22	10	3	15	Darrell Waltrip	193.819	38th
16	7/24/88	Pocono, PA	Bill Elliott	Ford	122.866	22	9	5	42	Morgan Shepherd	157.153	2nd
17	7/31/88	Talladega, AL	Ken Schrader	Chevrolet	154.505	30	14	8	1	Darrell Waltrip	196.274	7th
18	8/14/88	Watkins Glen, NY	Ricky Rudd	Buick	74.096	13	10	8	36	Geoff Bodine	120.541	6th
19	8/21/88	Brooklyn, MI	Davey Allison	Ford	156.863	21	9	2	9	Bill Elliott	174.940	4th
20	8/27/88	Bristol, TN	Dale Earnhardt	Chevrolet	78.775	23	13	14	83	Alan Kulwicki	116.893	5th
21	9/04/88	Darlington, SC	Bill Elliott	Ford	128.297	24	12	10	39	Bill Elliott	160.827	Pole
22	9/11/88	Richmond, VA	Davey Allison	Ford	95.770	14	7	5	42	Davey Allison	122.850	Pole
23	9/18/88	Dover, DE	Bill Elliott	Ford	109.349	22	8	14	84	Mark Martin	148.075	3rd
24	9/25/88	Martinsville, VA	Darrell Waltrip	Chevrolet	74.988	11	6	11	53	Rusty Wallace	91.372	20th
25	10/09/88	Charlotte, NC	Rusty Wallace	Pontiac	130.677	36	15	10	63	Alan Kulwicki	175.896	3rd
26	10/16/88	N.Wilkesboro, NC	Rusty Wallace	Pontiac	94.192	15	7	9	34	Bill Elliott	116.901	12th
27	10/23/88	Rockingham, NC	Rusty Wallace	Pontiac	111.557	18	10	11	76	Bill Elliott	148.359	3rd
28	11/06/88	Phoenix, AZ	Alan Kulwicki	Ford	90.457	14	7	6	53	Geoff Bodine	123.303	21st
29	11/20/88	Atlanta, GA	Rusty Wallace	Pontiac	129.024	33	15	9	55	Rusty Wallace	179.499	Pole

1989 NASCAR Winston Cup Series Season

No.	Date	Site	Race Winner	Car	Speed	Lead Chgs	Ldrs	Caut.	C.Laps	Pole Winner	Speed	Winner Started
1	2/19/89	Daytona Beach, FL	Darrell Waltrip	Chevrolet	148.466	26	12	7	30	Ken Schrader	196.996	2nd
2	3/05/89	Rockingham, NC	Rusty Wallace	Pontiac	115.122	29	11	10	64	Rusty Wallace	148.793	Pole
3	3/19/89	Atlanta, GA	Darrell Waltrip	Chevrolet	139.684	29	11	6	41	Alan Kulwicki	176.925	4th
4	3/26/89	Richmond, VA	Rusty Wallace	Pontiac	86.619	19	7	12	67	Geoff Bodine	120.573	2nd
5	4/02/89	Darlington, SC	Harry Gant	Olds	115.475	14	9	7	68	Mark Martin	161.111	10th
6	4/09/89	Bristol, TN	Rusty Wallace	Pontiac	76.034	34	16	20	98	Mark Martin	120.278	8th
7	4/16/89	N.Wilkesboro, NC	Dale Earnhardt	Chevrolet	89.937	10	5	10	49	Rusty Wallace	117.524	3rd
8	4/23/89	Martinsville, VA	Darrell Waltrip	Chevrolet	79.025	12	6	5	31	Geoff Bodine	93.097	10th
9	5/07/89	Talladega, AL	Davey Allison	Ford	155.869	28	9	7	26	Mark Martin	193.061	2nd

No.	Date	Site	Race Winner	Car	Speed	Lead Chgs	Ldrs	Caut.	C.Laps	Pole Winner	Speed	Winner Started
10	5/28/89	Charlotte, NC	Darrell Waltrip	Chevrolet	144.077	22	12	7	46	Alan Kulwicki	173.021	4th
11	6/04/89	Dover, DE	Dale Earnhardt	Chevrolet	121.670	20	7	6	36	Mark Martin	144.387	2nd
12	6/11/89	Sonoma, CA	Ricky Rudd	Buick	76.088	3	3	3	16	Rusty Wallace	90.041	4th
13	6/18/89	Pocono, PA	Terry Labonte	Ford	131.320	23	12	6	23	Rusty Wallace	157.489	23rd
14	6/25/89	Brooklyn, MI	Bill Elliott	Ford	139.023	13	6	5	23	Ken Schrader	174.728	2nd
15	7/01/89	Daytona Beach, FL	Davey Allison	Ford	132.207	28	11	12	42	Mark Martin	191.861	8th
16	7/23/89	Pocono, PA	Bill Elliott	Ford	117.847	28	14	9	42	Ken Schrader	157.809	14th
17	7/30/89	Talladega, AL	Terry Labonte	Ford	157.354	48	9	6	25	Mark Martin	194.800	5th
18	8/13/89	Watkins Glen, NY	Rusty Wallace	Pontiac	87.242	13	9	6	19	Morgan Shepherd	120.456	13th
19	8/20/89	Brooklyn, MI	Rusty Wallace	Pontiac	157.704	20	11	2	8	Geoff Bodine	175.962	2nd
20	8/26/89	Bristol, TN	Darrell Waltrip	Chevrolet	85.554	11	5	11	69	Alan Kulwicki	117.043	9th
21	9/03/89	Darlington, SC	Dale Earnhardt	Chevrolet	135.462	26	10	4	24	Alan Kulwicki	160.156	10th
22	9/10/89	Richmond, VA	Rusty Wallace	Pontiac	88.380	9	7	14	76	Bill Elliott	121.136	6th
23	9/17/89	Dover, DE	Dale Earnhardt	Chevrolet	122.909	18	7	5	31	Davey Allison	146.169	15th
24	9/24/89	Martinsville, VA	Darrell Waltrip	Chevrolet	76.751	19	7	8	46	Jimmy Hensley	91.913	2nd
25	10/08/89	Charlotte, NC	Ken Schrader	Chevrolet	149.863	19	9	4	21	Bill Elliott	174.081	2nd
26	10/15/89	N.Wilkesboro, NC	Geoff Bodine	Chevrolet	90.289	7	4	11	60	No Time Trials	NTT	11th
27	10/22/89	Rockingham, NC	Mark Martin	Ford	114.079	35	10	14	69	Alan Kulwicki	148.624	7th
28	11/05/89	Phoenix, AZ	Bill Elliott	Ford	105.683	17	9	5	24	Ken Schrader	124.645	13th
29	11/19/89	Atlanta, GA	Dale Earnhardt	Chevrolet	140.229	21	8	6	35	Alan Kulwicki	179.112	3rd

1990 NASCAR Winston Cup Series Season

No.	Date	Site	Race Winner	Car	Speed	Lead Chgs	Ldrs	Caut.	C.Laps	Pole Winner	Speed	Winner Started
1	2/18/90	Daytona Beach, FL	Derrike Cope	Chevrolet	165.761	27	13	3	15	Ken Schrader	196.515	12th
2	2/25/90	Richmond, VA	Mark Martin	Ford	92.158	18	8	12	75	Ricky Rudd	119.617	6th
3	3/04/90	Rockingham,NC	Kyle Petty	Pontiac	122.864	18	9	8	36	Kyle Petty	148.751	Pole
4	3/18/90	Atlanta, GA	Dale Earnhardt	Chevrolet	156.849	21	9	3	10	No Time Trials	NTT	Pole
5	4/01/90	Darlington, SC	Dale Earnhardt	Chevrolet	124.073	20	10	10	51	Geoff Bodine	162.996	15th
6	4/08/90	Bristol, TN	Davey Allison	Ford	87.258	11	9	13	65	Ernie Irvan	116.157	19th
7	4/22/90	N.Wilkesboro, NC	Brett Bodine	Buick	83.809	6	4	10	68	Mark Martin	117.475	20th
8	4/29/90	Martinsville, VA	Geoff Bodine	Ford	77.423	12	5	10	44	Geoff Bodine	91.726	Pole
9	5/06/90	Talladega, AL	Dale Earnhardt	Chevrolet	159.571	25	12	7	28	Bill Elliott	199.388	5th
10	5/27/90	Charlotte, NC	Rusty Wallace	Pontiac	137.650	15	10	11	48	Ken Schrader	173.963	9th
11	6/03/90	Dover, DE	Derrike Cope	Chevrolet	123.960	22	9	5	32	Dick Trickle	145.814	15th
12	6/10/90	Sonoma, CA	Rusty Wallace	Pontiac	69.245	8	6	9	24	Ricky Rudd	99.743	11th
13	6/17/90	Pocono, PA	Harry Gant	Olds	120.600	26	16	13	44	Ernie Irvan	158.750	16th
14	6/24/90	Brooklyn, MI	Dale Earnhardt	Chevrolet	150.219	16	7	4	16	No Time Trials	NTT	5th
15	7/07/90	Daytona Beach, FL	Dale Earnahrdt	Chevrolet	160.894	15	8	4	14	Greg Sacks	195.533	3rd
16	7/22/90	Pocono, PA	Geoff Bodine	Ford	124.070	22	9	10	35	Mark Matin	158.264	4th
17	7/29/90	Talladega, AL	Dale Earnhardt	Chevrolet	174.430	23	13	2	12	Dale Earnhardt	192.513	Pole
18	8/12/90	Watkins Glen, NY	Ricky Rudd	Chevrolet	92.452	11	8	5	15	Dale Earnhardt	121.190	12th
19	8/19/90	Brooklyn, MI	Mark Martin	Ford	138.822	23	11	6	26	Alan Kulwicki	174.982	5th
20	8/25/90	Bristol, TN	Ernie Irvan	Chevrolet	91.782	9	4	10	47	Dale Earnhardt	115.604	6th
21	9/02/90	Darlington, SC	Dale Earnhardt	Chevrolet	123.141	20	8	10	51	Dale Earnhardt	158.448	Pole
22	9/09/90	Richmond, VA	Dale Earnhardt	Chevrolet	90.567	17	6	9	55	Ernie Irvan	119.872	6th
23	9/16/90	Dover, DE	Bill Elliott	Ford	125.945	11	5	6	29	Bill Elliott	144.928	Pole
24	9/23/90	Martinsvile, VA	Geoff Bodine	Ford	76.386	16	10	11	57	Mark Martin	91.571	14th
25	9/30/90	N.Wilkesboro, NC	Mark Martin	Ford	93.818	6	4	9	40	Kyle Petty	116.387	2nd
26	10/07/90	Charlotte, NC	Davey Allison	Ford	137.428	14	10	6	37	Brett Bodine	174.385	5th
27	10/21/90	Rockingham, NC	Alan Kulwicki	Ford	126.452	21	8	7	28	Ken Schrader	147.814	3rd
28	11/04/90	Phoenix, AZ	Dale Earnhardt	Chevrolet	96.786	1	2	9	48	Rusty Wallace	124.443	3rd
29	11/18/90	Atlanta, GA	Morgan Shepherd	Ford	140.911	19	9	3	34	Rusty Wallace	175.222	20th

1991 NASCAR Winston Cup Series Season

No.	Date	Site	Race Winner	Car	Speed	Lead Chgs	Ldrs	Caut.	C.Laps	Pole Winner	Speed	Winner Started
1	2/17/91	Daytona Beach, FL	Ernie Irvan	Chevrolet	148.148	21	9	9	36	Davey Allison	195.955	2nd
2	2/24/91	Richmond, VA	Dale Earnhardt	Chevrolet	105.937	25	7	6	23	Davey Alison	120.428	19th
3	3/03/91	Rockingham, NC	Kyle Petty	Pontiac	124.083	13	5	7	29	Kyle Petty	149.205	Pole
4	3/19/91	Atlanta, GA	Ken Schrader	Chevrolet	140.470	16	9	4	33	Alan Kulwicki	174.413	5th
5	4/07/91	Darlington, SC	Ricky Rudd	Chevrolet	135.594	15	7	3	19	Geoff Bodine	161.939	13th
6	4/14/91	Bristol, TN	Rusty Wallace	Pontiac	72.809	40	8	19	133	Rusty Wallace	118.051	Pole
7	4/21/91	N.Wilkesboro, NC	Darrell Waltrip	Chevrolet	79.604	8	8	17	87	Brett Bodine	116.237	13th
8	4/28/91	Martinsville, VA	Dale Earnhardt	Chevrolet	75.139	13	4	11	53	Mark Martin	91.949	10th
9	5/06/91	Talladega, AL	Harry Gant	Olds	165.620	24	11	3	18	Ernie Irvan	195.186	2nd
10	5/26/91	Charlotte, NC	Davey Allison	Ford	138.951	22	10	9	54	Mark Martin	174.820	10th
11	6/02/91	Dover, DE	Ken Schrader	Chevrolet	120.152	22	9	6	42	Michael Waltrip	143.392	19th
12	6/09/91	Sonoma, CA	Davey Allison	Ford	72.970	9	7	5	14	Ricky Rudd	90.634	13th
13	6/16/91	Pocono, PA	Darrell Waltrip	Chevrolet	122.666	23	14	7	37	Mark Martin	161.996	13th
14	6/23/91	Brooklyn, MI	Davey Allison	Ford	160.912	31	11	1	4	Michael Waltrip	174.351	4th
15	7/06/91	Daytona Beach, FL	Bill Elliott	Ford	159.116	18	11	4	18	Sterling Marlin	190.331	10th
16	7/21/09	Pocono, PA	Rusty Wallace	Pontiac	115.459	21	11	11	48	Alan Kulwicki	161.473	10th
17	7/28/91	Talladega, AL	Dale Earnhardt	Chevrolet	147.383	32	13	7	43	Sterling Marlin	192.085	4th
18	8/11/91	Watkins Glen, NY	Ernie Irvan	Chevrolet	98.977	14	9	5	11	Terry Labonte	121.652	3rd
19	8/18/91	Brooklyn, MI	Dale Jarrett	Ford	142.972	24	12	4	22	Alan Kulwicki	173.431	11th
20	8/24/91	Bristol, TN	Alan Kulwicki	Ford	82.028	14	8	11	81	Bill Elliott	116.957	5th
21	9/01/91	Darlington, SC	Harry Gant	Olds	133.508	20	10	8	33	Davey Allison	162.506	5th
22	9/07/91	Richmond, VA	Harry Gant	Olds	101.361	15	9	9	43	Rusty Wallace	120.590	13th
23	9/15/91	Dover, DE	Harry Gant	Olds	110.179	10	7	9	71	Alan Kulwicki	146.825	10th
24	9/22/91	Martinsville, VA	Harry Gant	Olds	74.535	20	12	15	81	Mark Martin	93.711	12th
25	9/29/91	N.Wilkesboro, NC	Dale Earnhardt	Chevrolet	94.113	3	3	8	43	Harry Gant	116.871	16th
26	10/06/91	Charlotte, NC	Geoff Bodine	Ford	138.984	10	4	6	38	Mark Martin	176.499	6th
27	10/20/91	Rockingham, NC	Davey Allison	Ford	127.292	26	6	5	24	Kyle Petty	149.461	10th
28	11/03/09	Phoenix, AZ	Davey Allison	Ford	95.746	18	13	10	55	Geoff Bodine	127.589	13th
29	11/17/91	Atlanta, GA	Mark Martin	Ford	137.968	21	12	6	37	Bill Elliott	177.937	4th

1992 NASCAR Winston Cup Series Season

No.	Date	Site	Race Winner	Car	Speed	Lead Chgs	Ldrs	Caut.	C.Laps	Pole Winner	Speed	Winner Started
1	2/16/92	Daytona Beach, FL	Davey Allison	Ford	160.256	15	7	4	22	Sterling Marlin	192.213	6th
2	3/01/92	Rockingham, NC	Bill Elliott	Ford	126.125	11	5	7	28	Kyle Petty	149.926	2nd
3	3/08/92	Richmond, VA	Bill Elliott	Ford	104.378	5	4	4	23	Bill Elliott	121.337	Pole
4	3/15/92	Atlanta, GA	Bill Elliott	Ford	147.746	10	6	7	29	Mark Martin	179.923	4th
5	3/29/92	Darlington, SC	Bill Elliott	Ford	139.364	21	7	4	21	Sterling Marlin	163.067	2nd
6	4/05/92	Bristol, TN	Alan Kulwicki	Ford	83.316	11	7	10	75	Alan Kulwicki	122.474	Pole
7	4/12/92	N.Wilkesboro, NC	Davey Allison	Ford	90.653	8	6	9	55	Alan Kulwicki	117.242	7th
8	4/26/92	Martinsville, VA	Mark Martin	Ford	78.086	11	6	11	59	Darrell Waltrip	92.956	12th
9	5/03/92	Talladega, AL	Davey Allison	Ford	167.609	16	5	5	21	Ernie Irvan	192.831	2nd
10	5/24/92	Charlotte, NC	Dale Earnhardt	Chevrolet	132.980	27	14	12	62	Bill Elliott	175.479	13th
11	5/31/92	Dover, DE	Harry Gant	Olds	109.456	20	11	7	98	Brett Bodine	147.408	15th
12	6/07/92	Sonoma, CA	Ernie Irvan	Chevrolet	81.413	7	8	3	7	Ricky Rudd	90.985	2nd
13	6/14/92	Pocono, PA	Alan Kuwicki	Ford	144.023	26	11	3	13	Ken Schrader	162.499	6th
14	6/21/92	Brooklyn, MI	Davey Allison	Ford	152.672	14	6	4	13	Davey Allison	176.258	Pole
15	7/04/92	Daytona Beach, FL	Ernie Irvan	Chevrolet	170.457	17	8	2	8	Sterling Marlin	189.366	6th
16	7/19/92	Pocono, PA	Darrell Waltrip	Chevrolet	134.058	13	7	3	23	Davey Allison	162.022	8th
17	7/26/92	Talladega, AL	Ernie Irvan	Chevrolet	176.309	17	8	2	11	Sterling Marlin	190.586	7th
18	8/09/92	Watkins Glen, NY	Kyle Petty	Pontiac	88.980	6	4	3	13	Dale Earnhardt	116.882	2nd
19	8/16/92	Brooklyn, MI	Harry Gant	Olds	146.056	16	8	5	25	Alan Kulwicki	178.196	24th
20	8/29/92	Bristol, TN	Darrell Waltrip	Chevrolet	91.198	14	8	10	55	Ernie Irvan	120.535	9th
21	9/06/92	Darlington, SC	Darrell Waltrip	Chevrolet	129.114	23	11	5	28	Sterling Marlin	162.249	5th
22	9/12/92	Richmond, VA	Rusty Wallace	Pontiac	104.661	12	6	3	20	Ernie Irvan	120.784	3rd
23	9/20/92	Dover, DE	Ricky Rudd	Chevrolet	115.289	13	7	9	48	Alan Kulwicki	145.267	6th
24	9/28/92	Martinsville, VA	Geoff Bodine	Ford	75.424	12	8	12	67	Kyle Petty	92.497	7th
25	10/05/92	N.Wilkesboro, NC	Geoff Bodine	Ford	107.360	12	7	0	0	Alan Kulwicki	117.133	3rd
26	10/11/92	Charlotte, NC	Mark Martin	Ford	153.537	21	8	3	12	Alan Kulwicki	179.027	4th
27	10/25/92	Rockingham, NC	Kyle Petty	Pontiac	130.748	9	4	2	12	Kyle Petty	149.675	Pole
28	11/01/92	Phoenix, AZ	Davey Allison	Ford	103.885	8	7	6	34	Rusty Wallace	128.141	12th
29	11/15/92	Atlanta, GA	Bill Elliott	Ford	133.322	20	9	7	45	Rick Mast	180.183	11th

1993 NASCAR Winston Cup Series Season

No.	Date	Site	Race Winner	Car	Speed	Lead Chgs	Ldrs	Caut.	C.Laps	Pole Winner	Speed	Winner Started
1	2/14/93	Daytona Beach, FL	Dale Jarrett	Chevrolet	154.972	38	13	7	30	Kyle Petty	189.426	2nd
2	2/28/93	Rockingham, NC	Rusty Wallace	Pontiac	124.486	20	9	7	40	Mark Martin	149.547	10th
3	3/07/93	Richmond, VA	Davey Allison	Ford	107.709	12	6	3	19	Ken Schrader	123.164	14th
4	3/20/93	Atlanta, GA	Morgan Shepherd	Ford	150.442	19	9	4	19	Rusty Wallace	178.749	7th
5	3/28/93	Darlington, SC	Dale Earnhardt	Chevrolet	139.958	18	11	3	14	No Time Trials	NTT	Pole
6	4/04/93	Bristol, TN	Rusty Wallace	Pontiac	84.730	19	10	17	87	Rusty Wallace	120.938	Pole
7	4/18/93	N.Wikesboro, NC	Rusty Wallace	Pontiac	92.602	12	9	4	38	Brett Bodine	117.017	9th
8	4/25/93	Martinsville, VA	Rusty Walace	Pontiac	79.078	10	4	8	49	Geoff Bodine	93.887	5th
9	5/02/93	Talladega, AL	Ernie Irvan	Chevrolet	155.412	22	7	4	25	Dale Earnhardt	192.355	16th
10	5/16/93	Sonoma, CA	Geoff Bodine	Ford	77.013	9	6	5	11	Dale Earnhardt	91.838	3rd
11	5/30/93	Charlotte, NC	Dale Earnhardt	Chevrolet	145.504	29	10	7	33	Ken Schrader	177.352	14th
12	6/06/93	Dover, DE	Dale Earnhardt	Chevrolet	105.600	25	12	14	78	Ernie Irvan	151.541	8th
13	6/13/93	Pocono, PA	Kyle Petty	Pontiac	138.005	22	13	6	24	Ken Schrader	162.816	8th
14	6/20/93	Brooklyn, MI	Ricky Rudd	Chevrolet	148.484	16	8	5	20	Brett Bodine	175.456	2nd
15	7/03/93	Daytona Beach, FL	Dale Earnhardt	Chevrolet	151.755	28	13	6	22	Ernie Irvan	190.327	5th
16	7/11/93	Loudon, NH	Rusty Wallace	Pontiac	105.947	13	6	6	27	Mark Martin	126.871	33rd
17	7/18/93	Pocono, PA	Dale Earnhardt	Chevrolet	133.343	24	12	8	27	Ken Schrader	162.934	11th
18	7/25/93	Talladega, AL	Dale Earnhardt	Chevrolet	153.858	26	10	5	27	Bill Elliott	192.397	11th
19	8/08/93	Watkins Glen, NY	Mark Martin	Ford	84.771	8	4	7	20	Mark Martin	119.118	Pole
20	8/15/93	Brooklyn, MI	Mark Martin	Ford	144.564	15	8	8	27	Ken Schrader	180.750	12th
21	8/28/93	Bristol, TN	Mark Martin	Ford	88.172	8	4	11	71	Mark Martin	121.405	Pole
22	9/05/93	Darlington, SC	Mark Martin	Ford	137.932	21	10	3	16	Ken Schrader	161.259	4th
23	9/11/93	Richmond, VA	Rusty Wallace	Pontiac	99.917	12	6	8	47	Bobby Labonte	122.006	3rd
24	9/19/93	Dover, DE	Rusty Wallace	Pontiac	100.334	18	8	16	103	Rusty Wallace	151.564	Pole
25	9/26/93	Martinsville, VA	Ernie Irvan	Ford	74.102	10	4	11	73	Ernie Irvan	92.583	Pole
26	10/03/93	N.Wilkesboro, NC	Rusty Wallace	Pontiac	96.920	15	10	4	26	Ernie Irvan	116.786	11th
27	10/10/93	Charlotte, NC	Ernie Irvan	Ford	154.537	9	4	2	11	Jeff Gordon	177.684	2nd
28	10/24/93	Rockingham, NC	Rusty Wallace	Pontiac	114.036	23	11	8	54	Mark Martin	148.353	18th
29	10/31/93	Phoenix, AZ	Mark Martin	Ford	100.375	19	11	9	45	Bill Elliott	129.482	3rd
30	11/14/93	Atlanta, GA	Rusty Wallace	Pontiac	125.221	26	12	11	58	Harry Gant	176.902	20th

1994 NASCAR Winston Cup Series Season

No.	Date	Site	Race Winner	Car	Speed	Lead Chgs	Ldrs	Caut.	C.Laps	Pole Winner	Speed	Winner Started
1	22/0/94	Daytona Beach, FL	Sterling Marlin	Chevrolet	156.931	33	13	4	23	Loy Allen, Jr.	190.158	4th
2	2/27/94	Rockingham, NC	Rusty Wallace	Ford	125.239	19	8	5	38	Goeff Bodine	151.716	15th
3	3/06/94	Richmond, VA	Ernie Irvan	Ford	98.334	15	8	8	51	Ted Musgrave	123.474	7th
4	3/13/94	Atlanta, GA	Ernie Irvan	Ford	146.136	19	7	5	27	Loy Allen, Jr.	180.207	7th
5	3/27/94	Darlington, SC	Dale Earnhardt	Chevrolet	132.432	28	10	5	26	Bill Elliott	165.553	9th
6	4/10/94	Bristol, TN	Dale Earnhardt	Chevrolet	89.647	11	5	10	75	Chuck Bown	124.946	24th
7	4/17/94	N.Wilkesboro, NC	Terry Labonte	Chevrolet	95.816	8	6	6	35	Ernie Irvan	119.016	10th
8	4/24/94	Martinsville, VA	Rusty Wallace	Ford	76.700	11	5	11	65	Rusty Wallace	92.942	Pole
9	5/01/94	Talladega, AL	Dale Earnhardt	Chevrolet	157.478	30	11	4	23	Ernie Irvan	193.298	4th
10	5/15/94	Sonoma, CA	Ernie Irvan	Ford	77.458	7	5	4	10	Ernie Irvan	91.514	Pole
11	5/29/94	Charlotte, NC	Jeff Gordon	Chevrolet	139.445	24	8	9	47	Jeff Gordon	181.439	Pole
12	6/05/94	Dover, DE	Rusty Wallace	Ford	102.529	22	8	12	99	Ernie Irvan	151.956	6th
13	6/12/94	Pocono, PA	Rusty Wallace	Ford	128.801	22	12	5	35	Rusty Wallace	164.558	Pole
14	6/19/94	Brooklyn, MI	Rusty Wallace	Ford	125.022	13	7	7	52	Loy Allen, Jr.	180.641	3rd
15	7/02/94	Daytona Beach, FL	Jimmy Spencer	Ford	155.548	18	10	4	19	Dale Earnhardt	191.339	3rd
16	7/10/94	Loudon, NH	Ricky Rudd	Ford	87.599	19	11	17	78	Ernie Irvan	127.197	3rd
17	7/17/94	Pocono, PA	Geoff Bodine	Ford	136.075	18	9	5	23	Geoff Bodine	163.869	Pole
18	7/24/94	Talladega, AL	Jimmy Spencer	Ford	163.217	24	10	5	20	Dale Earnhardt	193.470	2nd
19	8/06/94	Indianapolis, IN	Jeff Gordon	Chevrolet	131.977	21	12	6	25	Rick Mast	172.414	3rd
20	8/14/94	Watkins Glen, NY	Mark Martin	Ford	93.752	7	5	4	11	Mark Martin	118.326	Pole
21	8/21/94	Brooklyn, MI	Geoff Bodine	Ford	139.914	14	8	5	30	Geoff Bodine	181.082	Pole

No.	Date	Site	Race Winner	Car	Speed	Lead Chgs	Ldrs	Caut.	C.Laps	Pole Winner	Speed	Winner Started
22	8/27/94	Bristol, TN	Rusty Wallace	Ford	91.363	16	10	12	73	Harry Gant	124.186	4th
23	9/04/94	Darlington, SC	Bill Elliott	Ford	127.952	28	10	6	42	Geoff Bodine	166.998	9th
24	9/10/94	Richmond, VA	Terry Labonte	Chevrolet	104.156	17	8	5	35	Ted Musgrave	124.052	3rd
25	9/18/94	Dover, DE	Rusty Wallace	Ford	112.556	26	12	13	72	Geoff Bodine	152.840	10th
26	9/25/94	Martinsville, VA	Rusty Wallace	Ford	77.139	18	9	11	62	Ted Musgrave	94.129	7th
27	10/02/94	N.Wilkesboro, NC	Geoff Bodine	Ford	98.522	6	6	4	25	Jimmy Spencer	118.588	18th
28	10/09/94	Charlotte, NC	Dale Jarrett	Chevrolet	145.922	30	16	7	34	Ward Burton	185.759	22nd
29	10/23/94	Rockingham, NC	Dale Earnhardt	Chevrolet	126.408	26	12	10	52	Ricky Rudd	157.099	20th
30	10/30/94	Phoenix, AZ	Terry Labonte	Chevrolet	107.463	13	9	4	27	Sterling Marlin	129.833	19th
31	11/13/94	Atlanta, GA	Mark Martin	Ford	148.982	30	13	4	27	Greg Sacks	185.830	5th

1995 NASCAR Winston Cup Series Season

No.	Date	Site	Race Winner	Car	Speed	Lead Chgs	Ldrs	Caut.	C.Laps	Pole Winner	Speed	Winner Started
1	2/19/95	Daytona Beach, FL	Sterling Marlin	Chevrolet	141.710	12	8	10	41	Dale Jarrett	193.498	3rd
2	2/26/95	Rockingham, NC	Jeff Gordon	Chevrolet	125.305	19	7	11	58	Jeff Gordon	157.620	Pole
3	3/05/95	Richmond, VA	Terry Labonte	Chevrolet	106.425	17	6	5	28	Jeff Gordon	124.757	24th
4	3/01/95	Atlanta, GA	Jeff Gordon	Chevrolet	150.115	9	7	5	27	Dale Earnhardt	185.077	3rd
5	3/26/95	Darlington, SC	Sterling Marlin	Chevrolet	111.392	16	11	15	87	Jeff Gordon	170.833	5th
6	4/02/95	Bristol, TN	Jeff Gordon	Chevrolet	92.011	12	5	7	65	Mark Martin	124.605	2nd
7	4/09/95	N.Wilkesboro, NC	Dale Earnhardt	Chevrolet	102.424	19	7	3	14	Jeff Gordon	118.765	5th
8	4/23/95	Martinsville, VA	Rusty Wallace	Ford	72.145	8	5	7	84	Bobby Labonte	93.308	15th
9	4/30/95	Talladega, AL	Mark Martin	Ford	178.902	24	10	2	8	Terry Labonte	196.532	3rd
10	5/07/95	Sonoma, CA	Dale Earnhardt	Chevrolet	70.681	4	4	5	14	Ricky Rudd	92.132	4th
11	5/28/95	Charlotte, NC	Bobby Labonte	Chevrolet	151.952	32	12	7	33	Jeff Gordon	183.861	2nd
12	6/04/95	Dover, DE	Kyle Petty	Pontiac	119.880	20	8	5	38	Jeff Gordon	153.669	37th
13	6/11/95	Pocono, PA	Terry Labonte	Chevrolet	137.720	24	11	6	20	Ken Schrader	163.375	27th
14	6/18/95	Brooklyn, MI	Bobby Labonte	Chevrolet	134.141	20	10	8	44	Jeff Gordon	186.611	19th
15	7/01/95	Daytona Beach, FL	Jeff Gordon	Chevrolet	166.976	8	4	3	11	Dale Earnhardt	191.355	3rd
16	7/09/95	Loudon, NH	Jeff Gordon	Chevrolet	106.999	16	8	6	29	Mark Martin	128.815	21st
17	7/16/95	Pocono, PA	Dale Jarrett	Ford	134.038	37	13	5	25	Bill Elliott	162.496	15th
18	7/23/95	Talladega, AL	Sterling Marlin	Chevrolet	173.187	21	9	2	11	Sterling Marlin	194.212	Pole
19	8/05/95	Indianapolis, IN	Dale Earnhardt	Chevrolet	155.206	17	11	1	4	Jeff Gordon	172.536	13th
20	8/13/95	Watkins Glen, NY	Mark Martin	Ford	103.030	7	6	3	7	Mark Martin	120.411	Pole
21	8/20/95	Brooklyn, MI	Bobby Labonte	Chevrolet	157.739	17	8	3	16	Bobby Labonte	184.403	Pole
22	8/26/95	Bristol, TN	Terry Labonte	Chevrolet	81.979	16	10	15	106	Mark Martin	125.093	2nd
23	9/03/95	Darlington, SC	Jeff Gordon	Chevrolet	121.231	21	11	12	75	John Andretti	167.379	5th
24	9/09/95	Richmond, VA	Rusty Wallace	Ford	104.448	15	7	4	30	Dale Earnhardt	122.543	7th
25	9/17/95	Dover, DE	Jeff Gordon	Chevrolet	124.740	10	7	5	34	Rick Mast	153.446	2nd
26	9/24/95	Martinsville, VA	Dale Earnhardt	Chevrolet	73.946	16	8	10	85	No Time Trials	NTT	2nd
27	10/01/95	N.Wilkesboro, NC	Mark Martin	Ford	102.998	28	13	2	10	Ted Musgrave	118.396	2nd
28	10/08/95	Charlotte, NC	Mark Martin	Ford	145.358	19	11	7	35	Ricky Rudd	180.578	5th
29	10/22/95	Rockingham, NC	Ward Burton	Pontiac	114.793	14	10	7	64	Hut Stricklin	155.379	3rd
30	10/29/95	Phoenix, AZ	Ricky Rudd	Ford	102.128	11	8	8	39	Bill Elliott	130.020	29th
31	11/12/95	Atlanta, GA	Dale Earnhardt	Chevrolet	163.633	22	8	2	11	Darrell Waltrip	185.046	11th

1996 NASCAR Winston Cup Series Season

No.	Date	Site	Race Winner	Car	Speed	Lead Chgs	Ldrs	Caut.	C.Laps	Pole Winner	Speed	Winner Started
1	2/18/96	Daytona Beach, FL	Dale Jarrett	Ford	154.308	32	15	6	26	Dale Earnhardt	189.510	7th
2	2/25/96	Rockingham, NC	Dale Earnhardt	Chevrolet	113.959	22	6	10	66	Terry Labonte	156.870	18th
3	3/03/96	Richmond, VA	Jeff Gordon	Chevrolet	102.750	25	11	8	36	Terry Labonte	123.728	2nd
4	3/10/96	Atlanta, GA	Dale Earnhardt	Chevrolet	161.298	30	12	3	13	Johnny Benson, Jr.	185.434	18th
5	3/24/96	Darlington, SC	Jeff Gordon	Chevrolet	124.792	15	9	11	56	Ward Burton	173.797	2nd
6	3/31/96	Bristol, TN	Jeff Gordon	Chevrolet	91.308	7	7	5	37	Mark Martin	123.578	8th
7	4/14/96	N.Wilkesboro, NC	Terry Labonte	Chevrolet	96.370	17	9	3	25	Terry Labonte	116.549	Pole
8	4/21/96	Martinsville, VA	Rusty Wallace	Ford	81.410	18	7	6	36	Ricky Craven	93.079	5th
9	4/28/96	Talladega, AL	Sterling Marlin	Chevrolet	149.999	24	14	6	31	Ernie Irvan	192.855	4th
10	5/05/96	Sonoma, CA	Rusty Wallace	Ford	77.673	9	7	5	10	Terry Labonte	92.524	7th
11	5/26/96	Charlotte, NC	Dale Jarrett	Ford	147.581	20	8	6	35	Jef Gordon	183.773	15th
12	6/02/96	Dover, DE	Jeff Gordon	Chevrolet	122.741	19	6	5	38	Jeff Gordon	154.785	Pole
13	6/16/96	Pocono, PA	Jeff Gordon	Chevrolet	139.104	26	12	4	23	Jeff Gordon	169.725	Pole
14	6/23/96	Brooklyn, MI	Rusty Wallace	Ford	166.033	17	9	2	8	Bobby Hamilton	185.166	18th
15	7/06/96	Daytona Beach, FL	Sterling Marlin	Chevrolet	161.602	9	6	3	11	Jeff Gordon	188.869	2nd
16	7/14/96	Loudon, NH	Ernie Irvan	Ford	98.930	23	15	8	49	Ricky Craven	129.379	6th
17	7/21/96	Pocono, PA	Rusty Wallace	Ford	144.892	23	12	4	17	Mark Martin	168.410	13th
18	7/28/96	Talladega, AL	Jeff Gordon	Chevrolet	133.387	24	10	5	35	Jeremy Mayfield	192.370	2nd
19	8/03/96	Indianapolis, IN	Dale Jarrett	Chevrolet	139.508	18	13	5	21	Jeff Gordon	176.419	24th
20	8/11/96	Watkins Glen, NY	Geoff Bodine	Ford	92.334	8	6	4	11	Dale Earnhardt	120.733	13th
21	8/18/96	Brooklyn, MI	Dale Jarrett	Ford	139.792	13	8	8	36	Jeff Burton	185.395	11th
22	8/24/96	Bristol, TN	Rusty Wallace	Ford	91.267	8	5	8	67	Mark Martin	124.857	5th
23	9/01/96	Darlington, SC	Jeff Gordon	Chevrolet	135.757	29	14	6	37	Dale Jarrett	170.993	2nd
24	9/07/96	Richmond, VA	Ernie Irvan	Ford	105.469	16	9	4	24	Mark Martin	122.744	16th
25	9/15/96	Dover, DE	Jeff Gordon	Chevrolet	105.646	28	12	14	91	Bobby Labonte	155.086	3rd
26	9/22/96	Martinsville, VA	Jeff Gordon	Chevrolet	82.223	11	4	7	35	Bobby Hamilton	94.120	10th
27	9/29/96	N.Wilkesboro, NC	Jeff Gordon	Chevrolet	96.837	18	8	4	29	Ted Musgrave	118.054	2nd
28	9/06/96	Charlotte, NC	Terry Labonte	Chevrolet	143.143	21	9	5	37	Bobby Labonte	184.068	16th
29	10/20/96	Rockingham, NC	Ricky Rudd	Ford	122.320	21	10	7	46	Dale Jarrett	157.194	2nd
30	10/27/96	Phoenix, AZ	Bobby Hamilton	Pontiac	109.709	19	9	5	25	Bobby Labonte	131.076	17th
31	11/10/96	Atlanta, GA	Bobby Labonte	Chevrolet	134.661	27	12	8	47	Bobby Labonte	185.887	Pole

1997 NASCAR Winston Cup Series Season

No.	Date	Site	Race Winner	Car	Speed	Lead Chgs	Ldrs	Caut.	C.Laps	Pole Winner	Speed	Winner Started
1	2/16/97	Daytona Beach, FL	Jeff Gordon	Chevrolet	148.295	12	9	8	29	Mike Skinner	189.813	6th
2	2/23/97	Rockingham, NC	Jeff Gordon	Chevrolet	121.371	9	6	7	47	Mark Martin	157.885	4th
3	3/02/97	Richmond, VA	Rusty Wallace	Ford	108.499	15	7	3	12	No Time Trials	NTT	7th

No.	Date	Site	Race Winner	Car	Speed	Lead Chgs	Ldrs	Caut.	C.Laps	Pole Winner	Speed	Winner Started
4	3/09/97	Atlanta, GA	Dale Jarrett	Ford	132.731	16	7	7	45	Robby Gordon	186.507	9th
5	3/23/97	Darlington, SC	Dale Jarrett	Ford	121.162	15	7	10	60	Dale Jarrett	171.095	Pole
6	4/06/97	Ft. Worth, TX	Jef Burton	Ford	125.111	19	10	10	73	No Time Trials	NTT	5th
7	4/13/97	Bristol, TN	Jeff Gordon	Chevrolet	75.035	13	6	20	132	Rusty Wallace	123.586	5th
8	4/20/97	Martinsville, VA	Jeff Gordon	Chevrolet	70.347	4	3	11	99	Kenny Wallace	93.961	4th
9	5/04/97	Sonoma, CA	Mark Martin	Ford	75.788	6	4	3	9	Mark Martin	92.807	Pole
10	4/27/97	Talladega, AL	Mark Martin	Ford	188.354	26	13	0	0	John Andretti	193.627	18th
11	5/25/97	Charlotte, NC	Jeff Gordon	Chevrolet	136.745	27	12	7	50	Jeff Gordon	184.300	Pole
12	6/01/97	Dover, DE	Ricky Rudd	Ford	114.635	23	13	8	54	Bobby Labonte	152.788	13th
13	6/08/97	Pocono, PA	Jeff Gordon	Chevrolet	139.828	25	15	4	22	Bobby Hamilton	168.089	11th
14	6/15/97	Brooklyn, MI	Ernie Irvan	Ford	153.338	26	11	3	18	Dale Jarrett	183.669	20th
15	6/22/97	Fontana, CA	Jeff Gordon	Chevrolet	155.025	21	12	4	22	Joe Nemechek	183.015	3rd
16	7/05/97	Daytona Beach, FL	John Andretti	Ford	157.791	16	11	4	116	Mike Skinner	189.777	3rd
17	7/13/97	Loudon, NH	Jeff Burton	Ford	117.194	14	8	2	10	Ken Schrader	129.423	15th
18	7/20/97	Pocono, PA	Dale Jarrett	Ford	142.068	23	14	4	18	Joe Nemechek	168.881	4th
19	8/02/97	Indianapolis, IN	Ricky Rudd	Ford	130.814	19	11	6	25	Ernie Irvan	177.736	7th
20	8/10/97	Watkins Glen, NY	Jef Gordon	Chevrolet	91.294	10	9	5	11	Todd Bodine	119.399	11th
21	8/17/97	Brooklyn, MI	Mark Martin	Ford	126.883	18	8	3	46	Johnny Benson, Jr.	183.332	2nd
22	8/23/97	Bristol, TN	Dale Jarrett	Ford	80.013	12	5	12	97	Kenny Wallace	123.039	3rd
23	8/31/97	Darlington, SC	Jeff Gordon	Chevrolet	121.149	9	7	11	67	Bobby Labonte	170.661	7th
24	9/06/97	Richmond, VA	Dale Jarrett	Ford	109.047	10	9	3	16	Bill Elliott	124.723	23rd
25	9/14/97	Loudon, NH	Jeff Gordon	Chevrolet	100.364	15	8	8	49	Ken Schrader	129.182	13th
26	9/21/97	Dover, DE	Mark Martin	Ford	132.719	10	4	1	11	Mark Martin	152.033	Pole
27	9/28/97	Martinsville, VA	Jeff Burton	Ford	73.078	17	7	11	91	Ward Burton	93.410	10th
28	10/05/97	Charlotte, NC	Dale Jarrett	Ford	144.323	20	9	4	33	Geoff Bodine	184.256	5th
29	10/12/97	Talladega, AL	Terry Labonte	Chevrolet	156.601	32	16	4	22	Ernie Irvan	193.271	6th
30	10/26/97	Rockingham, NC	Bobby Hamilton	Pontiac	121.730	20	9	5	40	Bobby Labonte	156.696	28th
31	11/02/97	Phoenix, AZ	Dale Jarrett	Ford	110.824	13	9	4	23	Bobby Hamilton	131.579	9th
32	11/16/97	Atlanta, GA	Bobby Labonte	Pontiac	159.904	24	11	4	25	Geoff Bodine	197.478	21st

1998 NASCAR Winston Cup Series Season

No.	Date	Site	Race Winner	Car	Speed	Lead Chgs	Ldrs	Caut.	C.Laps	Pole Winner	Speed	Winner Started
1	2/15/98	Daytona Beach, FL	Dale Earnhardt	Chevrolet	172.712	13	8	3	9	Bobby Labonte	189.498	4th
2	2/22/98	Rockingham, NC	Jeff Gordon	Chevrolet	117.065	27	12	6	50	Rick Mast	153.645	4th
3	3/01/98	Las Vegas, NV	Mark Martin	Ford	146.554	24	12	2	9	Dale Jarrett	168.224	7th
4	3/09/98	Atlanta, GA	Bobby Labonte	Pontiac	139.501	29	14	7	52	Todd Bodine	192.841	14th
5	3/22/98	Darlington, SC	Dale Jarrett	Ford	127.962	18	6	5	31	Mark Martin	168.665	3rd
6	3/29/98	Bristol, TN	Jeff Gordon	Chevrolet	82.850	19	10	14	88	Rusty Wallace	124.275	2nd
7	4/05/98	Ft. Worth, TX	Mark Martin	Ford	136.771	24	9	7	43	Jeremy Mayfield	185.906	7th
8	4/19/98	Martinsville, VA	Bobby Hamilton	Chevrolet	70.709	15	6	14	96	Bobby Hamilton	93.175	Pole
9	4/26/98	Talladega, AL	Bobby Labonte	Pontiac	142.428	19	9	3	16	Bobby Labonte	195.728	Pole
10	5/03/98	Fontana, CA	Mark Martin	Ford	140.220	18	8	6	35	Jeff Gordon	181.772	3rd
11	5/24/98	Charlotte, NC	Jeff Gordon	Chevrolet	136.424	33	12	8	49	Jeff Gordon	179.647	Pole
12	5/31/98	Dover, DE	Dale Jarrett	Ford	119.522	15	7	5	35	Rusty Wallace	153.807	4th
13	6/06/98	Richmond, VA	Terry Labonte	Chevrolet	97.044	17	8	7	47	Jeff Gordon	122.956	16th
14	6/14/98	Brooklyn, MI	Mark Martin	Ford	158.695	15	9	2	11	Ward Burton	182.927	7th
15	6/21/98	Pocono, PA	Jeremy Mayfield	Ford	117.809	19	12	9	48	Jeff Gordon	168.042	3rd
16	6/28/98	Sonoma, CA	Jeff Gordon	Chevrolet	72.387	9	9	5	23	Jeff Gordon	98.711	Pole
17	7/12/98	Loudon, NH	Jeff Burton	Ford	102.996	17	9	6	40	Ricky Craven	127.949	5th
18	7/26/98	Pocono, PA	Jeff Gordon	Chevrolet	134.660	10	7	5	25	Ward Burton	168.805	2nd
19	8/01/98	Indianapolis, IN	Jeff Gordon	Chevrolet	126.772	10	7	9	34	Ernie Irvan	179.394	3rd
20	8/09/98	Watkins Glen, NY	Jeff Gordon	Chevrolet	94.446	8	6	4	9	Jeff Gordon	120.331	Pole
21	8/16/98	Brooklyn, MI	Jeff Gordon	Chevrolet	151.955	22	9	3	17	Ernie Irvan	183.416	3rd
22	8/22/98	Bristol, TN	Mark Martin	Ford	86.949	12	7	13	86	Rusty Wallace	125.554	4th
23	8/30/98	Loudon, NH	Jeff Gordon	Chevrolet	112.078	11	9	4	25	Jeff Gordon	129.033	Pole
24	9/06/98	Darlington, SC	Jefff Gordon	Chevrolet	139.031	12	6	2	16	Dale Jarrett	168.879	5th
25	9/12/98	Richmond, VA	Jeff Burton	Ford	91.985	24	11	8	66	Rusty Wallace	125.377	3rd
26	9/20/98	Dover, DE	Mark Martin	Ford	113.834	11	5	7	47	Mark Martin	155.966	Pole
27	9/27/98	Martinsville, VA	Ricky Rudd	Ford	73.350	11	5	11	82	Ernie Irvan	92.655	2nd
28	10/04/98	Charlotte, NC	Mark Martin	Ford	123.188	17	8	11	65	Derrike Cope	181.690	2nd
29	10/11/98	Talladega, AL	Dale Jarrett	Ford	159.318	20	13	4	20	Ken Schrader	196.153	3rd
30	10/17/98	Daytona Beach, FL	Jeff Gordon	Chevrolet	144.549	16	9	6	26	Bobby Labonte	193.611	8th
31	10/25/98	Phoenix, AZ	Rusty Wallace	Ford	108.211	8	7	4	25	Ken Schrader	131.234	6th
32	11/01/98	Rockingham, NC	Jeff Gordon	Chevrolet	128.423	20	10	4	25	Mark Martin	156.502	9th
33	11/08/98	Atlanta, GA	Jeff Gordon	Chevrolet	114.915	10	8	5	68	Kenny Irwin	193.461	21st

1999 NASCAR Winston Cup Series Season

No.	Date	Site	Race Winner	Car	Speed	Lead Chgs	Ldrs	Caut.	C.Laps	Pole Winner	Speed	Winner Started
1	2/14/99	Daytona Beach, FL	Jeff Gordon	Chevy	161.551	14	7	4	20	Jeff Gordon	195.067	Pole
2	2/21/99	Rockingham, NC	Mark Martin	Ford	120.750	25	6	6	39	Ricky Rudd	157.241	5th
3	3/07/99	Las Vegas, NV	Jeff Burton	Ford	137.537	25	10	5	22	Bobby Labonte	170.643	19th
4	3/14/99	Atlanta, GA	Jeff Gordon	Chevy	143.284	25	10	6	44	Bobby Labonte	194.957	8th
5	3/21/99	Darlington, SC	Jeff Burton	Ford	121.294	13	8	3	19	Jeff Gordon	173.167	9th
6	3/28/99	Ft. Worth, TX	Terry Labonte	Chevy	144.276	24	11	8	39	Kenny Irwin	190.154	4th
7	4/11/99	Bristol, TN	Rusty Wallace	Ford	93.363	7	5	7	57	Rusty Wallace	125.142	Pole
8	4/18/99	Martinsville, VA	John Andretti	Pontiac	75.653	20	9	10	70	Tony Stewart	95.275	21st
9	4/25/99	Talladega, AL	Dale Earnhardt	Chevy	163.395	29	15	3	18	Ken Schrader	197.765	17th
10	5/02/99	Fontana, CA	Jeff Gordon	Chevy	150.276	28	13	5	23	No Time Trials	NTT	5th
11	5/15/99	Richmond, VA	Dale Jarrett	Ford	100.102	19	9	8	58	Jeff Gordon	126.499	21st
12	5/30/99	Charlotte, NC	Jeff Burton	Ford	151.367	23	9	5	23	Bobby Labonte	185.230	2nd
13	6/06/99	Dover, DE	Bobby Labonte	Pontiac	120.603	15	7	4	31	Bobby Labotne	159.320	Pole
14	6/13/99	Brooklyn, MI	Dale Jarrett	Ford	173.997	12	7	0	0	Jeff Gordon	186.945	6th
15	6/20/99	Pocono, PA	Bobby Labonte	Pontiac	118.898	22	13	11	46	Sterling Marlin	170.506	3rd
16	6/27/99	Sonoma, CA	Jeff Gordon	Chevy	70.378	7	4	7	26	Jeff Gordon	98.519	Pole
17	7/03/99	Daytona Beach, FL	Dale Jarrett	Ford	169.213	17	9	3	9	Joe Nemechek	194.860	12th
18	7/11/99	Loudon, NH	Jeff Burton	Ford	101.876	9	6	7	49	Jeff Gordon	131.171	38th
19	7/25/99	Pocono, PA	Bobby Labonte	Pontiac	116.982	27	15	9	49	Mike Skinner	170.451	4th
20	8/07/99	Indianapolis, IN	Dale Jarrett	Ford	148.194	13	6	3	12	Jeff Gordon	179.612	4th
21	8/15/99	Watkins Glen, NY	Jeff Gordon	Chevrolet	87.722	11	8	7	15	Rusty Wallace	121.234	3rd

22	8/22/99	Brooklyn, MI	Bobby Labonte	Pontiac	144.332	24	11	6	26	Ward Burton	188.843	19th
23	8/28/99	Bristol, TN	Dale Earnhardt	Chevrolet	91.276	11	5	10	60	Tony Stewart	124.589	26th
24	9/05/99	Darlington, SC	Jeff Burton	Ford	107.816	20	10	6	62	Kenny Irwin	170.970	15th
25	9/11/99	Richmond, VA	Tony Stewart	Pontiac	104.006	13	5	6	45	Mike Skinner	125.465	2nd
26	9/19/99	Loudon, NH	Joe Nemechek	Chevrolet	100.673	12	9	11	53	Rusty Wallace	129.820	11th
27	9/26/99	Dover, DE	Mark Martin	Ford	127.434	25	10	4	22	Rusty Wallace	159.964	8th
28	10/03/99	Martinsville, VA	Jeff Gordon	Chevrolet	72.624	17	11	8	75	Joe Nemechek	95.223	5th
29	10/10/99	Charlotte, NC	Jeff Gordon	Chevrolet	160.306	21	10	2	9	Bobby Labonte	185.682	22nd
30	10/17/99	Talladega, AL	Dale Earnhardt	Chevrolet	166.632	32	16	3	17	Joe Nemechek	198.331	27th
31	10/24/99	Rockingham, NC	Jeff Burton	Ford	131.103	18	8	3	18	Mark Martin	157.383	6th
32	11/07/99	Phoenix, AZ	Tony Stewart	Pontiac	118.132	12	6	2	10	John Andretti	132.714	11th
33	11/14/99	Homestead, FL	Tony Stewart	Pontiac	140.335	19	10	1	5	David Green	155.759	7th
34	11/21/99	Atlanta, GA	Bobby Labonte	Pontiac	137.932	38	15	8	53	Kevin Lepage	193.731	37th

2000 NASCAR Winston Cup Series Season

No.	Date	Site	Race Winner	Car	Speed	Lead Chgs	Ldrs	Caut.	C.Laps	Pole Winner	Speed	Winner Started
1	2/20/00	Daytona Beach, FL	Dale Jarrett	Ford	155.669	9	7	6	24	Dale Jarrett	191.091	Pole
2	2/27/00	Rockingham, NC	Bobby Labonte	Pontiac	127.875	22	10	4	22	Rusty Wallace	158.035	3rd
3	3/05/00	Las Vegas, NV	Jeff Burton	Ford	119.982	13	7	2	29	Ricky Rudd	172.563	11th
4	3/12/00	Atlanta, GA	Dale Earnhardt	Chevrolet	131.759	30	17	10	62	Dale Jarrett	192.574	35th
5	3/19/00	Darlington, SC	Ward Burton	Pontiac	128.076	13	7	5	30	Jeff Gordon	172.662	3rd
6	3/26/00	Bristol, TN	Rusty Wallace	Ford	88.018	18	9	11	76	Steve Park	126.370	6th
7	4/02/00	Ft. Worth, TX	Dale Earnhardt, Jr.	Chevrolet	131.152	29	17	12	62	Terry Labonte	192.137	4th
8	4/09/00	Martinsville, VA	Mark Martin	Ford	71.161	14	8	17	116	Rusty Wallace	94.827	21st
9	4/16/00	Talladega, AL	Jeff Gordon	Chevrolet	161.157	27	10	4	17	Jeremy Mayfield	186.969	36th
10	4/30/00	Fontana, CA	Jeremy Mayfield	Ford	149.378	20	15	5	22	Mike Skinner	186.061	24th
11	5/06/00	Richmond, VA	Dale Earnhardt, Jr.	Chevrolet	99.374	21	10	9	59	Rusty Wallace	124.740	5th
12	5/28/00	Charlotte, NC	Mett Kenseth	Ford	142.640	25	11	7	38	Dale Earnhardt, Jr.	186.034	21st
13	6/04/00	Dover, DE	Tony Stewart	Pontiac	109.514	14	10	10	58	Rusty Wallace	157.411	16th
14	6/11/00	Brooklyn, MI	Tony Stewart	Pontiac	143.926	19	11	4	20	Bobby Labonte	189.883	28th
15	6/18/00	Pocono, PA	Jeremy Mayfield	Ford	135.741	24	11	5	21	Rusty Wallace	171.625	22nd
16	6/25/00	Sonoma, CA	Jeff Gordon	Chevrolet	78.789	10	7	4	14	Rusty Wallace	99.309	5th
17	7/01/00	Daytona Beach, FL	Jeff Burton	Ford	148.576	10	8	5	23	Dale Jarrett	187.547	9th
18	7/09/00	Loudon, NH	Tony Stewart	Pontiac	103.145	12	12	5	38	Rusty Wallace	132.089	6th
19	7/23/00	Pocono, PA	Rusty Wallace	Ford	130.662	25	10	7	32	Tony Stewart	172.391	2nd
20	8/05/00	Indianapolis, IN	Bobby Labonte	Pontiac	155.912	9	5	2	7	Ricky Rudd	181.068	3rd
21	8/13/00	Watkins Glen, NY	Steve Park	Chevrolet	91.336	9	7	5	12	No Time Trials	NTT	18th
22	8/20/00	Brooklyn, MI	Rusty Wallace	Ford	132.597	21	8	8	38	Dale Earnhardt, Jr.	191.149	10th
23	8/26/00	Bristol, TN	Rusty Wallace	Ford	85.394	19	12	13	85	Rusty Wallace	125.477	Pole
24	9/03/00	Darlington, SC	Bobby Labonte	Pontiac	108.273	22	15	9	69	Jeremy Mayfield	169.444	37th
25	9/09/00	Richmond, VA	Jeff Gordon	Chevrolet	99.871	16	9	8	57	Jeff Burton	125.780	13th
26	9/17/00	Loudon, NH	Jeff Burton	Ford	102.003	1	1	7	42	Bobby Labonte	127.632	2nd
27	9/24/00	Dover, DE	Tony Stewart	Pontiac	115.191	25	13	8	45	Jeremy Mayfield	159.872	27th
28	10/01/00	Martinsville, VA	Tony Stewart	Pontiac	73.859	12	7	13	88	Tony Stewart	95.371	Pole
29	10/08/00	Charlotte, NC	Bobby Labonte	Pontiac	133.630	46	13	9	51	Jeff Gordon	185.561	2nd
30	10/15/00	Talladega, AL	Dale Earnhardt	Chevrolet	165.681	49	21	3	13	Joe Nemechek	190.279	20th
31	10/22/00	Rockingham, NC	Dale Jarrett	Ford	110.418	23	10	9	60	Jeremy Mayfield	157.342	21st
32	11/05/00	Phoenix, AZ	Jeff Burton	Ford	105.041	23	13	6	39	Rusty Wallace	134.178	2nd
33	11/12/00	Homestead, FL	Tony Stewart	Pontiac	127.480	15	7	4	25	Steve Park	156.440	13th
34	11/19/00	Atlanta, GA	Jerry Nadeau	Chevrolet	141.296	23	13	8	44	Jeff Gordon	194.274	2nd

2001 NASCAR Winston Cup Series Season

No.	Date	Site	Race Winner	Car	Speed	Lead Chgs	Ldrs	Caut.	C.Laps	Pole Winner	Speed	Winner Started
1	2/18/01	Daytona Beach, FL	Michael Waltrip	Chevrolet	161.783	49	14	3	14	Bill Elliott	183.565	19th
2	2/25/01	Rockingham, NC	Steve Park	Chevrolet	111.877	20	10	4	52	Jeff Gordon	156.455	2nd
3	3/04/01	Las Vegas, NV	Jeff Gordon	Chevrolet	135.546	20	13	6	25	Dale Jarrett	172.106	24th
4	3/11/01	Atlanta, GA	Kevin Harvick	Chevrolet	143.273	25	11	8	42	Dale Jarrett	192.748	5th
5	3/18/01	Darlington, SC	Dale Jarrett	Ford	126.557	12	7	7	38	No Time Trials	NTT	2nd
6	3/25/01	Bristol, TN	Elliott Sadler	Ford	86.949	18	10	13	87	Mark Martin	126.303	38th
7	4/01/01	Ft. Worth, TX	Dale Jarrett	Ford	141.804	18	7	10	44	Dale Earnhardt, Jr.	190.678	3rd
8	4/08/01	Martinsville, VA	Dale Jarrett	Ford	70.799	15	11	12	98	Jeff Gordon	94.081	13th
9	4/22/01	Talladega, AL	Bobby Hamilton	Chevrolet	184.003	37	26	0	0	Stacy Compton	184.861	14th
10	4/29/01	Fontana, CA	Rusty Wallace	Ford	143.118	23	14	6	29	Bobby Labonte	182.635	19th
11	5/05/01	Richmond, VA	Tony Stewart	Pontiac	95.872	12	5	8	58	Mark Martin	124.613	7th
12	5/27/01	Charlotte, NC	Jeff Burton	Ford	138.107	28	14	6	45	Ryan Newman	185.217	18th
13	6/03/01	Dover, DE	Jeff Gordon	Chevrolet	120.361	16	8	5	31	No Time Trials	NTT	2nd
14	6/10/01	Brooklyn, MI	Jeff Gordon	Chevrolet	134.203	17	7	8	34	Jeff Gordon	188.250	Pole
15	6/17/01	Pocono, PA	Ricky Rudd	Ford	134.389	13	5	7	26	Ricky Rudd	170.503	Pole
16	6/24/01	Sonoma, CA	Tony Stewart	Pontiac	75.889	10	8	5	16	Jeff Gordon	93.699	3rd
17	7/07/01	Daytona Beach, FL	Dale Earnhardt, Jr.	Chevrolet	157.601	14	9	3	15	Sterling Marlin	183.778	13th
18	7/15/01	Chicago, IL	Kevin Harvick	Chevrolet	121.200	14	10	10	56	Todd Bodine	183.717	6th
19	7/22/01	Loudon, NH	Dale Jarrett	Ford	102.131	10	8	10	51	Jeff Gordon	131.770	9th
20	7/29/01	Pocono, PA	Bobby Labonte	Pontiac	134.590	20	12	6	24	Todd Bodine	170.326	11th
21	8/05/01	Indianapolis, IN	Jeff Gordon	Chevrolet	130.790	18	12	7	28	Jimmy Spencer	179.666	27th
22	8/12/01	Watkins Glen, NY	Jeff Gordon	Chevrolet	89.081	13	11	5	13	Dale Jarrett	122.698	13th
23	8/19/01	Brooklyn, MI	Sterling Marlin	Dodge	140.513	16	8	3	18	Ricky Craven	188.127	15th
24	8/25/01	Bristol, TN	Tony Stewart	Pontiac	85.106	11	8	16	93	Jeff Green	123.674	18th
25	9/02/01	Darlington, SC	Ward Burton	Dodge	122.773	19	9	11	51	Kurt Busch	168.048	37th
26	9/08/01	Richmond, VA	Ricky Rudd	Ford	95.146	8	6	12	80	Jeff Gordon	124.902	9th
27	9/23/01	Dover, DE	Dale Earnhardt, Jr.	Chevrolet	101.559	13	7	11	71	Dale Jarrett	154.919	3rd
28	9/30/01	Kansas City, KS	Jeff Gordon	Chevrolet	110.576	19	12	13	70	Jason Leffler	176.499	2nd
29	10/07/01	Charlotte, NC	Sterling Marlin	Dodge	139.006	19	9	8	40	Jimmy Spencer	185.147	13th
30	10/14/01	Martinsville, VA	Ricky Craven	Ford	75.750	19	14	13	81	Todd Bodine	93.724	6th
31	10/21/01	Talladega, AL	Dale Earnhardt, Jr.	Chevrolet	164.185	32	13	3	16	Stacy Compton	185.240	6th
32	10/28/01	Phoenix, AZ	Jeff Burton	Ford	102.613	15	6	7	45	Casey Atwood	131.296	3rd
33	11/04/01	Rockingham, NC	Joe Nemechek	Chevrolet	128.941	16	6	2	16	Kenny Wallace	154.690	13th
34	11/11/01	Homestead, FL	Bill Elliott	Dodge	117.449	19	7	6	41	Bill Elliott	155.226	Pole

No.	Date	Site	Race Winner	Car	Speed	Lead Chgs	Ldrs	Caut.	C.Laps	Pole Winner	Speed	Winner Started
35	11/18/01	Atlanta, GA	Bobby Labonte	Pontiac	151.756	23	13	5	28	Dale Earnhardt, Jr.	192.047	39th
36	11/25/01	Loudon, NH	Robby Gordon	Chevrolet	103.594	10	5	7	43	No Time Trials	NTT	31st

2002 NASCAR Winston Cup Series Season

No.	Date	Site	Race Winner	Car	Speed	Lead Chgs	Ldrs	Caut.	C.Laps	Pole Winner	Speed	Winner Started
1	2/17/02	Daytona Beach, FL	Ward Burton	Dodge	142.971	20	12	9	38	Jimmie Johnson	185.831	19th
2	2/24/02	Rockingham, NC	Matt Kenseth	Ford	115.478	17	7	10	57	Ricky Craven	156.008	25th
3	3/03/02	Las Vegas, NV	Sterling Marlin	Dodge	136.754	21	13	6	25	Todd Bodine	172.850	24th
4	3/10/02	Atlanta, GA	Tony Stewart	Pontiac	148.443	34	8	7	37	Bill Elliott	191.542	9th
5	3/17/02	Darlington, SC	Sterling Marlin	Dodge	126.070	11	8	5	40	Ricky Craven	170.089	11th
6	3/24/02	Bristol, TN	Kurt Busch	Ford	82.281	14	6	14	101	Jeff Gordon	127.216	27th
7	4/08/02	Ft. Worth, TX	Matt Kenseth	Ford	142.435	24	15	7	41	Bill Elliott	194.224	31st
8	4/14/02	Martinsville, VA	Bobby Labonte	Pontiac	73.951	19	13	14	104	Jeff Gordon	94.181	15th
9	4/21/02	Talladega, AL	Dale Earnhardt, Jr.	Chevrolet	159.022	26	10	3	19	Jimmie Johnson	186.532	4th
10	4/28/02	Fontana, CA	Jimmie Johnson	Chevrolet	150.088	20	8	5	24	Ryan Newman	187.432	4th
11	5/04/02	Richmond, VA	Tony Stewart	Pontiac	86.824	13	10	14	103	Ward Burton	127.389	3rd
12	5/26/02	Charlotte, NC	Mark Martin	Ford	137.729	21	11	9	48	Jimmie Johnson	186.464	25th
13	6/02/02	Dover, DE	Jimmie Johnson	Chevrolet	117.551	14	8	7	40	Matt Kenseth	154.939	10th
14	6/09/02	Pocono, PA	Dale Jarrett	Ford	143.426	17	12	5	17	No Time Trials	NTT	13th
15	6/16/02	Brooklyn, MI	Matt Kenseth	Ford	154.822	15	10	4	16	Dale Jarrett	189.071	20th
16	6/23/02	Sonoma, CA	Ricky Rudd	Ford	81.007	10	9	3	9	Tony Stewart	93.476	7th
17	7/06/02	Daytona Beach, FL	Michael Waltrip	Chevrolet	135.932	6	6	9	39	Kevin Harvick	185.041	7th
18	7/14/02	Chicago, IL	Kevin Harvick	Chevrolet	136.832	19	11	7	35	Ryan Newman	183.051	32nd
19	7/21/02	Loudon, NH	Ward Burton	Dodge	92.342	23	12	14	77	Bill Elliott	131.469	31st
20	7/28/02	Pocono, PA	Bill Elliott	Dodge	125.809	17	11	5	29	Bill Elliott	170.568	Pole
21	8/04/02	Indianapolis, IN	Bill Elliott	Dodge	125.033	16	10	8	36	Tony Stewart	182.960	2nd
22	8/11/02	Watkins Glen, NY	Tony Stewart	Pontiac	82.208	12	9	7	18	Ricky Rudd	122.696	3rd
23	8/18/02	Brooklyn, MI	Dale Jarrett	Ford	140.555	23	12	7	30	Dale Earnhardt, Jr.	189.668	8th
24	8/24/02	Bristol, TN	Jeff Gordon	Chevrolet	77.097	10	7	15	118	Jeff Gordon	124.034	Pole
25	9/01/02	Darlington, SC	Jeff Gordon	Chevrolet	118.617	14	9	9	63	No Time Trials	NTT	3rd
26	9/07/02	Richmond, VA	Matt Kenseth	Ford	94.787	14	11	10	65	Jimmie Johnson	126.145	25th
27	9/15/02	Loudon, NH	Ryan Newman	Ford	105.081	7	6	3	24	Ryan Newman	132.241	Pole
28	9/22/02	Dover, DE	Jimmie Johnson	Chevrolet	120.805	15	7	6	37	Rusty Wallace	156.822	19th
29	9/29/02	Kansas City, KS	Jeff Gordon	Chevrolet	119.394	13	10	11	52	Dale Earnhardt, Jr.	177.924	10th
30	10/06/02	Talladega, AL	Dale Earnhardt, Jr.	Chevrolet	183.665	35	12	0	0	No Time Trials	NTT	10th
31	10/13/02	Charlotte, NC	Jamie McMurray	Dodge	141.586	23	11	5	33	No Timie Trials	NTT	5th
32	10/20/02	Martinsville, VA	Kurt Busch	Ford	74.651	12	9	12	65	Ryan Newman	92.837	36th
33	10/27/02	Atlanta, GA	Kurt Busch	Ford	127.519	19	9	5	50	No Time Trials	NTT	8th
34	11/03/02	Rockingham, NC	Johnny Benson, Jr.	Pontiac	128.526	22	9	4	18	Ryan Newman	155.836	26th
35	11/10/02	Phoenix, AZ	Matt Kenseth	Ford	113.857	14	9	4	18	Ryan Newman	132.655	28th
36	11/17/02	Homestead, FL	Kurt Busch	Ford	116.462	12	6	6	41	Kurt Busch	154.365	Pole

2003 NASCAR Winston Cup Series Season

No.	Date	Site	Race Winner	Car	Speed	Lead Chgs	Ldrs	Caut.	C.Laps	Pole Winner	Speed	Winner Started
1	2/16/03	Daytona Beach, FL	Michael Waltrip	Chevrolet	133.870	11	8	5	23	Jeff Green	186.606	4th
2	2/23/03	Rockingham, NC	Dale Jarrett	Ford	117.852	20	11	7	46	Dave Blaney	154.683	9th
3	3/02/03	Las Vegas, NV	Matt Kenseth	Ford	132.934	17	10	6	30	Bobby Labonte	173.016	17th
4	3/09/03	Atlanta, GA	Bobby Labonte	Chevrolet	146.037	23	10	7	34	Ryan Newman	191.417	4th
5	3/16/03	Darlington, SC	Ricky Craven	Pontiac	126.214	15	11	7	33	Elliott Sadler	170.147	31st
6	3/23/03	Bristol, TN	Kurt Busch	Ford	76.185	11	7	17	121	Ryan Newman	128.709	9th
7	3/30/03	Ft. Worth, TX	Ryan Newman	Dodge	134.517	19	11	10	52	Bobby Labonte	193.514	3rd
8	4/06/03	Talladega, AL	Dale Earnhardt, Jr.	Chevrolet	144.625	43	16	6	32	Jeremy Mayfield	186.489	13th
9	4/13/03	Martinsville, VA	Jeff Gordon	Chevrolet	75.557	14	9	11	64	Jeff Gordon	94.307	Pole
10	4/27/03	Fontana, CA	Kurt Busch	Ford	140.111	19	9	8	34	Steve Park	186.838	16th
11	5/03/03	Richmond, VA	Joe Nemechek	Chevrolet	87.134	20	10	15	91	Terry Labonte	126.511	2nd
12	5/25/03	Charlotte, NC	Jimmie Johnson	Chevrolet	126.198	16	8	8	46	Ryan Newman	185.312	37th
13	6/01/03	Dover, DE	Ryan Newman	Dodge	106.896	16	10	9	68	Ryan Newman	158.716	Pole
14	6/08/03	Pocono, PA	Tony Stewart	Chevrolet	134.892	28	16	5	25	Jimmie Johnson	170.645	4th
15	6/15/03	Brooklyn, MI	Kurt Busch	Ford	131.219	22	9	9	41	Bobby Labonte	190.365	4th
16	6/22/03	Sonoma, CA	Robby Gordon	Chevrolet	73.821	6	4	6	16	Boris Said	93.620	2nd
17	7/05/03	Daytona Beach, FL	Greg Biffle	Ford	166.109	17	11	2	10	Steve Park	184.752	30th
18	7/13/03	Chicago, IL	Ryan Newman	Dodge	134.059	13	7	7	36	Tony Stewart	184.786	14th
19	7/20/03	Loudon, NH	Jimmie Johnson	Chevrolet	96.024	14	9	12	63	No Time Trials	NTT	6th
20	7/27/03	Pocono, PA	Ryan Newman	Dodge	127.705	18	11	8	36	Ryan Newman	170.358	Pole
21	8/03/03	Indianapolis, IN	Kevin Harvick	Chevrolet	134.548	17	12	5	25	Kevin Harvick	184.343	Pole
22	8/10/03	Watkins Glen, NY	Robby Gordon	Chevrolet	90.441	7	7	6	14	Jeff Gordon	124.58	14th
23	8/17/03	Brooklyn, MI	Ryan Newman	Dodge	127.310	14	8	8	46	Bobby Labonte	190.24	2nd
24	8/23/03	Bristol, TN	Kurt Busch	Ford	77.421	11	8	20	119	Jeff Gordon	127.597	5th
25	8/31/03	Darlington, SC	Terry Labonte	Chevrolet	120.733	24	12	10	55	Ryan Newman	169.048	3rd
26	9/06/03	Richmond, VA	Ryan Newman	Dodge	94.945	20	12	14	76	Mike Skinner	125.792	4th
27	9/14/03	Loudon, NH	Jimmie Johnson	Chevrolet	106.580	20	11	6	38	Rayn Newman	133.357	8th
28	9/21/03	Dover, DE	Ryan Newman	Dodge	108.802	12	7	7	63	No Time Trials	NTT	5th
29	9/28/03	Talladega, AL	Michael Waltrip	Chevrolet	156.045	41	17	5	23	Elliott Sadler	189.943	18th
30	10/05/03	Kansas City, KS	Ryan Newman	Dodge	121.630	23	11	9	46	Jimmie Johnson	180.373	11th
31	10/11/03	Charlotte, NC	Tony Stewart	Chevrolet	142.871	15	8	5	31	Ryan Newman	186.657	6th
32	10/19/03	Martinsville, VA	Jeff Gordon	Chevrolet	67.653	9	8	15	117	Jeff Gordon	93.650	Pole
33	10/26/03	Atlanta, GA	Jeff Gordon	Chevrolet	127.769	28	12	10	63	Ryan Newman	194.295	19th
34	11/02/03	Phoenix, AZ	Dale Earnhardt, Jr.	Chevrolet	93.984	10	6	10	66	Ryan Newman	133.675	11th
35	11/09/03	Rockingham, NC	Bill Elliott	Dodge	111.677	14	5	10	65	Ryan Newman	155.577	5th
36	11/16/03	Homestead, FL	Bobby Labonte	Chevrolet	116.868	21	12	10	60	Jamie McMurray	181.111	2nd

2004 NASCAR NEXTEL Cup Series Season

No.	Date	Site	Race Winner	Car	Speed	Lead Chgs	Ldrs	Caut.	C.Laps	Pole Winner	Speed	Winner Started
1	2/15/04	Daytona Beach, FL	Dale Earnhardt, Jr.	Chevrolet	156.345	28	10	4	23	Greg Biffle	188.387	3rd
2	2/22/04	Rockingham, NC	Matt Kenseth	Ford	112.016	15	6	7	58	Ryan Newman	156.475	23rd
3	3/07/04	Las Vegas, NV	Matt Kenseth	Ford	128.790	18	10	6	37	Kasey Kahne	174.904	25th

617

No.	Date	Site	Race Winner	Car	Speed	Lead Chgs	Ldrs	Caut.	C.Laps	Pole Winner	Speed	Winner Started
4	3/14/04	Atlanta, GA	Dale Earnhardt, Jr.	Chevrolet	158.679	16	8	3	17	Ryan Newman	193.575	7th
5	3/21/04	Darlington, SC	Jimmie Johnson	Chevrolet	114.001	22	12	9	58	Kasey Kahne	171.716	11th
6	3/28/04	Bristol, TN	Kurt Busch	Ford	82.607	13	10	11	85	Ryan Newman	128.313	13th
7	4/04/04	Ft. Worth, TX	Elliott Sadler	Ford	138.845	24	12	7	45	Bobby Labonte	193.903	19th
8	4/18/04	Martinsville, VA	Rusty Wallace	Dodge	68.169	10	6	11	106	Jeff Gordon	93.502	17th
9	4/25/04	Talladega, AL	Jeff Gordon	Chevrolet	129.396	54	23	11	55	Ricky Rudd	191.180	11th
10	5/02/04	Fontana, CA	Jeff Gordon	Chevrolet	137.268	23	15	6	39	Kasey Kahne	186.940	16th
11	5/15/04	Richmond, VA	Dale Earnhardt, Jr.	Chevrolet	98.253	19	12	9	66	Brian Vickers	29.983	4th
12	5/30/04	Charlotte, NC	Jimmie Johnson	Chevrolet	142.763	16	7	7	37	Jimmie Johnson	187.052	Pole
13	6/06/04	Dover, DE	Mark Martin	Ford	97.042	13	9	11	90	Jeremy Mayfield	161.522	7th
14	6/13/04	Pocono, PA	Jimmie Johnson	Chevrolet	112.129	30	16	11	57	Kasey Kahne	172.533	5th
15	6/20/04	Brooklyn, MI	Ryan Newman	Dodge	139.292	17	10	9	33	Jeff Gordon	190.854	4th
16	6/27/04	Sonoma, CA	Jeff Gordon	Chevrolet	77.456	9	7	6	13	Jeff Gordon	94.303	Pole
17	7/03/04	Daytona Beach, FL	Jeff Gordon	Chevrolet	145.117	21	10	5	25	Jeff Gordon	188.660	Pole
18	7/11/04	Chicago, IL	Tony Stewart	Chevrolet	129.507	20	14	9	43	Jeff Gordon	186.942	10th
19	7/25/04	Loudon, NH	Kurt Busch	Ford	97.862	4	3	12	62	Ryan Newman	132.360	32nd
20	8/01/04	Pocono, PA	Jimmie Johnson	Chevrolet	126.271	16	10	9	35	Casey Mears	171.720	14th
21	8/08/04	Indianapolis, IN	Jeff Gordon	Chevrolet	115.037	9	6	13	47	Casey Mears	186.293	11th
22	8/15/04	Watkins Glen, NY	Tony Stewart	Chevrolet	92.249	13	9	5	11	No Time Trials	NTT	4th
23	8/22/04	Brooklyn, MI	Greg Biffle	Ford	139.063	25	13	9	33	No Time Trials	NTT	24th
24	8/28/04	Bristol, TN	Dale Earnhardt, Jr.	Chevrolet	88.538	18	10	9	63	Jeff Gordon	128.520	30th
25	9/05/04	Fontana, CA	Elliott Sadler	Ford	128.324	29	13	11	51	Brian Vickers	187.417	17th
26	9/11/04	Richmond, VA	Jeremy Mayfield	Dodge	98.946	20	9	10	57	Ryan Newman	128.700	7th
27	9/19/04	Loudon, NH	Kurt Busch	Ford	109.753	15	12	7	30	No Time Trials	NTT	7th
28	9/26/04	Dover, DE	Ryan Newman	Dodge	119.067	13	7	5	38	Jeremy Mayfield	159.405	2nd
29	10/03/04	Talladega, AL	Dale Earnhardt, Jr.	Chevrolet	156.929	47	20	5	22	Joe Nemechek	190.749	10th
30	10/10/04	Kansas City, KS	Joe Nemechek	Chevrolet	128.058	24	12	9	39	Joe Nemechek	180.156	Pole
31	10/16/04	Charlotte, NC	Jimmie Johnson	Chevrolet	130.214	18	9	11	53	Ryan Newman	188.877	9th
32	10/24/04	Martinsville, VA	Jimmie Johnson	Chevrolet	66.103	22	12	17	125	Ryan Newman	97.043	18th
33	10/31/04	Atlanta, GA	Jimmie Johnson	Chevrolet	145.847	16	7	6	33	Ryan Newman	191.575	8th
34	11/07/04	Phoenix, AZ	Dale Earnhardt, Jr.	Chevrolet	94.848	10	7	11	63	Rayn Newman	135.854	14th
35	11/14/04	Darlington, SC	Jimmie Johnson	Chevrolet	125.044	27	10	8	47	No Time Trials	NTT	4th
36	11/21/04	Homestead, FL	Greg Biffle	Ford	105.623	14	7	14	79	Kurt Busch	179.319	2nd

2005 NASCAR NEXTEL Cup Series Season

No.	Date	Site	Race Winner	Car	Speed	Lead Chgs	Ldrs	Caut.	C.Laps	Pole Winner	Speed	Winner Started
1	2/20/05	Daytona Beach, FL	Jeff Gordon	Chevrolet	135.173	22	12	11	45	Dale Jarrett	188.312	15th
2	2/27/05	Fontana, CA	Greg Biffle	Ford	139.697	26	14	7	40	Kyle Busch	188.245	5th
3	3/13/05	Las Vegas, NV	Jimmie Johnson	Chevrolet	121.038	25	12	10	46	Ryan Newman	173.745	9th
4	3/20/05	Atlanta, GA	Carl Edwards	Ford	143.478	27	7	8	40	Ryan Newman	194.690	4th
5	4/03/05	Bristol, TN	Kevin Harvick	Chevrolet	77.496	14	9	14	115	Elliott Sadler	127.733	13th
6	4/10/05	Martinsville, VA	Jeff Gordon	Chevrolet	72.099	17	11	16	91	Scott Riggs	96.671	16th
7	4/17/05	Ft. Worth, TX	Greg Biffle	Ford	130.055	25	14	11	56	Ryan Newman	192.582	5th
8	4/23/05	Phoenix, AZ	Kurt Busch	Ford	102.707	16	9	9	43	Jeff Gordon	133.675	2nd
9	5/01/05	Talladega, AL	Jeff Gordon	Chevrolet	146.904	33	16	8	30	Kevin Harvick	189.804	2nd
10	5/07/05	Darlington, SC	Greg Biffle	Ford	123.031	30	13	12	48	Kasey Kahne	170.024	3rd
11	5/14/05	Richmond, VA	Kasey Kahne	Dodge	100.316	21	6	9	53	Kasey Kahne	129.964	Pole
12	5/29/05	Charlotte, NC	Jimmie Johnson	Chevrolet	114.698	37	21	22	103	Ryan Newman	192.988	5th
13	6/05/05	Dover, DE	Greg Biffle	Ford	122.626	9	5	7	33	No Time Trials	NTT	2nd
14	6/12/05	Pocono, PA	Carl Edwards	Ford	129.177	14	7	7	32	Michael Waltrip	169.052	29th
15	6/19/05	Brooklyn, MI	Greg Biffle	Ford	150.596	20	11	4	23	Ryan Newman	194.232	25th
16	6/26/05	Sonoma, CA	Tony Stewart	Chevrolet	72.845	7	6	8	18	Jeff Gordon	94.325	7th
17	7/02/05	Daytona Beach, FL	Tony Stewart	Chevrolet	131.016	7	5	9	41	Tony Stewart	185.582	Pole
18	7/10/05	Chicago, IL	Dale Earnhardt, Jr.	Chevrolet	127.638	17	12	10	47	Jimmie Johnson	188.147	25th
19	7/17/05	Loudon, NH	Tony Stewart	Chevrolet	102.608	14	9	10	49	Brian Vickers	130.327	13th
20	7/24/05	Pocono, PA	Kurt Busch	Ford	125.283	13	8	13	40	Jamie McMurray	168.760	2nd
21	8/07/05	Indianapolis, IN	Tony Stewart	Chevrolet	118.782	15	10	10	43	Elliott Sadler	184.117	22nd
22	8/14/05	Watkins Glen, NY	Tony Stewart	Chevrolet	86.804	9	7	7	14	No Time Trials	NTT	Pole
23	8/21/05	Brooklyn, MI	Jeremy Mayfield	Dodge	141.551	19	13	7	30	Joe Nemechek	191.530	11th
24	8/27/05	Bristol, TN	Matt Kenseth	Ford	84.678	17	9	16	87	Matt Kenseth	127.300	Pole
25	9/04/05	Fontana, CA	Kyle Busch	Chevrolet	136.356	30	12	11	43	Carl Edwards	185.061	25th
26	9/10/05	Richmond, VA	Kurt Busch	Ford	98.567	23	10	12	60	Kevin Harvick	128.425	5th
27	9/18/05	Loudon, NH	Ryan Newman	Dodge	95.891	18	12	10	60	Tony Stewart	131.143	13th
28	9/25/05	Dover, DE	Jimmie Johnson	Chevrolet	115.054	15	7	11	50	Ryan Newman	158.103	5th
29	10/02/05	Talladega, AL	Dale Jarrett	Ford	143.818	50	20	10	34	Elliott Sadler	189.260	2nd
30	10/09/05	Kansas City, KS	Mark Martin	Ford	137.774	16	12	7	28	Matt Kenseth	180.856	19th
31	10/15/05	Charlotte, NC	Jimmie Johnson	Chevrolet	120.334	35	17	15	81	Elliott Sadler	193.216	3rd
32	10/23/05	Martinsville, VA	Jeff Gordon	Chevrolet	69.695	15	8	19	113	Tony Stewart	98.084	15th
33	10/30/05	Atlanta, GA	Carl Edwards	Ford	146.834	27	12	9	39	Ryan Newman	193.928	2nd
34	11/06/05	Ft. Worth, TX	Carl Edwards	Ford	151.055	23	11	6	27	Ryan Newman	192.947	30th
35	11/13/05	Phoenix, AZ	Kyle Busch	Chevrolet	102.641	10	5	9	44	Denny Hamlin	134.173	15th
36	11/20/05	Homestead, FL	Greg Biffle	Ford	131.431	21	12	8	37	Carl Edwards	176.051	7th

2006 NASCAR NEXTEL Cup Series Season

No.	Date	Site	Race Winner	Car	Speed	Lead Chgs	Ldrs	Caut.	C.Laps	Pole Winner	Speed	Winner Started
1	2/19/06	Daytona Beach, FL	Jimmie Johnson	Chevrolet	142.667	32	18	11	39	Jeff Burton	189.151	9th
2	2/26/06	Fontana, CA	Matt Kenseth	Ford	147.852	18	9	7	26	Kurt Busch	187.086	31st
3	3/12/06	Las Vegas, NV	Jimmie Johnson	Chevrolet	133.358	22	11	7	30	Greg Biffle	172.403	3rd
4	3/20/06	Atlanta, GA	Kasey Kahne	Dodge	144.098	27	12	8	43	Kasey Kahne	192.553	Pole
5	3/26/06	Bristol, TN	Kurt Busch	Dodge	79.427	19	8	18	105	No Time Trials	NTT	9th
6	4/02/06	Martinsville, VA	Tony Stewart	Chevrolet	72.741	12	6	16	87	Jimmie Johnson	96.736	3rd
7	4/09/06	Ft. Worth, TX	Kasey Kahne	Dodge	137.943	22	12	9	43	Kasey Kahne	190.315	Pole
8	4/22/06	Phoenix, AZ	Kevin Harvick	Chevrolet	107.063	20	11	7	29	Kyle Busch	133.745	15th
9	3/30/06	Talladega, AL	Jimmie Johnson	Chevrolet	142.880	56	22	8	34	Elliott Sadler	188.511	16th
10	5/06/06	Richmond, VA	Dale Earnhardt, Jr.	Chevrolet	97.061	12	6	11	61	Greg Biffle	127.395	10th
11	5/13/06	Darlington, SC	Greg Biffle	Ford	135.127	25	10	6	24	Kasey Kahne	169.013	9th
12	5/28/06	Charlotte, NC	Kasey Kahne	Dodge	128.840	37	16	15	66	Scott Riggs	187.865	9th

No.	Date	Site	Race Winner	Car	Speed	Lead Chgs	Ldrs	Caut.	C.Laps	Pole Winner	Speed	Winner Started
13	6/04/06	Dover, DE	Matt Kenseth	Ford	109.865	23	12	9	51	Ryan Newman	154.633	19th
14	6/11/06	Pocono, PA	Denny Hamlin	Chevrolet	131.656	25	13	7	28	Denny Hamlin	169.639	Pole
15	6/18/06	Brooklyn, MI	Kasey Kahne	Dodge	118.788	17	10	9	28	Kasey Kahne	185.644	Pole
16	6/25/06	Sonoma, CA	Jeff Gordon	Chevrolet	73.953	9	8	7	12	Kurt Busch	93.055	11th
17	7/01/06	Daytona Beach, FL	Tony Stewart	Chevrolet	151.143	29	15	6	19	Boris Said	186.143	2nd
18	7/09/06	Chicago, IL	Jeff Gordon	Chevrolet	132.077	18	10	8	34	Jeff Burton	181.647	13th
19	7/16/06	Loudon, NH	Kyle Busch	Chevrolet	101.384	21	11	11	49	Ryan Newman	129.683	4th
20	7/23/06	Pocono, PA	Denny Hamlin	Chevrolet	132.626	13	9	7	29	Denny Hamlin	169.287	Pole
21	8/06/06	Indianapolis, IN	Jimmie Johnson	Chevrolet	137.182	18	9	8	24	Jeff Burton	182.778	5th
22	8/13/06	Watkins Glen, NY	Kevin Harvick	Chevrolet	76.718	14	11	10	22	Kurt Busch	122.966	7th
23	8/20/06	Brooklyn, MI	Matt Kenseth	Ford	135.097	26	11	10	36	Jeff Burton	186.936	3rd
24	8/26/06	Bristol, TN	Matt Kenseth	Ford	90.025	18	7	10	62	Kurt Busch	124.906	4th
25	9/03/06	Fontana, CA	Kasey Kahne	Dodge	144.462	26	10	7	29	Kurt Busch	184.540	9th
26	9/09/06	Richmond, VA	Kevin Harvick	Chevrolet	101.342	16	8	7	48	Denny Hamlin	127.986	5th
27	9/17/06	Loudon, NH	Kevin Harvick	Chevrolet	102.195	17	10	10	47	Kevin Harvick	132.282	Pole
28	9/24/06	Dover, DE	Jeff Burton	Chevrolet	111.966	12	9	10	48	Jeff Gordon	156.162	19th
29	10/01/06	Kansas City, KS	Tony Stewart	Chevrolet	121.753	20	13	5	45	Kasey Kahne	178.377	21st
30	10/08/06	Talladega, AL	Brian Vickers	Chevrolet	157.602	63	23	6	22	David Gilliland	191.712	9th
31	10/14/06	Charlotte, NC	Kasey Kahne	Dodge	132.142	34	13	10	52	Scott Riggs	191.469	2nd
32	10/22/06	Martinsville, VA	Jimmie Johnson	Chevrolet	70.446	16	5	18	106	Kurt Busch	97.568	9th
33	10/29/06	Atlanta, GA	Tony Stewart	Chevrolet	143.421	24	7	9	39	No Time Trials	NTT	20th
34	11/05/06	Ft. Worth, TX	Tony Stewart	Chevrolet	134.891	23	13	12	51	Brian Vickers	196.235	8th
35	11/12/06	Phoenix, AZ	Kevin Harvick	Chevrolet	96.131	12	7	10	58	Jeff Gordon	134.464	2nd
36	11/19/06	Homestead, FL	Greg Biffle	Ford	125.375	15	10	11	43	Kasey Kahne	178.259	22nd

2007 NASCAR Sprint Cup Series Season

No.	Date	Site	Race Winner	Car	Speed	Lead Chgs	Ldrs	Caut.	C.Laps	Pole Winner	Speed	Winner Started
1	2/18/07	Daytona Beach, FL	Kevin Harvick	Chevrolet	143.355	13	9	6	26	David Gilliland	186.320	34th
2	2/25/07	Fontana, CA	Matt Kenseth	Ford	138.451	28	12	9	36	Jeff Gordon	185.735	25th
3	3/11/07	Las Vegas, NV	Jimmie Johnson	Chevrolet	128.183	28	16	9	40	Kasey Kahne	184.856	23rd
4	3/18/07	Atlanta, GA	Jimmie Johnson	Chevrolet	152.915	31	13	6	27	Ryan Newman	193.124	3rd
5	3/25/07	Bristol, TN	Kyle Busch	Toyota	81.969	14	10	15	90	Jeff Gordon	125.453	20th
6	4/01/07	Martinsville, VA	Jimmie Johnson	Chevrolet	70.258	14	9	13	93	Denny Hamlin	95.103	20th
7	4/15/07	Ft. Worth, TX	Jeff Burton	Chevrolet	143.359	13	9	7	33	No Time Trials	NTT	2nd
8	4/21/07	Phoenix, AZ	Jeff Gordon	Chevrolet	107.710	12	7	6	34	Jeff Gordon	133.136	Pole
9	4/29/07	Talladega, AL	Jeff Gordon	Chevrolet	154.167	42	20	8	28	Jeff Gordon	192.069	Pole
10	5/06/07	Richmond, VA	Jimmie Johnson	Chevrolet	91.270	24	12	14	80	Jeff Gordon	126.251	4th
11	5/13/07	Darlington, SC	Jeff Gordon	Chevrolet	124.383	21	10	10	44	Clint Bowyer	164.897	10th
12	5/27/07	Charlotte, NC	Casey Mears	Chevrolet	130.222	29	15	13	62	Ryan Newman	185.312	16th
13	6/04/07	Dover, DE	Martin Truex, Jr.	Chevrolet	118.950	18	6	7	35	Ryan Newman	152.925	26th
14	6/10/07	Pocono, PA	Jeff Gordon	Chevrolet	135.608	15	8	4	10	Ryan Newman	170.062	18th
15	6/17/07	Brooklyn, MI	Carl Edwards	Ford	148.072	22	11	4	19	J.J. Yeley	187.565	12th
16	6/24/07	Sonoma, CA	Juan Pablo Montoya	Dodge	74.547	11	8	7	14	Jamie McMurray	92.414	32nd
17	7/01/07	Loudon, NH	Denny Hamlin	Toyota	129.437	20	11	6	31	Dave Blaney	129.437	11th
18	7/07/07	Daytona Beach, FL	Jamie McMurray	Ford	138.983	27	11	8	30	No Time Trials	NTT	15th
19	7/14/07	Chicago, IL	Tony Stewart	Toyota	134.258	20	9	7	32	Casey Mears	182.556	19th
20	7/29/07	Indianapolis, IN	Tony Stewart	Toyota	117.379	14	6	9	43	Reed Sorenson	184.207	14th
21	8/05/07	Pocono, PA	Kurt Busch	Dodge	131.627	17	11	7	27	Dale Earnhardt, Jr.	169.975	2nd
22	8/12/07	Watkins Glen, NY	Tony Stewart	Toyota	77.535	9	6	8	20	No Time Trials	NTT	5th
23	8/21/07	Brooklyn, MI	Kurt Busch	Dodge	138.475	18	10	8	36	Jeff Gordon	189.026	15th
24	8/25/07	Bristol, TN	Carl Edwards	Ford	89.006	12	8	9	61	Kasey Kahne	119.805	6th
25	9/02/07	Fontana, CA	Jimmie Johnson	Chevrolet	131.502	30	16	11	43	Kurt Busch	182.399	2nd
26	9/08/07	Richmond, VA	Jimmie Johnson	Chevrolet	91.813	15	10	12	70	Jimmie Johnson	126.298	Pole
27	9/16/07	Loudon, NH	Clint Bowyer	Chevrolet	110.475	13	9	7	27	Clint Bowyer	130.412	Pole
28	9/23/07	Dover, DE	Carl Edwards	Ford	101.846	14	9	13	66	Jimmie Johnson	154.765	15th
29	9/30/07	Kansas City, KS	Greg Biffle	Ford	104.981	16	10	12	54	Jimmie Johnson	175.063	7th
30	10/07/07	Talladega, AL	Jeff Gordon	Chevrolet	143.438	42	22	9	34	Michael Waltrip	189.070	34th
31	10/13/07	Charlotte, NC	Jeff Gordon	Chevrolet	125.868	26	11	15	62	Ryan Newman	189.394	4th
32	10/21/07	Martinsville, VA	Jimmie Johnson	Chevrolet	66.608	12	7	21	127	Jeff Gordon	94.974	4th
33	10/28/07	Atlanta, GA	Jimmie Johnson	Chevrolet	135.260	19	11	14	55	Greg Biffle	192.453	6th
34	11/04/07	Ft. Worth, TX	Jimmie Johnson	Chevrolet	131.219	27	12	12	52	Martin Truex, Jr.	193.105	8th
35	11/11/07	Phoenix, AZ	Jimmie Johnson	Chevrolet	102.989	10	6	10	42	Carl Edwards	132.773	6th
36	11/19/07	Homestead, FL	Matt Kenseth	Ford	131.888	25	11	7	32	Jimmie Johnson	176.788	4th

2008 NASCAR Sprint Cup Series Season

No.	Date	Site	Race Winner	Car	Speed	Lead Chgs	Ldrs	Caut.	C.Laps	Pole Winner	Speed	Winner Started
1	2/17/08	Daytona Beach, FL	Ryan Newman	Dodge	152.672	42	17	7	23	Jimmie Johnson	187.085	7th
2	2/24/08	Fontana, CA	Carl Edwards	Ford	132.704	33	15	12	44	No Time Trials	NTT	9th
3	3/02/08	Las Vegas, NV	Carl Edwards	Ford	127.729	19	9	11	44	Kyle Busch	182.352	2nd
4	3/09/08	Atlanta, GA	Kyle Busch	Toyota	140.975	26	9	8	35	Jeff Gordon	185.251	6th
5	3/16/08	Bristol, TN	Jeff Burton	Chevrolet	89.775	17	8	10	68	No Time Trials	NTT	8th
6	3/30/08	Martinsville, VA	Denny Hamlin	Toyota	73.163	20	8	18	89	Jeff Gordon	96.288	2nd
7	4/06/08	Ft. Worth, TX	Carl Edwards	Ford	144.814	16	6	6	27	Dale Earnhardt, Jr.	190.907	2nd
8	4/12/08	Phoenix, AZ	Jimmie Johnson	Chevrolet	103.292	10	4	8	42	Ryan Newman	133.457	7th
9	4/27/08	Talladega, AL	Kyle Busch	Toyota	157.409	52	20	8	23	Joe Nemechek	187.386	5th
10	5/03/08	Richmond, VA	Clint Bowyer	Chevrolet	95.786	4	4	11	62	Denny Hamlin	126.198	31st
11	5/10/08	Darlington, SC	Kyle Busch	Toyota	140.350	35	15	8	31	Greg Biffle	179.442	6th
12	5/25/08	Charlotte, NC	Kasey Kahne	Dodge	135.772	37	16	11	50	Kyle Busch	185.443	2nd
13	6/01/08	Dover, DE	Kyle Busch	Toyota	121.171	15	9	5	26	Greg Biffle	155.214	3rd
14	6/08/08	Pocono, PA	Kasey Kahne	Dodge	125.209	23	12	10	36	Kasey Kahne	170.219	Pole
15	6/15/08	Brooklyn, MI	Dale Earnhardt, Jr.	Chevrolet	145.375	31	13	8	22	No Time Trials	NTT	3rd
16	6/22/08	Sonoma, CA	Kyle Busch	Toyota	76.445	5	5	6	14	Kasey Kahne	92.153	30th
17	6/29/08	Loudon, NH	Kurt Busch	Dodge	106.719	9	8	7	33	Patrick Carpentier	129.776	26th
18	7/05/08	Daytona Beach, FL	Kyle Busch	Toyota	138.554	21	10	11	33	Paul Menard	185.916	9th
19	7/12/08	Chicago, IL	Kyle Busch	Toyota	133.996	16	10	9	33	No Time Trials	NTT	Pole
20	7/27/08	Indianapolis, IN	Jimmie Johnson	Chevrolet	115.117	26	16	11	52	Jimmie Johnson	181.763	Pole
21	8/03/08	Pocono, PA	Carl Edwards	Ford	130.567	25	13	7	31	Jimmie Johnson	168.215	15th
22	8/10/08	Watkins Glen, NY	Kyle Busch	Toyota	97.148	8	5	4	9	No Time Trials	NTT	Pole
23	8/17/08	Brooklyn, MI	Carl Edwards	Ford	140.351	18	9	7	27	Brian Vickers	188.536	27th

No.	Date	Site	Race Winner	Car	Speed	Lead Chgs	Ldrs	Caut.	C.Laps	Pole Winner	Speed	Winner Started
24	8/23/08	Bristol, TN	Carl Edwards	Ford	91.581	4	3	8	56	Carl Edwards	121.860	Pole
25	8/31/08	Fontana, CA	Jimmie Johnson	Chevrolet	138.857	20	9	8	34	Jimmie Johnson	180.397	Pole
26	9/06/08	Richmond, VA	Jimmie Johnson	Chevrolet	92.680	22	10	14	71	No Time Trials	NTT	3rd
27	9/14/08	Loudon, NH	Greg Biffle	Ford	105.468	14	8	8	37	No Time Trials	NTT	9th
28	9/21/08	Dover, DE	Greg Biffle	Ford	114.168	15	9	10	45	Jeff Gordon	157.061	5th
29	9/28/08	Kansas City, KS	Jimmie Johnson	Chevrolet	133.549	16	10	7	25	Jimmie Johnson	172.007	Pole
30	10/05/08	Talladega, AL	Tony Stewart	Toyota	140.281	64	28	10	41	Travis Kvapil	187.364	34th
31	10/11/08	Charlotte, NC	Jeff Burton	Chevrolet	133.699	24	16	10	49	No Time Trials	NTT	4th
32	10/19/08	Martinsville, VA	Jimmie Johnson	Chevrolet	75.931	14	7	12	76	No Time Trials	NTT	Pole
33	10/26/08	Atlanta, GA	Carl Edwards	Ford	134.272	18	8	10	43	No Time Trials	NTT	4th
34	11/02/08	Fort Worth, TX	Carl Edwards	Ford	144.219	16	9	5	26	Jeff Gordon	188.469	16th
35	11/09/08	Phoenix, AZ	Jimmie Johnson	Chevrolet	97.804	9	5	10	55	Jimmie Johnson	134.725	Pole
36	11/16/08	Homestead, FL	Carl Edwards	Ford	129.472	15	8	7	31	David Reutimann	171.636	4th

2009 NASCAR Sprint Cup Series Season

No.	Date	Site	Race Winner	Car	Speed	Lead Chgs	Ldrs	Caut.	C.Laps	Pole Winner	Speed	Winner Started
1	2/15/09	Daytona Beach, FL	Matt Kenseth	Ford	132.816	9	9	8	35	Martin Truex, Jr.	188.001	39th
2	2/22/09	Fontana, CA	Matt Kenseth	Ford	135.839	19	11	5	43	Brian Vickers	183.439	24th
3	3/01/09	Las Vegas, NV	Kyle Busch	Toyota	119.515	16	12	14	66	Kyle Busch	185.995	19th
4	3/08/09	Atlanta, GA	Kurt Busch	Dodge	127.573	13	8	11	54	Mark Martin	187.045	2nd
5	3/22/09	Bristol, TN	Kyle Busch	Toyota	92.139	13	7	9	58	Mark Martin	125.773	19th
6	3/29/09	Martinsville, VA	Jimmie Johnson	Chevrolet	75.938	13	7	12	66	No Time Trials	NTT	9th
7	4/05/09	Ft. Worth, TX	Jeff Gordon	Chevrolet	146.372	28	14	6	30	David Reutimann	190.517	2nd
8	4/18/09	Phoenix, AZ	Mark Martin	Chevrolet	108.042	14	10	6	29	Mark Martin	133.814	Pole
9	4/26/09	Talladega, AL	Brad Keselowski	Chevrolet	147.565	57	25	9	33	Juan Pablo Montoya	188.171	9th
10	5/02/09	Richmond, VA	Kyle Busch	Toyota	90.627	21	8	15	79	Brian Vickers	127.131	14th
11	5/09/09	Darlington, SC	Mark Martin	Chevrolet	119.687	23	13	17	73	Matt Kenseth	179.514	12th
12	5/25/09	Charlotte, NC	David Reutimann	Toyota	120.899	14	10	6	40	Ryan Newman	188.475	21st
13	5/31/09	Dover, DE	Jimmie Johnson	Chevrolet	115.237	25	11	10	43	David Reutimann	156.794	8th
14	6/07/09	Pocono, PA	Tony Stewart	Chevrolet	138.515	22	12	5	20	No Time Trials	NTT	Pole
15	6/14/09	Brooklyn, MI	Mark Martin	Chevrolet	155.491	11	6	3	14	Brian Vickers	189.110	32nd
16	6/21/09	Sonoma, CA	Kasey Kahne	Dodge	71.012	10	8	7	20	Brian Vickers	93.678	5th
17	6/28/09	Loudon, NH	Joey Logano	Toyota	97.497	21	14	11	47	No Time Trials	NTT	24th
18	7/04/09	Daytona Beach, FL	Tony Stewart	Chevrolet	142.461	23	10	8	30	No Time Trials	NTT	Pole
19	7/11/09	Chicago, IL	Mark Martin	Chevrolet	133.810	10	6	7	30	Brian Vickers	184.162	14th
20	7/26/09	Indianapolis, IN	Jimmie Johnson	Chevrolet	145.882	9	7	3	14	Mark Martin	182.054	16th
21	8/03/09	Pocono, PA	Denny Hamlin	Toyota	126.396	17	11	10	39	No Time Trials	NTT	6th
22	8/10/09	Watkins Glen, NY	Tony Stewart	Chevrolet	90.297	12	7	5	13	Jimmie Johnson	123.633	13th
23	8/16/09	Brooklyn, MI	Brian Vickers	Toyota	131.531	25	14	7	36	Brian Vickers	187.242	Pole
24	8/22/09	Bristol, TN	Kyle Busch	Toyota	84.820	12	5	11	76	Mark Martin	124.484	15th
25	9/06/09	Atlanta, GA	Kasey Kahne	Dodge	134.033	31	13	9	42	Mark Truex, Jr.	184.149	2nd
26	9/12/09	Richmond, VA	Denny Hamlin	Toyota	96.601	12	4	10	56	Mark Martin	126.808	3rd
27	9/20/09	Loudon, NH	Mark Martin	Chevrolet	100.753	20	10	11	49	Juan Pablo Montoya	133.431	14th
28	9/27/09	Dover, DE	Jimmie Johnson	Chevrolet	118.704	6	4	9	38	Jimmie Johnson	157.356	Pole
29	10/04/09	Kansas City, KS	Tony Stewart	Chevrolet	137.144	26	14	6	23	Mark Martin	175.758	5th
30	10/11/09	Fontana, CA	Jimmie Johnson	Chevrolet	143.908	29	9	8	30	Denny Hamlin	183.870	3rd
31	10/17/09	Charlotte, NC	Jimmie Johnson	Chevrolet	137.658	22	9	10	42	Jimmie Johnson	192.376	Pole
32	10/25/09	Martinsville, VA	Denny Hamlin	Toyota	73.633	21	12	15	77	Ryan Newman	96.795	17th
33	11/01/09	Talladega, AL	Jamie McMurray	Ford	157.213	58	25	6	23	No Time Trials	NTT	22nd
34	11/08/09	Fort Worth, TX	Kurt Busch	Dodge	147.137	13	4	5	26	Jeff Gordon	191.117	3rd
35	11/15/09	Phoenix, AZ	Jimmie Johnson	Chevrolet	110.486	9	4	4	23	Martin Truex, Jr.	135.120	3rd
36	11/22/09	Homestead, FL	Denny Hamlin	Toyota	126.986	18	10	7	31	Jimmie Johnson	173.919	38th

2010 NASCAR Sprint Cup Series Season

No.	Date	Site	Race Winner	Car	Speed	Lead Chgs	Ldrs	Caut.	C.Laps	Pole Winner	Speed	Winner Started
1	2/14/10	Daytona Beach, FL	Jamie McMurray	Chevrolet	137.284	52	21	9	40	Mark Martin	191.188	13th
2	2/21/10	Fontana, CA	Jimmie Johnson	Chevrolet	141.911	26	13	6	30	Jamie McMurray	183.744	7th
3	2/28/10	Las Vegas, NV	Jimmie Johnson	Chevrolet	141.450	18	9	7	29	Kurt Busch	188.719	20th
4	3/07/10	Atlanta, GA	Kurt Busch	Dodge	131.294	31	13	11	53	Dale Earnhardt, Jr.	192.761	11th
5	3/21/10	Bristol, TN	Jimmie Johnson	Chevrolet	79.618	29	8	10	103	Joey Logano	124.630	4th
6	3/29/10	Martinsville, VA	Denny Hamlin	Toyota	73.180	24	8	13	79	No Time Trials	NTT	19th
7	4/10/10	Phoenix, AZ	Ryan Newman	Chevrolet	99.372	20	13	9	59	AJ Allmendinger	134.675	14th
8	4/19/10	Fort Worth, TX	Denny Hamlin	Toyota	146.230	29	12	7	32	Tony Stewart	191.327	29th
9	4/25/10	Talladega, AL	Kevin Harvick	Chevrolet	150.590	88	29	8	32	No Time Trials	NTT	4th
10	5/01/10	Richmond, VA	Kyle Busch	Toyota	99.567	12	8	6	37	Kyle Busch	127.077	Pole
11	5/08/10	Darlington, SC	Denny Hamlin	Toyota	126.605	20	11	11	56	Jamie McMurray	180.370	8th
12	5/16/10	Dover, DE	Kyle Busch	Toyota	128.790	20	8	5	24	Martin Truex, Jr.	157.315	4th
13	5/30/10	Concord, NC	Kurt Busch	Dodge	144.966	33	17	8	34	Ryan Newman	187.546	2nd
14	6/06/10	Pocono, PA	Denny Hamlin	Toyota	136.303	14	7	8	27	Kyle Busch	169.485	5th
15	6/13/10	Brooklyn, MI	Denny Hamlin	Toyota	156.386	18	9	4	14	Kurt Busch	189.984	7th
16	6/20/10	Sonoma, CA	Jimmie Johnson	Chevrolet	74.357	12	8	7	14	Kasey Kahne	93.893	2nd
17	6/27/10	Loudon, NH	Jimmie Johnson	Chevrolet	113.308	14	9	4	19	Juan Pablo Montoya	132.337	10th
18	7/03/10	Daytona Beach, FL	Kevin Harvick	Chevrolet	135.843	47	18	9	37	No Time Trials	NTT	Pole
19	7/10/10	Chicago, IL	David Reutimann	Toyota	145.138	10	7	4	21	Jamie McMurray	183.542	7th
20	7/25/10	Indianapolis, IN	Jamie McMurray	Chevrolet	136.054	14	10	6	25	Juan Pablo Montoya	182.278	4th
21	8/01/10	Pocono, PA	Greg Biffle	Ford	132.246	19	9	5	31	Tony Stewart	171.393	12th
22	8/08/10	Watkins Glen, NY	Juan Pablo Montoya	Chevrolet	91.960	10	5	5	13	Carl Edwards	124.432	3rd
23	8/15/10	Brooklyn, MI	Kevin Harvick	Chevrolet	144.029	17	9	5	25	Kasey Kahne	187.183	8th
24	8/21/10	Bristol, TN	Kyle Busch	Toyota	99.071	15	9	7	39	Jimmie Johnson	123.475	19th
25	9/05/10	Atlanta, GA	Tony Stewart	Chevrolet	129.041	22	7	8	53	Denny Hamlin	187.380	5th
26	9/11/10	Richmond, VA	Denny Hamlin	Toyota	104.096	14	6	3	28	Carl Edwards	127.762	14th
27	9/19/10	Loudon, NH	Clint Bowyer	Chevrolet	106.769	21	8	8	34	Brad Keselowski	133.572	2nd
28	9/26/10	Dover, DE	Jimmie Johnson	Chevrolet	131.543	16	10	4	19	Jimmie Johnson	155.736	Pole
29	10/03/10	Kansas City, KS	Greg Biffle	Ford	138.077	20	12	5	24	Kasey Kahne	174.644	5th
30	10/10/10	Fontana, CA	Tony Stewart	Chevrolet	131.953	23	14	9	36	Jamie McMurray	185.285	22nd
31	10/16/10	Charlotte, NC	Jamie McMurray	Chevrolet	140.391	27	19	9	39	Jeff Gordon	191.544	27th
32	10/24/10	Martinsville, VA	Denny Hamlin	Toyota	71.619	24	12	15	90	Denny Hamlin	97.018	Pole
33	10/31/10	Talladega, AL	Clint Bowyer	Chevrolet	163.618	87	26	6	19	Juan Pablo Montoya	184.640	2nd

34	11/7/10	Fort Worth, TX	Denny Hamlin	Toyota	140.456	33	13	9	40	Elliott Sadler	195.397	30th
35	11/14/10	Phoenix, AZ	Carl Edwards	Ford	110.758	13	6	5	25	Carl Edwards	136.389	Pole
36	11/21/10	Homestead, FL	Carl Edwards	Ford	126.585	22	8	10	41	Kasey Kahne	176.904	2nd

2011 NASCAR Sprint Cup Series Season

No.	Date	Site	Race Winner	Car	Speed	Lead Chgs	Ldrs	Caut.	C.Laps	Pole Winner	Speed	Winner Started
1	2/20/11	Daytona Beach, FL	Trevor Bayne	Ford	130.326	74	22	16	60	Dale Earnhardt, Jr.	186.089	32nd
2	2/27/11	Avondale, AZ	Jeff Gordon	Chevrolet	102.961	28	12	8	43	Carl Edwards	137.279	20th
3	3/06/11	Las Vegas, NV	Carl Edwards	Ford	135.508	21	14	7	35	Matt Kenseth	188.884	3rd
4	3/20/11	Bristol, TN	Kyle Busch	Toyota	91.941	17	8	10	57	Carl Edwards	128.014	12th
5	3/27/11	Fontana, CA	Kevin Harvick	Chevrolet	150.849	18	10	4	16	Juan Pablo Montoya	184.653	24th
6	4/03/11	Martinsville, VA	Kevin Harvick	Chevrolet	74.195	31	12	11	72	Jamie McMurray	96.509	9th
7	4/09/11	Fort Worth, TX	Matt Kenseth	Ford	149.231	31	13	5	24	David Ragan	189.82	4th
8	4/17/11	Talladega, AL	Jimmie Johnson	Chevrolet	156.261	88	26	6	24	Jeff Gordon	178.248	2nd
9	4/30/11	Richmond, VA	Kyle Busch	Toyota	95.280	14	10	8	60	Juan Pablo Montoya	128.693	20th
10	5/07/11	Darlington, SC	Regan Smith	Chevrolet	129.678	21	12	11	46	Kasey Kahne	181.254	23rd
11	5/15/11	Dover, DE	Matt Kenseth	Ford	125.578	23	11	6	28	No Time Trials	NTT	24th
12	5/29/11	Concord, NC	Kevin Harvick	Chevrolet	132.414	38	19	14	64	Brad Keselowski	192.089	28th
13	6/05/11	Kansas City, KS	Brad Keselowski	Dodge	137.184	17	9	5	22	Kurt Busch	174.752	25th
14	6/12/11	Long Pond, PA	Jeff Gordon	Chevrolet	145.384	18	10	4	14	Kurt Busch	171.579	3rd
15	6/19/11	Brooklyn, MI	Denny Hamlin	Toyota	153.029	21	12	5	18	Kurt Busch	188.699	10th
16	6/26/11	Sonoma, CA	Kurt Busch	Dodge	75.411	12	9	5	17	Joey Logano	93.236	11th
17	7/02/11	Daytona, FL	David Ragan	Ford	159.491	57	25	6	21	Mark Martin	182.065	5th
18	7/09/11	Sparta, KY	Kyle Busch	Toyota	137.314	20	12	6	32	No Time Trials	NTT	Pole
19	7/17/11	Loudon, NH	Ryan Newman	Chevrolet	104.100	21	14	10	44	Ryan Newman	135.232	Pole
20	7/31/11	Speedway, IN	Paul Menard	Chevrolet	140.762	22	13	5	21	David Ragan	182.994	15th
21	8/07/11	Long Pond, PA	Brad Keselowski	Dodge	137.878	23	10	5	21	Joey Logano	172.055	13th
22	8/14/11	Watkins Glen, NY	Marcos Ambrose	Ford	99.417	14	8	5	14	Kyle Busch	126.421	3rd
23	8/21/11	Brooklyn, MI	Kyle Busch	Toyota	150.898	20	10	5	21	Greg Biffle	190.345	17th
24	8/27/11	Bristol, TN	Brad Keselowski	Dodge	96.753	22	10	6	42	Ryan Newman	122.811	8th
25	9/04/11	Hampton, GA	Jeff Gordon	Chevrolet	124.623	35	14	9	64	Kasey Kahne	186.196	5th
26	9/10/11	Richmond, VA	Kevin Harvick	Chevrolet	89.910	11	7	15	85	David Reutimann	127.383	7th
27	9/18/11	Joliet, IL	Tony Stewart	Chevrolet	143.306	22	10	6	25	Matt Kenseth	183.243	26th
28	9/25/11	Loudon, NH	Tony Stewart	Chevrolet	116.679	19	15	3	14	Ryan Newman	135.002	20th
29	10/02/11	Dover, DE	Kurt Busch	Dodge	119.413	24	13	10	44	Martin Truex, Jr.	159.004	2nd
30	10/09/11	Kansas City, KS	Jimmie Johnson	Chevrolet	137.181	19	9	6	25	Greg Biffle	174.887	19th
31	10/15/11	Concord, NC	Matt Kenseth	Ford	146.194	16	10	8	34	Tony Stewart	191.959	2nd
32	10/23/11	Talladega, AL	Clint Bowyer	Chevrolet	143.404	72	26	9	37	Mark Martin	181.367	3rd
33	10/30/11	Martinsville, VA	Tony Stewart	Chevrolet	68.648	23	12	18	108	No Time Trials	NTT	4th
34	11/06/11	Fort Worth, TX	Tony Stewart	Chevrolet	152.705	23	10	5	21	Greg Biffle	193.736	5th
35	11/13/11	Avondale, AZ	Kasey Kahne	Toyota	112.918	14	7	8	30	Matt Kenseth	137.101	10th
36	11/20/11	Homestead, FL	Tony Stewart	Chevrolet	114.976	26	15	8	54	Carl Edwards	175.467	15th

2012 NASCAR Sprint Cup Series Season

No.	Date	Site	Race Winner	Car	Speed	Lead Chgs	Ldrs	Caut.	C.Laps	Pole Winner	Speed	Winner Started
1	2/27/12	Daytona Beach, FL	Matt Kenseth	Ford	140.256	25	13	10	42	Carl Edwards	194.738	4th
2	3/4/12	Avondale, AZ	Denny Hamlin	Toyota	110.085	25	15	7	37	Mark Martin	136.815	13th
3	3/11/12	Las Vegas, NV	Tony Stewart	Chevrolet	137.524	16	11	8	33	Kasey Kahne	109.456	7th
4	3/18/12	Bristol, TN	Brad Keselowski	Dodge	93.037	13	7	5	49	Greg Biffle	125.215	5th
5	3/25/12	Fontana, CA	Tony Stewart	Chevrolet	160.166	9	5	1	5	Denny Hamlin	186.403	9th
6	4/1/12	Martinsville, VA	Ryan Newman	Chevrolet	78.823	18	10	7	56	Kasey Kahne	97.128	5th
7	4/14/12	Fort Worth, TX	Greg Biffle	Ford	160.577	18	7	2	10	Martin Truex, Jr.	190.369	3rd
8	4/22/12	Kansas City, KS	Denny Hamlin	Toyota	144.122	14	9	3	18	AJ Allmendinger	175.993	4th
9	4/28/12	Richmond, VA	Kyle Busch	Toyota	105.202	14	7	5	31	Mark Martin	128.327	5th
10	5/6/12	Talladega, AL	Brad Keselowski	Dodge	160.192	33	17	5	24	Jeff Gordon	191.623	13th
11	5/12/12	Darlington, SC	Jimmie Johnson	Chevrolet	133.802	22	8	8	38	Greg Biffle	180.257	2nd
12	5/27/12	Concord, NC	Kasey Kahne	Chevrolet	155.687	31	11	5	23	Aric Almirola	192.940	7th
13	6/3/12	Dover, DE	Jimmie Johnson	Chevrolet	122.835	17	7	7	32	Mark Martin	158.297	2nd
14	6/10/12	Long Pond, PA	Joey Logano	Toyota	131.004	19	10	7	35	Joey Logano	179.598	Pole
15	6/17/12	Brooklyn, MI	Dale Earnhardt, Jr.	Chevrolet	139.144	23	14	8	39	Marcos Ambrose	203.241	17th
16	6/24/12	Sonoma, CA	Clint Bowyer	Toyota	83.624	8	5	2	7	Marcos Ambrose	95.262	6th
17	6/30/12	Sparta, KY	Brad Keselowski	Dodge	145.607	17	6	4	24	Jimmie Johnson	181.818	8th
18	7/7/12	Daytona Beach, FL	Tony Stewart	Chevrolet	157.653	12	9	6	23	Matt Kenseth	192.386	42nd
19	7/15/12	Loudon, NH	Kasey Kahne	Chevrolet	116.226	16	8	3	15	Kyle Busch	133.417	2nd
20	7/29/12	Speedway, IN	Jimmie Johnson	Chevrolet	137.680	17	9	5	25	Denny Hamlin	182.763	6th
21	8/5/12	Long Pond, PA	Jeff Gordon	Chevrolet	139.249	13	10	3	14	Juan Pablo Montoya	176.043	27th
22	8/12/12	Watkins Glen, NY	Marcos Ambrose	Ford	98.145	10	5	4	13	Juan Pablo Montoya	127.020	5th
23	8/19/12	Brooklyn, MI	Greg Biffle	Ford	144.662	26	13	8	35	Mark Martin	199.706	13th
24	8/25/12	Bristol, TN	Denny Hamlin	Toyota	84.402	22	13	13	87	No Time Trials	NTT	8th
25	9/2/12	Hampton, GA	Denny Hamlin	Toyota	142.020	18	7	6	31	Tony Stewart	186.121	7th
26	9/8/12	Richmond, VA	Clint Bowyer	Toyota	100.019	17	10	6	41	Dale Earnhardt, Jr.	127.023	4th
27	9/16/12	Joliet, IL	Brad Keselowski	Dodge	143.363	16	9	4	23	Jimmie Johnson	182.865	13th
28	9/23/12	Loudon, NH	Denny Hamlin	Toyota	116.810	17	10	4	17	Jeff Gordon	134.911	32nd
29	9/30/12	Dover, DE	Brad Keselowski	Dodge	125.076	11	6	5	28	Denny Hamlin	159.299	10th
30	10/7/12	Talladega, AL	Matt Kenseth	Ford	171.194	54	18	5	17	Kasey Kahne	191.455	15th
31	10/13/12	Concord, NC	Clint Bowyer	Toyota	154.935	20	8	5	23	Greg Biffle	193.708	4th
32	10/21/12	Kansas City, KS	Matt Kenseth	Ford	115.086	16	10	14	66	Kasey Kahne	191.360	12th
33	10/28/12	Martinsville, VA	Jimmie Johnson	Chevrolet	77.677	22	9	11	64	Jimmie Johnson	97.598	Pole
34	11/4/12	Fort Worth, TX	Jimmie Johnson	Chevrolet	136.117	20	7	9	49	Jimmie Johnson	191.076	Pole
35	11/11/12	Avondale, AZ	Kevin Harvick	Chevrolet	111.182	11	7	8	38	Kyle Busch	138.788	19th
36	11/18/12	Homestead, FL	Jeff Gordon	Chevrolet	142.245	19	8	3	17	Joey Logano	176.056	15th

2013 NASCAR Sprint Cup Series Season

No.	Date	Site	Race Winner	Car	Speed	Lead Chgs	Ldrs	Caut.	C.Laps	Pole Winner	Speed	Winner Started
1	2/24/13	Daytona Beach, FL	Jimmie Johnson	Chevrolet	159.250	28	14	6	24	Danica Patrick	196.434	9th
2	3/3/13	Avondale, AZ	Carl Edwards	Ford	105.187	12	9	8	43	Mark Martin	138.074	16th
3	3/10/13	Las Vegas, NV	Matt Kenseth	Toyota	146.287	22	8	5	25	Brad Keselowski	NTT	18th

Appendix

No.	Date	Site	Race Winner	Car	Speed	Lead Chgs	Ldrs	Caut.	C.Laps	Pole Winner	Speed	Winner Started
4	3/17/13	Bristol, TN	Kasey Kahne	Chevrolet	92.206	17	10	10	66	Kyle Busch	129.535	2nd
5	3/24/13	Fontana, CA	Kyle Busch	Toyota	135.351	17	8	9	35	Denny Hamlin	187.451	4th
6	4/7/13	Martinsville, VA	Jimmie Johnson	Chevrolet	72.066	12	5	12	85	Jimmie Johnson	98.400	Pole
7	4/13/13	Fort Worth, TX	Kyle Busch	Toyota	144.751	18	7	7	36	Kyle Busch	196.299	Pole
8	4/21/13	Kansas City, KS	Matt Kenseth	Toyota	133.611	13	8	8	40	Matt Kenseth	191.748	Pole
9	4/27/13	Richmond, VA	Kevin Harvick	Chevrolet	92.141	10	7	11	75	Matt Kenseth	130.334	17th
10	5/5/13	Talladega, AL	David Ragan	Ford	148.729	30	17	5	31	Carl Edwards	NTT	19th
11	5/11/13	Darlington, SC	Matt Kenseth	Toyota	141.383	9	4	5	25	Kurt Busch	181.918	15th
12	5/26/13	Concord, NC	Kevin Harvick	Chevrolet	130.521	24	12	11	61	Denny Hamlin	195.624	15th
13	6/2/13	Dover, DE	Tony Stewart	Chevrolet	123.172	21	11	7	32	Denny Hamlin	157.978	22nd
14	6/9/13	Long Pond, PA	Jimmie Johnson	Chevrolet	144.202	12	4	6	19	Jimmie Johnson	NTT	Pole
15	6/16/13	Brooklyn, MI	Greg Biffle	Ford	193.278	22	13	8	38	Carl Edwards	202.452	19th
16	6/23/13	Sonoma, CA	Martin Truex, Jr.	Toyota	76.658	10	8	7	19	Jamie McMurray	94.986	14th
17	6/29/13	Sparta, KY	Matt Kenseth	Toyota	131.948	11	6	10	42	Dale Earnhardt Jr.	183.636	16th
18	7/6/13	Daytona Beach, FL	Jimmie Johnson	Chevrolet	154.313	18	11	6	27	Kyle Busch	193.723	8th
19	7/14/13	Loudon, NH	Brian Vickers	Toyota	98.735	10	6	12	58	Brad Keselowski	135.922	13th
20	7/28/13	Speedway, IN	Ryan Newman	Chevrolet	153.485	20	12	3	14	Ryan Newman	187.531	Pole
21	8/4/13	Long Pond, PA	Kasey Kahne	Chevrolet	129.009	27	14	9	35	Jimmie Johnson	180.654	18th
22	8/11/13	Watkins Glen, NY	Kyle Busch	Toyota	87.001	5	5	8	21	Marcos Ambrose	128.241	5th
23	8/18/13	Brooklyn, MI	Joey Logano	Ford	144.593	20	13	9	34	Joey Logano	203.949	Pole
24	8/24/13	Bristol, TN	Matt Kenseth	Toyota	90.279	16	9	11	74	Denny Hamlin	128.959	5th
25	9/1/13	Hampton, GA	Kyle Busch	Toyota	135.128	28	13	9	47	Ricky Stenhouse, Jr.	189.688	9th
26	9/7/13	Richmond, VA	Carl Edwards	Ford	105.028	17	9	5	29	Jeff Gordon	130.599	26th
27	9/15/13	Joliet, IL	Matt Kenseth	Toyota	125.855	25	16	9	46	Joey Logano	189.414	10th
28	9/22/13	Loudon, NH	Matt Kenseth	Toyota	107.573	19	11	7	37	Ryan Newman	136.497	9th
29	9/29/13	Dover, DE	Jimmie Johnson	Chevrolet	130.909	19	8	4	21	Dale Earnhardt Jr.	161.849	8th
30	10/6/13	Kansas City, KS	Kevin Harvick	Chevrolet	114.884	24	12	15	71	Kevin Harvick	187.526	Pole
31	10/12/13	Concord, NC	Brad Keselowski	Ford	158.308	24	11	4	20	Jeff Gordon	194.308	23rd
32	10/20/13	Talladega, AL	Jamie McMurray	Chevrolet	178.795	52	20	3	10	Aric Almirola	NTT	9th
33	10/27/13	Martinsville, VA	Jeff Gordon	Chevrolet	70.337	15	8	17	111	Denny Hamlin	99.595	9th
34	11/3/13	Fort Worth, TX	Jimmie Johnson	Chevrolet	151.754	28	10	5	26	Carl Edwards	196.114	3rd
35	11/10/13	Avondale, AZ	Kevin Harvick	Chevrolet	105.733	23	13	8	49	Jimmie Johnson	139.222	9th
36	11/17/13	Homestead, FL	Denny Hamlin	Toyota	130.693	22	8	8	37	Matt Kenseth	177.667	5th

2014 NASCAR Sprint Cup Series Season

No.	Date	Site	Race Winner	Car	Speed	Lead Chgs	Ldrs	Caut.	C.Laps	Pole Winner	Speed	Winner Started
1	2/23/14	Daytona Beach, FL	Dale Earnhardt Jr.	Chevrolet	145.290	42	18	7	39	Austin Dillon	196.019	9th
2	3/2/14	Avondale, AZ	Kevin Harvick	Chevrolet	109.229	14	8	8	38	Brad Keselowski	139.394	13th
3	3/9/14	Las Vegas, NV	Brad Keselowski	Ford	154.633	21	10	4	18	Joey Logano	193.278	2nd
4	3/16/14	Bristol, TN	Carl Edwards	Ford	84.051	20	12	12	95	Denny Hamlin	129.991	12th
5	3/23/14	Fontana, CA	Kyle Busch	Toyota	132.987	35	15	9	42	Matt Kenseth	187.314	14th
6	3/30/14	Martinsville, VA	Kurt Busch	Chevrolet	72.176	33	12	14	92	Kyle Busch	99.674	22nd
7	4/6/14	Fort Worth, TX	Joey Logano	Ford	134.191	18	9	7	49	Tony Stewart	195.454	10th
8	4/12/14	Darlington, SC	Kevin Harvick	Chevrolet	131.191	22	12	11	50	Kevin Harvick	183.479	Pole
9	4/26/14	Richmond, VA	Joey Logano	Ford	93.369	20	8	9	66	Kyle Larson	NTT	17th
10	5/4/14	Talladega, AL	Denny Hamlin	Toyota	154.103	48	23	8	31	Brian Scott	198.290	34th
11	5/10/14	Kansas City, KS	Jeff Gordon	Chevrolet	128.149	25	10	8	47	Kevin Harvick	194.252	13th
12	5/25/14	Concord, NC	Jimmie Johnson	Chevrolet	145.484	34	9	8	44	Jimmie Johnson	194.911	Pole
13	6/1/14	Dover, DE	Jimmie Johnson	Chevrolet	117.724	18	6	8	41	Brad Keselowski	164.444	4th
14	6/8/14	Long Pond, PA	Dale Earnhardt Jr.	Chevrolet	139.440	21	10	7	26	Denny Hamlin	181.415	8th
15	6/15/14	Brooklyn, MI	Jimmie Johnson	Chevrolet	143.441	25	13	8	36	Kevin Harvick	204.557	7th
16	6/22/14	Sonoma, CA	Carl Edwards	Ford	76.583	11	9	6	19	Jamie McMurray	96.350	4th
17	6/28/14	Sparta, KY	Brad Keselowski	Ford	139.723	12	3	6	34	Brad Keselowski	188.791	Pole
18	7/6/14*	Daytona Beach, FL	Aric Almirola	Ford	130.014	21	14	6	29	David Gilliland	199.322	15th
19	7/13/14	Loudon, NH	Brad Keselowski	Ford	108.841	18	9	7	35	Kyle Busch	138.130	7th
20	7/27/14	Speedway, IN	Jeff Gordon	Chevrolet	150.297	15	9	4	16	Kevin Harvick	188.889	N/A
21	8/3/14	Long Pond, PA	Dale Earnhardt Jr.	Chevrolet	127.411	15	10	8	35	Kyle Larson	183.438	9th
22	8/10/14	Watkins Glen, NY	AJ Allmendinger	Chevrolet	N/A	7	6	6	17	Jeff Gordon	129.466	6th
23	8/17/14	Brooklyn, MI	Jeff Gordon	Chevrolet	141.788	20	8	8	37	Jeff Gordon	206.558	Pole
24	8/23/14	Bristol, TN	Joey Logano	Ford	92.965	16	9	9	64	Kevin Harvick	131.362	5th
25	8/31/14	Hampton, GA	Kasey Kahne	Chevrolet	131.514	21	6	10	56	Kevin Harvick	190.398	10th
26	9/6/14	Richmond, VA	Brad Keselowski	Ford	104.702	4	2	4	27	Brad Keselowski	126.618	Pole
27	9/14/14	Joliet, IL	Brad Keselowski	Ford	142.330	18	7	6	28	Kyle Busch	NTT	25th
28	9/21/14	Loudon, NH	Joey Logano	Ford	98.697	10	6	15	63	Brad Keselowski	140.598	7th
29	9/28/14	Dover, DE	Jeff Gordon	Chevrolet	130.541	10	7	5	23	Kevin Harvick	162.933	6th
30	10/5/14	Kansas City, KS	Joey Logano	Ford	141.951	25	9	8	34	Kevin Harvick	197.621	4th
31	10/11/14	Concord, NC	Kevin Harvick	Chevrolet	145.346	32	14	8	39	Kyle Busch	197.390	7th
32	10/19/14	Talladega, AL	Brad Keselowski	Ford	160.302	38	19	6	25	Brian Vickers	196.129	5th
33	10/26/14	Martinsville, VA	Dale Earnhardt Jr.	Chevrolet	70.525	24	11	15	105	Jamie McMurray	99.905	16th
34	11/2/14	Fort Worth, TX	Jimmie Johnson	Chevrolet	132.239	23	7	13	61	Matt Kenseth	199.299	3rd
35	11/9/14	Avondale, AZ	Kevin Harvick	Chevrolet	99.991	8	6	12	58	Denny Hamlin	142.113	3rd
36	11/16/14	Homestead, FL	Kevin Harvick	Chevrolet	122.280	18	5	13	52	Jeff Gordon	180.747	5th

* Race scheduled for 7/5/14 but postponed

2015 NASCAR Sprint Cup Series Season

No.	Date	Site	Race Winner	Car	Speed	Lead Chgs	Ldrs	Caut.	C.Laps	Pole Winner	Speed	Winner Started
1	2/22/15	Daytona Beach, FL	Joey Logano	Ford	161.939	27	12	7	26	Jeff Gordon	201.293	5th
2	3/1/15	Hampton, GA	Jimmie Johnson	Chevrolet	131.078	28	12	10	54	Joey Logano	194.683	7th
3	3/8/15	Las Vegas, NV	Kevin Harvick	Chevrolet	143.611	18	9	6	28	Jeff Gordon	194.679	18th
4	3/15/15	Avondale, AZ	Kevin Harvick	Chevrolet	105.753	8	4	10	53	Kevin Harvick	140.751	Pole
5	3/22/15	Fontana, CA	Brad Keselowski	Ford	140.662	19	9	7	31	Kurt Busch	185.142	8th
6	3/29/15	Martinsville, VA	Denny Hamlin	Toyota	68.843	31	13	16	112	Joey Logano	98.461	15th
7	4/11/15	Fort Worth, TX	Jimmie Johnson	Chevrolet	140.500	29	9	8	40	Kurt Busch	193.847	5th
8	4/19/15	Bristol, TN	Matt Kenseth	Toyota	74.997	21	6	11	117	Matt Kenseth	128.632	Pole
9	4/26/15*	Richmond, VA	Kurt Busch	Chevrolet	97.157	12	5	8	53	Joey Logano	127.071	3rd
10	5/3/15	Talladega, AL	Dale Earnhardt Jr.	Chevrolet	159.487	27	15	6	23	Jeff Gordon	194.793	4th
11	5/9/15	Kansas City, KS	Jimmie Johnson	Chevrolet	125.265	16	10	9	49	Joey Logano	192.387	16th

No.	Date	Site	Race Winner	Car	Speed	Lead Chgs	Ldrs	Caut.	C.Laps	Pole Winner	Speed	Winner Started
12	5/24/15	Concord, NC	Carl Edwards	Toyota	147.803	22	9	8	39	Matt Kenseth	194.252	3rd
13	5/31/15	Dover, DE	Jimmie Johnson	Chevrolet	119.547	15	9	7	40	Denny Hamlin	160.121	14th
14	6/7/15	Long Pond, PA	Martin Truex, Jr.	Chevrolet	134.266	12	6	8	31	Kurt Busch	177.599	3rd
15	6/14/15	Brooklyn, MI	Kurt Busch	Chevrolet	116.688	17	11	5	38	Kasey Kahne	201.992	24th
16	6/28/15	Sonoma, CA	Kyle Busch	Toyota	74.774	9	5	5	21	AJ Allmendinger	96.310	2nd
17	7/5/15	Daytona Beach, FL	Dale Earnhardt Jr.	Chevrolet	134.941	22	12	9	43	Dale Earnhardt Jr.	NTT	Pole
18	7/11/15	Sparta, KY	Kyle Busch	Toyota	129.402	13	8	11	49	Kyle Larson	NTT	9th
19	7/19/15	Loudon, NH	Kyle Busch	Toyota	108.504	9	7	7	34	Carl Edwards	135.164	4th
20	7/26/15	Speedway, IN	Kyle Busch	Toyota	131.656	16	6	9	36	Carl Edwards	183.464	9th
21	8/2/15	Long Pond, PA	Matt Kenseth	Toyota	132.159	18	13	8	32	Kyle Busch	178.416	7th
22	8/9/15	Watkins Glen, NY	Joey Logano	Ford	91.420	8	8	5	16	AJ Allmendinger	127.839	16th
23	8/16/15	Brooklyn, MI	Matt Kenseth	Toyota	143.455	16	8	8	31	Matt Kenseth	197.488	Pole
24	8/22/15	Bristol, TN	Joey Logano	Ford	96.890	14	5	8	52	Denny Hamlin	131.407	5th
25	9/6/15	Darlington, SC	Carl Edwards	Toyota	111.993	24	11	18	89	Brad Keselowski	178.874	13th
26	9/12/15	Richmond, VA	Matt Kenseth	Toyota	100.353	13	4	6	47	Joey Logano	126.470	2nd
27	9/20/15	Joliet, IL	Denny Hamlin	Toyota	140.117	17	10	6	28	Kevin Harvick	NTT	29th
28	9/27/15	Loudon, NH	Matt Kenseth	Toyota	106.480	16	7	9	41	Carl Edwards	137.980	13th
29	10/4/15	Dover, DE	Kevin Harvick	Chevrolet	119.870	14	3	8	43	Matt Kenseth	NTT	16th
30	10/11/15**	Concord, NC	Joey Logano	Ford	139.760	14	10	9	44	Matt Kenseth	194.532	3rd
31	10/18/15	Kansas City, KS	Joey Logano	Ford	135.732	21	9	7	39	Brad Keselowski	195.503	14th
32	10/25/15	Talladega, AL	Joey Logano	Ford	167.311	30	18	3	18	Jeff Gordon	194.500	10th
33	11/1/15	Martinsville, VA	Jeff Gordon	Chevrolet	69.643	21	9	18	109	Joey Logano	98.548	5th
34	11/8/15	Fort Worth, TX	Jimmie Johnson	Chevrolet	137.490	15	8	9	47	Brad Keselowski	196.929	8th
35	11/15/15	Avondale, AZ	Dale Earnhardt Jr.	Chevrolet	106.512	8	7	2	29	Jimmie Johnson	143.158	3rd
36	11/22/15	Homestead, FL	Kyle Busch	Toyota	131.755	18	8	7	30	Denny Hamlin	176.655	3rd

* Race scheduled for 4/25/15 but postponed
** Race scheduled for 10/10/15 but postponed

2016 NASCAR Sprint Cup Series Season

No.	Date	Site	Race Winner	Car	Speed	Lead Chgs	Ldrs	Caut.	C.Laps	Pole Winner	Speed	Winner Started
1	2/21/16	Daytona Beach, FL	Denny Hamlin	Toyota	157.549	20	15	6	31	Chase Elliott	196.314	11th
2	2/28/16	Hampton, GA	Jimmie Johnson	Chevrolet	155.863	28	8	3	13	Kurt Busch	191.582	19th
3	3/6/16	Las Vegas, NV	Brad Keselowski	Ford	138.17	20	10	6	36	Kurt Busch	196.328	4th
4	3/13/16	Avondale, AZ	Kevin Harvick	Chevrolet	113.212	7	4	5	30	Kyle Busch	138.387	18th
5	3/20/16	Fontana, CA	Jimmie Johnson	Chevrolet	137.213	26	8	6	33	Austin Dillon	188.511	19th
6	4/3/16	Martinsville, VA	Kyle Busch	Toyota	80.088	11	5	8	51	Joey Logano	97.043	7th
7	4/9/16	Fort Worth, TX	Kyle Busch	Toyota	138.355	17	8	7	41	Carl Edwards	194.609	15th
8	4/17/16	Bristol, TN	Carl Edwards	Toyota	81.637	16	7	15	102	Carl Edwards	127.997	Pole
9	4/24/16	Richmond, VA	Carl Edwards	Toyota	97.07	23	8	8	49	Kevin Harvick	NTT	4th
10	5/1/16	Talladega, AL	Brad Keselowski	Ford	140.046	37	17	10	41	Chase Elliott	192.661	7th
11	5/7/16	Kansas City, KS	Kyle Busch	Toyota	141.909	16	10	6	30	Martin Truex, Jr.	190.921	6th
12	5/15/16	Dover, DE	Matt Kenseth	Toyota	109.348	19	10	12	65	Kevin Harvick	NTT	10th
13	5/29/16	Concord, NC	Martin Truex, Jr.	Toyota	160.655	9	4	4	19	Martin Truex, Jr.	192.328	Pole
14	6/6/16*	Long Pond, PA	Kurt Busch	Chevrolet	125.49	14	10	10	40	Brad Keselowski	181.726	9th
15	6/12/16	Brooklyn, MI	Joey Logano	Ford	134.241	14	8	9	46	Joey Logano	199.557	Pole
16	6/26/16	Sonoma, CA	Tony Stewart	Chevrolet	80.966	12	8	4	10	Carl Edwards	95.777	10th
17	7/2/16	Daytona Beach, FL	Brad Keselowski	Ford	150.342	26	13	5	28	Greg Biffle	192.955	5th
18	7/9/16	Sparta, KY	Brad Keselowski	Ford	128.583	16	9	11	53	Kevin Harvick	NTT	2nd
19	7/17/16	Loudon, NH	Matt Kenseth	Toyota	107.416	13	6	7	36	Jimmie Johnson	133.971	18th
20	7/24/16	Speedway, IN	Kyle Busch	Toyota	128.940	4	3	8	34	Kyle Busch	184.634	Pole
21	8/1/16**	Long Pond, PA	Chris Buescher	Ford	127.581	19	11	7	31	Martin Truex, Jr.	179.244	22nd
22	8/7/16	Watkins Glen, NY	Denny Hamlin	Toyota	89.513	9	8	8	20	Carl Edwards	126.562	6th
23	8/20/16	Bristol, TN	Kevin Harvick	Chevrolet	77.968	20	8	9	106	Carl Edwards	131.407	24th
24	8/28/16	Brooklyn, MI	Kyle Larson	Chevrolet	162.73	20	13	4	17	Joey Logano	201.698	12th
25	9/4/16	Darlington, SC	Martin Truex, Jr.	Toyota	126.427	14	8	10	52	Kevin Harvick	NTT	8th
26	9/10/16	Richmond, VA	Denny Hamlin	Toyota	85.778	21	7	16	89	Denny Hamlin	122.344	Pole
27	9/18/16	Joliet, IL	Martin Truex, Jr.	Toyota	145.161	17	9	4	22	Kyle Busch	NTT	6th
28	9/25/16	Loudon, NH	Kevin Harvick	Chevrolet	109.291	14	8	6	31	Carl Edwards	135.453	19th
29	10/2/16	Dover, DE	Martin Truex, Jr.	Toyota	130.969	14	6	4	22	Brad Keselowski	NTT	2nd
30	10/8/16	Concord, NC	Jimmie Johnson	Chevrolet	134.929	17	9	8	51	Kevin Harvick	196.029	11th
31	10/16/16	Kansas City, KS	Kevin Harvick	Chevrolet	133.155	16	10	8	38	Matt Kenseth	192.089	11th
32	10/23/16	Talladega, AL	Joey Logano	Ford	159.905	31	14	6	25	Martin Truex, Jr.	193.423	16th
33	10/30/16	Martinsville, VA	Jimmie Johnson	Chevrolet	78.54	15	9	5	54	Martin Truex, Jr.	98.206	3rd
34	11/6/16	Fort Worth, TX	Carl Edwards	Toyota	134.541	12	8	8	37	Austin Dillon	192.301	9th
35	11/13/16	Avondale, AZ	Joey Logano	Ford	102.866	8	5	9	53	Alex Bowman	140.521	4th
36	11/20/16	Homestead, FL	Jimmie Johnson	Chevrolet	128.869	20	6	7	33	Kevin Harvick	177.637	14th

* Race scheduled for 6/5/16 but postponed
** Race scheduled for 7/31/16 but postponed

Index

Index

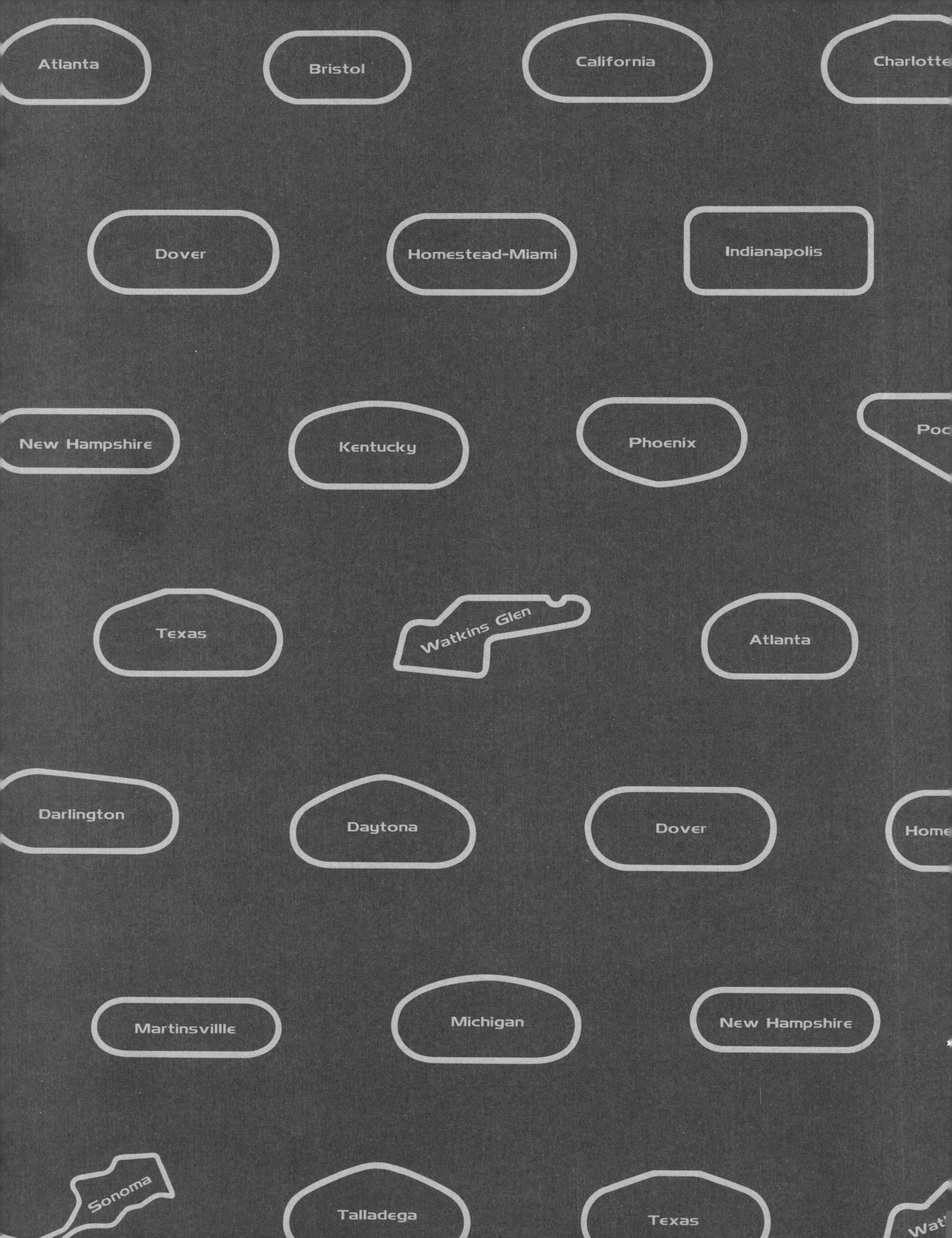